THE EXPERT

THE EXPERT

The Statistical Analyst in Litigation

Stephan Michelson

LRA Press
HENDERSONVILLE, NORTH CAROLINA
2006

ISBN 0-963-84660-4

Library of Congress Control Number: 2005910061

LRA Press
Longbranch Research Associates
1430 Valmont Drive
Hendersonville, North Carolina 28791

*"An expert is someone who wasn't there when it happened,
but who for a fee will gladly imagine what it must have been like."*

—Michael Tigar—

*"For litigants to have access to experts,
it may be necessary for some experts to concentrate on litigation."*

—Judge Edward Becker—

*"Statistical evidence is merely probabilistic evidence
coded in numbers rather than words."*

—Judge Richard Posner—

"Law is not mathematics."

—Aharon Barak—

"I didn't look at the big picture. I was just delighted to be doing these things."

—Al Kooper—

*"This is a book about the law, but it's presented from the standpoint
of one who has plodded and staggered in the furrow."*

—Gerry Spence—

*"I state things the way I consider appropriate,
not as might be desired by those who aspire to things remote from inner truth."*

—Mario Luís Rodríguez Cobos—

Contents

Preface

In the 1960s, when I was a research associate at the Brookings Institution, Bill Gorham invited me to join the initial staff of the Urban Institute in Washington, D.C., where he was the president. Instead, I joined another newly forming organization, the Center for Educational Policy Research at the Harvard Graduate School of Education. Gorham handwrote a note saying I could call on him at any time.

The purpose of the Harvard group was to employ empirical methods in the study of the "production" of education, inspired by the Coleman Report's empirical approach to relating school inputs to school outcomes. I was to become an economist of education and, with W. Norton Grubb, authored a book on public-school finance, an area in which I think economists can contribute positively. I came to think that economists—at least this one—had nothing of importance to contribute to education itself. Through litigation in education, especially the judicial enforcement of the concept of "equality" in education (first within a district and then among districts) I found my niche: using empirical analytic skills to enlighten courts on facts, to which they would apply the law to reach a decision.

I testified in federal district court on the impact of the National Teacher Exam in selecting teachers for Boston's schools. Boston claimed that the exam was a small contributor to the total point score used to evaluate prospective teachers. I showed that it was the dominant contributor to the *variation* in total point scores, hence to the ranking of candidates. Use of the National Teacher Exam to select teachers was disallowed by Judge W. Arthur Garrity in his famous Boston school-desegregation decisions.

In Chapter 3 I tell the story of my involvement with *Hobson v. Hansen*, a Washington, D.C., school-desegregation case. Two economists had defended the current allocation of school resources, claiming it was technologically determined. My explanation of why they were wrong was accepted by Judge J. Skelley Wright.

I enjoyed having contributed to the factual argument in lawsuits, having clarified the muddle that had been made of presumably relevant data. I was paid in no other way. The muddle in Boston had been created by the ignorance of the school committee. In the Washington case, the muddle had been created by "experts." Although I would have preferred to play the guitar, statistical analysis in litigation dominated the rest of my "professional" life.[1]

For some years I participated in cases "on the side." I became research director at the Center for Community Economic Development. I wanted the Center's research to inform the government how the federally financed program to support community-development organizations was operating, as I was informing courts: objectively, factually. Everyone in management above me, in the Center and in the Washington bureaucracy, wanted the Center's research to praise the failing federal program that funded it. I would not do that. After three years I called Bill Gorham who, without his or my referring to that now ten-year-old note, invited me to be senior fellow at the Urban Institute. The project we negotiated was the writing of this book. I started in March 1978.

Needless to say, I could not complete a book in one year. However, the work I did then remains in this text, now with close to thirty additional years of litigation history, my own personal experiences, and a certain distance and perspective.

In March 1979 I co-founded and became plurality owner of Econometric Research, Inc. (ERI) in Washington, D.C. A few years later I bought out the other founding partners of ERI, and continued doing business as Longbranch Research Associates (LRA). Our mission statement was "We derive fact and value from data." We did that almost exclusively in connection with litigation. As a businessman, meeting an annual payroll over a million dollars, I took the time to analyze my situation: what my product was and who my clients were. They did not match well. Clients did not want to purchase what LRA was selling. I called what we did "empirical analysis," the use of any tools available to determine fact as well as possible from relevant data wherever we could find them, and to measure how well we had done so. We were interested only in the truth. *Our* clients, on the other hand, wanted advocacy for *their* clients. It looked like the Center for Community Economic Development all over again.

I reduced the staff and reorganized the administration of LRA in 1990. In 1995 I sold the mainframe computer I had owned since 1980, further reducing the staff to just myself and my administrative assistant, Tanya Shields. By the middle of 2000, having participated in more than four hundred cases and broken new methodological ground in several areas, it was time to return to this book.

Over the years, I had come back to this material several times. I could expect no reward

---

1. Like many before me, I faced the reality of the difference between what I most enjoyed and what I was best at. Although my musical partners—Neil Hornick and David Cronin for folk, Backwards Sam Firk for blues, Beta Hat and Al Fabar for rock-and-roll—cannot share in the credit for the writing of this book, they deserve credit for keeping me sane enough to do it.

for such an effort. Part of the academic's job is to write books, but my job was to direct cases and a corporation. The point is made in the text that one should not regard *writings* on statistics and the law as reflecting the *knowledge* that workers in the field have of it. Most of the literature is produced by academics. Those with first-hand knowledge have neither time nor incentive to record it.

One example of this confusion between knowledge and writings is found in Chapter 5, on representation of the "community" among jurors. The ideas in that chapter evolved over many years, working with John A. Danaher, III, Deputy United States Attorney in Connecticut. John is a thinker and an honest truth seeker. He took the time to discuss the literature and cases. He encouraged the long reports I wrote laying out the new principles we evolved. He presented the materials I produced in *Fields* (1995) to the Second Circuit Court as part of the *Rioux* (1996) case. The strength of the language criticizing standard analyses, in the *Rioux* circuit-court opinion, is surely derived from my reports. John and I talked about writing an article together.

Harry Weller, Assistant State's Attorney in Connecticut, then joined the conversation. Harry supported further development of my views, which prevailed in *Gibbs* (1998). Perhaps all three of us should write the article, we said. But a private-sector expert, a United States Attorney, and a State's Attorney do not have time for that activity.

Harry recommended me to Rebecca Tedford Partington, an Assistant State's Attorney in Rhode Island, and to Gerald Mollen, District Attorney of Broome County, New York. Rebecca also accepted and contributed to my non-traditional viewpoint on how to analyze jury selection. Jerry made a number of provocative and helpful comments on a draft of Chapter 5, but none of my clients ever again spoke of joining in the writing. I had the time. They did not.

This book fulfills an intellectual obligation to myself, and an unstated but long-held obligation to Bill Gorham. Without that year at the Urban Institute, none of this would have happened. This expression of my appreciation for Bill's support just when I needed it comes perhaps late, perhaps unexpectedly.[2] Some experiences have life-changing impact. The time I had to study experts and the law in the abstract allowed me to contemplate my later experiences from a perspective I think no other expert had, a better knowledge of the history and evolution of the enterprise in which I was engaged.

---

2. Not that I did not "pay my way" as senior fellow. One day I asked Bill what made a book or report an "Urban Institute" product. What was the quality control, the unification not only in subject matter, but in substance, style, and quality? Bill's answer was perceived by both of us as lame. Shortly thereafter the Institute hired Robert Reischauer, a skilled and wise economist, knowledgeable in Washington political matters, to perform the very function I had outlined. I do not know how Bill perceived my year's stay, but I have always thought that, to the Institute, that one moment was worth the year's support. Apparently it was also to Reischauer, who succeeded Gorham as the Urban Institute's president.

Acknowledgments

This book was written entirely by me. I did all the research, all the writing, even the editing. I designed all tables and graphics, although some have been redrawn for this publication. I engaged John Laursen at Press-22 in Portland, Oregon, to transfer my WordPerfect files into Quark XPress, design the book this is, and institute consistency in form. He has gone beyond the bounds of the ordinary book designer, making occasional editorial suggestions. Except for his help, this is as close to a one-person show as I can imagine. No one but me is responsible for any errors or omissions.

Of course, in a deeper sense, one never functions alone. Marc Rosenblum has read several chapters and advised me on both content and form. He has also steered me to a number of sources, both cases and articles. Harry Weller read Chapter 5 and chewed me out for not understanding his strategy in *Gibbs*. I trust that it is accurately portrayed now. My brother, Mark Michelson, has read several chapters and prompted several rewrites, as has his son-in-law David Kahan. Clay R. Smith read the *Crow* section of Chapter 3 and made helpful comments, some of which I have effectuated. He has also read parts of Chapter 5, and again made interesting and helpful suggestions. Neil Vidmar refrained from commenting on the section from Chapter 10 that I sent him, but provided helpful references and pre-publication copies of two of his articles.

Mildred R. Howe and Clayton Mosher each suggested some of the references used here. Lynn S. Crook provided helpful comments on my section on repressed memory. Bethanne Knudson read through some early chapters and agreed that this is as difficult a book to read as I had thought. Ralph Pochoda's questions forced me to rewrite the Introduction and Chapter 1—twice. These people deserve separate mention because everyone named in the preceding paragraph is an attorney. My readership is not intended to be— and I hope is not—limited to attorneys, although I acknowledge that it is, indeed, limited. My intellectual debt to various members of my staff over the years—to Vicky Albright, Gail Blattenberger, Ani DiFazio, Kenneth Martin, Diane Steele, Lane Tapley, Joy Walzer, and especially Timothy Wyant—should be evident in several places in the text.

Most of the people who have read and commented on this work would like to see it become part of the conversation, even if they disagree in places. Some have tried to suppress it. Others, when they learn about it, will wish it had been suppressed. Egos may be bruised, but that is corollary damage, not my intent. I do not contend that all my analyses are perfect, or that my reforms would work exactly as I say. I do contend that what I have to say represents fresh, creative, and insightful work in this field, which only a fool would dismiss. Unfortunately, fools abound, but this work will outlive them. There are many new ideas here, both about statistics and about law. I thank those people who have disagreed as well as those who have agreed, but not those who have tried to keep my analyses out of public view.

Note on References

A List of Cases Cited and a Bibliography, both in alphabetical order, appear at the end of this book. Author names appear in the text, but literature references occur only in footnotes. They appear as name and parenthetical date in the note, such as Gibson (1950) or Wells (1911). The complete citation is in the bibliography, organized alphabetically by author, and within author by date. When I have not read the original source, but it is referenced in the source I do use, I cite the original in a footnote, and refer to my source listing in its Bibliography entry. I cite most newspaper and popular magazine (as opposed to scholarly journal) references fully in notes, not in the Bibliography, which is reserved for more-important sources. Most references to the *Oregonian* are to national news stories. I could have referenced a more widely available paper, but my library research was done at the Boley Library of the Northwest School of Law at Lewis & Clark College, and at the Reed College library. That I did much of the work on this book in Portland leaves its mark, for example, in the opening paragraph of Chapter 5.

Cases are organized in the List of Cases Cited by an abbreviated name in italics accompanied by a parenthetical date, such as *Gibson* (1896) or *Wells* (1985); and they are so referenced in both text and footnotes. I sometimes refer to a case using a date different from the one that appears in the heading in the List of Cases Cited. If so, the date indicates a particular (usually later) decision, included in the case description. For example, *Daubert* (1989) refers to the original summary judgment; *Daubert* (1991) to its affirmance by the appeals court; *Daubert* (1993) to the changing, by the Supreme Court, of standards for reviewing scientific testimony; and *Daubert* (1995) to the re-instatement, under the new standards, of the initial summary judgment. Only *Daubert* (1989) appears as an alphabetized heading, but all dates, referencing subsequent decisions, appear in the entry following.

In neither the Bibliography nor the List of Cases Cited do I strictly follow the form that one might see in law-review articles or legal briefs. I have tried to make both the attorney or professional law writer and the novice—the statistician, for example—comfortable. I spell out actions (such as "affirmed" or "vacated") where attorneys abbreviate them. I reserve italics for the case titles and legal Latin phrases (such as "*certiorari*"), leaving more-common terms (such as "et al.") in roman. This same rule is used in the text. Different sources for the same decision are separated by commas, whereas a semicolon, a punctuation not found in standard case citations, separates decisions.

Within a day or two of its filing, a decision may be found in Westlaw, an internet service available by subscription only. Westlaw provides consecutive numbers within year (such as 2004 WL ___). Some decisions are not reported further, or received more-formal publication after I had closed work on this book. Therefore there are some WL citations included herein. References are to sections numbered *1, *2, etc., as they appear in the WL print, placed there by Westlaw editors for this purpose, to allow specifying the approximate location of a quotation.

There are some references to online publications that have no pages. I refer then to section headings.

District-court opinions usually are indicated by ___ F.Supp. ___ (<u>volume</u> F.Supp. <u>page</u>), followed by the jurisdiction (always including the state) and year in parentheses. More-current decisions will refer to___ F.Supp.2d. ___. An appeals-court cite would be ___ F. ___ or ___ F.2d ___ or ___ F.3d ___ followed by the circuit number and year in parentheses. Supreme Court cites are ___ U.S. ___ (<u>volume</u> U.S. <u>page</u>) or ___ S.Ct. ___. Where a U.S. cite is available, I use it, but cases are published quicker in S.Ct., so some recent cases are referenced using that pagination.

Decisions that focus on federal rules may be published in the series Federal Rules Decisions, or F.R.D. Decisions in Fed.Appx. are considered unpublished. Military decisions are published in an M.D. series. I have read some cases in reporters, most often Fair Employment Practices Cases (FEP Cases), published by the Bureau of National Affairs. Some cases were published only in FEP cases, and are cited thereto, although some also have a WL number. If I know that a decision will be published in a preferred reference, I indicate that with underlined blank spaces. In almost every case, therefore, that a district court opinion has only a WL or FEP Cases citation, it has not been and will not be published in F.Supp. or F.R.D. As all Supreme Court cases are eventually published in the U.S. series, each such decision has a ___U.S.___ listing, even if no numbers are given.

I have made no attempt to list complete case histories. West publishes a case digest in which one can find complete case histories; or one can call up a history page from Westlaw online. For example, *Key* (1982) was preceded two days earlier by a decision I do not list, published in F.R.D., granting class certification. If I do not use a particular decision, I normally do not list it.

I do not always inform the reader when the case name has changed. This may occur when the head of a government agency is replaced, when criminal defendants plead guilty and drop out of a joint trial, or when the defendant appeals to the Supreme Court (at which point the parties are reversed). For the usual phrase "*sub nom.*" which means "under the name of," I write "as."

Following each bibliographical and case listing are numbers in brackets. They refer to the chapters—or, followed by "A," chapter appendices—in which the item is referenced. In this usage, "P" indicates Preface, "I" stands for Introduction, and "C" for Coda.

Formalities and mannerisms have changed over time. "Justice W" would, in the past, have been referred to as "Mr. Justice W." Some judges capitalize "Court" in their own opinions, which I respect when quoting. In my own writing, I capitalize "Court" only when referring to the U. S. Supreme Court. Currently, to refer to a specific page of an opinion, ZZ—let's say it is a Supreme Court opinion—one will write "*Title*, XX U. S. YY, ZZ (year)." This form splits the reference, inserting the specific page within it. I use the form "*Short Title* (year) at ZZ," which retains the citation the same in every reference, and refers the reader to my case list for the volume number and full name.

Currently, I see titles of journal articles referenced in italics. I do not follow that form. I reserve italics for the name of the publication. A book title is italicized, as is the name of the journal in which an article is published (as if the article were a chapter in that book). One consequence of the current use of italics to denote article titles is that if the title contains an italicized expression, that artifact is lost. Indeed, as here, case titles are usually italicized in an article title as it appears in the journal. In my form, one will see it that way.

It has also become the norm to refer only to the volume and page number of a journal article, followed by the year, such as 80 *Columbia Law Review* 1197 (1980). However, the journal volume was published one issue at a time. Some journals, such as *Law and Contemporary Problems*, paginate each issue from 1. Thus, when I have this information, I write 80 *Columbia Law Review* 6:1197 (1980), which is read as "Volume 80, Number 6, page 1197 in 1980." Similarly, in the Bibliography, I write out the name of every author (current form is the first author only), first name first. And I write out the name of the journal. I am not sure that B.U. L.R. or B. U. L. Rev. conveys the name *Boston University Law Review* to all readers.

Note on the Index of Experts Referenced

I include a third list, naming each expert witness to whom I refer. I indicate the chapter or appendix in which that referral is made, but not the page. An expert may appear more than once in a chapter, but be listed only once. You have to read the entire chapter to find out.

Some experts also are authors. For example, Alan Gelfand is prominent in the Appendix to Chapter 4. Yet he is listed in the Index of Experts as appearing only in Chapter 5, because the Index is a listing of references to experts, not all references to anyone who at any time was also an expert. In both the Index of Experts and the Bibliography I list the full name—that is, including middle name or middle initial—to the extent that I know it. This allows me to use only first and last names in the text. Therefore Janice Fanning Madden appears as Janice Madden, and Michael J. Saks appears as Michael Saks, except in these lists. Perhaps if I had a middle name I would be more sensitive, but I find these middle names and initials clumsy if not annoying, so I have omitted them.

NOTE ON PRONOUNS

I cannot undertake to reform a language that provides no easy gender-neutral reference. Some writers alternate pronouns, thereby referring to the same person as "he" in one reference, "she" in another. Faust Rossi, Samuel Gross, and Stephen Easton have published books or articles using the feminine pronoun exclusively.[3] I use the masculine. Thus persons of unknown gender are referred to as "he," meaning but not taking the time to write "he or she." I still think "they" is a plural form, not to be used to refer to a single person. "Data" is plural (the singular is datum).[4] Yes, sometimes I do feel like the little boy with his finger in the dike.

NOTE ON QUOTATIONS

Short quotations are placed in the text in quotation marks. Long quotations are indented. They appear in slightly smaller type. This distinction was not made by counting words, but by listening. If one voice, say my own, is narrating this story, a quotation that flows with the narrative remains in the text, in quotation marks. An indented quotation is meant to imply that it is being read by a different voice. I have tried hard to make this text readable, including by varying the voices in which it is made audible. If you do not hear voices in your head when you read, then this is all gibberish to you.

Initially I assigned a separate typeface to quotations from Supreme Court opinions. When the Supreme Court is not stating the solution, it is creating the problem. Members of the Supreme Court, if not always correct, at all times—even in dissent—are the most important voices in the conversation. Rather than being a short cut to the source of the quotation, the different typeface caused confusion. Valuing experience over theory, I abandoned the practice.

The Supreme Court makes many errors, and even recognizes some of them.[5] Nor is reversing formerly held positions a recent phenomenon.

> *Stare decisis* is not, like the rule of *res judicata*, universal inexorable command,[6]

---

3. Rossi (1991), Gross (1991), and Easton (2000).

4. I am not the lone holdout. This is the entire conclusion of Clermont and Eisenberg (2002) at 154: "Data are good."

5. In the summer of 2002, for example, the Supreme Court treated us to *Atkins* (2002), unabashedly reversing *Penry* (1989), now ruling execution of the mentally impaired unconstitutional. On March 1, 2005, in *Roper* (2005), the Court reversed its prior opinion in *Stanford* (1989), now barring execution of defendants under age eighteen, where the earlier age limit was sixteen.

6. *Coronado* (1932) at 405; following in-text quotation from footnote 1 at 406. Indeed, the Court reversed itself six years later:

wrote Justice Brandeis in dissent. He listed many cases that "overruled [the Court's] earlier decisions although correction might have been secured by legislation."

As Judge Rubin once wrote,

> When today's vibrant principle is obviously in conflict with yesterday's sterile precedent, trial courts need not follow the outgrown dogma.[7]

The Supreme Court vacated Judge Rubin's decision because it thought the issues therein were moot.[8] In a sense, though, that means it agreed. That is, sometimes lower courts tell the Supreme Court that it was wrong, and sometimes the Supreme Court listens. The Court stumbles a lot but, one could also say, it rights itself often.[9]

NOTE ON NOTES

This manuscript was written with footnotes, that is, with notes on the same page as the text itself. I then converted to endnotes, sensing that a book that looked like a long law-review

---

> We are of the opinion that the Coronado Case and the decision upon which it rested should be reconsidered in the light of our other decisions as to the taxing power.

7. *Healy* (1973) at 1117.

8. *Healy* (1975). Ruth Bader Ginsburg (now Justice Ginsburg) argued for appellees to sustain the decision.

9. I disagree with Brooks Adams (1913), at 83:

> For the court of last resort having once declared the meaning of a clause of the Constitution, that meaning remains fixed forever, unless the court either reverses itself, which is a disaster, or the Constitution can be amended by the states.

In most reversals, the "disaster" was the original opinion. In *Pokora* (1934), at 102, Justice Cardozo set out to "to clear the ground of brushwood" created by *Goodman* (1927). *Batson* (1986) was an admission that *Swain* (1965) had been decided incorrectly, following many law-review commentaries to that effect. *Atkins* (2002) was an admission that *Penry* (1989), which also had been widely criticized, had been incorrect. Was reversing *Plessy* (1896) with *Brown* (1954) a disaster? The terms of the law, on balance, are improving.

John Noonan (2002), among other commentators, might argue that Adams' view still holds. Look at the "trend" in decisions, they would say. The trend may be toward increasing federal power, and that may be bad. But the trend, even with a "conservative" court, is also towards what Justice Blackmun in *Collins* (1994) called, at 1132, "evolving standards of decency." *McGautha* (1971) allowed juries to prescribe the death penalty without clear standards. In *Furman* (1972) Justice Douglas wrote, at 248,

> We are now imprisoned in the *McGautha* holding.

But they weren't. *Furman* overturned *McGautha*. The dissenters echoed Brooks Adams, at 400:

> [I]f *stare decisis* means anything, [*McGautha*] should be regarded as a controlling pronouncement of law.

Although it took twenty-two years, one of those dissenters, Justice Blackmun, recanted, writing in *Collins* (1994), at 1131:

> There is little doubt now that *Furman*'s essential holding was correct.

I agree. Decisions get better.

article would be difficult for some people. I planned to have the book printed in two volumes, so a reader could hold one volume open to a chapter, the other to its notes. I began to notice, in my reading of other works, that I read every footnote, but only an occasional endnote. Although it made book design more difficult, I reverted to footnotes.

This business of notes has been considered by others, also. Rosemary Erickson and Rita Simon, for example, provide a minimum number of chapter endnotes, placing most citations in parentheses in the text. This leads them to the following sentence:

> As Lewis Coser discusses in *Masters of Sociological Thought* (1977), Max Weber contended that an empirical science can never advise people what they should do, though as Karl Mannheim points out in *Ideology and Utopia* (1936), Louis Wirth said that in studying what is, we cannot totally rule out what ought to be.[10]

The reader of this book will discover that Erickson and Simon are not alone in excessive, compulsive referencing; but I would have contrasted Weber and Wirth in the text, and referenced Coser and Mannheim in a note.

Jerry Spence and John Noonan eschew note indications in the text, requiring the page number and repetition of a phrase before each note, and leaving the text reader uncertain that there is one.[11] These are failed reforms. The reader should know, from an indication in the text, whether he will find a note. When a note exists, it should be easily found. Renumbering endnotes by chapter makes finding them difficult, if they are run together in a "Notes" section at the end of the book. When I had endnotes, I numbered consecutively, so one would not have to determine which chapter's notes one was looking at. There are over eighteen hundred of them. You don't have to know that, now that the notes, renumbered within each chapter, are easily found at the bottom of the text page.

To make notes easier and to minimize their number, one note sometimes contains several citations. Many notes in this book are parenthetical, illuminating, extended remarks. Some refer to literature nowhere else discussed. I consider reading the notes part of reading the text. The reader has the option of skipping them, but I am not going to make it easier to do so.

---

10. Erickson and Simon (1998) at 6.

11. See Spence (1989) and J. Noonan (2002).

THE EXPERT

Introduction

As early as there was a judicial system, someone surely found fault with it. The first critics of courts probably were the first losers of decisions. Now that courts have become—or have been perceived to become—more entangled in broad social issues, and therefore in the lives of more people, more institution-wide criticisms have emerged. The one of interest here is about how courts discern, absorb, and utilize "fact;" how they determine fact from what is presented to them as fact.

Starting in the late 1980s, critics cried that courts were allowing "junk science" conclusions into the system, presented to juries as if they were fact. The criticisms, in some instances, were correct. The Supreme Court responded, in rules and opinions, telling judges to screen technical testimony for its science content. Did that solve the problem? I argue that academically approved "good" science is often no better than easily recognized junk science. That puts me at odds with many members of the "scientific" community, but I debate the point on their terms in this book. If the all-inclusive subject is "science," my focus is on a smaller area, social science; and, smaller yet, statistics. I provide many examples of "junk" statistical analysis in this book, much of which has fooled both courts and commentators on courts.

I provide clues to how the judicial system can spot and deal with bad statistical analyses, both because statistical analysis is what I do, and because it lies at the heart of most "science" testimony. In this Introduction I provide some background for the discussion, and summarize some conclusions from the book. Chapter 1 provides a history of the expert witness, and therefore of the science (and statistical) expert witness. In Chapters 2 through 8 I make my case that the junk is still with us. I also try to determine why, which leads to an essay, in Chapter 9, about the institutions outside the judicial system that bring us the people who function within it. In Chapter 10 I propose what to do about it. There is also a laconic "Coda," an epilogue about lay misunderstanding of some of the issues discussed in previous chapters.

THE ACTIVIST COURT

We hear much about the "activist court." In one version, this is a court at any level that not only orders but implements desegregation, that not only finds employment discrimination but awards back-pay damages, that not only considers abortion a justiciable issue but finds in the constitution implicit guidance thereon. In another version, a court's merely finding fault with the way society operates, or acting as though judicial interference can make for a better world, is "activist" enough.[1] "The Warren Court has been the most activist in history," says Arthur S. Miller, defining activism as the creation of constitutional law.[2] The Supreme Court that "stole" the 2000 presidential election, according to Alan Dershowitz, was activist to a fault.[3] Jamin Raskin, who decried the "stupefying judicial activism" of the same *Bush* (2000) majority in *Shaw* (1993),[4] says the Court "actively carried out a partisan agenda":

> But behind *Bush v. Gore* lies a thick and unprincipled jurisprudence, hostile to
> popular democracy and protective of race privilege and corporate power.

Raskin, describing "fits of judicial activism," might argue that the Rehnquist court is the most activist in history.

Circuit-court judge Richard Posner, on the other hand, would say that, in *Bush*, the federal Supreme Court was preventing the unauthorized activism of Florida's Supreme Court:

> The state courts retain their ordinary powers but the U.S. Supreme Court is
> authorized to intervene if, in the guise of interpretation, the state courts
> rewrite the state election laws, usurping the legislature's authority.[5]

---

1. I include Glazer (1978) and Moynihan (1969) in the former group, Wolf (1976), Wolf (1978), and Horowitz (1977) in the latter.

2. Miller (1968) at 221. Or see R. Berger (1997) at 25, about *Brown* (1954):

> Put baldly, the Court had no popular mandate for its revolutionary decision but assumed
> the role of an Old Testament prophet, enhanced by the sanctions at its disposal.

3. Dershowitz (2001) is hysterical. He calls the Court's decisions "lawless," at 3; a "hijacking," at 11; "preposterous," at 43; and "corrupt," at 174. Better books on this topic, which direct their ire more at the participants in the debacle than at the court that put an end to it, can be found by Tapper (2001) and Sammon (2001). Dershowitz contends that the members of the Supreme Court voted in opposition to their usual principles. Tribe (2001) has a different view:

> Far from discrediting the justices in the *Bush v. Gore* majority for acting *out* of character, this Comment seeks to discredit them for acting *in* character.

Introductory footnote at 170. Perhaps it is to the Supreme Court's credit that its discreditors cannot agree. Tribe also provides an extensive collection of references on this topic.

4. Raskin (2003) at 74; following in-text quotation and indented quotation both at 3; then in-text quotation at 4.

5. Posner (2003) at 344. Posner defends the Court's decision, but not its reasoning. Charles Fried (2002), in contrast, considers the Court's rationale "reasonable."

"Activism" is usually defined in outcome terms. I extend its meaning here to methods of making decisions. Activist courts have as often been repressive as liberating. The "activist" court of John Marshall

> was to become a conservative and nationalistic bulwark against the dominant political forces of democracy and states' rights.[6]

The "activist" court of the late nineteenth and early twentieth centuries, abandoning the presumption that legislation was constitutional unless overwhelming proof was presented to the contrary, declared unconstitutional many legislative attempts to enlarge minority rights.[7] In the 1930s the "activist" court, in President Roosevelt's eyes, emasculated New Deal legislation. Posner, referring to the Supreme Court's decision to ban school segregation, opined "Restraint is not everything. *Brown v. Board of Education* was an activist decision, but a justifiable one."[8]

Assessing the judicial system from some political perspective, people judge it harshly when the court's perspective is different from their own.[9] For example, Henry Steele Commager concluded that

> judicial review has been a drag upon democracy and—what we may conceive to be the same thing—upon good government.[10]

Archibald Cox was happy with the activist court of the 1950s and 1960s.

> The use of constitutional adjudication as an instrument of reform made ours a freer, more equal, and more humane society.[11]

Although some would say it is a less constitutionally directed one.[12] As soon as decisions began to emanate from the full Reagan Court, they were decried as "conservative judicial

---

6. Kelly and Harbison, *The American Constitution,* third edition (1963) at 201, quoted in Kurland (1970) at 11.

7. See especially *Civil Rights* (1883), in which the Civil Rights Act of 1875 was vitiated, though not actually vacated.

8. Posner (1985) at 220. Paraphrasing Dahl (2002), Hendrik Hertzberg describes *Brown* (1954) as
> the exercise of unelected, unaccountable, unchecked, quasi-legislative judicial power.

"Framed Up" (a review of Dahl), *The New Yorker,* July 29, 2002, at 86.

9. R. Berger (1979) at 5:
> Commentary on the Court's decision frequently turns on whether they harmonize with the commentator's own predilections.

10. Commager (1943), in Levy (1967) at 73.

11. A. Cox (1987) at 182.

12. R. Berger (1997) at 22:
> In their zeal to ameliorate social injustice, academicians undermine the constitutionalism that undergirds our democratic system.

activism" by civil-rights attorneys—that is, by those who had supported liberal judicial activism.[13]

John Noonan would have us abandon the "activist"concept:

> The idea that "activism" is a helpful or accurate or meaningful category for judging the Supreme Court of the United States is an illusion.[14]

I disagree. Like a car, the Court has both direction and "velocity" (degrees of extremism). One can usually find more or less extreme positions the Court might have taken in the same direction. Noonan is so upset with the Court's current direction—limiting the federal government's authority vis-à-vis states—that he dismisses the concept of velocity when it might be more productive to measure it.

Why and in what ways the courts are active at present, and in what ways this differs from the past, is a subject of considerable historical interest, and considerable current discussion. Understanding the position of the expert witness requires considering the role the Supreme Court has assigned to lower courts, and how that role has been effectuated. Courts at one time were passive recipients of "expert" testimony, even—as we will see in Chapter 1—allowing experts to certify themselves. In its *Daubert* (1993) decision, the Supreme Court turned expert-activist. It instructed lower courts to screen technical and scientific expert testimony for methodological validity before allowing it to be presented at trial. This is a different kind of activism than is usually discussed under that term, but this book is a call for more of it.

EXPERT STATISTICAL ANALYSIS

This book is about empirical analytic expertise within and concerning the judicial system. The extent to which statistical inference should be considered "scientific" is explored in Chapter 10. My primary focus is on statistics as a tool of physical and social scientists, understanding that the label "scientist" does not necessarily imply the content "science." My attention is on the finding of fact in a judicial context. I bring together two areas of "expert" judgment. One is the expertise utilized within the arena of adversarial fact finding, voiced by "experts" as certified to be so by the court. The other is the expertise utilized to evaluate judicial findings of fact in articles, usually in law reviews, and books. Peculiarly, the formal study of "Law and Economics" has been distant from such expertise, despite the practical experience of many economists in the court-

---

13. In June 1989 the Supreme Court delivered a series of decisions limiting the ability of plaintiffs to prevail in equal-employment-opportunity cases. See Al Kamen, "Landmark Civil Rights Decision Narrowed," *Washington Post* (June 16, 1989) at A1 and A22.

14. J. Noonan (2002) at 10.

room.[15] This book is intended to be a contribution to the use and evaluation of statistics and social-science expertise within the judicial process, to be read by and to influence experts, attorneys, and judges, as well as university professors, students, and commentators.

If, in principle, the role of the expert is to elucidate fact, to derive useful information from data and explain it understandably to the lay court, we should ask whether that is what experts actually do. Actors in any system will be moved primarily by incentives. The intended roles of the players will not be their actual roles unless the rules of the game are designed to induce the players to adopt the system's assumed behaviors. The U.S. legal system produces incentives for attorneys to bring forward the worst experts, not the best; for competent experts to produce substandard work; for honest experts to leave the system. The principle is a myth.

The reality, besides being different from the myth, is ill-spirited:

> One of the most unfortunate consequences of our system of obtaining expert witnesses is that it breeds contempt all around.[16]

Why? Not because experts tell uncomfortable truths. It is because they tell uncomfortable lies.

Were someone "reform" minded, the first challenge would be to produce good experts, to train students to be able to discern good from bad analysis. The next challenge would be to find a way to get truly good experts engaged in the system. Those doing the engaging would have to understand analytic quality, *and want it*. Third, these good experts should be supported by their clients and the judiciary—given the resources and the respect they would then deserve. The fourth challenge would be for the judicial system, the expert's audience, to learn how to discard the tripe and digest real information. To different degrees, the system fails all of these challenges. I am not that reformer, but this book would be a good tool for such a reformer to have.

Only if better analysis is rewarded by judges will it be desired by attorneys. Thus judges cannot just complain about the experts the attorneys have provided. Throughout this book I will ask judges to be more active. I also ask them to be more intellectual, less technical. The meaning of that summary statement will evolve. Readers familiar with these ques-

---

15. The field called "Law and Economics" concerns principles from which judicial decisions "should" flow. Much of the study of law and economics concerns methods of coming to some "correct" allocation of rights and liabilities. My subject is less grand, and less abstract. It is more about the actual world than the optimal world. It is about how courts determine fact, not how they come to principles of law.

16. Gross (1991) at 1135. See also Jasanoff (1995) at 45:

> What the common law adjudicator sees in practice are two carefully constructed representations of reality, each resting on a foundation of expert knowledge but each profoundly conditioned by the culture of expert witnessing as it intersects with the interests, ingenuity, and resources of the proffering party.

tions will find my arguments novel, but not for novelty's sake. We need not only to be able to recognize junk when it is presented as fact, but to understand its nature and its source.

The message of this book is that empirical analysis often fails for conceptual—not technical—reasons. Sometimes the error is in the choice of methodology; sometimes, its execution. Just as often, the problem is the paradigm, the set-up of the issue. The expert is solving the wrong problem. The important implication of this understanding, for the judicial system, is that the skill judges need to deal with these studies is not technical. They need confidence in their own ability to discern when testimony is not making sense in the context of the case. That is the notion of "intellectuality," as contrasted with technical knowledge, that will emerge in the pages that follow.

Reality and This Book

That the real world does not live up to its mythic principles is hardly a surprise. My field, economics, perpetuates the myths of *homo economicus* (we all act only for ourselves, maximizing individual satisfaction) and perfect competition (consumers face small competitors who sell products—about which the consumers have complete knowledge—at their marginal cost), for example. Economists make policy recommendations from models that assume these myths.[17] Not all of that advice is helpful, but not all is as farcical as the assumptions on which it was built. Some conclusions may be "robust" to errors in assumptions, an important point to remember when we assess empirical studies offered to courts.[18] It facilitates discussion of the real system to set it against a model, even if the model is a myth. It also provides useful distinctions. And so I start with description, with conceptualization, with neat boundaries that will be blurred in practice, but define the language for the discussion that follows.

In Chapter 1 I outline three kinds of fact a court can find: constitutional, legislative, and adjudicative. I distinguish the "meta-debate" (the debate about principles of finding

---

17. From Coase (1988) the first chapter, written for the book (most of which is reprints of journal articles), at 28:

> The majority of economists . . . paint a picture of an ideal economic system, and then, comparing it with what they observe (or think they observe), they prescribe what is necessary to reach this ideal state without much consideration for how this could be done.

18. Box and Draper (1987) at 74:

> Remember that all models are wrong; the practical question is how wrong do they have to be to not be useful.

C. R. Rao:

> The current statistical methodology is mostly model-based, without any specific rules for model selection or validating a specified model.

Statistics: Reflections on the Past and Visions for the Future," *Amstat News* 327:2 (September 2004).

relevant information to answer a legal fact question—the choice of paradigm) from the methodological debate (the technical aspects of finding fact, assuming one has determined the broad principles—the questions that need to be answered).

I have to prove first that apparently "expert" analyses fail, and second that the root cause of such failures is the conceptions underlying them. I do so with explicit, challenging examples, in Chapters 2 through 5. Then I try to analyze the problem—the problem of poor analyses being offered to courts—from the point of view of the actors. It is easy enough to show that there are few incentives leading to presentation of penetrating analyses. Attorneys do not necessarily want them. In Chapter 6 I focus more on the attorney's interaction with data. Although I expose instances in which a judge was befuddled, Chapter 7 also applauds judges who understand and articulate the problem with the expert presentations they have suffered through. Chapter 8 is critical of experts, and demanding of the reader. It once again presents specific analyses in specific cases to establish my point. Although I expose technical failures, the more important defects are at a level more amenable to judicial rule.

Why do analysts misconceive litigation issues? I can only suggest, as I do in Chapter 9, that universities have become technologically—rather than conceptually—oriented. Professional experts reflect their training, and academic experts reflect their environments. If one's background matters, and if I have convinced the reader that social-science presentations in court lack intellectuality, more than methodology, then I should at least explore how this common university background affects expert presentations.

The Expert's Task

Laws are about procedures. Statistical studies are about outcomes. Many expert failures come down to such simple confusions. It is the job of the expert witness to start with a clear vision of what questions are appropriate given the complaint and the law. He should understand not only what questions can be asked within his expertise, but what questions *should* be asked. Then he can proceed to methodology: How can these questions be answered? Then he can proceed to conclusions: What are the answers to these relevant questions, and how strongly can one rely on those answers?

I illustrate in this book how badly experts perform these tasks. My material extends from library research to experience, from analysis of issues with which I have had no formal association to cases in which I have testified. My concern is always with the procedures by which we find "fact" in law, through statistical analysis.

Attorneys and Judges

One might think the adversary system is designed to ferret out expert flaws and biases. Some attorneys study statistics. They learn the language spoken by experts. I call for the expert to learn the language of litigation. In their briefs attorneys attack, rather than debate.

They often assault the person, not his work; or they engage in trivial sorties that, though technically meaningless, leave the impression of vulnerability. The attorney's search is for weakness, not error. His job is to destroy the other side's army. His own army is engaged for that purpose. Peacemakers (competent and unbiased experts) are seldom invited to the battle.

It is not the judge's job to pierce the veil of the expert's technology. His job is to determine whether that technology elucidates the fact issues before the court.

> All judges and most legislators and administrators come from the ranks of lawyers. These are people who typically ended up in law school because their prospects in science and math were dim.[19]

Judges know better than to believe experts. They should know better than to believe the attorney's representation of either his own expert's infallible study or the opposing expert's faulty one. Judges have an increasingly complex role as the "gatekeeper" of expert presentations.[20] They decide which studies shall become evidence. But once the gatekeeping decision has been made, and the expert is allowed into the process, the judge's real problems begin.

Do judges see through all of this and keep the experts straight? They can. Some do. I will discuss some opinions that indicate the apparent willingness of the bench to keep pace with the evolving complexity of statistics-based science evidence. I reject revising the required qualifications of the judiciary. Judges need not learn statistics. I argue, in Chapter 10, that basic statistics instruction does more harm than good. I call for stronger case management, and procedures that produce incentives for experts to be competent and honest. Judges may think attorney choice of expert is out of their hands. As a long-run proposition, I disagree.

THE FOLLOWING CHAPTERS

Chapter 1 contains a history of my profession. How did the introduction of "expertise" into a trial come about? Who does it? I will note some trends other than in the law that have contributed to the explosive growth in the use of statistical analysis as expertise in litigation.

The next two chapters appear to be organized by analysis method: selection and then regression. That is not the only way to see it. One point of Chapter 2 is to show that experts traditionally utilized incorrect statistical methods to solve a particular kind of selection problem. The major point, however, is that judges, although not having the tools to develop

---

19. Faigman (2000) at 53.

20. *Daubert* (1993) clearly imposed this role. The 1975 Federal Rules of Evidence had done so, but were not always understood that way.

a correct analysis, should have been able to reject faulty analyses. This chapter begins the demystification of statistical expertise in the courtroom. Where experts fail is in the relationship of the analysis to the law and institutions at issue.

In Chapter 3 I discuss how "experts" have bedazzled attorneys and judges alike with words that bear no relationship to their actual analyses, and "analyses" that are incapable of shedding light on the questions before the court. Regression is a fine statistical tool, but I show many instances in which neither experts nor their clients, and certainly not judges, understood it—not "understood" in the mathematical sense, but "understood" in the sense of realizing that the expert's results simply did not mean what he said they meant. I do not intend to condemn all experts, and certainly not all regression analyses. What Lizzy Borden did to her parents says nothing about the functionality of an axe. I do mean to demonstrate that there has been a lot less expertise than there pretends to be, and that the way to discern helpful from awful expert work is not through statistics, but through intelligent reasoning in law.

The story of Chapter 4 is how social scientists failed to grasp the moment in their harsh criticism of the Court's decisions on the size of the jury. Chapters 2 and 3 concern the failures and successes of social science in the courtroom. Chapter 4 concerns social scientists' failure in criticizing the lack of social science in the courtroom. I show that criticisms of a set of Supreme Court decisions on the size of the jury are themselves failed social science, because of a conceptually inappropriate approach to the question.

> Increased knowledge brings complexity rather than simplicity, uncertainty rather than certainty, frequently blurring distinctions rather than clarifying them. This knowledge thus becomes less helpful to the all-or-none, two-valued decision-making process of the law.[21]

The right approach might—just might—justify the Court's decisions on jury size. My work opens that possibility, creating doubt where self-satisfied social scientists expressed certainty. But, as I will express in several places, it is not the job of social science to draw lines for judges, only to provide some measures to inform judges what their line-drawing means.

Selection issues return in Chapter 5. Here I take on both in-court analysts and academic commentators. The subject is the composition of persons recruited to become jurors, with respect to constitutional provisions that jury-gathering be impartial. The Supreme Court (and federal law) thinks that means the outcome should be "representative" of some "community." When the Court substitutes "representative" for "impartial," it substitutes an outcome for what surely was originally seen as a procedural constraint on juror selection. When it substitutes "population" for "community," it also substitutes an

---

21. Diamond (1974) at 451.

outcome for a procedure in which who is in the "community" is determined within the jury-selection process. What is needed is to understand "impartial" and "community" as procedural terms.

One influential law-review article appeared to supply rigor to the Supreme Court's outcome-oriented direction. In the more than thirty-five years since its publication, neither the Court nor any academic in this field has seen its essential fallacy, or that of the entire line of jury-representation analyses and cases. Analysts posit a statistical model that cannot be estimated. Pretending to estimate it, they often obtain the wrong answer. I suggest an entirely different way to analyze jury representation issues, one that has infuriated opposing experts, but been accepted by every judge to whom it has been put forward.

Chapter 5 also forms the foundation for my assertion that experts should be more familiar with the laws under which they work. They should not accept the role of legal eunuch, the role that current rules and practices assign to them. I do not expand on that point until Chapter 8, however.

Here is another take on Chapters 2 through 5. Chapters 2 and 3 are about the failure of experts to understand their tools, using the wrong ones or using them improperly. They are about statistical methodology, but (it is my intention) framed in a way that attorneys and judges should understand. Chapters 4 and 5 take a larger view. They are about paradigms, approaches to legal questions. They are part of the meta-debate, how we go about finding relevant facts in law in a broad sense. Chapters 2 and 3 are as much about the analyst failing to answer well-framed questions, as their being the wrong questions. It can be read as about technical or conceptual error. Chapters 4 and 5 are more clearly about the framing itself. The analysts' answers may be correct, but their questions were not.

With these four chapters I intend to establish that many analyses considered good, even expert, are failures because the expert lacks the understanding necessary to produce relevant work in the litigation context. Attorneys want experts who seem to support them, even if they do so irrelevantly. Judges often decide the questions posed by the attorneys, rather than the questions posed by the law.

I will demonstrate that bringing academics into the system is no answer, because the best of academics are often the worst of experts. Chapters 6 through 8 use my experiences, the examples provided in Chapters 2 through 5, and research material to discuss attorneys as clients and adversaries, judges as determiners of good science, and experts as all too often not up to the task they have taken on.

In Chapter 9 I follow academic experts back to their home base, the university, wondering how they can get away with such bad work. One answer appears to be that they do not bring litigation back to school, at least not to educate. This is a loss to them and their students. I also illustrate just how badly some "experts" mangle their own work, and how they, their professional organizations, and publishers suppress exposure of it. Where

Chapter 9 most fits in the puzzle, however, is in my suggestion that academia was noticeably misdirected in the 1960s through 1980s towards technology, away from good thinking. This is a problem that suggests its own solution.

Chapter 10 is about the rules of expert-witness work in relation to attorneys and courts. I contribute to the discussion about procedures for dealing with "science" experts, an active subject in the law-review literature, and almost completely devoid of input from experts themselves. In previous chapters I have argued that the system is seriously flawed: Fact is hard to pull out of expert presentations, experts are not there to help, and judges are ill-equipped to function without the help the experts should—but fail to—provide. In Chapter 10 I try to develop a theory of how this dilemma is evolving, and suggest who can arrest it and how.

This book is not a cry for help. It is an offer of help. Chapter 10 is an attempt to move forward, draw conclusions, set some standards, and at least understand, perhaps improve, the system of fact finding in the courts. The most important part of Chapter 10 is the development of a framework for judicial assessment of expert presentations. Legal scholars have been asking how judges can assess experts under *Daubert* (1993). My answer is that there is no single way. I define four kinds of expert, which are distinguishable by and large easily and cleanly. This classification leads to different methods of assessing expert work.

I also suggest changes to procedures with the goal of improving discernment among judges, so that attorneys have more incentives to bring better expert work to trial. I offer no magic bullet, no single key to the king's gold.[22] Chapter 10 is long, difficult, and, I think, rewarding. Then again, I would characterize the entire book the same way.

You will do best reading all the chapters in order, with their footnotes. After each chapter that has an appendix, I suggest glancing at it. Appendix material supports and amplifies—but is not fundamental to—the rest of the book. The harried reader can get by with skipping the appendices entirely, skimming Chapters 1, 3, 4, 6, and 9, reading the others with more care. Chapter 2 demonstrates how badly experts mangle the simplest of statistical issues by faulty framing of the question. Chapter 5 is revolutionary, but requires some knowledge of the material in Chapter 2. Chapters 7 and 8 use lessons learned in Chapters 2 and 3 to explore the awful testimony provided in several fields, and judicial reaction thereto. Some stories begun in one chapter end in another, because the point is the lesson to be learned, not descriptions of cases. Chapter 10 is visionary, but will not make much sense without some knowledge of the preceding material. The Coda applies this book's lessons to two issues, pointing out the applicability of this seemingly dense technical work to the public interest.

---

22. At least I am not alone. Posner (1985), for example, wrote brilliantly about the expanding caseload confronting federal judges. He had little to offer in the way of remedy.

1

The Evolution of the Expert Witness

I define three kinds of fact, and therefore, with the same names, three debates, areas of arguments about proofs of fact:

> constitutional;
>
> legislative; and
>
> adjudicative (or "record").

These words are found in law books, and taught in law schools.[1] Both to bring non-attorneys along and to be clear how I am using these words—which might not be exactly how attorneys use them—I will explain my usage (and their importance) here.

Constitutional Fact

"Constitutional" fact is the meaning of the Constitution; the meaning of legislation; the meaning of precedent decisions. Finding these facts is the traditional and virtually exclusive province of people with law degrees, with some help from historians. I refer to constitutional debates as "strictly legal" debates,[2] because no data-based statistical evidence—the sort con-

---

1. Monaghan (1985) at 231, footnote 17:

> The term "constitutional fact" was first used by Professor Dickinson in his insightful analysis of *Crowell v. Benson*, 285 U.S. 22 (1932) and its antecedents

The Dickinson reference is 80 *University of Pennsylvania Law Review* 1055 (1932). The classic explication of legislative and adjudicative fact is by K. Davis (1942), though perhaps his later discussion in K. Davis (1955) is clearer. See also Marlow (1998). These distinctions are also used in Monahan and Walker (1986), Walker and Monahan (1987), and Walker and Monahan (1988).

2. The phrase "strictly legal" can be derived from Dahl (1957):

> To consider the Supreme Court of the United States strictly as a legal institution is to underestimate its significance in the American political system. . . . What is critical is the extent to which a court can and does make policy decisions by going outside established "legal" criteria found in precedent, statute, and constitution.

sidered to be "science" evidence in this book—is brought to bear on constitutional issues. Indeed, "constitutional fact" may be another term for "law." In principle there is a difference between fact and law. Judges, in their formal opinions, relate their findings about them separately. However, as I want to bring judges along to thinking that they can be part of the fact-finding process—even when it is statistical fact that is being found—it serves my purpose to explain that determining the law is finding a particular kind of fact.

Legislative Fact

"Legislative" facts are statements we believe about populations. They may be descriptive:

> Women are weak.

> Children are susceptible to temptation.

> Hispanics register to vote at a lower rate than non-Hispanics.

They may be implications derived from these descriptions:

> Because women are weak physically, long hours of work do more harm to them than to men.

> Because children are weak-willed, the state has a special duty to interfere with their decisions.

> Because Hispanics have a lower voter-registration rate, they will not appear on juries that are based on voter lists in proportion to their presence in the population.

The term "legislative fact" is derived, no doubt, from the lawmaking capacity of the judicial system.

> The Constitution lives on in a changing world because it grows not only by formal amendment but also by "interpretation"—a process in which the judiciary plays a large, yet by no means exclusive, role. Lawmaking, then, is an inherent and inevitable part of the judicial process.[3]

> It has been sometimes said that the Law is composed of two parts—legislative law and judge-made law, but in truth all the Law is judge-made law. The shape in which a statute is imposed on the community as a guide for conduct is that statute as interpreted by the courts.[4]

Reprint in Levy (1967) at 106. Here it is in use:

> The first question before the Supreme Court—a strictly legal question—was whether the drafters of the 1975 Federal Rules of Evidence had intended to incorporate *Frye* explicitly into the new rules. The Court [in *Daubert* (1993)] concluded they hadn't.

Foster and Huber (1997) at 13.

3. Mendelson (1967) at 3.

4. J. Gray (1960) at 125, quoted in Kurland (1970) at 69.

It is an admission that judges engage in the same kind of activity as legislators, and therefore require the same kind of information.

Legislative facts are generalizations about the world, not about the specific situation or people involved in the case at hand.[5] More broadly, as I will use the term in Chapter 10, someone who would have a particular type of evidence never be accepted in court (say, phrenology) is making a legislative-fact argument.

Adjudicative Fact

"Adjudicative" disputes concern facts about the parties to the case. Whether this butler did it, not whether butlers do it more than non-butlers.[6]

> Hence, "adjudicative facts" refers to facts established through testimony and physical exhibits introduced by the parties in an adversarial setting at hearings and trials.[7]

Expert witnesses express opinions about legislative fact in general (the world operates this way), but about adjudicative fact specifically (the parties in this case acted this way). The adjudicative-fact argument about phrenology testimony is whether this expert in this case can provide information about the particular events in dispute.

Of course these three different kinds of fact are abstractions, their boundaries blurred.[8] They raise the question: Where do facts come from? Or, where does the "fact finder" in litigation get his (or, if a jury, its) facts? Constitutional facts are argued by lawyers. Some facts are presented by non-expert ("lay") witnesses. These are almost always adjudicative facts,

---

5. *Sheehan* (1997) at 942:

> Everyone knows that younger people are on average more comfortable with computers than older people are, just as older people are on average more comfortable with manual-shift cars than younger people are.

Mister (1987) at 1432:

> People generally want jobs close to home.

6. Freund (1954), at 47, explains:

> A law forbidding the sale of beverages containing more than 3.2 percent of alcohol would raise a question of legislative fact, i.e., whether this standard has a reasonable relation to public health, morals, and the enforcement problem. A law forbidding the sale of intoxicating beverages (assuming it is not so vague as to require supplementation by rule-making) would raise a question of adjudicative fact, i.e., whether this or that beverage is intoxicating within the meaning of the statute and the limits on governmental action imposed by the Constitution.

7. Marlow (1998) at 303.

8. Monaghan (1985) at 231, footnote 16:

> Like other legal distinctions, the difference between adjudicative and legislative fact is one of degree, and for that reason the existence of borderline cases does not mean that the distinction is empty.

the witnesses being parties to the case or "fact" witnesses, persons with some knowledge of the events in dispute. Experts, then, are not the only source of judicial fact.

Facts can be adopted by judges without prompting from attorneys.[9] "Judicial notice" is the term under which a court accepts fact without requiring that experts debate it. Judicial notice is perhaps usually taken of an adjudicative fact, such as that there was a stop sign on a particular corner, or that the general speed limit in a city is thirty-five miles per hour, even if there is no sign in a particular place stating what that limit is. However, legislative fact, also, may be asserted by the judge, or brought to his attention by attorneys and then adopted by judicial notice.[10]

META-ARGUMENTS

Meta-arguments concern the kind of evidence that would be required to have a court accept something as fact. That there are meta-arguments in law is not a novel concept, only an important one. There are meta-arguments in all fields, sometimes called competing philosophies.

> There is no single philosophy of science to be understood and adopted, but rather a choice of positions, each representing a different account of science.[11]

---

9. Miller (1968) at 217:

> Information is garnered from wherever a Justice may find it—and according to his personal standards of relevance.

10. Imwinkelried (1995) at 71, quoting from Conrad, *Modern Trial Evidence* (1956):

> The traditional basis for judicial notice is that the proposition in question is a matter of common knowledge within the territorial jurisdiction of the court. "Courts should at least know what everybody else knows."

For example, *Local 638* (1975) at 481:

> It is a fact of which the court takes judicial notice that non-white persons obtain high school diplomas at a lower rate than do whites.

Peteet (1989) at 1432:

> We may take judicial notice that the facts relied on by Dr. Teitelbaum are those usually considered by medical experts.

McAsey (2002) at 1097:

> A court may take judicial notice of standard mortality tables.

The assertion of Cappalli (2002) at 101 that judicial notice operates "exclusively in the domain of adjudicative fact" is simply wrong. See Peggy Davis (1987) at 1540:

> [T]he legislative-fact concept has become firmly established within the judicial notice pigeonhole of evidence scholarship.

Kenneth Culp Davis wanted judicial notice to "extend to facts and sources that are disputable." K. Davis (1955) at 952.

11. Caudill and Redding (2000) at 702.

We will see, for example, that until the 1950s courts were loathe to accept adjudicative generalizations from samples. There was no methodological debate about how large a sample had to be, or how it should be drawn, or by whom. The decision was made at a grander level of argument, the meta-notion that inference from a sample was unacceptable no matter how it was done. I will briefly go through these three kinds of facts, outlining what kinds of meta-arguments they generate.

The Constitutional Argument

We can discern three constitutional paradigms, ways of approaching how to solve the constitutional dilemma, "What does the law say?"

> **Strict construction (or "original intent")**. The Constitution means what its Framers intended it to mean, or a law means what its congressional proponents explained it to mean, in terms of the activities protected or the rights adhering equally to all citizens.
>
> **Living Constitution.** Issues arise which the Framers could not have imagined, or social knowledge (see below) has so changed that the Constitution requires a fresh interpretation; laws that once seemed constitutional no longer are, etc.
>
> **Pragmatic.** Only the effect of a constitutional decision matters. Textual analysis both in a historical sense (what did the language mean then) and a current sense (what should it mean now) should give way to an examination of the effect of a decision.

Charles Black considers constitutional arguments the kind

> which the trained lawyer, as such, is skilled in dealing with . . . a question of the sort that lawyers deal with every day.[12]

Yet in a large part they are meta-arguments. They are arguments about what to debate, not the substantive debate itself.

The constitutional argument is about the right of government to interfere with actions by private parties, or the right of the judicial system to interfere with an action by private parties or other branches of government. If one chooses a strict-constructionist approach, then the "facts" in dispute are about what words or phrases meant to the Framers of the

---

12. C. Black (1960) at 173. Levy (1967) argues that "Lawyers . . . are poorly qualified to decide such questions." He suggests, for example, at 29, that economic issues "could be better settled by a panel of economists . . . than by a group of judges." Each profession seems to have more regard for the expertise of other professions than its own. I shudder at the thought of leaving economic questions to economists, I doubt that historians are the best people to analyze the history of the judicial system, and obviously I will not leave the study of litigation to lawyers and "legal scholars."

Constitution or its Amendments, or to legislators when bills were being formed into acts. The data, the material from which factual conclusions are drawn, are writings of the Framers, newspaper accounts of the times, transcripts or reports of legislative debates; and the antecedent material utilized by the Framers, such as the English common law, the *Commentaries* of Coke and Blackstone, existing state constitutions, etc.[13]

If one thinks the appropriate debate is, rather, how to interpret the constitution and legislation *now*, one does not engage in the strict-constructionist debate. "Living" Constitution debates are about social knowledge—what we think we, as a society, know, and how to apply that knowledge to the issue at hand. How we can re-interpret the words of the Constitution as if they were written today, not as the Framers meant then.

The pragmatic approach is the least formalized and least restricted of the constitutional debates. Everyone wants his solution to be "pragmatic."[14] Advocates of that standard, however, propose no principle by which that effect can be evaluated, and leave no principle in their wake by which the next issue can be determined. We are living in an era of the "pragmatic" Court, which says in *Grutter* (2003) that a little racial discrimination is OK, as long as it favors minorities and is called something else. When there is a principled decision, such as in *Blakely* (2004), the dissents worry about the impending fall of federal sentencing guidelines and other difficulties created for the bureaucracy. They do not argue that the principle is wrong—only impractical.

The Warren Court's interpretations of the Fourteenth Amendment were (and still are) criticized from a strict-constructionist viewpoint.[15] Believing that outcomes of previous constitutional debates should hold some authority for a current one—the principle

---

13. See Blackstone (1793). The first edition of his *Commentaries* was published in four volumes between 1765 and 1769.

14. Caudill and Redding (2000) at 688, for example, propose "a pragmatic approach to scientific evidence we call 'pragmatic constructivism,'" in discussing the implications of *Daubert* (1993), a case that will form part of the history, below, and much of Chapter 10. Pragmatic? Who could be against that? It could be that, when accosted by a police officer, a person should answer all "reasonable" questions. Or it could be that the police can ask, but "have no right to compel,"an answer; *Davis* (1969) at 727, a view reiterated in *Berkemer* (1984)—"the detainee is not obliged to respond," at 439—and other cases. Suddenly, in *Hiibel* (2004), the police *do* have the right to compel a person to identify himself, because "Asking questions is an essential part of police investigations." It is "a routine and accepted part" of traffic stops, 124 S.Ct. at 2458. No principle, as the dissenters point out, supports this sop to the police, this "special exception" to an otherwise "clear rule." Justice Breyer at 2466.

15. For example see Justice Harlan in dissent, *Reynolds* (1964) at 595:

The history of the adoption of the Fourteenth Amendment provides conclusive evidence that neither those who proposed nor those who ratified the Amendment believed that the Equal Protection Clause limited the power of the States to apportion their legislatures as they saw fit. Moreover, the history demonstrates that the intention to leave this power undisturbed was deliberate and was widely believed to be essential to the adoption of the Amendment.

of *stare decisis*—critics have noted the Warren Court's sharp breaks with precedent.

> [The Warren Court] has paid less heed to *stare decisis*—one of the features that Cardozo pointed out as distinguishing legislative legislation from judicial legislation—than any Supreme Court in History.[16]

"The task here undertaken is that of an historian, to attempt accurately and faithfully to assemble the facts," writes Raoul Berger, castigating "revisionist historians."[17] The Warren Court misrepresented the intentions of the Framers of the Fourteenth Amendment, Berger says. Those intentions form the correct basis on which to decide, are the basis on which the court pretended to decide, yet correct knowledge of them would lead one to different conclusions from the Court's.

These are irrelevant considerations if one takes a different position in the constitutional meta-debate. These days, much of the constitutional debater's energy is expended in the meta-debate, in discussing which debate to have. We thus often hear debates about the rules of the debate, not about the issues; about principles of decision making, not about principles of the decision.[18]

As tiresome as such arguments may be, they are also fundamental. Would that more such debates were generated about factual issues in particular cases. Much of what passes as legal argument is not resolvable by fact, as each party has a different view of what "fact" is relevant, though they might well agree on what each party's facts are. In Chapter 4, for example, we will see that the strict constructionist's view of fact—how many people the founding fathers considered constituted a jury—was never questioned. Its relevance to determining constitutional fact, was. The Supreme Court's acceptance of fewer than twelve jurors surely was a triumph of the pragmatic camp in the constitutional meta-debate.[19] But there was no analogous meta-debate in the legal and scientific literature regarding the mathematical models that led all commentators to declare that the Court had erred. As I show in Chapter 4, such a debate was called for.

Although I do no more than allude to it here, I think the rise of social-science "fact" in law and the decline of the strict-constructionist form of constitutional debate are related.

---

16. Kurland (1970) at 186.

17. R. Berger (1997) at 6.

18. See, for example, the sparring between Harriet Pilpel and Raoul Berger on the PBS television program *Firing Line*, October 5, 1977. Transcript (at one time) available from Southern Educational Communications Association. Reasoned debates about what principles should be used to make decisions are rarely seen or heard in popular media any more. Stanley Fish provides a badly flawed exception, arguing that only "original intent" survives scrutiny. See "Intentional Neglect," *New York Times*, op-ed, July 19, 2005.

19. The Supreme Court's upholding of the Election Contribution Reform Act, *McConnell* (2003), is another triumph of the pragmatic camp. That it came as a surprise is probably a hallmark of pragmatic decisions.

The rise of the social-science expert, the acceptance of his "fact" in resolving disputes, has provided a perhaps illusory acceptance of scientific "fact." Empirical social science has altered judicial concepts of "data," of "proof," and, hence, of "fact." Its entry into law has changed law, changed the debate about law, in ways that deserve more historical scrutiny than I can provide here.

The Legislative-Fact Argument

If the constitutional argument is about the meaning of the Constitution or legislation, any other argument would seem to be "extralegal." As the term is used, however, "extralegal" facts are those that enter the judicial process upon the motion of an attorney and acceptance by the judge, not through an expert subject to cross-examination. It is a procedural, not an analytic term. Over time the system has accepted, even required, more and more facts. They are sometimes debated, sometimes accepted without debate. What facts are "extralegal," therefore, is a historical phenomenon. Most important, recently, and most relevant to this book, some facts are not known, and are not even knowable by the direct participants in a particular case. To find these facts requires special skills. Hence, we have experts.

One meta-argument about legislative facts is whether they have to be correct—can legislation be overturned if the factual predicate for it is shown to be false—or merely believable—the legislature may rationally believe what it took to be fact, so the court does not have to determine if the legislature was correct. The decision on the meta-argument sets out an agenda for debate about fact. It would therefore be helpful if courts made their meta-argument determinations before asking the parties to present their factual arguments. Few courts operate that way, however. One of the inefficiencies in the judicial system is having parties prepare factual arguments that are *then* declared irrelevant through a decision at the meta-argument level.[20]

Chapter 4 presents a meta-argument that the critics of the Court's decisions on jury size did not consider. Once the constitutional questions had been answered—juries could have fewer than twelve members—the question became one of legislative fact: What effect would smaller juries have? No one pretends to know, or be able to find out, what effect jury size might have in a particular case. Courts legislate on generalities. The Appendix to

---

20. An example is *McCleskey* (1987), which I describe in Chapter 8. As Faigman (1989) summarizes, at 1094:

> The *McCleskey* decision exemplifies how, through a court's interpretation of the law, social science research can become irrelevant because the factual questions the research answers have become irrelevant.

Had that determination been known, plaintiffs would have been spared the considerable effort and expense of their empirical study of differential death penalties, depending on the races of perpetrator and victim.

Chapter 4 presents some notation that will be familiar to people who know the jury-size debate, and shows why that debate missed the mark. Chapter 4 itself contains a graphic demonstration that critics of the Supreme Court's acceptance of fewer than twelve jurors on a jury were asking the wrong questions.

Relevant Adjudicative Fact

One meta-argument about adjudicative fact, whether inferences can be drawn from sample data, was mentioned above. Another meta-argument is what data would be relevant to the judicial decision. For example, if a corporation posts a sign, "No Blacks May Apply," then surely one could not estimate from application data how many blacks a non-discriminating employer would have hired. However, suppose there is no such sign, but one party thinks that "too few" blacks have applied. That party will argue to substitute census data (so-called "availability analysis," discussed in Chapter 2) for applicant data. That was, in essence, the difference between the district court's finding from an inappropriate availability analysis in *Lamp* (1985) and the appeals court's reversal based partly on applicant data in *Lamp* (1991).

Thus, once—in meta-argument—the court accepts adjudicative fact in principle, the question becomes which adjudicative facts are relevant.[21] Only when the experts agree on the paradigm can they meaningfully debate the methodology that would provide the best answer. Chapter 5, concerning the empirical meaning of the constitutional requirement that a jury be "impartial," is fully in the meta-argument sphere. I have been willing to stipulate in trials that if the opposing expert wants to answer the question he is asking, his method applied to his data provides a sufficiently accurate answer—one the court should ignore on meta-argument grounds. Chapter 5 is longer than I wish it were because it is not about methodology, but about paradigm; and because it shows that the universally accepted paradigm is the wrong one.

Social Knowledge

How do meta-arguments get resolved? Surely judges have preconceptions, at least ideologies, which dictate to them the answers to the meta-questions of a case.[22] David Caudill asks,

---

21. In *Lamp* there were the expected methodological disputes about how to determine the "available" work force. The case exploded out of proportion to its intrinsic importance with the district court's insistence on substituting a particularly inappropriate measure for a plain adjudicative fact: The defendant hired blacks in excess of the proportion who applied. Fortunately, the Seventh Circuit got it right. I discuss *Lamp* in further detail in Chapter 7.

22. Susan U. Phillips claims to have decoded ideological differences among judges, in *Ideology in the Language of Judges: How Judges Practice Law, Politics, and Courtroom Control*, Oxford University Press (1998). Griffin (1999), in reviewing Phillips at 399, reports that "boredom with an uncomplicated procedure,

"How does one frame an inquiry into the social aspects of science?" Then he informs us:

> We do not even have a language, a discursive tradition, in legal literature
> concerning the matter.[23]

Paul Rosen argues that, overtly or not, courts always have some social and physical conceptions of the world. These are the filters through which evidence is passed.

> To be sure, the high bench from its outset has often made constitutional law
> on the basis of factual judgements that were not inherently legal. . . . As we shall
> see, the court has assessed and defined fact situations in terms of hypotheses,
> assumptions, and social data that were regarded legally as facts even though
> they were derived from disciplines or sources plainly not internal to law.[24]

For example, Kenneth Clark blamed the Supreme Court's decision in *Plessy* (1896), in which public accommodations segregated by race were declared constitutional as long as they were "equal," on then-current social-science teachings.

> One might assume that the *Plessy* decision was an implicit reflection of the
> social science theory and knowledge available at the close of the 19th Century.[25]

Kenneth Karst quotes Oliver Wendell Holmes to the effect that "in substance the growth of the law is legislative," and goes on to add:

> Uncomfortable as a court may be beyond the area of its special competence,
> the court's legislative function requires it to be informed on matters far
> beyond the facts of the particular case.[26]

Rosen concludes that:

> Since legislative facts are in effect a synonym for sociological analysis, it would
> seem inevitable that the legislature that formulated them, or the court that
> reviewed them, would take note of the social sciences.[27]

---

full dockets, or even dislike for one of the attorneys" may affect at least the language, if not the behavior of judges, but suggests that the idea that they differ ideologically—and that such differences matter in their opinions—is old news. So it is:

> Whatever may be thought of this holding as a piece of political ideology . . . I think it
> demonstrable that the Fourteenth Amendment does not impose this political tenet on the
> States or authorize this Court to do so.

Justice Harlan dissenting in *Reynolds* (1964) at 590.

23. Caudill (2002) at 1804.

24. P. Rosen (1972) at 12. Assisting courts' understanding and acceptance of "social facts" was the goal of Note (1948).

25. K. Clark (1953) at 5.

26. Karst (1960) at 76. The Holmes quotation is from *The Common Law* (1881) at 35. This same passage from Holmes is quoted by Kurland (1970) at 173.

27. P. Rosen (1972) at 53.

All societies utilize whatever knowledge they have, be it in the form of assumptions, conclusions, or religious faith, to structure their institutions. Court procedures reflect what we believe we know about how to determine what we "know" about the world. In the Middle Ages, for example,

> grand juries would indict and choose among the ordeals of fire, water, and iron as the fittest test of guilt or innocence in the particular case before them.[28]

Both the concept of trial by ordeal and the choice of the particularly relevant ordeal must have been governed by some commitment to a fact-finding process.

Chapters 4 and 5 concern the size and selection of the petit jury, a body often called upon to determine the facts of the case (some cases being decided by judges alone). The petit jury as fact finder is derived from fact-finding conceptions that had to be developed when the church banned the trial by ordeal early in the thirteenth century A.D. The notion of the independent jury—jurors selected for their a priori ignorance of the facts—was not clearly established in the English tradition until the seventeenth or eighteenth century. The concept that the accused could challenge some jurors preceded the independent jury ("He's not really a witness"), but its retention with the independent jury created an additional question. Any witness could be (and still can be) challenged, but how many "peremptory" challenges to independent jurors—dismissal at the discretion of one party—could there be? Societies have to answer these questions; they make a decision of the form, "X in general produces Y in the society in which we live."

The Supreme Court used this form of legislative fact, X leads to Y, to find segregation impermissible in the middle of the twentieth century, when it came to believe that racial segregation per se has bad societal consequences. The debate turned around again towards the end of the century when many black voices argued in favor of segregated schooling, including curricula tailored for the specialized students they think their children are.[29] California tried to institute gender-segregated schools although the Supreme Court has banned state-supported single-gender university education.[30] Has social knowledge changed? Have the facts changed? Has their importance changed? Do we not know what the facts are?

Are the facts relevant? Isn't segregation wrong—that is, neither a legitimate state function nor tolerable in public institutions—regardless of its consequence? Perhaps if we had

---

28. C. Wells (1911). Wells does not attempt to list (or describe) all ordeals, but these are all that he mentions by name. Trial by ordeal, trial by battle, proof by witness, and compurgation are the "four older methods of trial" mentioned by L. Rosenthal (1935) at 406. Tigar and Levy (1977) at 36 mention trial by ordeal, trial by battle, and "other mystical means of determining truth."

29. See for example, James S. Kunen, "Integration Forever?" 150 *Time* 3 (July 21, 1997).

30. As Justice Ginsburg noted for the Court, the trial about VMI's exclusion of females "involved an array of expert witnesses on each side." See *VMI* (1996) at 521.

a clearer view of when facts matter, we might spend less time in court trying to determine what they are.[31]

Courts evolve in their acceptance of fact, their determination of fact, their use of fact. In *Muller* (1908), it was argued that details about the physiology of women (X), led to physical harm (Y) under current labor practices. That legislatures could rationally believe this relationship to be fact permitted laws preventing the "equal" employment of women. However, in *Dothard* (1977), it was argued that the physiology of women, in this case the height and weight distribution of women (X), led to their disparate exclusion from employment as prison guards in Alabama under existing minimum qualifications (Y). Unless those qualifications were valid, this legislative fact argued that they should be struck down. And in *VMI* (1996), it was accepted as fact that some women *could* meet the physical requirements of the Virginia Military Institute, and so (accepting these standards as valid) such women should be admitted. The factual issue then became adjudicative, asking whether these particular plaintiffs were harmed by the requirements.[32]

The ways in which social knowledge becomes incorporated in judicial decisions can be arrayed from assumption (essentially, ideology), to judicial notice, to briefed arguments about legislative fact, to social-science assertions and judicial acceptance thereof with regard to legislative fact, to the more recent and more difficult statistical "proof" of adjudicative fact. Although this last area will dominate this text, learning how we got there is a relevant aspect of knowing where we are.

THE DETERMINATION OF LEGISLATIVE FACT

The facts, we are told, cry out for the decision that is being made.[33] If courts are to resolve the issues brought before them, they require some concept of fact to do so. Over and above the specific facts of the case are more general fact questions, like what is the accepted prac-

---

31. I will briefly touch on this issue in Chapter 3, discussing *Hobson II*. The problem with asserting "fact" as a rationale for action is that one acts as if the fact were certain, something one "knows." "Fact" that drives broad social decisions is a prediction, something one "thinks." Decisions based on principles, not facts, might be inherently more worthy.

32. The factual question in *Dothard* (1977) of whether the plaintiff Rawlinson herself was eliminated by physical requirements is merely an issue of her standing to represent others "similarly situated." The adjudicative issue is whether the regulation has unjustified adverse impact against women, under the theory set out in *Griggs* (1971). *VMI* (1996) is a throwback to the days of *de jure* segregation, but because military training is such a sacred cow, the Court had to do more than just say that a state's interest in segregating trainees cannot override *Brown* (1954).

33. For example, after a brief introduction to the legal issues, the opening paragraphs of *Goodridge* (2003), in which the Massachusetts Supreme Court allowed marriage between partners of the same sex, described the plaintiffs in some detail. Just the facts. The implication: These are good people, model citizens who would be denied their equal rights without the path-breaking decision this court was making.

tice, what is the relationship between this result and its alleged cause, etc. Courts require some procedure by which to obtain and assess science and social-science fact. In *Schollenberger* (1898) Justice Peckham, writing for the Court, referred to

> those facts which are so well and universally known that courts will take notice of them without particular proof being adduced in regard to them.[34]

He then referred to "encyclopedias of the day" and "official reports of the commissioner of agriculture," indicating that "every intelligent man knows" the truth of which the Court is taking notice. In *Holden*, earlier in the same year, the Court had explicitly utilized such facts, and *Holden* is subsequently cited in many cases in which judicial notice is taken of legislative fact.

The Legislative Brief

The first attorney to produce a legislative-fact argument to the Supreme Court apparently was Julius M. Mayer, attorney for the defendant (New York State) in *Lochner* (1905). Justice Harlan, in dissent (joined by White and Day), quotes from "Professor Hirt in his treatise on the 'Diseases of the Workers'" and other works presumably brought to his attention by Mayer's brief.[35] However, probably because Mayer lost the case, and possibly also because Mayer did not stress his legislative-fact arguments as much, credit for introducing this kind of argument before the Supreme Court has gone to Louis D. Brandeis. In *Muller* (1908), Brandeis successfully defended protective legislation by reminding the Court that it had expressed an openness to other than constitutional arguments. He then presented a legislative-fact argument, which the Court accepted:

> It may not be amiss, in the present case, before examining the constitutional question, to notice the course of legislation, as well as expressions of opinion from other than judicial sources.[36]

Paraphrasing the court's acceptance in *Holden* (1898), Justice Brewer for the *Muller* court rationalized this practice, saying, "We take judicial cognizance of all matters of general knowledge."

As Paul Rosen and others show, the Supreme Court started down the road toward findings of legislative fact when it accepted the notion of "substantive due process," which comes into play when the outcome of legislation contradicts some constitutional privilege.

---

34. *Schollenberger* (1898) at 8; following in-text quotations at 10.
35. *Lochner* (1905) at 70. The defense responded in kind. Collins (1978) concludes at 149 that biased research presented in the employer's brief circumvented the traditional standard and succeeded in influencing the majority of the court. Social research and development was off to a roaring start—on the wrong foot.
36. *Muller* (1908) at 419; following in-text quotation at 421.

In *Powell* (1888), the Court allowed Pennsylvania to ban manufacture or sale of oleo-margarine. The determination that the product was unworthy of sale may or may not have been scientifically correct, but it was legitimately the Pennsylvania legislature's decision to make, said the Court. On the other hand, in *Schollenberger* (1898), the Court prevented the same legislature from forbidding the importation of oleomargarine, because that legislation affected interstate commerce. *Powell* did not require the finding of fact, but rather the finding that the legislature could reasonably believe what it took to be the facts.[37] In *Schollenberger*, in contrast, the Court felt obliged to defend the wholesomeness of the product before inflicting it on the citizens of Pennsylvania.[38]

Muller was much like *Powell*. The Oregon legislature had passed protective legislation, in this instance limiting the hours of work for women to ten a day. However, although the authority of the legislature to protect its citizens was still formally intact,[39] it had suffered serious setbacks. In *Lochner*, New York legislation restricting the hours of bakery employees to ten a day had been struck down because it violated the "right of the individual to labor for such time as he may choose"[40] or, more generally, the

> right of the individual to his personal liberty or to enter into those contracts in relation to labor which may seem appropriate or necessary for the support of himself and his family.

---

37. Surely no one was fooled by all of this. The Pennsylvania legislature was acting to protect its butter industry. Justice Field's lone dissent in *Powell* (1888) was not based on a dispute of the facts, but on a meta-issue, an economic theory by which no facts could justify the legislative interference with free enterprise. See Mendelson (1967) at 19. On the evolution from substantive due process to finding legislative fact, see P. Rosen (1972) at 54.

38. In *New Energy* (1988), in contrast, the unanimous Court took judicial notice that all ethanol is the same. At 279:

> As far as ethanol use in Ohio itself is concerned, there is no reason to suppose that ethanol produced in a State that does not offer tax advantages to ethanol produced in Ohio is less healthy, and thus should have its importation into Ohio suppressed by denial of the otherwise standard tax credit.

State favoritism is still with us. Some states (for example, New York) allowed mail or internet purchase, and home delivery, of in-state wine, but denied those privileges for out-of-state wine. The Supreme Court put a stop to it in *Granholm* (2005).

39. *Holden* (1898) had upheld a Utah law restricting hours of work of miners, taking judicial notice of the extraordinary hazards involved in that occupation, but also remarking that the law excluded emergencies, when miners could not get out. Language in *Schollenberger* (1898) stressed that the reasoning of *Powell* (1888) still held. Pennsylvania could still forbid manufacture and sale, but not importation, of oleomargarine. If this were seriously true, the importers could not sell the product. But this would be a restriction on interstate commerce, so obviously sale of the imported product had to be allowed.

40. *Lochner* (1905) at 46; following indented quotation at 56. The Court displays an ignorance of the world (or, one might argue, a class bias) in language that appears to be solicitous of the rights of employees. Lochner was the proprietor of the bakery, as Muller was of the Grand Laundry in Portland, Oregon. In *Coppage* (1915) the Court upholds the right of the St. Louis and San Francisco Railway Company to

Since from *Lochner* one would believe that legislation limiting hours of work for all employees would not be sustained, Brandeis emphasized that only women were protected by the Oregon statute, and provided evidence that the physical difference of females called for legislative protection.

Didn't this violate the Fourteenth Amendment, which said that laws had to be equally applicable to everyone? Not if women had special needs, or at least if the Oregon legislature believed that they did. The Brandeis brief contained reviews of studies of women at work, and inspection reports providing detail on the nature of industrial life.[41] The court found that the difference between men and women "justifies a difference in legislation,"[42] and sustained an act that surely would neither be passed nor sustained if passed today. Aggressive presentation of social-science legislative fact had been accepted by the Supreme Court, and had proved decisive.

Although the Court had several times stated that it would take notice of legislative facts, that still left undetermined how they would come to its attention, and to what extent such facts would be utilized in a decision. *Muller* opened the door for attorneys to bring items to the Court that the Justices might otherwise overlook in their extralegal wanderings. The gathering and presentation of these facts required the employment of social scientists. Not only a fact commonly known by members of society, but also generalizable fact expressible in lay language but based on expert study, are both covered by the same

---

require employees to sign a document renouncing union membership, "conceding the full right of the individual to join the union," but noting that as long as the company had stated non-membership as a criterion for employment, the worker was free to accept or reject employment like any other contract. The Court laments the inequality of power here, but notes that contracts are often made among unequals. It is correct, but somewhat out of character, for the *Holden* Court to chide the employer for arguing that the Utah act

> works a particular hardship to his employees, whose right to labor as long as they please is alleged to be thereby violated. The argument would certainly come with better grace and cogency from the latter class.

Holden (1898) at 397.

41. The material for this brief, and subsequent "Brandeis briefs," was gathered by Brandeis' sister-in-law, Josephine Goldmark, and a team of researchers. Although an early pioneer social scientist, Goldmark is unlikely to be resurrected as a heroine among feminists, given the position she supported.

42. *Muller* (1908) at 423. Once a court has determined that some other party is the appropriate decision maker, it will still be reluctant to overturn a decision that appears rational, even if only weakly supported. In *Ferebee* (1984) at 1536:

> [I]f reasonable jurors could conclude from the expert testimony that paraquat more likely than not caused Ferebee's injury, the fact that another jury might reach the opposite conclusion or that science would require more evidence before conclusively considering the causation question resolved is irrelevant.

Thus, as Marlow (1998) points out, judges are more and more determining that *they* should make the decision in the first place. See the discussion on *Daubert* (1993) below and in Chapter 10.

term. Not all generalizable facts are obvious. The Court needs to get them from knowledge and method not ordinarily available to an attorney, or a judge, without the aid of experts.

THE RISE OF THE EXPERT WITNESS

In presentation to the Supreme Court, social-science evidence in *Muller* was contained in an appeals brief. The trail from acceptance of social-science legislative fact at the highest court to introduction of such evidence into lower courts, to the use of social scientists themselves to present such evidence, seems logical and obvious. But it is unrecorded. I have been unable to construct a definitive history of social-science expert testimony, although what that history would contain would be as much a matter of definition (at least of "social science") as events. Social-science testimony can take many forms, which will be the subject of Chapter 10. Here, and for most of this book, I deal with social science as knowledge that is derived from statistical analyses of data about people and their activities.

A National Academy of Sciences panel takes only eight pages to review the use of statistical evidence from the Talmud to the present, the earliest of their case studies having been decided in 1977. They note that "a more accepting attitude began to emerge"[43] in the 1950s, and refer to

> the limited, fragmentary, and suspicious attitude of much of the law to statistical forms of proof prior to 1960.

I would assert somewhat earlier dates, but I agree with the general point: Statistical studies presented by experts became common only in the second half of the twentieth century. To use this example again, courts were reluctant to substitute sample evidence for complete enumeration prior to the 1950s, but samples are commonly accepted today.[44]

Experts in Legislative Fact

Although the original expert-as-witness was clearly part of the adjudicative-fact debate, there were legislative-fact issues long before *Muller*. For example, the questioning of scholars about the meaning of Latin phrases, where the scholar is not asked to indicate anything

---

43. Fienberg (1989) at 6; following indented quotation also at 6, as well as in Appendix B at 218.

44. Judge Wyzanski drew his own sample of manufacturers.

> If antitrust trials are to be kept manageable, samples must be used, and a sample which is in general reasonable should not be rejected in the absence of the offer of a better sample.

Shoe (1953) at 305. In *Robins* (1988), the bankruptcy action forced by hundreds of thousands of claims for damages from use of the Dalkon Shield intra-uterine contraceptive device, Judge Merhige directed the taking of a sample of claimants by a special master and his staff.

about the particular contract in which the phrase was found, is a legislative-fact proceeding. In *Powell*, a witness was prepared to testify that the particular oleomargarine sold to the prosecuting witness was "clean and wholesome."[45] He was not allowed to do so. Several years earlier, however, experts had testified in state court to the wholesomeness of oleomargarine in general, i.e., as legislative fact.[46]

Before 1880, the Supreme Court accepted a loose definition of "expert," and seemed to take their appearance to explain legislative fact as unexceptional. Two experts discussed the characteristics of deer:

> A witness for the plaintiff, introduced as an expert, testified that he was a dentist, and resided in Albany; that he was to some extent acquainted with the habits and nature of the deer, and had hunted them; that in his opinion. . . .
>
> Another witness testified that he was a taxidermist, and had made natural history a study, and had read the standard authors in regard to the general characteristics of deer.[47]

Thus, the concept of legislative-fact presentation long preceded *Muller*. Expertise was a self-asserted "being acquainted" with the subjects (which most of us are not), or based on study. It should not be surprising, then, that when similar evidence on general characteristics were folded into a brief, authored by someone who had studied the subject, they were accepted. What is novel in *Muller* was that the presentation was about *social-science* legislative fact.

The inevitable succeeding step was to bring social scientists, as experts, into the courtroom to make the argument in person. By the mid-1950s, Jack Greenberg tells us:

> Social scientists have testified in recent cases on such questions as: What are the psychological effects of racial segregation? Are Negroes inherently intellectually inferior to white people?[48]

Arnold Rose, Kenneth Clark, and Jack Greenberg tell us that the first use of social-science testimony in school-desegregation cases occurred in *Sweatt* (1950).[49] The attorney who

---

45. *Powell* (1888) at 681, describing the district-court proceedings:
    The defendant then offered to prove by Prof. Hugo Blanck that he manufactured the article sold to the prosecuting witness; that it was made from pure animal fats; that the process of manufacture was clean and wholesome.

46. Professors Chandler and Morton testified in *People v. Marx*, 99 N.Y. 377 (1885), cited and quoted in *Schollenberger* (1898) at 11.

47. *Spring* (1878) at 647. This testimony convinced a jury that their owner was responsible for the harm one of them inflicted on a person the deer attacked on the owner's grounds, for he should have known the characteristics of these animals.

48. Greenberg (1956) at 953. From today's perspective, it is amazing that the Supreme Court allowed "fact" to be asserted by an expert (Goldmark, see note 41) in *Muller* (1908) without subjecting her to cross-examination. That procedure could not continue.

49. See Rose (1967), K. Clark (1953), and Greenberg (1956).

introduced this innovation was Thurgood Marshall. His first social-scientist expert, testifying about the harm of segregation, was Robert Redfield, chairman of the Department of Anthropology at the University of Chicago.[50]

Earlier social-science experts were, for the most part, economists.

> Of the social sciences proper, only economics seems to have been used extensively. . . . The testimony of economists in cases involving antitrust legislation, licensing, taxation, labor law, corporations, and trade regulations seems to be widely used and accepted in the courts.[51]

Lloyd Rosenthal tells us that

> but recently expert testimony was presented to the Surrogate of New York County dealing with the probability of inflation and the effect thereof on investments,[52]

as the executor of an estate apparently felt he could not protect the estate under current restrictions. In the 1930s expert social-science testimony was considered a novelty. It had as yet not made a major impact in federal court.

Social-science testimony occurred, but was still rare, in the 1950s and early 1960s. Despite a few adjudicative examples provided below, most such testimony was still part of the legislative-fact debate. Whether segregation was consonant with equality, whether the word "savings" is more advantageous than "thrift" when used by a bank, the credibility of eyewitness identification, whether the death penalty deters crime—these are the kinds of issues that brought the social scientist to court with data, statistical analysis, and knowledge derived from a profession's method, not just one's lay "understanding."

Rose describes testimony he presented in two cases, one of disputed parentage, the other involving the obligation of a state to provide services to a woman who had been a resident less than a year. In both cases, and in a third in which Rose was prepared to testify but was not called, his evidence was directed toward legislative fact. In the first he disclaimed the ability to determine who was the father of *this* child, but noted that one could not exclude a dark-skinned man (who wanted custody) as the biological father of a light-skinned child. In the second, he gave no mental test to the woman, but argued that those

---

50. See Kluger (1975). See also Chesler et al. (1988) who interviewed these early attorneys and experts. They also tell us who was contacted to testify but refused to do so.

51. Rose (1967) at 101 and 102. Louisell (1955) says, referring to Wigmore's *Evidence in Trials at Common Law*, third edition, 1940, that

> we search in vain for any substantial analysis, in Wigmore or elsewhere in American legal literature, of the psychologist functioning as an expert witness,

The National Academy panel, in Fienberg (1988) at 216, refers us to a discussion of the product rule for combining individual quantified pieces of evidence in Wigmore's *Science of Judicial Proof* (1937).

52. L. Rosenthal (1935) at 406.

characteristics on the record were jointly held by many competent people, so that there was no reason from knowledge of legislative fact to conclude that this person was mentally incompetent and would necessarily be a charge upon the city.[53]

Elizabeth Loftus and John Monahan similarly describe their legislative-fact testimony about eyewitness identification.[54] Decades earlier, Hugo Munsterberg had discussed the unreliability of observation in the context of eyewitness testimony, and apparently was involved in several cases. It is unclear whether he appeared as a witness, however, and I find no record in later times of psychologists impugning individual witnesses.[55] Legislative-fact experts cannot say how well a particular identification was made, although they have studied the problem of recognition. They point out, for example, that cross-race identification is particularly suspect, creating questions in many assault and rape cases. For another example, people may confuse identification of a particular person with identification of familiar people, so that a store clerk who has been robbed might see familiar features in a customer some time later and confuse that recognition with recognition of his assailant. This is legislative-fact knowledge, but it is not common knowledge. It requires presentation by experts.[56]

Loftus and Monahan provide some evidence, similar to that from Rita James, that jurors are not particularly moved by legislative-fact arguments from expert witnesses.

---

53. Rose (1967) gallantly notes that this woman *did* subsequently become a burden to the taxpayers, bearing several illegitimate children at public expense. Social-science evidence should never be presented or accepted as certain.

54. Loftus and Monahan (1980). These authors also discuss moral dilemmas facing experts presenting general evidence in relation to specific situations.

55. In discussing the acceptance of applied psychology as a field of inquiry, Munsterberg (1909) lists educators, physicians, artists, businessmen, politicians, naturalists, ministers, and officers as willing users. "The lawyer alone is obdurate," at 10. Wigmore (1909), in a parody of a report of a trial, defends his profession against Munsterberg's attack, calling it libelous. He informs us that the first suggestions of using psychological tests to determine the accuracy of testimony appear in the period 1898–1901, and the first practical proposals were made independently by Stern, Wertheimer, and Jung in the period 1902–1905.

56. There has been adjudicative-fact testimony concerning the competence of the witness, the larger subject of which eyewitness identification is a part. For example, in the famous Alger Hiss case, the credibility of Whittaker Chambers was attacked by a psychiatrist, who testified as an expert. See *Hiss* (1950). However, the more general rule is to exclude adjudicative opinion of this kind about witnesses, while receiving it about the defendant. See, for example, *Barnard* (1973), in which at 913 the Ninth Circuit, affirming exclusion, expresses its "grave doubt that the expert testimony would have helped the jury." The Ninth Circuit would have had no problem with legislative-fact testimony about the ability of children to be fact witnesses, in *Binder* (1985). However, at 602:

> The testimony of the experts in this case was not limited to references to psychological literature or experience or to a discussion of a class of victims generally. Rather the experts testified that these particular children in this particular case could be believed.

Admitting such adjudicative testimony was error, thus the conviction was reversed.

It may be that this form of evidence is more impressive to judges who, being professionals, believe "expert" testimony more readily than lay jurors.[57]

As mentioned above, the debate before the Court in *Brown* (1954) appeared to be constitutional. Did the Framers of the Fourteenth Amendment, which provides for equal protection, mean to include such state functions or human activities as education and marriage? Or did this part of the constitution merely provide that police and judicial procedures would be equal for all people? The phrase "equal protection" has two words. The strictly legal debate concerns the inclusiveness of "protection." The social-science argument concerns the meaning of the word "equal."[58] Jack Greenberg contends that the Supreme Court did not "affirm or reverse the findings below on the effect of segregation." The social-science evidence

> illuminated the issues and perhaps informed for the first time one or more
> members of the bench whose interest might not have led them earlier to
> acquire such information.[59]

That is, Greenberg sees the social-science evidence in *Brown* as not much more than a Brandeis brief, bringing information commonly available ("the general recognition of segregation's harm") to the attention of the Court. The Court had to define "equal," and did so by finding legislative fact—not fact about harm done to the children of Topeka, Kansas, but fact about harm done to children in general, under similar conditions.

---

57. Loftus and Monahan (1980) quote a juror at 274:
> (W)e felt that the experience of a subject in a psychologist's experiment and the experience of a person with a knife at his throat . . . they just aren't the same.

Rita James (1960) reports:
> It was almost because the jurors recognized that these men were experts, that they were members of a profession, that it gave the jurors license to grant them a certain degree of deference which did not also oblige them to accept the witnesses' statements as directives for their own actions.

Reprint in Lawrence M. Friedman and Stewart Macaulay, *Law and the Behavioral Sciences*, Bobbs-Merrill (1969), at 684. Hand (1901) reports, at 48, that a surgeon's opinion that the defendant was insane was given similar treatment in 1760:
> [T]he jury, i.e., the Lords, seem to have preferred their own inference to the surgeon's, and convicted the defendant.

58. Kurland (1970) at 98:
> The motif on the façade of the Supreme Court building reads: "Equal Justice under Law." If earlier courts emphasized the words "Law" or "Justice," the Warren Court has accentuated the word "Equal."

59. Greenberg (1956), all quotations at 965. Greenberg feared that social-science findings are ephemeral.
> If *the Court* had found "inequality" as facts are normally found in litigation, it would have left open the possibility of a future case in which there might be defense testimony that Negroes are psychologically better off in segregated schools.

Also at 965.

From *Muller* (1908) to *Brown* (1954) there was, on the surface, little progress. *Brown* represents a clear turning point, though like most such historical landmarks it was as much a product of its era as a creator of that era. *Brown* is significant both procedurally for the use of direct social-science testimony, and substantively for the apparent acceptance by the Court of a social-science legislative-fact argument supported by expert presentations.

Experts in Adjudicative Fact

Expert opinions on such things as cause of death were an accepted part of trials in "the colonies" and the earliest U.S. courts. What Neil Vidmar calls "the great toxicology trial of the nineteenth century" featured experts for prosecution and defense, one of whom had testified in earlier cases.[60] The Supreme Court encountered social-science adjudicative expert witnesses, "experts as they are called, though it is not clear they were of that character," as early as 1854. Greenberg's discussion of the rise of the expert witness takes no note of the kind of fact being presented. He goes on listing expert topics:

> Is a community's public opinion such that a defendant cannot receive a fair trial there? Is a label on a bottle of orange drink misleading? Are two trademarks likely to be confused? Is a book so obscene that it is likely to corrupt youth?[61]

Greenberg's list also introduces another consideration: derivation of the evidence (i.e., the research) specifically for litigation. Although Brandeis' use of an expert to gather data specifically for his case was a novel application, it came from an ancient heritage and evolved into a profession of litigation experts today. In 1935, Lloyd Rosenthal listed "Some of the many matters upon which such testimony has been admitted" as including:

medicine;

X rays;

chemistry;

radio tubes;

nautical skill;

growth of trees;

---

60. *People v. Hendrikson*, Albany County, New York (1853), is described in Vidmar (2001) at 1 and in Vidmar and Diamond (2001) at 1123. For additional examples, they refer the reader to Kenneth A. Deville, *Medical Malpractice in Nineteenth-Century America: Origins and Legacy*, New York University Press (1990). Following Supreme Court quotation from *Catharine* (1854) at 174. It will be interesting to remember, as this book progresses, that in this possibly first encounter, the Court found the experts' conception of their task wanting, not so much its execution. The experts had estimated the expense to raise and repair a sunken boat. But the boat had been raised and repaired. Why, wondered the Court, are we dealing with estimates of a cost that is now known?

61. Greenberg (1956) at 954.

handwriting;

ballistics;

curative powers of mineral water;

alteration of coat;

fingerprints;

mental condition;

watertightness of cellar;

operation of street cars; and

electricity and electric lights.[62]

Three broad areas are clear here. One is tort law, finding an entity liable for a personal injury. Another is criminal proof or excuse. A third is contract law, did the buyer get what he paid for. If there is not overt statistical analysis in our early history, there is certainly "science," to which one state supreme court reacted strongly in 1899:

> Experts are nowadays often the mere paid advocates or partisans of those who employ and pay them, as much so as the attorneys who conduct the suit. There is hardly anything, not palpably absurd on its face, that cannot now be proved by some so-called "experts."[63]

However disliked they may be, though, experts should have knowledge and experience beyond that of jurors. This is what one state supreme court thought of the practice in 1942:

> In the early days of court procedure there was less need of expert opinion testimony. But with the complexity of modern life and with the amazing growth and advancement of a myriad matters of science, art, mechanics, discovery, invention, and industry, which touch our daily life constantly on every side, a failure to make the fullest use of expert opinions in court procedure means in a great many cases a denial of proof and necessarily a denial of justice.[64]

Handwriting, fingerprints, and ballistics are more clearly probabilistic than the other items on Rosenthal's list, but none comes close to requiring the kind of expertise that is commonly employed today. Contrast the previous two lists of expert subject matter with this more modern one:

neutron-activation analysis;

sound spectrometry (voiceprints);

psycholinguistics;

---

62. L. Rosenthal (1935) at 405, cites omitted.

63. *Keegan* (1899) at 95.

64. *Grismore* (1942) at 343.

atomic absorption;

remote electromagnet sensing; and

bitemark comparisons.[65]

History and Heritage

We have seen that the evolution of the social-science expert, a presenter of statistical gen-eralities the judge or jury would not otherwise know, was built on an acceptance of the concept of an expert who informed an independent fact finder. I have hinted above that the key ingredient in this concept was the evolution, in England, of the jury from witnesses to non-witnesses. Let's go back further, now, and see how that concept evolved, filling in the pre-United-States history.

Possibly the earliest use of the expert in England was to translate Latin terms in contracts. An independent legal profession was developing in the thirteenth century. The original advocates, like those of today, were licensed. They possessed a virtual monopoly on access to the system. Roman law had spread prior to 400 A.D., and in essence seems to have survived well past the Norman invasion of 1066. It provided the basis for a battle between ecclesiastical and secular law, parallel to the struggle for control of govern-mental authority. The Normans failed to establish French as a common language. Most advocates were trained by the Church, and most legal documents, as was Magna Carta, were written in Latin. This was especially true for contracts among merchants, who may themselves have spoken different languages. Thus, the contracts were drawn up by the advocates in a language familiar to neither of the parties and sometimes, it appears, not even to the judge.[66]

The role of the expert, in these early trade cases, was to clarify the trade usage of cer-tain terms left imprecise in these contracts. Experts, then, were persons as familiar with the items being traded as the buyers or sellers. Lloyd Rosenthal notes that the earliest appear-ance of individuals whose testimony is based on their special skills, not their knowledge of a particular incident, probably occurred at the instigation of the court in its fact-finding role. These "prototypes of the modern expert witness" apparently advised the judge in private.[67] The judge then instructed the jury on the basis of this expert information. It requires the evolution of the jury as a body independent of the events in question, and therefore the concept of "witness" as different from "trier of fact," before the modern con-cept of the *expert* witness was to take shape.

---

65. Giannelli (1980) at 1198.

66. See Tigar and Levy (1977), especially at 155–164.

67. L. Rosenthal (1935) at 408.

The Independent Jury

In some sense, those who observe an incident are most expert about it. These experts at first were the accusers, the origin of today's grand jury. Fact was determined by a contest between plaintiff and defendant, where the more persons a party could bring forth agreeing to his side of the dispute, the better.[68] Through several centuries of development, the concepts of "witness" and "juror" were interwoven. They were to some extent one and the same. For example, coroners' juries were formed from close-by townships, from people "more likely to know the facts of any occurrence."[69]

The concept of the independent jury is sometimes attributed to Magna Carta, which did include the right of trial by peers; but the history of that document would indicate that the idea of peer judgment had been in the air for some time before King John promised it as a right—though only for some—in 1215.[70] Although that right was extended to common people ("villains") only sixty years later, still the institution of the independent jury that would hear witnesses evolved over a long period of time.[71]

Parallel to the jury of observers of the incident is the jury of experts, people experienced in the general issue. Especially in commerce, the earliest experts were used not individually, but in a group. However, they were answering adjudicative questions. A common dispute about the fulfillment of contracts, for example, was the quality of the delivered goods. Learned Hand writes that in urban communities

> the practice was well established in the 14th Century of having the issue actually decided by people especially qualified.[72]

Rosenthal lists these issues for which special juries, "summoned from tradesmen or craftsmen" were created:

> whether hides were improperly tanned;

---

68. What C. Wells (1911) called "proof by witness," Tribe (1971a) describes as "a starkly numerical jurisprudence," at 1329. On this topic see also Holdsworth (1903), Volume I, at 302.

69. Holdsworth (1903), Volume I, at 85.

70. Magna Carta assured trial by jury only for "freemen," which meant property owners; and as the jury was to be composed of their "peers," it too was limited to property owners.

71. There were clearly criminal juries in the thirteenth century, which just as clearly were composed of persons with knowledge of the crime. Although there is some disagreement about when and how the "self-informing" jury gave way to the uninformed jury, there should be little question that such an evolution occurred. See Klerman (2003). The First Statute of Westminster, in 1275, while establishing the court system, either deliberately or by later interpretation, also conferred the right of trial by jury to all. Some writers, Helmholz (1999) for example, use the spelling "villein." I use the American spelling because equating lack of property with lack of character survived well into the twentieth century in requirements for jurors. See Chapter 5.

72. Hand (1901) at 42.

whether the meshes of fishing nets were smaller than required by the trade
   ordinance;

whether tapestry was false;

whether hats and caps were improper;

whether wine was false;

whether putrid victuals had been sold; and

whether a surgeon was guilty of malpractice.[73]

   The independent jury was evolving. In this first step the jury were no longer witnesses
to the event but were especially qualified to judge it. This is the "blue ribbon jury" concept,
which remains alive today, although I will disparage it in Chapters 5 and 10. The next step
was to separate those experts out of the jury, instead of having them compose it. And with
that step came the need for their testimony.

   Not until the middle of the 15th Century was even the practice of summon-
   ing witnesses well settled as an incident to the trial.[74]

But even though the concept of a "witness" and even an "expert witness" was contemporaneous, the jury with prior knowledge of the facts did not disappear. The notion of the
jury as a body drawn from a given community to decide the facts based upon their own
knowledge persisted.

   English jurors before the fifteenth century, like ancient jurors in Greece and
   Rome, did not have to be impartial.[75]

Thus, the report of a case in 1550 contains the observation:

   Some of the jurors knew this to be true.[76]

   The independent jury and, hence, the necessity for expertise outside the jury, seems
finally to have been established in the seventeenth century. Learned Hand's examples from
early in that century include expert testimony about both legislative fact (could a woman
bear a child more than forty-one weeks after conception?) and adjudicative fact (what was
the cause of death?). As Lawrence Friedman summarizes:

   In medieval times, the jury had been a panel of neighbors—knowing busy-
   bodies, who perhaps had personal knowledge of the case. When the function
   of the jury changed to that of an impartial panel of listeners, the law of evidence underwent explosive growth.[77]

---

73. L. Rosenthal (1935) at 407, cites omitted.

74. Hand (1901) at 44.

75. Pizzi and Hoffman (2001) at 406.

76. Tigar and Levy (1977) at 267.

77. Friedman (1985) at 153.

The first experts were jurors, and when the jurors were not sufficiently expert the judge sought independent advice. In the next evolutionary step, attorneys directed the judge to particular experts either by suggesting which experts should be consulted or by quoting them. At some point a determined advocate brought his own expert into court. Rosemary Erickson and Rita Simon tell us that the first such expert was "a civil engineer, John Smeaton, who testified in *Folkes v. Chadd* in 1782." More likely, Smeaton is the first expert whose name we know.[78] We understand from Hand that experts were being called by attorneys, not only by judges, at the end of the seventeenth century; but we know little before that time.

The expert is tied inextricably into the law of evidence, the rules that say what information can and cannot be brought before the determiner of fact, in what form, by whom. As witness-jurors became harder to find, and non-participant (expert) witnesses were allowed, examination and cross-examination evolved to transmit their knowledge to the jurors. Thus, by the sixteenth century, attention was being paid to the nature of witnesses and procedures allowing their testimony, requiring a change in the definition of "hearsay," which had heretofore meant anything other than direct observation.

Probability and Statistics

Probability theory entered the law almost as soon as it entered man's consciousness. Gottfried Wilhelm von Leibnitz

> wanted to know what kinds of combinations of conditions, none complete in themselves, would justify a conclusion of unconditional right. He even put this theory to work when in 1669 he had to prepare a brief on that bizarre intertwining of conditional rights, the disputed throne of Poland.[79]

Jacques Bernouilli was concerned with legal applications of probability, even urging that there be a common legal standard of "moral certainty," which is a high probability that one's belief is correct (a standard that has not been set to this day).[80] Nicolas Bernouilli, Jacques' nephew, was interested in the confidence with which courts could determine fact, such as the death of a long-missing person,

---

78. Erickson and Simon (1998) at 19. The case is from England, *Folkes v. Chadd*, 3 Dougl. 157 (1782). See *Minner* (2000), where the early history of experts is discussed; and see also Hand (1901).

79. Hacking (1975) at 88. Although Leibnitz is now known for his developments in mathematics, he earned his living as a lawyer. Hacking calls him the "first philosopher of probability," at 185. Formal probability theory was in its first decade when Leibnitz became involved with it.

80. J. Bernouilli in *Ars Conjectandi*, published posthumously in 1713. Apparently no complete English translation exists. The information in the text comes from Hacking (1975) at 146. The phrase "moral certainty" appears from time to time in jury instructions. Used without clarification, it has led to the overturning of convictions, such as in *Cage* (1990). It is not defined, however, as a probability. For example,

> At petitioner's trial, the judge elaborated upon the phrase "moral certainty," defining it as "a deep, abiding conviction" as to the defendant's guilt.

the value of annuities, marine insurance, the veracity of testimony, and the probability of innocence.[81]

More than a century later, Siméon Poisson investigated the probability of error in jury determination of guilt, an issue that resurfaced in the 1970s, again commanding the attention of prominent statisticians.[82] A debate on the use of probabilistic proof in criminal cases, sparked by such an attempt in a state court, raged in the *Harvard Law Review* in the early 1970s. Only in the late 1970s was statistics and law first discussed in book form.[83]

Although some concept of science evidence entered through the legislative-fact door, some issues called for adjudicative-fact determination. Consider identification through handwriting, which covers forgery, especially of wills.

> It would seem that, right down to the end of the seventeenth century, it was very doubtful whether any evidence to prove that X had written a given document was admissible, other than the evidence of a witness who had actually seen him write the document in question.[84]

Handwriting analysts, excluded by this tradition, insisted that their opinions were worth considering. In 1854 the British Parliament moved to allow

> evidence of persons who merely got their knowledge from a comparison of the disputed document with genuine documents for the purposes of the trial.

Whether that comparison is craft or science, valid or not, it is brought to court in the testimony of an expert.[85]

The first statistician to provide an expert adjudicative analysis in the United States was Professor Benjamin Peirce of Harvard, in 1868. In question was the legitimacy of the will of Sylvia Ann Howland. Peirce estimated that the probability of two signatures being as alike as a known real one and the suspect one, by anything other than "design," was minute.[86]

Mattson (2002) at *1. When so explained, although it does not seem like an explanation to me, the term "moral certainty" may be used. See my discussion of g*, a threshold probability for a juror's determination of guilt, in the Appendix to Chapter 4.

81. Fienberg (1989) at 211. See Finkelstein (1978) at 2.

82. See, for example, the series of articles by Gelfand and Solomon, and the brief debate between Fabian (1977) and Gelfand and Solomon (1977b) in the *Journal of the American Statistical Association*. This question is explored further in Chapter 4 of the present work.

83. See Finkelstein and Fairley (1970), Tribe (1971a), Finkelstein and Fairley (1971), and Tribe (1971b), some articles reprinted in Finkelstein (1978), which is also the first major book dedicated to statistical proof in law. A section of Fairley and Mosteller (1977) also discusses this subject. For statistics in a civil context see, for example, Baldus and Cole (1977), Morris (1979), Baldus and Cole (1980), and Saks and Baron (1980).

84. Holdsworth (1903), Volume IX, at 212; following indented quotation at 214.

85. What should be considered "science" in litigation, and especially whether "forensic science" is appropriately named, is discussed in Chapter 10.

86. *Howland* (1868). Hetty Robinson produced a will that differed from that in the possession of Mandell,

A similar kind of calculation was made in *Risley* (1915), in which reference was made to the Howland will calculations.[87] In *Risley* the question concerned the identification of a typewriter apparently used to add words to a document. The calculations assumed that all characteristics tested were independent, a feature that became prominent again in discussions of a probabilistic identification of a suspect in California in 1968.[88] In these cases (as it had been in *Muller*), the role of the expert was to accept the theory of the case provided by his client, and lend expertise to those calculations his client needed to present his argument. As we will see in Chapter 6, at least from the point of view of the attorney who engages an expert, little has changed. In Chapter 8 I argue that change is due.

The "statistics" of antitrust cases in the early 1900s, in contrast, were for the most part merely data summaries, requiring definitions of terms according to social-science concepts. By and large these studies did not involve statistical testing.[89] Quantitative analysis in antitrust matters appears to have been initiated by a judge! I find no hint of expert input to the sample drawn by Judge Wyzanski in *Shoe* (1953), nor expert analysis of the data collected.[90]

---

the estate's executor. Mandell called in Peirce. His testimony is described in Meier and Zabell (1980), and in Kaye (2001). Another claim of forgery—to mask the defendant's handwriting—was made in the Dreyfus trial in France in 1899. See Tribe (1971a).

87. *Risley* (1915). On both cases, *Howland* (1868) and *Risley*, see Kaye (2001) at 1940, Barnes and Conley (1986) at 4, and Collins (1978) at 154. Both cases were also discussed in Albert A. Osborn, *Questioned Documents* (1929), by Wigmore in *Science of Judicial Proof* (1937), and in McCormick's *Handbook of Evidence* (1954), according to the historical survey in Fienberg (1989).

88. *Collins* (1968). The California Supreme Court understood not only that independence was assumed, but that assuming independence among all characteristics (for example, between being a male and having a moustache) was unacceptable. Less well known, but earlier, is *Sneed* (1966). The New Mexico Supreme Court reversed a criminal conviction:

> We hold that mathematical odds are not admissible as evidence to identify a defendant in a criminal proceeding so long as the odds are based on estimates, the validity of which have not been demonstrated.

At 862.

89. See Lozowick et al. (1968). This study, supporting the defendants in an antitrust charge against a bank merger, was not presented to the court because the case was dismissed on strictly legal grounds. The detailed, didactic presentation of an elementary (but presumably novel to the law) econometric study prepared for an antitrust case in the early 1960s lends weight to the conclusion, in text, that multivariate methods were rare in antitrust litigation.

90. See *Shoe* (1953). Where were the experts? At 305:

> The Court arbitrarily selected from a standard directory of shoe manufacturers, the first fifteen names that began with the first letter of the alphabet, the first fifteen names that began with the eleventh letter of the alphabet, all eight of the names that began with the twenty-first letter of the alphabet, and the first seven of the names that began with the twenty-second letter of the alphabet. This sample covers 3 percent of the shoe manufacturers.

Even administrative law judges now pass on the quality of samples. See, for example, John O. Cunningham, "Carrier's 'Bad Math' Nixes Bid To Recover Overpayments" (*Massachusetts Lawyers Weekly,*

A daring attempt to determine the association between race and sentence in rape cases did not convince an Arkansas court in 1966, nor the Supreme Court in 1970.[91] A more thorough study, concluding that the combination of black perpetrator and white victim more likely resulted in the death penalty than other race combinations, statistically controlling for other aspects of the crime, failed to sway the Court in 1987.[92]

The first appearance of quantitative social-science evidence for adjudicative fact, other than antitrust, seems to have been from polling data. Julian L. Woodward of the Roper Organization was engaged to assist the defendant in his motion for a change of venue.

> We cannot approve this method of determining the likelihood of a defendant's
> being unable to receive a fair trial in a given community.[93]

Thus wrote the Florida Supreme Court in 1953, also doubting its accuracy because Roper had projected a Thomas Dewey victory in the 1948 presidential election. Jack Greenberg discusses a poll presented by the U.S. government to show that people thought Bireley's Orange Beverage contained more than the 6 percent fruit juice it actually had.[94] He also mentions expert testimony on the obscenity of particular books and movies.[95] David Louisell describes a poll taken of patrons of a particular theater, to ascertain (from their addresses) whether that theater drew only from the immediate area, and (from their responses to questions) whether these patrons would pay higher prices for first-run pictures at this theater.[96]

Anthropologists have appeared in adjudicative-fact settings although not, as far as I can determine, utilizing formal statistical analysis. The earliest issues involved fitting American Indian culture into the Anglo legal framework before the Indian Claims Commission.[97] By

---

May 12, 2003) describing *In re: Gavigan*, in which a Medicare insurance carrier had sued a doctor, alleging overpayments on the basis of a sample audit. Dawn Lieb, a Social Security Administration administrative law judge, determined (on advice of defendant's statistical expert) that the audit sample was not representative, and rejected extrapolation from it.

91. See *Maxwell* (1966) and *Maxwell* (1970). For a description of the issues, and reflections of the expert, see Wolfgang (1974).

92. See *McCleskey* (1987). As noted above, the Court declared at a meta-level that no statistical study would convince it to alter McCleskey's death sentence. That is, it wanted adjudicative fact (that race played a role in this sentence), not legislative fact.

93. *Irvin* (1953) at 291.

94. *Bireley's* (1951); Greenberg (1956) at 957.

95. Included here is the earliest reference I have found to expert social-science testimony, *Larsen* (1938).

96. Louisell (1955) at 250. The theater brought suit in a local court against Warner Brothers for considering it a neighborhood theater, and therefore not allowing it to show first-run pictures.

> In view of the apparent paucity of published material on the actual functioning of the
> psychologist as an expert witness,

Louisell reproduces (at 258–272) the expert testimony of Kenneth E. Clark, who conducted the poll.

97. See L. Rosen (1977).

the mid-1950s, anthropologists had written about their experiences before the Commission, which had been established in 1946.[98] Anthropologists, like the Latin scholars before them, have testified in U.S. district courts about issues involving the meaning of terms in a contract, specifically, Indian treaties. In the late 1970s, for example, anthropologists were called upon to help define the term "tribe," when Indian tribal claims to aboriginal ownership of land in Mashpee, Massachusetts and other New England sites essentially froze all land sales.

Large financial claims have led to an increased use of experts. Management consultants and academics are used to demonstrate that corporate management was or was not negligent.[99] Journalism professors testify about the propriety of methods used by journalists.[100] Economists calculate the value of damages, even attempting to project the expected future earnings of people who, because of someone's alleged negligence, will not reach the heights that would have been available to them.[101] In the Dalkon Shield litigation, the value of damages was derived statistically from previously settled and litigated cases. Tobacco litigation by states has produced damages in the billions of dollars, based on expert estimates of state expenditures generated by misdeeds of tobacco companies.[102] We are told that business executives testify in legislative-fact situations only—offering what in Chapters 8 and 10 I will call "wisdom"—but Enron and other twenty-first-century scandals may break down that barrier.[103]

MODERN TIMES

Two legal areas that loom large in reviewing cases using statistical expertise are product liability and antitrust. I have not tried to trace their histories separately, although I refer

---

98. See, for example, Lurie (1955), Ray (1955), and Steward (1955).

99. See Ranii (1980). Jeffrey Toobin, "The Man Chasing Enron," *The New Yorker* (September 9, 2002) at 88:

> Securities cases are often decided by battles among experts, who duel over such issues as whether a company's management behaved in line with normal business practices.

100. See Al Kamen, "More Journalists Ushered Into Court: Welcome to World of Expert Witness," *Washington Post* (January 26, 1981), Business Section at 23. It is not clear from this report whether the expert witness, Philip Robbins, was issuing "legislative" guidelines for reporter behavior, or was commenting on the difference between a particular reporter's behavior and the standard.

101. For example, see my discussion of an expert's projection expected future earnings in *Eymard* (1986), and the court's rejection thereof, in Chapter 7.

102. See, for example, plaintiffs' experts Zeger et al. (2000), and defendants' expert Rubin (2000), in tobacco litigation in Minnesota.

103. "How to Be An Expert Witness," *Business Week* (March 30, 1981), at 147:

> Expert witnesses are put on the stand not for what they know about the facts in a specific controversy but for what they know about general business practices that shed light on the matter at hand.

to cases from both of those fields in subsequent chapters. Here I quickly review three other areas that use social-science adjudicative fact-experts: civil rights, education, and voter issues.

Civil Rights

Courts have relied on determining the lawfulness of a process by observing its results. Such processes include selecting persons for jury duty; minority and female hiring, pay, and promotion; termination based on age; etc. Expert analysis is called upon to assist in estimating the probability of finding the known results had a "fair" process been in operation.

In *Griggs* (1971), the Court distinguished "disparate impact" from "disparate treatment," and in so doing opened the floodgates to a torrent of statistical proofs. Disparate *treatment* is direct discrimination. In its original form, it was overt. "White only" and "colored" restaurant counters or bathrooms are examples, as are strictly segregated jobs. Disparate *impact* claims require only that the result of a behavior, however neutral that behavior may appear on its face, affect distinct definable and measurable population subgroups differently. An employer either did or did not define jobs so as to exclude minorities or females, although determining whether he did so may be difficult. That's treatment. But whether a test or screening device does or does not differentially select out minorities or females is inherently a statistical question. It is not answerable by direct observation without the application of statistical method. That's disparate impact. It requires a different concept of fact, and experts to discern it.

In *Griggs*, no complicated statistical test was called for. The facts were not in dispute. Blacks had been excluded from a particular job, said defendant Duke Power Company, because they did not have the requisite education. Neither the fact of exclusion nor its basis was in doubt. However, employees with lower education had performed that job as well as any employees. Requiring education for those jobs did not distinguish better from worse workers. It had the effect of keeping blacks out, and an unjustifiable requirement with a disparate impact must fall.[104]

Does a process "exclude" a certain kind of person when *some* of those people pass the screen? The Supreme Court first faced this question in jury-selection cases. With the passing of cases with the "inexorable zero," i.e., the absolute bar to blacks on juries, in jobs, and in other places they have a right to be, the Court faced the task of determining when there was effective exclusion, a different chance for some people to be hired, for non-work-related

---

104. Disparate-impact analysis, and its rebuttal, have come a long way since *Griggs* (1971). Primus (2003) finds the principle in conflict with other strands of Supreme Court thinking, especially the difference between individual rights and class identification. His discussion is interesting, even provocative. However, *Griggs* itself is more simple than Primus allows, and clearly correct.

reasons. As the Court had had to define "equal" in *Brown*, it now had to define "unequal" as in "unequal probability of a black and a white being selected" for a job or a jury.

The Supreme Court had been approaching a probabilistic definition of jury selection for more than thirty-five years. In *Smith* (1940), the representation of blacks among those summoned for grand-jury duty was contrasted with what "chance and accident alone" would have produced.[105] Over an eight-year period, eighteen blacks were summoned, and five served, out of 512 persons summoned and 384 serving, in all. Not many, but not zero. The Court did not perform a formal statistical test on these numbers, but subsequently W. S. Robinson did, comparing them to the numbers a "fair" population sampling would have produced. Robinson also showed how the Court's view of "representation" of the population on juries expanded to include socio-economic status.[106] The Court makes clear that *each* jury need not be representative, but the jury *system* must be. Whether it is, this statistical argument goes, can be determined from an analysis of the overall composition of those called for jury duty over time.

Castaneda (1977) is much like *Smith*. Mexican-Americans constituted 79 percent of the Hidalgo County, Texas, population; but over the eleven years studied by the Court, 39 percent of those summoned for grand-jury duty (339 of 870) were Mexican-American. Footnote 17 in *Castaneda* accepts a statistical measure of disparate impact, measuring the difference between the "expected" and "actual" number of Mexican-Americans in standard deviation units. There is no record of this analysis having been presented by an expert. The history from *Muller* (1908) in legislative fact was relived in adjudicative fact. The Court has taken notice of a kind of evidence, and now attorneys will introduce that evidence. Unfortunately, the entire line of decisions from and including *Castaneda* is ill-conceived. Although a boon to statisticians, ultimately, as I demonstrate in Chapter 5, the kinds of analyses prompted by *Castaneda*, insofar as the subject matter is jury representation, are statistical failures.[107]

History has not repeated itself in the lag time between the Court's acceptance of the notion of statistical evidence and attorney control of that evidence by the use of experts. *Griggs* opened the door. *Teamsters* (1977) and *Hazelwood* (1977), following quickly after *Castaneda*, represent the Supreme Court's clear acceptance of expert-presented adjudicative statistical argument.[108] The statistical expert became a fixture in class-action litigation.

---

105. *Smith* (1940) at 131.

106. See Robinson (1950).

107. Chapter 5 is dedicated to proving this assertion. The entire text of *Castaneda* (1977) footnote 17 appears there.

108. In subsequent chapters I will show that the empirical analysis in *Teamsters* (1977) was correct, but that in *Hazelwood* (1977) was not.

Education

The opportunity for an historic use of social-science-based empirical analysis presented itself in *Rodriguez* (1973). At issue was the allocation of public-school funds by a state. The state laws allowed unequal distribution of such funds, and therefore made an "accident of birth"—the wealth of the school district in which a child lived—a determinant of the state resources applied to that child's education. This was not a legitimate state function, argued the plaintiffs.

That argument had been successful in state courts. In *Serrano* (1971), experts produced a factual case that the state supported unequal education, the California Supreme Court affirmed it, and the legislature was required to devise a more equal school-fund distribution. A movement for *Serrano*-like cases formed within the legal community, and in several other states results similar to *Serrano* were obtained.[109] In *Rodriguez*, however, the federal courts were asked to overturn the Texas public-school-finance system as a violation of the federal constitution. Experts presented evidence that the wealth of the school district and the per-pupil expenditures in that district were related. Ultimately the Supreme Court did not find that evidence convincing as law, though it may have been as fact.

Usually only cases in which the plaintiffs have emerged victorious are taken as milestones, indicating a change of direction. However, important points have been made by defendants' experts, and accepted by courts.[110] With statistically laden opinions being written in lower forums,[111] it was in the late 1970s when these analyses reached the Supreme Court.[112]

As if anticipating such an eventuality, the Supreme Court began warning litigants that analyses brought to it must be directly relevant. In *Hazelwood*, the Court suggested that

---

109. I participated in one of them. See *Robinson* (1973).

110. A successful defense of controversial legislation may be as "historic" as plaintiff victories disallowing legislation. See, for example, *McConnell* (2003), sustaining Congress' authority to control campaign finance.

111. Examples that received attention among statistical experts and interested commentators include *Greenspan* (1980), *Vuyanich* (1980), *Harris Bank* (1981), and *Chang* (1985).

112. Some people thought the opportunity was at hand in *Bazemore* (1986) for a mature, definitive pronouncement about statistical evidence. Although the Court did reach the right conclusion in that case, it was not aided by the plaintiffs' inept statistical analyses. Thus, although *Bazemore* stands as a watershed for procedural argument (stating, for example, that one side's criticism of the other side's statistical presentation cannot just procedurally nit-pick; it must show that the procedural flaws led to conclusions that would be greatly altered if they were corrected), it represents very little in the way of a statistical analysis that demonstrates fact to the Supreme Court. A more detailed description of the statistical mess made of *Bazemore* appears in this book in Chapter 2 (explaining the analysis that should have been performed) and Chapter 3 (explaining the analysis that was performed).

data—the kind of summary data the Court accepted in principle the same day in *Dothard* (1977)—had to be shown to be the most relevant data available. The potential supply of teachers to one school district might be affected by actions of another district, and, at any rate, teacher hiring must be compared with teacher supply, not with the race of pupils. In *Beazer* (1979), the Court rejected an argument that the New York Transit Authority's refusal to hire methadone-maintained conductors had a disparate racial impact just because the majority of methadone-maintained people in New York City were minorities (even accepting this statement as legislative fact). The data had to show that the race composition of the Transit Authority's work force *was* affected, not *might have been* affected. Fact had to be adjudicative.

Testimony utilizing statistical analysis began to be decisive. The Court was learning some statistics and the rudiments of data analysis. Heavy guns were firing in the district courts. Heavy guns were also firing outside courtroom doors, as will be discussed in Chapter 4, in response to judicial use of data analysis to determine fact. Determining which were firing real bullets, which blanks, became the judge's problem.[113]

Electoral Politics

The power of the judicial system was brought home to many people who had not thought about it when the vote for President in Florida, in November 2000, seemed about to be determined by the Florida Supreme Court—and then was determined by the U.S. Supreme Court.[114] Neither body made outcome determinations. They did what courts usually do, they made procedural determinations. As it happened, by any procedure, the outcome would have been the same.[115] As important as expert testimony was in the lower courts,

---

113. See, for example, Horowitz (1977), Morris (1979), Saks and Baron (1980), Huber (1992), Jasanoff (1995), and Faigman (2000).

114. See *Bush* (2000).

115. Democrats, who lost, will object to this statement. Surely most Floridians who voted *meant* to vote for Gore. See Gore Vidal, "*Times* Cries Eke! Buries Al Gore," 273 *The Nation* 20 (December 17, 2001). But that is irrelevant to the court cases, as Posner (2003) notes at 225:

> The traditional and on the whole salutary American distrust of officials makes it unacceptable to determine the winner of an election by analytical means, whether statistical inference from a sample (as in polling) or informed speculation about the intentions of voters who spoiled their ballots with the result that the tabulating machinery did not record them as votes.

The only issue before the courts in December 2000 was whether to let several counties continue recounting under very dubious and, indeed, changing standards. The Florida court said yes, the federal court said no. The *Miami Herald* then provided a way to recount under many standards, by categorizing the disputed ballots (the "undercount," not ballots with multiple choices). If one uses the *Herald*'s information to recount as the state court would have allowed, George Bush still emerged the winner. Other

where the (apparently correct) view that recounting would not affect the outcome prevailed, it played no role in the high courts' decisions.

The re-dividing of a state into election districts, which follows each decennial census, has been the subject of many a complaint. In *Hunt* (2001) the Court appeared to write a two-party system into the Constitution, deciding *de novo* between two expert reports that redistricting to provide a safe Democrat seat is proper, whereas redistricting to provide a safe black seat is not.[116] In previous cases concerning the same district (North Carolina's Twelfth), the Supreme Court had held that the state had deliberately created a majority black district.[117] Now, faced with a lower-court finding that North Carolina had done the same thing again, the Court read the expert reports and testimony, reversed the lower court's decision on the facts, and allowed the district to stand.

In the history of Supreme Court decisions, this case, decided after the 2000 U.S. Census, just before redistricting was to start again, is minor. But as an exemplar of how far statistical expert witnesses have come—from a footnote in *Brown* to the focal point of Court attention in 2001—it is stunning. Fact finding is generally the province of the lower court, unless egregiously incorrect.[118] Where in *Castaneda* the Court apparently was willing to do its own analysis, it is not willing to step aside when faced with expert reports and testimony (and lower court evaluations thereof). The review standard is "clear error," meaning the courts below must have just plain gotten it wrong. It does not seem to me that the error in

---

standards might have produced other outcomes, but they were not "in play" at the time. The National Opinion Research Center sponsored a careful recount, including tests of inter-coder reliability. Although Bush emerged victorious in only three of the nine scenarios considered (including that endorsed by the Florida Supreme Court, and that espoused by Gore, but *not* that espoused by Bush at the time), the authors note that an intensive study such as theirs "was not an option in the hectic days following the presidential election." See Wolter et al. (2003) at 12.

116. The United States shows its British heritage—remember, where Latin became the language of law—and it does not hurt to use a Latin phrase now and then to show that non-lawyers can see through the masquerade. *De novo* means "anew," that is, not deciding on the judge's interpretation of the studies, but on the studies themselves. As Justice Thomas wrote in dissent, in *Hunt* (2001) at 260:

> [T]he Court ignores its role as a reviewing court and engages in its own factfinding enterprise.

117. *Shaw* (1993) and *Shaw* (1996). In addition, in *Hunt* (1999) the Supreme Court had sent the Twelfth District back to the lower court for further consideration, holding that summary judgment for plaintiff was ill-advised. The district court panel then held, as they originally had in summary judgment and as was clearly true, that the Twelfth District's boundaries were based on race. That opinion was reversed in *Hunt* (2001).

118. For a reversal of the lower court's bland acceptance of an incorrect expert, see the Fifth Circuit's opinion in *James* (1977). *Daubert* (1993) is an example of the more traditional approach, providing guidelines by which the lower court should review the facts. Then in *Kumho* (1999) the Supreme Court again reviewed the expert testimony and, rather than remanding, made its own determination that such testimony could not pass standards enunciated in *Daubert*.

courts below *Hunt* was clear, if it was error at all.[119] Supreme Court Justices do not have the ability to make that determination. But when a higher court wants to determine fact, it does.

As important as statistical evidence has become, it is not, and perhaps should not be, dominant. The *Hunt* Court in 2001 was probably driven more by feedback from its intervention in Florida than by its sophistication in evaluating expert testimony. Ronald Weber's expert conclusion for plaintiffs, that the important factor was race, appears to be more substantial than the Court's:

> Dr. Weber's calculated tiny percentage differences are simply too small to carry significant evidentiary weight.[120]

As we will see throughout this book, determining what difference is "tiny," like determining what "equality" means, remains a judicial function. It is not one courts exercise expertly, or even consistently.

INTO THE TWENTY-FIRST CENTURY

The end of the twentieth century was a boom time for science-oriented experts—quite a contrast with the first three-quarters of the century. Here is one summary from 1978:

> Throughout this century, courts have been generally unreceptive to expert probability and statistical testimony. . . . Although the volume of statistical and probability evidence has grown since the 1960s, the skepticism of the courts has increased correspondingly, with legitimate justifications.[121]

Statistics is a tool, where classifications of expertise are by subject matter. Statistics was not mentioned in the "more modern" list of expert topics, quoted above. Nor is it among

---

119. The Court's decision in *Hunt* (2001) was statistically arbitrary. The state's expert, David Peterson, showed that race and party affiliation are hard to distinguish. Blacks register 95 percent as Democrats, and are less likely to vote against their affiliation than Democrat whites. Thus a black district is a reliably Democrat district, and both party affiliation and preserving incumbent seats are legitimate bases for districting. As a statistical matter, the apportionment *was* based on race, regardless how the Court chose to see it. When combined with the higher burden placed on plaintiffs—they must show that the predominant decision factor was race, whereas the state does not have to show that it was otherwise, only to show that plaintiffs' evidence is not conclusive—the Court's opinion seems to offer a safe "let them do what they want" sop to states.

120. *Hunt* (2001) at 247. *I.e.*, the Court's conclusion may have been wrong as a matter of statistics, but the decision cannot be called "wrong" on that account, as judges get to decide where to "draw the line."

121. Collins (1978) at 161. In her survey of cases, which includes jury bias, jury size, school segregation, sentencing bias, and pre-trial detention, Collins for the most part (except for testing) misses equal-employment opportunity. By the time she was writing her article, it should have been clear to any observer that courts were receptive to statistical arguments generalizing from well-defined populations (applicants or employees). Collins does not differentiate between legislative-fact and adjudicative-fact arguments, a distinction that might have led her to see the trend that was well underway.

the topics covered in a 1982 compendium of experts in civil actions from the Practising
Law Institute:

> contract actions;
>
> construction cases;
>
> real estate;
>
> patent infringement;
>
> matrimonial actions;
>
> medical;
>
> tax;
>
> antitrust;
>
> securities; and
>
> copyright.[122]

Sheila Jasonoff writes separate chapters on the following late twentieth century "science
and technology" subject areas:

> toxic torts;
>
> genetic engineering;
>
> family affairs; and
>
> definitions of life and death.[123]

These subjects, which include abortion, adoption, assisted suicide, and in-vitro fertil-
ization, make uncomfortable decision makers of lay judges. They look to experts for help.
Few social commentators have contrasted the certain expert—the one with the binary
conclusion, "he did it" or "no, he didn't"—with the expert whose very expertise includes a
probability of error: the statistical expert. All evidence is ultimately probabilistic. Statistics
stands nearly alone in saying that it is. In Chapter 10 I recommend methods by which
uncertainty can become a more prominent part of expert testimony.

A recent *Yale Law Journal* note tells us:

> Historians have testified in a range of cases: Indian rights; land claims; gender
> discrimination; deportation of alleged Holocaust participants; voting rights;
> and gay rights, among others.[124]

---

122. Kraft (1982). This is the complete list of chapter headings. One might note that these are areas of
law, and so statistics would be an inappropriate heading. But this is my point. Attorneys assumed that
experts were legal-subject-matter oriented. They did not have a structure in which to consider expert
skill sets as transcending such subjects.

123. See Jasanoff (1995).

124. Case Note (2001) at 1536.

Michael Saks:

> In short, fact-finders are called upon to make evaluations of more complex
> evidence all the time.[125]

Certain or not, and correct or not, experts have helped the judicial system come to conclusions, or at least to rationalize them. Ultimately, Nancy Cruzan and Terry Schiavo were allowed to stop breathing.[126] Hitherto-unknown life forms can be patented.[127] Maternity disputes, when one woman carries another's conception to term, or when a child is reclaimed from an adoption, can be settled. Whether one finds these decisions "correct," it is satisfying that they are made; and it is reasonable to understand that they were made in consultation with experts. It is also scary. Much of what is called science in courts—not "junk science," but academically approved science—is so wrong and so irrelevant that it inspired this book. Nonetheless, one must also be struck by how badly many courts have used the science presented to them, even when that science was adequate to the task.[128]

Issues and Language

Many of these new issues have generated strange debates. Consider, for example, the extent to which the state can act to protect an "unborn child," surely an oxymoronic phrase. Terminating a fetus is not a problem; killing an "unborn child" is. People who would allow a mother to die rather than abort her fetus are called "pro-life." People who would prefer there to be no abortions, but most of all prefer that the pregnant woman has the right to decide, call themselves "pro-choice," but are nonetheless labeled "pro-abortion" by others. The probability that a person who has been in a coma for twenty years will come out of it is not zero. But calling a person "brain *dead*" beforehand provides language by which pulling the plug is not "murder."[129] The political right uses the term "nazi" to describe people who oppose their smoking in public places,[130] a term at least as applicable to their lack

---

125. Saks (1990) at 1028.

126. Nancy Cruzan lay in a coma, with no measurable brain activity, for years. No doctor was willing to "pull the plug" for fear of being prosecuted for murder. In *Cruzan* (1990), the Supreme Court allowed the Missouri courts to prevent disconnecting Cruzan from life support, absent sufficiently compelling proof that it would have been her wish to do so. However, the Missouri courts were ultimately satisfied, and allowed the life-support apparatus to be disconnected. See also *Schiavo* (2005).

127. *Diamond* (1980).

128. See, for example, Annas (1992). Some of the examples in the following chapters of this book make the same point, that judges may be misled by opposing analyses even when one of them is quite good.

129. The concept of "brain death" was formalized in 1968 and used, for example, in *Goldston* (1977) to deny the appeal of a murderer who wanted to blame the doctor who took the victim off a respirator.

130. Peggy Noonan (1990) at 189 described as "health nazis" those who wished she would not smoke in a restaurant. Victor Crawford, a paid tobacco-industry lobbyist, claimed credit for inventing that term

of concern for the nuisance, and possible health risk, they have become. In law and politics both, language often substitutes for thought.

David Faigman discusses a Tennessee case in which the "ownership" of frozen, fertilized embryos was at issue.

> Judge Young . . . relied almost exclusively on the expert testimony of Dr. Jerome LeJeune, the director of the French National Center of Scientific Research, the discoverer of the genetic cause of Down's syndrome and an ardent "pro-life" advocate.[131]

The judge therefore determined that these four-cell pre-embryos were tiny human beings who needed the "protection" of their mother, even though she had previously failed to bring several implanted embryos through to birth. Neither science nor the unlikelihood that this woman could convert these cell masses into a human state—no factual issue, that is—appeared to be relevant.

In *Barefoot* (1983) the Supreme Court was not ready to take on clearly fanciful pseudo-scientific psychobabble, the prediction of future dangerousness, decried by the American Psychiatric Association and lower-court judges alike as bearing no relationship to reality. Two psychiatrists

> testified that petitioner would probably commit further acts of violence and represent a continuing threat to society.[132]

The jury had to believe that was true before it could impose the death penalty. It did.

> The upshot was that Thomas Barefoot, his future dangerousness suitably certified by a credentialed expert, was executed by lethal injection.[133]

In *Wells* (1985) the allegation that Ortho-Gynol Contraceptive Jelly caused birth defects won the plaintiff several million dollars, on the basis of "expert" testimony that could not have concluded, scientifically, what the experts claimed.

> In most respects, Judge Shoob's opinion in Wells is a first rate specimen of judicial craft. It is clear, detailed and carefully reasoned. . . . Unfortunately, Judge Shoob's opinion is absolutely wrong. There is no scientifically credible evidence that Ortho-Gynol Contraceptive Jelly ever causes birth defects.[134]

I do not envy the modern courts having to deal with such issues. I ascribe at least some

---

to deflect efforts to regulate tobacco consumption in an interview by Leslie Stahl on *60 Minutes*, CBS television, March 19, 1995. Rush Limbaugh expanded the terminology to include "gestapo." Refer to his radio programs of September 26, 1994, December 15, 1994, and June 27, 1995, for example.

131. Quotation from Faigman (2000) at 43, referring to *Davis* (1992).

132. *Barefoot* (1982) at 884, Justice White for the Court.

133. Huber (1991) at 220. See also my broader discussion of experts divining the future, in Chapter 10.

134. Gross (1991) at 1122.

of the lack of the courts' ability to handle them to the lack of expertise among experts. It would be easy enough for an expert to say, "This is just a language issue, your honor. You may define, under law, when an embryo becomes a person, but please do not rely on an expert for that information." Let me suggest this testimony:

> No expert can define when life begins, or, for a certainty, what it is. There are debates right now whether micro-bacteria, which appear to be too small to contain DNA, can be called a life form, even though they can be cultured; that is, they can reproduce. 'Brain dead' is therefore not a scientific term. The court may decide that a comatose existence with no measurable brain activity is not worth the resources it takes to sustain it, but scientific 'expertise' cannot be relied on to come to that decision.

Social decisions masquerade as scientific decisions. The experts appear to be as confused as the courts about them.

Even if a cogent scientific debate can be had on such subjects, there is little evidence that the courts can absorb it, utilize it, bring forth a compelling scientific opinion. Judge Jack Weinstein's granting of defendants' motion to dismiss the complaints of the *Agent Orange* "opt-out" class declared plaintiffs' evidence to be worthless.[135] His opinion is convincing. Weinstein's intervention is widely praised as beneficial judicial activism, stopping a farce before it got out of hand. It is a model of judicial handling of "science" experts that deserves to be studied.

As reported by Scott Zeger, Timothy Wyant, Leonard Miller, and Jonathan Samet, the methodological dispute between Minnesota and the tobacco companies it was suing for tobacco-related costs was resolved by Judge Fitzpatrick. He found it "abhorrent and horrendously contrary to public policy" to allow damages to be reduced because the death of an ill Minnesotan reduced the state's cost.[136] Where Weinstein's *Agent Orange* decisions were rational and thorough, Fitzpatrick's was emotional and abusive. There is clear precedent opposing Fitzpatrick's ruling: The Dalkon Shield payments in the A. H. Robins bankruptcy were smaller for death than for lingering illness, because that had been the history of prior settlements and jury awards. Heirs of persons killed by wrongful acts of tobacco companies could try to collect damages. They were harmed by the death, and could pursue compensation on their own. The state, however, truly incurred less expenditure on that account, and therefore should have received a smaller reimbursement. Judge Fitzpatrick's decision makes no sense. Facts should matter.

---

135. *Agent Orange* (1985). See also a follow-up opinion, *McMillan* (2003), in which Judge Weinstein does not allow challenge to National Academy of Sciences studies of the effects of Agent Orange. I briefly discuss this case in Chapter 10. There, also, I will comment on Judge Weinstein's current strategy of allowing all expert testimony, declaring some to be right, some wrong, but none invalid.

136. The court ordered the defense not to raise "any defense so predicated." See Zeger et al. (2000) at 317.

Standards of Assessment

As indicated above, the expert witness is part of the evidentiary process, and "process" implies rules. What are the rules for judicial evaluation of "science" testimony? Where did they come from? When?

Before Articulation

Situations requiring rules often precede the rules themselves. We cope. Michael Saks has a theory of how the rules—at first implicit, then explicit—evolved to deal with science evidence. He starts with the idea that before there were articulated standards there was a "commercial marketplace test":

> The implicit test of expertise was whether there was a commercial market for the witness's learning. If a person could make a living selling the knowledge at issue, then expertise presumably existed.[137]

One can see the derivation of Saks' hypothesis in this early opinion accepting the expertise of a handwriting expert:

> It is a question of skill and experience, depending upon a practiced eye, experience, judgment, and habit, arising from being constantly employed to examine signatures and detect forgeries.[138]

Although one court saw one skill this way, I do not think it is easily generalizable. Many a charlatan made a living—no doubt many still do—positing the absurd. I doubt that, on those grounds alone, courts would have accepted evidence from, for example, phrenologists. It is also unclear what this "marketplace" was. For example, the *Jennings* (1911) court not only tells us that it is probably the first U.S. court to accept fingerprint evidence, but that British courts had been accepting it for at least two years, and police departments had been using it for seven. The use by government agencies (foreign, federal, and local) impressed the court, but was hardly a "commercial marketplace" test.[139]

There is some early judicial language about the characteristics desired in experts.

---

137. Saks (1998) at 1074. This view of the evolution of science standards in courts was initially articulated in Faigman et al. (1994), of which Saks is a co-author.

138. *Moody* (1835) at 496. The Court also explains that "such persons by their situation, employment, and habits of observation" "may be presumed to have such art and skill."

139. Unfortunately, writers passing through this topic quickly often fail to question what they have read. So, for example, Owen (2002) covers "early common law" in one paragraph, at 354, and summarizes the Saks-Faigman theory as if it were fact.

> Loose general opinions on the subject, entitled to very little more respect in
> the ascertainment of facts than the conjectures of witnesses, are of themselves
> undeserving of consideration.[140]

That these experts' opinions rise above "conjecture" apparently is determined by their
"education and experience." In short, an expert had to have the appearance, the accouter-
ments of expertise. Erica Beecher-Monas thinks that "whether the evidence purported to
reflect a consensus of the relevant scientific community" was the evidentiary criterion at
least since the early part of the twentieth century.[141] This, as we are about to see, is no
standard at all.

Frye (1923)

The district-court judge did not allow James Alphonso Frye, on trial for murder, to present evidence from a systolic-pressure lie detector, "a progenitor of today's polygraph
test."[142] Frye, protesting his innocence, offered to take such a test live, in front of the jury.
Denied. He offered the test administrator as an expert witness. Denied. Obviously, if there
were no correlation between this instrument's measurement and the subject's mendacity,
such a demonstration would be just a show, one a gullible member of the jury might
believe. The court thought it had to decide, in advance, if such a test would be valid.[143]
How was an appeals court to do that, assuming that denying Frye his test affected the jury's
verdict? The court ruled:

> [W]hile courts will go a long way in admitting expert testimony deduced from
> a well-recognized scientific principle or discovery, the thing from which the
> deduction is made must be sufficiently established to have gained general
> acceptance in the particular field in which it belongs.[144]

As "general acceptance" surely comes long after a scientific proposition is enunciated
(consider, for example, the theory of evolution), this is a conservative position. The *Frye*
standard raised as many questions as it answered. What degree of affirmation comprises
"general acceptance"?[145] Who decides what the "field" is, who is in it, and what their con-

---

140. *Catharine* (1854) at 175.

141. Beecher-Monas (2000) at footnote 1.

142. Kesan (1996) at 1989.

143. Despite the abuse that *Frye* principles have received in recent years, this one is right on: Decide
meta-issues first. We will see in later chapters, especially Chapter 7, that assessing the validity of a defendant's "explanation" is one of the key functions of a judge faced with statistical evidence.

144. *Frye* (1923) at 1114.

145. Gianelli (1980) at 1210:

> The percentage of those in the field who must accept the technique has never been clearly
> delineated.

sensus opinion is? How? By survey, by literature review? Usually the expert is asked: "Is this a generally accepted practice in your field, Dr. X?" "Yes, it is," the initial expert would assert; but "No, it is not," would be part of the rebuttal by Dr. Y. Thus the "general acceptance" rule generates yet another debate among experts. Then what?

Whether one thinks that the prior standard was based on some market test or on scientists validating themselves, *Frye* represents a benchmark.

> *Frye* replaced buyers with sellers as assessors of the validity of what was being offered.[146]

Courts continued to defer to some external authority or mechanism. To determine what was good science, what bad, was not the judge's responsibility.

The *Frye* "rule" or, better, the general-acceptance principle, became amended or dropped by different federal circuits over time. It was also accepted by some state courts, rejected by others. Such a conservative rule was too slow, in an age of innovation. For example, in 1991, the New Jersey Supreme Court reversed a lower court's rejection of expert testimony about the cause of cancers. Lower-court judges could

> rely on scientific theories of causation that have not yet reached general acceptance as long as they are based on information generally relied on by experts.[147]

Neither the multiple-pools approach to selection nor survival analysis, both discussed in Chapter 2, were "generally accepted" when I introduced them to courts. The procedural analysis of jury selection that I explain in Chapter 5 is still not "generally accepted" by experts, although it has been by both federal and state courts. This extension of *Frye*, to generally accepted "principles" instead of generally accepted method, is the door through which courts managed reasonably well under rules that appeared to tell them not to.

Focus on procedure is also what has allowed bad statistical analyses to masquerade as informative. The "urn" model of selection—comparing observed colors of selected beads to what would have been found, on the average, had selection been made blindly from an urn containing known proportions of different-colored beads—and the use of the normal distribution to approximate the binomial, are universally accepted statistical procedures. As we will see in Chapter 2, they are often inappropriately applied to selection situations.

---

146. Faigman et al. (1994) at 1807. They elucidate:

> The commercial marketplace test, even with its serious weaknesses, had the virtue of allowing buyers to assess the value of purported expertise and whether it was, "therefore," valid. Under the *Frye* variant, that control was transferred to the people who produced the knowledge and offered it (and themselves) to the courts.

Identical language appears in Saks (1998) at 1075. I presume it originated in the co-authored piece with Saks himself.

147. "In Trenton, Court Takes On Toxic Damages Cases," *New York Times* (September 16, 1991), at B2. The opinion is *Rubanick* (1991).

Regression is a generally accepted statistical method but, as we will see in Chapter 3, it may be inappropriate to the issues.

Jack Weinstein notes:

> Hardly a case of importance is tried today in the federal courts without the involvement of a number of expert witnesses.[148]

As evidenced by his *Agent Orange* decision, he does not think much of them. Writing shortly thereafter:

> An expert can be found to testify to the truth of almost any factual theory, no matter how frivolous, thus validating the case sufficiently to avoid summary judgment and force the matter to trial. At the trial itself the expert's testimony can be used to obfuscate what would otherwise be a simple case. . . . Juries and judges can be, and sometimes are, misled by the expert-for-hire.

We have already seen that this is an old complaint. Another nineteenth-century example:

> Experience has shown that opposite opinions of persons professing to be experts may be obtained to any amount . . . and perplexing, instead of eluci-dating, the questions involved in the issue.[149]

Despite the growth of expert presentation of fact, and the importance of rules for handling such evidence, the federal courts had no rules of evidence until 1975. Weinstein cites the Federal Rules of Evidence as the death knell for federal application of the *Frye* standard.[150] Although those rules did specifically recognize expert witnesses, and accord them a certain leeway not given to other witnesses, they did not set new standards for determining when the court might exclude proffered experts. Rather, they said a judge could take "scientific, technical, or other specialized knowledge" from expert opinion, if it "will assist the trier of fact."[151] That approach left discretion in the hands of the judge, but offered no guidelines for its use. The evidence would assist the trier of fact if it validly made a distinction important to the case at hand (such as whether Mr. Frye was lying when he declared his innocence). How would the judge determine the validity of the science?

There is still no good answer to this question. The *Frye* standard provided language

---

148. Weinstein (1986) at 473; following indented quotation at 482.

149. *Winans* (1858) at 101. We saw a similar view expressed above from *Keegan* (1854). The point is that for over 150 years it has been common for judges to see their experts as badly motivated, and on this account badly serving the court.

150. Walsh (1999), agreeing in retrospect, calls the Federal Rules "the greatest barrier to *Frye*'s contin-ued viability." At 141.

151. Federal Rule of Evidence 702.

for attorneys arguing that a court should or should not hear certain evidence, but courts were inconsistent. Weinstein's proclamation notwithstanding, as it allowed judges to use others' judgments about the quality of the work being presented, the *Frye* standard continued to rule in some federal jurisdictions into the 1990s, and in some states into the twenty-first century.[152]

There are two reasons the *Frye* standard deserves more than the two lines it is accorded in most books. One is that its original subject, the polygraph (lie-detector) test, reappeared in *Scheffer* (1998), which I will discuss below. Second, in retrospect, it appears that Frye's expert was correct, though we do not know if he or his machine was up to the task. Systolic pressure changes when one is lying. In a well-administered lie-detector test a baseline is established for each individual, from which false answers can be detected with some probability of error.[153] Although the court correctly questioned the validity of Frye's machine, it seems not to have been willing to take evidence on that subject. If it was as good as current polygraphs, Frye should have been allowed to take his test and use it as evidence of his innocence, just as Scheffer should have been able to present his polygraph results in his defense.[154] What is required is an understanding of probabilistic evidence, as I explain in Chapter 10.[155]

---

152. Seven years after Weinstein was writing, ten of the thirteen federal circuits still followed *Frye*, according to Kesan (1996) at 1990 (footnote 26). See also Rossi (1991), Chapter 2. Also,

Frye is not dead. Many courts continue to adhere to the *Frye* test by name.

Lewin (1992) at 187. Cheesebro (1993) lists twenty states that adhere to the *Frye* standard. David Bernstein (2001) lists seventeen, but New Jersey is erroneously one of them. The Nebraska Supreme Court does not even mention *Daubert* in affirming the admission of DNA evidence under *Frye* in *Freeman* (1997). The next year they remembered that they had "expanded the *Frye* test to ensure maximum reliability with regard to DNA evidence," but still did not adopt *Daubert*. See *Carter* (1998). The Alaska Supreme Court first adopted *Daubert* standards in *Coon* (1999). The Arizona Supreme Court reaffirmed its reliance on *Frye* in *Logerquist* (2000). The Minnesota Supreme Court reaffirmed its reliance on *Frye*—modified by its own state rulings (adding a reliability test)—in *Goeb* (2000). The Mississippi Supreme Court held to *Frye* until October 2003. See *McLemore* (2003). David Bernstein (2003) tells us, at 23, that at least California, Florida, New York, Illinois, and Pennsylvania continued to adhere to the "general acceptance standard" in 2003. The Alabama Supreme Court has declined to adopt *Daubert*. See *Martin* (2004), and references therein. Figure 1 in Cheng and Yoon (2005) shows twelve states still adhering to *Frye*.

153. Widacki and Horvath (1978) provide an example of how one might derive the probability of an accurate polygraph reading, and in their test find it quite reliable in differentiating between guilty and innocent suspects. A National Academy of Science panel, having reviewed many studies, declared that the polygraph's accuracy was "well above chance, though well below perfection." See Committee (2002) at 3.

154. Gallai (1999) argues against allowing polygraph testimony. I discuss such blanket (legislative-fact) assertions in Chapter 10.

155. Scientific conclusions are probabilistic, and so I agree with Moreno (2002) that the fundamental skill judges need to acquire is statistics, not science. But judges do not need to know technical aspects of statistics. I write more about this in Chapter 7 on judges, and Chapter 10 on procedures.

Daubert (1993)

Jason Daubert's attorneys alleged that his birth defects were caused by his mother's inges-
tion of Bendectin. Eight experts were prepared to state their opinions that this was so, even
though there is little scientific evidence to that effect as legislative fact, and it seems beyond
science to establish it as adjudicative fact. Daubert's attorneys argued that a reasonable jury
could find that Merrill Dow was at fault—similar to Brandeis' argument in *Muller* (1908)—
and therefore that a jury should be allowed to hear the evidence that Merrill Dow wanted
suppressed. The question before the Supreme Court was on what basis the district-court
judge could exclude this "evidence." While disavowing that these factors applied to any other
case, the Court enunciated a four-factor test that scientific evidence would have to pass:

> The hypothesis (propounded here by plaintiff, the connection between
>   the medicine and the defects) is testable and has been tested.
>
> The "error rate" associated with the relationship is not too great.
>
> The basic research has been published in a peer-reviewed journal.
>
> The science supporting the opinion is generally accepted in a relevant
>   scientific community.[156]

There is something strikingly familiar about this "revolutionary" doctrine. The third
factor requires that there be a "field," and gives some power to others in it to determine the
worth of this expert's ideas. The fourth factor reiterates the *Frye* test![157] Presumably, failure to pass any one of these qualifications could be grounds to prevent the expert's testimony. Thus the *Frye* rule has been supplemented, not supplanted.[158]

---

156. *Daubert* (1993) at 590. *Daubert* was hardly the first suit against Merrell Dow over side-effects of
Bendectin, nor the first in which plaintiffs' expert's testimony had been disallowed or severely restricted.
Kesan (1996) at 2004 writes,

> Over 1,900 Bendectin cases were filed in state and federal courts between 1977 and 1988.

As the circuits disagreed on the admissibility of plaintiffs' experts' testimony, it was clear even to a reluctant Supreme Court that it was time to set expert standards.

157. As New York Judge Sweet quickly noted, in *Maiorana* (1993) at 1033,

> The decision in *Daubert* kills *Frye* and then resurrects its ghost.

158. The Third Circuit immediately doubled the number of factors:

> Specifically, there are eight criteria to determine the reliability of expert testimony: (1)
> whether a method consists of a testable hypothesis; (2) whether the method has been sub-
> ject to peer review; (3) the known or potential rate of error; (4) the existence and main-
> tenance of standards controlling the technique's operation; (5) whether the method is
> generally accepted; (6) the relationship of the technique to methods which have been
> established to be reliable; (7) the qualifications of the expert witness testifying based on
> the methodology; and (8) the non-judicial uses to which the method has been put.

Williams (2002) footnote 5. These eight factors were originally presented in *Paoli II* (1994) footnote 8.

The Court was placing the burden of determining acceptable science—good enough to be heard at trial—on trial judges. Not on marketplace buyers of "scientific" advice. Not on "scientists" themselves.[159] Even today, the implication of an internal standard is not fully appreciated. Most commentators still think the task is to judge a field—handwriting analysis, tool markings, fingerprint identification—for its credibility as science. I will argue in Chapter 10 that such a broad focus misses the point. "Good" science must be identified in the particular proffered testimony.[160]

The judge became the "gatekeeper." He had to decide what was "scientific" evidence, and whether that evidence, if scientific, was relevant and helpful to the trier of fact in this particular case. Novel science possibly could pass such tests.

As Marc Rosenblum points out, this gatekeeping function had recently become more important in civil rights cases, as the 1991 Civil Rights Act moved fact determination of discrimination from the judge to a jury. Andrew Gavil notes the conjunction of *Daubert* and the increased reliance of the court on economists in antitrust cases. *Daubert* hearings may well have an impact in these and other fields.[161] From the point of view of this book, it means that expert testimony will receive more scrutiny from trial courts. Such scrutiny is welcome. Whether judges can meaningfully provide it is one question. Whether attorney or expert behavior will be modified by this scrutiny is another question. I tackle these questions in Chapters 6, 7, 8, and 10.

Daubert was an amplification of Title 7 of the Federal Rules of Evidence, especially Rule 702 concerning expert qualifications and Rule 703 concerning what the expert can say. It instructed judges to use Title 7 in situations where they might have used Title 4, to allow trials to proceed using parts of proffered testimony, rather than grant summary judgment.[162]

The *Daubert* decision did not come out of thin air, unanticipated. Weinstein's treatise on evidence had long held that Rule 702 obviated *Frye*. Paul Giannelli had reviewed over half a century of the application of *Frye*, and found it wanting as a standard for 1980s cases.

---

159. For example, the Third Circuit concluded

> that the precept . . . that the principal arbiters of the reasonableness of reliance upon inadmissible evidence are the experts and not the trial judge, does not survive *Daubert*.

Paoli II (1994) at 732.

160. As summarized by the Third Circuit,

> even if an expert's proposed testimony constitutes scientific knowledge, his or her testimony will be excluded if it is not scientific knowledge *for purposes of the case*.

Paoli II (1994) at 743, emphasis in original.

161. See Rosenblum (2000) and Gavil (1997). In Chapter 8 I will characterize the economist's antitrust expertise as "craft" more than science, at least with reference to *Microsoft*.

162. Gavil (1997) appears to think that *Daubert* applies Rule 702 only to the methodology in some generic sense, and not to its effectuation in this case by this expert. No court that I know of has interpreted it this way.

The Third Circuit, referring to Weinstein's and Giannelli's work, had suggested "a more flexible approach to the admissibility of novel scientific evidence" based on an assessment of its reliability. Peter Huber popularized the issue, coining the phrase "junk science" and holding courts responsible for admitting it.[163] The world of litigation was ready for a Supreme Court pronouncement on the subject.

Daubert and its "progeny," especially *Joiner* (1997) and *Kumho* (1999), have created an industry in the publication of law-review articles, as well as in litigation.[164] Gavil, less enthusiastic than most commentators, writes:

> *Daubert* has contributed yet another layer of expensive and time consuming satellite litigation to the already encumbered process of litigating antitrust cases.[165]

He then asks whether the benefits have exceeded the costs. On a not very analytic basis—let us call it suggestive—Gavil concludes in the negative. The *Daubert* hearing occurs for the benefit of, and at the discretion of, the judge. As long as their work is accepted into evidence, *Daubert* is not the experts' concern.[166] I conclude, in Chapter 10, that *Daubert*'s lasting impact will be on procedure, the *Daubert* hearing—that other "layer of . . . satellite litigation"—in which the expert's work is scrutinized. I support that procedure, and suggest some modification to achieve its desired end.

Daubert Progeny

Because *Daubert* was about science (indeed, it was at heart a statistical case), some courts questioned whether the same gatekeeper function should be applied to more "technical" experts. The question in *Kumho* was whether plaintiffs could use a person clearly experienced and expert in the automobile-tire business to identify a particular tire blowout as due to a manufacturing defect. Whereas *Daubert* had been remanded back to lower courts,[167] in *Kumho* the Court decided the question directly: The judge's exclusion of

---

163. Weinstein (2001) listed in the bibliography is a late version of his second edition. This edition always had a section on Rule 702, and always suggested that it was more liberal than the *Frye* test. See Giannelli (1980). The Third Circuit case is *Downing* (1985), quotation from 1237. See Huber (1991).

164. Margaret Berger (1994) at 1345 says *Daubert* "will probably appear in every evidence casebook," that is, will become part of every law school's curriculum. In 1996, a digest of *Daubert* cases—usually one or two sentences per case—comprised fifty-five law-review pages. See Fenner (1996). No one would attempt such a task today, but the flow of cases is monitored at http://daubertontheweb.com.

165. Gavil (2000) at 876.

166. In *Venator* (2002), for example, defendant moved to exclude testimony from plaintiffs' economist expert, Janice Madden. Madden had to articulate the reasoning behind each of her challenged decisions, but any expert should expect to do so. She did. Motion denied.

167. See *Daubert* (1995), where the Ninth Circuit determined that the evidence against Merrill Dow did not pass the Supreme Court's standard.

plaintiff's tire expert was reasonable and fitting, following his gatekeeper role.

Kumho provided no insight into how technical or craft experts should be evaluated. The Court implied that the same standard applied to technical as to scientific expert testimony, although it has never been clear what that standard is. In Chapter 10 I suggest that science and craft testimony require different standards and different procedures.

In *Scheffer*, the defendant, a military officer, had been administered a polygraph test a few days after he had been found to have drugs in his urine. He denied that he had taken any drugs, and the polygraph test could not distinguish his denial from the truth. He wanted that test result submitted as evidence. However, polygraph evidence is prohibited under military law. In 1996, the Military Appeals Court declared that prohibition unconstitutional. In 1998, the Supreme Court reversed:

> The *Scheffer* Court concluded that science has boundaries, and since polygraph test results fall outside the boundaries of science, they can be excluded by the legislature without employing a *Daubert* analysis.[168]

Although concurring opinions noted that the Court was ducking the obvious application of *Daubert*, only Justice Stevens dissented. Stevens would have found that the exclusion rule violated military code, and not reached the constitutional question. He also argued (alone) that the rule was clearly unconstitutional, that defendants have a right to defend, or at least to try to. *Daubert* should be a vehicle for just such a defense.

A number of commentators have noted that *Scheffer* (1998) makes no sense coming after *Barefoot* (1983) (psychiatrists may predict one's future behavior) and *Rock* (1987) (the state cannot proscribe, on a blanket basis, the augmentation of a witness's memory by hypnosis).[169] It is *Barefoot* that should be questioned. *Scheffer* makes no sense, period. There is no reason to continue the bad example of *Frye*, excluding polygraph tests, as long as standards can be set, individual examiners tested, and probabilities of erroneous interpretation calculated. I hold out the hope that the *Scheffer* aberration is due to the Court's reluctance to interfere with the military justice system, except that it did so by overruling a military court.

Joiner (1997) concerns the grounds on which an appeals court can reverse a trial judge's exclusion of expert testimony. Both parties and the Court agreed that the proper standard for review is "abuse of discretion." The district-court judge's decision will be given great deference, unless it can be shown that he went too far, or did not in fact judge the science behind the expert's views.

> [Joiner] claims that because the District Court's disagreement was with the conclusion that the experts drew from the studies, the District Court com-

---

168. Moreno (2002) at 1046.

169. *Rock* (1987) at 49:

> Petitioner's claim that her testimony was impermissibly excluded is bottomed on her constitutional right to testify in her own defense.

mitted legal error and was properly reversed by the Court of Appeals. But conclusions and methodology are not entirely distinct from one another.[170]

I agree again with the lone dissent by Justice Stevens, who thinks methodology and conclusions *are* distinguishable. He asks:

> When qualified experts have reached relevant conclusions on the basis of an acceptable methodology, why are their opinions inadmissible?[171]

One of the *amicus* briefs in *Daubert* contained this phrase:

> It is *how* the conclusions are reached, not *what* the conclusions are, that makes them "good science."[172]

That is the distinction Justice Stevens would like to maintain, as would I.

The question is *not* did the expert use a methodology that is praised in textbooks. The question is whether the expert asked relevant questions and understood the data, the institutions from which they came, and the legal issues the data analysis should illuminate. The question first is whether the expert did a good job of analysis, and second whether he did a good job of interpretation. As we will see in Chapter 3 on regression, the methodology itself does exactly what it claims to do, and in a sense tells you how well (from the data at hand) it has done it. But regression is often used where it is inappropriate, through expert misunderstanding of the question, or of the method. Passing on the value of "fields" or "methods" outside the particular case at hand is a waste of judicial resources, and asks the judge to be something he is not.

Passing on the use of methods in this particular case may seem more difficult, more technical. In this book I explain why that is not so.

No matter how well a study appears to have been done in some technical sense, the expert's conclusions still may not follow.[173] District-court judges will have to learn to make this distinction.[174] Once again, although it may seem that drawing conclusions from a

---

170. *Joiner* (1997), majority opinion by Justice Rehnquist at 146.

171. *Joiner* (1997), Stevens dissent (to Part III) at 154. This will be exactly my point in Chapter 5: If juries are gathered following every rule the jury administrators are supposed to follow, rules condoned by the Court, how can any court second-guess the result? Saks (2000a) agrees that the distinction between methodology and conclusions should stand, but is disturbed by *Joiner*'s implication that district courts can re-litigate in fields the scientific merit of which has been determined by the Supreme Court. To the extent that *Joiner* does this, I agree with it, and not with Saks. But I think *Joiner* is more about the particular effectuation than the general merit of a procedure. Regression passes, but does *this* regression?

172. *Amicus* brief for Nicolaas Bloembergen et al., the so-called "Nobel Laureates" brief, at 22. This quotation appears in Imwinkelreid (1993) at 62.

173. Several examples of this phenomenon appear in this book. I recommend particularly my discussion in Chapter 3 of Mark Killingsworth's regression in *I-NET* and my discussion in Chapter 8 of the illogic behind the "market" defense in *Nassau* (1992).

174. Dixon and Gill (2002) at 301:

statistical study is the most technical of tasks, I show in the chapters that follow that it is a task similar to the finding of constitutional fact, which is at the heart of the judge's abilities.

The system will not come to a halt if judges are not statistical experts. Judges need to be intelligent and open-minded, but not skilled in statistics methodology. They may require procedural help, sometimes the assistance of their own expert, but not statistics education. Again I leave demonstration of these points to Chapters 2 through 5, and my argument to Chapters 6 through 10.

TECHNOLOGY AND COURTS

The expert witness has come a long way, from an observer of the event to a knower of legislative fact to a data analyst. A complete picture of the emergence of the statistical expert would include at least these additional historical strands:

> The inevitable statistical interpretation of "due process," propelled by legislation directed at behavior patterns, not individual actions (such as discrimination and antitrust behavior).
>
> The development of econometrics, the statistical testing of social-science models, and other statistical-analysis methods.
>
> The development of computer technology, which allows analysis of large data sets with a reasonable amount of resources; and the same technology which creates those data sets in the course of business.
>
> Public-interest-law organizations with the funds and foresight to support social-science analyses.

I cannot cover all of this material here. How to ascertain and understand fact in a modern, computer-based, data-driven era is one of the great struggles within the justice system. The movement toward the courts' determination of fact based on a social-science methodology beyond the courts' expertise can be discussed in two parts. First, courts have always had to make determinations of fact in areas beyond their immediate knowledge. Second, quantitative social-science methods have expanded at an enormous rate since, say, the 1970s. As long as courts are called upon to decide what relationships hold in society or in some limited set of events, they must rely on social-science statistical analysis. That analysis relies on computer-manipulated data bases. So the evolution toward accepting social-

---

Judges may be more actively evaluating reliability, but we do not know whether they are doing so in ways that produce better outcomes. Judges may feel compelled to evaluate reliability and yet not be knowledgeable enough in the relevant field to make accurate determinations.

science "proof" involves acceptance of statistical generalities not even determinable three or four decades ago.[175] It is the inexorable future.

Advances in computer technology are so obvious they require no explanation.[176] As computer technology has advanced, computer power has become less and less expensive. With such cost reduction, computers have replaced paper in some functions, such as the maintenance of corporate personnel files, hospital files, and bank and brokerage financial files. Data bases constructed for management purposes were quickly exploited in litigation, as demonstrated in 2002 and 2003 by the use of e-mail archives to show that brokerage analysts were condemning internally stocks that they were praising publicly. As governments and corporations computerize more of their operations they are creating more grist for the data analyst's mill. In short, changes in the form in which ordinary business records are kept has played a large role in changing the methods of analysis in dispute situations.

At the start of the computer age, only large institutions could process automated data sets. Now it is commonplace. The Dalkon Shield litigation required the processing of hundreds of thousands of records. I processed over six million automobile-driver records to assess patterns of mobility in *Gibbs* (1998). The state's experts in the Minnesota tobacco litigation processed hundreds of millions of medical records.[177]

The laws themselves now require statistical analysis. What is "discrimination," when does a product "cause" harm, with what certainty does a forensic identification method identify the perpetrator of a crime? These relationships are not seen directly. They are inferred from outcomes. The expert using statistical tools may provide essential guidance to the court. Alternatively, as I show in the following chapters, his analysis may be incorrect, despite his elegant credentials and use of approved methodologies.

Be it deliberately or through lack of skill, experts hide very bad "analyses" under the name of scientifically approved technique. That is why Chapters 2 and 3 appear difficult: They are about piercing the skin of the method to its meaning. There we see that many analyses do not mean what they are interpreted to mean by statistical "experts." The remainder of this book unmasks the experts. I hope it helps judges do so, also.

---

175. The National Academy of Sciences panel puts it this way, in Fienberg (1989) at 218:

> The recent and expanding resort to statistics by the courts may therefore be seen as merely the reflection and logical outcome of the now ubiquitous use of statistics in accounting, marketing, political science, psychology, economics, and throughout the social sciences generally.

176. For a collection of articles about the early use of computers to assist attorneys, see Cwiklo (1979). The *entire* history of the computer, from the first vacuum-tube-based hard-wired calculator through the Pentium fast central processor on a chip, has occurred during my lifetime. We can have no idea what technological changes will affect the generation and presentation of expert evidence in courts in even livable spans of time.

177. Zeger et al. (2000).

2

Analyzing Selection Issues

They called themselves Progressive Citizens of America. It made sense to them that if Lucky Stores' clientele was 50 percent black, 50 percent of its clerks should be black. They picketed a Lucky in Contra Costa County, California, demanding that as white clerks resign, blacks be hired in their place, to achieve this goal. Lucky asked for and got an injunction to stop the picketing. The injunction was upheld by the California and U.S. Supreme Courts.[1] Hiring to fill a quota is racial discrimination. Picketing to enforce quota hiring is not protected free speech.[2]

A few years earlier, the Supreme Court had upheld a grand-jury-selection system in which, when the jury commissioners had selected one black person, they admitted, they stopped considering blacks for the remaining positions.[3] Apparently, at least at that time, some quotas were legal, some were not. I think they never are, and the Court's allowing them exemplified their lack of a procedural language in which they could define "fair."

WHAT IS "FAIR"?

Selection is a process. The word "fair" usually is taken to mean that certain characteristics, say race or gender, were not considered in that process; that only characteristics related

---

1. See *Hughes* (1950). Many cases are more about what protagonists are doing or proposing to do to obtain quota-based selection than about the existing selection process itself. For example, as described in *PEPCO* (1962), the Council on Racial Equality (CORE) issued stamps to customers which, if affixed to bills as directed, made them unreadable by electronic machines. CORE's stated purpose was to support "merit hiring," but sabotage, as it was described by the court, is not a protected labor activity.

2. In the September 3, 2001 issue of *The Nation*, letter-writer David Wilson says,

> The right has the money and the media. The progressives have the brains and the moral highroad.

In this case, in 1950, the progressives had neither.

3. See *Akins* (1945).

to performance in the position for which one is being selected (student, athlete, juror, worker) are used to determine selection. Statistical analysis is usually based on data from the *outcome* of a process. A statistical analyst tells us what outcomes a process would produce, with what frequency, from a model of "fair selection" that he "builds," depicting the way he or his client thinks the world should be. One then judges whether the actual outcome was so improbable, as a result of this model of a fair process, that we should not believe that the actual process was fair at all. That is, statistically, unfairness is not observed. It is inferred by comparing outcomes with those "expected" most of the time from a model of fair selection. The expectation from an inappropriate model, even if correctly calculated, can lead to an incorrect inference.

Fair selection might be by merit, as perceived without bias by the selectors; or, if there are no merit considerations, either randomly or by a neutral procedure, such as first-come, first-served. Selection to achieve a certain result cannot be "fair" by statistical criteria, regardless by what other criteria people may think that it is. If we *know* that the procedure was manipulated to produce a certain outcome, there is no statistical inference to be drawn. If we do not know what procedure was used, an appropriate statistical review of the outcome might lead us to suspect that it was manipulated, but such a suspicion may, or may not, be correct.

In most cases, the court would be better served judging procedures directly, something it is more capable of doing than understanding the tenuous connection between a probability model and reality. Outcomes are only relevant if the procedures cannot be judged on their own. Like the attorneys that bring them cases, and the experts who participate in them, the Supreme Court is confused about how to analyze selections. It is also confused about what "fair" means or, more in their area, what "constitutional" means.

Justice Scalia, dissenting from a decision that in effect reversed the principles of the Lucky Stores example by sustaining "affirmative action" over merit hiring, demonstrated a clarity of understanding:

> The Court today completes the process of converting this from a guarantee that race or sex will not be the basis for employment determinations, to a guarantee that it often will. Ever so subtly, without even alluding to the last obstacles preserved by earlier opinions that we now push out of our path, we effectively replace the goal of a discrimination-free society with the quite incompatible goal of proportionate representation by race and by sex in the workplace.[4]

In the selection process there is a "pool" of "candidates" from which selection is made. "Fair" surely should be defined with reference to that pool. If a police department needs to recruit someone who speaks Chinese, then it is unlikely that selection will look fair when

---

4. *Johnson* (1987), dissent at 658.

the pool is considered to be all police applicants. The pool should be Chinese-speaking applicants, among whom Chinese-origin people may have an advantage of understanding colloquialisms. Analyzing the outcome based on something other than the appropriate pool—say, defining a desired outcome of the race of clerks from the race of customers—is never a statistical issue.[5] Some people, even some courts, prefer such outcomes. They should not want statistical tests of fair hiring to support them.

In what Judge Garza thought "was probably the last case filed by the Johnson administration," the United States sued to integrate Longshoremen's unions in Texas. Most unions, regardless of origin, opposed integration. Blacks argued that their populations were relatively small in some areas, and therefore the 50 percent of the work they obtained in agreement with other unions benefitted them.

> They are off target in their argument. It is not the racial composition of the community that should control, but the number of Blacks and Whites that make themselves available for longshore work that counts.[6]

The pool, Judge Garza noted, was badly measured by the "community." In Chapter 5, we will see how difficult it is to measure the "community." Here, more than half of longshoremen were blacks. The result was that only 50 percent of the work had been allocated to over 50 percent of the longshoremen, leaving blacks worse off than they would have been with integrated hiring. The judge's arithmetic was correct, but his reasoning was not. Allocating longshoreman jobs by race is not a fair procedure. It cannot be legal, as the Fifth Circuit said in this case some years later, regardless who benefits.[7]

I was engaged by the Equal Employment Opportunity Commission to analyze hiring of workers into the Tempel Steel plant in Chicago. The owner was a Polish immigrant, dedicated to the proposition that the United States was the promised land. He helped other Polish families immigrate, giving them jobs in his mill. This seemed right to him. He was helping his kind, just as the Progressive Citizens of America were "helping" blacks in California. He misunderstood. The essence of "equal opportunity" is that one cannot favor one's own, or any kind. The steel-mill owner didn't need a lawsuit; he needed a lecture. The Progressive Citizens of America needed the same lecture. I know that Mr. Tempel got his lecture,

---

5. Thus, for example, the Board of Education of Hendersonville, North Carolina, when forced to integrate, proposed that it would be "fair" to have faculty "represent" the proportion black among students. That led to reducing the number of black teachers on the basis of their race. The court had a more appropriate concept of "fair." See *Chambers* (1966). Plaintiffs objected to the ratio of minority among supervisors, compared with minority among children in New York City schools. The judge was correctly "unimpressed." See *Chance* (1971).

6. *ILA* (1971) at 979; preceding in-text quotation at 977.

7. See *ILA* (1975). Allocating jobs by race *implicitly* is not legal, either. See, for example, *Steamship* (1995) in which new members of Steamship Clerks Union Local 1066 had to be nominated by old members— all of whom were white. No surprise, all nominations were white.

and I believe he understood it (he settled the case). I don't know if the Progressive Citizens of America ever realized how unprogressive their cause was. When I arrived in northern California ten years later, Lucky was still considered, by "progressives," to be a discriminatory employer, though they were never found to have unfairly rejected black applicants.

Early Equal-Opportunity Laws

By 1961, twenty states had some form of fair-labor practices or equal-employment-opportunity law.[8] Other states had broad anti-discrimination laws.[9] These laws established commissions with the right to review complaints and order compliance. Thus, through the 1940s, 1950s, and 1960s, many firms and government agencies experienced the discomfort of hiring people they had rejected for employment. And many individuals got jobs they had been discriminatorily denied. On occasion, constitutional issues were raised, such as whether a state could enforce an anti-discrimination law on a company engaged in interstate commerce. Some commission rulings for plaintiff thus made their way to federal courts, where most were upheld.[10]

The first federal anti-discrimination laws were passed after the Civil War. Laws such as U.S. Code 42 §1981 and §1983, still in use today, allowed federal intervention into the affairs of business and government agencies, although not providing for compensation, as did later civil-rights laws. The 1970s prosecution of one such case, against the Philadelphia Police, demonstrates some important facets of statistical argument. Bias against blacks in hiring and promotion was alleged. In the district court decision we find the information in Figure 1 regarding promotion examinations.[11]

	White	Black
Sergeant	18.4%	11.7%
Detective	27.2%	17.7%
Corporal	36.2%	23.8%

FIGURE 1: Pass Rates for the Philadelphia Police Exam, 1968–1970

Plaintiffs' expert was Bernard Siskin, then an assistant professor at Temple University, later a professional statistical analyst in litigation. The court does not tell us how many

8. The Michigan Supreme Court lists these laws in *Highland Park* (1961).

9. For example, see *Hall* (1878).

10. See, for example, *Colorado* (1963).

11. *O'Neill* (1972) at 1101, 4 FEP Cases at 982.

individuals were involved. As statistical inference is based on the outcome of events, the more events there were the better. It is inconceivable that Siskin, if he knew them, did not reveal the number of observations on which these pass rates were based. It is equally inconceivable that he would not have provided some measure of the improbability of these differences from a population in which white and black pass rates were equal. We are told early in the opinion that 20 percent of the police force is black. Using this ratio, depending how the number of takers is distributed among the exams, it requires over eight hundred test takers to find that these pass rates are different at the 0.05 level of probability (or, better, improbability). In other words, if this experiment were run many times, from a population in which there were equal black and white pass rates, we would find differences at least this large only one time in twenty from chance variation, assuming at least eight hundred test takers each time. If there were sufficiently many test takers, most people would take the leap, believing that this is not one of those rare times that equal pass rates would generate this result. They would infer that the pass rates differ.

Surely district-court judge Fullam had some idea of the number of test takers, but he provided no figure in his discussion regarding promotion. He nonetheless found for plaintiffs, and ordered that blacks and whites be promoted in a fixed ratio: one black for every two whites. This order was vacated by the court of appeals, as the pass-rate differences were untested for "statistical significance."[12] Plaintiffs need more than different pass rates to challenge an exam. They need different pass rates *improbable from chance, following a fair procedure.* The defendant has an opportunity to show that the exam selects those who will be the better officers, so that those who fail can be said to lack sufficient merit for promotion. The Philadelphia police were unable to make that showing. Plaintiffs would have won with a more persuasive statistical presentation. If there were not yet enough test takers to make a statistical case, Siskin should have recommended that plaintiffs defer the case through another exam period or two.

With only 108 observations of persons taking the Sergeant test in Mobile, Alabama, the court correctly found that the black and white pass rates (14 percent and 60 percent) differed.[13] The more different are the rates, the fewer the observations required to obtain a low probability of finding this disparity, from chance, from an equal pass-rate population. However, in this case, the exam was determined to have sensibly asked job-related questions. As another court explained:

---

12. *O'Neill* (1973). Curiously, the Supreme Court did not require statistical tests of race-based differences in several 1977 cases, including *Dothard* and, for some issues, *Teamsters.* Thus, a later district court in the Third Circuit declared that the rule of *O'Neill* was no longer in force. See *Dickerson* (1977).

13. *Allen* (1971).

> A hiring practice related to ability to perform is not itself unfair even if it means that disadvantaged minorities are in fact adversely affected.[14]

Again, it is the process that must be judged. One infers bias from the statistic only if one assumes that the populations are equal. Disparate pass rates, from a test that correctly measures abilities to perform on the job, tell us these categories of applicants are systematically different. The result of that statistical comparison is information about the populations, not about the test. We will come across this non-invidious interpretation of a statistical difference again, in Chapter 5's study of juror selection.

THE BASICS OF TESTING

Most tests have many questions resulting in one score. Ultimately, we think that two people who score the same have equal "XYZ"—the name of what is being tested here. That name has certain connotations. The language by which we refer to the test means more than "test score." After all, that is the point of the test. The relationship between the test score and its connotation—the ability of the test to describe who actually is or will be better at XYZ—is called *validity*. Validity is the ability to use the name of the test meaningfully. To base a decision on a test score, surely the test must have some high level of validity. What is "high" is liberally interpreted in this context,[15] because an employer has a right to employ the best applicants he can find, even if he makes that judgment with error, as long as he does not make it with bias.

Because the test has many questions, and because which questions are answered correctly is disguised in the score, it is important that the different questions be testing the same concept, whatever that may be. The ability of questions to substitute for each other, to provide measures of the same thing, is called *reliability*. Reliability is essentially consistency, although of course we do not want a test to have identically answerable questions (in which only all wrong and all right scores are obtained). Reliability is tested by asking if an individual gets the same score on one set of questions as he does on

---

14. *Arrington* (1969) at 1358, 2 FEP Cases at 373.

15. Risinger et al. (1989) at 737:
> Validity refers to the extent to which a test measures what it purports to measure.

Also, *Williams* (1999) at 536:
> Both the initial study and a supplemental study demonstrated a correlation of 0.30 between the test battery score and overall job performance rating.

At 546:
> It is undisputed that a correlation coefficient of 0.30 is statistically significant and sufficient to establish job-relatedness.

Validity scores are typically 0.30 or lower. See, for example, *Delaware* (2004).

another.[16] It is usually a correlation coefficient, and is expected to be very high (greater than 0.90) in a professional test. If there is high agreement, then the two sets of questions are reliable. They measure the same thing. What that thing is, particularly whether we can *call* it by a connotative name (such as intelligence, police skills, law-school aptitude, psychological stability, XYZ), is a separate question, the question of validity.

Both reliability and validity are obvious and easily understood concepts, but difficult to achieve in practice. That is why testing is a profession, and, like statistical analysis, a difficult, misunderstood, and under-utilized profession. It is also a profession I do not trust in most litigation circumstances, because it faces an often insurmountable problem: To know if a test is a valid predictor of performance, we need 1) to have a measure of that performance, and 2) to observe that measure on both passers *and failers* of the test. Indeed, we do not know what "pass" or "fail" should mean (at what score an applicant becomes an acceptable candidate for a position) without a range of scores and their post-score performance measures. Validity is often calculated by comparing the range of scores of those who passed to later performance ratings. That calculation is incomplete without performance scores of test failers.

For example, the U.S. Civil Service Commission financed a validation study of entry-level-firefighter examinations in California and New Mexico.[17] Test takers from seventy-three jurisdictions had from one to six years of experience on the job. Their test scores were correlated with supervisor ratings on nine criteria. The test questions concerned basic mechanical and tool knowledge. Needless to say, the test makers declared it to be valid. Persons who scored higher on the test, in general, had higher supervisory ratings. However, as the test questions concerned knowledge one would expect to acquire on the job, Judge Ferguson correctly found it not a valid predictor of success among firefighter appli-

---

16. Mosher et al. (2002) at 105:

> Reliability is the extent to which the same results are obtained each time the measure is used.

Risinger et al. (1989) at footnote 22:

> A truly inconsistent or "unreliable" test could not produce valid results, but a consistent or "reliable" test can produce invalid results because it is consistently testing some factor other than the one the tester believes is being tested.

These same terms may be used by attorneys with different meanings. See, for example, B. Black (1988) at 599:

> As used in this Article, reliability means that a successful outcome, or a correct answer, is sufficiently probable for a given situation. In contrast to reliability, validity means that which results from sound and cogent reasoning.

By Black's definition, reasoning in law can be valid but not reliable. Redefining terms that already have precise meanings is not helpful.

17. All of my information on this validity study comes from *League* (1976).

cants.[18] A question into which the judge did not inquire is interobserver reliability: To what extent were supervisor ratings in one jurisdiction comparable to those in another?[19]

Strictly speaking, test developers can do their work well only if they at first fail to do it, and pass persons who do not perform well. Test developers have found ways to circumvent this dilemma, but testing persons on the job for skills they acquired on the job is not one of them. Over and above "face validity" (does the test *seem* to ask relevant questions?) they have devised the concepts of "content validity" and "construct validity." Questions are based on job content or job processes. Real validity, comparing scores with job performance, has become relegated to the term "criterion validity."

Although test construction is a profession, I doubt that it is a science or even a technical exercise in the *Daubert* sense that we can assess its accuracy. How many times have "content-valid" test scores been ignored, generating observations of persons with a range of scores who either did or did not perform well on the job? How is a judge to assess the accuracy, in terms of criterion validity, of a content-valid test?

This issue was joined, and then ignored, in *Mexican* (1996). Starting in 1983, passing the California Basic Educational Skills Test (CBEST) was required for a certificate to teach most classes in a California public school, or to be an administrator in a California public-school system. That the test had a disparate impact against black and Latino test takers was not in doubt. The question therefore became, was it valid?

The CBEST had been validated on content only. Judge Orrick took it to be "a measure of basic skills," testing

> a minimum threshold of competency that one would not expect to be positively correlated with job performance, any more than one would expect the written driver's examination to predict which candidates will be good drivers on the road.[20]

---

18. *League* (1976) at 904:
> Since each and every participant in the study had at least one year's experience as a firefighter, the study could not account for the crucial variable: experience as a firefighter versus no experience as a firefighter.

19. Consider a multi-office firm, in which bonuses or promotions are derived from valid evaluation forms. The Los Angeles office could generate more bonuses and promotions simply by being more liberal in their evaluations than the New York or London offices. A Wall Street investment-banking firm asked me to investigate this possibility when their New York employees complained. There was sufficient joint venturing among offices that many agents had been evaluated by different offices. I reported that there was indeed an inter-observer reliability problem, that Los Angeles' evaluation standards were more generous than New York's, which in turn were more generous than London's. It also appeared that the Los Angeles agents really were the best, but not as far above the others as their at-home evaluations would lead the head office to believe.

20. *Mexican* (1996) at 1411, 80 FEP Cases at 487.

It may be true that, among those who pass, there is no correlation between driver's-test score and driving ability, but we certainly *do* expect that a driver's test keeps the worst drivers off the road. Yet we do not allow some of those who have failed the test to drive, to find out if, at this level of basic competence, the test is valid. Similarly, California was not willing to risk letting persons who failed the CBEST teach. Therefore, we cannot evaluate whether the CBEST eliminated the incompetent. What "validity" comes down to in litigation is whether the test *seems* to test skills the employer *reasonably* would like persons on the job to have. Judges (correctly, I think) are loath to make either judgment. "Reasonably" comes from the job-content study. "Seems" is a professional-tester call, usually made by asking a panel of experts (say, supervisors) what skills they think are important for the jobs at issue.

Although there are few examples of test failers performing on the job, there are some. The most notable is *Griggs* (1971), described in Chapter 1. The "test" was a certain level of education. Persons who had not achieved that level had been hired in the past and performed their tasks well.[21] The education requirement was not valid. Thus for "test" we should substitute the term "screening device." We should see *Daubert* challenges to experts who justify the use of such devices from other than criterion validity.

Distribution of Scores

Another problem is hinted at by my indicating that the words "pass" and "fail" have no definitive meaning. In Figure 2 I show scores on a fictional test (horizontal axis). The display is a frequency-distribution "histogram," showing vertically the number of people at each score on the test. As I made up this distribution, there are no numbers on the vertical axis. All that matters is the relationship: taller is "more." I have constructed this example to suit my purpose, but it represents a common finding. On most tests there are clear winners, clear losers, and a lot of people in between.

Are winners on the test really "winners" in some other sense? That is, is the test valid? As I have made up the number of persons who achieve each test score, I also have created scores on a five-part assessment. My correlation between test score and this "rating" is 0.785, exceptionally high for validity. By and large the higher scorers on this test get the better ratings. We can give this test to people for whom we have no ratings, and have some

---

21. In *Delaware* (2004), plaintiffs found ninety-seven individuals who failed the "Alert" test to be state police, but successfully became police elsewhere, including elsewhere in Delaware. Judge Jordan determined that the state's minimum "pass" score was too high. In *Thompson* (1979) at 1155, defendant's expert Irwin Lazarus "concluded that a high school education was necessary to adjust the relatively simple two knife Round Cornering machines" at the Government Printing Office. However, over half of the bookbinders hired from outside the GPO had not completed high school. Why wouldn't an expert know this, know *Griggs*, and not let himself look so foolish? I discuss this aspect of litigation expertise in Chapter 8.

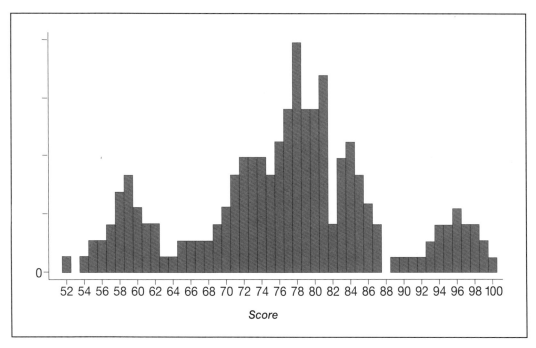

FIGURE 2: Hypothetical Distribution of Test Scores

confidence that if we select the higher scorers, we will select the better performers. But on this, as on most tests, the extent to which that is true depends on how many applicants we will select. We can get an impression of what the result of selecting from this valid test looks like, in Figure 3.

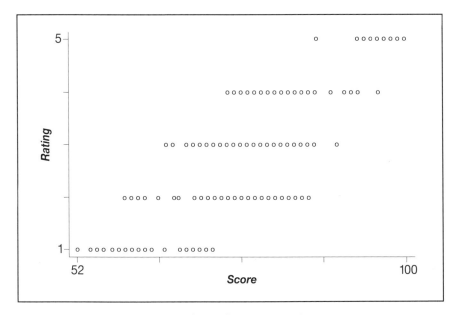

FIGURE 3: Hypothetical Ratings and Test Scores

Figure 3 displays test scores against the ratings that validated the test. We do not know how many people occupy the same place in this graphic, as some symbols lie on top of others. That information is not critical to the points that follow.

The correlation between score and rating, if we exclude ratings 1 and 5, is 0.374. The correlation using only ratings 1 and 5 is 0.961. We have a lot of confidence in who is very good and who is very bad, but less confidence about who will perform better in the middle of the test-score range. We cannot pick only the best performers from their test scores. As we move from right to left, picking the highest scores, we get some 4 performance ratings, even some 3 ratings, before we exhaust the 5 ratings. By score, we confidently select good over very bad, but not always the best. All valid screening devices share this characteristic: Starting at the highest test score and proceeding in order, we find the higher-performing people *in general*, but not *in particular*.

This was surely the construct behind the testimony of Norman Henderson. "A crummy test can get by if you only had a 2 percent selection ratio," he said. You can "sacrifice some validity when the selection ratio is small."[22] The fewer selections you make, the lower the validity can be, and you still will be selecting from those most likely to be among the best performers.

The "passing score" cannot be set by the test constructors. The "passing score" turns out to be the score the last applicant you are hiring (the last student you are admitting, etc.) has. In a range around the passing score on most tests, if there are many selections (that is, if the passing score is somewhat down from the top), you can have no confidence that a higher score selects a better performer. The single metric supplied for the test as a whole is least applicable around the lowest "passing" score.

Most courts assess the "validity" of a test, its ability to select the best performers in general, without reference to how many selections there will be from how many applicants with what distribution of scores.

> The difficult issue in situations such as these is the determination of the level of business relevance necessary to justify the utilization of a test.[23]

It is more difficult than that. If plaintiffs were minorities, whose scores were below the "passing" score (lowest score of a winner), they might still have been better candidates. But now, because the defendant has won a discrimination suit based on a valid screening

---

22. *Shield Club* (1974), both quotations at 546. An example is profiling to investigate the possibility that an individual is a threat, or engaging in illegal activity, such as among passengers at an airport. Finkelstein and Levin (2003) at 275 suggest that courts might "accept a valid profile as a rational and sufficient basis for a stop." Few passengers will be selected, but a "valid" profile will make the exercise more efficient than selecting people randomly. They do not suggest how such a profile would be validated.

23. *Arrington* (1969) at 1358, 2 FEP Cases at 373. Error around the passing score, the generation of "false negatives," is discussed by Judge Jordan in *Delaware* (2004).

device, it cannot deviate from that device to select an applicant it thinks will perform well. To do so would invite a discrimination suit (or "reverse-discrimination" suit) even if race had nothing to do with the decision.[24]

In sum, too much is made of measured validity. It is usually measured only on those who pass, and then applied to the pass-fail border, where virtually no test can discriminate well. One could determine the validity of a test *near the passing score* from the test developer's raw validation data. It would be lower than the reported validity. Yet I have never seen an expert make this point.[25] No court has been faced with a challenge to the validity score as presented, based on the range of scores in that measure compared with the range of scores at issue.

The Concept of "Pool"

Selection is from something to something. We generally organize analyses around a common "to." For example, if a firm hires engineers and shipping clerks, and it is alleged that it does so unfairly—let us say based on race—an expert analyst would perform separate analyses for hiring into these two positions. It is not likely that the same criteria are used for both, that the same applicants apply to both. Similarly, one might think that women are under-selected into graduate school at a particular university. They are, in fact, admitted to departments. Men and women apply to different departments in different proportions, and departments accept different proportions of applicants. Any sensible analysis would account for the different ratios of male and female applicants to the different departments; would, in short, organize an analysis by "to" groups.[26]

In the best of all possible worlds we would know who applied for which opening. We do not always have this information. Judith Stoikov defined as the promotion pool for each promotion, in a gender-discrimination case, that position from which the person who was appointed had come.[27] As I noted, in response:

> Suppose, for example, that 100 females and 100 males are in one group from
> which ten promotions are observed (five female and five male) and 100 males

---

24. The world is waiting for a criterion-validity study showing that university entrance committees are selecting better candidates when they deviate from selecting those with the highest College Board or professional (such as LSAT) scores. Instead, minority selection is defended as bringing "other values" ("diversity") to the campus. It might just be that schools could select better students, deviating from their scores more, the lower the scores are. If so, those superior but lower-scoring students do not appear to be minorities, or we would be told that the schools are "beating the tests" in this manner.

25. I have seen this point made in arguments for "affirmative action," but it is inapposite there. A lottery among those scoring near the "passing" grade would be fair. Selection by race is not.

26. See Bickel et al. (1975) for a study of graduate admissions at the University of California, Berkeley.

27. Judith Stoikov, affidavit opposing class certification, May 25, 1984 in *Holden* (1987).

are in the second group from which 100 promotions are made. Dr. Stoikov's methodology would indicate that exactly as many female promotions were observed as one would expect.[28]

That is, allowing defendant to define the sending pool as that which *did* send the winner, not those which *might* have, would validate discriminatory selection. Stoikov's analysis was not credited by the court.

I have almost always created pools from all source groups that *ever* sent a member to the receiving position. This approach can be biased against either party. It might fail to see the skill pool the firm is segregating and discriminating against. It might consider many persons as "applicants" for a position they could never get. Management might find a particularly talented person in a source group that does not ordinarily prepare employees for the particular "to" job. My approach not only inhibits searching for such talent, it induces an employer to *never* dip into a source group that contains many minorities, or many females. This could hurt the best of employers. The issue is complex. I describe below a modification of this approach, which makes the statistical solution better, but not necessarily good. The real answer lies in better management—better hiring and advancement procedures that delineate eligible candidates and their qualifications separately for each opening.

Situations vs. Events

Worse than manipulating the definition of the pool is not recognizing the pool concept at all. Because this is such a fundamental point, which has been and continues to be so misunderstood by statistical analysts, I discuss the concepts "situations" and "events" in this chapter and also in the next.

"Selection" is an event. Discrimination is an event. The employer must *do* something. Situations are like "snapshots," descriptions of placement, pay, etc. A situation may be that someone is dead, whereas whether he is so by murder, suicide, accident, or natural causes is a description of the event. A situation might be that there are no blacks in Department X. But several may have just resigned, and offers may have been made to others. In *Eagle* (1976), the Equal Employment Opportunity Commission's expert Louis St. Peter inferred a hiring rate from the racial composition of the firm. The judge pointed out that as blacks were in higher-turnover jobs, their hiring rate was presumably higher than St. Peter gave the firm credit for.

The situation often provides no information about events.

[P]laintiffs' witness Alan Fechter compared the percentage of blacks in various job classifications at Allison with the percentage of blacks available for

---

28. Stephan Michelson and Rebecca Klemm, affidavit supporting class certification, June 19, 1984, in *Holden* (1987) at 12.

such positions in the Indianapolis SMSA and the United States as a whole. These figures do not satisfy the second phase of the Court's test of statistical evidence since they do not compare the placement of new hires to the relevant labor pool, i.e., those actually hired.[29]

Three Columbia University professors analyzed a promotion case from situation data, presumably because they did not understand how to construct an events analysis. Defendant was the Navy Resale System Office (NAVRESO) in Brooklyn. For the plaintiffs, these analysts confused where people were in an organization with how they got there. They presented Figure 4 as if it were evidence that blacks were denied promotion to high grades, calculating the probability from a Fisher's exact test as 0.0515.[30]

	Non-Black Males	Others
Grade 12+	10	0
Grade 11−	67	25

FIGURE 4: Grade at Entry of NAVRESO Management Employees

This was the only hiring "analysis" presented by plaintiffs. Like Fechter, they describe a situation. We might say Figure 4 is organized by selections "to" (to higher or lower management grades). But there is no "from." There are no pools. There are no events.

It is instructive to realize that persons of high repute sometimes just don't get it. These academics, expert in mathematics and statistics, did not know how to analyze this legal issue.

THE PRETTY GOOD CANDIDATE

Applicant X knows he is an above-average candidate. He is, let us say, at the thirtieth percentile from the top of the pool of people who might apply for a particular position. He is superior to seven out of ten candidates. Pretty good, indeed. Knowing his reasonably high

---

29. *Diesel* (1978) at 581.

30. Herbert E. Robbins, Gerard E. Dallal, and Stephen J. Finch, "Initial Analysis of NAVRESO Personnel Practices," December 17, 1981, Table 16, in *Verdell* (1985). They made the same mistake that St. Peter had made. Their data describe grade at entry *then* of persons who are employed *now*. Their population is not those to whom an event occurred—who was selected to what grade—but a subset of that population (those still employed at the firm) that may or may not be representative of assignments. Furthermore, there is no count of persons to whom the event did *not* occur, even though they were eligible.

  If the number of winners is fixed, Fisher's exact test calculates the proportion of selections of that number from the applicant pool that would result in no more than the number of minorities selected that were in fact selected. It is inherently a one-tail test. See Gastwirth (1988) at 217. Other tests from a 2 x 2 table, such as chi-square or the Z-score, are two-tail approximations of Fisher's exact test.

status, he does not expect to get his desired position right away, or easily. But he does expect eventual success. He applies over and over again, never winning. He has some characteristic that he might think is unfairly limiting the view of those selecting the winners. Let's say— for this was the charge in the actual case I have in mind—he was (and was known to be) a socialist. He had applied for over eighty openings before he finally filed charges alleging discrimination against his political beliefs. He contended that, as a thirtieth-percentile candidate, he surely could be expected to win at least one competition in eighty!

He hires a statistical expert who ascertains that typically there are twenty applicants for each position to which the plaintiff had applied. He reasons: Let us suppose that every hire is a selection from a bowl in which there is one blue marble and nineteen green marbles. What is the probability that eighty times in a row ("with replacement"—starting every time from the same set of marbles), *without looking*, the blue marble is never selected? Having set up the problem this way, the expert provides the answer:

$$\text{probability that no blue marble is selected} = (1 - \frac{1}{20})^{80} = 0.95^{80} = 0.0165$$

If there is a low probability that the plaintiff was never selected, under this model, then perhaps the answer is that someone did look, that the characteristic he claims distinguished him was indeed used against him

The expert does not want to characterize his analysis further, but the attorney can now plead his case. "That is a small probability," X's attorney argues. "It means that this result essentially would occur by chance fewer than two times in one hundred tries. It is 'significant at the 2 percent level.' We contend that it didn't occur by chance, that it occurred because this candidates was, and was known to be, a socialist."

Does this seem like a reasonable approach? This is the sort of analysis just about every statistical analyst who has ever testified would do. It is wrong.

In order to win a competition that is fairly judged, you have to be the best candidate in that pool. If the average opening announcement receives twenty applications, of which Applicant X is one, then the remaining nineteen must all come from the bottom 70 percent of possible applicants if X, who is at the thirtieth percentile in the universe, is to win. The probability of that occurring in a given competition, if application is random with respect to rank, is:

$$\text{probability of winning on this try} = 0.7^{19} = 0.00114$$

Applicant X might expect to win one competition in a thousand. The probability that he would not win, not even once in eighty tries, is the probability of losing all eighty competitions:

$$\text{probability of never winning through eighty tries} = (1 - 0.00114)^{80} = 0.913$$

More than nine times in ten that this candidate would apply to eighty openings, he would be selected to none of them. Having lost eighty is not evidence of adverse selection.[31]

Let's make the issue more stark. Applicant X gets five other socialists, who also rank at the thirtieth percentile, to apply with him. The socialist applicants think that the more of them there are, the more likely selection of one of them will be (in a fair system), because their expert's analysis supports that view. Their expert reasons the same way he did before, but with different numbers. "What is the probability that in eighty competitions in which six of twenty-five candidates are socialists, not a single socialist is ever selected?" he asks.

This is his answer:

$$\text{probability of no socialist being selected} = (1 - \frac{6}{25})^{80} = 0.76^{80} = 0.00000000029$$

X now has a class-action lawsuit. "That is a *very* small number," X's attorney pleads. "It is 'significant' at well below the 1 percent level. This result essentially would never occur by chance. It occurred because these candidates were, and were known to be, socialists."

Wrong again. The average number of applicants per position is now twenty-five, but we *know* that six of them rank at the thirtieth percentile from the top of the relevant applicant population. The correct math stays the same. The probability of any one of the six socialists ever winning is the probability that all nineteen other applicants will be lower ranked at least once.

I have never seen any analysis like this in any case or in any literature about the statistics of hiring.[32] What I have hypothesized that Applicant X's "expert" statistician would do is what all statistical experts do. He assumed that all candidates were otherwise equal, the only distinguishing characteristic being their politics. He tested only his client's theory, and got his client's answer. I will provide many examples of this expert behavior, of not considering alternative explanations, in Chapter 8.

Because defendant attorney's search process fails to uncover my firm (about which I will have more to say in Chapter 6), and therefore is unable to find a statistical expert who will offer a supportive analysis, the defense proceeds without an expert. "Which competition should a socialist have won?" defendant asks, prepared to defend every se-

---

31. Calculating the probability of success on multiple independent tries was, at least in one version of the story, the original problem that led to probability theory. In 1654, Blaise Pascal and Pierre de Fermat solved the problem posed by the dice player Antoine Gombaud, to determine the chance of rolling twelve (two sixes) throwing two dice twenty-four times. Both experts in the example in text use the Fermat-Pascal formula. What differs between them is how they set up the problem.

32. The one exception is my presentation of this analysis in an administrative law hearing responding to this socialist's complaint. Defendant prevailed. Timothy Wyant, then a senior analyst at Longbranch Research Associates, first developed the insights of this section.

lection. Plaintiffs' attorney replies: "Being that specific would put too much of a burden on plaintiff. Can't we just see how unlikely it is that this employer never selected a socialist? That is what our expert has done." Plaintiffs may win such a case, although they never should.

My calculation assumed a fact (X and his friends all ranked at the thirtieth percentile down from the best candidates) that we are unlikely to know. But X's expert assumed a fact that not only we are unlikely to know, it is unlikely to be true: All applicants were otherwise equal (or unknowably different) on all factors other than being a socialist. This is the most common of assumptions. In Chapter 8 we will encounter an equally incorrect analysis, unrelated to employment—concerning the race of drivers stopped for speeding—that is the direct descendant of this use of the wrong selection model in employment litigation.

The assumption that all applicants are essentially alike—which is to say, in its more sophisticated form, that of course applicants differ, but the distributions of difference are assumed to be unrelated to the characteristic at issue, here political belief—has a reasonable heritage in selecting applicants for unskilled work. We should pay homage to its use in the 1960s and 1970s, to its often correct discernment of bias in hiring. For most positions, though, the assumptions that the job requires no special abilities, or that abilities are distributed equally throughout every sub-population, and that the employer has no other information from which to make an informed selection, are false.

Introduction to Multiple Pools

First, one correction. The ordinary statistical expert might not frame his calculation as I did for him. I framed it as we know it to have been, as many instances of single selections from separate "pools" of applicants. This is the way most hires are made, but not the way most hires have been analyzed. Recognition and analysis of separate competitions began in the 1980s, and still remains unknown to the majority of analysts.

The traditional statistical analyst would more likely have said:

> "Over the time period we are considering there were 80 selections from 2,000 applicants (80 times 25), of which 480 were known to have been socialists. No socialist was ever selected. From the binomial distribution we can calculate the probability of zero selections out of eighty when one selection has $p = 0.24$ (from $480 \div 2,000$). That probability is $p = 0.00000000029$."

In this example, the outcome is the same as from the separate-pools approach, because I set up the example assuming that every pool was constituted the same way. In practice, the pools will be different, and the multiple-pools probability calculation will be different from the single-aggregate-pool calculation. Joseph Gastwirth notes that

> [When] the selection probabilities and racial composition of eligibles (appli-
> cants) are substantially different in each table [each competition], the simple
> addition method leads to an erroneous inference.[33]

Experts' models often bear no resemblance to the mechanism and criteria of the selection. The result is that their impressive low probabilities are meaningless not because of
errors in mathematics, but because their models are discordant with reality. That is one
reason why, throughout this book, I will defend the proposition that judges, without statistics training, can perfectly well evaluate most statistical cases. The error lies in how the
problem is stated, not how its solution is calculated.

ATTORNEYS WITHOUT EXPERTS

In the early 1970s, when it became clear that one could establish a *prima facie* case with
a statistical showing, many attorneys made the statistical argument themselves. In almost
all cases they compared situations. For example, they would compare the percent minority in a work force with the percent minority in a population defined by geographic
area and perhaps skill level. Attorneys at Legal Services in Philadelphia sued the state of
Pennsylvania, and some development authorities, seeking to stop a loan to the Chilton
Company.

> Plaintiffs . . . urge that since 35% of Philadelphia's population is Black, Chilton
> must be discriminating unless 35% of its employees are black.[34]

Judge Ditter did not think much of this approach. With more than a touch of sarcasm
he wondered:

> Perhaps had a statistician testified or had there been some other evidence to
> show why the number of children, old people, the disabled, and all others not
> available to work should be ignored when evaluating the ratio between Black
> population and Black employees at Chilton, a different result might be pos-
> sible. On the present record, however, a mere comparison between jobs and
> population proves nothing.[35]

Similarly, the D.C. Circuit did not find the Federal Communications Commission
negligent in allowing television station WMAL to continue broadcasting. The court refused
to accept plaintiff's assertion that WMAL's employment, 7 percent black, in an area 70
percent black, indicated discrimination in hiring. The recruitment area, said the court,

---

33. Gastwirth (1988) at 236.

34. The Legal Services attorneys were joined by attorneys from the Lawyers Committee for Civil Rights
Under Law, another group of well-meaning but non-comprehending attorneys. See *Louis* (1974) at 885.

35. *Louis* (1974) at 885.

was more like 24 percent black, and we do not know the race of qualified applicants.[36]

In California,

> Expert witness Flanagan, called by defendant and the only expert to be called by either party at trial, testified that defendant's workforce data is the best evidence available to establish whether or not defendant is discriminating against blacks with respect to hiring. . . .
>
> Based upon the foregoing, this court finds and concludes that plaintiffs' statistical evidence is in this case insufficient to establish a *prima facie* case of hiring discrimination.[37]

Apparently Robert Flanagan tested seven or eight separate categories of workers, finding the proportion black within two standard deviations of the expected value, where the expectation came from census data, in all of them. In addition to the data fallacy—measuring the race of employees, not hires—there is no summary calculation. The probability is less than 0.01 that the difference would have the same sign (that a coin would come up only heads or only tails) in seven tries, had selection been random from Flanagan's criterion population. It would be even smaller, less than 0.001, if we knew that the smallest black hiring deficit was one standard deviation, a level at which defendant could deny that it under-hired blacks in each individual job group, while clearly under-hiring blacks overall.

Flanagan may have steered the judge towards the best analysis of the data. Or he may have been flat-out wrong. We will never know. Plaintiff's attorney, by not engaging an expert, deprived the court of an alternative view.[38] It may be, as Gerry Spence tells us, that

> The spectacle of pitting purchased experts against each other in the court-room, the best performer taking all, is a barbarous throwback to the days of trial by duel.[39]

But the spectacle of an attorney taking on a statistical expert without one of his own is more like throwing the Christians to the lions.[40]

---

36. *Stone* (1972). In 2000, the Federal Communications Commission proposed a rule "requiring licensees to achieve a 'broad outreach' in their recruiting efforts." *Broadcasters* (2001) at 16. Essentially, they would have required "affirmative action" recruitment, that is, expansion of the proportion minority in a pool. The inevitable result would have been to find discrimination in selection from that pool. The circuit court vacated that rule in *Broadcasters*, at 23.

37. *Patterson* (1976) at 775.

38. We do not know that plaintiff did not engage another expert, only that he did not present one.

39. Spence (1989) at 272.

40. Discussing a regression study in *Petruzzi* (1993), the Third Circuit notes (at 1238) that
> while the defendants did try to poke holes in the value of the study during the depositions, they have not supplied any experts who testified that the study's methodology was fatally flawed.

Therefore the testimony was admissible, summary judgment for defendant was reversed.

Fact in Law

"Fact" is as much a matter of law as of empirical truth. For example, when a burglar puts his arm through a window, he has entered. This may not be the lay understanding of "entry," but the law has its own definitions, and this is one of them.[41] What the expert takes as "fact" often is not so under the law. Attorneys do not understand the importance of this distinction to their expert's presentation.

Early cases under the Age Discrimination in Employment Act were argued by showing that the average age of employees decreased after a layoff.[42] Apparently no one pointed out to attorneys or judges that in comparing two means, no person should appear in both. The difference between before and after average age as calculated was affected by how many people were selected; the fewer, the smaller the difference. A competent statistical analyst would at least have compared the average age of those terminated with the average age of those not terminated.

However, there is more than an arithmetic problem with comparing average ages.[43] Because the law does not recognize age differences under forty, it should not accept as "fact" any calculation made using those ages. Both the average age and its standard deviation incorporate "facts" that should not be seen as facts in a court of law.

In *Mastie* (1976), an exact test was available. Twenty candidates for termination are listed in age order. The two selected for termination were among the oldest five. A simple test would be:[44]

$$\text{probability of two selections at least this old} = \frac{5}{20} \times \frac{4}{19} = 0.0526$$

Although the selection of the two plaintiffs might have been made for any reason, as a statistical matter their selection is suspiciously related to age. Presented with only the

---

41. This snippet of "fact" comes from Zuckerman (1986), in a debate with Nessen (1985). It also became newsworthy when O. J. Simpson stuck his hand through the (open) window of someone else's car, in Florida, and was surprised to learn later that he had thereby "entered" that person's property.

42. See, for example, *Stringfellow* (1970) and *Mastie* (1976). In *MacDissi* (1988), at 1057, circuit-court judge Arnold expressed his dislike for the average-age comparisons in the record:

> Both parties have complicated the quantitative aspects of this case by relying on involved statistical comparisons to describe relatively simple facts.

The "relatively simple facts" were that the two persons terminated were the oldest of those who might have been terminated.

43. The court reports an incorrect mean age for those remaining after termination in *Mastie* (1976).

44. Here is another way to think about this. There are ten combinations of two people one could select from the five oldest. There are 190 combinations of two people one could select from all twenty. The probability of selecting both from the oldest five is ten divided by 190, which gives the same answer as that provided more simply in the text.

before-and-after average ages, Judge Guy made his determination:

> The court concludes that a decrease of 1.29 years in the average age of employ-
> ees remaining employed by a company following termination of some em-
> ployees does not establish even a prima facie case of age discrimination.[45]

Some plaintiffs did prevail making statistical cases about discriminatory selection without expert help. In the 1970s and 1980s, especially in the South, racially discrim-inatory labor practices were not eliminated without judicial intervention. A common scenario was the district-court judge finding for defendant, that decision reversed by the circuit court.[46] Whether better statistical presentations would have obviated some appeals, we cannot know. More important than the history is its living legacy among judges and among experts, both of whom learned the wrong statistical lessons from the "successes" of the past.

Selection from a Single Pool

Seldom does an employer make many offers from a single pool of applicants. It is varia-tion in the composition of applicants among different pools that makes analysis difficult, multiple-pools analysis necessary. One situation in which all pools are thought to be the same is where we have no data on actual applicants. We construct an "availability" pool of likely candidates, which might be seen, in the language of Chapter 1, as substituting a legislative fact for an adjudicative fact. If that availability pool is the same throughout the hiring period, it does no further damage to assume that hires are made at one time, from that one pool.

The Uncountable Pool

Suppose an employer, accused of insufficient hiring of blacks, has no record of how many people applied, or has no record of their race. "Availability" analysis was conceived to accomplish two purposes: 1) to thwart ignorance or failure to take minority applica-tions as a defense, and 2) to allow preliminary review of employment data without ob-taining detailed applicant data.[47] Availability analysis is, or should be, a calculation based on hires (better, offers) from an infinite pool with a proportion of persons with plain-tiff's characteristic—let's say black—derived from some believable data source. Given the

---

45. *Mastie* (1976) at 1319.

46. See, for example, *Pettway* (1967), which took a over a decade to resolve on its third trip to the Fifth Circuit in *Pettway* (1978).

47. Section 703(j) of the Civil Rights Act of 1964 (42 U.S. Code §2000e-2(j)) refers to the "available work force" of an area, prompting courts to find a way to determine what that is.

proportion black in the availability pool, p_b, then where n_b is the number of black hires, n is the number of hires (all races), we make three easy calculations:

$$\text{expected hires} = p_b \times n$$

$$\text{difference} = \text{actual hires} - \text{expected hires} = n_b - (p_b \times n)$$

$$\text{standard deviation} = \sqrt{n \times p_b \times (1 - p_b)}$$

Drawing randomly from an uncountably large pool of two-valued (either black or white) items is called "binomial selection." The size of each draw is n. The statistic that is the outcome of the draw can be thought of as either n_b or the difference, $n_b - (p_b \times n)$.[48] That statistic has a "distribution," which just means it has a different value on each draw. The standard deviation is a measure of the distribution of random differences between expected black hires and actual black hires. The distribution of the binomial statistic is *approximately* normal (the bell-shaped curve), if n is reasonably large (the smaller p_b, the larger n should be, but think fifty draws or more). What is commonly done, then, is to calculate a "Z-score":

$$Z = \frac{\text{difference}}{\text{standard deviation}} = \frac{n_b - (p_b \times n)}{\sqrt{n \times p_b \times (1 - p_b)}}$$

which expresses the difference in standard-deviation units. One obtains the probability of finding at least this large a difference by looking up the conversion from numbers of standard deviations to probability (it is called the "tail" probability because it describes this large *or larger*) in a table of the normal distribution. So, for example, if that ratio is 2.0 or larger, one would call the difference "significant at the 0.05 level" because two standard deviations is associated with a probability below 0.05. That means that had there been no difference between the proportion of blacks among selectees and in the population, with this standard deviation, random selection alone would bring about a difference at least as large as the difference we calculated in a proportion smaller than one time in twenty.

This is the basic language of selection, in sample size (or draw size, n), difference from expected, standard-deviation, Z-score, probability. But now that we have reached the end, this probability from a table of the normal distribution, what do we know? We know how often a draw would produce such a large difference, or larger, over many draws, if the model is correct—if we have performed relevant calculations. Assessing this probability is

---

48. It does not make any difference whether the "statistic" is seen as the number of blacks hired or the difference between that number and the expected number, as long as the expected number remains the same throughout the period. The expected number, from any size draw, is a constant. We will see, in Chapter 7, that there are no inferences to be made from constants (despite one judge's insistence that there are). The distribution of "difference" looks identical to the distribution of n_b.

a complex issue, some discussion of which appears in this chapter. I will return to it in Chapter 7.

The Countable Pool

We saw one example of a countable-pool analysis above, in my exact-probability calcu-lation of the tail of the distribution of ages (for that is what selection from among the oldest is) in *Mastie* (1976). That is a special kind of countable pool, however, because, as it was about age, we can *order* it. The more typical single countable pool is composed of applicants who differ in a characteristic such as gender or race. They can be divided into two groups by that characteristic, each of which is subdivided by whether they were selected or not. Thus the countable-single-pool data can be presented in a 2 x 2 table as in the prison parole data in Figure 5.

	Paroled	Not Paroled
Majority	506	319
Minority	29	48

FIGURE 5: Selection from a Countable Pool

The pool is the sum of all four cells, the population from which whether to parole was determined.[49] About one-third of the minorities are paroled (37.7 percent), compared with three-fifths of the majority (61.3 percent). A statistical test should tell us how likely that would be, from chance, were the selection rates "really" equal in a very large population. We can calculate a Z-score. Because this is a countable pool, the standard deviation of the difference in proportions is smaller than the binomial standard deviation above.[50] Qualitatively one gets the same answer by any calculation, so we will worry about being more precise later. This would be a very unlikely race distribution of paroles from selection random with respect to race, *if* we otherwise believe that race is the only distin-guishing factor.

Plaintiffs constructed a similar table, describing requests for transfer by gender at the

---

49. The data come from Sugrue and Fairley (1983). "Majority" here are whites and blacks; "minority" are Mexicans and native American Indians. A chi-square analysis of the original 4 x 2 table showed clear disproportionalities in parole. Peeking at the data then is allowable, to determine a reasonable way to separate winners from losers. Different races treated similarly can be aggregated. See *Paige* (2002) at 1148. Why Sugrue and Fairley did not proceed this way I do not know. This case is discussed again in Chapter 5.

50. The probability calculated from a two-tailed normal distribution is 0.0000526. This is not an instruc-tion book, but I will provide the "finite-population correction" and explain distribution tails, below. For more instruction on calculation see Gastwirth (1988) at 212.

National Labor Relations Board in the early 1980s. They drew the same conclusion: Few requests were granted to female applicants compared with male applicants. However, almost all the female requests were made by Ms. Smith, the plaintiff.[51] As defendant's expert, I informed Judge Gasch that, in my opinion, this issue was not amenable to a statistical test. The question was whether the agency made a reasonable decision not to inflict Ms. Smith on another office. He could answer that question more easily from her testimony than from data. Judge Gasch agreed with my approach, and with the agency's decision.

In summary, the single-pool analysis serves as the backbone of selection analysis. Calculation is easy. Non-countable pools are usually formed from some availability estimate. A binomial Z-score gets us a pretty good picture of what this simple model tells us, even if the pool is countable and better statistics are available.

There is a problem here. Usually selections are made from different pools, on the basis of measurable criteria such as date of application, test score, etc., that distinguish candidates. The assumptions behind single-pool single-variable analysis are hardly ever correct. The method of analyzing selection that dominates almost every instruction book written for attorneys and judges is based on facts that almost never exist. How unreal is the model is often a more important question than how large is the difference between the model's expectation and actual selections. The role of the expert is not to calculate—computers do that—but to frame the calculation so its results are meaningful. Let's take a step in that direction.

MULTIVARIATE SINGLE-POOL ANALYSIS

Suppose we want to estimate the influence of certain characteristics on selection, one of which is gender, race, even age. We would like to estimate an equation:

probability of selection = f(characteristic at issue, other characteristics)

which is read: "The probability of selection is a function of (is determined by) the characteristic at issue plus other characteristics that relate validly to expected job performance." In interpretation, most analysts say they "control" for the other characteristics, and "test" for the importance of the characteristic at issue in the case. In fact, all coefficients are estimated, simultaneously, the same way. Because we are estimating something that we will interpret as a probability, the estimation procedure has to be sure the estimates

---

51. See *Smith* (1982). Also:

> Thus almost half of all garnishments of black firemen are attributable to two individual firemen.

Friend (1981) at 365, 18 FEP Cases at 1033.

are bounded by (do not go beyond) zero and one. The most common analytic method is logit analysis.

In logit what is estimated are the coefficients b in:

$$\ln\left(\frac{p}{1-p}\right) = b_0 + b_1 x_1 + b_2 x_2 + \ldots$$

where the x_i are the independent variables, the characteristics for which each observation has values in our data. "ln" denotes the natural logarithm. As $\frac{p}{1-p}$ is the odds of success, logit estimates the "log odds." The data behind p are values one and zero based on "selected" or "not," which we think of as the dependent variable. The logit program estimates the "best" set of coefficients in the sense of finding those coefficients that best predict the actual log odds. In that estimation we can determine how important each variable is, how much knowing its value affects our estimation of the odds of success.

Logit-estimation routines appear in all statistical computer packages. Both parties' experts, given the same data, should derive the same coefficients from the same "model," that is, the same variables in the same form. The issue, as with all of these methods, is whether the logit that was estimated was appropriate to the legal question.

Promotions at Polaroid

Plaintiffs alleged discrimination in pay, through failure to promote females from Grade 5 to Grade 8 at Polaroid, in Massachusetts state court. Plaintiffs' expert, Rich Goldstein, performed an analysis using a peculiar sample of Polaroid employees.[52] He used situation data, asking: "What grade are males and females at?" That was not the question before the court.

I took as a base all Grade 5 employees on December 31, 1977 who were also employed (in salaried, non-technical positions) on December 31, 1979. I then identified which of these people had been promoted to Grade 8 in the interim. I found the promotion numbers in Figure 6.

	Still Grade 5	Now Grade 8
Males	211	52
Females	80	19

FIGURE 6: Salaried Non-Technical Promotions at Polaroid, 1977–1979

52. See *Polaroid* (1981). Goldstein actually used a discriminant analysis, but the choice of method was irrelevant.

Males have been promoted at a 19.8 percent rate, females at 19.2 percent. A difference of proportions this large or larger, from this many observations, would occur ninety-six times out of one hundred by chance from a population in which the "true" proportions were exactly equal.[53] The difference appears to be small, easily a chance observation having nothing to do with gender.

Perhaps women were more qualified than men. If they were, then being promoted at only the male rate would not be justifiable. These promotions were "in line," or made without application and without competition. We will learn another way to analyze such promotions, below, but in the Polaroid case what I wanted was a straightforward multivariate extension of Figure 6. I had no direct measures of performance, but I had some data that might indicate performance differences, might affect management's decisions, and might be accepted by a court as reasonably doing so.

Some people came to Polaroid as hourly employees and worked their way up to salaried jobs. They might perform salaried jobs adequately but, because of their background, not advance as rapidly as those who started as salaried employees. Some people moved from technical jobs to non-technical jobs. In a different aspect of this case I noticed that senior buyers, the people who order laboratory and manufacturing supplies, most often had worked in the laboratory or manufacturing facility. Polaroid had determined that such support personnel could relate to the people they were supporting, and knew the materials they were purchasing.[54] Another characteristic, gaps in Polaroid employment, might raise questions at promotion time. Polaroid liberally allowed employees to leave and return, but it did not prefer to advance employees whose work history was spotty.

I estimated the logit equation in Figure 7 to best "explain" (except for the gender variable) who had and had not been promoted by the end of 1977. We can "expect" a coefficient to be zero, and calculate a Z-score subtracting the expected from the observed coefficient, dividing by its standard error. An alternative is to estimate the model with and without each variable, and calculate how much the variable contributes to the overall fit of the equation to the data. By this more elaborate criterion, Number of Leaves appeared to be important. In most cases the Z-score and this goodness-of-fit test agree closely.

---

53. This statement comes from Fisher's exact test. Calculating a Z-score with the finite population correction that I will explain below, looking up the probability from a table of the normal distribution, one would say this disparity would occur ninety-one times in a hundred by chance from no relationship in fact.

54. It is also possible that people who moved from the laboratory to purchasing were not stars where they had been. Movement to a support position was their only way to advance. Is that bad? It made life hard for the Buyer who wanted to become a Senior Buyer, to be constantly beat out for that position by a lateral mover, but it seemed to serve other interests well, and not be clearly unfair.

	Coefficient	Standard Error	Z-Score
Hire Age	−0.028	0.012	−2.36
Time Hourly	−0.073	0.018	−4.07
Ever Technical	0.389	0.226	1.72
Number of Leaves	−8.116	415.420	−0.02
Gender: Female	−0.042	0.184	−0.23

FIGURE 7: Logit Estimate of Salaried Non-Technical Promotions at Polaroid, 1977–1979

The equation in Figure 7 tells us that persons hired later in life, and as hourly employees, were less likely to be promoted. People with a technical background were more likely to be promoted. The more leaves probably the less likely was a promotion. There was no relationship between gender and promotion. Defendant prevailed.

Because promotions were made in this job-advancement path, we sort of have the correct pool. It is deficient in that we have not correctly identified either the different pools of persons who might have been promoted when each promotion was made, nor necessarily identified all promotions. Both counts should include persons who subsequently left Polaroid or were promoted to Grade 5. We also do not observe persons hired since our initial observation date, but perhaps they were not yet eligible for promotion. As noted above, basing an analysis on before-and-after situations may misrepresent the events and the persons eligible for the events. However, one does not walk away from a question because the data are not perfectly suited to it. Rather, one gets as close as possible to event data from the situation data at hand. The Polaroid work force was stable over those years, so that the pool implicit in this analysis was almost all-inclusive. Plaintiffs, having attempted to analyze only current employees themselves, could hardly object to my doing so.

SELECTION FROM MULTIPLE POOLS

Let us take a step back, to a one-variable analysis, but forward, to analyzing selection from multiple pools. I have constructed an example. Let's say blacks and whites take four tests, perhaps for different advanced positions in a fire or police department. Although judges like to see the total number of test takers and who passed, a statistical analyst would rather portray the data as pass-fail by white-black, four 2 x 2 tables, one for each exam. I present the data this way in Figure 8.

	Fail	Pass
Test One		
Black	60	5
White	60	5
Test Two		
Black	60	3
White	20	1
Test Three		
Black	10	4
White	60	24
Test Four		
Black	40	10
White	200	50

FIGURE 8: Hypothetical Multiple Pools

Calculation As If a Single Pool

In Figure 9 I have added together the winners and losers of Figure 8, by race, over all the pools. There could be many reasons why an analyst would use the data from Figure 9, including these being the only data available (individual test results having been lost). The black pass rate is 0.105. The white pass rate is 0.181. Are these rates far apart? Let's set up a Z-score. The overall pass rate is

$$\text{pass rate} = \frac{22 + 80}{22 + 80 + 170 + 340} = 0.167$$

So the expected number of blacks passing is

$$E(\text{blacks}) = 0.167 \times (22 + 170) = 32.064$$

This is read: "The expected number of blacks who pass is the proportion of all persons who pass times the number of blacks who applied, equals thirty-two blacks."

	Fail	Pass
Black	170	22
White	340	80

FIGURE 9: Aggregate Data from Hypothetical Multiple Pools

This is not a binomial selection—we can count the number of people in the pool—but the number of applicants is large, so as a first approximation let's calculate the binomial standard deviation. Recall that 102 persons have passed the test. The binomial assumption is that the number of passers is fixed, and this is realistic if we say that the passing score was set to select 102 people. The number of persons who failed the test does not appear in the binomial calculations, as the assumption is that we do not know it.

$$\text{binomial standard deviation} = \sqrt{n \times p \times (1 - p)} = \sqrt{102 \times 0.167 \times 0.833} = 3.764$$

The difference between actual and "expected" black passers, divided by this standard deviation, is:

$$Z = \frac{\text{difference}}{\text{standard deviation}} = \frac{-10}{3.764} = -2.66$$

This analyst declares that blacks fall short of expectations by well over two standard deviations, a large amount in that there is a low probability of a difference this large appearing randomly if the value in the population is zero. We can adjust this calculation because we do know the size of the pool. We multiply the standard deviation by the "finite-population correction":

$$\sqrt{\frac{N - n}{N - 1}} = 0.914$$

where N is the number of people in the pool, the number we do not know in the binomial calculation. Multiplying the denominator of the Z-score by a number less than one increases the Z-score. The deficit of blacks passing these exams is seen to be 2.91 standard deviations, an impressively large number (in this context). The number -2.91 might not appear in a printed table of probabilities associated with standard deviations in the normal distribution, but that is a task of the past. We can obtain the probability on almost any computer. The probability of finding a difference this large, or larger, this expert will say, when there is no differences among the population, is p = 0.0036.[55]

Now please return to Figure 8 and find the exams where the black deficit was created. There is no deficit in any exam! Pass rates are different in the different exams, and the proportion of test takers who are black varies, but blacks pass each exam at exactly the same rate as whites. Figure 8 illustrates the proposition I had stated above, that a single-pool test cannot substitute for a multiple-pools test when pools differ in composition. An "expert" who calculates a single-aggregate test from data such as these is no expert at all.

---

55. In Excel, for example, type the following into any cell:

=normdist(−2.91,0,1,true)

and hit the return key. You use "true" because you want the entire tail probability, the probability of finding a difference this large *or larger* if the difference in the population is zero. The result in the cell is now one tail of the distribution. Multiply it by two to get the two-tail probability (this large a difference in either direction) in the text.

Calculation As If Multiple Pools

To calculate the multiple-pools test that is called for by the data in Figure 8, first calculate the Z-score components (difference and standard deviation) for each sub-table. If there is a selection deficit of blacks, it must be the sum of the deficits (including surpluses, if any) over all the pools. In this example the deficit in each pool is zero, so the sum over all pools is zero. Now just trust me: The variance of a sum of independent random variables is the sum of their variances. The variance is the square of the standard deviation. The finite population-corrected variance for each pool is

$$\text{variance} = n \times p \times (1 - p) \times \frac{N - n}{N - 1}$$

That may look like a handful, but remembering that p, which we interpret as the overall probability of winning, is the proportion of winners in the entire pool (passers divided by all takers), it is easy to calculate. In this book "p" always means "probability," but it is often estimated by a proportion.

Add up the deficits, pool by pool. That's the multiple-pools numerator. Add up the variances, and then take the square root of that sum. That's the multiple-pools denominator. Divide. That's the multiple-pools Z-score. Then use a spreadsheet to derive the probability from the normal distribution. Multiply whatever answer you get by two, because most courts are familiar with two-tail probabilities, which is the probability of a difference as large in absolute value (i.e., a deficit or a surplus this large) as the one you are testing.

The point of this story—the reason I took you through a calculation—is that it's really easy. In the early 1980s, my firm developed software to calculate an exact multiple-pools test, a user add-on to the SAS mainframe statistical package, called MULPOOLS™. Exact is better than approximate, but not nearly the improvement that a multiple-pools test is over a single-pool test, where the events are in fact selections from multiple pools. The approximate test is available to any expert with a hand calculator. So why don't they do it?

Fire Department Promotions in *Rizzo* (1979)

Tests were given for three leadership positions in the fire department: assistant chief, deputy chief, and battalion chief. By the principles expressed above, the "passing" score should have been that which admitted the number of persons to fill the number of openings.

> On August 30, 1977, a special meeting was convened at the office of Commissioner Rizzo for the purpose of establishing the cut-off score. . . . At the meeting, the parties agreed that the likelihood of minority representation

would be enhanced if the cut-off points were lowered so that more examinees could be included on the ultimate list.[56]

We know that, even from a valid test, the superior candidates may not have obtained the very highest scores. A lower cutoff score with other, but fair and valid criteria, selecting the winners from these finalists (see Figure 3 and its discussion, above) could be supported. Lowering the cutoff to include more minorities, however, is selection by race.

To be free of the charge that the score was lowered for racial reasons (although later, in court, they admitted that it was) those at the meeting did not first look at the scores attained by the test takers. Lowering the cutoff did not achieve its purpose. The results are presented in Figure 10. Plaintiffs asked the court to enjoin the City of Philadelphia from using the results of these tests to promote into these positions. Each side brought forward statistical and testing experts. Not one of them analyzed the data appropriately.

	Fail	Pass
Assistant Chief		
Black	2	0
White	17	8
Deputy Chief		
Black	1	0
White	30	15
Battalion Chief		
Black	6	0
White	59	40

FIGURE 10: Leadership Exam Test Results, Philadelphia Fire Department

The statistical question is whether these data, from three tests, provide evidence that they have a disparate impact against blacks. Plaintiffs thought there were two ways they could "analyze" these results: separately for each test or aggregated among all three tests. Justifying aggregation was the task of their test expert, Felix Lopez. He testified

> with some understandable equivocation, that from the point of view of test content and structure there was sufficient similarity in the three Fire Command series examinations to aggregate the results for the purpose of performing a statistical analysis to determine adverse impact.[57]

Following Lopez' testimony, Jagbir Singh, plaintiff's statistician, testified that the "probability of having . . . all the fifty-eight passing candidates be white is 0.014 or 1.4 percent."

---

56. *Rizzo* (1979) at 1223, 20 FEP Cases at 132.

57. *Rizzo* (1979) at 1224, 20 FEP Cases at 133; following in-text quotation at 1229, 20 FEP Cases at 137.

I will discuss the meaning of these calculated probabilities, the language one *should* use with them, in Chapter 7. As this is the judge's translation, it may be that Singh's language was different in ways the judge did not understand.

Now let's look at Singh's statement and Figure 10 again. What does he mean, "the fifty-eight passing candidates"? From Figure 10 I count sixty-three passing candidates!

Singh was worried about individuals who took more than one test. He aggregated over persons, not test takers. Apparently every test taker either passed or failed all tests, or else it would have been impossible to collapse the data this way. Singh's concern was worthy, but misplaced. If we can keep the test data separate, but aggregate the results, we can assume that each person taking each test was an independent observation. Regardless of Lopez' client-serving testimony, these must be considered different test pools.[58] The question, which Singh did not posit, should have been how to keep the tests separate, and derive a conclusion from the three "pools" from which there have been zero black "selections."

That is the essence of multiple-pools analysis. Aggregating data from the three exams was wrong, even if they were the same exam, because we have three pools of competitors for different positions, just as if they were applying to different departments in graduate school. In this instance, what we find is presented in Figure 11.

One-Tail Probability	
Aggregate	0.017
Multiple Pools	0.148

FIGURE 11: Aggregate and Multiple-Pools Probabilities in *Rizzo*

I have not doubled the probabilities into a two-tail test. A one-tail probability is appropriate, as no one had any expectation that the tests would have a disparate impact against whites. That is an important detail in the conception of the case, but it has no practical import in this example. By any standard, the aggregate result suggests a small probability of these results from a test with no impact. From an appropriate multiple-pools calculation, this "obvious" conclusion is not well supported. Most experts and most judges, given the appropriate test, would say the statistics favor the defendant. The experts needed better tools, but more important, they needed to know that they needed better tools.

Judge Bechtle's concern about the sample size was also misplaced, because the probabilities are calculated taking sample size into account. However, he wisely considered a "sensitivity" test, asking how much damage to the conclusion would have been done if just

---

58. Although the test events should be analyzed separately, what data we have tell us that these are the same test, in the sense that they are reliable—a person who fails one fails another.

one black passed any exam. In the first two exams, the judge notes that the disparate impact would have been the other way, against whites. Sensitivity considerations are appropriate in social data, where the happenstance of who took these tests is not controlled by the "experimenter," and where we cannot have fractional people. It would have been an unnecessary exploration, however, had the experts performed the correct aggregation, by multiple pools, in the first place. In this case, the ruling did not suffer: Plaintiffs did not make a *prima facie* case, motion for injunction denied.

With an appropriate calculation, an expert should have advised plaintiffs to wait another year. If blacks would have fared better on the next year's exams, good for them. If not, good for the lawsuit. Plaintiffs' attorneys went forward with bad advice based on bad analysis, and lost.

Police Promotions in *Montgomery* (1979)

Although both sides made what Judge Johnson referred to as statistical arguments, there is no hint that the judge had any professional advice (that the parties offered statistical experts) in reviewing success on police-sergeant examinations in *Montgomery*. The exams were given on three dates with at least two years between any two tests. Given this time lapse, I think it does not matter if the same people took the tests at different times. All observations can be considered independent. One could argue that the results of three takings of the same test surely can be added. I think it would be wiser to use a multiple-pools approach, again because in these different years the test takers were competing with different people for different positions. One black appointee to a community-relations position reserved for blacks is dropped from the data. Otherwise, the three pools are summarized in Figure 12.[59]

	No	Yes
November 21, 1973		
Black	6	1
White	107	16
August 16, 1976		
Black	12	0
White	142	19
September 12, 1978		
Black	13	0
White	124	7

FIGURE 12: Appointments to Police Sergeant in *Montgomery*

59. Data from *Montgomery* (1979) at 487.

The original language is somewhat awkward. "No" and "Yes" refer to being appointed. There was a test-score cutoff, but more whites than were appointed scored above it. The score without the appointment meant nothing, so the labels are helpful, but they do not reflect the disparity in test results. As plaintiffs were challenging the test, not the promotion, they would have done better placing the passing and failing score data in the record. Perhaps they did, but the data in Figure 12 are what Judge Johnson chose to show and discuss. My calculations are presented in Figure 13.

	One-Tail Probability
Aggregate	0.128
Multiple Pools	0.165

FIGURE 13: Statistical Results from Different Analyses in *Montgomery*

Again, I show one-tail probabilities. The "aggregate" test is Fisher's exact test. The "two or three standard deviation" difference that the Supreme Court enunciated in *Castaneda* (1977) as required for a finding of "significant difference" refers to a probability of 0.025 or smaller.[60] By that criterion we would say that, just as in *Rizzo*, there have not yet been enough black applicants to make a statistical determination from this sample that in the population blacks score far below whites.

Judge Johnson calculated "promotion rates" from aggregate data.

> Thus, the white promotional rate is ten percent (42 out of 415) whereas the black promotional rate is approximately 3 percent (1 out of 32), which means the black promotional rate is only 30 percent that of the white promotional rate.[61]

He lacked an understanding of the concept of statistics, of a sample from a population, as a probabilistic inference to that population based on characteristics of the sample. He lacked the concept of uncertainty one would expect to find in a court. Judge Johnson ruled that plaintiffs had shown disparate impact. Defendant failed to show that the test was valid. I don't doubt that the police department of Montgomery, Alabama was a difficult place in which a black might receive a promotion, but on the statistics, following the guidelines of federal cases, this one was decided incorrectly. The city might have prevailed had it engaged a statistical expert, though no expert used multiple-pools methods at the time.

---

60. The influence of *Castaneda* (1977) on judicial acceptance of binomial selection statistics, and the "conventional wisdom" of what constitutes a "large" difference that followed, is discussed in Chapter 5.

61. *Montgomery* (1979) at 488.

Hiring in *AmNat* (1979)

The Equal Employment Opportunity Commission (EEOC) compared employees of American National Bank with availability estimates, collapsing both into three categories: officials and managers, service workers, and office and clerical.[62] The answer to availability analysis—especially one so ill-conceived—should be applicant-flow analysis: Who applied, and who among them was hired? That was the bank's and their Richmond law firm's approach to their defense, but they did it badly.

We are told that applications are alive for six months. Therefore, at any point at which a job is filled, we should be able to review the previous six months of applications, create a relevant applicant pool, and build up data for a multiple-pools analysis. The bank did not keep all applications of failed candidates. Courts do not look kindly on missing data, especially data that went missing after the EEOC had notified them that it was investigating their employment practices. What applicant data the bank did have, it presented in yearly summaries. At least in 1979—but we will find this mistake made in 2002, also—data often were not presented for analysis in a form representing how they were used to make decisions. I see no reference to a statistical expert, but Judge Clarke does say that

> Defendant has attempted to apply the *Castaneda-Hazelwood* method to statistics concerning the persons it hired between 1969 and 1975.[63]

Did the attorneys perform that calculation themselves? Surely it was done on aggregate data, and surely that was wrong.

Judge Clarke himself calculated binomial standard deviations for both availability and hiring data. He found the differences between expected and actual black workers not sufficiently large to survive rebuttal by applicant data. The Fourth Circuit disagreed.[64] As presented in the district court's opinion, the applicant data are shown in Figure 14. Data from earlier years at Portsmouth are missing.

It is not clear what the bank thought it was proving with the data in Figure 14. I agree with the circuit court that these applicant data cannot rebut a presumption from an availability analysis, not because the availability analysis is persuasive, but because the applicant data are so badly put together.

---

62. See *AmNat* (1979).

63. *AmNat* (1979), 21 FEP Cases at 1559. The reference is to the single-pool binomial calculation, as accepted by the Supreme Court in *Castaneda* (1977) and *Hazelwood* (1977). *Castaneda*, a jury-selection case, is discussed in some detail in Chapter 5.

64. See *AmNat* (1981).

| | Number of Applications | | Number of Hirees | |
	White	Black	White	Black
Suffolk				
1969	23	7	5	1
1970	41	6	3	0
1971	59	30	1	1
1972	11	5	4	2
1973	60	19	7	0
1974	62	35	6	1
1975	40	7	6	2
Portsmouth				
1975	379	115	24	3

FIGURE 14: Applications for Employment in *AmNat*

Judge Clarke was influenced by finding that, in some years, hiring from black applicants appears to exceed that from white applicants. Because we do not know which applications were "alive" at the time the hire was made, it is not clear that the bank really did this. Whites may have applied when there were no offers to be made. However, defining yearly pools is surely better than aggregating over all years, which is what the defendant, the district court, and the circuit court all did.

The circuit court also limited its view to office and clerical workers. In Figure 15 I have made aggregate and multiple-pools calculations from the data as the district court and as the Fourth Circuit saw or would have seen them.

	One-Tail Probability
District Court	
Aggregate	0.049
Multiple Pools	0.005
Circuit Court	
Aggregate	0.0088
Multiple Pools	0.0001

FIGURE 15: Aggregate Results Compared to Multiple-Pools Analysis in *AmNat*

District-court judge Clarke obviously was given no guidance. His largely aggregate view, aided by variation among years, seemed to constitute a defense. Under-hiring of blacks appears to fall about 1.65 standard deviations from expected. Because these are not the real pools, I have no trouble throwing out the bank's data and deciding from the availability analysis alone. But a competent EEOC analyst could have shown that the bank's data worked better for plaintiffs than for defendant, when analyzed by multiple pools that come as close to reality as we can get.

If the Fourth Circuit was correct to limit the data, then it was correct to find against the bank by any calculation method. Remember, "fact" is a legal concept. Here, the "fact" of under-hiring is determined by establishing which data are legally relevant. The legal concept seems to be highly influenced by what the court is told by experts. The circuit court is wary of aggregating applicant data across job groups. Their concern is legitimate. Once again, though, if we had applicant-pool data, and wanted to reach a conclusion about the firm as a whole, multiple-pools methods would have satisfied the court's concern. Who competed against whom is lost in aggregation. The Fourth Circuit stumbled to what seems like the right conclusion, but it worked too hard, and worried unnecessarily about issues that would have been resolved with an appropriate statistical analysis.

Promotion in *Bazemore* (1982)

Bazemore v. Friday concerned pay received by black and white agents of the North Carolina Extension Service. One might think that, as the issue is pay, the method of analysis would be regression. We will indeed encounter this case again in Chapter 3. However pay in the Extension Service depends on rank, and rank depends on promotion. Therefore we consider the promotion aspect of this case here.

The Fourth Circuit opinion, affirming the unpublished district court's finding of no harm, no foul, is a model of emasculation of both statistics and law. For example, we read that the two segregated divisions of the Extension Service had been merged on August 1, 1965, one month after the effective date of Title VII of the Equal Employment Opportunity Act of 1964. The decision notes:

> Salary disparities which had existed between the two branches were not immediately eliminated. By 1972, however, when public employers such as the Extension Service were required to comply with Title VII, it had already been operating on a non-discriminatory basis for about 6 years. Some pre-existing salary disparities continued to linger on nevertheless.[65]

If, six years after integration, salary disparities were still evident, why is the merger characterized as "non-discriminatory"? As of March 24, 1972, the effective date of the modification of Title VII to include public employers, the *situation* of blacks and whites was admittedly unequal. As of that date, salaries should have been modified to eliminate racial discrimination. Whether salaries of blacks and whites would have been made equal would depend on how salaries were set. Non-discrimination means fairness, not equality.

---

65. See *Bazemore* (1984) at 666, 36 FEP Cases at 837, cite omitted.

The Fourth Circuit saw salary *increases* as events, and asked that increases be fair, even if the underlying base from which the increases occurred was discriminatory. It would call equal rates of increase "non-discriminatory," no matter how one might evaluate the salary.[66] Title VII says otherwise, as the Supreme Court unanimously determined.[67]

In addition to rank (which was uncontested) and the lingering effects of pre-Act discrimination in salary—which did not affect persons hired since August 1965—there was one factor the parties agreed affected salary. That was placement into performance quartiles by the District Extension Chairman. If placed in the fourth (lowest) quartile, the agent received no merit pay increase. Thus under Title VII selection-analysis procedures, the plaintiffs should show that this placement was disparate, and then the defendant could attempt to justify the placements, show that they were justified by performance.

Apparently Charles Mann, plaintiffs' expert, did not present such an analysis. The Fourth Circuit undertook its own. They provided the data in Figure 16.[68] Then they approached their analysis with language that may sound familiar, but numbers that are wrong.

	Quartile I		Quartile II		Quartile III		Quartile IV	
	White	Black	White	Black	White	Black	White	Black
District								
North Central	17	5	16	7	14	12	12	9
Northeast	12	2	13	3	10	5	8	3
Northwest	19	1	21	1	17	3	9	4
Southeast	22	1	18	9	14	6	10	7
Southwest	20	3	21	2	18	2	12	4
West	16	0	16	0	15	0	13	0

FIGURE 16: Quartile Rankings by District and Race in *Bazemore*

The Fourth Circuit correctly combined the first three quartiles, so that racial comparison in each district would be based on the proportion in the first three quartiles or its complement, the proportion in the fourth. They presented the correct formula for the standard deviation, but did not calculate it correctly. Their arithmetic, however, is not the

---

66. Several prospective clients of mine held the Fourth Circuit's theory. I tell how I reacted to their requests to utilize it in Chapter 8.

67. See *Bazemore* (1986). Thompson Powers, the lead equal-employment-opportunity attorney at Steptoe & Johnson, a major Washington D.C. equal-employment-opportunity law firm, predicted that the Fourth Circuit's decision would be sustained, lecturing to attorneys at an educational seminar I attended. I had also attended the oral argument at the Supreme Court. I knew they should reverse, and thought they would, as they did.

68. *Bazemore* (1984) at 673.

problem. The initial problem is that they find a black deficit in each of the five "competitive" districts (all but West), but report only each district's Z-score. They view each district as if it constituted a separate lawsuit, to be analyzed separately and never seen as a piece of a larger picture.

Even an aggregate test would have shown that the "fourth quartile" comes from 30 percent of the blacks, but 17 percent of the whites. Plaintiffs' expert, who did not have a multiple-pools solution in his tool kit, could have presented these differences in enough ways that the court would have had to acknowledge them. A binomial approximation (ignoring the fact that we can count losers as well as winners) to the aggregate distribution provides $p = 0.008$. Fisher's exact test provides $p = 0.007$, a chi-square $p = 0.005$. The aggregate distribution is highly improbable from a universe in which whites and blacks are assigned to the fourth quartile equally. Only a misinformed court could find otherwise.

A better approach would utilize a multiple-pools analysis. An approximate multiple-pools probability, calculated following my instructions from above, is $p = 0.003$. Thus the correct probability is even smaller than that derived from aggregate data. Any summary statistic tells you that blacks are differentially placed in the fourth quartile. Apparently no expert testimony to this effect was offered by plaintiffs.

Promotions at Hackley Bank

In 1980, the Office of Federal Contract Compliance Programs (OFCCP) declared that Hackley Bank in Michigan was out of compliance with federal contracting requirements, and demanded that reparations be paid to females. I was invited to analyze the bank by their attorney, Walter Connolly. I explained a mathematical error in the OFCCP's back-pay calculation, explained multiple-pools analysis and why there was no back-pay calculation to make. No other analyst had ever used multiple pools in litigation.[69] The OFCCP crept back under their rock, suitably chastised.

Although the OFCCP challenged pay to females, my question was what events led females to be at their grade. Can we analyze the fairness of those events? The OFCCP made no allegation that females were under-hired, only that they were underpaid. Pay clearly was "fair" by grade, so the only way in which females could be underpaid was if they were assigned to too low a grade upon hire, or if they failed to advance. There being no allegation about mis-placement at hire, I took position at hire as given and analyzed promotion.

Reading this in the twenty-first century, one might be surprised how lethargically, how sloppily firms were managed before they had to account, in an equal-employment-

---

69. Although, in *Hackley Bank*, I was clearly the first expert to use multiple-pools analysis in litigation, Joe Gastwirth and I first entered such analyses as evidence in court in separate cases at about the same time. I do not know whose was earlier.

opportunity sense, for their actions. Every opening should be announced internally (even if also externally), and filled from applications submitted by the closing date. Just play fair. This is the kind of advice attorneys were giving to firms from the 1970s, from the time when it became clear that a firm without strict procedures for hiring and promoting would be subjected to mythical "availability" pools of non-applicants. That advice went unheeded. Hackley Bank had no such procedures in place.

If a person was hired into the correct grade and a promotion was made from that grade the next week, surely this new hire was not "eligible" for that promotion, and should not be included in the pool of candidates. As Hackley Bank had no formal eligibility criteria in most of the period I studied, November 1, 1976 through September 30, 1980, I had to create informal but realistic ones.[70] In June 1980 they formally required one year in grades 71 through 79 before an employee could be promoted to a higher grade. I found no one promoted quicker in my data, so I adopted that rule over the entire time period.

The promotions will be analyzed as selections from different pools, aggregated by job promoted *to*. As described above, the path of least resistance in pool creation is to consider all people in any job classification that *ever* supplied a person to the receiving job, to be eligible for that job. Even though we could see "typical" and "atypical" feeder groups, with an agency as incompetent and irrational as the OFCCP, the fewer analytic constructs the better. We did refer to "atypical" feeders at one grade, but did not incorporate a weighting scheme (so that a person in a typical feeder group would have more "applicantness" for any selection than a person in an atypical feeder group) into this analysis. That modification appeared in later cases.

Figure 17 contains an illustration of the promotions and pools of eligibles that we found, at one grade. The totals are at the bottom. To construct a statistical test, we will have to subtract winners from "pool members" to count "losers." The most naive "analysis" of these data would be a test on the column totals. For example, using the finite-population-corrected binomial, females are under-promoted by three standard deviations. Even the Fourth Circuit, in *Bazemore*, could see that pools without competition should be dropped from the analysis. Using bottom-line numbers, from competitive pools only, generates a Z-score of -2.08. Females appear to be under-promoted by more than two standard deviations, enough to make OFCCP analysts salivate.

That finding is clearly wrong. A female was promoted from every large pool. In the aggregate-single-pool analysis, the "losers" appear to lose over and over again, most of them females. In the real world they lost once, to a female winner.

---

70. We will see a similar situation, below, in which the question is how long are applicants to positions in the City of Gallup, New Mexico, to be considered "active." The answer there will be more complicated than it is here.

| Pool Members | | Winners | |
Female	Male	Female	Male
0	1		1
3	0	1	
7	0	1	
39	2	1	
3	2		1
2	0	1	
3	0	1	
0	11		1
0	4		1
0	3		1
3	1		1
37	2	1	
27	1	1	
16	2	1	
2	0	1	
2	0	1	
Totals 144	29	10	6

FIGURE 17: Promotion to Grade 79 at Hackley Bank

The multiple-pools Z-score, using finite population-corrected-pool variances, is -1.59; not small, but below the two-standard-deviation level the OFCCP considered critical.[71] Once again the single-pool calculation—the one that appears in all the textbooks and cases—provides not only the wrong Z-score, but a qualitatively wrong answer.

A complete analysis would include an aggregation of single-grade results over all grades. As there are no control variables, this would be most easily accomplished by just doing one multiple-pools analysis over all grades.

The multiple-pools approach as so far presented is simplistic. It assumes that all persons in a pool are equally qualified. This is not likely to be the case; but one thing at a time. In reality, individuals compete with only certain other individuals for any opening. Now I have established that analysts typically do not model this multiple-pool selection correctly, nor do courts object to the unrealistic single-pool analysis. Most important, I have established that multiple-pools methods are easily calculated in commonly available

---

71. I did an exact calculation in 1980, the first use of Longbranch Research Associates' MULPOOLS™ program. I retain only one report, which just describes the statistic and generalizes about its outcome. Sloppy writing? I doubt it. I suspect this approach was determined by my client, to tell the OFCCP what we were doing but hold back the details.

software, and often provide different answers from single-pool statistics. I promise to explain the logic behind multiple-pools selection analysis *with control variables* before the end of this chapter.

SELECTION OVER TIME

Although hires must be selections from competitive pools, promotions need not be. Many large organizations, including the federal government, place most entry positions in "career ladders." The career ladder is a series of grade levels, usually reaching a maximum at Grade 9 or 11, that one can anticipate moving through in one's "career." It makes sense to tell entering employees that there is a future with the agency or firm, that one can advance without competition by performing well and learning.

The Logic and Language of Survival Analysis

This book is more about using statistical tools properly than about the tools themselves. Nonetheless, as I have briefly explained selection, and will introduce regression in Chapter 3, let us look at a clever field of statistics called "survival analysis."[72] I will explain why it was needed, how it operates, and what some of its terms mean.

The naive analyst studying promotion equality, say between males and females, may gather data over a long period of time and compare the mean time a person waits for promotion between the two groups. Problems arise immediately: What about people who have not been promoted, or not *yet* been promoted? What about people who leave the firm or transfer to another department before the observation period ends, not having been promoted? Most experts have floundered under the burden of these questions.

The driving force for survival analysis, as its name implies, was asking how long one has to wait to know if a medical treatment is efficacious. How many in the placebo group have to die before we decide that a drug is keeping members of the treatment group alive? If someone dies of a non-related cause (not the disease the drug is supposed to remedy), is he lost to the study? Can we gain no information from the fact that he survived for some time?

The cleverness of survival analysis is the formation of a pool of "applicants" every time there is an event. In medical research, the event is death from the disease. There are two kinds of applicants: those receiving the medication, and those receiving a placebo. The researcher needs to know everyone's situation at the time of each event. For example, if one member of the study group died in an automobile accident last month, and someone dies

---

72. The seminal publication in this field is E. Kaplan and Meier (1958). The multivariate version of survival analysis has other names, but "survival analysis" as a term describing an analytic approach should cover both univariate and multivariate survival-analysis methods.

from the disease this month, then the accident victim is not an "applicant" for *this* death. He was, however, an applicant for all deaths that occurred while he was alive—an applicant who was not selected. This person is "censored," dropped from all events after he leaves the study. Similarly, when the study ends, some people are still alive. They, too, are censored from that time.[73] A censored observation is in every pool up to the time he is censored, and then just does not appear in subsequent pools, if there are any.

Persons in the study see themselves as part of a flow. It is the analyst who creates the event concept. The analyst has to know who applied for each event, how long he has been in the applicant pool (time since diagnosis, treatment, or supposed disease onset), and what group he was in (placebo or medication). Breaking the flow of time into events, converting the problem to one that could use all the information available from one in which researchers helplessly waited for enough deaths from both groups to draw a conclusion, was a remarkable intellectual achievement.

In its simplest form, survival analysis is a multiple-pools method. The more pools (the more death events) the stronger the analysis will be, but an analysis can be done at any time there have been some events. The statistic is developed asking if the probability of "selection" (death) among these otherwise equal candidates (in waiting time, anyway) depends on whether one was in the experimental group or the control group, the medicated group or the placebo group. In the discrimination context, we ask if blacks (for example) wait longer for their promotions than non-blacks, not if they are never promoted. However, rather than being able to average the waiting times of only those persons who have been promoted, we are able to use our knowledge at the time of each promotion that others waited this long, also, and were not promoted.

The usefulness of this kind of analysis for the study of waiting time until promotion was seen immediately when survival analysis was presented to the statistics profession in the 1950s. However, there were few uses of the method in employment litigation before the 1980s. My firm developed expertise in survival analysis because we were often engaged in promotion-discrimination cases involving federal government agencies which had non-competitive promotion plans.

The concept of a survival-analysis average waiting time is complicated. For example, in any study we have more observations early on, declining as the events (death, promotion) occur, or people are censored (leave the study). If we weight the waiting time at each event by the number of people involved, the early observations will dominate. On the other

---

73. We might say that people whose start date is known, and do not have an event occur to them, are "right censored" at some point. We indicate to the computer program what that point is—after how much elapsed time—and if there are any events to the right of that point, these censored observations are not in the pools formed to analyze those selections. There is a parallel concept of left censoring, when we do not know the start time, but we still consider people applicants for some events.

hand, there may be few differences between treatment and control group at the early events, so perhaps "average waiting time" should be calculated to give more weight to later events. There are, therefore, different legitimate concepts of how best to calculate and compare waiting-time means.

That there may be no simple metric describing which category waits longer for promotion—that different metrics may provide different answers—is one reason it takes expert analysts to understand, use, and explain these procedures. The explanation must be understandable to lay people (judges) not so much in its technical details, but in its coverage of the events at issue, and how these methods help us understand those events.[74]

Faculty Promotion at Swarthmore

Barbara Presseisen's appointment as an assistant professor at Swarthmore College was not renewed in 1972. She parlayed that event into a class-action discrimination suit that included, as part of the class, females who had not been hired, and female associate professors waiting to be promoted to full professor.[75] Courts vary widely on the extent to which plaintiffs must represent the class, and this is one of the more liberal allowances, but it had the advantage of inducing a broad range of statistical analyses.

Plaintiffs' experts included John de Cani. Defendants' experts included Gudmund Iverson and Paul Meier, a co-inventor of the Kaplan-Meier procedure, the first iteration of survival analysis. No mention is made of survival-analysis methods in Judge Bechtle's decision, but the telltale signs are there.

De Cani had measured mean and median time from highest degree to promotion or appointment as associate professor, for males and females. He used simple arithmetic, excluding persons at lower rank still waiting for their associate-professor appointment. Iverson excluded forty-seven people who had been promoted before 1966, but counted waiting time of those promoted later (or not), even if some of that time occurred before 1966. I am not sure that he appropriately allowed for the enactment of Title VII of the Equal Employment Opportunity Act, but I appreciate his concern.

The judge, also, was appreciative of the effort, although I am not sure he understood it. He writes:

> However, only four of those forty-seven [excluded] people were women.[76]

---

74. For example, from *Craik* (1984), majority opinion at 476:
   There is some argumentation in the briefs about the relative merits of multiple linear regression and logistic fitting analysis. Neither side, however, either in the briefs or at the oral argument, bothered to explain, in intelligible terms or otherwise, what these terms mean.

75. See *Presseisen* (1977).

76. *Presseisen* (1977) at 610; following indented quotation also at 610. In *Ottaviani* (1988), at 300,

Waiting-time statistics are comparative. He may have meant to say that the average waiting time of females was hardly affected, but what counts is their time compared to that of males, and male waiting time (implicitly) was affected.

The key sentence in the decision, for the discussion here, is this:

> However, [de Cani] only studies time of promotion and did not study time in rank for those persons still in rank, as did the studies of Dr. Iverson.

It is survival analysis that counts waiting time of those who are still waiting when the data are collected. I take it, therefore, that *Presseisen* represents the first use of survival-analysis methods in equal-employment-opportunity litigation—possibly in any litigation. Defendant used a better concept of waiting time (time from one rank to another, separately by rank), and a better measure of that time (survival-analysis means), than plaintiff. Defendant found no male-female difference in waiting time to promotion, and prevailed.

Career-Ladder Advancement in the Maritime Administration

The U.S. Maritime Administration says that

> [Career-ladder employees] are given grade-building experience and may be promoted as they demonstrate ability at the next higher level until they reach their full performance levels.[77]

If we assume that blacks and whites who enter such a plan are equivalent—they have different abilities as individuals, but equal as a group—then an appropriate measure of equal treatment is the time they take to get from one grade to another. That time might be related to calendar time (due to budget considerations) or other factors, but as a start it is reasonable to expect that, if promotion is fair, there will be no distinction by race in time to promotion, on the average, from the same starting grade, in the same career ladder.

Blacks claimed that they were promoted unequally, either more slowly or not at all, compared with whites. Plaintiffs' expert, John Van Ryzin, understood that waiting times might reasonably differ by grade. He studied promotion rates of blacks and whites separately for each grade. He used survival-analysis averages to measure how long each group apparently waited until promotion. He concluded that, in general, blacks waited longer.

Remember that "waiting longer" does not mean he observed blacks being promoted after a long time. One can say they "waited longer" even if they were never promoted. That is the power of survival analysis, but also its danger. The analyst has to understand his data.

> Dr. Gray compared the average years to promotion for men and women promoted from 1973–1984.

That is, more than a decade later, "experts" still did not know to use survival analysis to incorporate waiting time of persons not yet promoted. Mary Gray's analysis of promotion was rejected.

77. Maritime Administration Order 730-335, at 4.

Van Ryzin's conclusion about blacks waiting longer for promotion, at some grades, was due to their being censored. They never were promoted. Was bias in promotion that stark?

The censored observations came about because these employees were at their career-ladder ceilings. Some such people advanced by winning competitions. Van Ryzin should not have included competitive promotions in his analysis of career-ladder progression.

Van Ryzin also combined lines of progression with different ceiling grades. Thus it appeared to him that some people were not being promoted, and others were, from the same grade, when many of those who stayed behind were already at their ceiling grade.[78]

Finally, different job groups may have different rates of promotion independent of race. If whites are in a promotion plan where promotion is swift, and blacks in one where promotion is slow, one may question selection into the more progressive plan. However, there is no reason for a court to assert that promotion must occur at the same rate in different job lines.

For all these reasons—to avoid comparing in-line with competitive promotions, to avoid comparing in-line with impossible promotions, and to avoid comparing two rates of progress that are inherently different—survival methods for promotion analysis make sense only when comparing people in the same grade *and career ladder* (promotion path), and only at a grade below the ceiling. Van Ryzin had selected the right tool, but did not know how to use it.

My survival analyses was limited to career-ladder employees below their ceiling grade. I showed that there was no difference between black and white advancement rates.[79] In such a formal system as the federal government's, there was also the problem of transfer-in. Some people were seen waiting a long time in a grade below career-ladder ceiling. They had transferred to the Maritime Administration in grade, usually for the express purpose of getting into the career ladder they were now in. They had to wait in grade in this agency until they were ready for promotion. Van Ryzin incorrectly counted all of their time in grade.

The "pretty good candidate" who can expect never to win a competition above entry level would be well advised to find a career ladder and rise to its ceiling. Many do just that. The analyst who does not recognize the different promotion opportunities, who includes

---

78. *Harrison* (1982). Fifteen years later, Harriet Zellner also failed to ask if blacks were in positions from which they could be promoted, when she claimed that they were not being promoted at the same rate as whites. See *Robinson* (1997) or, for a more complete discussion, *Caridad* (1999) at 288. Janice Madden, also, "did not compare similarly situated individuals" when she failed to consider "typical lines of promotion within departments and job families." *Cooper* (2001c) at 614. Madden used a multiple-pools exact test, but had constructed the wrong pools.

79. There were two clerical ladders in which blacks, for no reason I could determine, failed to advance. I notified my client, the United States Attorney, that unless they had a good explanation, they should admit the violation and, more important, take corrective action within the agency. Being able to find no explanation, he too concluded that discrimination was the operating force, and admitted so to the judge.

persons not in career ladders, or persons competing out of career ladders, as observations of career-ladder waiting time, whether for plaintiff or defendant, fails his client, and the court. Defendant prevailed.

Promotion at the Naval Air Rework Facility

The issue was promotions of females by the Naval Air Rework Facility in Oakland, California.[80] Rather than learn how one got to be promoted in this agency, John Freeman, plaintiffs' statistical expert, invented his own promotion concept. To Freeman, all persons in a grade ever during a time period were "eligible" for all promotions to the next grade. So, for example, if females were entering certain grades at a high rate, and being promoted out fairly, after serving their time in each grade, he would conclude that they were being promoted out *un*fairly, because many would appear not promoted from his "pool" of eligibles.

Freeman constructed his analysis (promoted or not from a single pool), by collapsing grades. So, for example, his merged data assumed that females in Grade 5 were passed over every time there was a promotion from Grade 11 to Grade 12. I explained:

> What model of a "fair" world does Freeman posit, against which he contrasts the NARF world? Freeman is careful to say that his findings are consistent with discrimination. I agree. A statistical analysis, however, ought to do more. It ought to show some apparent inconsistency with a nondiscriminatory world. Freeman's does not.
>
> The simplest model of a fair world is consistent with Freeman's description of the grade distribution of males and females. One can calculate the following percentages from Freeman's Table B:

	Percent Female	
	1978	1981
Grade 9 and below	23.3	23.4
Grade 10 and above	3.5	5.2

> Female representation has increased by 43 percent at the high grades, while remaining constant at the lower grades. Does this mean there has been rampant favoritism for females? From Freeman's logic it does, but I do not think so. We still need to know what actions NARF could have taken. We need a statistical test that contrasts actual actions with expected (sex-neutral) actions. Telling us that most females begin and end at low grades provides no such test.[81]

---

80. *Moore* (1981). What happened to this case is a mystery. The district-court decision was never published. The Ninth Circuit affirmed without a written opinion.

81. Stephan Michelson, "Review of Affidavit of John H. Freeman," November 12, 1982, in *Moore* (1981) at 6.

Freeman expressed a distressing level of statistical illiteracy. However, my affidavit was well-meant, encouraging plaintiffs to study actions of the agency, and bring forth evidence (if there was any) that the agency was not fair to females. My affidavit did persuade the court that Freeman provided no basis from which to issue a summary judgment for plaintiffs. One would expect that plaintiffs and their expert would have seriously considered my criticisms of their approach.

They did not. In a September 1983 affidavit, Freeman's definition of promotion was still being taken from grade at the end of year and, as I had warned in 1982, not all persons in Freeman's data may vie for any particular promotion. The Navy had a special apprentice program in which it trained people to repair the equipment brought into this facility, expecting them then to advance to full-time positions. Females had fared well within that program. Survival analysis might have been an appropriate way to analyze promotion out of the apprentice program, though one could as well have considered each "class" a pool, and asked who succeeded, who did not. It would seem reasonable to assume that all apprentices are implicitly "applicants" for the journeyman job to which apprenticeships led. Freeman, however, decided that promotions through the apprentice program did not count!

Freeman continued to perform an "availability" analysis, considering all persons ever at a grade available for every promotion from that grade. He added a "waiting time" model in which he counted time to promotion for persons promoted, and time until the end of the observation period (at the end of 1979) for those not promoted. This is the amateur's analysis. It creates the very fallacies survival analysis was designed to avoid.

It was not surprising, as I pointed out in my affidavit of January 13, 1984, that a logit analysis Freeman performed implied that the shorter the waiting time the more likely the promotion. In survival analysis, an individual's waiting time is different at the date of each promotion. But Freeman calculated a single waiting time for all people for all promotions. Those who were promoted had a shorter waiting time than those who were not, leading to his absurd result.

His method was worse than that. How did Freeman handle the employee who left before the end of the period? Was he still considered a candidate for all promotions? With what waiting time? Or for none, even though he was there for some? No solution, in the context of his analysis, would have been correct.

This was a small case many years ago. It is not important in the grand scheme of the history of litigation. But it is an excellent example of a typical phenomenon: Judge Patel needed only to inquire about how plaintiffs' analysis was constructed to see that it bore no relationship to the institutional facts.

Freeman justified his method:

It simply makes little sense to take for granted that only those who go through the process of formally applying for a promotion are "available for promotion."[82]

The opposite is true: When considering a competitive promotion, it makes sense to consider *only* those who have applied for it as available for it, except when one has entered a special program to achieve the promotion. The only "candidates" one could infer had applied were the apprentices, whom Freeman chose not to study. Otherwise, as I describe in Chapter 6, there were indeed applications for promotion. I reveal there what information they contained that convinced me the Navy's position was indefensible, and what the Navy did when it received my analysis.

MULTIVARIATE WAITING-TIME ANALYSIS

We have a patient population, we know when they started in the study (or were diagnosed, etc.), we know who is in the experiment, who in the control group, and who is censored (leaves the study) when. We know how to analyze waiting time, to compare rates of survival of the experimental group with the control group, not having to wait until they die to make the calculations. But the simple survival analysis assumes that, otherwise, all patients are equal.

All patients are not otherwise equal. They never are. Some are males, some females. They are of different ages. They have different education levels, dietary histories, genetic histories (age at death of parents, for example). We cannot do anything about these differences. By randomly assigning persons to experiment and control groups the experimenter tries to mitigate their effect, but it is essentially impossible to control for all variables by construction. We need to test for the possible effects of other inputs on the outcome of interest.

As employers do not see their promotion plans as survival experiments, employee differences will have to be accounted for statistically. For example, entrance might have required "passing" a valid test, but even though all employees passed, they did not all receive the same score. Might a valid predictor of performance also predict differences in waiting time to promotion?[83] Employees could differ on a number of factors other than

---

82. Quoted in my affidavit, "Comments on 'Analysis of Mobility Patterns for Men and Women in the Avionics Division of the Naval Air Rework Facility-Alameda' by John H. Freeman," January 13, 1984, in *Moore* (1981).

83. It would be important, for interpretation, that those making the promotion decision not know the entrance-exam score of the employees. That could happen. For example, score on the Foreign Service Entrance Exam is not part of a Foreign Service Officer's record. No decision maker at the Department of State would know it. State was willing to concede that its exam had not been validated, although I found a high correlation between exam score and success (such as rate of advancement). I never could

the one defining the plaintiff class. Surely we want to compare "otherwise equal" employ- ees with the same waiting time in the same grade of the same promotion ladder, when we ask if a certain characteristic affected the probability of promotion.

It was over a decade after survival analysis had been "invented" before a multivariate form—a form that could measure the effect of other characteristics on the result—was developed. It is sometimes referred to as "Cox regression" after its developer, or more in- formatively "conditional logit."[84] It is, indeed, a multivariate multiple-pools logit analysis.

Multivariate Multiple-Pools Analysis

By the late 1970s, sophisticated mainframe statistical computer packages contained the mathematics for multivariate multiple-pools solutions, conditional logit, usually under the name "proportional-hazards" models. If statistics were grouped by their use, it would be listed as a biostatistical survival-analysis tool. If used very carefully, such a program would print out multivariate multiple-pools solutions for promotion analyses, though it would list those promoted as "dead" and have other printout anomalies best not brought into the courtroom. Longbranch Research Associates created MULQUALS™, a multiple-pools events-analysis program, from proportional-hazards routines.[85] We then made it available to our competitors, for a fee, to squelch cries that only we could do such an analysis, how could anyone check our work. The major statistical experts in employment-discrimination litigation purchased MULQUALS™ along with our exact univariate multiple-pools soft- ware, MULPOOLS™. Our policy of sharing our software led to a smooth transition— among many professionals, at least—to more advanced methods of selection analysis than previously had been available.

As explained above, the key intellectual achievement of survival analysis was turning what seemed like a continuous-measure problem (average waiting time) into events. Al- though conditional logit was then developed in a survival (time) framework, it was, true to its origins, an events-analysis method. The function of MULQUALS™ was to transform data

---

convince State or the Department of Justice attorneys defending them that, except for the usual exclu- sion of those who had not passed, I had performed a criterion-validity study, that the exam was valid.

84. D. Cox (1972). For the technically minded: Regression, the subject of Chapter 3, has an analytic solu- tion. Cox "regression" is a maximum-likelihood procedure without an analytic solution. One iterates to a solution (the values of its coefficients), that is, estimates, modifies coefficients, and re-estimates, until the differences from one run to the next are "small" by parameters set within the program. Similarly, "logit" analysis is often called, to my distaste, "logistic regression."

85. We learned that the PHGLM proportional hazards procedure, written for SAS by Frank Harrell, was in the public domain. MULQUALS™, as was PHGLM, was written in PL1, and therefore was a valid addition to SAS through Version 5. When SAS converted its programming to the C language, we did not upgrade MULQUALS™.

into pools, and then estimate the importance of factors leading to selection from these pools.

By "transform data into pools" I mean the researcher did not have to specify the content of each pool, if he could specify rules. The program must put this person as a loser in every pool for which he was eligible and not hired, and then put him as a winner in the pool for which he was eligible and hired, and then not put him in any more pools. Our MULQUALS™ program did that, creating the pools and then running the estimation.

An application for employment may expire after a given number of days. A person who had received some promotions might leave the firm, becoming ineligible for others. As in standard survival analysis, people who leave without experiencing the event are called "censored." People who are still alive when the study ends—or who are still applicants when we stop recording hiring data, or still employees when we stop recording promotion data—are also censored. They can be given a "censor date" of the day after the last event, and the computer program will know that they are in pools but never selected.

An application might expire slowly, that is, become less and less likely to result in promotion as it ages. In this multivariate world, we do not need to assume that all pool members are equally likely to be selected, any more than we assume that all medical subjects are equally likely to die, regardless when they reached the critical stage. We can create "time since application" as a variable, to be recalculated in every pool.

This approach solves the great dilemma of age-discrimination analysis. Almost all analyses of this subject ever done have struggled to define who was how old when the events occurred, if they did not all occur on a single day. Almost all age-discrimination studies have assumed a single pool, where each pool member had a characteristic and was hired, terminated, promoted (whatever the study is about), or not. In fact, not only is each person's age different at every event, so is his outcome. A person might survive the first round of reduction in force, but be terminated six months later in a second round. That is information conditional logit estimates can use.

The solution is to recalculate age at each event. Only a multiple-pools approach can cope with the fact that people have different ages at different times. Yet, in 1997, Judge Chin refused to allow the presentation of a proportional-hazards model because, he thought, it had never been used in an age-discrimination case. Judge Chin was wrong on two counts. First, in this post-*Daubert* world, science is supposed to be evaluated by its merits. The proportional-hazards model was the best statistical approach to the issue before the court. Second, he was historically wrong. Why the experts did not refer him to my cases, I do not know.[86]

---

86. See *Wyche* (1997). Because the procedure has so many names, one can miss its use from a name search. I had used MULQUALS™, which is to say proportional hazards, in *Koger* (1994) and several other age-discrimination cases. See my description of *Koger* in Chapter 6.

Hiring in *Gallup* (1986)

The Department of Justice alleged that the City of Gallup, New Mexico, discriminated in hiring against females and American Indians in the 1970s and 1980s. Engaged by plaintiffs, I found no evidence supporting their gender claim, but substantial evidence for their "race" claim.

The first task was to determine who was an applicant for each job.

> We have found over 2,000 separate "job applied for" titles, but fewer than 300 titles of positions into which persons were hired. If we measure strictly from these job titles, most employees were hired into a job other than the one for which they applied.
>
> I have chosen to collapse jobs into job groups or categories. I do this by connecting jobs applied for to jobs received, and using common sense to interpret abbreviations and general terms. Still, I find some records of persons who apply to Category X, but are hired into Category Y. Applicants to X are to some extent applicants for Y positions. However, they need not be equal in applicant status to persons who applied in the Y category. By controlling for position into which one applied while testing the position into which one is hired, I allow an X applicant to be less of an applicant for a Y position than a Y applicant.[87]

This is a major advance over the traditional hiring analysis in which one is an applicant or not, or in the "availability pool" or not. Firms sometimes hire or promote people out of line. We saw this problem at Hackley Bank. There I was concerned that I was making the employer's pool too large, including people it would not consider, just because it once considered one person from an unlikely source for a particular position. Here we see the solution: We can add that unlikely source, but account for its unlikeliness. Everyone in that source is a candidate for future positions, but not a strong one.

To bring this point home to the judge, I can express my findings as giving each applicant tickets in a lottery. Some legitimately have more tickets than others, have a better chance to be selected, depending on such characteristics as what position they currently have, and how long they have been there. In *Gallup*, how many tickets an applicant had for the next available job depended in part on to which job he had applied.

The next issue in *Gallup* was race. We plumbed many sources, including Navajo Election Commission data and affidavits from tribe members, as well as information on application forms, to verify who was an Indian. A failed applicant was not an Indian unless we could identify him as such, so that errors would be biased for defendant.

The final important variable was date of application. Some applications were completed *after* hire, and some persons were hired without a formal application in the record.

---

87. Stephan Michelson, "A Study of Hiring of The City of Gallup," at 10, in *Gallup* (1986).

These are the everyday problems of litigation data. Once again, we did not have to determine an application life, whether a person was an applicant or not. We let the "applicantness" of an application slowly fade as time passed, determined in our estimating equation. For all practical purposes, even though in a pool, applications over five hundred days old had no chance of being selected. Except that four were—all non-Indians.

Following a discussion of the advantage of being a non-Indian, in terms of having more "tickets" in the job application lottery, I expressed results in this case not as coefficients, but as "relative preference." Non-Indian preference is the probability of being selected with baseline characteristics if the applicant is not Indian, divided by that probability if he is Indian. My multivariate multiple-pools results are shown in Figure 18.

Position	Non-Indian Preference	Standard Deviations	One-Tail Probability	Hires	Indian Deficit
Clerical	8.00	−5.94	0.00	128	−37
Animal Control	3.22	−1.70	0.04	13	−4
Recreation	3.35	−1.95	0.03	63	−5
Labor / Low Skill	3.13	−8.14	0.00	362	−81
Dispatcher	10.38	−2.23	0.01	30	−5
Lineman	0.44	0.78	1.00	11	0
Equipment Operator	5.42	−3.25	0.00	30	−9
Fire	15.96	−2.74	0.00	81	−12
Jailer	1.11	−0.34	1.00	55	0
Sewer Technician	2.66	−0.90	0.83	13	−1
Mechanic / Welder	3.19	−2.47	0.02	26	−5
Police	3.06	−2.73	0.00	57	−9
Traffic	1.60	−0.48	0.95	11	−1
Teacher	1.23	−0.41	0.85	24	−1
Combined Remainder	1.80	−1.48	0.17	50	−4
Totals			0.00	954	−174

FIGURE 18: Summary of Analysis of City of Gallup Hiring, 1973–1983

I did a separate study of police hires, an area in which specific skills might be important, but still found a relative preference for non-Indians exceeding three to one. It seems unlikely that the facts were other than as I described them, a sloppy municipal-employment system that paid little attention to application life, and exercised a striking preference for non-Indian employees. The City of Gallup settled, paying money damages.

Defendant's expert in *Gallup* was Finis Welch. Through depositions and reports, we held a conversation. Finis expressed skepticism about my methods, and questioned some aspects of them. Expert questions should be welcome, but so should answers. Some professorial experts simply assert disagreement, which helps neither their clients nor the court. Some experts, when challenged, will just say, "Well, I think this provides information," without saying what information that is. Those kinds of exchanges can be ended quickly. Others, such as occurred in *Gallup*, are enlightening.

The appendix to this chapter contains excerpts from my *Gallup* report, in which I rebut Finis' challenges to my work. They deserve reproduction because his questions were good, and my answers are informative about characteristics of conditional logit estimation. However, the material in that appendix lies outside the flow of this book. It is an example of the kind of exchange that can take place between the experts that the attorneys need not try to understand. Having it "on the record"does not assist the court. In Chapter 10 I suggest that experts should meet to resolve such issues off the record.

Layoffs at Polaroid

A second Polaroid case is another example of a discussion between experts, of worthy questions being answered. The issue was layoffs from the Polaroid work force in the eighteen months from the middle of 1974 through 1975. Rich Goldstein was again plaintiffs' statistical expert. I derived data from Polaroid's personnel data files, carefully distinguished between hourly and monthly employees, dropped those monthly employees who voluntarily resigned, and produced the summary bottom-line picture of Figure 19 and the following comment.

	Hourly Employees	
	Black	**Non-Black**
Laid Off	284	766
Not Laid Off	1,193	5,877
	Monthly Employees	
	Black	**Non-Black**
Laid Off	39	217
Not Laid Off	218	3,064

FIGURE 19: Impact of Layoffs at Polaroid, 1974–1975

Most analysts would conclude that these tables show some ultimate relationship between being black or not, and being laid off or not. I concur. Whatever decisions were made, whatever rights existed or were exercised, whatever individual characteristics were considered, blacks were laid off in excess of their proportion in the Polaroid work force.[88]

---

88. Stephan Michelson, "Polaroid Corporation Layoffs 1974 Through 1975 by Race," in *Polaroid* (1983), November 11, 1982; quotation at 13, tables at 15.

There is a difference between Polaroid's decision to lay off a person and who ultimately left. That difference was a bona fide seniority system with bumping rights, as spelled out in Polaroid's personnel-policy manual. Seniority rights are protected in the language of the federal law under which this suit was brought. Thus I started my report by agreeing with plaintiffs that the layoffs had a disparate *impact* on blacks, but proposing that Polaroid was immune from attack if I could show that there was no disparate *treatment*. Fair treatment filtered through a bona fide seniority plan wins for defense, regardless who was terminated.

Managers manage. Managers must have a concept of what structure is needed to run their business at any scale. At Polaroid, the central authority determined how many jobs would be eliminated from each division. Which jobs were eliminated was then determined by division managers. There was no trading between divisions. If a division was to be reduced by twenty-seven positions, then the division manager could select which twenty-seven, but not argue about the number. That is, the divisions became pools, and within the divisions there were additional job-specific pools. Selection of individuals to receive lay-off notices—those holding the jobs that would be eliminated—was competitive within division but not among divisions, within job but not among jobs.

Who received termination notices? Probably because the individual decisions were decentralized, there was no data file indicating who (that is, the holders of which jobs) were sent layoff notices. No company would undertake a large layoff without legal advice. Why wasn't Polaroid advised to keep careful records of who was notified that his job had been eliminated? See Chapter 6: Attorneys do not know what is important, especially when it comes to "data." Defendant had not retained termination notices, and plaintiffs spent no effort on the question. Neither side's attorneys seem to have understood the difference between receiving a termination notice and being terminated.

Although the termination notices could not be found, employee behavior upon receiving such notices could be. Hourly employees had bumping rights, and there was bumping. But it was not limited to hourly employees, because, as we saw above in *Polaroid* (1981), some salaried employees had been hired as hourly. They retained whatever seniority rights they had accrued as hourly employees.

Those who received termination notices either were terminated or did something not to be. That something would appear in personnel data. The trail was obvious. First, out of 363 notices sent to monthly employees, 111 who had hourly seniority returned to hourly status. They did that in exactly the same time frame as those who did not move to hourly were terminated. There were essentially no such personnel actions in any other proximate time frame. In Figure 20[89] I show as MTOH (move to hourly), the time series of such moves,

---

89. The Polaroid graphics in Figures 20 and 21 are not remakes, but are scans of the original graphics, which were produced by a mainframe graphics program driving a pen plotter. Originally each graphic

superimposed on a graph of layoffs, persons who terminated (and whose records indicated layoff, excluding those Polaroid could prove were voluntary). The scale is on the right.

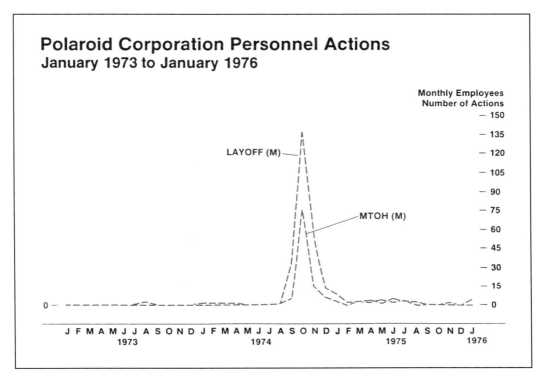

FIGURE 20

Clearly—I received no resistance from plaintiffs about this interpretation—the persons who received layoff notices are identified by the sum of the monthly layoffs and the MTOH that occurred at exactly the same time. Only one of these 111 employees who returned to their former hourly position was ultimately terminated. Thus 110 monthly employees told to leave, did not; which means that 110 *other* hourly employees were laid off. Those terminated were not those selected for termination and, the key, the race of those selected was quite different—far fewer blacks—than the race of those who ultimately were forced to leave.

Managers manage within the constraints of the system, including laws, regulations, and union contracts. For example, from the ultimate result one would think that proportionately more hourly than monthly employees had been selected for termination. The opposite was true.

Within the hourly ranks, rights also led to personnel actions other than termination.

---

consumed an 8½-by-11-inch page. They were also photographed and enlarged to poster-size images for courtroom presentation.

One would see only one action in the records of monthly employees, MTOH, whereas one bump led to another among hourly workers. Thus the hourly data provided more problems to solve. In Figure 21 I show three of the four data series I used to create a measure of those sent termination letters. XFER and XOUT are both transfers, the former just to another position, the latter to another department. Each transfer, some caused by the inflow of MTOH actions, created a second wave of layoff actions.

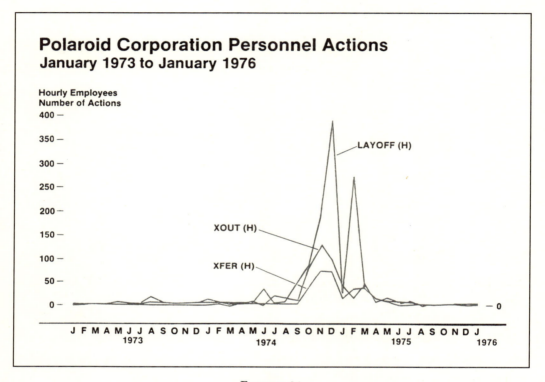

FIGURE 21

The personnel actions I identify as indicating a reaction to a termination notice (or to being bumped) occur, to some extent, all the time. I analyzed this as a signal-noise problem and, as with all such problems, admitted that my "signal" undoubtedly contained some error. I minimized that error, and provided an estimate of it. Plaintiffs expressed no objection to my identifications.

I emphasized to my clients the importance of establishing that all termination decisions were made within division, that persons in one division were not "eligible" for layoffs from another. It was not important for my clients to have understood conditional logit. They surely did not. It was important that I communicate to them their responsibility in establishing the predicate for my analysis. The structure of decision making was an incidental part of the story they told. I suspect the judge saw no reason for their emphasis on the isolation of each division until I referred back to that management testimony in my own.

Plaintiffs had estimated terminations through a logit equation, where "terminations" were those who had been laid off. As we have just seen, those were the wrong observations. Although this is a classic multiple-pools case, where not all employees compete together for termination, the key aspect of my analysis was not its statistical methodology. It was understanding the factual issue under the law. Even a logit of the sort plaintiffs prepared, though methodologically incorrect, would have shown no race effect, a zero coefficient for the variable "black," had it been estimated from the appropriate data.

I showed that seniority explained the entire race disparity among who was terminated, that race was not a factor in the selection of persons for termination. Polaroid had been an aggressive affirmative-action employer, bringing blacks into hourly jobs and helping them move up. There was more turnover than average among such employees, so the resulting black work force had low seniority. Polaroid had bent over backwards to avoid terminating blacks. Why plaintiffs did not know that, I cannot say. They came away from this litigation with nothing, as their expert should have told them they would.

A LITTLE BIT OF HISTORY

Many of the examples I have used to introduce multiple-pools and survival methods are from cases in the 1970s and 1980s. Is it fair to criticize experts of that era for not knowing how to solve (indeed, how to articulate) the problems they faced? Is it fair to leave an impression of incompetence derived from that era, now in the twenty-first century?

There was a smattering of discussion in the statistics literature, in the 1930s and 1940s, about how to combine the results from separate tests. To a large extent, the impetus for this investigation was the desire to use previous literature as information, a task now called "meta-analysis." Why should each new study on a topic have to substitute for all previous studies? Why can't it *add* to knowledge?

This literature was given a boost by R. A. Fisher's testing the sum of $-2\log(p)$, where p is the tail probability calculated from each individual study, against the chi-square distribution.[90] The twist in this concept is that it can be calculated regardless what statistical test generated the individual probabilities. However, summing probabilities is inherently flawed unless they all come from findings in the same direction. If any of the individual tests differs in sign, which we have seen confuses many a judge, the results of applying Fisher's transformation can be nonsense.[91] The magic of this statistic was seen to

---

90. See R. Fisher (1948). This is called Fisher's transformation.

91. For example, in *AmNat* (1979), see Judge Clarke's sympathy for the defendant, American National Bank, when it appeared that in some years they hired blacks at a higher rate than whites. Fisher's transformation could not have been used in such a circumstance.

be sleight of hand when it was discovered that it was biased towards too high (i.e., defendant-favoring) probabilities.[92] Nonetheless, there was an era, in the late 1970s and early 1980s, when one did find this approach to aggregation of results in courts.[93]

The question of combining studies, of adding information rather than substituting information, was paramount in medicine, in testing drugs and protocols, where initial studies come from small samples. The issue seems far from litigation, in which the analyst gets only one shot. But, as we have seen, events may call for an aggregation, for a summary statistic from multiple tests. The key breakthrough came from the National Cancer Institute at the National Institutes of Health. The results of several cancer treatment studies were combined by an aggregation of chi-square statistics. The paper is difficult to read to this day (more difficult than the material itself), and published in a journal few people could obtain.[94] Nonetheless, the "Mantel-Haenszel" method (or statistic) did creep into the general statistics literature.

Anyone posing as an "expert" in statistical analysis in litigation should have known about methods of aggregating independent tests—as well as knowing that Fisher's transformation was a particularly bad method—by the 1970s. I do not know how much time it "should" take for statistical innovations to be disseminated, but I am giving the Mantel-Haenszel statistic over a decade to get into the hands of "experts." If they really are experts, I think that is fair.

Each field acquires statistical procedures in its own literature. Information tends to remain field-specific until it is brought from one to another, usually by a member of the receiving field who happens to have learned about it. One example is Michael Finkelstein's bringing the binomial distribution, the most common and well known of statistics tests—two-hundred-year-old knowledge—to the legal profession and the Supreme Court through a law-review article.[95] Gregory Harper was able to publish a law-review article as a student, introducing the legal profession to a non-parametric statistic for analyzing age discrimination.[96] "[T]he advances of game theory have been slower to diffuse into legal reasoning than other economic contributions," writes Ian Ayres, noting that game theory might lead

---

92. This flaw was well-known by the late 1950s.

93. See, for example, *Brown* (1980). Plaintiff's expert, Betty Goldsberry, so mishandled data that it did not matter what her analysis was. Defendant's expert, Carl Hoffman, used Fisher's transformation, which was accepted by the court. I know of few other cases accepting Fisher's transformation. In particular, J. Wanzer Drane used it for many a defendant, none of whom (I believe) prevailed.

94. See Mantel and Haenszel (1959).

95. See Finkelstein (1966). Even Gilbert and Sullivan's modern major general of *The Pirates of Penzance* knew about the binomial distribution, to hear him brag of it, in the nineteenth century. But it was news to lawyers in the twentieth.

96. See Harper (1981).

to "different policies than other modes of law and economic analysis."[97] Without such in-dividual efforts, knowledge stays in place. Ayres underestimates: Inter-field dissemination is *always* slow. In a 1978 review of methods to combine the results from several studies, written for psychologists, there is no mention of the two-decades-old Mantel-Haenszel statistic.[98] Experts in litigation *should* do better than that.

The multiple-pools exact test that Timothy Wyant and I developed was more a prod-uct of technology than innovation. It required that the mainframe computer be invented, and be accessible to analysts. The reason most experts did not and do not know how to conduct a multiple-pools analysis, I am convinced, is that statistics in law is not a "field." Experts came to the court from "fields," whereas Wyant and I were full-time professional litigation analysts. Our profession had no association, no meetings, no journal, no "field" identity, or communication. Nor does it today. The professional expert has to be aggres-sive, to seek out information on both law and statistics. There is no natural route by which it will otherwise come to him.

Survival analysis was introduced to the world in 1958, in a major statistics journal.[99] There must be time for the importance of this innovation to sink in. One way to measure time, to get a view of how long it takes for information to disseminate, is to know that the extension of survival analysis to a usable, generally acceptable multivariate form, took another fourteen years.[100] It took this long for people to work through some of the issues with survival analysis that have been mentioned here, such as weighting the early ob-servations compared with the later ones, and become immersed in the analysis that could be done. It took that long for someone to conceive how to put survival analysis in a maximum-likelihood form that could be estimated with control variables.

Long? I would say that developing the multivariate proportional-hazards model, which requires understanding what compromises are worth making to achieve that goal, took *only* fourteen years. The creation and development of survival analysis is a modern story of brilliant people doing brilliant work. But dissemination outside the bio-medical community took another ten years. Biometricians had their own statistical package, BMDP. Proportional hazards was a free add-on to SAS, one of the two most popular mainframe statistical software packages of the day. That is, it was not a routine the SAS Institute itself thought needed to be in the package. To my knowledge it did not exist at all in SPSS, the other popular statistics software package, in the 1980s.

I came to this task with a Ph.D. in economics. Not one of these methods—multiple-

---

97. Ayres (1990) at 1292, then 1317.

98. See R. Rosenthal (1978).

99. As noted above, see E. Kaplan and Meier (1958).

100. Again, see D. Cox (1972).

pools analysis, Mantel-Haenszel aggregation, Kaplan-Meier survival analysis or Cox's con-ditional logit—was known in my field. So why was I in some instances the first person, in others nearly the first, to use them in litigation? Because I knew that the tools I started with were inadequate to solve the problems before me. I could articulate the question, look in my tool chest for the right tool, and recognize that none in there was satisfactory. Ninety percent of the problem, you can quote me on this, is not understanding that there is a problem. The secret of my success was not that I had solutions in hand, and not that I cre-ated them, but that I knew I needed them and sought them out.

Hiring in *Anderson* (1994)

OK, that's history. We did badly two decades ago. We're all sorry. Now let's get on with it.

Not so fast. No data are presented in *Anderson*, and the district court opinion is unpublished. But in the circuit court opinion we are told that Douglas & Lomason's appli-cant pools were tightly controlled. When there was not an opening, no applications were taken. When they were, they stayed "alive" for six months. When the defendant had "enough" applicants for a position, applications again were not taken.

> Thus, it was possible for individuals to be told that D & L was not taking appli-cations both when the Company was and was not hiring.[101]

This procedure requires a multiple-pools analysis. Neither side performed one.[102] Here is how defendant's expert, Joan Haworth, analyzed the data:

> Dr. Haworth divided the applications into six "pools," which reflected each hir-ing event, and compared the percentage of blacks and whites hired from the applicants in each pool. Only one hiring pool—pool 5, which covered the one-month period of October, 1984—reflected a statistically significant standard deviation. Haworth also analyzed the pools on an aggregate basis, comparing the percentage of blacks hired who applied from April 1984 through mid-January 1985. She found what the parties agree to be a statistically significant standard deviation. Haworth testified, however, that pool 5 largely accounted for the deviation. When she excluded pool 5 from the analysis, she found the standard deviation to be statistically insignificant.[103]

First, let's forgive Judge Garza his statistical illiteracy. When he talks about a "signifi-cant standard deviation," he means the Z-score, the *number* of standard deviations by

---

101. *Anderson* (1994) at 1282, 69 FEP Cases at 135.

102. Plaintiffs' attorney, Richard Seymour, had been working in this field for decades by the time this case came to him. His expert in this case, as usual, was Marc Bendick. Seymour has never appreciated the differences in quality among experts, only the differences in their billing rates. So he got what he deserved, though whether his clients did, I do not know.

103. *Anderson* (1994) footnote 15 at 1288, 69 FEP Cases at 139.

which actual and expected selections differs. Less forgivable is his discussion of the effects of pool 5 being in, compared with out, of the aggregation. It is just this problem, the assumption that all workers available for that promotion were available for all promotions, that should have indicated that this was the wrong analytic method. There should have been no aggregation of pool members, and therefore no discussion of the place of pool 5. No matter what training a judge gets in statistics, we cannot expect him to ask about Mantel-Haenszel aggregation or an exact multiple-pools test. We *can* expect him to ask if the analyses incorporate the real-world events at issue in the litigation. He should reject any analysis that does not.

Haworth went on to analyze hiring under a different regime in the same way, pool by pool and aggregated over pools. The first method is called "divide and conquer," and has long been discredited.[104] The fallacy of her second method, aggregating competition pools to a single measure, was shown by several examples above. Haworth's repertoire appears not to include a multiple-pools method.[105]

Layoffs in *Reid Jr.* (2001)

In *Reid Jr.*, plaintiffs' expert Thomas Daymont analyzed layoffs throughout an entire plant with a single-pool analysis, even articulating his "everyone is equally situated" assumption. Defendant's expert Bernard Siskin determined that layoffs were made by department, as at Polaroid, and offered a twelve-department multiple-pools analysis. Daymont responded that in most of those departments, more above-median-age employees were laid off than below-median-age employees. The court appointed its own expert, whose report concludes that

> the analysis of "median age [within each department]" does not directly address the legally protected class of employees 40 years of age and older.[106]

True enough, but there is a more important point here. If decisions were made by department, the analysis should be by department. Multiple-pools methods were called for. Siskin was right. Daymont was under-equipped. More than two decades after I introduced

---

104. See *Capaci* (1983), where this phrase first appears. In *Rendon* (1989), plaintiff's expert William Schucany testified that "it's certainly a proper statistical approach to break an analysis into groups. But it is equally important to recombine the results of those separate tests to get the overall picture." At 397, 50 FEP Cases at 1594.

105. Haworth should not take instruction from *Rendon* (1989), however, where Schucany used the inappropriate Fisher's transformation to aggregate across pools.

106. *Reid Jr.* (2001) at 502. William Schucany appears here as the court's expert. Siskin recognized the value of multiple-pools methods from the beginning, purchasing MULPOOLS™ and MULQUALS™ from Longbranch Research Associates.

multiple-pools methods in equal-employment litigation, and offered software to perform them, at least some experts and attorneys still don't have a clue.

Hiring in *Yapp* (2004) and *Rhodes* (2002)

In *Yapp*, defendant Union Pacific Railroad suggested that a multivariate procedure, where variables differed by department, was necessary to analyze selection from applicants. They would thus analyze selection in each department separately, the "divide and conquer" method mentioned above. Where would their variables come from? To determine that procedures were different in different departments, Michael Ward and Nathan Woods interviewed certain employees "chosen by Defendant's counsel" in only some of the departments at issue.

> Ward and Woods predicated their entire analysis on their understanding of the hiring and selection processes used at UPRR, and a failure to ground that analysis in a reliable method for understanding those processes undercuts the validity of their entire effort.[107]

For variables to enter into the study, they must be valid. They must be measured independent of defendant and its counsel even before asking if they relate to job performance. Assessing the experts' work by their procedures, Judge Limbaugh correctly excluded the testimony of these two would-be experts.

Plaintiffs' expert, Edwin Bradley, may have utilized a multiple-pools method—one cannot tell from the limited discussion of his work—but his argument that a multivariate method was not required because he had eliminated applicants who did not meet minimum requirements is specious. Bradley assumes that the distribution of selection characteristics is the same among minimally qualified white and black applicants. As plaintiffs did not challenge the minimum position requirements, whether quantities of those characteristics above the minimum (education, experience, seniority, for example) differed by race, and affected selection, was a relevant and testable question

We know that Bradley was aware of multiple-pools methods from the report by Magistrate Judge Walter E. Johnson in *Rhodes*. Referring to Bradley and his co-author Liesl Fox, Judge Johnson writes:

> Using a multiple-pools analysis, these experts found that 9,221 more African Americans were hired into the dishwasher position than one would have

---

107. *Yapp* (2004) at 1036; preceding in-text phrase at 1033. As outrageous as it seems for an expert to rely on his clients to choose whom to interview, one expert relied on his clients for the questions themselves. In *Dentsply* (2003), at 435, we read about a survey of dental labs taken by the Department of Justice expert, Yoram Wind.

> Prof. Wind relied on Dr. Reitman and the DOJ's lead trial counsel, William Berlin, as the principal questionnaire designers.

expected on the basis of their representation in the counties where their stores were located.[108]

Defendant Cracker Barrel took applications for openings in front or in back. Based on their application, blacks and whites were hired equally: More than 90 percent of hired applicants, regardless of race, were hired into their preferred position. Foregoing tips, blacks preferred back-room jobs (cook, dishwasher, etc.) where they were better paid. In response, plaintiffs formulated an availability analysis based on persons currently working in similar positions in each county, even though they knew that experience was not a requirement for the jobs.

The Bradley and Fox multiple-pools analysis was as badly conceived as John Van Ryzin's survival analysis in *Harrison* (1982). Using an appropriate statistical method should be a requirement for expert testimony, but is hardly sufficient. More important is understanding the application of law to the events in question, in the institutional context of the defendant. Plaintiffs' availability analysis in *Rhodes* was hopeless, in the light of application data, and not credited by the court. Class certification was denied.

Promotions in *Wal-Mart* (2004)

In the summer of 2004, plaintiffs achieved class certification in their employment-discrimination suit against Wal-Mart. Issues included differential compensation and slower promotion of females. If high positions were filled by competitions, promotion should be analyzed from applicants to high positions, "controlling" for current position and time (seniority, time at position, etc.). It is not clear that Wal-Mart has consistently practiced what attorneys have been preaching since the 1970s, to have open announcements and limited pools. For class certification at least, plaintiffs' analysis, and the court's quandary about it, are stated as follows:

> The Court observes, however, that Dr. Drogin's data shows that while female Co-Managers received fewer promotions than similarly situated men in 37 of 40 regions across the country, the disparity was of a statistically significant value in only 22 regions. Furthermore, while the data shows that for Store Manager positions women received fewer promotions than men in 34 of 40 regions, the disparity was of statistically significant value in only 13 regions.
>
> Although Defendant has not made an issue of the number of regions lacking a statistically significant gender differential at the higher level in-store managerial jobs, the Court became concerned that this evidence raises the question of whether a nation-wide class should be narrowed to lower level in-store managers (Support Managers and Management Trainees) with respect

---

108. *Rhodes* (2002) at *34.

to promotions. The Court raised this issue with counsel at oral argument, and Plaintiffs responded by arguing that the wide-spread discrimination at the lower levels carries through to the upper levels, especially where most promotions are made from within.[109]

Suppose female promotions lagged male promotions in all forty regions, in both positions, but in no region was the result "statistically significant." Could plaintiffs not prevail? The answer requires asking what the probability would be, if the "true" proportion of regions in which female promotions were in deficit was 50 percent, that one would find data as disparate as these. We can consider the two jobs as separate, but test them together in a multiple-pools sense (two sets of forty regions). If we "expect" twenty regions to show female deficits, for each position, in a world where only chance was operating, the data are 6.9 standard deviations from that expectation.

That is, "significance" of individual region disparities need not, and should not be an issue. The judge posed a good question. That plaintiffs did not provide a statistical answer, a multiple-pools answer, indicates the continued low level of expertise in litigation. In Chapter 6, with reference to Figure 58, I discuss how I handled a similar question more than twenty years before *Wal-Mart* was argued.

THE GOVERNMENT AS PLAINTIFF

The analysis evolution from defining an amorphous pool of theoretical "applicants," to attempting to count real applicants, to understanding that people apply for specific jobs, at specific times—the development of multivariate multiple-pools methods—all presupposes an events-based analysis, hiring or promoting or terminating from well-constructed (realistic) pools. This development from availability analysis (compare work force with labor force) to hiring analysis (compare offers to applicants) to multiple-pools hiring analysis (compare offers to applicants per opening and then aggregate, rather than aggregating applicants and then comparing) was true progress. Better statistical methods helped the court better ascertain fact.

Executive-Branch Ignorance

Unfortunately, at least two government agencies do not understand this progress: the Office of Federal Contract Compliance Programs (OFCCP) and the Equal Employment Opportunity Commission (EEOC). In the context of selection, what is important here is the OFCCP's concept of "utilization." A federal contractor has to compare each major division

---

109. *Dukes* (2004) from footnote 33.

of its work force with an availability estimate, and be in "compliance," although the OFCCP has no fixed definition of that term. Basically, to obtain federal contracts, the employer has to operate on a quota system, and show an approvable work-force composition. Then it has to pay "fairly," a requirement one cannot oppose in its language, although one can oppose the OFCCP's view of what "fair" is. We will see under the heading "Promotion and Salaries at I-NET," in Chapter 3, that the OFCCP has no standards for determining if salaries are "fair."

Nor does it have standards for workforce compliance. Nor should it. The work force is a situation, the result of applications, offers, hires, terminations (voluntary and not), promotions and transfers. The OFCCP should be assessing events, and it should have standards by which it does that. In Chapter 3 I will discuss a mid-1990s case in which I was the OFCCP's expert. In this chapter I have presented the Hackley Bank case from 1980. Here are two sentences from page one of my report in that case:

> OFCCP has not made clear what actions of the bank have been unfair to women, or when those actions occurred. However, OFCCP has presented a formula for the calculation of back pay for the alleged affected class.

Nothing has changed. They don't sense a need for a rational analysis. They just want to claim "success" in squeezing money out of another employer.[110] Regardless how imbecilic is the OFCCP's rationale, contractors by and large cave in, for anything is cheaper than litigating against the deep pockets of a government agency.

Thus we have the judicial branch improving, because some better-equipped experts make better presentations, and more-informed judges accept them; and at the same time the executive branch continues in the dark ages. I bring it up here to exempt the OFCCP's view of the world from any general words of praise. I do not know if the administrative law judges who hear OFCCP cases have followed advances in the federal judiciary. The OFCCP would claim that they follow different rules. But there are not two sets of rules about what is a good statistical analysis of events, asking if they look discriminatory. I have seldom seen a case in which the OFCCP, or the EEOC for that matter, cared about the quality of the analysis they set forth. Just like the discriminating firm that hires an expert to say it isn't, these agencies want to find that the employer discriminated whether it did or did not. As a taxpayer, I would prefer that federal agencies seek truth, not victory.

Affirmative Action

Government actors are quick to declare that they want to "do better" than equality. This is dangerous territory. Anything other than equality is inequality. There may be special

---

110. Charles Mann was also quick to spot the deficiencies in the OFCCP's practice. See C. Mann (1981).

qualifications (language, technical or cultural knowledge) that require special hires. Others argue that "affirmatively" hiring minorities *is* equality. If so, it is not an equality that can be analyzed by any method discussed in this book. The Supreme Court has not been helpful, because they lack a clear view of their role as guardians of procedure. In *Grutter* (2003), they caved in to a feel-good kind of unfairness that does them no credit. I delve more deeply into selection fairness, how any standard but equality is no standard at all, in Chapters 5 and 10.

The most sophisticated "affirmative action" concept involves fair selection from a stacked pool. If you recruit heavily enough, this argument goes, you will find superior minority candidates.[111] This comes down to finding some procedure that gets the outcome you want, and therefore is not amenable to statistical testing. In most cases, it backfires: Stacking the pool with minorities, asking as many minorities to apply as possible, hoping to find some that will prevail, will generate many more additional minority losers than winners. Almost regardless of the results, the employer will have to defend procedures that look discriminatory against minorities, though they were designed to be discriminatory against the majority.[112]

Some persons have suggested that different standards should be used to select minorities for jobs, or for entrance to school. The United States took this position in at least one case. Finding that blacks scored lower than whites on valid tests, the Attorney General apparently suggested that the court should order use of a lower scale for black candidates.[113]

Schools are encouraged to discriminate in this manner because, we are told, "diversity" benefits all students. We have seen that strict selection by a valid screening device will not bring in the best performers; but the diversity argument does not claim to improve merit-based selection. Is there more "value" to a given student from having a fellow black student, or from having a fellow *good* student? If the latter, then just admit the best students, regard-

---

111. See, for example, my comments on Marilyn vos Savant's articulation, in the Coda.

112. See my discussion of *Broadcasters* (2001) in note 36, above. I had one such case in Monroe County, New York. The county had induced barely qualified minorities to take an exam, and then faced the fact that most of them failed. My client and I decided that there was no statistical defense. If the exam was valid, prove it. I had to take the pool of applicants as it was, and though I could show that disproportionately many minorities were likely to fail, from their other characteristics, that had nothing to do with the individuals who did or did not fail. The county's strategy, though well-meaning, was legally stupid.

113. See *Porter* (1970). The suggestion that "fairness" would call for a lower standard for blacks was first made by the Attorney General's expert witness, Richard Barrett. Whether tests need to be validated for different races and genders may be an interesting question. These days it is often applied to Scholastic Aptitude Tests for college admissions. Setting different criteria by "race" would clearly be wrong, and I trust just as clearly illegal. Some schools are abandoning the SAT, and so generating classes with a wider variation in SAT score than we have found in the past. Perhaps someone will analyze the success of those who enter despite not having "passed" the test, i.e., perform a true validity study.

less what they look like, to the extent that one can fairly determine who they are. Most rationales for anything but straight-up fairness make no sense.[114] Using different standards for entry into the pool, by race, is discrimination. Calling it "affirmative" changes nothing.

EXPERT ANALYSIS OF SELECTION

Selection has traditionally been considered the easy analysis in equal-employment opportunity; so easy that attorneys thought they could offer selection analyses without engaging an expert. That view often sufficed in the early civil-rights era, say the first decade following the passage of Title VII of the Equal Employment Opportunity Act of 1964. Reading case after case of blacks suing trucking companies for the opportunity to take long hauls, blatant discrimination against clearly qualified drivers is evident. All long-haul drivers: white. All short-haul drivers: black. Blacks had been asking for long hauls for years. Judgment for plaintiffs. Similar displays of job segregation occurred in mills, factories, banks, etc. A hundred years after the Civil War there was not equality of opportunity in the work place. I have not tested this proposition, but it could be that much of the startling increase of labor productivity of the 1980s and 1990s was due to forcing employers to value merit; to hire, pay, and promote fairly, based on valid objective standards.

Unfortunately, the presentation of the allocation of the work force between long and short haul, between clerical and management, between labor and learn-on-the-job craft, became called a "statistical" presentation. It contained no statistical analysis of events, only descriptions of situations. Discrimination was *proved* by the defendant's refusal to allow black drivers to take long hauls, females to be "management trainees," Hispanics to be other than janitors.

Courts said that "statistics" on gender and racial composition of jobs would be adequate to make a *prima facie* case for plaintiffs. That shifted the burden (perhaps of persuasion, perhaps only of production, never of proof—that burden was always on the plaintiffs) to the defendant. Failing to justify the racial differences, defendant lost the case, was enjoined from making similar decisions in the future, and often paid back-pay damages. Thus some early employment-selection cases came out right on the merits—often not until the circuit court level—but failed to establish good precedents for the handling of selection issues. We will see the same sequence of proofs in jury-selection cases in Chapter 5.

---

114. Consider the enormous farm-subsidy bill signed by President Bush in May 2002. The purpose of such subsidies is not to correct "inequities," but to generate Republican votes for Congress in 2002. This is the level of intellectuality we live with, sadly, in politics. All too often courts do no better. May 2002 was a bad month for those looking for logical thought and rational decisions. It was also the month of *Grutter* (2002), the Sixth Circuit's upholding affirmative-action admissions at the law school of the University of Michigan, later affirmed by the Supreme Court.

The earliest opinions appear to be correct, in the sense that they identified, uncovered, and prevented further blatant discrimination. But they set an unfortunate reasoning in place that has failed since the 1930s, as it does today.

Statistical experts have by and large not helped the matter. As I will show in Chapter 3, as presaged by the *Bazemore* discussion above, many more cases should have been seen as selection cases than were analyzed that way. Experts did not make the fundamental distinction between situations and events. Experts did not model decision making. Many a judge did see that equal-employment-opportunity laws are about *acts* of the employer, whereas the expert's analysis was not. Many a judge was thereby faced with only irrelevant statistical presentations.

Evidence of the paucity of selection tools available to most experts—evidence beyond reading the cases—can be seen in the statistical-instruction articles in the *Reference Manual on Scientific Evidence*. Here the Federal Judicial Center tries to ease judges into the kinds of analyses they will see. No explanation of survival analysis or multiple pools appears, even though most selection complaints are about waiting time or selection from applicant pools. The lesser expert thus will present analyses for which the judge is prepared, and the better expert will have to convince the judge that, even though those analyses seem to bear Federal Judicial Center credentials, they are inadequate for the task at hand. The Federal Judicial Center should not have tried to create such instructional materials. Having done so, however, it had an obligation—which it has failed—to prepare judges for less simple, more realistic analyses.[115]

With senior analysts Gail Blattenberger at first, and then Timothy Wyant, Longbranch Research Associates revolutionized selection analysis in litigation by being open to the failings of our first impressions. After carefully articulating the issues, we came to see that the methodology employed by all experts, including ourselves, was insufficient, even erroneous. The failure of litigation experts has been their lack of humility in the face of a real-world problem. (Have they conceptualized the problem so the answer will assist the court? Are the tools they know adequate to the task?) Not understanding how their solutions failed, they did not look for solutions that might succeed. The simple observation that statistical experts often fail *and do not know it* summarizes not only this chapter, but the following three chapters as well; and the state of statistical analysis in litigation today.

---

115. As introductions to what they introduce, these articles are quite good. As indicators to judges of the kinds of analyses they might encounter, they are misleading. These comments apply also to Chapter 15, "Statistical Evidence," in Giannelli and Imwinkelried (1999). Their analysis of selection issues is paltry, as if "statistical evidence" is almost exclusively regression.

3

Regression Analysis

"Regression" is a statistical method for estimating the shape and strength of the relationship between "independent" variables and a "dependent" variable. Regression is widely used by statistical experts in litigation. Too widely used, and often badly used. I will describe cases in which regression, though offered by an expert, was not the right tool for the job; and cases in which an expert so badly handled regression he got the wrong results. I will show more subtle errors. But I am not going to explain regression itself. No more than this:

We write a regression "equation" first as a generality, such as

$$\text{dependent} = f(\text{independent}_1, \text{independent}_2, \ldots)$$

There is a dependent variable which is related to (whose values can be estimated by, or "is a function of") values of independent variables when combined in some mathematical relationship. The actual equation might include transforms of variables, such as logarithms or powers. For example:

$$\text{dependent} = b_0 + b_1\text{independent}_1 + b_2\text{independent}_2 + b_3\text{independent}_2{}^2 + e_i$$

This equation has a constant, b_0, a coefficient b_j for each of the j "independent variables" in the equation, and an error term, e_i, where i represents each observation (each data element). The coefficients are numbers that we will derive. It is understood that they are multiplied by the values (different for each data element) of the independent variables—"understood" because there is no explicit multiplication symbol.

As the terms (coefficient times variable value) are added, this procedure is sometimes called "linear" regression. An observation's "error," e_i, is the difference between its actual dependent-variable value and the value estimated by this equation.[1] It is also called the

---

1. As the subscript in e_i refers to an observation, whereas all other subscripts refer to the equation as a whole, I will place e with no subscript at the end of following equations. This is standard notation, but

"residual," or the "unexplained" portion of the ith individual's salary, the ith school's test score, whatever it is we are estimating. This equation is fit, that is, the coefficients b_j are determined, to minimize the sum of the squares of these residuals. So the procedure is also called "least squares" regression.

The regression procedure estimates only the functional form the analyst specifies. It does not, on its own, try to figure out how variables are best related. The analyst specifies the variables and the equation. The procedure generates statistics that inform the analyst how well those variables in that form fit the data. There may be another form that fits the data better; and there may be other variables whose use would reduce the sum of squared errors even more. Finding that equation which does best fit the data is not necessarily the criterion by which the "best" equation is determined. What I would consider "good" use of this tool requires also that the equation make sense in the real world. Like all statistical analysis, it is not just mathematics. Although I will determine in Chapter 10 that statistics is "science"—as that term is used in litigation—it is also craft.

Not only are the relationships not necessarily linear (as the squared term indicates), they are not necessarily separable. The equation can contain "interaction" terms, for example:

$$\text{interaction term} = b_k(\text{independent}_m \times \text{independent}_n)$$

The effect of this interaction—its coefficient b_k—cannot be associated with variable m or variable n, only with both together. The world is sometimes messy that way.

TEST SCORES IN BOSTON-AREA SCHOOLS

There are many ways to picture a regression equation. Typically, the vertical axis is in units of the dependent variable, and the horizontal axis is in units of an independent variable. If the variable of the horizontal axis appears in two terms (for example, linear and squared), the plot combines them. It is supposed to be a plot of the relationship, not of a coefficient. Also, if there are many variables, when we plot a two-dimensional graph, the result is not necessarily even a smooth line.

In Figure 22 I estimate average scores on a Massachusetts high school test, by school. Craig Bolon had suggested that only per-capita income was related to test scores—that academic tests were essentially measures of wealth.[2] A regression following his idea is pictured in Figure 22 as a solid line. One can write the equation of this line as

$$\text{average school score 1999} = 190.4 + 1.7(\text{town per-capita income}) + e$$

---

it does allow one to forget that the value of e, like the values of the variables in the data—but unlike the values of the coefficients—is different for each observation.

2. See Bolon (2001).

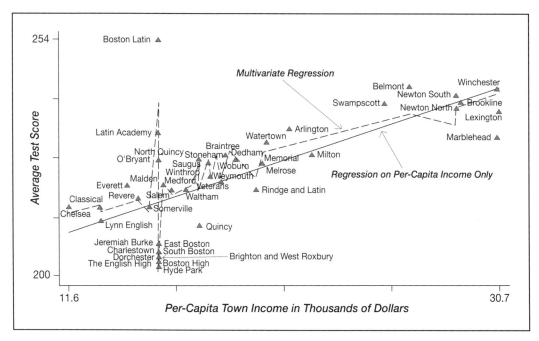

FIGURE 22: Two Regression Estimates of School Test Score

Every school starts with 190.4 points, and then its score increases (as a general rule) 1.7 points for every thousand dollars of the town's per-capita income.

Adding four other variables, I derived the equation pictured in Figure 22 by the dashed line. Per-capita income and test score are indeed correlated, although the regression cannot tell us why. However, income *alone* is a biased correlate of test score: Bolon's regression estimates scores that are too low for low-income towns, too high for high-income towns. Other things matter.

Although the higher the income of a town, the higher will their students score on this test, the highest-scoring students, at Boston Latin, come from a poor town. Is the school producing the high scores, or just selecting the students who get them? The regression is not descriptive of the process by which the facts came about, only of the facts as they are, the situation as it is. Nothing about this regression suggests that the test scores are "valid" or "invalid," predictive or not of something (success in college? in life?), although Bolon's purpose seems to have been to find the test invalid in some way.

Sometimes what is important is what does not appear in the equation. For example, ethnic measures (such as percent Hispanic) had no effect on these scores. What Massachusetts hopes to achieve by subjecting all of its students to these tests, I do not know. Neither do I know what the study's author intended to accomplish by asserting that only income contains information predicting average school score. As Figure 22 shows, that is clearly not true.

REGRESSION CAUTIONS

The mathematics of regression were formulated in the late nineteenth century. Calculation, however, was arduous. When I entered graduate school in 1960, my research-assistant job consisted of performing regression calculations, by hand, on a mechanical calculator, with unknown accuracy. Each regression (deriving the coefficients from the data) took hours to calculate. Mainframe computers, and programs to calculate regression in seconds, became available later in the 1960s. Both the computers and the programs improved for the next two decades, but were largely inaccessible outside large institutions. Only late in the 1980s were personal computers and statistics programs widely available, and not until the mid-1990s were they fast, accurate, and easy to use.

Non-Homogeneous Effects

As computing power and data became available to provide quantitative answers to policy questions, regression became an oft-used tool. In the 1960s, many estimates were made of the effect that more-equal education would have on the incomes of blacks and whites. All contained a similar error. The "income effect" of education can be thought of as the increase in earnings with the increase in years of school. If we use only one variable to measure schooling, we can obtain its coefficient in a regression on earnings, "corrected" for age and other factors. It is easy to estimate this coefficient, and multiply it by the difference between the mean years of school of whites and blacks, to estimate how much more blacks would earn if they had the schooling of whites.

That is what economists did. They were wrong to do it. I call the error the assumption of "homogeneity." All analysts estimated a single relationship between schooling and income, the slope (the regression coefficient) being the same for blacks and whites. They assumed that a black whose education increased would raise his earnings by the same amount (dollars or percentage) as whites—that schooling had the same income effect on the margin for whites and blacks—at least white and black males.[3]

To illustrate this problem, I have made up data at six levels of schooling. I duplicated the data for whites (indicated by "W" in Figure 23) several times, so there would be many more whites than blacks in the data. In a regression of the form:

$$\text{earnings} = b_0 + b_1 \text{schooling} + b_2 \text{other} + \ldots + b_k \text{race} + e$$

---

3. Giora Hanoch pioneered in the use of census data to estimate an "earnings generation function." In his Ph.D. dissertation, "Personal Earnings and Investment in Schooling," (University of Chicago, 1965), he estimated what characteristics contributed how much to individual income. Apparently few people understood that Hanoch utilized data on *white males* only. He tried to estimate a relationship between schooling and earnings for black males, but found none. He never looked at female earnings.

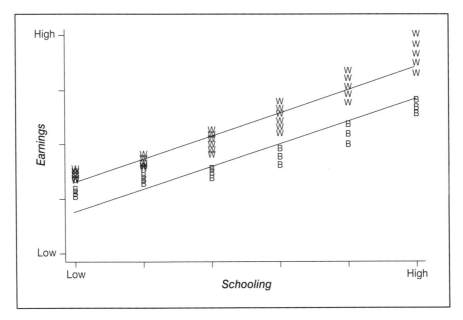

FIGURE 23: Schooling and Earnings Assuming Effects Homogeneous by Race

where race is a binary variable, let's say 1 = black, 0 = white, I estimated parallel earnings loci, whites earning more than blacks at every schooling level, as in Figure 23.[4]

The distance between the two regression lines, which is the value of the race coefficient b_k, is interpreted as the "race effect," the average disparity between black and white earnings, given their schooling. Notice, however, that the line supposedly estimating incomes of blacks lies above the highest-earning black in the top three schooling categories, and below the lowest-earning black in the lowest two schooling categories. The earnings of blacks are not as responsive to schooling as the equation implies. There being many more whites than blacks, the slope, the schooling coefficient, takes on close to the white value.

The income effect of schooling was estimated, in the 1960s, by locating the white average schooling level on the black regression line, to the right of actual black average schooling, and measuring the implied increase in mean black earnings on the vertical axis. The conclusion from Figure 23: Equal education would close one-third of the income gap.

Effectively, it was *assumed* that black and white incomes reacted to schooling in the same way. That was not true in real life, nor is it in the fictitious data here. The regression can be reformulated to observe this phenomenon by allowing both the slope and the intercept to differ by race. I do that in Figure 24.

---

4. This form of two-value variable is called an "indicator" variable (it indicates race), or a "dummy" variable. Although most analysts name the variable "race" (or, as we will see below, "gender,"), one provides more information to the reader if the variable takes the name of whatever is assigned the value 1. I would call this variable "black," and a gender variable "female."

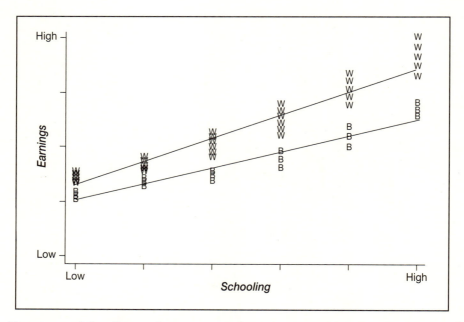

FIGURE 24: Schooling and Earnings with Homogeneity Assumption Relaxed

The estimate of the impact of equalized schooling on incomes of blacks now moves along a less steeply inclined locus. The implied increase in earnings is smaller in Figure 24. Failing to recognize non-homogeneity of schooling effects among races, researchers thought that education would be an effective anti-poverty and anti-racial-inequality strategy. When nominal black and white schooling became equal, years later, the income gap had closed by about 10 percent, which is what I had predicted from dropping the homogeneity assumption.

The lack of homogeneity, that is, differential reaction of the dependent variable to one independent variable, depending on the value of another independent variable, appears still to be little understood. The expert who says that he "controls" for many factors by simply adding variables to his equation may be incorrect, depending on what the real relationships are. Yet this is what analysts do, and what they say.[5] It is what courts believe.[6]

---

5. See, for example, *Greenspan* (1980) and the I-NET section of this chapter. Defendant's expert made the same mistake in *Wilkins* (1981), using one regression over all departments of the University of Houston. Lempert (2000), not understanding the homogeneity fallacy of the regression in *Wilkins*, supports plaintiffs' interpretation of defendant's regression. Lempert is unsure of the most salient feature of the case, that plaintiffs' attorney, not an expert, argued unsuccessfully for this alternative interpretation of defendant's expert's work. The technical lesson of *Wilkins* is that analysts still do not understand the perverting effect of non-homogeneity on regression estimates. The legal lesson, as we will again see in Chapter 6, is that statistical arguments should be made by experts, not attorneys.

6. In *Greenspan* (1980) at 1061:

> To the extent that Dr. Killingsworth has sought to include in his regression equation all of the pre-employment factors he can characterize as having a possible effect on a

Earnings Regressions

Judith Stoikov, for defendant Burlington Northern Railroad, devised an argument that certain named plaintiffs in a sex-discrimination case could not represent (were not "typical" of) the defined class. It was a curious enough use of regression to deserve mention here.

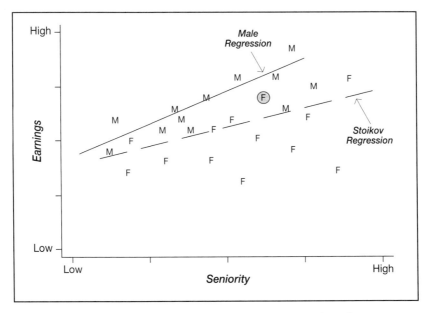

FIGURE 25: Wages at Burlington Northern Railroad, 1984

Stoikov's argument was that certain named plaintiffs earned more than expected, based on a regression of only females. In my response to her, I provided Figure 25. Stoikov's regression was designed to show that the named plaintiff, circled, earned well above the female regression line. As I wrote in 1984:

> Such a methodology is clearly faulty. If the named plaintiff were paid the highest among similarly situated females, and yet these females were generally paid less than the similarly situated males with the same length of service and within the same grade or ICC code, then the named plaintiff would appear

---

> person's salary, he is anticipating and (Plaintiffs contend) negating any legitimate, non-discriminatory explanation of salary differential which Defendants might wish to raise along these lines.

In *Appalachian* (1998) at 804:

> It is commonly understood that the more variables that are included in the regression analysis, the more likely it is that the model describes accurately the phenomenon it is being used to explain.

Good (2001), at 181, quotes *Appalachian*, apparently accepting it as correct. I will further explain, below in this chapter, why it is not.

to be overpaid when, in fact, she and similarly situated females were under-paid relative to the similarly situated males.[7]

Thus—a theme of this book—the judge does not need to understand technical aspects of the methodology to discern its misuse. Plaintiffs achieved their class certification.

I do not know how John Ullman tried to estimate back-pay from regression; whether by a single gender variable or a more complicated procedure not assuming homogeneity. I do not know whether his study or its explanation is at fault here, but Judge Stern appears not to have been capable of understanding complicated proofs or estimates, in *Kyriazi* (1978). Selecting the right tool is a part of the expert's job. He also has to use it well and explain it clearly:

> The Court, at least at this stage, is not prepared to accept or adopt the regres-sion analysis of plaintiff's expert, Dr. John Ullman. The Court found Dr. Ull-man's testimony unhelpful in determining this [back-pay] issue in large part because his criteria and their valuations were quite arbitrary and subjective, and, frankly, in larger part because his testimony was simply not comprehen-sible to the Court.[8]

Faculty Salaries

A typical analysis of equal pay by gender, in a complex institution, starts with a compari-son of the average salaries of the groups of interest. Females typically earn less than males, and the remainder of the study is an attempt to determine why. I was engaged by the De-partment of Labor, and then the Equal Employment Opportunity Commission, to inves-tigate allegations of Equal Pay Act violations among faculty salaries at Framingham State College.

University pay is largely based on rank and time in rank. I developed a recursive sys-tem, in which I first asked if gender affected rank (full professor or lower) and secondly if gender affected salary given rank. This is a solution to the question, "Do I hold rank con-stant or not?" in a regression context.[9] Although treating attainment of rank as an event—

---

7. Figure 25 from Stephan Michelson and Rebecca Klemm, "Second Affidavit Supporting Class Certifi-cation," June 19, 1984, in *Holden* (1987), at 19; quotation at 18. "ICC Code" is a labor categorization into which all railroad jobs are coded. Stoikov's assertions are found in her affidavit opposing class certifi-cation, May 25, 1984. I do not discuss the expert's role in class-certification hearings in any single place in this book, but the subject does appear again. Defendants stress the differences among putative class members in an effort not only to defeat the class, but to undermine plaintiffs' expert's statistical analy-sis, which depends on similarities among plaintiffs. See, for example, *Cardizem* (2001) at 349:

> Despite Defendants' claims to the contrary, the use of an aggregate approach to measure class-wide damages is appropriate.

8. *Kyriazi* (1978) at 913, 18 FEP Cases 924 at 938.

9. I mention this approach in my "Critique of Plaintiff's Statistical Studies" in *Polaroid* (1981), October

using the events tools of Chapter 2—would be a better approach, many experts have used regression for this purpose, but not this way. Let's explore this recursive method a little further.[10]

In a recursive system we first estimate

$$\text{rank} = a_0 + a_1 \text{degree} + a_2 \text{other} + \ldots + a_j \text{female} + e_a$$

where the variable "rank" is equal to 1 if the individual is at a certain level (say, associate professor) or higher. Then

$$\text{earnings} = b_0 + b_1 \text{rank} + b_2 \text{other} + \ldots + b_k \text{female} + e_b$$

The variable "female" has the value 1 if the person is female, and 0 if male. We substitute the first equation for the variable rank in the second equation. This appears to be complicated, and should be done with due regard for the error terms. In practice, we care only about terms that include gender. In the recursive system we ultimately estimate the gender effect as

$$\text{earnings difference} = ((b_1 \times a_j) + b_k) \text{female} + ((b_1 \times e_a) + e_b)$$

We don't really care about the effect of degree or other variables on rank; we care only to "control" for these effects in estimating the effect of gender on rank. A variable will do so if its effect is homogeneous across all other variables, especially gender.

The rank regression estimates a binary (two-value) dependent variable. Regression on a binary dependent variable is frowned upon in graduate econometrics courses. I would avoid it in most situations (using logit, as described in Chapter 2). However, the binary-regression phobia is overdone.[11] Its statistics (standard errors, goodness of fit) are not reliable, because assumptions underlying them are violated, but the parameters are not bad on that account, just unknowably good. Regression has never given me a different qualitative answer from logit. In this case the Ph.D. degree affected attaining the professor position, but had no separate effect on salary within rank, and no differential effect by gender.

What made this case interesting was that, from the raw data, average male and female salaries were statistically indistinguishable. On this account, the data drew an unusual picture. In no year was the t-statistic, the number of standard deviations difference between average male salaries and average female salaries, greater than 1.40. As the t-statistic ap-

---

28, 1980. There I say that I had developed this method in an even earlier case, most likely *Tufts* (1977). The problem of controlling for rank has loomed large in many faculty cases, including *Presseisen* (1977) as discussed in Chapter 2. More advanced methods than the recursive system explained here have since been devised, but they do not differ in principle.

10. In *Craik* (1984), for example, plaintiffs used regression—I would say appallingly badly—to analyze rank, whereas defendant used logit. I will revisit *Craik* at the end of this chapter.

11. See L. Goodman (1975), or J. Goodman (1976).

proximates the normal distribution, as with Z-scores of Chapter 2, courts generally look for values above 2.00 from plaintiffs. I wrote:

> If we had found that women have significantly lower average salaries than men, we would not necessarily conclude that female faculty members were paid less than comparable male faculty members. Similarly, we cannot conclude that comparable faculty members are paid equally from the equal mean salaries.[12]

In salary regressions with several independent variables, the gender dummy variable had a large negative coefficient.

> Although this preliminary finding indicated that there was a sex-based salary deficit, that is, females were paid less than men alike in other respects measured by our data, it did not help us understand how such a deficit came about.[13]

This is where most equal-employment-opportunity regressions fail. They do not relate to the decisions that must have been made if there was discrimination. It was possible, but unlikely, that administrators just took $1,000 from the salary of each female. The question of what characteristic was rewarded differently, by gender, can be written, "Is the relationship between each characteristic and salary homogeneous by gender?" I determined that seniority gained by female faculty at Framingham State College was valued more than $200 per year less than the seniority gained by male faculty.[14] Valuing female seniority as if it were held by males generated estimates of female "salaries" more than $1,200 larger per year than the salaries female faculty actually earned. The recursive approach, with an explicit test for non-homogeneity of seniority, told us how the pay disparity had come about.

Defendant engaged Richard Freeman, an economics professor at Harvard. Freeman produced a salary regression for one year with a single gender variable, in which the female coefficient was "insignificant," though negative. He speculated that the difference in result was explained by data differences, but he did not show in what way my data (or procedure) may have been faulty and, if so, how correcting them would reduce the value or confidence of my results. The burden is generally placed on the defendant not only to describe plaintiffs' errors, but to demonstrate their importance. In this case, Freeman's study contained none of the subtlety of mine, and assumed the homogeneity in the school's treatment of seniority that I found did not exist. Judge Zobel accepted my results. Plaintiffs prevailed.[15]

---

12. Stephan Michelson, "Faculty Salaries At Framingham State College: An Econometric Analysis," in *McCarthy* (1982), February 25, 1982, at 30. In Chapter 7 I will argue that experts should not characterize their findings as "significant" or not. Twenty years ago, I had not come to this understanding.

13. Michelson on Framingham State at 33. Seeking this additional understanding is missing from most encomia for regression in assessment of faculty salaries. See, for example, Greenfield (1977).

14. A similar seniority differential was found in a multi-university study of 1972–73 data. See Tuckman et al. (1977), especially Figure 2 at 700.

15. See *McCarthy* (1983).

Modeling the System

Although no statistical approach can perfectly reflect the system it is meant to analyze, modeling that system is still the goal. A judge can well understand if an analyst is being relevant, without understanding how to estimate a regression. Here is a good example:

> The starting point is to understand that salary increases at Vassar are based upon merit and seniority. Merit increases are determined on a scale of 0–8 points, based on the criteria of scholarship (0–3 points), teaching (0–3 points) and service (0–2 points). [Plaintiff's expert] Gray's regression analysis, however, does not even purport to account for two of these major variables—teaching and service.[16]

I described in Chapter 2 how Judge Bechtle determined that Swarthmore College had not discriminated in waiting time to promotion, in *Presseisen* (1977). John de Cani, plaintiff's statistical expert, "admitted several times in his testimony, once you hold rank constant, there is no significant disparity in the average salaries of men and women." Without showing differences in attaining high rank, plaintiffs could not prove differences in salaries, for if rank was fairly attained, it is fairly used to "explain" salary.[17] In addition, de Cani assumed that the relationship between seniority and salary was homogeneous among divisions of the school. Paul Meier's rebuttal, although not using my term, made my point:

> Finally, Dr. Meier testified that, although the regression analysis allows for different intercepts, it does not allow for possibly different slopes, or different rates of change of salary in different divisions.[18]

Defendant prevailed on the question of salary, as it had on promotion.

Situations or Events

Consider this articulation of the basis for a statistical analysis:

> Females are clustered at the bottom few levels; male employees, on the other hand, advance rather uniformly up the entire progression ladder.[19]

This is not a satisfactory description. It lacks parallelism. We are told that the females are

---

16. *Bickerstaff* (1999) at 633, with reference to *Atonio* (1989), in which matching the analysis to the defendant's practices is discussed by the Supreme Court.

17. The de Cani quotation is from *Presseisen* (1977) at 614, 15 FEP Cases at 1484. See also *Ottaviani* (1989) at 368:
> The district court's rejection of plaintiffs' claims as to discrimination in rank . . . "validated" academic rank as one of the legitimate factors to consider in accounting for salary disparities between male and female faculty members.

18. *Presseisen* (1977) at 615, 15 FEP Cases at 1486.

19. First hypothetical in Note (1975) at 388.

at low levels, not that they have remained at low levels over a long time. We are not told whether these low levels the females are in are precursors of the higher levels the males are in. Are these males and females arguably fungible? Reading through the inarticulateness in this *Harvard Law Review* note, let us assume that the complaint is that females advance at a slower rate than males. Is there a post-and-bid promotion system? Did females apply for posted jobs? Who won which jobs? Or do people advance just by waiting? We know from Chapter 2 how to analyze either type of event, but the above articulation of the problem does not tell us which it is. In no interpretation should this description lead to analysis by regression, though the law-review editors who wrote it thought that it did.

Differential pay for persons performing essentially the same tasks is a different conceptual creature. Even if you want to consider receiving a pay check an event, it is described by a number (the pay amount), not an action ("selected" or not). Being *assigned* to a pay rate is the relevant event. One's current pay rate is a "situation." Regression analyzes situations, such as gender differences in current pay. The job assignment you have is a situation, but the assignment event is what should be analyzed.

Sandra Day O'Connor was paid less than others with whom she had graduated from Stanford Law School not because of discrimination in attorney salaries, but because the only job she could get was as a secretary. The selection decisions—not the pay decisions—were biased. Many of the actors in those decisions (others who got the jobs she wanted, and still others who didn't) are not in her current-situation data. Plaintiffs may not know who all the relevant people are. If the firm has not maintained data on rejected job applicants, the events may be difficult to reconstruct. However, the difficulty of obtaining data describing events does not justify using the wrong kind of analysis.

Mark Killingsworth wrote a report for plaintiffs, the Office of Federal Contract Compliance Programs:

> [W]omen are statistically significantly much less likely to be in high grade
> levels, and much more likely to be in lower grade levels, than are otherwise-
> similar white men. This unequal access to better-paid work has substantial
> effects on pay.[20]

A situation—females are in lower grades—has become a generalization about the nature of events that the analyst concludes led there ("unequal access"). This is speculation, not analysis. The data generalization was correct: Women were in lower grades than men. Did they have the qualifications to be in higher grades? Had they been denied such positions? If so, justly or not? Killingsworth knew none of this; nor could he learn the answers from regression.

---

20. I received this report, undated and untitled, on January 13, 1997. I discuss Killingsworth's "analysis" in several places, particularly later in this chapter. The case, *I-NET*, is discussed in Chapters 6 and 7.

I wrote in response:

> In fact, different job groups have different grade spans, and it is entirely pos-
> sible that the groups the lower-grade females are in do not contain the higher
> grades possessed by males in other job groups. Without knowing that these
> people compete for these grades, that the same span of grades is available to
> all of them, no statement about "access" can be made.[21]

Regression, the tool of this chapter, can tell us a lot about situations, and can suggest
how they came about. The tools of Chapter 2 apply to the decisions that created the situation, to events. Most apparently situational disputes—such as job grade—are actually disputes about events, about the decisions that led to the current situation. They should be
analyzed using those events tools. Unfortunately, situation tools (such as regression) are
often employed, incorrectly, to "analyze" event complaints.

The Institutional Origin of Data

My final preliminary caution about regression is the importance of understanding how the
data one is using came about. In equal-employment opportunity, this means the structure
of the organization, the rules and decisions that produced the data. I started making this
point in Chapter 2, describing how those who were laid off from Polaroid were not those
who were selected to be laid off, because of the operation of a seniority plan. To illustrate
this point in the regression context, Figure 26 presents two salary histories, as seen by a
reviewing agency or plaintiffs' analyst.

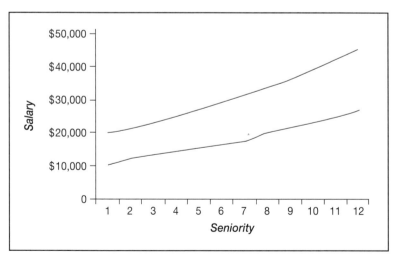

FIGURE 26: Misleading Graphic of the Relationship Between Seniority and Earnings

---

21. My response is dated February 10, 1997. It is unlikely that it was ever delivered to the OFCCP or to
Killingsworth, as will be discussed in Chapter 6.

The top line in Figure 26 appears to show higher pay at each year of seniority than the lower line. Let us say that these lines represent the salaries of a male and a female. These lines are drawn so that the pay histories are the same (in nominal dollars), counting seniority *within grade*. The lower line shows a female gaining experience enough to be eligible for the higher grade, and earning exactly what the male did once she got there in year eight.

A regression on data such as these, "controlling for (total) seniority," will "show" that females have lower salary than males, even though the firm recognizes merit and promotes people equally to higher grades. Suppose females do not get promoted to higher grades, and their salaries do not rise as fast as those of males. Is that proof that females are mistreated? As we saw in Chapter 2, and I explained in response to Killingsworth, persons might be in different job groups, and not all job groups encompass all grades; sometimes higher-level jobs are achieved by winning a competition, for which not all eligible employees become candidates. Being good is not good enough, if another candidate is better. Whether through merit increases or competition, it is unlikely that employees rise through the ranks at the same rate in all job groups. The same issues that we had to understand to investigate waiting time in grade re-appear when we investigate the salary consequence of trying to attain a higher grade. We have to know what "fair" would be if we are to uncover "unfair." To study the salary situation in the firm represented in Figure 26 we have to study events, the attainment of grade. Obvious? Not to many "experts."

HOBSON V. HANSEN

Despite figures produced by some researchers, no one knows how many cases have included statistical arguments or, more specifically, regression analyses at any level of court, state or federal. The easiest way to count regression presentations is to search in decisions for the word "regression." However, "regression" is also a psychological term. The earliest reports of the number of "regression" cases, from single-word searches, were exaggerated. Multiple-word searches fare no better. The word "correlation" appears in *Hobson I*, and I have seen that case cited as including statistical methods, presumably on that account. It did not. The word "correlation" appears there in the judge's informal sense of "apparent relationship" between income of parents and the percent of public-school students in college tracks. Finally, not all decisions are published, and some judges, in published opinions, not wanting to take a side on competing analyses, avoid statistical words altogether.[22]

---

22. Similarly, "correlation" appears in Justice Thomas' dissent in *Miller-El* (2003), again in the sense of a relationship, not a calculation. Fienberg (1989) at 7–8 presents figures based on word searches in cases. At an early stage in their work, I pointed out these problems to the Panel on Statistical Assessment As Evidence in Courts, as well as that they were counting the same case several times because of appeals (the same case at different court levels) and remands (the same case reappearing in district court). I do not believe these problems were corrected.

Any systematic attempt to measure appearances of regression at different points of time, however, probably well conveys the explosion in its use, even if the counts themselves are suspect. By any count, regression analyses abound, and have increased in frequency since the early 1970s. The first regression in litigation may have appeared in the late 1960s or early 1970s—eighty or so years after the procedure was developed—but I do not know that anyone can determine which was the first case, who was the first judge to be presented with (subjected to) a regression analysis. This case, however, *Hobson II*, might be it.

Economies of Scale

Julius Hobson had sued the Washington, D.C. school district in the 1960s to try to eliminate segregated schools. That was *Hobson I*. Because the "white" area was west of Rock Creek Park, in the northwest part of the city, and the poorest black area was in Anacostia, the far southeast, desegregation by bussing was impractical. So Hobson went back to court to ask for the next best thing, equality in per-pupil expenditures. The American Civil Liberties Union assisted him in this quest. That case became *Hobson II*.

Plaintiffs compiled figures showing that the average per pupil expenditure in schools west of Rock Creek was higher than that in schools elsewhere in the city. That demonstration, with the findings from *Hobson I*, seemed to be sufficient, especially as the District schools had no coherent explanation why it occurred. On October 15, 1970, an article appeared in the *Washington Post* under the title, "The Division of D.C. School Funds." Written by economists June O'Neil and Arlene Holen, it purported to present an "expert" analysis showing that funds were distributed by size of school, not the race of students. The crux of the argument was contained in one bar chart, redrawn from the original in Figure 27.

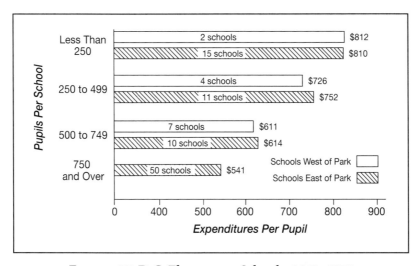

FIGURE 27: D.C. Elementary Schools, 1969–1970

Economies of scale! Spreading fixed costs over more pupils reduces apparent per-pupil expenditure. "When schools of equal size are compared" wrote O'Neil and Holen, "it is clear there are no significant east-west differences." This article became the focus of the defense.

> Defendants do not offer the article as evidence. Defendants do, however, offer the article as *argument* and adopt the reasoning contained in the article and incorporate it in this memorandum by reference.[23]

So the school system was handed a "plausible alternative explanation" for why per-pupil expenditure appeared to vary by race, and adopted it immediately.

Peter Rousselot, a pro bono attorney for Hobson, contacted me. The *Post* article has some obvious weakness, for example that half of the District's schools, and more than half of its students, are in the bottom bar, in large schools east of the park. One might ask what has been averaged out—how much variation is there within each clustering that contradicts the impression formed from comparing cluster averages. But, as the school system's lawyers later said, the argument has plausibility. It's just that this is not what economy of scale is.

Economies of scale occur when with larger facilities there are lower costs per unit of *output*. O'Neil and Holen had only shown that larger schools spend less per unit of one of the *inputs*, the children themselves. O'Neil and Holen illustrate their point:

> For example, school principals get similar salaries, but in larger schools the principal's salary cost per pupil will be much lower.

Not only cost, but both teacher and pupil interaction with the principal is lower in the larger school. Does the educational outcome suffer? I do not know, but O'Neil and Holen have assumed that the only consequence from having more pupils per principal is to lower cost. They do not even inquire about the educational result of the size of schools. Without further investigation, we cannot say that this is an economy of scale, expending fewer resources for the same education. It is just an economy, expending fewer resources.

To know if there are economies of scale you have to ask if input cost is reduced when the school is larger *and it produces the same education*, whatever that is. "Could one ascertain the extent, if any, of economies of scale?" Rousselot asked. We could use test scores as outcomes, socioeconomic measures per school district as controls for background, and assess the impact of size on per-pupil expenditure, holding background and outcome "constant," by regression, I asserted. It turned out that I could not do these things. I did not think the data were sufficient, once I set to the task. But first I found that two other economists had tried to assess economies of scale in schooling, by regression, in literature that O'Neil and Holen should have known.[24] I would not appear to the judge to be some abstract critic

23. "Defendants' Memorandum to the Court" in *Hobson II*, November 17, 1970, at 18.

24. Cohn (1968) and Riew (1966). See also Osburn (1970), on which Riew (1972) comments much as I

or academic upstart. And finally it happened that I was working on similar issues, under the name "educational production function." I signed on to do the litigation work and created a graduate course out of it, which is to say, gathered no-cost research assistance.

Regression Estimates

A more sophisticated approach to cost than O'Neil and Holen provided would appear to use regression, based on data from individual schools:

$$\text{per-pupil cost} = b_0 + b_1 \text{pupils} + \ldots + b_j \text{independent}_j + e_i$$

where "j" denotes the number of independent variables. There are several reasons why it is not a good idea to define the dependent variable as a ratio (cost divided by number of pupils), especially when the denominator also appears as an independent variable.[25] It is both better for a number of mathematical reasons, and more informative, to estimate the effect of scale on cost:

$$\text{cost} = b_0 + b_1 \text{pupils} + b_2 \text{pupils}^2 + \ldots + b_j \text{independent}_j + e_i$$

O'Neil and Holen would want the coefficient b_2 to be negative, so that (within the relevant range of school size) cost would be seen to increase at a decreasing rate as school size increases.

What would such estimates mean? The ability to describe a relationship mathematically provides no evidence that it is due to technology. It might be due to management discretion. Further investigation is required. However, having quantified the economies of scale, we could then ask how much of the actual expenditure differential was "explained" thereby. We could estimate the number that O'Neil and Holen assumed to be 100 percent, even not knowing why it occurred.

We might like schools to "make up" for deficiencies at home, but the existence of Head Start and other remedial programs is our admission that schools cannot do that. What we ask of schools is to add to or multiply the learning children receive at home—to "add value." If we are to estimate educational outcomes, we should estimate the improvement in skills brought about by different schools, not the level of skills that children in different schools have.

One way to achieve such an estimate would be to select schools with the same average outcomes—better, the same value added—but different sizes, and ask if the larger

---

would have.Other studies purporting to be about economies of scale in schooling were part of the school-consolidation literature. Their subject was district size, not school size.

25. Although ratios as independent variables are frowned upon, I find that objection unimportant when the ratio itself is a common metric, such as percent Hispanic. There is little reason ever to allow the dependent variable to be a ratio, however, when one can estimate the effect of the denominator by defining one or more independent variables from it.

schools produced this equal outcome less expensively than the smaller schools. In Washington, D.C., too many important characteristics were correlated with outcome, so that restricting the data by outcome would fail to test the relationships among cost, outcome, size, and race of students. A statistical control such as by regression was required. If we do not know starting test scores, we know correlates thereof, socioeconomic indicators like family income, parental education, a measure of educational resources in the home, whether the child had been to the library, to book stores, etc. A cost estimate that included outcome variables and indicators for non-school effects might look like this:

$$\text{cost} = b_0 + b_1 \text{pupils} + b_2 \text{pupils}^2 + b_3 \text{test} + b_4 \text{home} + \ldots + b_j \text{independent}_j + e_i$$

To my knowledge, more than thirty-five years later, no one has performed a satisfactory study of this type. The data requirements are too difficult to meet.[26] It is not clear how one would gather information on variables measuring non-school inputs, or what is the appropriate unit of observation. This is a problem we have to live with: The question may be too complex to arrive at a definitive statistical answer, ever, and surely is so within the restraints of the time and budget allowed in litigation.

Interpreting Regression Results

However, a statistical analysis can still be informative. In my report to the court, I took some space to discuss the legitimacy of including certain variables. I discussed, first, a "decision function":

> It will be true that costs are related to capacity utilization. This relationship is strong and negative: the heavier the utilization, the lower the per pupil costs. But capacity utilization is itself directly under the control of the D.C. Superintendent of Schools. In asking whether the Superintendent favors schools west of the park, it is not sensible to control out of the equation the *means* by which he does this. It is like asking a football coach to ignore the size of his players in choosing his starting team. While we recognize the concept of a smaller player being better *given his size*, football games are won or lost as they are played.[27]

I distinguished this kind of estimation, looking at options for decisions, from the technical question, "Are there economies of scale?" For that estimation, as indicated above, I would control for more variables. The point here is not what estimates I made, but that I tried to engage the judge about the logic of what I was doing, as opposed to the mechanics or mathematics. Each variable has to mean something, and the equation has

---

26. For example, Lazear (2001) discusses why one cannot even conclude, from the literature, that class size affects student outcome. Findings are inconsistent, he thinks, because personalities of the students (some of whom do better in large classes, some in small) have not been considered.

27. In *Hobson II*: Stephan Michelson, "A Research Report for Plaintiffs," December 28, 1970, at 102.

to mean something, and we have to agree what that is.

My conclusion:

> It should be clear that defendants' case for economies of scale, while both
> plausible and possible, has been highly exaggerated.[28]

Although I provided full regression equations, perhaps the most understandable figure I gave was the "effect of size" on per-pupil teacher expenditure for a seven-hundred-pupil school, which is the reduction in per-pupil cost with the addition of one more pupil. When only average daily membership (and its square) is accounted for, that figure is $0.168. This could be interpreted as an estimate of the effect posited by O'Neil and Holen, calculated at this school size, although they provided no such measure. When other aspects of the school were accounted for, such as the proportion of special students, whether it was a "model" school, and capacity utilization, this effect was reduced to under $0.10. Thus I showed, by regression, that much of the lower cost of larger schools, attributed by O'Neil and Holen from grouped data to a size-cost relationship, was better associated with other expenditure characteristics. And I showed that in many cases those characteristics were discretionary, under the control of the superintendent.

> We will make one last observation about these regressions. The size variables
> "explained" 28% of the variation in expenditures per pupil themselves. Our
> most complete equation . . . explains 52% of the variation. How much of that
> can be attributed uniquely to scale? An answer is found by estimating the
> amount of variation explained by the other variables in the equation, without
> the size variables. These variables can account for over 44% of the variation
> themselves, leaving 7.5% "uniquely" attributable to size. Thus . . . size of school
> may unambiguously be said to account for one thirteenth of the variation in
> per pupil teacher expenditures in District schools in Fiscal 1970. Hardly the
> magnificent explainer claimed by June O'Neil, Arlene Holen, and defendants!

There appeared to be some economy of scale at the school level, some efficiency not lost by lower educational outcomes. O'Neil and Holen had a legitimate insight, but they presented it as explaining cost differences among schools without testing the extent to which it did. Their article should have raised the question rather than purporting to provide the answer.

An idea about a factor that *might* explain what is being complained about is not a defense.[29] Judge J. Skelly Wright ordered equalization among schools, within 5 percent bounds, for per-pupil teacher expenditures. He cited the "Michelson Analysis" for support

---

28. "A Research Report for Plaintiffs," at 107; following indented quotation at 116.

29. *Holiday* (2002) at 1310:

> Production of evidence to show that something could happen creates no inference that it
> did happen.

denying, as was the judicial tradition for many years thereafter, that he had critically relied on it. The judge does not want to pass on the merits of opposing analyses presented in a language foreign to him. Yet, that is his job. So he tries to mask his thinking in the language of his opinion.

Ex Post Review

Donald Horowitz had an interesting take on the dilemma facing the court presented with econometric analyses, at least in the amorphous context of education:

> Each legal question turned on the resolution of an empirical question, which then turned out to have another legal question embedded within it. The legal question of inequality depended in part on the empirical question of economies of scale. Whether there were genuine economies of scale depended in turn on the legal question of exactly what scale-related disparities the school system was to be held "responsible" for. But what disparities the system was to be held responsible for depended on the empirical question of whether the disparities had any effect on education. This factual question was finally resolved by resort to a legal question: who bore the burden of proof on such questions?[30]

What do we do with this insight? In Chapters 8 and 10 I suggest that rather than being deliberately ignorant of the law, which is almost demanded of experts in today's courtroom environment, the expert needs to understand the law in the particular field in which he is testifying. If the judge needs a legal predicate to accept a statistical fact, or to decide between two experts' views of statistical fact, the expert needs to be aware of it, and be sure it is produced.

Horowitz also suggested that I was duplicitous in arguing for equalization of public school resources while, in other forums, disavowing the findings from the "educational production function" literature. Not at all. The question is what face does government present to citizens when it is ignorant, when it does not know the consequence of unequal (by some measure) provision of services. This is not a statistical question. The Supreme Court made clear the difference between a continuing principle of law and a remedy given violation of that principle, in *Montgomery* (1969). In the circumstances of *Hobson II*, that mandate would be to equalize per-pupil expenditures, as was ordered, just as in *Montgomery* the Court ordered reshuffling of teachers to achieve a racial balance in each school, but only as a remedy for past segregation. It was my opinion during *Hobson II*, and is now, that once the "economies of scale" and any other technological excuse for unequal resource allocation was shown to be false, the court had to order equalization along lines we could

---

30. Horowitz (1977) at 133. See all of Chapter 4, "*Hobson v. Hansen*: The Calculus of Equality in School Resources."

measure—such as dollars—as a statement to citizens that equality is what their government stood for. I know of no evidence that this court-ordered equalization had an educational consequence, positive or negative. Nor did I ever predict that it would. It was simply the right thing to do.[31]

EQUAL-EMPLOYMENT OPPORTUNITY

Most early equal-employment-opportunity cases were about selection, the subject of Chapter 2 of this book. One might think that regression would have been a popular method of proof of Equal Pay Act claims, but I will explain here why they were not appropriate to the firm structures of the earliest cases. Regression in equal-employment-opportunity litigation developed largely after the 1972 amendments to the Equal Employment Opportunity Act.[32] Inspiration for its use, that is, how attorneys became aware of regression as a tool in their litigation, is usually credited to the AT&T consent decree of 1973, and the 1975 *Harvard Law Review* note quoted above.

The AT&T Consent Decree

In 1970, "Ma Bell," the monopoly long-distance carrier AT&T, filed with the Federal Communications Commission (FCC) to obtain a long-distance rate increase. The Equal Em-

---

31. As Judge Wright wrote in *Hobson I* in 1970, at 497:

> Whatever the law was once, it is a testament to our maturing concept of equality that, with the help of Supreme Court decisions in the last decade, we now firmly recognize that the arbitrary quality of thoughtlessness can be as disastrous and unfair to private rights and the public interest as the perversity of a willful scheme.

If Wright seems to be asserting a consequentialist view—we want equality because of what follows if we don't have it—let me be clear that my approach is deontological. Without empirical evidence that equal expenditures per pupil is a false measure—which was O'Neil and Holen's assertion—the equal-expenditure solution

> arises not from a desire to achieve the best state of affairs or otherwise "do good" in the world, but simply from a belief that pursuing prescriptive equality is the right thing to do, that equal treatment is a good in itself.

Peters (2000) at 1097. Peters argues against this notion, in favor of a consequentialist one. However, he considers only known consequences. In the context of this book, deontological equality is observable, whereas consequences are estimated with a probability of error. The question is: What standard should apply when the consequences are *not* known?

32. The Equal Pay Act of 1963 was an amendment to the Fair Labor Standard Act, 29 U.S. Code §206(d)(1). The Equal Employment Opportunity Act of 1972 is 86 Stat. 103, which amended 42 U.S. Code §2000(e) et seq. In this Act, §3 rescinds the former exemption of teachers in educational institutions, as well as including state and local governments. Most important, the 1972 equal-employment-opportunity amendments gave the Equal Employment Opportunity Commission the right to sue. It could now be the plaintiff.

ployment Opportunity Commission (EEOC), petitioned to intervene, on the basis that AT&T discriminated in its employment practices. That petition was denied, but it achieved its purpose in inducing the FCC to instigate its own investigation, at which the EEOC could appear. In January, 1973, during a suspension of hearings, the FCC, AT&T, and the EEOC announced a settlement that, for the most part, was approved by courts following appeals by civil-rights groups.[33] One of the pieces of the EEOC's evidence was Ronald Oaxaca's regression analysis of earnings. The settlement can be characterized as revamping assignment practices (which is why we see female installers and hear male operators—formerly gender-segregated jobs—for example) and bringing wages to race and gender parity in a revised job structure.

For many reasons, Oaxaca's study would not be accepted as expert testimony today. One is that the data did not come from the defendant firm, but from the 1967 "Survey of Economic Opportunity." From this sixty-thousand-person survey, Oaxaca extracted the 92 males and 124 females among white or black urban workers who reported their industry as "telephone communications." Surely some of these people did not work for AT&T. The calculation "the worker's age minus his or her level of education minus six years" was used to represent "experience," thereby equating experience outside the firm with experience inside the firm (seniority), and assuming no gender difference in actual work experience since school.[34] Most important, only four years had passed since the passage of the Equal Pay Act, three years since Title VII, the Equal Employment Opportunity Act. Yet the average female had almost fourteen years of experience, the average male almost seventeen. Thus through most of their working lives, what later came to be called discriminatory acts (in assignment, promotion, or pay) had not been illegal.

With sufficient data, situation-based analyses can correct for pre-Act or pre-employer decisions by controlling for each employee's characteristics before hire or before the Act. This information was not available in Oaxaca's "snapshot" survey. Today, controlling for laws enacted in the 1960s would be much effort for little gain. Almost all work events expe-

---

33. See in general Wallace (1976) and Northrup and Larson (1979).

34. The quotation is from Oaxaca (1976) at 29. Oaxaca says that adding the number of children as a variable "corrects" for differential male/female labor market experience, but that cannot be true. The variable "number of children" was not in the male equation. Thus when female characteristics were entered into an equation based on males, the number of children they had was not one of them. Using "potential experience" as a substitute for experience in a wage equation assumes homogeneity—assumes that males and females have been equally employed prior to this moment, and therefore should be rewarded equally for that time. It has been explicitly disallowed in litigation. See, for example, *Valentino* (1982). In *Key* (1982) at 1619, Judge Caffrey says that substituting time for experience is "unreasonable, circular, and even a bit dishonest," given that the equal-employment laws have been passed

> to correct a cultural situation which results more often than not in men being able to achieve far greater experience than women of equal age.

rienced by anyone occurred after the effective date of the Equal Employment Opportunity Acts. In the early days, in the 1960s and 1970s, failure to control for each individual's skills and position as of the effective date of the law was a major conceptual error by analysts, unperceived by most attorneys. The more lasting and more important "situation" vs. "event" distinction was also not understood by anyone in the process—experts, attorneys, or judges. And so Oaxaca's clearly fallacious regressions—suggestive for research, but unacceptable as evidence in law—impressed the world with the existence of a powerful tool plaintiffs might wield in court.

Oaxaca himself concluded,

> The reason why females received less than the wage predicted on the basis of the male wage structure has more to do with the types of jobs they held than with unequal pay for equal work.[35]

That is, most of the complaints were about job assignment, not pay per job. Job assignment is a selection event. It should have been analyzed using selection tools. That AT&T had gender-segregated jobs was clear. The threat of Oaxaca's regressions seems to have had a righteous effect. But the regressions themselves, and the estimates of discriminatory wage differentials derived therefrom, bore no relationship to the analyses called for by the relevant laws.

The *Harvard* Note

The 1975 *Harvard Law Review* note, from which I quoted above, was amateurish. Worse than that, it was incorrect. It seems that its authors knew about, and were taken in by, Oaxaca's work. Like Oaxaca's regressions, the note was effective in bringing awareness of regression to the eyes of attorneys and judges. Like the AT&T review, the issues discussed in the note are events. More events than just those that occurred to the obvious population may be at issue. Rejected job offers are not reflected in "hires" data; are not reflected in any data about persons ever employed by this firm. Thus the note publicized regression in the wrong way, for the wrong reasons, for complaints about which it was the wrong tool.[36]

Possibly the note authors were also impressed with the effectiveness of a regression presentation in *Readers Digest* (1974) which, like AT&T, concluded with a settlement, not a trial. In addition, by the time of this note, regressions had been presented in courts

---

35. Oaxaca (1976) at 34.

36. The *Harvard* note (1975) centered on two hypotheticals. Part of the description of the first has been quoted above. The second hypothetical was also about movement up a progression ladder, not about differential pay at the ladder's steps. The note's authors distinguish the two examples by asking if a bona fide occupation qualification explains the second one. Neither hypothetical called for regression.

and discussed in opinions.[37] Thus one should not credit the *Harvard* writers with initiating the idea, but reporting ideas is important. For example, one can agree or not with Peter Huber's generalizations, but coining the phrase "junk science" and making courts aware that theirs was a prime forum for it, was a service.[38] That the *Harvard* editors misrepresented regression is unfortunate, but could have been cleared up by good expert use and subsequent expert writing. The misuse and abuse that followed cannot be laid at the feet of the *Harvard* editors or attorneys who wanted regression to do for their clients what it had done for AT&T and *Readers Digest* employees. No, the blame for what followed rests squarely on the "experts."

A Legal-Literature Explosion

The *Harvard* note also reported incorrectly about regression methods, for example finding the use of qualitative variables "difficult." Gender is itself a qualitative variable, but we define a female indicator variable and there is nothing difficult about it at all, conceptually or technically. Rich Goldstein, my colleague at the time at the Center for Community Economic Development, wrote to the *Harvard Law Review* about their errors. Susan Estrich, then president of the *Law Review*, asked Thomas J. Campbell, editor (and presumably the note's author), to respond. His response contained more errors, prompting a second letter from Goldstein, who wrote:

> Lawyers need . . . the ability to question statisticians, both witnesses and prospective consultants. They also need some ability to converse with their consultant so that strategy can be better devised. They do not need the ability to compute statistics or even to choose between several possible appropriate statistics.[39]

In 1980 David Baldus and James Cole published a lawyer's manual for use of statistics in equal-employment-opportunity cases, with much on regression. The *Columbia Law Review* devoted its May 1980 issue to the subject.[40] In 1981 Arthur Smith and Thomas Abram suggested regression analysis and asserted that statistics could be used as "proof" of discrimination. The next year the *Columbia Law Review* published a full length discussion of regression by Jean Manning. *Law and Contemporary Problems* devoted its Autumn 1983 issue to a symposium on statistical issues, more accurately characterized as a self-advertising forum for a number of experts. Not getting the point, the Federal Judicial

---

37. *Hobson II* is one clear example of regression preceding the *Harvard* note, but as the *Harvard* authors were concerned about employment, they may not have noticed it.

38. See Huber (1991). I will have more to say about Huber's writing in later chapters.

39. Letter from Richard Goldstein to Thomas J. Campbell, June 30, 1976.

40. See especially Finkelstein (1980) and Fisher (1980).

Center has sponsored elementary explanations of some statistical concepts, including regression.[41]

As noted in Chapter 2, most people in a field are engaged in a conversation with other members of that field. They do not have the time to explore other fields. Thus each field of application explains common statistical methods to its own constituency. The articles listed in the previous paragraph are a sampling of law-talk about statistics. I think most of this technical discussion in law journals can be of no help to attorneys who, as Goldstein wisely stated, need concepts, not formulas. It is especially aggravating when the articles contain such basic errors as the confusion between situations and events.

Campbell, for example, subsequent to his Harvard-student days, suggested that one should estimate two salary equations, one for the plaintiff class, one for others, instead of one with a dummy variable for the class.[42] The problem he saw was non-homogeneous effects. That indeed is a problem, but Campbell provided no method to compare the coefficients, lamely indicating that one might find them far apart by their listed standard errors. He also chided courts for not paying attention to goodness of fit—R^2—without setting out either any standard by which to evaluate that statistic, or use to make of it.

The Equal Pay Act

Early Equal Pay Act claims largely concerned nominally different job titles for males and females, in which the work performed was the same. For example, in *Behrens* (1973), a drug company paid male "sales trainees" more to learn the work that female "Order Clerks" were doing than they paid the order clerks. This is a classic Equal Pay Act violation, which we will encounter in a federal contracting context in *Harris Bank* (1981), below.

When two jobs require different skills, if only on the margin, then they are different jobs that could command different pay. See for example *Cain-Sloan* (1973), in which marking clothes for alteration was considered a separate skill justifying higher compensation for male sales clerks than for most female sales positions. However, that logic led also to finding that clerks for upscale women's clothing, who did mark for alteration, required equal compensation.

In short, unequal wages was undisputed. Plaintiffs had to pierce the veil of segregated jobs to prove that the functions were the same. We find few statistical presentations of any kind in these early cases. The issue was whether the different titles represented seriously different jobs requiring different skills.

---

41. See A. Smith and Abram (1981), and Manning (1982). For the Federal Judicial Center document, see *Reference Manual* (1994). The *Reference Manual* was revised in 2000. The articles in it are perhaps most easily available in Faigman et al. (2002).

42. See T. Campbell (1984).

Although somewhat later, a startling and classic example of sex-segregating jobs to keep salaries of females low (and to keep authority with males), explained in great detail by the judge, is *Kyriazi* (1978). Not only was recruitment designated by gender within Western Electric, documents were falsified to hide this fact. Employees then lied, denying the falsification. Plaintiffs who understand the mechanism by which male salaries are kept above female salaries fare best if they explain this mechanism and focus their statistics on it, as did Judith Vladeck, Kyriazi's attorney.[43]

Job titles are seldom differentiated by gender in college faculties, though certain departments are historically one-gender dominated. Many college faculties have systematized salary schedules, with ranges at each level that would allow for consideration of other factors, or discrimination by race or gender. Data on faculty qualifications are usually easy to find, often published in a school's catalog of course offerings. In January 1977 I testified for plaintiffs in a case in which Tufts University was alleged to have discriminated against female faculty in salary determination.[44] I presented regression analyses showing that females were paid less than males, accounting for the kinds of things universities value (highest degree, seniority at this institution, prior experience), even considering department. Apparently overwhelmed, Judge Murray retired without deciding the case. It withered away into a settlement years later.

In *Keyes* (1976) we find one of the earliest academic cases that could have used a regression analysis. But there wasn't one. Annie Laurie Keyes' major contention was that her contract as professor of education, renewed annually since 1968–69, should have been renewed for 1973–74 even though she had reached age sixty-five. Alleging salary discrimination against females, she argued that she should have been paid more, also. She offered such evidence as the rank order of the highest-paid female, by year—but not, as far as I can tell, even a comparison of mean salary by title. The defense was particular, explaining why every male above the highest-paid female deserved a higher salary. A more general affirmative case would have required a more general defense. The particularized defense was appropriate given the complaint and "evidence." Keyes lost every point.

Sweeney (1977) also included a faculty-salary issue. Although the decisions mention "statistics," it appears that what was presented to the court were data—salaries and titles of

---

43. In Chapter 5 I make this same point in illustrating that the defense against the statistical charge that jurors did not "represent" populations from which they were drawn was not so much statistical as descriptive. "This is what we do. What are we doing wrong?" is a good defense if "we" are doing nothing wrong. "This is what they do, and this is why it is wrong," is a good offense when they are doing something wrong. Statistics is overrated as "proof" when there is a good story to be told.

44. *Tufts* (1977). Many female faculty at Tufts were wives of faculty at other Boston-area colleges. Plaintiffs' theory was that Tufts knew the females could not threaten to move elsewhere. By gathering this personal information I might have tested the theory—distinguishing wives of other area faculty from other females—and now wish I had, but I did not.

Keene State College faculty for each year from 1965–66 through 1975–76—except two years for which the court reports finding "only blank sheets."[45] Judge Bownes went quite far from only this slim presentation, noting that "there is bound to be discrimination against females," given the school's lack of standards for determining salary. Having been provided no regression analysis, he concluded that "plaintiff has not proven that her salary as an associate professor was less than that of other male associate professors with the same qualifications and responsibilities."

Regression in Equal-Employment-Opportunity Cases

In an equal-employment-opportunity case, regression converts a disparate-treatment case to a disparate-impact case. Many attorneys think that if a regression equation can "explain" disparities, say between salaries of male and female faculty, then the case is over, defense wins. No it doesn't.

"See, there really is no male-female difference," says the defendant's expert of his regression output. But there is, or he would not have needed a regression to "explain" it. The question, as in Chapter 2, is whether his explanation is valid. Before I amplify that concept in this regression context, I use a hypothetical data set to illustrate how experts might go at each other with dueling regressions. Figure 28 contains the coefficient of the gender variable (0 if male, 1 if female) under different "specifications," which means different sets of observations and variables.

	t-test	All Faculty	Only Assistant Professors	Only Associate Professors	Only Full Professors
Coefficient	−7,130	−442	−823	−89	−1,479
Probability	0.011	0.159	0.303	0.883	0.008
n	30	30	14	8	8
R^2 (adjusted)	0.180	0.994	0.779	0.903	0.999

FIGURE 28: Regressions on Hypothetical Faculty Data

Plaintiffs' expert begins with a t-test. This is a statistical test of the difference in means between two variables, here salaries of male faculty and salaries of female faculty. Later we will see one judge criticize an expert for performing a t-test, not a regression. There is no

---

45. *Sweeney* (1977), 14 FEP Cases at 1229; following in-text quotations at 1230. Sweeney had been promoted to full professor before this trial. She was complaining about not having been promoted earlier, and so arguably should have brought forward a waiting-time-to-promotion (events) analysis. The court finds equivalently that her salary as a full professor had not been shown to be discriminatorily low.

difference.[46] The smaller the probability, the less likely it would be to find a difference of this size or larger, in a data set of this size, by chance, if there were no difference in fact. This interpretation assumes that there is a larger population of observations of which this is a sample. There has been a lot of fruitless discussion about this concept, some people arguing that as this *is* the population, any difference is "significant." This is a sample of persons whose salaries might be set by whoever sets them, and from this sample we are trying to infer behavior of these decision makers towards females.[47] It is a sample of the decisions that might be made, and therefore a sampling of the decision process. So the smaller the probability, the better for plaintiff, provided the difference has a negative sign (females have lower salaries than males).

No judge would accept this t-test as evidence of an illegal pay difference between males and females. At the very least we should control for seniority and prior experience. Should we control also for faculty rank? Let us say that promotion is not at issue here, our data include assistant, associate and full professors, and the experts agree to control for rank.

The "All Faculty" regression controls for seniority and its square, and for rank by having a dummy variable for full professor (1 if professor, otherwise 0) and another dummy variable for associate professor. Assistant professors are uniquely defined by a zero value for both rank variables. In the remaining three regressions in Figure 28 I control only for seniority by variable. Rank has been controlled by selecting the samples.

Defendant will argue that the All Faculty regression shows that, while it appears to be true that females earn less than males, this difference lies well within the bounds of chance and unexplained variation due to variables not in the regression. Plaintiffs will counter that the gender-based salary difference is overwhelming at the full-professor rank, and will amend their complaint to be about salary discrimination among full professors. If one thinks that regressions don't lie, that otherwise equal (same rank and seniority) women are paid almost $1,500 less than comparable men, then plaintiffs win at that level.

---

46. Strictly speaking there are two ways to calculate a t-test, and only one of them produces the same answer as the regression. I do not think a judge (or expert) who distinguishes a t-test from a regression does so from this level of sophistication. He does so from ignorance.

47. Levin and Robbins (1983) at 264 comment on the proposition

> that in a completely observed finite population any differences between groups are significant. While true in a strict sampling sense, this narrow attitude is not useful because it fails to allow for any variation in the way things might have been.

I agree with this statement, but not with Levin and Robbins' urn-model approach, which essentially says the distribution of salaries (strictly, of the "unexplained" regression residuals) is given, and all that might have varied is who got them. That is a selection issue. There is no point to recasting regression as selection and then not using selection analysis tools.

Litigation Strategy

That is an incorrect conclusion from these data. Plaintiffs are willing to abandon their case at the lower levels, where most faculty, and especially most females (thirteen of sixteen) are found. Should defendant accept this reduction in the number of plaintiffs? Robert Follett and Finis Welch don't think so:

> There are obvious economies to be realized from reducing the scope of a case, both for plaintiffs and defendants. From a statistical perspective, however, such a procedure may be counter to correct inference. . . . Judging a company's guilt or innocence based on its statistically most damning employment practice is similar to estimating a family's average height by measuring the tallest member.[48]

I agree. In fact, defendant attorneys should be wary about any litigation against a part of a firm. Deposition questions to plaintiffs' expert should probe for the studies that were done to reduce the scope of the original conception of the case. Whether it happens before or during litigation, selecting areas of a firm to represent that firm's decisions may be a biased plaintiff tactic. I will review this issue of altering the scope of the case based on statistical analysis again in Chapter 8.

Defendant's attorney may think it is good practice to minimize the risk to his client—how much harm can three females do, compared with sixteen?—and may accept the amended complaint. The defendant's expert should try to prevent this acceptance. The defense in this case is not a regression equation, it is a picture. The picture in Figure 29.

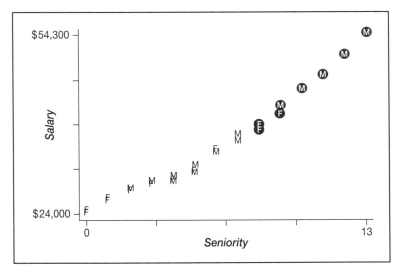

FIGURE 29: Graphic of the Hypothetical Faculty Data from Figure 28

48. Follett and Welch (1983) at 183.

Males and females are distinguished by the first letter of their gender. Full professors are shown in white letters on a black circle. Viewed as a whole, the situation appears to be what the All Faculty regression said it was. Regression among only full professors is hampered by the very small seniority overlap between males and females. The school should explain only two observations, the full-professor male and female with the same seniority, where the male earns a higher salary. Defense should not accept the amended complaint, because to do so would prevent it from showing that all other males and females are on the same salary path.

Multiple Tests

Like the probabilities in Chapter 2, the statistics reported with regression mean what they are said to mean only if the investigator looks once. The analyst is supposed to set out a theoretical basis for the regression and estimate it. He might then adjust the "specification," drop some variables that do not contribute to the fit, try terms with higher powers to capture non-linearities, etc.; but he may not (legitimately) cast about for some specification or subset of observation that "works." I do not want to judge this hypothetical situation too harshly. It is legitimate to ask if the same coefficients apply over the entire range of faculty, in other words, to "control" for faculty rank by separating the data. But having looked at three ranks, it is wrong to present each as if it had been the only rank investigated. This is a complex issue, rarely ventured into in litigation, although it parallels a topic of great concern, "shopping" for experts. The existence of many tests may reflect an expert "shopping" for a client-conforming analysis.

The regression based only on full professors in this example misrepresents the facts. The judge should not be cowed by the mathematics of regression. He needs to probe at the level he can understand. It is the more important level, anyway: What does this really mean? In this example the full-professor regression means essentially nothing, especially as it was not what the complaint was about.

Regression and Disparate Treatment

In equal-employment-opportunity cases, "disparate treatment" is direct discrimination against a subject group. It is an action taken in response to the characteristic of the individual. "Disparate impact" achieves the same result through an intermediary, some requirement for pay or selection that is held unequally between the subject group and the "majority." The classic example, from *Griggs* (1971), was mentioned in Chapter 2 in connection with validity.[49]

---

49. One might say that "affirmative action" or "race preference" in selection has, on its face, disparate impact against those who do not receive preferential treatment. When the Supreme Court accepts such procedures, as in *Grutter* (2003), it must be declaring race a valid selection mechanism. This is a

Regression converts a disparate-treatment case to a disparate-impact case by identifying other factors that "explain" the observed salary differences by gender. As stated above, it is a defense only if these other factors are valid. Seniority will almost always be considered a legitimate criterion for compensation differences, so much so that it was written into equal-employment-opportunity law. Other variables need to be questioned. That they have the effect of reducing the gender (or race) coefficient does not mean that they belong in a regression equation. Faculty rank might not be objective. Even department. See, for example, universities in which fiber arts or textile courses are offered under "home economics," to keep their female faculty from being compared with male professors in the art department. As we will see below in *James* (1975), neither job title nor department nor a variable called "skill" should be allowed to "explain" compensation when they are manipulated in a segregated environment to justify lower wages for minorities.

Layoffs in *Diehl* (1996)

In *Diehl*, defendant Xerox Corporation, it was alleged, selected persons for layoff on the basis of age and gender. I consider only gender here. Plaintiffs' expert showed a relationship between gender and layoff, according to the judge, by means of a t-test. On its face, that is not possible: Layoff is an event. A t-test compares situation means. Plaintiffs' t-test compared the mean scores of males and females on a "skills" continuum. Plaintiffs accepted that the score was used as the basis for termination, but to effectuate their own conception they should have used a rank-order test. As explained in Chapter 2, means are irrelevant in selection. Only rank order (who is better than whom) should matter.

Judge Telesca criticized plaintiffs' expert for not using a "regression." As stated above, a t-test *is* a regression with one dependent and one independent variable. One might question whether plaintiffs' regression was adequate, but not whether they did one. Defendant's expert David Bloom offered a regression in which other variables "explained" the termination. Those other variables were previous "performance" ratings. Plaintiffs' expert Marjorie Honig said she did not use those ratings because they are subjective. Bloom said he did use them because they are correlated over time—the same workers were rated high in review after review. And because they are correlated also with the final "skill" rating, they "explained" that rating. Performance, not gender or age, "explains" the skill rating by which persons were selected for termination, said defendant's expert. The judge agreed.

Not so easy. Plaintiff says the following model holds:

$$skill = f(gender)$$

---

peculiar notion—that race itself is a valid explainer of race differences in selection. The answer, I think, is that affirmative action, racial preference, should never be allowed. Primus (2003) sees something like the same contradiction, but chooses to conclude that therefore the disparate-impact concept fails.

Skill, as Xerox sees it, can be predicted by gender. Defendant says this model is better:

$$\text{skill} = f(\text{gender, prior-performance ratings})$$

Skill can be predicted by prior-performance ratings and, when it is, gender adds no predictive power. The gender coefficient is zero. Defendant has shown that "prior-performance rating" has a disparate impact on selection for termination, and defends the variable because it was created before management knew there would be a layoff.

Honig says "prior-performance ratings" should not be used in the model because they are a surrogate for gender.[50]

$$\text{performance rating} = g(\text{gender})$$

Substituting,

$$\text{skill} = f(\text{gender, } g(\text{gender}))$$

where "skill" is to be interpreted as "perceived skill." Thus, plaintiff asserts, all decisions are based on gender.

Who is correct? The issue seems not to be resolvable by statistics, at least not the statistical analyses employed by these experts.[51] If the question is whether a variable should be allowed in an explanatory model, what characteristics should a variable have to allow its inclusion? What does the judge need to know to decide this question? He needs two terms I introduced in Chapter 2: *reliability* and *validity*. In the *Diehl* context, "skill" means the ability to perform work at Xerox. The question is whether the measure that becomes a regression variable is a valid indicator of that skill.

That question was never asked. Although Xerox argued that prior assessments were independent of knowledge of the layoff, it apparently offered no evidence that they were made independent of gender. Bloom asserted only reliability, not validity. Judge Telesca

---

50. In a separate case based on this same set of layoffs, plaintiffs' expert, Philip A. Smethurst, made essentially the same argument. Judge Larimer excluded his testimony for failure to look for reasons other than gender and age that might explain who was terminated. See *Wado* (1998) and a quotation therefrom below in Chapter 8.

51. Honig was chair of the department of economics at Hunter College, City University of New York; Bloom, professor of economics at Columbia University. Neither expert apparently understood that layoffs are better analyzed with a multiple-pools-selection procedure, as described in Chapter 2. According to Bloom, Honig made an irredeemable error: She included the wrong people in her selection pool, including employees at other sites who were not subject to these layoffs. Honig, the consummate academic,

> testified that the usual division of labor for statistical purposes is based upon the Federal Labor Standard Act's designation of exempt versus non-exempt workers.

Diehl (1996) at 1163. As discussed in Chapter 2, the appropriate division in litigation is into pools defining competitions for the same layoff. Bloom's criticism was probably correct. My discussion in text is not about the merits of the outcome of *Diehl* (1996), only about the failure of the experts and judge to understand the role of validity in regression, although regression was not called for.

cannot be exonerated just because the appropriate issue was not presented to him. He allowed a debate about statistical methodology to overwhelm meaning.

Wages in _James_ (1975)

In the earliest well-known equal-employment-opportunity case utilizing regression, _James_, only defendant presented a statistical analysis. The local Alabama judge not only "bought" the regression, produced by James Gwartney and Joan Haworth of Florida State University, he adopted defendant's proposed finding of facts essentially verbatim, much to the annoyance of the Fifth Circuit. The more well-known and correct opinion is the Fifth Circuit's reversal in 1977. It showed that regression could be misused, and that such misuse could be detected.

Stockham Valves' plants in Birmingham, Alabama, were segregated even as the trial was proceeding. As was typical of the day, blacks usually held the hardest (in the steel mill, the hottest) jobs, with the lowest pay. Where blacks and whites worked together, a white person was a supervisor. Stockham's practices were what equal-employment laws were designed to prevent.

Defendant's experts saw the allegation as one of lower wages of blacks. From a regression they argued that the difference was due to the impact of "productivity characteristics," of which whites had more than blacks. Gwartney's independent variables, used to explain earnings, all but race being "productivity characteristics," were these:

> years of schooling;
>
> seniority;
>
> skill level;
>
> outside craft experience;
>
> outside operative experience;
>
> absenteeism;
>
> merit rating;
>
> achievement; and
>
> race (black or white).

Gwartney starts by assuming that more schooling "should" generate more income, homogeneously, across all jobs. If there is such a relationship, there is no reason to assume homogeneity, but there is no reason to believe that additional schooling generates additional income within a job. The existence of different levels of schooling on the same job is better evidence that schooling does _not_ matter. But whites at Stockham Valves had more of it, and earned higher pay. Gwartney argued, and Judge Guin agreed, that schooling was a relevant factor to help "explain" differential salaries as reflecting differential productivity, essentially because more schooling indicates more of the kind of employee employers want.

How could such factors as "skill" and "merit" and "achievement" not be relevant determiners of salary? If people are not prepared to do better work—if they are less productive—they should be paid less. It may be too bad that race is correlated with poorer "productivity" factors, but is that the fault of this one firm? This seems like a convincing defense. Why it was no defense at all, therefore, is instructional.

Judge Wisdom, in the Fifth Circuit's reversal, explained the fallacy of Gwartney's regression:

> The rub comes with how these factors were defined in Dr. Gwartney's study. . . . "Skill level" was derived from an employee's job class; he had "skill" only if he worked in a job with a rating between JC 10 and 13. The systematic exclusion of blacks from promotion and training opportunities for such jobs, as is alleged here, will automatically produce no black employees with "skill level." . . .
>
> Dr. Gwartney used the merit ratings of Stockham supervisors, who are overwhelmingly white, for his "merit rating" factor. . . . If there is racial bias in the subjective evaluations of white supervisors, then that bias will be injected into Dr. Gwartney's earnings analysis.
>
> Further, Dr. Gwartney included education as one of his productivity factors, even though education is not a job requirement at Stockham, because, according to the defendant, "an individual's educational level, regardless of race, impacts earnings." The fallacy in this conclusion stems from two facts: (1) as the defendant concedes, education is not a job requirement at Stockham, and (2) white employees at Stockham have more education than blacks. Thus, adjusting for education in a regression analysis where education is not related to job performance and where one race is more educationally disadvantaged than another, masks racial differences in earnings that may be explainable on the basis of discrimination. Certainly such differences cannot fairly be explained on the basis of a factor, such as education, concededly irrelevant to adequate job performance.[52]

One would think that plaintiffs in *Diehl* (1996) would have cited this case. The judge does not, implying that either plaintiffs also did not, or the judge dismissed it out of hand. In Chapter 8 I will suggest that a truly expert "expert" should know about such precedents, and bring them to the attention of his often less-knowledgeable client.

Not only does job determine wage, and not only were jobs segregated, but, as Judge Wisdom noted,

> Job vacancies have never been posted at Stockham and the company does not have a formal bidding system.[53]

---

52. *James* (1977) at 332, 15 FEP Cases at 844.

53. *James* (1977) at 316, 15 FEP Cases at 831; following two indented quotations at 334, 15 FEP Cases at 846; fourth indented quotation at 359, 15 FEP Cases at 867.

First,

> over two-thirds of Stockham's work force were assigned to jobs without assignment requests.

Second, blacks applying for traditionally white jobs were not hired. Third, there were

> blacks who sought to transfer to jobs in traditionally white departments after having worked for a time at Stockham.

This case was about job assignments, not wages per job. The Fifth Circuit's conclusion makes clear the real issues:

> The record in this case reveals that the defendant Stockham is guilty of unlawful racial discrimination in the segregation of facilities and programs, the allocation of jobs, craft training and selection, promotion, and supervisory recruitment and training.

Regression was not called for. Plaintiffs should have offered an expert to say that not only was Gwartney's regression fallacious (as Judge Wisdom explained), it was irrelevant.

Gwartney and Haworth defended themselves. They expressed their undying belief in the rationality of employers, in theory over reality:

> It is important to remember that cost-conscious employers will not compensate employees for skill factors that do not increase employee productivity.[54]

They excuse their lack of empirical work, citing the "impracticality and infeasibility of strict validation procedures." They enunciate the "warm body" hypothesis, which they claim the Fifth Circuit had accepted:

> According to the warm body hypothesis, all persons who have a warm body are equally qualified. The warm body approach denies the importance of qualitative degrees of competency.

The "warm body" hypothesis is equivalent to using quotas, or body counts, to determine discrimination. Gwartney and his cohorts were in a sense prescient, predicting that just counting bodies (by race or gender) would satisfy bureaucrats administering equal-employment-opportunity laws. As Gwartney had used a situation analysis to defend against allegations of biased events, and admittedly ignored whether his variables were valid, this insight does not redeem his work.

David Barnes' take on *James* (1975) either requires a loose definition of "regression" or is itself as peculiar (and incorrect) as Gwartney's equation:

> If blacks were unable, due to discrimination, to obtain higher-paying jobs, then the productivity factors offered by the defendant are irrelevant. The statistician's response to this criticism should be to perform a multiple-

---

54. Gwartney et al. (1979) at 658; following in-text quotation also at 658; then indented quotation at 643.

regression analysis of the factors influencing job assignment. In such a regression equation, job assignment would be the dependent variable and various explanatory factors—both legitimate, such as appropriate measure of skill level, and impermissible, such as race—would be the dependent variables.[55]

Barnes does not specify how he would construct a "job-assignment" regression. What would the observations be? Surely not the work force as it is. Assignments are made when there are openings. People may be in an inappropriate position through no bias on the part of the company, because of what jobs were available when they applied, or because of the job they applied to, perhaps underrating their own skills. Barnes is inappropriately advocating a situation analysis for an events complaint.

If viewed as an assignment case, *James* called for a multiple-pools test, defining pools by sources that could have fed each job, not just the sources that did. Aside from the implication that Gwartney should have approached this as an assignment case, there is nothing correct about Barnes' view. Barnes would analyze assignments from observations only on those who got them, not those who competed for them. Yet Barnes' book purports to be an instructional text "designed to help the practicing attorney present simple factual arguments in a mathematical form familiar to courts."[56] Simple is good. Relevant would be good, too.

THE CROW TRIBE AND THE STATE OF MONTANA

Montana taxes the separation of coal from the ground. On behalf of plaintiffs the Crow Tribe, National Economic Research Associates, Inc. (NERA) presented a report alleging, among other issues, that Montana's separation tax of 1979 made their coal non-competitive.[57] The Crow Tribe had leased land to Westmoreland Coal Company, on which Westmoreland opened the Absoloka Mine. Westmoreland paid Montana's separation tax, which reduced the payments they made to the Tribe. The Tribe then sued in federal court, arguing that the tax was unfairly high.

The effect of Montana's tax on coal sales takes up roughly a quarter of NERA's report, Section III and Attachment 1. NERA—in the persons of Mark Berkman and Fred Dunbar—compare the output of coal from Montana with that of Wyoming. From their regression study, the authors conclude that "Montana's coal taxes regulate the output of Crow coal." That is, the final price of coal produced by the Crow Tribe is dominated by Montana state taxes, so that output is "regulated" by the demand response to that price. My critique incorporated economics (modeling response to tax), legal concepts (what is "compliance" coal),

---

55. Barnes (1983) at 355.

56. Barnes (1983) at 1.

57. Mark Berkman and Fred C. Dunbar, "Expert Witness Report," corrected version, dated January 6, 1984, in *Crow II*.

and criticism of NERA's statistics methodology.[58] What my critique did not say, but I will here, is that regression was an inappropriate tool for the question NERA proposed to answer.

Faulty Conception

In Figure 30 I show Montana compliance and noncompliance coal sales, along with Wyoming noncompliance coal sales and coal sales from Utah and Colorado, over time.[59] Montana does not seem to fare badly and, particularly, nothing untoward happens to Montana, vis-à-vis these other data series, in 1975 or thereafter. It is obvious from Figure 30 that Montana's 1975 severance tax had no effect on Montana's coal sales. Even NERA's data showed that the price increased by only half of the tax; the other half was absorbed by producers and distributors. The tax might have had some effect on long-term sales, but it requires a model of the anticipated future tax, as seen by purchasers, to draw such a conclusion. NERA did not study that question, and does not say that it did.

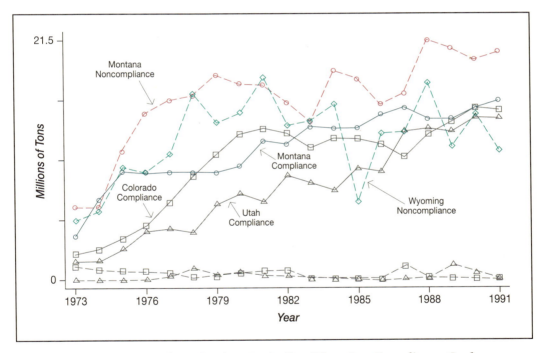

FIGURE 30: Coal Production, Excluding Wyoming Compliance Coal

---

58. Stephan Michelson, "The NERA Statistical Analysis: A Critical Review," June 10, 1993, in *Crow III*. "Compliance" refers to the sulfur content of coal, which is regulated by the Clean Air Act of 1970. Because not all plants operate under the same rules, one cannot actually know what is "compliance" coal from the chemical composition of the coal alone. I use the standard definition of "compliance," coal that will generate no more than 1.2 pounds. of SO_2 per million BTU. The Absoloka Mine produced noncompliance coal.

59. The two unlabeled lines in Figure 30 are noncompliance sales from Colorado and Utah.

Berkman and Dunbar did not show such a multi-state comparison. They presented no data from states other than Montana and Wyoming.[60] Nor did they study noncompliance coal sales.

I omitted Wyoming compliance coal sales in Figure 30. Wyoming sales grew so large that the scale would obscure year-to-year production variation in other states. In Figure 31 I show all coal sales from Wyoming and Montana. The oddball, the phenomenon to be explained, is the increase in Wyoming's compliance coal sales, not a reduction in Montana's coal sales.

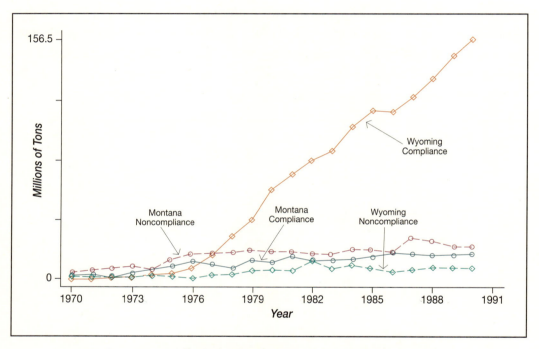

FIGURE 31: All Coal Sales from Montana and Wyoming

"Time" As an Explanatory Factor

The data NERA used, and NERA's estimates thereof, are contained in Figure 32. NERA tried to formulate a regression equation that would "explain" Wyoming and Montana coal sales over time. In Figures 30 through 32, the diamonds represent Wyoming's annual coal sales;

---

60. Selection of data to make an expert's point has a long history. For example, Peter Max, estimating damages due to his client, developed a formula that included the percentage of gross sales that became profits. In evaluation, he then used the 1946 figure of 19.81 percent,

> by all odds the highest ratio of profits to sales ever experienced by Schwabe . . . and nearly six times the average, 3.3%, during the years 1954–1959, for which damages were being computed.

Schwabe (1962) at 912. Max's evidence was rejected, as Berkman-Dunbar's should have been.

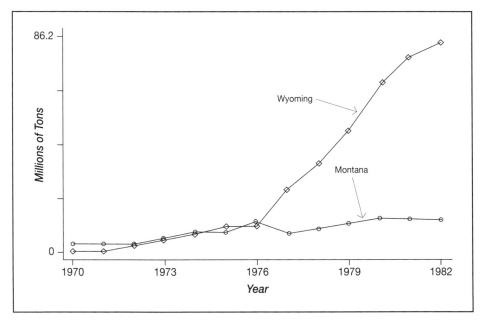

FIGURE 32: NERA's Regression Estimates of Wyoming and Montana Coal Sales

the circles, Montana's. The data and their estimates are points. I have connected them with lines to clarify the trends at issue in this case.

NERA's estimating equation was:

$$\ln\left(\frac{MS}{WS}\right) = 0.12071 - 0.91707\left((T_{M(t-2)} - T_{W(t-2)}) \times t\right)$$

where ln means natural logarithm, MS and WS are Montana and Wyoming shares of their combined total coal sales (in the Powder River Basin only), T represents taxes, t represents time and the subscript t−2 indicates a two-year lag (coal shipments respond to taxes in effect two years earlier).

The ratio of shares equals the ratio of tons:

$$\ln\left(\frac{MS}{WS}\right) = \ln\left(\frac{MO}{WO}\right)$$

where "O" indicates output, tonnage. I used NERA's equation to estimate the ratio, and then calculated what each state's tonnage would be, given the total.

Although the dependent variable was constructed from two states, NERA attempted to assign to Montana (in its tax rate or anything else) all credit (or blame) for whatever occurred between them. It would be like adding the heights of two children (although there were four or more children in the family), calculating each child's "share" of their total inches, and then assigning to one child the responsibility for his declining share of this total. Could it be that the other child had a growth spurt while the blamed child grew perfectly well on his own?

I will spend some space on this example because its source is unusual (not employ-ment discrimination, not antitrust, not product liability) and because there are so many lessons to draw from it. There are even more, in the appendix to this chapter. One lesson is that client-oriented experts made no attempt to ask what was happening, what real-world events generated the data. They attempted only to develop a statistical presentation that supported their client. However, looking closely, one can see that they failed even at that. Therefore another lesson is about the failure of the court to ask elementary questions, to figure out that Crow's experts had produced a classic example of junk science.

Interpretation

Berkman and Dunbar's independent variable is a tax difference multiplied by time. The operating force in this equation is time. The small effect of the tax difference created error in estimates for just those years of greatest concern, 1975 through 1977. Nor does NERA's discussion lead to a hypothesis that one would see the reaction to taxes two years later.

> Taxes increase price which in turn reduces demand and production. Histori-cal coal production trends support this theory. Montana's slow coal produc-tion growth since the imposition of the coal taxes is explained in large part by the tax.[61]

Actually, the 1975 tax explains *none* of the relatively slow growth of Montana coal sales in the late 1970s.

The tax and time data that NERA used to predict outputs are contained in Figure 33. "Tax Difference" is the Montana tax rate less the Wyoming tax rate. One might consider that the difference in tax rates between Montana and Wyoming was essentially constant in 1971 and 1972, and then again from 1975 through 1982. Or, avoiding such a judgment, one can surely say that the difference in tax rates was constant from 1977 through 1982 (from NERA's data). Apparently NERA believed that demand is instantaneous, but supply reacts two years late. This is almost equivalent to saying that Montana and Wyoming coal are sold predominantly on the spot market.[62] That is not true today, and was not true in the 1970s.[63]

---

61. NERA report at vii, figure reference omitted.

62. Most long-term contracts allow purchases above a minimum tonnage at a predetermined price (plus taxes). The purchaser can also obtain coal in the spot market. I call the combination of spot and above-minimum purchases the "short-term" market. As Montana coal was cheaper, at the mine mouth, than Wyoming's, a higher Montana tax *rate* did not necessarily produce more tax cost, to the purchaser, per ton.

63. From Federal Energy Regulatory Commission reports of public-utility coal purchases I get the fol-lowing amounts, in millions of tons:

	Montana Tax Rate	Wyoming Tax Rate	Tax Difference	Time
1970	0.069	0.066	0.003	1
1971	0.089	0.066	0.023	2
1972	0.086	0.066	0.020	3
1973	0.153	0.088	0.065	4
1974	0.142	0.148	−0.006	5
1975	0.329	0.152	0.177	6
1976	0.329	0.156	0.173	7
1977	0.329	0.161	0.168	8
1978	0.329	0.161	0.168	9
1979	0.329	0.161	0.168	10
1980	0.329	0.161	0.168	11
1981	0.329	0.161	0.168	12
1982	0.329	0.161	0.168	13

FIGURE 33: Independent Variables in NERA's Regression

Until 1975 there were fast-changing small and large tax differences. It is difficult to believe that coal supply reacts to changes in demand two years earlier. It is statistically impossible to measure the reaction of coal mines to changes in tax differences when the tax difference does not change.

Montana Coal Production

That Montana coal sales are not sensitive to Montana's tax rate—that NERA's relationship is idiosyncratic, dominated by the time variable, and not a description of the structure of the coal market—can be seen by extending the data and NERA's equation over time. I do that in Figure 34.

Asking whether an expert's equation predicts data outside the estimation period is common in antitrust litigation.[64] It should be clear from Figure 34 that NERA's equation is just an arithmetic fit to numbers, not an estimate of a real-world structure.[65]

Year	Montana	Percent Spot	Wyoming	Percent Spot
1973	10.315	3.13	13.113	5.08
1975	21.077	3.32	21.608	3.39
1978	26.009	0.83	53.464	6.14

64. See, for example, F. Fisher (1986), graphs at 283–284.

65. That the taxes change in fiscal years, and production data cover calendar years, makes accurate tracking from one to the other impossible. NERA seems not to have noticed this incomparability in its data.

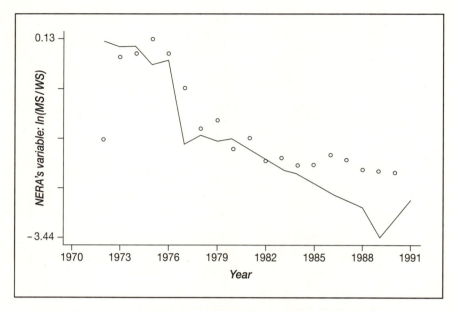

FIGURE 34: Projecting NERA's Equation to Later Data

The astute reader has spotted a problem with NERA's dependent variable: It is the log-arithm of a ratio. The ratio ties Montana and Wyoming sales together. In interpreting their regression, NERA says the result is a Montana tax influencing Montana sales. In fact, tax has nothing to do with their fit.

Note that

$$\ln\left(\frac{\text{MO}}{\text{WO}}\right) = \ln(\text{MO}) - \ln(\text{WO})$$

Berkman and Dunbar could easily have done what I did in *Hobson II*, put the denomina-tor on the right side of the equation. The key reason why one does not want a regression's dependent variable to be a ratio is that you don't know if it is the numerator or the denom-inator creating the variation that is estimated by the independent variables. By adding $\ln(\text{WO})$ to both sides of the equation—placing Wyoming's sales on the right side—we can estimate Montana sales. We ask if, as one might infer from Figure 31, Montana and Wyo-ming are simply on different growth paths in their coal production.

I could "explain" Montana's sales from Wyoming's sales, and when I did so, NERA's tax/time variable had no impact. Of course Montana sales were not *caused by* Wyoming's sales. I just as easily estimated Wyoming's sales from Montana's. These demonstrations are commonly employed to show that two outputs are responding to the same influences, albeit differently. NERA's theory is that the sum of the two states' sales will have a common explanation, and taxes explain the distribution between them. A better theory is that both states' sales are influenced by the same factors, except that something created a higher rate of growth of sales of compliance coal in Wyoming. The "share" of one is just an arti-fact of adding the two states together. The difference between the two states, whatever determines the higher sales and faster growth in Wyoming, was not changing over this time period in any way measured by NERA's variables. Whatever was "regulating" Montana's coal production was neither time nor taxes. The NERA regression is incompetent at the level of defining their dependent variable. Their interpretation is nonsense.

The Outcome of the Crow Coal Litigation

My report is dated nine years after NERA's. At the original trial, Montana presented no statistical expert to rebut NERA's study. The state's attorneys may have correctly assessed NERA's study as absurd, but they did not correctly anticipate the Ninth Circuit Court of Appeals' reaction to it. Attorneys who believe that courts will listen to their rebuttal of a statistical expert are playing with fire. Montana got burned.[66]

NERA's thesis (that greater growth in Wyoming compliance coal sales was due to Montana's tax) was the sole basis on which the court determined that Montana's tax had "cost" the Crow Tribe coal sales it otherwise would have had. In dictum in another case, in which it upheld the right of a state to tax coal severance from Indian lands, the Supreme Court alluded to how large Montana's tax had been as the reason Montana's tax had been declared invalid.[67] NERA had seemed to prove that this high tax had the consequence of reducing Crow's coal sales, so that by the time it reached the Supreme Court the proposition was accepted essentially without further review. As described later by that Court,

> Montana's taxes were "extraordinarily high" and the Ninth Circuit [recognized] that "the state taxes had a negative effect on the marketability of coal produced in Montana."[68]

---

66. Although Kaye (2003) thinks little of expert Richard Leftwich's regression analysis in *Conwood* (2000), he fails to note that defendant United States Tobacco, which "thoroughly cross-examined Leftwich about his opinions and theories" (at *6), apparently also offered no expert in rebuttal. Defendant's expert offered alternative regressions in the liability phase of the trial. Leftwich claimed to have employed all variables suggested by Tobacco's expert in his estimate of damages. See *Conwood* (2002) at 793. Kaye cites an *amicus* brief by several prominent statisticians and economists, submitted to but presumably not read by the Supreme Court (which did not grant *certiorari*), as support for his position that Leftwich's regression analysis was flawed. He (and they) may well be correct, but they write from an academic perspective. Like New Jersey's expert in *Soto* (1996), whom we will meet in Chapter 8, United States Tobacco's expert apparently offered no testimony directly confronting Leftwich's model, directly countering Leftwich's claim to have incorporated his suggestions.

Most important, United States Tobacco, arguing that it did not violate antitrust laws, was left without an alternative damages calculation. Once the jurors determined that throwing out Conwood's displays, moving their stock to United States Tobacco's displays (and other vandalous acts) were antitrust violations, they had only Leftwich's regressions to guide them in determining a monetary award. That was United States Tobacco's—their attorneys'—mistake; one that Montana, in the round of *Crow* in which I was engaged, did not make.

67. See *Cotton* (1989).

68. *Crow IV* (1998) at 715, quoting *Cotton* (1989) at 186, footnote 17.

The Supreme Court accurately summarized the Ninth Circuit's conclusion. Unfortunately, the Ninth Circuit had been snookered. NERA could be satisfied that they had served their client, even though they did not serve the judicial system's pursuit of the truth.[69]

Restitution

The facts never were analyzed correctly. First, let us look, in Figure 35, at the components of the spot price (yearly averages) of coal. The light patch in the middle of each bar, the state's tax, is a very small part of the final price of coal. It could still be that tax determined the distribution in sales among states, if its variation were large. In fact, compared with the mine-mouth price and the freight cost of coal, taxes are both small and invariant.

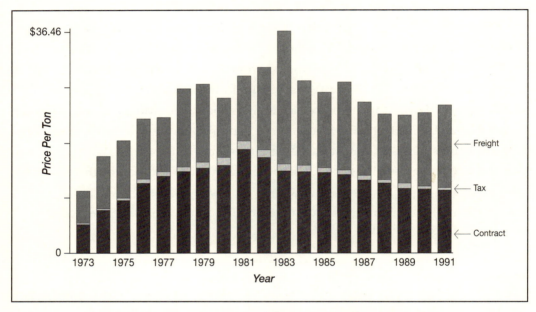

FIGURE 35: Components of the Delivered Price of Coal

---

69. Montana's attorneys question my assertion that the Ninth Circuit credited NERA's regression analysis. It did reject the district court's conclusion that transportation costs were predominant considerations in the marketability of Westmoreland's coal. *Crow II* (1987) at 900. It further reasoned that

> the taxes imposed are the components that differ most clearly between Montana and Wyoming,

and that

> The timing of the loss in coal production in Montana and the losses sustained by the Crow Tribe correspond exactly with the imposition of the taxes.

There was, of course, no "loss in coal production in Montana." From Figure 32 one can discern that Montana production exceeded Wyoming's in 1976. NERA's two-year lag was required to align the increase in tax rate with Wyoming's growth spurt. Montana's compliance and noncompliance coal

What about freight? NERA never considered any factor other than the tax to estimate Montana's "share" of the combined coal shipments. In Chapter 8 I reproduce well-deserved disparaging remarks by judges faced with analyses that allow no alternatives. That view should have applied in this case. These simple elements—the components of the delivered price and some coal chemistry—would lead one to ask if something besides taxes changed in 1977.

Something did change. Burlington Northern opened a new rail line near where Wyoming compliance coal was mined. Getting Wyoming coal to market became much less expensive. In Figure 35 we can understand that a large change in taxes will have a small effect on sales, but a small change in freight rates could have a large impact, tempered by the length of existing contracts. It is because Wyoming suddenly had a freight-rate advantage that its shipments soared. Had NERA looked for explanations of the surge in Wyoming's compliance coal sales, it might have found one, but not the one their clients needed to support their case.

The district court, in an unpublished opinion, decided that it was bound by the Ninth Circuit's 1987 determination that the severance tax

> burdened the Tribe's economic interests by increasing the costs of production by coal producers, which reduced royalties received by the Tribe.[70]

It determined, however, that whatever the precise impact of the tax on the Absoloka Mine's sales, the equities of the situation did not justify allowing the Tribe to recoup Westmoreland's tax payments. As the Supreme Court's final opinion reversed the circuit court's reversal of the district court, we can take this non-decision as the judicial system's penultimate word (lacking, still, a settlement and final order).

Why did the Crow Tribe never sell compliance coal? I do not know enough to provide a definitive answer. The Tribe at one time had a contract with Shell to open a compliance mine, but Shell extricated itself from that arrangement.[71] I believe the Crow Tribe failed to sell compliance coal because no coal company wanted to deal with them. They preferred to sue rather than improve their business skills.

---

production each increased in absolute terms over the period between 1975 and the time of the 1984 trial, the evidence from which was reviewed in the 1987 Ninth Circuit decision. The court of appeals ultimately tried to save face with the holding that

> Montana has failed to rebut that the taxes had at least some negative impact on the coal's marketability.

70. *Crow II* (1987), 819 F.2d at 899.

71. *Crow IV* (1996) at 831:

> Shell officials were concerned about internal conflicts among the Tribe's leaders and disputes as to who had authority to represent the Tribe in negotiations with Shell.

A Relevant Analysis

Crow coal should have been analyzed as a multiple-pools-selection issue. The spot market was and is trivial. Most of the variation in demand occurs within long-term contracts. We can characterize the selling of coal as the selection of a vendor (a mine) by a public utility. The utility has made a decision about what kind of boiler to build, looking at the market as a whole. It now needs gas, compliance coal or noncompliance coal, whatever its boiler requires. It will take bids from potential vendors. It will select one based on measurable characteristics such as mode (or modes) of transport, mine-mouth cost, transport cost, taxes, coal chemistry, ability of the mine to produce the quantity likely to be demanded, etc.

One can assume that all producers of compliance coal, actual or potential, "compete" for each contract. They form a pool of competitors, each one with its bundle of characteristics. If Crow's complaint was that their compliance mine did not open because of the tax, we would have to consider theirs *and other* not-opened mines as potential suppliers. We would have had to construct data on transport mode and cost from mines—Crow's and others—some of which did not (or did not yet) exist. Although the data would have been attacked as "speculative," modeling the long-term-contract decision would have been the only way to assess the effect on sales, if any, of variation in taxes. I discussed this approach with coal experts, and I believe that credible data could have been constructed.

The unit would be the contract. Those contracts had to be made, just as when there is an employment opening, someone will get the job. Given the frequency of tax changes, we would have had to construct an "expected tax" which could be highly influenced by current tax. As the analysis was being made years later, we might have used as the expected future tax, in one pass, an average actual tax over the life of the contract, as if the utilities were omniscient. Interviews with public-utility executives might have gleaned a convincing way to estimate future taxes as future costs. Unfortunately for such a project—and more so for NERA's theory—most state regulatory agencies allow taxes to be passed through to consumers as rate changes. Thus although utilities are obligated to minimize cost, they are not asked to anticipate future tax legislation in the state from which they purchase coal.

A pool of competitors would be formed for each contract that occurred, and the winner identified. Using multivariate multiple-pools methods, as outlined in Chapter 2, we would estimate the impact of different characteristics on selection, based on the actual contract-winners compared with the contract-losers. Each potential supplier would have a tax rate as a data element, and that tax either would or would not be seen to be important in selection. Where NERA's analysis tells us nothing, because time is the only variable that is related to output, the selection analysis would not have a time variable. Each pool would contain data relevant at its time—such as the tax rates when the contract was made—but time itself, which so confuses the NERA analysis, would not be an explicit variable. With our parameter estimates in hand, we would substitute lower tax rates for Montana's, to determine which contracts would have been located differently, if any; to estimate how much more coal would have been sold from Montana had its taxes been lower.

There was no issue in this case amenable to regression analysis. Either Berkman and Dunbar knew that their regression was inappropriate, in which case they were deliberately producing a faulty analysis for the benefit of their clients; or they did not, in which case they were incompetent.

PROMOTION AND SALARIES AT I-NET

I introduced some of Mark Killingsworth's sense of what one could learn from cross-section data earlier in this chapter. He concluded that females did not have "equal access" to high-level jobs in a firm because few females were seen there. The firm was named I-NET. It was purchased by Wang during its struggles with the Office of Federal Contract Compliance Programs (OFCCP), leaving me with an attorney story to tell in Chapter 6. The story for this chapter is Killingsworth's view of how to perform salary regressions to ask equal-employment-opportunity questions.

The Single-Regression Equation

At one time the OFCCP and I-NET had signed a conciliation agreement, I-NET promising to pay females and minorities fairly. In their compliance review, the OFCCP had divided the firm by job group. It calculated some mean salaries and concluded that females were underpaid. The females were in lower grades, with lower pay, but unfairly so? I was engaged by Anita Barondes of Seyfarth, Shaw, Fairweather and Geraldson in September 1993. I wrote a scathing report, excoriating the OFCCP for such a flimsy "analysis." Then they engaged Killingsworth.

Abandoning their more relevant job-group approach, the OFCCP apparently instructed Killingsworth to analyze by grade—but not all grades. In his report to the OFCCP Killingsworth complies:

> I have now analyzed the I-NET data for employees in grades E-01 through E-04, E-08, E-09, and E-13.[72]

There is no explanation for this selection of grades. Except at grade 12, lack of observations could not be the reason: There were 291 employees in grades 5 through 7. Grade 11 contained only white males, some of whom were in job groups containing females at lower

---

72. Killingsworth's report was undoubtedly dated, but that information was deleted from the copy provided to me, by fax, on January 13, 1997, the same day it was received by Seyfarth, Shaw. At 1.

grades. They were legitimate grist for an analyst's mill, but could not be included in Kill-ingsworth's analysis as he structured it.

He reported results his clients surely liked:

> Women and nonwhite men are paid substantially less than white men who are the same in terms of seniority and a great number of other pay-related back-ground characteristics (educational attainment, prior work experience, mili-tary service, etc.) *and* are in the same pay grade. This difference is statistically significant at conventional test levels for women; for nonwhite men, the sta-tistical significance of this difference is somewhat weaker.[73]

These results are incorrect. They come from a sloppy, mechanical approach to regres-sion in which the analyst just throws variables at the problem.[74] In particular, Killings-worth's results come first from the biased selection of those grades in which, the OFCCP had already determined, females and minorities appeared to fare badly; second, from not under-standing that the basic unit of the firm was the job group; and third, from not understand-ing what his results mean. Persons in the same grade, in different job groups, performed different work. They were not "the same" in any way a court should accept as formulating a legitimate comparison. Persons in different grades but in the same job group were doing in many ways the same work, at different levels. They could be compared, the constituents of their pay estimated by regression. Whether grade should be "held constant," would best be answered by an events analysis to determine if there was gender bias in the attainment of grade. If attainment of grade was not challenged, which seemed to be the OFCCP's posi-tion, then grade should have been allowed as an explanation of salary, within job group.

The same six job groups that appear in grade 4 appear in the omitted grades 5, 6, and 7. Three of them continue to grade 8, two to grade 9, and one to grade 10. Killingsworth's

---

73. Same Killingsworth transmission to the OFCCP, also at 1. This is Killingsworth's finding 3. The first presents a simple comparison of means; the second controls for some characteristics, but not grade.

74. This approach was Killingsworth's trademark. In *Greenspan* (1980), as noted above, he had estimated salaries—as here, across non-comparable job groups—using 128 variables. In *Melani* (1983) at 774:

> The regression analyses in plaintiffs' Study II included as many as 98 independent variables.

Do experts tell judges to think that the more variables, the finer the control? Consider this précis of Fred Dunbar's testimony in a bankruptcy case, referring to a study by Timothy Wyant:

> [Wyant] used, at best, nine parameters whereas NERA uses 70 for a small producer and 2,500 for producers with a number of occupations. Because he used so many more parameters, he was able to account for things like, age, jurisdiction and occupation that Dr. Wyant's model did not consider.

Combustion (2003) at 487. I make no judgment about the studies in this case, but the argument is fal-lacious. Some variables may "account" for what they claim to, and others might introduce spurious asso-ciations that corrupt the entire estimate, as happened in *I-NET*. Thinking that "more variables" equals "better study" might come from an introductory statistics course. Judges need help, but not that kind.

approach systematically deprives us of the opportunity to see people moving up the lines of progression. In the post-*Daubert* world one would hope that a judge would exclude this study because grade selection emasculates the very relationship—salary success by grade increase within job group—Killingsworth should be estimating. The OFCCP imposed the grade selectivity I suggested, above, that a smart defendant would argue against. I also suggested that an expert should see the fallacy under which the OFCCP was operating.

Third, Killingsworth's conclusion comes from an assumed homogeneity of effect of seniority, when that effect differs by grade and job group. This homogeneity assumption— that whatever the job group, whatever the grade, one additional year at the firm should increase one's salary by the same proportion—would still have ruined Killingsworth's regression even if he had used data from all grades.

To understand the homogeneity fallacy in these data, let's take Killingsworth on his own terms—analyzing the mandated grades, ignoring job group—and ask if he even looked within grade adequately. Using seniority variables, but not interacting them with grade, Killingsworth asked that salary in every grade have the same relationship with time at I-NET; and, as we will see, a very peculiar relationship. Constraining his estimating equation this way, Killingsworth forced other variables to pick up salary differences that are in fact due to persons being in different grades.

When discussing litigation in academic circles, Killingsworth has noted:

> In employment-discrimination cases as in other kinds of litigation, rival economists present analyses that lawyers (and even other economists) regard as dauntingly technical and esoteric. Each side's lawyers then praise their own economist's analyses and cite what they view as fatal flaws in the other's work. Only rarely do they attempt to show that the alleged flaws actually explain why the results diverge.[75]

I take this as a worthy aspiration for the analysis that follows.

We have seen that economists think that education and seniority *should* have a positive relationship with salary. They expect this relationship from logic and empirical results when the observations are *among* firms. Within a firm, when analyzing discrimination, having "similar" characteristics means having similar relevant characteristics. If education is not a requirement for—or at least a valid predictor of performance in—the position, then all levels of education are "similar," because "fact" is a legal as well as empirical concept.

The law asks only that everyone be treated like others similarly situated, which means that within job groups (lines of similar work), hiring, placement, promotion, and pay should be indistinguishable among persons with similar characteristics. There is no re-

---

75. Killingsworth (1993) at 71. These remarks would have been applicable, for example, to Richard Freeman's work in *McCarthy* (1983), as described above.

quirement, and there should be no expectation, that the rate of advancement in one job group is the same as in another—that a member of the clerical staff would advance as rapidly, for example, as a member of the financial staff into executive positions with executive pay; that a machine operator would see the same proportionate annual pay increases as a systems programmer.

As his other litigation work demonstrates, Killingsworth was unaware of the homogeneity problem. Killingsworth assumes he has "controlled" for grade by adding variables into a single equation. If we are going to proceed with only certain grades, knowing that they span different skills, we should ask whether we can combine them into a single regression before doing so. Here, in one graph, is why his approach is an estimation disaster. In Figure 36 I show the relationship between salary and seniority in each grade, as well as in a combined regression.[76] The small numbers along the horizontal axis are years of seniority. No employee in Killingsworth's data had more than seven years of seniority. We are looking at the partial relationships, the relationship between seniority and salary given a statistical equality in other variables.

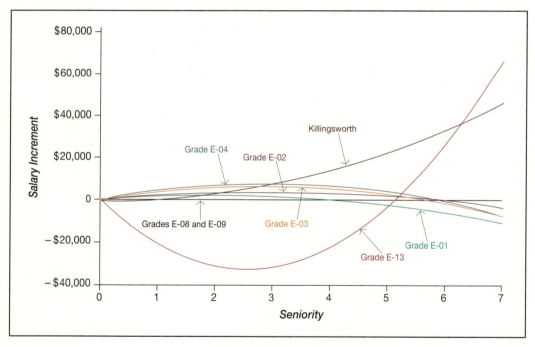

FIGURE 36: Indexed Salary by Grade at I-NET

---

76. Killingsworth's dependent variable was the logarithm of salary. I use seniority and seniority-squared as variables explaining salary. Thus what I report as "Killingsworth" is in fact my replication of his equation in my form. There is no essential difference—I found what he found—except that I can relate my equation to dollars, a decided advantage in litigation, I think.

The salaries in Figure 36 are indexed. They are set equal at the far left, just as one might compare two stock-market securities for differential price increases over time. The scale of the vertical axis is dollars. The plotted lines indicate increase or decrease in salary, from their initial values at zero seniority, "due to" seniority, measured on the horizontal axis.

Because it might be confusing to see just what the "Grades E-08 and E-09" label is pointing at, I start with it. There is *no* relationship between seniority and salary at those two grades. The arrow is pointing at the horizontal axis, at a picture of zero relationship.

There is an interesting consistency in the four bottom grades. Salary rises, then falls with seniority. Falls? Not for most individuals. This is a cross-section view: We are observing different people at each seniority level and grade. Only the losers—those who have not been promoted to a higher grade—remain in a lower grade with high seniority. Their salary has not gone down, but their average salary is lower than those in the middle—different people—some of whom will soon be promoted up. At I-NET one should want to be promoted out of each of the bottom four grades before achieving four years of seniority. Most people are, but at different rates depending on their job group.

Were promotions "fair"? I do not know. One cannot ask that question from these data. Promotion was worthy of an events analysis, but Killingsworth did not perform one. In a post-*Daubert* world, he should not be allowed to make any comment about females being unable to attain high grade. That is a statement about events he has not studied.

Grade 13 contains an entirely different relationship between seniority and salary from that in the lower grades. Surely a spurious one. We can see that it is spurious in the decline in salary from zero years. It takes five years to climb back to one's starting salary at this grade. This is not a very likely description of the reward for seniority. It simply describes these people. Grade 13, containing twenty-six males and two females, is the entire job group "officials and managers." Where salaries increase in other job groups by moving up in grade, salary in this job group is determined without regard to grade. These salaries are assumed, by Killingsworth, to have the same relationship to seniority—different by only a constant (or a constant percentage)—as the engineers in grades 2 through 4, or the technical-professionals in grades 1 through 4.

Because of the spurious grade-13 relationship, and Killingsworth's assumption that additional seniority will generate the same proportionate salary increases in all grades and job groups, his multi-grade regression expects high-seniority employees in every grade to be very highly paid, relative to their grade-level peers. We know that exactly the opposite relationship holds. We know why it holds, that pay increases at lower grades come with advancement to a higher grade. Employees at grade 13 have no higher grade to be promoted into. Killingsworth's "control" for grade by dummy variables fails because the relationship between seniority and salary is not homogeneous among grades. His constraining the equation to find one shape for that relationship over all grades creates a space for other variables to "explain" variance that seniority, if correctly specified, would explain.

If the highest-seniority employees in the lower grades are females—which they are—then the regression will attach a large negative value to being female. The regression algorithm relates the variable "female" with the lower salaries that, as we see in Figure 36, are reasonable for the grades most females occupy. Killingsworth then reports that gender explains salary. Killingsworth's expectation that employees in grades 1 through 4 as well as grades 8 and 9 would be paid "like" those in grade 13—of course at a lower level, but "like" in having the same relationship to seniority—has led him to a clearly erroneous result.[77]

"Clearly erroneous" is a legal term, the basis on which an appeals court can overturn a district court's finding of fact. Would an administrative law judge have found for the OFCCP?[78] If so, would a higher court have reversed? To know that would have required that I-NET's attorneys understood the issue and pursued their defense. They did not. That is the story of Chapter 6.

Influential Observations

It is reasonable to ask why the grade-13 relationship would so influence the regression coefficients, for surely there are more employees in the lower grades. Indeed, there were 539 employees in grades 1 through 4 and 8 through 9. How could the twenty-eight at grade 13 so dominate the relationship between salary and seniority, to so pervert the finding of a combined-grade regression? The answer is that the salaries for the high-seniority employees in grade 13 were so out of line with the salaries of persons in the other grades that the data points from grade 13 have a high "influence" on the regression slope. It is easy enough to understand why.

Ignore for now the quadratic term, seniority-squared. Assume we are estimating a straight-line relationship between individual salaries and seniority. You have an X-Y-axis system in front of you, with a scatter of points. Now hold a pencil at its middle, with two fingers. Place your fingers, and therefore the pencil, at the point made by the intersection of mean salary and mean seniority. You are now allowed only to twist the pencil, not move it up or down, to "fit" the data. The pencil must touch the point defined by the mean of salary and the mean of seniority.

Error is the vertical distance between the regression line and each data point. Remem-

---

77. In a short note in *Science*, Leroy Wolins suggested that if there is a male/female difference in salaries, one ought to be able to see it in an appropriate graph of the data. Even today there is an appalling lack of the use of visual information to ask if the numbers appear to make sense. Killingsworth could have used that advice. See Wolins (1978).

78. With I-NET, as in *Harris Bank*, to be reviewed below, the "lower court" is an administrative law judge. My experience with these judges has been positive. I have no reason to believe an administrative law judge would be seduced by a Killingsworth-type analysis, if the fallacies were explained to him.

ber, we are minimizing the square of error, which means that large errors get very large, and therefore are to be avoided in twisting the pencil to fit the data.

Data points near the mean of the variable on the horizontal axis—here seniority—no matter how many there are, have very little influence on the slope of the regression line. Those points affect the height at which you placed your pencil—the equation constant—but not the slope. Salaries at high or low seniority will "influence" how you twist the pencil.[79] Thus the high salaries held by employees who happen to have high seniority, in grade 13, dominate the seniority coefficients. To fail to estimate them would create large errors—differences between salary and estimated salary. No other variable explains them, so they are related to seniority. The now seemingly low salaries of females with high seniority in lower grades then becomes "explained" by their gender. The error is not in the mathematics of regression, it is in the analyst's structuring of the equation.

The highest-seniority person in the data set is a female at grade 2 with average (for that grade) pay. In grade 9—which contains two job groups with quite different salary structures—the highest-seniority person, paid well among those in the lower-paid group, is a female. These points—high pay, high seniority in grade 13, and "low" pay, high seniority in lower grades—are highly influential. The former generate the seniority-salary relationship that Killingsworth found; the latter, the gender-salary relationship. Both relationships are incorrect.

To maintain as much consistency as possible with the OFCCP's approach, I formulated a general model, and then fine-tuned it for each grade. There is a danger that in creating a different equation for each grade one might be fitting error, not generality. Even though all of this is wrong, the regressions should be by job group with variables for grade, I was careful to make salaries in adjacent grades be based on similar factors. My by-grade regression results are presented in Figure 37.[80] A version of the equations estimated in Figure 37 that always included seniority variables generated the loci of Figure 36.

At each grade, and in all grades aggregated over the company, there is no gender-related salary differential to be found. The variables are pretty much the same in each grade, except that seniority plays no role in determining salary at grades 8, 9, and 13. Entry

---

79. The highest-paid employee—the owners have been excluded from these regressions—is a technical manager at grade 9. In general, persons at grade 13 have high salaries, but this person's salary towers above theirs. The OFCCP surely has a right to ask on what basis he is paid, but Killingsworth should have dropped him from regressions whose purpose was to estimate ordinary gender-pay relationships. He has average seniority, and therefore does not affect the seniority-salary relationship. But he is a male, and therefore does affect the estimated gender-salary relationship. See the discussion of "outlier analysis" in *Penk* (1985) at *49.

80. The variables in each equation, other than "Female," are cryptically indicated. "Logist" is logistician, "prog" is programmer, and "progsr" is senior programmer. Other job titles should be obvious: "ntrysal" is salary upon hire, and "entry_n" indicates if the employee's first job at I-NET was non-exempt.

Grade	N	Female	t-stat	Other Variables	Adjusted R^2
1	50	445.36	0.45	sen, sen2, prog, logist, priorsal, ntrysal, entry_n	0.620
2	126	236.46	0.35	sen, sen2, engineer, priorsal, ntrysal, entry_n	0.213
3	204	−1,147.22	−1.25	sen, sen2, system, prog priorsal, ntrysal, entry_n'	0.438
4	132	−753.15	−0.62	sen, sen2, engineer, network, ntrysal	0.421
5	117	−1,455.89	−1.01	sen, sen2, progsr	0.272
6	73	1,675.99	0.76	sen, sen2, admin, engineer, analyst, system	0.308
7	101	722.69	0.24	sen, sen2	0.082
8	12	−4,001.20	−0.98	(no control variables)	−0.004
9	15	2,081.64	0.21	sectese, priorsal, ntrysal	0.824
10	24	3,877.75	0.70	sen, dirman	0.097
13	28	2,998.04	0.23	vp, ntrysal	0.043
All Grades	882	4,680.46	0.26		

FIGURE 37: Variables and Results from Separate I-NET Regressions by Grade

salary and being a vice-president seem to matter, but (from the R^2 column on the right) we cannot really explain salaries at grade 13 at all. (I dropped seniority from that grade's regression not because it was not "significant," but because it was nonsense.) Killingsworth thinks that he "controls" for differences in function, in relationship between seniority and pay, by adding variables to his equation. It just doesn't work that way.

Summary Statistics

Before we leave this sad affair, we should not let me "divide and conquer," a traditional defendant's technique. It is often proper to divide a firm into units of comparable people, whose salaries should grow without relationship to gender or race, but with different relationships to prior experience, education, time at the company, and time in grade. However, it is then an analyst's obligation to recombine the results, to present one set of summary statistics.

Here are some measures of variance explained (R^2):

Adjusted R^2 Killingsworth   0.279

Adjusted R^2 Michelson, K's grades   0.516

Adjusted R^2 Michelson, all grades   0.406

Had I not "explained" so much more variation than Killingsworth, my theoretical objections to his work would have had no practical import. The difference between his R^2 and mine, over the same grades, is a measure of the distortion he created in not accounting for non-homogeneity of the effects of variables across grades.

Adding to the study the grades that Killingsworth had omitted (shaded in Figure 37) reduced R^2. Additional observations bring their own variation with them. It is more difficult to explain salaries, by regression, in the grades Killingsworth omitted than in the grades he included. But this is a hopeless exercise to begin with. People increase in grade as a mechanism for increasing pay, within job groups. The data should have been organized by job group, not by grade.

I calculated a joint t-test, a firm-wide summary of differential pay. It is reported at the bottom of Figure 37. Over all the grades, females seem to earn slightly more than comparable males, but really we should interpret the difference as zero. Any difference from zero is well within the bounds of chance. The OFCCP was dead wrong. A competent and honest analyst would have told them so, although he probably never would have been engaged by them again.

GROUPED DATA

The first figure in this chapter showed a regression based on grouped data. Many data sources provide summary information from groups of individuals. Housing permits, for example, are counted by town. We can relate the number of permits to other town data. We might estimate housing permits by the number, average age, and income of residents in the town. Suppose we find that the higher the average resident's income, the more permits, holding size of town constant. Can we say that the higher one's income the more likely he is to build a home? That is a conclusion about individuals, whereas the data were groups of individuals.

Grouped data come with their own problems. First, there are data-definition issues. Much grouped data come from the U.S. Census, which in 2000, for the first time, allowed persons to be identified as of more than one race. There has always been an "other race" category in census data, but it has always been small. Many "other race" individuals in 1990 were Hispanics who answered the race question by writing "Hispanic" (or "Latino" or something else interpreted as Hispanic). Census took the information from the race question, used it to complete the Hispanic question, and called their race "other." In a strictly race analysis, we did not know if they were "white" Hispanics or "black" Hispanics; but they were counted correctly in an analysis of "minorities."

The 2000 U.S. Census is not reported as it was collected. Rather, data are collapsed into alternative race groups. To count blacks, one can select persons who said they were black only, or black in any combination with any other race. We do not know what combinations we are seeing, nor how comparable this collapse of the data is to earlier censuses. A lot of political pressure and arbitrary decisions led to this tepid conclusion from the fiery start of this decade's population count.

There is another problem with defining variables in grouped data, although to some extent this is just a problem of defining variables, not a problem of grouping observations. We have these large race categories, say non-black non-Hispanic, non-black Hispanic, and everyone else. All of our analysis occurs by these categories. Others, however, may occupy the same "niche" as those defined by a race variable, in some economic or behavioral sense. For example, when estimating driver's-license registration by race, using Connecticut towns as observations, I estimated that when one hundred Hispanics moved into a town (holding size of town constant, that is, displacing others) the number of licenses declined by more than one hundred. How could this be? Not everyone drives. The hundred people conceptually displaced by Hispanics did not have one hundred licenses to begin with. How can adding Hispanics take away licenses held by non-Hispanics?

The answer comes in a word we use to designate when we know that what we have measured is not a direct measure of the force that is operating: "proxy" variable. Others besides Hispanics occupy the same economic niche as many Hispanics in Connecticut: transient day-laborers. When we observe a same-size town with one hundred more Hispanics, there are other ethnic differences not measured by the Hispanic variable. There are more Haitians, more Ethiopians, more Middle-Easterners, perhaps more Southern whites —more people who also will have fewer driver's licenses. They work in the same jobs as Hispanics, live in the same places, and in these fundamental attributes are an uncounted "Hispanic" block. Our "Hispanic" measure is a proxy for the economic niche in which others, though they are not Hispanic, function in the same way as Hispanics. When we hold the town size constant but substitute one hundred Hispanics, we are implicitly substituting perhaps two hundred others who move with Hispanics for persons unlike them. It is from these three hundred or more Hispanic and other substitutions that we then find more than one hundred fewer driver's licenses.

This is another "validity" lesson: Be careful about accepting labels, the words we apply to numbers. The census question was, "Are you Hispanic?" and so applying the word "Hispanic" seems correct enough. But the effect of origin may not be what you are measuring. In the case of housing permits, the purchasers of the houses may not be current town residents. They might be outsiders who want to live near wealthy people. If so, the regression estimating permits from income—which would generate a "significant" income coefficient—would not be describing the behavior of wealthy people, at least not these wealthy people.

Using grouped data to infer individual characteristics has its own language. Some people call this "ecological inference." It may reflect "Simpson's paradox" or "the ecological fallacy," which are essentially non sequiturs generated by the data grouping. That inference from grouped data *may* be incorrect is not assurance that it *is*. The incorrect inference in the 1960s, from data grouped by state, that increased education of blacks would close the income gap by 30 percent or more, came from regressions in which percent black and the distribution of education were independent variables in an equation estimating earnings. The correct inference—that equal formal education would close only ten percent of the income gap—was available from those state observations, from regressions that contained interaction variables.

Although it always deserves to be questioned, an analysis based on grouped data can lead to correct insights. Consider a regression based on geographical units—precincts or districts—in which there are two candidates, one black and one white, where we can (if only approximately, from census data) determine the race of voters. We want to determine if there is "racially polarized voting," whether the race of the candidate appears to influence the voter. Despite other factors—who the candidates are, for example—two regressions (one for white candidates, one for black) should show us how individuals vote, although the data are grouped:

votes for one candidate = f(number of blacks, number of whites, . . .)

The ellipses allow for other variables that might differentiate districts. As there are more blacks and whites than votes, the coefficients of the independent race variables will each be less than one. The coefficients can be interpreted as the "propensity" of a black or white member of the population to vote for a candidate of the race of the dependent variable. The coefficients from each equation should be reasonable, in light of the other equation, or they are not estimating what the analyst says they are.

We would attribute these "propensities" to individuals, even though they were derived from grouped data. Would we be wrong? The Supreme Court did not think so in *Gingles* (1986), based on regressions presented by Bernard Grofman.[81] I agree with Grofman, and the Court. Inferring individual characteristics from grouped data is something at which regression is particularly good. It requires skill in addition to knowledge of statistical method. It requires some understanding of the real world, some craft. But it can be done.

---

81. Grofman's regressions may not have been exactly in my form. He apparently did not run them on candidates of both races, reporting only regressions based on black candidates. See *Gingles* (1984). If two possible regressions should tell the analyst the same thing, he should estimate them both to be sure that they do. See also Grilliches and Grunfield (1960).

Modeling the Complaint

Some airplane production by McDonnell Douglas Corporation, it was alleged, was charged to the wrong contract. When one contract was "over budget," charges would be applied to an "under-budget" contract. I put these phrases in quotations, because they will require definition in a statistical study. An analyst will have to argue that persons being tested as acting on that information had it, and used it as he defined it.

Defendant's expert was Franklin Fisher. My only mandate in this case for the plaintiff, the Department of Justice, was to devise a sample which the government would substitute for complete data in its analysis, whatever that was to be. I did have the opportunity to review Fisher's work, but I believe the government was caught off-guard, and never employed its own analytic expert, neither me nor anyone else. This case would have been a good vehicle for the discussion forum I advocate in Chapter 10, but it settled without anyone getting to the bottom of Fisher's work.

Workers punched in, or "rang," for each task. To mischarge, they would ring for a small time period on the over-budget job, and for a longer time on another job (which they did quickly) to an under-budget project. In this way they charged to the under-budget project work that they did for the over-budget project. Defendant claimed that the "ring" data were not maintained in sequence, so that one could not identify proximate long and short rings; but the data could identify the worker and the day, the project charged and the elapsed time.

Fisher figured that, if there was such cheating, the record would show a lot of work getting done on the short ring, because it was really done on a long ring charged elsewhere.

> We would expect to observe higher average efficiencies of short rings charged (to over-budget programs) when the same employee also charges to under-budget programs on the same day than when the employee charged only to over-budget programs.[82]

He defined a binary independent variable to denote when a short ring on an over-budget project occurred on the same day as at least one long ring on an under-budget project. Fisher's regression will compare "efficiency," the dependent variable, over all short rings on days during which only over-budget work is done, to the efficiency over all short rings on days during which both under- and over-budget work is done.

A simple comparison of means would have sufficed, except that Fisher added other variables in case average efficiency differed by project. He ran a separate regression for each worker. Item 43 of the complaint discusses how employees are "instructed by foremen"

---

82. Fisher's report in *O'Keefe* (1996), at 4. "'Produced hours' is the number of work pieces completed multiplied by the target hours. 'Efficiency' is the produced hours divided by the expended hours" in McDonnell Douglas' data. Fisher report at 2.

to mischarge. It is foremen "and other supervisors and managers" who read the reports, who knew which projects were over or under budget.[83] There is a mechanism lurking in here, describing (perhaps some foremen did it, others did not?) where we should look to find mischarges. Fisher did not look there. His analysis does not seem to be consistent with the complaint.

Because mischarging must be a rare event, differential efficiency can be swamped by simply misidentifying suspect charges. Fisher understands that most of the charges will be correct and vary around "average" efficiency. His point is not that the signal is strong, but that it is isolated, that it occurs only under the conditions of short charge to over-budget project and long charge to under-budget project on the same day. If there is a lot of random high and low efficiency on both suspect and non-suspect days, we should still be able to detect high-efficiency short rings indicating mischarging if they occur *only* on the days he has indicated as over budget. If he has defined "over budget" and "under budget" correctly. Regression is certainly the proper tool with which to test Fisher's model. Indeed, this is one of the most subtle and expert uses of regression I have ever seen in litigation.

Budget: Short-Term View

Subtle, expert, and also irrelevant, probably flat-out wrong. Fisher assigned over-budget and under-budget status to projects for a week, based on their Sunday data. Let us look at the data and understand how Fisher derived the measure that drove his study. And then let us ask, though this measure drives his study, if it plausibly drove shop-floor behavior.

In Figure 38 I show the budget entries for one department for March 5, 1989. Fisher's program compared the Sunday value, if there was one, to the value in the column marked "Budget," and used the difference to determine "over-budget" (or not) status for the entire week. If there was no Sunday value, Fisher's computer program used the Saturday value, and kept going backwards until it found a day-associated value.

"Model" in Figure 38 is an indication of the project to which these data apply. Budget is a daily figure. Fisher did not average the daily values to reach a generalization about the week, or retain the daily comparison for use with daily labor charge records. He used a one-day comparison, usually Sunday, to determine the budget status for that week.

The first row under the headings, in Figure 38, contains data for Model 3. Fisher compared the value on Sunday (333) with the value for Budget (826) and declared that this project was under budget. On this account, the indicator variable that separated suspect from non-suspect short rings was given the value zero for Model 3 short rings during the

---

83. Quotation from the complaint, item 52. See also item 53, "Foremen . . . determined which [contracts] were over, under or on target," or the district court's summary of the complaint, "employees . . . have been instructed by supervisors. . . ." *O'Keefe* (1986) at 1341.

Model	Budget	Sun	Mon	Tues	Wed	Thurs	Fri	Sat
3	826	333	1,100	1,131	934	906	805	871
4	1,711	1,845	2,710	2,227	2,299	2,441	2,114	2,055
30	7,504	6,593	12,613	10,559	9,081	8,732	8,700	8,713
7	0	0	0	0	0	0	0	0

FIGURE 38: Sample of the Budget Data in *O'Keefe*

week following this budget. Model 3 long rings were available to be the suspect long rings should there have been suspect short rings (to other projects) on the same day. Besides Sunday, only Friday was also under budget. On five days the project was over budget, and if the daily figures can be summed or averaged, the week was clearly over budget.

How often does Fisher mischaracterize the week like this? I count a week as having a conflict if there is a conflict between any day in the week and the day Fisher utilizes. I find at least one day's budget comparison in conflict with Fisher's view of the week in more than one-third of the budget-weeks in this department and the one other that I investigated. When there is a conflict in a week, on average there are 2.4 days of them in the first department, 2.0 of them in the other. Remembering that no more than six days can be in conflict, sometimes (when Sunday is not the budget day) fewer, the conclusion is that over 11 percent (more than a third of a third) of Fisher's "over-" or "under-budget" declarations would be incorrect if one took a daily rather than a weekly view.

A review of Figure 38 should raise at least one other question, this one with a good answer. Does Fisher think behavior will be affected by *any* amount of budget overage or budget underage? Because of the subtleties of his hypothesis, the answer is no. Fisher does not claim that mischarging might be triggered by any budget overage. He claims only that it will *not* be triggered in the week after a particular project is *under* budget.[84] Identifying, isolating when mischarging might occur is critical to Fisher's model; but its occurring in those weeks is not.

Budget: Long-Term View

Why would foremen, if they are to cheat, regard a day or a week as the proper unit within which to determine budget status? Fisher's implicit behavioral model, that mischarging occurs only during weeks defined by budget data for the previous week, is not plaintiff's model. A more telling picture, one surely known by foremen, might take a longer view.

Figure 39 displays Fisher's weekly budget data for one airplane project. A weekly "over-

---

84. Fisher tells us little about the budget data, but does clearly say they reflect the budget and charges "for that week." Fisher report at 2.

budget" condition exists in weeks when the data lie below the zero line. A budget "surplus"—as defined by Fisher—occurs when the plotted bar is above the line. Why would mischarging from this budget occur for only one week after an over-budget week? The correction might go on for another week, violating Fisher's assumptions. The regression requires that mischarging occurs only where Fisher has assumed it will be, although no reasonable observer would expect it to be only there.

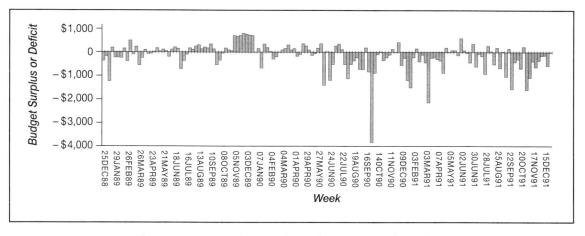

FIGURE 39: Long-Term View of One Project's Budget

Consider the end of November 1990 for example. The project has been over budget for several weeks. If there is mischarging, it might occur over several later weeks, regardless of the previous week's budget status. Consider the fall of 1991. Once again the project in general is over its budget. Its status changes from week to week as Fisher measures it, but would the basis for mischarging follow such an erratic course? I think not. One week of being under budget would not have changed a general over-budget impression.

If the time horizon of those directing the mischarging was either broader or narrower than the one week Fisher gives them to act, then his study does not test their behavior or its results. There could be mischarges aplenty, but no relationship between them and Fisher's findings. His sine qua non, his requirement of when mischarging would occur, fatally corrodes his analysis.

Departments and Centers

A center is composed of several departments. The two departments I have been using as illustrations are under the same center. We can use the budget data Fisher provides to suppose that whoever directs the mischarging is motivated not by the department budget, but by the center budget.

If the data for one department are positively correlated with data for the other—if when a particular project is over budget in one department it is usually over budget in the other—then we might believe that Fisher's use of departmental data does little harm. In Figure 40 I have plotted the budget differences in the two departments. Each point represents the budget surplus or deficit in the same week. A positive correlation would be indicated by the scatter of points sloping upwards, bottom left to top right. Had that occurred, then perhaps one department's data could have been used as an indicator of both departments together, and maybe the center. But it did not. Anyone concerned with the center's budget might have cheated in one department to balance an over-budget condition in another. The complaint did not specify that cheating was confined to a weekly budget condition in each department, isolated from the budget condition of the project. Only Fisher's model contained these restrictions.

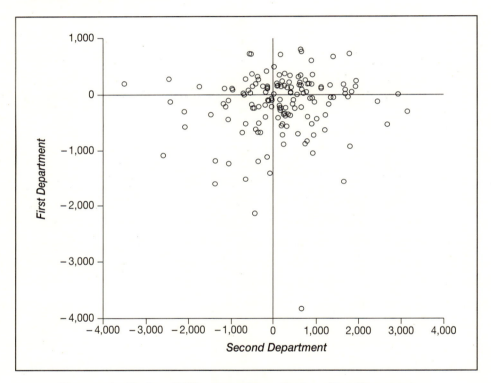

FIGURE 40: Budget Differences, Same Project, Two Departments

There is another side to Fisher's theory. If "efficiency" was inordinately high on the suspect short rings, it should have been inordinately low on the under-budget long rings. One would think that Fisher, who has criticized one-sided studies when performed by others, would have modeled and tested both propositions. Indeed, he tested the proposition that some projects were favored by receiving work not charged to them. Surely the government's complaint is the other side of this picture, that some projects were charged for work from which they did not benefit. Those are the long rings with inordinately low efficiency, which Fisher did not explore. It is also troubling that "budget status" not only may drive mischarging, but might be the *result* of mischarging. Using the result of a system as if it were an independent input to the system is surely a dangerous practice in any statistical analysis.

One could review a distribution of short-ring efficiencies, looking for a suspicious tail, highly efficient short rings that do not appear to fall within the bounds of a random distribution. One could do the same analysis of long rings, looking for those that were suspiciously inefficient.[85] Worker-days on which both conditions occurred would become a data set in which one would look for project patterns related to overall budget. Where Fisher imposed a theory upon his study of when cheating occurred, I would have looked for that theory to reveal itself in the data. At some point regression might have been used, but perhaps not. Perhaps Fisher, like so many others, used the tool he knew in a situation that did not call for it.

I leave discussion of Fisher's reported results to Chapter 8, because his interpretation struck me as peculiar. Here, what seemed at first like a very strong regression study now appears not to be. But Fisher has had no chance to respond to my critique. Thus my questions remain questions, my skepticism merely inquiry. In a seminar, the burden would be on Fisher to defend his study. A court, however, wants more than supposition from critics. The burden might have been on the government to demonstrate that Fisher's incorrect model led to incorrect or inconsistent results, that a better model would have indicated more cheating. I was not engaged to do such work, and never had the data to perform it.

The important points from this example for this chapter are first that regression can be well done, clever, and possibly informative; and second that even an expert and innovative analysis may provide the wrong answer, or the answer to the wrong question. The overarching point is that the questions the court needs answered rarely are esoteric or technical. Here, it is a matter of asking whether Fisher's model confronts the complaint, or tests a believable model of worker behavior. As Fisher will contend that the information from his study is that he looked for cheating and found little, one must ask, "How hard did you look? Where?" The Justice Department's lawyer was not interested in or prepared to understand what Fisher had done, or what might be wrong with it. In Fisher's deposition, he asked none of the questions raised here, although I had written them out for him.

REVERSE REGRESSION

For the Department of Labor, I was plaintiffs' expert in *Harris Bank* (1981). Harry Roberts, a well-known statistician, was the bank's expert. There were two complaints in this OFCCP

---

85. Work was accounted for in hours and tenths of hours. The parties agreed that the "short ring" in this scenario would be one-tenth of an hour, but I saw no evidence on the length to expect in a "long ring."

administrative charge, threatening Harris Bank's function as a federal repository. One was that females were not promoted at the same rate as males. The other was that females were paid less than males performing the same work. For example females, hired as tellers, performed the same tasks for a lower salary than males, hired as "managers-in-training," who in the teller booth performed teller-like functions. The males were promoted to higher level positions as the female tellers lagged behind.

To the extent that this description covers the argument, one may wonder why it was not treated as a selection case. Let the bank articulate why some people were called "managers" and others "tellers," and why they were paid differently for the same work. Using perhaps a logit analysis, does the bank's rationale work? Can we distinguish tellers from managers-to-be by their characteristics upon hire, other than gender? The "situation" analysis that called for regression estimation of salaries was imposed by my clients' legal theory. My analysis had to be consistent with their legal approach, even though I explained to them at the time that I thought their approach was wrong, and why.

Roberts initially divided the work force into cohorts by date of hire, and estimated wages (by standard regression) in different years trying to find variables that would explain away the male/female differences. He called these "mini-regressions." He was clear about his goals. He instructed his assistants to look for specifications that would reduce the gender variable to "insignificance." Roberts paid no attention to the "multiple-test" issue (divide and conquer) I raised above. He was prepared to interpret each regression as if it had been the only one ever estimated.[86] His goal was just to bring something to court that countered my regressions, in which I found that otherwise comparable males and females were paid differently.

Roberts never did find a bank-exonerating equation specification. Shortly before trial he devised a new approach, reverse regression. In order to hinder plaintiff's rebuttal preparation, the bank refused to obey the order of the administrative law judge to exchange all expert work. The administrative law judge then barred the bank from putting on a statistical defense. Or so he thought. The bank presented Roberts' testimony not as a defense, but as a rebuttal to my analysis for plaintiffs.

So the bank's chicanery succeeded procedurally. But not substantively. The administrative law judge rejected Roberts' critique. The finding for plaintiffs was upheld on appeal to the district court. I believe the bank's penalty for failing to follow the court's order should have been more severe. Roberts should not have been allowed to testify at

---

86. Roberts was aware, as F. Fisher (1980) wrote at 715, that if one "casts about for a good-looking relationship by trying all sorts of possibilities" he "is very likely to come up with relationships where none exist." As defendant's expert, though, all Roberts had to do was cast enough doubt on my regressions, by presenting alternatives without gender-based differentials, to dissuade the judge from finding mine persuasive.

all.[87] What happened in the *Harris Bank* proceedings, even though the bank ultimately failed, encouraged defendant's attorneys to defy rules instructing the experts to cooperate, and thereby discouraged courts from imposing such rules. In Chapters 7 and 10, where I write more about the role judges do and should play, I will advocate more judge involvement and harsher penalties for recalcitrant experts.

Harris Bank's Defense

Here is Roberts' method as summarized by the National Research Council panel:

> [T]he defendant's expert argued that the plaintiff's regressions, which were of the standard direct form, were inappropriate, and that reverse regressions (in which the roles of salary and productivity, the dependent and explanatory variables, respectively, are reversed) were called for to properly take into account the measurement error in the explanatory variables, which were imperfect proxies for productivity variables. This reverse-regression approach attempted to address in a novel fashion a statistical problem known as "attenuation," in which the regression coefficient of an imperfectly measured explanatory variable is inflated in magnitude when nothing is done to take the measurement error into account.[88]

David Peterson describes conditions that must hold to justify this reverse-regression approach:

> First, the proportion of females who are highly productive must be less than the proportion of males who are highly productive. Second, the proxy must not measure productivity correctly in some cases.[89]

The "proxy" is at least one variable used to explain productivity (hence, salary) differences, such as education, seniority, or experience. This problem remains: The theory contends that the firm pays strictly according to productivity, but cannot measure it. The firm knows individual productivity well enough to pay for it, without bias, but not well enough to tell us what it is. That is what a judge needs to know: not the mathematics, but the illogic of the theory.

Roberts' argument, somewhat different from both summaries, above, was based on omitted variables, not badly measured variables. There were "other factors in the employment process that are not specified by the model."

> Models of the employment process are generally crude approximations to the factors that enter into actual employment decisions. There is always concern

---

87. In *Penk* (1985) two statistical experts were not allowed to testify for violation of scheduling orders. See *Penk* (1987) at 466.

88. Fienberg (1989) at 97.

89. Peterson (1986) at 111.

> that important factors used by the employer to arrive at salary and job deci-
> sions may be omitted from the model.[90]

Although different in nuance, this explanation is not different in its contradiction: The firm knows why it pays what it pays, for it is disclaiming that gender is a factor. Why would measures of "important factors used by the employer to arrive at salary and job decisions" not be available to its expert? Let us not forget that these factors must be *valid*.

That plaintiffs' expert may have left out important variables used by the firm is plausible, although one must ask: Did defendant not provide these crucial data elements? The way for defendant to correct this flaw is to insert the variables in plaintiffs' equation and see if they affect the gender coefficient. Defendant expert's attempted to do that in *Diehl* (1996), although his explanatory variable was not necessarily valid. In *Presseisen* (1977), defendant's expert added variables to plaintiffs' regression, reducing the gender coefficient to "insignificance."[91] Plaintiffs were unable to convince the court that the additional variables were improper.

What problem does reverse regression solve? If plaintiffs' model is incorrect because it lacks variables used by the bank in its salary determination, then produce the data, add the variables.[92] If the data contain errors, then how does the firm rationalize basing pay on them? If the data cannot be produced, then perhaps plaintiffs' implicit assumption, that other factors are distributed among employees unrelated to gender, *and unrelated to compensation*, is proper and indeed true. Why should we believe there are errors in the direct regression, which bias its results, without any evidence?

Why Reverse Regression Fails

Reverse regression also poses some technical issues. The theory starts as Gwartney explained it. Wages are determined by productivity. Therefore we might write a direct-regression equation as:

$$salary = b_0 + b_1 productivity + b_2 female + e_{bi}$$

where the b in e_{bi} is meant to indicate *this equation's* error term. The test, then, is whether there is a non-zero—particularly negative—b_2 coefficient. Gwartney's error in *James* (1977) was to use decisions by the company (such as job grade) as if they were objective measures of productivity. That is, he *defined* the firm as fair, and then "found" that it was. Roberts knew (and quoted) Gwartney's work. He did not repeat Gwartney's errors.

---

90. Conway and Roberts (1986) at 157; preceding in-text quotation at 117.

91. See, for example, *Tagatz* (1988). When number of publications was added to the salary regression, remuneration differentials between Catholic and non-Catholic faculty disappeared.

92. Some courts, bless them, have approached defendants' criticisms this way. See, for example, *Sobel* (1988).

The "reverse regression" is

$$\text{productivity} = g_0 + g_1 \text{salary} + g_2 \text{female} + e_{gi}$$

The reverse question is whether females with the same salary have the same productivity as males. A positive g_2 coefficient implies that, at a given salary, females have less productivity (they need a productivity boost in the equation) than males.

Individual production is easily measured in piecework and commission sales. If the employer pays at a different rate for pieces produced by females than by males, say a different rate per pound of peaches picked, then the employer discriminates. Plaintiff does not need a statistical analysis in such a case. Sales commissions are product, but not necessarily productivity, as territories differ in their sales potential or sales difficulty. Employees at Harris Bank were salaried. Had they been formally assessed, the bank would have added an assessment metric as a variable in a regression such as mine. The argument would have been about the admission of that variable, its validity and objectivity.

To pursue the reverse-regression model, one must find a way to express productivity as a single variable. When we do not know productivity, we commonly assume that it is related to factors (experience, seniority, education, training) that imply productivity if they do not directly measure it. This is where measurement error enters, as these "productivity proxies" are productivity with error. Thus the strange logic of reverse regression starts by condemning plaintiffs for using "proxies" as variables, and then must devise some form of production index from many salary factors for its own purposes.

A regression operates better when the error is in the dependent variable, because then it can be incorporated into the error term e_g. To that extent, Roberts was on to something. But as productivity in reverse regression must be measured by a single variable, how did Roberts propose to get it?

He wants to express "productivity" as a function of the productivity proxies, a weighted average. One way to obtain weights is to hold to the productivity model of earnings, and estimate the regression:

$$\text{salary} = d_0 + d_1 \text{productivity}_1 + d_2 \text{productivity}_2 + \ldots + d_j \text{productivity}_j + e_{di}$$

using only males as observations. Then salary*—this equation's estimate of salary, not salary itself—is an estimate of productivity, presumably not biased by gender. This requires a great leap in logic: In order to test whether salary is productivity-based, we must first assume that, within gender, it is. The only non-productivity factor must be between genders. The reverse-regression equation is:

$$\text{salary}^\star = c_0 + c_1 \text{salary} + c_2 \text{female} + e_{ci}$$

Note that the estimate "salary*" differs from "salary," for males, by e_{di}, the errors from the salary equation. Those errors sum to zero. So the coefficient c_2 will be determined by whether the same equation generates a zero mean error for females. The coefficient c_2 will take the value that brings about this condition, a zero mean e_c.[93]

The reverse regression, therefore, is not nonsense. But neither is it necessary, as I have explained above. Nor does it have any intuitive meaning. And, although I have not seen this noted elsewhere in the literature, neither is it unique. One could as cogently argue that the salary regression to weight productivity factors should be estimated on females. Females may be paid on a lower scale, but why wouldn't the rational employer pay more-productive females better than less-productive females? Economic theory says the "rational" *competitive* employer will pay all people their marginal productivity, so the reverse-regression argument that starts with an employer rewarding productivity and then tests for whether he does so is suspect. There must be collusion in the firm so that males share the benefit of the artificially low female wage. If there is discrimination, then male wages do not represent productivity. One must assume the absence of discrimination to test for it by reverse regression!

The banking industry was regulated, competition limited, at the time of the *Harris Bank* litigation. There was an economic rent to be had, and once again no theory dictates that all such rent accrued to the firm. If some went to males—which one can infer from the fact that male wages fell more than female wages subsequent to banking deregulation—then again measuring productivity from males is suspect.[94] One could argue that a better productivity equation would be based on females. Their errors, their e_{di}, will not be the same as from the equation in which the male-based equation was used, and the reverse-regression gender coefficient will not necessarily have the same absolute value. There are two possible reverse regressions! Proponents can hope they are consistent, but as a method supposedly as telling as direct regression, it has this problem to overcome, that the two estimates might not agree.[95]

---

93. Using the data from my academic example, made-up data, I estimated salary = f(seniority, seniority squared) for males, to get my "productivity" equation, and then salary* = f(salary, gender) as my reverse regression. The gender coefficient is $1,389 with a probability of 0.002. Using the reverse-regression logic, defendant does not have to explain that one equal-seniority comparison where the male is paid more. Males are "significantly" underpaid.

94. The most reasonable assumption would be that male workers (especially white male workers) and the firm collude to divide the excess product of underpaid females and minorities, and any monopoly rent the firm may garner. We do not have to leave this at the level of theory, however. Sandra Black and Philip Strahan (2001) found that "rents were shared with labor" in the pre-1990s regulated banking industry. At 814:

> [F]irms were able to discriminate against women by sharing those rents disproportionately within male workers.

95. From my made-up academic data, the reverse regression from a salary* based on females provides a gender coefficient of $1,048 with a probability of 0.006. Not the same coefficient, but consistent. That's it, females are overpaid!

That what seems like a reasonable analytic method has a duality, another way of being estimated, is not unique in the annals of litigation. We saw an example in *O'Keefe* (1996), where Franklin Fisher tested for inordinately high efficiency, but not inordinately low efficiency, which was the complaint. In *Corrugated* (1977), a price-fixing case, plaintiffs' expert fit a regression model to prices during the "collusion" time period. He then calculated "would be" prices in a later, competitive period. The projected prices were higher than the actual prices, apparently confirming that the model had captured the collusion which no longer existed. Defendant's expert estimated a regression model from the competitive period and then projected it back to the earlier period. Lo and behold, it projected higher prices during the "collusion" period. As the model specification had come from the period plaintiffs admitted was competitive, and the actual "collusion" prices were lower, perhaps there was no collusion after all. The jury agreed.[96]

Arlene Ash produced a refreshing, straightforward analysis of reverse regression. She pointed out that the failure of the employer to have good measures of relevant employee qualifications, "Q,"

> introduces extra scatter in the data, and increases the likelihood that reverse regression will fail to detect real cases of discrimination. Likewise, the better our knowledge of Q the less opportunity there is for direct regression to falsely detect discrimination. So the use of reverse regression rewards the employer for poor recordkeeping, while the methodology of direct regression provides an incentive for the maintenance of accurate records.[97]

Ash followed Conway and Roberts in assuming that employees in two jobs, professional and clerical, will be analyzed in one regression. The mathematics is correct without this language, but the language should distress any astute reader, for there is no reason to expect an employer to reward qualifications in both professions the same way. As we saw with *I-NET*, a single regression covering multiple skills not in the same line of progression should be looked at skeptically by a judge, be it reverse or direct.

Reading through this unfortunate choice of language, we see that reverse regression will find "unfairness" in only a subset of salary conditions most people would call "unfair."

---

96. Although this is a good story, it is also curious. Both sides' experts (John Beyer for plaintiffs, Franklin Fisher for defendant) must have assumed that the structure of pricing, not just the level, was different in collusion and competitive periods. Otherwise, why not estimate a single model over the entire time period, with a "dummy" variable to distinguish the two periods? As many defendants settled prior to trial, one wonders if Fisher's criticisms of plaintiffs' model, technically correct as they may have been, contributed to a just result. For this and other antitrust cases involving regression, see Finkelstein and Levenbach (1983). I disagree with their suggestion that a dummy variable would have had an "under-adjustment bias." Beyer's equation did not contain a time trend, although prices for corrugated cardboard were rising throughout both periods. A quadratic trend variable would have solved the problem.

97. Ash (1986) at 93; following indented and in-text quotations both at 94.

Ash produces an example in which

> there is, in fact, *no* distribution of 40 qualified and 60 less-well-qualified wom-
> en to jobs which reverse regression would find unfair to them,

calling this result "astonishing."

Finally, Ash shows that an employer with reverse regression in mind can easily and consistently pay females less than males below the reverse-regression-detection threshold. Reverse regression is therefore inherently biased against finding "unfairness" to the lower-paid class.

Reverse regression ultimately drowns in a sea of incoherence. There was no rationale for Roberts' use of reverse regression in the *Harris Bank* case. The bank would have been better off arguing that my regressions contained a legal error than that they contained a statistical error. The legal error is that my regression analyses included the salary effects of decisions that were made prior to there being laws against them, as explained with reference to the AT&T case, above. So, for example, it may have been unfair that females were placed in inferior jobs, but not clearly a violation of law until women were included in the Equal Employment Opportunity Act, in 1972 amendments.[98] The Equal Pay Act, enacted in 1963, does not cover unfair assignments subsequent to work as a teller, but should have easily covered the teller/manager pay differential. Harris Bank should have reviewed its pay and promotion procedures in 1972, but females with inferior experience because of the earlier unfair assignment decisions would not have deserved immediate promotion. Even though it was the bank's doing, the bank could not be held responsible for the fact that their experience in 1972 and thereafter *was* inferior to that of males hired at the same time, years earlier.

One must ask why Harry Roberts brought this confusing and self-contradictory reverse regression forward. The answer would appear to lie in his mini-regression failures. Roberts' job, as he saw it—as did Gwartney and Haworth before him, Berkman, Dunbar and Killingsworth after him—was to find some way to prove his client correct. Gwartney's efforts in *James* (1975) and Roberts' in *Harris Bank* (1981) simply were not expert analyses of fact situations based on a viable legal theory and acceptable statistical analysis. It is a credit to the judicial system that both were rejected.

---

98. *Harris Bank* (1981) was a contract-compliance hearing pursuant to Executive Order 11,246, first promulgated in 1948. Plaintiffs may therefore have a point that all previous differential behavior toward females was covered. But contractors have a right to know what would be impermissible behavior, which they only surely knew with the passage of civil-rights legislation. I am satisfied with my role in showing that the bank discriminated, which no doubt it did, but uncomfortable that my regressions were used as a basis for generating what surely was excessive "back-pay" for female employees.

Harris Bank's Appeal

The Department of Labor did not utilize my services in the bank's appeal. Being deposed by the bank and no longer employed by the plaintiff, I made this point: "Your defense is all wrong. Your expert, by raising a technical issue, is blinding you to the legal issue. He is not helping you."[99] They ignored my advice, and lost their appeal, also.

Paul White and Michael Piette discuss reverse regression, but add nothing.[100] They do not inform us that no expert ever prevailed in court using it. That history should not of itself condemn the technique, but it should alert a client to ask questions about it. Although the "reverse regression" submitted by defendants in *Delaware* (2004) was not the complicated two-stage affair developed by Roberts—it simply reversed dependent and independent variables in a one-variable regression—Judge Jordan dismissed it:

> Thus, use of the reverse-regression method in this context is mathematically guaranteed to arrive at a result favorable to Defendants.[101]

The context was a search for a cutoff point for a screening device. As there were few scores below the existing cutoff, the equation's constant was above that level, and with a positive slope, the regression line never passed through a lower point. Reverse regression may not be nonsense in theory, but in most litigation situations it provides no help to the judge.

MISSED OPPORTUNITIES

A major thesis of this chapter is that many regressions in litigation are the wrong tool for the job. This is a sub-thesis to my larger one, that most errors in statistical analysis are the way in which the problem was conceived, not the technical finesse of the analysis given that erroneous concept. Thus it is important for a judge to know what regression does, but not important for him to know how it does it. The experts should correct each other on technical matters, leaving the conceptual matters for adjudication. Here are two examples of courts dealing with the low level of presentation with which they are faced, the mechanical application of regression. After them, I present one case in which regression was the solution, but no one seemed to know it.

---

99. I articulated this point in my article, Michelson (1986). My "situation"-based analysis—consistent with my client's legal theory—should have been countered with an "event"-based analysis, showing fair (if it was fair) selection for the higher-level positions that created the salary differential. I concluded, at 180:

> I am free to express my long-standing disappointment that the bank's expert chose to attack the *form* of my regression rather than the *fact* of my regression. . . . After all these years, allegations of discrimination at Harris Bank remain unanalyzed.

100. See P. White and Piette (1998).

101. *Delaware* (2004), paragraph 77 at *18.

Salaries in *Craik* (1984)

Females alleged in *Craik* that they had been discriminated against in initial rank assignment, promotion, and salary. Their major tool was regression. For example, to argue that women were in low ranks, plaintiffs offered a regression in which rank was assigned a numeric scale in order to be a single dependent variable.

> The defendants argue that multiple linear regression is an inappropriate method for examining discrepancies in rank. . . . Accordingly, they presented studies based on logistic regression fitting analysis, which showed that when five degree categories—Ph.D., M.A. + 90 quarter-hour credits, M.A. + 45 quarter-hour credits, M.A., and B.A.—were controlled for, sex was not a statistically significant factor in rank differentials.[102]

Defendant's methodological critique is correct, but the solution is evasive. The question is, how did faculty get to be at the rank at which they were observed? They were assigned, or they waited in one rank for promotion to the next. Faculty competed for a limited number of high-level appointments.[103] They were in different departments, which had different openings at different times. It apparently did not occur to either side's experts that current faculty did not represent all the choices open to the administration at the time decisions were made. No expert tried to determine who the candidates for each position were, from which data a multiple-pools-selection test would have been appropriate.[104]

The only conceptually appropriate use of regression was in estimating salary given rank that, when restricted to full-time faculty, showed no male-female difference. Whether the same factors are appropriate, and whether they should have the same coefficients (that old homogeneity problem) regardless of department, are questions that should have been asked. The appeals court majority seems to have found convincing that 77 percent of the females, but 87 percent of males, were hired as assistant professors—the difference presumably reflecting female hires as instructor—without assessing differences in qualifications. On the basis of the poor analyses offered by both sides, I would have found for

---

102. *Craik* (1984), majority opinion at 476, 34 FEP Cases at 658.

103. Faculty did compete for chair positions, and females did not apply proportionately. In his dissent, Judge Swygert tried to analyze five chair appointments in different years, different departments. "If all of these candidates were pooled and chance were the sole determinant of outcome," he explains his clearly incorrect test at 494, 34 FEP Cases at 672. A multiple-pools analysis would not have contradicted his result, however. Finding no females appointed to chair departments was not an improbable result from chance.

104. Plaintiffs offered "flow" analyses in which they argued that among those "eligible" for promotion at any time, women were less likely to be selected. But plaintiffs apparently considered all eligible *equally* eligible, which would always show a deficit of the group that was increasing its presence, because at any time, among the eligible, they would be the most junior.

defendant, Judge Swygert's dissent being more convincing than the majority opinion by Judge Arnold.

Perhaps the most telling line in the majority's opinion is this: "It is clear that the defendants' practices changed after this lawsuit was filed."[105] So maybe it is harsh to see this as a statistical case wrongly decided. The circuit court accepted inappropriate analyses and discredited the only arguably correct regression, but statistics are not the whole story.

Salaries in *Bazemore* (1986)

As discussed in Chapter 2, *Bazemore* established important principles, though the presentation of regression was inappropriate and the analysis of selection was faulty. Black and white divisions of the North Carolina Agricultural Extension Service had merged in 1965, without equalizing the separate and unequal salary structures. The first important principle established in this case is that equal rates of increase of salary do not constitute equality, if the base salaries were discriminatory. It is similar to the court's argument in *Craik* that, if female faculty were initially assigned to a low rank, subsequent "fair" promotions do not make them equally placed later.

This logic seems so obvious that it is embarrassing that attorneys argued against it, and appalling that courts had to struggle to come to it. The problem in *Craik* was not the logic, but the lack of proof that females were in fact unequally placed initially. In *Bazemore*, disparate starting positions and salaries were not in dispute.

> At trial, petitioners relied heavily on multiple regression analyses designed to demonstrate that blacks were paid less than similarly situated whites.[106]

Defendant complained that plaintiffs' regressions did not include all relevant variables. As in the discussions above, say in *Harris Bank*, defendant's responsibility is obvious: If they paid according to factors that plaintiff has not considered, then provide an analysis that does consider them.

> The Court of Appeals erred in stating that petitioners' regression analyses were "unacceptable as evidence of discrimination" because they did not include "all measurable variables thought to have an effect on salary level.". . . A plaintiff in a Title VII suit need not prove discrimination with scientific certainty; rather, his or her burden is to prove discrimination by a preponderance of the evidence.

Defendant is instructed to be more substantive. As bewildering as the lack of insight by plaintiffs' experts about what regression does, was the carping by defendants' experts about

---

105. *Craik* (1984) at 477, 34 FEP Cases at 659.

106. *Bazemore* (1986) at 398, 41 FEP Cases at 98; following indented quotation at 400, 41 FEP Cases at 99. *Bazemore* has been held not to apply to summary judgment motions. See *VCU* (1996).

"flaws" in regressions offered by plaintiffs. *Bazemore* stands for the worthy proposition that statistical critics should put up or shut up.

Remedy in *Arkansas* (1971)

The Board of Education of Portland, Arkansas, adopted a unified salary schedule, starting in the fall of 1968. Black teachers wanted back-pay for earlier salary discrimination. Judge Harris denied it:

> The Court is of the opinion and so holds that during these years employment of each teacher, white and black, historically was on the basis of private negotiation with each teacher individually; that substantial salary variations occurred not only between black and white teachers, but also between white teachers based on the needs of the district and the availability of individual teachers; and that there is no credible evidence in the record from which the Court could fix any amount of claimed damages.[107]

The evidence on the record included characteristics of forty-five teachers, and their salaries for the three years starting 1966–67. Not every teacher had a salary in every year, but still there were males, females, whites, blacks, administrators, and non-administrators with both local and total teaching experience from zero to at least twenty-five years. One might think the court could "fix" damages by regression. Judge Harris, however, thought there were no damages to fix.

The Eighth Circuit thought differently, reproducing the data, and suggesting that although determining race-based salary differential might be difficult, "the record is not totally lacking in evidence from which the trial court may make its determination."[108] Thus the lower court was implicitly instructed to award the black teachers back-pay.

From the data listing I could tell that there were some errors, or at least unexplained circumstances. Two salaries were clearly part-year, though not indicated as such. One person, whose salary went from $4,800 in 1967–68 to $6,700 in 1968–69, with half the experience of those making less, must have become an administrator. The first thing an expert can do is recognize when the data are probably not correct, and go back for clarification.

I generated the regression described in Figure 41 for salaries in 1966–67.[109] The variable "Except" was used to identify the data exceptions (only one in this equation). The variable "D-years" is years of teaching in this district, whereas "T-years" is years of teaching experience elsewhere. I thought district years would be more valuable than years spent else-

---

107. *Arkansas* (1970) 3 FEP Cases 798 at 800.

108. *Arkansas* (1971) 3 FEP cases 800 at 805.

109. Figure 41 is an abbreviated form of a standard regression output. In the Appendix to Chapter 3 I show the full form, and explain the elements, including those shown here.

where, but the opposite was true. I thought high-school teachers might be paid more than elementary-school teachers, administrators more than just teachers, and persons with masters degrees more than persons without. All of these hypotheses appear to have been correct.

			Number of Obs	31
			$F(7, 23)$	3.22
			Prob > F	0.0000
			R^2	0.8761
			Adjusted R^2	0.8383
			Root MSE	468.41
1966 Salary	**Coefficient**	**Standard Error**	**t**	**P > |t|**
Black	− 734.022	263.449	− 2.786	0.010
High	691.128	238.621	2.896	0.008
Admin	1194.133	356.672	3.348	0.003
master	830.653	340.560	2.439	0.023
D-years	39.689	12.460	3.185	0.004
T-years	76.212	24.380	3.126	0.005
Except	− 1831.038	504.911	− 3.626	0.001
_Cons	3671.270	405.977	9.043	0.000

FIGURE 41: Regression Output from Data from Portland, Arkansas, 1966–1967

What about special features? Let's look.

The two white observations substantially above the regression line in Figure 42 were in fact predicted by the equation. So was the highest-paid black. They are all administrators. The extremely low-paid black was the exception in this equation, I believe not receiving a full year's pay. That point was fitted perfectly by the "except" variable, and therefore plays no role in the calculation of the race-based differential. In this graphic I have smoothed out the black and white locus lines to better show the generality of the differences in salary by race. A dummy-variable approach works well. I think an award of $734 per black teacher would have been appropriate for 1966–67, plus interest for not having received their just pay at that time. Similarly, the differential for 1967–68, from the same regression specification, was $884. In 1968–69 I found a differential of $267, but with a probability of 0.19. As the parties had stipulated that there was no differential in that year, finding none validates the general regression approach as well as their impressions.

There is no published record of what the district court did on remand. Judge Harris was surely not prepared to try to make sense of these data. Nor should he have been expected to do so on his own. The numbers the circuit court wanted were easy to derive, even in the early 1970s. All the court needed was a reasonably competent expert.

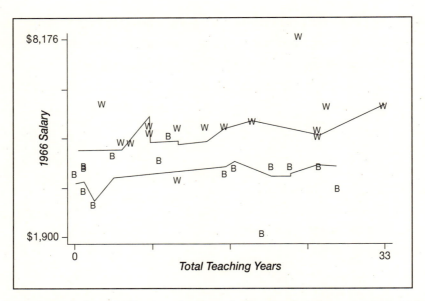

FIGURE 42: Salary Differences by Race in Portland, Arkansas, 1966–1967

A MISUNDERSTOOD, MISUSED TOOL

Regression can inform the court about relationships of importance to the ultimate decision. We will see examples in Chapter 5 on jury representation. Lack of homogeneity in one variable can be corrected by interaction terms, but for clear equations and interpretation, non-homogeneity leads to separate regressions. The results of these multiple tests can then be aggregated, as I did in the I-NET case. Aggregation of results unfortunately is seldom discussed in books purporting to instruct attorneys and judges about statistics.[110]

Much of what I call non-homogeneity is simply different meanings some words have in different situations. Would number of publications have the same impact on salary in the economics and physics departments of a university? Should paintings or weavings or sculptures in the art department be counted like publications in other departments? Art-department personnel also write articles, but what is considered their professional product? A physics experiment may take years to construct, perform, analyze, write up. Meanwhile an economist has downloaded data sets and written several articles and op-ed pieces. Why should "publication" be a common measure between these two departments? And

---

110. For example, Gastwirth (1988), who in general is good about discussing the need for separate tests and an aggregated summary statistic, does not mention the topic in his section on regression, at 362–436. He appears to accept the use of binary variables to adjust for departments in a university-wide salary regression, not questioning whether faculty characteristics have—or even should be expected to have—the same impact on salary in all departments. That question would have lead to suggesting several regressions, and then to the need for a summary statistic.

what about good teachers? No faculty-salary regression presented in litigation has ever considered that the primary purpose of the job is supposed to be education!

There is no reason why years of schooling should have the same impact on salaries of doctors, nurses, and secretaries. If there are no male secretaries, salaries of male doctors hardly provides information on what their salaries would be. If the secretaries have medical degrees and the allegation is that they should have higher salaries because they should have different positions, the analyst should turn to selection models. Regression is inappropriate. "Experts" commonly ignore these issues, throwing data into the computer and generating impressive-looking regression printouts.

Some number of famous regression cases, *Bazemore* and *Harris Bank* among them, should have been analyzed as selection cases. *Crow* should have been analyzed by simulation, which is selection where all data but the selectee's is estimated. The first question to ask, when an expert suggests that regression will be his main analytic tool, is whether it is the right tool for the job; whether the expert understands the legal issues and the data— and regression itself.

We have also seen that the expert's description of what he learned from his data may bear little relationship to the information actually contained therein. We will see more in later chapters. Harry Roberts called what reverse regression was testing "fairness 2," ignoring that his method was biased towards always finding it, and thus was unfair. Mark Berkman's interpretation of his regression in *Crow* bore no relationship to the equation itself. In the case of I-NET, Mark Killingsworth reported that females were underpaid when "education" was held constant, even though six different skills (lines of progression, job groups) appeared in some grades. What these people did for a living did not seem to matter to him. Franklin Fisher allowed last week's cheating to determine whether he would find any cheating this week, as if persons trying to balance budgets would do so from weekly data that they have just manipulated. In short, we have seen substantial differences between what a regression did and what the expert said it did.

Expert, attorney, and judge all fail to ask, "What does this mean?" In later chapters we will encounter a "market" variable that measured nothing about the market, but carried that name, and carried the day. That a class representative earned more than other females hardly made her unfit to complain about salaries in comparison with males. What was Judith Stoikov thinking? Many regressions should not be run in the first place, others are run badly (wrong functional form, wrong observations, wrong variables) and others claim to provide information they do not in fact provide. Yet, despite being presented with improper regressions badly explained and badly rebutted, most judges make some sense of it all. They often do so despite the experts, not because of them. ·

4

The Size of the Jury

From the beginning of the federal judicial system questions arose about what a judge may say (or must say) to a jury, what size a jury must be to render a fair verdict, what kinds of cases could be appealed and whether a higher court *must* or only *could* hear the appeal, what kinds of cases belonged in federal courts, what laws were applicable, to what extent judges may or should utilize knowledge other than that presented to them, etc.[1] The structure of federal and state court systems evolved slowly through acts of Congress, decisions and rules of the courts, state legislation, and committees of the American Bar Association. For over 130 years there was no formal mechanism by which judges even could discuss court structure or procedures.

> The Judiciary Act of 1922 marks the beginning of a new chapter in the administration of the federal courts. It is the first recognition by Congressional legislation that effective and economic adjudication is to no small measure dependent upon the ways in which the federal courts transact business.[2]

The Judiciary Act established an annual conference at which judges from around the country would gather to discuss their experiences. First called the Conference of Senior Circuit Judges, this institution survives today as the Judicial Conference of the United States.

> Conference duties include: conducting comprehensive surveys of the condition of federal court business, continually monitoring the operation and effect of the rules of procedure, and recommending to Congress legislation designed to improve the operation of the federal courts.[3]

The Conference only partially answered the criticisms of scholars such as Roscoe Pound and Benjamin Cardozo, who called for

---

1. The federal courts were established by the seventy-third law passed under the U.S. Constitution, in the Act of September 24,1789. State courts, of course, had existed before the Revolution.

2. Frankfurter and Landis (1928) at 242.

3. Judicial Center (1977), at 54.

some man or group of men to watch the law in action, observe the manner of its functioning, and report the changes needed when function is deranged.[4]

The Conference itself has recognized the need for help, suggesting the creation of the Administrative Office of the United States Courts (1939) to gather data and provide administrative services, and later the Federal Judicial Center (1967); the dates being those of the passage of enabling legislation by Congress. Other watchdog functions have been taken up by law reviews and journals, to which courts now routinely refer.

Yet the ability of the legal system to generate responsible and appropriate research at the proper time is still seriously in doubt. Although a role of the aggressive attorney is to bring new forms of argument before the court, there is a time lag between the availability of relevant expertise and the use of that expertise in the law. At times (such as Gottfried Wilhelm von Leibnitz' use of probability) the gap is short, but at others (such as the lag between the use of social-science-expert reports and the use of social-science-expert witnesses) it seems long. Finally, the court's ability to evaluate new concepts of proof is as in doubt as the appropriateness and validity of the research itself. These problems are no less apparent when we deal with judicial procedures than when we deal with substance.

Many areas of judicial procedure have become subjects for adjudication. The most obvious of these is the notion of a "fair trial," which includes "trial by jury." Litigation about jury selection, jury size, and jury vote (whether unanimity is required) have raised operating procedure to the level of common law or constitutional issues.

The most common procedural issue in popular literature is juror selection from the *voir dire* panel.[5] In technical literature, perhaps the most well-known is that of discrimination in the composition of juries, the subject of the next chapter of this book. The least studied is that of the determinative vote.[6] The issue provoking the strongest and most immediate response within legal literature, though remaining obscure outside of that

---

4. Cardozo (1921) at 114. Roscoe Pound, and before him Jeremy Bentham and others, are credited by Cardozo with initiating the idea of a Ministry of Justice that would somehow see when the Court had gone astray (because, suggests Cardozo, of its excessive reliance on precedent) and would articulate alternative procedures or legislation to correct judicial errors. This institution is discussed in Chapter 10, along with other ideas for judicial reform.

5. A panel of potential jurors is presented to the court, and may be examined by the judge and the attorneys in a process known as *voir dire*. Whether to allow "scientific jury selection"—the use of prediction equations to help attorneys challenge potential jurors they think they will fail to convince—was at one time a subject of debate. See Schulman et al. (1973) and Shapley (1974). For an interesting view that selecting juries through social-science research will eventually work to the disadvantage of defendants, who are now its prime sponsors, see Etzioni (1974). If Etzioni's fear of state use of "scientific selection" is realized, it is sure to be the subject of litigation. However, more than twenty-five years later, it appears that Etzioni was wrong, as usual.

6. Although most people surely think that jury votes always need to be unanimous, even today that is not always true. In federal court, a determinative jury must be unanimous, but an advisory jury was

literature, has been the size of the jury.[7] Despite wide initial interest, an adequate analysis of the effect of jury size on the outcomes of trials has never been produced.[8] The analysis below is the first to consider the benefits of different sizes of jury within the context of a social-science model.

HISTORY AND ISSUES

Trial by jury is considered to be a fundamental protection for citizens against the excesses of government.

> We have had it with us for so long that any sense of surprise over its main characteristics has perhaps somewhat dulled.[9]

The civil jury is older than the criminal jury. In English history the existence, for criminal proceedings, of a grand jury—the accusing or "presentment" jury—precedes the trial or petit jury. But, as described in Chapter 1, when trial by ordeal was banned by the Church in 1219 A.D., the petit jury evolved as a determiner of facts in criminal cases.

> The evolution of the jury was not brought about by a series of legislative enactments and royal ordinances, but by the practices of the justices itinerant in meeting the various cases that came before them.[10]

Juries were not unique to England, though the English system is the precedent for the American jury. It is of interest to learn that citizen participation in the legal-justice system historically preceded participation in legislative or administrative functions. During the Crusades:

---

instructed that the court would accept a verdict agreed to by at least 10 jurors—that is, a verdict that was unanimous, 11–1, or 10–2.

Acusport (2003) at 466. *Apodaca* (1972) allowed majorities of eleven to one and ten to two in state courts with twelve jurors. The definitive decision is *Johnson* (1972) which upheld a nine-to-three jury vote and said that smaller majorities were not acceptable. In *Burch* (1979), the Court declared that if the state uses a six-person jury and the trial is for non-petty offenses, the jurors must be unanimous to convict.

7. *Williams* (1970), *Colgrove* (1973), and *Ballew* (1978) are the major decisions on jury size.

8. Indeed, years later, the initial criticisms of the Supreme Court continued to be summarized but not analyzed. See, for example, Penrod and Hastie (1979), Sperlich (1979), and Grofman (1980).

9. Kalven and Zeisel (1966) at 3.

10. C. Wells (1911) at 360. Leonard Levy (1999) tells us, at 16,

> The Fourth Lateran Council in 1215 forbade the participation of the clergy in the administration of ordeals,

which may not have been a ban, but ended the practice. The 1219 date may come from the king's writ of 1219 that instructs circuit judges to deal with trials, given the church's prohibition of clergy participation. Levy credits King Henry II for paving the way for this reform, having offered alternatives to ordeals. Henry insisted that serious crimes be settled in the king's courts, over which he had some procedural control.

> Everything possible was done to bridge the gap between the Franks and their
> subjects, and to conciliate local feeling. In the courts, Muslims were permitted
> to take the oath on the Koran, and in the *Cours de la fonde* which tried com-
> mercial and civil suits it was the rule that, in a jury of six, four should be
> natives.[11]

More recently, although Saddam Hussein was deposed and captured by foreign forces, there
were no judicial proceedings against him until he was brought before an Iraqi judge in 2004.

Jury size obviously has varied throughout history. We can ask what the framers meant
the U.S. Constitution to require when they wrote:

> In all criminal prosecutions, the accused shall enjoy the right to a speedy and
> public trial by an impartial jury.[12]

or when they wrote:

> In suits at common law . . . the right of trial by jury shall be preserved.[13]

Charles Wells found records of juries with

> from twenty-four to eighty-four jurors, and the number became embarrass-
> ingly large and unwieldy, and the sense of the personal responsibility of each
> juror was in danger of being lost.[14]

Speculating on why the trial jury came to be composed of twelve people, Wells cannot provide a definitive answer.

> Various more or less fanciful reasons for the number twelve have been given,
> but they were all brought forward after the number was fixed.

Keith Mossman writes, with an air of certainty:

> The present system of twelve jurors and unanimous verdicts in criminal cases
> . . . arose as a means of proof to establish a fact, not as a means of judging.
> Twelve oaths were required in order to establish the proof, and twelve wit-
> nesses were required to support the winning party. For that purpose, their tes-
> timony had to be unanimous.[15]

Although the history of the twelve-person jury is not that clear, we do know something
about it. We know of twelve tribes of Israel, twelve apostles, and, in general, a favorable and
frequent use of the number twelve in religion. Leonard Levy describes communal determinations in the twelfth century:

---

11. Fedden (1950) at 43.

12. Sixth Amendment to the U.S. Constitution.

13. Seventh Amendment to the U.S. Constitution.

14. C. Wells (1911) at 356; following indented quotation at 357.

15. Mossman (1974) at 23. I have found no other source of the twelve-oath theory of the origin of the
jury except C. Wells (1911). Mossman does not give a citation.

> Twelve men from each hundred of the county and four from each vill or township of the hundred were to be summoned by the sheriff to attend the public eyre.
>
> The Constitutions of Clarendon in 1164 provided the precedent for turning to twelve men of the countryside for a verdict on a question concerning property rights.
>
> [G]radually only twelve jurors were selected to try the indictment, but they always included among their number some of the original jury of present-ment. The unfairness inherent in this practice, and the theory that the accused must consent to this jury, eventually led to a complete separation of the grand jury and the trial jury.[16]

The separation of the grand and petit juries, and the establishment of twelve as the size of the latter, thus is clearly evident before Magna Carta.

Even though juries varied in size in the pre-Constitution United States, twelve was the accepted standard. Whether the framers of the Constitution meant to fix the size of jury at twelve, they surely thought of juries as having twelve people. To what extent that binds contemporary judicial practice is a matter of history. "We hold that the twelve-man panel is not a necessary ingredient of 'trial by jury,'" said the Supreme Court in *Williams* (1970).[17]

Then the storm broke. Hans Zeisel reviewed the evidence and concluded that "it would appear that the Court's holding in *Williams* rests on a poor foundation."[18] David Walbert presented the first modern probabilistic model of the jury, reserving for a footnote his question, equally apt today, "whether the Justices, their clerks, and the attorneys are capable of correctly using available knowledge."[19] In the text, he concluded that they were not:

> To summarize the court's analysis of jury size, one can only say that the reasoning is superficial and the conclusions are unsupported. . . . The number of jurors significantly affects the likelihood of conviction.

Herbert Friedman discussed a similar model without condemning the Court, but finding that

---

16. Levy (1999) at 11, 13, and 19. Levy goes on to note how differently the English system evolved from that on the Continent. The important element, to Levy, is the "accusatorial" form, as opposed to an inquisition. At 50:

> One system presumed the guilt of the accused; the other, requiring the prosecution to prove its case to a jury, did not.

In *Blakely* (2004), 125 S.Ct. at 2536, Justice Scalia reminds us of Blackstone's assertion that fact was found by "the unanimous suffrage of twelve of [a defendant's] equals and neighbours," citing *Commentaries on the Laws of England* (1769 edition) volume 4 at 343.

17. Justice White for the Court in *Williams* (1970) at 86.

18. Zeisel (1971) at 720. Pabst (1973), seldom referred to, raises more interesting questions.

19. Walbert (1971) at 531, note 8; following indented quotation at 537, 547.

> Conviction patterns for an eleven out of twelve and a unanimous six out of
> six criterion are similar and intermediate between the twelve out of twelve and
> ten out of twelve results.[20]

Alan Gelfand and Herbert Solomon produced a series of articles using a more complex probability model.[21]

The Supreme Court, meanwhile, was extending its *Williams* decision, which applied strictly to state courts, in *Colgrove* (1973) to federal courts, based partly on additional studies apparently verifying that size did not affect jury performance. Hans Zeisel and Shari Diamond struck out:

> Again the court was misled; the four studies do not support this proposition.
> This failure to evaluate empirical research properly raises serious questions.[22]

Michael Saks was even less restrained:

> The quality of social science scholarship displayed in these decisions would
> not win a passing grade in a high school psychology class.[23]

What was all this commotion about? What had the court held, and how had it come to hold it? Did the Supreme Court misunderstand the experts? Did the experts understand the issue? We look first at why the decision was such a surprise, and then at the reasoning behind it.

Legal Precedents

On May 24, 1779, John Holmes was convicted of violating a New Jersey statute that made it unlawful to bring goods

> from within the lines or encampments or any place in possession of the sub-
> jects or troops of the King of Great Britain.[24]

Following procedures set out in a 1775 statute, Holmes was tried before a six-man jury. Holmes appealed the conviction to the New Jersey Supreme Court, on the argument that the state's constitution, which guaranteed "the inestimable right of trial by jury," meant a

---

20. Friedman (1972) at 22. Friedman presents no model of his own, but extends Feinberg (1971), whose didactic discussion of Type I and Type II errors in the judicial system did not deal with the question of varying jury size or voting procedure.

21. Gelfand and Solomon (1973) and (1974) refer to *Williams* (1970), and Walbert's (1971) and Zeisel's (1971) critiques. Eventually they summarized their work in the legal literature, Gelfand and Solomon (1977a).

22. Zeisel and Diamond (1974) at 282.

23. Saks (1974) at 18.

24. Excerpts from the law and all details of the case come from Scott (1899). It is arguable that the *Williams* Court did not know this history; but also that they would not have been impressed if they did, as they were intent on contravening it.

jury of twelve. On September 7, 1780, the Supreme Court of the state of New Jersey agreed, sending the case back for retrial.[25]

This was a momentous decision, the first exercise of "judicial review," the power of the court to invalidate an act of the legislature. Some people trace the origin of that powerful notion to Alexander Hamilton in *The Federalist*.[26] Chief Justice Marshall's enunciation in *Marbury* (1803) is the first use of review power by the federal judiciary. But the first telling application of the principle was in this case concerning the size of the jury,[27] protecting the interpretation of trial by jury as requiring a jury of twelve.

The Supreme Court overturned convictions by juries with fewer than twelve members in 1898, in 1899, and again in 1900.[28] The issue emerged again in the 1930s, with the same results.[29] All federal juries or state juries hearing criminal cases, if smaller than twelve, were thought to be incorrectly constituted, until *Williams* (1970). Williams, convicted of robbery, contended that he should have had a twelve-member jury, although Florida law called for a six-member jury. The U.S. Supreme Court upheld his conviction.[30]

---

25. Scott (1899) traces the subsequent careers of major figures in this drama. Chief Justice Brearly, for example, was a delegate at the Constitutional Convention. However, we do not learn whether Holmes was convicted at his retrial. Under this and other "seizure" acts, anyone who had the power to stop the violator was granted the authority to do so and retain part, if not all, of the loot. That should explain who Walton was.

26. *The Federalist Papers* (Viking Penguin, 1987), No. 78:

> Whenever a particular statute contravenes the Constitution, it will be the duty of the judicial tribunals to adhere to the latter and disregard the former.

It might be noted that this power of the court is not mentioned in any other Federalist Paper, nor did Hamilton offer it in any explicit form to the Constitutional Convention.

27. In Corwin (1925), 1964 reprint at 10:

> As a practice, judicial review made its initial appearance in independent America in 1780, in the case of *Holmes v. Walton*. . . . Although the opinion of the court apparently was never published, the force of the example may have been considerable.

Holmes v. Walton is one of seven cases cited by Haines (1914) as state precedents for judicial review at the federal level and one of nine cited by Crosskey (1953), in both cases the earliest. Levy (1967) asserts that some of these precedents are "spurious," though *Holmes* is not. Levy's argument, at 8, that *Holmes* is not precedent for judicial review because there is no record of Brearly's endorsing that concept at the Constitutional Convention cannot be taken seriously.

28. *Thompson* (1898), *Traction* (1899), and *Maxwell* (1900). Justice Brennan dismisses these precedents as "clearly dictum" in *Colgrove* (1973) at 157.

29. See, for example, *Patton* (1930), in which it was held that defendant had the right to a twelve-person jury, although it was a right the defendant could (and did) waive.

30. Other commentators have noted that past decisions of the Court on this subject led people to believe that it would not suddenly validate the six-member jury in a criminal case. However, there is another reason why this case went unnoticed until it was decided. Williams also contended that a Florida statute that required him to reveal his alibi, if he had one, before the trial, violated his right against self-incrimination guaranteed by the Fifth Amendment. Most of the *Williams* opinion, and much of the dissent, is on this point. Briefs, also, were dominated by this issue. The Court held that, since he was not required

The Decisions

The *Williams* Court first considered whether the framers of the Constitution had a twelve-person jury in mind. Admitting that they did, the Court then looked for a way to make that admission irrelevant:

> In short, while sometime in the 14th Century the size of the jury at common law came to be fixed generally at twelve, that particular feature of the jury system appears to have been a historical accident, unrelated to the great purposes which gave rise to the jury in the first place.[31]

What difference would it make, anyway, if the jury were smaller?

> [C]ertainly the reliability of the jury as a fact finder hardly seems likely to be a function of its size.[32]

How should we determine the appropriate size of the jury?

> To be sure, the number should probably be large enough to promote group deliberation, free from outside attempts at intimidation, and to provide a fair possibility for obtaining a representative cross-section of the community.

The court, then, has set the following standards:

A jury must be a group;

it must be independent; and

it must be drawn fairly from the community.

In social-science-modeling jargon, these conditions are constraints on the objective function: Maximize discovery and articulation of fact (minimize error). The question then is to what extent lowering the size of the first constraint reduces achievement of the objective.

In *Williams* (1970) and *Colgrove* (1973), the Court allowed the jury size to fall below twelve, saying the determination of fact would not be greatly affected. In *Ballew* (1978),

---

to have an alibi, and therefore was not required to provide any information, the state could properly demand to know what his alibi would be *if* he were to have one. When one comes across *Williams* citations in current legal research, it is on the due-process question, whether the state can require that a defendant articulate his alibi before trial.

31. *Williams* (1970) at 89. Whether a common practice's "accidental" basis is sufficient reason to discard it can be debated. R. Berger (1997), for example, argues at 448 that

> Adherence to a practice for 600 years renders its "accidental" origin irrelevant, for as Coke stated, "usage and ancient course maketh law."

One thinks immediately of other "historical accidents," such as the age at which a person is considered to be an adult, as suddenly vulnerable. The following analysis could be adapted to that question, and I, for one (disagreeing with Berger), think that such lines *should* be analytically, not historically, defined.

32. *Williams* (1970) at 100; following indented quotation also at 100. See also *Ballew* (1978) at 229 for similar, though not identical, language.

they would not let it go to five. Referring to studies published between *Williams* and *Ballew*, Justice Blackmun, writing for the Court, said:

> These writings do not draw or identify a bright line below which the number of jurors would not be able to function as required by the standards enumerated in *Williams*. On the other hand, they raise significant questions about the wisdom and constitutionality of a reduction below six.[33]

In a concurring opinion, Justice Powell admits (reluctantly) that "a line has to be drawn somewhere if the substance of the jury trial is to be preserved," but questions the Court's reliance on the literature:

> I have reservations as to the wisdom—as well as the necessity—of Mr. Justice Blackmun's heavy reliance on numerology derived from statistical studies. Moreover, neither the validity nor the methodology employed by the studies cited was subjected to the traditional testing mechanisms of the adversary process.

Twenty years later, Hans Zeisel (posthumously) and David Kaye praised Blackmun's opinion, saying he "relied on empirical research and statistical reasoning."[34]

> The opinion correctly insisted that smaller juries are inferior in two respects: they are less likely to represent minorities within the community, and they are more likely to arrive at an erroneous verdict.

Social scientists have held the position summarized by Zeisel and Kaye consistently and unanimously for decades.

The Aftermath

Two reactions followed quickly upon the *Williams* and *Colgrove* decisions. One was the surge of interest by social scientists in statistical models of the jury process. The Court articulated its belief that jury verdicts would not be affected by jury size, at least not in the range from six to twelve. Yet, this range is large in statistical terms. One would expect the standard deviation of any measure to be larger the smaller the sample size.[35] Although the average decision might appear to be unchanged, one might expect there to be more variation in outcome. Thus if the average decision is "correct," then one expects a smaller jury to pro-

---

33. Justice Blackmun for the Court in *Ballew* (1978) at 231; following in-text and indented quotations both from *Ballew* at 246.

34. Zeisel and Kaye (1997) at 176; following indented quotation also at 176.

35. For example, the standard deviation of the integers 1 through 6 is 1.871. But the standard deviation of two sets of these numbers (1, 1, 2, 2, etc.)—the same numbers distributed the same way—is 1.784, and of three sets is 1.757. The more observations, the smaller the standard deviation. The statement in text comes from drawing samples of different sizes from the same distribution, which implies that the standard deviation of random outcomes from six jurors will be 42 percent larger than that from twelve jurors, regardless of the underlying distribution. See Zeisel (1971). But are jury outcomes random?

duce more error. It is not clear to what extent the Court in *Williams* and *Colgrove* relies on there being no difference between the twelve-person jury and six-person jury, or there being not much of a difference. David Walbert argues that *Williams* is defective by either interpretation and should be reconsidered. Other critics do not make this distinction.

The other reaction was the speedy adoption of smaller juries. By the time the *Colgrove* decision was announced, fifty-six federal districts had adopted six-person juries for some or all civil proceedings. By July 1978, only ten districts required the twelve-person jury for all cases; and of the eighty-five districts allowing smaller juries for some cases, seventy-six provided for juries of six in all civil cases.[36]

Thus, the six-person jury is a reality. Is it an evil we must live with because the Court did not know how to ask for social-science help on a social-science issue? My support for the smaller jury stands alone. But, though I reach a different conclusion from the critics of the *Williams* and *Colgrove* decisions, I agree that the Court's understanding of the issue was not sophisticated. Furthermore, and more important, had it consulted with "experts" of the day it would have received unhelpful—I would say incorrect—advice.

METHOD OF ANALYSIS

In dissenting from the *Colgrove* opinion, Justice Marshall set out a concept of the functions of the legislative and judicial branches:

> Normally, in our system we leave the inevitable process of arbitrary line draw-ing to the Legislative Branch, which is far better equipped to make ad hoc compromises. . . . Today, the court turns this practice inside out.[37]

Marshall's dilemma, however, is unfounded. The judiciary often must draw lines when deciding constitutional issues.

> What is "due" process of law, a "speedy" trial, an "impartial" jury, an "unrea-sonable" search, an "excessive" bail, a "cruel" or "unusual" punishment, or an "establishment" of religion?[38]

The list can be extended: When is a fetus a person, or a child an adult, for example?[39] Of interest in Chapter 5: When (or of what) is a jury "representative"? Of interest in Chap-

---

36. Data from Director's Report (1973) and later records (tabulated but unpublished) at the Adminis-trative Office of the United States Courts.

37. Marshall dissent, *Colgrove* (1973), at 182, 183.

38. Levy (1972) at 8.

39. Following Brown (1943), one could say that the Court establishes a rule of law against which one tests the facts. In order to create a factual issue, resolvable in lower courts, the Supreme Court must define the law so that determination of the facts sufficiently indicates what the decision should be. That is, it must draw a line.

ter 8: When is a police officer's suspicion reasonable enough to allow searching a car for drugs? Of interest in Chapter 10: When does an expert presentation contain enough "science" that it should be permitted under the Federal Rules of Evidence, as mandated by *Daubert* (1993)? When is a potential class "numerous" enough, its issues "common" enough, its representatives "typical" enough to allow class certification? As has been made clear in Senate hearings concerning nominations for Supreme Court justice, the *job* of the Supreme Court justice is to draw lines. Thus it is appropriate to review the Supreme Court's decision in terms of their drawing a line at six jury members.

I start graphically. Figure 43 presents a coordinate system that will allow us to draw the relationship between jury size (the horizontal axis) and benefits (the vertical axis). I leave aside for now how to evaluate benefits. That is discussed below. The relationship between jury size and benefits will be some curve, presumably not decreasing as size increases, at least not decreasing as jury size increases from one to twelve or a somewhat larger number. I draw it as increasing at a decreasing rate, asserting that this general shape is what most people would agree holds, even if they disagree on the definition of "benefit." The more jurors (in this range) the more benefit, but each additional juror adds less benefit than the preceding juror (in terms of their number).

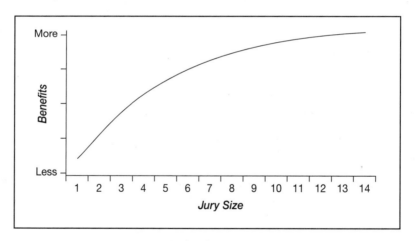

FIGURE 43: Benefits from Larger Jury Size

To determine an optimum jury size, we would also need a curve measuring costs. If costs (including opportunity cost) are below benefits at small sizes, but increase faster than benefits, then it is to society's advantage to increase jury size until no more benefits can be gained from shifting resources into this use. However, determining the optimum jury size is a function reserved for legislatures, or for judicial systems in their internal rule making. The constitutional issue is: What is the smallest *permissible* jury? This question may or may not require a measure of benefits, but it is independent of costs.

Do we even need to measure benefits? If the argument is framed as a matter of constitutional (strictly legal) fact, then the relationship between jury size and benefits is not at issue. Raoul Berger, for example, discusses no issue but the one admitted in Justice White's majority opinion in *Williams*, that twelve was the accepted size of the jury to the authors of the Constitution.[40] Graphically, one would show a strictly legal decision by drawing a straight vertical line at the jury size intended by the framers of the Constitution. All commentators agree that, if the line is to be drawn this way—if a strictly legal decision is to be made—it would be drawn at the number twelve.

There must be some fact in contention other than constitutional fact for the Court to have held that the minimum permissible jury size was fewer than twelve. They did not discuss the particular juries in these cases, nor would such discussion have been appropriate. Thus, we are concerned with the characteristics of juries in general. We are in the realm of legislative fact and, indeed, statistical fact: the benefits derived from juries of different sizes, on the average, and the variation therein. That question should be amenable to social-science analysis.

The Benefit-Size Relationship

A social-science analysis can start with the assumption that the framers of the Constitution meant to assure a minimum level of benefits from the jury system. That level can be specified as the benefits resulting from a jury as it was known at the Constitutional Convention. Thus, our goal is to describe the size-benefits relationship. We already know one point on that locus: In 1787, a jury of twelve provided the minimum (or slightly more than the minimum) allowable benefit. There are two ways in which a smaller jury could now provide at least the minimum benefit (or, as we will see, the minimum value of benefits):

> The shape of the curve now is essentially flat between twelve and six, whatever its shape may have been then.
>
> The location of the curve has changed over time; specifically, it has moved higher so that minimum benefits are provided today with fewer jurors, although twelve jurors were required to produce that benefit in the late eighteenth century.

The decision in *Ballew* (1978) indicates that (as the Supreme Court sees it) the benefits curve must lie below the minimum line at jury sizes less than six. The Court, therefore, says that the benefits curve now crosses the minimum benefits line between five and six jurors. The decisions do not require that the curve then be flat, but the opinions, say the critics, are based on the assumption that larger juries provide no additional benefits. The benefits curve as seen by the Supreme Court, *as interpreted by its critics*, is shown in Figure 44.

---

40. R. Berger (1977) at 401, 405. Pabst (1973), in contrast, focuses on benefits.

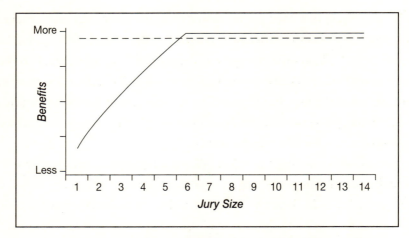

FIGURE 44: No Additional Benefits from More Than Six Jurors

The critics' assumption that the curve must be of this shape to support the Court's opinion is unfounded. Nonetheless, I will show that benefits could look like this. The critics are wrong in two ways: The benefits curve could be flat between twelve jurors and six with reasonable assumptions, and it need not be flat in this range to support the Court's position.

Moving the Curve

The possibility that the present-day benefits curve could be different from that of 1787 has never before been explored, although the distinction between movements *along* a relationship and movements *of* the relationship is fundamental to social science. It is easy enough to draw benefits curves "then" and "now," having the shape posited above. I do so in Figure 45. Minimum benefits may have been obtainable with no fewer than twelve jurors in 1787, yet be obtainable with six jurors today.

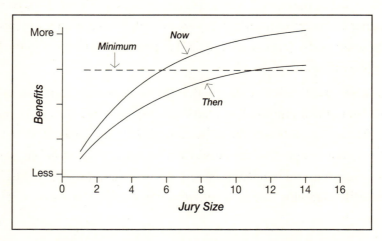

FIGURE 45: Benefits Function May Change Over Time

Graphically, either Figure 44 or Figure 45 supports the Court. It is a start to understand that there is a concept, indeed, a standard social-science concept, by which the Court's critics could be shown to be wrong. One must do more than just draw such curves, however. The curves should plausibly describe reality.[41] Evidence supporting either argument would be sufficient to exonerate the Court and silence the critics. Thus, I will proceed in a form adopted from legal briefs, arguing first that the benefits curve is, or may reasonably be believed to be (remembering the oleomargarine cases) flat; and second that, even if it isn't and has never been flat, it now rests (or may reasonably be believed to rest) where minimum benefits are provided by juries of six.

MEASURING BENEFITS

What benefit do we expect from juries? In setting out standards for the size of the jury, the Supreme Court did not address the question of why we have a jury in the first place. Selecting each jury separately for each trial implies both that we will not know in advance who (or what class of people) will decide the issues, and that whoever it is will not be "professional" at making these decisions.[42] Choosing one citizen at random would accomplish these ends, but has three drawbacks:

> Most individuals do not want the burden of determining, alone, the outcome of a case.
>
> Groups make fewer errors than individuals.[43]
>
> The "luck of the draw" would appear to play too large a part in the outcome, weakening public acceptance of the outcome and the system.

These points argue for the Court's requirement that the jury must be a group, but they do little to specify that group's size.

It is commonly held that the primary function of the jury is to determine fact. The right of review of higher courts is limited to review of the law,[44] or grossly incorrect fact

---

41. If we apply the Court's logic in *Purkett* (1995) to this situation, we need not even assert plausibility. Apparently courts may accept proffered reasons even if they are ridiculous (as, for example, in peremptory juror challenge). The sine qua non is that the reason can be articulated.

42. There is ordinarily no rule against having experienced people—persons who have served on previous juries—on a jury. The typical juror-selection procedure of "sampling with replacement" virtually assures that some people will be called twice for jury duty before everyone is called once. See Pabst and Munsterman (1975) and Kennebeck (1975).

43. See Taylor and Faust (1952). Larger groups do not do better than smaller groups, however.

44. The Seventh Amendment to the U.S. Constitution:

> [N]o fact tried by a jury, shall be otherwise re-examined in any court of the United States, than according to the rules of the common law.

determination. Incorrect fact reasonably held does not constitute legal error. As we would prefer that the jury be correct, not just reasonable, we might want to compare jury decisions to some absolute standard. Recent determinations from DNA evidence that many jury findings of criminal guilt were in error should instruct us to make objective determinations wherever possible. Unfortunately, no such standard exists in most cases.[45]

Jury Nullification

Besides, we don't always want juries to be objectively correct. A newspaper publisher, John Peter Zenger, was tried in 1735 for libel against the incumbent royal governor, William Cosby. The judges charged the jury with the responsibility for determining only whether Zenger had made the statements which he obviously had made, not whether they were true. Although the fact of publication could hardly have been in doubt, the jury found Zenger not guilty.[46] In modern times juries can either find defendants "temporarily insane," or otherwise follow the time-honored tradition of acquitting when they do not want to bring in a conviction. This is called "jury nullification."[47]

To be fair, it is not only juries that nullify. Prosecutors do not bring cases on the basis of guilt or innocence, as they see it, but on the basis of convictability. This concept turns out to be useful in the mathematical modeling in the Appendix to Chapter 4, but might

---

45. Note that all capital cases are tried before twelve-person juries. The number of innocent people who have been convicted by twelve-person juries should make us aware that, regardless of size, the jury as determiner of fact is not nearly as good as it should be. For example, see S. Cohen (2003).

46. See Hyman and Tarrant (1975) and Brody (1995). Levy (1999) emphasizes that two grand juries had refused to indict Zenger, his trial following an independent government prosecution by the royal governor Zenger had criticized. The jury decided that the truth of Zenger's criticisms outweighed any law against his voicing them.

47. *Local 36* (1949) at 339:

> However, in flagrant instances, the jury has always exercised the pardoning power, notwithstanding the law, which is their actual prerogative.

Paul Newman's character says to the jury in *The Verdict* (Fox, 1982), "Today, *you* are the law." Marilyn vos-Savant agrees:

> Although your obligation as a juror is to follow the law as given, when it comes to voting, people may vote their conscience. This is one of the ways in which we, the people, keep our legislators from having too much power.

"Ask Marilyn," *Parade* magazine, July 20, 1997, at 12. Wenger and Hoffman (2003) write, at 1119, that "nullificatory juries protect us from rule by legal economists." Judges do not inform jurors of their nullification rights.

> I argue that a nullification instruction is more likely to lead juries to exercise their nullification power in the appropriate cases, and the absence of an instruction causes more social harm than good.

Brody (1995) at 108. Spence (1989) is annoyed that civil-jury nullification is often overturned on appeal, but in criminal law the jury, as Paul Newman should have said, determines fact, not law.

lead a reader to wonder why the mathematicians bother. It has lead one commentator to coin the phrase "pre-emptive nullification," the failure to prosecute.[48]

One standard by which to assess a jury decision is how the judge would have voted. In Figure 46 I reproduce information on that question, from a 1966 study.

	Percentage
Disagree on	
Facts Alone	34
Values and Facts	45
Values Alone	21
Facts	79
Values	66

FIGURE 46: Causes of Juror Disagreement

> The conventional and official role of the jury, although it is not clear that any-one believes this, is that it is the trier of facts and nothing else. [This table] tells us that in only one-third of the cases is the jury's fact finding the sole source of judge-jury disagreement; in the remaining two-thirds of the cases the sources of disagreement are seen fully only by looking beyond the official role of the jury.[49]

Thus, one of the characteristics of a jury is that it provides the flexibility which, if exercised by professional jurists, we would call "arbitrary abuse of power," but when used by lay jurors we call "humanitarian" or "the voice of the community."

THE JURY AS REPRESENTING ALL POSSIBLE JURIES

John Kaplan's analysis of decision making on the jury shows how

> under various circumstances a rational fact finder might believe it better to acquit a defendant who he felt was certainly guilty than to convict him.[50]

This view, that the "correct" verdict is not an absolute rendering of guilt or innocence (or, in civil cases, the finding of wrong or harm), can be formalized: a correct verdict is

---

48. Conrad (1998) at 178. A recent famous criminal case, the allegation that basketball star Kobe Bryant forcibly raped a woman in Colorado, ended this way.

49. Kalven and Zeisel (1966) at 116. Figure 46, based on 962 cases, is their Table 30, also at 116. Kalven and Zeisel do not contend that one party or the other is correct. Only the differences are of interest.

50. J. Kaplan (1968) at 1076.

as close as possible to the typical verdict that would be returned by all possible jury subsets of the full community if each one had viewed the trial.[51]

Correct by this interpretation means "representative." Hans Zeisel's critique of *Williams* is based entirely on a demonstration that the variation in representation of the six-person jury is larger than that of the twelve-person jury.[52] As courts have consistently refused to overturn verdicts on the basis of the composition of the particular juries that reached them,[53] it is not clear why the increased variation in representativeness of the personnel in the smaller jury, and therefore presumably of its decisions, would be an argument against it.

There may be a difference between juries being representative in their composition and being representative in their decisions. Decision representation has been formally explained:

> Perhaps a fairer way to describe the juror's responsibility is for him to determine whether the accused is "convictable" or not. This is the definition of "guilty" that we imply. Thus, e.g., if we calculate the probability of an erroneous conviction that is not the same as the probability that an innocent defendant is convicted.[54]

Although this definition was constructed to provide empirical estimation, not to include functions of the jury other than determining "fact,"[55] it can usefully serve both purposes. Convictable by whom? By a representative jury. Error occurs when a particular jury's decision differs from the "norm." Not knowing what the norm of decisions is, analysts look at the norm of jury characteristics. However, none has shown that jury decisions are affected by variation in these characteristics, and thus that a demographically "unrepresentative" jury produces an unrepresentative decision.[56]

---

51. Walbert (1971) at 548, note 68. This is not necessarily Walbert's standard. It is what he infers the Court's standard to be, citing *Smith* (1940).

52. Zeisel (1971) at 716:

> It is clear, then, that however limited a twelve-member jury is in representing the full spectrum of the community, the six-member jury is even more limited, and not by a "negligible" margin.

Since, on the average, even a one-person jury is representative, Zeisel's language is misleading. His proof that smaller juries have more variance in representation should not sound like a statement about the expected verdict from that representation, or its variation.

53. For example, see *Rives* (1879). In *Castaneda* (1977) jury data was aggregated over eleven years. The composition of the jury that indicted the defendant is never mentioned. Investigation of the system of which the jury is a part, rather than the jury itself, was initiated in *Smith* (1940).

54. Gelfand and Solomon (1977a) at 301.

55. [T]he juror's charge is not to render a decision as to the guilt of the defendant but rather whether the evidence is sufficiently convincing to establish a very strong probability of guilt." Gelfand and Solomon (1977a) at 300.

56. As attorneys shop for advantageous forums and use jury-composition experts to assist in manipulating jury composition, they also insist that it is answers to *voir dire* questions and socioeconomic or

The norm is not a jury representative of the population. The peremptory-challenge system in the United States is clear evidence that we do not insist, even on average, that juries should be representative, or its surrogate, random.[57] Studies of the occupational distribution of jurors indicate that, whether measured before or after challenge, juries are not statistically representative of the nation.[58] As I argue in Chapter 5, neither should they be. Assessing juries by their composition is not the same as assessing the fairness of the system that recruited them. I will find that juries fairly assembled do not look like "representative" juries, in the sense that "representative" is typically measured. Similarly, I hold that any jury-size study that is based on the same faulty "representative" concept is itself flawed.

Criticisms of *Williams* are all based on there being greater "error" in representation from a distribution of small juries than from a distribution of large juries. They did not inquire whether that "error" had been, or could be, ameliorated by other changes in the jury system. No critic has attempted to measure the unrepresentativeness of juries—or of their decisions—attributing some of it to jury size. Nor has anyone assessed the possibility that alternative reforms could bring the system back to its twelve-member-jury distribution of representation (of all jury findings) with smaller juries, if they have not already achieved that standard.

In short, critics of the allowance of smaller juries compared jury size with some theory about juries. They neglected to examine juries historically. They neglected to ask if the benefits of the modern six-person jury were lower than the twelve-person jury assumed by the framers of the Constitution. They assumed that the framers' concept was of numbers, not of benefits. Indeed, the critics have not dealt with the issue of benefits at all.

FROM ERROR TO BENEFITS TO VALUATION

My aim is not to convince anyone that the Supreme Court's decisions in the jury-size cases were correct, though I think that argument can be made. I will show only that they were defendable. There is insufficient evidence for a definitive finding about either the shape or the location of the benefits curve; but there *is* sufficient evidence to find both of my arguments plausible, that is to say, rationally and reasonably held by the Supreme Court. It requires understanding *what* curve (what function of jury size) we should be discussing.

---

observed characteristics—but not "protected" characteristics such as age, race, or gender—that are related to how a juror will vote. At least they are so instructed by *Batson* (1986). But again see *Purkett* (1995), in which the Court says the proffered explanation does not have to be plausible.

57. In amending the Federal Rules of Criminal Procedure, Congress in 1977 declined to adopt the Supreme Court's proposal to reduce the number of peremptory challenges. See Zeisel and Diamond (1978).

58. See E. Mills (1962) and Robinson (1950).

Valuing Benefits from Reduced Error

As much as statistics is concerned with estimation, it is concerned with error. Two types of error have standard definitions:

> **Type I error.** The false positive—convicting an innocent person or finding for the plaintiff when the defendant is blameless.

> **Type II error.** The false negative—acquitting a guilty person or finding for the defendant when he has wronged the plaintiff.

These two types of errors have different consequences.

> One of the fundamental feelings of our society is that it is far more serious to convict an innocent man than to let a guilty man go free.[59]

Similar though perhaps less strong feelings apply to civil cases. Thus, Type I error should be weighted several times Type II error on the benefit scale. How many times? Stuart Nagel and Marian Neef, following Sir William Blackstone, create a compound benefit measure in which Type I error is ten times more serious than Type II error.[60] John Kaplan, however, informs us that we can find equally august sources for ratios of five to one and twenty to one.[61] It seems unnecessary to choose a specific weighting scheme in a theoretical exposition. Indeed, it seems more likely that a comprehensive "benefits" measure would value Type I and Type II errors differently depending at least on the nature of the crime (or civil complaint). To make the benefits scale accord with our accustomed sense of direction, we should at first think of benefits as related to the complement of error, although we will find benefits to be more complicated than this:

$$\text{benefit} = f(1 - \text{weighted probable error})$$

That is, benefits are not necessarily directly measured by the chance of getting it right. They may be a positively valued *function* of the chance of getting it right. For example, we might weight convicting a serial murderer higher than convicting a once-only murderer, from an objective count of the number of lives lost. Benefits are measurable, at least in principle, although people can disagree about what to measure, or how.

---

59. J. Kaplan (1968) at 1073.

60. Nagel and Neef (1977), at 86, justify their choice as follows:
> In view of the influence of Blackstone on the founding fathers of the American Constitution when it came to legal matters, that trade-off weight of ten can therefore be considered as roughly reflecting their constitutional intent.

61. J. Kaplan (1968), at 1077, citing M. Hale, *Pleas of the Crown* (W. Stokes and E. Ingersoll ed., 1847) volume 2 at 288, and J. Fortescue, *Commendation of the Laws of England* (F. Grigor, translator, 1917). The Blackstone cite is *Commentaries on the Laws of England* (1769 edition) volume 4 at 358.

This definition is sufficient to get us from Figures 43 through 45. What we want to know is not how much error is reduced by some procedure, but how much society values the measurable benefits engendered by that reduction in error.[62] Valuation is a subjective reaction to benefits. Valuation can be more completely defined as an indexed-value function:[63]

$$\text{Valuation} = V_1 + V_2 - V_3 - V_4$$

where

V_1 = f(benefit from correct convictions);

V_2 = f(benefit from correct acquittals, including discretionary acquits of some "guilty" parties);

V_3 = f(negative benefit from incorrect convictions [Type I error]); and

V_4 = f(negative benefit from incorrect acquittals [Type II error]).

As many commentators have noted, we do formally value incorrect criminal convictions more highly than incorrect civil findings for plaintiff, when we require proof "beyond reasonable doubt" for a criminal conviction, but only the "preponderance of the evidence" in civil cases. Where "benefit" is some measurable characteristic, "valuation" is society's assessment of how much it wants increasingly more benefit, implicitly understanding that it must pay for it. Thus, the way society values error in its judicial system is important, and what seems like a mathematical abstraction is what we actually do in determining the parameters of the judicial system.[64] Equally important is how society values the absence of error.

At the very least, we would expect society's valuation of correct convictions to depend on the frequency of correct convictions. If the system already is correct most of the time, then an additional increment of correctness might not be as highly valued as when the system is incorrect most of the time. If each V_i is a nonlinear function of its argument, the sum is likely to be nonlinear with respect to some parameter that changes the arguments of the V_i. In particular, if variation in jury size affects the proportion of cases that falls into each of these four categories, an overall valuation curve can be described.

---

62. Confusing error with its societal evaluation, or ignoring the value of error, is a fundamental mistake made by many analysts, including Nagel and Neef (1977). Ignoring the problem of aggregation of individual values to society's "values" is a simplification forced on anyone who wishes to write one book at a time.

63. By "indexed" I mean that there is a common metric that allows comparisons. This is how money functions, allowing comparison between steak and potatoes, shoes and video rentals. But if steak is more valuable than potatoes, why do we ever eat the latter? It must be that the value of a next ounce of steak is less than the value of the previous ounce. Valuation is too difficult to go into more detail here. We have to be satisfied, for now, with understanding that my exposition is deeper than anyone before me ever went.

64. See Posner (1972) at 334 for a discussion of the cost (hence, the value) of error in civil procedures.

An argument that the societal valuation curve is flat within some range of benefits (say, that flowing from six-person or larger juries) could follow directly. It could also follow from a more detailed derivation of these value functions. I do not want to interrupt the flow of the logic of this chapter to bring mathematical models of jury decisions into this discussion. That material appears in the Appendix to Chapter 4. The interested reader would find this a convenient place to consult that appendix.

The Relationships Among Jury Size, Benefits, and Valuation

When we realize the complexity of error in judicial outcomes, and the many levels of valuation that must be combined into a rule about how jurors should vote in the face of uncertainty, we see that the critics' simple assertion that smaller juries make more errors is not sufficient, or even correct. Actually, their own models show that larger juries are more dominated by error if unanimity is required, although it is the presumably lightly valued error of acquitting the guilty. An increase in society's ability to bring guilty people to trial would reduce the probability that an innocent person was convicted by any size jury. If the error in bringing innocent people to trial has been reduced, and if the error in convicting innocent people dominates society's weights, then a modern six-person jury could be as efficient in avoiding this error as a twelve-person jury of 1787.

The critics of *Williams* and *Colgrove*, by focusing on error, simply missed a fundamental tenet of social science. An individual's demand curve, for example, is not a statement of how much better off he will be, by some objective measure, if he purchases more of a good at a lower price. It is a measure of how much that individual values that increased well-being. The aggregate-demand curve reflects desires of many individuals, the anticipated value from the perceived benefit of a good or service; not the benefit itself.[65] The critics were stuck on the mathematics of error, where what counts is the sociology of error. We should at least be skeptical, at this point, that the Court's critics, harping on a presumed increase in variance of personal characteristics within smaller juries, have come to grips with what I take to be the constitutional question, the provision of minimal societal *value* from the benefits of juries.[66]

---

65. Another way to see this is that the metric of "value" must be currency, because value will be compared with cost. The metric of benefit, however, is something else. Thus we can measure amounts of different antacid treatments in their own units (say, pills or tablespoons), and their benefits in units of result, the reduction of stomach acid or the discomfort therefrom. However, an individual must go to the next step, to *value* these differences in dollar terms, in order to decide what kind to purchase, given their prices.

66. In the twelfth century, proof "was not a burden but a benefit," we are told by Holdsworth (1903) at 302. "Better proof" meant more witnesses for one side than the other. How would one get more witnesses? Ultimately, we call the ability to prove one's case before a jury a benefit because it was paid for!

THE SHAPE OF THE VALUATION CURVE

As reducing Type I error may result in an increase in Type II error, and vice versa, one could hope to find a jury-size or jury-voting scheme that produced minimum weighted error, for a given set of weights.[67] This optimum would be sensitive to assumptions about the parameters of the model and the relative weights of Type I and Type II error, as well as weights for correct decisions. However, explicit weighting is not necessary to demonstrate the difference between a socioeconomic analysis and the probability models used to criticize the *Williams* decision. I will show a locus on the assumption that there is a weighting system, without further description of what that system is or how we determine it.

In Figure 47, three relationships are pictured. Start in the upper left quadrant. The curve there is the same curve that appears in Figure 43. It expresses the same relationship between jury size and benefits, a larger jury providing measurably higher benefits than a smaller one. The graph is derived from decreasing incremental error as the size of the jury increases, which is the common concept underlying all mathematical models of error.

I do not place values on the vertical axis. We have no metric for benefits. The only concept of importance here is that benefits increase at a decreasing rate as jury size increases.

The upper right quadrant expresses our valuation of these increased benefits (say, the increased value of the increased reduction in variation among jury decisions compared with the average jury). Its vertical axis is the same benefit scale as in the upper left quadrant, and its horizontal axis is the value of benefits, which also is unlabeled to indicate that we do not have a metric for this concept, in the jury context, either. It may help to view this graph by turning the page 90 degrees counter-clockwise. Remember, however, that benefits seen this way increase from right to left. (The graph will look "correct" in a mirror.) It is reasonable to assume that as benefits increase we value each addition less than the prior addition. That is, this function also contains diminishing increments of the value of whatever it is valuing (here, the benefit from reduced error).

Unlike benefits, which we can model (say, by verdict error), I have to posit (I cannot derive) that increments to benefit are less and less valued, on the margin. I can argue for it, however. For example, as we add lanes to highways, we may decrease congestion, even if the number of cars increases. We can measure this decrease in congestion, which we can call the "benefit" of the added lanes. The reduction in congestion presumably is largest from one lane to two, smaller from two to three, etc. But beyond the measurable decrease in congestion is society's valuation of it, so that even if four lanes to five would decrease

---

67. Nagel and Neef (1975) explore this possibility, but quickly leave it. Their analysis is based on the one-parameter model.

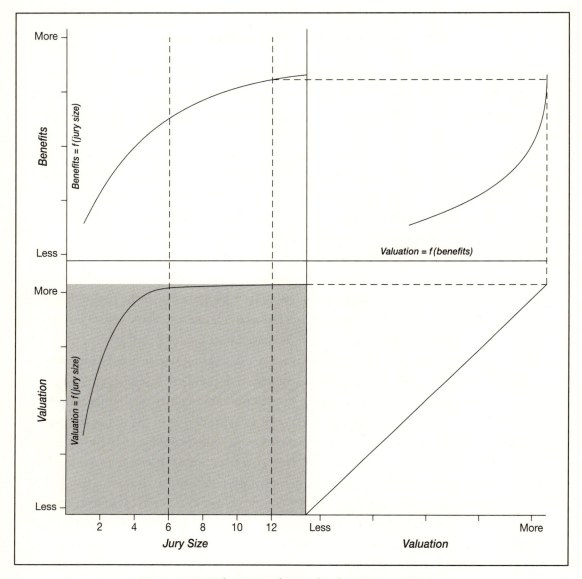

FIGURE 47: Valuation of Benefits from Larger Juries

congestion by the same amount as three lanes to four, we might decide to stop at four lanes because our valuation of the decrease in congestion decreases. Where the decrement in congestion from three lanes to four was worth the cost, an equivalent additional decrement may not be, even if the additional cost would be the same. That decreasing valuation of additional benefits is pictured in the upper right quadrant of Figure 47. Increasingly more benefits are required to gain each additional unit of valuation.

I contend that neither the benefits curve nor the valuation curve is extreme. They look about like most people think the world is, with decreasing incremental benefits, and decreasing incremental valuation of increased benefits. Running another mile might do you some better, but not as much as the last mile; and even if the additional benefit were the same as that from the last mile, you don't value it enough to continue.

The bottom right quadrant of Figure 47 contains a 45-degree line. Its purpose is to bring the horizontal axis of the valuation curve to the vertical axis of the lower half of the graphic. The lower left quadrant, then, plots the valuation against that which generated the benefits, increased jury size. I have shaded the bottom left quadrant to bring the reader's attention to it. I trace these functions from benefits to jury size for a jury of twelve persons. This is the picture of the societal valuation of different benefits generated by different size juries. Its shape is what we are after.

The result is a curve that is flatter than critics of the Court's jury-size decisions imagined. Their imagination was hampered by forgetting that societal decisions are based on valuation of benefits from reduced error, not on the reduction of error itself.

The notion that successive improvements have less value is incorporated regularly in police and regulatory behavior, and perhaps more critically in budget discussions about police and regulators. First, an additional policeman probably will not reduce crime by the same amount as the last policeman. Second, even if the crime reduction would be the same, its value to us would be lower.

Some readers may find difficult the concept of placing two relationships in graph quadrants, and following their effect on each other around the axes. This form of economic analysis appears to be extinct, but in the early decades of the twentieth century this is how economics was done. As economics becomes more empirical, it seems to become less visual. I applaud the former, but not the latter. Easy empiricism has led to lazy conceptualization. I see this often in statistical analyses in litigation. As in the preceding two chapters, I will time and again, throughout this book, find technically correct but conceptually faulty use of statistical methods. There is no shortage of intelligence in the expert community. Given the common failure to conceptualize the problem adequately, I conclude that there is a dearth of intellectuality.

Hey, It's Good Enough

Classical economists might argue that the "value" of reducing error should be calculated from the opportunity cost of putting innocent people in jail, plus the damage done to society by freeing miscreants.[68] Unless there is a reason to believe that the next guilty person who is convicted by the better jury, or the next innocent person freed, has different opportunity costs from those treated incorrectly by the less accurate (smaller) jury, the classical argument would have the "value" function be a straight line.

---

68. Most economists who delve into legal studies are "classical" in this sense. See D. Martin (1972), Posner (1972), and Landes (1971).

I don't have to argue against the view that individual costs should be counted. It is sufficient to argue that there are social benefits to maintaining an accepted judicial system. The system is accepted if it keeps errors below some point. Doing better than that point has some value, to be sure, but not as much value as getting there, no matter which individuals benefit from the correct decisions or suffer from the error. I recommend the United States' occupation of Iraq in 2003 and thereafter as an example. Whatever "establishing security" means, it is not the elimination of crime. Nonetheless, everyone appears to agree that there is some level of "security" below which the economy and the society do not function, above which they do.

A traditional analytic result of positing a fixed benefit (after some point) is that average and marginal benefits diverge, even if marginal benefits do not change. The marginal benefit of additional reduction of error will be below the average benefit after the system reaches the critical level of acceptability. Thus I could make the final valuation-jury curve flat without violating any cherished economic assumption. Society's valuation of the benefits of a larger jury cannot be less than of a smaller jury, one would think, but it might not be greater at all.

THE LOCATION OF THE VALUATION CURVE

There are both logical and empirical grounds for believing that the 2005 six-member jury provides as much benefit—and a fortiori as much value—as the 1787 twelve-member jury. What would be required for this to be true? From the models in this chapter's appendix, one can derive two answers:

> If the police and state's attorneys are better able to discern guilt and innocence before trial, so that a higher proportion of those brought to trial are guilty, then society can achieve the 1787 rate of correct and incorrect convictions with smaller juries.

> If individual jurors are better able to discern guilt when they see it, and if the system is at least as good in bringing guilty people before juries, then a given level of benefits should be accessible with a smaller jury.

The questions then are:

> How much better do the police authorities have to be to allow more variation in smaller modern juries to come out at about the same place larger juries came out over two hundred years ago?

> How much better do current juries have to be in order for current six-member juries to provide the benefits of 1787 twelve-member juries?

> Is there any evidence that current police or current juries *are* this much better?

> Is there any reason to think that we value jury benefits so much less now
> that we require the greater benefits of the twelve-person jury to com-
> pensate, even if benefits from the smaller jury are now what those from
> the larger jury were then?

Police Quality

There is no evidence that the proportion of those brought to trial who are convicted has
increased over time. This may not be as sad a statement about the police as it appears to
be. Legislatures have burdened the police with many new kinds of "crimes," some of which
(especially "victimless" crimes, such as possession of small amounts of drugs) lead often to
jury nullification. It means only that we cannot rely on increased quality of the initiating
system to relieve the burden on jurors to distinguish guilty from not-guilty defendants.

Juror Quality

Charles W. Joiner, U. S. district judge in the Eastern District of Michigan, thinks jurors have
improved perceptibly during his tenure:

> I have noted that jurors today appear to be more highly qualified than they
> were thirty years ago. This seems to be the result of three factors: (1) The key
> number system . . . results in fewer old and unemployed persons on our jury
> panels and brings to these same panels the vigorous young or middle-aged
> persons. . . . (2) The increased mobility of people . . . has an impact on their
> ability to make decisions and to deal with ideas and facts that may be strange
> to them. (3) Finally, television has increased the knowledge of almost all of
> us . . . about the world and how it operates.[69]

The "key number" system is a form of random selection of jurors from source lists, as will
be described in Chapter 5. It is being contrasted with the "key man" system, in which jurors
are selected by a commissioner. Although this statement may help establish the plausibility that jurors have improved over time, it is hardly evidence. That there *is* evidence on this
proposition is quite as remarkable as the fact that it has never been used within the context of a model allowing shifts of the benefit curve over time.

The studies by Alan Gelfand and Herbert Solomon, discussed in the Appendix to
Chapter 4, were designed for empirical estimation. I emphasized above that their careful
definition of guilty as "convictable" was required for estimation of the model's parameters
from conviction data. Mathematically, the parameters could have been defined as

---

69. Joiner (1975) at 149. Whatever weight one gives Joiner's impression of the quality of the jury, the
causal factors are just guesses. Interestingly, he does not mention either the quality or quantity of education, although average education levels rose markedly over the thirty years he was a judge.

$$g° = \text{probability of conviction if tried by average jury}$$

and

$$\mu = \text{jurors' ability or desire to emulate } g°$$

where μ is the Greek letter "mu."

Employing their mathematics (but not their statistics), I could derive David Walbert's model as a limiting case of Gelfand and Solomon's. I do that in this chapter's appendix. Here I am talking about estimates from the model. Since I found the Gelfand and Solomon definitions to be functionally equivalent to a "representative" view of guilt, I think no more than the caveat in this paragraph is necessary to bring out the limited meaning of these parameter estimates.

Gelfand and Solomon estimate their parameters from data recorded by Siméon Poisson, referring to the 1820s and 1830s in France. At this point I should provide evidence that however good or bad jurors were in early nineteenth-century France, they were not worse than jurors in the United States in the late eighteenth century. If there is any bias, then, it would be against finding that twenty-first-century jurors are sufficiently better than the jurors known to our Founding Fathers to justify the smaller jury. I will provide no such evidence, though I suppose by some inferences (from education and other data) a comparison could be made. I leave the matter at the level of argument.

Current estimates come from the same 225 observations, reported by Harry Kalven and Hans Zeisel, that everyone else has used. The French rules allowing conviction by majority vote, the interest of French mathematicians in the jury process, and the limited information gathered by the Chicago jury project before it was determined that they should not know initial jury votes,[70] conspire to provide us sufficient information to make some estimates of both system and juror parameters. This is how Gelfand and Solomon describe their findings:

> It would appear that . . . the probable guilt of an accused on being brought to trial has remained constant despite a considerable difference in the criminal justice systems and differences in societal factors. . . . However, it also appears that juries have improved considerably in terms of not making errors in verdicts since μ . . . is significantly larger today. Of course, more analysis and interpretation would be required before one could place strong faith in these conclusions.[71]

Their estimates of μ are presented in Figure 48.[72]

---

70. Kalven and Zeisel (1966) describe their run-in with the American Bar Association and discuss the difficulties of research on secret processes. A clever solution to this lack of data is the "shadow jury." See Zeisel and Diamond (1978).

71. Gelfand and Solomon (1974) at 36.

72. In Gelfand and Solomon (1973) several estimates are made from French data, including separation

	μ
France, 1825–1830	0.75
United States, 1966	0.90

FIGURE 48: Two Estimates of Juror Quality

I will calculate probabilities assuming that 70 percent of those brought to trial will be found guilty, to avoid having two causes for the resultant figures. In Figure 49 I calculate the joint probability of guilty and convicted. I have shaded the figures of most interest, from the values in Figure 48. Gelfand and Solomon's estimates show that the present-day U.S. system, if different from that of nineteenth-century France, is better.

μ	Jury of Five	Jury of Six	Jury of Twelve
0.65	0.5354	0.4530	0.5511
0.70	0.5858	0.5210	0.6175
0.75	0.6275	0.5814	0.6619
0.80	0.6595	0.6308	0.6864
0.85	0.6814	0.6669	0.6968
0.90	0.6940	0.6889	0.6996
0.95	0.6992	0.6984	0.7000

FIGURE 49: Probabilities of Guilty and Convicted; Majority Rules

The perfect jury will achieve a joint probability guilty and convicted equal to 0.70, because this calculation requires that the defendant be guilty and the jury discern it. A 1787 jury of twelve would have failed to convict thirty-eight out of seven hundred guilty defendants. The twenty-first-century jury of six would fail to convict only one of seven hundred guilty defendants. To the extent that we value convicting the guilty, the existing evidence supports the Supreme Court's decisions in *Williams* (1970) and *Colgrove* (1973).

What about *Ballew* (1978)? Is five too small? The calculation presented in Figure 49 for the five-person jury with μ = 0.90 indicates that five is not too small a jury, compared with the twelve-person jury where μ = 0.75. Indeed, by this calculation the five-person jury is "smarter" than the six-person jury. That is because it requires only three out of five jurors (60 percent) to be correct, whereas the six-person jury requires that four out of six (67

---

by crime and using various levels of judgment. In Gelfand and Solomon (1974) these estimates are summarized as here. Several estimates from the U.S. data were made from solutions to different sets of equations. The figures shown here were also used by Gelfand and Solomon (1974) at 36 as a summary of those separate calculations.

percent) be correct, in these models where the majority usually wins over (convinces) the minority.

We value more than just convicting the guilty. Figure 50 shows the joint probability of conviction when not guilty, multiplied by one thousand to avoid printing many zeros. This is a calculation of Type I error when seen from the system's point of view. The smaller the jury, the easier it is to make a mistake in convicting the innocent, because large juries have a hard time convicting at all. One reason for the twelve-person jury may well have been the large weighting we place on not convicting the innocent. Although the six-person jury of today avoids that error less well than the twelve-person jury of 1787, in both cases the amount of error is very small.

μ	Jury of Five	Jury of Six	Jury of Twelve
0.65	1.57566	0.55148	0.00101
0.70	0.72900	0.21870	0.00016
0.75	0.29297	0.07324	0.00002
0.80	0.09600	0.01920	0.00000
0.85	0.02278	0.00342	0.00000
0.90	0.00300	0.00030	0.00000
0.95	0.00009	0.00000	0.00000

FIGURE 50: Probabilities of Not Guilty and Convicted (Times 1,000); Majority Rules

Although the smaller jury "loses" in this measure, the Court's decision must be based on the benefits, or the value thereof, not the measures themselves. From reasonable weightings of the benefits from not making these errors, the Court could rationally declare that six-person juries were not too small, but five-person juries were. The valuation of benefits ultimately is a legislative function. The most reasonable stance in the Court's weighting the value of the benefits derived from different size juries, as benefits change over time, is that valuation remains constant. With a constant valuation scale of increased benefits at every jury size, the Court's decision was properly permissive.

Had our values changed so that we now required the greater benefits of the twelve-person jury, it would have been appropriate for legislatures to retain the larger juries. It would seem, from the rapid adoption of the smaller jury described above, that the value of the benefits from more-accurate jury decisions did not increase. The only argument against this conclusion is that legislatures ultimately compare value to cost. So there is room to quibble, to fancy that valuations did change. There is no room to argue that the Court's decision was wrong on that account. If legislators thought that accuracy would improve with larger juries, they did not, however, value this increased accuracy enough to pay for it.

But . . .

The arguments presented here have distressed people to whom they have been presented, all of whom were committed to viewing the Supreme Court's use of social-science evidence negatively. Criticizing the Court's inadequate consideration of social-science method is a well-founded industry. Nothing in this chapter is intended as praise for the Court's abilities in social-science analysis. Alas, neither have I been able to praise the critics. This has not made the critics happy.

Michael Saks has presented two arguments defending his criticism of the Court.[73] One is that the sole criterion for jury selection is representativeness. As I have pointed out above, the average jury would be equally representative if it is only one person as at any other size, if that person is randomly selected. Saks would counter that a particular jury has more chance of being representative if it is larger than if it is smaller. He is correct: The variance of non-representativeness decreases the larger is the jury. So, is this an argument for juries of twenty? Thirty?

What counts, we now know, is the *value* of diminishing variation in representation among juries. It is the Supreme Court's insistence that the jury *system* must be representative, not the specific jury, that obviates the representation argument. There may be some value in reducing demographic variation among juries, but the Court has never expressed it. The constitution overtly requires only impartiality.

Given the poor procedures by which juries historically have been recruited, juries today are probably more representative than ever before. Increases in the ability of the jury system to gather people randomly from the eligible population—indeed, just a broader definition of "eligible," which only since the 1970s includes minorities and females—would argue once again that the Court was correct in allowing jury size to diminish while the benefits at least remained equivalent to those in 1787. Furthermore, though the Court proclaims the primacy of representativeness of the jury,[74] it clearly does not mean it. The single most effective way to make juries more representative of venires would be to eliminate the peremptory challenge.[75] I do not think critics can rely on representativeness of juries to argue that their size should be twelve.

---

73. These points can be found in some writings by Michael Saks in the 1970s, and come also from private conversations. Those conversations took place decades ago—as did the initial draft of this chapter—and may or may not reflect Saks' current views.

74. See, for example, *Smith* (1940), but see Chapter 5 for my critique of the Court's measurement of this jury representativeness.

75. The venire is a group of potential jurors assembled by a clerk of the court, and directed to a particular courtroom that needs a jury. Venire members are interviewed by the judge and attorneys, accepted, excused, dismissed for cause or dismissed by the peremptory challenge of one of the parties. Each party

In my analysis, the objective of the jury is finding fact. Representativeness is either a means to fact finding or a constraint on achievement of that objective. Saks' position is functionally equivalent to asserting the strictly legal issue, about which there is no debate: The framers of the Constitution meant "twelve." Thus Saks is not wrong; he simply leaves no room for social-science analysis.

A more interesting argument is that fact finding requires contention, and small groups are too tame.[76] The larger group does have a better chance of having a contentious member, but that means larger juries will find it more difficult to reach conclusions, which is not necessarily an argument in their favor. Saks means that the *same* people will be more contentious in a larger group. This could be a powerful argument if it is shown that 1) it is true; and 2) contention leads to better fact finding. By Saks' argument, the "smarter" people of today will not reach their potential in groups of six, and therefore my secondary calculations are incorrect. More important, the flat value-of-benefits curve I was able to generate as jury size varies ignored the problem of production. Benefits may be valued as I show them, but perhaps they cannot be obtained as I show them.

This argument is clever. It might even be correct. However, there is no evidence for it. Indeed, evidence on the efficacy of group processes suggests that groups of six or even twelve do not solve problems better than groups of three. Saks contends that smaller juries produce fewer serious arguments for conviction or acquittal than larger juries, a conclusion I believe cannot be drawn from empirical evidence about group behavior.[77]

Decades ago, Bernard Grofman proposed the interesting theoretical argument that groups can get better by admitting even inferior members. Recently, James Surowiecki has put forth the same idea in a more popular forum.[78] Both, however, rely on each individual's estimate of the "correct" answer being independent of the other individuals. As applicable as this theory may be to such results of multiple-independent-actor behavior as stock prices, it provides no information about jury decisions, which follow from juror interactions.

My presentation suffers from the same fault. It is static. It does not incorporate group processes.[79] Therefore, it is potentially vulnerable to such a process as Saks describes and even the fine-tuning that Grofman and perhaps Surowiecki would add, should groups of interacting individuals actually behave that way. We do not know that they do.

---

is allowed a fixed number of peremptory challenges, which is the space wherein jury selection "experts" ply their trade. The jury, then, is a (non-representative) subset of the venire.

76. The Supreme Court was much taken with this argument in *Ballew* (1978) at 235.

77. See Saks (1975).

78. See Grofman (1975) and Surowiecki (2004).

79. I suggest that the static nature of arguing from individual characteristics, without analyzing how those individuals interact, turns vigorous arguments in support of an "elite" democracy flaccid. The results of interaction are missing, for example, from Posner (2003). See Strodtbeck et al. (1957) and Strodtbeck and Hook (1961).

The deliberation-process model by Steven Penrod and Reid Hastie includes the concept that the more outnumbered a person is, the more likely it is that he will change his vote.[80] In the larger jury there are more possibilities for a lopsided vote distribution, but also more possibilities for a juror to change his mind (there being more minds that are changed, in their model, by a random number generator affected by the previous votes). Though they are critical of the six-person jury with a non-unanimous-conviction system, Penrod and Hastie do not find that the smaller jury per se is inferior.

Several people have contended that although jurors get smarter, cases get harder. I made that suggestion above, referring to the kinds of laws that lead jurors not to want to convict. However, that does not speak to my argument that society may have a flat valuation curve, in the relevant range, out of the additional benefits from a not-flat error curve. Furthermore, to the extent that evidence of the superiority of today's jurors is derived from cases in two different time periods, changes in the severity of the cases has already been controlled for. Therefore either jurors are better, or cases are *easier*, or both; or cases are harder and jurors have improved by more than we measure. I suspect that the last is the best interpretation.

So? What Happened?

In the more than thirty years since juries of six have been allowed, society has not fallen apart. Many juries still have twelve members, but many have only six. Research on jury decision making has continued, but none of the early impressions has been changed. Most verdicts can be predicted from the majority of the initial vote, and the more lopsided that majority, the more likely it is to prevail. Research has delved into other factors, such as the receptivity of juries to expert testimony, whether jurors can submit questions to witnesses, the impact of the strength of the evidence, the definition of terms in the judge's instructions, even whether the jurors are informed about their ability to nullify the law, and just decide as they wish.[81] It appears to me that the jury-size issue has essentially disappeared, as it should have.

Though there surely is public criticism of jury verdicts, it, too, does not revolve around jury size. I think this public view is correct. Today's juries of six are as good as juries of twelve were in 1787. They provide the benefits we value, probably because jurors have gotten better, but also because even if the benefits of a jury of twelve are higher than those from a jury of six, society's basic criteria for juries are now satisfied at six. Society might have been satisfied with five-member juries, but although one may think the Court was wrong to prohibit them, it is a close call. The Supreme Court got it about right. It is the critics who did not.

---

80. See Penrod and Hastie (1980).

81. Devine et al. (2001) provide a massive review of forty-five years of studies of jury deliberations.

5

The Composition of the Jury

SPECIAL REPORT

Some lawyers say minorities underused on juries

So the *Oregonian* introduced a story in 1999, explaining why attorney Frank Stoller argued that his client in a felony theft case, Francisco Bermudez, could not get a fair trial in Yamhill County, Oregon.

> Yamhill County has 7,300 Latino residents, but in a preliminary hearing last month, Stoller argued that only a handful had served on county juries in the past few decades.
>
> "In Yamhill County, 9 percent of the population is Hispanic," he said in an interview. "We don't get that percentage of Hispanics on the juries, and in particular, not on the grand juries."

The allegation is typical: Jurors do not look like the people we see on the streets. Yamhill County's district attorney, Brad Berry, defended: "Latinos may not be in the pool from which jurors are selected in the first place if they lack a driver's license or voter registration."[1]

---

1. The *Oregonian*, August 27, 1999, at C1, continued at C8. This is a quotation of the *Oregonian*'s summary of Mr. Berry's position, not of him. There is no follow-up to this story. In a telephone conversation with Mr. Berry, August 9, 2001, I learned that the case was settled without trial, and therefore the jury question was not litigated.

Should jurors look like the local population? Do lists that are used for jury selection—"source lists"—contain Hispanics in the same proportion as some measure of the population? Even if so, will Hispanics be found eligible for jury service in the same proportions? Will they appear for service in the same proportions? And if not, should the jury system be held accountable?

There is a long history of litigation in this area. The major thrust of this chapter is to show that in trying to determine whether jury recruitment was biased by race or gender, statistical and legal analysts led the courts down the wrong road, and came out at the wrong place, where they remain to this day.

MEN OF HIGH CHARACTER

In Chapter 1 I outlined the evolution of the jury to an independent body of non-observers, the essential leap in British law that allowed room for such people as independent experts. I amplified that story in Chapter 4. A little more detail is relevant here, where the jury is again the subject.

By 1275 everyone in England, property holder ("freeman") or not ("villain"), had a right to a trial by a jury of his peers. However, the jury continued to be persons with knowledge of the facts. This system presupposes a stable society with little privacy, a society even then beginning to disappear. An appeal to a body of twenty-four knights could result in overturning the jury verdict. Such a result could lead to fines of the original jurors, called "attaint." As those jurors had been witnesses, a finding of attaint was a finding of perjury. Whether this system operated to force jurors to tell the truth, or to tell a "truth" they expected a panel of knights would want to hear, no one knows. But one suspects that villains of the day did not expect much from their judicial system.[2]

The rise of the merchant class brought about the need for experts with knowledge of the rules of trade. Such people testified or advised the traveling judges about standards to be used for products in commercial disputes. Only at the beginning of the fourteenth century did the English Parliament license attorneys, beginning to wrest this function from the Church. In another 150 years printing and cheap paper allowed the English-law concept of "precedent"—case law—to flourish. Thus at the same time that fact finding was undergoing change, so was determination of the law. The jury evolved to be persons independent of the events, who would be instructed by experts about relevant terms of trade, and by judges about the law.

If the jurors would not be identified by their association with the facts, how would they

---

2. McCart (1966) writes: "The threat of attaint must have brought about many verdicts based on expediency."

be identified? On what basis would they be appointed? Even the attaint jury that heard appeals became more representative, no longer restricted to knights. By the time of Blackstone, character replaced station. The attaint jury

> is to consist of twenty-four of the best men in the country, who are called the *grand* jury in the attaint, to distinguish them from the first or *petit* jury.[3]

The tradition that jurors would be independent men (yes, men) of high character moved across the Atlantic with the settlers.[4] That jurors had to be of upright character required that some persons in authority exercise some discretion. Despite the federal Constitution's requirement of impartiality, the establishment of jury commissioners with the mandate to screen potential jurors for their character appeared in the original constitution of every state of the United States except Louisiana which, by law rather than by constitution, constructed a jury system like other states.

State judicial systems are not supervised by the federal judiciary, but the Fourteenth Amendment holds states to providing all rights guaranteed by the federal constitution. Thus, since that amendment's adoption in 1865, federal courts have had oversight of state courts, to the extent that federal constitutional issues were raised. State jury systems came under federal review when it was alleged, in post-Civil-War federal courts, that the commissioners refused to acknowledge the good moral character of any but white males. As will be described below, even into the 1970s jury commissioners in some states were making "character" decisions about prospective jurors.

Through most of this time, the federal system was deferential to state systems. Not until 1968 do we find fundamental change in the federal system of jury selection, followed in the next twenty years by similar revisions to state procedures. Litigation about the fair-

---

3. Blackstone (1783) volume III at 351. Later, a person who had been convicted was called "attainted" when he had exhausted all of his appeals. Volume IV at 380:

> He is then called attaint, *attinctus*, stained or blackened. He is no longer of any credit or reputation.

4. Constitutional interpretation very much relies on this English heritage. Thus, for example, in *Wood* (1936), Chief Justice Hughes (for the Court) asks, at 134:

> (1) Whether, in the practice in England prior to the adoption of the Amendment, or in the colonies, there was an absolute disqualification of governmental employees to serve on juries in criminal cases, and (2) whether, either because of that practice, or in reason, such a disqualification should be regarded as essential to the impartiality of the jury and hence beyond the reach of the legislative power.

He answers, at 137:

> [I]t is manifest, to say the least, that there was no settled practice under the English law establishing an absolute disqualification of governmental employees to serve as jurors in criminal cases. And such a disqualification cannot, upon the ground of such a practice, be treated as embedded in the Sixth Amendment.

For some reason, the Court in *Crawford* (1909) had not understood this history.

ness of juror selection continues into the twenty-first century. That, then, is the subject of this chapter: recruiting and qualifying jurors.

Availability Analysis

I discussed the evolution of statistical analysis of employment-selection claims, from hiring to assignment to layoff, in Chapter 2. Initial analyses of hiring compared some version of the population, some estimate of the "relevant" labor force, to the work force of the firm whose practices were being challenged. Over time, it became clear that the theoretical underpinnings of this comparison were weak. Who was to say that this "labor force" correctly measured the people who wanted to or could perform these particular jobs, at this location, for this pay, at this time?

The other side of the comparison was no better conceived. The employer's work force had been hired over many years. The work force was what remained of many hires and many terminations, voluntary and not. The stock of accumulated hires, minus departures, on its face says nothing about hiring practices; and the labor force now might say nothing about who was available when hires were made. What can a comparison mean if both sides are so flawed?

The formation of juries would seem more amenable to traditional selection analysis. We do not care who "wants" to be a juror.[5] We are drafting juries, not hiring them. It seems reasonable to consider everyone equally available. The selection is made and service is performed over a relatively short period of time. Unlike a work force, a jury does not change its composition. Analyzing juries as selections from an availability pool is more like analyzing hires than analyzing work forces. Directing attention at those selected to be potential jurors, as opposed to those who serve, would cure another flaw, being similar to analysis of offers, not hires. It seems that most of the arguments by which availability analysis of hiring has fallen into ill repute do not apply. Jury duty, apparently, remains an area where the government is supposed to make fair "offers" to an "available" population, where "available" is not just a surrogate measure of applicants, but is the very pool from which jurors will be drafted.

---

5. In *Barksdale* (1980), the percent black among the male population of Orleans Parish was accepted as the basis of an availability comparison. Females could be jurors, but only if they affirmatively requested to be so. In footnote 16 at 255, the court concludes that "so few women asked to be placed on jury duty that the male population was the relevant one." Though this opinion was reversed *en banc* in *Barksdale* (1981), the full court also accepted the male population as the relevant population.

Where source lists were at issue in New York state, defendants suggested that labor unions could provide lists of names. Judge Learned Hand scoffed at the idea. Union members did not want to serve on juries any more than anyone else, he said. See *Dennis* (1950).

That is what analysts, attorneys, and judges think, reinforced by all prior literature on this subject. However, analyzing juries as selection from a population pool is still a fatally flawed approach. Statistical experts and courts routinely evaluate jury systems this way, and doing so, they get it wrong. It is time to see this approach as the error it has been. The solution: to analyze jury selection as a process, not an outcome.

What Should Juries Look Like?

Juries are supposed to be representative of their communities.[6] The Constitution does not say so,[7] but the Supreme Court thinks it does. Laws say so.[8] What does it mean?

It sounds like an outcome statement: Juries should "look like" a representative cross-section of the "community," like persons we see on the street. And in mental hospitals? In jails? In schools? Visitors? Transients? Non-citizens?

Well, no, of course not. We don't mean children, or felons, or persons certified to be incapable of reasoning rationally. It's not clear that we want people attending college in our

---

6. *Smith* (1940) at 130:

> It is part of the established tradition in the use of juries as instruments of public justice that the jury be a body truly representative of the community.

Fifty years later, in *Holland* (1990) at 480, the Court came to its senses:

> The Sixth Amendment requirement of a fair cross-section on the venire is a means of assuring, not a *representative* jury (which the Constitution does not demand), but an *impartial* one (which it does).

However, the "fair cross-section" is still of the "community." As the Ninth Circuit wrote—though any court might have—"This court is loath to attempt to discover or define communities, in Southern California or anywhere else." *Bradley* (1976) at 417. Later, we will discover that the Supreme Court has sort of defined "community," but its definition contradicts every measure the courts have ever accepted.

7. The Fifth Amendment to the Constitution requires a grand-jury indictment, but does not address the composition of the grand jury except to say that persons cannot be punished "without due process of law." The Sixth Amendment requires an "impartial jury" for criminal matters. The Fourteenth Amendment brings states under the requirement for due process, adding an "equal protection" (of all people) clause. Nowhere in the Constitution is the question of who is eligible for jury duty addressed. In 1789, when the Constitution was adopted, jury eligibility was reserved by economic class and, in many states, by race. That, it seems to me, is sufficient reason to reject a "strict constructionist" (or "originalist") interpretation of the Constitution.

8. The Federal Judiciary Act of 1968 incorporated the phrase "representative of the community" for the first time into law. Judges and legal analysts trace lines of reasoning by the specific laws, rules, regulations, or articles of the Constitution with which they are associated. Although an expert should understand the law under which he is operating—a topic to be discussed in some detail in Chapters 8 and 10—the various lines of analysis, all of which are asking a jury to be "fairly" drawn, are more confusing than helpful. They have blinded the courts to the fact that there is only one question, the answer to which should have one analytical foundation. See Beale (1983) for an opposing view. In this discussion I will not make distinctions among decisions based on the Fifth, Sixth, or Fourteenth Amendments, and various state and federal statutes. In his essay on jury decisions, Gewin (1975) makes the same simplification.

town to be judging people who have a more permanent association with it. We want juries to look like the *rest* of us, you know, the people—the adults—we think of as "the community." Or do we?

Joseph Gastwirth writes:

> Since there are few, if any, special skills required of jurors, courts typically determine the minority share of eligible persons from census figures for the appropriate age segment of the population in the relevant jurisdiction (city, county).[9]

What is this word "eligible"? Do analysts know "the minority share of *eligible* persons" against which to compare jurors?

Though they may be part of the community, we do not allow non-citizens to make state-authorized decisions about citizens.[10] Felons and institutionalized persons are systematically excluded from jury service. And what about people who do not speak English well enough to understand the trial proceedings, even if they are citizens? That's more of a practical problem, raising such questions as how would we translate for them, and could the translator be in the jury room during deliberations.[11] Most jurisdictions exclude them.

The most important and least recognized practical problem is mobility. To the extent that they are populated with strangers, the streets may look the same today as they did yesterday; but some individuals have been replaced by others. How do we identify and select individuals from an ever-changing population? Will they still be here when their time to serve on a jury comes around? Are transients part of the "community," or just part of the population?[12] Are more-mobile persons in general different from more-stable persons such that, without them, we will think something is amiss in our selection procedures?

---

9. Gastwirth (1998) at 154.

10. We could. There is no constitutional prohibition against non-citizens being on juries. S. Clark (1999) argues that a community is different from a "mere assemblage," and that the jury is an important forum for expression of our community values and acceptance of community responsibilities. In this context, the cavalier expert use of population data to describe the community appears all too typically thoughtless, ill considered, unintellectual.

11. I think excluding persons who don't speak English is legitimate, and some jurisdictions do so. Even though local Puerto Rico courts operate in Spanish, the federal district court operates in English, excluding jurors who do not speak it. See *Valentine* (1968). Some jurisdictions provide interpreters for deaf jurors, and let them go into the jury-deliberation room, while excluding hearing persons who do not speak English. Others also allow translation for non-English speakers. Although it seems unfair to exclude persons from jury duty because of a handicap, such as deafness, I would have thought translators violated the sanctity of the jury as selected.

12. Not understanding the availability-analysis context, what few critics there have been have gotten their criticism wrong. For example,

> Since it is self-evident that the process of selection is not, nor is it desirable to be, random, it is far from clear why either the social scientist or the Supreme Court should look upon

The decennial census counts persons, telling us how many are citizens; how many are in institutions; how many are felons; how many speak English well, passably, and not at all. It counts some college students at their college residence, though they might think of themselves as part of a different community; and some college students at "home" even though they are not physically there. The census does provide information on citizenship separately for Hispanics and non-Hispanics; and it does tell us something about institutional status and language ability, but perhaps not exactly what the jury system wants to know, and not by race, ethnic background, religion, citizenship, or command of the English language. The census does not tell us how many or what kind of people who are counted on April 1 of each census year will not be there at some later date, although it does provide some clues.

Surely, one would think, the census is not an appropriate basis by which courts could accurately assess fairness in jury selection. It will tell us that we "should" include people whom we purposely exclude; that we have done something wrong by following constitutional rules. We should not confuse the process of selecting jurors, which should be fair, with the outcome, about which we should have no preconception. Yet statistical analysis of this issue has been based on outcome, on census comparisons, only.

Finding Jurors

Before we investigate the jury, let's review its formation. We start with a practical problem: How are we going to find the people who constitute this "community"? We don't require people to register when they move into a town.[13] We expect them to be included on juries, but have no simple mechanism to get them there. After a brief diversion to place jury selection in the context of sampling, I discuss the practicalities of obtaining juries, and their evaluation by courts. To bring home my critique of the Supreme Court and the writers who have led it astray, I have created an Appendix to Chapter 5 containing summaries of two analyses from litigation in which my clients, states' attorneys, prevailed. Analyses of the

---

a standard based on randomness as appropriate to assess the likelihood of purposeful discrimination.

Meier (1986) at 271. To be fair, Meier refers to both *Castaneda* (1977), a jury case, and *Hazelwood* (1977), a hiring case. Perhaps he means to limit this comment to hiring. To get to the qualified jury pool, random selection is exactly what we want. But in focusing on the selectees Meier misses the real problem: their selection *from what pool*? Kairys et al. (1977) also eschew a statistical for an arithmetic solution, again missing the point that the comparison is at fault regardless what measures are used to make it.

13. Perhaps I do not sufficiently fear Big Brother, but I would not object to having to register in a place I have chosen as my residence. I have to declare a principal residence to the Internal Revenue Service, and every ten years to the census, but apparently I do not have to tell authorities in the locale of that residence that I have done so—except in Massachusetts, where municipalities maintain lists of residents, revised each January 1. Those lists have been used as a source for juries. See Zeisel (1969).

kind I advocate in this chapter are doable, relevant, and enlightening. Judges find them convincing. Yet I am the only expert who approaches the problem this way.

Sampling

At this point, an academic course would divert to a discussion of sampling. That is the subject we need to know now. We do not need to know much about it, though. We need to discuss sampling because "the community" does not sit in judgment. Much as we do not all constitute a legislature—we select "representatives" to perform that function—our juries are supposed to be representative of the community.

Our legislators "represent" the community whether they "look like" the community or not. We accept our legislators because they got to be where they are by a process we find acceptable. Apparently courts think juries are to "represent" the community in some other sense. Jurors, again, are drafted, not elected. The military draft was made from complete lists, on which all adult males placed themselves by law. Although in some sense the drafted army was supposed to be representative, soldiers had to meet certain qualifications. Some potential soldiers were exempted, either by their activities (such as being students) or because they failed to pass some qualification. Even starting from a universal base, by gender, race, and social class, American soldiers have never "looked like" the civilians they represented.

The sense in which we expect representation among jurors needs to be defined. We need to discuss the pool from which jurors are drafted, the process, and the characteristics that make some people "unqualified" for jury duty. I will show that no adjustment of census data tells us what the availability pool looks like. Even if testing the fairness of selection from its outcome were a reasonable procedure, it cannot be accomplished.

It is not a reasonable procedure. I will show that testing the process from its outcome leads to a dilemma. If the representatives do not "look like" the availability pool—the population, however corrected—do we adjust the process to achieve this "representative" outcome? Or do we adjust the outcome directly, substituting some for others until the jury "looks" right?

These are not "academic" (meaning "not serious") issues. This outcome mindset permeates legal and statistical literature. Both rigging the process and adjusting the outcome have been advocated and effectuated! The goal of this chapter is to convince you, the reader, that assessing juries by what they look like, rather than by how they were formed, is seriously wrongheaded. I propose that a fair process produces a fair jury regardless of what it looks like. We should accept juries in the same way we accept as legislators those who win procedurally unbiased elections, whatever their gender or ethnicity.

The Selection Model

Sampling is less of an issue than courts think, because more important than defining "representation" is defining "community" in the first place. Defining "community" is not the same as measuring it. As with "eligibility," the need for a definition and feasible calculation of "community" has escaped notice.

Traditional analyses of jury composition substitute "population" for "community," select a demographic characteristic that courts might certify as defining a "distinctive" group (by gender, age, race, or occupation, for example), and then ask if those qualified to be on juries have the census proportion of that characteristic. This is the availability approach. The composition of the sample of jurors is compared to the composition of the population, asking if the difference, defined only in relation to this one characteristic, is "large" relative to what might easily occur if the jurors had been selected by chance. I call this the "selection model" in the same sense that I used the term in Chapter 2.

Because the characteristics of the population from which the sample is drawn are supposedly known from the census, the data problems, as most analysts see them, lie in determining the characteristics (gender, race, ethnicity) of the jurors. It turns out to be relatively easy to make good estimates of these characteristics from questionnaires, addresses, and/or names. The truly difficult problem is that which analysts ignore: determining the same characteristics among a population of "eligible" and available jurors —persons who, if selected, would be qualified to serve and, if we care about actual jurors (not just those called for jury duty), would actually do so.[14] People who make up the "community."

The Survey Model

The idea behind the word "representative," as commonly used, is an outcome comparison: The sample is to "look like" the whole (more precisely, those sampled are to look like those not sampled), in whatever characteristics we choose to measure, with whatever error we will tolerate. How do we know if we have a representative sample from a population—say of seeds from which to determine crop yields? We select *randomly*. We cannot know if the seeds we plant really are representative of the ones we do not plant, but we rely on ignorance as a substitute. Rather than measure sun and moisture, to assure equality between test and control, we randomize planting locations. There will be no systematic variation in

---

14. From *Johnson* (1997), footnote 7 of the magistrate judge's report:
    It is important to note that the U.S. Census data does not reflect those persons in each racial category who are ineligible to serve on a jury because they cannot speak or read English or have been convicted of a felony.

growing conditions that we might confuse with differences in seeds. When testing the seeds, we infer their population characteristics from the results of the experiment.

Surveys are similar to crop experiments. In the selection model, we act as if we know the population characteristic at issue. In a survey, we recognize that we do *not* know it. We take measurements from our sample and associate that measurement with the population. We do not know in advance which seed population yields more fruit, and so we sample and test to find out. We do not know how many people, among those eligible, will vote and, if so, for which presidential candidate, until we sample and ask. In the survey model we infer the characteristics of the population from the sample.

If what we want is a representative sample, but we do not know representative of what (we do not know what the population looks like), we take a *random* sample. We do this for seeds, for planting locations, for voters, and for jurors. Random is a *procedure* we use to get close to representative most of the time. We substitute a procedure for an outcome in surveys to get around our ignorance, to pierce through the enormous data problems that "representative" would present.

In polling, we take a random sample of the population, or at least a random sample of that part of the population that gets on our source list. To pare that sample down to one of voters (continuing that analogy), the survey starts by asking whether the respondent is registered to vote, and if so, whether he intends to. A random sample of the population is only the beginning. What we want is a *representative* sample of *voters*. To the extent that voters do not "look like" the population, neither should the sample.[15] The headline "Dewey Wins" and the television-network pronouncement "Gore Takes Florida" were not incorrect because of last-minute changes of voter preference, but because sampling was not representative of voting.

Law is about procedure, not outcome. Here we are concerned only with pre-trial processes, not "procedure" during a trial. The U.S. Code proclaims its goal as obtaining "representative" jurors, but states as its procedure random selection from persons qualified for the position. If these two facets conflict, procedure should rule. If we did it right, then it is right. If it seems wrong, then find the procedure that failed; and if you can't, then it didn't.

I therefore propose that "random" should not be considered a substitute for "rep-

---

15. The "screening" questions in a survey are analogous to the procedure by which the jury-selection system determines who is jury-qualified. In *Dentsply* (2003) at 436 we see the rejection of a survey because it screened for the wrong population:

> The survey's screening questionnaire does not distinguish between those technicians who make purchasing decisions, and those who merely select teeth from the labs' inventory for use in a particular denture case.

resentative." Random is really what we want.[16] Because persons eligible for jury duty are not necessarily "representative" of the population, there is no reason to expect a random selection of eligible jurors, from an approved source list, to be so.[17] If a disparity from "representative" is a benign result from fair selection of jurors, then finding such a disparity cannot indict the selection procedure. Ultimately, it is that simple. Comparing jurors with the population tells us nothing about juror selection. We can still draw fairly from eligibles in the community even if we do not know in advance what the community looks like.

Uniform-Random Sampling

I will not define "random" precisely here. We all know what it means in practical terms: Draw blindfolded from a container filled with markers that cannot be distinguished by touch. Throw fair dice without trickery. Draw a card from a shuffled deck. Choose in some way that is not associated with the outcome. The selection, then, is a matter of "chance."

If I buy more lottery tickets than you, I have a better chance of winning, even if the selection of numbers is fair.[18] We need a word that specifies that each individual has the same number of markers in the jury box,[19] the same chance of being selected. That word is "uniform." Let's simplify. We will say that a uniform-random sample is a blind draw among indistinguishable markers, where everyone in the relevant population has *one and only one* marker in the container.[20] I think uniform-random sampling would be a universally accepted principle by which to select potential jurors, subject to later excuses and exemptions, if only we could solve the "from what population" question. It is, at any rate, a procedural standard, not an outcome standard.

---

16. The question of "representative" comes up in class-action suits, where the defendant challenges the plaintiffs as not being "representative" of the class. The plaintiffs are certainly not randomly selected from the class. I have seen defendants prepare elaborate charts of the kinds of persons in the class—by race, gender, union affiliation, age, etc.—to argue that the plaintiffs do not represent them; but short of clear conflicts courts appear to be generous in allowing some to represent others.

17. As Judge Wodbury put it, "it has never been the law that a jury must represent a true cross-section of the community." *Gorin* (1963) at 644.

18. In the *Gallup* (1986) example in Chapter 2 I explained the result of conditional logit as determining that non-Indians had more tickets in the employment lottery than otherwise equivalent Indians. A statistician might say that I increase my chances of winning a lottery the more tickets I buy, but an economist will say that I increase the expected value of losing. In most lotteries, betting on every possible outcome will guarantee that one spends more than he receives in prize money, even though it guarantees the prize money, also. Some huge lotteries do pay out more than the cost of every combination, but they get so large because they have sold many tickets, increasing the chance that a winner will have to share.

19. The "jury box" in this context is not where jurors sit, but where their names were placed to be drawn.

20. This is a simplification because it would also be uniform-random selection if we each had ten markers in the box.

The Eligible Population

Let us call those who could serve on juries under the rules—they are over eighteen, citizens, non-felons, speak English—"presumptively eligible."[21] Can we formulate a list with just those names? Currently, we get jury names from source lists. Voter and tax lists have long been used for this purpose. More recently driver's licenses, welfare, and other government-service lists have been added. Source lists provide as many names of eligibles as possible, even at the expense of obtaining many names of persons who are not eligible. A major task of the jury-selection system is to weed out ineligibles from source lists. Until it does its job, we do not know what the pool from which jurors will be selected looks like.

Source lists contain two populations—E (eligible) and N (non-eligible)—mixed together. Let's say our population is made up of green balls and red balls. Inside each ball is a slip of paper marked "E" or "N." If we took the time to open every ball we could separate out the balls into the two categories we care about, and then sample from the E balls. In this hypothetical population—although we do not know it yet—80 percent of the red balls contain "E," and 40 percent of the green balls contain "E." Finally, two out of three balls are red. There are many balls, tens of thousands of them.

Determining the content of every ball would be an enormous task. Instead, let's take a simple random sample of three thousand balls. We find that one thousand of the balls we selected are green. No complaint that we have under-sampled green balls. Not in this example. However we do not care about the color of the balls. For juries, what counts is only the letter they contain inside. As we do not have that information until we look, we have drawn our sample from all balls. A "fair" sample of green and red balls should provide a "fair" sample of "E" and "N" balls. So let's open the balls in our sample and see what we get.

The number eligible we would expect to get, on the average over many such random draws, is:

$$\text{number eligible} = (0.8 \times 2000 \text{ red}) + (0.4 \times 1000 \text{ green}) = 2000$$

Let us say that this is exactly what we do find, having opened the three thousand balls and checked for E and N inside. Two out of three balls contain "E." The composition of the eligibles is 75 percent red, 25 percent green.

---

21. *Barksdale* (1980) at 262:

> Because the disparity is generally altered when one turns from general population data to statistics concerning the portion of the population which is presumptively eligible to serve on juries, it is crucial to hold constant the statistics being used when comparing cases.

More common is to find discussion of the "eligible" when "presumptively eligible" would be more appropriate language.

The green balls are outraged. They sue. The system is corrupt, they claim. You can tell from the outcome. One of three balls in the population is green, but only one of four jurors will be green. Green balls have been discriminated against, lost to the system. It's unfair.

We want a random—not a representative—sample of balls because we do not know what a representative sample of E balls looks like, in terms of red and green, until we actually select balls and look at their slips of paper. What we did was take a random sample of (E + N) balls. It should be obvious, and in any case is mathematically correct, that a random sample of (E + N) is a random sample of E. The N balls are an expense. They are "noise." They are non-voters in a sample survey designed to ask questions of voters. They force us to take a larger sample than we want, as every jury administrator knows, but they do not undo the randomness of the sample of E balls. We just have to understand that we will have a smaller number of E balls than of all balls in our sample, and that the E balls may not "look like" the source lists by some characteristic—say, their color.

The complaint is filed. Green's statistical expert explains that the difference between the population (one-third green) and those found eligible for jury duty (one-fourth green) is twenty-two standard deviations.[22] We would never observe a difference this large in a real world in which selection of jurors was "fair," he explains. The judge says that the challenger has made a *prima facie* case and turns to the state for rebuttal.

The state's expert cannot fault the challenger's mathematics. The state's attorney can argue that not all courts accept this statistical measure. The difference between 33 percent representation of green balls in the population and 25 percent on the jury list is not "substantial," as concluded by many courts. Its "absolute impact" is below the critical level. I will discuss these and other commonly used measures below. The discussion is misdirected. It has become about outcomes. A fair procedure has produced a fair result, but the parties, using the wrong model, measuring the wrong thing, don't know it.

The Survey As Information

Using the survey model, we have now learned (or at least estimated) that green and red balls are eligible at different rates. As long as the red and green balls really were randomly selected from source lists representative of the population, we can infer that these different eligibility rates describe the red and green world in which we live. Those who utilize the selection model, complaining that for some unknown reason we have too few green

---

22. Traditional availability analyses measure the sample parameter against a fixed number, assuming that census figures are certainties. Here we are comparing two estimates, and so a joint standard deviation was calculated.

balls among the E population, are assuming a fact (equal rates of eligibility) that the survey model has just shown almost certainly to be false.

If the desired outcome is red and green E in the same proportions we found red and green in the population, we will have to over-sample green balls to get more green E. That would violate the criterion of uniform-random sampling, where every ball has the same chance of being chosen. It would violate what many regard as the "equal protection" guarantee of the Constitution. As noted above, some writers and even some courts have suggested that we *should* do non-uniform sampling. More seriously, some legislatures have written non-uniform-random sampling into law. They want an outcome standard, and will bend the procedures to obtain it. I think they do not understand the procedural basis of a constitutionally governed democracy. I return to outcome advocacy at the end of this chapter.

The remainder of my analysis will assume that we agree that a uniform-random sample of E balls (presumptively eligible potential jurors), drawn from a list of people who have been fairly allowed to participate in the community and have done so, is the procedural standard we want jury-selection systems to meet. I warned in Chapter 1 that many discussions in law are about what discussion to have. It should be clear that analyzing the composition of source lists in terms of red and green would be irrelevant. Yet when source lists are discussed, it is always in the context of whether they contain a "representative" sample of red and green balls. The point is not that courts get the wrong answer. They allow the discussion to be about the wrong question.

Irrelevant Comparisons

The quotation from Joseph Gastwirth earlier in this chapter summarizes traditional thought in this area: Compare a measure of jurors with a measure of the population. The problem is well known in statistics literature.

> The proper choice of the method and the resulting inferences depend upon a model and assumptions that describe how the observations have come about. For statistical inferences, there is always a formal representation of a model, whether implicit or explicit.[23]

If the model is wrong, the answer is likely to be wrong. Traditional thought ignores "how the observations have come about," which is selection from persons eligible to be jurors. Gastwirth uses the word "eligible" without any operational concept of what it means.

In December 2000, the Miami-Dade Election Commission had stopped recounting presidential votes, realizing that they could not conclude within the time set by the Florida secretary of state. The Democrats, who had called for the recount in three counties, and

---

23. Fienberg et al. (1995) at 12.

were still behind in the vote count after two were complete, went to court to obtain an order for the recount to continue, to extend the time limit.

The Democrats' expert was Nicholas Hengartner, an associate professor of statistics at Yale University. He claimed that he could project, from the 22 percent of the precincts already recounted, that if the net increase in Gore votes continued apace, six hundred would be added to Gore's statewide total. That would be enough to change the election result. The election results were in the balance; the Miami-Dade recount was too important to stop now.

This projection was not credible. Laurentius Marais, engaged by the Republicans, pointed out that in the precincts recounted, Gore had won 75 percent of the pre-recount votes. In the county as a whole, he had won 48 percent. So the recount up to the point at which it stopped was unlikely to be representative in the additional votes Gore would get were it completed. The sample was biased. A linear projection exaggerated the benefit Gore would obtain from the complete recount.[24] Like these projections, selection models rely critically on an assumption about the population from which the selection is being made. If that assumption is wrong, as was Hengartner's, then the analysis is worthless.

Those who have passed through the system far enough to be determined not to be obviously ineligible constitute the "qualified wheel."[25] Analysts who use jurors as their comparison data confuse characteristics of the jury-selection system with the behavior of other actors, including potential jurors themselves, ascribing both to the jury administrators.[26] A uniform-random sample of those as eligible as we can know them to be (at the stage at which the qualified wheel is measured) among members of fairly composed source lists, will produce a fair qualified wheel. Not all of these people are in fact qualified, and not all of them will serve when asked, either on their own volition (they fail to appear, or appear and ask to be excused) or someone else's (they are never called into a venire, they are dismissed by the judge or by a party's attorney). Thus those who serve as jurors may again not "look like" the qualified wheel, under the fairest of procedures.

---

24. Marais was correct. The "recount" produced by a consortium of newspapers, reported a year later, showed that had Miami-Dade continued, Bush still would have won in that county, and the state overall. Finkelstein and Levin (2004) contend, at 183, that the statistical experts "testified about a matter entirely peripheral to who would win if a recount were to occur." Either they did not see the live C-SPAN broadcast or they forgot it. I videotaped it.

25. *Reyes* (1996) at 556:

> The names of persons who complete and return the questionnaire (and who are found
> to be qualified as jurors) constitute the qualified jury wheels.

26. Unfortunately, judges use whatever data are handed to them. The following decisions—and many more—refer to venires: *Arnold* (1964), *McAnderson* (1990), *Ireland* (1995), *Six* (1995), *Rioux* (1996), *Schanbarger* (1996), *Miller* (1997), *Truesdale* (1998). A proper measure would include persons who have been excused from service. They do not appear in the venire.

From Source Lists to Master List

When the English jury was composed of witnesses, obtaining the jury was relatively simple. One could contest whether a particular person was enough a witness to be part of the jury, but the population from which the jury could be drawn was small. When the issue of selection followed the concept of an independent jury, the sheriff took that responsibility. To facilitate acceptance of the jury's decision, jurors were expected to be "upstanding" citizens, persons of "good character" and all that. This was the English heritage that we adopted.

The "key-man" system that evolved allowed the sheriff to delegate actual selection. He would appoint one or more "key men" who would bring in potential jurors.[27] As the sheriff was in a sense the prosecutor, the system evolved to allow other upright citizens to be responsible for obtaining impartial juries. They were called "jury commissioners." When a jury was needed, the commissioners went out to find members of the "community" as the city fathers knew it. The commissioner system, whether directly appointing jurors or doing so through key men, survived in the United States for well over 150 years. Most jurisdictions still retain the title "jury commissioner," though such people are responsible today for operating an anonymous and objective system, not for finding people of good character, like themselves.

In the South—*de jure* before the Civil War, *de facto* thereafter—neither the commissioner nor his key men considered black people to be of such character as to be eligible to be jurors. By and large, the same thinking excluded females. Progressive litigation questioned whether such a system could provide an "impartial" jury as required by the Constitution.[28]

The evolution from commissioners and key men, to commissioners selecting from source lists, to a more-objective random draw from a single list, involves adopting the dem-

---

27. Equivalent in form, Nebraska called theirs the "suggestor" system, emphasizing that the key men "suggested" more than enough potential jurors, from whom actual jurors were selected at random. See *Pope* (1967).

28. It took a long time for the judicial system to recognize that the right to a fairly drawn jury is independent of the race and gender of the defendant. The North Carolina Supreme Court wrote in *Koritz* (1947) at 556, for example:

> In no event could the defendant Koritz profit from, or be hurt by, the alleged discrimination against the Negro race, as he is a member of the White race.

Peters (1972) is the first case in which the Supreme Court faced a challenge to the jury by a white defendant, alleging that he was harmed by the exclusion of blacks. The Court found, correctly, that if there was such exclusion, he could properly claim to have been harmed by it; but three justices dissented. Three years later, in *Taylor* (1975), where the issue of exclusion of women was raised by a male, only Justice Rehnquist still held the position that the defendant had no standing to raise the issue. See more at the end of this chapter under the heading "Evaluating Procedure, Not Outcome."

ocratic view that everyone should be presumed to have the capacity to sit in judgment. As technology has advanced, most current litigation concerns selection from computerized source lists. Still, a review of litigation concerning key-man systems is essential to understanding how the Court so badly missed the boat, and why it struggles today under case law that leads it down blind outcome alleys.

Jury-Gathering Systems

The concept of the jury may have come to England in 1066 with the Normans, who got it from the Romans. Less than two centuries later, a limited form of jury was written into Magna Carta. Thereafter it evolved as discussed in earlier chapters. As Judge Fee wrote:

> For centuries the jury was subject to intimidation by judges and by the crown and in later times by popular violence. But after the revolutions of 1649 and 1688, in the form in which we have received it in America, it has become a bulwark against encroachments by the government and a protection of the rights of individual citizens.[29]

Roger Kuhn succinctly introduces us to middle American history:

> On March 1, 1875, the Congress of the United States made it a crime to "exclude or fail to summon" a qualified citizen for jury service on account of his race. Five years later to the day, the Supreme Court sustained a Virginia judge's conviction of this crime, and held in three cases that exclusion of Negroes from jury service on account of race contravenes the fourteenth amendment of the United States Constitution.[30]

In the First Judiciary Act of 1789, the criterion for becoming a federal juror was set as that for being a juror in the highest state court that held jury trials. Thus different standards were used to select federal jurors in different states.

New York "required a freehold of the value of $150 or personal property of like amount; which was raised in 1830 to $250 for personal property, where it has since remained."[31] In addition, according to state law, a juror in New York City was to be

> in possession of his or her natural faculties and not infirm or decrepit; not convicted of a felony or a misdemeanor involving moral turpitude; intelligent; of sound mind and good character; well-informed; able to read and write the English language understandingly,

---

29. *Local 36* (1949) at 339.

30. R. Kuhn (1968) at 235, the opening sentences of his article. He refers to the Civil Rights Act of 1875, which became 18 U.S. Code §243; *Virginia* (1879); and then *Strauder* (1879) and two other cases.

31. *Dennis* (1950) at 220. In Puerto Rico, since 1901, a person had to show "on the last assessment roll of the district or county on property of the value of at least $200, belonging to him." The law as quoted and upheld in *Crowley* (1904) at 463.

and not a member of certain exempt occupations.[32] As late as the 1960s New York maintained an overt class requirement for jurors.

New York was not alone. Not only did every state system at one time include a judgment about the character of the juror, others besides New York also placed an economic requirement on them.[33] Early jury-gathering systems were defined by their exclusions. Illinois excluded women until 1939, California until 1944. Mississippi, Alabama, and South Carolina did not allow females to be qualified for jury duty until the 1960s. Florida, Louisiana, and New Hampshire maintained "opt-in" systems, whereby women could register for jury duty if they wanted to, but would not otherwise be called. Georgia, Louisiana, New York,[34] and other states maintained "opt-out" provisions, whereby females would be excused upon request.

Here is a closer look at the Alabama system that excluded half the population a priori, as it operated in Lowndes County:

> The Jury commissioners are required to place on the jury roll "the names of all male citizens of the county who are generally reputed to be honest and intelligent men and are esteemed in the community for their integrity, good character, and sound judgment."[35]

Names were printed on cards and placed in the jury box, from which the presiding judge would draw the venire. Voting lists, which contained no blacks, were supposed to be the

---

32. *Fay* (1947) at 266, quoting state law, which is also quoted less extensively in *Dennis* (1950). With the apparent blessing of the Supreme Court, from *Fay*, the Second Circuit steadfastly allowed New York jury commissioners to judge "character." Justice Harlan for the Court in *Flynn* (1954) at 388:

> We observed in *Dennis*, and need only repeat here, that "cross-section" means not proportional representation of all groups within the community but rather a fair sample, tempered and limited by the eligibility standards imposed upon the jury clerks by applicable federal and state laws, such as age, character, intelligence, integrity, etc.

Greenberg (1961) at 396:

> The use of the voter-registration lists and the procedures followed by the jury commissioner and the deputy clerk in selecting names from them was reasonably designed to produce an array which was a representative cross-section of the community and no group or class was systematically excluded.

In the South, reliance on voter registration was misplaced, as "character" judgments were used to keep blacks from voting until the federal Voting Rights Act of 1965 outlawed the practice.

33. The economic requirement might be implicit, such as gathering names from property-tax rolls. *Brown* (1953) and *Arnold* (1964) describe such a procedure in Forsyth County, North Carolina; and *Whitus I* (1967) describes one existing through 1953 in Mitchell County, Georgia.

34. *Fay* (1947) at 267:

> Women [in New York] are equally qualified with men, but as they also are granted exemption, a woman drawn may serve or not, as she chooses.

35. *White* (1966) at 405, quoting the Code of Alabama (1958), Title 30, Section 21; following in-text quotation also at 405.

primary source. In fact, the same very few people were consistently called for jury duty. Almost everyone in the county was excluded from jury service, in particular, "No Negro has ever served on a civil or criminal petit jury in Lowndes County, Alabama."

The key-man system in Maine was described in *Bryant* (1968). Unlike the typical Southern system, in which the sheriff named someone he knew to be a key man, in Maine the key man was selected from the Maine register. This document named officials in each town. Usually the town clerk would be selected and therefore, the *Bryant* court notes, one-third of these "key men" were women.

Each key man recommended four or five persons, screened to meet statutory requirements. By the 1960s, Maine did not ask for character qualifications. Those nominees were sent questionnaires from which it was determined who was exempt and who just didn't want to do it. "The Commission proceeded to 'weed out' those who appeared to be too old or in bad health," and those who would suffer personal hardship (women with small children, sole proprietors, etc.).[36] Juries were then selected randomly from this pool.

Such a system clearly excluded people out of the mainstream of Maine communities. Although it was one step removed from purely discretionary systems, subjective decisions were still being made.[37] Uniform-random selection this was not.

A typical Southern system, showing how late such systems survived, is described in *Foster* (1975). The six jury commissioners of Quitman County, Georgia,

> compile a traverse jury list of "intelligent and upright citizens of the county," and from this list select "the most experienced, intelligent, and upright persons" of 21 years of age and older for the grand jury list.[38]

Apparently they tried to "cream" the list for grand jurors, but eventually drew randomly from the remainder of each list for petit jurors.

In several Georgia cases we read that names were put in the jury box on different colors of paper, white for whites and yellow for blacks.[39] This did not seem like an overt act to the jury commissioners, because they took names from the tax rolls, which were on similarly color-coded paper. Jury commissioners testified in many cases that they did not take race into account. Such non-credible assertions satisfied many a local federal district-court judge, but not higher federal courts.

Florida became famous for its female opt-in system because it defended that system,

---

36. *Bryant* (1968) at 545.

37. Differences between the juries and a selection model standard were "explained" to the satisfaction of the district and circuit courts. The circuit-court decision is *Bryant* (as *Butera*) (1970), but is considered by Gewin (1975) as something of an anomaly.

38. *Foster* (1975) at 807, quoting from the Georgia Code that authorized this process.

39. See *Avery* (1953), *Williams* (1955), and *Whitus I* (1967).

and won in the Supreme Court![40] However, recognizing that blacks were systematically prevented from voting, and that the Supreme Court would not condone exclusion of blacks, at least some counties included "Negro citizens recommended by local Negro ministers and business leaders,"[41] and thus passed outcome-based judicial review.

In Massachusetts, election commissioners used voter lists, then "weeded out" those exempt by law using information on police lists, which apparently included age and occupation.[42] The commissioners then dropped those who could not speak English, and persons who (in their judgment) were otherwise handicapped. The system was unsuccessfully challenged in the early 1960s for excluding citizens not registered to vote.[43]

As one court noted,

> From 1789 to 1948 Congress made few inroads upon the discretion of federal judicial officials and state governments in development and application of jury qualifications.[44]

The federal Judicial Code of 1948 did say the jury should be "truly representative of the community," and urged that all "social groups" be "represented"; but it also called for jurors to have "a high degree of intelligence, morality, integrity, and common sense," thus leaving the commissioners with the discretion they had so abused for 159 years.[45] Although perhaps intending to set uniform minimum federal standards, the 1948 Act in fact left juror qualifications up to the states. The California Code called for "fair character and approved integrity and of sound judgment" at that time.[46] Even progressive states still had a long way to go.

Moving Towards Objectivity

The Civil Rights Act of 1957 at last struck down the federal obeisance to state juror qualifications. A Fifth Circuit panel concluded that

---

40. See *Hoyt* (1961). This was not a surprise. *Crowley* (1904) had left jury standards up to local law. *Muller* (1908) allowed different work standards for women. *Ballard* (1946) had found that as a matter of congressional intent, federal juries should be formed inclusive of women, but *Hoyt* was about a state system.

41. *Chance* (1963) at 202.

42. Zeisel (1969) tells us that the police lists were the source. He refers to *Spock* (1969), which contains no mention of a jury-selection issue. "Local-resident lists" are still used today to recruit jurors.

43. See *Gorin* (1963).

44. *Rabinowitz* (1966) at 45. I think a better last date would be 1957.

45. The Knox Committee, which led to the 1948 revisions of the Judicial Code is discussed in *Rabinowitz* (1966) Appendix A, starting at 60, from which my quotations are taken. Appendix B, starting at 67, discusses the "Legislative History of the 1957 Civil Rights Act as it relates to the qualifications for federal jurors."

46. California Code of Civil Procedure §205, quoted in *Local 36* (1949) at 338.

> Congress intended to set uniform qualifications for jurors in federal courts
> without vesting discretion in jury commissioners to either set higher or lower
> qualifications.[47]

This court had to go through some logical hoops to reach this conclusion. Arguing that
"discretion" was a form of authority that had been taken by jury commissioners, the court
decided:

> It would seem anomalous for Congress to create elaborate procedures for the
> district judge to excuse or exclude persons from jury service and at the same
> time to silently vest even broader discretion in the unregulated hands of the
> clerk and the jury commissioner.

Few other circuits agreed with this logic. Additional legislation brought uniform standards—but not uniform procedures—to federal selection of jurors. The Jury Selection and
Service Act of 1968, P.L. 90-274, required every federal judicial district to devise a plan for
fairly recruiting jurors, to be approved by each circuit court. Congress understood that
local courts, even local federal courts, could not be trusted to do this fairly, without review,
but apparently it was unwilling simply to impose uniform procedures on them. The strong
implication was that each plan should provide for random sampling from voter lists, with
the possible addition of other lists if the voter lists appeared insufficiently inclusive. Governmental divisions within the judicial district were required to be proportionately represented, and persons were to be "fairly" represented.[48]

Hans Zeisel announced:

> The new law orders random selection of jurors, primarily from voter lists, to
> guarantee a true cross-section of the population eligible for jury service.[49]

I would like to think Zeisel was saying that we would determine, from the survey model,
what the eligible population looked like. Unfortunately, his other writing, and the way the
concept of eligibility has been ignored, imply that he was only making a prediction: "Now
blacks will appear on juries in their population proportion." Would that Zeisel had said,
"Stop litigating about outcome, once we have a sound procedure."[50]

Before the random-selection models were fully formed, some jurisdictions had moved
from "Whom do you know?" to "Whom can you find?" to drawing from published lists

---

47. *Rabinowitz* (1966) at 72; following indented quotation at 53.

48. This Act amended 28 U.S. Code §1861–71; it is sometimes referred to in opinions as "1861."

49. Zeisel (1969) at 16. As Zeisel had testified before Congress in support of the legislation, his enthusiasm is not entirely an objective assessment. He clearly foresaw the computerization of voter lists, hence
of jury selection.

50. Zeisel's last words on this topic, issued posthumously in Zeisel and Kaye (1997), show that neither he
nor David Kaye, his heir apparent, ever made that intellectual leap from selection model to survey model.

as part of objectifying the jury-selection process. The problem always has been to obtain names and addresses of persons who live in the area, although originally it was to find acceptable (blacks and poor whites need not apply) men (literally) to represent "the community," in evolving conceptions of that term.

A telephone book or, better, telephone-company records (to include unlisted numbers) might be a good place to start. The police lists used in Massachusetts could not be trusted to be kept systematically, and were known to be slow in revision. Perhaps many people did not have telephones.[51] We do not know if all people with telephones meet other criteria— say, whether they are old enough—but any source list has the problem that it contains ineligibles. Some people have more than one telephone number, so duplicates would have to be eliminated before sampling, but the use of several source lists creates this problem also. Probably the issue is the other way around: One phone serves many people. Telephone directories may have been a common source for jury lists at one time,[52] but few systems use them now, and system critics who support multiple source lists do not propose that one.

The most common source lists for jury service now are voter registration and driver's licenses (including Department of Motor Vehicle identification cards).[53] Connecticut has added "residents subject to taxation on personal income under chapter 229 and recipients of unemployment compensation under chapter 567."[54] Massachusetts has added resident college students. New York uses five source lists (voter, driver, tax, unemployment, and welfare), merging them and purging them of duplicates at the state level, and distributing these names of presumptive eligibles to the counties. There is thus no rule that these source lists must contain only or all the kinds of people we think are in the "community" of persons who might be jurors. If lists were initially selected to reduce N, states are now going the other way, paying the cost of many N, desperately seeking minority E. No one has yet produced a definitive study examining the impact of additional lists on the composition of *eligible* prospective jurors, or examining their cost, but the general finding is that multiple source lists do not increase representation of minorities on qualified wheels.[55] Why am I not surprised?

---

51. The problem is not so much the number of people without telephones as it is their characteristics. A telephone survey is a biased survey, as the Montana jury system found in *LaMere* (2000).

52. Greene County, Alabama, used telephone books as a jury source in the 1960s; see *Carter* (1970). Lafayette Parish, Louisiana, did so in the early 1970s, according to *Alexander* (1972). New York used telephone directories to supplement voter lists at least through the 1950s; see *Greenberg* (1961). So did California, at least through the 1940s; see *Local 36* (1947).

53. Saunders (1997) provides the source lists for all states, as of 1997, in his Appendix B. Voters are included in every state. Appendix B shows the minimum. In text, Saunders discusses Pennsylvania, which allows local districts to supplement the voter lists, but only voters are indicated in Appendix B.

54. Connecticut Public Act 97-200, §6(b). The practical meaning of this law is that the list of welfare recipients now is merged in with voters and drivers. Quotation from *Ferguson* (2002), footnote 18.

55. "Not only is supplementation ineffective, but it is also quite costly." Bueker (1997) at 392.

Source-List Litigation

The first case in which voter lists alone were affirmed to be a reasonable source of jurors appears to be *Gibson* (1896).[56] Courts routinely reject complaints about the voter list as the source of juries, unless accompanied by a complaint about the structure of that list.[57] To do otherwise now would be to invalidate the federal adoption of that standard in 1968. The Court therefore has entered into making procedural determinations about the jury-selection system, about the acceptability of lists from which, if the system draws randomly, we do not care what the result looks like.[58]

How old can a list be? Persons who turn eighteen during the use of a source list are not on it, so an old list is an age-biased list. In *Hamling* (1974), the Court rejected the argument that a four-year-old voter list was too old. The claim was that jurors from such a list would be older than the population they were supposed to represent; *Hamling* was an obscenity case, for which younger jurors would presumably have been more-liberal

---

56. The voter list was not an issue in this case. It was assumed as a basis that "no person should be a grand or petit juror unless he was a qualified elector and able to read and write." The question was whether the state could impose the additional qualifications "that persons selected for jury service should possess good intelligence, sound judgment, and fair character." Both quotations from *Gibson* (1896) at 589.

57. In *Test* (1975), the Court accepted that blacks and Chicanos might not register to vote at the same rate as others. In *Thompson* (1974), plaintiffs had achieved the reform of drawing from the voter list, but then did not like the outcome. In both cases, not having shown chicanery, the challenger lost. In *Gorin* (1963), the voter list was challenged specifically for excluding non-voters from juries. That challenge failed, also. In *Louisiana* (1965) at 148, the state constitution

> required that an applicant for registration be able to "give a reasonable interpretation" of any clause in the Louisiana Constitution or the Constitution of the United States.

That registration scheme was struck down. A current articulation is this:

> The use of voter-registration lists as the sole source of the names of potential jurors is not constitutionally invalid, absent a showing of discrimination in the compiling of such voter-registration lists.

Gordon (1980) at 820, repeated in *Young* (1987) at 1239.

58. The embodiment of the Federal Judiciary Act of 1968, 28 U.S. Code §1861, does call for supplemental lists if the voter list is found to be too restrictive. In *Hamling* (1974) the adequacy of the voter list seems already settled. In *Ireland* (1995), the Eighth Circuit said the defendant had to show that something was wrong with voter-registration requirements to void use of that list for juries. In *Schanbarger* (1996), the Second Circuit said the defendant had to show irregularities in the voter-registration process such that some groups were hindered from registering. The Second Circuit tied voter registration to the key word "community" in *Biaggi* (1990) at 677:

> Giving up one's community of residence is a major dislocation. Registering to vote is a simple task of minimal inconvenience, viewed by many as an obligation of citizenship.

One would think it automatically acceptable to use the voter list *plus other lists*, but if there is doubt see *Warren* (1994) or *Johnston* (2000).

jurors.[59] In addition, new arrivals to the community are excluded from an old list.

> But some play in the joints of the jury-selection process is necessary in order
> to accommodate the practical problems of judicial administration.[60]

A four-year-old list may not be representative of some ideal jury pool, but random draws from it provide an acceptable sample under the law, even though that sample could not possibly be representative of census counts.

In sum, what source lists may be representative of we do not know. They are procedurally not a random sample of any known population. I call such a list a "deterministic" sample because being on it is determined by the individual's behavior. We may decide that, as a matter of law, persons on source lists "represent" our notion of the "community" that is supposed to people juries, plus some ineligibles. But as a matter of statistics, we do not know what the population from which those on source lists were drawn looks like. We have no measure of that "community" independent of the people we find on the source lists, and no measure of "eligibles" other than those who remain on the list after an initial screening. I call persons on source lists "participants." They have participated in society in some way that identifies them to jury commissioners as possible members of the community. Residents not on any of the jurisdiction's source lists are "non-participants."

In Figure 51 I indicate the progression from population to source list by arrows leaving one rectangular container, going into another. The left diagram represents older, subjective systems; the right diagram, newer, objective systems. The diagram's containers leak, illustrated by arrows that lead to elliptical (oval-shaped) bins. In the diagrams in this chapter, every rectangle represents people who stay in the jury-recruitment system through that stage, and every ellipse represents people who fall out of the system at that stage.

My analysis will concern the behavior of jury administrators. Thus I need to differentiate their actions from those of others. Blue indicates the result of actions by individuals; green, actions (or failures to act) by the jury-selection system.[61] We start with a colorless

---

59. Different attitudes would have to be proved. Although it came later, whether age was related to differences in attitude was discussed in *Test* (1976) at 591:

> There is no evidence in the record before us suggesting that persons between the ages of twenty-one and thirty-nine hold attitudes which are distinctive from those held by the rest of the population.

The Court would have gone outside that record had it wanted to. As we know from Chapter 1, when a court wants to accept something as fact, it just does. The Court did not need authority to find, in *Bryant* (as *Butera*) (1970) at 571, that "males and females can have sufficiently different points of view to be considered legally cognizable groups for purposes of defendant's *prima facie* case."

60. *Hamling* (1974), Justice Rehnquist for the Court at 138. In *Bailey* (1996) the Tenth Circuit did not find a clerk's errors sufficiently "substantial" to exclude the juries. Unfortunately for my point, the Court determined this lack of importance of the errors by comparing the outcome to the census.

61. In black-and-white photocopies, the blue should be clear, and the green shaded.

population. In early systems, selection lists were subjective and based on the knowledge and behavior of the jury commissioners. The result is illustrated by the green source-list box in the left diagram of Figure 51. People either participate or not. If they do, they get on a list that will be used by the jury system to recruit jurors. Thus in the more modern systems illustrated in the right diagram, whether the source lists are proper or not, so far there is no commissioner discretion. On the right, there is no green.

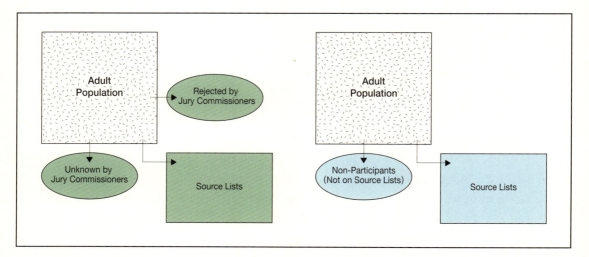

FIGURE 51: Two Versions of the Progression from Population to Source Lists

The Master List

Source lists are just names and addresses of people. The list from which notices to appear are mailed is called the "master list." The Supreme Court forgot to tell us to screen out persons who will be too young to serve on a jury,[62] but jury administrators do it anyway. Otherwise, the master list contains both E and N, from which the system eventually will delete the N.

The master list comes from collecting source lists from the district's component parts and, if there is more than one kind of list, attempting to find and eliminate duplicates. Merging is adding all the names together from various sources, and purging is deleting the duplicate names that result from merging, or were in a list to begin with. Thus the master list may be called the merged-purged list. In some systems the master list is a subset of the merged-purged source lists. In other systems the original source lists are sampled first, so

---

62. This chapter will contain a strong criticism of one of the Court's most famous and praised decisions, *Castaneda* (1977), which was based on total-population data. My critique is not based on their confusion about age. It may be that not using the adult population as a basis of comparison with grand juries (the issue is the percentage of Hispanics thereon) was just an oversight, but to this day attorneys pleading non-representation of juries use *Castaneda* as a Supreme Court statement that the total population should be the basis of comparison statistics. Lower courts always reject that argument, as they should.

the merged-purged list is itself a sum of samples. I assume here—and in practice I test for this—that the master list is a representative draw (by town or other geographic entity) from the merged-purged source lists. Geographic representation at this stage is required in federal systems, and is a reasonable expectation for the master list from any system.

Whether the sample of merged-purged source lists is further refined prior to sending a summons to appear for jury duty varies among jurisdictions. Some systems send summonses directly from the master list. Some send a questionnaire asking whether the person is a non-citizen, a felon, or otherwise unable to perform the duties of a juror. The list from which summonses are sent then contains only those persons who pass this first round of elimination. This smaller list of not-so-far ineligibles is the qualified wheel. It is the empirical realization of the concept of "presumptively eligible."

The graphic principle in Figure 51 is that when one box follows from another, as source lists follow from the population, we do not know how much "alike" they should look, because there is "leakage" (an ellipse) from the sending rectangle. The standard analysis compares the compositions of two rectangles. It sets as a standard that succeeding rectangles *should* "look like" preceding rectangles, while the process tells us they will not.

Evaluating Source Lists

By ruling on the validity of source lists, courts ventured down the path of procedure: If you follow these rules your jury is acceptable. Simultaneously, it ruled on outcomes: If your juries look very disparate, they are *not* acceptable. Jury challengers have noted the two different kinds of argument, and so have pursued both.[63] Although courts have accepted the voter list as usually minimally sufficient to maintain a credible jury-gathering system, analysts have not been satisfied. Not surprisingly, the voter list often can be shown to be unrepresentative of the population. Litigation based on the statistical showing that red and green balls in the system are not in proportion to the population follows. The debate becomes how different the jury proportions must be for a court to declare the system invalid. Once again, resources wasted on the wrong question.

David Kairys, Joseph Kadane, and John Lehoczky provide a categorization of ways to look at the jury-composition issue. They note that

> standards governing challenges to jury-selection systems have usually been formulated in terms of prohibiting discrimination rather than requiring representativeness. This theoretical choice has significant consequences. If

---

63. Challenges have been made to the source list, for example *Test* (1975) or *Ramseur* (1992), and also to those who remain on the list after questionnaires have been sent out. "One of the pertinent criticisms here then is the fact that for this jury panel no one is drawn who does not return his questionnaire." *Local 36* (1949) at 339. If this complaint seems absurd, as it did to the *Local 36* court, keep it in mind when I discuss recent Connecticut and Rhode Island challenges in the Appendix to Chapter 5.

discrimination is the focus, the actions, intent, and perhaps even motives of selection officials are crucial in determining the validity of the selection system. If representativeness is the guiding principle, state and federal governments have a duty to provide representative sources and pools, and the presence or absence of discriminatory intent is irrelevant.[64]

They then choose the representativeness principle, leading them to advocate affirmative selection by race (or age, gender, etc.) to achieve it.[65] Both the logical and factual premises on which these authors base their suggestions are faulty. They claim that

> Analysis of the evidence presented in support of [jury] challenges reveals that most of the proven unrepresentativeness is attributable to the source list. Indeed, statistical data indicates that no single available list, including voter registration lists, the most widely used source, adequately represents a cross-section of our communities.[66]

Their evidence comes from comparison of population proportion, source-list proportion, and jury-wheel proportion of seven categories over four cases. I reproduce their data summary in Figure 52.[67]

Case	Group	Percent of Population	Percent of Source	Percent of Wheel
1	Blacks	30.2	18.9	17.0
2	Age under 30	25.5	17.2	18.6
	Age under 40	41.8	32.2	33.3
	Nonwhites	15.7	11.7	12.8
3	Blacks	22.8	16.3	16.0
4	Blacks	8.4	6.5	5.1
	Age 21–29	20.7	4.5	3.4
	Females	53.0	53.0	16.7

FIGURE 52: Source List Disparities from Kairys et al., Table B

Kairys et al. conclude that the decline in percentage from the population (of the group specified on the left) to the source list far exceeds that from the source list to the qualified wheel. But in the fourth case, there is no decline from population to source list for females; and the declines for blacks may be seen as essentially equal (the source list is 77.4 percent

---

64. Kairys et al. (1977) at 783.

65. "The representativeness principle places an affirmative duty on selection officials." Kairys et al. (1977) at 816, note 195.

66. Kairys et al. (1977) at 777.

67. Kairys et al. (1977) at 804, Table B.

of the population proportion, and the jury wheel is 78.5 percent of the source). Yes, you count eight categories, but "Age under 30" and "Age under 40" are not independent. They are two measures of the same thing, alleged exclusion of young people. Besides illustrating that Kairys et al. do not know what the community looks like—they treat it as synonymous with the population—this small collection of data is not the overwhelming evidence they say it is. In the Rhode Island example in the Appendix to Chapter 5, the source lists *over*-represent "minorities," the allegedly excluded group, compared with the population.

Alan Gelfand testified that

> reliance on voter lists will inevitably result in the under-representation of His-panics and Puerto Ricans in the New Haven and Hartford Divisions, because many members of these groups do not register to vote.[68]

However, Gelfand did not know if non-voters were citizens, non-felons, or long-term res-idents. Using the selection model, Gelfand needed a measure of eligibles, the very measure he did not have. Without that knowledge, he did not know if any group had been "under-represented" on qualified wheels.

From Master List to Jury

If we think of the master-list process as utilizing all the information we know about people —which is that they participated and sometimes their age—then next we must try to bring some of those people into the jury-selection process where more can be learned about them. That information can be used to separate the E from the N. As above, this first step can be a questionnaire (the responses to which determine the qualified wheel); or a summons to appear in court (where eligibility will be determined by answering a clerk's questions).

Persons whose status is such that the jury system does not want to include them are called "disqualified." I use the term "ineligible" to mean those who *would be* disqualified if we knew their characteristics. "Eligibility" for jury duty then is a theoretical construct, and "qualified" is the effectuation of that construct on real people. Those who are not eli-gible, when we learn their characteristics, will be disqualified. They are noise, N.

If we are looking for an availability pool on which to apply the selection model, we must mean persons who could be called to serve, *and who would serve if called*. Non-citizens, non-English speakers, felons, persons about to leave the jurisdiction, or those who have left, all may be over eighteen and drive. Until we know that they are not qualified we must communicate with them fairly. But they surely are not in anything we would think of as the "jury pool." If they no longer reside here, then they are not eligible; which means

---

68. *Gerena* (1987) at 1269; following in-text quotation also at 1269. This is Judge Clarie's summary, not necessarily Gelfand's words.

that when we know their station we will declare them not qualified.

Others may be eligible, but will not become qualified because they will fail to appear when summoned. We will declare them "not present" or "no-show." Showing up is part of the process. Persons who are not there or not cooperative may be presumptively eligible, and therefore may appear on a qualified wheel, but they will never appear on a jury. I use the joint term "eligible and present" to identify the pool of could-be jurors, from the system's point of view. The system, if it knew all their characteristics, would consider them qualified, because they pass the qualifications, *including living in the jurisdiction at the time of proposed service.* I use the term "eligible, present, and cooperative" to indicate those who would be allowed to serve on a jury *and would do so when asked.* There is no way other than through the jury-selection system itself to determine what this pool of eligible, present, and cooperative would-be jurors looks like. Only the qualification and summons process ascertains this information. The jury-selection system takes a survey. Its fairness should be judged as surveys are judged, not as selection from a known pool would be judged.

Some summoned people are excused from duty. As "excuse" is supposed to be at a judge's discretion, whereas "not qualified" is based on laws and rules governing the district, persons who will be excused should first be determined to be qualified. Where this is not done, and that is in many jurisdictions, we never can know, even after the juror survey, what the eligible, present, and cooperative population looks like.

The First Mailing

Ordinarily a judge is in charge of providing juries. He instructs a clerk how many people to produce for venires—the pools from which individual juries are drawn—in the next few weeks. The clerks know to ask for more people than that. They direct a mailing from the master list. Analysts should investigate the procedures used to sample master lists, but customarily this is done in some way we can accept as "random."[69] Thus each mailing list is a random sample of the master list, and can be used as if it (or, better, the accumulated mailings) were representative thereof.

From the mailing, some envelopes are returned by the Postal Service as "not delivered." In Contra Costa County, California, for example, we are told that, in 1982 over 26 percent of the questionnaires mailed were not returned.[70] The addresses from which no response

---

69. Some legislatures have codified how this is done, usually by drawing every nth name after some formulaic start, the "key number" referenced in Chapter 4. Historically this detail may have been a safeguard against finding that the jury-system personnel devised some faulty method for extracting samples. Today, lists can be randomly ordered by common computer programs, and for reasons explained below, should be.

70. *Pervoe* (1984) at 352. All subsequent references to Contra Costa County jury data are to this case at this page.

was forthcoming will not be randomly distributed with respect to the mailing. If we take a non-random sample away from a random sample, what is left is a non-random sample. Therefore, delivered notices usually are not a representative sample of the mailing. Seriously so? That depends on the extent of the non-delivery, and how skewed it is; but between non-delivery and non-response, those entering the system are not a "random sample" of the mailing, and usually are not a "representative" sample, either.

Joseph Kadane has some ideas about why some people do not respond to this mailing.

> In some jurisdictions, the proportion of returned questionnaires is very low, stemming from (1) poor-quality lists, (2) a tradition of seeing jury service as a tax-in-kind, . . . and (3) long required service, making it a burden.[71]

Presumably by "poor-quality lists" he means that people no longer live at the list address. "Poor quality" implies selection-system error, whereas in many cases those residents have simply moved elsewhere. As for his third item, I know of no evidence that shorter jury duty ("one day or one trial," for example) induces better questionnaire response, though Kadane's is a worthy guess that it might.

Kadane fails to mention *disparate* non-response. With respect to Hispanics, Eugene Ericksen provides three answers, as summarized by Judge Bartle:

> First, many Hispanics are poor. Like other poor people, they are apt to move more frequently than the more affluent, with their mail not being forwarded to their new address. Secondly, poor people in general have less-reliable mail service. Finally, Ericksen reported that Hispanics were found to be less likely to return census questionnaires and thus presumably less likely to send back jury questionnaires.[72]

The judge correctly determined that it was not the behavior of the jury-selection system that created what appeared to be a numeric under-representation of Hispanics. It was the behavior of Hispanics themselves.

I have found that non-response is strongly related to mobile populations, and that mobility can be anticipated from demographic characteristics: renters as opposed to homeowners, or single persons as opposed to married persons, for example. There is no evidence that objective source lists (such as voter registration) have ever been a problem, unless they were discriminatorily maintained. However frequently lists are revised, if there is differential mobility there will be differential response. Multiple source lists have not affected jury composition because they have increased N, and therefore expense, rather than E.[73]

---

71. Kadane (2000) at 355.

72. *Ortiz* (1995) at 204. Interestingly, Ericksen was defendant's expert, not the state's. I know of no study showing that "reliability" of mail service is correlated with income.

73. See Bueker (1997). Jury systems I have consulted with report that not only have multiple source lists increased the proportion of the mailing that turns out not to be qualified, they have increased non-

In Figure 53 we see that the mailing list is the result of some actions made by the jury-selection system (in green), and some actions made by members of the population (in blue). In the absence of a mechanical error, mailing lists should give us a good picture of source lists from which under-age participants and duplicates have been culled. Therefore the difference between where mail was sent and where adults live measures the difference between the population and participants. For example, we might find that central cities appear "under-represented" in mailings. Central-city residents are less likely to register to vote and less likely to have local driver's licenses than persons of equal age who live elsewhere.[74] But would these central-city non-participants be E, or N?

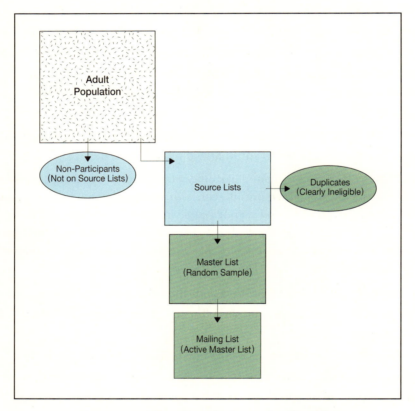

FIGURE 53: From Population to Mailing List

delivery of their notices and no-shows, also. Fairfax County, Virginia, found that the voter list alone was over 44 percent more productive of jurors than the merged list of voters and drivers. See Tom Jackman, "Fairfax Uses Voter Lists, not DMV, for Jury Pools," the *Washington Post*, February 15, 2003, at B-2.

74. The census regularly publishes studies of persons registering to vote by place, which can be compared with that place's population over age eighteen, excluding non-citizens. Similarly, minorities (blacks, Hispanics, Asians) congregate in central cities, and census studies show lower propensities to drive and vote among these groups. Data in the table below come from the appendix to Justice Douglas' dissent in denial of *certiorari* in *Donaldson* (1971). "Adults" here are age twenty-one or more. The bold figures in the shaded background at the bottom are my calculated rates, showing that Hispanics and blacks, at

We might calculate that the mailing list was not a likely product of a random draw from the population. But it *wasn't* a random draw from the population. It was drawn from participants. Suppose the challenger accepts the source list. Then he should correct any subsequent comparison between jurors and the population for the difference between the population and the source list. If the source list is acceptable, then the percent black (say) on the source list, not the percent black in the population, should be the standard.

This seems obvious. Yet I have never seen it done. I have never seen a challenger's expert understand that if his client is not challenging the source list, he should use the distribution of his categories on the source list as a standard. It would still be wrong. It is still an outcome comparison. We still do not know the composition of eligibles on the source list. But from *his* point of view there is no argument against it. Where there are fewer minorities on the source lists than in the census, his statistical presentation holds the jury system responsible for the failure of the unchallenged source lists to include minorities. Such an analysis should be excluded as irrelevant. It does not match his client's complaint.

Generating the Qualified Wheel

Figure 54 is a generalized picture of the processes that occur between the development of source lists and the creation of juries. Although actual systems differ in details, all follow this general structure. We see many ellipses. Whatever rectangle we measure is reduced by leakage from the preceding rectangle, not by accident, but by construction. The system is weeding out the N, finding the E.

The events that cause most of the loss to the jury system from the mailing are persons leaving the system and nonresponse from persons still in the jurisdiction. It is not always possible to tell the difference. In some systems the mailing is a summons to appear at a certain court on a certain day. People who do not respond by mail are considered qualified because they have not shown that they are not qualified. This is a mistake that works to the detriment of the system itself. When such persons are declared "no-shows," it will seem that

---

least in this instance, neither registered to vote nor responded to a jury notice at even two-thirds the rate of middle-class whites. How voter lists are maintained—how often they are purged—will affect this kind of comparison.

	Long Beach (White)	Wilmington (48 Percent Spanish)	Central Long Beach (55 Percent Black)
Adults	11,522	18,002	13,423
Voters	8,991	8,945	5,747
Notices	315	163	110
Responses	216	68	46
Voter Rate	78.0	49.7	42.8
Notice Rate	3.5	1.8	1.9
Response Rate	68.6	41.7	41.8

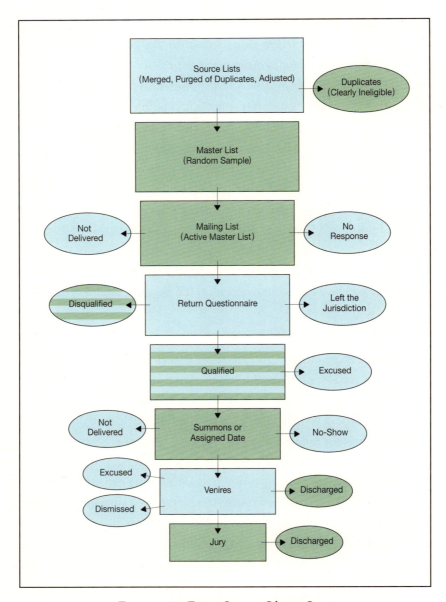

FIGURE 54: From Source List to Jury

they are flouting the system. In fact, many of them simply are no longer in the jurisdiction. Thus the categories of leakage from the system in Figure 54 are not all easily distinguished because of the uninformed manner in which systems create and maintain data. But they exist whether we can identify them or not. Because cooperation is at the heart of being qualified to be a juror, people on the mailing list should be considered not qualified until it is determined that they are, not the other way around.[75]

75. A naive expert might accept these no-shows as part of the qualified wheel which, because many

The "qualified" rectangle represents the application of a jury-system rule to the characteristics of the individual as listed in his questionnaire response. Whether the rules are fair, and whether the application (the way the jury-selection system determines who is disqualified) is fair, can be challenged.[76] It could turn out that disqualification is a potential juror characteristic, or a jury-selection-system action, or both. Therefore, for this general picture, I show both colors for both the "qualified" rectangle and the "disqualified" ellipse that precedes it. Determining which color should prevail in a particular case is a task for the analyst.

This "qualified" rectangle is the qualified wheel, the *presumptively* qualified. In a two-step procedure, those who did not receive or did not return the questionnaire have been dropped. In Contra Costa County over 20 percent of those who responded to the first mailing were deemed unqualified. They were not sent a second mailing.

Non-delivery almost always means the person is no longer in the judicial district. Non-return may mean the person has left the jurisdiction, or that he would be found otherwise unqualified, or that he would not appear for service. We cannot hold the jury commissioners responsible for persons who are no longer in the jurisdiction or are unqualified or uncooperative.[77] Yet that is what the analyst does by using some earlier rectangle than post-questionnaire qualified to measure characteristics of persons captured in the system's draft.

Generating Juries

Although I place excuses after determination of qualification, where it should be, some systems (Rhode Island, for one) allow clerks to grant excuses without assessing whether the individual is qualified. The arrow, then, should come from the "Return Questionnaire" rectangle. Excuse would be a leakage between returning the questionnaire and forming the qualified wheel.

---

of them are minorities, makes the system look as though it corrals more minorities on to juries than it does. In my experience the naive expert does not know to measure the qualified wheel, much less how to.

76. *Eubanks* (1958) at 586:

> Petitioner does not challenge this system of choosing grand jurors, as such, but he does contend that it has been administered by the local judges so that members of the Negro race have been systematically excluded from grand jury service.

77. In Michigan,

> The Kent Circuit Court Administrator testified that for persons who did not respond to this [second] letter, the standard process was to request that they appear in court to show cause why they had not responded. Those who further failed to appear generally became the subject of bench warrants, although law-enforcement agencies refuse to serve the warrants because the warrants lack personal information necessary for their service.

Smith (2000a) at 210, footnote 4 of Judge Cavanagh's concurring opinion.

"Excused" is a discretionary act of the system in response to the application by an individual.[78] Because the individual must ask to be excused, and have a characteristic reasonably qualifying for excuse, I have on balance called this individual behavior.[79] Courts are
reluctant to excuse blacks and Hispanics. Not that judges are biased against minorities, less
believing of their reasons to be excused. Judges are driven by the "body-count" aspect of
conventional, outcome-driven, jury analyses. They are not expert enough in the analysis of
their own system to understand that even with an incorrect outcome comparison, jury
wheel to population, excused jurors should count as jurors in the same way that offers
should count as hires.[80]

A second mailing asks some of those on the qualified wheel to appear at a certain court
at a specified date and time. Some do not. In Contra Costa County, for example, 9 percent
from the October 1982 mailing failed to appear. There are more no-shows in Connecticut,
which sends the second mailing to those who did not respond to the first mailing. In *Gibbs*
(1998) I was able to infer that a large number of those who were considered "no-shows,"
disproportionately Hispanic, were unlikely still to have been in the jurisdiction. Defendant's
expert, like the state, considered them qualified. Working for the state, I was in the apparently anomalous position of saying that the actual percent Hispanic among qualified
potential jurors was even smaller than defendant was claiming. If one is making a comparison to the census, my estimate seemed to argue against my client's interest. In fact, I
was showing that the system did not drop Hispanics. Hispanics dropped themselves.

---

78. In most systems there are also some people who are exempt from jury duty. In Massachusetts, for
example, police and fire personnel are exempt. As "exempt" is simply an automatic excuse, those found
exempt can be considered to be in the "excused" ellipse.

79. In female opt-in or opt-out systems, analysis had to be based on males, because one could not know
how many females took themselves out of the qualified population. See *Barksdale* (1980) and *Barksdale*
(1981). Given *Healey* (1973), I cannot understand why the absence of females was not part of challenger's
objection to the Louisiana system in *Barksdale*. The Supreme Court has understood that individual
behavior vitiates population comparisons only in female opt-in systems, but the Court came to this
understanding late. See *Taylor* (1975), which reverses the Court's position in *Hoyt* (1961).

80. Judge Spada, the state judge in *Gibbs* (1998), admitted to being reluctant to excuse Hispanics, after
I testified that the data implied this behavior among Connecticut state judges. See also *Barksdale* (1981)
at 1128:

> Several of the judges testified that they had to make special efforts to find at least two
> blacks who were eligible to serve and did not have to be excused because of occupation
> or hardship.

In *Hare* (2004), at 966, the arresting officer

> testified that he was so concerned with the issue of racial discrimination that he would
> sometimes intentionally refrain from stopping minority motorists who had committed
> traffic violations in an attempt to avoid being perceived as a racist.

That is, how we measure—how participants think we measure—has behavioral consequences.

Becoming a qualified potential juror who shows up for duty requires an action on the part of the citizen. Therefore I have colored venires blue in Figure 54. Persons who do not actually serve on a jury because they were excused, or were not placed on a venire, or were discharged (not selected from the venire for a jury) have performed their duty. In many jurisdictions, where recent service is a disqualification or excuse later, they are allowed to say they have served on that date.

Potential jurors have been told to appear at courthouses where trials are scheduled. Unless all trials have been cancelled, they are assembled into groups and sent to court-rooms. Each group is now a venire. In some systems, some people may be excused at this point. The potential jurors enter the courtroom for the *voir dire* process, in which they are questioned by the judge and attorneys. Some people may be dismissed for cause, others with peremptory challenges. The final result of that process is the formation of the jury.

No defendant has a right to a representative jury.[81] His constitutional right is to "an impartial jury." The Supreme Court would have this mean that some large pool of potential jurors—usually larger than the venire, but always larger than the jury—is "representative" of something. Figure 54 should demonstrate that we cannot measure the "something" of which this potential-juror pool is supposed to be representative, except in jury-selection data. Yet, it is the jury data that are being questioned in this litigation. Defendant's attorney would argue that jury-selection data cannot be the basis on which juries are evaluated. He would be wrong. They are the *only* basis on which whether selection was fair can be evaluated.

EVALUATING JURIES: EARLY METRICS AND STANDARDS

That source lists reduce the proportion of minorities in the jury-selection system, compared with the population, was Yamhill County's conjecture in the *Oregonian* article that heads this chapter. That has been the theory of those who have sponsored increasing the number of source lists. However, the Supreme Court requires no more than the voter list. By speaking to both input and outcome standards, the Court is in a vise that some day will close. It will be faced with an acceptable list, pristine procedures slavishly followed, and an unacceptable outcome. Lower-level judges have found a solution—the "third prong" of

---

81. *Goldsby* (1959) at 81:

> The United States Constitution does not guarantee to a defendant in a State court a trial before a jury in which his race is proportionately represented, nor a trial before a jury composed in any part of members of his race. . . . It does assure him of equal treatment under the law and that, so long as the State elects to accord jury trials, it must not systematically exclude from jury service qualified persons of his race.

Duren (1979)—to which I will get. First, let's review how such a confusing, unnecessarily complex, and ultimately unsatisfactory system of evaluation evolved.

Earliest Cases

Before we go back to the early jury cases, let's consider an important employment case, *Teamsters* (1977). The complaint was that T.I.M.E.-D.C., Inc., a trucking company, in collusion with the Teamsters union,

> had engaged in a pattern or practice of discriminating against minorities in hiring so-called line drivers. Those Negroes and Spanish-surnamed persons who had been hired, the Government alleged, were given lower-paying, less-desirable jobs as servicemen or local city drivers, and were thereafter discriminated against with respect to promotions and transfers.[82]

Part of the government's proof had been a comparison between the proportion black among drivers and

> the proportion of blacks in the city or Standard Metropolitan Statistical Area, where T.I.M.E.-D.C. operates terminals.[83]

That is a comparison of a stock with a stock, a situation, employees (work force) against a census-defined labor force, a classic availability analysis. The government also contrasted hires with this same labor force, comparing flow with stock. It prevailed, over defendant's objection that the availability concept was too vague. As the circuit court concluded,

> the inability [of the employer] to rebut came not from the lack of an informed standard. Rather, in most instances for L[ine] D[river]s, the inability came from the inexorable zero.

It was thus from the Fifth Circuit that the Supreme Court picked up this phrase, "the inexorable zero," in its famous footnote 23 of *Teamsters* (1977).[84] But though the term was new in the 1970s, the concept was old. It came from jury-composition cases in which blacks had been excluded, totally.

To stretch a point, we can go back to 1879. It is a stretch because we deal here not with just an observed absence of blacks on juries, but with overt exclusion, a West Virginia law

---

82. Justice Stewart for the Court, *Teamsters* (1977) at 329.

83. Chief Judge John R. Brown of the Fifth Circuit Court of Appeals, for the circuit court in *Teamsters* (1975) at 315; following indented quotation also at 315. The phrase should be "proportion black," not "proportion of blacks."

84. Another famous quotation from the Court's opinion in *Teamsters* (1977), at 340:

> We caution only that statistics are not irrefutable; they come in infinite variety and, like any other kind of evidence, they may be rebutted. In short, their usefulness depends on all of the surrounding facts and circumstances.

that restricted jurors to "all white male persons who are twenty-one years of age and who are citizens of this State." [85] Such a law clearly violated the newly adopted Fourteenth Amendment to the Constitution. The Court had no trouble with that question, only with establishing its jurisdiction to enforce the federal Constitution during a state trial for violation of a state law. This activist Supreme Court held that the Constitution was meaningless if it did not apply within a state court, that equal protection was a federal right regardless of state jurisdiction over its own crimes. But if blacks could not be excluded from juries *de jure*, could they be *de facto*?

The Court first tackled the problem of exclusion of blacks from juries one year later:

> [T]he fact (so generally known that the court felt obliged to take judicial notice of it) that no colored citizen had ever been summoned as a juror in the courts of the State—although its colored population exceeded twenty thousand in 1870, and in 1880 exceeded twenty-six thousand, in a total population of less than one hundred and fifty thousand—presented a *prima facie* case of denial, by the officers charged with the selection of grand and petit jurors, of that equality of protection which has been secured by the Constitution and laws of the United States. It was, we think, under all the circumstances, a violent presumption which the State court indulged, that such uniform exclusion of that race from juries, during a period of many years, was solely because, in the judgment of those officers, fairly exercised, the black race in Delaware were utterly disqualified, by want of intelligence, experience, or moral integrity, to sit on juries. [86]

And, if there were any question about total exclusion, the Court settled it in 1900:

> Whenever by any action of a state, whether through its legislature, through its courts, or through its executive or administrative officers, all persons of the African race are excluded, solely because of their race or color, from serving as grand jurors in the criminal prosecution of a person of the African race, the equal protection of the laws is denied to him, contrary to the Fourteenth Amendment of the Constitution of the United States. [87]

Elsewhere, minorities were provided "separate but equal" facilities. [88] As one could not conceive of separate but equal juries, they would have to be integrated.

Zero black draws from a mixed availability pool makes a *prima facie* case that something is wrong with the drawing process. A showing of the total exclusion of blacks from

---

85. West Virginia Acts of 1872–73 at 102, quoted in *Strauder* (1879) at 305.

86. *Neal* (1880) at 397. Although standard procedure and language today, the articulation of defendant's burden to make a "*prima facie*" case, with the state's opportunity to rebut it, is attributed to this decision. See, for example, *Hill* (1942) at 405–406.

87. Justice Gray delivered the opinion of the Court in *Carter* (1900) at 447.

88. See *Plessy* (1896), which allowed separate (by race) railroad passenger cars.

juries in areas where blacks live cannot be countered by white assertions that the blacks were not really qualified. Their availability for the job at hand (here, jury duty) is to be presumed, absent a persuasive showing to the contrary. No standards for the denominator (the pool being drawn from) were given, but zero was a compelling numerator for close to a hundred years.

The question was visited many times. For example, in the famous Scottsboro Boys case, with regard to the grand jury:

> We think that the evidence that for a generation or longer no negro had been called for service on any jury in Jackson county, that there were negroes qualified for jury service, that according to the practice of the jury commission their names would normally appear on the preliminary list of male citizens of the requisite age but that no names of negroes were placed on the jury roll, and the testimony with respect to the lack of appropriate consideration of the qualifications of negroes, established the discrimination which the Constitution forbids.[89]

Similarly, discussing the venire,

> The population of Morgan county, where the trial was had, was larger than that of Jackson county, and the proportion of negroes was much greater. The total population of Morgan county in 1930 was 46,176, and of this number 8,311 were negroes.

There were no blacks on the venire or, indeed, on any venire in the memory of anyone who testified on this point.

When broadening the notion of a "distinct class" that could be discriminated against, the Court applied the same logic:

> Circumstances or chance may well dictate that no persons in a certain class will serve on a particular jury or during some particular period. But it taxes our credulity to say that mere chance resulted in there being no members of this class among the over six thousand jurors called in the past 25 years.[90]

Availability analysis seemed to work at this level: There were enough minorities available that surely some of them would have been selected, were it not for racial bias.

Less than Total Exclusion

Laws that disallowed minorities on juries were repealed. As the states learned that zero minorities drawn from a substantial availability pool (whatever "substantial" might mean)

---

89. Chief Justice Hughes for the Court in *Norris* (1935) at 596; following indented quotation also at 596.
90. *Hernandez* (1954) at 482.

would doom their system, they moved away from zero to few. Numbers such as these were presented to the Court:[91]

> (Stock or pool) Blacks were:
>   20% of population
>   10% of poll-tax payers.
>
> (Flow of selections) Blacks were:
>   18 of 512 summoned for grand-jury duty
>   (13 of these 18 were the last on 16-person lists)
>   5 of 384 on grand jury.

Or, put another way, 28 percent of the blacks on the lists served, as opposed to 77 percent of the whites. The Court found that the law itself was not unfair, but the discretion it allowed apparently had been abused.

> Chance and accident alone could hardly have brought about the listing for grand jury service of so few negroes from among the thousands shown by the undisputed evidence to possess the legal qualifications for jury service. Nor could chance and accident have been responsible for the combination of circumstances under which a negro's name, when listed at all, almost invariably appeared as number 16, and under which number 16 was never called for service unless it proved impossible to obtain the required jurors from the first 15 names on the list.[92]

This is not a statistical conclusion. It is about procedure, about "the wide discretion permissible in the various steps of the plan." Few blacks were on service lists, most were placed last on ordered lists, therefore few were chosen to serve. Even though the jury-selection scheme "is capable of being carried out with no racial discrimination," it was not.

Discrimination did not necessarily require overt action on the part of the jury selectors.

> Where jury commissioners limit those from whom grand juries are selected to their own personal acquaintance, discrimination can arise from commissioners who know no negroes as well as from commissioners who know but eliminate them.[93]

One might say that procedures neutral on their face (select people you know) would fall when they had a disparate impact on blacks, and could not otherwise be justified. This logic evolved into the principle under which Duke Power, in *Griggs* (1971), was found to have discriminated by imposing employment standards that were unrelated to performance in the low-level jobs at issue, and had the effect of excluding blacks. In the 1940s, rather

---

91. *Smith* (1940), Justice Black for the unanimous Court.

92. *Smith* (1940) at 131; following in-text quotations at 131 and 130.

93. *Smith* (1940) at 130.

than substituting for intent, this yet-unnamed disparate impact was taken as *evidence* of intent.[94]

Of course Texas juries were deliberately, intentionally devoid of black members. That is why the commissioners had discretion. It was there to disqualify blacks. Courts did not yet believe that they could determine intent from the procedure itself. Yet they required intent to reverse. A solution would have been to prohibit discretionary procedure per se, without regard to what the discretion produced. Instead, they judged the jury-composition outcome, which meant both measuring it and applying some standard to that measure. The Court was traveling down the outcome road by 1940.

The Court juggles procedure and outcome, concerned with both:

> At each term of court, three grand jury commissioners are appointed; at the time they are sworn in, the judge instructs them as to their duties; they are required to take an oath not knowingly to select a grand juror whom they believe unfit or unqualified; they must then retire to a room in the courthouse, taking the county assessment roll with them; while in that room they must select a grand jury of 16 men from different parts of the county; they must next seal in an envelope the list of the 16 names selected; thirty days before court meets the clerk is required to make a copy of the list and deliver it to the sheriff; thereupon the sheriff must summon the jurors.[95]

The system was capable of discretion, and the results of selections imply that the discretion was used adversely to blacks. Not only did these early decisions identify a specific mechanism that could result in a small number of minorities on juries, they did so *first*. Procedure was paramount, though it mattered only if the effect was bad; so there had to be a finding that the number of blacks was unexpectedly small. Finally the Court associated the paucity of blacks with the discretion that allowed it.[96] Bad process led to bad outcome. It was unconstitutional.

As the Court itself noted in 1972, the facts were becoming less stark. In *Alexander* (1972) it explained:

---

94. See, for example, *Akins* (1945) at 403, referring back to *Smith* (1940):

> The mere fact of inequality in the number selected does not in itself show discrimination. A purpose to discriminate must be present which may be proven by systematic exclusion of eligible jurymen of the proscribed race or by unequal application of the law to such an extent as to show intentional discrimination.

95. *Smith* (1940) footnote 5.

96. That courts assumed that discretion-caused disparity is illustrated by cases in which there is a similar disparity, but no selection discretion. See, for example, the district-court opinion in *Grisham* (1994). The Eleventh Circuit did not understand this subtlety, and applied a "statistical" test. See *Grisham* (1995). The Second Circuit came closer in *Rioux* (1996). The Supreme Court still has not dealt with the no-discretion situation.

This is not a case where it is claimed that there have been no Negroes called for service within the last 30 years; only one Negro chosen within the last 40 years; or no Negroes selected "within the memory of witnesses who had lived (in the area) all their lives." Rather, petitioner argues that, in his case, there has been a consistent process of progressive and disproportionate reduction of the number of Negroes eligible to serve on the grand jury at each stage of the selection process until ultimately an all-white grand jury was selected to indict him.[97]

The Court presented these statistics:

(Stock or pool) Blacks were:
    21% of population over age 21.

(Flow of selections) Blacks were:
    14% of those on prospective-juror list
    7% of those summoned for grand-jury duty
    5% on petitioner's grand-jury venire
    zero on grand jury.

Still not having a standard of comparison, the Court nonetheless stated:

The progressive decimation of potential Negro grand jurors is indeed striking here, but we do not rest our conclusion that petitioner has demonstrated a *prima facie* case of invidious racial discrimination on statistical improbability alone, for the selection procedures themselves were not racially neutral. The racial designation on both the questionnaire and the information card provided a clear and easy opportunity for racial discrimination.

Non-neutral selection procedures are an integral part of the finding.

This Court has never announced mathematical standards for the demonstration of "systematic" exclusion of blacks.

So wrote Justice White for the Court. As we will see, it soon did.

The increase in case complexity is well illustrated by the difference between *Whitus I*—in which the accepted fact was that there had never been a black juror from 45-percent-lack Mitchell County, Georgia—and *Whitus II*. In 1967 the Court goes through its litany—many available blacks, few on juries—and once again finds the system to be fraught with race identification and discretion. Names still came from segregated tax records, and were written on color-coded slips of paper. It was easy enough to find that the jury-selection system discriminated against blacks. The selection system was flawed, racially biased, and discretionary; and petitioner showed a statistical disparity between expected and actual blacks that constituted a *prima facie* case.

In *Whitus II*, for the first time, the outcome comparison—the statistical showing and

---

97. *Alexander* (1972) at 628. Data are presented in the text at 627; the following two indented quotations are both at 630.

the *prima facie* case—was described *first*, before the procedural weakness that allowed discrimination. The Court did seem to require the explanation of why the system was so flawed, but it did so to say the state failed to rebut the *prima facie* statistics.

Thus, in 1967, the logic of the argument became reversed. As reinforced later in *Alexander* (1972) and similar cases, by the late 1960s the statistical conclusion was enunciated first, the procedural flaw, second. Result became paramount, process, subsidiary. By placing the statistical comparison first, over time the logic associating the statistics with the flaw was lost. The Court was looking at outcomes. Therefore the justices sensed that they needed an outcome standard. What they actually needed was someone to tell them that their entire approach was wrong. No one did.

Introducing the Binomial Distribution

All of these early jury cases utilized an informal availability analysis. At various times judges at different levels speculated that due to differences in demographics, losing blacks or Hispanics from census to jury hardly seems surprising. However, the only evidence taken was anecdotal, liberally quoting from witnesses to establish that not a single black person served on a jury in the memory of anyone alive.

The Court was the victim of a method that could not call the close ones. In *Smith* (1940) it relied on no method at all, just assertion. *Teamsters* (1977) referred to the good old days of "the inexorable zero" because that was no longer the fact pattern in these cases. The Court was looking to improve availability analysis to cover the situation where there were some—but seemingly too few—minorities on juries, in jobs, wherever availability analysis (by whatever name) was applied. What the Court thought it needed was a tool to analyze these new situations. In 1966, Michael Finkelstein provided it.[98]

The Finkelstein Rationale

Finkelstein's contribution, especially given its use by the Supreme Court, is universally acclaimed as a triumph of the acceptance of modern statistical methods in the judicial process. Within ten years it had been proclaimed a "classic."[99] I agree that his is a sophisticated, clear, informative article that everyone interested in this topic should read. I also think it was seriously in error. Its acceptance as the solution to the Court's problem has kept the Court off track for decades. Analysts are correct to pay homage to Finkelstein's effort; but they are incorrect to follow it.

---

98. See Finkelstein (1966). This article was edited and reproduced in Finkelstein (1978). As this is a historical review, I refer to the original version.

99. Sperlich and Jaspovice (1975) at 83.

Great interest had been focused on the Supreme Court's analysis of jury representation by their decision in *Swain* (1965):

> It is wholly obvious that Alabama has not totally excluded a racial group from
> either grand or petit jury panels. . . . Moreover, we do not consider an aver-
> age of six to eight Negroes on these panels as constituting forbidden token
> inclusion within the meaning of the cases in this Court. Nor do we consider
> the evidence in this case to make out a *prima facie* case of invidious discrim-
> ination under the Fourteenth Amendment.[100]

Given the facts and attitudes in Alabama, this decision was a travesty. A spontaneous outcry emerged to tell the Court how wrong it had been. The *Virginia Law Review* commented that *Swain* "handed the states a blank check for discrimination."[101] The *Yale Law Journal* was quick to conclude:

> In the recent case of *Swain v. Alabama* the Supreme Court served notice that
> it is not ready to wage a final campaign against exclusion of Negroes from
> juries.[102]

That such a campaign was necessary was clear to at least one Fifth Circuit panel:

> The impression was general in the South at the time of Goins' trial that the
> constitutional requirement was met if Negroes were simply represented on the
> grand jury.[103]

Finkelstein's article appeared a year after the *Yale Law Journal* suggested that something more should be done to achieve fair jury selection. Finkelstein was politely disparaging of the *Swain* decision. The Court did seem impressed that *some* blacks were on jury panels, having no tools by which to ask if "enough" were. Finally, in *Swain*, the Court was unwilling to censure attorneys for using their peremptory challenges to exclude those few blacks who were on venires. It would take another twenty years to get there.[104]

Finkelstein adopted the Court's outcome approach. He took no issue with looking to differences in race composition between juries and the population. The Court needed a method, he thought; a way to deal with "few." He introduced the Court to the wonders of the binomial and chi-square statistics, from which one could calculate the probability of selecting no more blacks than had been selected (or the probability of their distribution

---

100. *Swain* (1965) at 206.

101. Comment (1966) at 1175.

102. Note (1965a) at 322.

103. *Goins* (1968) at 696.

104. See *Batson* (1986) and then for females, *JEB* (1994), and Hispanics in *Hernandez* (1991). Some state courts were well ahead. See, for example, *Soares* (1979), in which the Massachusetts Supreme Court recognizes the criticisms of *Swain* (1965) and essentially rejects it.

among juries) had they been randomly selected from a large pool of known composition. And so, because we do *not* know the composition of the pool, he failed the Court by agreeing with it.[105]

Without question, Finkelstein is the major contributor to the development of statistics in law, probably ever, and surely in the 1960s through 1980s. His view of the appropriate comparisons required to test jury composition has been unchallenged except for some technical matters. That is a failure of the combined profession of analysts in the law and analysts of the law. Although I will disagree with Finkelstein's calculation, his important error lies in the concept that drives it. Everyone since Finkelstein has followed his lead. The elaborate detail of this chapter is dictated by its uniqueness in challenging this received doctrine.

Eligible Jurors

The later experts, and the courts, failed also by avoiding a subject about which Finkelstein is clear. Finkelstein wants to test selections from a pool of persons "eligible" for jury duty. Lacking sufficient data, he turns the test around, asking how unqualified would blacks have to be, relative to whites, to rationalize their low appearance in jury pools. He finds that ratio, and then leaves it to the Court to decide whether it is a likely representation of fact.

> The results [in *Swain*] could not be justified by any lack of qualifications for jury service among Negroes unless it was assumed that the rate of Negro qualifications with respect to such subjective factors as lack of integrity was little more than half the rate of white qualification.[106]

Finkelstein gets to this point by correcting census population figures for sixth-grade education, to account for the other requirement for jury service, literacy. That appears to leave one qualification, integrity. But what is the answer? It seems to me that a jury system in which some people have the right to assess the "integrity" of others should fail on that ground alone. One should not have to make outcome arguments or look to education data for proxy measures. The process of some people *deciding* on a case-by-case basis who can be a juror is the opposite of random. Finkelstein's mathematics just leaves a question—could blacks be qualified at only half the rate of whites?—without any way to get to an answer. It may *seem* unlikely that blacks are so different from whites, but the promise of mathematical certainty disappears when it must be resolved by a guess about the value of an abstraction.

---

105. Mathematically, the binomial test is as applicable to zero black selections as to "few." It is only as a matter of relevance in law that it is not applicable in either case. I admire Michael Finkelstein in person as well as in his writing. He was thoroughly honest and would never have compromised his work for Supreme Court praise. He was simply wrong.

106. Finkelstein (1966) at 374.

Finkelstein's calculation is incorrect in any case. As we have seen, there is another qualification for jury service: being present when the time comes. I do not know if blacks were more mobile than whites in Alabama in the 1960s. Nor does Finkelstein. His proof is no proof at all, for it lacks required facts. That those facts were required is a telling defect of this outcome approach.

Roger Kuhn, reacting to *Swain*, and also recommending Finkelstein's binomial test, was quick to spot the defect in the logic as long as character qualifications were allowed to stand. I will disagree later with where Kuhn takes his argument, but I agree with his premise:

> No one familiar with the history of discrimination will believe, however, that the Old South is on the threshold of full compliance with the mandate of the Constitution.[107]

Eliminating character requirements might have led Kuhn to consider other procedural solutions. Recognizing that the Southern establishment would place as few blacks on juries as they could get away with was a good start. However, substituting objective eligibility characteristics for a "character" judgment, which is where I would have gone, would have vitiated the use of statistical analysis of outcomes that Kuhn, like Finkelstein, espoused.

Finkelstein was an attorney, building on precedent, making a contribution on the margin. He just wanted to introduce the Court to "various methods of applying mathematical techniques to problems of jury discrimination."[108] His exposition follows from the early cases of *de jure* exclusion of blacks from juries, to *Norris* (1935), which Finkelstein cites as the earliest use of numerical evidence that qualified blacks abounded in the population, but not on juries.[109] After a compelling critique of the Court's refusal to review the evidence in *Swain*, Finkelstein states the problem as finding "a rational way of determining which disparities were large enough to be evidence of design."[110]

> Since the judges have recognized that not every variation from proportionate numbers is evidence of design, they are confronted with the harder problem of drawing a line between significant and insignificant variations and the related problem of determining the effect to be given to "explanations" for significant variations.

So Finkelstein will not provide an answer after all. He would still use outcome disparity as a measure of intent, asking the Court to set a standard based on statistical "significance." All he is providing is a measurement. Taking a lawyer's tack, Finkelstein summarizes cases of total exclusion of blacks from juries, demonstrates the Court's confusion

---

107. R. Kuhn (1968) at 237.

108. Finkelstein (1966) at 340.

109. What happened to *Neal* (1880), or *Carter* (1900)?

110. Finkelstein (1966) at 348; following indented quotation at 349.

when presented with partial exclusion, and buys in to the comparison of jury pools with the population. What we need, he says, is "an analysis of the data which will expose the true legal issues." [111]

That worthy goal remained unmet. The "true legal issues" cannot be analyzed from outcomes. The standards on which the Court needed help were procedural standards, not outcome standards. I agree that the Court needed a way to discern bad systems and find them unconstitutional. Finkelstein's approach, unfortunately, cannot do that.

Finkelstein comes close to understanding the "denominator" (jurors compared to what?) issue:

> But within the pool of eligibles, however restricted in size, the selection must still be made without reference to race, and this means that the racial population of jury venires is—or should be—the result of random selection and consequently an appropriate subject for probability theory analysis.

He misses the mark. Despite his homage to "eligibles," and his analysis of qualifications, Finkelstein is stuck on comparing the numerator, the *outcome* of "random" selection, to a census-based availability pool. In *Swain*,

> neither Court nor counsel offered a rational way of determining which disparities were large enough to be considered evidence of design.

After presenting a first course on statistics of selection, Finkelstein summarizes:

> A basic legal principle in the jury-discrimination cases is that the selection of an improbably small number of Negroes is evidence of discrimination. . . . The second legal principle controlling these cases is that disparity between the proportion of Negroes on venires and in the population generally is evidence of the improbability of random selection. [112]

His role, as he saw it, was to calculate these "improbabilities." Because we do not know the composition of the eligible, present, and cooperative population, that is something no one can do.

Discretion

As the editor of the *Virginia Law Review* noted, one could take another lesson from the cases Finkelstein reviewed:

> While some state laws are discriminatory on their face, without question the greatest source of problems is the almost complete discretion vested in local

---

111. Finkelstein (1966) at 349; following indented quotation at 350; second indented quotation at 348.

112. Finkelstein (1966) at 374. Note that Finkelstein accepts the comparison of population to venires. He missed his opportunity to make the correction that venires usually follow excusals, and excused persons must be considered selections or their requests to be excused will not be considered fairly.

jury commissioners, who select the list on the basis of such vague and subjective criteria as good character, integrity, and sound judgment.[113]

This point can be approached another way. See, for example, *Theil* (1946):

> Recognition must be given to the fact that those eligible for jury service are to be found in every stratum of society. Jury competence is an individual rather than a group or class matter.[114]

or *Cassell* (1950):

> [J]urymen should be selected as individuals . . . and not as members of a race.

The Court has been stunningly consistent, over time and issue, in considering people as individuals, not bound by their race or gender. Using life tables, insurance companies had noted that females live longer than males, on average. Pension funds were collecting money to guarantee a stream of future income that would last as long as one lived. Because the average female would live longer, and therefore take more money out of such a fund, the fund managers thought it was right to make females put more in. The Court disagreed in *Manhart* (1978). Rights adhere to individuals, not to characteristics such as gender. You cannot charge a female more because she *might* live longer, that is, because she is like people who statistically do live longer.

Shortly thereafter, in *Teal* (1982), the Court once again disassociated individuals from their group. In following an employment procedure, blacks had been disproportionately eliminated by a test, and then disproportionately selected among those who survived the test. Overall, selections of blacks were at their proportion of application. Could those who had been screened out by the test complain? Yes, said the Court. Discrimination by race occurs to individuals. The characteristic may be collective, but the actions are against individuals; and these individuals have a right to complain about being discriminated against by the test, even though other individuals like them were hired in great numbers.[115]

---

113. Note (1966) at 1071. Although listed in the *Virginia Law Review* as a note, it is signed by initials that identify the editor, Earl C. Dudley, Jr.

114. *Theil* (1946) at 220; following quotation from *Cassell* (1950) at 286.

115. I state my disappointment in several places in this book that this great principle of law was not followed in *Grutter* (2003), the decision allowing the law school at the University of Michigan to assess individuals of different races differently. Following the "pragmatic" law creation espoused by Richard Posner (2003), *Grutter* is an example of the failure of the Court to enunciate and live by clear principles. As Posner summarizes in *Lust* (2004) at 583,

> the anti-discrimination laws entitle individuals to be evaluated as individuals rather than as members of groups having certain average characteristics.

If procedure should rule, which is the point of this chapter, then it should rule fairly. I cannot imagine eliminating "discretion" from graduate-school admissions. In *Grutter*, the Court missed its opportunity to make race an impermissible factor of that discretion.

Yet in the jury cases we are counting people by their race, and wondering if qualifications are different enough, by race, to "explain" different selection. A *Teal* approach would have required the jury-selection system to indicate how many minorities were dropped at each stage. The state would then have to defend any "test" that had a disparate impact, arguing that the measure was valid—reasonably related to the purpose at hand, getting qualified jurors. Requiring valid screening procedures at every stage surely would have put an end to character judgments.

That the Court could not utilize Finkelstein's approach to qualifications, determining whether minorities had so few of them as to have been plausibly treated equally, became evident in *Carter* (1970), another Alabama case. The system not only contained discretion, the clerks did not follow the rules. The Court was asked to declare Alabama jury-selection laws invalid on their face, for allowing such discretion and for structuring it so that clerks could make biased decisions. But the Court could understand how upright citizens (self-indulgent pause required here) might operate a discretionary system fairly. And who would not want jurors to have integrity and good character?

> Again, in *Smith v. Texas*, we dealt with a statute leaving a wide range of choice to the commissioners. Yet we expressly upheld the validity of the law. The statutory scheme was not in itself unfair; it was "capable of being carried out with no racial discrimination whatsoever." [116]

This approach made no sense to Justice Douglas:

> There comes a time when an organ or agency of state law has proved itself to have such a racist mission that it should not survive constitutional challenge.

I agree. The Court's failure to strike the statute in *Smith* (1940) was an error. Finkelstein should have taken that position. Following *Carter*, challengers would have to prove that the discretion, which was placed there by the state to be used differentially by race, was so, judicial district by judicial district. A better approach would have been to disallow the discretion, declaring the state law and therefore all of its systems unconstitutional. [117]

Consider, for example, the oath taken by jury commissioners in Virginia, placed in the

---

116. *Carter* (1970) at 335, quoting from *Smith* (1940); following indented quotation from *Carter* (1970), Douglas dissent at 341.

117. The Supreme Court of Connecticut adopted this position in *Ferguson* (2002). They assert, at 18, that *Gibbs* (1998), which is discussed in the Appendix to Chapter 5, is sufficient to cover other jurisdictions in the state, because

> The procedures for summoning persons to serve on juries in Connecticut is [*sic*] the same throughout the state and, therefore, it makes little difference that our decision in *Gibbs* was based on a case from the judicial district of Hartford-New Britain, while the defendant's case originated in the Stamford-Norwalk judicial district. We will not engage in a piecemeal evaluation of jury-array procedures for each of the state's judicial districts.

code in 1919. Each commissioner swears to include only "persons whom I believe to be of good repute for intelligence and honesty."[118] Under a procedural review requiring that there be only objective standards, a jury-selection system requiring such an oath would be invalid.

THE BINOMIAL IN USE

It did not take long for Finkelstein's sense that calculations could be made from this model to attract the attention of the Supreme Court. The model, after all, *was* the Court's. Finkelstein provided a tool, not a concept. The first Supreme Court reference to Finkelstein's 1966 article came the next year, in *Whitus II*:

> While unnecessary to our disposition of the instant case, it is interesting to note the "probability" involved in the situation before the Court.
>
> The record does not indicate how many Negroes were actually on the "revised" jury list of approximately 600 names. One jury commissioner, however, said his best estimate was 25% to 30%, which is in close proximity to the 27.1% who were admittedly on the tax digest for 1964. Assuming that 27% of the list was made up of the names of qualified Negroes, the mathematical probability of having seven Negroes on a venire of 90 is 0.000006.[119]

The difference between nine black jurors and the "expected" 24.3 (27 percent of 90) is 4.1 standard deviations. And that is too many, following Finkelstein, as the Court later declared.[120] It shyly put its foot into statistical waters in *Whitus*. In *Castaneda* it took the plunge.

Castaneda (1977)

Claudio Castaneda, sheriff of Hidalgo County, Texas, arrested Rodrigo Partida for burglary and attempted rape. Partida was tried and convicted in the state court, and then argued

---

118. Quoted in Tucker (1966) at 738.

119. This is the entire footnote 2 of *Whitus II*, at 552, except for its overt citation to Finkelstein (1966). The probability is not precisely correct, but the number of zeros is.

120. Perhaps one should not hold Finkelstein responsible for the fact that this calculation is not appropriate in these circumstances. The normal approximation to the binomial distribution advocated by Finkelstein assumes that draws are made from a fixed, known composition of potential jurors. I have shown in this chapter that in fact we do *not* know the composition of the pool of "eligible jurors." But let's suppose that although we do not *know* its composition, we have some estimate of it. Then we are comparing two proportions, both of which are estimates. The standard deviation between them is larger than the standard deviation used by the Court, and therefore the distance between numerator and denominator is smaller. We need some measure of how good our estimate is. If we assume that the estimation error is equivalent to the sampling error, then seven blacks are 2.9 standard deviations from the expected 24.3, p = 0.0009. Some courts have rejected disparities of this size as "not significant."

in federal court that his indictment was invalid. The jury system was unduly constituted because it omitted Hispanics, he claimed. Grand juries were formed much as in *Smith* (1940), using the "key-man" system, even though the Texas jury-selection laws had been rewritten. The numbers were undisputed.[121]

> (Stock or pool) Hispanics were:
>> 79.1% of population
>> 10% of poll-tax payers.
>
> (Flow of selections) Hispanics were:
>> 50% of grand-juror lists
>> 39% of grand jurors
>> 45.5% of petit jurors.

Although these figures were undisputed, there was some discussion about how they were defined. "Hispanics" in the numerator were persons of Hispanic surname. Some might have been Anglos who married Hispanics, said the state appeals court, affirming the conviction.[122] The federal district court denied the petition for *habeas corpus*, although granting that the defendant had made a *prima facie* case of discrimination in jury selection from the census comparisons. The *prima facie* case was weak, said Judge Garza, because "the census statistics did not reflect the true situation accurately."[123] Furthermore, the challenger had more of a burden.

> After proving a discriminatory result, the Petitioner must further prove this result was accompanied by some particular discriminatory act or failure to act; or accompanied by token inclusion or total exclusion; or accompanied by a jury-selection system containing a significant danger of abuse; or by proving that the discriminatory result was representative of the result obtained in a history of the cases in the particular jurisdiction in which the trial occurred, this being strong circumstantial evidence of discriminatory jury selection.[124]

Judge Garza saw the whole picture: Census data were a poor measure of the relevant

---

121. These numbers were taken from the Supreme Court opinion, *Castaneda* (1977), though they appear in text, not in a table. They can be found, also, in the circuit court opinion, *Castaneda* (1975).

122. *Castaneda* (1974a). In fact, a count of Hispanic last names is usually quite accurate, despite a large error in specific identification, because just about as many Hispanic women marry non-Hispanics as non-Hispanic women marry Hispanics.

123. This is the Supreme Court's precis of district-court judge Garza's reasoning, *Castaneda* (1977) at 491. Judge Garza, in *Castaneda* (1974b) at 89, stated the issue: "[I]t must be remembered that this area is unique in that it has a larger ineligible migrant and illegal-alien population than other areas." Unfortunately, this is just extra-legal speculation. If the state had the burden to present it as an argument, with data, it failed to do so.

124. Judge Garza in *Castaneda* (1974b) at 87.

eligible juror base, and causality required more than an assertion. His logic was correct. Given the Supreme Court's prior decisions, one could argue that so was his law.

The Fifth Circuit reversed Judge Garza, attorneys would say, because once the challenger has made a *prima facie* case (from the statistical comparison), the burden is on the state to explain its system. The real reason is that the Supreme Court consistently allowed systems with abusive discretion to function, requiring what it thought was micro-analysis of the exercise of that discretion.

> While the Texas system of selecting grand jurors is constitutional, the unbridled discretion afforded the jury commissioners to prepare the grand jury lists requires close scrutiny of the disparities and the proof offered to explain them. Here, the disparities are too great and the proof offered too paltry.[125]

Had *Smith* (1940) banned unchecked discretion, there would have been no *Castaneda* (1977).

As the circuit court saw it, the challenger makes a *prima facie* case

> by showing a disparity between (1) the percentage which his ethnic or racial group constitutes of the persons from whom a jury list is drawn and (2) the percentage which that group constitutes of the jury list compiled. Once a defendant establishes his *prima facie* case, the burden shifts to the State to offer a satisfactory explanation why the disparity exists.[126]

The error is in (1). The census does not measure "the persons from whom a jury list is drawn." The census provides (E + N). The jury list is drawn from participating, cooperating E. The former does not provide a basis from which to measure the percentage Hispanic in the latter.

Perhaps a more fundamental error is the failure to associate the disparity between population and jury with any systematic flaw. Here is how a Sixth Circuit panel summarized the *Castaneda* process many years later:

> Specifically, to establish a *prima facie* case of discrimination, a petitioner must satisfy a three-part test. First, he must establish that the group excluded from the grand jury is one that is a recognizable, distinct class capable of being singled out for different treatment under the laws. Second, he must establish that the selection procedure used by the state to select grand juries is susceptible to abuse or is not racially neutral. Finally, he must establish the degree of underrepresentation occurring over a significant period of time by comparing the

---

125. *Castaneda* (1975) at 484. A better decision would have been to reverse only Judge Garza's finding that the challenger had made a *prima facie* case. Had the Fifth Circuit affirmed the district court's finding disallowing the *habeas corpus* decision because it was challenger's responsibility to associate cause with effect, would the Supreme Court have reversed to introduce statistical "proof"?

126. *Castaneda* (1975) at 483.

proportion of the excluded group in the total population to the proportion
serving as grand jurors.[127]

The association of this under-representation with a procedure "susceptible to abuse" is
implicit. Proof that the procedure caused the disparity is not required.

The effect of *Castaneda* was to allow a challenger to place the burden of persuasion on
the state with the flimsiest of statistical demonstrations. The Court was so taken with its
newfound ability to measure that it did not ask if the measurement made sense. Discretion
was apparent in two sections of Texas state law. A juror had to be literate and, "He must be
of sound mind and good moral character." [128] Following my logic, the system should have
failed on that ground alone. Although, as in other areas, some wiggle room must be allowed,
in principle I would have agreed with the challenger in *Singleton* (1974) whose position was

> that the mere existence of a jury-selection system in which discrimination is
> possible constitutes grounds for reversal.[129]

The Fifth Circuit in that case, reading the procedures the Supreme Court had enunciated,
disagreed.

> Absent some proof of the reasons underlying the absence of Negroes from the
> petit jury in his case, appellant failed to show the existence of a racially dis-
> criminatory jury-selection practice existing in Jefferson County at the time of
> his trial.

In short, prior to *Castaneda* (1975), the Fifth Circuit thought that the jury challenger
had an obligation to associate the jury disparity with a jury-selection mechanism that
could be biased. My concept that the existence of subjective judgments should be unconstitutional regardless of the outcome had been explicitly rejected. My second preference
appeared to be in force: The challenger could not just assert an "improbable" statistical
comparison within a system with discretion. He had to show (at least to argue) that the
discretion was used to create the measured disparity. Judge Garza thought this was the law
in *Castaneda* (1974b).

That all changed with the Supreme Court's affirmation of the circuit court in *Castaneda* (1977). The statistical disparity became sufficient to make a *prima facie* case, and
the burden was shifted to the state to explain that it was *not* related to selection procedures.

Castaneda introduced three new elements. The first was the reason the Supreme Court
accepted it. Hidalgo County government was dominated by Hispanics. The sheriff himself
was Hispanic. Could the Court's model of discrimination from discretion be applied to

---

127. *Jefferson* (1992) at 1188, omitting references to *Castaneda* (1977).

128. *Castaneda* (1974a) at 211.

129. *Singleton* (1974) at 679; following indented quotation also at 679.

Hispanics discriminating against Hispanics?[130] A split Court, in a silly debate, thought it could. Of course.

The second new element, as just explained, was the disassociation of cause from effect. The outcome disparity became the primary focus. Defendant did not have to explicitly associate the disparity with a procedural flaw.

The third new element was the determination of when disparities are "large." From *Whitus II* (1967) the Supreme Court's logic became: First measure the disparity between census and juries, then discuss a systemic flaw, be it only discretion, the chance for jury selectors to discriminate. Following this order, the *Castaneda* Court, in its footnote 17, accepted the standards Finkelstein had proposed. That footnote is reproduced in its entirety (except for references to statistical texts and to Finkelstein) here:

> If the jurors were drawn randomly from the general population, then the number of Mexican-Americans in the sample could be modeled by a binomial distribution. Given that 79.1% of the population is Mexican-American, the expected number of Mexican-Americans among the 870 persons summoned to serve as grand jurors over the 11-year period is approximately 688. The observed number is 339. Of course, in any given drawing some fluctuation from the expected number is predicted. The important point, however, is that the statistical model shows that the results of a random drawing are likely to fall in the vicinity of the expected value. The measure of the predicted fluctuations from the expected value is the standard deviation, defined for the binomial distribution as the square root of the product of the total number in the sample (here 870) times the probability of selecting a Mexican-American (0.791) times the probability of selecting a non-Mexican-American (0.209). Thus, in this case the standard deviation is approximately 12. As a general rule for such large samples, if the difference between the expected value and the observed number is greater than two or three standard deviations, then the hypothesis that the jury drawing was random would be suspect to a social scientist. The 11-year data here reflect a difference between the expected and observed number of Mexican-Americans of approximately 29 standard deviations. A detailed calculation reveals that the likelihood that such a substantial departure from the expected value would occur by chance is less than 1 in 10,140.
>
> The data for the 2½-year period during which the State District Judge supervised the selection process similarly support the inference that the exclusion of Mexican-Americans did not occur by chance. Of 220 persons called

---

130. *Castaneda* (1977) at 492:

> We granted *certiorari* to consider whether the existence of a "governing majority" in itself can rebut a *prima facie* case of discrimination in grand jury selection, and, if not, whether the State otherwise met its burden of proof.

to serve as grand jurors, only 100 were Mexican-Americans. The expected Mexican-American representation is approximately 174 and the standard deviation, as calculated from the binomial model, is approximately six. The discrepancy between the expected and observed values is more than 12 standard deviations. Again, a detailed calculation shows that the likelihood of drawing not more than 100 Mexican-Americans by chance is negligible, being less than 1 in 1,025.[131]

The selection-model disparity—the availability analysis—now makes a *prima facie* case for the challenging party. The challenger no longer has to describe the mechanism by which the state had discriminated. This is not disparate treatment, nor disparate impact. Disparate outcome is sufficient. The burden to describe its race-neutral mechanism has become the state's, to rebut, to show that it did not discriminate. The Court offered no guidance how to do this, saying only:

> We emphasize, however, that we are not saying that the statistical disparities proved here could never be explained in another case; we are simply saying that the State did not do so in this case.

Neither did they inform experts how to make this explanation nor, more important, have experts instructed the Court.

That the burden to rebut a simple availability analysis is on the state, that the challenger does not have the burden to cover his bases, is made clear from seeing how the state court had handled the availability analysis. The state court thought the challenger had to show more than a comparison between jurors and the population:

> How many of those listed in the census figures with Mexican-American names were not citizens of the state, but were so-called "wet-backs" from the south side of the Rio Grande; how many were migrant workers and not residents of Hidalgo County; how many were illiterate and could not read and write; how many were not of sound mind and good moral character; how many had been convicted of a felony or were under legal indictment or legal accusation for theft or a felony; none of these facts appear in the record. Their absence renders the disparity of the percentages of little force or effect.[132]

It may seem that the state court, as the federal court, assumed (if only implicitly) that all those called to serve appeared. On closer inspection, what the court has done is skip over how persons make their non-qualification apparent. Residents of other countries, other states, and other counties might appear and be found unqualified—or might have returned home.

---

131. *Castaneda* (1977) at 496, footnote 17; following indented quotation at 499.
132. *Castaneda* (1974a) as *Partida v. State*, at 211.

That the Supreme Court needed a new approach, not a new tool, is seen in Chief Justice Burger's dissent in *Castaneda*:

> The decisions of this Court suggest, and common sense demands, that eligible population statistics, not gross population figures, provide the relevant starting point. In *Alexander* (1972), for example, the Court in an opinion by Mr. Justice White looked to the "proportion of blacks in the *eligible* population." [133]

Correct as Burger is, the larger issue is not the burden, but the statistical model. The challenger could never meet the burden proposed by Burger, because eligible-population data did not then and do not now and never can exist to compare with jury data.[134] Rather, the jury-selection process itself is the best source of the very statistic Burger wants to see, the proportion minority among eligibles including, had he thought of it, people who remain in the community and will—do—show up when called for jury service.

OTHER METRICS AND STANDARDS

After the Supreme Court said it would accept the binomial selection model, three things occurred. First, lower courts followed that instruction. Second, academic articles, praising this advance on principle, criticized the way these courts did so. Third, other calculations and standards were developed. Many of the criticisms of the mathematics of courts' decisions were correct enough, but the fundamental flaw of the comparison went unnoticed.

Paul Sigal proposed a neat way to make a calculation that Michael Finkelstein had found difficult, but endorsed Finkelstein's approach.[135] Mary Gray described statistical analysis of jury-representation cases as "simply an application of a binomial model,"[136] a view that lingers almost universally among statistical experts today. John de Cani, who would have testified in *Swain* had the district court not excluded his data as hearsay, approached the problem the same way as Finkelstein, but advocated a one-tail test.[137]

Other experts thought the paradigm was correct—the outcome measure, the compar-

---

133. *Castaneda* (1977) at 504, emphasis added. Burger was joined by Powell and Rehnquist. That population was a poor proxy for eligibility had been articulated even earlier than Burger notes. Consider Judge MacKenzie's dissent in *Witcher* (1969) at 731:

> The proper inquiry to raise a *prima facie* case, in my judgment, is to reflect the number of Negroes chosen for jury service against the number of Negroes qualified and eligible for jury service and not the total number of Negro inhabitants of the County.

134. The First Circuit had figured out how hard it would be to predetermine eligibles long before Burger opined that one should. See *Bryant* (as *Butera*) (1970) at 570, footnote 13.

135. Sigal (1969), see footnote 17.

136. M. Gray (1983) at 76.

137. De Cani (1974) at 237. De Cani is too kind to the judge.

ison of jury wheel to census—but proposed modifications to the calculation. Consider the point made by Thomas Sugrue and Will Fairley.[138] Their primary complaint is that when the population is small, successive draws of the majority population increase the probability that the next random draw will be of a minority. By holding the probability constant, as the binomial calculation does, few minority selections are not seen to be as improbable as they are. They present one case in which this error seems to have been made, to the detriment of complainants, and propose a "difference between proportions" statistical test.[139] They are in one sense correct: If we accept as a pool those eligible for parole, the minorities do appear to have been under-paroled in a way that the reviewing courts did not understand. On the other hand, as I demonstrated in Chapter 2, Sugrue and Fairley do not need their new test to show that the courts were mistaken: The *Castaneda* binomial approximation based on two groups (blacks and whites on one hand, Mexican and Native Americans on the other) would suffice.[140] The problem, rather, is that we do not know if all persons "eligible for parole" should be considered equally likely to get it. We do not know the "community" from which to expect representative selections.[141] Sugrue and Fairley do not consider this issue.

David Kaye suggests relative chance, odds ratios, and Mantel-Haenszel aggregation of multi-year data. Although he is not against adjusting census data, or substituting voter data, he thinks that

> general population data may give a perfectly adequate indication of a substantial degree of discrimination.[142]

He reports that correcting the census data used in *Castaneda* for literacy, approximated by a seventh-grade education, still left under-representation of Hispanics "blatantly large." However, he does not know if those Hispanics were citizens, how many participated on source lists, or if those that had were still present at the time of Partida's trial.

Courts have not waited for experts to tell them how to measure disparities between jurors and populations. Nor has some independent expert panel ever taken on this task.

---

138. See Sugrue and Fairley (1983).

139. Sugrue and Fairley (1983) refer to *Greenholtz* (1976). This case illustrates another problem, which they discuss, of appropriate calculations when there are multiple minority groups.

140. The *Castaneda*-type calculation yields 2.58 standard deviations between expected and actual minority paroles, with a probability of 0.01. I think it is easy to justify this test from a chi-square test on a 4 x 2 table. The attorney should present some anecdotal evidence justifying the combining of whites and blacks as "majority," even if it is not strictly necessary for the statistics.

141. Justice Marshall once noted that blacks are "executed far more often than whites in proportion to their percentage of the population." That information may form a reasonable basis for questions, but not, as it was to Marshall, an answer. See *Furman* (1972) at 364.

142. Kaye (1986) at 22; following in-text phrase at 23.

Just as well, as it would only have reinforced the false paradigm that "discrimination" in juror selection can be measured from population or voter-registration data. One would have thought, though, that someone would systematically deal with the issues of what should be measured, and how. Perhaps Kaye thought he did that, but I do not think so. Kairys, Kadane, and Lehoczky reviewed the mathematical formulas described below, and even chose one.[143] Fortunately, their suggestion has not been heeded. Their substitution of the word "population" for "community" evades the issue of what should be measured.

Peter Detre provided a review almost in passing.[144] He presented common measures based on venires, reinforcing the tradition that attorneys, when they write about statistics, make legal errors. Pre-qualified no-shows and persons excused should be counted as jurors in all outcome calculations. Not to count them is to attribute their failure to serve to the jury-selection system that summoned them.

Detre's summary was merely a platform. After criticizing other measures, he added yet another to the literature. He would calculate the expected number of juries with one or more minorities, two or more, etc., and contrast that with the actual number of juries that had one or more, two or more, etc. minorities. Detre is testing something else, not under-representation, but the distribution of the few minorities among juries. There is nothing new in this measure: Finkelstein proposed a formal test of the frequency with which minorities accumulated on juries, as did Paul Sigal.[145] Kaye discusses it under the heading, "Statistical Analysis of Peculiarities."[146] As I have never seen Detre's measure accepted by a court, and I think it is both clumsy and silly (unless a distribution complaint is made), I will not further discuss it.

It was apparently courts themselves that came up with these other measures of the disparity from the population in jury-representation cases. All disparity measures assume there are two groups. All disparity calculations compare two proportions: minorities from a standard (most often the latest census) and minorities in the pool that is used to represent jurors. Most measures require some other number, a count. I will define these counts as I get to them.

My symbols are as follows:

C = proportion of the subscript class in the census or other source of population data.

Q = proportion of the subscript class in jury data, preferably the qualified wheel.

---

143. See Kairys et al. (1977).

144. See Detre (1994). A review of measures also appears in *Villafane* (1980).

145. See Finkelstein (1966) and Sigal (1969).

146. This appears in Kaye (1986). See also Sperlich and Jaspovice (1979).

Absolute Disparity

The "absolute disparity" is the difference between the percentage minority in the population and the percentage in the data. It is calculated:[147]

$$\text{absolute disparity} = 100 \times (C - Q)$$

The "100" converts proportions to percentages. Following the exposition above, C is the proportion black in the population as reported by the census, and Q is the proportion black as surveyed or otherwise estimated in the jury. Obviously, when C is small, the absolute disparity can never become large.

Absolute Impact

The "absolute impact" is the difference in number of minorities on an average panel—here, a jury of twelve—drawn from the population or from the data. It is a number multiplied by people, and therefore is expressed in units of people. It is calculated:[148]

$$\text{absolute impact} = 12 \times (C - Q)$$

Except for scale, this measure is the same as the first. It appears to be the difference in numbers of people appearing on a representative jury, and if that formulation appeals to a judge, who am I to tell him it is meaningless? It would be easier if absolute impact referred to a general formula:

$$\text{absolute impact} = J \times (C - Q)$$

where "J" would refer to some measure of the jury size. However, as we will see, this same essential formula carries other names as J is defined differently.

Relative Disparity

The "relative disparity" (or "comparative disparity") expresses the percentage-point difference of the absolute disparity as a percentage of the census percent minority. It is, again, a percentage measure:[149]

$$\text{relative disparity} = 100 \times \frac{C - Q}{C} = \frac{\text{absolute disparity}}{C}$$

---

147. See *Swain* (1965); or *Hubbard* (1996) at 501:
> The absolute disparity test measures representatives by the difference between the percentage of a certain population group eligible for jury duty and the percentage of that group who actually appear in the venire.

148. See *Yazee* (1981).

149. See *Clifford* (1981). Or *Ramseur* (1992) at 1231: "Comparative disparity is calculated by dividing the absolute disparity by the population figure for a population group."

Absolute Numbers

"Absolute numbers" is the difference in number of minorities on a venire, rather than a jury. It is the same calculation as that made for the absolute impact, except that as the venire (the size of which I denote by the symbol "V") is larger than the jury, all differences must be larger in this measure. One reason to present this formula here is that a colleague of Detre's at Yale, Ian Ayres, presented it in a case on which I was the other side's expert.[150]

$$\text{absolute numbers} = V \times (C - Q)$$

"Statistical"

The "statistical" measure is called "statistical decision theory" by Detre, after Finkelstein.[151] Simply calculating the normal approximation to the binomial distribution, and using a 0.05 probability cutoff, is hardly what "statistical decision theory" is about.[152]

The "statistical" measure is presented as the probability of randomly drawing a difference of this magnitude or greater between Hispanics on the qualified wheel and the census standard, under the assumption that the census measures the pool from which the qualified wheel is drawn. We need another symbol, "L," to represent the qualified wheel, a number far larger than a jury or a venire:

$$\text{statistical measure of disparity} = \frac{L \times (C - Q)}{\sqrt{L \times C \times (1 - C)}}$$

The numerator is a count of the difference between the number of Hispanics in the data and the number we would have expected ("expectation" implies on average) from a random draw from the census. The denominator is the binomial standard deviation of the expected value of Q over many such draws. The standard deviation is calculated from the population parameter (C) and the size of the sample. The result of this formula is the number of standard-deviation units by which the number of minorities in the data differs from its "expected" average value. It is the Z-score from Chapter 2.

Other measures are in units of percentages or people. Faced with this measure, in units of standard deviation or converted to probabilities, courts have asked for help in interpretation. I discuss their dilemma, and the answers they have received, in Chapter 7.

---

150. *United States v. Danna*, D. Conn. No. 3:94-CR-00158, Ayres' testimony of October 10, 1995.

151. Chapter 2, "Jury Discrimination," in Finkelstein (1978).

152. In one of the applications of statistical decision theory, in factory production, a rule is formulated based on this statistic. Products are sampled and tested. When the sample falls more than two standard deviations outside the specification, the batch is rejected and the production line is halted until the "problem" is "fixed." It is in this context, making a decision based on a sample statistic, that the phrase "statistical decision theory" was coined. I think courts will not find this context analogous to their own.

Non-Probabilistic Standards

Not all writers have jumped on the statistical bandwagon. Paul Meier, Jerome Sacks, and Sandy Zabell suggested that statistical-significance testing alone was inappropriate in law, because relatively small differences would be "significant" with a large enough sample size. They accepted the comparison of the "qualified wheel" to the population, just not the measure of disparity. They supported the Equal Employment Opportunity Commission's administrative standard: Statistically "significant" differences plus the minority must be selected at a rate less than 80 percent that of the majority.[153]

Kairys, Kadane, and Lehoczky advocated use of the comparative-disparity standard, and acceptance of a *prima facie* case when that metric exceeds 15 percent. They were determined to achieve population representation regardless of the characteristics of the populations including, apparently, citizenship. So if half the Hispanics in the region are not citizens, they would have the other half do double duty. I think the non-citizen half are not in the community, and imposing a responsibility on citizen Hispanics because others who share this same ethnic characteristic live close by is a violation of due process and common sense. The concept that some people should be selected by their ethnic status to compensate for the behavior of others of that status violates the individualistic precepts of *Theil* (1946), *Cassell* (1950), *Manhart* (1978), and *Teal* (1982).

Roger Kuhn, though supporting a statistical approach, also advocated "compensatory" selections of minorities to achieve a parity that would occur improbably from random draws:

> If random selection in combination with tests of juror quality, hardship excuses, or other factors in the system produce unrepresentative juries, the end of fairness is not achieved and the appearance of fairness vanishes.[154]

The "end" to Kuhn is juries representative of the population. If random selection does not get the system there, then use deliberate selection.

Kuhn was not alone, nor even the first to prefer an outcome standard to a procedural standard. Hugh Gibson had argued along the same lines many years earlier:

> This end [rooting out prejudice] cannot be accomplished by the court's requirement of a process of selection of jurors which will make any ascertainable racial representation completely dependent on chance.[155]

S. W. Tucker tells us that, in response to *Norris* (1935), a judge of Virginia's Third Judicial Circuit directed the jury commissioners to add names of blacks to the essentially white

---

153. See Meier et al. (1984). The EEOC's standard is commonly referred to as "the four-fifths rule."

154. R. Kuhn (1968) at 316.

155. Gibson (1950) at 38. The Fifth Circuit, in *Labat* (1966), also called for compensatory over-selection of blacks.

(because the commissioners had to swear that persons on the list were honorable) 1935–36 jury lists. The goal was to achieve, on the source list, the same proportion as blacks "qualified, and not exempt from" jury service. Names of blacks were placed on lists, but apparently on the bottom.[156] No black was called for jury duty until 1940.

Outcome-Oriented Solutions

Not content to develop an objective, impartial jury-selection system, Virginia ultimately went too far the other way. In a 1965 Virginia trial, a jury commissioner says, "You have to consider the element of race in order not to be discriminatory." The commissioner's oath was still on the books. More distressing than the commissioner's view (which probably only reflected what he thought he had to do to avoid the wrath of the federal courts) is Tucker's agreement:

> It is only by the adoption of the second suggestion of this jury commissioner— that the element of race be consciously considered in the selection process— that the discriminatory effect of Virginia's [intelligence and honesty] requirement can be counteracted.[157]

As noted above, Kairys et al. argued that the basis of litigation should be the failure of the jury pool to represent the population. Complainant should not need to describe an act of discrimination. Jury commissioners should mold the pool to force representation, they say, regardless of the composition of the source list or any other measure of "the community."

Let us picture the meeting of commissioners, at which they face the task of balancing the jury wheel (or the juries themselves—see below). "Here, we need seventeen blacks," says one commissioner. "But, oh, these are males over age forty. That will throw the gender and age categories out of balance," says another. A third notes: "These six are black Hispanics. Must be careful not to over-include Hispanics. After all, representativeness is at issue." A similar scene was envisioned by Judge Hall, where the challenge was to the occupational distribution of jurors:

---

156. Tucker (1966) at 740. As the Fourth Circuit described it in *Witcher* (1967) at 709:

> The Commissioners chose names from each of the county's seven magisterial districts, invariably designating the few Negroes selected as "(Col.)." In one district, no Negro names were picked and in four of the districts, the names of Negroes were placed at the end of each list, clearly identified as such.

157. Tucker (1966) at 749. The case is *Witcher* (1966). Tucker's quotation of the jury commissioner, from the trial transcript, is also on his page 749. This overt manipulation is not described in the three published decisions, but its result is, as quoted in footnote 155, above. The Fourth Circuit twice reversed the lower court's dismissal of the writ for *habeas corpus*, eventually vacating Witcher's jury conviction because of discrimination in juror selection.

And if all occupations were represented, which in the practicalities of life is actually impossible, unless the number of jurors is going to be increased far beyond 12 and actually to mob size, would not then someone make a classification of the religions of those selected, or their social connections, or their sex, or their race, or their geographical location, and come up with a statistical abstract which showed disproportionate distributions or exclusions of any of the multitude of religions represented in this community, or a disproportionate distribution or exclusion of any group which might be classified by any other common characteristic?[158]

One can appreciate Justice Douglas' frustration, given the discriminatory systems that came before him time and time again. Yet his proposed cure is as bad as the disease. Dissenting in *Carter* (1970) he suggested deliberately race-selecting the commissioners:

I cannot see any solution to the present problem, unless the jury commission is by law required to be biracial. In the Kingdom of Heaven, an all-white or an all-black commission could be expected to do equal justice to all races in the selection of people "generally reputed to be honest and intelligent" and "esteemed in the community for their integrity, good character, and sound judgment." But, where there exists a pattern of discrimination, an all-white or all-black jury commission in these times probably means that the race in power retains authority to control the community's official life, and that no jury will likely be selected that is a true cross-section of the community.[159]

Douglas was operating within the constraints of the discrimination model, as the Court had defined the issue. He articulated that model in a most unfortunate way:

The law only requires that the panel not be purposely unrepresentative.[160]

Even though stated in dissent, this sentence has been the underpinning of many a suggestion that deliberate representation was the solution to "under-representation." The qualified wheel could not be purposely *un*representative, but could it be purposely representative? That is where Douglas took it:

---

158. *Local 36* (1947) at 796. There is nothing fanciful in imagining that "activists" reach deeper and deeper to find outcome inequality. Although most people would consider them "fringe" thinkers, Lani Guinier and Henry Louis Gates, Jr,. have been given a platform by Harvard University. Now that Harvard admits many people with dark skin, Guinier and Gates worry that their ancestry is not representative. See Sara Rimer and Karen W. Arenson, "Top Colleges Take More Blacks, but Which Ones," *New York Times*, June 24, 2004. David E. Bernstein has articulated the fear that excessive outcome-accounting violates civil liberties in *You Can't Say That!: The Growing Threat to Civil Liberties from Antidiscrimination Laws*, Cato Institute, 2003.

159. *Carter* (1970) at 342. Citations from Alabama Code, Title 30, §21 (Supp. 1967).

160. *Carter* (1970) at 343; following indented quotation at 345. As above, Douglas is not proposing that juries be proportional, but that commissions be.

> Where the challenged state agency, dealing with the rights and liberties of the citizen, has a record of racial discrimination, the corrective remedy is proportional representation. Under our Constitution that would indeed seem to be the only effective control over the type of racial discrimination long practiced in this case.

I disagree. Deliberate racial selection of jurors or jury commissions is no more a solution to juror discrimination than quota systems are to employment discrimination. The remedy for unfairness is fairness.[161] The remedy for juries that have been rigged to be white, or upper class, is to un-rig them; to let them be selected randomly, not deliberately.

Against Random Selection

In _Brooks_ (1966) the Fifth Circuit, recognizing that it was abandoning the neutral stance (race cannot be used in juror selection) it had enunciated in _Collins_ (1964), approved purposeful inclusion of blacks on juries. As long as outcomes are at issue, students at the _Yale Law Journal_ were free to call for prescribed all-black juries, gained by gerrymandering jurisdictions and making deliberate selections. They proposed to

> establish a formula that makes the number of black jurors dependent on both the degree to which race is central to the decision and the number of jurors necessary to bring about an equitable result.[162]

It's not that procedural standards had not been discussed. Thirty years prior to Justice Douglas' unfortunate one-sided statement, the Court had stated the procedural issue correctly:

> An accused is entitled to have charges against him considered by a jury in the selection of which there has been neither inclusion nor exclusion because of race.[163]

The Fifth Circuit expressed some malaise at the prevailing outcome approach:

> At the most, the notion of a jury as a cross-section of the community is a conceptual one. A literal cross-section is neither required nor desired.[164]

Twenty-five years after Douglas, a district court concluded that

---

161. The remedy for the _results_ of prior discrimination may require more than fairness, if the position at issue is long lasting. See, for example, _Croson_ (1989) and the discussion on employment, below. Juries are different. With fair procedures, the results will be just what we want.

162. Note (1970) at 549.

163. _Cassell_ (1950) at 287.

164. _Chance_ (1963) at 204. This was a clearly faulty decision, one of many upholding an "opt-in" system for females. I quote it because of its good wording, not for any value as precedent.

the Sixth Amendment requires only a cross-section that is fair and not one perfectly attuned to multiple variables.[165]

Others, however, argued against random selection of jurors. Judge Learned Hand asserted

> that jurors . . . are to be deliberately chosen on the basis of qualities which are assumed not to be in the possession of all citizens.

He found unobjectionable the New York law that called for selection of jurors by quality.[166] Judge Wisdom, writing for a Fifth Circuit panel, expressed a similar opinion.[167]

Here, describing another concept of non-random selection, in effect in Dallas County, Texas, is Justice Kennedy writing for the Supreme Court:

> A 1963 circular by the District Attorney's Office instructed its prosecutors to exercise peremptory strikes against minorities: "Do not take Jews, Negroes, Dagos, Mexicans, or a member of any minority race on a jury, no matter how rich or how well educated." A manual entitled "Jury Selection in a Criminal Case" was distributed to prosecutors. It contained an article authored by a former prosecutor (and later a judge) under the direction of his superiors in the District Attorney's Office, outlining the reasoning for excluding minorities from jury service. Although the manual was written in 1968, it remained in circulation until 1976, if not later.[168]

So there are "good guys" arguing against random selection, and there are "bad guys" arguing against random selection. Either we have to judge who the "good guys" and "bad guys" are, which is what I decried about the character judgments made by the early jury commissioners, or we abandon that approach and adopt random selection as the rule.

DUREN (1979): THE BURDEN SHIFTS

Where *Taylor* (1975) disallowed a jury system to which females had to opt in, *Duren* (1979) considered, and disallowed, an opt-out system. The availability analysis was standard: 54 percent of the adult population—but only 14.5 percent of venire members—were female. What is important about *Duren* is the articulation of a challenger's three-prong burden:

---

165. *Greer* (1995) at 958.

166. *Dennis* (1950) at 220. Hand was leaning over backwards to accept the New York rules, which by federal law determined who could be federal jurors. In this McCarthy-era case, defendants had been convicted of being Marxists, and Hand was not about to let that decision be reversed.

167. *Labat* (1966).

168. *Miller-El* (2003) at 334. Internal reference omitted and punctuation slightly changed on that account.

In order to establish a *prima facie* violation of the fair-cross-section requirement, the defendant must show (1) that the group alleged to be excluded is a
"distinctive" group in the community; (2) that the representation of this group
in venires from which juries are selected is not fair and reasonable in relation
to the number of such persons in the community; and (3) that this under-
representation is due to systematic exclusion of the group in the jury-selection
process.[169]

As we have seen, the Court had been making the association called for in the third
prong, between the "under-representation" and the procedural flaw, on its own. And it had
placed the burden on the state to rebut that presumed association. In *Duren* the Court put
the burden of making this association on the challenger of the system. Surely this is where
that burden always should have been.

With the phrase "systematic exclusion," and the requirement that the measure of disparity be associated with its cause, the Court is almost asking for the analysis I propose.
If the lists are acceptable and the procedures are neutral (even random), then the safest
assumption is that differences between census and jury compositions are due to the leakages shown as blue ellipses in Figure 54, that is, to individual behavior. By counting at each
event, one can state just where the serious leakages occur, and then ask if it was the "fault"
of the jury-selection system. The challenger should find the system doing something
wrong, or lose. Yet, if *Duren* so clearly asked for a procedural analysis, why have experts
failed to produce it?

Perhaps the *Duren* prongs are not that clear. What is "the community"? What is "systematic" exclusion? Is it disparate impact? Mailing notices proportionately around a jurisdiction has a disparate impact on mobile populations, which are usually new immigrant
groups. Once it was Europeans, then blacks, then Asians; today it is Hispanics and Haitians;
tomorrow it may be Middle-Easterners or sub-Saharan Africans. Is the fact that some
group will "systematically" fail to respond a failing of first-class mail? The Supreme Court
must say no, differential impact of reasonable and neutral procedures, on different populations, based on their own behavior, should not be the concern of jury administrators.[170]

Interestingly, the Supreme Court *has* clarified what it means by "community," although

---

169. *Duren* (1979) at 364. What happened to the qualified wheel? If we read these prongs literally, then
granting excuses fairly can condemn a system based on rational and fair behavior of judges, as allowing
minorities to be excused surely can be interpreted by some court as "systematic exclusion." I know of no
court that has yet been this literal, but the Supreme Court's language is sloppy.

170. The Federal Judicial Center reviewed first class mail vs. certified mail. Response to delivered certified mail was better, but fewer were delivered. The net returns were the same. They suggested that first
class mail, being less expensive in postage and clerical effort, was superior. See Shapard (1981). After I
explained the disparate impact on renters in *Tremblay* (1993), defendant argued that such an impact was
unconstitutional, the state should lose on that account. The judge did not see it that way.

no legal researcher has noticed it. Justice White, who wrote many of the major decisions in this area, took pains to discuss the population "presumptively eligible" in *Alexander* (1972). In *Taylor* (1975), he wanted representation from "the local population otherwise eligible for jury service." In *Duren* (1979), it is "the population eligible for jury service."[171] However, Justice White, like Chief Justice Burger before him, dissenting in *Castaneda* (1977), does not know how to identify (and therefore count) the eligible population.

Ultimately the three *Duren* prongs fail because they still allow the challenger to create trouble from an outcome disparity. That failure is illustrated by what I think is a farcical debate in an obscure case, *Osorio* (1992). The federal jury-selection system in Connecticut was marred by computer errors. In certain cities in the Hartford jurisdiction (including Hartford and Bridgeport) all names were shifted one column to the right, leaving the first column in the name field blank. In the computer program that read the names, a blank in column one was read as "dead." All residents of Hartford, Bridgeport, and twenty-five other cities were considered deceased. None was sent a notice for jury service. If the standard for jury selection were that each participating resident had an equal chance of being contacted, or each participating and eligible resident had an equal chance of being asked to serve, there would be nothing more to say. A system that excludes twenty-seven towns cannot be used to formulate juries.

Because of the second prong of *Duren*, which followed from *Castaneda*, challengers had to show that there was a distinct class of people that had been disproportionately excluded by this computer error. Despite the 1968 requirement for geographical representation on federal juries, being a resident in these towns apparently was not such a class. Because twenty-five almost exclusively Anglo towns had been excluded, along with two minority-rich central cities, the proportion black and Hispanic on jury wheels was essentially what it would have been had all towns been included. Two wrongs, the United States Attorney argued, made it right.

Neither the *Osorio* trial nor any others from that wheel, following this discovery, could be held in the Hartford Division because whether justified under *Duren* or not, the district court would not accept it. I think that decision was correct. But litigation went on for years on *habeas corpus* petitions filed by those who had been convicted before the *Osorio* hearing, from the same jury wheel.[172] Experts were brought in by the challengers to show that when you exclude Hartford and Bridgeport you exclude minorities. The United States Attorney's expert—usually me—then showed that the other twenty-five town exclusions balanced the racial expectations and actualities of the juries.

---

171. These expressions are found in *Alexander* (1972) at 627, in *Taylor* (1975) at 537, and in *Duren* (1979) at 364.

172. See, for example, *Jackman* (1995).

Would the Connecticut system have been acceptable if Hartford and Bridgeport had not been excluded, if only twenty-five small white towns had been? Under the discrimination model, perhaps so. Yet it is silly to try to answer this question. The issue is not that no residents appear from some towns. That is an outcome. Procedurally, Connecticut failed to give everyone in the judicial district a chance to be a juror. The system could not pretend to uniform-random selection. In my view, that's it. End of story. The process is flawed. The system that through clerical error eliminates whole towns fails the constitutional test. Neither bad intent nor a "bad" outcome should be required.

A more recent example may lead one to the same conclusion. The story in the *Miami Herald* began:

> An accused Opa-locka drug dealer has won a new trial with an only-in-Miami argument: The jury pool contained too many people whose last names start with the letter "G." Of 38 potential jurors in the pool, 21 had surnames starting with "G" and 14 of those were of Hispanic origin: six Garcias, two Gomezes, two Gonzalezes, two Guerras, a Gutierrez, and a Goldares.[173]

The suspect, a black man, had been acquitted of most charges by an all-black jury, so this mostly Hispanic jury looked threatening on the remaining charge. "There is no way Mr. Carter can get a fair cross-section of the community. That's especially true in this case where the overwhelmingly majority of G surnames are Hispanic," the *Herald* reports defendant's attorney as saying. It's all about outcome.

How did so many people whose names start with "G" get into the jury pool? Venires are to be drawn randomly from an active qualified wheel of approximately four hundred names, which is renewed every two weeks. Any spreadsheet program would randomize four hundred names in an instant. A small fee to a local statistician would have created a defendable procedure. But some clerk decided to randomly draw a letter of the alphabet, use all members of the wheel with that letter, and continue drawing letters until there would be around forty persons who constitute the venire. That procedure is not defendable. It took an outcome to bring to the court's attention that the draws were not random, but it is the procedure that is bad. The jurors should have been drawn randomly.

The third prong of *Duren* should be framed not in terms of explaining a disparity, but in terms of finding a procedural error, a non-neutrality in the jury-selection system, a way in which the system, not the behavior of potential jurors, is rendering the qualified wheel unrepresentative. Then drop the first two prongs. The procedural test should be the *only* test of whether there is a flaw. Measurement can be used to determine whether the

---

173. Larry Lebowitz, "'G' names in jury pool win suspect a new trial," *Miami Herald* (online), posted June 7, 2002.

error, in its current form, is "harmless"; but a procedural error should nonetheless be noted and corrected, if only in the future. I will return to this concept in a section on harmless error, below.

Employment: A Parallel Path

The confusion between the individual and the group, the uncertain requirement for a showing of procedure creating some "disparity," and just about every issue that has come to the Supreme Court in jury formation, has arisen in equal-employment opportunity, also. It is not so much the juror, but the defendant, who is harmed if his jury is improperly constituted.

Remediation would be a just concept if it went from the harmer to the harmed. That has never been the solution to a jury-discrimination case, and often is not to employment discrimination. Employers are often forced to open their doors wide. That was what happened in *Teamsters* (1977) and several other famous cases: Hire blacks excessively until some "parity" is achieved, after which hire fairly. We do not need precision. We need a sense of justice. But in more-complex cases, such as *Croson* (1989), neither was the employer the malefactor (the discriminator) nor were the workers who now will benefit those who had been harmed. *Croson*, which allowed minority set-asides when there had been prior discrimination by the local government, was therefore tentative, calling for "strict scrutiny" and a clear sunset, an ending of the favoritism.

The Court seemed to waver in *Metro* (1990), relaxing the standard required for such remediation, where neither had the employer been the harmer nor his employees, old or new, the harmed. In *Adarand* (1990), in the same year, the Court quickly recovered its senses, in essence apologizing for being so casual about racial favoritism. In *Grutter* (2003) the Court backslid, once again allowing "compensation" by a non-discriminating university to students selected by race, not by prior victimhood, and not compensating for prior discriminatory admissions.

In these matters, it seems clear that few members of the Supreme Court have guiding principles; and fewer have guiding principles deserving respect. I recommend that the jury cases, because they are easier in that remediation is never at issue, would be a good place to start trying to find some principled legs to stand on.[174] I suggest that the principle be that fair procedure, not some predetermined numeric outcome, should carry the day.

---

174. Reversing a conviction might be considered "remediation" for an improper jury, but it is not. Defendant only gets another trial. Except in those cases where there was rampant prejudice from the beginning, where jury formation is simply the handle the federal government used to intervene, most defendants are re-tried and re-convicted.

"Expert" Analyses

Expert presentations are almost all identical. Analysts usually use the measure of "disparity" that their client perceives to be the "prevailing standard" in the jurisdiction. Today all analysts also calculate the statistical measure, and recommend it to the court as the best measure available. It seems so . . . scientific.

The only difficult question, as most analysts see it, is how to measure the percent minority in the jury system. That is usually done by "geocoding," whether formally or informally, although Hispanics can also be identified by their last names.[175] Just as the Supreme Court defined "enumeration" as counting each person, one by one (not by sampling), judges are reluctant to believe that anyone can know the ethnicity of prospective jurors without their responding to a questionnaire. Here is the amateur skepticism of one judge:

> The surname approach has [the] result of failing to account for "Hispanics" who either through marriage or adoption obtain an English surname. Similarly, surname classifications fail to consider "Hispanics" whose surnames are not commonly considered Spanish, whose surnames are a result of varied European ancestry, whose surnames have been Anglicized, or whose surnames are derived from other than Castillian Spain. . . . Non-Spanish surnames (e.g., Banchs, Dols, Galtieri, Cristiani, Domecq) are frequently found among Latin Americans but are not found in the Spanish-surname lists.[176]

Experts who have studied the inference of "Hispanic" from surname, or from residence, have found that the race and ethnic identification of groups of people (such as prospective jurors) is very good, as good as is required for the jury-representation question. But judges do not ask experts, or they do not believe them. The Massachusetts Supreme Court, for example, has instructed its jury selectors to devise a *required* questionnaire to ascertain race and ethnicity.[177] What will the court do to the recalcitrant recruit? Not allow him to serve on a jury if he does not answer the question? Hold him in contempt of court?

---

175. Residentially, we are a largely segregated society. Nine out of ten persons on the jury list from a 90 percent white neighborhood can be assumed to be white, and a similar assumption can be made about persons from black, Hispanic, etc. neighborhoods. These percentages can be derived from the census, and are reasonably stable within a ten-year period. From his address, each individual in the qualified wheel can be assigned a fractional indicator of race or ethnicity. Every single fractional identification will contain error. Nonetheless, the pool of potential jurors can be well described by calculating the averages of these characteristics. That is the essence of "geocoding."

176. *Alen* (1992) at 1093. Also quoted in *Arriaga* (1992) at 564 (1263).

177. *Arriaga* (2003) at 572 (1268).

As all systems send mail to prospective jurors, we can start with their addresses. Where other data have been available, geocoding has been found to well describe the ethnic composition of the source lists. And where the question has been asked, the source list overall does not "look like" the population. The reconciliation between these two statements is this: Within mini-communities—Zip codes or census tracts or towns in a jurisdiction—individuals on source lists are representative. People look like their neighbors. But the proportion of the population on source lists varies among these mini-communities. Thus the source list as a whole does not represent the population, even though each mini-community sends representatives to the jury.

In their analyses, experts continue to use the population as a basis of their expectations. They do not correct for source-list disparities, even if the source list is clearly constitutional and is not being challenged. Expecting jurors to reflect either population or source-list demography ties up state resources defending that which needs no defense, and not investigating procedures, which may. By insisting on enumerated ethnicity data, courts stick to their outcome orientation and expend resources solving the wrong problem.

A good example appears in *Reyes* (1996), featuring two traditional experts, Andrew Beveridge for the defendant, Bernard Siskin for the government. Judge Scheindlin thought himself instructed by *Biaggi* (1990) to use the absolute-disparity test. The judge explains:

> Whether the unreturned questionnaires are included or excluded affects the degree of disparity that the defendant can demonstrate.[178]

Because ultimately the issue is one of arithmetic, as Judge Scheindlin sees it, he follows this false logic:

> [P]eople who choose not to serve—whether because they simply do not want to serve or because they think they are unqualified—are still part of the potential jury pool. They could be considered for service if they returned the questionnaire.

This is fantasy land. The judge now must determine how many of the undelivered or unreturned questionnaires represent people who have died or left the jurisdiction—as opposed to those who are uncooperative—with a guess at how many of them would have been found unqualified. None of this matters if the "community" of those from whom jurors are to be selected is defined as eligible *and cooperating* participants. From that definition, however, there would be no work for experts, or at least not Siskin and Beveridge. If the system is facially neutral (and free of subjective judgments), and performed essentially without error by clerical personnel, then its results should not be second-guessed by outcome measures. Experts who like to derive measures from data, for the court to make

---

178. *Reyes* (1996) at 561; following indented quotation at 562.

judgments therefrom, will not support my approach to jury-system evaluation. At least, none ever has.

COLLATERAL DISPUTES

There are, in summary, *three* standards by which jury composition can be evaluated.

> **Discrimination.** There must be an outcome which is by some measure substantially different from the outcome that "fair" selection by some measure would produce. If so, then under this standard someone did something wrong. The remedy must be to change some procedure to end discrimination.

> **Representation.** Again, by some measure, jurors do not "look like" what we expect from "fair" selection. Regardless of cause, the outcome may be unacceptable. The remedy includes direct appointment of jurors to achieve representation.

> **Random selection.** This effectuates the survey model. Outcome is not at issue. Source lists have to be valid, that is, acceptably reflective of those who can participate and want to do so. Draws from the source list must be uniform-random. If procedures are fair, juries are fair.

In *Turner* (1970), discretion was directly tested, à la Michael Finkelstein. Ninety-six percent of "those rejected as unintelligent or not upright were Negroes."[179] If the Court is not going to ban systems for their subjectivity, then it should, as in *Turner*, test the exercise of subjective determination directly. However, once again we are in a land of no standards. *Turner* was a case of blatant discrimination. Standards become important when the discriminatory behavior is not so stark, or nonexistent, despite what appear to be outcome anomalies.

Preliminary Hearings

An efficient approach would be to hold a preliminary hearing to take offers of proof, and defer bringing completed studies and practiced testimony to an OK Corral showdown. The judge could quickly determine if the challenger has identified a potentially unacceptable procedure. As it stands now, the challenger need only show an "unacceptable" *result*, a disparity between jurors and the population (in percent minority, say), and the dispute goes on to trial. With procedural standards, most challenges would disappear at an early stage, if they were brought at all.

---

179. Justice Stewart for a unanimous Court, *Turner* (1970) at 358.

Procedural Standards

Defenders of the Court could say that my critique is more economic (decrying the needless expenditure of resources) than legal, and in any case is not fundamental. As I have just outlined it, the Court's procedures allow my reasoning to prevail at trial. The third prong of *Duren* requires more than a statistical disparity. It requires a relationship between that disparity and some exclusionary procedure. What's the problem?

The Court still allows subjective systems, where some people judge the qualifications of others for jury service. If such systems *might* produce acceptable outcomes, courts have to judge them. They do so by the discrimination standard, which (as *Osorio* illustrates) may not support a challenge even if the system has unarguably faulty procedures. There is a *voir dire* of prospective jury members, there are for-cause dismissals by the judge, and there are peremptory "challenges" by the parties. There is adequate protection in the system against a feebleminded voter (for example) making it to the jury. Yet, bypassing the qualified wheel, ignoring no-shows, *Duren* compares population to venires. That's not just wrong, it's stupid.

The Court is engaged in discerning which categories (race, gender, what next?) require special notice, and the standards by which it will assess "deficits" of different categories of people.[180] Procedural standards would get the Court out of this dilemma.

Does Guilt Matter?

Some writers have urged another criterion for federal-court review of convictions from questionable state-jury systems. Judge Friendly of the Second Circuit wrote:

> My theme is that, with a few important exceptions, convictions should be subject to collateral attack only when the prisoner supplements his constitutional plea with a colorable claim of innocence.[181]

Judge Friendly was concerned that appeals courts overturn sentences of clearly guilty defendants, and use considerable judicial resources to do so. He was not alone. Paul Bator had earlier asked, "When should state determinations, subject to direct Supreme Court review, not be final?" He stated, much in line with the thinking in this chapter, that only procedural error should be grounds for reversal. Yet his article is internally contradictory, due to Bator's frustration at and dislike of pleas for federal reversal of state convictions of

---

180. See, for example, *JEB* (1994) on peremptory strikes. As Leipold (1998) puts it at 991:

> It is difficult to explain why gender-based strikes—which receive only intermediary scrutiny—are barred by the Equal Protection Clause, but viewpoint discrimination—subject to strict scrutiny—is not.

181. This is from a law-review article, not a judicial opinion. See Friendly (1970) at 142.

clearly guilty defendants. As referenced above, one circuit panel was so disapproving of the crime of the defendants—being Marxists—that any jury that convicted them, arrived at by any means, would have been approved.[182]

In *Barksdale* (1981) Judge Ainsworth, who had written the original panel decision in 1980, now in dissent *en banc*, wonders whether defendant Blackburn's clear, admitted, unrefuted guilt should play a role in deciding on the merit of a technical dispute. Judge Gewin, a conservative Fifth Circuit judge active in the jury-composition debate, clearly thought guilt mattered:

> This case, involving one of the most heinous crimes ever committed in the rich and varied history of New Orleans, Louisiana, has been lost in the "nice, sharp quillets of the law."[183]

Gewin's impatience with everlasting collateral litigation shows even more clearly in another dissent in the same year:

> In this matter of jury composition, I would hope that in some way we can get back to the true pole star, which is that when any party litigant has been heard by a fair, impartial, intelligent jury, he should have no further room to complain.[184]

---

182. See Bator (1963), quotation at 456. But here is his conclusion, at 527, which argues for considering the outcome:

> [W]here a federal constitutional question has been fully canvassed by fair state process, and meaningfully submitted for possible Supreme Court review, then the federal district judge on *habeas*, though entitled to redetermine the merits, has a large discretion to decide whether the federal error, if any, was prejudicial, whether justice will be served by releasing the prisoner, taking into account in the largest sense all the relevant factors, including his conscientious appraisal of the guilt or innocence of the accused on the basis of the full record before him.

See *Dennis* (1950), a disappointing decision by the legendary conservative judge Learned Hand.

183. Dissent in *Labat* (1966) at 729. The internal quotation is from Shakespeare, *King Henry VI*, Part I, Act II, Scene 4. The jury commissioners had excluded persons who worked for a daily wage, which had the "disparate impact" (to use later terminology) of excluding blacks. Gewin could not see that discrimination could be accomplished through a correlated variable. Dealing with exclusion of wage earners "goes beyond the mandate of the Supreme Court which directed consideration of the race issue only." Footnote 3a at 730.

184. *Rabinowitz* (1966) at 92. Joni Rabinowitz, a field representative in Albany, Georgia for the Student Nonviolent Coordinating Committee, clearly was innocent. She had been accused of lying to the grand jury about her knowledge of a picketing event. She said she knew only what she had read. Eyewitnesses said she was there, but all agreed there was only one white female at the event, and another girl said it was she. No matter, Rabinowitz was found guilty. Apparently there was no way for the federal court to overturn the state-court verdict simply because it was wrong, but *that* is the problem. This is a most inappropriate case in which to advocate a "convict 'em, punish 'em" standard. Judge Gewin must have understood that the Fifth Circuit panel was only using the jury route to get someone out of jail who never should have been there.

Although one cannot object to these words, whether the jury *was* "fair" and "impartial" is the question at issue. Gewin, in effect, wants to call violation of pre-trial jury-selection procedures "harmless" error. As we will see below, the Supreme Court is moving in this direction. What I seek is that clearly guilty defendants (for example, those who have voluntarily confessed) may induce correction of poor jury-formation procedures without having their convictions reversed on that account.

The dogged insistence by the federal courts—so far—that defendants deserve fair trials, guilty or innocent, reinforces my bewilderment that they use outcome standards to determine "fair." It is not the outcome of the trial that matters, it is its fairness. It should not be the outcome of jury selection that matters, only the objectivity and randomness of the procedures that created it.

We see remnants of Judge Friendly's argument—unless defendant claims that the jury's finding was wrong, who cares?—in Justice Rehnquist's dissent in *Taylor* (1975). The Court's determination that the defendant can complain of an improper jury, even if it is not people like him who have been excluded from it, was based on asking whether Taylor had been hurt by the jury's composition. Rehnquist thought the defendant could be harmed only if the excluded juror was of his race. They were debating the wrong question.

Intent

We have seen that unequal outcome does not substitute for intent, but has been accepted as a measure of intent. More overt proof of intent is still at issue.[185] In some instances—first-degree murder, for one—intent is intrinsic to the finding. Intent may affect one's view of an outcome, but it should not be relevant when assessing procedure. Preference for one type of person is discrimination against another. There is no mathematical difference between exclusion and inclusion, though some judges have hung their decisions on thinking that there is. The phrase "intentional and systematic" appears in several jury-composition cases.[186] Systematic should be sufficient, although Justice Murphy claims a constitutional mandate for intent in his dissent in *Fay* (1947):

> The equal protection clause of the Fourteenth Amendment prohibits a state from convicting any person by use of a jury which is not impartially drawn from a cross-section of the community. That means that juries must be chosen without systematic and intentional exclusion of any otherwise qualified group of individuals. Only in that way can the democratic traditions of the jury system be preserved.[187]

---

185. See, for example, *Bakke* (1978).

186. See, for example, *Theil* (1946) and *Ballard* (1946).

187. *Fay* (1947) at 296. Justices Black, Douglas, and Rutledge joined. Cites omitted.

Although "impartial" comes from the Constitution, "drawn from a cross-section of the community" does not. It would be reasonable language if it implied a procedure, but as long as courts think it implies an outcome, which they can observe and judge, I must complain that they have confused the Constitution's language with their own.

I have not discussed the "blue-ribbon" or "special" jury. Such a jury is derived from pure intent—the intent *not* to formulate a jury by random selection from "the community." Under the constitutional standard of impartiality, one would be hard pressed to argue against it. That is, a special jury might be shown to lack impartiality, but on what basis would one assume that it does? Although it is an overt violation of the "cross-section" standard of the Supreme Court, one might be surprised to learn that special juries have been consistently allowed. As Judge Hall in *Local 36* (1947) noted, one must be circumspect in applying the cross-section standard too literally. Richard Lempert advocates a blue-ribbon jury as a last resort, if none of his other suggestions produces impartial results.[188] His topic is how to make decisions in complex cases—the kind that use experts. He, too, wants to assess juries from their decisions, not from the procedures by which they were formed.

Parties who think a common jury cannot decide their case can waive the jury, letting the judge be the finder of fact. No one in this discussion contends that the size of the jury matters, which I take as some confirmation of my position, in Chapter 4, that today's jury of six is easily the equal of the jury of twelve from two hundred years ago. In any case, although I will revisit the issue in Chapter 10, I accept the implication of my own uniform-random-selection standard that there should be no blue-ribbon juries.

The *Harvard Law Review* editors looked at this subject before *Fay* had been reviewed by the Supreme Court. They could see no rationale for special juries.

> [C]ontinued dissatisfaction voiced by able critics indicates that even though superior mental equipment be conceded to the special jury, this tampering with the composition of the ordinary jury has disrupted psychological and political functions which are fully as important as efficient fact-finding. The courts, nevertheless, have repeatedly sustained the special jury.[189]

Fay (1947) continued this tradition and affirmed the conviction of "labor bosses" by a jury that contained no laborers, by design. I see no reason for an intent standard, no reason to consider the guilt or innocence of the defendant, and no room for special juries. Refusing to reverse the decision because the jury was deliberately structured, insisting on an outcome analysis, the Court had it backward.

---

188. See Lempert (1981).

189. Note (1947) at 613.

HARMLESS ERROR

We are imperfect humans. Calling for perfection in trial procedure is calling for a trial never to occur, or never to end. Thus Rule of Civil Procedure 61 instructs the judge to ignore errors "in either the admission or the exclusion of evidence" and indeed, "in anything done or omitted by the court or by any of the parties," unless to do otherwise would be "inconsistent with substantial judgment." Rule 61 concludes:

> The court at every stage in the proceeding must disregard any error or defect in the proceeding which does not affect the substantial rights of the parties.

This practical approach to trial procedure was not always the rule, however.

Courts not only established their right to review legislation for "constitutionality"; they established their right to review each other, as described in Chapter 4. Into the twentieth century, lower-court decisions, especially criminal convictions, would be overturned for failure to comply strictly with some required procedure. As we inherited the practice from England, procedure was, in a sense, king; but a touchy and seemingly absurd king. "Parliament enacted a law in 1873 that set forth a standard for assessing harmless error," but the U.S. courts stuck with impractical exactitude.[190]

The situation became intolerable.

> So great was the threat of reversal, in many jurisdictions, that criminal trial became a game for sowing reversible error in the record, only to have repeated the same matching of wits when a new trial had been thus obtained.[191]

Congress acted in 1919, asking reviewing courts to examine "the entire record before the court, without regard to technical errors."[192] The Supreme Court took the law to mean what it said:

> It comes down on its face to a very plain admonition: "Do not be technical, where technicality does not really hurt the party whose rights in the trial and in its outcome the technicality affects."[193]

This section of the U.S. Code reached its current form in its only revision, in 1949:

---

190. Carter (1993) at 127. An exception is *Motes* (1900) in which, as we will see became a common theme (sometimes only in dissent), overwhelming evidence of guilt made reversal unacceptable, and, therefore, the error harmless. At 476:

> It would be trifling with the administration of the criminal law to award [Motes] a new trial because of a particular error committed by the trial court, when in effect he has stated under oath that he was guilty of the charge preferred against him.

191. *Kotteakos* (1946) at 759.

192. Quoting from the Act of Feb. 26, 1919, Chapter 48, 40 Statutes 1181.

193. *Kotteakos* (1946) at 760.

> On the hearing of any appeal or writ of *certiorari* in any case, the court shall give judgment after an examination of the record without regard to errors or defects which do not affect the substantial rights of the parties.[194]

Rule 61 is a paraphrase of this law. No longer do the errors have to be "technical," which is to say, no longer does the reviewing court have to determine what "technical" means in this context. In theory, the question is not whether the verdict was correct, and not even whether the verdict was arguably altered because of the error, but whether "rights" were affected.[195] Only "substantial" rights, substantially affected. How can we determine if rights are "substantially" affected? One obvious way would be by asking whether the verdict was altered by the error. And so we come full circle, admitting by obfuscation that which we clearly denied. So much in law is like this.

There are four reasons to bring up this line of legal thought in the context of jury formation. First, it is the essence of the application of law to facts to come to a binary decision from continuous information. Determining "harmless" error is a standard exercise in judicial line-drawing. Second, the error is one of procedure, but the harm is (sometimes) measured by an outcome, the influence of the error on the decision maker (the jurors). Does "harmless" mean zero harm, or *not very much* harm? It appears to mean not enough to change the jurors' minds. The incorrect material or process can affect the jurors, but not affect their vote. That is, it cannot affect the line-drawing, much as it may affect sentiment on one side or the other of the line. Not only is some error OK, so is some harm. Just not very much, and only of a certain (non-binary-conclusion-affecting) kind.

Third, this is exactly the jury-formation problem. Juries are not to be thrown out because they weren't perfectly formed. They are to be rejected if they were so badly formed that "substantial rights" were affected. The Sixth Amendment calls for an "impartial" jury, but impartiality is never measured directly. The indirect measures are rough, and are given some leeway, as we have seen, before they indicate an unconstitutional system, to the Court.

Fourth, despite this concordance between the concept of "harmless error" and the decision to find jury formation constitutional or not, and despite the fact that both lines consider Sixth Amendment issues, the two judicial concepts of law have passed each other virtually unconnected. In this section I will explain why these two lines of cases have remained isolated—why the phrase "harmless error" is never applied when the constitutionality of a jury is at issue—and show that the reason involves the Court's misconception about what statistics can do for the law.

---

194. 28 U.S. Code §2111.

195. *Fahy* (1963) at 86:

> We are not concerned here with whether there was sufficient evidence on which the petitioner could have been convicted without the evidence complained of."

Constitutional and "Structural" Errors

From its earliest encounters with harmless error, the Supreme Court tried to carve out an exception, an area in which any error was fatal to the proceedings in which it occurred.

> If, when all is said and done, the conviction is sure that the error did not influence the jury, or had but very slight effect, the verdict and the judgment should stand, *except perhaps where the departure is from a constitutional norm or a specific command of Congress.*[196]

The legislation does not contain this exception, but the judiciary has its own role, including to guard the Constitution *from* the legislature. The Court is pointing out that the legislature may not overrule the Constitution with a law, that "perhaps" a constitutional violation therefore cannot be "harmless."

The "constitutional" vs. "other" distinction did not take hold in any meaningful way. The trend has been first to include more issues as amenable to "harmless-error" analysis, and second to impose a more lenient standard, allowing more errors to be harmless. Yet the Court has tried to articulate a categorization by which some errors cannot be harmless. A major step toward this breakdown of strict reversal faced with procedural error came in *Chapman* (1967), where the Court first clearly articulated that "constitutional" questions were *not* automatically immune from "harmless-error" analysis:

> We conclude that there may be some constitutional errors which in the setting of a particular case are so unimportant and insignificant that they may, consistent with the Federal Constitution, be deemed harmless, not requiring the automatic reversal of the conviction.[197]

Showing error shifts the burden:

> Certainly error, constitutional error, in illegally admitting highly prejudicial evidence or comments, casts on someone other than the person prejudiced by it a burden to show that it was harmless.

What it takes to overcome that burden was then the subject of further litigation.

Now that constitutional errors could be harmless, analysts asked what kind of error remained sacrosanct. Philip Mause explained that the import of *Chapman* was informing state courts that federal rules would apply to determination of harmless federal-Constitution error, although that did not help much if no one knew what those rules were.[198] In *Harrington* (1969) the Court reaffirmed that the error must have been "harmless beyond

---

196. *Kotteakos* (1946) at 764, emphasis added.

197. *Chapman* (1967) at 22; following indented quotation at 23.

198. See Mause (1969).

a reasonable doubt" because "the case against Harrington was so overwhelming."[199] They articulated the obvious again ten years later:

> Assessing the strength of the prosecution's evidence against the defendant is, of course, one step in applying a harmless-error standard.[200]

Steven Goldberg, understanding that the harmless-error disease was spreading, called it "among the most insidious of legal doctrines,"[201] although it was not clear what that doctrine was. Unalloyed guilt, above all, allowed improper procedure to be waived. The Tenth Circuit, in 1985, declared that the prosecutor's "conduct is plain, fundamental error"[202] for asking an impermissible question. Yet,

> After carefully reviewing the record as a whole, we are convinced beyond a reasonable doubt that the error was harmless.

A principle began to be formed in the late 1980s. In *Satterwhite* (1988):

> We have permitted harmless error analysis in both capital and noncapital cases where the evil caused by a Sixth Amendment violation is limited to the erroneous admission of particular evidence at trial.[203]

One might think that an incident can be forgiven if it is not a decision that "infects" the whole trial. In *Fulminante* (1991), Chief Justice Rehnquist spoke for the Court in putting forward this distinction. As

> the Court has applied harmless-error analysis to a wide range of errors and has recognized that most constitutional errors can be harmless,[204]

Rehnquist suggests that the contrast should be between "structural errors" and "trial errors." Structural errors affect

> the framework within which the trial proceeds, rather than simply an error in the trial process itself.

The language is clumsy, the distinction unconvincing. Charles Ogletree considers a faulty jury instruction:

> It is no coincidence that the Court has not subjected the failure to instruct on the reasonable doubt standard to harmless error analysis, but Chief Justice Rehnquist did not address this inconsistency.[205]

---

199. *Harrington* (1969) at 254.

200. *Holloway* (1978) at 478.

201. Goldberg (1980) at 421.

202. *Remigio* (1985) at 735; following indented quotation at 736.

203. *Satterwhite* (1988) at 257.

204. *Fulminante* (1991), Rehnquist at 306; following indented quotation at 310.

205. Ogletree (1991) at 163; following indented quotation at 164.

Although rightly bothered by Rehnquist's poor attempt to articulate a principle, Ogletree seems perplexed that "line-drawing" is the Court's job:

> The opinion never clearly articulates the structure that the structural errors undermine. The structure, I assert, is the fair trial. Thus, the Chief Justice's distinction can never be more than a distinction of degree.

Of course; but somewhere there is a binary-choice line, the case is reversed or not. "Harmless" error is no different from "substantial" disparity, except that disparities seem to come packaged as numerical measures. As we know that those measures are vacuous—any standard would be arbitrary—we are down to judgments either about the error itself or about the harm the error has done, when there is any procedural flaw.[206]

However, if any flaw can be considered "structural," surely it is the formation of the jury that occurs before the first day of trial. Thus, even though the Court has allowed many a procedural error to infect the composition of the jury, it could not associate those flaws with the "harmless-error" doctrine, because they are just not the kinds of at-trial error that had traditionally been covered thereby.

What Is Covered by This Doctrine?

To apply harmless-error standards, a court must first determine that an issue is subject to harmless-error analysis. In *Glasser* (1942), for example, the Supreme Court held that "assistance of counsel" was denied when two codefendants, who had and articulated conflicting interests, were unable to obtain different attorneys. Could such an error even be considered under harmless-error rules? Over thirty years later, the question was still being debated:

> Some courts and commentators have argued, however, that appellate courts should not reverse automatically in such cases but rather should affirm unless the defendant can demonstrate prejudice.[207]

Reversing this conviction, and thus sustaining *Glasser*, the Court nonetheless provided the wiggle room it needed:

> We read the Court's opinion in *Glasser*, however, as holding that whenever a trial court improperly requires joint representation over timely objection reversal is automatic.

---

206. Following upon the *Fulminante* distinction, Justice Scalia phrases the trial-error question as "whether the guilty verdict actually rendered in *this* trial was surely unattributable to the error." See *Sullivan* (1993) at 279. This line of thinking is the direct precedent for the string of decisions such as *Apprendi* (2000), *Ring* (2002), and *Blakely* (2004), in which facts upon which sentencing will be based have to be found by a jury, not a judge. If harmless error is limited to the trial, then the absence of a trial about a question of fact must be structural. I discuss this line of cases further, below.

207. *Holloway* (1978) at 487, Chief Justice Burger for the Court; following indented quotation at 488.

The joint representation must be improper, and the objection must follow proper procedure.

Thus some procedural flaws, such as joint representation of defendants with conflicting interests, are analyzed directly as procedure. No measure of harm is proposed, none assessed. But the Court cannot avoid the question: How much procedural violation is constitutional violation? If it is not harm that is being measured, it is the extent of the procedural violation itself. There is always a continuum. The Court is always drawing a line.

To assess the impact of a psychiatric report on the jury's assessment of defendant's mental state, the Supreme Court of Kentucky used the obvious measure: Was the outcome affected?

> The evidence of the competency report did not affect the ultimate outcome of the trial.[208]

In their review, the U.S. Supreme Court accepted the Kentucky court's finding that

> if the admission of the competency report had been an error, it was harmless, given petitioner's confession and the overwhelming evidence of his guilt.

It wasn't error (a direct procedural finding), but if it was it was harmless.

This is often the solution: Cover the bases. "Even if we were to assume error, it would be harmless."[209]

> Assuming, arguendo, that the challenged testimony should have been excluded, the record clearly reveals that any error in its admission was harmless beyond a reasonable doubt. The jury, in addition to hearing the challenged testimony, was presented with overwhelming evidence of petitioner's guilt.

Either it's error or, maybe it's not; but if it is, well, the guy was clearly guilty.

Error in forming the jury cannot be harmless. It is as structural as it gets.

> Similarly, when a petit jury has been selected upon improper criteria or has been exposed to prejudicial publicity, we have required reversal of the conviction because the effect of the violation cannot be ascertained. Like these fundamental flaws, which never have been thought harmless, discrimination in the grand jury undermines the structural integrity of the criminal tribunal itself, and is not amenable to harmless-error review.[210]

Is the illogic apparent yet? Some errors require a judgment whether they are serious or not.

---

208. *Buchanan* (1985) at 213; following indented quotation from *Buchanan* (1987) at 414. *Buchanan* is better known for its other issue, whether one defendant is harmed by "death-qualifying" the jurors, when the death penalty could not be imposed on him (but could be on his codefendant). See below.

209. *Robledo* (2002) at *2; following indented quotation from *Milton* (1972), Chief Justice Burger for the Court at 372.

210. *Hillery* (1986) at 263, Justice Marshall for the Court.

Serious errors require reversal. If they are not serious, practical judicial administration says let them go. Some errors—those committed in jury formation, for example—cannot be let go, even if by no criterion are they serious. Error means reversal. Is a court's decision process any different? Of course not. Now the Court ponders whether there really was an error by asking how serious this non-error is. If not serious ("substantial") the Court cannot say there was one but it was harmless. It concludes that there was no error at all!

Standards for Assessing Error

Fulminante (1991) provided language more than a concept. It allowed the Court to contend that some errors were "trial" errors and thus amenable to harmless-error analysis. This is nothing more than a tautology: "We will decide which errors may be harmless," the Court is saying, "and apply to them the label 'trial error.'"

Gregory Mitchell articulates two tests, which coexist. One is the "contribution-to-conviction test" which he also calls the "*Chapman* (1967) test." The conviction is reversed if the error contributed (how much?) to the conviction. This does call for reading the minds of the jurors, or what in other contexts would be called "speculation." The other test is the "overwhelming-evidence-of-guilt test," or the "*Harrington* (1969) test."[211] True, in *Harrington*, the Court had found the evidence overwhelming; but it also reiterated the standard *Chapman* test:

> We of course do not know the jurors who sat. Our judgment must be based on our own reading of the record and on what seems to us to have been the probable impact of the two confessions on the minds of an average jury.[212]

Mitchell's distinctions, then, may not be as clear as he indicates. Nonetheless, he tells us that a conviction is more likely to be reversed if a reviewing court follows the *Chapman* standard than if it follows the *Harrington* standard. He also notes that the *Harrington* standard allows the reviewing court to assess the evidence—a role not usually in its purview. Would we prefer that the Court delve into the psychology of the jurors? I suspect that, regardless what any jurist writes, none does that. The decision is always based on the evidence of guilt excepting that evidence which should not have been entered. Mitchell follows a long tradition of confusing language with reason. He is confusing the judge's rationale with his thinking. When a judge wants to reverse a conviction, he does so by saying that jurors' judgments were affected; and when he wants to affirm he says, "The evidence of guilt was overwhelming." In that judge's opinion, no reasonable juror would have decided the case differently had the erroneous evidence been excluded.

---

211. Mitchell (1994), both phrases defined at 1341.

212. *Harrington* (1969) at 254.

Judges Posner and Easterbrook, writing separate concurring opinions in an *en banc* decision, question what standards are appropriate in what issue, and why. As each joined the other's opinion, I will attribute authorship only in notes, and consider these comments joint.

> Every court that has applied a harmless error test to a *Doyle* problem has assumed that *Chapman* supplies the appropriate standard. Not one case discusses why.[213]

A "*Doyle*" issue arises when a prosecutor refers disparagingly to the defendant's silence after a *Miranda* warning—a notification that anything he says will be held against him but that his silence will not be.[214]

> *Doyle v. Ohio* is a questionable interpretation of the self-incrimination clause. . . . The element of sanction is less an argument for forbidding the use of silence to impeach testimony by someone who received *Miranda* warnings than it is an argument against *Miranda*.
>
> A state may not deprive a person of his liberty without due process of law. But it is not obvious that a prosecutor's comment (if that is what it was in this case) on a defendant's failure to try to exculpate himself when he was arrested denies the defendant due process of law, even expansively construed.

Or, in more simple terms, let's call the error, if it was one, harmless.

The Supreme Court is moving in Posner's and Easterbrook's direction. With its newfound categorization, the Court later defined *Doyle* issues as "trial" error, apparently lessening the difficulty of finding error harmless. Justice O'Connor notes the changing standard:

> In *Chapman*'s place, the Court substitutes the less rigorous standard of *Kotteakos v. United States* (1946).[215]

And she doesn't like it:

> By now it goes without saying that harmless-error review is of almost universal application; there are few errors that may not be forgiven as harmless.

---

213. Easterbrook in *Phelps* (1985) at 1421. See *Miranda* (1966).

214. See *Doyle* (1976). Following indented quotations from Posner in *Phelps* (1985) at 1416 and then 1417.

215. O'Connor's dissent in *Brecht* (1993) at 652; following quotation also at 652. As usual, I am not concerned with issues that some attorneys would emphasize, such as under what auspices the case is before a federal court. Both *Phelps* and *Brecht* were *habeas corpus* petitions. Courts are concerned about what issues can be considered when reviewing state actions, as well as what standards apply. To a lay person, or at least to me, having different standards apply to the same issue before the same court, depending on the route it took to get there, is absurd, as is basing the standard on which article of the Constitution is claimed to have been violated, when several apply.

The Logical Fallacy

Despite Justice O'Connor's observation, there are some errors that no court is willing to call "harmless." One appears to be "any error that impinges on the integrity of the jury."[216] But there is *always* a continuum, *always* a line drawn. As I noted above, what the Court does is place that line earlier in the process, in the determination whether there was an error. It hides the error, finding it so small (dare I say "harmless"?) that it concludes there is no error at all. This is nothing but a word game, as illustrated in Figure 55.

	Not Really Error	OK, It's Error
Affirm	**Not Substantial**	**Harmless Error**
Reverse	**Substantial**	**Not Harmless**

FIGURE 55: The Language of Error

Although the Court makes one decision, it actually draws two lines. The first line is the decision; the second is what it calls the decision. The Court will be faced with a continuum, from a trivial error in language to the denial of a right or an event that may affect jurors' verdicts. The Court will either affirm or reverse. It places this case above or below the horizontal line in Figure 55.

But what to call it? Suppose the allegation was that the jury was selected with racial bias, and indeed there is some evidence to that effect—but not enough to reverse. The Court cannot say the error was harmless. Error in the formation of the jury cannot be tolerated. So it places the case to the left of the vertical line, where it is categorized as "not error." And so the emperor puts on his new clothes.[217]

---

216. This language is common, but here quoted in context from Mause (1969) at 541. At 542:

> [Any] error which goes to the integrity of the jury which convicted the defendant, should invoke the application of an automatic reversal rule.

217. This phenomenon, finding language to obscure fact, runs rampant throughout law. For example, consider *Oneonta* (2000). Rather than concluding that describing a suspect as "black" was racial classification, but legitimate, the circuit court chose to determine that it was not racial classification at all. Primus (2003) asks, at 512:

> *Oneonta* raises the question of why a court staffed with intelligent judges would deny the existence of a racial classification in that case.

Dissenting in *Blakely* (2004), Justice Breyer limits arbitrary line-drawing to the legislature:

> I agree that, classically speaking, the difference between a traditional sentencing factor and an element of a greater offense often comes down to a legislative choice about which label to affix.

124 S.Ct. at 2552. Would that justices were so frank about admitting their own arbitrary lines.

In jury selection, the Court has asked that statistical analysis draw the line for it. Along came statistics with its "significance" language. Why most courts have veered off to a more error-looking concept of "substantial" I do not know, but as I will explain in Chapter 7, "significance," like substantiality, is in the eye of the beholder. There is no scientific line to be drawn.[218]

This word game has deleterious consequences. By not labeling as flawed the process that produced a barely passing qualified wheel, the Court gives up its ability to correct it. The Court has to wait until the outcome is egregious. Only then does it criticize the system that produced it. Had the Court taken my procedural view, it could have said, "We'll call the error harmless, and let you use this particular jury, but correct the procedures or next time we will not allow it."

Warning from the Higher Court

It is not unheard of. Had *Barefoot* (1983) come after *Daubert* (1993), it would no doubt have been reversed.[219] While affirming, the Supreme Court expressed its doubts:

> That the Court of Appeals' handling of this case was tolerable under our precedents is not to suggest that its course should be accepted as the norm or as the preferred procedure.[220]

What had the circuit court done? At one point it writes:

> Nevertheless, the testimony of Mary Richards, one way or the other, cannot and could not affect the determination of Barefoot's guilt.

This bears the mark of "harmless-error" thinking, though the term never appears in any opinion in this case.

The Supreme Court's dissenters were strong:

> A death sentence cannot rest on highly dubious predictions secretly based on a factual foundation of hearsay and pure conjecture.[221]

---

218. Courts would like to adhere to "objective" lines, but such lines do not exist.

> Whether persons are to be held responsible for their crazy behavior is not a scientific matter to be determined by experts. It is a moral, social, and legal matter to be determined by the legislatures and the courts, the legal and political representatives of society. Moreover, the line drawn reflects a moral judgment that is not compelled by scientific findings.

Morse (1978) at 589. More on the limitations of science appears in Chapter 10.

219. Beecher-Monas and Garcia-Rill (2003) at 1856:

> The standards set out in the *Daubert* trilogy, however, were not met by the *Barefoot* experts, nor by any experts offering clinical judgments about future dangerousness since.

220. *Barefoot* (1983) 463 U.S. at 892; following indented quotation from the Fifth Circuit opinion, 697 F. 2d at 599. Mary Richards was a fact witness.

221. Dissent by Blackmun, joined by Brennan and Marshall, *Barefoot* (1983) 463 U.S. at 922, footnote 5.

A psychologist's conjecture about the future behavior of the defendant was instrumental in the jury's sentence of death, but the discussion was about whether allowing it was error, not whether it was harmless. I will provide a framework for assessing such testimony in Chapter 10. Of course it was error and, when seen that way, it was not harmless. Mr. Barefoot was executed.

In *Roman* (1987), the main prosecution witness was black, so the prosecutor used his peremptory challenges to strike white jurors. The circuit court agreed that his action was discriminatory, but found that it did not affect the outcome because 1) defendant had also challenged two whites; 2) the county was 34 percent white, the jury was 25 percent white, difference of one white juror; and 3) most Bronx county juries were majority black and Hispanic. That is, it drew a line based on outcome, not procedure, and called it "not error":

> Though the prosecutor's actions are to be condemned, the defendant's conviction before a jury that was in fact a fair cross-section should be allowed to stand.[222]

Writes Judge Frank Easterbrook:

> *Ex parte* contacts of the sort to which [then-prosecutor] Tuite admits are forbidden. . . . Condemning *ex parte* contacts and issuing a writ of *habeas corpus* are different matters, however.[223]

The prosecutor had tried to influence the judge, but failed to do so. Defendants would not pay the bribe the judge wanted, and so the prosecution prevailed anyway.

> Did the *ex parte* contact work to Branion's "actual and substantial disadvantage, infecting [the] entire trial with error of constitutional dimensions"? No. It did not affect the trial at all. Branion had a fair trial, after which the jury rendered its verdict of guilt.

Seems like harmless error to me, but this kind of wheeling and dealing cannot be called harmless error, so it is called not error.

Harmless Error in Jury Formation

Except for excuses, pre-trial jury selection is carried out by clerks following rules. Resources can be used to be sure the rules minimize discretion,[224] drawing a uniform-random sample from reasonable source lists. Once the rules have been judicially approved, all that can be challenged is whether they are being followed.

There should be some flexibility in the rules themselves. So, for example, jurisdictions

---

222. *Roman* (1987) at 230.

223. *Branion* (1988) at 1267; following indented quotation at 1268.

224. I prefer that there be no sub-judicial discretion, but many systems are overwhelmed by requests to be excused. That decision is delegated to clerks where it could indeed be abused.

currently can use a voter list for four years. Perhaps the maximum should be two years, but new lists need not be formed every day. Thus there is a sort of "harmless-error" concept in making the rules broad enough that they can be followed by clerical personnel. Not all source lists need be struck on the same day. Courts can determine how close they must be, and within that range they are "close enough." Some people will pass through to the merged list more than once, because their names are not spelled the same on all source lists. Strictly speaking, duplicates nullify the "uniform-random" rule. Nonetheless, if the merge-purge procedure is recognized to be quite good, then the rule should be to use it. That occasionally duplicates slip through is, let's say, harmless.

Whatever room for variation is built into the rules, there will be variation outside them. The new list is a week late. What is the system to do? It is to admit its error. If a defendant appeals, a reviewing court should be able to chastise the jury-selection system, let it know it is serious, and assist in fixing the problem. Look at the efforts systems have taken to "fix" "problems" that did not exist, that were considered problems because of out-come measurement! Confining "structural" variation to stay within the rules is a management task. If the procedures are objective, aimed toward supplying a uniform-random selection of community participants, what few errors outside the rules there may be should be harmless. I would not obfuscate any more: Call them harmless and get on with it.

THE BEAT GOES ON . . .

The reader for whom this material is new may have reached this point wondering why I have worked so hard to get here. It is not difficult. Indeed, it is obvious. We should begin with a reasonable view of persons in "the community" who have most of the qualifications for jury duty. The voter list might do. Persons on it are citizens, probably are not under court supervision for having committed a felony, are likely to be literate and stable. Supplementation with driver's licenses and other lists, other than increasing cost, does no harm. It generates the expense of merging and purging duplicates, and more expense for printing and mailing questionnaires to non-eligibles, and then the additional expense of handling these nonproductive names, taking them off jury lists. For political reasons, however, having these additional names on source lists may be worth the expense. Most are N being added to E. Statistically, they are irrelevant, unless one formulates the wrong test. Ultimately, whatever the source lists, select randomly, send questionnaires mechanically. What's the problem?

The problem is that analysts and judges think "the community" is measured by a census count of the population. My idea, that we measure the community in the very act of fair, uniform-random selection, either is beyond the understanding of everyone else who has written on this topic, or is unacceptable to them. Why?

Writing that supplementation of source lists does not work—in the sense of finding more minorities to be jurors—John Bueker refers to "the problem of minority under-representation," noting that "the source list from which potential jurors are selected may not be representative of the community." Yet he articulates no concept, and no measure, of this "community." He means the source lists do not look like the census view of the population. Source lists having fewer minorities than the population is an "abuse" of the selection process, he says.[225] If source lists capture the names of participating minorities who will be in the jurisdiction when they are called, there is no problem. Someone with Bueker's preconceptions, however, will still think there is one.

I am proposing a paradigm shift in the way people conceive of jury selection. Such shifts are always difficult. Writers who start with the notion that there is a "problem," by comparing jurors with census counts, are forced to counter that "problem" by instituting make-up procedures. They are driven to achieve outcome goals that will not result from fair, uniform procedures. Rather than question the goal, they question the procedures. Ultimately "fair" gets lost. It's body-count time: *Where are my minorities?* Even the Supreme Court seems confused about whether the constitutional question is about outcome or process. It is willing to decide about both.

The standard I would have the Court impose is that every member of the presumptive community, as indicated by some level of presence and participation, should have an equal chance of being drawn for any qualified wheel. We cannot characterize the "community" beforehand. We will learn what the community is by taking the juror survey.

This procedural standard is in direct conflict with the outcome standard. The commentators, as far as I can tell, do not understand this conflict. They have not come to realize that rigging the outcome bastardizes the process. Even if they understood this conflict, they might still want an outcome standard. If so, we can agree to disagree. If we were to engage in a political debate, I would gladly defend my concept of democracy and equality. But there is no debate. The outcome approach that I am saying is disastrous is taken for granted by all "intellectuals" in this field. They have not come to appreciate that there is a question, and so I have to both explain that there is one and answer it in the same chapter.

The Importance of Participation

OK, not literally *all* persons who have gotten involved have been obtuse. Judge Shubb in California perhaps puts his dictum in his mouth:

> What is clear to this court is that supplementation of the list of registered voters with the names of persons who for whatever reasons have chosen not to register to vote will increase the percentage of apathetic individuals in the venire.[226]

---

225. Bueker (1997). Quoted phrases, in order, at 392, 394, and 395.

226. *Luong* (2003) at 1129.

Probably not. A more likely result is an increase in the numbers of no-shows.

It is not necessary to discuss motivation or personality. It is sufficient to define "participation," as I have, as part of the differentiation between "population" and "community."[227] For this reason, I would suggest (if lists are being merged at all) adding the local-library list, or asking persons applying for a library card if they would allow this participation to bring them into the jury pool. As Judge Shubb continues:

> It would also be a mistake to assume that forcing jury service upon persons who do not have enough public spirit even to register to vote would promote the policy that all citizens be afforded the opportunity to be considered for jury service.[228]

I am open to other forms of participation. Any list is fine with me. Use of other lists will not force jury service on anyone who doesn't want to do it. Getting more people on lists will not much affect who populates juries, and that is *not* a problem.

Motives

Not that there is never establishment chicanery. We can find examples where the concept of "community" has been manipulated. In Florida, communities are counties, except that a large county can determine to be more than one community, for the purpose of forming juries. A county with a population exceeding fifty thousand can divide into jury districts, provided that none has fewer than six thousand people in it.[229] When such division was implemented in Palm Beach County, the districts in Figure 56 were created.[230]

Geographic Area	Total	Blacks	Percentage Black
Palm Beach County as a Whole	398,797	29,859	7.487
Western (Belle Glade) Jury District	9,549	4,974	52.080
Eastern (West Palm Beach) Jury District	389,248	24,885	6.393

FIGURE 56: Divisions of the Palm Beach County District

---

227. The other differentiations are eligibility and being present, not having moved between source list and trial date.

228. *Luong* (2003) at 1129.

229. See Florida Statutes §40.015. That's right: The first standard is based on population, the second on registered voters.

230. A peculiarity of this division was that if a crime were committed in the eastern part, it would be tried there, but if it were committed in the western part, the defendant could choose where the trial would be held. A black from the west, committing a crime in the east, would be tried in the east, whereas a white from the east, committing a crime in the west, could choose to be tried closer to home, in the east. *Spencer* (1989), table at 1354.

The Florida Supreme Court found this division to be unconstitutional. What seemed like a way to reduce juror distance between home and court masked a deliberate reduction of blacks on eastern juries below the county average. Why should race matter? If uniform-random selection from the county is the standard, then it should be enforced regardless of racial consequences. The procedural standard requires no determination of juror characteristics and allows no measure of disparity.

There is room for innovation in procedure. Joe Kadane suggests:

> [S]end questionnaires from a random sample from, for instance, a list of registered voters and a list of licensed drivers, ask the drivers whether they are registered, and if so, discard these as duplicates.[231]

This solution adds "also on voter list" to reasons for ineligibility, because driver-voters had two chances to be selected. It is clever and simple. Aside from differential cheating, when and how to delete duplicates is an accounting issue.[232] That is the only kind of issue that a jury-selection system should have.

Outcome Manipulation

Although I think the procedural approach makes most sense, directly analyzing and even manipulating the outcome remains in vogue. Hiroshi Fukurai, Edgar Butler, and Richard Krooth compare what I would consider fair systems, and condemn their outcomes. They note, for example, that Hispanics are less likely to register to vote than others, and propose to over-sample Hispanics to get them better represented on juries. Like Alan Gelfand, Fukurai et al. do not even consider that many of these non-registered Hispanics are not citizens, do not speak English, or are mobile. They take the body-count approach—the approach endorsed by the Supreme Court and Michael Finkelstein—to its absurd extreme. They recommend "probability proportionate to size"—cluster sampling, based on population (not source lists)—to get more minorities on juries. People in different clusters would have different probabilities of being selected for jury duty depending on cluster size and rate of participation.[233] There is a perverse concept of fair procedure here, where uniform-random selection is anathema. Outcome rules.

---

231. Kadane is so paraphrased in Boatright and Krauss (2001) at 146.

232. Initially, it would be difficult to estimate how many notices to send. With some experience a system could estimate the cost of processing these additional questionnaires and alternatively the cost of purging earlier in the process. I expect the less-expensive procedure will be merging and purging earlier in the process, as those are computerized functions with zero marginal cost. It is ultimately an empirical question.

233. See Fukurai et al. (1993). In contrast, as we are told in *Johnson* (1998) at 333, federal juries in New York come from stratified samples of voter-registration lists, but in constructing the master wheel, names are "taken from each county in proportion to the number of registered voters." Stratification pre-

As if only to provide more evidence that judges should not play with numbers, the federal jury system in Connecticut was put under the control of Magistrate Judge Joan Glazer Margolis in December, 1992. Following the plan under which she worked, Judge Margolis plumbed the depths of her source lists, looking for minorities.

> In previous Reports and letters, I included detailed tables which indicated that Hispanics are disproportionately disqualified from jury service, relative to Whites and Blacks, due to lack of citizenship or fluency.[234]

Had that conclusion been correct, it should have ended the issue. These people are N, not even presumptively eligible. The responsibility of the system is only to contact them, to determine, but not to make up for, their jury-ineligible characteristics.

To Judge Margolis, however, this was a statement of the problem, not the response to critics. She devised a formula, approved by the judges, by which in July 1995 a special supplemental mailing was sent to only three cities in the New Haven district: New Haven, Meriden, and Waterbury (86.8 percent to New Haven). Judge Margolis sent questionnaires to only Hartford, New Britain, and Windham in the Hartford district (77.8 percent to Hartford); and to only Bridgeport in the Bridgeport district. Her reports contain arithmetic and interpretation errors, and disappointment. Alas, trolling for Hispanics, she had nary a nibble. Attributing her inability to increase the percent Hispanic on the qualified wheel to having used up the available Hispanics,[235] making no assessment of the ethnicity of the ever-increasing non-delivered notices, Judge Margolis missed the point. The count of Hispanics may have increased in each jurisdiction, but the actual Hispanics on her source lists were no longer present.

She and the entire Connecticut judiciary were solving a non-problem. True, they would be attacked with census comparisons. A response was at hand: "Our process is fair; it is the characteristics and behavior of Hispanics that are keeping them off the qualified wheel." The judges chose not to respond, but to violate the basic uniform-randomness of their own approved plan by selecting certain cities for their mailings. They had learned nothing from *Osorio* (1992), where skipping whole cities was the problem. Now they proposed the same thing as the solution!

---

serves the criterion that each registered voter has the same chance of selection, reducing the variance. Connecticut, however, follows the Fukurai et al. approach, weighting areas by the census count of population, not by their own counts of persons on source lists.

234. Magistrate's report of November 9, 1995, at 3. Margolis' reports surely are public documents, but to my knowledge have not been "published." I received them as litigation materials.

235. Magistrate's report of November 9, 1995, at 7. This is either an absurd conclusion or plain fact. The only way to "use up" Hispanics is to bring them into the courthouse out of turn. That had not been done. On the other hand, that there were fewer "available" Hispanics the older the list, is correct. From the day a list is struck, relatively more Hispanics will leave the jurisdiction and therefore not be "available" for duty.

Chief Judge Sapala in Wayne County, Michigan, expressed concern about the paucity of residents from Detroit on juries. We can read "black," but all witnesses expressed themselves as being concerned with geographic distribution, not racial balance. However Judge Sapala perceived this "problem," the solution was worse. In the fall of 2000, after a standard mailing from a uniform sampling of drivers, he sent an additional 122,000 questionnaires to Detroit.

> As a result of these measures, Chief Judge Sapala claimed that the percentage of Detroit residents in Wayne County jury arrays now closely matches the percentage of jury-eligible Detroit residents in Wayne County.[236]

The "problem" that Judge Sapala was solving was explained by James McCree, director of jury services for the Wayne County Circuit Court.

> The source list Wayne County received in 2000 contained the names of 1,285,732 individuals and revealed that 621,373 of these people were residents of Detroit. Thus, he claimed that approximately 48 percent of the jury-eligible population in Wayne County were Detroit residents. According to the number of questionnaires sent out, Mr. McCree stated that approximately 34 percent of residents throughout the county qualified as jury-eligible. He claimed that the percentage of jury-eligible Detroit residents was close to the county average.

Only through outcome-oriented eyes is this a problem. Mr. McCree does *not* know who is jury-eligible. He has confused the presumptively eligible—those we do not know are not eligible—with an actual count. We do not know that these people are actually eligible, or that they are even still present.

Even if they are, do we want recalcitrant jurors? Judge Shubb thinks we do not. I think a person who has shown himself willing to resist an order of the court to return a questionnaire and appear for jury service should be ineligible on that account alone. Perhaps such a person should be put in jail, but not on a jury.

However, Detroit residents were less likely to be eligible than residents in other parts of the county.

> Mr. McCree testified that 51.3 percent of the prospective jurors throughout Wayne County returned their questionnaires. According to Mr. McCree, prospective Detroit jurors returned their questionnaires at approximately the same rate, 47.44 percent. Mr. McCree claimed that after the questionnaires were returned, but before summonses were mailed out, some potential jurors were disqualified from duty pursuant to statute. According to Mr. McCree, Detroit residents typically disqualified for jury duty at a higher rate than other communities in Wayne County.

---

236. *Wallace* (2003) at *2; following two indented quotations from the same source, one footnote omitted from each; fourth indented quotation at *3.

First, 720,840 questionnaires were mailed, of which 285,902 were mailed to Detroit. Mr. McCree has made a mistake I described in age-discrimination cases, in Chapter 2: He has compared a part of the population with the whole. The correct comparison is between the two parts. The return rate for non-Detroit Wayne County was 53.84 percent. The difference between this return rate and the 47.44 percent rate of Detroit is over one hundred standard deviations. The return rates were not close to "approximately the same." Mr. McCree's testimony was either ignorant or politically motivated. Either way, it was grossly incorrect.

Second, we have not accounted for differential no-shows. Where judges think the problem will be recalcitrant jurors, there are in fact non-jurors.

> However, Mr. McCree explained that these percentages took into account only those people that received summonses. On August 28, 2000, the day of defendant's trial, 389 jurors were drawn. Ninety-six of these jurors were residents of Detroit. Thus, Mr. McCree estimated that 25 percent of the jurors drawn that day were Detroit residents.

So Judge Sapala wants to make up for the ineligibility of and lack of cooperation by Detroit residents by over-sampling those who are eligible. In essence, eligible and cooperative Detroit residents pay a jury tax: They have an increased probability of being selected for a county jury because they live in the same area as many ineligibles and no-shows who get on source lists and are counted by the census. This makes sense? It is a procedural outrage, but it does make outcome sense. "Fairness" to cooperative citizens simply is not an issue in this discussion. The criterion is to make jurors look like (E + N). I say jury pools should look like E, like the community, as the Supreme Court has directed.

The federal plan adopted in 1992 in Eastern Michigan called for adjustment of the jury pool by "subtraction." From implementing Administrative Order 92-AO-080:

> [T]he Clerk of the Court shall remove by a random process the names of 877 White and Other Qualified Jurors from the 4,829 total qualified jurors in the 1992 wheel. . . . As a result of this procedure, the 1992 qualified Bay City wheel shall be composed of 166 Black qualified jurors and 3,786 White and Other qualified jurors.[237]

Reviewing this scheme, and its rejection by the Sixth Circuit, Leslie Ellis and Shari Diamond conclude:

> The barrier is the use of membership in a cognizable group as the basis for jury selection. The same logic would preclude privileging the qualification questionnaires of certain jurors on the basis of race or gender, or oversampling from districts based on their higher percentages of minority residents.[238]

---

237. This order is quoted in *Ovalle* (1998), in which it was found to violate the Judicial Selection and Service Act of 1968.

238. Ellis and Diamond (2003) at 1055.

This is some progress. Overt manipulation, weighting advocated by Fukurai et al., and the geographic search for Hispanics practiced by Judges Margolis and Sapala, are all seen to be race-based, and therefore unacceptable. Ellis and Diamond also see through the "jural districting" scheme proposed by Kim Forde-Mazrui.[239] However, it is very little progress. Rather than abandon outcome manipulation, Ellis and Diamond suggest masking it. To add minorities to jury pools, they propose a "stratified and weighted random draw of juror names from the potentially eligible population." The weighting this year would come from last year's responses to the initial questionnaire mailing:

> If a particular political district or ZIP code X accounted for 4% of the mailed questionnaires, but only 2% of the qualified jurors who appeared in the courthouse were from district or ZIP code X, that "under-yield" would be adjusted in the next mailing. The mailed questionnaires to district or ZIP code X would represent 8% of the total mailed, with a predicted yield of 4% that would reflect the actual distribution in initial list.[240]

The problem, as usual, is starting with the belief that there is a problem. The proposed solution is to "tax" people differently (if jury service is seen as a tax on one's time) depending on where they live. That does not seem outrageous, because people *are* taxed differently in different locations. Identical property may have different valuations, the property and sales tax rates may be different and, among states, income tax rates differ. Indeed, if one were to calculate the probability of a random eligible adult being noticed for jury duty, state or federal, it surely would vary across jurisdictions. However, *within* a jurisdiction, the Ellis-Diamond scheme, like all the other outcome-manipulation schemes, violates the "uniform-random selection" criterion that I suggested would be an acceptable (indeed, the only acceptable) procedural standard. It violates procedural equity, and should not be allowed.

---

239. Forde-Mazrui (1999) also thinks that juries should "look like" the census, that their not doing so is a problem. At 365:
> The reality, however, is that jury selection procedures have resulted in juries that underrepresent distinct groups, especially racial minorities, with serious consequences.

He then proposes a system based on "electoral districting principles." At 389:
> Under a strict model of jural districting, a jury district would be divided into twelve subdistricts of approximately equal population. Each petit jury would be required to contain one juror from each sub-district.

Finally, he asserts, at 404, that
> jural districting would avoid many of the constitutional difficulties facing other race-conscious affirmative selection proposals.

I trust that is not true. Ellis and Diamond are correct. Jurors are not meant to be representatives of constituencies. Forde-Mazrui's proposal is to select juries by quota. One could call this a procedural approach, but it is a bad one, designed to achieve an outcome goal.

240. Ellis and Diamond (2003) at 1056; preceding in-text quotation at 1053.

. . . AND ON

It is impossible for a book to be strictly "current." Nonetheless, a reader might wonder what is going on in this area in general—not just with some examples—in later years. Before returning to juries, here is evidence that the outcome orientation that has plagued the Supreme Court is alive and well in the public at large. Catherine Seipp wrote an end-of-year 2004 article on notable (to her) events concerning the media, one per month. This is May:

> I go to a Media Bistro party here in L.A. and get into a conversation about blogs with some guy from KPFK, the lefty Pacifica Radio station. A recent Blogads survey indicates that 80 percent of blog readers are men. "More women should write blogs!" the KPFK guy exclaims. "Then more women would read them."
>
> "Should we make women read blogs even if they don't want to?" I asked. "Should we limit the amount of male blog readers . . . or prevent more men from starting blogs, since there are already so many?"
>
> "Well . . . yes."[241]

Louisiana

Lip service is paid to having a race-blind process, but judges see through and write through that façade. They know, or at least they think, that they will be held to a race-conscious outcome standard. Judge Alarcon, who selected grand jurors, testified at the hearing in which they were contested.

> He was concerned that the African American population as well as males and females were represented on the grand jury. He expressly denied engaging in any type of scientific method of selection. He testified that he "basically looked for a balance on the grand jury that was consistent with the Orleans Parish demographics."[242]

But that is OK, says the Louisiana appeals court:

> Although Judge Alarcon candidly acknowledged that he was concerned about race and gender and attempted to achieve a balance on this grand jury, that type of concern is not discriminatory.

People looking over the judge's shoulder will be comparing the composition of the grand jury with that of the "community." Trying to get the former to look like the latter cannot be discrimination, if that is also the goal, reasons this court.

---

241. Catherine Seipp, "From the Left Coast," *National Review Online*, December 30, 2004 (http://www.nationalreview.com/seipp/seipp200412300854.asp).

242. *Fleming* (2003), both quotations at 121 (the first at *4, the second at *5). This state court, having learned nothing in thirty-seven years, cites *Brooks* (1966) for its rationale.

New York City

One might think, from press reports, that the Second Circuit got it exactly right in *Nelson* (2002). After a Jewish driver hit a black pedestrian, a mob formed, roaming the Brooklyn streets, looking for Jews. They found one, Yankel Rosenbaum. He identified Lemrick Nelson as having stabbed him, before he died of his wounds. In state court, with an exclusively non-Jewish jury, the perpetrators were found not guilty of murder. Now in federal court on the charge of impeding access to a public facility, based on "race," district-court judge Trager did what many have advocated, and what I excoriated above: He deliberately manipulated the jury composition. Following a trial that ended in a hung jury, Judge Trager stated that "the first jury did not represent the community." Said the Second Circuit:

> The [district] court relatedly and repeatedly expressed its desire to *empanel* a jury (and not merely *begin from a venire*) "that represents this community." [243]

More from the district court:

> I have an agenda here which I have made very clear from the very beginning, to end up with a jury that represents the community that will have moral validity.

When one juror reported ill, Judge Trager selected two alternates out of order, one black, one Jewish. He created the second opening *sua sponte*, dismissing a white juror whom neither side had challenged. To Judge Trager, the phrase "representative of the community" meant "that the jury should contain appropriate numbers of African Americans and Jews." [244] The jury pool had few Jews in it, relative to the "community" as Trager saw it on the streets. As if the system were responsible for that difference, Judge Trager tried to rectify it.

The appeals court could have and it seems would have struck down the jury verdict on this basis alone. But it didn't have to. The Jewish juror, number 108, had declared in *voir dire* that he was not sure that he could give the defendants a fair trial. He should have been excluded for cause.

> We conclude that the district court erred in declining to remove Juror 108 from the jury for actual bias, and that the defendants' acceptance of the district court's jury-packing scheme (which placed Juror 108 on the jury) did not constitute a valid waiver. [245]

---

243. Both in-text quotations from *Nelson* (2002) at 172, quoting from the trial transcript at 628, emphasis in the source; following indented quotation also at 172, from the trial transcript at 759.

244. *Nelson* (2002) at 199.

245. *Nelson* (2002) at 211. Judge Straub, in partial dissent, says the facts were overwhelming, they are guilty, at 218. Echoes of Friendly (1970). Following in-text quotations at 201 and 207.

Not that the Second Circuit failed to understand the fallacy of jury packing. They called the trial court's procedure "illegal." Why is defendants' waiver irrelevant? *Batson* (1986) forbade peremptory juror dismissals based on race. "What the district court could not allow the parties to do, it could not also do of its own motion even with the consent of the parties." Thus we can believe that deliberate manipulation of the jury to achieve representation of the "community" will not be tolerated by the Second Circuit; but it is not quite right to cite *Nelson* (2002) to that effect.

New Jersey

Let us listen to a state judge in Essex County, New Jersey, in perhaps 1990 or 1991:

> I don't mind telling you, ladies and gentlemen of the jury or the panel of the grand jury, I am trying to get a cross-section; and as you've probably noticed, I have asked two of the blacks who have indicated a willingness to serve to sit in the body of the courtroom. I am deliberately trying to get an even mix of people from background and races, and things like that. And if any of you think I am in any way being sneaky about it, please understand that I am not. I am telling you like it is, and that is the reason I have done what I have done.[246]

State law called for random selection of jurors, but judges deliberately formulated the jury on the basis of race, to achieve that magic "cross-section." Defendant Ramseur's jury was thus not an exception, but the rule.

> The random-selection procedure set forth in the New Jersey statute was routinely ignored by the assignment judges of Essex County at the time Ramseur's jury was chosen.[247]

After an *en banc* rehearing, the Third Circuit told the district court, seven to three, that it should not do that, that *Cassell* (1950), at the very least, forbade stopping the selection of minorities when "enough" had been seated. Forbade racial quotas on juries. On the other hand, this racial manipulation occurred at the grand-jury stage. So the question is, should a properly found conviction be overturned because it was based on a faulty indictment? In this case, the Third Circuit said no, let the conviction stand, and by the way, please don't form juries this way again.

Ramseur (1992) either influenced or provided a rationale for other courts to be equally cavalier. It is cited in *Wallace* (2003), one of the Michigan cases, and *Fleming* (2003), the Louisiana case above. Judge Alito, concurring in the *Ramseur* opinion, expresses hostility towards *Cassell* (1950), and suggests a rationale for deliberate manipulation of the jury's composition. He thinks that

---

246. *Ramseur* (1992). The trial judge is quoted by the majority at 1222.

247. *Ramseur* (1992) at 1223.

the use of cross-section grand juries seems likely to result in *more equal* treatment for potential defendants than the use of randomly selected grand juries.
The racial and ethnic composition of most randomly [selected] grand juries
does not mirror that of the community at large.[248]

There would be less variation, and a mean equal to the population proportion for each minority about which judges were conscious, if they just appointed jurors on that basis. There should be no question about the arithmetic: If we really want an outcome standard, it will take outcome-oriented procedures to achieve it. As in my play script above, deliberate outcome manipulation is complicated. But that is not my argument. It should be rejected because it violates equal protection by selecting jurors based on their race..

Thus I agree with Judge Cowen, who wrote the *Ramseur* dissent:

Ramseur is a very unsympathetic defendant, having murdered his girlfriend
in front of six witnesses, but the seriousness of his crime is irrelevant to the
resolution of his equal-protection claim.

The indictment should have been invalidated based on the way in which the grand jury was formed. I am sympathetic with the concept of a reviewing court's instructing lower courts to "cut it out," without imposing extreme burdens on the system. But this flaw was egregious. It is easily distinguishable from a clerical error, a failure of the system to quite come up to its own good rules. Ramseur would have been convicted in a retrial. The Third Circuit should have reversed.

Vermont

The Vermont Supreme Court easily came to my conclusion in 1986, on essentially the same grounds (with much less publicity) that the Second Circuit used in *Nelson* (2002).[249] Asked if he could impartially evaluate testimony of a doctor, whom he knew, "The prospective juror responded: 'I certainly could try to be impartial but I'm not saying that I could.'"[250] Yet the trial judge refused to excuse this juror for cause. Defendant used a peremptory challenge. Before the jury had been seated defendant had used all the peremptories he was permitted, so

he was in effect deprived of one peremptory challenge. . . . On appeal, the Vermont Supreme Court reversed the conviction and remanded for a new trial.
Such an error, said the court, is automatic reversible error.

---

248. *Ramseur* (1992) at 1243; following indented quotation from dissent at 1246.

249. *Doleszny* (1986). I learned of this case from Pizzy and Hoffman (2001), who also cite a case in which the Idaho Supreme Court found that a "curative" peremptory challenge created no error. Thus state courts disagree on this issue.

250. *Doleszny* (1986) at 622 (694). Following indented quotation from Pizzy and Hoffman (2001) at 1392.

Pennsylvania

The following item was on the Associated Press wire on June 12, 2003. I have not seen it in any newspaper.

> **Murder Trial Delayed for Lack of Black Jurors**
>
> A Pennsylvania judge's decision to let a murder defendant delay trial until African Americans make up at least 10 percent of the jury pool is spurring debate about how people of color are picked for juries and whether the judge's remedy is practical.
>
> Under state law, potential jurors are drawn at random from voter registration lists. Counties may use driver's license and telephone records. Citizens can also volunteer for jury duty.
>
> The defense attorney in the case argued that a five-month study by the Allegheny County Public Defender's Office found that fewer than 5 percent of the people who appear for jury duty are African American, although 12 percent of the county's population is African American, a disparity which the defense argues violates the defendant's Sixth Amendment right to an impartial jury.
>
> While some analysts say the ruling contradicts the ideal of colorblind justice, others believe Judge Lester Nauhaus' decision was needed to spur jury reforms.

Massachusetts

The magnificent district-court opinion in *Royal* (1998) was trivialized, though its outcome was affirmed, by the First Circuit in *Royal* (1999). Judge Keeton had said, in effect, "Sure, blacks do not appear on juries in the same proportion as they are listed in the census, but what has the jury-selection system done that is correctable error?" He denied the defendant even a *prima facie* case, for failing to specify a faulty procedure that was bringing about this outcome. To Judge Keeton, the outcome was a flag, not the basis of a determination. Judge Keeton saw it correctly.

What did the First Circuit do with it?

> In the end, any dispute over the facts is essentially moot. This case turns on the choice of statistical methodology to determine whether there is under-representation of black persons.[251]

Procedure be damned. Just measure the outcome.

---

251. *Royal* (1999) at 5.

Although, under First Circuit standards, the disparity facing her does not call for action, Judge Gertner, unswayed by Judge Keeton's logic, doesn't like what she sees. She has ordered resampling—sending additional letters—by Zip code.[252] Each Zip code will be sent the same number of additional letters as they had letters returned undelivered. Thus the higher the proportion of N in a Zip code, the greater will the chance be of an E individual being selected for jury service. That E individual's chances are affected not by his characteristics, but by those of the people he lives near.

Judge Gertner sees only the outcome, and is determined to change it. She embraces the homogeneity of Zip codes, that the person who ultimately does respond will "look like" those who did not. That her resampling procedure creates differential probabilities of jury service—higher for E individuals in high-N Zip codes—is not even discussed. Outcome-oriented judges will do what they can to get the outcome they think is "right," even though from the viewpoint of procedural fairness, that outcome will always be wrong.

Connecticut

The best articulation of a way to place the thread of my procedural concept into the needle eye of judicial-think was made in *Purdy* (1996), a federal case in Connecticut. Although the United States Attorney's office in Hartford is a long-time client of mine, I had nothing to do with this case. Apparently no expert was involved on either side. Judge Arterton explains:

> Here, the government urges the court to adopt a measure of community population which is based not on the entire voting age population, but the qualified voting-age population. That is, the government requests that the court compare the proportion of Blacks and Hispanics in the relevant jury pool with the proportion of Blacks and Hispanics in that segment of the voting-age population which meets the various qualifications for jury service, including the English fluency requirement. The advantage to measuring community population in this fashion, according to the government, is that it enables the court to factor out of its measure of under-representation the impact of factors which do not implicate constitutional or statutory guarantees.[253]

The court notes that, however reasonable this standard is, it cannot be measured. One appears to have been offered:

> [T]he measure relies upon speculative estimates regarding the proportion and makeup of the population which satisfies the qualifications for jury service.

Had I been consulted I would have suggested not providing a measure, for this very reason. I would have suggested using an expert to provide a record for the court explaining why sta-

---

252. *Green* (2005).

253. *Purdy* (1996) at 1100; following indented quotation also at 1100.

tistical analysis of outcomes cannot answer the procedural question being asked. Reluctant as Judge Arterton was to deviate from precedent,[254] he seems to have been concerned with procedure, finding no evidence of the "systematic exclusion" called for in *Duren*'s third prong. Some day a more courageous judge will accept the procedural argument as given, and let the defendant argue in a higher venue that precedent should trump common sense.

The Supreme Court

Disturbingly, the Supreme Court, mired where the First Circuit seems to be, has not achieved the jury-composition clarity of the Second Circuit or Vermont. In *Martinez* (2000), Justice Ginsburg, writing for the Court, decried collateral litigation. This looks more like the Vermont case than like the New York case. Defendant had used a peremptory juror dismissal when the trial judge failed to dismiss a biased juror for cause, and had run out of peremptory challenges before the end of juror *voir dire*. Because the biased juror did not get on the jury, the issue became whether a peremptory substituting for a "for-cause" juror dismissal deprived the defendant of some constitutional right. The majority opinion said no, implying that since seating a biased juror is clearly out of bounds, defendant could perhaps *not* use his peremptory when a biased juror is seated, and challenge the outcome later. Justice Scalia would not approve that tactic. Writing in dissent, he argued that defendant cannot appeal from a circumstance he could have prevented. The Second Circuit thinks he can.

The lack of clarity in judicial thinking on this topic is understandable, given the outcome-oriented view the Court established early, and then affirmed with faulty statistical analysis in *Castaneda* (1977). The literature asking whether innocence matters, whether court efficiency demands that procedural flaws be tolerated, is similarly, mistakenly, outcome-oriented. This confusion continues to plague Supreme Court opinions.

Consider two death-penalty cases decided in the summer of 2002. *Ring* (2002) followed the procedural logic of *Apprendi* (2000) in limiting the penalty imposed on a defendant to the maximum allowable under the jury's verdict. Ring's jury had not found him guilty of premeditated murder. He had been sentenced to death by the judge following a post-trial hearing on aggravating factors, following Arizona procedure that had been reviewed and found acceptable in *Walton* (1990). But the Court found that *Apprendi*'s reasoning

> is irreconcilable with *Walton*'s holding in this regard, and today we overrule *Walton* in relevant part. Capital defendants, no less than non-capital defendants, we conclude, are entitled to a jury determination of any fact on which the legislature conditions an increase in their maximum punishment.[255]

---

254. *Purdy* (1996). "[N]either the Second Circuit nor any Court in this district has utilized the measure which the Government proposes . . ." at 1100; "Bound by Second Circuit precedent . . ." at 1102.

255. *Ring* (2002) at 2432. Justice Ginsburg, writing for the Court in *Ring*, reminds us that Justice Kennedy

And so the earlier decision was unceremoniously scrapped.

Ring is not about the death penalty. It is about who gets to determine the facts. It is a strikingly good decision. It follows the principle I enunciated, in response to Judge Friendly's 1980 question, that guilt is not at issue. Only procedure is.[256] Ring was clearly guilty not only of an armed robbery in which a man had been killed, but of planning the robbery (premeditation) and of the actual killing. The Arizona judge's reasoning for imposing the death penalty was faultless, but his authority was lacking. Only a jury, says the Court in *Ring*, can determine facts that lead to the defendant's penalty.

Justice Scalia, concurring in *Ring*, most clearly sees the procedural element that I am emphasizing:

> What today's decision says is that the jury must find the existence of the fact that an aggravating factor existed. Those States that leave the ultimate life-or-death decision to the judge may continue to do so—by requiring a prior jury finding of aggravating factor in the sentencing phase or, more simply, by placing the aggravating-factor determination (where it logically belongs anyway) in the guilt phase.[257]

Four days before releasing *Ring*, the Supreme Court determined an outcome in *Atkins* (2002). The Court would say that it determined the criterion for an outcome—that mentally retarded people could not receive a death penalty. That criterion is meaningless in *Atkins*, where a jury heard the defendant's attorney describe his client's mental abilities, and still determined that he should receive the death penalty. That is, the trial outcome in *Atkins* followed the rules of *Ring*, but was nonetheless reversed. Justice Scalia complained, in dissent:

> Seldom has an opinion of this Court rested so obviously upon nothing but the personal views of its members.[258]

But jury decisions rest upon the personal view of *their* members. The question, as Scalia's and Chief Justice Rehnquist's dissents both emphasize, is *how* the judicial system

---

had correctly observed (in dissent) a discordance between the decision in *Jones* (1999) and *Walton* (1990). If the Court was going to limit sentences depending on the jury's finding, why did it not do so in *Walton*, Kennedy asks. *Apprendi* came hard on the heels of *Jones*, making the decision in *Ring* inevitable.

256. Justice O'Connor, in dissent in *Ring* (2002), notes the number of appeals of sentence following *Apprendi* (2000), and predicts a deluge to follow. Similarly, in *Blakely* (2004), which supported and extended *Ring*'s conclusion that facts used in sentencing must be found by juries, O'Connor warns of the "far-reaching" as well as "disturbing" consequences. She envisions challenges to federal sentencing guidelines, which followed immediately. See *Booker* (2004), in which the Seventh Circuit declared those guidelines unconstitutional; *Hammoud* (2004), in which the Fourth Circuit found exactly the opposite; and *Penaranda* (2004), in which the Second Circuit certified the question to the Supreme Court. She may be factually correct, but since when does good procedure give way when following it is burdensome? Is that really what being "pragmatic" means?

257. Scalia concurrence in *Ring* (2002) at 2445.

258. Scalia dissent in *Atkins* (2002) at 338.

should take the measure of public standards. Strange stuff from "originalists," opponents of the "living Constitution" concept.

As *Atkins* provides a safe haven from the death penalty for murderers, Christopher Hitchens foresees

> an arena where the unscrupulous lawyer will appear for the shifty, remorse-free, lowbrow killer, and the charlatan tester will appear as an expert for the state. Or the other way around.[259]

He predicts another standardless battle of the experts. Surely presentation of expert opinions requires standards—the derivation of which is the concern of Chapter 10. But let's not confuse standards for assessing experts with the usefulness of experts in the first place. As difficult as it may be to assess mental deficiency, surely the majority in *Atkins* was correct: Executing the mentally retarded is cruel, and violates the Eighth Amendment. Until all capital punishment is described that way, the jury should be empowered to draw its conclusion about the defendant's mental capacity, advised by true experts. Why the Court thought the *Atkins* jury did not do that is the mystery in this case.

EVALUATING PROCEDURE, NOT OUTCOME

I am arguing in this chapter for the simplest of propositions: that jury-selection law is about procedure. Procedure can be judged on its own merits.[260] There are those who think that the rule of procedure is malicious. A character in Daniel Koshland's theater-script editorial in *Science* sarcastically says, "Truth has its place, but only if due process and judicial precedent are on its side."[261] His derision comes from thinking that legal procedures obfuscate the truth. In jury selection, there is no known truth—we do not know what the relevant "community," which is supposed to be mirrored on juries, looks like. We have only procedure to guide us.

In drawing jurors in Georgia, Justice Frankfurter informs us that "the aperture in the box was sufficiently wide to make open to view the color of the slips."[262] Absent an outcome finding—too few blacks on juries—the Georgia system was not declared unconstitutional. Its challengers had to "prove" that race was used in decisions, jurisdiction by jurisdiction. The other direction would have been more fruitful: The system was procedurally corrupt. It should have been invalidated for allowing race to be a factor, if only for all future trials.

Courts rightly ask whether a charging party has an interest, whether he (or it) has

---

259. Christopher Hitchens, "Tinkering With the Death Machine," 275 *The Nation* 4:9, July 22/29, 2002.

260. Noting the difficulty lawyers have with science: "The scientist's emphasis on progress is replaced by the lawyer's emphasis on process." Goldberg (1987) at 1345. Would that it were so.

261. Koshland (1994).

262. *Avery* (1953) at 564.

suffered harm. For example, only harmed parties can sue for antitrust damages; without a claim for damages, the judicial system is not interested.[263] Application of this principle to jury composition has led to such embarrassing positions as that expressed by Justices Scalia and Rehnquist, years after this concept was rebuffed in *Peters* (1972), referring to *Strauder* (1879):

> The statute did not exclude members of *his* race, and thus did not deprive *him* of the equal protection of the laws.[264]

When the subject is the action of the state, the organization of its judicial system, *everyone* is harmed if it is not fair. To this extent, the majority got it right, rejecting Scalia and Rehnquist's assertion that only black defendants suffer when the jury is stripped of blacks:

> The discriminatory use of peremptory challenges by the prosecution causes a criminal defendant cognizable injury, and the defendant has a concrete interest in challenging the practice.

This position hardly goes far enough. The process is not impartial if it is subjective, regardless whether we can tell, in a particular circumstance, that the subjectivity has been used to select on an illegitimate basis.[265] In Louisiana:

> Obviously the judges have broad discretion in selecting from the list provided by the Commission. Several of them interview a substantial number of prospective jurors before making their choice.[266]

Where the prospective jurors were not interviewed, they were assessed by "personal knowledge or reputation in the community." Neither the jury challenger nor the Court found, in this procedure, sufficient reason to declare the system unconstitutional. They had to find district by district, as in Georgia, that this discretion had been used to cause "harm" to the defendant, by excluding members of his race.

Of a Missouri defendant, the Eighth Circuit wrote:

> O'Neal did not demonstrate that the grand jury, consisting of seven men and five women, ten whites and two blacks, excluded any distinctive group *to which he belonged* or failed to draw from the townships of Butler County in proportion to their size, as then required by state law.[267]

---

263. See *Brick* (1977) or *Utilicorp* (1990), for example.

264. *Powers* (1991) dissent by Scalia, joined by Rehnquist, at 417. *Powers* allowed the complaint against racially biased peremptories—which in *Batson* (1986) had been made by a black man—to be raised by anyone. The following quotation is from the majority opinion at 411.

265. R. Thompson (1991) at 770:
> Jury-selection methods which seek a decision making biased in favor of one side of the case are [an] . . . effort to secure a result divorced from impartial evaluation of information.

266. *Eubanks* (1958) at 586; following in-text quotation also at 586.

267. *O'Neal* (1995) at 662, emphasis added; following in-text quotation also at 662.

The sheriff had used "maps, phone books, and personal references to construct the jury list." The system was procedurally corrupt, but survived on its numbers. Personal references! The jury-selection system should have been ruled unconstitutional on its face. For appellate judges not to understand, in 1995, that the defendant's race and gender are irrelevant to his claim, is disgraceful.

Name cards in Jefferson County, Texas, identified each prospective juror by race ("c" or "w") and gender; but without statistical evidence that this information was used to oversample the "w" cards, the Fifth Circuit refused to allow the jury composition to become a federal issue.[268]

The replacement procedures in Georgia were no improvement:

> In DeKalb County, Georgia, jury lists are divided into thirty-six demographic groups before a computer algorithm generates a venire designed to reflect a proportional representation of these groups.[269]

Allowing establishment elites to pass judgment on the character of citizens is bad process, whatever one thinks of the juries that result. Strait-jacketing a system to achieve racial proportionality misses the point. The race of the last juror is determined by formula. That juror has been selected by his race. The system fails the uniform-random-selection test.

A simple approach, in principle like mine, was recommended by the dissenting justices in *Fay* (1947):

> The Court demonstrates rather convincingly that it is difficult to prove that the particular petitioners were prejudiced by the discrimination practiced in this case. Yet that should not excuse the failure to comply with the constitutional standard of jury selection.[270]

Justice Douglas did not see the need to assert that jury outcomes would differ with the inclusion of females:

> The truth is that the two sexes are not fungible; a community made up exclusively of one is different from a community composed of both; the subtle interplay of influence one on the other is among the imponderables. To insulate the courtroom from either may not in a given case make an iota of difference. Yet a flavor, a distinct quality is lost if either sex is excluded.[271]

---

268. See *Singleton* (1974).

269. Saunders (1997) at 65. Saunders does not say proportional to what, but I presume to census counts. This is an appalling outcome solution to a non-problem. It is selection of jurors by race.

270. *Fay* (1947) at 300, dissent by Murphy, joined by Black, Douglas, and Rutledge.

271. *Ballard* (1946) at 193.

Constitutionality rides on "flavor," on a "distinct quality"? Of course not. It rides on uni-form-random sampling from a source list of participants—of "the community," not the population.

I have not avoided the problem of practicality. I am not seeking immediate perfection here. A reasonable compromise is to see random selection, judged by its procedures, as the goal. In a specific case, where the procedures are not quite right, the solution is not nec-essarily to throw it out (i.e., disallow all past grand and petit juries). Sometimes the system can operate for now, and be corrected for the future. Unfortunately, the prospect of hav-ing the court thank the defendant for pointing out a real error, while not granting him relief, will deter some litigation that might otherwise bring imperfections to light. None-theless, as an expert, I do not want my clients, on either side, thinking that if I find the slightest non-randomness in a jury-selection system, the court will be required to dissolve it.[272] My goal is to move the basis of judgments from arbitrary and contradictory outcome measures to procedural fairness. We can accomplish that without closing down reasonably good systems—as long as we also set out to improve them.

The Fifth Circuit expressed the goal almost brilliantly:

> We conclude that a jury list drawn objectively, mechanically, and at random from the entire voting list of a county is entitled to the presumption that it is drawn from a source which is a fairly representative cross-section of the inhabitants of that jurisdiction.[273]

Once one deviates from random selection of jurors from among those presumptively eligible, trouble ensues. Having procedural standards frees the courts from the pretense of a mathematically precise representation of a "community" we cannot measure. As Jus-tice Murphy succinctly stated it in 1946:

> The undisputed evidence in this case demonstrates a failure to abide by the proper rules and principles of jury selection.[274]

When that happens so that selection is "unfair," the jury is invalid. A procedural assessment, allowing a little room for harmless error, is what the experts should have been suggesting, and what the courts should provide.

---

272. This question, or dilemma, has been in the air for a long time. Consider, for example, this language from the dissent by Justices Burger, Blackmun, and Rehnquist in *Peters* (1972) at 507, referring to an unconstitutionally formed grand jury:

> The real issue is whether such illegality necessarily voids a criminal conviction, absent any demonstration of prejudice, or basis for presuming prejudice, to the accused.

273. *Thompson* (1974) at 833. The Fifth Circuit itself recognized the intelligence of this phrasing, quot-ing it in *Barksdale* (1980) at 263. If only it had used the word "community"! "Inhabitants," of course, is wrong.

274. *Theil* (1946) at 222.

6

Attorneys

It is a standing joke among statistical experts that lawyers went to law school because they lacked skill with numbers. When I tell this to lawyers they invariably, seriously, agree.

> Judges and lawyers usually react to science with all the enthusiasm of a child about to get a tetanus shot. They know it's painful and believe it's necessary, but haven't the foggiest idea how or why it works.

> The average lawyer is not merely ignorant of science, he or she has an affirmative aversion to it. . . . Indeed, nothing puts a class of law students to sleep faster than putting numbers on the chalkboard.[1]

Yet when alone or, worse, in small groups, lawyers say to themselves, "Hey, it's just numbers, we can do that." Noting that a 1972 firefighter examination

> contained problems involving cubed roots, square roots, and the square root of fractions which neither the Court, the Court's staff, nor learned counsel were able to perform,[2]

Judge Teitelbaum declared it not job-related. How could firefighters be asked to perform calculations beyond the comprehension of attorneys and judges? And so, incautious about their inability to swim, attorneys leap unaided into numerical waters. I described some of the consequences of their going it alone in Chapters 2 and 3.

---

1. First quotation from B. Black et al. (1994) at 716; second from Faigman (2000) preface at xi. Both quotations are sufficiently general ("usually" and "average"), as is my discussion, that I trust no one will think that exceptions (Ian Ayres, with an economics Ph.D.; Laurence Tribe, a college mathematics major; or Eugene Volokh, who received a B.S. in mathematics and computer science at age fifteen, for examples) disprove the rule.

2. *Glickman* (1974) at 733, 7 FEP Cases at 605. I do not mean to imply that the court's decision was frivolous or incorrect. I just found this reference to the bafflement of attorneys irresistible.

Some attorneys intend to call an expert later. If they do, it is even later than that.[3] The late-arriving expert tries to help, but his work almost always contains serious errors traceable to this process. Experts sign on to these cases sometimes not knowing the damage that has been done to them, sometimes not knowing the damage they are doing, sometimes bearing it in the struggle for survival.

In its title this chapter is about attorneys, both the ones who are my clients and those who cross-examine me.

> When it comes to lawyer-bashing, there is not much new under the sun. Hostility toward lawyers is perennial.[4]

At least part of this hostility is explained in the evolution of the expert, which I described in Chapter 1. As Jack Weinstein summarizes, initially

> expert witnesses were considered to be assistants of the court. By the seventeenth century, experts began to be treated as witnesses.[5]

After at first being called to assist the judge, *by* the judge, experts were called by attorneys, to assist the parties. I am interested in the corrupting influence of attorneys on experts, and therefore on the judicial process.[6] This presentation will lead to proposals, which I make in Chapter 10, for procedures more conducive to allowing expertise to emanate from experts. Here and in Chapter 8 I warn experts: Fend for yourselves. Don't count on your client.

Attorneys have a role to play, and I do not demean that role or them for playing it. I mean only to point out that it is not what experts or the public might like it to be.

> It is the business of lawyers to tolerate and master artifice. After all, technical difficulty is the sole social excuse for the lawyer's monopoly, his stranglehold on court work, on the drafting of documents, on the counseling of clients.[7]

---

3. For example, attorneys at the St. Louis Equal Housing Opportunity Commission were involved in testing whether real estate agents "steered" parties to different homes based on their race. Yet their input consisted largely of being sure materials used in the test were maintained, not that they constituted a credible case. In *EHOC* (2001) at 1084 we learn the consequence:

> There simply was no standardized protocol utilized in the design and execution of the EHOC tests. The Court is not dismissing the fact that tester evidence is probably the best means by which to demonstrate fair housing violations. However, the production of such evidence must be done under some set of standards which assure a reasonable level of validity and reliability.

4. Galanter (1994) at 634.

5. Weinstein (1986) at 474.

6. After defining categories of experts, Saks (1987), at 44, wonders if one kind of expert is systematically better than another. "Unfortunately, each category of experts is vulnerable to the possibly distorting influence of lawyers."

7. Friedman (1985) at 24. On this line, see my discussion of law-school education in Chapter 9.

This artifice is not practiced only at the expense of the opposing party. Experts are selected, instructed, and often manipulated by their attorney clients.[8] Judges beware. You are correct to mistrust even honest experts.

INFORMATION

More important than not trusting what his client tells him, the expert should at least wonder what his client does *not* tell him. Consider this advice to attorneys:

> It is important to remember, however, that virtually everything that has been said to the consulting expert from the beginning of her involvement in the case will become discoverable once she is designated as a testifying expert. Thus, any unfavorable tests or laboratory results from tests conducted by consulting experts should not be disclosed to testifying experts unless you are willing to risk discovery.[9]

Lawyers are told to keep information from their expert, and that is what they do. Often the expert cannot be expected to have framed the right question in the light of misinformation or non-information. In a case discussed in Chapter 1, the Supreme Court wondered why one expert had not considered alternative explanations for the basis of redistricting—that political party, not race, may have determined where lines were drawn:

> Dr. Weber said, for example, that he had developed these conclusions while under the erroneous impression that the legislature's computer-based districting program provided information about racial, but not political, balance.[10]

Ultimately, the failure to know what was in the computer program used to draw district lines is that of the expert. Ultimately, a "scientific" investigation of a phenomenon that does not consider alternative explanations is not scientific at all. But also, clearly, the challengers, who based their case on race, did not inform Weber about alternative theories of what factor was in play, or what data were available to the persons who drew the district lines.

Nicholas Hengartner, Al Gore's expert in *Bush* (2000), explained the rationale for some of his vote projections. He needed to know which contests appeared on the right side, which

---

8. See the subsection "Marionettes" in Chapter 8, and cases cited therein, for examples of client manipulation of experts and their data.

9. Meyers and Albers (1991) at 499. This particular advice is being provided within the context of the construction industry, but it is typical, and is followed. George Harris (2000) at 37 tells us:

> The common practice is to engage an expert as a "consulting" expert only and not to identify the expert as a "testifying" expert until such time as it is clear that the expert will offer testimony helpful to the party's case.

10. *Hunt* (2001) at 249.

on the left side of the ballot.[11] On cross-examination it became apparent that he had not seen the actual ballot. He had been informed by his client—not surprisingly, incorrectly.

Litigation is designed by and for attorneys. So, for example, when an attorney is involved with counseling a plaintiff or defendant, person or firm, the communication is "privileged." The other side may not ascertain what information passed from client to attorney, or what advice passed from attorney to client. The 1993 revision of Rule 26 (a) (2) (B) of the Federal Rules of Civil Procedure instructs the testifying expert to reveal, in a report, all data and information he "considered." Earlier versions called for disclosure only of information "relied upon." The attorney's job has become to protect his expert from "considering" the wrong things.

If the expert gains access to information the party does not want made public, the expert is prevented from testifying.[12] The attorney is under no such constraint to tell all. This privilege, any lawyer will say, is his client's.

> The reason why Courts, both of law and equity, refuse the production of confidential communications is, not for the advantage of the attorney, but the privilege of the client.[13]

So the attorney may discuss the case openly with his client, but must be circumspect discussing the case with an expert. It seems a logical difference to attorneys, but when dealing with an expert whose job is to "explain" events, it is pernicious. The information the expert needs to form his opinion may be denied to him because it loses any privilege it had once the expert sees it.[14]

This is settled law, but an incorrect interpretation of mathematical interaction. If the privilege is the client's, why not have the client present when the attorney talks to the expert? Because the presence of the expert nullifies the client's privilege. Thus, though any attorney will stress that the privilege is the client's, not his, the fact is that the privilege is the client's in relationship to the attorney alone, and so it is as much the attorney's.[15]

---

11. *Bush* (2001). This testimony was broadcast live on C-SPAN.

12. See, for example, *Construction* (2002), particularly at 53:
> If chronology was determinative, the opportunity for parties to shield disclosure of otherwise discoverable documents considered by their experts simply by hiring those individuals first as consultants and later as experts would be too great.

13. *Knight* (1836) at 40 (160 English Reports at 303). Morgan and Maguire (1937), at 910, refer to the lawyer-client privilege as "the privilege of suppressing truth."

14. The investigative expert, looking for an explanation of events, is more credible the more he knows the details of the case. The expert who merely performs a technical task, such as identification experts, "forensic scientists" in handwriting, DNA, or fingerprint analysis, should be treated in exactly the opposite manner. Their work is less credible the more they know outside their technical area.

15. I explain this conclusion mathematically in Chapter 10. Attorneys use the privilege to protect themselves as much as their clients. For example, speaking of Kidde's attorney Charles Oslakovic, "Thus, he

On two issues the expert will have ultimate responsibility: data and method. Yet an analysis depends on many other assumptions, many of them legal. Ultimately, the important questions are about law and fact. Indeed, as I have been saying since Chapter 2, only fact that is relevant under the law is fact *in* the law. My position on the expert and law stands in stark contrast with what any attorney would advise: As statistical fact depends critically on being legally relevant fact, the expert must understand the law. He cannot assume that the attorney who engages him understands the law he needs to know. My position places an additional burden on the expert, but it follows from this simple proposition: Statistical facts—data, method, model, conclusion—are the expert's to gather, devise, and explain. The rare expert who is more concerned with the quality of his work than with the quantity of his bank account needs to be prepared to reject his client's view of any of these elements.

Yet I think the sincere attorney's version of fact must be respected. Several times my client's opposition to my analysis, his conviction that I had the facts wrong, has led me to rethink and re-do my work. Law and fact both interact with data and method. Expert and client should be interacting in both areas, also. As much of earlier chapters has been about method, the emphasis in this chapter is on data. As much in the earlier chapters has been technical, this chapter is more conceptual. It is less about law, more about people who do law.

FINDING THE EXPERT

One might think that finding the "right" expert is a difficult task, one that lawyers and law firms take seriously, as a service to their clients. This should be true whatever "right" means to an attorney, in a particular case. To me, "right" should mean competent in his field, honest, innovative, understanding not only the relevant analytic tools but the relevant law; in short, truly expert. No book of helpful hints for attorneys defines "right" that way, and very few attorneys think these are the elements of the "right" expert.

Few firms put much effort into defining what Mr. or Ms. Right would be like, or into looking for him or her. It's simpler than that. The purpose of an expert is to present a case for the client in a particular field. The attorney has given up understanding what the expert does, except to presume that it will support him. Therefore that support, and of course having expert-like characteristics (university degrees, fluid speech, assuredness, availability), become the only criteria for retention.[16] Few attorneys seek excellence. All seek compliance.

---

marked several of the e-mails with 'attorney-client privilege' so no one could get to them." *X-It* (2002) at 547. Oslakovic was at the same time posing as a neutral party to X-It products, Inc.

16. Danner and Varn (2002), at 66, instruct:

It is absolutely essential that an expert who is expected to testify at the trial appear honest, credible, and attractive as a witness.

The scientific community is large and heterogeneous, and a Ph.D. can be found to swear to almost any "expert" proposition, no matter how false or foolish.

The lawyers invite potential witnesses to their offices for interviews and pepper them with questions, but the question they care most about is, "Can you prove my case?"

Most often witnesses are not chosen for their knowledge but for their ability to persuade.

[T]he too-frequent surfacing of the ubiquitous journeyman expert who will fashion his credentials as well as his conclusions "to fit the crime" is lamentably predictive of a superficial conclusion.[17]

There are expert-finding services. They may charge those on both sides of this transaction, the expert to appear in a listing in a book or web site, the attorney to obtain the listing.[18] Having no way to evaluate either party, the service becomes like a list of local eateries in a hotel lobby. There might be good restaurants on such a list, but they are there because they paid to be, not because they were evaluated to be.

Some membership organizations gather lists as a service to their members. For example, Gerry Spence tells us:

The Defense Institute, an organization of lawyers who defend personal-injury cases for the insurance industry, has a computer bank listing willing witnesses in every conceivable field of expertise.[19]

Douglas Danner and Larry Varn suggest contacting professional organizations and local universities. The American Statistical Association does not appear in their listing, which covers over twenty-one pages of association names and addresses. Richard Posner suggests that professional associations should maintain lists of experts who testify, some-

---

17. First quotation, Huber (1985) at 333; second quotation, Moss (2003) at 52; third quotation, Spence (1989) at 270; fourth quotation, Donaher et al. (1974) at 1311. Of medical experts, Sink (1956), at 197, writes:

Of all the many experts available [the litigant] chooses the most favorable to him, not necessarily the one who most accurately represents informed medical opinion.

George Harris (2000), at 43, notes:

Parties unquestionably continue to "shop" for experts favorable to their case. Indeed, under our present system counsel who failed to do sufficient shopping would be negligent in her duties to her client.

18. For example, SEAK, in Falmouth, Massachusetts, publishes medical and non-medical directories of experts. The 2004 non-medical edition, they say, contains over sixteen hundred expert listings, and is "mailed to over forty thousand law firms nationwide." How many firms asked for or use this directory is not known. Jonathan D. Glater mentions this type of service in "More and More, Expert Witnesses Make The Difference," *New York Times*, August 19, 2005, at C7.

19. Spence (1989) at 272.

how monitoring what they say against what they do.[20] Such a list would have the subsidiary effect of advertising to attorneys who has what courtroom experience. It would have the appearance of objectivity. It is the worst idea I have ever seen from Posner.

Not all experts are members of all relevant professional associations. Most such associations are dominated by academics, many of whom, as the previous three chapters have demonstrated and Chapter 8 amplifies, are not fit to perform or evaluate litigation analyses. Surely they do not have the skill to evaluate their members, much less non-members; and what about those who object to the list's practices? People who rise in the ranks of professional associations have their own reasons to do so, unrelated to merit as a litigation expert. Inclusion would be based on credentials rather than abilities. Such a list might make it easy for an attorney to choose an expert, but less likely that he would choose appropriately for his client. The subject of an association-prepared list arises again in Chapter 10, with regard to how judges find their own experts. There should be no association-maintained expert lists.

As an example of a web site, www.Law.com lists eight experts in statistics, all of whom, I presume, have paid to have themselves included. Three such listings are shown in Figure 57.[21] Although I searched for "statistics," few of the eight listings and none of these three mentions it. There must be additional key words lurking in the background. Heler lists types of damage claims in detail, whereas Andersen covers damages with one word, emphasizing more their "wisdom," their presumed experience and knowledge. JurisSolutions comes complete with logo and advertising slogan, I presume at additional cost.

Becoming known to potential clients is difficult. Experts advertise in the *American Bar Association Journal*, and Findlaw, at www.Findlaw.com, which is part of Westgroup.[22] They advertise indirectly by writing articles for local legal newsletters, and directly by sending reprints of such articles to attorneys.[23] My approach was to produce seminars in employ-

---

20. See Danner and Varn (2002) and Posner (1999a). One of the secrets behind Posner's prolific output is his word-for-word repetition. The same suggestion is made in Posner (2001b) at 407. In Posner (1999b) he specifically nominates the American Economic Association. Michael Saks (1987) notes, however, at 45: "Professional associations are in business to insure their members' well-being more than to police them."

21. These listings were obtained on April 17, 2002.

22. Richey (1994) describes this process at 540. It is perhaps different now. Findlaw claims to be the premier web site for such purposes, having "over 56,000,000 page views and 3,300,000 unique visitors per month" (in December 2002). Findlaw charges $1,495 a year for a listing, but twice that to be among those who rotate at the top of a listing. I found forty-one listings under "statistics," again in December 2002.

23. For example, Elizabeth Becker and Charles Diamond co-authored "Assessing Class-wide Claims of Unfair Employment Conditions" in 28 *New York State Bar Association Labor and Employment Newsletter* 2 (Summer 2003). Becker then included that article in a mass mailing to attorneys (September 3, 2003), with the opening line: "I am writing to tell you about a highly favorable resolution for my client in a recent Title VII class-action matter."

Arthur Andersen LLP
Location of Expert: CA
Expert Areas: forensic accounting, business litigation, trial strategy, damages analysis, document analysis, assets appraisals/valuations, litigation technology, accounting, appraisals, economics, more. . . .
Expert States: CA

JurisSolutions, Inc.
Location of Expert: National
"Put Your Expert Needs in Our Expert Hands"
Expert Areas: cancer missed diagnosis, psycho-therapy, vehicles accident investigation & reconstruction, seat belt analysis, actuaries appraisals/valuations, insurance disability claims, long-term disability, automotive accident investigation & reconstruction, vehicles failure analysis, traffic accident analysis, more . . . .

Edward Heler, Ph.D., Consultant in Forensic Economics
Location of Expert: IN
Expert Areas: long term disability, loss of income, loss of productivity, lost wages, manpower, market research, medical devices/equipment appraisals/valuations, medical insurance, personal injury, racial discrimination, more . . . .
Expert States: All

FIGURE 57: Three Expert Listings from www.Law.com

ment discrimination, a burgeoning field for both attorneys and experts in the early 1980s. The seminars gave platforms to prominent attorneys, who did their own marketing, and to members of my staff. We purchased attorney lists from the American Bar Association, by their designated subject (such as "labor law"), and sent thousands of notices for each seminar to get perhaps twenty attendees. We produced seminars in places people would want to go, including Washington, D.C., where we were located.

The purpose of this exercise was to enter into the word-of-mouth forum. An attorney, being asked about experts, might say, "I don't have one, but I have heard of Econometric Research, Inc." Over time, even the referencing attorney might not remember that he had heard of Econometric Research only through a seminar announcement that crossed his desk every six months—the design always as in Figure 58, the color and detailed information different each mailing. It is hard to know how well the campaign worked. In response to, "How did you hear of us?" many clients gave vague replies, like, "Oh, you are well known." If so, it was because of our seminars, and especially because of our seminar announcements.

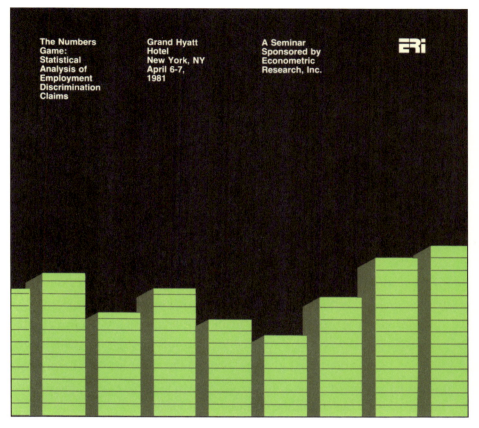

The Numbers Game: Statistical Analysis of Employment Discrimination Claims

Grand Hyatt Hotel New York, NY April 6-7, 1981

A Seminar Sponsored by Econometric Research, Inc.

FIGURE 58: The ERI Seminar Brochure

At the same time, I also participated in seminars produced by others. Whether an expert gets that exposure is partly the luck of the draw—whom he knows—and partly political. At one such seminar I was enraged by a presenter advocating the use of misleading graphics.[24] I took advantage of my later presentation to expose him. I was not invited back.

Attorneys continue to delve into local universities. Even though I think one almost never gets the best expert from such a source, for small cases—for which the search cost for a truly professional expert might be prohibitive—I cannot gainsay probing for eager, earnest assistance.

THE INITIAL PHONE CALL

I was asked to take a small case. As usual, it started with, "Time is short; trial begins in three weeks; can you tolerate that schedule?" Yes, I can work under pressure, but why? "We have

---

24. Apparently the presenter was unaware that some of the graphics that he advocated were similar to those criticized in Huff (1954). Mine is not the only opinion that his graphical ideas were poor.

a theory of mitigation for which we have begun gathering the data." That is, I was not invited to participate in deriving the theory that would control the calculation I was to make. I declined the invitation. I'm willing to listen to their theory, but not willing for them to be committed to it before my participation. And I don't want their data.

Defendant's attorney asked me to take a case in which plaintiff had indicated he might call an expert. I reviewed materials and suggested key concepts to look for in any further plaintiff papers. I suggested one direction in which the plaintiff had not yet gone which, in my experience, would create problems for defendants. If plaintiff goes in this direction, I indicated, think in terms of settlement before you spend more money on me. Armed with my advice, my client talked plaintiffs' attorney out of his proposed duel.

Similarly, in two hours of consulting with Queens County, New York, I outlined a response to defendant's motion containing what appeared to the Assistant District Attorney to be a strong (as well as mathematically correct) argument. He formulated a brief around my logic and defendant's motion was denied. In these and other cases, by quickly and wisely spending some money, my client saved much more.

David Baldus kindly recommended me to an attorney. I had time to work on the case, I had no conflicts, and my rate was acceptable. That was enough for the attorney; let's begin. "Hold on," I said, and started into my "prepare the client for who I am" speech:

> You cannot expect me a priori to support your side of the case. You have to hire me with the understanding that, to me, the judge is my ultimate client. I am looking for facts. If, when I find them, I think I can do you no good, I will recommend that you fire me. . . .

I was dis-engaged on the spot. Baldus never recommended me again.

An Assistant United States Attorney called to inquire if I was available to assess the representativeness of juries. Yes I was, I said. "We can win on the standard numbers" he said. I informed him, à la Chapter 5, that I would not do the standard numbers. As he wanted only to win the case, whereas I wanted to revolutionize the law, we agreed that we were a bad fit.

Too Late, Too Late [25]

I am happy to report that I am not alone in believing that the system should be about finding fact and applying law. That this is what many judges think, I have no doubt. But this chapter is about attorneys, whose decision-making processes do not reflect such goals. Richard Lempert provides this opinion:

---

25. Document Records tried to produce complete CD compilations of pre-World-War-II blues records, by artist. Sometimes a record came to light subsequent to their issuance of an artist's "complete" works. So they started a "Too Late, Too Late" series. They have more of an excuse for incomplete versions of "complete works" than most attorneys do for failing to call an expert when an expert is needed.

> I expect that before [an employment-discrimination] case reaches the point
> of a substantial investment in a careful statistical analysis (often at the expense
> of the plaintiff's attorney), it appears to someone that there is a high proba-
> bility that the defendant company has been discriminating.[26]

It is possible that some plaintiffs' attorneys think about fact this way, but not those I have known. One, whose Caribbean-based yacht was named "Class Action," considered only the probability of getting far enough that defendant would settle. What he wanted from his expert was a strong case, not necessarily a winning case, and only irrelevantly a correct case. He was willing to go to trial if that was what it took. He was always surprised when he got there, which was seldom; but when he went to trial, he acted as if he had wanted to be there all along. By demonstrating his willingness to cost the company a lot of money in court, he most often got them to spend somewhat less—but some of it on him— without a trial.[27]

Nor is the government as plaintiff any better towards its experts. In *O'Keefe* (1996), dis-cussed in Chapter 3, my task was limited to drawing a sample of individual work charges from which others in the government would build estimates of the mischarging. I never formed an opinion about whether there was the kind of cheating the government alleged, or if not, how the firm explained whistle blowers who admitted doing it.[28] The government expressed no interest in pursuing the fact question through statistical analysis, or even engaging an expert to analyze defendant's statistical presentation.

Judge Blair understood that the data he had been presented by plaintiff's expert, pur-porting to be of hires into a department since 1972, in fact were hire data only of those remaining in that department on a single date in 1978. How did the expert, Gittlesohn, make such an error?

> These exhibits were assembled by Ms. Jacqueline Hardy, a research assistant
> employed by plaintiffs' attorney.[29]

---

26. Lempert (1985) at 1114.

27. The attorney is Paul Sprenger. An example is *Beckman* (2000), in which Judge Frank pleaded, at 620, after certifying a class:

> All parties are aware that a trial of this action would be extended and complex. Further-more, a short review of the procedural history of this case reveals that massive expendi-tures of resources have been made and will likely continue to be made before the matter even reaches a trial. The Court believes that all parties would benefit by closely scruti-nizing their positions and seeking a settlement at this time.

Exactly where Sprenger wants to be. It was interesting to watch his Minneapolis partnership dissolve as he coolly bet the firm against Burlington Northern Railroad—and won. I thought the facts were on his side, but I also sensed that he did not care. The parties settled shortly after I testified.

28. For more on this case, *O'Keefe* (1996), see below and Chapter 8.

29. *Queen* (1978) at 264, 21 FEP Cases at 769; following indented quotation at 265, 21 FEP Cases at 770.

At the very least Gittlesohn should have examined the material provided to him with more of a skeptical eye. Better, he should not have taken the case nine days before trial with no ability to develop his own data. Even though the judge knew how the errors came about, they were (correctly) ascribed to the expert:

> In sum, this court finds Dr. Gittelsohn's testimony relating to initial assignments to be utterly without probative value for the reason that it was based on misleading and incomplete data.

Some government agencies contracted with Better Homes and Gardens to move employees and sell their old homes for them. There were complaints that the contractor was not performing well, which brought the Justice Department into the picture. And they brought me into it, but long after they had built a "data base." The data were in Symphony, a spreadsheet program of which most readers of this book have never heard, with good reason. They used the symbol "*" as data. However, "*" is the universal computer symbol for "anything." We would never have used it to represent information.

It is hard for someone who does not understand a subject to know when someone he hires does. It seems—but is not—so much more cost-effective, in any large setting, private or government, to utilize resources that are already being paid for: employees. My view is that although hiring an "expert" is often a mistake, using the law firm's labor to save the cost of hiring an expert is *always* a mistake. Hiring *an* expert is probably never a mistake, although hiring a *particular* expert may be.

UNDERSTANDING THE LAW

Plaintiffs' bar has lived for many years on the deserved good reputation it acquired in obtaining damages for some egregious corporate behavior, and in the "civil rights era." The central organizing body for that struggle was the NAACP Legal Defense Fund, which ultimately separated from the NAACP. We see their footprints in cases scattered throughout the country.[30]

---

30. For example, in Virginia, in the 1960s, local attorney Henry L. Marsh, III, was assisted by Jack Greenberg and Leroy D. Clark of New York, New York, in an attempt to break down barriers to job transfer within Philip Morris. See *Quarles* (1968). Judging from the number of references to Quarles, it was either a very influential district-court opinion or a clear expression of principles later courts wanted to follow. Greenberg also authored the appeals briefs in *Griggs* (1970) and *Griggs* (1971). He is listed as appearing in many cases. See *Chambers* (1966), with Derrick A. Bell, or *Montgomery* (1969) or *Cypress* (1967), both with James M. Nabrit, III. *Chambers* established that public-school faculty could not be hired in proportion to race of pupils. *Montgomery* allowed school-faculty allocation by race, once, as a remedy, to achieve desegregation *now*. *Cypress* reversed the district court's failure to require the hospital to admit black doctors to staff privileges.

Most experts get their entrée into litigation through plaintiffs. Kenneth Clark's testimony in *Brown* (1954) is a notable example of brilliant civil-rights lawyering, bringing relevant expertise to the attention of the Court. Marian Wright Edelman had been a plaintiffs' civil rights attorney before she started building institutions. One, where we met, was the Center for Law and Education at Harvard University. She was a delight to work for, as long as my ideas sounded like hers. I learned to be silent when I thought she was wrong about something. I think that is common to the early civil-rights attorneys: First, in the civil-rights era, they generally *were* right. They certainly thought so, and were not especially tolerant of other views. Second, they were fighting for the good guys against the bad guys. Even the descendants of the bad guys agree about that today. Third, they were steeped in the law. The only reasonable position for a young statistical expert to take in those days, working for one of them, was that all legal questions were the attorney's to answer, all strategy decisions the attorney's to make.

That I no longer hold that view is due as much to changes in who lawyers are as to who I am. As I will argue in more detail in Chapter 8, the truly expert "expert" had better know a lot about law. First, where the early civil-rights attorneys were pushing the edges of the law, attorneys today generally do not know where that edge is. Few of those who do try to push at it. Second, the expert has to talk to a judge. He needs to know how the judge sees things, right or wrong, to communicate with him. Third, the law frames all aspects of the expert's work, from data gathering to analysis to presentation. The following case is an example where an unknowledgeable attorney and a not-very-expert "expert" conspired to lose when the law and the facts were on their side.

Competitive Promotions in *Koger* (1994)

Koger v. Reno was a class-action case in which older GS-11 U.S. Marshals complained, under the Age Discrimination in Employment Act, that they were under-selected for promotion to GS-12 positions. To be promoted, a marshal had to apply for a specific opening. Applications contained information from which applicants were scored. The three highest-scoring applicants (or more if the announcement contained more than one position, or if there were ties for third place) then were forwarded to the selecting official, who selected among them. This two-stage process, "certification" through an application-scoring system followed by "selection" from only those certified, is the most common method of competitive hiring and promotion within the federal government. I use the word "competitive" as I did in Chapter 2, to mean that there was a fixed number of openings to which applicants applied in response to specific vacancy announcements.

The primary reason the older marshals were under-selected, plaintiffs claimed, was the Service's reliance on a physical "fitness" test, the primary component of which was a mile-

and-a-half run (the "run test"). A secondary complaint was that education had lower weight the further in the past it was obtained.

Plaintiffs asked the Marshals Service for data indicating who applied for each vacancy announcement, their scores, and the outcomes of the process. Copies of all relevant paper were provided in boxes of vacancy announcements. Each announcement packet contained the announcement itself, scoring sheets, a certification list (indicating who among those certified was finally selected), and applications. Plaintiffs' expert Mary Gray key-entered the data herself.

Unforgivably, but typically, I was engaged by the defendant after it had delivered data to plaintiffs. The Service had made only one copy of vacancy-announcement folders, which they gave to plaintiffs. They did not retain even a log of those materials. The source boxes continued to be used (announcements pulled, results updated, etc.) subsequent to the data delivery. Thus I did not have information about the same vacancy announcements that plaintiffs had, nor necessarily the same information even when I had the announcement.

In her record layout, Gray did not provide for information that would have allowed grouping applicants by vacancy announcement. Nor did she denote which applicants had been certified. For each position she entered each applicant's component scores, the applicant's age, and whether the applicant was selected or not.[31] She did not key data when all applicants were either over or under age forty.[32] She presented the following "findings:"

> Older applicants are not under-selected on the face of it, not accounting for any other variables.
>
> However, when their scores on other variables are accounted for, they are under-selected. That is, they are under-selected given their characteristics other than age.

With plaintiffs agreeing that older applicants were selected in proportion to their rate of application, Judge Oberdorfer granted summary judgment for defendant on plaintiffs' claim of disparate impact.[33]

---

31. As the application process takes some time, age should be determined on some consistent date. I presume the selection date would be relevant under the law, as it is the date of the employer's action. Because selection was determined from a retrospective entry on the certification list, the date of selection was not always known. I used the certification date to calculate age, as each certification list had a date. I also had access to computerized personnel data which contained the date of the promotion, but not the date of the decision to promote. Mary Gray did not use a consistent date, sometimes using an age provided by the Marshals Service without inquiring about the date on which that age calculation was based.

32. A list where all applicants are over age forty still contains information indicating whether age is a factor in selection, and should be included.

33. *Koger v. Reno*, Order of March 15, 1994.

The case went to trial on plaintiffs' disparate-treatment claim: Older applicants who otherwise "look like" younger applicants are under-selected based on their age. This logic is the opposite of that posited by plaintiffs in their complaint, that older applicants are harmed by the run test and conventions of scoring education. Did Gray knowingly disagree with her clients, or did she screw up?

Four serious errors led Mary Gray to believe that older applicants fared badly, controlling for score, when in fact they fared well. Her first error came from not understanding the law. The Age Discrimination in Employment Act does not recognize age variation under age forty. Plaintiffs first must choose an age (at least forty) above which they complain discrimination has occurred. Above that age, one can still count as "discrimination" the selection of a younger applicant instead of an older applicant. Thus, even if forty is the demarcation, a forty-five-year-old winner can be evidence of discrimination if the losers were over forty-five. Discarding announcements in which no applicant was younger than forty was a mistake.

Gray's second error came from a similar misunderstanding. A thirty-year-old winner does not support youth favoritism more than a thirty-nine-year-old winner. All applicants under the selected age have the same age in the eyes of the law. That an analysis should not recognize age variation below age forty is not a difficult point to attorneys, only to experts.[34] Judge Oberdorfer immediately accepted it:

> Dr. Gray performed a regression analysis in which variation in age under age 40 affected her conclusions. However, such a variation is no basis for liability under the Age Discrimination in Employment Act.[35]

Few lawyers would figure out that Mary Gray's regression and correlation analyses were incompatible with applicable law. Neither her client nor mine perceived this error on his own. It is up to the expert to understand the nuances of the law as they apply to the statistical analysis, and to inform his client when something is amiss.

As Gray had also converted age into a binary variable (age forty and above = 1, otherwise = 0), she was allowed to present those analyses. They were marred by Gray's third error. She had ignored the institutional phenomenon of vacancy announcements. In her single-pool analyses, all applicants were competing for all openings; a marshal who applied for more than one opening competed against *himself* for promotion. A multiple-

---

34. For example, Harriet Zellner argued to use a continuous measure of age (claiming that experts incorrectly use binary variables) in an article "When Is It Really Age Discrimination?" *New York Law Journal*, November 4, 1993. Zellner did not realize that her continuous variable would be incorrect if used on people below age forty, under federal law. Some state age-discrimination acts do not have the "cutoff" age contained in the federal legislation. Zellner's article could be helpful in such a circumstance. Once again, the expert must understand the law under which she is operating.

35. *Koger v. Reno*, typescript of June 6, 1994, memorandum opinion at 17; following indented quotation at 16.

pools world was analyzed with inappropriate single-pool statistical methods.

A statistical analysis of employer decisions should be consistent with the institutional context in which those decisions were being made. Judge Oberdorfer understood:

> Dr. Gray ignored the requirement that selections be made from among those in individual vacancy-announcement pools. Thus, her analysis treated as "losers" applicants who had high scores in comparison to the entire pool of applicants for all vacancies but whose scores were not sufficient to gain promotion to the particular position for which the applicants applied.

Although when I first encountered employment-selection issues no analyst's toolkit included multiple-pools methods, I would have expected all analysts to understand the problem *and its solution* by 1994. My firm's software had been available for over a decade, and had been purchased by most experts in equal employment. Furthermore, by 1994, most commercial statistical packages (including Systat, which Gray used) offered appropriate software, though usually only at extra cost.[36]

As Gray had analyzed selection from applicants with and without controls for component scores, I followed her lead. Holding age below forty constant for legal integrity, I maintained competition integrity by using the multiple-pools methods described in Chapter 2. I found:

> Older applicants were selected proportionately.
>
> Given their application scores, older applicants were selected in *greater* proportion than younger applicants.

The implication of these findings was that older applicants had lower scores than younger applicants. When we know their scores, our "expectation" of the success of older applicants is lowered, so proportional success is unexpectedly high. Although this finding directly contradicts plaintiffs' own expert's findings, it supports their argument. It is also a correct description of the facts.

Gray's fourth error was her most egregious. She ignored the certification stage of the promotion process. As described in Chapter 5, in *Teal* (1982) a "bottom-line" analysis of hires from applicants showed that blacks were hired in proportion to their application. However, blacks failed an initial exam at an excessive rate. The question was whether excessive selection of blacks from the remaining candidates compensated blacks as a group for

---

36. All such programs produced approximate calculations. Of course I made much of having an "exact" test at my disposal. Opposing experts who did not had to admit that my calculations were "more accurate." But this is all foolishness. Data inaccuracies and the arbitrariness of the "relevant time period" overwhelm any difference between exact and approximate multiple-pool calculations. I never found a case where the two disagreed qualitatively, and if they had I would not have wanted to see a judicial decision based on the small differences between them.

the disparate impact of the test. The court's answer was that the individual blacks who failed the test may have been discriminated against (unless the test was shown to have been valid), regardless of the success of *other* blacks. As I noted in Chapter 5, *Teal* is an exemplar: Civil rights adhere to individuals, not the group.

Koger's facts were close to those of *Teal*. The Marshals Service operated just as anyone familiar with such institutions would have expected. There was an "old-boy" network, in the most literal sense. An older applicant who could survive to a certification list was likely to be selected for promotion—more likely than a similarly situated younger applicant. However, just as plaintiffs claimed, older applicants were less likely to be certified, largely because of their failure on—the disparate impact of—the run test.[37]

Gray's data collection was not erroneous in a technical sense. It was erroneous in a conceptual sense. She failed to test her client's theory. The system had no way to bring the most appropriate analysis to the attention of the court.[38] The culprit here is either the adversarial system or incompetence within it. But if there is no protection from incompetence then the culprit, eventually, is indeed the system itself, that is, the biases inherent in associating experts with contestants.

On technical issues the expert is alone. His client relies on him to do his job. In contrast, an expert who does not perform a *conceptually* correct analysis of the issues presented by his clients has not failed alone. This is the area attorneys and experts should be discussing. Does the expert understand all prevailing law? Has that law been incorporated into the analysis? Does she (in this case) understand the mechanism of selection, and where in that mechanism her clients claim to have been discriminated against, so the analysis of selection can be relevant to their complaint? Does the attorney have the same understanding, so he can explain his case and where the expert's work fits in? An attorney who does not spend the time with his expert to evolve an analysis that correctly portrays the institution, the law, and the complaint is not doing his job.

On the published record, plaintiffs' expert's failure in *Koger* appears to be one of statistical method. As in *Polaroid* (1983), discussed in Chapter 2, that is not the lesson to learn. Plaintiffs' failure was conceptual, and thus it was the attorney's failure as much as the expert's. There is a final reason why this case so well demonstrates the failure of the expert, the attorney, and the attorney-expert relationship: Plaintiffs cited *Teal* (1982) in their

---

37. I did not test plaintiffs' allegations about the scoring of education. To do so would have required data on those components of education plaintiffs claimed were undervalued, and the proposal of an alternative scoring system. Older applicants did not score noticeably lower than younger applicants in education, but whether they should have scored higher I cannot say.

38. I described these plaintiff failings to my client, an Assistant United States Attorney. He did not think it was his job as defendants' attorney, or mine as his expert, to make plaintiffs' case. He did prepare a validity defense of the run test.

pleadings! They did not fail to know about the case, and its relevance to *Koger*. They just failed, utterly, to connect it to the work of their expert.

Hospital Closures in *Bryan* (1980)

In the late 1970s, the City of New York announced that they would close three municipal hospitals. The NAACP Legal Defense Fund contacted me. They claimed that such closures would be racially discriminatory. The intent of the selection of hospitals to be closed, they said, was to deprive the black community of medical services.

Of all potential clients, the righteous plaintiff is the most difficult. By this time I was seeing the civil-rights legal apparatus in decline. I was not asked to test a proposition, but to support one, and to do so on essentially no budget.

The analysis appeared to be difficult because data on the racial composition of hospital patients differed. Why different counts disagreed is one point of this story, but it can wait.

There were thirteen municipal hospitals. Not only were the racial compositions different among data sources, so were the placement of individual hospitals in rank order of "blackness," of serving blacks. One hospital may have appeared to serve the third-whitest population by one measure, but the fifth-whitest in another. However, the three hospitals to be closed, by switching places, happened to occupy the same rank positions in the two racial measures available. I used a simple rank-order statistic to calculate the improbability of selecting hospitals as black as these (or more so), by chance. The particular hospitals selected were not a strikingly improbable result from random selection.

I thought I performed the service I should have been expected to perform, by informing my client that further use of statistical expert services would not be cost-effective. I received no thanks. Obviously I was not on "their team." I was never again contacted by the NAACP Legal Defense Fund for any purpose. They did not even have the courtesy to inform me, later, that the court had agreed with my view, not theirs.

As Judge Sofaer understood it, the experts argued about data accuracy. He was unhappy at bickering about data because the three selected hospitals were easily characterizable as serving minorities. Perhaps, but data concepts, not accuracy, should have been at issue.[39] They will ultimately take over this chapter.

Will Fairley, expert for the city, describes plaintiff's approach in contrast to his own.[40]

---

39. *Bryan* (1980) at 219:

> Disputes as to the relative accuracy of these data sets have raged needlessly since this case was filed.

40. See Sugrue and Fairley (1983). Thomas Sugrue may also have been an expert, in which case I apologize for the singular reference to Fairley. Sugrue is not mentioned in either decision. I knew that Fairley had performed such services for the City of New York. I respected his abilities, and warned the Legal Defense Fund that he would easily see what I had seen.

Plaintiffs' expert Richard Faust, the Fund's team player, performed a binomial test, using the numbers of beds (prorated by percent minority of the hospital) as his counts. Fairley countered that patients are not selected "independently," as required by the binomial test. Patients come bundled with hospitals. As closing was a hospital decision, not a patient decision, the unit of analysis should be the hospital, not the patient.

Foster-Care Placement in *Wilder*

As an employee of the Center for Law and Education in the early 1970s, I was asked to help frame interrogatories to obtain basic information for *Wilder I*. Plaintiffs were represented by the Children's Rights Project.[41] Defendant was the foster-care system of New York City. In the 1980s, the Project came back to me for help in their analysis in *Wilder II*. By this time Ms. Wilder, who had been in the foster-care system when the suit was filed, was an adult, whose child had been removed from her home and placed in the system.

The Project alleged that foster-care placement associated the religion of the child with the religion of the foster-care giver. This practice not only violated the constitutional prohibition on state action to support religion, said the Project; it resulted in inferior services for black children. In settlement, the city agreed that foster-care placements would no longer associate the religion of the child with the religion of the care giving institution. The Project failed to get the City of New York to honor the settlement, however, which opens a seriously interesting topic I do not explore in this book: the limits of judicial intervention.[42] Or, "So you won, now what?"

The city's "experts" were going to defend the institutional child-care system on the basis that there were many providers.[43] A separate statistical test, they said, should be run on each. When many tests are made, the likelihood that one of them will appear "improbable" increases. Therefore, the analyst applies a correction, that is, raises the bar, makes "improbability" surpass a higher barrier.[44] Multiple tests is a sophisticated subject that

---

41. This case caused the Children's Rights Project to split off from the New York Civil Liberties Union, many contributors to which thought religious freedom included religion-specific home care. The objective of *Wilder* was to prevent such religion-directed care. Not only did *Wilder I* continue through *Wilder IV* (as listed in the case list), plaintiffs' larger thrust, to improve New York City's provision of foster care and welfare services to children, continued in *Marisol* (1996) with decisions through at least 2001. That is, it became a three-decades-long industry.

42. N. Bernstein (2001)—I trust no relative of the one-time defendant—provides one view of this case, but not of the opposing statistical analyses discussed here.

43. Defendant's experts were professors of statistics at Columbia University. Their work was not just bad, but, I have to believe, deliberately wrong. It was junk, presented by those who some would have be arbiters of the quality of statistical presentations.

44. See Finkelstein and Levin (1990) at 209 for the Bonferroni method of "correcting the nominal error rate in multiple or simultaneous tests of significance." They also discuss the multiple-comparisons problem, and the Bonferroni correction, in Finkelstein and Levin (2003), particularly footnote 44 at 279.

deserves serious attention in courts, and receives much attention in this book. It deserved no attention in this case. The city had one foster-care system with many care providers.

That there was an association between the religion of the parents of children who were entering the system with the religion of the institution into which the child was placed could not have been disputed. That was the clear practice that the city was defending. The question was whether children were segregated by race when placed by religion, and whether, thereafter, Protestant (black) children received worse service than Catholic or Jewish (white) children.[45] These placement decisions were made by the system. The placement data were observations, outcomes of that decision process. The quality data, assessed independently per institution, indicated the results of that placement. The test was whether placement by religion had a disparate impact such that minority children received inferior care.

Once the child is placed, the foster-care question becomes like one of hospitals or schools, asking if variation in an institution's resources is related to some child outcome. Echos of *Bryan* (1980), or of *Hobson II* (discussed in Chapter 3), children are bundled with institutions. In the assignment analysis there is a single allocator of children to an institution (each child, each allocation is an observation). In the quality-of-care analysis there is a measure of the average characteristic of children and a measure of the quality of care they receive (each institution is an observation). Correctly analyzed, there is no multiple-test issue.

I felt secure in my ability to convince any judge that defendant's position was chicanery, not analysis. I think the city's attorney saw the same problem. They settled, burying this sad record of academic experts going too far for their clients.

THE CONCEPTUAL BASIS OF DATA

Although Thomas Sugrue and William Fairley chose not to discuss it, the data issue is more interesting than the analytic issue on which they easily prevailed in *Bryan* (1980). Why did different data sources produce such widely varying counts of race of patients at hospitals? Were samples taken at such different times that demographics had changed? Were some studies poorly done? Was it, as the judge determined, a question of accuracy?

None of the above. The surveys differed because they had different *conceptions* of what they were counting. The issue with defining "race" at a hospital is length of stay. Consider a hypothetical hospital with two divisions: children's cancer and emergency. The cancer patients, 120 of them, are white, young by definition, stay an average of six months. The

45. Although one-third of the black children were not (or not known to be) Protestants, well over 90 percent of the Protestant children were black. Placement by religion was placement by race, even though many of the same race were not so placed. However, I was able to show non-random placement into a specific agency by race even within religion. That is, the non-Protestant black children were segregated directly by race, whereas the Protestant black children were segregated by race through their religion.

trauma patients, twenty arriving each day, are black, have wounds or automobile accident injuries, and stay an average of six days.

Two measures of patients are devised: One survey will randomly select several days during the year. On each day, each patient is an observation. His or her characteristics are noted, and the average of these observations is reported as the demographics of those served by the hospital. On a typical day the hospital will serve 120 cancer patients and 120 trauma patients. The survey will find a ratio of one white for every black served, one child for every adult served, one long-term-care patient for every trauma patient served.

The second survey will be taken over a period of time, let us say one month. Each patient will constitute an observation. In that month we can expect one-sixth of the long-term patients to leave and be replaced, so the survey will see 140 young white cancer patients—120 at the start, and twenty new ones in that month. In thirty days it will see at least seven hundred adult black trauma patients—twenty new ones entering each day, plus one hundred remaining from the six days preceding the first day of observation. This survey will report five blacks for each white served, five adults for each child served, five trauma patients for each long-term patient served. The first survey is correct in terms of patient-days, whereas the second survey is correct in terms of individuals, patients. Is this an equal white/black young/old hospital, or does it serve the adult black community predominantly?

An expert cannot assume that treating twelve different patients on each of ten days is more or less important than providing ten days of treatment to a fixed group of 120 patients. The call to the expert to use data on the populations of hospitals, to the attorney apparently simple, is in fact complex. The expert who does not treat it as complex may be hurting his client, and is surely not providing expert assistance to the trier of fact.

Social Rehabilitation Services

Despite successfully thwarting defendant's false statistical finesse in *Wilder II*, I did not hear from the Children's Rights Project again until 1992. I was called to offer advice on how to deal with a coding project gone awry. I will provide excerpts first from attorney Chris Hansen's six-and-a-half-page letter explaining the issues to me, and then from my twelve-page reply. The defendant was the Social Rehabilitation Services (SRS) of a particular state, but which state is immaterial.

Here is a letter from the Project to me (excerpted and slightly edited):

Stefan Michaelson

Dear Stefan,

We represent a class of all children who are in state custody as a result of abuse or neglect by their parents or those who are at risk of such custody. We allege that the state child welfare agency does not meet minimal standards set by law and the social work profession in the way in which it cares for children.

Which measures of adequacy of care are relevant depends on the goal established for the child. Most child-welfare agencies have little data available on the quality or quantity of services they provide. To determine these factors we do case readings. We identify the universe of children affected by the child-welfare system, draw a sample, and code answers to questions from the folders of that sample. The state did the same thing. We have identified a number of methodological questions that we have been unable to resolve.

Plaintiffs' Case Reading

The universe was limited to children in state custody, because there is no way to identify children at risk of such custody but not in it. The sample was drawn on May 31, 1991. No data entered after May 28, 1991, is included, because of key-entry delays. The universe was 5,344 children.

We designed a stratified sample with sample sizes as follows:

Plaintiffs' Sample Design

	Goal	Universe	Sample	Coded	Actual	Final
1a	Return to parents, trial discharge		150	64		
1b	Return to parents, discharge	4,140	150	238	244	192
2	Adoption	617	200	201	171	158
3	Permanent foster care	309	150	148	146	137
4	Independent living	198	120	118	118	95
5	No plan	41	41	41	1	
6	Awaiting placement	39	39	39		
7	Place with relatives				17	
8	Life maintenance				3	
9	Sheltered living				2	
10	Other				147	188

The first category was proportionately divided between cases on trial discharge and those not on trial discharge. The total of both categories is shown on line 1b. The sample was also stratified by geography, with each of the state's regions represented proportionately.

We ended up reading 849 cases. We weighted the data by goal type as indicated on the May 28, 1991, computer list from which the sample was drawn. Only weighted results were reported.

Questions were goal-dependent. We read the cases over a period of several weeks beginning July 8, 1991. The goals for many children had changed between May 28 and our reading. We utilized the current goal, not the goal as of the date the sample was drawn, in deciding which questions to answer for a particular child. The actual goals at the time of coding are reflected in the table above. Our expert's estimate is that about one-third of all cases had a change in the goal from the time the sample was pulled until the date it was read.

In addition, 188 children at the time of the reading were found not to be in state physical custody (in a foster home or whatever) but in state legal custody and living with their own parents. We thought it made no sense to treat those cases the same as cases where the child was out of the home. For example, how do you measure parent/child visitation as you would for an out-of-the-home case if the child is in the home? Accordingly, we took those 188 cases out and looked at them in a totally separate section of the report. In addition, cases with "other" goals of "life maintenance" or "sheltered living" were counted in totals but they do not appear in analyses by goal type. Finally, "placement with relative" was counted as "return home" in analyses. We ended up with the numbers in the "Final" column in the table above. "Other" for this column means "In Own Home."

Defendants' Case Reading

Defendants used the sample we drew, read the same folders, specified goals, and devised sample weights from those goals. They report the numbers in the following table. It appears (although we are not sure) that "goal" was derived from a hard copy of the computer form found in the record at the time the case was read. Alternatively, they did a computer run in July or August, from which they derived goal as of May 28. Because of delay in entering data into the computer, this might be a different goal from the one attributed to the same date from an earlier printout. At any rate, these are two possible explanations for why, reading the same cases, their sample looks different from ours.

Defendants' Sample Design

	Goal	Universe	Sample	Read
1	Return to parents	4,173	326	221
2	Adoption	618	187	174
3	Permanent foster care	310	136	125
4	Independent living	202	155	127
5	No plan	41	35	38
6	Life maintenance	23	3	2
7	Sheltered living	40	7	2
8	Place with relatives			10
9	Other			43

Defendant reports 106 cases not applicable, and one goal missing. However, when they report analyses by specific goals, they do not report the numbers in the above table. They have up to 190 answers to "adoption" questions, for example. We do not know where such numbers come from.

Questions

We have another expert who has both data sets and wants to do some new analyses. Our questions are:

- What errors, if any, did we make?
- What errors, if any, did they make?
- How should our expert do his analysis?

Both expert reports were sorry affairs not only because they lacked conceptual under-pinnings, but because they were boring. With many questions coded under many goals, plaintiffs' expert presented 127 tables. Defendant's expert presented 163 tables plus 474 detailed backup tables. In short, both experts described, neither analyzed.

The problems started well before the case readings. The first problem is that neither party had thought about the concept of the "population" and, therefore, how to sample it. The second problem is that neither party had considered what "data accuracy" should mean, and for that reason they do not describe the concepts they are trying to capture.

What Is Data Accuracy?

I started my response with an obvious "attitude," engendered by the folly of the situation. I tried to explain what "accuracy" might mean in the context of this case reading, and then why their sample most likely was meaningless.

Dear Chris:

I am responding to your April 30 letter (regarding the SRS) even though you mis-spelled both of my names. . . .

The two sets of experts agree that they worked together, but then disagree on the basic elements of their sample. Plaintiff says, "The universe consisted of all open cases as of May 28, 1991, and encompassed 5,344 cases" [page 1]. Defendant says, "The pop-ulation was further defined as all open cases as of May 31, 1991, a total of 5,407 cases" [page 7]. Defendant states that the first stratification was Area Office and then, within Office, by type of plan and current placement. Plaintiff's writing is less clear, but implies that the first stratification was on "permanent plan." Where "letter" refers to your letter of April 30, the sample and population are given as:

	Plaintiffs			Defendants	
	Population	Sample	Letter	Population	Sample
Return to Parents / Place with relatives	4,140	300	302	4,173	326
Adoption	617	200	201	617	187
Long-Term Foster Care	309	150	148	310	136
Independent Living	198	120	118	202	155
Remainder	180	79	80	104	45

Plaintiffs then go on to say they will present weighted percentages and the num-ber in the sample. Defendants say their unweighted figures are to be ignored; "all analy-ses and interpretations involve **weighted frequencies**" [page 11, bold in original].

So the parties agree that results should be weighted, but disagree on the weights. It is unfortunate that the two parties diverged this early in the process. They should not have. There is a clear correct way to proceed. I will stop here to explain how the process should have gone to this point. In this explanation I assume the parties have agreed to sample active cases on a given day. (Did defendant count non-active cases in the population?) That is not the only possible sample, and it may well be a biased sample. I will return to this point below. For now, the parties agree that they will sample cases active on May 28—or is it May 31? Your letter, which says that May 28 and May 31 should have produced the same figures, only confuses the issue further, since the dates and figures both are reported differently by the two parties. I suggest that later entries effective by May 31 may have created the difference. If so, defendants are using data to which plaintiffs had no access.

The population should have been frozen on a particular day, and there should be no dispute about the day or the population. The population should be identified as of that day, but whether the data for the sample should be drawn then or later depends on a concept that appears to have not been considered at all.

Every researcher says he wants his data to be "accurate," but few say accurate what. Here are two concepts of accuracy leading to different samples. Record accuracy means the "fact" you are trying to measure is the computer records on that day. Data accuracy means the "fact" you are trying to measure is the data as of that day, regardless when they achieve the status of a computerized record. The former may be of interest if you believe decision makers obtain their information from the computerized record. Then you are measuring what was known on that day, and you should define the sample by recorded case plan as of that date.

In most institutions, facts are known before they are recorded. A clearer view of input to decisions, or the decisions themselves, is from the effective date of data, not its date of entry. The parties could have agreed on a reasonable time to allow recording to occur. Defendant should have been willing to suspend data purges for that period. Then, say two weeks later (whatever is agreed), the population identified on the freeze day should have been extracted (i.e., delete new entrants). From that file, the parties would draw the sample, based on the now recorded region and plan effective on the freeze day.

There could be many hitches in such a scheme. For example the recording system may not be transaction oriented (where every change of data is a transaction with an effective date). If the computer-indicated plan could be changed merely by changing it, then you would not know two weeks later what plan was in effect on the freeze date. The solution here is to have saved the file on the freeze date as well as on the later agreed-upon date. Then, two weeks later, the parties can determine all instances of plan change, investigate them from the paper files, place them where they belong, and proceed.

Your disagreement on the date of freezing probably explains the difference in the populations, but not the disagreement about where to place observations within the sample. Not having agreed what you are trying to capture, recording or fact, you are starting down different paths. Assuming again that you want to sample the facts on May 28, you should define the plan as of that date, derive the sample as of that date, and keep observations in the stratum into which they were sampled. This last statement introduces a new point, so let's see how the parties proceeded before we come back to my comments.

Defendants state, Table 3 on page 11, that they used inverse weights of the sample, as drawn. Defendant provides "standard errors" per stratum, as if all questions were binomial p = 0.5. They are calculated using the finite-population correction. This sophistication breaks down when the standard error for the total is incorrectly calculated as if based on a simple random sample. (A reasonable calculation of their total standard error, derived from independent stratum samples, is 0.079, about five times larger than the standard error they report.) Defendant then ignores its standard errors in its presentations.

It is clear that defendants observed the data as of May 31, 1991. They use the word "current" often. When they report "Current Service Plan," Table 15 (page 21), they report the same frequencies that were drawn from the sample. "Current" to defendant in this instance means as of the sample date. Later, it seems to mean current as of coding. I understand your confusion.

Plaintiff and defendant cannot even agree on the gender of the children being served (defendant: 50.6 percent female; plaintiff: 53.3 percent female). Such a figure does not depend on different concepts of the plan (i.e., when the plan is to be observed), or on appropriate weighting method. If not due to coding errors, it must be due either to the disagreement between May 28 and May 31 populations or to defendant's deleting certain observations as "irrelevant." This level of difference, not being able to report the identical sample identically by gender (or ethnicity), will infuriate a judge. These are your check totals, the numbers on which the parties should agree before proceeding. It serves neither party to allow differences at this level. There is no way for me to say who is right here. Under proper procedures, no such dispute would have arisen.

Plaintiffs accepted the plan at the date of the reading, which you say (your letter, page 3) may be different in as many as one-third of the sample. (But plaintiffs' report says the goal changed in only 9 percent of the cases, see page 80.) They are then weighted by their original sample weight, using the argument that different observations had different probabilities of being drawn into the sample (page 80).

Although the weighting statement is correct enough, plaintiffs are wrong on several counts. First, I see no calculation of standard errors. Neither party seems to be aware that the standard error of a variable measured from a stratified sample is larger than from a random sample if the strata are not critical to understanding the measure. One should be sure of the importance of one's strata before using them to sample.

Plaintiffs' argument that it is all right to change the observation's plan category prevents one from making any sense out of the sample. In the following graphic, time flows from the bottom to the top. I have indicated May 28 (sample date) and July 8 (begin-reading date). There is no unit along the horizontal axis: I just show nine observations (cases). A horizontal tick at an end of each observation's time line indicates a start or end date of this custody, within the limits of the time shown. For example, observation 1 starts before this picture, and ends after this picture, whereas observation 9 starts and ends within the time shown. The final symbol, •, indicates a date of setting or changing the case's plan, which plaintiff report states should have been accomplished within 60 days of entry into the system.

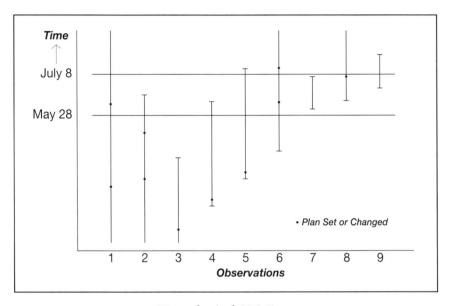

Hypothetical SRS Data

Observation 1 has a plan change between May 28 and July 8. One of your main questions is, what plan should have been coded? My answer is: the plan effective May 28. Much of this discussion is aimed at showing you why. Observation 2 also had a plan change, but the second plan occurred before May 28, so both parties will code the same plan. On the other hand, this case has left the SRS. Do plaintiffs ignore it? If plaintiffs code this case with its May 28 plan, do plaintiffs recognize that it was not in the system from May 28 through July 8, and thus did not have the same chance to have its plan changed as observation 1?

Neither party codes observation 3, which has left the system prior to May 28. Presumably neither party codes observations 7, 8, and 9, either. Yet plaintiffs purport to say what percentage of a stock—a day's snapshot—is in which plan, or no plan. Observation 8 is in a plan on July 8, but is not counted. Plaintiffs' description of the distribution among plans does not accurately reflect May 28, because it uses the July 8 plan; but neither does it reflect the population on July 8.

Observation 4 is in a plan on May 28, but has left the system by July 8. Observation 5 is similar, but survives just past July 8. How observation 6 is coded depends on when it was coded. The plan changes after May 28, but then again shortly after July 8. Plaintiff could code "plan" one way, and defendants code "current plan" another way. One might think there is something wrong with the coding, but what is wrong is the coding instruction: If coded as of May 28, the parties would agree.

I think these nine observations present the cases worth considering in setting out a sampling plan, except that I did not include leaving and re-entering the SRS system. By coding live folders at different times, some differences between coding could be due to differences in the folders themselves (especially counts of actions). Wasn't the point of agreeing on a sample to confine differences to coding form? As you no longer have the same samples, the point of the agreement has been lost.

Observations 4 and 5 differ from Observation 2 because they had only one plan. Neither party seems to account for plan changes, though defendants do better than plaintiffs in acknowledging them. Plaintiffs apparently will hold SRS to a higher performance standard for observation 2 (which has been in the system longer) than for observations 4 or 5. Yet there has been less time for the system to effectuate its current plan on observation 2. Does your coding differentiate between these cases?

Only observations 1, 2, 4, 5, and 6 will be in the sample. Observations 1 and 6 will look different on July 8, from May 28, and a strict July 8 coding will drop observation 2. All of this leaves us with no picture of a cross-section of SRS cases on any day. But such a picture must have been the point of the sample. Why else would both parties, though disagreeing on the number, refer to and weight according to the population on a given day? Plaintiffs neither code a picture of July 8 (ignoring observations 7, 8, 9) nor of May 28 (incorrectly coding plan of observations 1 and 6, and possibly not coding 2 at all). Plaintiffs show a picture of nothing intelligible. Defendant may have made all the same mistakes, but they describe their process so badly one can't really tell.

Two parties can both code the same documents "accurately" and yet disagree, because they are looking for conceptually different data elements under the same name. In over thirty-five years of data analysis in litigation, I have never seen a public discussion of the *concept* of accuracy, what idea is meant to be represented by data. There is no such discussion, I think, because both attorneys and experts lack an intellectual approach to what they are doing. They think of the task as technical.[46] In this SRS case, plaintiffs and defendants appear to have different concepts—if any concepts at all—about what their data are to represent. What seemed obvious to my client, to code plan as of the case reading, was inappropriate. What "accuracy" might mean thereafter is not important. It would be accurate nonsense.

Data When?

Is the computer a data-recording device or an instrument of decision making? Where the same people who use the data have generated it, the best working assumption is that the participants know the facts even if the computer does not. In the State Department case discussed in Chapter 8, I will run into this problem of the appropriate concept of accuracy in a different institutional context again, with different answers. If engaged in this SRS case

---

46. The reader may recall my discussion of *O'Keefe* (1996) in Chapter 3. Franklin Fisher's regression model was technically brilliant. However, his definition of "over" or "under" budget was suspect and, like Gray's work in *Koger* (1994), his model did not reflect the complaint. The problem lay not in the "accuracy" of his data, but in its conceptual relevance to the issues in the case.

I would have tried to determine if my supposition that decision makers have information before the computer does is correct. I would spend a day at the institution determining how the data are recorded, and how recorded data are accessed and used. I would estimate the time between an event or a decision and its reflection in the computer record, and not access the records relating to a set date until that time for recording had elapsed. Here I assume that information in a computer printout of May 28 might be incorrect, and be known to be incorrect by all decision makers at the time. What, then, should be done in coding?

It might be that by the time of the case readings in July, all data relevant for a May 28 observation had been coded, and could be discerned. Suppose, for example, that goals are coded with a goal-effective date. Then one looks in a July printout for the last goal-effective date prior to May 28, to retrieve *data*-accurate information. On the other hand, if all decisions are made from computer data (printout or screen), then *record* accuracy is wanted. In this circumstance, coding should have been done from a May 28 printout. The experts need to know how record keeping interacts with decision making, and therefore how to derive from the records the "knowledge" utilized by decision makers as of May 28, 1991.

If my supposition that the computer acts as a data-recording device is correct, then some actions taken after May 28 may not have appeared appropriate to the goal of record because another as yet unrecorded goal was known to be in effect. Changing goal itself might have been a reasonable focus of the study. The appropriate stratification might have been by *initial* goal. What was required was that the attorneys sit down with analysis experts, probably for days, discussing what was already known about the institution, and what was its alleged failure. Perhaps a "mini study" should have been designed, to let the experts follow through on some thoughts for which the attorneys did not have sufficient answers.

Not all computerized record systems give up relevant analytic information easily. For example, the most "advanced" federal jury software overwrites a person's address when he notifies the court that it has changed.[47] The result is that an analyst cannot determine where notifications have been mailed, and therefore cannot test the jury-notification mailing for representativeness. This result easily could have been avoided, both old and new addresses maintained.[48] The software could have been designed to accomplish this purpose had the concept of "address accuracy" been discussed. Accurately reflecting where

---

47. This is the JARA system in place, in 1996, in a few select areas. I do not know what has happened to this system since that date, or even what "JARA" stood for.

48. Retaining Zip code mailed to would have required only one additional field. Modern data bases build separate tables that are merged when necessary. A table with two elements—juror number and old Zip code—would only have as many observations as there were changes, and therefore would be even more efficient than an additional field on every record.

mailings were sent is different from accurately reflecting where people now live, both important concepts for different purposes, and both attainable in a single data base with forethought.

Similarly, the coders of SRS data needed a concept of "plan accuracy" relevant to the issues of the litigation. As the parties in the SRS case were agreeing on the sample, I would have urged coding to proceed in two steps. By agreeing on fundamental data concepts, such as the meaning of "accuracy," there would have been no need to code basic data twice. It could have been coded once, the parties sharing the costs. The parties would then exchange check totals (number of observations by plan as of a certain date, gender, etc.) to be sure they were both reading the same data the same way.

It would follow that the parties would necessarily agree, at least initially, on who is in the sample, their gender, ethnicity, initial goal, age, date of entry into the system, status vis-à-vis the system on May 28, and other particulars. Each side's experts then could generate their own coding form, starting with basic information filled in. They would then go on to code different data elements. While doing so, each party would check the joint coding, and some questions would undoubtedly be raised. As certain data elements have been agreed to be agreed upon, the course of action is clear: If either party raises a question about the original coding, the parties will have devised a dispute-resolution mechanism. The parties could then come to court agreeing on every detail of the basic sample, and disagreeing where their concepts of what to code diverged. Agreeing on the sampling concept, the sine qua non of this approach, requires understanding that there *are* such concepts.

Damages from the Dalkon Shield

In the A. H. Robins bankruptcy litigation, over three hundred thousand individuals claimed damages from use of the Dalkon Shield (their own or their partner's). The total amount of damages, obviously a statistical estimate, had to be set aside before the residue of the Robins company could be sold (as it was, eventually, to American Home Products, now Wyeth). The general procedure by which this would be done was obvious to all:

> From resolved cases (jury decisions and settlements) determine which
>   characteristics found in the data relate to the size of the award.
>
> Draw a sample of claimants.
>
> Design a survey instrument to collect data from the claimant sample,
>   under penalty of perjury, on the characteristics found to have been
>   important in the resolved-cases study.

As the parties might disagree on which characteristics relate to damages, and as only one survey instrument was to be imposed on claimants, the solution was to ask any question that either party deemed important to his case. Defendant wanted to ask questions about prior sexual history that plaintiffs found objectionable. These conflicts were resolved with arbitration, where necessary, by a special master appointed by the court. The parties agreed on a simple random sample of valid claims. After the survey questionnaire was negotiated by the parties, it was administered, collected and coded by a neutral third party under the supervision of the special master. Thus the parties disagreed at trial only on their analyses, not on the data.

Sample What? SRS Continued

Recall, here, the lessons learned from my experience with the closing of New York City hospitals. I do not mean the lesson that the expert's clients do not appreciate good advice. I mean the lesson that, if one samples such an institution on a single day, one counts short-term stayers at the expense of long-term stayers. There is no single "correct" answer to the question, "Whom does the hospital serve?" It depends on how you look at it.

The SRS clearly had the same characteristics, some short-term and some long-term stayers. Thus, my letter continued questioning the sample:

Perhaps 20 percent or so of cases are in the system under 6 months (see plaintiffs' Table II.7). If one were to sample all persons ever seen by the system over a period, say May 28 to July 8, you would pick up observations 7, 8, and 9, not in the May 28 sample. These short-term placements may be very different in age, in plan, and in other aspects of service. If you are trying to describe persons serviced by the system, you are under-counting these people, and, if they are different, under-representing their characteristics.

I think a description of cases on a particular day misstates the characteristics of the case load as seen by SRS. As defendant agreed on a single-day sample, I take it there is no reason to raise this issue. I suggest, however, that you review the 78 closed cases for differences in characteristics among short-term and long-term stayers. If you find such a difference, you may want to re-think doing any further work on this sample.

Referring again to my figure, the only way you can provide a cross-section look at SRS is by coding as of May 28. Reading the cases on July 8 is no excuse for violating the sample scheme. It leaves you with nothing: neither a picture of July 8 nor a picture of May 28. Meanwhile, you lost the opportunity to show, in addition to a May 28 cross-section, an additional month or more of activities. You could measure, for example, inactivity on plan as of May 28 against observed later change of plan. Such a correlation would imply doubt within the system that the plan was correct, or knowledge that it was going to be changed. You could measure the effect of plan changes (or incorrect plan setting, or whatever is going on), which may be preventing SRS from providing adequate services. Now, you can measure none of this.

In short, your problem is not the weighting, it is the case reading, the coding. I will provide several suggestions, none of which I like. Perhaps the best your additional expert could do now is to throw out observations whose plan changed between May 28 and coding, re-weighting the remainder. However, this procedure requires the assumption that such plan changes were random, which I doubt.

Can we find some guidance from standard procedures? Finding that a person is not in the correct stratum must be a common occurrence. One always stratifies from a weaker data source than he codes from, and coding must often, though marginally, show that some cases were misclassified in the stratification data source. What do you do?

First, you can keep each observation in his original stratum, and code him as incorrectly stratified thereby. I.e., he is a sample of a problem, namely, misidentification of proper stratum. You could then report his data in his original stratum. This would correctly report on information you would find stratifying by the original data source. For example, if you want to know the incomes of CEOs of small companies, as reported by *Inc.* magazine, you would report each CEO's income even if, in the questionnaire, you determined that his company no longer fit *Inc.*'s definition of "small." You might keep his income even if he were no longer CEO. The answers would properly represent information derived from the stratum, which is a reasonable focus of a study.

However, suppose you are trying to report information not vis a vis a data source, but vis a vis a population. Suppose, also, you believe the correction obtained in the questionnaire. You want to know CEO income by size of company, you sampled this guy in one stratum but he belongs in another. The answer is: do what both experts said they did. As long as he keeps his weight with him, you put him into the correct stratum, and you calculate means and standard errors using weights, then you are doing the best you can.

The reason this approach does not save you is that it is based on the concept of correction of error, not change of data. Your work is more like using *Inc.* magazine's list of companies and CEOs from three years ago to ask current questions. Then, when the person is in a different current stratum, you move him, with his weight, and report as if you had sampled current CEOs. You do not have a sample of current CEOs. If there is not much change over time, it won't much matter; and if children did not come into and leave SRS, it would not much matter for you, either. But I believe they do. I believe children who left are coded differently from children who remain, and children recently entered are sampled with probability = 0. You can get away with carrying original stratum weights into new strata, but I don't see how your results can be interpreted. They do not represent May 28, they do not represent July 8, or September, when reading was still going on.

If you did have a concept of the population, an alternative procedure would be to estimate (from cases of mis-stratification) the correct distribution of the population, and re-weight the correctly coded sample accordingly. Again, the critical assumption is that incorrect stratification is random; i.e., that an incorrectly coded case could end up anywhere.

Given marginal differences between stratification and response to the stratification question, move observations to their correct stratum with their old stratum weight. That solution doesn't really apply here. In your case, an action of the agency under study—not random error—caused the changed stratum. I think that is quite different.

If that damage has been done, keeping the original weights in the new strata is the best you can do. But it is wrong. The study should have been organized to reach a definitive stratification from correct (waiting for the records to be computerized) relevant (applicable to May 28) data. You should not have to re-stratify.

After responding to specific questions, I wiped my hands of this disaster. I have never heard what happened thereafter. Just as the failure to code separate competitions and selection stages in *Koger* doomed any future analysis to failure, so too did the failure to prepare for SRS coding doom the Children's Rights Project's study. The attorney cries about the constraint of his budget. A better expert can make more of a smaller sample. It is almost always cost-effective to allocate funds to thinking, even if less is left for the doing.

MORE ON THE PLAINTIFFS' BAR

In *O'Keefe* (1996), remember from earlier in this chapter and from Chapter 3, the Justice Department alleged that McDonnell Douglas mischarged one project's work to another. Data did not exist in computer form, because some government attorney thought he had done his job by writing into a contract with a defense supplier that data had to be maintained—but not that they had to be maintained in a standard electronic form that could be transferred to and read by others. Data existed only on microfiche images of computer printout.[49]

The Justice Department attorney came to me with a question: Did he have to enter all the microfiche cards, or could he recreate the data from a sample with sufficient accuracy for his case? I asked how many tasks a worker did in a day, how many workers did Justice think mischarged, and how often. (The more rare the event, the larger the sample required to find it.) Was there a time period where they suspected more mischarges?

A key parameter would come from an investigator's determination which charges were false, from interviews of workers. "He will only be able to do hundreds of interviews at most," said my client. "I can project if he only does tens," I said. "The key element is how credible is his determination of falseness in charges."

The case would under any circumstance come down to the identification of mischarges more than the projection from identified mischarges to a total. I think my client's funds were well spent on devising simulations and consulting among three experts (myself and two Department of Defense statisticians) to determine the characteristics of the sampling. As I urged at the time, if the government was not going to expend these resources on these tasks, it should abandon the case.

---

49. I have no doubt that saving the files on microfiche was an attorney's idea. No data-oriented person, no computer person, would have suggested it.

Managing Public-Interest Suits

Do-good agencies serve their clients poorly by employing low-priced "experts." "We do not have the funds" does not wash. Agencies have funds. They do not like to see those funds go to "outside" vendors. If agency leaders mean what they say, then it is wiser to pursue fewer cases and succeed than to pursue more cases and fail. The way to succeed is first to have a deserving case and second to use the services of persons who know what they are doing.

I was once asked to work for the Church of Scientology, although I do not remember the issue. Having no prejudice, I gave my "I work for truth, beauty, and the American way" speech, and prepared for a meeting in Washington, D.C. The Scientologists could barely keep their eyes open. To save money, they had flown on a "red-eye special" overnight from Los Angeles. I did not want to work for people who had so little regard for their own state of mind, who did not understand the importance of being awake when they dealt with their expert.

Agencies chartered to bring salvation to the world often think they know the way, and anyone who disagrees should not be engaged in the struggle. Nonetheless, it is reasonable to think that the NAACP Legal Defense Fund is not as irrational as I portrayed it in the hospital-closure case, *Bryan* (1980). I presume that there are criteria for bringing cases to court other than that the complainant was truly hurt, that the closure decision was truly biased, or that the complainant even thought it was. The Fund was not concerned with the merits of its statistical expert, only with his willingness to support its preconceived positions. It may have considered the political consequence of going back to its constituents, who were asking for action to stop the closings, using my analysis as a reason not to pursue litigation. It may have decided that, politically, it would do better by litigating, even if losing. The Fund's management comes complete with built-in excuses. They could say they had tried, it was the courts' fault for not listening. Or the expert's.

Any client, human or organization, may have its own agenda, in which winning isn't everything, and being right is irrelevant. In addition, the people in the organization may have an agenda different from that of the organization itself. Clients are complex. An expert who just wants to do a good job, including telling the client when he is playing a losing hand, may be engaged in an entirely different game from that of the people who hired him.

The Equal Employment Opportunity Commission

Working in the civil-rights field in the 1980s, I understood that the Legal Defense Fund no longer commanded moral authority in litigation. The Equal Employment Opportunity Commission (EEOC) had their own problems. It did not know how to let go, to declare victory or accept the reality of having been wrong and move on to other things. I saw the EEOC squandering resources on trivial cases, where I thought it should have been organizing resources for important cases. I thought that perhaps Clarence Thomas, as chairman of the EEOC, could take on the required strategic leadership unknown since the days of Thurgood Marshall and Jack Greenberg.

I persevered enough to get an interview with Chairman Thomas. I explained my understanding of the brilliance of the Legal Defense Fund's school-desegregation strategy.[50] I propounded my desire to see the EEOC take conceptual leadership of the push for equal-employment opportunity. It needed to gather resources to pursue such a strategy, and to do that it should stop spending money on the kind of work I was doing. A number of contracts I had with the EEOC were petty and unprogressive. I suggested that I would not object if he canceled them and instead did something important with the funds. I wanted to give money *back* to the EEOC and take my chances that I would get to work on "the big one." Just to put the money to better use would have satisfied me.

Chairman Thomas thanked me for my concern with a patronizing "my boy, you clearly don't understand" tone. I was in and out in ten minutes. When I persevered in my efforts to rationalize the EEOC's behavior, in discussion with "movement" attorneys, I was asked, "Have you taken these concerns to the chairman?" Yes, I had. That was the end of it. Thomas, exercising his political savvy, had nullified my attempt to affect EEOC strategy.

I foolishly thought the EEOC was a civil-rights-litigation agency. It was, and is—what else could it be?—a political agency. The EEOC was doling out funds, a little here, a little there, a case in the North, a case in the South; black, Hispanic, female issues—all at once. This was a political strategy, not a litigation strategy. Its goal was not to break new paths in the law, but to make paths for individual power brokers. This is the politics of buying friends with government money.[51] In its pursuit of those goals I was correctly perceived as a functionary, not a player; a nuisance, not an asset.

---

50. Historically, plaintiffs have been the more innovative party. See my discussion of Mayer's reasoning in *Lochner* (1905), Brandeis' in *Muller* (1908), Thurgood Marshall's in *Brown* (1954), etc., in Chapter 1. The forces leading to greater innovation by plaintiffs should be obvious. Defendants are, by and large, defending the status quo. Innovation is required for change, not for maintenance. In addition, many members of the plaintiffs' civil bar earn a living only by winning, whereas members of defendants' bar earn a living merely by working.

The NAACP's use of the Fourteenth Amendment to overturn the separate-but-equal doctrine was devised by Charles Houston. It was effectuated by Legal Defense Fund attorneys led by Thurgood Marshall and then (from 1961 to 1984) by Jack Greenberg. The strategy was to start at graduate school and move down the grades, as explained in Kluger (1975). At the elementary-school level, the strategy of selecting defendant states in different regions is told as part of the story in Kluger's two volumes, but is also told succinctly and with admiration by an attorney for the defendant state, Kansas, in Wilson (1995).

51. It is always so. Describing the distribution of federal funds to help "potential terrorist targets prepare for a second attack," Elizabeth Kolbert tells us that "40 percent of the money would be divided equally

The Commissioner's Charge

In the most peculiar institutional arrangement in Washington, the general counsel of the EEOC works for the President of the United States, not for the commissioners of his own agency. Thus there is always a tension, a power struggle, between the two. Commissioners may bring charges, which must be approved (after some investigation) by the general counsel. Once a case is approved, there appears to be no way to stop it. Facts, certainly, do not affect the pursuit.

I worked on *EEOC v. Luby Cafeterias*. Luby constructed a cafeteria-manager position at which most people would fail, so that they not only seemed to prevent upward mobility of minorities, but always lacked managers of their cafeterias. The promised pot was not at the end of a rainbow, but at the end of a hellish several years of day-and-night work that broke most applicants.

The commissioner's charge was reasonable: Luby did not seem to have minority managers. And its approval by the general counsel was reasonable: He saw that many minorities tried and failed to become cafeteria managers. On closer analysis, there was nothing racial about it. Luby would have been happy had minorities survived to become cafeteria managers. They accepted minorities in proportion to their application, but the minorities (indeed, most trainees of any kind) failed. It is not good management to make the course so hard that the company is always short of trained lower-management personnel, but bad management is not necessarily illegal. I described this view of the reality behind the EEOC's perceptions to my clients.

Luby's practices may well have had some disparate impact, but they may have been justifiable by a validity study, understanding the fallacy (explained in Chapter 2) that only survivors could be seen in the job. The company surely would have been smart enough to sign some kind of non-discrimination declaration, and revise its probation-period practices, in return for peace. But, though I inquired, and made clear that I thought the EEOC could not prevail at a trial, I found no mechanism by which a commissioner's charge, once approved, could be halted. This might have been more true in practice (no one wants to tell a commissioner his instinct was wrong) than in the rules, but to me, an outsider, it made no difference.

The inability to stop when the facts demand it surely is not exclusive to the EEOC, but it is endemic at that agency. One court decision contains this irate outburst:

---

among the states, without regard to their needs or the likelihood that they would ever be attacked." The remainder went to the Department of Homeland Security, where Secretary Tom Ridge, in the Clarence Thomas tradition, followed "the politically more expedient path of making awards solely on the basis of population." See "Risk Management" under "The Talk Of The Town" in *The New Yorker*, May 31, 2004, at 27.

> The Court is of the strong opinion that this case should never have been insti-
> tuted and, once commenced, it should not have gone to trial.[52]

The EEOC had to pay defendant's costs for this litigation. The commissioner's charge is an inducement for some people to serve in that position. It allows commissioners to appear to be "fighting" for their constituents. It would work against any chairman who would devise a strategy to eradicate only some forms of discrimination.

Two things stand out in the recent history of the derivation and presentation of social-science quantitative fact in law: First, attorneys in the field of equal-employment opportunity inspired many advances in its use. No other area has had the influence labor issues have had in establishing the utility of statistical fact in law.[53] Second, the federal agency most involved in that field has had nothing to do with these advances. Some spectacular failures come to mind, but not a single success based on creative use of statistical analysis.[54] Perhaps one could find some historical evidence that the EEOC has been an important, progressive agency, but from my observation it has been stupidly organized, managed for personal gain, and staffed by attorneys for the most part incapable of obtaining a private-sector job. A good case can be made that it practices as much racial bias as it prevents. Indeed white agency attorneys have sued it and won.[55] The EEOC has been a drag on progress for equal opportunity and a drag on the intelligent use of social-science evidence in courts. It never became an intellectual force and deserves, at this point, to be quietly put to sleep.

THE DEFENSE BAR

One of my private-sector defendant clients said to me: "You just don't understand. You think my objective is to win my case. You are wrong. My objective is to keep my clients."[56] I think this is equally true for the private sector, the public sector (as the EEOC), and

---

52. *Eagle* (1976) at 250, 14 FEP Cases at 544. I have been unable to find a reported decision in *EEOC v. Luby's Cafeterias.* Perhaps they did settle.

53. Epidemiology, the association of cause with illness or disease, has possibly been the most criticized area of statistical analysis in law. It is not surprising that it was the false association of Bendectin with birth defects that led to the Supreme Court's telling judges to screen experts, in *Daubert* (1993).

54. Let us not forget *Sears* (1986), a massive statistical case based more on speculation than evidence. Claiming that the lack of female salespeople in large items—tires, refrigerators, etc.—was evidence of sex discrimination, the EEOC failed to call a single woman to say she had been denied such a position. The entire case confused outcome—there were indeed few female salespeople in the designated areas— with the process of taking applications and assessing applicants.

55. See, for example, *Wexler* (1983).

56. My client was Wayne Barlow. His client was the Stater Brothers grocery chain in southern California.

the non-profit sector (as the NAACP Legal Defense Fund). They keep their clients, their supporters, by putting up a fight, even when it is expensive and futile. They look for scapegoats—the judge or the legal system are against them, you know, and that expert just wasn't up to it—rather than for progress.

The Equal Employment Opportunity Commission vs. IBM

The EEOC's Baltimore office had sued IBM for failure to promote blacks. They had engaged a local professor and IBM had engaged a Harvard professor whom I knew to be bright, but conventional. He was good enough, apparently, to have demolished the work of the local low-bid neophyte. The EEOC asked me for help. They offered me IBM's report. When they also offered me their own I asked, incredulously, "You really don't want me to read this, do you?"

"Huh?"

"Look, if I read your expert's report, I can be asked questions about it. If I don't, I can't. Now, should I read your expert's report?"

They decided that no, I shouldn't, after all.

IBM took in stride their losing a motion to have me suppressed. I wanted access to some data directly from IBM. I did not know if it was different from the data used by the EEOC's initial expert. We requested and received data tapes. They arrived in an obscure format that required modulo mathematics to decode. That was just a little defendant's trick, one of the stories to which I will return when I discuss the role of the judge. Defendants' bar is peopled by nasty critters.[57]

One variable was especially difficult to extract correctly. In principle, the deposing attorney's job is to get information from me while not providing any to me. In fact, I always learn from being deposed. IBM's attorney—knowing that his programmers had made the task as difficult as possible—had me explain how I extracted data from his tape. He paused longer after one explanation than after the others. I recognized that I must have extracted the data incorrectly. Though I cannot explain how this happened, the solution came to me on reading the deposition transcript, remembering the event. We re-extracted the data from their difficult transmission. When I testified, my data were not challenged.

I would think it would be gratifying to make data as easy to understand as possible. I tell several stories in this book of how I try to do that. I cannot understand the mindset in which making data difficult for someone else to use is enjoyable. That is because I seek truth, a different goal from that of IBM's employees. My staff understood what lowlife we

---

57. Barry J. Nace, plaintiffs' attorney in several Bendectin cases, describes defendant's attorneys' behavior: "I learned that . . . their favorite time to make deliveries to my office was 5 o'clock on Friday afternoons." 29 *Trial Magazine* (September 1993) at 7.

had dealt with. Defendant's staff surely understood what lowlife they had been, but it was not a negative value to them.[58]

Insurance Executives

Fox and Grove decided to advise a client to settle. Kalvin Fox got me into a high-level insurance-company-executive meeting to inform the executives that they were clearly going to lose the case they had hired me for.[59] "Sure, sure," one executive said, "But let's go through the scenario."

So they figured how long the trial would take, and then the appeal. How long before they would have to pay millions of dollars in damages. It turned out that as long as they thought they might drag it out, this executive would still not have reached retirement. What he wanted to achieve was that the shit would not hit the fan on his watch. Not what's right, not what's good for the insured or for the company, not what's smart strategically. His vote to settle was based on not otherwise being able to accomplish his personal objective.

Client Failure

I explained some of the I-NET situation in Chapter 3. The Office of Federal Contract Compliance Programs (OFCCP) had done a compliance review, asking that male and female salaries be equal within job group, not controlling for grade or any other factor. My report strongly condemned their approach, and affirmatively showed no male/female (or majority/minority) salary differences.[60] The OFCCP engaged Mark Killingsworth to prove that they were right.

This dispute lasted several years, during which time I-NET was purchased by Wang Corporation. There was some question whether my client, Seyfarth Shaw Fairweather & Geraldson, would retain I-NET's labor-law business. My reports argued that Killingsworth's study was a farce, that it was not only incorrect but manipulated, and that a company could not afford to let the OFCCP get away with it. On July 31, 1997—changing only the figure number—I wrote in a client memorandum:

---

58. One could fill books on just this aspect of legal practice, the scurrilous practices of defendants' attorneys. Yes, plaintiffs' attorneys are not saints, but much of the work of defendants' attorneys, uniquely, is hiding from discovery. See, for example, how General Motors' attorneys kept denying that there were certain documents when there were, in fact, hundreds of them, in *Baker* (1996), and then continued to protest the release of other documents that impeached one of their witnesses, in *Baker* (1999). Reminds one of *Kyriazi* (1978), described in Chapter 3.

59. It will become interesting that Fox and Grove continued to use my services after this incident, because the next time I told them they would lose, I was fired forever. I tell that story below.

60. I-NET was owned by the Indian Bajaj family, requiring the OFCCP to devise a novel on-the-fly redefinition of "minority."

By pre-selecting grades that they think will show salary deficits, the OFCCP hopes to rig the sign test. But the only fair test is of all grades, or all that can be analyzed. We see that there are four negative and seven positive signs in Figure 37. Although there are more positive than negative gender-salary relationships, this distribution is well within the bounds of chance when there is no relationship at all. The female coin is about as fair as the sign test can find it to be.

Had all of the OFCCP's grades shown a female salary deficit, and all those they did not consider shown a female salary surplus, I-NET still would have passed the sign test. It was only by suppressing four grades that the OFCCP could hope to convince anyone that there are female salary deficits at I-NET. Even then, females are "advantaged" in four of their seven grades. The OFCCP can only find otherwise by confusing the relationships in a single equation.

This is why it is so important, as I have been saying for years, to refuse to let the OFCCP define the terms of the dispute. It is critically important not to give in to their "we're willing to reduce your exposure" argument. You want more exposure, because three out of four of the grades they did not analyze are female surplus grades. You cannot let them obscure this fact by pre-selecting not to study these grades. Besides, when it comes to damages, the OFCCP forgets that they haven't studied the firm. They want to generalize from only what they think are salary deficit grades. I-NET would have to be stupid to let them do that. . . .

In short, females and minorities look randomly distributed in terms of having higher or lower salaries than white males. Only by pre-selecting not to review Grades 5 through 7 and 10 can one begin to think that there is anything other than a random distribution of the sign of the salary difference, only for blacks. The OFCCP needed an "expert" to obscure these simple facts. Killingsworth's "finding" is phony, built in by "controlling" for seniority (and other variables) in a way that expects everyone to be paid like people in Grade 13 are paid.

I do not know if it was Seyfarth Shaw, the attorneys for Wang, or Wang itself that decided not to fight the OFCCP. Nor do I know any details of how they capitulated, or whether it was associated with Wang's subsequent bankruptcy. I never heard from them again.

Jean-Luc Calvez used a regression to estimate damages for thirty-eight claimants who, they said, had lost money they otherwise would have made but for the oil spilled by the *Amoco-Cadiz* in the spring of 1978. District-court judge McGarr preferred a simple averaging presented by William Wecker for Amoco. On appeal, Amoco argued that it was "inappropriate . . . to award damages on the basis of the defendant's calculations."[61] In the future, Amoco's attorneys will be sure that their expert finds no damages at all.

Plaintiffs did not appeal their damage award. On review, the Seventh Circuit went out of its way to chastise plaintiffs' attorneys for not pursuing their interests:

---

61. *Amoco-Cadiz* (1992) at 1320; following indented quotation also at 1320.

> Had the private parties pursued this matter on appeal, we would have
> been inclined to instruct the district court to base its award on the Calvez
> computations.

Regression was appropriate. Neither the court nor Amoco found fault with Calvez' use of
the method. Only his own clients did.

WHAT DO CLIENTS WANT?

David Copus once engaged both my firm and Joan Haworth's firm on the same employment-discrimination case, for defendant. He gave us the same data and authorized the
same preliminary analysis. I found that plaintiffs could not support their complaint as filed,
but if they amended their complaint, they might get somewhere. I suggested some changes
in personnel practice defendant might institute before plaintiffs got wise. Copus told me
he thought my analysis was far superior, but he "liked what Haworth said" better.

I understand. Joan Haworth is one of the least-competent analysts I have ever come
across, but she is by far the best advocate-witness. She adopts her client's position and finds
some numeric manipulation that appears to support it. She presents it in a plain and simple manner, as if it makes sense, indeed, as if anyone else would do and find just what she
did. When the other side's expert must resort to some proof of the absurdity of Haworth's
"analysis," the judge gets lost. The judge thinks this expert must be pulling a fast one—it
was so obvious when Haworth explained it.

Copus asked me to help defend a Southern bank against an allegation of race discrimination in hiring. He came with me to talk to bank officials about data. My approach is elementary: Start at the beginning of the process and identify all places where some information was recorded. Perhaps a file folder is created when a letter of application is received. OK,
let's track every action that can put information into that folder. And let's see the folders.

That is what we did, systematically going through each step in recruitment and handling of applications. When we got to the folders, on site, we saw photographs. "Photographs?" asked Copus. "We took them out of the copies we sent to you," said his client,
innocent in demeanor. The whole case changed. The ability to say no one knows the race
of the applicant just disappeared. I do not know if Copus alone would have gotten this
information, or when. By engaging an expert in data retrieval he found the smoking gun
before plaintiffs did.

Know the Law

Copus cared about what his expert knew. He sat me down one day, with my partner at the
time, Farrell Bloch, to scold us. "What you don't know about the law is hurting you, and
therefore is hurting me," he said, and proceeded to give us a lecture on the law.

Later, I got to reward him for that advice. His client was Firestone, which had been sued for race discrimination—for "under-utilization," an availability-analysis term—by the OFCCP. Copus said the rules required Firestone to produce a "utilization analysis" for every division. "No they don't," I said. "Yes they do," he said, exasperatedly reaching for the published rules. And that was when he first recognized the word "major," as in "every *major* division" required a utilization analysis. What was "major"? That is the kind of word that requires clarification, without which employers do not know what the rules are. Indeed, it was on the OFCCP's failure to have defined "major" that Firestone prevailed legally.[62]

Firestone also prevailed factually, on an issue I mentioned earlier in this chapter. The OFCCP had compared the percent black employment in seventeen divisions against some availability figures, and had found "under-utilization" in one of them. At the "0.05 level of probability" it found fewer black employees than it expected. It then threatened to prevent Firestone from having any federal contracts unless it brought that division into compliance. Here is the simple mathematics of the problem.

What is the chance of one division being out of compliance at the 0.05 level, by chance, if there is only one division and the division is not in fact out of compliance? This is a trick question. The answer is 0.05. Randomly, one time in twenty, a compliant division will look out of compliance at the 0.05 level. That is what the 0.05 level *means*. It's a trick question because there is no trick: 0.05 means 0.05.

Now let us apply the 0.05 level to two divisions, assuming that they operate independently. What is the chance that at least one of them will appear to be out of compliance, by chance at the 0.05 level, when in fact it is in compliance? The probability of a particular division being out of compliance, by chance, is 0.05, while the other division has a 0.95 chance of being in compliance:

$$p = 0.05 \times 0.95 = 0.0475$$

The total probability of finding at least one division out of compliance, by chance, when neither is, is 0.0475 for the first alone, plus 0.0475 for the second alone, plus 0.0025 for the rare chance that they are both randomly found out of compliance. The sum is 0.0975. Even though one says that the probability of finding one division out of compliance is 0.05, by chance, when they are not out of compliance, when two are studied the probability is almost twice as large.

What does it mean to say we find a division out of compliance, "by chance," when it is in compliance? Where does chance enter in? Chance is in measurements (do we think we have everyone's race correct?); in the comparison (is the availability figure immune to

---

62. See *Firestone* (1981).

error?); in timing (perhaps two more blacks were hired the next day)[63]; in omitted variables (we do not know how applicants appeared in interviews, for example); and in the confusion of outcome with process (perhaps two blacks resigned voluntarily the day before, or were offered positions they did not take). "Chance" is at issue because we can never have more than a sample of the behavioral response of a firm to an applicant characteristic, even if we have appropriately and correctly measured that characteristic on all actual applicants within the relevant time frame. When we obtain a low probability in one test we think, quite reasonably, that this is unlikely to be one of those rare times where chance is dominating. Thus because the finding we have would be rare *assuming* no under-utilization, we prefer to believe that there is under-utilization.

If we do seventeen tests, the probability that we will find at least one test "significant at the 0.05 level," when there is no under-utilization, is 0.58. That is, in firms the OFCCP might study, each with seventeen divisions, all in compliance, it would by chance declare more than half to be out of compliance. Two divisions would falsely show under-utilization slightly over 5 percent of the time. Strictly speaking, then, the OFCCP would have to find three divisions out of compliance to assert that it had found noncompliance "at the 0.05 level" in a seventeen-division firm.[64]

To demonstrate this point in court, I purchased a roll of quarters, which I presumed to be "fair."[65] I had two research assistants toss them into the air, let them hit the floor, and count heads and tails. They did this seventeen times and plotted the results. We say we expect fifty heads each time, but actually we expect a range of values. The standard deviation is five, that is, five heads too many or two few. So the two-standard-deviation—that is, $p = 0.05$—level is fewer than forty or more than sixty heads. But although a disparity this great from the average of fifty heads is a rare event if we toss one hundred coins once, in seventeen tosses we actually expect to find at least one such occurrence.

And we did. I brought to the hearing a histogram (bar chart) showing the number of heads on each toss, with lines at the forty- and sixty-heads levels. One of the seventeen was

---

63. In *Ochoa* (1971), the district-court judge notes, not as a part of his finding but as a "See, I told you so" punctuation, that Monsanto hired many Hispanics just after the period used by plaintiffs to make their case, but before they knew there would be litigation about hiring Hispanics. In *Roman* (1976), plaintiffs sought to limit the time period to before June 1971.

> In December 1971, the first month after May 1971 in which ESB hired, there were 11 blacks
> hired, and only two whites. In January 1972, there were 14 blacks hired and eight whites.

At 1353, 14 FEP Cases at 244.

64. This is a practical demonstration of the operation of the Bonferroni correction, mentioned above. When there are multiple tests, the height of the hurdle over which one must pass to appear "improbable" is raised.

65. No other assumption is tenable. See Gelman and Nolan (2000).

higher than the 0.05 level—just as was true at Firestone. I do not still have that original chart. Figure 59, in which I have shaded the area of most-expected random variation, was derived similarly, from random numbers.[66] The OFCCP would declare the sixth "division" in Figure 59 "significantly" out of compliance, although the difference from fifty, in its height, is due to chance alone. I don't think the OFCCP has ever understood the fallacy of their mechanical approach to probability. The I-NET case occurred more than a decade later. The OFCCP was still doing the same kind of multiple tests, interpreting random variation as noncompliance.

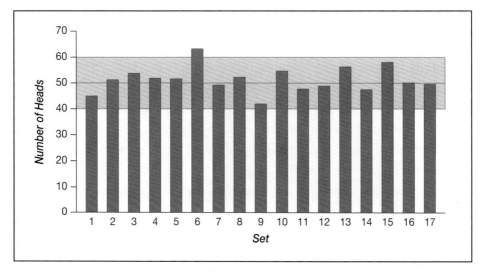

FIGURE 59: Seventeen Sets of One Hundred Random "Coin Flips"

The Price of Honesty

In the A. H. Robins bankruptcy proceedings, instigated by the extent of damages claims stemming from the Dalkon Shield intrauterine birth-control device, Committees formed to represent different interests. One, called the "Claimants' Committee," more formally the "Otherwise Unrepresented Claimants' Committee," engaged Murray Drabkin of the Washington office of Cadwalader, Wickersham & Taft, as its counsel.[67] It was my impression that

---

66. Figure 59 was created in Excel, using the random-number-generation tool in the data-analysis pack. I have shaded the plus-and-minus-two-standard-deviations band around the mean. It might be noted that Excel's algorithms, although criticized by many statisticians, are satisfactory for illustrative purposes, if not precise to many decimal places.

67. As it was the mounting Dalkon Shield claims that put Robins in bankruptcy, the initial claimants, perhaps two thousand of them, had attorneys. Ultimately over two hundred thousand additional claims were accepted by the court. The Claimants' Committee was their voice, whereas the represented claimants elected a different representative to speak for them.

Drabkin was more in control of the committee than they of him. He had no interest in statistical experts. Drabkin had opposed the way the case was going—towards a pot of funds put aside for Dalkon Shield claimants, then a no-liability sale of the remaining assets of the company. But if it was going in that direction, then Drabkin and the Claimants' Committee would work for the largest pot they could get. Their expert was simply a means toward that end.

Years before, I had met, liked, and engaged Robert Lasky of Cadwalader as my firm's attorney. I was an inconsequential client, but Lasky seemed to enjoy the relationship, and the break from his more typical high-finance work. Lasky arranged for me to be interviewed by the Claimants' Committee. Later that day he took me aside. "Why did you do that?" he asked, referring to my customary preliminary remarks. He conveyed no other information except that I had done the unthinkable, declared myself to be for hire only to do honest work.

The Claimants' Committee engaged someone else. I did not know this, because a week after my interview I got the job. I assumed they took a week to make the decision. In fact, they had decided against me on the day of my interview, as Lasky surely knew. They brought their expert to a meeting in Richmond, where he proved not up to the task. Only reluctantly did they then accept the package deal, honest work from someone who could handle the job.

That speech is how I screen my clients. I incorrectly thought the Claimants' Committee had passed my test. I barely ever saw Drabkin. My client became Mark Ellenberg, a junior partner at Cadwalader. He seemed to sleepwalk through the processes that concerned me, until eventually I quit for lack of support. Had I known that the Claimants' Committee had rejected me on the first day, in revulsion at the suggestion that I would seek a just solution, I would not have taken the case.

More on Attorneys and Data

The curse of the expert is the client with theory and "data" in hand. David Copus should be a model: His attitude was, "Let's find the data together." Richard Caro, Assistant United States Attorney in the Eastern District of New York, had the same approach. We had to find who had applied for certain positions at the Navy Resale and Services Support Office, at the Brooklyn Navy Yard. It had been sued for racial discrimination in hiring and promotion.[68] To study hiring, as indicated in Chapter 2, plaintiffs would traditionally describe the current work force and perform an availability analysis, making up who "should" have

---

68. The case as it finally went to trial, without class claims, is *Verdell* (1985). I discuss in Chapter 8, for it is a story about experts, why the class claims were dropped.

applied and been hired from population data. We wanted to know who actually had applied. We were told that no data existed.

Well, let's see. What does an applicant do? An applicant fills out a form. Can we see the form? Yes, this is the form.

This form has three pages with carbon paper between: a blue, a pink, and a yellow page. What happens to these pages? The blue page is the official application, it goes here and there and to a selection official and, if you win, it remains in your personnel file. If you lose, when the process is over, it is destroyed. As I told you, there are no data.

The pink page? Well, if you win, the pink page goes to payroll. They use it to initiate a record. Only the winners. Then they discard it, but remember the blue page is safe in the personnel folder.

The yellow page? All the yellow pages go to Mary Beth, down at the end of the hall. We don't know why, or what she does with them. OK, let's go see Mary Beth.

Whereupon Mary Beth tells us that she has saved every yellow page that has come into her office for the last ten years. Here they are in cardboard cartons stacked around the room. Although any Navy official Caro might have asked would have told him that they did not exist, we found our applicant data, and did our selection analysis.

Post Office Change of Address

The amount of money the State of Connecticut was spending for my expert services in *Gibbs* (1998) clearly exceeded their prior experience or their expectations. The challenge to their jury system, described in the Appendix to Chapter 5, boiled down to making the state responsible for the higher non-delivery rate of summonses to Hispanics than to non-Hispanics. It seemed obvious that a Hispanic is more likely to move out of the judicial district than a non-Hispanic, and reasonable to believe that the court would accept mobility—not living there when the summons arrived—as an innocent explanation of the mail-delivery disparity. The State's Attorney's office had lined up personnel from the public-school system and various welfare agencies to document the higher Hispanic turnover.

I studied driver's-license renewals (associating address with ethnicity through census data summarizing ethnicity by Zip code), and census data on recent moves. We knew of a third data base, the National Change of Address (NCOA) data retained by the Postal Service.

To save funds—possibly the only cheap action in this case and, not at all coincidentally, the only one that created data problems—a state's attorney obtained the "data" and transmitted them to me. I found these categories:

> residence;
>
> business; and
>
> post office box.

As both businesses and individuals can have boxes, and as I care only about individuals, I ended up doing a number of "sensitivity analyses" (what if X percent of the boxes are individuals, etc.) to determine if my results were robust to possible errors in data. Doing so cluttered my presentation, and required more hesitance in my conclusions than the data in fact warranted.

I finally could talk with someone from the NCOA program at the trial. I asked him about the post-office-box confusion, and he said he thought that was intrinsic to the data. They were not collecting data for the purpose to which I was putting them. Before he testified, however, we were both shown an affidavit from the NCOA person who had provided the data. That person stated that he had deleted all business post-office boxes from the "box" category. The data separated businesses from persons very well, and allowed us to separate persons by box or residence. Excellent. That separation called for a sensitivity analysis itself, but one created by the intrinsic nature of the data: We do not know where box holders live. I was associating the number of moves per Zip code (as a ratio of number of units, itself a confusing and ill-defined concept) with the percentage Hispanic among households in the Zip code. Box holders might live in a different Zip. It appears that not enough do to affect conclusions, but you have to check.

I should have known better than to let a client provide data. As described above, attorneys are trained to give as little information as possible to their expert. That, no doubt, was why the affidavit had been hidden from me. Even in the best of client relationships, with the best of clients, this attitude worked against my client's real interest. The standard advice may keep embarrassing facts from the court, but it is deleterious to good statistical analysis.

Obtaining Dalkon Shield Data

A. H. Robins had lost to or settled with over a thousand plaintiffs prior to the Dalkon Shield class action. Robins maintained a computerized file of these settlements, as well as claims frozen by the bankruptcy. The file contained systematic data culled from settled cases so that Robins could assess future settlements for reasonableness (from their point of view) and consistency. I wanted those data, and believed they should be available through ordinary discovery. Mark Ellenberg had dismissed the file as "worthless."

In a general plea for more cooperation from my clients, I wrote, "I think data questions should be left to me. It is hardly worthless."[69] Indeed, the settled-claims data turned out to be the core of every expert's estimation of the amount to be set aside for claimants in bankruptcy. They served as the basis of debundling characteristics, valuing in compensation and punitive dollars the various harms that had befallen claimants from their or

---

69. Michelson memorandum to Murray Drabkin and Mark Ellenberg, July 14, 1986. The following two indented quotations are from this same memorandum.

their partners' use of the Dalkon Shield. Applying those values to a sample of claims out-
standing, and then projecting that valuation to the population, was the general approach
envisioned by the court, and taken by every expert. Ellenberg, dragging his feet because the
Claimants' Committee did not want to be in this process of estimation, only made my
job harder.

I described to Ellenberg the steps I had gone through with Francis McGovern, the special master, to obtain the tape file. Ultimately, the expert can do nothing. All procedures
are attorney procedures. I explained:

> It is standard in litigation to exchange computerized data. Just give them to us.
> There is no reason for McGovern, and certainly none for his obviously inex-
> perienced and not very qualified helpers, to invent some process. Mark Peter-
> son, a McGovern myrmidon, says he has to determine "what is in the file" to
> select how to distribute it. That is nonsense.

What was going on was a struggle for power. The special master and his staff were not
interested in a process in which they mediated among and facilitated the parties' experts.
They wanted to be players. To gain that position, they would control the data.

Robins had paid to remove the Dalkon Shield from some women, and also maintained
a file of that expense. My memorandum to my clients continued:

> The Removal File identifies people who, Robins cannot contest, used the
> Shield. It may also identify persons who said they did but, upon removal,
> didn't. You may expect Robins to employ those data to cast doubt on some
> claims, but not to use them to support claims. I believe that file could lead to
> a more powerful sampling plan to get at the value of pending claims, and I
> believe Robins knows very well that this is a potential use of the file. Once
> again, they gain from delay. And they have been successful in getting the delay.

As far as I could see, my clients were being out-lawyered at every turn. What I did not yet
understand was that they did not care. Their goal was to keep *their* client, and to maintain a high profile as bankruptcy attorneys.

I did not realize that "keeping their client" to Murray Drabkin meant eventually
becoming the attorney for the Claimants' Trust. Usually, plaintiffs' attorneys would have
no further connection with a case when a trust has been established to receive and settle
claims. Drabkin thought big, and for a time got his way. The former Claimants' Committee was represented among the trustees, who in due course appointed Cadwalader as their
counsel.[70]

That August 1988 victory was short-lived. There were power struggles all around,
and in the struggle between an attorney and a judge, the attorney is almost always the

---

70. For details on how this came about, how each trustee voted, etc., see Sobol (1991) at 288.

loser.[71] Drabkin, knowing that Judge Merhige, with the power to determine the trust's attorney, would not appoint him, opposed the judge's having that power. As the Fourth Circuit had given Merhige carte blanche in this case—if they would not remove him for meeting privately with the head of the company, they would tolerate anything—I don't see how Drabkin thought he had a chance.

That power struggle is not my story. Richard Sobol tells it better than I could.[72] My story is how Drabkin cared not a whit for honest assessment of the data, did not support his expert, did not even attempt to provide his expert with the material to do his work.

What Are "Data"?

We need to have a broad concept of "data," the grist for the analyst's mill. We need this broad concept partly because the expert is allowed to inform a court about his view of the case, and therefore the court is free to inquire how he came to this view. Consider, for example, the sorry experience of the dean of the School of Business Administration at Rutgers, Horace J. DePodwin:

> What DePodwin has in essence done is to examine the myriad documents supplied to him by plaintiffs' counsel, to quote liberally from these documents, and to conclude, "Aha! Cartel! Conspiracy! Illegal concerted action!"[73]

DePodwin let his client select his data. At least that was the impression left with Judge Becker.[74]

Sheila Jasanoff lays much of the blame for the poor showing of experts at the feet of attorneys:

> Expert witnesses in U.S. courts are sought out, trained, and compensated by the disputing parties. Unlike civil-law tribunals, the judge in a classic common-law proceeding plays little or no part in managing the production of evidence, structuring its presentation, or examining witnesses, except to exclude material that is deemed inadmissible by law.[75]

---

71. Sobol outlines these other power issues, stated as Judge Merhige wanted them: Hiring Michael Shepherd, the clerk of the bankruptcy court in Richmond, as keeper of the Trust's files (at double his previous salary), and engaging a Richmond bank rather than a New York bank to handle the Trust's funds. Merhige got everything he wanted, including the ouster of Cadwalader.

72. See Sobol (1991).

73. *Zenith* (1981) at 1349. It is not clear that DePodwin should be considered an academic, if we are keeping score, because he also had a consulting firm.

74. The appeals court disagreed with Judge Becker's characterization of DePodwin's work, reinstated it and reversed the summary judgment. See *Zenith* (1983). The Supreme Court reversed the appeals court, resuscitating Judge Becker's interpretation and, more important in litigation history, establishing the ability of the trial court to dispose of such cases by summary judgment. See *Zenith* (1985).

75. Jasanoff (1995) at 45.

This expert-client relationship is what Samuel Gross was writing about:

> Frequently attorneys do more than limit and select the information their experts receive; they shape the experts' work product as well.[76]

Timothy Perrin agrees:

> The lawyer decides what information the expert receives, what issues the expert testifies about, and, in some instances, the words the expert uses in stating her opinions.[77]

Peter Huber thinks the problem goes deeper than the attorney selecting the data, and deeper than the attorney dictating the outcome and language of the analysis. He notes that, at least at times, the case has been constructed by the attorney, by his selecting plaintiffs rather than plaintiffs selecting him. "The plaintiffs' lawyer, through careful selection of a particular group of plaintiffs, a single product, and a single disease" can create a statistical case of product liability.[78]

Huber's suggestion is not fanciful. David Bernstein, for example, discusses the problem of "expert" credibility under just this circumstance, in asbestos litigation:

> [P]laintiffs' law firms seeking clients transport physicians they have hired to workplaces and union halls, where the physicians test workers for asbestos exposure. The attorneys, often working with labor unions and other organizations, offer free X-rays to the workers in exchange for the workers signing an agreement saying that the attorneys will get forty percent of the recovery if

---

76. Gross (1991) at 1145.

77. Perrin (1995) at 1418. Recall also the examples from *Dentsply* (2003) and *Yapp* (2004) in Chapter 2, in text and in footnote 107, of attorneys manipulating their experts' data.

78. Huber (1985) at 324. Hager (1990), at 540, describes Huber (1988) as "a book riddled with flaws and errors—factual, historical, logical, philosophical, and moral." Regarding Huber's major work (1991), Lewin (1992) notes, at 186:

> Huber fails to prove his contentions about the extent and origins of the problem of junk science because his own methodology is little better than that of the charlatans he criticizes.

Cheesebro (1993), at 1643, quoting Huber (1991) at 3, declares that

> Galileo's Revenge is perfectly described with Huber's own words as "a catalog of every conceivable kind of error: data dredging, wishful thinking, truculent dogmatism, and, now and again, outright fraud."

Yes, these lawyers can get catty. Consider this about Huber from Faigman et al. (1994), footnote 38 at 811:

> Unfortunately, he does not advance our knowledge on the question [whether there is an "upsurge of unreliable scientific testimony"] because his own methodology is a form of junk social science (that is, he uses no systematic empirical evidence or analysis, merely anecdotes).

Although Huber's statistics are unsupported and probably incorrect, no one questions his examples. The complaint is that they are overgeneralized.

they turn out to have a lung abnormality related to asbestos. . . . [T]he doctors involved are by no means neutral, detached experts, but instead are hired guns looking to gain clients for their employers by finding an asbestos-related abnormality on an X-ray.[79]

The ultimate strategy in the struggle of the attorney to keep his client surely is to create the client in the first place. In December 2004, CNBC broadcasts are interrupted time and again with white lettering on a blue screen, accompanied by a disembodied voice informing us that James Sokolove has already filed for reimbursement if we had stock losses due to broker fraud. No longer does the client come first, selecting among attorneys. Sokolove is the attorney. Are you deserving enough to be one of his clients?

ATTORNEYS AND ANALYSIS

Kalvin Fox was cross-examining Joe Donovan of the EEOC, who had performed a regression analysis in *Kouba v. Allstate* (1982, on remand). Kal came running over to the attorneys' table, where I was seated. "What do I do now?" he asked of me. No prior discussion of what this witness was going to do, what we, defendants, wanted to get from his testimony, how to get it. Just, blow-by-blow, "What do I do now?" "Settle," I thought, but did not say. Shortly thereafter, they settled.

Termination from AAA Michigan

It was alleged that Allstate Insurance had discriminated in hiring based on gender, in Toledo, Ohio. Plaintiffs and Allstate at first contended that there were no data relevant to the issue. I found that a copy had been sent to Allstate's research facility in Menlo Park, California, prior to their having been destroyed in Toledo. I retrieved the data from Menlo Park, and was able to reconcile slight discrepancies between the number of observations in the data and that expected from Toledo records. That is, I was able to show that if this was not a perfect representation of the missing data, it was at least a reasonable and believably unbiased representation of them. My analysis supported Allstate's contention that gender was not a factor in the hiring decision. I testified. Allstate prevailed.[80]

Convinced that I was "on the team," Fox and Grove retained me in defense of Allstate in *Kouba*. The company conducted a training institute, during which it paid female prospective agents at a lower rate than male prospective agents. That seems like a difficult proposition to defend, but I had an interesting take on it.

There was no set compensation rate for trainees. There was no rule that females would

---

79. D. Bernstein (2003) at 12. Also: "[T]his is a lawyer-driven lawsuit." *DeMarco* (2004b) at *1.

80. See *Bechtel* (1984).

be paid less than males. Nonetheless, plaintiffs could allege disparate treatment of females first because the Supreme Court had made it clear that statistics alone could stand as proof in such cases,[81] and second because the regression analysis any expert would do—the one Joe Donovan did—would show a negative relationship between being female and pay rate.

Recall, however, the role of defendant's expert in disparate-treatment discrimination cases: Convert the disparate-treatment claim (a relationship between result and gender) to an impact finding (a relationship between result and some measurable characteristic). That leaves the problem of justifying the factor that has impact as a "business necessity," or as "reasonable," or whatever standard applies at the time. In its first round of litigation, All-state had claimed that trainee pay had been based on prior pay which, it happened, was lower for females than males. The Ninth Circuit did not rule out such a defense, writing that

> a factor used to effectuate some business policy is not prohibited simply because a wage differential results.[82]

But that was not the defense I was offering, at least partly because I did not have data on prior pay. The persons who set the training compensation told me they were predicting *future* performance as agents, for which I did have data. I found that these predictions were valid: Those whom they paid less in training did in fact perform less well, regardless of gender. The "screening device" was subjective, but accurate.

Although subjective screening criteria did not sit well with courts, none had ever before been shown to be a valid predictor of performance.[83] Few situations produce performance data, and even commission sales as a performance measure should be controlled for differences in "territory." Still, in my view, the case could possibly be defended by showing that what appeared to be disparate treatment was disparate impact, that the item that created the impact had been stated in advance (it was not an ex post facto analyst's creation) and was valid.

This defense might not have succeeded on legal grounds. The Court had struck down other valid predictors of performance on the basis that antidiscrimination law protects individuals, not groups.[84] But there was a difference between this case and previous cases:

---

81. See *Teamsters* (1977) and *Hazelwood* (1977).

82. *Kouba* (1982) at 876.

83. Just a few years later the Supreme Court did affirm that subjective employment-screening devices could be analyzed under disparate-impact theory. If they could be shown to be valid, the outcome was excused by the procedure. See *Watson* (1988).

84. See *Manhart* (1978) as well as the aforementioned *Teal* (1982). The Ninth Circuit was one of many circuits that accepted "disparate-impact" analysis of subjective employment practices, which allows for their validation. See *Atonio* (1987) at 1482. Although at the time my theory was novel—and not understood by my clients—apparently I am not the only analyst who thinks testing the validity of a subjective system makes sense. I hope it is not too out-of-context to quote David Kaye: "Methods that involve some

Allstate personnel insisted that the predictions were made individually. They only happened to correlate with gender. If Allstate personnel could reliably predict which trainees would do better after training, independent of gender, why would paying them differently based on that prediction not be acceptable?

Although what I had created was a novel *legal* defense—the analysis was straightforward once one had thought of it—Kal Grove never seemed to understand its logic. He was not a contemplative attorney. We did not discuss the evolution of equal-employment-opportunity law, where my theory fit in, what legal research was needed to support it. Nor, as it turned out, was pursuing my approach just to see how far we could go with it a relevant consideration. There were anecdotes about abusive behavior toward female trainees that Allstate preferred not to have told in open court. Although Fox and Grove had no comprehension of my sophisticated and complex argument, they were satisfied that I was still "on the team." In the face of what seemed like a hopeless set of facts, I had written a report that defended them. I was their guy.

Another large client of theirs was the American Automobile Association of Michigan. Although in name and origin an automobile service firm, the AAA/M had become a huge insurance company. It had a staff of insurance agents, some of whom it had terminated on the basis of an unvalidated formula. I was told that forty-eight cases alleging discrimination based on age had been filed against the AAA/M, each of which had to be litigated separately. I was provided with relevant data, the formula, the actions, and the jury-trial date for the first of these cases.

Unfortunately, I did not understand the nature of my relationship with Fox and Grove. I had acted honestly, competently, and creatively in several cases. Here was one, and perhaps forty-seven more, in which I intended to continue in that mode. To Kalvin Grove, however, I had acted in support of his client, making him look good and, in the one case that was litigated, successful. The difference between these two understandings of my role in the relationship was bound to create conflict.

I could not validate the method the AAA/M had used to select the two people they terminated. By any logical view of sales quality, my staff and I found two younger salespersons who should have been terminated first. Without a valid selection device, given these facts, the AAA/M would lose an age-discrimination complaint.

I told Kal that I should come to Michigan to explain my results. "I'm sure you will be presenting good news," he said. I did not understand his statement to be an instruction. "I don't think so. Have only the most-necessary people at the meeting," I replied. "Keep it small."

---

subjectivity can be validated." "Expert Testimony on Fingerprints: An Internet Exchange," 43 *Jurimetrics Journal* 1:91 (2002). Kaye's remark is from January 15, 2002.

The meeting was held in a very large conference room. More than a dozen executives from the AAA/M were there. Oh well. I presented my results, explaining the fallacy in their formula, naming the two employees who should have been terminated and why they were clearly poorer salespersons than those who were now suing. Kal Grove was not happy. "We're waiting for the good news," he said. "I don't have any," I replied. "Settle this case."

Recognizing that I was not "their guy" after all, Grove fired me. From all forty-eight cases. We have not exchanged a word since then. However, a junior associate sent me a letter. They had gone to trial without presenting a statistical case, the other side had identified the same two other people as clearly inferior salespersons, and the jury had found for plaintiffs.

Kal Grove did not listen. In my view, and as I think the junior associate came to understand, I was what Fox and Grove needed, if not what they wanted. Had they followed my advice, they would have settled the first AAA/M case, and let me analyze the data behind the second case. But handling the case well was not what I had been hired to do. Finding the truth was not the point. Keeping the client was. Kal succeeded in that end. I failed.

Promotions at the Naval Air Rework Facility

To some extent, United States Attorneys are immune from this "keep the client" mentality of private defendant attorneys, and the "make a buck" mentality of private plaintiff attorneys. Although in a sense United States Attorneys have federal agencies as clients, they have a monopoly on that role. The agency's attorney must defend—he has to continue to work with the accused malefactors—but the United States Attorney can stand back, judge, and act to bring about a reasonable resolution based on facts.

Sometimes agencies do not cooperate. It is worth reporting that the two most distasteful experiences I had through the United States Attorney in Washington, D.C. were with the Federal Bureau of Investigation and the Bureau of Alcohol, Tobacco, and Firearms of the Department of Treasury. In cases at both agencies, after it became clear that I would not "join the team," but would, instead, work to determine the facts, I was eased out. It makes sense. This "join the team or get out" mentality originates in the military, in the conception of activity as life or death, win or lose, you're "fer" us or "agin" us. Both the FBI and the ATF were outstandingly non-cooperative. The very idea that an outsider could come into their territory, ask questions that might lead to finding anything wrong with their behavior, was contrary to the way those agencies operate. Both cases settled.[85]

---

85. The *Oregonian*, July 10, 1996, at A11:

> The federal Bureau of Alcohol, Tobacco, and Firearms announced Tuesday that it has agreed to a $5.9 million settlement in a discrimination lawsuit brought by black agents.

But here we go again: "Treasury Dept. Faces Suit by Minority Agents," *New York Times*, May 17, 2002 at A19. Plaintiffs include black agents from the ATF.

In *Moore* (1984),[86] this dynamic relationship between United States and agency attorneys was worked out by letting the Navy run its own case. I had worked for the Navy before, in their appeal of *Trout* (1981). Once again, because my findings supported the defendant, the Navy's attorney, Daniel O'Connell, assumed that I was "on the team." Once again, when they found out otherwise, rather than settle the case, they terminated our relationship and continued in their fight.

The issue in *Moore* was a complaint by females that they had been passed over for promotion in a rework facility in Oakland, California. "Rework" is the repair and rebuilding of airplane parts. It is an indoor workbench-oriented mechanical job that requires very little heavy lifting or other activities in which males could be expected to be generally superior. Applicants for promotion filled out forms, by hand, describing their qualifications. I could find no way to quantify and test the use of these qualifications that obviated gender-based selection for promotion. That is, I could not convert a plain finding of disparate treatment of females to one of disparate impact.

During this time, plaintiffs' expert, John H. Freeman, filed several documents that illustrated his inability to perform a competent analysis. His analyses and my comments on them were presented in Chapter 2. Thus it was easy enough for me to appear to be on the Navy's team in my critiques of plaintiffs' arguments. However, I was finding that although plaintiffs' statistical analyses were hopelessly inadequate, their complaint was correct.

As a final test, I sent a staff member to Oakland with copies of completed application forms, names obliterated. Even without the names, the forms contained facts that should have revealed identities to reviewers, in the applicants' handwriting. We wanted to see in what order those who had made the original promotion decisions would rank these applicants now. Thus, when we showed these forms to the original reviewers, replicating the original competitions, one would have thought the reviewers—who must have known who got the promotions—could substantially replicate the original rank ordering of the applications. At least at the extremes: winners and losers.

They could not. Their new rankings were unrelated to their original rankings.

To convert a disparate-treatment case to a defendable disparate-impact case requires not only that items with impact be found, but that those factors in some sense be validated. As described in Chapter 2, validity (the relationship between a measure and a criterion) requires reliability (the relationship between a measure and itself, that is, consistency in measurement). The Navy had an unreliable evaluation system which, therefore, could not be valid. As females were less likely than males to be promoted, the court would infer that

---

86. *Moore* (1981). I do not know the final disposition of this case. There is an unpublished opinion I have not seen, and a curt Ninth Circuit affirmation.

gender itself had played a role in selection. It was time for the Navy to derive objective and performance-related criteria for promotion in this facility. Meanwhile, their best course would be to settle this case.

I was fired.[87] The Navy engaged the American Institute for Research to replace me. However, the Institute did not have the technical expertise to perform its task. In particular, it did not understand the conditional logit estimation I had used to derive a generality about behavior from a set of competitions. The Navy engaged me to teach this method to the Institute.

The only software available to effectuate multivariate multiple-pools analysis was my firm's MULQUALS™ routine in mainframe SAS, as explained in Chapter 2. Even though the Navy had been willing to pay me to teach this method to the Institute, it was unwilling to purchase my software, perhaps because it could not handle the overt contradiction between firing me and using my product. The Navy supported the Institute's writing of equivalent software, which cost many times as much as purchasing mine would have. As my software was the standard effectuation of conditional logit for equal-employment-opportunity cases, the Institute had to validate its own. Thus, in its literature, it claimed that its software should be considered accurate because it produced the same results on test data as MULQUALS™!

Attorneys and Trial

"So you're a professional expert witness, eh?" I am asked. "No. I'm a professional expert. Even though this is a full-time job, I spend very little of it as a witness." The misunderstanding, probably based on seeing too many "Perry Mason" programs, applies to attorneys as well as experts. Even trial lawyers spend relatively little time in court. Fewer than one case in ten in which I am engaged actually goes to trial. In many cases, keeping it out of court represents my success. I am a better expert than expert witness. Many attorneys are better in their office than in the courtroom. When they are not good trial performers, they can not only hurt their case, but hurt their expert, as well. Some of my suggestions in Chapter 10 concern how badly an expert's work can be mangled by his client.

---

87. There is much much more to this story, of course. Although it would not be my concern if a private client wasted money fighting indefensible cases, as a taxpayer I could not let this flagrant misuse of public funds go unchallenged. I complained to O'Connell's Navy superiors that he was not pursuing truth, that he was defending the indefensible. In short, I blew the whistle, and received what whistle blowers get: My complaint was rejected, my contract terminated. I was never engaged by the Navy again, a loss to my firm of millions of dollars of revenue, and a loss to taxpayers of the kind of advice they deserved, but that would not be listened to by Navy attorneys.

Making the Trivial Difficult

I do not remember the attorney's name—he worked for the EEOC; it was many years ago. The issue was at what probability level an analyst thinks there is a relationship between a dependent and an independent variable. I will describe in detail, in Chapter 7, the origin of the "bright-line" demarcation of a "significant" coefficient. It is arcane, but it lingers on.

The defendant's expert was going to claim that my finding was "not significant." I spent an evening coaching my client on why that was not a responsible way to view the finding, and how to bring the person he was cross-examining to agree with me that my finding was respectable, even "significant" if one must use that term.

Unfortunately, I do not remember the expert's name, either. He did his job well. He saw where my client was going with his questions, and that he, the expert, would ultimately go there, also. So he just did. "Oh, sure, you could call that a statistically significant finding," he said. This is exactly right. When an expert is going to lose a point, he should lose it quickly.

My client stood there, mute. After some time the judge asked him to continue, but he remained frozen in his tracks. Eventually the judge told him to sit down. The poor guy had stayed up all night practicing his cross-examination, concentrating on getting the expert to finally admit one small thing. When he achieved the point quickly and easily, the lawyer had nothing more to say. He had let a small technical point become the object of his examination, not something to get past to focus on substance.

This was an extreme example, but the problem is common. The lawyer, as I indicated at the beginning of this chapter, does not know how to engage in a discussion with the expert, either his own or the opposing party's. Some lawyers study statistical texts and learn the language, but they usually get too tied up in the language to understand the ideas. Unless the case is very simple—as, for example, *Bush* (2000) on projecting Dade County partial-voting results—the attorney is quite capable of blowing it, even if his expert did a fine job, and even if his client is right. Experts do fail their clients, to be sure; but at least as often it is the client who fails his expert.

Comparable Worth and *Nassau* (1992)

Joel Klein, who later became prominent as the Justice Department attorney who brought an antitrust action against Microsoft, had co-founded a "boutique" law firm in Washington, staffed exclusively by former Supreme Court law clerks.[88] This would have been an

---

88. The firm was Onek, Klein and Farr. One of its associates was Peter Huber, who had clerked for Justice O'Connor, and who later coined the phrase "junk science."

interesting approach for taking on appellate work but, as we will see, made no sense for what would become a trial firm. They captured a big client, the American Federation of State, County, and Municipal Employees (AFSCME) with a big case: allegations that pay scales had been devised in Nassau County, New York, so that female-dominated jobs were paid unfairly low.[89] It sounds like a "comparable-worth" argument, but Klein smartly avoided that term. Klein initially alleged intent, a deliberate downgrading of female-dominated positions. That allegation disappeared as the trial progressed.

"Comparable worth" developed as a concept when economists, attorneys, whoever it was, created a logical extension of the Equal Pay Act. As noted in Chapter 2, what Equal Pay Act complaints required as proof was descriptive, not statistical. If an employer had fabricated two different job titles for the same work, and plaintiffs could show that it was the same work, then the employer had to pay the same wages. What if the work was demonstrably not the same, but had overlapping elements? The theory, an extension of "hedonic pricing," became that those elements would have to be paid for at the same rate in male-dominated jobs and female-dominated ones. Under Title VII of the Equal Employment Opportunity Act, differences in pay would have to be justified by the values of the differences in the elements.[90]

The concept of hedonic pricing goes back to the 1960s. Using regression, one estimates the value of each component of a bundle, even though the components cannot be purchased separately. For example, horsepower, wheelbase, and turning ratio of an automobile can each be accorded a "price," by extracting the variation in total automobile cost as these factors vary.[91]

Jobs also are bundled. In a government agency or large corporation, each job has a formal description. Most items in most job descriptions appear also in other job descriptions,

---

89. See *Nassau* (1992).

90. The extension of the Equal Pay Act is simple. Suppose two jobs are the same except for who inhabits them and one task in the one that is held by males; and except for their pay. By the mid-1980s courts had concluded the obvious: A firm could not fabricate a "different" job to avoid the Equal Pay Act. The wage differential would have to be commensurate with equality plus reasonable compensation for the additional task in the male job. See, for example, *Wheaton Glass* (1970). Comparable worth just draws this out to two characteristics different, then three, etc. See Becker (1984) and Becker (1986).

91. Zvi Grilliches is the father of the concept of "hedonic pricing." For example, see Grilliches (1961) and Grilliches (1971a). Despite referring to statistical cases, Freed and Polsby (1984) seem to be unaware of what hedonic pricing does—evaluating characteristics as this employer pays for them. Fischel and Lazear (1986) inexplicably (given Lazear's other writings) avoid the topic. They argue that if wages in occupation X are low because women, prevented from entering Y, flood to X, then the solution is to reduce the barriers to entering Y. That line of analysis misses the point that comparable-worth valuations come from one employer, asking that it pay equally for characteristics wherever they appear. Its Equal Pay Act heritage virtually demands that Equal Pay Act defenses be unrelated to market-wage measures. No attorney or judge seemed to understand that in this case. See Nelson and Bridges (1999).

though bundled differently. The employer can be hanged by his own words if one can show that he paid differently for the same job characteristic depending on the gender of the employee. One could presumably ask how much pay was associated with supervisory responsibility, for example, and even how much additional pay could be attributed to each additional person supervised, as long as the job description contained that information. Doesn't the job description tell us what the employer is paying for, and the wage rate tell us how much?

I had used such information to develop a "comparable-worth" regression analysis of pay of Washington State employees. I had testified for plaintiffs, who prevailed at the district court and agreed with the state on pay-scale adjustments before their victory was reversed on appeal.[92] The state had engaged a rebuttal expert who attended the trial but did not testify.

Although both cases had the same ultimate client, AFSCME, the law firms were different.[93] Klein interviewed a number of experts, but ultimately selected me for the Nassau County job. The county engaged Joan Haworth. I warned Klein that Haworth was a good witness. She would find some way to defend her client, and some way to make it sound sensible, whether it was or not. If trial preparation and trial lawyering were not first-class, Haworth's ability to persuade the judge would determine the outcome.

It was the historical twist, that gender composition *then* affects wage rates *now*, that made my analysis different from traditional comparable-worth analyses. I could not rely only on the current gender composition of jobs, because relative rates had been determined by a contractor some years before.[94] Of course there were procedures for revising rates every year, but equally "of course" such a procedure did not include, "Increase rates more if the percentage of males in the job class has increased." Plaintiffs would have to show the relationship between gender and pay, holding job characteristics constant, not only statistically, but historically, as a deliberate (though not explicit) policy of the original wage-setting contractor.

The county could not incorporate gender bias into a rigid wage structure if the gender composition of jobs changed rapidly. The story, not just the statistics, had to make sense. Thus I needed, obtained, and utilized both historical and current job-holder information. I coded job descriptions, and, by regression, established prices for them. Then I

---

92. *AFSCME* (1985).

93. Winn Newman, who essentially invented comparable-worth lawsuits, was my client in Washington. How he lost AFSCME as a client, I do not know.

94. Judge Glasser's opinion in *Nassau* (1992) is confused about this. He says I used only current gender composition, but then disapproves of my historical data. In general, this is a well-written opinion. You have to look hard for these hints at what really went on at the trial.

asked if the pay for a given characteristic was different between historically male and historically female jobs. Was there an implicit price for the characteristic "maleness"?

I found that, accounting for written job characteristics, the presence of many females was a negatively valued additional characteristic apparently built into the wage structure. Indeed, the relationship was so clear that even Haworth did not try to refute it. She tried to justify it.

The defense was the disparate impact of "the market." Haworth, we knew, would find some variable that, when entered into the equation, reduced the absolute value and improbability of the "female" coefficient to "insignificance." Whatever it was, she would *call* it a measure of market wages. However, as we went to trial, Haworth had not revealed her market variable, how she derived it, what it would do. One can give Haworth credit: Keeping her key variable secret was designed to prevent me from rebutting it, and she got away with it.

Not that I didn't have an answer. The *Nassau* trial is a story first of defendant's obfuscation, second of a judge's bias. I will discuss the merits and the judge's role in Chapter 7. The story for this chapter is attorney incompetence, not understanding what arguments must be made by an expert.

I was plaintiff's first witness. Arranging the trial order is not my business, but I knew that was a mistake. You have to tell a story. You have to bring a judge to where you want him to get, point by point. Klein had the opposite view: Let's impress him with the extent of the differences in wages, and how inexplicable they are except by gender composition. It reminds me of a mistake I once made in testifying before a jury. "I won't mention the other side's expert [who had already testified]," I said. "I will just present my analysis, which bears no relationship to his." Wrong. The jury had worked to understand and believe the other expert. I would have to start by explaining his errors, if I were to get anywhere. Indeed, I should have scuttled my analysis, and just demonstrated how fallacious his was. I clung to my way, where I should have modified my approach to deal with the jury. My client lost that case. It was my fault.

Judge Glasser, in *Nassau*, was rude. In cross-examination he instructed me to answer only "yes" or "no." I said "no" a lot because Nassau's attorney did not phrase his questions as I would have phrased my answers. Glasser then wrote that my answers were "evasive." No, the questions were badly phrased; my answers were correct. The situation was bad.

Otherwise, the case progressed: Plaintiff's expert produced evidence that, other things being equal, females are paid less. A multiple regression on wage rates, using written job characteristics as independent variables, attributes a wage difference to gender. Defendant's expert comes up with a variable no one has seen before which has the effect of substituting for gender. The variable's *name* was "the market," but was it valid? Was it, in fact, a reliably measured, meaningful concept independent of gender itself?

I told Klein I was ready to re-enter the pit, to face the judge to present my rebuttal. He said he would do it in argument. Did Klein not know that only an expert can rebut an expert? That's not true, you say. In *James* (1977), attorney argument on appeal reversed the case. The Fifth Circuit knew the problem of local judges ratifying local discrimination in jury-selection and employment cases. I also knew, as perhaps did the Fifth Circuit, that behind the attorney's appeal brief in *James* was a considerable amount of economist expertise, too late to testify, but embedded in the lawyers' argument.[95] It was just argument, however, interpretation of regression results. I had new evidence. The only way you can introduce rebuttal statistical evidence is through an expert.

I tried to tell Klein about a precedent case in which, without expert rebuttal, a clearly erroneous study (admitted to be so by the person who did it!) was accepted as the last evidentiary word.[96] He told me he did not like what happened when I was on the stand. Neither did I, but without entering rebuttal evidence, what chance would Klein have on appeal? It was obvious that Klein was back-pedaling as fast as possible. Support his expert? Argue on appeal? AFSCME never did appeal the merits of the decision, only the legal fees that had been assessed.[97] If there were conferences to assess plaintiffs' position, I was not included. That Haworth was wrong, that I could show that she was (as I do in Chapter 7), that without my recalculation of her "market" variable they could not argue against it, never became part of a conversation. Klein was into "keep my client" mode.[98] Decision for defendant.

THE POST-TRIAL BRIEF

After the trial, the attorney organizes his argument based on the evidence. In doing so, he summarizes the weakness of the opposing expert's analysis, and the strengths of his expert's analysis. These summaries are never correct. I do not know what the attorney thinks he gains by mischaracterizing the other side's argument, but what the judge gets

---

95. At least Lester Thurow and Marc Rosenblum were involved in advising plaintiff's attorneys in *James* (1977). They deserve credit in the story, as they get none in the opinions.

96. See *Wilkins* (1979). The requirement that statistical evidence be accompanied by expert testimony has been reinforced over the years. For example, in *Janes* (2002) at *3,

> the Court finds that the proffered statistical evidence would not be admissible unless supported or interpreted somehow by an expert pursuant to Rule 702. The suggestion that somehow it would be admissible and more or less speak for itself is rejected by the Court.

The "statistical evidence" offered by the plaintiff here is tables from defendant's published reports. The court wants the interpretation of these tables to be provided by an expert.

97. "No appeal was taken on any issue of liability." *Nassau* (1996) at 649. In *Nassau*, the "reversed in part" was the circuit saying that AFSCME does not have to pay Nassau County's litigation costs. I presume Klein's firm did the work to reverse that finding for free.

98. Klein was aware of his weakness as a trial attorney. Paul Smith from his firm did the trial work always, it appeared to me, under Joel's thumb. In *Microsoft*, Klein engaged David Boies for trial work.

is confusion masquerading as clarification.

Let's look at three sentences from defendant's attorney Michael Courtney's post-trial brief in *Gibbs* (1998):

> According to JIS [Judicial Information System] data, *twice* as many non-Hispanics as Hispanics are disqualified for having left the district, but Michelson says that Hispanics have left the district. This court, in order to accept Michelson's conclusions has to reject both the JIS data *and* the census estimate of Hispanic population. (If they moved out then one must wonder why Michelson can claim that the source lists contain less Hispanics, (5.38%), than the Hispanic population, (6.6% (1990)) and yet the master list Hispanic population increased between 92–93 and 96–97).[99]

Whether this was written in ignorance or maliciousness, I cannot say, but if legal argument consists of setting up straw positions to deride, it is a waste of time. What I had shown was that, although the count of Hispanics was rising, so was turnover. We see more and more Hispanics on the streets of Hartford, but they are different people from one month to the next, possibly not part of the "community," and at any rate impossible to draft on to juries.

I had said that Hispanics leave the system *without informing anyone*. They do not appear in the Judicial Information System data as having left because the JIS does not know that they have. They appear in the JIS data as undelivered mail or "no-shows." The master list contains an inflated number of Hispanics because, as I demonstrated at trial, Connecticut weights towns to discriminate in favor of bringing Hispanics into the jury system. It also purges names slowly, which exaggerates the count of the most transient group. The weighting fails to achieve its objective because many Hispanics leave between the date of the master list and the date of their supposed duty. That other Hispanics have moved in has no bearing on the disposition of those on the master list.

This is not difficult to follow. Mail does not reach Hispanics because they are not there, but as the system does not know that they have left, they are not "disqualified for having left the District." There is no "remedy" because no one has done anything wrong, least of all the jury-recruitment system. Judge Spada understood that there was no fallacy in Michelson's testimony.

Judge Scheindlin compared plaintiffs' filing with their own expert's report, and found that the numbers stated by the attorney could not be supported.

> The question arises whether [plaintiffs' attorney] Mr. Ratner is intentionally trying to deceive the Court or if he simply cannot grasp the findings of his own expert's report.[100]

---

99. Defendant's Brief to the Superior Court, CR93-0089935, April 27, 1998, at 13.

100. *Bonton* (2004), footnote 8.

The lawyer feels free to distort the plain facts of the trial because he is never penalized for doing so. Would attorneys create a system that held them to the standards to which they hold others? Of course not. The attorney takes no oath to tell the truth. He seldom consults with his expert about his summary of either expert's testimony. It cannot assist the judge to have this kind of distortion presented as argument.

THE LAWYER'S ECONOMICS OF EXPERTS

Timothy Perrin describes the situation as virtually all commentators see it:

> Lawyers look for experts who will work with the lawyer in shaping the expert's opinions, then label those same experts as "whores" or "hired guns" for doing so; lawyers aggressively cross examine opposing experts about their fees and suggest the expert's opinions were purchased, but still pay their own experts the same exorbitant fees; lawyers hire experts to give opinions in every case, including opinions about the most mundane, speculative or unreliable matters, and then vigorously disparage the "battle of the experts" that they created.[101]

He asks lawyers to change. He knows they won't.

I *require* that lawyers change, those who engage my services. The attorney does not know what questions to ask of the data, and does not even know when he has the answers to an important question. The attorney who tries to save his client money by obtaining the data himself is doing no service. I don't want their data.

But here is the problem. I have raised this in discussions with some attorneys. All say I am wrong. I don't think so.

The attorney makes no money from the activities of an expert. He does from the activities of his own staff. Regardless what the attorney charges for his own labor, real money is made from billable hours of junior staff. Lead attorneys make money from directing cases, not from performing on them. To engage an expert, some lawyers think, is to export funds that could go into their law firm. On the other hand, going it alone, formulating a mitigation theory, designing a coding form, obtaining "data"—these activities pass money through the firm.

"At heart, economics reduces to the proposition that incentives matter."[102] Why did Gerry Spence decide to become a lawyer? Only the lawyer in his town had a car. "Oh, to be a lawyer. Oh, to have a new black Chevy!" he thought.[103] Jesse "Baby Face" Thomas saw

---

101. Perrin (1995) at 1441.

102. Gary Galles, "Back-to-school just Economics 101," The *Oregonian*, "Reader Forum" section, August 15, 1998, at B9. Galles is identified as "a professor of economics at Pepperdine University in Malibu, California."

103. Spence (1989) at 33.

Lonnie Johnson play the guitar. Inspired by the music? Perhaps. When he told me about it, he said he was most impressed by Johnson's clothes! Wanting clothes like that, he learned to play Lonnie Johnson material. Then he was told by record companies, "We already have this kind of material. Do something different." So he did. Jesse Thomas became one of the most creative, interesting, distinctive blues musicians ever recorded. To improve his wardrobe. Incentives matter.

A solution to the monetary incentive to perform work in the law firm is obvious: Put a "service charge" of perhaps 5 percent on top of an expert's bill. That money could support some overhead, such as maintaining files of experts with attorney comments. I think it would be money well spent by the ultimate client, to redress the bad incentives operating currently. The attorneys who deny that they are affected by those incentives are the same attorneys who tell me, "My objective is to keep my client." Attorneys are unaffected by income considerations? Sure.

Going Too Far

Most of my clients tried to do a fair job. Some did not. I think it is important to tell their stories, a few anecdotes about scurrilous attorneys, to clarify the expert/attorney relationship.

Misrepresentation in *Miller* (1980)

I did some regression estimates of damages. My equation had an interaction variable, perhaps (black × seniority), as well as a variable for blacks. When this occurs, you cannot tell from looking at the equation what the total damages will be. In Chapter 3 I tried to distinguish "fishing" for variables from producing a final specification. There is a final stage in the preparation of regressions, as I do them, in which I may drop variables or adjust their form and interactions, test for the influence of specific observations, etc. This is refinement, after I already know my results. At one point in *Miller*, while adjusting the specification of the model, I reported to my client the number of blacks times the black coefficient as the total damages. That was wrong. Blacks were in more than one variable. The "deficit" had to be calculated from all the variables in which blacks appeared.

Finis Welch was the expert on defendants' side. In response to this last piece of information, he told my client that I was interpreting my own equation incorrectly. My client—whose name I do not remember, or I surely would expose him here—reported Welch's comment to me. I immediately agreed. I stopped billing until the error was corrected. My client had already been charged for the work. I would not charge him again to get it right.

I provided the correct damages figures to my client. The case was settled. I thought no more of it for years.

Finis was on the other side of *Gallup* (1986), discussed in Chapter 2. Shortly thereafter he and I were in the same place at the same time and sat down for a beer together. "You sure got me on that one," he said, alluding to *Gallup*. "But I sure got you in *Miller*, didn't I?" "You certainly did," I replied.

Finis was surprised at my response. My client had not reported back that I agreed to having made an error. Instead, he said a trial would bring forth a battle of the experts, that Michelson would explain his estimates and deny Welch's criticism. In Chapter 10 I will recommend that in many cases the experts should meet face to face when there are issues like this.[104] The attorneys may not understand the technical dispute. Or, they may lie about it.

Interference in *Firestone* (1987)

David Copus moved to Jones, Day, Reavis & Pogue, a large Cleveland firm with a Washington, D.C. office, along with Dan Karnes, with whom I had also worked on the earlier Firestone case. Apparently they took Firestone as a client with them. Karnes engaged my firm. As summary judgment was granted for defendant, one might say our work was successful.

It was also done on time, a joint affidavit by me and Bliss Cartwright of my staff, under duress. The duress was a particularly officious Jones, Day attorney—not Karnes, but one whose name I have suppressed forever. He practiced an unseemly micromanagement, marking up drafts, calling for redefinitions and other changes at that depth. I appreciate editorial help from clients, as they better than I know how to communicate with a judge. But *what* we are communicating must be my work.

My client's markings created the need for me to review everything in more detail than I would have liked, because Bliss was caught between providing a service for a client—an important part of business—and maintaining the independence that I required. Not only did this attorney ask for changes, he did not like those he got. We received back furious notes decrying changes *he* had made, "correcting" them with our original wording! Need-

---

104. Misinterpretation, or the failure to be clear about interpretation, happens frequently. One can hope a face-to-face session between experts would cure most of it. In a regression estimating salary, plaintiff in *Eastland* (1983) had two "race" variables, one for blacks, one for other non-whites. Defendant's expert formulated regressions by job schedule, not accounting for the fact that he did many of them. In all of them, the only race variable was "black." Defendant was comparing black salaries to those of the combined white and other non-white group. Plaintiffs' "black" variable made a starker contrast, whites against blacks. If, as was often the case, those "others" had lower salaries than whites, but not as low as blacks, defendant's regressions may have masked real racial differences. This is difficult stuff for attorney argument. It should be put to one expert by the other.

less to say, all this useless back-and-forth increased our bills which, when the case was over, Jones, Day refused to pay.

I sued. Not for the money, but for the principle. At a cost of $100,000 in attorney fees, I pried $100,000 more from Jones, Day, a deal I would make any time. You can't let clients get away with this kind of behavior. Of course I have never worked for them again. Their loss.

Getting Paid for *Holden* (1987)

Paul Sprenger called me from Minnesota, told me the only thing between him and a settlement with Burlington Northern Railroad was my bill. I didn't believe him, but I wanted the settlement. I gave him a little and then said "no more." He mentioned in passing that of course I would return Burlington Northern's data tapes. I understood that Burlington Northern had made return of the data a condition of the settlement. So I told him I would return them after I had been paid.

To the end, Paul tried to whittle down my fees. We finally arranged to meet in my attorney's office, where he tried one more time to reduce the amount.

"I'm trying to give you a million dollars," he said.

"No you're not. You owe me the million. You're trying to rob me of $100,000."

He wrote out the check for the amount I had specified. I never worked for him again.

Lawyers know no bounds. It's just as Perrin described it. They want you to lie for them, then to lie about lying. They want you to have a high billing rate so they can impress the judge with what an expert you are. Then they don't want to pay it.

Advocacy

All lawyers advocate for their clients. That is their job. IBM's attorney at Covington & Burling was in on the confused way in which they presented data to us. I trust he was suitably impressed, at trial, that my firm had figured out everything, the modulo arithmetic, the disguised codes, the whole thing. But such games are not only not necessary, they are expensive. Much of what attorneys do is designed to cost the other side. In Chapter 10 I will suggest that there should not be "full disclosure" of expert materials, the only consequence of which is to increase cost. It is not an efficient or effective way to learn what the other side did and did not do. Parties that manipulate their data to make it difficult for the other side to decode it, however, should be exposed to and sanctioned by the court.

The OFCCP is the reason Home Depot, and I am sure other firms, will not sell to the federal government. The OFCCP is supposed to support an executive order that commands contractors' labor practices to have no regard to race or gender bias. But they require race- and gender-conscious decisions at all levels. They bring nonsense concepts like "utilization" to the table, based on a fictitious "availability" figure that cannot be refuted by applicant data.[105] Few companies go to trial to resist the OFCCP, because bad relations with a government monitor can lead only to bad consequences. The OFCCP is advocacy run amuck.

Like statistics, lawyers come in all kinds. We are the most lawyered country the world has ever seen. Gerry Spence has an exaggerated view. He tells us, "Two-thirds of the lawyers on earth live in the United States."[106] More reasonably,

> Counting conservatively, American lawyers probably make up somewhere between 25 and 35 percent of all the world's lawyers.[107]

Whether attorneys are brainwashed or forced by circumstances, by the structure of the system, to fight each other when there is a clear right-thinking view, I do not know. Spence describes "that nearly irresistible need for lawyers to smear their adversary."[108] Paul Wilson's tale is indicative of the brainwashing attorneys undergo in the name of "due process," the concept that justice is derived from advocacy. He was a minor attorney for the State of Kansas, a defendant in *Brown* (1954). He knew he was on the wrong side, making clear that he thought so in the title of a humble little book he wrote about his experiences. But see how he rationalizes his behavior:

> As a human being applying personal standards of conscience and rationality, I felt that the position of the state of Kansas was indefensible. At the same time I did not regard my personal view and bias as relevant. The issue was one of law.[109]

I find this expression as sad as the virtuous but inept views of pretenders to moral superiority, including the "progressives" with which I started Chapter 2, and religious fanatics who would like to regulate (if not obliterate) non-religious life. Kansas was defending school segregation, in the same way that Dan O'Connell was defending the Navy's discrimination against females in promotion. O'Connell was wrong. His work as Navy's counsel did not require that he defend improper behavior. Kansas was wrong. In the name of advocacy for his "client," Wilson defines the issue, and his work thereon, as something outside himself, distant, not to be evaluated. I think his job should have been to argue that the state should admit the facts and gracefully lose. Integration by vote would not occur in his lifetime. Losing the case was a better outcome for Kansas than winning. Yes, guilty

---

105. See the Seventh Circuit's opinion in *Lamp* (1991), for an articulation of the court's preference for applicant data over availability data.

106. Spence (1989) at 27.

107. Galanter (1994) at 647.

108. Spence (1989) at 147.

109. Wilson (1995) at 227.

defendants should have legal assistance, but that assistance should be directed toward getting them to plead guilty.[110]

The Real Economics of Experts

It is not only attorneys who learn the lesson that the "name of the game" is to get, and keep, clients. Although repeat business can come from client attorneys bringing different client plaintiffs or defendants, new cases are continually filed by inexperienced attorneys. The expert has to keep getting additional clients. An implication is that the expert is getting new clients *who have never before used a statistical expert*. More and more, the professional expert is more experienced than his client.

As the quotations in an early section of this chapter, "Finding the Expert," attest, attorneys by and large view the expert as a commodity. His compliance, not his expertise, is paramount.[111] It makes sense for the attorney not to try to inquire if the expert is "good," both because he doesn't care, and because he could not assess quality if he did care. Most important, though, quality of the expert *as a determiner of fact* is not what interests the attorney.

This is not to say that no assessment of quality is made. An expert who will adopt the client's point of view and convince the court that it is correct—whether it is or not—will gain more new clients than one who always supports the client but never convinces the court. As the ability to gather and analyze data relevant to the legal question is not the client's predominant criterion, it must be, and is, a diminishing characteristic of experts.

The Inevitable Consequence

Although I think many markets fail for many reasons, and although there are many imperfections in the market for statistical expertise, I am willing to assume that the market for statistical experts works well. The result of a market in which the valued good is support

---

110. I understand and commiserate with medical personnel who, regardless how mistakenly, would like to choose which procedures to perform, or which patients to assist, on other than medical grounds. The answer to their bigotry is not to force them to act against their conscience, but to refuse to employ them if they will not follow the rules of the non-discriminating institution. Employees need not participate in what they consider immoral acts of their employer, but neither can they stay employed by them. Attorney General Elliot Richardson and Deputy Attorney General William Ruckelshaus resigned, in October 1973, rather than obey the order from President Nixon to fire Special Prosecutor Archibald Cox. Robert Bork did the deed, informing us about who he is. State Department personnel have resigned to protest foreign-policy decisions. In Chapter 9 I describe the resignation of Kenneth Maxwell from the Council on Foreign Relations, and that of five editors from Climate Research. That is what medical personnel who do not want to attend to minorities should do, and what Wilson should have done.

111. Under the federal rules, admission by an expert that he thought of himself as "on the team" would be grounds for exclusion. The attorney wants his expert to violate that rule, and then deny it.

of an advocate's position, in the guise of objective "scientific" analysis, is that the best analysts are driven out. This is not the working of Gresham's law, where the "inferior" good chases out the "superior" good. Gresham's law is about commodities with intrinsic value and incorrect prices. The market for experts reflects the values of attorneys. In their view the supply of their preferred commodity is increasing. The prices are correct, in the market sense that they reflect the values of the purchasers. Only in *my* eyes are the "good" experts driven out. I simply hold to old-fashioned values, like the search for truth in the resolution of disputes. Those characteristics are not valued in the expert marketplace.

I do not contend, however, that anything has changed, that the "old values" have been swept away by flimsier ones. I managed to survive as long as my results served my client's interests, not because my clients valued honesty or skill. I got enough winning cases to make a career. When the case was a loser—and I told my client—I lost him forever.

If one were to attempt to measure the statistical expertise offered in courts, over time, I suspect that by any measure it has gotten better. Yet I just concluded that it would be getting worse. Is my conclusion about the trend wrong? No, the trend exists just as I have laid it out. But we have seen a technological boom. Better statistical algorithms and better graphics are available for a fraction of the cost of the crude mainframe packages of only two decades ago. Sample design can be automated. Exact tests can be run on more accurate data. Color graphics easily can be printed and photocopied. In addition, one should understand the improvement in the statistics profession since I started doing litigation work in the 1960s. Like other sciences, statistics itself is simply better. We have better statistical tests, and know more about them, about errors, bias in data, etc. In both substance and form, surely expert presentations have improved.

The rate of improvement in science theory and the hardware and software to effectuate it cannot keep up with the adverse selection of professional experts. The improvement he gets from even faster chips, busses, and data interchange will hardly be noticeable to the future statistical expert in litigation, except to automate data transfer and make fancier graphics even easier to produce.[112] If we measure relative to the increasing skill level available today, expertise in litigation has gotten noticeably worse. While serving his client, the expert fails to serve the judicial system, to further its goals of fact determination. In standard market terms, neither the "people" nor the judge are the clients, because they do not expend funds. A view of the expert marketplace within the judicial system as serving any-

---

112. In twenty years, analysts have been relieved from mainframes and 9-track tape by PCs with 32-bit operating systems, inexpensive usable memory, and massive hard drives. The impact of forthcoming 64-bit operating systems will be trivial in comparison. Software incorporates new knowledge in statistics. Simply by upgrading, an analyst could be introduced to improved methods of analysis, and tests of the characteristics thereof. It seems apparent that analysts in litigation take little advantage of this source of information.

one other than those who pay the bills misses the point. The market does not fail. The bill payers are getting what they want.

Sometimes experts are correct even though analytically unsound. A flawed analysis does not necessarily imply incorrect conclusions.[113] Sometimes the analyst does not have the expertise he claims; sometimes the analyst has approached the issue in such a biased way that he does not allow himself the use of his skills; sometimes to do a proper analysis in this case, even though it would favor a client, contradicts what he has done in another case where an honest approach would have backfired. If the name of the game for the defendant attorney is to keep the client, and for the plaintiff attorney is to get far enough to force a settlement that includes his fees, the name of the game for the "expert" is to provide inputs to the process that produces those outcomes for the client. No other behavior will be consistently rewarded.

Stephen Easton asks us to construct, in theory, a system to provide really bad, corrupt, expert witnesses:

> For starters, why not let attorneys select, hire and pay the important witnesses? Make sure these witnesses are hired under "at will" employment contracts that allow the attorneys to fire the witnesses as soon as they do or say anything that is not completely consistent with the position the attorney wants them to take.[114]

In short, construct the system we have.

Although it has taken, and will continue to take, some time for this process to work itself out, this is our system and it is heading toward its inevitable result. The structure of the marketplace for statistical expertise, where the parties' attorneys are the buyers, guarantees that no statistical expert should be trusted to have done an honest job of data collection or analysis. No client, other than some United States or state's attorneys, would engage him to do so. As the honest-yet-competent-expert supply diminishes, even the few remaining truth-seeking clients may have a hard time finding the expert they want.

---

113. The best example remains *Bazemore* (1986), in which a hopelessly inadequate analysis supported the party that deserved to and did win. When explaining, in Chapter 2, why multiple-pools methods better match the institution they are modeling, I noted that sometimes one does not get a qualitatively incorrect answer from the incorrect single-pool approach. I do not know which side was right in *Greenspan* (1980). Mark Killingsworth's regressions for plaintiffs were as overloaded with variables, as aggregated in non-homogeneous effects as those he did in *I-NET*, described in Chapter 3. But defendant's expert, J. Wanzer Drane, asked, at 1063, "whether female employees progress in salary at different rates than similarly situated male employees." That was the defense the Supreme Court later declared unacceptable, in *Bazemore*. At least Killingsworth addressed the right question, however badly. His client prevailed.

114. Easton (2000) at 469.

7

Judges

Judges were once lawyers and few lawyers, as we learned in Chapter 6, are whizzes at science. Bluntly:

> All judges and most legislators and administrators come from the ranks of lawyers. These are people who typically ended up in law school because their prospects in science and math were dim.[1]

More delicately:

> In matters of science, most lawyers, including many appointed to the bench, lack any extensive scientific training.[2]

A judicial opinion tells us three things. It determines jurisdiction: By what authority, what law or constitutional doctrine, this court gets to make this decision. Then it finds fact, which might be a jury or a judge function, but it is the court's function for sure. Finally it rules on law, which is to say, comes to a judgment about the complaint. A fourth element—the sentence in criminal cases, the penalty in civil cases—is not only contingent on the legal ruling, but might be made separately. Once jurisdiction has been established, fact and law go tumbling in the hay together. As I have indicated earlier, "fact" is not readily definable outside the legal context in which it stands to be found. The two terms are hardly independent, law always operating on fact.[3]

---

1. Faigman (2000) at 53.

2. Imwinkelried (1995) at 64.

3. From Lempert (2000) at 266:
   > Although people usually think that evidence leads to legal rulings, it is equally true that legal rules shape the evidence produced.

In Chapter 4 I described the 1735 case of John Peter Zenger, the classic example of jury nullification. One can view that case as the jury deciding to rule on the law, not just find fact. Juries do that all the time, even though they are instructed not to, partly because they find the distinction between fact and law arbitrary.

Most judges pretend otherwise. Findings on one must be written before rulings on the other, but a cautious judge can cover himself as did Judge Lake:

> In the event that any of the foregoing Findings of Fact are Conclusions of Law, they are adopted as such. In the event that any of the foregoing Conclusions of Law are Findings of Fact, they are adopted as such.[4]

In our system, judges, among the least scientifically inclined members of the population, will determine what is fact, and then determine how the law applies in the context of the allegation. I say they can do it.[5]

Michael Saks warns:

> Few judges are trained in statistics, demography, psychoanalysis, cognitive psychology, or whatever the relevant social science material may be. There is

---

4. *Wilkins* (1989) at 336. Judge Jordan expressed a similar caution in *Delaware* (2004) at *22:

> To the extent that any of my findings of fact may be considered conclusions of law, such findings are incorporated herein.

Justice Scalia (1989) at 1182 is equally confused: "I frankly do not know why we treat some of these questions as matters of fact and others as matters of law." Richard Posner (2001b) at 379 agrees: "But the line between a question of fact and a question of law is not always clear". When considering jury composition, the Third District Court of Appeals in Florida says, "Whether or not a group is cognizable is a question of fact," finding that Hispanics are. *Alen* (1992) at 1085. But a Rhode Island court found that renters are not in *Tremblay* (2003). If the issue had been rent control, surely both decisions would have been the opposite from what they were.

There are disputes within the Supreme Court about what is fact, what is law. Justice Powell, writing for the Court in *Biggers* (1972), footnote 3 at 193:

> This rule of practice, under which the Court does not lightly overturn the concurrent findings of fact of two lower federal courts, is a salutary one to be followed where applicable. We think it inapplicable here where the dispute between the parties is not so much over the elemental facts as over the constitutional significance to be attached to them.

Justice Brennan, in dissent, quotes from this passage of the majority opinion, and continues, at 203:

> I cannot agree. Even a cursory examination of the Court's opinion reveals that its concern is not limited solely to the proper application of legal principles but, rather, extends to an essentially *de novo* inquiry into such "elemental facts" as the nature of the victim's opportunity to observe the assailant and the type of description the victim gave the police at the time of the crime.

5. I am not alone. Note (1995) at 1556:

> An examination of opinions in which courts have made the effort to evaluate the reliability and relevance of scientific evidence suggests that this responsibility is fully commensurate with judicial capabilities.

Poulter (1992), at 195, asserts that "scientific reasoning and legal fact finding employ the same rules of logic. Thus, lay judges need not fear that examination of scientific evidence to determine whether it is soundly reasoned and reliable is beyond their capabilities." I do not deny the existence of incompetent and bigoted judges. They and, if federal, their life tenure, are a problem; but they are not the norm.

plenty of reason to be concerned about judges' and the law's ability to evaluate proffered knowledge.[6]

He concludes, as do I, that "The answer is to find ways to facilitate judicial evaluations."

Scott Brewer defines "intellectual due process," contends that juries and judges not trained in scientific method cannot do it, and then tells us that describing "the consequences of this analysis for institutional and doctrinal revision and transformation"—translation: procedural remedies—"are beyond the scope of my current project." He argues from epistemology that the current system does not work, but will not say what to do about it.[7] I argue from experience that it usually does work, but we need to understand the slim post on which the system stands. In Chapter 10 I do say what to do about it.

Gerry Spence, also, is skeptical. Good judges, he says, "are the few giant trees in the forest—but the weeds, not the majestic cedars, choke us." The bad systematically outnumber the good, so that "after one subtracts the small margin of great judges, there is something wrong with the remaining lot of them." The problem is not dishonesty, but their "parentage," the class bias in judge selection. "[W]e must find a better way to choose our judges."[8]

Robert Bork warns:

> Men and women given unaccountable power will often use it to further their own ends, not the ends of the polity which they exist to serve.[9]

True enough, and this chapter comes complete with a description of my experience of just such wayward power wielded by Judge Robert Merhige in the Dalkon Shield bankruptcy litigation. Perhaps that they can so easily misuse their station is even more reason to be impressed with the quality of the judiciary, as I have experienced it, from county to state to federal levels.[10]

---

6. Saks (1990) at 1026; following in-text quotation at 1027.

7. Brewer (1998) at 1677. Actually, Brewer does go on to hint at a few solutions, which I will visit in Chapter 10.

8. Spence (1989) at 102, 110, and 111.

9. Robert H. Bork in the Foreword to Boot (1998), at v. Robert Thompson (1991) at 738, using himself as an example, asserts that "A state judge is a lawyer who had a governor as a friend, and in the case of a federal district judge the friend was a senator." However, he quickly concedes, at 739, that many "judges reach the bench by popular election, and most of those who are initially appointed are subjected to electoral accountability in one degree or another." Bork and Boot see "electoral accountability" as the problem. Thompson, as did Ashman (1973), sees elected judges as the solution.

10. In May 2004, Chief Justice Rehnquist formed "a high-level panel to investigate the federal courts' handling of judicial misconduct," chaired by Justice Breyer, according to Mike Allen and Brian Faler, "Judicial Discipline to Be Examined," the *Washington Post*, May 26, 2004, at A02. However, both the *Post* article and the next day's *New York Times* editorial, "Judicial Ethics Under Review," erroneously implied that this panel would investigate ethical issues at the Supreme Court. The panel was formed under the Judicial Conduct and Disability Act of 1980 (revised in 2003), which specifies that complaints about

The Judicial View of Experts

We know that a party in a dispute can be his own witness. Can a party be his own *expert* witness? It would seem not. The expert, as we saw in Chapter 1, is supposed to be and sometimes is considered to be objective, disinterested, uninvolved, not knowledgeable of the facts or incidents except through his study thereof.

Nonetheless, the Seventh Circuit did allow a party to be his own expert witness. It overcame the hurdle of objectivity not by finding that the party was objective, but by finding that experts aren't! Judge Richard Posner, at one time a social-science expert himself, wrote:

> [H]ired experts, who generally are highly compensated—and by the party on whose behalf they are testifying—are not notably disinterested.[11]

Experts, like attorneys, want to keep their clients; and to do that, they want to keep their clients happy. There is essentially universal agreement about the problem. I think the solution has to come from judges, the subject of this chapter.

Judges and Statistics

What kind of person would take a job in which he must find "fact" in areas of which he has little knowledge? Illustrations of judicial ineptness in this book are meant only to indicate problems, not to measure the extent of those problems. Judges think in certain ways. Evidence, to be convincing, needs to be presented to them in those ways. Part of the job lawyers do, or should do, is to be sensitive about how individual judges receive informa-

---

federal judges are to be accepted and evaluated by judicial councils formed within each circuit. John W. Dean tells us:

> The process has worked for corrupt judges and some conspicuously egregious misconduct. But the run-of-the-mill bad judge can escape its reach.

See http://writ.news.findlaw.com/dean/20040813.html, "Thoughts on the Law Addressing Bad Federal Judges."

Dean notes that attorneys are deterred from filing complaints both because most are dismissed, and because that judge (or others) can invoke retribution. Thus a count of complaints produces a downwardly biased view of malaise within the bar. Nonetheless, Dean also notes that states are doing better than the federal courts in bringing sunshine to judicial behavior (with open hearings). It may be that one cannot expect much to come of Breyer's panel, but the subject of egregious federal judicial behavior is now open. I do not mean to dismiss it in text. However, judicial mishandling of statistical expert testimony is seldom a sign of judicial misconduct. It is usually well-meaning judicial inadequacy.

11. *Tagatz* (1988) at 1042, 50 FEP Cases at 100. Posner later cited this decision referring to a gang member who had testified as an expert on the gang's code:

> There was no pretense that he was impartial, or a member of a learned profession. Neither condition is required to qualify a person as an expert witness under the current rules of evidence.

Williams (1996) at 1441.

tion. A number of my clients have described their judges to me, to assist me in writing my reports. Most attorneys do not think of such things, however.

I could argue that when a judge is faced with statistical experts, he should have one of his own. In Chapter 10 I will go farther, suggesting that a judge might want a statistical expert even if no party's expert is one. Almost any science-based expert will present statistical evidence, whether he himself is a geologist, medical researcher, economist, etc. We saw in Chapter 5 that non-experts, such as jury commissioners, present findings (such as that X is "not very different" from Y) that a statistical expert can show to be incorrect. Statistics is a tool experts and non-experts use, often badly. It is one that few experts, and fewer judges, understand. The solution does not lie in the judge "learning" statistics. It lies in giving him access to skilled advice although, as we have already seen, and as I will additionally explore in Chapter 8, that is a rare commodity.

Future Earnings

Let's start with the judge as economist.[12] Ted Eymard had been a successful entrepreneur. His income had been growing at 40 percent a year. He was earning about $368,000 a year in 1982, when he was killed in an airplane crash, at age twenty-five. If defendant is liable, what was Eymard's family owed? First they were owed that part of his income that would have been spent on them. Then they would be owed that part of his income that he would have saved, and its accumulation if reasonably invested, discounted back to "now" (sometime in 1986), if he lived a "normal" life longer than theirs. All of this would be discounted by the probability that Eymard would have met some other life-shortening fate, if not this one.[13]

I will assume the calculations are made in nominal dollars, that the economist had enough trouble without also projecting inflation forward for forty years, that "real" income in this decision means discounted to present value. The economist, who is not named, did

---

12. Actually, let's start with the judge as *Daubert* gatekeeper. Fradella et al. (2004) summarize, at 338:

> Some courts prohibit any testimony from forensic accountants or economists on the issue of damages calculations. In stark contrast to such an outright ban, other courts welcome such testimony.

Surely expert testimony on damages would assist the jury, as long as the jury had some way to evaluate how expert the testimony was.

As for the judge as an economist, George Thomas (2001) explains, in footnote 1:

> What I mean by the title is that a background in economics is neither required nor even thought necessarily useful for judges.

13. Many experts calculate income to a person's "life expectancy." It may seem obvious to do so, but because the value of money now depends on when it would be earned later, that procedure is incorrect in a compensation forum. As David Hemenway (2004) informs us, at 10, "More than half of all Americans who die before the age of forty die from injuries rather than disease." The expert should reduce expected income by the probability of surviving each successive year, to discount all future risk in one calculation.

not assume that Eymard's 40 percent annual rate of income increase would continue. He projected that his income would increase at 8 percent a year. The district court did not agree. The appeals court supported the district court:

> Despite the testimony concerning Ted Eymard's business acumen, we find an assumed 8% salary increase continuing over almost 40 years to be unsupported by the record and completely incredible.[14]

Starting with my first full-time professional job in 1964, my income increased at an average compound annual rate exceeding 9 percent over the next forty years. Eymard starts at a higher base, but by this projection he would have earned $1.7 million a year in 2002, which seems unextraordinary, given what we know of him and CEO salaries.[15] So far, there is nothing "incredible" about it at all, except stating it as a certainty. That is, the damages specialist should project a reasonable best case (continued business success), and then reduce it by the risk of failure, and the risk of death.

Circuit judge Patrick Higginbotham did not like the rate of 8 percent per year, but did not remark on the expert's *immediately* reducing Eymard's earnings increases to it. Let's satisfy both reality and Judge Higginbotham. Eymard's earnings increased from 1981 to 1982 at a rate of 40 percent. Let's assume that the next year they increased by 35 percent, and then the next by 30 percent, etc. From 1989 on his income would increase 5 percent each year, well below the 8 percent rate that so irritated the judges. At a straight 8 percent rate of increase, through 2021, Eymard would have earned over $95 million; but under the sliding scale just enumerated, he would have earned over $108 million. This has to be expressed as a present value. A discount rate of 5 percent would mean Eymard's "real" earnings would not increase at all starting in 1988. Surely the court would assume a discount rate below Eymard's rate of increase of earnings, or under 5 percent. Let's say 3 percent. Then the defendant airline would owe approximately $11 million more calculating my way, despite assuming a slower equilibrium growth rate than did the nameless economist. What is Judge Higginbotham's problem?

---

14. *Eymard* (1986) at 1234.

15. *The Economist*, October 11, 2003:

> In 2002, the median base salary of the CEOs of the S&P 500 companies was $925,000. The median total compensation for that year, on the other hand, was $3.65 [million].

369 *The Economist* 8345, at 85. Courts are legitimately cautious about projecting business revenues forward indefinitely, when there is a natural limit to growth. See, for example, *Boxhorn* (1986) at 1023:

> Rates of growth are subject to moderating influences, and a computation of damages that assumes exponential growth must take these influences into account.

The business in *Boxhorn* was use of a trapshooting range, and the court correctly asked how many trapshooters there could be in the area. No description of Eymard's business, no rational questioning of the limit of its growth, appears in *Eymard* (1986). There is nothing exceptional about the rate of increase of my income. The *whole point* of investing in "human capital" is that it provides a good return.

I suspect the economist irritated the court with his assumption that Eymard's tax rate would continue to be 5 percent, which Eymard had achieved through depreciation write-offs. This is a feature of judges that we should not take lightly. As they are to a large extent bewildered by the expert's work, when they find something that they can understand to be fallacious, they are likely to assess the entire work through that lens. The court rightly saw that such a low tax rate could not continue. I am not sure the court appreciated that assets already in place would continue to shelter Eymard's income for years into the future; but it did understand that *increased* depreciation requires massive increases in investment, which Eymard was unlikely to make. On the other hand,

> While the Eymards had no virtually no savings or money in retirement plans at the time of their deaths, the economist assumed, without any objective basis for doing so, that they would begin saving in 1990 at a rate of 5% of total income and increase their rate of savings to 20% from the year 2000 on.[16]

There are many "objective" rationales for such estimates. As a general proposition, the savings rate increases with income. I find nothing intrinsically wrong with these assumptions. What is wrong is that they seem to have been pulled out of the air. Each should have been justified by reference to earnings and savings tables. Furthermore, as noted above, not only might Eymard not have continued to be successful, he might have died by some other means. However, Higginbotham's conclusion seems unjustified:

> In sum we find the assumptions of plaintiffs' economist so abusive of the known facts, and so removed from any area of demonstrated expertise, as to provide no reasonable basis for calculating how much of Ted Eymard's income would have found its way into assets or savings to be inherited by his children.

My impression: It was not the calculation (except for taxes), or the sums (unless they were not reduced by their probabilistic nature) that bothered both trial and appeals-court judges. It was the lack of documented justification, and the single bad misstep of assuming an unrealistically low tax rate. The judges obviously did not understand how generous the assumed constant 8 percent earnings increase was to defendant.[17] The judge does not know what is a realistic assumption. He needs a crutch, a document, a study: something that allows the economist to say he is not setting the parameters, his research has led him to them.[18]

---

16. *Eymard* (1986) at 1235; following indented quotation also at 1235.

17. There is always time between the liability and its compensation, time the heirs waited without the income that the court now determines they would have had but for the airline's malfeasance. That time requires its own compensation, "pre-judgment interest," which should have increased the award. See Knoll (1996).

18. There are guidebooks for every task in the law. The expert should know about them, inform the judge, and indicate where and why he has diverged from them. G. Martin and Clay (1981) or an earlier edition of Speiser (1988), for example, surely would have been available to Eymard's expert.

Correlation

In Virginia, Judge Michael looked suspiciously at Seth Schwartz's credentials. Schwartz received his B.A. in geological engineering from Princeton in 1977, and since then had worked for a living. He has years of experience in "market research analysis, including identifying and forecasting prices as well as business analysis for investment decisions." Some of that work involved testifying, although "none of these cases involved antitrust matters requiring the rigorous defining of a relevant market." It is easy to find a professional wanting in academic credentials. "Schwartz never has authored a book or article dealing with antitrust matters or vermiculite."[19] The world does not need more résumé-aggrandizing books. It needs more experienced experts.

Furthermore, who but a person in the employ of a vermiculite mining company would study the vermiculite market? Such minute specialties are found almost exclusively in the current or past employ of a firm likely to be a defendant. I agree with William Donaher, Henry Piehler, Aaron Twerski, and Alvin Weinstein, writing (fruitlessly, it seems) thirty years ago:

> In short, it is time for courts to recognize the realities of technological expertise and insist that the capability for and acquisition of self-education be demonstrated. Once self-education has been recognized as a legitimate basis for expert qualification, the courts have a duty to prevent its debasement by reckless cross-examination.[20]

The primary defendant in Judge Michael's court was W. R. Grace. Co-defendant Historic Green Springs, Inc., moved to reject Schwartz. A *Daubert* hearing was scheduled.

> Grace withheld a memorandum to support its motion [to join Historic Green Springs] until the late afternoon of March 2 [2000], giving the court and the plaintiffs only one business day to consider Grace's arguments before the hearing was to begin on March 6.[21]

I know this kind of chicanery well. It is through rigorous scheduling meticulously enforced that a court can—and should—stop it. Not this court. The hearing was adjourned until March 29.

At the hearing, defendants produced a snap quiz for the unsuspecting Schwartz, who apparently had been performing satisfactory professional work for over ten years:

---

19. *Vermiculite* (2000), three quotations at 730–731.

20. Donaher et al. (1974) at 1326. This article, as one can deduce from the quotation, is about and most related to product liability. Nonetheless, it introduces the possibility that one may be an expert without credentials, and that persons with credentials are not always "disinterested."

21. *Vermiculite* (2000) at 731; followed indented quotation at 734 (internal references omitted); and then in-text quotation at 732.

Furthermore, Schwartz seems to be confused about the concept of price correlation. Correlation refers to how pieces of different products move in relation to each other over time. In considering two different vermiculite concentrate size grades (what Schwartz has labeled as small and ultrasmall), Schwartz was unable to draw any conclusion about the price correlation of the two products as the prices did not change. He stated, "[The unchanging prices] provide no empirical evidence from a statistical basis of any kind to demonstrate that these two prices are, in fact, correlated; it merely demonstrates that those prices are unchanged, not that they would move in the same direction, let alone by the same magnitude of correlation." However, by simple definition, no change over the years in the two products' prices indicates perfect correlation.

Here we have Judge Michael making up his own definition of "correlation," fulminating when he should have been learning. Schwartz was correct. The correlation between two constants is undefined, because it would require division by zero. Why would Judge Michael display his ignorance like this? He concluded that "Schwartz lacks the requisite educational background for an expert witness."

I find the fact of this academic quiz more irritating than the judge's giving a failing grade to a correct answer. What does it have to do with Schwartz's testimony? If a concept that Schwartz does not know is important, then Schwartz's analysis will be deficient. Why not bring it up at that point? The qualifications threshold has turned cross-examining attorneys into "Truth or Consequences" quiz masters. If they allow it, judges are playing the wrong game. What should be assessed is the worthiness of the statistical expert's testimony, not of the expert.

In *Local 38* (1969) the issue was whether the union was continuing to discriminate against black applicants for apprenticeship. Judge Green considered the data on the left side of Figure 60, in which

"IQ" is the score on an IQ test;

"Mech" is the score on a mechanical-aptitude test;

"EJAC" is the score on the union's competence test; and

"Oral" is the score on the union's oral exam.

Judge Green concluded:

It appears to the Court from these results that there is at least a strong possibility of a direct correlation between achievement on the direct mechanical aptitude test and the EJAC mechanical aptitude tests.[22]

---

22. *Local 38* (1969), 1 FEP Cases at 690.

Applicant Number	IQ	Mech	EJAC	Oral		IQ	Mech	EJAC	Oral
140	6	0	10	25	**IQ**	1.000			
85	6	10	5	27	**Mech**	0.315	1.000		
181	6	0	5	28		0.447			
156	2	4	5	15					
99	2	0	5	20	**EJAC**	0.408	−0.155	1.000	
37	2	0	10	25		0.315	0.715		
118	8	0	10	21	**Oral**	0.202	−0.163	−0.029	1.000
125	8	9	10	18		0.632	0.700	0.946	

FIGURE 60: Data and Correlations, *Local 38*

On the right side of Figure 60 I have calculated the correlations between the variables. Beneath each correlation, shaded, is the probability of finding a correlation at least this large had the true correlation been zero. All probabilities are above 0.3, which is to say that correlations of these sizes are likely, by chance, from uncorrelated data, in samples of this size. The correlation Judge Green thinks is positive is negative, but the sign is of no consequence. The correlation cannot be differentiated from zero. From the paucity of observations and lack of variation in the scores, any statistical expert would have anticipated that there would be no correlation, made the calculation, and informed the judge. This judge preferred to guess.

Selection

As I reported in Chapter 2, Judge Chin did not allow a statistical procedure that had not been accepted, in this use, in any court before—to his knowledge. At one time credit cards operated under the same conundrum: You couldn't get one unless you already had one.

> Defendant has not demonstrated that the "proportional hazards model" has generally been accepted in the scientific community.[23]

Use of proportional hazards had been suggested by Michael Finkelstein and Bruce Levin, but argued against by Douglas Herbert and Lani Shelton essentially because juries would not understand it. Nowhere does Judge Chin ask if this might simply be the best way to analyze the case before him, as contended by defendant's expert James Halavin. That is what the judge is supposed to do under *Daubert* (1993). Apparently no participant

---

23. *Wyche* (1997) at 1601. This may seem to be a little late for relying on *Frye* criteria, but remember that *Frye* (1923) was incorporated into *Daubert* (1993), not obviated by it.

understood that MULQUALS™ estimates *are* proportional hazards.[24] By 1997 the method had been widely used in age-discrimination and other selection cases, as Finkelstein and Levin should have known, and as Halavin should have known and informed Judge Chin.

Judge Maxine Chesney excluded statistical evidence of racial bias in selection. As described by the affirming Ninth Circuit panel:

> Zottola's direct evidence of discrimination consisted of statistics showing that the eight black candidates interviewed by Panel L—the panel that interviewed Zottola—scored significantly higher than the 30 white candidates interviewed by the panel, and that all three members of the panel were black. Although statistical evidence is relevant in disparate treatment cases . . . the sample size in Zottola's case is too small, standing alone, to establish a *prima facie* case of intentional discrimination.[25]

The probability of selecting eight persons of one race to be the top scorers, one after another, by chance, when they are the only members of that race among thirty-eight candidates, is $p = 0.00000002$. When the panel is made up of members of only that race, and the screening device is a subjective oral examination, such an unlikely result needs to be explained. There is nothing "too small" about this sample size, if selection from it can achieve such low probabilities.

We will encounter a similar situation, with a not much larger sample, concerning promotion of Washington D.C. firefighters, in Chapter 10. The fire chief could adjust scores to elevate black firefighters above otherwise higher-scoring whites—and did. Perhaps it is fortunate that those parties settled before a judge could ask if there were too few promotions from which to draw a conclusion.

These examples of judicial error are interesting and instructive, but nonetheless anecdotes. A judge can look foolish trying to be "scientific," while nonetheless getting the law right. Judge Robinson, for example:

> A confidence interval is a measure of percent of people who respond in a certain way.[26]

---

24. See Finkelstein and Levin (1990) and Herbert and Shelton (1996). Long before Finkelstein and Levin "proposed" it, I had presented proportional-hazards results to juries in age-discrimination cases. See, for example, *Shulton* (1983). It was also my primary methodology in *Koger* (1994), an age-discrimination case not heard before a jury, but well-known and often cited. Both Judge Chin and Herbert and Shelton have it backwards: Proportional hazards should be used because it is the only method that accounts for multiple pools in which the same people may appear at different ages. And it is not that difficult to explain (see Chapter 2).

25. *Zottola* (2002) at 309.

26. *Dentsply* (2003) at 439. The judge is correct that "failure to calculate a standard error measurement for the survey result has rendered the survey data uninformative." Professor Wind appar-

Not even close. The judge does not have to know precisely what a "confidence interval" is, or how it is obtained. He needs to know something about its use. Some measure of the variation one might expect randomly is required in an expert's presentation—and was missing in this one.

Judge Warren rejected "statistical" evidence that pay raises for non-Catholic faculty were smaller than the pay raises of Catholics. As the Seventh Circuit explained, affirming:

> All that the data show is that there is in all likelihood a real, not a spurious, difference between the means of the samples compared. The data do not show that the difference is due to a particular attribute (namely, being Catholic) which the members of the better-off group have and the members of the worse-off group lack. Correlation is not causation.[27]

The Professional Expert

Judge Smalkin allowed Lilly Ann Gordon to testify for plaintiff as an expert on damages. The jury awarded plaintiff over $2 million in Robinson-Patman Act damages. After the trial, defendant Lorillard objected, as described by circuit-court judge Chapman:

> During her entire career Gordon had published only one article, a piece which had nothing to do with price discrimination, credit, or anti-trust generally. Her work experience was limited largely to analyses of companies' financial health. Gordon stated that her present employer devoted most of its efforts to providing expert testimony in trials of complex business cases.[28]

Like Seth Schwartz, Ms. Gordon was a professional. She didn't have time to write articles; she was too busy doing what the articles others write are about.

> Although it would be incorrect to conclude that Gordon's occupation as a professional expert alone requires exclusion of her testimony, it would be absurd to conclude that one can become an expert simply by accumulating experience in testifying.

Wrong. Testifying is a minute part of any expert's work. I can think of no better way for Ms. Gordon to have become expert at calculating damages than to have been employed to do so, if her employer knew the craft and helped her learn it. Being unable to prove her wrong, Lorillard appealed that it was the judge who was wrong. I agree with dissenting judge Sprouse, who would have let Gordon's testimony stand.

---

ently used proprietary software, which he was unwilling to share, and which made no such calculation. The judge's skepticism was well-founded. It did not rely on his knowing what a standard error was.

27. *Tagatz* (1988) at 1044.

28. *Kline* (1989) at 799; following indented quotation at 800.

Statistical "Significance"

One of the things judges think they know is that an expert needs to say his finding is "statistically significant." That is an unfortunate and obsolete phrase that does more harm than good.[29] Furthermore, judges misstate probability in most cases, so we have the nonsense word "significant" mixed with a nonsense description of its meaning.

"Significance" Explained

First, the probability that is reported in court is almost always a "classic" (or "frequentist") probability. I won't describe Bayesian probability here, although courts will see more of it. The expert who presents a Bayesian estimate has a *lot* of explaining to do.[30] I count on judges to ask questions.

We report classic probabilities as if they describe the estimated parameters. A better view is that they evaluate the data in a particular way. If I report a probability of 0.045 associated with a regression coefficient, I mean that:

The size of the data set has been taken into consideration in making this calculation.

We are estimating, from this one sample, the parameter value in a larger data set (the "universe") and the variation we would find estimating that value from repeated samples of this size from that universe.

Given that sampling variation, these data would generate a parameter value at least as different from a stated comparison value than the value we have estimated, forty-five times in one thousand, if the actual co-

---

29. Ziliak and McCloskey (2004) tell us that the phrase "statistically significant" first appeared in Francis Y. Edgeworth, "Methods of Statistics," in *Jubilee Volume of the Statistical Society*, Royal Statistical Society of Britain (1885), at 181.

30. For an attempt to explain Bayesian statistics to a lay audience, although overly enthusiastic about its use in litigation, see Malakoff (1999). David Kaye (1987) suggests, at 54, that Bayesian probability estimates are the "reigning" formulation in litigation. He is free to argue, as he does at 55, that

[Bayesian statistics] provide a pleasing and harmonious interpretation of civil litigation's usual requirement of proof by a preponderance of the evidence.

He is not free to assert what clearly was not a fact in 1987, and is not a fact in 2005. Bayesian statistics are found in some presentations of DNA evidence, and seldom elsewhere.

Classical or "frequentist" probabilities are so predominant in litigation that Bayesian methods receive virtually no attention in most books about statistics in law, including this one. From Stephen Fienberg, an unabashed Bayesian, in Fienberg (2001) §6.0:

It is worth noting that Bayesian methods in expert testimony are gaining increasing currency in the courts although the progress is slower than in the statistical and econometric literatures.

efficient in the universe were the comparison value, and if we have constructed a reasonably correct model.

The comparison or test value is usually, but not always, zero. A t-test is the difference between the coefficient and the test value for that coefficient, divided by the estimated standard error of that difference:

$$t = \frac{\text{coefficient} - \text{test value}}{\text{standard error}}$$

We saw t-tests in Chapter 3, associated with regression coefficients. A t-statistic, like the Z-score of Chapter 2, calculates how many standard deviations (a standard error is the standard deviation of a mean, and the coefficient is, in this usage, a mean value, and no one ever calls it the "estimated" standard error, even though that is what it is) the estimated coefficient is from the value we are testing.[31]

So we do compare the coefficient against some predetermined value. What we are able to say about it is how unlikely it would be to derive this coefficient from our sample, had the *real* relationship been the test value (zero). We then have to ask: Do we think the population is appropriately described by the test value, or do we reject the test value and think the population is better described by some value closer to the estimated coefficient?

A classical test never concludes with a probability that there is or is not a relationship, or how large it is. We *assume* a relationship (usually zero, a *lack* of relationship), and then test the frequency with which sample data would show what they do if that relationship holds. We are describing the population's ability to generate sample data that would mislead us into thinking there is a relationship when there is none. It is a test of the data—or of our assumptions about the data—but surely you now understand why no one tries to explain it that way.

Let's suppose we find a $3,000 gap between earnings of otherwise equal males and females. If our model is acceptable, have we established that the earnings difference is $3,000? No. Let's say we report a t-statistic of 2.6—which has an associated probability of 0.0093. A population with a zero salary gap would generate a coefficient this different from zero (or more so) only ninety-three times in a thousand. But if the test value were $2,000, the t-statistic would be 0.867, the associated probability, 0.388. More than a third of the time when the true coefficient is $2,000, we would estimate it as $3,000, by chance.

If we are not very confident that the real relationship is $3,000, what are we confident of? As the first test value was zero, we are confident of the *sign* of the real relationship. The coefficient is as undetectably different from $4,000 as it is from $2,000, so $3,000 remains our best estimate; but our confidence, the probability we report, is about the sign of the

---

31. The test value is called the "null hypothesis" in statistics-speak. I do not think that language is necessary or even helpful, and I do not use it in court.

coefficient, its difference from zero, an unlikely difference to find if in the population there is really a zero relationship.

Experts who contend that the t-test evaluates our confidence in *this coefficient* do not know what they are talking about. Many "experts" would tell you that a t-test is the coefficient divided by its standard error—not that it is the coefficient *minus a test value* all divided by its standard error. That the test value is zero *means* that what is being tested is the sign, not the value, of the estimated coefficient. As experts seem not to understand this simple concept, neither do they relay it to judges in their crash courses in elementary statistics.[32] It is one reason why I would prefer that judges not take those courses.

"Significance" Interpreted

I expounded a rule in Chapter 5: There is always a continuum. The judge would like the science expert to make his binary choice for him, to proclaim that something is and something else is not. We cannot (and therefore should not pretend to) do that. The answer to a statistical test is a probability, a number that lies between zero and one.

Suppose in one study the probability reported is 0.046, and in another, 0.054. It's just about the same thing. Yet the former would be called "statistically significant at the 5 percent level," and the latter would not.[33] There is something wrong with this manner of reporting. There is no bright line here. The language might indicate that there is, but I will explain below the historical accident by which that language was developed. It was such a difference that generated the story in Chapter 6 of my client who became mute when the opposing expert sensibly agreed to call p = 0.054 "significant."

The bright-line language needs to be abandoned for two reasons. First, it makes some findings appear far stronger than others, when they are only marginally so. Second, it allows the expert to testify to a binary conclusion ("Yes, there is a relationship," or "No, there is not") when he has only probabilistic knowledge. I will suggest, in Chapters 8 and 10, that probabilistic evidence be presented in its probabilistic form. Let the court convert it to a binary finding.

---

32. Hubbard and Bayarri (2003) at 177.

> It is disturbing that the ubiquitous p-value cannot be correctly interpreted by the majority of researchers.

33. According to Judge Murphy in *Rhodes* (2003), at 669,

> Defendant's experts . . . calculated the exact number of standard deviations as −1.915, which is not statistically significant.

The experts could not have done that. Using the hypergeometric distribution, they calculated an exact probability, and translated it back to a standard deviation metric. However, the hypergeometric distribution is not symmetric. It produces a one-tail test. It is likely that they calculated a one-tail probability of 0.0277, which they did not want to report. The question should have been whether it was meaningful, not whether it was "significant."

Judges take the language presented to them as something they must understand.

> The term "significant" is yet another statistical concept. It is generally accepted that this means the relationship must be sufficiently high as to have a probability of not more than 1 in 20 to have occurred by chance. Stated differently, the relationship must be "significant at the 5 per cent level."[34]

The arbitrary has become a rule.

A statistic has a distribution, a range of values (that would be found from different samples from the same universe) with associated probabilities. The estimate of that statistic has a value, so it would be natural to try to determine the probability associated with that value. The probability of a statistic achieving any particular value is tiny. We care about the "tail" of the distribution, the probability of finding a number this large *or larger* (or larger than its absolute value, called "this extreme"). In the past, the analyst would translate a statistic to its tail probability using a published table.

A table with every possible value of a statistic, let us say the t-statistic as an illustration, would be impossibly large.[35] Thus tables select probability values as benchmarks, and tell us the associated statistic for only those. The phraseology "significant at the X level" came about because one did not know the probability associated with his test, given the parameter value he estimated, but knew that his value was greater than the value just at the 0.05 level. The higher the t-statistic or Z-score, the lower the probability. A Z-score larger than 1.96, from enough observations (let's say fifty or more), is reported as "significant at the 0.05 level" in a two-tail test.

Many experts have commented on the anachronism of using this bright-line language when we now can calculate probabilities. No one who has written about it supports the "significant" language, or the 0.05 level as a meaningful benchmark. When David Peterson and John Conley say the 0.05 level of "significance" is "based more on tradition than rational principle," they are referring to the language that was generated from look-up tables.[36]

Whether a statistic is "significant" or not should be the conclusion of the fact finder, not the expert. Significance is a judgment, which should be made based on the model as well as the data, and perhaps on other evidence in the case.[37] For example, in Chapter 3,

---

34. *Kinsey* (1974) at 1084.

35. As there is an infinite number of possible coefficient values (hence, associated probabilities), such a table would literally be impossible. We actually derive probabilities from statistics by means of an estimating equation. There is no point in asking that equation to provide a "precise" probability beyond its own estimation error, and in any case, from social-science data, probabilities beyond two, perhaps three decimal places are meaningless.

36. Peterson and Conley (2001) at 228.

37. Recall, for example, from Chapter 5, that many an expert found a "significant" difference between census population and jurors. The difference between these two measures was large by any statistical standard. And meaningless.

the relationship between seniority and salary at Grade 13 of I-NET would be called "significant" from the computer printout. But the relationship was absurd, clearly an artifact of the salaries and seniority of individuals whose salary was set on some other basis entirely. It was not "significant" at all, in the sense that a judge should recognize it.

The 0.05 Standard

Once an expert has explained that his findings are "significant," or "statistically significant," or "statistically significant at the 0.05 level," the judge wants to know what to make of that information. He asks: "What is the standard?" Most people report: "0.05 is the most common standard." We now know how that happened: 0.05 was simply a "critical level" for which values were printed in tables, when a table look-up was the only way we could evaluate our parameters. It became the standard by which publishers decided to release "findings" to the world. Of what relevance is that to a court in the twenty-first century?

Probability is better seen as a dimmer switch than as a toggle: It is a "more or less" measure, not "on or off." The statistical presentation may be evidence, but it is not proof, and should be judged in the light of other evidence. What should be considered "evidence" in court is a very different question from what one might say about one's results in a publication. In neither forum should the phrase "statistically significant" be used today.

Judge Posner writes, "The 5 percent test is arbitrary."[38] David Barnes says, "There is no magic to the 5 percent value."[39] Richard Lempert:

> For a decade I have questioned the unthinking use of the 0.05 level of statistical significance to evaluate the importance of empirical research results to legal proceedings. In an earlier article, I noted that the values of social science are not the values of law, and that the 0.05 level reflects the social scientist's conservatism with respect to Type I error.[40]

Daniel Rubinfeld agrees:

> Courts often accept conventional practices of the statistics profession without considering whether such practices are valid in the context of litigation.[41]

Posner argues that

> to exclude *from a trial* statistical evidence that failed to reach the 5 percent significance level would imply that eyewitness testimony, too, should be in-

---

38. Posner's decision in *Kadas* (2001) at 362.

39. Barnes (2001) at 198.

40. Lempert (1985) at 1098. Like me, he objects, at 1101, to using the term "significant." Type I and Type II errors were explained in Chapter 4.

41. Rubinfeld (1985) at 1050.

admissible unless the probability that the testimony would have been given even if the event testified to had not occurred was less than 5 percent.[42]

Posner also notes that

> The convention is rooted in considerations that have no direct relevance to litigation, such as the need to ration pages in scientific journals.[43]

Joelle Anne Moreno is certainly correct in emphasizing that science results are statistical, and so fact finders need to understand statistics more than science:

> Legal scholars and practitioners who must assess the quality of scientific evidence must also acquire a basic understanding of core statistical concepts.[44]

Then she completely loses it when discussing "significance" and the 0.05 level:

> Only a statistically significant relationship between variables helps to determine causation. . . . A p-value factor of 0.05 does not mean that the hypothesis has a 95% chance of being correct. It means only that the result observed has a 95% chance of being valid.

Huh? What does that mean? We know from Chapter 2 that validity is the relationship between our measures and the language we want to apply to them. It cannot be used to explain the meaning of a probability. Moreno's statement comes under the subheading, "How To Improve Our Understanding of Basic Statistics." I don't think so.

Other writers have used equally inappropriate language. Joseph Kadane and Caroline Mitchell confuse the standard deviation with the number of standard deviations, that is, the Z-score explained in Chapter 2. First they tell us:

> The standard deviation of the disparity in female hiring was 1.12. Thus the statistics alone did not support the inference that women were not being hired for reasons other than their lack of representation in the available applicant pool.[45]

Although, in Chapter 2, I forgave Judge Garza for being so statistically illiterate, I cannot so easily forgive statisticians. Kadane and Mitchell mean "the number of standard deviations," as confirmed by a succeeding and equally incorrect statement:

---

42. Posner (1999a) at 1511. Also, from *Kadas* (2001) at 362:

> Litigation generally is not fussy about evidence; much eyewitness and other nonquantitative evidence is subject to significant possibility of error, yet no effort is made to exclude it if it doesn't satisfy some counterpart to the 5 percent significance test.

43. Posner (1999b) at 95. See also Malakoff (1999) at 1463:

> For decades, many journals would only publish results with a p-value of less than 0.05.

44. Moreno (2001) at 1018; following indented quotation also at 1018.

45. Kadane and Mitchell (2000) at 252; following indented quotation also at 252; third indented quotation at 253.

The expert concluded that the standard deviation of the disparity was 2.55, which exceeded the two standard deviation rule.

And then, from other data:

[T]he standard deviation of disparity in hiring females was 3.75 standard deviations.

Where was the editor? It is hard to blame judges both for getting the language wrong and for thinking that statistics has produced a magic threshold for them, when the "experts" are so confused, so incoherent.

Joseph Kadane is concerned with the wrong issue:

Essentially, the problem is that by testing at a fixed level, like 0.05, with a small sample size virtually no hypothesis is rejected; while with a large sample size, virtually every null hypothesis is rejected. Thus, far from measuring the verisimilitude of the hypothesis, the procedure is measuring sample size, for which there are simpler measures.[46]

See my examples, in Chapter 2, of "significant" differences in test-passing rates for blacks and whites with few observations. I also suggested there that some suits should have been deferred to gather more observations. Probability is a function of both the size of the difference and the power of the test to detect it. A large difference may be apparent from few observations. When there is a small difference, requiring many observations to be "significant," perhaps it isn't very important.

The Classical Test

The meaning of the probability reported in classical (virtually all) tests is difficult to grasp. How many readers' eyes glazed over when I tried to explain it, albeit differently from most, above? People get it wrong. Bert Black, for example:

Before drawing inferences from comparisons between exposed and non-exposed populations, scientists typically require that there be only a five percent probability that a difference between the two populations occurred by random chance.[47]

---

46. Kadane (2000) at 354. Rejecting a similar canard in *MacDissi* (1988), Judge Arnold wrote, at 1058:

There is no minimum sample size prescribed either in federal law or in statistical theory: the adequacy of numerical comparisons within small sets of data depends on the degree of certainty the factfinder requires, as well as the type of inference the statistics are meant to demonstrate.

Kadane and Judge Arnold would probably agree that one problem is the fixed level of probability. One might add that a statistical conclusion also depends on the magnitude of the observed difference, and the judgment that the particular observations are representative of the issue being considered.

47. B. Black (1994) at 2133.

No they don't. The probability is that *if* chance had been the factor, then we would have found data as extreme as we did find in fewer than 5 percent of the times we looked.

David Barnes does only somewhat better:

> Varying between 0 and 1.00, the p-value measures the likelihood that it is the happenstance of selection of the particular individuals included in the study, rather than any relationship in the underlying population, that accounts for the observed relationship.[48]

Barnes understands that the probability is a statement about the data, but it is not this statement. The "p-value" does not measure the likelihood that the data are unrepresentative. It measures the difference of the data from the *assumption* that there is no relationship.

Peter Detre misstated the result from the "statistical decision theory" test of jury disparity, explained in Chapter 5:

> SDT calculates the probability that the observed underrepresentation of the group on the jury wheel was the result of chance.[49]

Detre's misguided articulation has been quoted in briefs calling for the use of this measure. Thus, the infection spreads.

John Bueker similarly misleads his readers. Discussing the "standard deviation" test (read: Z-score) of jury composition:

> The test measures the likelihood that the disparity resulted from random chance, but does not indicate anything about the magnitude of the disparity.[50]

Both parts of this sentence are wrong. The test does not measure the likelihood that the disparity occurred randomly. A Bayesian statistic might attempt to do that, but a classic statistic does not. And the standard deviation test does indeed indicate the magnitude of the disparity. The units of a standard deviation are the same as what the standard deviation is of—points of a test score, numbers of hires, etc.

As not all legal commentators get it right, neither do all judges. New Jersey superior-court judge Francis states that defendants' expert John Lamberth "opined it is highly unlikely such statistics could have occurred randomly or by chance."[51] Lamberth may have made that error, but I would prefer to believe that Judge Francis did not understand the subtle difference between what Lamberth said and what the judge wrote. Judge Batchelder, writing for a Sixth Circuit panel accepting a 0.30 validity coefficient (as noted in Chapter 2):

---

48. Barnes (2001) at 198.

49. Detre (1994) at 1918.

50. Bueker (1997) at 404.

51. *Soto* (1996) at 71.

Specifically, the HR study found that the 0.30 correlation coefficient was statistically significant at the 0.01 level, which means that there is less than one chance in one hundred that the 0.30 correlation coefficient was the product of chance.[52]

No, it doesn't mean that.

Circuit-court judge Kleinfeld wrote, in a dissent:

[A] result is commonly treated as statistically significant when one can be 95% confident that it didn't occur by chance.[53]

He then compounded this error by moving from probabilities to absolutes:

A statistically insignificant difference is one where chance cannot be ruled out as explaining the result.

We expect our most sophisticated judges to formulate an acceptable expression of statistical "significance." It would be better if they could see through the binary nature of this language and be content with the probabilities. Judge Weinstein goes the other way, correctly defining "significance" but dispensing with a measure of the probability:

A "statistically significant" difference is one that, under the assumptions made in the study and the laws of probability, would be unlikely to occur if there were no true difference and no biases.[54]

At one time even Judge Posner provided an incorrect interpretation of a finding that was "significant at the 0.05 level:"

This means . . . that there is a probability of less than 5 in 1,000 that the difference is due to chance.[55]

In later writings, he phrased it correctly:

[I]n other words, unless there is no more than a 5 percent probability that we would observe a statistical correlation between the dependent variable . . . and the independent variable . . . even if the variables were uncorrelated in the population from which the sample was drawn.[56]

The probability is of finding data like these in a sample from a zero-relationship (or other test value) world. It is a test of the data in a model with assumed parameters. It is therefore not a test of the parameters. It is a test of the likelihood of finding a parameter that large

---

52. *Williams* (1999), in footnote 13 at 546.

53. *Rudebusch* (2002) at 527; following indented quotation at 528.

54. *McMillan* (2003) at 310. I trust that "not true difference" is a typographical error, where "no true difference" was intended.

55. *Tagatz* (1988) at 1044, 50 FEP Cases at 102.

56. *Kadas* (2001) at 362.

were the true parameter some other number. When that other number is zero, the analyst has tested the likelihood of finding data that generated an estimated parameter of this sign when the true population parameter was zero. The statistical test, in short, tells us far less than experts claim it does.

Why It Matters

This convoluted meaning of these "frequentist" probabilities lies behind Richard Lempert's statement that "frequentist statistics are inherently unsuited to the forensic context."[57] He continues, noting that

> the statistics usually presented to juries are not directly related to the question that the jury must resolve, and the relationship between the question the statistics can answer and the one the jury must answer may be unclear or prone to confuse.

It is therefore important that a judge, though not necessarily knowing how to compute them, understand what these statistics mean. The best way is to have an expert by his side, skeptical though I remain about the expertise of most experts.

The Society of Forensic Ink Analysis determined that its members could call a difference in age of ink "significant" if two samples differed by more than one standard deviation. Thus Erich Speckin, a Society member, would have reported to the jury "to a high degree of scientific certainty" that a critical letter was not written on the date claimed by the writer. Judge O'Malley responded:

> That a small number of analysts got together and agreed that statistical significance in ink dating is acceptable at the level of one standard deviation, however, does not make it so.[58]

I do not question Judge O'Malley's exclusion of Speckin's testimony, but by demonstrating her knowledge of the translation of standard deviations to probability (assuming the normal distribution) she misses the point. The expert should not be allowed to use either the phrase "statistically significant" or "to a high degree of scientific certainty," when he can report and be cross-examined on the probability itself. Writes the judge:

> A high degree of scientific certainty *may* be attained by tests using a 2 STD measure of statistical significance.

She is not objecting to the language the expert proposed to use, but to the standard his test must reach to use it. I am objecting to the language itself.

---

57. Lempert (1991) at 315; following indented quotation also at 315.

58. *Ethan Allen* (2003) at 634; preceding in-text quotation also at 634; following indented quotation at 635.

The Concept of Expected Value

As explained and illustrated in Chapter 6, we do not expect to find exactly fifty heads and fifty tails when we flip a coin one hundred times. We do expect to find the results usually confined to a range. If we repeat these one hundred flips seventeen times, one result *outside* the two-standard-deviation range should not surprise us. We "expect" a result only in that it is the most frequent result. Not finding that exact result is not "unexpected." Sometimes we will find no out-of-range flips, sometimes more than one. The litigation analyst supposes he is facing a randomly selected experiment, and so has fifty heads as his *expected value*, but does not hold that expectation singularly—he describes the expected range around it.

Judge Parker in Louisiana did not grasp the concept at all.

> Dr. Daymont declares that in tossing a "fair" coin twelve times, "we would expect about six heads" and that a result of eleven out of twelve would be statistical evidence that the coin is not "fair", and by analogy statistical evidence that the position elimination process in the twelve departments was not age-neutral.
>
> The court is independently aware that Dr. Daymont's expectations in his coin-tossing analogy are not supported by scientific principle or published scientific data.[59]

We saw in Chapter 1 that judges may use knowledge they have gained elsewhere to evaluate evidence, but how would the court be "aware" of something as erroneous as this? Judge Parker quotes John Paulos and Darrell Huff to the effect that one does not usually get five heads out of ten flips of a coin, apparently not understanding that Thomas Daymont did not assume that one would.[60] Daymont's language is perhaps too casual, but not incorrect. In a two-tail setting (where high and low values are equally unexpected), using a fair coin, the probability of having nine or more heads out of twelve flips is 0.042, and ten or more heads is 0.010. In nine out of ten of these experiments (twelve flips each) one usually expects between four and eight heads. What Daymont meant by expecting "about six" is "six plus or minus no more than two, most of the time."

Judge Parker would have fared better had he concentrated on the meaning of Daymont's model. He did not need to understand the mathematics. The popular books he consulted were saying something important, but not something that contradicted Daymont's work. As described in Chapter 2, the problem with Daymont's testimony did not lie in his numbers, but in his concept of how one tests for age bias.

Some judges do have a sophisticated understanding of some key statistical issues. In

59. *Reid Jr.* (2001) at 504.

60. See Huff (1954) and Paulos (1990).

sending a gender-discrimination case back for trial (reversing summary judgment), Judge Frank Easterbrook shows his mastery of one of the conundrums to which I refer often in this book, multiple tests:

> Suppose the University hired blindly from a pool that is 62% women. How likely is it that exactly seven of twelve would be female? What the University appears to have in mind is a world in which the absence of discrimination means that every department would exactly mirror the population from which its members are hired. But that is statistical nonsense. Suppose a university has 64 departments or faculties, each with five members; that half of all persons meeting its standards for appointment are women; and that the university makes appointments by drawing blindly from an urn containing infinitely many balls, each representing a candidate. Then the most likely outcome is that two of the 64 departments would be all male and two would be all female. Ten of the 64 departments would be 80% male, and another ten 80% female. The remaining forty would have three men and two women, or three women and two men. The existence at this hypothetical university of 24 departments that were composed 80% or more of one sex would do nothing at all to imply discrimination or a need for corrective action; such a distribution is simply the result of chance.[61]

That is, asking each department separately, precisely, to achieve some gender "balance," is essentially setting a quota system, and is therefore illegal. But a judge who cannot make Judge Easterbrook's calculation still can understand the *concept* of a statistical distribution, the fallacy of imposing statistical measures on individual appointments.

Judge Easterbrook may seem unkind to this expert, but is too kind to others:

> Dean Ross wanted to look at the Psychology Department in isolation, which no statistician would do, and to collapse the distribution by compelling every academic department to mimic the population from which it was hired.[62]

"Which no statistician would do"? Would that were the case.

What Does "Explain" Mean?

Plaintiffs' statistical analyst will show that the phenomenon under investigation, say inequality in salaries, can be "explained" by the characteristic at issue, say, gender. Defendant's statistical analyst will say that he is able to "explain" the alleged phenomenon by other factors and, having done so, the subject factor (gender) "explains" nothing.

---

61. *Hill* (1999) at 591. I have omitted an inexplicable "(25 = 32)" in the Westlaw version of this opinion. Judge Easterbrook started out his adult life as an economist.

62. *Hill* (1999) at 592. Dean Howard Ross was the defendant, not an expert.

Does "explain" mean "cause"? Almost all analysts will agree that in some ultimate sense one cannot determine "cause" statistically. A statistical analysis is evidence, not "proof."[63] The expert witness should never state ultimate conclusions with certainty because he does not know them with certainty. He knows them with some uncertainty that should be explained.

Judge Easterbrook holds up an academic model, though, as above, I think an imaginary one:

> Professor Bryan would not accept from his students or those who submit papers to his journal an essay containing neither facts nor reasons; why should a court rely on the sort of exposition the scholar would not tolerate in his professional life?[64]

Who is to say whether the expert's professional work is better than his court work? The relevant question is whether the expert's analysis has contributed to understanding the facts. I wrote Chapter 9 partly because I doubt that most experts do better in the classroom than in court. In any event, how an expert performs elsewhere is irrelevant. That is why the *Daubert* hearing should be about the proffered testimony, not the expert.

Validity

As described in Chapter 3, James Gwartney used the ratings of supervisors to justify the lack of authority positions and the low wages accorded to blacks at Stockham Valves.[65] The district-court judge thought that made sense. The Fifth Circuit did not. Using race- or gender-related supervisory ratings to justify personnel actions is a tricky business. They might be correct assessments of the personnel, their outcomes correlated with a "protected class." Alternatively, they might incorporate prejudice. How is a court to know?

In *Diehl* (1996), also discussed in Chapter 3, a regression with one independent variable established that there was a correlation between gender and skill. Defendant proposed adding another independent variable, asking whether skill was still related to gender when supervisory ratings were accounted for. That is an appropriate procedure *if and only if* supervisor rating is validly related to performance. Validity is essential to an expert's claim that prior performance "explains" current skill assessment. Validity is what the judge needs to establish in order to answer the question before him, which is whether he should allow defendant's variable. Yet defendant's expert in *Diehl* never asserted that his added measure was valid, and the judge never asked.[66]

---

63. Apparently Barnes (1983) and Baldus and Cole (1980) do not agree. See B. Black et al. (1994) on the nature of science as falsification, not as proof.

64. *Mid-State* (1989) at 1339.

65. See *James* (1975).

66. Apparently neither plaintiffs' attorney nor plaintiffs' expert brought the example of *James* (1975) to the attention of the judge. Did they not know the literature?

The judge does not need to know how to calculate a regression or a validity coefficient. He needs to know whose burden it is—defendant's to assert validity, or plaintiffs' to assert non-validity—and then hold that party to it. The judge does not need to be more skilled in statistics. Let the experts expose each others' technical errors. He needs to know what the expert should be telling him, and know when he isn't getting it.

Unless applicant flow is perverted by action of the employer (one can imagine, for example, advertising job openings in only white-supremacist literature), most analysts, most attorneys, and most judges consider it a superior measure of interest in positions to availability, a statistical guess. The Equal Employment Opportunity Commission suggested otherwise in their complaint against Chicago Miniature Lamp, a manufacturer of, yes, miniature lamps. They employed Hekmat Elkhanialy to derive availability figures. Judge Shadur thought he could do better, and asked her to make some calculations for him.

Defendant's expert, Barry Chiswick, followed a reasonable path of weighting Zip codes by the proportion of people who applied therefrom for Lamp jobs.

> One consequence of Dr. Chiswick's obviously flawed methodology was that because of the total absence of applications from blacks in certain zip code areas, *the entire black labor force in numerous Chicago zip code areas was totally excluded from what he defined as Chicago Miniature's relevant labor market.*[67]

Obviously flawed? I don't think so. Using addresses of *employees* would be obviously flawed, as it would incorporate the hiring decision in the data being used to test it. Availability figures are imaginary. The advantage of applicant figures is that they represent people who, we can believe, would have taken jobs if offered. As the Seventh Circuit later summarized, "Interest in the jobs at issue is therefore ordinarily an important consideration for proof of a Title VII pattern or practice case."[68] Lamp offered jobs to a higher percentage of blacks who applied than to others. Judge Shadur wanted more.

Judge Shadur was overtly hostile towards Chiswick, as the above gratuitous (and incorrect) remark indicates. If that extract is not sufficient evidence, perhaps this will be:

> In sharp contrast to his unwillingness to acknowledge obviously relevant factors that should have changed his analytical method entirely (thus wholly revising his quantitative statistical analysis), Dr. Chiswick maintains that shift preference and immigrant status, and a related lack of English language fluency, were factors that would "qualitatively" [sic] *decrease* the proportion of black representation in Chicago Miniature's relevant labor market.[69]

Chiswick was correct. The plant was located in an Asian community, where the short

67. *Lamp* (1985) at 1300, 39 FEP Cases at 311; italics in original
68. *Lamp* (1991) at 302, 57 FEP Cases at 415.
69. *Lamp* (1985) at 1301, 39 FEP Cases at 311; "[sic]" and italics both in original.

commute, often at night, combined with no requirement to speak English in most positions, made Lamp's jobs desirable to local residents. Lamp seldom had to advertise an opening. Any reasonable view of "availability," as Chiswick said, would produce a smaller proportion of blacks than Judge Shadur obviously wanted to see.

Sometimes, perhaps for no known reason, the judge just dislikes an expert. I describe my experience as the recipient of judicial wrath in *Nassau* (1992), below. I do not know if Chiswick did something to irritate the judge or if Shadur, like Judge Merhige, whom we will also meet later in this chapter, simply had his own agenda, and Chiswick was in the way.

The Seventh Circuit, reversing the district-court opinion, had no trouble with Chiswick's "obviously irrelevant factors." The circuit court explained:

> Because the jobs did not require English language fluency, they had some special attraction to those persons who did not speak English as a primary language.[70]

Chiswick had performed a careful analysis of hires from applicants *and* an availability analysis based on actions by persons interested in the jobs. Judge Shadur rejected both in favor of an analysis he contrived under the guise of preferring the Equal Employment Opportunity Commission's expert. The judge should learn from his experts, not try to manipulate them. Ultimately, one of them tells a more credible story than the other. In *Lamp*, it was Barry Chiswick.

Availability

Judge Richey had ruled against plaintiffs, suing the Voice of America for failing to employ them on the basis of gender.[71] The Voice of America had not retained applicant data, a big mistake. So two experts argued about the gender of the availability pool. Judge Richey found for defendant, but he was reversed by the D.C. Circuit. The prevailing, court-approved availability estimate came from plaintiffs' expert, Marc Rosenblum.

The case was back in court on two bases: damages and continuing violation. A new census had been published, calling for a new availability estimate. For the defendant, I was willing to accept Rosenblum's update, which I assumed plaintiffs would provide. Instead, plaintiffs brought forth Bernard Siskin—no better at availability than I. Where was Rosenblum?

In Washington, D.C. It was easy enough for me to subcontract the availability work to Rosenblum. Indeed, he discovered—as I would not have and Siskin did not—that one

---

70. *Lamp* (1991) at 295. I was engaged by defendant's law firm, Jenner & Block, to write an affidavit in their appeal. As well as re-analyzing the data, my affidavit explained basic precepts of equal-employment-opportunity analysis, including the superiority of applicant-hire data to availability-workforce data. At that time I did not know either expert, but was concerned that the district-court opinion was so erroneous that failure to reverse it would do serious harm to future expert analysis.

71. *Hartman* (1988).

occupation group that formed his analysis, fire-department radio operators, had been moved by the Bureau of the Census from one category to another. Siskin replicated the earlier calculation, but Rosenblum reconfigured it to get at the same underlying workers. This is a good example of *why* one (a statistical analyst, a judge) wants truly expert advice. I engaged Rosenblum with the approval of my client, a pleasant but dull Assistant United States Attorney.

I concluded that there was no continuing violation, and there were zero damages. My analysis was not an attempt to change the rules, but to follow them. I used the circuit court's preferred expert's work, in the availability context that they sanctioned, as the basis of my calculations.

Plaintiffs' attorney complained about my use of Rosenblum, and the judge hit the roof. Indeed, he hit it so hard that the record of the discussion among attorneys in chambers was sealed. I will never know what was said there. Plaintiffs' attorney alleged that Rosenblum could have told me strategic secrets, that surely his switching sides was improper, etc. And Judge Richey bought it all.

Whatever Rosenblum knew was about a trial that had come and gone years before. We never discussed it, because what bearing could such knowledge have now? Over and above plaintiffs' attorney's theory, what had I actually done that evidenced any secret inside information I should not have? Richey should have posed that question directly to plaintiffs' attorney, as I anticipated he would: "Show me some harm that could possibly have occurred." How would defendant gain had Rosenblum given me detailed plans for a battle that it won, on which there is a record?[72] In contrast, the benefit from having Rosenblum develop the availability is obvious. The record shows that Rosenblum knew what he was doing, where Siskin and I did not.

Lawyers may see this some other way, but this one is simple to me. I was presenting expert estimates on which Rosenblum would testify, if asked (he was in the courtroom). As I have throughout this book, I plead here to stick to the basics. It's just like being bogged down in credentials, a subject for Chapters 8 and 10. If Siskin had a problem with Rosenblum's availability figures, then challenge them. When attorneys have nothing substantive to say, they attack the expert, not his work. Plaintiffs' lawyer had no challenge to the availability estimates I was about to use, so he challenged that they came from his own former

---

72. Can a juror from a hung-jury mistrial be engaged as an advisor for either party during the subsequent trial? I believe the answer is "yes." One might argue that the juror knew only public information, but that is not true: He knew how the jurors had reacted to that information. Having this knowledge does not disqualify him. In Chapter 6 I raised a question about the attorney's view of "privilege," and in Chapter 10 I will prove how wrong that view is; but that the expert does not share it is not in doubt. Having been an expert in the preceding case, Rosenblum was not exposed to secrets. Quite the opposite: He was shielded from them!

expert. The appropriate response from the judge would have been to move the trial on. If the objection has no substance, deny it.

Much though I support judges in general, they certainly can be pompous asses. None more than Judge Richey. None of my exhibits based on Rosenblum's availability estimates was allowed to be entered into the record. I had shown that Siskin's data also provided no evidence of "continuing violation," and that became the finding of the court. Judge Richey's outburst did not affect the outcome, but was nonetheless way off base.

In another case I saw Judge Richey strut into his courtroom, packed with attorneys and experts, ready for trial. "Apparently I am the best lawyer in this room," he announced. There was an unresolved motion in the case, which neither party had brought up recently. The judge's preparation, making sure everything was in order for today's showdown, was admirable. Both parties' lawyers agreed to drop the motion. But not the judge. He called off the trial for that day, caring nothing for either the financial or emotional cost on the fully prepared parties.[73]

The Market

Market solutions are the subject of many a judicial paean, the hallmark of the kind of "objective" decision judges love, because they do not have to make it. The prominence of market solutions underlies our antitrust laws. It is not surprising that they have found their way into equal-employment-opportunity law.

> We find nothing in the text and history of Title VII suggesting that Congress intended to abrogate the laws of supply and demand or other economic principles that determine wage rates for various kinds of work. We do not interpret Title VII as requiring an employer to ignore the market in setting wage rates for genuinely different work classifications.[74]

The question becomes, as with supervisory ratings, how would we determine when a "market" variable is truly measuring the market? Is the measure put forward by an expert a valid indicator of a market phenomenon? What evidence allows us to apply that language, "market," to this measure?

Although judges faced with such a complex situation probably should obtain assis-

---

73. I have been advocating rigorous scheduling. Rigorous scheduling means that every motion not decided when raised must be set for a hearing, or briefs, and a decision time. It was the judge's fault that the motion had not been resolved. See the October 1987 ruling in *Foster* (1987).

74. *Christensen* (1977) at 356, 16 FEP Cases at 235. The Equal Pay Act, in contrast, cannot be countered by a "market" defense. Yet "comparable worth" is just an extension of the Equal Pay Act, not Title VII. It comes from asking how alike do two jobs have to be to be considered the same under the Equal Pay Act—and if they have characteristics in common, shouldn't those characteristics receive equal pay? See Freed and Polsby (1984).

tance, they might be able to figure out whether it is the chalice from the palace or the flagon with the dragon that holds the brew that is true by sticking to what they know. "What judges know" is procedure. What judges should know is to ask the expert for evidence that his proposed market measure is valid. Just as with the work-force measures discussed above, there will not be a formal "validity test" associated with a measure made up by an economist for litigation. The proposing witness, defendant's expert, has some freedom to make an argument. But he should make one. In rebuttal, plaintiffs' expert should be able to question the validity of defendant's expert's "market" measure. The debate is not about the statistical method by which this measure is found to "explain" wage disparities. It is about the association of language with numbers. It is about concepts with which the judge is familiar.

I introduced *Nassau* (1992) in Chapter 6. Let's deal with two items here. One is the content of defendant's expert Joan Haworth's measure of the market. The other is how Judge Glasser saw that content.

In Chapter 6 I explained that I had coded the language in Nassau County's job descriptions. Judge Glasser challenged the validity of my coding, my ability to say that a variable represented the meaning I gave to it. That is exactly what the judge should do, where the judge should focus. In this case his questioning seemed a bit absurd, first because the language and the numbers both were the county's to begin with, and second because Joan Haworth, defendant's expert, generally accepted my codings. She agreed that I was measuring correctly, that my measures were valid.[75] Where she did not, she had an obligation to demonstrate that I was wrong, and/or that it mattered. She did neither. She did offer "corrections," which I accepted without argument.

Haworth's additional variable was based on salaries for comparable jobs in three nearby counties. She could not calculate "market" salary rates for all Nassau County positions. No mind, says the judge, with a wave of the hand. There was still a gender coefficient to be explained in the reduced data set. And so half of the male/female salary difference disappeared. It was never "explained." Some judges would say that plaintiff wins on that ground alone, that plaintiffs have shown a gender-based difference which defendant cannot explain away. Not Judge Glasser.

"When a market variable was added to the regression analysis, however, Dr. Haworth found"[76] is the kind of conclusion I did not allow students to reach without explanation. What makes this a "market" variable? Why should we accept Haworth's metric as valid? Why should we repeat that she "found" something just because she says she did?

---

75. The judge has to protect himself against accepting something that is wrong even though both parties' experts agree to it. "Is this measure valid?" "What study allows you to use the language that you associate with this measure?" These are always reasonable questions.

76. *Nassau* (1992) at 1401; following indented quotation at 1402.

> The results of Dr. Haworth's refinements to Dr. Michelson's regression analysis
> confirm that the labor market is a determinant of salary in Nassau County of
> which Dr. Michelson should have taken account. Her analysis also demonstrates
> that the labor market variable may well explain the salary differential that Dr.
> Michelson attributed to the sex dominance of job titles and of career lines.

There is not a hint in the opinion that Judge Glasser questioned the association
between Haworth's measure and her label, "market salary." I will explain here what
Haworth did, and why she was wrong. Despite Judge Glasser's hostility, we have to be careful not to assume that he would have been opaque to my rebuttal. As I described in Chapter 6, Joel Klein, my client, did not let me return to the witness stand to offer my critique.

The Fifth Circuit had stated the issue correctly in *Wilkins* (1981):

> Ideally, when a multiple-regression analysis is used, it will be the subject of
> expert testimony and knowledgeable cross-examination from both sides. In
> this manner, the validity of the model and the significance of its results will be
> fully developed at trial, allowing the trial judge to make an informed decision
> as to the probative value of the analysis.[77]

In *Wilkins*, plaintiffs had called males and females equivalent if they had the same age, rank,
and length of service, whereas defendant said one must also control for department at the
University of Houston. Defendant's expert argued that department was a valid differen-
tiator of the market—that competition in one department did not affect salaries in another.
Plaintiffs' expert, says the court, did not try to validate his model.

I knew the *Wilkins* case; Joel Klein did not. He suggested that he would make validity
arguments in his brief. I replied that *Wilkins* also represented the proposition that the court
would not listen to such an argument. Not letting his expert explain that Haworth's "market" variable was not valid was Joel Klein's mistake. Still, not questioning its validity was
Judge Glasser's mistake.

Haworth had obtained job descriptions in three proximate counties. Because Nassau
County delivered some services that the other counties did not—their cities did—Haworth
knew that she would lose some Nassau County jobs. Because she eliminated high grades,
she also knew, a priori, that her deletions would reduce the male/female salary difference.
Missing data had the effect of wiping out that which she has been called upon to explain.
Judge Glasser was not inclined to see through this chicanery.

Haworth then took an average—a simple arithmetic average—of the wage rates for the
jobs in the comparison counties. Not all counties had all jobs, and so her average wage was

---

77. *Wilkins* (1981) at 403. Although *Wilkins* was vacated by the Supreme Court for reconsideration following recent Court decisions, only one small finding—not the general finding for defendant—was
affected. See *Wilkins* (1983).

not always derived from three counties—sometimes one, sometimes two, sometimes three. However many counties contributed to her index for a particular job, each received equal weight (that is, 33.3 percent, or 50 percent, or 100 percent). That was her market index, which the judge did not question.

He didn't know to. But I did. There was at the time only one article in the literature about how to do this kind of thing, how to get information from multiple geographic areas and put them together into one index. By the time of this trial it was a well-known, often-cited piece, not in dispute. The authors, Joseph Gastwirth and Sheldon Haber, instruct us to weight the areas:

> Since people prefer to work nearer home, in describing a firm's labor market
> greater importance should be given to nearby areas than to distant ones.[78]

Although that is a principle to consider, Gastwirth and Haber realized it was not sufficient for two reasons. First, people think in terms of commute time, not distance. Second, an area farther away may be larger, and therefore present more applicants. Thus we need an empirical way to measure how much weight each other county should contribute to an empirical "market" measure for Nassau County. Despite their preference for applicant-flow data, Gastwirth and Haber concluded that "the data on commuting patterns reported in the census can be used."[79]

> From the 1970 Census of Population it is possible to obtain data on commuter
> flows from place of residence to place of work. The basic premise in using
> these data is that commuting patterns of employed workers reflect desires as
> to where individuals wish to work.

It is fair to say that by the time of the *Nassau* trial, no skilled economist would assert that the best available measure of the "market" was an arithmetic average of any characteristic (number of people, wage rate, etc.) from a few proximate counties. In *Lamp*, for example, Barry Chiswick had correctly weighted areas by interest shown—by applicants.

My revision of Haworth's measure, as it was restricted to her data, is not completely satisfactory. Like Chiswick, like Gastwirth and Haber, I would have preferred to measure Nassau County's market by the rate of applications from various places. And I would have preferred to discuss the quasi-monopoly that any employer has, in that commute time is expensive. Most people will take a lower wage to work closer to home. Indeed, the largest supplier of labor to Nassau County, by far, was Nassau County itself. Judge Glasser, however, did not ask Haworth how she factored local supply into her "market" measure.

---

78. Gastwirth and Haber (1976) at 33. Gastwirth's later article on this topic, Gastwirth (1981), is more about distinguishing flow (hires) from stock (employees), and finding flow data from which to calculate availability for hire.

79. Gastwirth and Haber (1976) at 34; indented quotation also at 34.

The 1990 U.S. Census, like its predecessors, contained data on journey to work. Each person who worked was asked where he went to do it. We could easily derive the distribution of places people work, given that they live in a particular location. Unfortunately, except for Nassau County itself, this is the opposite of the information we want. Census tabulations provide "from" summaries, because they are simple counts. What we needed were "to" compilations. Not what proportion of those who lived in Manhattan worked in Nassau County, but what proportion of those who worked in Nassau County came from Manhattan, for example.

As many people are interested in the tabulation aggregated by "to" counties, by work location, a government agency had made this inversion. It was available to anyone who knew to ask for it. Haworth could have used it. I reproduce the first seven sending counties, in order, in Figure 61.

County	State	Commuters	Weight 1	Weight 2
Nassau	NY	340,448	72.1	72.8
Suffolk	NY	76,950	16.3	16.4
Queens	NY	38,256	0.1	8.2
Kings	NY	6,334	0.0	1.4
New York	NY	2,991	0.0	0.6
Bronx	NY	1,691	0.0	0.4
Westchester	NY	1,238	0.0	0.3

FIGURE 61: Commuters to Nassau County, 1990 U.S. Census

I do not remember from which counties Haworth collected data, but they were not the top three (after Nassau). "Weight 1" in Figure 61 represents the proportion of *all* workers from each of these seven sites. "Weight 2" represents the proportion of *these* workers, of the total accounted for by these seven counties. These are all the counties sending over a thousand workers to Nassau, and would have represented a good view of Nassau's labor market.

Note that the natural weightings are disparate. Suffolk County, for example, sends twice the number that come from Queens, and over twenty-five times the number from New York (Manhattan). Weighting Haworth's haphazardly selected counties equally represents no economic concept.

I weighted Haworth's wage data by each county's importance in Nassau County's labor market. No surprise: This reconstructed market variable reduced only slightly the gender coefficient I had previously estimated. Had Haworth followed the advice in the literature, she would have generated no defense at all. An expert is not bound to follow previous literature, but should explain why she is not following it.

One reason the census inversion is unsatisfactory is that it is not job-specific. Haworth called for *the same* weighting of other counties regardless of job. My procedure generated weights by source, but not by job; closer to what we want, but admittedly not there. Yet if we agree, as the compromise the data force us to make, that the market metric for every job shall be the same weighting of salaries at other counties, the importance of what that weighting is, where it came from, grows even larger. Was Haworth's "market" measure valid? It wasn't even close.

Walter Connolly and his co-authors present a complicated version of a labor market based on distance to the work site.[80] That has the disadvantage of not accounting for travel routes, but the advantage of not allowing the fact that people do not go there now to affect the estimate of who might do so.

> It is hard to imagine that an expert witness seeking to determine the percentage of the labor pool composed of minority individuals in the context of a suit alleging purposeful discrimination (particularly in membership) would ever seek to define that labor pool by the characteristics of current members. Such an analysis obviously tends to beg the question raised by this suit and therefore must be rejected.[81]

The *Nassau* case was not about hiring, and so was immune to this criticism.

Applicant data would have solved the problem that both commute and distance weights are the same for every job. Haworth, as defendant's expert, was in a good position to get the county to keep applicant data and use it to weight wage data. Joe Gastwirth lists cases in which a weighted labor-pool calculation was accepted as superior to some arithmetic average.[82] Haworth's "market" measure bore no relationship to any thoughtful measure of the market.

Although the arguments offered above should prevail—it was Haworth's burden to validate her measure; all the literature argued against it, preferring applicant data; and the one literature-based recalculation I could make produced results dramatically different from hers—Haworth's "market" measure of wages was more fallacious than that. Let's say we are in the south in the 1960s, at a plant like Stockham Valves. Let's develop job descriptions. We will find that blacks work closer to the furnace than whites. And they are paid less. Is their pay based on race? We find these same jobs in other factories, from which we obtain similar job descriptions and wage rates, but not race data. In every one of them, the higher the temperature, the lower the wage. We put the variable we call "market" wage (for each job) into our regression estimating wages in this plant. The coefficient of the variable

---

80. See Connolly et al. (2001), Chapter 5, "Approaches to Estimating the Racial Composition of An Employer's Labor Pool." This is David Peterson's work, the same approach he developed in *Mister* (1986), on which see below.

81. *Local 542* (1979) at 1594.

82. Gastwirth (1998) at 172.

"black" becomes indistinguishable from zero. The "market" for people to work in the hot jobs explains the wage rates at Stockham Valves![83]

It is not traditionally acceptable to allow wages elsewhere to be used to assess wages in the subject place, because they might all be set discriminatorily. Haworth found one county, with a tiny contribution to Nassau's work force, that paid female-dominated jobs quite as badly as did Nassau. Then, using high-school arithmetic, she gave it the weight of one-third, sometimes one-half, sometimes one, and called it the "market" wage. Nassau County's wages were thereby "explained" by "the market"? I think not.

JUDGES' SUGGESTIONS

In *Harrison* (1982), my client was the United States Attorney of the District of Columbia, defending the Maritime Administration. As described in Chapter 2, plaintiffs' expert was John Van Ryzin. As I wrote in a post-trial memorandum:

> Van Ryzin, claiming that my methodology contained an "inherent problem," produced an even more biased analysis of selection by adding rejected females to the analysis previously based on race-known applicants. I have shown, on pages 60 through 65 of my February 22 [1982] Report and in trial, that Van Ryzin's method is almost guaranteed to produce plaintiff-oriented results. Van Ryzin's method includes neither analysis of the bias in the race-known sample nor any attempt to correct for that bias.[84]

Van Ryzin speculated that a certain test that I had performed might mask an effect favorable to plaintiffs, without providing any evidence that it did. When asked in cross-examination if such a masking *could* occur, I of course said yes, without being able to say, in that forum, that I had tested for it and the posited effect did not occur in these data. That explanation had to come in re-direct, which requires that my client understand to ask the right question, to bring out answers that I could not give in cross-examination.

If the objective is to get information to the judge when it is relevant, this procedure fails. The procedures are not designed for that purpose, but to maintain attorney control. These courtroom rules make statistical argument difficult. An expert who wants to defend,

---

83. There is now a literature describing the phenomenon I have illustrated above, the fallacy of using "market" variables as benchmarks for setting or assessing wages in female-dominated jobs. The sham arises from ignoring that the benchmarks, too, are female-dominated. Nelson and Bridges (1999) at 236 contend that the variables used in defense of Sears—another Joan Haworth study—"were of dubious business value." They dissect the market defense with respect to the Ninth Circuit's reversal of *AFSCME* (1985), finding (as had the district court, from my testimony) that the Washington State pay schedule was biased against females in its construction by just this method: basing female-dominated job remuneration on other female-dominated jobs.

84. Stephan Michelson, "Post Trial Report" in *Harrison* (1982), at 13.

"I thought of that, tested for it, and your supposition is incorrect," is silenced before he can do so. It is not responsive to the question, many judges will say: "Answer yes or no." In Chapter 10 I recommend a discussion among experts as more productively bringing information to the judge.

Still, under current procedures, a judge might ask plaintiffs' attorney, "Do you have any evidence that this effect occurs? Are you leading to a showing that Dr. Michelson's findings are erroneous?" When told no, the judge might ask, "But you do have Dr. Michelson's data, do you not? You could have tested for this fallacy?" Soon a probing judge would be telling the cross-examining attorney to stop speculating about what he should know, to bring out errors, not suppositions. The judge does not have to know statistics to do this.

Judge Oberdorfer, before whom I appeared several times, participated actively in *Harrison*, as usual. He did not engage in the fantasy dialogue imagined above, but he did inquire about missing data. Many applicants to the Maritime Administration were not race-identified in Maritime Administration data. I had gone to records in the Office of Personnel Management on the theory that people applying to one federal agency are likely to have applied to others. Ultimately, one-third of my race identifications came from Office of Personnel Management data. No expert in federal litigation had ever done anything like that (found race identifications outside of the specific application process under consideration). Still, most race identifications came from the Maritime Administration, which meant that I had more complete race information about hires than about rejected applicants.

I had presented statistical tests of hires using random assignment of race to persons whose race was unknown, in the same proportion as the races of those I did know, stratified by gender and job applied for. As most race-unknowns were rejects, Judge Oberdorfer suggested I assign race randomly to rejects using the same stratification, but based on known race of rejects only. I followed his suggestion in my supplemental report.

Isn't that what Judge Shadur did, you ask? Why do I praise Oberdorfer, but castigate Shadur? The difference is that Judge Oberdorfer was asking, gave me a forum to tell him what I thought of his idea. He listened. He asked for information, not capitulation. Judge Shadur was instructing. The difference is between being overbearing and being involved. Judge Oberdorfer always was impartial, but intellectually curious. It was always a delight to be on his witness stand.

A Special Master

David Peterson was defendant's expert for damages in *Mister* (1987), as he had been for liability in *Mister* (1986). Illinois Central Gulf Railroad had been building track and other facilities. It hired, the railroad said, according to distance from home to site. There were no written hiring instructions to that effect, and the data showed otherwise, especially considering the small number of blacks employed to work around East St. Louis. Nonetheless Peterson persisted, developing fancy maps to support a case he had already lost. I used an applicant-flow measure, thinking that all people who got to the hiring hall (there was only one) should have had the same chance to be hired for the next opening as whites. The two experts were going down very different paths in an attempt to develop monetary damages. The judge had originally found for the railroad. He had been reversed. He was not interested in the outcome of this struggle. He engaged a special master to oversee the calculations.

Each side made detailed presentations of its methodology and results. Many decisions were required, as the data were hardly clear about who applied when, who was qualified for what, how long each job lasted, etc. I could see a master asking the experts to codify these decisions, and their differences. This one, however, decided that he could do it better. He devised his own methodology, and selected Peterson's staff to make his calculations. They would then turn the computer program over to us for review.

As we went through Peterson's program and the master's instructions, we noticed a factor that Peterson inserted, and evaluated, that the master had not called for. More seriously, it made no appearance in Peterson's presentation of his work.

I don't doubt that the master's instructions were incomplete, that an additional factor was required to make sense of them. Lesson one: The master should choose one expert's view.[85] The scheme imposed by this master followed neither Peterson's nor my logic. Besides being internally non-calculatable, it was a conceptual mess.

Lesson two: If the expert deviates in any way from the special master's instructions, he should be clear about what he did, and why.

Lesson three: The review process worked, in the sense that we exposed Peterson's new factor, loud and clear. As he should have been, the master was livid. Not surprisingly, the parties settled shortly thereafter for just about the kind of money we had estimated. I am sure that my client promised to take Peterson's defiance of the special master's instructions (that is how he would characterize it) to the judge. The railroad wanted to avoid that grief.

When selecting a special master in such a situation, the judge should:

Engage a litigation-savvy economist, not an attorney.

Instruct him on the findings of the case so far, and not to accept re-litigation of settled points.

Delineate and explain the master's role. Either he is or is not to formulate his own plan. I suggest not.

---

85. By and large, this is a good rule for judges, also. A classic case is *Markey* (1977). Judge Sear calculated an employer's labor market by weighting census areas by the proportion of the employer's work force that came from them. The Fifth Circuit, in *Markey* (1981), explained, at 500:

> The trial court's approach would permit an employer to limit the number of blacks in his employ merely by recruiting and hiring from predominantly white areas.

It is well-known in negotiation theory that if the decision maker mediates—compromises between the parties' positions—the parties will find it profitable to move apart. If the rule is that an arbitrator is to accept one position or the other, whole hog, the opposing parties converge. As I will discuss in Chapter 10, it is not wrong for a skilled special master to perform his own calculations and recommend them to (not impose them on) the parties. Ultimately, though, he should not only choose one position or the other, but make clear in advance that this is what he will do. The master in *Mister* did not have such skills.

A Bankruptcy Master

I had experience also with a special master in the A. H. Robins bankruptcy: Francis Mc-Govern, a minor law professor with big ambitions. McGovern was manipulative, mendacious, and successful. The biggest concern my client had was that a questionnaire sent to a sample of claimants would contain questions about their sexual history. I thought that, if those questions would have been allowable in a trial, they should be allowable in the questionnaire. My clients argued, but provided no evidence, that such questions would deter claimants. My position, in contrast, was that people applying for thousands of dollars of damages will jump through the court's hoops to get it.

McGovern promised time and time again that those questions would not appear in the final draft. They remained in draft after draft, while McGovern assured the Claimants' Committee that he had a plan to eliminate them. He had no such plan. The questions stayed. A straightforward declaration that the questions would be allowed would have been a better way to handle them. Why McGovern took the more underhanded route of telling us what he knew not to be true, I cannot say.

More important, as told in Chapter 6, McGovern brought in a staff, who quickly established that they were the decision makers with respect to data. As we participated in sessions in which we, the experts, thought we would negotiate solutions to various problems, it became clear that McGovern's staff had a different view. We would discuss and suggest, but they would decide. As in *Mister*, the roles evolved, and evolved badly. The judge had no control—wanted none, at this level—and so power drifted to the master and his staff. The *point* was a good one: There were no data conflicts at trial, only different methodologies, among the parties. But the *process* was not. Still, the more interesting story about the A. H. Robins bankruptcy centers on Judge Merhige, not on his master.

The Dalkon Shield Bankruptcy

The Fourth Circuit allowed claims against A. H. Robins for damages due to the Dalkon Shield to be consolidated in bankruptcy proceedings at the Richmond, Virginia, court of Judge Robert R. Merhige. Plaintiffs' counsels had opposed this consolidation, among other reasons, because of Judge Merhige's personal friendship with his neighbor E. Claiborne Robins, Sr. Writing in support of strong judge roles, but seemingly blind to the circumstances of this case, Jack Weinstein predicted that Judge Merhige's

> knowledge of the medical problems will be of great assistance to the parties in his management of the A. H. Robins litigation and bankruptcy.[86]

In fact, Merhige bludgeoned his way to a solution. When discussing this case in Chapter 6, with concern for my relationship with my client, I alluded to some of Merhige's criteria, which included maintaining the wealth of the Robins family, maintaining banking control in Richmond, rewarding a friend, and maintaining the Robins production facility—that is, jobs—in Richmond. And, oh yes, compensating victims.

Merhige exhibited no special knowledge. One example should be sufficient. One task in settling damages claims is to determine who is eligible. The amounts can be determined later, but you have to start with a population. The judge notified all persons who had filed claims, and in media advertisements all those who might, that to be on the final rolls each claimant had to apply through his process, which included completing his questionnaire. I do mean *his* questionnaire. The parties were not asked to help devise a preliminary document such as this, and I do not believe any special master—there were several—was, either.

The quality of the judge's questionnaire—the only document that contained information about every claimant—can be assessed by the fact that no party used it. At the time I called it "an embarrassment." Here is one example. Judge Merhige asked if the claimant had ever received funds from A. H. Robins. After years of denying that the Dalkon Shield was flawed, Robins had begun to reimburse the cost of removing it—creating the "removal file" mentioned in Chapter 6. Thus persons only reimbursed for a small medical procedure were indistinguishable in this questionnaire from those who had been paid damages or had worked for the firm. Meanwhile, those who had filed claims before Robins declared bankruptcy, but were now not allowed to pursue their individual cases ("frozen claims"), and even some people who had been awarded damages but not received them—two groups of people we would have liked to distinguish in the data—could not be identified. They just answered "no," no funds received. All future work would refer back to this population, the definitive claimant population, without knowing who they were in the terms of the case.

Another example of Judge Merhige's lack of respect for experts came in Robins' attorneys' questioning of me. Experts were asked to submit "budgets," an estimate of expenditures. No one's estimate came close to their final figures, but mine, at over $500,000, was the highest. It became clear to Robins' attorneys that, among the various parties' statistical teams, I was their biggest threat. I knew something about the scope of the case, what it

---

86. Weinstein (1986) at 495.

would take to produce competent estimates of damages. So they attacked my "budget." Curiously, they aimed most at computer costs, which I had most seriously underestimated.

Robins succeeded in getting everyone suspicious, aided, for sure, by my client's inattention to what was going on. Eventually the FBI was called to investigate my computer charges and the fact that I personally owned the company's computer (without which we would not have had one). The judge engaged a "computer expert" to compare my rates to those of time-sharing services.

Of course neither the FBI nor Merhige's expert found anything untoward in my arrangements and rates, which had always favored my clients in comparison to rates charged by time-sharing services. For the court, that ended the matter. Not for me. I had incurred extraordinary, uncalled-for expenses, including engaging a lawyer to defend me. More important, for this is what Robins wanted, I could not expend effort on the substance of the case, and I had no desire to continue in a process that took so lightly the abuse it was laying on me. Where I was looking to the judge for some relief from what I considered harassment by Robins' attorneys, I got none.[87]

I should feel lucky. When Judge Lord in Minneapolis lectured A. H. Robins about the harm the Dalkon Shield had done to thousands of women, Robins launched "a head-on assault against the judge himself."[88] Who knows to what lengths Robins might have gone against me? Uninterested in living my life this way, and unsupported by either my client or the judge, I quit. Robins had stonewalled, protested, lied, and blustered enough to get me out. But I do not blame the Robins attorneys. They effectuated a successful strategy. In Chapter 6 I laid some blame on my clients, who didn't want me in the case in the first place. And, I opposed some of their positions. They failed to assist me in my dealings with the special master. Ultimately, Judge Merhige is directly responsible for letting the only expert who had insisted on producing honest estimates leave the case.

The experts had one job: to estimate the amount that should be placed in a trust fund to cover Dalkon Shield claims. In Figure 62 I list the estimates ultimately produced by each party.[89] Robins' estimate, as expected, was the lowest, followed closely by those who would only be paid if enough were left over after the pot was put aside, the various creditors. Aetna was involved because they insured Robins against such liabilities, though not to the extent of the Dalkon Shield claims. The Claimants' Committee's estimates were high. Absurdly high. I do not know who they got to replace me, but he did what the Committee wanted:

---

87. I will not dwell on the absurdity of the judge's "cost control." For one example, as I tried to point out at the time, attorneys were being reimbursed 25¢ per page for photocopying—of which they do a lot. My local copy shop was charging 2¢ a page, paper included. So while objecting to my below-market computer cost, Merhige was generating a slush fund for attorneys.

88. Spence (1989) at 202.

89. *Robins* (1988) at 747.

he came in with big numbers. He made his clients (Cadwalader, Wickersham & Taft) look good to their clients (the Claimants' Committee), while not assisting the trier of fact at all.

Claimant	Low	High
Robins	$0.8 Billion	$1.3 Billion
Equity Security Holders	$1.03 Billion	
Unsecured Creditors	$1.54 Billion	
Aetna	$2.2 Billion	$2.5 Billion
Claimants' Committee	$4.2 Billion	$7.0 Billion

FIGURE 62: Estimates of the Dalkon Shield Damages Pot

The Committee's high estimates were dismissed by Judge Merhige, and increased the friction between him and Murray Drabkin. Eventually Drabkin was removed as attorney for the trust fund that dispensed the money. I have been told that Merhige had some nasty things to say about the Claimants' Committee's expert at a hearing, but no such remarks appear in the written record. Merhige never seemed to connect his allowing the awful behavior by Robins' attorneys towards me—which I had pointed out in my resignation letter—with the substitute expert's estimates. If you allow the competent, independent expert to be hounded out, what do you think you will get? Merhige had no one to blame but himself.

The bankruptcy opinion refers to a $2.475 billion trust fund, while the circuit court refers to a $2.3 billion trust.[90] Whatever the number was, however it was derived, American Home Products offered enough for the remnants of A. H. Robins that Merhige could satisfy all claims and leave the Robins family wealthy. Richard Sobol says the damages pot was larger than any claimant representative had hoped for. The statistical estimates were a charade.[91] Merhige could have gotten to his figure by arithmetic—by subtracting from the buyout price to achieve his objectives—and probably did.

THE SYSTEM

Although individuals are often heroic, as a society we turn our backs on crises every day.[92] Analyses of systems are difficult, because most systems operate by imposing incentives on individuals, and so all that we perceive is the individual actions. How do we determine whether they occur because of or in spite of the system?

---

90. See *Robins* (1989) at 770. The difference might be accrued interest.

91. See Sobol (1991).

92. We know about Lenny Skutnick diving into the Potomac, saving a drowning woman after an airplane crash. A helicopter also crashed into the Potomac, trapping passengers inside. Civilian divers

The judicial system asks judges to do that which they did not do well in school, and did not expect to do ever again: follow a statistical argument, and determine who has the better one. But I praise judges. We do not have a well-functioning judicial system, in the areas of my concern. But we have, by and large, intelligent, well-meaning, honest, sincere, and hard-working men and women in the judiciary. Like me, Erica Beecher-Monas thinks they are up to the tasks assigned to them:

> I strongly believe that most judges are capable of understanding the logic and evaluating the merit of scientific arguments.[93]

As the press to some extent watches them, they have an additional incentive to "get it right." But as the press, guided by academic analysts, may be wrong (as noted in Chapters 4 and 5; and see Chapters 8 and 9), judges are essentially alone.

The Courtroom

My senior analyst Gail Blattenberger was on the witness stand in Judge Jack Weinstein's court in Brooklyn, during the *Caulfield* (1979) trial. The case concerned the allocation of education resources in New York City. Our client was Richard Caro, an Assistant United States Attorney. Gail had explained some statistical relationship involving education variables which, had she been an expert in education, would have given her a doorway into a line of testimony Weinstein did not want to hear. He wanted to close that door now, with Gail on the stand. "Are you also an expert in education?" he asked. Gail did not understand the import of the question, and wondered silently if, with her economics Ph.D., having studied education in a couple of cases, she might indeed be such an expert. As she hesitated, Judge Weinstein called a brief recess.

Gail and Richard had established good rapport. When I joined them at the front of the court room they were chatting away, as if Judge Weinstein's recess had been called to relieve his bladder. "Do you not understand what just happened?" I asked. "He wants you to say no, you are not an expert in *why* this relationship exists, only in finding that it does." "Oh, I suppose that *is* what just happened," said Richard. Judge Weinstein returned, called the court to order, reminded Gail of the question that was open, and showed obvious pleasure at her firm "No" answer.

---

were close by, offered to try to rescue them, but were rebuffed by police, who had called their own. Half an hour later police divers arrived and got the now-lifeless passengers out. In *Joy* (1993) their relatives were not allowed to sue the city for damages, even though the city was clearly culpable. A similar incident occurred on the Manistee River in Michigan in 1995. The sheriff's department prevented a private rescue team from functioning, even though its own divers comprised only a body-recovery team. The Sixth Circuit in this instance did allow the decedent's family to sue the county. See *Beck* (2004).

93. Beecher-Monas (2002) at 1815.

I wonder how many judges try to manipulate trial proceedings this way, but fail because the other participants do not get the clues. Weinstein has a reputation as a solid trial judge, not just in his opinions, but in his court room. I concur. Calling a recess to let Richard explain the context to Gail was good trial management. An inexperienced or inattentive lawyer may not get it, but it is always worth trying.

It is this level of engagement I ask from the judge. It is what I got from Oberdorfer in Washington, D.C., Judges Zobel and Skinner in Boston, and Weinstein when I appeared before him.[94] The judge understands the lines of argument that might be made in this case. The interactive judge can control those arguments, so they are always made to him or, in a jury case, to the jury. The passive judge, who leaves the courtroom proceedings in the hands of the attorneys, will end up making decisions about experts on bases the experts themselves would agree are not fundamental. The arrogant judge, like Richey or Merhige, is too impressed with himself to participate openly. Questions such as, "What should this mean to me?" or, "Where are you going with this?" or, "Explain why I should accept your measures as valid," are always in order. Too few judges ask them.

"Work It Out"

Telling one side or the other to come forward with a solution to some problem can be effective management. Telling *both* sides to solve their own problems is a favorite but poor judicial tactic. It induces bad behavior. I can understand why a judge thinks he is being confronted with childish bickering, and wants to tell the parties to stop it; but his unwillingness to determine who has created the problem only brings forth more of it.

Disclosure of expert materials creates issues. Each party tries to comport with the letter of the law, while at the same time making it as difficult as possible for the other side to understand what it has been given. Behind the judge's back there is turmoil, created by persons of bad will. The judge does not want to hear about it. "Work it out," he says. Yet, if the issue has come before him, it is because at least one of the experts or attorneys has not approached the issue of disclosure with the intent to disclose. "Work it out" empowers the wrong people, the obfuscators. The more mean-spirited one is, the more he gains from a command to "work it out."

Judge Duomar was appalled at the behavior of the parties before him:

> In the nearly fifty years that the undersigned has been a member of the bar, working almost always in litigation, of which twenty years have been on the bench, the undersigned has never seen a case which entailed more rancor between attorneys handling a case or involved in the case. Never have so many

---

94. For Oberdorfer see *Harrison* (1982) or *Koger* (1994). For Zobel see *McCarthy* (1982). For Skinner see *Polaroid* (1983). For Weinstein, see *Caulfield* (1979).

objections, obstructions, and motions been put forward by both sides than in any prior case seen by the undersigned during those almost fifty years.[95]

But Judge Duomar knew who was at fault. Consider his summary of his findings:

> In essence, Kidde pulled the rug out from under X-It, a promising young company with an innovative product, package, and an aggressive marketing plan. In the aftermath of Kidde's having stolen both X-It's product, package, and its marketing, as well as having willfully deceived X-It's management, X-It lost all its forward momentum and began to fall apart. Absent the intervention of the courts, Kidde had succeeded in its scheme to practically destroy an up and coming rival through deceit.

Kidde stole X-It's product, its packaging (including photographs of relatives of X-It's executives!), and its customers. Who does Judge Duomar think was being an obstructionist in the judicial process? Why did he do nothing about it?

Disclosure is a procedural issue about which the judge need not understand the technical details. If one side says they provided the raw data, the judge thinks that is just fine. When the recipient complains that he wants the analytic files, the data created by a program from the raw files, the judge is bewildered. "We'll even provide the program," says the obfuscator. The judge does not understand that the "program" is uncalled for and may be useless. It may not be in a language the other side's expert "speaks." It may have site-specific references (and software calls) that may not work on someone else's computer. In short, if the parties are to exchange data, each should provide that which the other asks for.

There is only one way to "work out" a data exchange, and that is to have a rule that the recipient can specify data elements and the physical format, among those formats to which the provider acknowledges he can convert the data. This suggestion does not ask the provider to gain additional capabilities, only to use those he has to make the exchange smooth. The provider might say there is no "analytic" data base, because the program that converts data from raw to usable is run anew with each program. Not to save their analytic data was Charles River Associates' policy in litigation, determined by meanness, not by statistical expertise. A judge should see through this, tell the party to stop obstructing, save the data in its usable form, and produce it.[96]

It doesn't work between Israelis and Palestinians, regardless who you think the bad guys are. Nonetheless, President George Bush tells them to "work it out":

> With a dedicated effort, this [Palestinian] state could rise rapidly as it comes to terms with Israel, Egypt and Jordan on practical issues such as security. The

---

95. *X-It* (2002) at 500; following indented quotation at 501.

96. The Equal Employment Opportunity Commission notes, at 457, "that there exists no comprehensive, common database in" *Morgan Stanley* (2004). In a large and important case like this, that should never be true.

final borders, the capital, and other aspects of this state's sovereignty will be negotiated between the parties as part of a final settlement. Arab states have offered their help in this process, and their help is needed.[97]

Palestine and Israel work out their borders? That is a doomed policy, and it isn't the real policy anyway. Israel is unilaterally determining the borders, with our acquiescence. The Serbs and the Croats couldn't work it out in Yugoslavia, nor could the Hutus and Tutsis in Rwanda. The government of Angola found it could not work anything out with Jonas Savimbi, but peace and cooperation prevailed after they found him and killed him. Liberian movements for democracy could not "work out" a democratic solution with Charles Taylor. Ultimately, he was bribed to leave by a coalition of neighboring states and the United States. Without third-party intervention, there would have been only war. We did not ask Haitian rebels to "work out" their dispute with the elected government. We removed President Jean-Bertrand Aristide. You can agree or disagree with these policies, but the lesson is that "Work it out" fails; "Do this now," if stated with authority, succeeds.

Could the United Nations armaments inspectors "work out" their operation with a recalcitrant Iraq? Not in 1998, when the U.N. withdrew them. Not in 2003 when the United States decided to become an activist judge. It didn't work between blacks and whites in the United States through the executive and legislative branches. Only when strong judges laid down the law, and shamed the executive branch into enforcing it, did segregation begin to fall away.

Yes, of course, these are extreme examples; but examples nonetheless.[98] They are examples of an unstructured "work it out" mentality, which encourages each side to wreak havoc on the other. India and Pakistan "work out" Kashmir, absent the United Nations or some other strong neutral authority setting out procedures and sanctioning those who do not follow them? If it happens, which remains unlikely, it will be because both countries have atomic bombs, to which there is no litigation analogy. We need strong judges, yes, but they need help, and they need tools. They need to be more involved with the daily mangling of truth-seeking that is the inevitable result of adversary attorney control of the expert process.

The Individual Judge

I had occasion to bring a small suit in a local court in Montgomery County, Maryland. The judge took his time to ascertain the facts, not all of which I had known coming into the

---

97. *New York Times* transcript of a June 24, 2002, speech outlining Middle East proposals, www.nytimes.com, June 25, 2002.

98. Lester Thurow says, "Scandals are endemic to capitalism." "Government Can't Make the Market Fair," *New York Times*, July 23, 2002. More important, the kind of corrupt behavior that, when it is exposed, we call a scandal, is endemic to competitive, adversarial systems.

courtroom (because pre-trial fact finding is too expensive in these small matters). He made, I thought, an excellent judgment. I stayed afterwards to tell him about my experience in state and federal courts. I told him the job I had seen him do was as good as any I had ever seen at any level. That may not be true in the kinds of legal scholarship in which I have little expertise, but in pursuing his role as a fact finder and administrator of justice, he was impressive.[99]

If you look at enough cases, you read some in which the judge was clearly wrong. In some, the judge may have been taken in by an expert with more form than substance. In some the fault lies with the attorneys, through whom all argument must flow. In some, surely, the local judge was "in bed" with some of the parties. And as my criticism of the Supreme Court on jury representation shows, sometimes the courts just get bound into an incorrect logic, or find that years earlier they had taken a wrong turn. But if you take a large view of the judicial system, I think a fair conclusion is that judges do a spectacularly good job.

The system itself also has some good points. Expensive though it is, the appeals process gives the district court loser a chance to reframe his argument. The appellant has a hard hill to climb to reverse lower-court fact finding. He must show "clear error," not just marginally incorrect thinking. But it can be done. *James* (1975), *Mister* (1987), and *Lamp* (1991) are examples of appeals-court reversals of incompetent findings into just findings, reversals of the findings of fact, not just the rulings of law. The *Washington Post* reveals that "around the Alexandria [Virginia] federal courthouse, Judge Hilton is notorious for his hostility to discrimination cases," describing his rejection of a complaint of racial discrimination because the plaintiff still held his job. However, the Fourth Circuit reversed, and a jury awarded damages.[100]

The general thrust of this book is that the system's incentives are wrong. Much that goes on in a courtroom is tone. If for whatever reason the judge just doesn't like one expert, that expert's position is doomed, be it right or wrong. The judge has to decide between experts on some basis. He too easily chooses the wrong basis, and therefore the wrong expert. Still, the U.S. judicial systems, at every level, are viable, vibrant, successful institu-

---

99. Montgomery County is wealthy. One might expect a good judiciary there. I had similar experiences in Polk County, North Carolina, one of North Carolina's poorest, and Henderson County, which may represent the middle. Not that small-claims-court judges are intellectuals, or legal scholars. Yet, in a direct way, each got through to the facts, and applied the law honestly. When we hear about how other countries operate, we should remind ourselves how fortunate we are in our dispute-resolution forums.

100. "Racism's Redoubts," *Washington Post* editorial, January 2, 2005, at B06. As the Fourth Circuit noted in *White* (2004), in footnote 6 at 298,

> One need not sacrifice one's job (and a steady source of income) in order to prove that racial harassment in the workplace rose to the level of an actionable hostile work environment.

tions. Yet systemically bad? Yes, bad as a *system*—in this particular niche of determining statistical fact—regardless of the outcome.

Judge Matthew Kennelly in the U.S. district court in Chicago read *Bazemore* (1986) and understood it. R. R. Donnelley & Sons wanted to exclude plaintiffs' statistical expert, Christopher Ross, because he did not enter into a regression all the explanatory variables Donnelley would wish. Judge Kennelley concluded:

> The fact that Ross did not conduct his analysis in the same way as Donnelley's expert does not make Ross' testimony inadmissible. Donnelley may cross-examine Ross on weaknesses it alleges exist in his regression analysis model and may argue the point to the jury.[101]

Although this passage indicates what lawyers will do with *Daubert* hearings—make extreme arguments with no merit in hope of winning a few of them—it also indicates what a judge can do with them. Judge Kennelley clearly does not know what a regression is. Whatever defendant said about regression cannot be discerned from Kennelley's botched paraphrase, not reproduced here. Just as clearly, it does not matter. He could see that Donnelley's expert just had a different view, not a devastating critique.[102]

EDUCATING JUDGES

One might conclude that the solution to the problem of the individual judge being misled by the advocate expert is education—education in science, technology, and, most important, statistics. This is the view of the Carnegie Commission on Science, Technology, and Government.[103] It is a role, probably initiated by that Commission, taken up by the Federal Judicial Center.

Thinking that in order to assess the probabilities that statistical experts report, the court must understand them, the Federal Judicial Center produced its *Reference Manual on Scientific Evidence*, a collection of articles it thinks a judge will read, understand, and apply. I think it fails, as I mentioned in Chapter 2 and will amplify somewhat in Chapter 10, but not because the individual articles are poor. When one reads other attempts to write statistics primers, one appreciates the effort the writers of the *Reference Manual* put in. I am not alone in thinking that effort was misdirected:

---

101. *Gerlib* (2002), 2002 WL 1182434 at *6. Although this seems to be a powerful point, many judges do not get it. The Ninth Circuit did, in *GenTel* (1989) at 581:

> [D]efendant cannot rebut an inference of discrimination by merely pointing to flaws in the plaintiff's statistics.

102. See also *Tyler* (2002), in which defendant Unocal contended that its expert's critique of plaintiffs' expert was devastating. Not so, said the Fifth Circuit, affirming the jury's decision for plaintiffs.

103. See Carnegie (1993).

It is unclear, however, whether a judge, without any prior formal training in statistics, could fully comprehend the material presented in these sections. Moreover, because the chapters contain only introductory material, they do not cover many of the more advanced techniques and principles presented by statisticians in trial.[104]

The Carnegie Commission recommends:

> Scientific and technical issues should be integrated into traditional judicial educational programs, "modules" should be developed that can be appended to existing programs, and intensive programs should be supported.[105]

One could not oppose such an innocuous, committee-constructed proposal. Perhaps judges need to know about probabilities in the sense of what they mean and the importance of model assumptions. I am opposed to "training" judges in *how* these probabilities have been estimated. Correcting technical errors is best left to the experts. When people try to produce materials to explain these technical manipulations, judges become more confused than enlightened.

Judges may be the wrong people to ask about this. In one survey many judges responded that they had taken continuing legal education courses, and felt ready to handle science issues under the *Daubert* mandate. Yet, they

> were unable to provide responses that reflected a scientifically appropriate understanding of the *Daubert* guidelines, especially for the concepts of falsifiability and error rate.[106]

The "*Daubert* guidelines" are the four factors articulated in *Daubert*, which can hardly be considered clear, and like most judicial "guidelines" present no standards, just a vague idea of what to look for.

Thus we visit, again, a central theme of this book: Errors that statistical experts make, for the most part, are conceptual, not technical. Training judges to look at scatter diagrams

---

104. Tam Cho and Yoon (2001) at 248. The two articles to which they refer, in *Reference Manual* (1994), are David H. Kaye and David A. Freedman, "Reference Guide on Statistics," at 331; and Daniel L Rubinfeld, "Reference Guide on Multiple Regression," at 415. The *Reference Manual* writers got two attributions out of their work as, revised only slightly, they appear also in Faigman et al. (2002). The statement in text is not a blanket endorsement. I take issue with much in these articles. For example there is a wimpy discussion of the 0.05 level as if it were meaningful in Kaye and Friedman (1994) at 380. No article in the *Reference Manual*, as I pointed out in Chapter 2, mentions multiple-pools methods. I do, however, appreciate the difficulty of their task, and criticize more the existence of the *Reference Manual* than the articles within it.

105. Carnegie (1993) at 51; also in summary at 17.

106. Shirley A. Dobbin, Sophia I. Gatowski, James T. Richardson, Gerald P. Ginsburg, Mara L. Merlino, and Veronica Dahir, "Applying Daubert," 85 *Judicature* 5:244 (March-April 2002), at 247. The *Daubert* factors are reproduced in Chapter 1 of this book.

and "see" regression lines may help some of them feel more comfortable with the way in which the computer has found the "best" line to fit the scatter of observations; but that is seldom the point. Let's assume that Mark Berkman's regressions for NERA were this "best fit" to accurate, even relevant data.[107] So what? None of it meant what Berkman said it meant (that Montana's taxes "controlled" the state's production of coal). Joan Haworth's regression in *Nassau*, in which her "market" variable drove the gender variable to zero, was technically correct. It was, after all, my regression with an added variable (and, hence, fewer observations). No course in statistics would teach a judge how to deal with the real issue, which was the validity of her "market" measure. It is, in any case, one expert's job to explain to the judge why the other expert's work was incorrect. It is the judge's job to understand the logic, not necessarily the science.

So, for example, it is disappointing to read:

> A pools analysis looks to pools of similarly situated employees to determine how the promotion success of a certain pool—here, African American would-be promotees—stacks up against that of a control group, such as all other would-be promotees.[108]

Remember, from Chapter 2, that pools are "applicants" to promotion events, grouped by receiving position and date. Judge Huvelle needs a different word, "success of a certain *group*," to avoid confusion. Blacks are not a pool in a multiple-pools analysis. The judge can more simply find that one expert's methodology was superior, and adopt his results. When the judge tries to explain the methodology, he screws up.

It is not surprising that the Carnegie Commission recommends education: 40 percent of its members were from academia. It is the content of that education that I question. Of course a commission report leaves it vague, but the *Reference Manual* convinces me that education in the form of statistics primers, which is what follows from such a recommendation, will serve few judges in their daily work. I return to this topic, with a suggestion, in Chapter 9.

KEEPERS OF THE GATE

I will discuss the standard by which experts are deemed to be expert, in federal court, in Chapter 10. There I will also discuss the judge's role as gatekeeper, as the person who determines whether the proposed "expert" is expert enough to speak to the court. I will describe various historical changes in standards in Chapter 10, also: allowing the expert to testify to ultimate fact, increasing the scope of discovery, etc.

---

107. See *Crow II* and my discussion thereof in Chapter 3.

108. *McReynolds* (2004a) at 8.

As noted above, to some, "education" is the answer to everything, even gatekeeping.

> Thus, the practical value of *Daubert* for judges may never be fully realized unless judges are provided with sufficient judicial scientific education to allow them to perform their gatekeeping role.[109]

We certainly should be concerned with the judge's ability to pass through the informative expert, while censoring the crackpot. I think we should look first at who these judges are and how they respond to experts. Again, I do not think the kind of education these commentators espouse is the missing ingredient.

Judges Who Get It

Judge Reed phrases his objection to expert testimony in easy-to-understand procedural language. Fire-expert Richard B. Thomas passed the qualifications test, but not the testimony test:

> The method applied by Thomas in his investigation of the alleged manufacturing defect appears to have consisted of a testable hypothesis, but Thomas never tested his hypothesis. . . . Thomas never attempted to recreate this phenomenon with a similar or identical toaster, something that he conceded could have been done.[110]

Therefore

> The court was presented with no evidence aside from Thomas' assurances that others use the methodology he applied in investigating the cause of this electrical fire.

Summary judgment for defendant. Note that Judge Reed is not assessing the specifics, the technical details. He just wants assurance that in Thomas' methodology the word "cause" can be validated. Failing that, it is rejected.

Similarly, Judge Selya is looking for reliability from William Bleuel:

> Expert opinions, however, are no better than the data and methodology that undergird them—and on this score, Dr. Bleuel's conclusions are highly suspect. . . . Dr. Bleuel did not conduct a customer satisfaction survey. . . . Then, citing to sources which it neither attaches nor discusses, the report concludes that DEC's customer-satisfaction ratings have been declining. Dr. Bleuel's conclusions may or may not be correct, but an expert must vouchsafe the reliability of the data on which he relies and explain how the cumulation of that data was consistent with standards of the expert's profession.[111]

---

109. Gatowski et al. (2001) at 453.

110. *Booth* (2001) at 219; following indented quotation at 220.

111. *SMS* (1999) at 25.

The phrasing here is exactly correct: Judge Selya does not want to take a stand on the ultimate issue, but he will reject the expert's opinion if the expert cannot justify it. As Judge Easterbrook put it, "An expert who supplies nothing but a bottom line supplies nothing of value to the judicial process."[112]

In another context:

> Yet the finer points of significance testing are pertinent only if the analyst has formulated the hypothesis correctly and decided what pattern (if established) will confirm or refute that hypothesis. The first, hardest, and often the only task is deciding what to look for.[113]

Judge Hochberg dealt with the motion to exclude David Ozonoff's testimony. Ozonoff was plaintiffs' primary expert on cause in a toxic tort suit. On his credentials, Ozonoff was admitted to testify, but a *Daubert* hearing was called to assess the testimony itself. The judge asked him to explain why he did what he did:

> However, Dr. Ozonoff still did not offer any scientific method to guide what weight he had accorded each piece of evidence nor did he explain why he weighted as he did nor how, given the body of evidence before him, he arrived at his ultimate conclusion. . . . [A]fter three days of testimony, no reliable scientific method for conducting the weighting of the evidence was offered by Dr. Ozonoff.[114]

Judge Hochberg did not determine that the "weight-of-the-evidence" method (a way to summarize others' studies, a way to weight them to a conclusion) was impermissible. That is, he made no judgment about Ozonoff's choice of methodology. He assessed what Ozonoff could say about how he had effectuated it. The judge stuck to his level of review, and granted the motion to exclude Ozonoff.

The magistrate judge had allowed plaintiff's medical doctor, Mary Reyna, to testify that a fall in Food Lion "caused physical trauma to Black, which caused 'hormonal changes,' which caused Black's fibromyalgia."[115] Incredulous, the Fifth Circuit panel concluded: "Dr. Reyna's testimony does not bear the necessary indicia of intellectual rigor." I will discuss the phenomenon of medical doctors, as expert as they may be in diagnosis of the problem, providing testimony as to cause, in Chapter 10.

In the bankruptcy proceedings of Armstrong World Industries, the question arose how much airborne asbestos there was in buildings that were claimed to have been damaged by Armstrong flooring. Expert measurements, made by the "indirect method," were

---

112. *Mid-State* (1989) at 1339.

113. *Mister* (1987) at 1431.

114. *Magistrini* (2002) at 601.

115. *Black* (1999) at 309; following in-text quotation at 312.

challenged.[116] Judge Newsome held a *Daubert* hearing on the subject.

There are three problems with the indirect method. First, it reports finding more asbestos than the "direct method," described in the National Institute of Occupational Safety and Health's *Manual of Analytical Methods*. The direct method measures asbestos in the air, whereas the indirect method attempts to infer airborne asbestos from dust on the floor. Second, there is no known relationship between the counts by the two methods, nor an agreed theory as to why they differ. Third, and surely most important,

> there has never been a controlled statistical analysis of the relationship between asbestos counts using the indirect method and actual airborne concentrations.[117]

As only airborne asbestos is harmful,[118] it is the quantity of airborne asbestos that must be measured to assess harm to building occupants, which generates a claim on Armstrong's assets. Measurements by the unvalidated indirect method were not allowed into evidence.[119]

Attitude

Let us suppose this is a binary world. There are only two values, zero and one. Plaintiffs' expert always says the defendant is zero, and defendant's expert always says he is one. The judge has to find fact, and can only choose zero or one, plaintiff's view or defendant's. So one of the experts is correct, or closer to the truth, or better. One expert will be vindicated. That expert may have been prepared to lie, cheat, and steal for his client, and he may have done so, through ignorance or habit. Nonetheless, his client was right. He was right.

Judges take the reasonable attitude that all experts are corrupt. But they *cannot* hold that all experts are *wrong*. In my zero/one world, half of all expert testimony supports the right side, even if illogically. Whatever attitude the judge has about the credentials and character of the witness, he should not hold, a priori, about his testimony. The guy just might have come to the correct conclusion, even if he had predetermined to do so.

The judge comes to work each day to face people who have focused their energies for months toward this moment. The intensity of the judge's workplace is exhausting. The judge must look for ways to simplify, to negotiate around the technicalities.

---

116. "Indirect method" is short for "Standard Method for Microvacuum Sampling and Indirect Analysis of Dust by Transmission Electron Microscopy for Asbestos Structure Number Concentrations," American Society for Testing and Materials, D5755.

117. *Armstrong* (2002) at 869.

118. *Armstrong* (2002) at 867:

> It is generally agreed that the risk of harm from asbestos stems from inhaling fibers, not from how much asbestos is on the surfaces of a room.

119. A curious omission in Judge Newsome's discussion is sampling. Environmental measurements are samples, and come therefore not as numbers but as probable ranges.

An expert can be found to testify to the truth of almost any factual theory, no matter how frivolous, thus validating the case sufficiently to avoid summary judgment and force the matter to trial. At the trial itself an expert's testimony can be used to obfuscate what would otherwise be a simple case.[120]

Samuel Gross describes the result:

The contempt of judges for experts is famous. They regularly describe expert witnesses as prostitutes, people who live by selling services that should not be for sale. . . . This attitude is not compatible with the serious attention to evidence these presumably untrustworthy witnesses provide.[121]

Stephen Chewning, expert for a driver whose vehicle hit the defendant from behind, had the unenviable task of explaining why the vehicle his client hit was at fault. Magistrate Judge Dohnal was taken by the explanation of Roland Ruhl, the victim's expert, that Chewning's analysis "results in the impossible conclusion that the plaintiff vehicle was going faster *after* the impact than the defendant vehicle."[122] Apparently they were joined, and therefore moving at the same speed. Chewning argues that defendant's car was moving too slowly. The magistrate concludes that Chewning's analysis "is best described as a patchwork of unreliable estimations blended with what is otherwise accepted science."

Judge Posner gives us two contradictory views of experts on the same page:

Because most expert witnesses, unlike most lay witnesses, are repeat players, they have a financial interest in creating and preserving a reputation for being honest and competent.

[I]t is also the repeat player who has an incentive to please his client, so that he will be hired in the future.[123]

The second view (in my opinion) dominates. The honest expert does not get to be a repeat player, as I described in Chapter 6. Still, the view that "expert witnesses are intruders who disrupt the judicial search for truth" dismisses whatever help is available.[124] Dismissive remarks should be reserved for experts who are excluded, whose testimony is determined to be worthless on a quality scale. Of Helen Morrison, one court said:

Her testimony seems illogical, inconsistent and, in considerable part, incomprehensible, and lacks any basis in fact.[125]

---

120. Weinstein (1986) at 482.

121. Gross (1991) at 1135.

122. *Hauling* (2000) at 772; following in-text quotation also at 772.

123. Posner (1999a), both quotations at 1537. The same two views are presented in Posner (1999b).

124. Gross (1991) at 1114. He takes this impression from "comments of lawyers and judges."

125. *Davis* (1985) at 1344.

Morrison may have needed science training, but the judge did fine without.

If the professional expert poses problems for judges, the academic fares no better. Academics

> tend to be unworldly. They are, most of them anyway, the people who have never left school. Their milieu is postadolescent. Because they are tenured and work mostly by themselves . . . they don't have to get along with colleagues; some of them don't get along with anybody.[126]

A judge should not start out with an assumption that the academic or the professional expert will better serve him. Judge Spada in *Gibbs* (1998), thrilled to have a Yale professor in his courtroom, was surprised when he ended up agreeing with me, the professional. I would prefer to see judges start with an attitude of respect for all experts, and lose that respect only for cause. In particular, having made a life decision to be a professional analyst, I am distressed that judges more distrust the professional's testimony.

And yet, I agree. To be a repeat player, the professional needs to please his client. Presenting honest, capable analysis is not the pathway toward that end. In short, the professional expert on the one hand is likely to be more capable than the academic expert; and on the other hand, he could be trying to achieve a corporate goal that has nothing to do with presenting a good analysis, with valid data. As Frankel concludes, "The advocate's prime loyalty is to his client, not to truth as such."[127] It should be assumed that the expert, professional or academic, holds this view. But that does not mean he is wrong. You just don't know until you listen.[128]

Judges and *Daubert*

David Peterson and John Conley think *Daubert* changed the role of the judge. *Daubert* and its progeny "redefine the duties of trial courts as arbiters of good scientific evidence." They "thrust" the judge "into an active 'gatekeeping' role."[129] Margaret Berger uses similar language, saying a consequence of *Daubert* was "the new role it thrust upon the district

---

126. Posner (2001a) at 73.

127. Frankel (1975) at 1035.

128. Philosophers describe the "genetic fallacy," using the origin of an idea to attack or defend that idea's validity. It is a fallacy because although history can illuminate, we can assess the value of individual behaviors without knowing where they come from. (Indeed, having made that assessment, one does not reject it if its origin is then shown to have been ignorance or evil. The act is still the act.) Avoiding the genetic fallacy is also Justice Scalia's argument for not caring about legislative history. He is less an "originalist," more a "literalist." One might say that philosophy is an investigation of rules for making intrinsic judgments about actions and thoughts. The judicial parallel to the genetic fallacy is the credential fallacy—accepting what an expert says not on its merits, but on his.

129. Peterson and Conley (2001) at 213.

judge."[130] I think this goes too far, as do Lloyd Dixon and Brian Gill, who conclude that the judge's duty to assess expert testimony, and the standards of assessment, were clear in the federal rules *Daubert* told judges to follow.[131] Not only are judges free to define their roles within broad outlines, they have been gatekeepers since before the Federal Rules of Evidence were adopted in 1975. Indeed, *Frye* (1923) is a famous example of a judge closing the gate on expert testimony, having decided that the court would not be hearing "good scientific evidence." The role of the judge has not changed. How he performs it has.

Margaret Berger early on also saw the procedural importance of *Daubert*.

> Although *Daubert* interprets the Federal Rules of Evidence, reflects an evidentiary concern for accuracy in the courtroom, and will probably appear in every evidence casebook, its impact will in large measure be affected and mediated by the procedural settings in which scientific evidence is proffered.[132]

I agree. The importance of *Daubert* lies not in the role of the judge, but in the introduction of a procedure to effectuate it, the *Daubert* hearing. Gatekeeping has been facilitated by making it the focus of a separate event. And it has been improved, by focusing on the testimony, not the testifier; the information, not the informant.

JUDGES AND SCIENCE

I have dropped hints throughout this chapter that there are several suggestions I would make to judges. One is to schedule all expert events, and enforce it. The last-minute "market" measure produced by Joan Haworth should have been grounds for exclusion of her testimony. The last-minute motion by W. R. Grace to join in the examination of plaintiff's proposed expert should have been denied. Both parties should have known in advance whether defendant Tremblay's expert would get a shot at rebuttal, and whether the state's expert would be allowed a rejoinder.[133] Instead, procedures were made up on the fly, motion by motion.

---

130. M. Berger (2001) at 293.

131. Dixon and Gill (2002) at 298:

> The *Daubert* decision did not change the standards for the relevance of expert evidence, for the expert's qualifications, or for other considerations that enter into a judge's assessment of whether to admit expert evidence, but it did affirm that judges should act as gatekeepers.

Either because judges had been encouraged by the Supreme Court to be more aggressive, or because they now thought they would be supported, "Challenges to expert evidence increasingly resulted in summary judgment after *Daubert*."

132. M. Berger (1994) at 1345.

133. See *Tremblay* (2002); see also Chapter 10 and the Appendix to Chapter 5.

A second suggestion is to be the problem resolver. Rather than wave off disputes, hear them. No one wants to have a dispute resolved against him. "Even-handedness" is being fair, not being equal. Lawyers will start off thinking that the other side has been winning, so I'll win this one. Not if you are wrong. Pretty soon, the obstructionist should cease and desist, if the judge provides the other party a refuge from his tactics.

Ultimately, money talks. Attorneys who are not cooperating, as the judge sees it, should be fined. When the issue is data exchange, if plaintiff's expert has clearly stated the form in which he wants to receive data—and which data they are; if defendant has said it would not be a burden to produce the data that way, it understands what is wanted (even if it is a data set defendant's expert deliberately has not saved); then produce the data by a set date or pay a fine for not having done so. If the issue is disclosure of witnesses, disclose or pay up. I once started to tell Judge Sand why it would be difficult for me to be in a certain place at a certain time. He cut me off. He had a schedule. I had to comply with it. I did.

My third suggestion is to engage experts in discussion. Courtroom procedure is designed to fragment the expert presentations. It would be easier if the judge could devise a forum to bring the experts together, to have explicitly the discussion that remains implicit under current procedure. I will outline a trial procedure toward that end in Chapter 10.

A fourth suggestion is to choose among the material provided by the experts. Do not try to create your own. If the judge engages a special master, be clear whether that master is to mediate, arbitrate, or participate. If the parties' experts just don't get it, perhaps they need a lecture, but it is still up to them to do their work. The master should see to it that the data are common, and the analytic methods are not so far afield as to be rejected out of hand. The master might do his own analysis, but only as a guide to his questions or lecture, not as a substitute for the parties' experts.

The short summary of these recommendations is to stay engaged. As Judge Frankel warned:

> Many judges, withdrawn from the fray, watch it with benign and detached affection, chuckling nostalgically now and then as the truth suffers injury or death in the process.[134]

Although in less detail, the Carnegie Commission reiterated the same concept:

> Judges should take an active role in managing the presentation of science and technology issues in litigation, whenever appropriate.[135]

A case large enough to have experts is large enough to have a schedule, and regular

---

134. Frankel (1975) at 1034.

135. Carnegie (1993) at 50; also in summary at 16.

conferences at which the judge can inquire which party is causing the other problems. He can begin to learn what roles the parties think the experts are playing, what the logic of each expert's argument is. If the judge first encounters the expert debate in court, say at a *Daubert* hearing, he will be ill-prepared to deal with it.

Finally, I recommend to the judge that he stay within his area of competence. He does not need to know what a correlation is, or how to calculate it. The judge does not need to be an expert on validity studies, either. He just needs to know that without validity, it does not matter what correlation is obtained, what the regression coefficient is, etc. So he needs to ask why he should believe the expert's results, not questioning the mathematics (that is the opposing expert's job), but questioning the concepts.

Like Gerry Spence, quoted at the beginning of this chapter, Max Boot asserts: "Bad judges will always outnumber good ones."[136] He follows the Peter Huber tradition of generalizing from anecdotes, of sensationalizing without analyzing. There is no way to assess this conclusion. There are bad judges, as many appointed as elected. My praise has come mostly from the limited perspective of the handling of statistical evidence. Judges as I have seen them, for the most part, are hard-working, sincere, and smart. The question is, how can we help them? Elementary statistics training, superficial as it must be, does more harm than good. Rather, I would want expert testimony judged by the logic it follows, by whether the language used to summarize it is justified by the work itself. The judge needs a few logical rules, not technical paradigms.

As will be amplified in Chapter 8, models need to allow explanations other than the one offered. The expert should come to his position by rejecting others, not by just asking if what his client sees could be. There would have been no Bendectin lawsuits had experts worked this way. Economic parameters in damages calculations—like projected rate of income, survival, business success—need to be based on experience, that is, on generalizable data. Results need to be stated probabilistically, with a clear explanation of where those probabilities come from. Judges can make these assessments. They need to know to do so. The judge does not need to learn how to be a statistician. He should not try.[137] He needs to learn how to be a judge.[138]

---

136. Boot (1998) at 30. In addition to providing us no way to count the "bad" vs. the "good," Boot comes up short on citations. It is difficult to check his anecdotes. It is to Robert Bork's discredit that he allowed himself to be associated with this book. Ashman (1973), though offering specific examples of corrupt judges, by name, tells us about too few of them to convince us that they are in the majority.

137. Beecher-Monas (2000) at 1570:

   While judges do need a mental framework for this analysis, they do not need to be trained scientists.

138. Barak (2002) at 1216:

   Judging is not merely a job. It is a way of life.

8

Experts

In Chapter 3, in the section "Modeling the Complaint," I described a regression study by Franklin Fisher in *O'Keefe* (1996). Airplane production tasks were left in bins, from which they were fetched by workers. Punching in and out for a task created a "ring," a work-charge observation. Fisher estimated a regression model in which observations were such charges from worker daily time records. "Efficiency" (a production measure divided by expended time) was the dependent variable. An independent variable denoted the existence of a short ring to an over-budget project (as Fisher determined it) on the same day as a long ring to an under-budget project. If large and of the correct sign, its coefficient, said Fisher, would have been consistent with allegations of mischarging, of doing one project's work on another project's budget.

Fisher estimated the same regression model for each worker. He found a "significant" coefficient in some of his regressions, something like thirteen out of more than three hundred, and presented his "not significant" regressions as evidence how few workers mischarged. It was a daring and innovative use of regression. In Chapter 3 I suggested also that it was a failure. Fisher's model required that individuals would act only on his definition of budget status. Other, more compelling definitions were available, as was an approach that did not require commitment to a budget concept in advance. Fisher's budget-status metric would have been affected by the worker actions supposedly based upon it, a serious circularity. I doubted that his elegant statistical model shed any light on the facts of the case, which settled without a full airing.

Fisher also missed the boat—his own boat—in interpretation. As he was testing all production workers, the number of "significant" regression coefficients he found was not implausibly different from chance at the 0.05 level he espoused. While willing to assert that lack of "significance" was evidence of non-cheating, he might have asserted that so few "significant" equations was itself an "insignificant"—not improbable—finding when no cheating occurred.

During my deposition I asked defendant's attorney what he was going to do about Fisher's results. He said he'd live with it; some people cheated. In Fisher's deposition, my client asked about the interpretation of coefficients under multiple testing. Just as Fisher had not thought of this issue himself, he seemed oblivious to it when it was suggested.

It was the government's responsibility to identify the wrongdoers, who according to the complaint would have been foremen. Fisher, for the defendant, specifically disclaimed "data-mining" aspirations. Among the "significant" coefficients was the main whistleblower, but not most in the "group of seven" alleged to have committed the same infractions. Obtaining a coefficient when there should be none is as faulty as not obtaining the co-efficient when there should be one. If proceeding this way at all, I would have run the regression on two sets of observations: those alleged to have cheated, and those not. Finding the same small proportion of "significant" coefficients in each set, one could conclude that the model had no ability to detect the fraud, that there was no fraud to detect, or that the model was correct and the government had named the wrong perpetrators.[1] What "should" have been done can be debated, but what *was* done was to let the computer churn away while the expert ignored the statistical as well as the legal basis of what the computer was doing.

WHO SETS THE PARAMETERS?

The American Booksellers Association and several independent bookstores in California alleged antitrust violations against Barnes & Noble and Borders Books. Franklin Fisher was the primary economic expert for the plaintiffs. The allegation was that

> defendants receive secret discounts and other favorable terms from book publishers and distributors that are not available to independent bookstores.[2]

To obtain damages, plaintiffs had to show that they were harmed, and by how much. Fisher's "economic simulation model" was the only evidence of this harm offered by plaintiffs. Apparently no attempt was made to find someone who said he had purchased a book at Barnes & Noble, or Borders—having also shopped at an independent bookstore—based on price. The Booksellers Association's case was like the Equal Employment Opportunity Commission's contention that Sears discriminated against females by not placing them in large-appliance (tires, refrigerators, etc.) sales positions. The EEOC presented no female who had applied for but was denied that job. Sears prevailed.[3]

---

1. If the government's ability to identify perpetrators was faulty, we would be back to the original point: From all workers, the number who failed Fisher's test was not an improbable result from chance variation under a no-fraud condition.

2. *Booksellers* (2001) at 1035.

3. See *Sears* (1988) at 311:

One would think that in an econometric analysis of the loss to some booksellers from (undisputed) wholesale discounts available only to other booksellers, an expert would include first a discussion of defendant firms' price policies (how much of the discount was passed to the store price?) and second an estimate of the price elasticity of the books in question (to what extent did a lower price draw customers away from plaintiffs?). Estimating price elasticity has often been an important task of an antitrust expert.[4]

Judge Orrick asked if Fisher considered how close the plaintiff bookstores were to defendants' stores, more distance allowing plaintiffs more price discretion. What the "retention ratio" is, the court does not explain, but that "Fisher acknowledged that he arbitrarily set the retention ratios at 0.5, without attempting to determine what those ratios actually were in the real world" would seem to be important.[5]

> The Fisher model contains entirely too many assumptions and simplifications that are not supported by real-world evidence. As a result, its conclusions that the discounts defendants received caused actual injury to the individual plain-

---

> Plaintiffs did not present in evidence even one specific instance of discrimination. There was no individual to testify how defendant discriminated against him.

"Him"? Plaintiffs were female by definition. The impact of failing to present live, presumably harmed witnesses is psychological. The dissent by Judge Cudahy provides a more sophisticated view of the statistical evidence than does the majority opinion. Yet he concedes, at 360,

> The EEOC as much as gave the case away by failing to produce any flesh and blood victims of discrimination.

Similarly, in *EHOC* (2001), footnote 8 at 1078:

> At no time during this hearing or in any papers filed with the Court has any person been identified as a victim of alleged housing discrimination in the City of Florissant.

In *Autozone* (2001), not only was no one presented who had inadvertently entered Radio Shack's Powerzone, Michael Rappeport's expert presentation for Autozone did not try to find such confusion:

> Oddly, during the survey, Rappeport never showed the survey respondents the POWERZONE mark. Therefore, the Rappeport survey gives no indication that customers will mistakenly believe that Tandy's use of the POWERZONE mark means that the AutoZone stores are somehow affiliated or connected.

The Sixth Circuit agreed, *Autozone* (2004) at 799: "AutoZone has failed to present any evidence of actual confusion."

4. For example, Richard Staelin "makes unsupported assumptions about the elasticities of demand in various markets" in assessing the impact of automobile fleet allowance programs. *Merit* (1977) at 673 (upholding summary judgment). Robert Lucas' estimation of price elasticity was found to be fatally flawed for lack of a good model of competition among pharmacies. *Drugs* (1999) at 788. Faced with a collusive prior price, John Beyer, plaintiffs' expert economist, proposes to demonstrate the effect of collusive prices from "a reasonable range of supply and demand elasticities." *Telephone* (2004) at 676.

5. *Booksellers* (2001) at 1041; following indented quotation also at 1041, citations omitted. A "retention ratio" usually would be the proportion of net earnings remaining with a firm after it pays dividends. It is the complement of the "pay-out ratio." Here, it more likely refers to what percentage of first-time customers return to make another purchase.

tiffs, and the amount of damages caused by that injury, are entirely too speculative to support a jury verdict.

Whatever the price differential between plaintiffs and defendants might have been, for
a given book, not all of it would necessarily have violated the law. If defendants were low-
cost producers, they have a right—to that extent—to be low-price sellers. Yet Fisher testified (in deposition) that *he had been asked* to assume that the entire price difference was
illegal. Judge Orrick excluded Fisher's study from plaintiffs' proof and calculation of damages, leading to summary judgment for defendant. It should not be on Fisher's head that
his clients made an assumption that the court found unjustified.

Or should it?

The Line Between Lawyer and Expert

As explained in Chapter 6, I once drew clear lines: Legal questions were to be answered
by my client; statistical or economics questions, by me. However, much of economics
involves law, and much of law involves understanding economics. Much of law is about
fact, but what is fact depends upon the law. It is not clear where one ends and the other
begins. When asked to defend employers who paid blacks and whites unequally, by showing that a "pre-Act" differential had been preserved (but not exacerbated) by equal rates of
increase in compensation for blacks and whites, I refused. Equal-employment-opportunity
laws instructed employers to pay without regard to race—not to *increase* pay, but to *pay*—
I said. I would not present testimony about the wrong metric. Some years later the
Supreme Court agreed.[6] My unwillingness to accede to my clients' view of the law no doubt
engendered a reputation as being "uncooperative." Yet it saved me from appearing to support a clearly bad (not to mention immoral) legal argument.

Justice Peter Lauriat was mandated to determine the competence of a Franciscan
friar to stand trial for committing "unnatural and lascivious acts with a child under sixteen"
and other offenses. Both the state and defendant produced expert psychological witnesses.

> The court further finds that the defendant's experts' conclusion that he is
> incompetent to stand trial reflects an incomplete understanding of and famil-
> iarity with the legal standard for competency, and a well-intended, but never-
> theless flawed attempt to elevate legal competency to a higher threshold of
> competence than the law requires.[7]

---

6. *Bazemore* (1986).

7. *DeBerardinis* (2004) at *4. Some readers will react that these experts should not be drawing conclusions about competence, because that is a legal determination, not a factual one. Such a position illustrates the confusion between fact and law that I am discussing. The entire hearing was about this question. Consider the "Martone Report" from *Stevens* (2004), which contains this expert conclusion,

That is, the fact to be determined depends on the law, and defendant's experts had the law wrong.

Adrian Zuckerman holds that law and fact are separable, distinct entities:

> The facts of the case are either admitted by the parties or ascertained by the court; either way, they are not governed by the law. The law determines which types of facts give rise to rights and duties; the facts of the individual case are not themselves created by the law, but exist in a world that lies beyond the law.[8]

On the contrary. That only some facts are relevant in law, and that some are *defined* by the law, is what makes law and fact *in*separable and, as I showed in Chapter 7, confusing even to judges. What fact is "fact" in law is a creature of law, or the legal process of discovery. As the expert's job is to assist the finder of fact, he must know something about the law, about the legal process within which he works. An analysis based on irrelevancies, however based on some other concept of fact, will be dismissed.[9]

My position now extends the *Firestone* (1981) lesson of Chapter 6, in which I brought a facet of the law to the attention of my client. The expert must make his own decisions regarding the law. The wise attorney will listen to the sophisticated expert's concept of the relevant law, and either educate the expert or change his own mind. My view does not allow the expert the excuse of having adopted an incorrect position because his clients wanted it. The responsibility is his.

Timothy Nantell was engaged by Hexamedics to estimate damages due it from Guidant Corporation, following an alleged breach of contract. His lower estimate survived a *Daubert* hearing. His higher estimate did not because, the court found, it was based on French law that would have applied only through a French subsidiary of Guidant. Nantell stated in deposition that "it was his understanding" that some "statutory protection applied to Hexamedics."[10] We know where he got that understanding.

---

reported at 605: "The defendant is competent to stand trial." Of course the fact finder sometimes solicits ultimate opinions from experts, as well as the premises of those opinions.

8. Zuckerman (1986) at 487.

9. Heaven forbid an expert should actually state his legal assumptions. *Carpenter* (2004), footnote 5:

> Dr. Siskin states in his report that the statistically significant disparities against females before April 2, 1999, create a "burden of proof" which is not overcome by the subsequent data. This contention . . . shades into an opinion of law. That point aside. . . .

Judge Brown does not like what he sees as an invasion of his turf, whereas Siskin, who has been through this process many more times than the judge, is merely explaining his reasoning in the context of the case. A more fair-minded judge could consider and reject Siskin's point without being irked by it, but such a judge, if one exists at all, is a rare creature.

10. *Hexamedics* (2003) at *4.

Hexamedics' attorneys had failed to file an amended complaint that joined the French subsidiary, although it seems that at one point they intended to. The court ruled that Nantell's higher estimate was fundamentally based on French law, and that French law did not apply. French law may not have been necessary to Nantell's estimate, but defendant is entitled to know on what information Nantell relied. He had claimed French law as his predicate. Had Nantell been more wary of his client, and had he understood what defendant's attorneys were asking, he would have explained initially that French law supported his estimate, but was not a basis of it.

In *Harcros* (1995), Judge Guin excluded plaintiffs' statistical expert, James McClave, but denied defendant's motion to exclude Robert Lanzillotti, an economist. Plaintiffs appealed the exclusion of McClave. Defendant did not appeal the non-exclusion of Lanzillotti. The Eleventh Circuit panel went out of its way to say that they should have.

> Lanzillotti's professed market definition is clearly wrong. Lanzillotti stated in his report that "[t]he relevant geographic market is the largest market for which data are available and facilitate a more comprehensive understanding of what transpired in the State of Alabama." This is contrary to law and scholarship; the relevant geographic market is the market that includes "producers that provide customers of a defendant firm (or firms) with alternative sources for the defendant's product or services."[11]

Lanzillotti cannot analyze the chlorine market *in litigation* without a law-savvy definition of his subject. Much of McClave's testimony was resuscitated, but not that which included Florida data. The scope of the analysis has to be consistent with the scope of the complaint, which was confined to Alabama.

There is hardly a case in which the proper litigation view of "fact" is not influenced by law. Yet another Franklin Fisher example also illustrates the point. Fisher was a prominent government witness in the Microsoft antitrust litigation. Although he is not referenced by name in the district court's findings of fact, his testimony can be read in its language. Fisher asserted that Microsoft, abusing monopoly power, sells its Windows operating system above its "competitive" price. He does not tell us what that price is, or, equivalently, how much of the price of Windows is due to Microsoft's monopoly position. Furthermore, Fisher says, "Despite the huge browser-related costs it was incurring, Microsoft distributed its browser at a negative price."[12]

---

11. *Harcros* (1998), footnote 27 at 567. The court is quoting from *Levine* (1996) at 1552. In *Citizens* (2004), at 121, we read about other restrictions on the scope of a survey for litigation: "The court should limit survey evidence in reverse confusion cases to the customers of the senior user."

12. Fisher's testimony is F. Fisher (1998). The district court's findings of fact are *Microsoft III* (1999). See paragraph 123.

The issue was tying Internet Explorer into the Windows operating system. Perhaps the Windows price includes a competitive price for both products but, like automobiles come with radios, one buys them together. It would be more expensive to buy a new car without a radio than with one, and therefore the radio seems to bear a negative price. Homogenization is an extra step in the production of milk, but non-homogenized milk is more expensive. Is milk homogenized at a loss? Is the automobile's radio given away? Or, rather, are there such economies in bundling items most consumers want that all of them receive positive prices, but lower prices than the unbundled products would have? Rejecting Fisher's argument, the circuit court concluded that "the separate-products test is a poor proxy for net efficiency from newly integrated products." It remanded the bundling question for consideration under the rule of reason.[13]

The D.C. Circuit also provides an instruction on standards of proof when challenging exclusive contracts, which are not anti-competitive per se.

> Though what is "significant" may vary depending upon the antitrust provision under which an exclusive deal is challenged, it is clear that in all cases the plaintiff must both define the relevant market and prove the degree of foreclosure.

This is surely as much an instruction for the plaintiff's expert as for its attorney.

Franklin Fisher does a lot of litigation work creating, in his wake, good examples of conceptual failure and failure to conform to law. My using these examples (here and in Chapter 3) should not be perceived as disrespect. It is because of the high technical quality of Fisher's econometrics that my point about what is missing becomes clear.

Wholesalers and distributors of tobacco products alleged that tobacco companies conspired to fix prices. They relied heavily on Fisher's expertise:

> The failure of Plaintiffs' expert to distinguish conscious parallelism from cartel behavior makes his subsequent opinion inadmissible as he finds inferences of collusion where the law finds none. . . . Because of his flawed view of the law, this testimony is inadmissible.[14]

---

13. *Microsoft III* (2001) at 92; following indented quotation at 69. Before it became the common form, homogenized milk was more expensive than milk that separated into cream and skim milk.

14. *Holiday* (2002) at 1321. Affirming in *Holiday* (2003), the Eleventh Circuit explained the problem at 1323. Fisher

> did not differentiate between legal and illegal pricing behavior, and instead simply grouped both of these phenomena under the umbrella of illegal, collusive price fixing. This testimony could not have aided a finder of fact to determine whether appellees' behavior was or was not legal, and the district court properly excluded it.

Several months after the *Holiday* (2002) decision, apparently without perceiving the irony (or mistakenly thinking *Holiday* would be reversed), Fisher co-authored an *amicus* brief that criticized another expert who, these authors say,

I visited an International Paper plant in Maine. Each paper-making machine was unique, I had been told by my client. A worker from one could not transfer to another, as they were different beasts.

Really? Never transfer? Machines four and five look sort of the same.

Well, yes, they actually are similar to each other. One worker did once move from a position on four to a higher position on five, I ultimately learned by repeating this question in more and more detail. So when I create availability "pools" for positions on these machines, I should include all workers in lower positions on *both* machines? Uh, yes, maybe that's right.

My clients had been suggesting a separation that, with some digging, I determined to be incorrect. Incorrect as a matter of relevant fact under the laws that generated my presence there in the first place. On a daily level at the plant, the machines were distinct. A sick worker on one machine was never replaced with a worker from the other machine. But as a promotion pool, that separation was untenable.[15] The expert will be held accountable for it all: the legal theory, the facts. He has to determine—at least support or feel comfortable with—the legal as well as the factual basis for his analysis.

Keith Leffler was plaintiffs' expert in an antitrust litigation alleging that Atlantic Richfield Oil Co. was selling petroleum products below its cost.[16] And what was its cost? Leffler argued that, as Atlantic Richfield at times traded oil, the marginal cost in use was the market price, the revenue that would have been available from trade. Under Leffler's approach, all producers had the same cost of production. However, the law is structured to reward low-cost producers. Leffler should have known that opportunity cost, though a sound economic concept, was not an acceptable measure of marginal cost in antitrust litigation.[17]

Marionettes

For the defendant, where race had been alleged to be a factor determining salaries, Jessica Pollner estimated salary by a regression based on all employees, even though only managerial personnel were at issue. The regression contained no variable for race. She then

---

simply defined an impact and assumed that any (and only) acts eventually found to be unlawful, whatever their identity and extent, created that impact.

"Brief of Washington Legal Foundation, Stephen E. Fienberg, Franklin M. Fisher, Daniel L. McFadden, and Daniel L. Rubinfeld as Amici Curiae in Support of Petitioners," in *Conwood* (2003), at 10.

15. Although apparently not investigated as carefully, constructing the appropriate pool for termination required understanding who, experienced on one machine, could be used on another, in *Mastie* (1976).

16. *Rebel* (1998). I refer to this case again in Chapter 10.

17. See, for example, *Continental* (1993).

estimated the difference between salaries of blacks and salaries estimated by her regression. In a race-discrimination case, one would ordinarily compare black salaries to the regression-estimated salaries of "comparable" whites. Pollner did not then subtract black earnings from that predicted by this biased regression estimate, to "compensate" all blacks earning below what the regression would expect. She

> adjusted the salary of 28 class members who were underpaid at the 90% confidence level to within the 90% confidence level.[18]

That is, she would compensate only blacks paid "significantly" low, and increase their salary only by that which would get them to this border of "significance," not to equality. Compensation is meant to make otherwise equal people equal in income, not just less different. Judge Sullivan, correctly, did not allow Pollner's figures to stand.

Countering an allegation of gender discrimination in compensation, Louis Wilde's expert report refers often to equal "rates of growth" or "percentage increases in compensation."[19] Equal rates of growth of compensation was North Carolina's losing defense in *Bazemore* (1986), the defense I had refused to incorporate into my work. Did Wilde so blatantly ignore the Supreme Court's ruling from ignorance, or instruction?

Joan Haworth, as plaintiffs' expert, made a presentation to my client, the United States Attorney in Washington, D.C., concerning a settlement demand for black officers of the Foreign Service. To calculate damages she subtracted each black officer's income from the mean white income. She then summed these differences *only among blacks whose income was below the white mean*. My clients were incredulous. After all, approximately half of the white officers earn below the same mean. Haworth would have calculated a black "deficit" even had blacks earned *more* than whites, on the average, as long as some blacks earned less than the average white. An Assistant United States Attorney asked her why she would make such a calculation, and present it as a "damages" estimate. "My clients asked me to," she said.[20]

The experience of courts with marionette experts, where the attorney is pulling the strings, is common enough that one court warned:

---

18. *McLaurin* (2004) at 64. This would upset me more, Pollner having at one time been my employee, had I not fired her for this kind of incompetence. This level of work is comparable to her "opportunistic rummaging within the data set" to construct a biased sample in *Reynolds* (2004) or *Reynolds* (2005) at *5. Client-oriented and indefensible.

19. Wilde's report, with only a 2002 date, was protected by a court order. I presume that protection no longer applies, as the case has been settled. See *Morgan Stanley* (2004).

20. This is a different issue from, say, pre-judgment interest. My view on whether pre-judgment interest is allowed in a particular case is irrelevant. Any calculation that I can do separately, so that a judge can decide if it belongs in the total, I will gladly do for my client. But my client cannot dictate the method by which I do it.

In all cases, however, the district court must ensure that it is dealing with an expert, not just a hired gun.[21]

That he is being paid should not be held against the expert. Nor should his agreement with his client's position. Most experts' opinions will agree with those of their clients, or they would not have been offered as witnesses. The court should care only about the expert's independence; and if courts would take that view, then perhaps fewer experts would let their clients make their assumptions for them.[22]

WHAT DOES MY CLIENT KNOW?

Many lawyers specialize, but is that to their advantage? Were the *Booksellers* (2001) attorneys specialists in antitrust? Is that why they did not know that the *Sears* (1988) court

---

21. *Tyus* (1996) at 263.
22. Referring to defendant's experts in *Yapp* (2004), Judge Limbaugh notes, at 1033:

> The survey questions were first drawn up by Dr. Ward and Mr. Woods, but were then subject to editing by Defendant's Counsel,

and, at 1034, that interviews with defendant's personnel

> were conducted in the presence of Mr. Woods, Defendant's outside counsel, and [defendant's] house counsel.

The judge found, at 1037, that

> the heavy involvement of defense counsel in the design and conduct of a survey used to guide expert statistical analyses indicates a lack of independence and thus a lack of scientific validity.

In *Rowe* (2003) at *2, Judge Patterson was aghast at counsel's involvement with providing a sample of concert-promotion contracts to expert Gerald Jaynes:

> In support of his position that the sample was fair and representative, Dr. Jaynes reasoned that as Plaintiffs and Plaintiffs' counsel were unaware of how he would conduct his analysis when they selected the contracts, they would not know how to create a biased group of contracts.

In *Electric* (2004), at 235, Magistrate Judge Francis was also concerned that Fred Dunbar, plaintiffs' expert, had used data selected by his clients. That selection was not itself fatal, but led to the presumption that the data were flawed:

> Finally, Dr. Dunbar performed no analysis that might rebut the finding of apparent bias.

Judge Francis even suggested his own sensitivity analysis that Dunbar had failed to make. Thus although counsel involvement implies lack of expert independence, in Judge Francis' thinking (as well as Judge Patterson's), that implication may be rebutted by showing that the data are representative.

In *Lauzon* (2001), plaintiff's engineer expert, H. Boulter Kelsey, refuted his client's testimony. He testified, at 684:

> Mr. Lauzon's testimony that he believed the gun was some 4 to 5 inches above the plywood surface when the accident occurred can only be an error on his part.

He argued that there was a design flaw, not a manufacturing defect, in the roof nailer that sent a nail through Mr. Lauzon's hand. Judge Rosenbaum did not appreciate Kelsey's independence, but the Eighth Circuit did.

essentially instructed plaintiffs to bring forward examples of persons harmed by defendant's actions? A sophisticated attorney may know what *he* does quite well, but still have a limited grasp of the law concerning his statistical expert. That expert may assist his client, but if only to cover his rear, he should understand the law, the rules of the arena in which is about to do combat.[23]

Most attorneys have no understanding of the issues the expert faces, or that they face because they have engaged a statistical expert. Most experts do not understand their clients' limitations. It was Franklin Fisher's responsibility first to understand the language of the publication industry and second to impose on it economic rigor (what is the relationship between wholesale discount and retail price; what is the relationship between retail price and sales). He could either try to obtain data to calculate parameters or, at the very least, provide a range of damage estimates based on a reasonable range of parameters (such as price elasticities). Disparaging other experts, in 1986, Fisher warned that

> the world has quite enough poor statistical and econometric testimony without serious statisticians and econometricians adding to the stock.[24]

I would add that the world also has quite enough experts with insufficient understanding of the legal framework within which they will perform their task.

The Expert and Fact

This caution, from the National Research Council panel:

> Expert witnesses proffering statistical testimony thus should be prepared not only to present the substantive evidence but also to advise courts on the acceptability of the evidence from both parties.[25]

is followed by this footnote:

> Such language does not attempt a fit with legally established criteria, a practice that judges might see as an usurpation of the court's authority.

This is absurd. Wigmore deals with it with a swipe of the hand:

> The "usurpation" theory . . . has done much to befog the bench and bar, and assist in producing some of the confusion which attends the precedents.[26]

---

23. Gross (1991) at 1120:

> Judging from 1985–86 cases, when an attorney examines an expert in a civil jury trial in California, the expert is twice as likely to have testified in another such case in the preceding six months as the attorney is to have tried one (42% to 21%).

24. F. Fisher (1986) at 285. As this book and this chapter in particular make clear, Fisher's plea was to no avail.

25. Fienberg et al. (1995) at 10; following indented quotation from footnote 31.

26. Wigmore (1935) §673, at 936 of Volume II, Chadbourn Revision, 1979. This is not a passing comment. It is a summary from a diatribe:

The "usurpation theory" can concern a witness providing his opinion about either the ultimate fact that remains to be determined or the ultimate legal conclusion.[27] Lay witnesses may not express themselves on either, but experts may on the former:

> *Federal Rule of Evidence 704*: Except as provided in subdivision (b), testimony in the form of an opinion or inference otherwise admissible is not objectionable because it embraces an ultimate issue to be decided by the trier of fact.[28]

This rule was recast into its current formulation, allowing the expert to speak to the "ultimate issue" of fact, in 1984. Allowance in a rule is not always allowance in the courtroom. Judge Brotman determined that plaintiff's handwriting expert could testify, but defendant's expert, skeptical that handwriting analysts can make the distinctions they claim to make, could not. Having determined

> that there are standard procedures in the field of handwriting analysis, [this court] refused to admit the testimony of Professor Denbeaux to contradict the court's legal conclusion.[29]

The Third Circuit easily reversed. A court cannot frame its fact opinion as one of law, and on that ground refuse to hear expert testimony that contradicts it.

Illinois judge Baker prevented the testimony of one psychologist, and restricted that of another, both of whom would have supported defendant's assertion that his own confession had been coerced and was false. Judge Baker concluded that such testimony "would in some respects usurp the jury's role and thus that it would not *properly* assist the jury in its task."[30] Finding that "expert testimony may be particularly important when the facts

---

> But the expert is not trying to usurp that function, and could not if he would. He is not trying to usurp it, because his error, if any, is merely the common one of witnesses, that of presenting as knowledge that which is really not knowledge. And he could not usurp it if he would, because the jury may still reject his testimony and accept his opponent's, and no legal power, not even the judge's order, can compel them to accept the witness' statement against their will.

27. Saks (1998), misguidedly casting the admissibility of scientific evidence as a legislative-fact question, also falls prey to the notion that expressions of opinion usurp the court's function. Referring, at 1116, to another National Academy panel report:

> Although the Report wisely declined to make a specific recommendation concerning admissibility—appreciating that to do so called for value judgments that should be made by the law, not usurped by scientists. . . .

28. As if eyewitness identification is not a statement about ultimate fact! Subdivision (b) prohibits the expert "testifying with respect to the mental state or condition of a defendant in a criminal case" from concluding that such a defendant did or did not have "the mental state or condition constituting an element of the crime charged or of defense thereto."

29. *Velasquez* (1995) at 847, quoting from the trial judge's Order and Memorandum.

30. *Hall* (1996a) at 1342; following in-text quotation at 1343.

suggest a person is suffering from a psychological disorder," a unanimous Seventh Circuit panel vacated the defendant's sentence and remanded the case with the implicit instruction that, if there were to be a retrial, the experts should be allowed to testify.

Christopher Mueller and Laird Kirkpatrick note:

> Typically the "ultimate issue" objection was framed in terms of "usurping the function of the jury," and the fear was that lay factfinders would give up their responsibility to look critically at testimony and just take the word of the witness. But the fear was overstated, since juries have the power and authority to reject even decisive and informed testimony and are told as much before deliberating.[31]

A turkey farmer had sued a feed manufacturer (and his sales agent) for the death of turkeys using their feed, following their instructions. Defendant objected to plaintiff's experts' conclusion that the feed caused the injury, arguing that

> the opinion would usurp the functions of the jury, or would determine the very fact or a vital fact inhering in the jury's verdict, or in short that it would pass upon and decide the ultimate fact.[32]

The Iowa Supreme Court thought otherwise:

> Since opinion testimony is an exception to the rule that only fact testimony shall be received, it should, with respect to its reception, be treated the same as fact testimony, and no one has ever contended that testimony as to a fact was inadmissible simply because it might be decisive of an ultimate fact.

Judge Richard Posner agrees:

> An eyewitness does not usurp the jury's function if he testifies that he is positive that he saw the defendant strike a match, and it would make no

---

31. Mueller and Kirkpatrick (1999) §7.12 at 921.

32. *Grismore* (1942) at 344; following indented quotation also at 344. I do not mean to imply that all courts agree, but I do mean to imply that those that don't sound ridiculous. For example, twelve years earlier, in *Steffen* (1930) at 538, the same court that decided *Grismore* had stated that

> while an expert may be permitted to express his opinion, or even his belief, he cannot testify to the ultimate fact that must be determined by the jury. Such testimony would invade the province of the jury and determine the very issue which they must decide.

In *Champ* (2001), defendant, having been convicted of rape largely through DNA evidence, argued against allowing the state's expert to frame his conclusion probabilistically:

> [T]here must be a limit so the function of the jury to be a fact finder is not supplanted by a State's expert in a white lab coat who spews out a number of a billion to one while offering a completely unintelligible explanation for that number.

Defendant's appeals brief at 36, quoted at *6. I will argue in Chapter 10 that the expert *must* state his conclusion probabilistically, that this expert, whose testimony was permitted, provided information, not usurpation.

difference if he said that he is "99 percent" positive. The significant question would be the accuracy of the estimate.[33]

Nonetheless, fear of usurpation persists. The state court system of Pennsylvania does not permit witnesses to inform juries about the fallibility of eyewitness identification, for example.[34] Such witnesses would *not* be stating their opinions on ultimate fact. They would present only legislative fact, conclusions drawn from research studies. I will discuss the role of such a "wisdom" expert below, and place it into my *Daubert* framework in Chapter 10. There I will argue that excluding social scientists who could inform a jury about relationships derived from research usually is deleterious to fact finding.

The Expert and Law

Although the rules of evidence allow the expert to assert an ultimate conclusion of *fact*, the Federal Rules of Civil Procedure instruct the expert witness not to make any statement about ultimate conclusions of *law*.[35] An extreme case can illustrate the rule. Burton Malkiel

> was asked to reach legal conclusions regarding those ultimate issues: whether Merrill and DLJ complied with the PSA Agreements, whether they adhered to the covenant of good faith and fair dealing, and whether they conducted the liquidations in a commercially reasonable manner. The terms employed in defining Malkiel's project are identical to the legal terms defining elements of the counts in this case.[36]

Concluding that "the Malkiel report is permeated with inadmissible legal opinions and conclusions directed at telling the jury what result to reach," Judge Sweet excluded it from the evidence of the case.

We have seen that it is not always this clear, not even to a judge, what is fact and what is law. Yet the distinction is a critical part of the rules. Perhaps the expert should not assert a conclusion to either, because there is other evidence besides his. We saw in Chapter 6 that attorneys are advised to keep the expert ignorant of some facts. Any expert should assume that his client has done just that. The important point, however, is that no matter how conclusive the expert's statement may be, and no matter how certainly held, it may be wrong.

---

33. *Veysey* (2003) at 606. Regarding eyewitness identification: "Research indicates that the correlation between certainty and accuracy is modest, at best." Bradfield and Wells (2000) at 592. The difference Posner notes, between the witness' assertion of his accuracy and an independent measure of it, will play a role in my *Daubert* framework, in Chapter 10.

34. The Pennsylvania Supreme Court stated this rule in *Simmons* (1995). That it survives is indicated by *Bormack* (2003).

35. Federal Rules of Civil Procedure 26(e).

36. *Primavera* (2001) at 528; following in-text quotation at 529.

The ultimate finder of fact knows that expert opinions are uncertain. The relevant question, then, is how uncertain.

PROBABILISTIC FACT

A "science" or "technical" expert has only probabilistic knowledge about the facts he has studied. In Chapter 10 I will urge judges to require that a science or technical expert's conclusion on fact be accompanied by an empirical probability. A handwriting expert, for example, should not say, "X wrote this document," without an estimate of his fallibility, the probability that he has misidentified the writer. Here the question what kind of fact the expert "knows" arises in the context of the distinction between law and fact.

Is the forum a factor? Should the expert operate differently between civil and criminal cases? William Haney thinks so: A liberal standard should apply in civil cases, but a conservative (defendant-oriented) standard should apply in criminal cases, he asserts.[37] All commentators see the expert's conclusory testimony as binary: He did it or he didn't.

In contrast, I assert that an expert in a criminal case should not say, "That guy did it," as if he had certain knowledge. He has only probabilistic evidence to that effect, and "did it" in the context of the case may be broader than the expert's knowledge. In the antitrust context, one might argue, an expert does little good if he provides a metric of monopoly power and draws no line about which we can ask whether the defendant firm crossed it. This argument would conclude: Let him say that Microsoft is a monopolist, or not, and why. But is that a determination of fact or a conclusion of law? And how certain is it?

Paul Giannelli noticed "neglect of the problems of expert testimony in criminal prosecutions" calling it "deplorable, if not inexplicable."[38] Five years later Margaret Berger concluded that the forum—civil or criminal—had mattered, in practice, and in the opposite direction from that advocated by Haney:

> [A] prosecutor's forensic expert is allowed to testify against the criminal defendant, but the plaintiff's expert is disqualified from testifying against the civil corporate defendant.[39]

Jennifer Mnookin also notes that, given its origin in civil litigation, attention to the scientific basis of criminal evidence lagged behind. "Today, at the turn of a new millennium, it is forensic science that is receiving greater public scrutiny."[40] Handwriting and fingerprint

---

37. Haney (1994).

38. Giannelli (1993) at 1100.

39. M. Berger (1998) at 1181.

40. Mnookin (2001b) at 1725.

analysis are under attack in the literature and in the courts. Some courts have excluded such evidence. Others have limited what the proffered expert could say.[41] In Chapter 10 I will argue that the implicit framework used by judges and forensic science critics is misdirected. I will provide a novel, alternative framework there.

Wisdom

The concept that scientific experts must have probabilistic answers to the questions they are asked runs afoul of some traditional lines of expertise-by-wisdom. In *Local 36* (1949), an expert witness had been offered to establish that the "businesses" cited for conspiring were, in fact, laborers. Not allowing the expert to testify was one of the grounds for appeal. Whether

> a fisherman is a laboring producer . . . was a question of fact, not a matter of opinion. As such question of fact, it was submitted to the jury, who found against appellants. It would, of course, have been improper to allow an expert to advise the jury on a matter not subject of opinion testimony.[42]

The jury is always the fact finder. Witnesses are always the fact suggestors. Why a court wanted the jury to determine the nature of work relationships without hearing from experts who could have clarified what they were, when such experts were offered, is a mystery to me. The question was one of a legal interpretation of an economic relationship. Truly expert witnesses—with knowledge of both economics and law—could have assisted the jury.

Similarly, in *Amaral* (1973), defendant offered Bertram Raven to testify "in regards to the effect of stress on perception and, more generally, regarding the unreliability of eyewitness identification."[43] Such legislative-fact testimony is often offered today, though not always allowed. In *Amaral*, trial judge Friendly ruled:

---

41. See reviews in Risinger et al. (1989), Risinger and Saks (1996), Giannelli (1997a), Saks (1998), Mnookin (2001a), Mnookin (2001b), Risinger et al. (2002), Epstein (2002), and Sombat (2002). *Mitchell* (1998) was the first *Daubert* challenge to fingerprint evidence. The first consideration of such a challenge by a circuit court is generally considered to have occurred in *Havvard* (2001). The Seventh Circuit affirmation of the judge's refusal to exclude the testimony prompted an objection by the *Harvard Law Review* in Case Note (2002). Earlier circuit courts had considered the issue in the trial court's rejection of defendants' attempts to refute forensic evidence with their own witness. See, for example, *Velasquez* (1995) and *Paul* (1999).

42. *Local 36* (1949) at 333. There is then a citation to *Farris* (1941). However, at 412, "These witnesses were not qualified as experts." That is a different finding. *Local 36* at 337:

> The court did instruct that, if the appellants were in fact businessmen who conspired to fix the price, then it was immaterial "whether the price so fixed by agreement among the defendants was reasonable or unreasonable."

43. *Amaral* (1973) at 1153; following indented quotation also at 1153.

> [I]t would not be appropriate to take from the jury their own determination
> as to what weight or effect to give to the evidence of the eyewitness and iden-
> tifying witnesses and to have that determination put before them on the basis
> of the expert witness testimony as proffered.

So factual determination should be made by juries with neither conceptual assistance nor knowledge of empirical research results? We want juries to operate at the least learned, most naive intellectual level possible?

It is becoming common for defendants to call academics to educate the jury on the fallibility of "forensic science" (fingerprints, handwriting, voiceprint, DNA) identification. In Chapter 4 I introduced the notion that there are many commentators on judicial procedure who are not themselves litigation "experts." Similarly, one should not have to be a forensic examiner to acquire expertise about the hazards of such identification.[44] Expertise which is the result of research and experience will not be directed specifically at the evidence in the current case. It is legislative-fact testimony. As long it stays on that side of the line, it should be welcome. It is a different kind of expertise from that required to make the identification itself, but just as likely to be helpful to jurors. I give it the name "wisdom."

So there is a kind of expert who can bring wisdom, experience, accumulated knowledge to the fact finder.[45] A live version of the "Brandeis brief" in *Muller* (1908). That person is not, and should not be considered, a "science" witness. We can readily tell who this is, because he will not present adjudicative conclusions. He will present generalizations. They should be stated with a description of the variation they contain. I discuss this category of expert testimony in my *Daubert* framework in Chapter 10.

---

44. In 2004 we were treated to an example of forensic document examination in the question whether memoranda relating to President George W. Bush's National Guard service, exposed by CBS, were forgeries. See, for example, articles in the *Washington Post* by Michael Dobbs and Howard Kurtz, September 14 and 15, 2004. "Experts" asserted that a 1972 typewriter could not make a superscript "th," or print with proportional spacing. These assertions are incorrect; typewriters had done both since the 1950s. On the other hand, the memos contain a kerning that software performs, but typewriters did not. One should understand, in the context of this book, that this is the level of "expertise," though not the level of attention, brought into courtrooms. Perhaps this example supports the "discussion" forum I advocate for experts in Chapter 10. It certainly does not enhance the reputation of forensic document examiners, even though CBS ultimately (on September 19) withdrew its backing for the documents' authenticity.

45. Gavil (1997) at 663:

> Litigating an antitrust case absent the aid of an economist has become an increasingly perilous proposition.

Could a drug addict propose another as a wisdom expert? *Pedraza* (1995) at 197:

> Pedraza asserts that [Antonio] Marquez is an expert on heroin withdrawals because of his thirty-years experience as a heroin addict.

Marquez' affidavit was assessed on *Daubert* science principles, and no doubt properly excluded on those grounds. But it is not beyond the realm of possibility that Marquez could have enlightened the court. It was only beyond the realm of present procedure and convention.

Language

The statistical case is only one piece of evidence among many. Yet a race variable in an earnings regression, indicating that otherwise comparable minorities earned X dollars less than their white counterparts, is more than a suggestion of discrimination; it is a figure for back-pay. The defendant's expert, whose regression coefficient is zero, is implying that "There is no discrimination in pay." These experts aren't speaking to the ultimate rulings of law?

The government's expert clearly stated that Microsoft had and used monopoly power. Defendant's expert just as clearly stated the opposite.[46] These statements were framed so that their attorneys could characterize them as economic-fact conclusions, but they were as much about law as about fact.

Thus whether the expert actually states his conclusion on the legal issue, or not, may be an artificial distinction. The implications for the legal determination are clear in the experts' positions. The distinction between the Rules of Evidence (fact conclusion—yes) and the Rules of Procedure (legal conclusion—no) may produce some objections in the courtroom, but no one is fooled, least of all members of the jury. The way to understand these rules is to see them as about language, and ultimately about turf, keeping the expert in his place. The rule that the expert must not suggest a legal conclusion to the judge or jury is circumvented in practice by euphemism and metaphor, innuendo and implication. It is not enforceable. What is needed is a rule that expert conclusions be stated with a contestable measure of their fallibility. Such a rule would be enforceable.

Marvin Wolfgang describes how he advocated, to his clients, keeping the word "discrimination" out of his testimony until the end.

> I felt secure as a social scientist asserting in court and in depositions that so clearly differential and disproportionate had been the sentencing that there was historically a pattern of discrimination in the imposition of the death penalty.[47]

---

46. Paragraph 17 of F. Fisher (1998) begins:
> Microsoft has achieved monopoly power in the market for operating systems for Intel-compatible desktop personal computers.

Point number 2 of the third paragraph of Schmalensee (1999) begins:
> Microsoft does not have monopoly power in the PC operating system market alleged by Plaintiffs—or in any relevant antitrust market in which Windows is licensed.

47. Wolfgang (1974) at 243, on *Maxwell* (1966), which concerned the imposition of the death sentence on persons convicted of rape, presumably more harshly on blacks if the victim was white. One can question Wolfgang's analysis by reference to *Davis* (1984) at 615:
> Dr. Wolfgang would testify . . . that defendant was a likely candidate "for a thirty-year sentence instead of a death sentence" because empirical studies demonstrate that a defendant

The courts that reviewed his material, however, thought that his analysis did not contain enough variables to draw a conclusion about discrimination. Again, no matter how certain the expert may be, his is only part of the picture. It is not because of the rule, but from common sense, that he should not be discussing the ultimate legal issue.

Lawyers seem not to understand how foolish they appear to the lay public, arguing about an expert's language, when his meaning is clear. One could assert that, as the expert will find a way to articulate his view, perhaps he should be able to do it openly, without artifice. I need not go that far here, though I have seen the exasperation on jurors' faces as attorneys and judges attempt to manipulate the expert's statement of an opinion the jury has firmly grasped. What we want of our experts is that they offer evidence without thinking that it is proof. "Discrimination" carries too much emotion with it, and is an ultimate legal conclusion requiring more than statistical evidence. I would not have used the word.[48]

EXPERT STANDARDS

That the client may not understand the legal issues of importance to the expert requires that the expert "train" his client before they appear together in court. Attorneys, however, are advised to train their experts, not to receive training from them. The expert needs feedback, not instruction.[49] He knows what his client wants to hear. But what the client wants and what the data support, filtered through a legal theory, may be quite different. The expert will have to find his own language with which to represent his data, methods, and conclusions—or else sound like the marionette he has become.

The expert and his client should hold a consistent view of both fact and law. It may not be possible or advisable for the expert to tell the judge about his legal premise, but it is possible for the expert to discuss such things with his client, for him to refuse to testify if he thinks the client's premises harm the expert's work, and for them to agree how to inform the court what the legal and factual premises of the testimony are.

---

    sharing Mr. Davis' statistical profile "would never again commit another serious crime of any kind" after serving the mandatory minimum thirty-year term.
Perhaps he simply opposed the death penalty.

48. In a re-analysis of *Moultrie* (1982), Good (2001) states, at 133: "As statisticians, we conclude that the results yield a pattern of discrimination." I think other language would be preferable, such as "are more consistent with a finding for plaintiffs than the court's finding for defendant."

49. If he does need instruction, several writers have offered their services. For example, Stanley L. Brodsky has published two books through the American Psychological Association: *Testifying in Court: Guidelines and Maxims for the Expert Witness* (1991), and *The Expert Expert Witness: More Maxims and Guidelines for Testifying in Court* (1999).

The Impact of *Daubert*

The expert needs to understand the standards of evidence the court expects. *Frye* (1923), discussed in Chapter 1, was a circuit-court opinion. We would not expect it to have immediate impact. Some current writers contend that it did not seem important at the time. "No contemporary law-review articles were written about it, commentators ignored it, and other courts did not cite it."[50] Even though *Daubert* (1993) was a Supreme Court decision, thereby automatically receiving more attention, the contrast, as described by Margaret Berger, is striking:

> In little more than five years, the *Daubert* opinion has been cited so often that it has its own database and has become the centerpiece of numerous symposia and other educational efforts aimed at enhancing an understanding of science.[51]

One difference is due to the frequency with which science issues come before courts, and with them, expert witnesses. Another difference is that, prior to the 1980s, few law schools had any non-lawyer faculty. Now many do, though I will question why in Chapter 9. They publish in law reviews.

"Expert witnesses are increasingly a fixture in litigation."[52] Federal Rules of Evidence 702 through 705 set the rules under which they operate. *Daubert* merely told judges to follow the rules, to limit testimony to that which would be helpful to ultimate fact determination. What is interesting about *Daubert*, as Margaret Berger has suggested, is the procedures that have been developed to accommodate it.[53] The *Daubert* hearing, I contend, is less a dramatic reinterpretation of the rules surrounding the expert witness than a restructuring of how those rules will be effectuated.

The consequences of *Daubert* and subsequent case law have been and will continue to be much discussed. For example, Edward Imwinkelreid opines:

> Some of the most important long-term consequences of *Daubert* may flow not from the formal holding in the case but rather from Justice Blackmun's adoption of the modern conception of the limits of scientific investigation.[54]

If this is a prediction that many *Daubert* hearings will result in the exclusion of expert testimony because the expert's conclusions are not methodologically justified, it appears to

---

50. Faigman et al. (1994) at 1808.

51. M. Berger (1999) at 336.

52. Posner (2001a) at 11.

53. See the quotation from Berger under the subsection "*Daubert* (1993)" in Chapter 7, at 472.

54. Imwinkelreid (1995) at 78.

be correct.[55] To some people, it came as a surprise. "Jason and Eric will get their day in court," wrote their attorney, Barry Nace, of the *Daubert* plaintiffs.[56]

> The company spin doctors were at work again after the *Daubert* decision, but the children, of course, were the clear winners. The children had argued that the *Frye* rule could not take precedence over the Federal Rules of Evidence. The Court accepted that argument.

Subsequently, plaintiffs' experts were excluded. Summary judgment was granted for defendant. The children were the clear losers. Jason and Eric were unfortunate accidents of the birth process, not of Bendectin. They deserved no day in court, and got none.

Reid (2001)

Burt Barnow blew it, as I'm sure he would admit. His trusted assistant re-assigned some work to someone not so capable. The work wasn't checked by Barnow's assistant or by him. And so:

> Dr. Barnow admitted in his deposition that his reports contain numerous errors including mathematical mistakes, the inclusion of wrong and misleading tables, counting as zero disparities that were not really zeros, and missing an implied decimal that rendered some of the disparities incorrect and changed some of the variances.[57]

Barnow's distance from the project and his failure to check the work handed him by assistants troubled Judge Forrester who, sticking to a timetable that had been accepted by all parties, refused to consider revised plaintiff reports. Frank Landy, another of plaintiffs' experts, relied on Barnow's study, and therefore incorporated all of Barnow's errors.

---

55. "The resulting effects of *Daubert* have been decidedly pro-defendant." Cheng and Yoon (2005) at 3. These authors also conclude that the major impact of *Daubert* has been on raising the consciousness and activeness of judges to control the quality of expert testimony. They find no difference in rates of removal of tort claims from state to federal court based on whether the initial state held to *Frye* or *Daubert*, whereas the rate of removal did vary among states. They interpret the finding as indicating that the quality and receptivity of the judiciaries may vary, but not in accordance with the name given to their practice.

56. In-text quotation and the following indented quotation both from 29 *Trial Magazine* 7, October 1993. Barry Nace "has been counsel for the plaintiff in almost every reported federal Bendectin case." *Oxendine* (1996) at *3. Subsequent to *Daubert*, Merrell achieved reversals of what had appeared to be plaintiff victories. *Oxendine* at *34:

> The science that existed in 1983 has changed and it would, in these circumstances, be inappropriate to allow the 1983 judgment to stand or to do anything other than enter a judgment mandated by the state of scientific knowledge.

Other drugs, such as Clomid, were successfully defended. See, for example, *Lust* (1996).

57. *Reid* (2001) at 661; following indented quotation also at 661.

Finally, much of Dr. Landy's opinion concerns the work culture and climate at Lockheed's Marietta facility, even though he admittedly has never been to that facility or interviewed anyone at that facility.

If a case ever called for exclusion of experts under the Rules of Evidence (702), before or after *Daubert*, *Reid* is it. While denying class certification, which accomplished defendant's primary goal, Judge Forrester did not grant defendant's motion to exclude these experts.

I would relax the rules on who could be heard as an expert, while being more stringent in assessing their testimony. That is, I would make it easier for any proffered expert to enter the screening process, and more difficult for his work to pass through it. Barnow will pass any test of "qualifications." Nonetheless, his work and that of Landy, in this case, was unacceptable and should have been excluded.[58]

DRIVING WHILE BLACK[59]

In Chapter 5 I discussed the common use of the "selection model" of Chapter 2 in analysis of jury representation. I suggested that this model, which assumes that we know what juries "should" look like and assesses selection against that standard, produces the wrong answers. It does so because we do *not* know what juries "should" look like, under fair selection. I proposed an alternative approach, the "survey" model, in which we assess the procedures and, if we do not find them to have been biased, we accept their outcome as information about the population.

I suggested in Chapter 5 that assessing a procedure from its outcomes was a precarious exercise, fraught with assumptions that could be incorrect. Allegations of bias in the issuance of speeding tickets have also been analyzed with the selection model. Doing so assumes both that we know what "fair" stops would look like, and that the police have prior knowledge of the race (ethnicity, gender, etc.) of those upon whom they have acted. The "driving-while-black" literature, including expert presentation to courts, is fatally flawed by false assumptions and mismeasurement.

---

58. In *DeMarco* (2004a), Judge Rakoff in footnote 3 cites a study by Frank Torchio, who "isolated the statements of the particular analyst there involved (Jack Grubman) on days in which there was no confounding information" from the stock issuer. In this case, against Michael Stanek, another security analyst, the expert did not make such a distinction, and therefore his results are unreliable. That the expert was again Torchio is not relevant. The judge cares more that this is bad work than that it is contradictory work.

59. An early version of some of this material appeared in Michelson (2004).

The Issue Defined

The phrase "driving while black" reflects a belief that traffic laws are enforced excessively against black drivers because of their race.[60] If we were to look for statistical evidence supporting that belief we would ask whether

(1)   traffic stop = f(speed, condition of car, driving behavior); or

(2)   traffic stop = f(speed, condition of car, driving behavior, race); or

(3)   traffic stop = f(race).

Is being stopped for a traffic violation a function (1) of the officer's perception of such a violation; (2) of such a perception modified by the officer's perception of the driver's race; or (3) of race alone, everything else being pretext? Although no doubt some people hold the third view, that at least some blacks are stopped for no reason other than who they are (not what they are doing), the data base for such an analysis would have to contain only persons who violated no traffic laws.[61] As we will see, statistical analysts assert the opposite, that *all* moving cars are violating some traffic law. Driving while black is discussed in the legal literature as differential enforcement among drivers with equal cause. The statistical question is, does equation (1) or equation (2) describe police actions?

---

60. Adherents of this view assume this selection bias to be fact. The statement often appears in a dependent clause, such as, "Because traffic laws are arbitrarily enforced against minorities. . . ." Oliver (2000) at 1412. See also Hall (1998) and D. Harris (1999). David Harris (1997) writes, at 546:

> In fact, the stopping of black drivers, just to see what officers can find, has become so common in some places that this practice has its own name: African-Americans sometimes say they have been stopped for the offense of "driving while black."

"Driving while black" is a subset of a larger concept describing interactions between police and citizens, often called "racial profiling." White police officers, it is said, make assumptions about black citizens that lead to differential behavior towards them. No doubt some police are racists, and act that way, but some (indeed, disproportionately many) blacks are criminals and drug dealers. A dispassionate look at the record would be in order, but is a far larger task than I undertake here. John McWhorter (2003) uses empiricism (facts) to free himself from the "victim" mentality of traditional (or "left") black leadership. Yet, at 62, he refers to "the naked realities of racial profiling." He offers no measure, and no evidence that what he senses are raced-based police behaviors are disproportionately or without probable cause applied to blacks.

   Now accepted as a phenomenon of interest, there exist at least two web sites devoted to tracking legislation, litigation and other activities around the phrase "racial profiling": http://www.racial profilinganalysis.neu.edu at Northeastern University, and http://www1.umn.edu/irp/publications/racial profiling.html at the University of Minnesota.

61. Peso Chavez claimed that he broke no laws, and in particular that he signaled the lane change for which he was stopped; but as he had deliberately emulated drug-trafficking behavior, with open maps, sandwiches, air freshener etc. in a rental car that had crossed the Mexico border several times, there was reasonable suspicion for an investigatory stop. See *Chavez* (2001) particularly at 623–624. Gregory Lee, who joined the *Chavez* case, posed a better case for stop without cause, but could not show that

Academic and popular literature is replete with driving-while-black anecdotes, quite enough to think (without a closer look) that something is amiss. Some authors provide, as support, quotations from other authors. Assertions of police bias therefore are more numerous than *independent* studies thereof.[62] Although the driving-while-black hypothesis is believable, it is not obvious. Nor, it turns out, is it supported by the studies that say it is.[63]

What happens *after* a traffic stop is a separate question from what induced the stop

---

similarly situated whites were not stopped. Christopher Jiminez, whose request to join the *Chavez* case was denied, does not fit this third model. His (white, non-Hispanic) fiancée was driving, admittedly above the speed limit.

Linda Johnson alleged that she violated no traffic rule in *Johnson* (2003). She was driving a four-year-old Lexus, up-scale automobiles driven by blacks being a target as this "no-violation" model is generally propounded. The Eighth Circuit majority determined, at 1000:

> When the claim is selective enforcement of the traffic laws or a racially motivated arrest, the plaintiff must normally prove that similarly situated individuals were not stopped or arrested in order to show the requisite discriminatory effect and purpose.

This is an absolutist (as opposed to probabilistic) statement. We do not know how a showing that blacks are *more likely* to be stopped than whites, in the same circumstances, would be received by this court. The Seventh Circuit does not hold the complainant to such a high standard, noting that "plaintiffs do not have to provide the court with the name of an individual who was not stopped," but may use statistical analysis instead. The offered statistical analysis, however, was inadequate. See *Chavez* (2001) at 640.

Jimmie Marshall alleged that Rodney Porter, a police officer for the city of Hobbs, New Mexico, arrested him for no reason other than race. *Marshall* (2003) at 1169:

> Mr. Marshall testified, and Officer Porter did not deny, that the officer made eye contact with him while stopped at the intersection prior to activating his emergency lights. From these facts it might reasonably be inferred that Officer Porter was ascertaining Mr. Marshall's race.

Because Officer Porter knew that Marshall was black prior to initiating his action, the trial court's granting of summary judgment was surely inappropriate, as the Tenth Circuit found. But, with respect to this book, Marshall's allegations concern one officer, whose employment was subsequently terminated for improper behavior, especially in connection with minority defendants. Marshall made no generalization, and offered no data. That there are bad cops there can be no doubt, but is not the point.

62. See, for example, Richard Morin, "The Latest on DWB," *Washington Post*, February 16, 2003, at B5. Morin discusses a study in which minorities perceive themselves as targeted by police."But do records and other evidence support what his interviewers were told?" he asked. Whereupon one author cited the New Jersey study by Lamberth, which is discussed below, as empirical evidence that the opinions were well founded. See Lundman and Kaufman (2003). Meeks (2000) compiles driving-while-black stories, not one of which is new. Gross and Livingston (2002) refer, at 1420, to "infamous racial profiling," and, at 1431, to "overwhelming evidence," citing only the Maryland and New Jersey studies that are dissected below. Not only are these studies not overwhelming, they are fallacious.

63. I am not alone in questioning the conclusion so many assume. PERF (2001) at 118:

> [T]here are legitimate questions as to whether there are, at present, cost-effective methods for interpreting these [traffic stop] data to reach valid, meaningful conclusions.

These authors, also, thought *they* were not alone. PERF (2001) at 136:

itself. All driving-while-black allegations and, we will see, "studies," assume that the officer has observed (or inferred) the driver's race while the offending car was in motion. After the car has been stopped, and after some interaction between officer and driver, we can safely presume that the driver's race is known (to the accuracy of observation) by the police officer. Thus studies of post-stop police behavior cannot be taken as evidence of pre-stop bias, but they avoid one of the flaws of stopping studies.

A Model of "Fair" Ticketing

By this point in this book we know to be wary about the analyst's assumptions, stated or not. As the laws at issue are about behavior, and the data are of results (be they hires or jurors or speeding tickets), what is required to intermediate between process and outcome is a "model." The implicit model in availability analyses is that there is a single pool of known composition, from which draws are to be made randomly with respect to a characteristic (such as race) described by a two-valued variable (such as black and non-black). The analyst measures how different actual draws have been from those that would have been generated by this model. In the real world, as discussed in Chapter 2, selections are made from different pools. There is an opening, for which there are applicants, and then another opening, for which there are different applicants. The availability model assumes that all pools look alike. If the pools are different, then the single-pool test could easily produce the wrong answer.

Many other assumptions affect the validity of the conclusion of what seem to be straightforward, simple selection analyses. The only driving-while-black model tested has been of random selection from a single pool in which driving speed is unrelated to driver's race. An alternative model might consider that selection is not random, but is based on a valid factor, say speed. That model has been assumed away. It has not been tested.

It would be a strange model of employment that suggested that hiring officials had no function other than clerical—that they did not try to hire the *best* of the applicants. In the case of speeding tickets, the "best" applicants for selection are the fastest drivers. At one time a car going seventy-five miles per hour will be the fastest. At another time, that same driver in that same car going that same speed would be passed by someone driving eighty-five miles per hour. We might think that his being stopped for speeding would be less

---

As stated in a U.S. General Accounting Office report (2000), because of methodological challenges, "we cannot determine whether the rate at which African-Americans or other minorities are stopped is disproportionate to the rate at which they commit violations that put them at risk of being stopped" (p. 18).

Such words of caution do not appear in the law-review literature, Michelson (2004) being the first law-review article to question what all previous writers took for granted. The only other writing seriously and systematically questioning statistical methodology on this subject is Mac Donald (2001).

likely in the second circumstance, that a multiple-pools approach is required to test police behavior. The fair likelihood of being stopped for speeding should be portrayed as a function of one's speed and the speeds of all proximate cars. This fair model would test whether the police stop the fastest cars. The single-pool selection model tests whether police stop the same proportion of cars driven by blacks as driven by whites, asking us to conclude that when the answer is negative, what hasn't been tested for (fair stops) has not happened. How bizarre![64]

Application of the Selection Model

John Lamberth tells about his analysis of arrests of black and white drivers on the New Jersey Turnpike in the *Washington Post*.[65] Lamberth had been engaged as a statistical expert on behalf of seventeen defendants who had been arrested for drug possession after being stopped for speeding on the New Jersey Turnpike.[66] Defendants complained that black drivers were stopped excessively by the New Jersey police. Lamberth summarized the question:

> Since arrests for drug offenses occurred after traffic stops on the highway, was it possible that so many blacks were arrested because the police were disproportionately stopping them?

And he summarized his answer:

> African Americans made up 13.5 percent of the turnpike's population and 15 percent of the speeders. But they represented 35 percent of those pulled over. In stark numbers, blacks were 4.85 times as likely to be stopped as were others.

---

64. Is it more bizarre that this approach has been used by statistical experts, or that it has not been laughed out of court? In *Caridad* (1999), for example, plaintiffs' expert Harriet Zellner, at 288,

  concluded that the "effect of being black on number of disciplinary charges over the 1990-to-1994 period was positive and highly significant statistically."

However, she did not ask if blacks *deserved* such charges. David Evans, defendant's expert, at 289,

  concluded that for two infractions that can be objectively documented—substance abuse and failure to remit—the higher rates of discipline of Blacks corresponded to the higher incidence of infractions by Blacks.

65. See Lamberth (1998). The following two indented quotations are from this article. The report on which it is based is Lamberth (1996). In 2000, Lamberth founded Lamberth Consulting, specializing in analysis of police "racial profiling." Unfortunately, as we will see, his firm has continued to employ the faulty methodology described in the *Post* article.

66. Defendants in *Soto* (1996) complain both that searching speeders' cars for drugs was unwarranted without probable cause, and that being stopped for speeding was racially determined. On the former see also *Carty* (2002). My comments refer only to the latter complaint. *Soto* was hardly the end. The issue of racial profiling by New Jersey state police "has consumed New Jersey's State and Federal Courts for the better part of six years." *White* (2002) at 125.

How did Lamberth identify race in the availability pool? Data were collected from April 1988 through May 1991 in two surveys, as described in the state-court opinion. The first is called the traffic survey.

> Teams supervised by Fred Last, Esq., of the Office of the Public Defender observed and recorded the number of vehicles that passed them except for large trucks, tractor trailers, buses, and government vehicles, how many contained a "black" occupant and the state of origin of each vehicle. Of the 42,706 vehicles counted, 13.5% had a black occupant.[67]

The second, called the "violator survey," was taken driving at sixty miles per hour,

> and observing and recording the number of vehicles that passed him, the number of vehicles he passed, and how many had a black occupant. Mr. Last counted a total of 2,096 vehicles other than large trucks, tractor trailers, buses, and government vehicles of which 2,062 or 98.1% passed him going in excess of sixty miles per hour including 306 with a black occupant equaling about 15% of those vehicles clearly speeding.

Judge Francis correctly describes the surveys as being of an "occupant." All cars "with a black occupant," regardless of the race of the driver, were considered black. The police officer is assumed to have noted, while they were moving, the races of all occupants. Later in the opinion Judge Francis simply refers to blacks, not persons driving a car with a black occupant. I will discuss Lamberth's New Jersey study as if it was about black drivers, as most people think that is the subject of interest.[68]

For the hypothesis of race-conscious behavior by the police, the actual race of the driver is of little importance. What matters is what the police officer *thinks* the driver's race is.[69] Lamberth does not assert that his "race" variable validly measures either the officer's view of the driver's race, or the driver's view of his own.

---

67. *Soto* (1996) at 70, footnote 13; following indented quotation also from footnote 13.

68. Note the word "Traveler" in the title of Lamberth (1996). The distinction between "driver" and "traveler" is not trivial. Christopher Jiminez, for example, as noted above, alleged discrimination based on his being Hispanic, even though he was a passenger in a car driven by a non-Hispanic. See *Chavez* (2001).

69. The New Jersey officers are supposed "to communicate by radio to their respective stations the race of all occupants of vehicles stopped prior to any contact." *Soto* (1996), footnote 5. That transmission is surely made while both cars are still. Those challenging the stops must assume—I would say must prove—that the officer determines the race of a moving car's occupants while it is moving.
    The PERF (2001) authors note, at 129:

> To the extent that officers make stopping decisions based on race, they do so based on their perceptions of race, not on the basis of driver's license information that they have not yet seen.

Then they report, at 133:

The first problem, then, is that Lamberth does not have a concept of the measure of race that accords with his model of police behavior, or with the requirements of the law. The second problem is that Lamberth's research team claims to have identified the race of all occupants of each car, some passing a stationary site at more than sixty miles per hour, *with certainty*. To what extent Lamberth's observer's identification is correlated with self-identified race, or with police-officer identification, with what error, with what bias, we do not know.

The difficulty of identifying the race of drivers is illustrated by a later study in New Jersey. Cars were photographed using "specially designed radar-gun cameras in a variety of locations on the turnpike."

> Researchers then showed the photographs of 38,747 drivers to teams of three evaluators who tried to determine each driver's race, without knowing whether the driver had been speeding. At least two of the evaluators were able to agree on the race of 26,334 of the drivers.[70]

Trying to suppress this second New Jersey study, a Department of Justice attorney expressed his skepticism about its racial identifications, citing windshield glare as one confusing factor.[71] If glare confused the photograph, might it not equally confuse the officer trying to peer inside the speeding car to determine, by the race of the driver, whether to stop it? How does the officer identify the race of the driver of a speeding car at night?

We need to know how well a police officer can make the racial identification that analysts assume he has made. In the only study that asks this question, 93.6 percent of

---

In our focus groups, many officers expressed great frustration at accusations of racial bias, and lamented that they were so accused even when it was clearly impossible for them to discern driver characteristics before a stop.

It should have been critical for defendants to show that the officer *could* make some determination before acting to stop the speeding car, and equally important for the state to show that he couldn't, or didn't. This issue seems not to have been raised by either side in *Soto* (1996). In *Mesa-Roche* (2003), *Arellano* (2004), and *Duque-Nava* (2004) we will see courts make exactly this point, rejecting another Lamberth Consulting study, Lamberth (2003).

70. Iver Peterson, "Racial Study of Speeders Is Released In New Jersey," *New York Times*, March 27, 2002. The "study" is apparently James E. Lange, Kenneth Blackman, and Mark Johnson, "Speed Violation Survey of the New Jersey Turnpike: Final Report" published by the Public Service Research Institute in December 2001. Accuracy of racial identification is difficult, but at least in this study a bold attempt was made, using multiple observers. In Lamberth (2003), "The researchers did nothing to verify the accuracy of the [arrest] information they received from the police agencies." And, in their own data collection, to determine a benchmark, "there was no verification of the accuracy of the observer, by spot check, by multiple observations of the same vehicle, or otherwise." Quotations from Judge Robinson's opinion in *Duque-Nava* (2004) at 1157 and 1158.

71. The attorney, Mark Posner, is quoted in David Kocieniewski, "Study Suggests Racial Gap in Speeding in New Jersey," *New York Times*, March 21, 2002, as well as in the Iver Peterson article cited in the previous note, and in a CNN news story about the release of this report from around that time.

the officers appear to have said that they had no preconception of the driver's race.[72] Again, skepticism is in order. Not only is that answer self-serving, it is the default in the data base. The officer may simply not have answered the question. However, it is a start: One analyst at least had the smarts to inquire about what all previous writers had assumed.[73]

The third and perhaps most egregious problem with Lamberth's study is that he fails to ask if blacks and whites drive at the same speeds. He will say that he did, but "speeding" is defined as exceeding five miles per hour over the speed limit in his study. In my "fair" model, police try to stop the fastest cars—or at least select from among them. Unless that possibility is tested, how can the analyst conclude that speed was *not* the determining

---

72. The study is of 24,491 traffic stops made by the Vancouver, Washington, police department over a one-year period beginning in February 2002. It is described in Mosher (2003). No results from the question on initial race impression appear in that paper. Mosher transmitted that information to me on June 4, 2003, two days after I requested it.

73. As indicated above, this omission caught up with Lamberth. In *Mesa-Roche* (2003) at 1194, referring to Lamberth (2003):

> The Lamberth study does not measure the officer's perception of race or ethnicity before making the stop.

Some participants in this Kansas study did record race prior to stopping, contrary to instruction. Restricting his comment to those mistaken observations, Judge Robinson reports in *Duque-Nava* (2004), at footnote 42:

> Because the officers were trained to record "unknown" if they weren't sure, the data includes a high number of unknowns.

In *Arellano* (2004) at 1234:

> Without proof of the officer's knowledge of a driver's race, an intent to discriminate against a driver because of his race can rarely, if ever, be shown.

Thus Lamberth's study could not be used as evidence of intent, a critical part of a Fourteenth Amendment "equal protection" claim. Judge Kopf noted in *Hare* (2004), at 963, that

> no discovery should be permitted unless the defendant can make a threshold showing that both the "effect" and "intent" prongs of *Armstrong* [1996] might reasonably be said to exist.

Judges are seeing through the flimsy legal basis, as well as the flimsy statistical basis, of defendants' "driving-while-black" arguments.

Judge Crow also questioned the reliability of Lamberth's identification of the ethnicity of drivers. He notes in *Arellano*, at 1230:

> Thus some persons who, when stopped, were reported in stop data as Hispanic, could have been recorded in the benchmark data as White because of their appearance as such to the surveyors.

Judge Crow credits Brian Withrow, an expert for the state, for piercing through Lamberth's methods, convincingly arguing that they proved nothing. From the point of view of this book, only my multiple-pools criticism (which Withrow apparently did not make) might be seen as technical, beyond a judge's ability to initiate. Any judge should be asking if the measures are valid, whether the officers had the knowledge required by intent, if the pool from which selections are made in the model is the pool from which selections are made in reality.

factor?[74] If we do not know the race of these fastest drivers, how can we draw any conclusion about the impact of race on the decision whom to stop?

Suppose a distribution of speeds of cars looks like Figure 63.[75] This distribution, showing mid-points of five-miles-per-hour-wide categories, accords with Lamberth's information that only 1.3 percent of all drivers were not speeding. His research team counted a higher percentage of blacks among speeders than among drivers, comparing results from the two surveys. Thus from Lamberth's own information it would be reasonable to infer that blacks, in general, are faster drivers.[76]

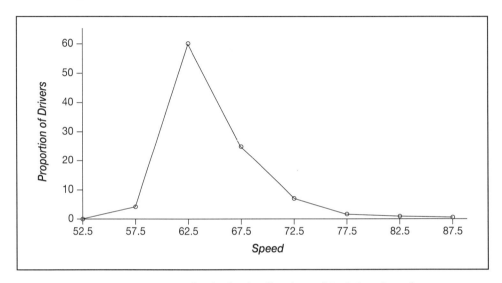

FIGURE 63: Hypothetical Distribution of Driving Speeds

---

74. As William Smith et al. (2003) state at 25, and is the simplest of concepts:

> Simple differences in racial composition of stops do not demonstrate the presence or absence of police bias. Rather, we should suspect racial bias only after accounting for racial/ethnic differences in driving behavior.

75. This distribution is essentially that provided by Terrin and Kadane (1998), defending Lamberth's survey. Terrin and Kadane do not allow for anyone driving under the posted speed limit of fifty-five miles per hour, so I split their lowest five-miles-per-hour category onto two parts. Nor did they or Lamberth notice that it is *impossible* for a population that is 13.5 percent of a distribution to be more than 13.8 percent of the top 98.1 percent of it. Lamberth has measured two different populations of drivers, and so cannot compare "speeders" with "total" as if they were from the same distribution. Because almost everyone speeds, say Terrin and Kadane at 26, "Therefore the police can practically stop whomever they choose." Mr. Last's car was going five miles per hour over the speed limit. Did he think he risked arrest for speeding?

76. It was disingenuous of defendants to switch sources to rebut this proposition: Referring to the state's expert:

> In any event, his supposition that maybe blacks drive faster than whites above the speed limit was repudiated by all State Police members called by the State who were questioned

Using the information that the slowest drivers are whites, I hypothesize that the distributions of speeds, by race, are as in Figure 64. These two distributions sum to the one in Figure 63, but lead to a very different interpretation of Lamberth's findings. Although these racial differences are conjecture, showing that a reasonable set of facts consistent with the known data would lead to a contrary conclusion from Lamberth's is a standard form of logical "disproof." It should be sufficient to establish that Lamberth cannot draw his conclusions from his data.[77]

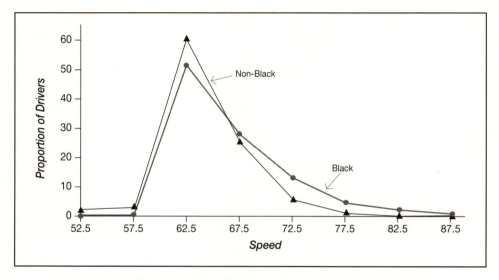

FIGURE 64: The Same Distribution of Speeds, Displayed by Race

Here blacks are 14.2 percent of the speeders as Lamberth sees them (sixty miles per hour or greater), but they are 35 percent of those driving seventy-five miles per hour or faster. These fastest speeders are 3 percent of all drivers, many times the proportion of cars stopped for speeding. Finding that 35 percent of those stopped were black would be consistent with these facts—that is, consistent with unbiased police behavior.

Defining "speeding" as fifteen miles per hour or more over the speed limit—looking

---

about it. Colonel Clinton Pagano, Trooper Donald Nemeth, Trooper Stephen Baumann, and Detective Timothy Grant each testified that blacks drive indistinguishably from whites.

Soto (1996) at 74. Politically correct, yes; but true? The data suggest not.

77. Note 184, below, lists law-review debates over how probabilistic evidence should be utilized in decision making. Some commentators would not accept that devising "facts consistent with the data," but inconsistent with Lamberth's conclusion, nullifies his conclusion. They would want to know which set of facts is more probable. As the later data confirmed, it is more likely that blacks drive faster than whites (possibly because blacks are younger) than that they drive at equal speeds. My assumption is more probably true than Lamberth's. His data should have led him to the same conclusion.

at the right tail of the distribution—the later New Jersey study (which identified driver race from photographs) found that 2.7 percent of the black drivers were speeding, as opposed to 1.4 percent of the white drivers. If these figures apply uniformly at higher speeds, we would expect that 25 percent of the stops for speeding would be of blacks. However, "the disparity between white and black drivers widened at higher speeds."[78] Stopping the fastest cars, regardless of race of driver, could easily lead to 35 percent of those stopped being blacks.

Litigation and Politics

We are told that the state's expert in *Soto* (1996), Leonard Cuppingood, "had no genuine criticism of the defense traffic survey."[79] More likely, Judge Francis defined Cuppingood's criticisms as "not genuine," just as Judge Shadur discredited Barry Chiswick's excellent work in *Lamp* (1985). Cuppingood had wanted the state to study the upper tail of the speed distribution, but it did so only after losing *Soto*. As the burden was on defendants to prove racial bias, Cuppingood should not have implied that he needed data to refute their assertion. Lamberth tested no hypothesis that differentiated between the state's view and defendants'. His claim that he had is an example of an expert's interpretation that is not supported by his own study. Judge Francis accepted what the expert said, as opposed to what he did.

Understanding what press reaction would be, New Jersey initially held its later study of the fastest speeders secret. When it was released, it was criticized for its racial identification data![80] Where were those critics when the first study appeared?

Lamberth's *Washington Post* article reports that police training videos "disproportionately portrayed minorities as perpetrators" and that New Jersey troopers "had been coached to make race-based 'profile' stops to increase their criminal arrests." He does not mention that it was the federal government that produced those materials and did the coaching.[81]

---

78. Iver Peterson's *New York Times* article of March 27, 2002. Kocieniewski, cited above in note 71, tells us that, in sixty-five-miles-per-hour zones, blacks constituted 16 percent of the drivers, 25 percent of the speeders, and 23 percent of the traffic citations. The same figures are reported in *Mesa-Roche* (2003) at footnote 10, attributed to the Lange et al. study cited above in note 70. This view is starkly different from Lamberth's. Kocieniewski also tells us that the report of this study was suppressed, at least in part, because

> the data could be used by defenders of the state police to argue that one reason black drivers are stopped more often than whites is that they are more likely to speed.

See Chapter 9 for more stories of politically inspired suppression of one side of a scientific debate.

79. *Soto* (1996) at 73.

80. In addition to the U.S. Department of Justice criticism cited above, see Robert Hanley, "N.A.A.C.P. Head Criticizes Study of Turnpike Arrests," *New York Times*, March 28, 2002, at B5.

81. This information can be found in Gross and Barnes (2002).

Nor do we know that such training and coaching was effective. If it was, then why do we not believe that, when the police were later told to do no such thing, they did not follow that instruction, also? One might think that such materials would have different effects depending on the race of the police officer, but no calculations are provided in the New Jersey study, nor the Maryland study described below, by officer race.

If the object is to slow speeders, and to put criminals in jail, profiling on the basis of race alone is not only unconstitutional, it is also unlikely to be efficacious. Despite it being more difficult to effectuate profiling at night, time of day is not accounted for in any study related to litigation. That stops for speeding correlate with race does not imply that race was the reason.[82] Lamberth concluded (and the court accepted) that the stops were based on race from a model that allowed no other explanation, a common expert error, many more examples of which appear below in this chapter. To someone like me, who sets his highway speed somewhat slower than the fastest proximate car, Lamberth's study not only is technically deficient, it seems silly.[83]

New Jersey signed a consent decree to end federal litigation. Despite adverse state-level decisions based on Lamberth's testimony, New Jersey did not admit to having done anything wrong, while promising to do everything right.[84] For New Jersey to have truncated the Justice Department's inquiry by agreeing to be "fair" is, as they say, a "no-brainer." It is not evidence that the defendants' experts in *Soto* were correct.

Maryland: A Similar-Selection-Model Study

Lamberth also provides the data in Figure 65 about the Maryland State Police.

---

82. For example, Mosher et al. (2004) find the number of citations issued to blacks stopped in forty Washington State districts disproportionate, compared with citations issued to whites who had also been stopped. However, they write,

> when racial/ethnic differences in the commission of traffic violations are taken into account, the initial effects of race/ethnicity on the probability of receiving a citation are greatly attenuated.

Studies that do not account for differential behavior, by race, should not be credited in the literature, and should not pass a *Daubert* screening in litigation.

83. Remembering "judicial notice" from Chapter 1, courts can and do take cognizance of "knowledge" that comes from everyday life. "To get out of a vehicle and reconnoitre is an uncommon precaution, as everyday experience informs us," wrote Justice Cardozo in *Pokora* (1934) at 104, discussing what standard of caution should prevail to find a driver negligent when he was hit by an unseeable train. Statistical analysts ought do no less.

84. See *NJ Consent* (1999). Item 4 reads:

> The State denies that the State Police has engaged in a pattern or practice of conduct that deprives persons of rights, privileges, or immunities secured or protected by the Constitution and laws of the United States.

In Item 8 the state agrees "to support vigorous, lawful, and nondiscriminatory traffic enforcement."

	Search	Arrest
Non-Black	287	80
Black	713	200

FIGURE 65: Cars Stopped on Interstate 95 in Maryland

The data in Figure 65 show that, although the Maryland police may well stop more blacks than their proportion among drivers, the police later think they are correct in their suspicions in the same proportion among blacks and non-blacks. Twenty-eight percent of those in both searched populations are arrested. Without additional information describing the results of these arrests, we have to interpret these figures as showing that the police were fair. I do not understand why Lamberth would have us think otherwise.

Samuel Gross and Katherine Barnes, using the same Maryland data, discuss the officer's required foreknowledge of race:

> Highway stops are stylized; the officer chooses his target based on the few facts
> he can see from a distance, one of which is race.[85]

No evidence is presented that the officer can in fact determine race at this distance. The one fact about the moving vehicle we are certain that the officer with a radar gun knows is its speed. Gross and Barnes pass over this candidate (without testing it) to implicate a characteristic the officer may not know.

John Knowles, Nicola Persico, and Petra Todd have a more enlightened but not necessarily relevant view of "fairness" in pretext arrests (in which the real objective is to find drugs, not to fine speeders) than other analysts. If police and drivers both react to differential probabilities (of being searched, of finding contraband), then finding contraband per search, they assert, should move toward an equilibrium equality between blacks and whites.

> Our model implies that at equilibrium, both races should have the same probability of carrying drugs, but one race may be searched more than another. In fact, searching some groups more often than others may be *necessary* to sustain equality in the proportions guilty across group.[86]

---

85. Gross and Barnes (2002) at 749. These data appear to have convinced the U.S. district court in Maryland that there was "relevant evidence that minority motorists were treated differently from whites, at least for a period of time on a portion of I-95." *MD-NAACP* (1999) at 566. I say "appear to" because the case in which the evidence was submitted is *Wilkins v. Maryland State Police*, Civil Case No. CCB-93-468, on which I can find no published opinion.

86. Knowles et al. (2001) at 227; following in-text quotation at 222. The deduced principle that an outcome equality requires a stopping inequality if different population sub-groups commit crimes in different frequencies contrasts with Albert Alschuler's contention that

As essentially equal proportions of white and black drivers stopped by the Maryland police carried contraband, "our findings suggest that police search behavior is not biased against African-American drivers."

It is hard to believe that finding a small amount of marijuana in a car has the same importance to police as finding a large amount of crack cocaine. Knowles et al., like other analysts, have been tripped up by the measures they use. Drug laws (or at least prosecutions) are quantity-based, the object being to catch dealers, not users.[87]

> the Court should hold that when a police practice systematically subjects minorities to searches and seizures at a higher rate than the rate at which these minorities commit crimes, this practice violates the Fourth Amendment unless it is appropriately tailored to advance a significant state interest.

Alschuler (2002) at 165, restated somewhat differently at 268. At least Alschuler wants to set criminal activity as a standard for searches. Attorneys like Alschuler might want to consult social scientists about the implications of their arithmetic before they publish such foolishness. He needs to consider police behavior in general, as well as criminal behavior, to set a standard of differential search and seizure.

Harcourt (2004) disagrees with the conclusions of Knowles et al. From a more complicated model, he writes, at 1313 and 1329:

> [W]hen the hit rates are 34 percent for African-American motorists and 32 percent for white motorists along Maryland I-95, we do not know if the police have searched African-American motorists simply based on their race and white motorists because of five other suspicious traits. . . . Equal hit rates could mean narrow efficiency, but they could also signal racial discrimination.

I will provide a third interpretation below. Later, Harcourt is less conditional, discussing, at 1373, the "present conditions of racial profilings" in Maryland. As interesting as Harcourt's theoretical musings are, about which I will have more to say, he demonstrates a lack of skill at describing as well as interpreting statistical results. For example, he asserts, at 1285, "that minority motorists offend at higher rates than white motorists" is an assumption of economic models. It is, rather, an empirical finding. He repeats results from Mitchell Pickerill, Clayton Mosher, Michael Gaffney, and Nicholas Lovrich in "Search and Seizure, Racial Profiling and Traffic Stops on Washington State Highways 15-26," unpublished paper prepared for annual meeting of the Law and Society Association, Pittsburgh, Pennsylvania, June 5–8, 2003. In private correspondence, I pointed out to one of these authors that the race/ethnicity effect they report from a single regression coefficient is incorrect, as race/ethnicity also appears in an interaction term. Harcourt reports what the authors said, not what they did. I comment further on this phenomenon, repeating rather than investigating stated conclusions, in Chapter 9.

87. The United States Attorney's guidelines regarding prosecution for drug offenses are based on
    race-neutral criteria, including the quantity of drugs or the presence of aggravating
    circumstances, such as subjects with prior felony convictions.

Turner (1997) at 1183. The role of blacks servicing the white population's craving for drugs is well chronicled. Cab Calloway's "The Man From Harlem" (Banner 32866, 1932) tells about whites waiting for the arrival of their connection. "The Stuff Is Here," sung by both Cleo Brown (Decca 410, 1935) and Georgia White (Decca 7436, 1937), describes the end of that wait. In Newport News, Virginia, responding to a defendant's claim of selective prosecution, because 260 of 285 cases had involved black defendants, Assistant United States Attorney Kevin Comstock explained,

As in New Jersey, most people on Interstate 95 in Maryland drive over the posted speed limit. Also as in New Jersey, the slowest drivers are white:

> Blacks are underrepresented among the few law-abiding drivers on I-95: 3.6% of black drivers are in this category, and 7.9% of whites.[88]

Gross and Barnes take pains to rationalize their measure of the "pool," from which blacks are "selected" disproportionately:

> The laws regulating driving are so elaborate, so detailed, and so unrealistic that virtually every driver violates one or another almost all the time—or at least there is probable cause to believe she might be, which is all that's required to justify a stop.

Thus to an empirical question—Do the fastest cars get ticketed?—Gross and Barnes, like Lamberth, like Norma Terrin and Joseph Kadane (whose articles support Lamberth), provide a theoretical answer: Anyone *can* get a ticket. They all understand that the selection model requires a measure of the composition of the pool. Like using population data to represent the pool of qualified jurors, like using availability data to measure applicants for employment, they use all-driver data to represent the pool of very fast drivers. Though it may be suggestive in research, this pool construct should be unacceptable as evidence in court.[89]

> the percentage of blacks indicted for crack cocaine offenses was high because blacks primarily were involved in the distribution of crack cocaine.

Olvis (1996) at 742.

> In Los Angeles, federal agents used drug arrests to attack street gangs. *Turner* (1997) at 1184:
>> Of 149 defendants charged with these offenses, 109 (74.4%) were black, 28 (19.2%) were Hispanic, and 8 (5.5%) were Asian. Three were unclassified and only one defendant was white.

Although defendants alleged selective prosecution, the Ninth Circuit, having been instructed in these matters by *Armstrong* (1996), rejected the argument that this apparent racial imbalance was driven by the behavior of the police. *Turner* (1997) at 1186:

> In effect, [defendants argue] that the minorities of the inner city of Los Angeles must be denied the protection of law enforcement by the federal government because the likely suspects are overwhelmingly apt to be members of the minority living in that area.

88. Gross and Barnes (2002) at 687; following indented quotation at 670.

89. In a study of Rhode Island, traffic-stop data were compared with population data. See A. Farrell et al. (2003). In litigation in Illinois, pool (driver) data were estimated from population data. *Chavez* (2001) at 626:

> Plaintiffs' experts compared the percentage of whites, African-Americans, and Hispanics in the ISP databases with the percent that each race is present in the Illinois population, based on data from the 1990 Census, and present on Illinois roads, as estimated by the Nationwide Personal Transportation Survey (NPTS).

However, at 641:

Knowles et al. ask whether police stops are "fair" in terms of finding drugs, and conclude that, in Maryland, they are. That skirts around the legal issues (whether there is reasonable suspicion to stop the car, or probable cause to search for drugs) as well as the economic issue (whether stopping drivers on interstate highways is an efficient way to do battle with the drug trade). Drugs should not be at issue in analyses of driving while black. Traffic violations are the issue, and "fair" is whether those violations are handled without regard for race. We are trying to distinguish between equation (1) and equation (2). Finding that, among drivers, more blacks are stopped for speeding, is not up to that task. We need to know how fast they, and the cars around them, were going.[90]

Faulty Expectations

The speed of the violator is recorded on every speeding citation. None of the analyses cited above looked at them. The mean speed and distribution of speeds on tickets could be compared to the mean speed and distribution of speeds of all cars to determine if tickets appear to be a random sample from the car population. We expect that it isn't.[91] If the average speed on a ticket is higher than the average speed of drivers, even of drivers exceeding the posted limit, then those given speeding tickets are not selected from all drivers (or all "speeders") any more than hires or school admissions are made from all applicants. We expect hires to be made from the *best* applicants. That was the lesson of "The Pretty Good Candidate" section of Chapter 2. The racial composition of the others does not matter, which is why availability analysis usually fails to determine if there was discrimination in

---

As we have noted, expert analysis must be both relevant and reliable, and the statistics here are neither.

"The crux of the matter lies in the population benchmarks" the court said, noting, at 643, that these population benchmarks can not provide an adequate backdrop for assessing the racial composition of drivers.

90. It is the driver caught with drugs who most needs to exclude evidence on the basis that it was improperly collected. The issue of driving while black is the vehicle for that showing, for that exclusion. Therefore the issue as I am analyzing it is about driving, even though the issue of most litigation is possession of illegal drugs. David Harris (1999), at 277, calls Lamberth's report in *Soto* "a virtual tutorial on how to apply statistical analysis to this type of problem." We should interpret this remark as an indictment of Harris' ability to evaluate statistical analysis, not as a credible compliment to Lamberth.

91. I requested the New Jersey data from one of the participants in *Soto* (1996), to make this calculation. I have received no reply. This review of speeds on tickets should precede the data collection. If not restricting the selection pool to the speeds of ticketed drivers seems strange, recall that jury analysts do not subtract non-citizens from their "availability" pools, either. Non-citizens are not available for jury duty in any jurisdiction, and are enumerated (by race) in the same census tabulations these analysts are using. Why are they still counted in the pool from which juror selections are said to have been made? Why is "speeding" not defined as driving fast enough to get a ticket? Are experts really this blind to the data they are using? Unfortunately, yes.

hiring. Similarly, comparing the proportion of blacks among all applicants to those admitted to a school tells us nothing, unless we really believe admissions should be random. Many faulty expectations, based on unreal assumptions about input equality, are used as the basis to call for "remedy" of processes that select fairly to begin with.

To the extent that stopping and searching Soto's car was legally unwarranted, race is irrelevant.[92] If that occurred, the police behavior was unacceptable, and that evidence should not be admitted. Nowhere does Lamberth suggest that his New Jersey clients did not possess drugs, nor that they were not speeding. If they were among the fastest cars on the road, they should have no cause to complain about being stopped. They never asserted otherwise. There was no reason to address this case as one of racial bias, except the defendants' apparent inability to prevail on any other ground.[93] *Soto* (1996) was *McCleskey* (1987) writ small, and should have been handled the same way.[94]

---

92. See *Whren* (1996) at 819:

> For the run-of-the-mine case, which this surely is, we think there is no realistic alternative to the traditional common-law rule that probable cause justifies a search and seizure.

Probable cause is the sine qua non for a legitimate search. At 813:

> Subjective intentions play no role in ordinary, probable-cause Fourth Amendment analysis.

Not surprisingly, many commentators disagree. See Glantz (1997), for example, or D. Harris (1997). Hall (1998), at 1096, characterizes reaction to *Whren* as "shock and outrage." Whren has hardly given the police free rein to search at will. Under the probable-cause standard, drug evidence obtained from *Freeman* (2000) and *Page* (2001), and surely many others, has been suppressed.

93. As one dealer services many clients, we can expect that more whites than blacks can be found with drugs; but not necessarily more whites in proportion to their larger population. Even if whites are disproportionately (not just numerically) more abundant holders of drugs, a race-blind policy of ignoring small users, like "slow" speeders, will appear (incorrectly) race-biased to the casual statistical analyst. Gross and Barnes (2002) say that the large drug hauls in Maryland were from blacks, but they also suggest that those stops may have been from tips, not from speeding.

94. In *McCleskey* (1987), like *Soto* a Fourteenth Amendment case, the defendant offered a study by David Baldus apparently showing that, in general, punishment for a black who murders a white is excessively harsh. McCleskey (black) had killed a policeman (white) while robbing a furniture store. This was the wrong case in which to make a civil-rights argument. Following its individualist principles, the Supreme Court said that the defendant had to show that *he* was being discriminated against, not that many black people are. Similarly,

> To establish a discriminatory effect in a race case, the claimant must show that similarly situated individuals of a different race were not prosecuted.

Armstrong (1996) at 465. For an example of a discussion of who is "similarly situated," see *Chavez* (1998) at 1066. Chavez was similarly situated to a white person who had been stopped (and found to be transporting drugs). Indeed, Chavez, a private detective, had been engaged to copy that person's attributes, except that Chavez was Hispanic. He was stopped. What could that prove except equal treatment by police? Judge Francis would have been better off following the *McCleskey*/*Armstrong* approach with the *Soto* defendants.

The Burden of Proof

Lamberth says his New Jersey findings are "bolstered by an analysis" by Joseph Kadane, who offered a Bayesian study that estimated missing data values. Those estimates were used by Lamberth as "data."[95] Not only did Lamberth not account for error in the data he collected, he did not account for error in the additional "data" that Kadane fabricated!

Judge Francis tells us:

> Dr. Kadane testified that in his opinion both the traffic and violator surveys were well designed, carefully performed, and statistically reliable for analysis.[96]

A car that would pass a stationary officer, at some distance, at seventy-five miles per hour, passed Mr. Last's car at a differential speed of fifteen miles per hour, one or two lanes away. The survey neither replicated the view of a patrol officer nor validated race identification against an officer's perception, nor even tried to determine if officers had any foreknowledge of the race of the driver. The survey made no attempt to differentiate cars going sixty-one miles per hour from cars going eighty-one miles per hour. The surveys were clearly unreliable, the analysis invalid. The piling on of "experts" testifying otherwise should be an embarrassment to the statistics profession.[97]

Relating race to speed in the relevant range was defendants' burden. Equality of driver behavior was an assumption, and apparently an incorrect one.[98] Defendant should

---

95. In *Soto* (1996), the race of 617 of the recipients of the 892 subject speeding tickets was estimated. Apparently Judge Francis disagreed with Ninth Circuit dictum that "courts are not free to decide legal propositions on hypothetical evidence." *Penk* (1987) at 465, footnote 1.

96. *Soto* (1996) at 71.

97. Can a judge determine when a survey has been badly designed, badly executed, and badly analyzed? In addition to the Kansas cases cited above in note 73, rejecting a Lamberth study similar to that in *Soto*, I recommend Judge Robinson's conclusion in *Dentsply* (2003) at 454, that "the survey" by Yoram Wind "is entitled to no weight and [is] inadmissible under the Federal Rules of Evidence."

98. From W. Smith et al. (2003) at 398 (in Appendix G):

> We can see that African Americans are over-represented among those who are speeding above the point at which speeding citations are likely. We can say that this pattern is "robust" across definitions of speeding thresholds in the sense that the pattern is the same regardless of how the thresholds are defined.

That is, blacks drive faster than whites where it counts—at speeds that induce tickets—on fourteen observed sections of four-lane highways in North Carolina.

In *Hare* (2004), at 999, Judge Kopf provides an example of the misimpression that one can derive from statistics that assume equal behavior:

> The defendants claim a canine was called to the traffic scene at a substantially higher rate for minority traffic stops. However, a significantly higher percent of minority drivers denied consent. While the raw statistics reflect a distinct disparity in the percent of cases where canine assistance was requested in minority traffic stops, the data also reflects that once consent was denied, minority and non-minority drivers were treated the same.

not be able to create a burden to refute this assumption simply by failing to collect relevant data.[99]

Other Literature

David Harris tells us about Volusia County. The *Orlando Sentinel*, he says, by reviewing tapes from sheriff's cars, counted eleven hundred stops:

> [E]ven though African-Americans and Hispanics make up only about five percent of the drivers on the county's stretch of I-95, more than seventy percent of all drivers stopped were either African-American or Hispanic.[100]

How police know that a driver is Hispanic, as cars pass at well over sixty miles per hour, Harris does not say, though it is imperative for his conclusion that they do. Harris implicitly assumes that driving speed is independent of ethnicity and race. He presents no credible evidence supporting the proposition that racial bias, as opposed to driver behavior, explains the proportion of stopped cars driven by minorities.

Harris provides the additional information that

---

99. Judge Robinson, in *Mesa-Roche* (2003), put the burden on the state to disprove defendant's assumption that driving speed is uncorrelated with race. He is wrong. Judge Crow got it right in *Arellano* (2004) noting, at 1231, that the Lamberth study

> is based upon an assumption that the incidence of traffic violations for all racial and ethnic groups is the same. The court is similarly unaware of any evidence in support of this assumption, which may or may not be valid.

Magistrate Judge Francis states the general proposition in *Electric* (2004) at 235:

> As the proponents of the expert, it is the plaintiffs' burden to demonstrate the reliability of his data.

Or, more generally yet, it is the burden of a party offering statistical evidence to demonstrate its relevance, and the validity of its measures.

Discussing the statistics behind *Hazelwood* (1977), Browne (1993) notes, at 483:

> The assumption underlying such a comparison is that within the class of certified teachers the average qualifications of blacks and whites are equal and that blacks and whites would be equally interested in obtaining a job in the school district at issue. The difficulty with this sort of assumption in general is that not only is it almost always unproved, it is often both demonstrably false as a matter of fact and inconsistent with other important assumptions of discrimination law.

Browne is correct that analyses are driven by false assumptions, but even he articulates the wrong ones. Equal average qualifications is *not* the assumption being made in a selection case, even though most analysts will say that it is. All blacks could be equal to the average "pretty good" white teacher applicant and, like that average white, never be selected in a merit-based, discrimination-free world. See "The Pretty Good Candidate" in Chapter 2.

100. D. Harris (1997) at 561, note 1; following indented quotation also from note 1. On Volusia County, see also Hall (1998).

the tapes showed that police followed a stop with a search roughly half the time; eighty percent of the cars searched belonged to Black or Hispanic drivers.

Harris does not assess the difference between the proportion minority among stops and searches. Let's make a rough single-pool calculation, understanding that the driver's race (ethnicity) is now known. Starting with p = 0.7 (the proportion black or Hispanic among stops), we calculate the standard deviation of percent black or Hispanic if searches were unrelated to race:

$$\text{binomial standard deviation} = \sqrt{0.7 \times 0.3 \times 550} = 10.7$$

We would "expect" 385 searches of minority cars (70 percent of 550), if search is unrelated to race; but we observe 440 (80 percent of 550). The difference is fifty-five. Thus the number of minority cars searched is over five standard deviations greater than the number of minority cars we would expect to have been searched, had searches been unrelated to race except randomly.[101]

Is this a *prima facie* case of racially biased searches? Or is it a survey that finds probable cause appearing disproportionately in behavior of minority drivers? If drugs were found among searched minorities in the same proportion as among whites, this higher propensity to search minorities would appear to be justified, following the reasoning of Knowles et al. That reasoning is clearly wrong, however. It could be that "X" percent of all people carry drugs, unrelated to their driving behavior. The driving-while-black literature is confused by looking to one illegal activity (driving) as an indicator of another (carrying drugs). There is no evidence that driving behavior indicates drug behavior, and that therefore the survey of speeders is anything but a random survey of the drug-carrying population.

If the survey of speeders is random with respect to drugs, it provides an estimate of "X," much as the juror survey of Chapter 5 determined what the eligible population looked like. Finding the same "X" in whites, blacks, and Hispanics might simply mean that "X" is not associated with race. Finding different values might simply mean that "X" *is* different by race. Finding an "unexpectedly" high proportion of minorities in the survey may be due to their dominance on the "source list," which is very fast drivers. Without a good measure of the violator pools, no inference about police behavior can be derived from the data. The only inference available is about driver behavior.

---

101. Obviously the difference is still large if 550 is not exactly the number of searches. A more precise calculation, taking into account the finiteness of the pool from which cars to be searched were drawn, would show an even larger difference. However, the data do not necessarily deserve closer scrutiny. We do not know how race was determined, or have descriptions of behavior prior to searches (and non-searches). A rough—and conservative—calculation is sufficient to raise questions about the behavior of the deputy sheriffs of this county.

The *Boston Globe* obtained data on 764,065 traffic tickets given by 367 different police departments from April 2001 through November 2002. They, too, compared traffic stops with a population:

> Blacks and Hispanics are ticketed at about twice their share of the population. Although blacks account for 4.6 percent of the state's driving-age population, they receive 10.0 percent of tickets to state residents. Hispanics make up 5.6 percent of the population, but get 9.6 percent of tickets.[102]

As usual, that comparison means nothing. It is an example of single-pool statistics being used in a clearly multiple-pools situation. Whether single or multiple, the pool is mis-defined as all drivers, not accounting for how much, how well, or where they drive, at what speed. Nor do the authors ask where the police are, or why. The *Globe* quotes the governor's secretary of public safety:

> Crime-plagued urban communities often plead for more-aggressive police patrols, but civil-rights groups accuse police of disproportionately stopping or arresting minorities in those neighborhoods.

The *Globe* also found that, among those searched, proportionately more whites than others possessed drugs, but does not tell us if those blacks with drugs possessed larger quantities, on the average, as was true in Maryland. Thus we still do not know if there is bias in determining how far to take a traffic stop. Matching town of arrest with town of residence, the *Globe* authors tell us:

> Minorities face greater policing even at home. In more than half the state's communities, minorities get a greater share of tickets in the town where they live from the town police than their share of the town's driving-age population.

"More than half" as an improbable finding from chance with race-neutral behavior? The sidebar states this number as "about half" of the communities, which is what one would expect from chance if there were equality of citizen behavior and unbiased ticketing by police.

In July 2003, the authors of the January *Globe* article, Bill Dedman and Francie Latour, reported on "an analysis of 166,000 tickets and warnings from every police department in the state in a two-month period, April and May of 2001."[103]

---

102. Bill Dedman and Francie Latour, "Traffic Citations Reveal Disparity in Police Searches," *Boston Globe*, January 6, 2003, at A1; this and the following two indented quotations are from the internet version of the article.

103. Bill Dedman and Francie Latour wrote a three-part report under the general title, "Speed Trap: Who Gets a Ticket, Who Gets a Break?" *Boston Globe*, July 20, 21, and 22, 2003. The July 20 article quoted here carries the subheading, "Race, sex, and age drive ticketing." No pages are referenced because I have this article from http://www.boston.com/globe/metro/packages/tickets/072003.shtml.

> Statistics professor Elaine I. Allen of Babson College, commissioned by the
> *Globe* to review the data, found that the racial, gender, and age patterns dis-
> cerned by the *Globe* are statistically significant.

Although Dedman and Latour provide the obligatory cautionary paragraph—many things
we don't know, etc.—they also summarize:

> When factors of race and sex are considered together, the records reveal a
> tiered system of ticketing. Local police allow white women to drive faster with-
> out penalty, while reserving the harshest treatment for minority men.

Elaine Allen apparently was engaged after the *Globe* had collected the data and formulated
its findings. Isn't this what I warned against in Chapter 6? We are told nothing about how
Allen came to these conclusions. However, limiting the observations to those stopped did
control for a number of factors. The officer knows (or presumes) race and gender. Regardless what other cars were not stopped, and why, the subject cars all have a similarity of circumstance and different (ticket vs. warning) treatments. Therefore, it is of some interest
that the state police were exempt from criticism:

> The records show that troopers gave almost exactly equal treatment to all driv-
> ers, regardless of race, sex, or age. No local police department of any size was
> as fair as the State Police.[104]

In May 2004 the Northeastern Institute on Race and Justice released its report, financed by the Massachusetts legislature, on bias in traffic stops in Massachusetts. It was
announced by an article in the *Boston Globe*, and supported by a *Globe* editorial the next
day.[105] The editorial opens:

> The 249 police departments in Massachusetts cited for apparent racial profil-
> ing in a major study released yesterday should resist defensiveness and accept
> the value of a data-driven approach to overcoming this significant impedi-
> ment to a just society.

Neither the 1.6 million traffic stops examined by the Northeastern Institute nor their
benchmark comparisons were "data-driven" to the extent that one should accept that the
report's conclusions are correct. The "stop" data included only those stops that resulted

---

104. In addition to this quotation from their July 20, 2003 article, Dedman and Latour feature the fairness of state troopers in their July 22, 2003, *Boston Globe* report, "Troopers fair, tough in traffic encounters." See http://www.boston.com/globe/metro/packages/tickets/072203.shtml.

105. The report is A. Farrell et al. (2004). The *Globe* announcement, now by Bill Dedman writing alone,
was again under the heading, "Speed Trap: Who Gets a Ticket, Who Gets a Break," the subheading being
"Racial profiling is confirmed." See http://www.boston.com/globe/metro/packages/tickets/050504_folo.
shtml. A follow-up article the next day, also by Dedman, carried the subheading, "Police Chiefs decry
profiling study." The editorial is available at http://www.boston.com/globe/metro/packages/tickets/
050504_editorial.shtml.

in a citation. Although locations differ in the extent to which they call for police action, the Northeastern Institute authors note that they do not know the location of a citation, only the jurisdiction. They comment that

> The lack of specific neighborhood information limits our ability to determine if certain neighborhoods in a city have greater levels of disparity than others.[106]

That misses the point. Police are not allocated uniformly throughout a jurisdiction. In a fair world, citations are created by supply (police presence and decisions) and demand (the incidence of law violation). The Northeastern Institute researchers make the most elemental mistake of assigning "cause" of interactions between supply and demand only to supply, the willingness of police to issue tickets, without accounting for either supply or demand variation.[107]

What were their benchmark comparisons? There were two. The first compared citations by a jurisdiction to its residents, measured by the population over age eighteen. That is a strange measure to apply in a state where driving licenses are issued starting at age sixteen. In any event, it is a measure of those who could drive, not those who do; and if it measured those who do drive, it would still not measure how fast, with what other violations of law, when, and where.

Rather than take a census—a difficult task in a study covering hundreds of jurisdictions—the authors' second benchmark was "driving population estimates" by race.

> To create the pool of contributing cities for each target city in Massachusetts we began with the assumption that the driving population of a jurisdiction is primarily influenced by communities that fall within a 30-minute drive time perimeter.[108]

The reader might recall from my discussion of *Nassau* (1992), in Chapter 7, that geographic proximity is one factor determining who commutes to work. From the same discussion we should remember that there is no need to estimate such flows.[109] While trying to capture other reasons for driving, including shopping and recreation, the Northeastern Institute researchers ignored direct data on commuting. They appear to do better at predicting des-

---

106. A. Farrell et al. (2004) at 8.

107. In a fair world, the police supply tickets to those who demand it, who act in such a way (as does a purchaser of any service) to have it issued to them by the service provider.

108. A. Farrell et al. (2004) at 12.

109. One indication of the confusion in the minds of the Northeastern researchers is footnote 15:

> No driving population estimate calculations were conducted for the sex of the driving population demographics because the distribution of male and female residents is nearly identical in most Massachusetts communities.

Is the distribution of male and female *drivers* the same everywhere? I mean, other than by assumption?

tination than route—who is going where, not where else he drives to get there—but they made no study of how good their estimates of drivers are.[110] If they had, it would still be an estimate of the wrong pool, of all drivers (à la Lamberth), not traffic-law violators.

Whose Bias?

It is conceivable that there have been biased cops who could tell the race of speeding drivers (or passengers) and used that information to decide whom to stop. It is conceivable that, by randomizing assignments (day of the week, time of day, place) among officers, and by associating each stop with an officer in the data base, deviant behavior could be detected. "Bias" must mean enforcement of laws against blacks *more than against similarly situated whites*. If citizen behavior has not been accounted for in data collection, it can be "controlled" by design, such that different results among different officers would likely be explained by *their* differences, not by pool differences. We could make a preliminary assessment of individual officers this way, but only compared with other officers. To test bias among officers as a whole we still need to know what kind of people drive very fast, the data no analyst has collected.

As was suggested in the January 2003 *Boston Globe* article, there is a police-resource-allocation question here. Would it be wrong to position police according to where people speed, or to where there are crimes? In San Jose, California:

> African Americans comprised 5 percent of San Jose's population but 7 percent of the vehicle stops; Hispanics were 31 percent of the city's population but constituted 43 percent of the stops. However, San Jose police officials asserted that there were two reasons for these racial/ethnic disproportions in stops: (1) the number of officers per capita was higher in police districts that contained

---

110. This estimate of drivers had been used in the Rhode Island study, A. Farrell et al. (2003), referenced above at note 89. It may be a worthwhile attempt to improve on population figures, but surely it is not sufficiently robust to use as a basis for policy or litigation. Heather Mac Donald questioned the Northeastern Institute methods and findings in an op-ed piece in the *Boston Globe* on May 19, 2004:

> The Northeastern study makes no effort to determine driving habits among its target groups; it thus has no basis for judging whether police stop rates are disproportionate.

She may go too far, saying that "Northeastern's method for determining road demographics is laughable," but only slightly. The problem is not their attempt to determine a driving population without taking a survey. It is that, even if their population were validated, it would be irrelevant. They fail to differentiate between legal and illegal driving behavior, and present tenuous, hypothetical, and ultimately fallacious conclusions as if they were fact.

To assess state troopers, the Northeastern Institute team did a "rolling road survey" as described in Lamberth (1998). Unfortunately, these authors used John Lamberth's work in Kansas as a model, apparently unaware that it was rejected in *Mesa-Roche* (2003), *Arellano* (2004), and *Duque-Nava* (2004). The Northeastern Institute research personnel should not have had to be told by federal judges that Lamberth's Kansas work—and therefore their own—was methodologically flawed.

a higher percentage of minorities, and (2) socioeconomic factors in minority neighborhoods resulted in more calls for service and resultant interactions with police.[111]

Even if no deliberate resource-allocation decision has been made, standards differ at least among different jurisdictions and, I would bet, among different locations in the same jurisdiction.[112] The first problem is that single-pool analysis with "average" pool characteristics is the wrong statistical method. It provides the wrong answer, because the pools from which selections are being made are mismeasured. The second problem is that reaction to the same circumstance can differ because police presence differs. Each individual cop can have the same, unbiased, propensity to react to a given set of circumstances; yet if there are more of them in one location than another, with the same violations, the one more densely patrolled will generate more citations.

One final problem is publication bias. Police have been collecting racial data from traffic stops in North Carolina since 1999. As in Florida, it appears that stopped minorities are excessively searched. There is no evidence that minorities are excessively stopped in the first place.[113] Yet we hear little about that finding.

David Harris tells the story of Peso Chavez and the Illinois police. His story ends:

> Chavez is now the named plaintiff in a lawsuit in federal court that seeks injunctive relief against the State Police to stop racially based searches and seizures, as well as other relief and damages. The suit seeks certification of a class of persons subjected to the same treatment.[114]

Two years later Harris referred to this litigation as ongoing.[115] In fact, plaintiffs changed their minds about some allegations, and "sought a dismissal with prejudice on the eve of

---

111. Mosher et al. (2002) at 185. Also, from *Duque-Nava* (2004) at footnote 43,

> Greater police presence translates into greater investigative presence, and surely some effect on the incidences of arrests and prosecutions.

112. See "Punishment varies by town and officer," Part 2 of the Dedman-Latour series, July 21, 2003.

113. See Ramirez et al. (2000). Zingraff et al. (2000)

> caution the reader from jumping to the conclusion that the racial disparity evidence should be dismissed as "minimal."

This phraseology smacks of a political agenda. Why not warn against over-interpretation of the small differences they do find, given that they have measured neither the race of drivers nor the race of speeders? See W. Smith et al. (2003) at 251:

> In general, NCSHP stop behavior of speeders seems to be determined by vehicular driving behavior.

"NCSHP" is the North Carolina State Highway Patrol, and race of driver is not indicated as a reason to stop a vehicle.

114. D. Harris (1997) at 568.

115. D. Harris (1999).

trial after five years of vigorous and costly pursuit of these (and other) claims."[116] They agreed to pay over $22,000 in costs.

A Note on Theory

It is all too easy for analysts to assume that characteristics and skills and behaviors are equal by race, and therefore too easy to believe from outcome statistics alone that employers discriminate in hiring, jury systems in selecting, and the police in stopping cars. These characteristics are measurable. When measured, and the outcomes appropriately tested against them, these assumptions often have been shown to be incorrect.

Bernard Harcourt has tried to develop a model accounting for differences of behavior. He assumes that police use racial profiling, and asks under what conditions it could be justified.[117] Except for the denials by police that they act this way, his is a reasonable approach. However, it is difficult to discern what Harcourt thinks should be accomplished by the police, or how they might go about it. Criticizing economic models, he tells us:

> The proper goal for the police is to minimize the social cost of crime—in this case, to minimize the transportation of drug contraband on the highways and the social cost of policing.[118]

His first model asserts a different goal:

> A proper model of police behavior would assume that police departments and police officers seek first and foremost to minimize the number of persons carrying drug contraband on the highway.

More likely they want to minimize the amount of contraband, or catch dealers, which are

---

116. *Chavez* (2000) at *1.

117. See Harcourt (2004). In his opening paragraph Harcourt notes the common empirical finding of disproportionate searches of African-American and Hispanic motorists in relation to their estimated representation on the road.

This definition of "disproportionality" is a nonsensical place to start. It comes from the selection model with a badly defined pool. However, it quickly leads to the conclusion that such disproportionality is justified if the rate of offending is greater among minorities than among whites. Unfortunately, "offending" is not so carefully defined.

What allows Harcourt to continue beyond such an obvious preliminary conclusion is his notion that whites might be induced to commit more crimes if police are more likely to search minorities. Besides being fanciful (Are criminals that calculating? Are they that well informed?) Harcourt's analysis accepts the assumption that everyone provides reasonable suspicion—everyone speeds or has a vehicle malfunction—and that therefore it is an "internal" rate of search (preference for stopping minorities) that drives differential police behavior. Harcourt does not even consider that there is no such internal rate, that police respond equally to equal behavior and do not even know, until the stop, the race of the driver.

118. Harcourt (2004) at 1295; the following indented quotations are, in order, at 1300, 1303, 1335, and 1280.

different things. Why is *his* model the "proper" straw to blow away? Harcourt offers an alternative model that reverts to his original concept:

> In order to model police behavior properly, we must focus not on maximizing search success rates, but on minimizing the costs associated with the profiled crime, including the social costs of the crime itself and of the policing technique.

This is a grand scheme in which police do not expend resources solving small crimes. If there is a "criminal set," people who commit crimes as opposed to others who do not, letting petty crimes go would be bad police policy. Again, however, Harcourt doesn't mean it:

> The proper question to ask, at the empirical level, is . . . whether it reduces the profiled crime—namely the illicit transportation of drug contraband on the highways—without creating a ratchet.

Whether persons, crimes, the quantity of contraband, or social cost should be the focus of attention is a complex issue. Just what Harcourt thinks "proper" analysis entails is, to say the least, unclear.

Also:

> For the more effective and efficient policing policy to be acceptable, it . . . must not produce a racial imbalance in the supervised or carceral population relative to the racial breakdown of offenders.

If blacks receive longer sentences, say because they are transporting larger quantities of drugs, they will be disproportionately represented among the incarcerated, relative to their propensity to commit a crime. This will be true even if they are arrested and convicted proportionately to their propensity to offend. The problem I discussed with relation to hospital surveys in Chapter 6, under "The Conceptual Basis of Data," keeps tripping people up.

Despite going off in many wrong directions, including not recognizing the difference between police behavior and its perception by the public, Harcourt's model does appear to justify racial profiling under some believable conditions.[119] However, Harcourt's efforts

---

119. Harcourt depends on whites and blacks having different elasticities—propensities to revert to criminal behavior when the likelihood of being caught goes down—to generate an argument against profiling. He assumes that minorities are relatively inelastic; they will be criminals no matter what police do. White behavior is elastic—whites are more opportunistic. As in Chapter 6, incentives matter. But the notion that there will be more drug crime under racial profiling—because minorities will continue apace and whites will join in—is divorced, in Harcourt's model, from such incidental issues as supply and demand for the drugs themselves, and barriers to market entry (such as by murder). I appreciate Harcourt's effort. I agree that if blacks had better alternatives, there might be fewer (and more highly paid) drug runners. But whites substitute for blacks as a reaction to racial profiling? That's a stretch. This kind of theory cannot be taken seriously.

It is never clear, in Harcourt's analysis, what an "offender" does. Police would say an offender first violates a traffic law, and then is found to be violating a narcotics law. Much of Harcourt's analysis is based on nonsense hypotheses such as, at 1331:

shed no light on my "null hypothesis," that police respond to reasonable suspicion of violations when stopping cars, seldom (and again only with reason) to suspicion of drug activity —and that they do so without knowing the race of the driver. No study has rejected this model.

It is curious that such good theoretical work is being done—that Harcourt fails does not impugn his effort—when most empirical work has been so shoddy. I am not trying either to justify or to discredit racial profiling as a police practice. I am just trying to determine whether it exists. Except for John Knowles and Clayton Mosher and their various co-authors, analysts assume that it does. Although one gullible judge bought into it, in *Soto*, no one has ever introduced convincing statistical evidence of it into a court of law.

DATA ACCURACY

Measurement is better than assumption. Of course data should be accurate, and unfortunately they never are. Therefore one of the expert's jobs is to evaluate and, to the extent possible, correct the data.[120] As much of the material of Chapter 6 showed, it's neither that simple nor that boring. The data used by Lamberth (and Kadane), as discussed above, are unsatisfactory not just because we should be uncomfortable with their collection, but because we should be uncomfortable with their conception. Lamberth's data seem tailored to reach his conclusion. No alternative hypotheses were considered.[121]

> if the police engage in race-neutral policing and take a random sample of the total motorist population.

Regardless of driver behavior? Harcourt writes, at 1348:

> If the police are going to engage in discrimination by searching a disproportionate number of minority motorists, then they should have the burden of proving that this will promote a compelling state interest.

Why is this "discrimination"? Police already have the burden to demonstrate why they stopped the car, and such reasons may or may not be equal by race. If police "are going to engage in discrimination" they should be fired. In Harcourt's mind, discrimination and disproportionality are the same thing. I say that differential searching is not troubling if cause varies by race, and police correctly judge cause. Shouldn't our effort be turned to determining what the facts are? Harcourt cites Michelson (2004), but either disagrees or has not read it or did not understand it.

120. I provided a small example in Chapter 3, from data published in *Arkansas* (1970).

121. Apparently Lamberth's New Jersey crew did not measure any characteristic but speed of car, state in which it is registered, and race of occupants. Gross and Barnes (2002) acknowledge, at 670, other legitimate reasons why cars are stopped:

> But even the rare driver who doesn't speed may be stopped if an officer has probable cause to believe that he has a burned-out license-plate light, an obscured tag or rear-view mirror, a cracked windshield, misaligned headlights, or is not wearing a seat-belt.

Some of these items were measured in the Maryland study.

Assessing Accuracy

The purpose of statistics, the way in which conclusions are drawn from data, is to see signal through noise, to measure and assess that signal's strength. Variables being measured and used in decisions, which are unrecorded in our data, appear as noise to the analyst. Another part of the noise is errors. Being "accurate" as attorneys use the term, though important, is not as important as they think. What is important is *assessing* the level of accuracy of the data, incorporating that assessment into one's estimates, and informing the legal decision maker about the effect inaccuracy could have on one's conclusions.

When the Equal Employment Opportunity Commission's Chicago office provided me with a list of companies with a certain standard industrial classification code, within a given radius of the subject firm, my staff checked it. We purchased a detailed map of that part of Chicago, drew concentric circles around the subject firm's location, and placed pins at the addresses of other firms with the same classification code. It would have taken nothing for defendant to destroy the credibility of the EEOC's data, there being firms on the list that were outside the area, and firms inside the area that were not on the list. Of course data should pass such scrutiny. But statistical experts should ask for more of their data, and courts should ask more of their experts.

In *Nassau*, my coding of job-description data was criticized on the grounds that persons higher in a hierarchy, say police lieutenants as compared with sergeants, should be considered to have all the positive attributes of the lower rank, plus others derived from their job descriptions. For example, even if the job description of the lieutenant did not say he had to be skilled in the use of firearms, one could infer that this was a required skill for his job, as it was, explicitly, for the lower-level job. I think this criticism had merit.[122] I had taken "qualifications" data to be a mechanical translation of written requirements. What was called for was a more creative understanding of what requirements were actually being sought.

Understanding the Institution

On purchasing Westwood One, Mutual Broadcasting reduced the size of the combined sales staff. As defendant's expert, I tried to make the record clear who was and who was not

---

122. It would have been easy enough for defendant's expert to correct the data in this regard and show that my analysis was seriously flawed (i.e., the results differed qualitatively, in this case, in terms of pay being related to percent female in the job), if it was. The law was clear that the burden should have been placed on defendant—in line with *Bazemore* (1986)—to show that this "error" affected the conclusion. I also think that, had we made those inferences, defendant would have criticized our data for having done so, for having gone beyond the wording of the job description. And I think this judge would have quoted that criticism in justification for his finding for defendant.

terminated. As usual, however, it was the conceptual basis of the data (and the analysis) that dominated my argument.

Plaintiffs' expert combined all personnel into a single selection pool, be they in Los Angeles, Detroit, or elsewhere; be they top-level sales personnel or clerical sales assistants. He then tested no hypothesis other than the relationship between age and termination. He did not consider the obvious other alternative, favoritism towards one's own, towards Mutual employees.[123] My analysis defined competitions for the jobs that would remain, among people who were logical alternatives, using the multiple-pools procedures described in Chapter 2. That is, I assumed that Mutual had in mind a final structure, so many sales personnel at different levels in different offices, so many secretaries, etc. I also tested the two competing explanations, age and prior association with Mutual. Prior association determined who stayed and who left.[124]

In *Coker* (1991), plaintiff complained of racial discrimination in hiring school principals. Both experts agreed that, in fact, relative to the number of blacks and whites who applied for principal positions, Charleston appeared to hire a proportionate number of blacks. The complaint changed to one of distribution: For which schools were blacks hired? Plaintiffs' expert, David Peterson, showed that the race of the principal was associated with the race of the students: black students, black principal; white students, white principal.

On the margin, there were the usual data-accuracy questions: how is "race of school" determined, and when, for example. But the basic problem was Peterson's concept of what data were relevant. First, Peterson compared situations, when at issue were events. It does not matter how many white schools have white principals. It matters how many white schools' principals were appointed during the relevant time period. Second, it does not matter who was appointed where, unless we control for who applied where. Appointment to principal was not made from a general pool, but from application to specific openings. Blacks applied largely to schools that had black students, and whites applied largely to schools that had white students. Third, are all applicants equal? The best analysis, I thought, occurred when persons who eventually did get a principal position competed against each other. The school board has certified all of these people to be qualified for a principal position and so, to this extent, we have controlled for "quality." There was no indication either that the board favored a white applicant over a black applicant, or that the racial composition of the student body predicted the race of the winner, in such competitions. When

---

123. Failure to test hypotheses other than that espoused by their client is the most common failure among plaintiff experts. Judge Weinstein notes this failure among *Agent Orange* (1985) experts, for example. See below in this chapter for additional examples.

124. *Yoder* (1988). The parties settled immediately after expert depositions.

the analysis was otherwise consistent with how decisions were made, the decisions were seen to have been race-neutral.[125]

In Chapter 2 I explained how I determined from personnel actions who at Polaroid had received a termination letter.[126] Understanding how the system worked led to the creation of a data element that had been lost: who was *selected* to be terminated, as opposed to who ultimately was terminated. This data element was derived with error. But for plaintiffs to challenge it, they would have to show that one could derive a different version of who received a termination letter, reasonably, and obtain a different analytic result. It did not matter that the data were not perfect. The ultimate flaw was plaintiffs' conceptual approach to the questions of the case.

Defining "Assignment" at the State Department

Plaintiffs alleged discrimination against black generalist Foreign Service officers in the State Department.[127] As expert for defendant, I convinced my clients to provide data to plaintiffs in a cleaner form than was available in original State Department records. We called this the "stipulated data base," by which we meant that we would not challenge the language used to count from this data base.

For example, the word "assignment" was sure to be misused by plaintiffs unless we controlled it by having an "assignment" field in the data. Foreign Service officers can be seen doing different activities, most of which are "duties." Assignments can be made only through a particular competitive assignment process. I could wait until trial, where I would explain that plaintiffs' analysis of "assignments" was meaningless because they had misdefined the term. Better, I thought, would be to provide a common language so the parties could debate the facts rather than the definitions.

Plaintiffs never agreed to this process. However, *de facto*, once we handed them a "stipulated" data set, they had no choice but to use it. Plaintiffs then misrepresented the data, saying defendant had stipulated *that they were accurate*. It never occurred to them to ask in what sense they might be accurate.

Although any Foreign Service officer would describe the promotion process as one of competing before promotion boards, quite a few promotions are made in other ways. The

---

125. See *Coker* (1991). The court credited my analysis, not Peterson's.

126. *Polaroid* (1983), discussed in Chapter 2.

127. *Thomas* (1991). The last name changes with the Secretary of State. The State Department has both Foreign Service and Civil Service personnel. Furthermore, among Foreign Service officers are specialists, for example in electronic communications, and generalists. It should also be no secret that some "Foreign Service officers" are in fact CIA agents. (The secret is which ones.) The parties agreed to rid the data of all of these difficult cases, except that specialists who competed for generalist positions were included in the analysis of promotion.

most common alternative route to promotion is a grievance. When a promotion is made as the result of a grievance, it is made retroactive to when it was denied. The "accurate" record now reflects a "fact"—the person's grade—that was not a "fact" at the time it now pretends to have been.

A person assigned to a position that carries a grade different from his own is said to have received a "stretch" assignment. Comparing the grade of a position with the grade of the officer inhabiting it to determine "down-stretch" will view those Foreign Service officers whose promotions were made retroactively as having been in down-stretch positions, although they were considered to be at grade at the time. As these assignments would not have been considered "down-stretch" when the decisions were made, they should not be considered to be down-stretch assignments in an assignment analysis. We needed a promotion-route-sensitive definition of "stretch" assignment which plaintiffs, applying the rules to the assignments and positions as they now saw them, would not produce on their own.

That the language used about the firm in litigation should be the language of the firm in operation is not universally understood, or perhaps not accepted. Here, the defendant in an equal-employment-opportunity suit is Sodexho-Marriott. Plaintiffs' expert is Bernard Siskin:

> Defendant argues that Siskin . . . does not know how different divisions in the company function. . . . Plaintiffs respond that Siskin's analyses did not require intimate familiarity with the inner workings of Sodexho, because as a statistician, his job was to look to the company's own internal data in determining what constituted a promotion.[128]

Plaintiffs concept of "accuracy" is that their expert can reflect back the numbers he was provided, even if he does not know what they mean. A judge should reject this kind of argument, asking if Siskin is using the word "promotion" with the same meaning it has at the firm. Judge Huvelle does not see it my way:

> As a statistician working with company-supplied data, Siskin does not need an understanding of "what the laundry operation does or how it conducts its operations."

---

128. McReynolds (2004b) at 38; following indented quotation also at 38, with internal quotation from Defendant's Motion to Exclude Plaintiffs' Expert at 22, note 7. Plaintiffs, also, complain that defendant's expert does not apply the appropriate data to her language:

> Plaintiffs strongly object to defendant's definition of promotion on the grounds that it is inconsistent with the company's own definition of a promotion, which requires that a candidate change jobs.

McReynolds (2004a), footnote 7. A word like "promotion" should have an agreed meaning prior to the submission of expert reports, even if that meaning is context-sensitive.

This is completely wrong, but understandable. Nowhere could the judge have found literature about the concepts of "accuracy" I have introduced in this book. The judge assumes that the expert manipulates numbers—I do mean "manipulates"—for the good of his client. Why does an expert have to actually know anything? And, indeed, this is the expectation experts live up to.

There is another problem about State Department data, which I suggested in Chapter 6 might have been true at the Social Rehabilitation Services, also. Recording often occurs long after the event occurred. Key-entry delays of six months are common at State. Worse, new entries are often erroneous. The errors are discovered and corrected again months later. So now, looking at the computerized data, we know that a particular officer was at Grade A and in location X on a given date. No one looking at the data at the time would have known that, however. Which is accurate, the situation as it *was* at any particular time, or the situation as it was *recorded* in the data source at the time? Plaintiff's expert, Joan Haworth, had no idea what I was talking about. "Just give us accurate data," she said, perturbed that I could not understand and comply with such a simple request.

Because, during the assignment process, the Foreign Service officer makes clear to his career development officer his true state of affairs, we might expect that correct information was in front of decision makers. To analyze assignments, then, we want to have a concept of accuracy that correctly places the Foreign Service officer where he was, and accords to him the skills he had acquired (language and other training, for example). "Accuracy" in assignment is what was, not what documents then said was, and not what documents now say was.

The papers that go before a promotion board are derived from the computer files. Both retroactive actions and late key-entry changes distort the record as it appeared to members of the promotion board. To some extent the officer is allowed to doctor his paper, perhaps in some awareness that the computer file is not always accurate, but preventing us from knowing what the promotion board sees unless we code directly from promotion folders. Although we know that some of this doctoring is done, not all Foreign Service officers are around Washington to do it. They have no local advocate in the promotion process, as they do in the assignment process.

We should call for a different concept of "accuracy" if we want to test bias in decisions by the promotion board. We should test those decisions against the paper those board members would have seen, which is likely to be closer to the computer files of that date (contemporaneous accuracy) than the facts of that date (historical accuracy). The computer files as later corrected (current accuracy) may be of some use, for some people; but as revised through grievance they would distort our picture of the decision process at the time decisions were made.

Not only data leading to the promotion, but the promotion decision itself, requires conceptualization. "Promotion" is an event on one's record, isn't it? Not necessarily. Selection for promotion by a promotion board only starts a process, which involves several other stages (including a greater language-skill requirement) that some Foreign Service officers failed. No one ever complained that these later processes were racially biased. Others, who should have been considered "promoted" as a management decision, left the foreign service before all other requirements had been met. Therefore, selection for promotion was a better definition of "promotion," for purposes of analyzing discrimination, than promotion itself, much as "offer" is a better measure of "hire" than hire records, and "selected for termination" was better than "terminated" at Polaroid.

Joan Haworth and her staff understood none of these issues. My proposal required her understanding, because unless both experts agreed to use different data for different issues—and agreed why they did so—the conflicting data concepts were certain to cause confusion. Plaintiffs would show that a person was at one grade for one of my analyses, at a different grade at the same time in a different analysis. "Michelson's data cannot be relied upon," they would say, "and therefore neither can his conclusions." Few judges would then let me explain why, and fewer yet would understand. I insisted that plaintiffs needed to agree about these things. They never did.

For good reason. It was better for them as protagonists if they just held out for "accurate" data, as the data correctly used supported nothing they claimed. "Accuracy" sounds important to a judge, and my different-grades-depending-on-the-analysis data base would be deemed to be inaccurate. Nuance, sophistication: Forget about it. Think of the litigation debate as on the level of political debates. The best one-liner wins. As I wrote in Chapter 6, the process would be better if data transfer were smooth, including the transfer of relevant information about how to use the data. But that assumes that the parties, at least the experts, are striving to determine the truth. My attempt to convince the Washington, D. C., United States Attorney's office that it would be more efficient to cooperate with plaintiffs on data issues failed. They never again provided "stipulated" data to plaintiffs. I don't blame them.

What's in a Name?

If litigation is about procedures, so should remedy be. Not only the experts, but the parties too focus on outcomes. The black plaintiffs in *Thomas* (1991) did not want equal promotion procedures, they wanted proportionate promotions. As "promotion" in the State Department is many procedures, there is no remedy unless one knows which procedure is failing, if any is. This is why my approach in the promotion cases was to chart out *all* the ways one could get a promotion, analyze each one separately, and then appropriately aggregate to one summary conclusion. Plaintiffs' approach—no surprise—was to define a simple promotion metric and show that blacks did not get "their share" of them.[129]

The first thing the expert should do is pierce through the attorney's language, much of which may be the language of the attorney's client, to determine what the complaint is about, what the law is about, and therefore what the real variables of interest are. Litigation in which a statistical expert is involved is almost always about procedure. Data are about events or outcomes. Stating the issue as "accuracy" fails to see the problem. The issue, rather, is tailoring the analysis to the complaint, finding data that reflect the procedures being complained about. Litigation experts seem to be particularly inept at this task.

ASSESSING THE EXPERT

Charles Mann presents himself as an honest expert. Describing the litigation environment, he wisely notes:

> Not surprisingly, an adversarial relationship may develop between the statistician and opposing counsel. More surprisingly, an adversarial relationship may develop between the statistician and the opposing statistician. Most surprising, however, is that a form of adversarial relationship may develop between the consultant and the retaining attorneys (those by whom he has been hired).[130]

Mann then wants us to be sympathetic with the weakness of the expert's position:

> The attorneys seek to present their client's case. The statistician might like to present what he considers to be the best explanation and interpretation of the data, but is generally allowed only that which counsel considers to be supportive of the client's cause.

---

129. Blacks sued Honda of America, Inc., alleging unequal promotion. To be promoted to team leader, one had to spend a year as a production associate in the same department. Plaintiffs' expert James Mc-Clave ignored the departmental distribution of blacks, seniority, and requests for promotion (which called for a multiple-pools analysis). He asked only that blacks be promoted in proportion to their presence in the work force. McClave also ignored the requirement for on-time attendance. *Bacon* (2004) at 577:

> Plaintiffs' expert found that more African-Americans than other employees were noted as being late or absent. . . . Plaintiffs overlook the fact that the basic attendance records are generated by computer time clocks.

They were counted as late because they were late. Outcome thinking begets outcome activism. Eugene Volokh tells us that Laura Blackburne, when chief counsel for the New York NAACP,

> sued Rupert Murdoch on grounds that it wasn't fair to let a foreigner own a TV station when so few blacks owned TV stations.

She later became Justice Laura Blackburne, a New York State judge. See the archives of *The Volokh Conspiracy*, http://volokh.com, from June 15, 2004.

130. C. Mann (2000) at 246; following indented quotation also at 246.

During cross-examination, the expert cannot control the questions that are asked, and judges want short, simple answers. In that forum, I agree with Mann. But the expert should control his own direct examination; and in one's report one not only may but should offer a complete picture. However, the system's incentives argue against it.

> An expert witness who truly believes that there are persuasive arguments on both sides of the case, and who is determined to present both sides to the best degree possible, is very unlikely to appear as a witness for either side.[131]

Mann agrees, stating that

> a statistician who insists on providing a report identifying all observations and conclusions, both supporting and opposing his client's position, should expect to be replaced.[132]

While analyzing Rhode Island's jury selection, for example, my draft report contained the following sentence:

> If defendant is looking for a procedure that has a disparate impact on minorities, however, first-class mailing of questionnaires appears to be one.

A reviewer in the attorney general's office wrote: "Why give this to them?" My answer: Because it is true. Indeed, because it is obvious. I properly defined my client's job: Argue that, though it does have a disparate impact, first-class mail is the most efficient reasonable way to send jury notices to residents.[133] The disparate impact occurs from the transient behavior of minorities, not from anyone's discriminatory behavior. I have done *my* job, determining what element in the system lines up with the reduction in Hispanics and blacks from source lists to juries. The statement remained in my report.[134]

Form vs. Substance

As a general rule, I find the following indicia related to expert performance.

> **Conception.** Has the problem been well-framed, so that the statistical work has a chance of informing the judge about what he wants to know?
>
> **Data.** Are the data well-conceived and well-gathered, about the best information one could find at reasonable cost?

---

131. Chesler et al. (1988) at 120.

132. C. Mann (2000) at 246.

133. As noted in Chapter 5, the Federal Judicial Center has recommended first-class mailing. See Shapard (1981).

134. The judge made nothing of it. See *Tremblay* (2003). Judge Posner thought the fact that drug companies were price discriminators was so obvious he wondered why expert-in-waiting Robert Lucas billed for forty hours of work to find that out. See *Drugs* (1999). Lucas, as plaintiffs' expert, surely thought his pronouncement would be dismissed if he made it without study. The expert can be ridiculed either way.

Method. Has the expert selected a statistical procedure well-fitted to the issue and data, one that has a chance to answer the question being asked?

Technique. Is the work well-done? Were the issues that come up in an analysis, large and small, well-handled and well-explained?

Interpretation. Does the language reflect the work done? Does it properly describe conclusions and the strength with which they can be held?

Presentation. Is the report well-organized and carefully produced? Is it readable as a story? Does it contain clean, clear, appropriate graphics?

When I saw Richard Levins' report in *Gerena* (1987), from a nine-pin dot-matrix printer with bad punctuation and misspellings, I was sure the content would be flawed. It was. After my response, he was dropped from the case.[135] There were so many inaccuracies and incomprehensible sentences in Andrew Beveridge's analysis of Rhode Island jury selection that I created a separate appendix to deal with them.[136]

Following these principles, I did not hire job applicants to my firm whose résumé contained any error. Grammar, spelling, non-uniformity of presentation: Any error eliminated the candidate. My view was that if you are not a perfectionist when presenting yourself, what chance do I have of getting you to do careful analyses for my clients? But is this really a job-related measure, a valid screening device? I could not test it extensively, but I did once hire a senior analyst despite errors in her résumé. She was the worst hire I ever made at that level. I asked her to leave, and followed my disqualification rule rigorously thereafter.

National Economic Research Associates (NERA), in *Crow I*, also failed my indexes. In addition to my problems with Mark Berkman's regression analysis—described in Chapter 3 under "Crow Coal"—and the sloppy appearance of his report, I could not derive his data from his sources, his equation from his data, nor his estimates from his equation. In Berkman's data there was no production in Montana in 1970 and 1971, then 0.8 million tons in 1972 and 4.2 million tons in 1973. These shipments came from one mine, the Decker mine, which first shipped coal on August 22, 1972.[137] What is the measure of coal

---

135. My response was contained in a joint affidavit with Timothy Wyant, April 8, 1987. This observation, that form implies content, is not unique to me or to this field. Neil Hornick, a professional literary consultant, writes in the December 19/26, 2003, issue of *The Bookseller* (Bookseller Publications, VNU Business Publications, London), in an article titled, "'Have I Wet Your Appetite?'" at 24:

> Most professional readers will confirm that you don't necessarily have to read a word of a typescript to be able to tell that it's a hopeless case.

136. Exhibit C of "Affidavit of Stephan Michelson" in *Tremblay* (2003), dated January 7, 2002. Bad writing reflects bad thinking. Although Judge Krause did not appreciate my efforts, I do not see how, faced with an expert's errors, I can let them go without making a record. That record, though, is properly appendix material.

137. This information is in the Keystone manual, and thus was easily available to NERA.

supposed to represent? Is annual data supposed to represent a rate of coal flow? If so, it would be reasonable to inflate the partial-year production to represent the annual rate at which Montana was shipping coal in 1972. Berkman needed a data *concept*, but, like most experts, he thought data were just numbers.

As *Crow* was about the effect of Montana's tax rate on coal production, the other data element that should have been "accurate" was the tax rate. Determining effective tax rate is difficult. Some coal is taxed by weight, other coal by price, though by different prices (mine-mouth, delivered, etc.). Different experts could honestly bring different tax series into court. A judge would find this frustrating, to say the least. If the parties cannot agree on what the tax rate was, how can he rule on its effect? I disagreed with NERA's calculations. Had I been part of that case from the beginning, I would have argued to try to reach agreement with plaintiffs on each effective tax rate. Perhaps I would have failed as badly as I did with State Department data. I still believe, however, that experts should try to agree on fundamental metrics. They should not be debating at trial how to determine when an employee receives a promotion. If they cannot get to this agreement, and use common data, the judge's first order of business should be to determine whose data shall be accepted.

Multiple Tests 1

I have mentioned several times, particularly in Chapter 6 and at the start of this chapter, that multiple tests cause a problem. The probabilities that are reported in computer printout, and then attached to one's work, are simply incorrect if one does multiple tests. Richard Lempert points out:

> If one looks at twenty independent random samples for an effect, it is not unusual for one to find a sample in which the effect appears at the 0.05 level simply as a result of random variation.[138]

David Kaye and David Freedman warn federal judges:

> Repeated applications of significance testing complicate the interpretation of a significance level. If enough studies are conducted, random error almost guarantees that some will yield significant findings, even when there is no real effect.[139]

They go on to advise that "There are statistical methods for coping with multiple looks at the data, which permit the calculation of meaningful p-values in certain cases." I doubt that most judges can make sense of this on its own, but perhaps it gives an expert something to

---

138. Lempert (1985) at 1114. Unfortunately, Lempert is talking about finding "too few" women in a work force. His statement about probability is correct, but he misses the point of the law, which is about events (hires), not situations (employees).

139. Kaye and Freedman in *Reference Manual* (1994) at 383.

refer to when making a point about interpretation of probabilities.

Kaye and Freedman are concerned that an expert may have done several studies before the one presented to the court. Robert Follett and Finis Welch go further back, questioning which cases are brought.

> If the 0.05 rule were applied separately to two independent employment practices tests in tests for discrimination, the chance that one of the two would fail—even with neutral treatment—is about 0.10. In fact, if the 0.05 rule were applied to fourteen independent practices, the chance is about 50-50 that one or more would fail, even with neutral treatment.[140]

A review of potential defendants, and selection of a few of them, can occur before the plaintiffs' expert has been engaged.

> Thus, analysis of an individual practice in isolation can lead to a mistaken inference of discrimination if the practice that is scrutinized is chosen because it presents the statistics that are least favorable to an employer.

> This selection of the most unflattering practices for analysis is exactly what happens in many EEO law suits.

The Office of Federal Contract Compliance Programs does thousands of "utilization" reviews regularly, and objects when any division of any firm has a "significant" disparity, as it sees the world, from the "available" labor force. The result is essentially a quota system. Faced with only these data, not inquiring how this case came about, an expert engaged by the OFCCP will report probabilities as if they were the result of a single test. The expert who asks if this case is the result of prior statistical testing, and adjusts his probabilities on that basis, will not be invited back.

Unfortunately, there is now literature suggesting that the OFCCP is under no obligation to adjust its "screening" for multiple tests. Supposing that a particular fiber is found at a crime scene, Michael Finkelstein and Bruce Levin ask if a match of a carpet fiber in a suspect's home, one of twenty samples, can be associated with the known frequency of such fibers in carpets, one in five hundred. Their (correct) answer is no, because taking twenty samples reduces the probability of finding this fiber by chance to one in twenty-five. If I were designing the sample, I would specify it in two stages—multiple samples taken from each of multiple carpets. Perhaps one sample per carpet is sufficient if the sample is large enough, but they carelessly write as if each sample is of but one thread, and seem to assume one sample per carpet.[141] The only issue here is existence, and that is what

---

140. Follett and Welch (1983) at 175; following indented quotation also at 175; third indented quotation at 183.

141. As I am surely the only statistical analyst on the planet who produces fabrics from his own industrial looms, Finkelstein and Levin are playing on my turf. As I warned above, the expert should

the sample should be designed to detect: Did the suspect have access to the critical fibers? The testing affirms that he did.

Finkelstein and Levin then offer this alternative example:

> One fiber is collected from each of the 20 homes in the neighborhood, and one of the fibers, that of neighbor Jones, is found to match the crime scene evidence.[142]

They conclude that the chance probability one in five hundred need not be reduced for Jones,

> because in this case the probability in question is not whether *any* one of twenty matches would be made, but whether Jones' fiber would match.

They argue that finding Jones from a random search is the statistical equivalent of taking one sample from Jones' home *after* having identified him as a suspect. The chance probability remains one in five hundred. I disagree. There is no such equivalence.

Apparently Finkelstein and Levin would agree with my *Firestone* (1981) example in Chapter 6, where seventeen samples were taken inside one firm; but apparently they would uphold the OFCCP's inter-firm search practice. Suppose the OFCCP searches the files of one thousand firms and finds a work force more than two standard deviations different from their "availability" measure in fifty of them. They take action against half of those firms. "This large a difference would be found, by chance, in only fifty firms in a thousand non-discriminating firms," their expert would state at each trial, ignoring the fact that it *was* found in only fifty out of a thousand firms.[143]

---

indeed know his subject matter. Let's say the basic unit of manufacture is a thread. A thread may be composed of different kinds of fibers, but not necessarily all that are in the rug. Threads serve different functions in woven rugs, such as warp, weft color, weft binder, etc., and that is not considering any special treatment at the edge. Rugs may be constructed in other ways, such as "hand-tufting," where threads are shot through a backing by a special gun. Without sampling the backing, one has not sampled the rug.

In weaving, many weft threads are available at each "pick," each pass of the shuttle or rapier. The frequency with which any one is used depends on the design. A sample wide enough to capture every warp yarn may not be tall enough to capture every weft yarn. There is no mechanical restriction on where and how often particular fibers are used in either woven or tufted rugs. That is, a random sample is the wrong kind of sample to take in this situation.

142. Finkelstein and Levin (2003) at 267; following indented quotation and then in-text quotation also at 267.

143. As Judge Easterbrook wrote in *Mister* (1987), at 1437:

> In a world with 1,000 employers, 50 will meet this [0.05] criterion of significance by chance. These will become targets of litigation, and courts are apt to find discrimination in all 50 cases even though by hypothesis none of the 1,000 employers is discriminating.

If the 0.05 "significance" level is a two-tail probability, only half of those disparities will appear adverse to minorities. Thus only twenty-five cases will be filed.

Finkelstein and Levin might also agree with Franklin Fisher's use of unadjusted statistics in regression after regression on individual workers in *O'Keefe* (1996), with which I opened this chapter, "because there were no multiple comparisons *for the identified individual.*"[144] The laws of probability, they would have us believe, work differently if you flip one coin twenty times, from flipping twenty coins once each. Not so.

The Finkelstein-Levin example can be distinguished from the OFCCP example because Finkelstein and Levin know that a crime has been committed. The OFCCP does not know if a "crime" has been committed. That is what they want to determine. We know that they will find evidence of one, even if there has been none, if they look in enough places. That is why Fisher, also, should have accounted for multiple tests, even though they were made on different individuals. Perhaps no worker cheated.

Finding a fiber in Jones' house that is similar to that at the crime scene only satisfies an existence criterion in all of Finkelstein and Levin's examples. Every fiber match creates a suspect, no matter how it was derived, no matter how many other suspects there are, from whatever other evidence. From the fiber match alone, we do not know how good a suspect any one of them is, or even if the guilty party is among them, even though we know there has been a crime. No probability calculation is called for.[145]

Whatever distinction Finkelstein and Levin might legitimately make, the one they articulate is wrong. They come close to the correct answer by suggesting that a large search is made from a population that certainly (this is a hypothetical, after all) includes the guilty party. Ten similar fibers are found, including Jones'. Now, they say, the probability that Jones did it is one in ten. Even accepting their impossible knowledge that the guilty party is among those sampled, I still don't agree.[146] If their point is that it makes no difference

---

144. Finkelstein and Levin (2003) at 289, emphasis in the original.

145. When photographs appeared showing O. J. Simpson wearing Bruno Magli shoes—the kind his wife's murderer wore, which he had denied owning—the general reaction was correct: This information showed that he could have been the murderer, but did not inform us about the probability that he was. Taking the other side for a moment, suppose only one pair of those shoes (at that size) had been made, and sold to Simpson. Then he was the murderer. Suppose two pair were made, and sold to different people. Then one of them is the murderer. If the police can track every pair ever made, then they have a complete list of suspects; and if they cannot, they have an incomplete list of suspects, but suspects nonetheless.

Suppose too many shoes were made to track. We survey the three hundred closest houses and find two other pair. Again, existence: Simpson or one of the others could have been the murderer, but they all might not be. If we double the sample size and find only one more pair, we have one more suspect, and that is all. The shoes satisfy a necessary condition, but do not provide probabilistic information. The size of our sample and the number of pairs of those shoes sold (if large) are both irrelevant.

146. They have not accounted for sampling error. Their footnote 8 discusses only testing error, which I (with them) am willing to assume away. Sampling error is more important.

how large a sample they took, and it makes no difference what the "prior" odds were, they are correct. We do not know how many members of the population have those fibers although, as in Chapter 5, we have done a survey and can make an estimate. More important, the sampling may have missed the fibers that would have fingered the guilty party. The guilty party is in the population, but not necessarily among those for whom we have found consistent fibers. All ten, including Jones, may be innocent, which means that Finkelstein and Levin's probability calculation must be incorrect.

Their ill-conceived example is of little practical import. Still, it illustrates that in many situations the information in a match itself cannot be quantified. In such cases there is no multiple-test correction to be made, not made, or argued about. If they are nonetheless determined to use the fiber match in a probability model, Finkelstein and Levin should not ignore that they did a lot of looking. To find a matching fiber from many looks is not as improbable as a matter of chance as if they had found it with only one look. Probability does not matter if the match leads you to the guilty party. But all matches might be coincidence, and the guilty party may have been missed in the vagaries of sampling. Finkelstein and Levin should know that.[147]

Multiple Tests 2

Recall the discussion of *Harris Bank* (1981) in Chapter 3. Defendant's expert Harry Roberts tested many "micro-regressions," defining sub-populations based on entry cohort to see if there was any way to dissolve the variable that kept showing that females, other things considered, were underpaid. I saw no discussion in his papers of the fact that he was doing many tests. The probabilities associated with the female coefficients in different regressions were not correct, there being so many of them. A summary statistic over all cohort regressions was needed. Roberts never offered one.

Can the implications from multiple tests be put to some advantage? Not as easily as Peter Sperlich and Martin Jaspovice think. They suggest a way to test discrimination in the composition of juries from a series of venires.

> The fact that at a 0.05 level of significance, an unbiased selection system on the average will produce by chance only one significant outcome in twenty separate selections defines the optimal number of panels for a serial test: *twenty*. A

147. Finkelstein and Levin (2003) continue their example, arguing for a Bayesian approach to assessing the probability of Jones' guilt. They start with the multiple test issue because they want to justify the one-in-five-hundred figure as the basis of their likelihood ratio, not corrected for the fact that they found Jones through a multiple-test procedure. Although I reject the logic by which they reject a multiple-test correction, I recommend their article both as a good introduction to the Bayesian approach to evidence, and as a good example of why, despite much fanfare, and some use in DNA evidence presentations, few Bayesian arguments are heard in courts to this day.

> sequence of twenty panels containing no significant outcome or only one significant outcome cannot be interpreted as discriminatory. A sequence of twenty panels must be interpreted as discriminatory if it contains two or more significant outcomes.[148]

Once again we have, to put it politely, nonsense.

There will never be "an optimum number" of observations in any study, except with regard to cost. A general principle is that the statistical benefit of a survey increases with the square root of the number of observations. More observations are *always* better, but additional accuracy, precision, power, whatever you want to measure, is more and more expensive on the margin. It is the budget constraint, physical constraints, and time constraints that force evidence gathering to stop.[149]

To penetrate the error by Sperlich and Jaspovice, we can easily calculate the likelihood of finding two or more green balls (their "significant outcomes") by chance, from twenty independent random selections from a large pool of 95 percent red and 5 percent green balls. The probability of zero or more green balls, of course, is 1.00. We can calculate the probability of one or more green balls by subtracting the probability of exactly zero (0.3585) to obtain 0.6415.[150] Subtracting the probability of exactly one green ball (0.3773) from that number[151] then leaves the probability of two or more: 0.2642. More than one time in four, random selection will look like discrimination under Sperlich and Jaspovice's test. These authors nonetheless would pass the Rule 702 criterion of having published their theory in a refereed journal!

The Test and the Model

No matter how many tests are done, whether correcting for multiple tests or not, the exercise is meaningless if the model is not appropriate. As Stephen Fienberg noted:

> Expert witnesses and judges often fail to take cognizance of the extent to which statistical models used to analyze employment data fail to capture the relevant aspects of the employment process. When they do so, standard tests of significance that ignore these aspects may be of little or no use, even as benchmarks. The burden of demonstrating the relevance of a statistical model

---

148. Sperlich and Jaspovice (1979) at 803.

149. Judge Jack Weinstein in *Agent Orange* (1985), at 1259:

   Courts cannot wait forever. They must decide cases now.

Oliver Wendell Holmes for the majority in *CB&Q* (1907), at 598:

   Somewhere there must be an end.

150. The large pool assures that draws from it do not affect the proportions of red and green balls remaining. To draw no green balls, we have to draw a red ball twenty times, or $p(0 \text{ green}) = 0.95^{20} = 0.3585$.

151. There are twenty chances to draw that one green ball, so $p(1) = 20 \times 0.95^{19} \times 0.05 = 0.3773$.

of the employment process should rest on the shoulders of those who would use the model for statistical purposes.[152]

We have seen expert after expert fail this simple criterion. Not "junk science" experts. Experts with serious credentials, presenting purportedly serious studies using widely accepted statistical procedures, finding "statistically significant" coefficients in meaningless regressions. Here is an illustration of Fienberg's concern.

When discrimination is alleged, over and above the rules in a collective bargaining agreement (CBA), one might expect the analyst, as does the foreman, to look first to those rules.

> For example, under the CBAs managers must normally offer overtime to employees who are present on the day of assignment, and Defendant alleges that the assignments for weekend overtime are typically made by Thursdays. . . . Dr. Siskin, however, considered only whether an employee had been present on Fridays.[153]

Finding other such dissimilarities between Siskin's analysis and how the plant actually operated, Judge Brown concluded:

> A statistical analysis which fails to control for equally plausible non-discriminatory factors overstates the comparison group and, under the facts of this case, cannot raise a question of fact for trial regarding discriminatory impact.

He then granted defendant's motion for summary judgment.

Single-pool selection studies show "significant" differences between plaintiffs and others that bear no relationship to the multiple-pools nature of the selection decisions. "Availability" analyses find "significant" differences between two stocks (employees and labor force, jurors and population) that bear no relationship to the events at issue. Like Lamberth's test of the race composition of arrests against the average "speeder," the results mean nothing because the comparison is faulty, even were the data not. A claim of "statistical significance" masks its meaninglessness when the model is not testing a legally relevant proposition from a realistic model of decision making with conceptually relevant and reasonably accurate data.

In litigation surrounding the tanker *Amoco-Cadiz*:

> Lewis Perl . . . presented a regression model by which he attempted to infer the lost consumer surplus—that is, the reduction in enjoyment consumers ob-

---

152. Fienberg (1986) at 44.

153. *Carpenter* (2004) at *11; following indented quotation also at *11. In considering a motion for summary judgment, the judge should assume that disputed facts are as the non-moving side states them. Therefore Judge Brown's grant of Boeing's motion did not rest solely on Siskin's failure to delve into procedural explanations for the disparities he found. Rather, Siskin's analysis supported only some of plaintiffs' claims. "Dr. Siskin's statistical analysis obviously places into question the viability of the Class," says the judge, at *3, and the opinion went downhill from there, from plaintiffs' view.

tained when they took their vacations in resorts other than their preferred destinations in Brittany.[154]

Consumers, however, were not parties in the case. Claimants were resorts which had lost business. Where did this expert get the idea that they could collect damages for the reduced satisfaction obtained by consumers in less-preferred venues? Did Perl's clients understand what he was doing?

THE EXPERT IN COURT

In Chapter 6 I explained that a client screens potential experts for compliance, for willingness to work towards this client's end. Filtered information is then provided to the expert to ensure that he will not learn anything the client thinks he "should not know." The expert and his client seldom engage in the "intellectual" exercise of defining the issues to obtain concepts of data and analysis that will seek out what can be learned about the controversy as a court will view it. Many experts fail to understand the institutional context of the data. The expert and his client do not interact on legal issues, only on factual issues, where the client determines which are which, and what the expert should be allowed to know.

A Catalog of Errors

Although presented with respect to forensic experts captive to their clients, the categorization of errors formulated by Michael Risinger, Michael Saks, William Thompson, and Robert Rosenthal is appropriate to statistical expertise, also:[155]

> Errors of apprehending (errors that occur at the stage of initial perception);
>
> Errors of recording (errors that creep in at the stage where what is observed is recorded, assuming a record beyond memory is even made);
>
> Errors of memory (errors that are induced by both desires and the need for schematic consistency, and that escalate over time when memory is relied on);
>
> Errors of computation (errors that occur when correct observations accurately recorded or remembered are transformed into incorrect results when calculations are performed on them); and

---

154. *Amoco-Cadiz* (1992) at 1321. Equally convincing to the Court was the notion that vacation trade lost to one venue was captured by another, and damages are to be awarded for loss, not for redistribution.

155. Risinger et al. (2002) at 25.

Errors of interpretation (errors that occur when examiners draw incorrect conclusions from the data).

These authors suggest, and I agree, that forensic experts should have little prior knowledge of the surrounding issues in a case. That is the opposite of what I call for with regard
to the privately engaged "science" expert. They also urge, and I also agree, that forensic analysts be given alternatives, so that their task would be to ferret out the relevant just as innocent people appear in an eyewitness "lineup" as a kind of control. Thus the captive forensic expert is a different creature from the experts that are the main subject of this book. He
will have his own section in Chapter 10.

Keeping the statistical analyst ignorant is not a healthy way to proceed with discovery. Risinger et al. make no attempt to apply their model beyond their forensic bounds.
Nonetheless, this categorization is informative and generally applicable to the kinds of errors
I have been exposing in statistical analyses. If keeping the expert ignorant is a safeguard for
one kind of expert, yet inapplicable to the statistical analyst, what can substitute for it?

Alternative Explanations

Plaintiff's attorney has more than a hypothesis. He has a complaint. The complaint is that
X causes Y. Like too many forensic analysts, many a statistical analyst thinks that finding
a relationship between X and Y assists his client. He does not ask, "What causes Y?" He asks,
"Is there any evidence that X causes Y?" The result is a failure to test alternative explanations for Y.[156] The forensic expert should be provided with alternative subjects in addition
to the suspect. The science, social-science, or statistical expert has to dig deeply to find and
test plausible alternatives. His client will not provide them.

William Mitchell was engaged by William Cooper in his suit claiming damages from use
of the Rogozinski System to fuse his spine. It took three operations to accomplish the task,
during which time (as for twenty-five years previously) Cooper smoked a pack of cigarettes
a day (a well-known inhibitor of spinal fusion), despite the pleas of his doctors to quit.

> Dr. Mitchell's methodology simply failed to provide any medical evidence as
> to what caused Cooper's specific injuries. Rather, Dr. Mitchell seems to have
> inferred causation from the existence of a nonunion alone.[157]

One of the pedicle screws put in place was found, two years later, to have fractured.
Mitchell assumed that the fracture was a fault, and a cause of the failed union.

---

156. "The courts distrust arguments predicated on the presence or absence of a single factor." Good
(2001) at 209. Indeed, the Advisory Committee notes accompanying modification of Federal Rule of
Evidence 702, in 2000, included asking whether the expert had considered alternative explanations as a
factor for survival of the testimony under *Daubert*.

157. Cooper (2001a) at 201; following indented quotations at 201 and 202.

Dr. Mitchell's causation theory failed to address the possibility that the screw fracture was caused by the nonunion.

Thus, if an expert utterly fails to consider alternative causes or fails to offer an explanation for why the proffered alternative cause was not the sole cause, a district court is justified in excluding the expert's testimony.

Margaret Schmerling had "been plagued with back problems since the age of eleven," for which she had undergone at least six operations, including four spinal fusions all utilizing pedicle screws. She engaged James Woessner, who produced a report of summary conclusions supporting her contention of fraudulent misrepresentation and a host of other errors by the manufacturer of the fourth set of rods and screws. Despite her history, "Dr. Woessner does not attempt to rule out alternate causes for her symptoms." As her case lacked "sufficient competent evidence," Judge Waldman dismissed it.[158]

The Supreme Court was correctly unimpressed by a "study" of twenty-four arrests of minorities for drug charges, when defendants alleged selective prosecution.

The study failed to identify individuals who were not black and could have been prosecuted for the offenses for which respondents were charged, but were not so prosecuted.[159]

To show that prosecution was racially "selective" requires describing a pool from which they were selected. The pool should contain persons of another race "similarly situated" but treated differently. This decision, *Armstrong* (1996), has set the standard by which lower courts approach seemingly disparate outcomes that might have been affected by disparate individual behavior. Unfortunately, some experts seem not to understand it, if they even know about it.

One New Jersey judge, we have seen, thought that all cars driving on the same road were "similarly situated." However, the point of stopping a speeding car is that it is *not* like other cars. The standard selection model, comparing who was selected to who among otherwise equals might have been, is inappropriate. John Lamberth, the expert in *Soto* (1996), the New Jersey case, did not learn from *Armstrong*. Engaged by two black defendants, Lamberth placed his staff in Chicago's Union Station over a period of twelve days in 1999. They counted 726 travelers, of whom 119 were black, of whom two, a black couple, were accosted and escorted away by Amtrak police. Lamberth reported

---

158. *Schmerling* (1999), first two quotations at *6, the last at *10. A similar situation, in which a screw fracture was assigned, by plaintiff's experts, to faulty manufacture, can be found in *Muller* (2001). Her experts, also, were excluded. See also *McCorvey* (2002), at 1256, concerning an erupted catheter, in which an engineering expert "did not consider or test possibilities for failure that could have come from sources outside the product."

159. *Armstrong* (1996) at 470. This case was referred to in my discussion of "driving while black." See, for example, notes 73, 87, and 94, above.

the probability that all four individuals approached would be African American to be less than 8 times in 10,000.[160]

Besides this being irrelevant (the defendants had been arrested by federal officials, not Amtrak police), both district-court and appeals-court judges understood that not all passengers were "equally situated" with the defendants, who had been caught hauling cocaine. Lamberth had tested no reason other than race why the police might have approached these people.[161] His clients went to jail.

In *Porter* (1992), a pharmacologist, David Benjamin, was prepared to testify that ibuprofen caused plaintiff's fatal disease. There were of course other possible causes (indeed, it is not clear that ibuprofen could be one), but Benjamin did not consider them. His "evidence" was blatantly unreliable, and so he was not allowed to testify. When Kenneth Court looked only at ordinary use by its owner to explain how a ladder (on a boat that had been chartered out!) had become bent, the Fourth Circuit noted:

> There are too many alternate theories of causation for Mr. Court's theory to establish causation by a preponderance of the evidence.[162]

---

160. *Barlow* (2002) at 1011. These are the circuit court's words, not necessarily Lamberth's. To what extent the staff's racial identification was reliable is unreported. Four individuals? Lamberth added the defendants, and so counted four persons accosted by police. (He was in fact engaged by only one of them, a detail too fine for the text.) This is absurd. We do not know four of how many. (If you use two observations from 1999, surely selecting which ones by their outcome cannot be justified). Judge Zagel appropriately called the procedure "statistically indefensible." See *Barlow* (2004) at *2.

Lamberth is not the first "expert" to select his clients as his observations in a study purporting to reach general conclusions. For example, in *Valentine* (1996), at 676, plaintiffs' expert Kaye Kilburn

> studied only seven people, all of whom, incidentally, were, at least at one point, involved in the litigation arising out of the accident.

Kilburn's testimony was excluded.

Experts and those assessing them should heed Judge Goodwin's dictum in *CSX* (2004), at 851:

> The purpose of using statistical tests is to eliminate guesswork and to give inductive logic a mathematical footing. This means that statistical tests must remain completely objective, and the choices made by a statistician in constructing a test must be supported by some evidence or data.

161. Although it is overkill, I will mention other issues.

First, Lamberth added the plaintiffs to his count of those selected, but failed to add those not selected to the pool from which selections were made. The selections Lamberth observed were only 1.2 standard deviations from race-proportional, although as we "expect" selection of fractional people, even this difference requires interpretation.

Second, what was the stopping rule of the sample? Did the study end when blacks were arrested?

Third, it is not clear that an "individual" is the proper unit of analysis, just as "patients" was not the proper unit of analysis in *Bryan* (1980), discussed in Chapter 6. In both cases of police interaction, the two individuals accosted were traveling together. The four people are covered by only two events. Lamberth's study fails at the level of determining what to measure.

162. *Higginbotham* (2004) at 916.

Similarly, a court did not appreciate that Robert Hall, a Stanford professor and plaintiff's expert, looked at only one explanation for overcharging:

> The only independent variable in [Hall's] formula [to determine over-charge] was Brunswick's stern drive market share.[163]

Natalie Calhoun's parents alleged that the throttle design on a Yamaha Wavejammer jet ski caused her fatal accident. One of their experts "possessed expertise in relevant fields, [but] failed to apply this expertise to the matter at hand."

> Dr. Warren acknowledged he could have conducted tests to evaluate the relative merits of alternative throttle designs but did not do so.[164]

In an age-discrimination case, Philip A. Smethurst

> failed to account for possible nondiscriminatory reasons for the disparities that he found. . . . [T]he failure to account for possible nondiscriminatory reasons for statistical disparities can render an expert's opinion practically worthless.[165]

In another, plaintiffs offered the testimony of Richard Wertheimer, a labor economist.

> Wertheimer's analysis fails to account for any other independent variable that might explain the association between age and termination rates, including job skills, education, experience, or self-selection.[166]

When Hispanics complained of being under-promoted, their expert, Benz,

> admitted to failing to consider other variables such as education and experience as explanations for any observed discrepancy between promotion rates.[167]

His testimony was excluded.

Alan Baquet, an agricultural economist who was "an adequately qualified expert witness" acknowledged "that he had neglected to consider any variables other than the introduction of the Risinger fullbloods" to explain the price decline for full-blood Simmental cows.[168] He, too, was not allowed to testify.

---

163. *Concord Boat* (2000) at 1047.

> Dr. Hall postulated that in a stern drive market that was competitive, Brunswick and some other firm would maintain a 50% market share. Under his theory, any market share over 50% would be evidence of anticompetitive behavior on Brunswick's part.

164. *Calhoun* (2003) at 324.

165. *Wado* (1998) at 184 and 185, 75 FEP Cases at 1812. This opinion also contains a review of other cases in which an expert failed to consider alternative explanations for an apparent disparity.

166. *Adams* (1998) at 1101. Motion to exclude Wertheimer's testimony was granted.

167. *Muñoz* (2000) at 301.

168. *Blue Dane* (1999) at 1040.

Harriet Zellner had noted that, among families investigated by New York City's Administration of Child Services (ACS), a higher percentage of children from black families than from white families were remanded to foster care.

> Zellner's statistical evidence does not make it any more or less likely that it is ACS's policy or custom to discriminate against African-Americans. . . . The reason for this is that other factors may account for the disparity. . . . Courts have repeatedly held that statistical analyses that fail, as Zellner's does, to control for any nondiscriminatory explanations are inadmissible.[169]

Years before *Daubert*, the analyses in a famous antitrust case did

> not even purport to take into account any characteristics of defendants' television receivers other than screen size and monochrome and color status, thus ignoring both technical differences among models of receivers sold domestically or exported and other differences such as cabinet size and style.[170]

This single-minded view was unacceptable to the court, and ended in the failure of plaintiffs to prove that Zenith was dumping, rather than meeting market competition.

Experts in medicine and discrimination seem particularly shortsighted in asking what "caused" their client's real problems. Excluding the testimony of Grace Ziem, although "there are no real questions as to Dr. Ziem's qualifications to testify as an expert,"[171] Judge Quillen wrote:

> The fatal flaw in Dr. Ziem's temporal association with the building is that she refused to adequately consider, and eliminate, other possible causes of the Plaintiffs' illnesses through a definitive scientific process.

From three discrimination cases:

> In *Sheehan* the court held that the plaintiff's statistical expert had . . . failed to consider that anything other than age could have contributed to the company's employment decisions.

> The EEOC's expert used a very simple demographic model. Applicant's race was the only variable considered in the model. . . . In this case, the underlying hypothesis is faulty because considerations of applicant preference were totally ignored.

> [The expert's] so-called "preliminary" statistical analysis of race taint in the CEQs makes *no effort* to account for nondiscriminatory explanations for

---

169. *Bonton* (2004) at *3 and *4. It is not clear if Judge Scheindlin is paraphrasing defendant's expert, Philip Bobko, or going off on his own, based on Kaye and Freedman (1994). He is correct to call for a multivariate analysis, but regression, which he suggests, would be inappropriate. His error is discussed in Chapter 3, that of trying to apply a situation analysis to selection events.

170. *Zenith* (1981) at 1353.

171. *Minner* (2000) at 848; following indented quotation at 854.

the disparity, such as class size or class level. Without attempting to control for such other causes, her assumption that race bias affected the CEQs is untenable.[172]

Characters in a Play

I am not as bothered by "corrupt" attorneys as one might infer from Chapter 6. Reforming that profession is not on my agenda. Attorneys want the most that they can get from their "experts," the least of which is expertise.

> There is no reason to hire an expert, for example, who will tell the jury that a client's losses are worth $150,000 if an attorney can find an equally credible expert willing to testify that the true figure is $300,000.[173]

Perhaps their duty as advocates requires plaintiffs' attorney to hire experts who aim high, and defendants' attorneys to hire experts who aim low. It's the system. *Whadya gonna do?*

Attorneys are corrupt only in the sense that they do not seek truth. But neither do they claim to. They are not the bad guys of my story. Judges are clearly the good guys. Some screw up, usually because they fail to apply basic rules. (For example: Either party must show that the other's errors affect the outcome of the study. To "explain," a variable must be valid. Data need not be perfect, but error should be accounted for in one's statistical presentation.) Their motivations are good, their brainpower is enormous, and they are human. They react to other things than just the evidence. I wish it were not so; perhaps *they* wish it were not so. But it is.

The bad guys in this drama are the experts, most of whom fit a case into a procrustean mold created by the limits of their methodological knowledge and their client's position. Donald McCloskey writes:

> Economists spend a lot of time worrying whether their metaphors—they call them "models"—meet rigorous standards of logic. They worry less whether their stories—they call them "stylized facts," a phrase that makes tiresome trips to the library unnecessary—meet rigorous standards of fact.[174]

Even if you grant him his premise (that economists' models are rigorous)—which I do not —this is not good preparation to be a fact expert in litigation.

Because the expert is told to be ignorant of the law, his methods, besides being in-

---

172. First quotation from *Gerlib* (2002) at *7, referring to *Sheehan* (1997); second quotation from *Lamp* (1991) at 301, 57 FEP Cases at 415; third quotation from *Bickerstaff* (1999) at 450, 81 FEP Cases at 633. "CEQs" are course-evaluation questionnaires. The court in *Sheehan*, at 942, criticized the proffered expert for "his equating a simple statistical correlation to a causal relation." See also *Janes* (2002), where a similar point is made, also quoting *Sheehan*.

173. D. Bernstein (2001) at 403.

174. McCloskey (1990) at 23.

stitutionally irrelevant, may well be legally irrelevant. Yet some courts feel free to disparage experienced experts, preferring what they call the "academic," whom I refer to as the "amateur." Where else are less applied knowledge and less practical experience preferred traits?

Well-meaning, predisposed to believe that his plaintiff-client had been harmed, we encounter an expert named Gittelson:

> Dr. Gittelson testified that he had no knowledge of the meaning or accuracy of the data he was given. . . . Dr. Gittleson's testimony on the statistical significance of data compiled from Exhibits 103 and 104 can only be significant if the data are correct.[175]

Is this the same man, despite the difference in spelling, we saw in Chapter 6? The expert who accepted another case nine days before trial?

> Furthermore, the data furnished to Dr. Gittelsohn was not reviewed at all by him until the morning of the day on which he gave his testimony.[176]

Consider the presentation by George Bardwell:

> As a matter of "probability theory," Dr. Bardwell found that the chances of drawing a sample which contains 4.88% Chicanos from a jury wheel which actually contained 8.93% Chicanos is approximately seven chances in ten million. Although this figure is, to say the least, impressive, we believe it has little if any relevance to the legal issues now before us.[177]

And Charles Cranny:

> Dr. Cranny's criticisms of the content-validity study are entirely conclusory, are unsupported by any specific data, and are premised on the unsupportable factual assertion that the data were collected after the test had been administered.[178]

If it isn't relevant it cannot assist the trier of fact; and if it is of no assistance, it can be excluded.[179] The rules hold for professionals and academics alike.

Gene Fisher did not charge for his services, he said, because he is a college professor.

---

175. *Friend* (1977) at 365, 18 FEP Cases at 1033.

176. *Queen* (1978) at 264, 21 FEP Cases at 769. Gittelsohn is identified as an expert in biostatistics.

177. *Test* (1975) at 694. In *Drake* (2005), Charles Mann implied that there was something untoward about re-sampling his client for drug tests, although Judge Block noticed that Mann's own calculation showed that there wasn't.

178. *Williams* (1999) at 1182.

179. I paraphrase Rothstein (2002), interpreting the Federal Rules of Evidence, at 360. Weinstein (2001) states it more formally, at 704:

> Testimony admissible under Rule 704(a) may be excluded under Rule 403 when the probative value of an opinion on an ultimate issue is substantially outweighed by the risk of prejudice, confusion, or waste of time.

He took his litigation work to be part of his academic job. To estimate race of potential jurors, Fisher at first modified the population count by voter registration, per town. After I praised the adjustment, and showed that the data supported my client's position, he reverted to unadjusted data. I think he charged what his work was worth.[180]

The Professional Expert

The cliché that history is written by the winners is inapplicable to litigation. History is written by those who have the time and incentive to write, be they winners, losers, or observers: social scientists, law-school faculty, and other academics. The work-a-day experts, professionals, are the most-informed but least-heard voices in this conversation.[181]

By "professional expert" I do *not* mean people employed by a party, such as forensic experts engaged by government criminal laboratories. I have mentioned above how different they are. Well-documented problems of tainted evidence and hasty prosecution-favoring conclusions need no repetition here.[182] By "professional" I mean those who make a living selling analytic services to plaintiff and defendant alike, and preferably to parties outside of litigation, also. Not all of them, of course. Though this is a generalization with exceptions, I still see them—us—as different from academic amateurs, dabblers. We have the capacity to question our clients' theories, to propose alternative explanations, to understand the legal requirements of the statistical case we are to make, to make mistakes, learn from them, and do better the next time. Unfortunately, as the market for our services is structured, we have little incentive to use this expertise, and less to write it up for the benefit of others.

In consequence, there is no discussion forum by, for, or even about experts. Professionals neither have the time nor do they see advantage in improving their "profession." The view that they are competitors dominates any view that they are engaged in a com-

---

180. See *Pugliano* (2004). Neither Fisher's testimony, nor mine, is discussed in an opinion as of this writing. Fisher acknowledged that this was his first experience as an expert, *and his last*. I have seen others express this same sentiment, Earl Balis, for example, in *Rubanick* (1991) at 426.

181. Although a bit strong, Hagen (1997) gets her voice heard, as does Charles Mann (2000).

182. Giannelli (1997a) at 441:

> Too many experts in the criminal justice system manifest a police-prosecution bias, a willingness to shade or distort opinions to support the state's case. Similarly, too many prosecutors seek out such experts.

Risinger et al. (2002) are more forgiving, at 11:

> If permitted to run uncontrolled through forensic practice, observer effects can lead competent and honest forensic scientists, using well-validated techniques, to offer sincere conclusions that are, nevertheless, distorted and inaccurate. Such results may occur in large numbers, completely without examiner awareness, much less with any wrongful intent.

mon activity.[183] The most penetrating characteristic of statistical expertise as practiced is its lack of intellectuality, its lack of conceptual thought. Whether that is a cause or an effect of the lack of communication among experts, I do not know.[184] It is surely an effect of the structure of the "industry."

Judges go out of their way to notice that an expert is a professional, as if non-professionals were not also being paid for their services. Judge Posner describes "[the] professional expert witness who testifies with scant regard for the truth," referring to an un-named playground consultant.[185] The professional expert is a creature of the judicial system, not of the professions themselves. I will have more to say about the contrast between the "professional" expert and the non-professional one, as judges see them in the credentials battle, in Chapter 10. Just as important, I discuss the scant regard other forums have for the truth, in Chapter 9. Litigation is just a messy part of a messy world. Trying to get by, people comply with the incentives that exist to move them in the direction others want them to go.

---

183. I instituted a discussion group among professional experts in Washington, D.C., in the late 1970s. Barbara Bergmann, from the University of Maryland, was the speaker at one session. Charles Mann, her opposing expert in a forthcoming case, would not agree not to use anything that transpired at that meeting, against her. Bergmann then refused to continue. There were no more meetings.

184. *Jurimetrics Journal* may have been intended to be such a forum, but is not. I have not discussed debates on the use of mathematics in courts. In particular, the debate about how to draw legal conclusions from probabilistic evidence is not a central concern of this book, although perhaps it should be required reading in a course on statistics in law. See Finkelstein and Fairley (1970), Tribe (1971a). Finkelstein and Fairley (1971), and Tribe (1971b). The subject continued with N. Cohen (1985), Kaye (1987), and N. Cohen (1987); and then Shaviro (1989), Callen (1991), and Shaviro (1991). The third article of three always asserts, as did Shaviro (1991), at 499, that his critic "addresses only a fictional Shaviro, not the real one." See also Nesson (1986) and other comments in the May–July 1986 *Boston University Law Review*.

These debaters consider only explicitly probabilistic questions, such as whether a bus line that operates most of the buses on a street can be held liable for an accident in which the perpetrating bus (the "blue bus") was unidentified. Suppose an eyewitness said, "Yes, that was a bus from Company X." Isn't that equally probabilistic evidence? Wouldn't it be probabilistic even if it were the only evidence? As Allen (1991) notes, all evidence is probabilistic. The debate about overtly probabilistic evidence is premised on a false distinction. Richard Posner has a different explanation why the blue bus example says nothing about how statistical evidence should be received. See *Veysey* (2003) at 605.

The blue bus example is derived from *Smith* (1945). Interestingly, had the color of that bus actually been part of plaintiff's description, the outcome might have been more favorable for her. A similar case, in which the Hertz Corporation may or may not have owned the truck at issue, gave a Michigan appeals court no trouble at all:

> It cannot be said that the preponderance of the evidence showed non-ownership of the truck by Hertz, when the facts stipulated showed 90 percent of the vehicles bearing the Hertz logo are owned by Hertz.

Kaminsky (1980) at 358. Judge Posner discussed these bus decisions also in "a charming miniature of a case," *Howard* (1998) at 358. Agreeing, at 360, that "all evidence can be expressed in probabilistic terms," Posner believes that the jury makes its own probability determinations. That is, one cannot assume that the jury is deciding on the probabilities given to it by experts.

185. *Albers* (1983) at 858.

9

Education

This chapter is about "education" in a broad sense. It concerns people who work in education (professors who become experts) and people who pass through (students who become experts or attorneys), as well as people in the media. Some comments on the university might be expected, following my differentiation between professional and "academic" experts. I have worked in universities, government, research institutions, and private enterprise. I write here from the perspective—perhaps the bias—of someone who found this last position the most satisfying.[1]

The critics whose work I described in Chapter 4 thought the Supreme Court had no basis on which to decide that juries could be any size but twelve. The conventional analytical path I fustigated in Chapter 5 confused process with outcome. The "Driving While Black" section of Chapter 8 shows how current and pervasive these analytic misconceptions are. Had I agreed with how these issues had been conventionally analyzed, I would have written nothing about them. That is true of most critical commentary: It is about examples, not the norm. One cannot determine from critiques, mine or anyone else's, whether most academic writing on law, or statistics, or statistics in law, contributes much or little to our knowledge.[2]

It would be easy to define "junk science" as that which is not accepted in academia; but, at least in statistical analysis in law, much of what *is* approved in academia is equally uninformed and non-informing. Some findings considered baseless by academics appear,

---

1. Rossi (1991) points out that "the learned treatise," that is, books and articles, are admissible as evidence. Few are written outside academia. So academics get to be experts even inadvertently. However, recently, use of such third-party expertise has been frowned upon. See, for example, *Hambsch* (1984), *Hutchinson* (1991), or *Spensieri* (1999). For a discussion, see Michael Hoenig, "Questions About Experts and 'Reliable' Hearsay," *New York Law Journal*, July 8, 2002.

2. This is one reason one should read overly critical books such as Huber (1991) and Boot (1998) with caution. Their examples may be correct, but are they generic?

after all, to have merit.[3] Judges may continue to hold that the academic standard is the best available. I think I have proved otherwise in my work and in this book. The "academy" is simply a place that sponsors writing, and therefore much writing comes from it. That says nothing about its quality.

Although my illustrations have appeared to be technical and practical, based on case experience, I have been trying to bring an intellectuality to the subject of statistics in law. I have dared—for an economist, a non-lawyer, it is indeed daring—to express my opinions about the law. Most statistical writing on the subject is didactic. We are told how things are, not why, not what the consequences are, not whether they should be as they are or how they might be different.

There is also a small literature of first-person narratives of legal experiences by non-lawyers.[4] Experiences count, and some who have had them have recounted them sensitively. The more-abstract literature, the lectures by famous professors, may have technical merit, but are not a basis for an intellectual approach, a serious analysis of the theory and practice of experts in law.[5] They are written as technical instructions.[6]

I have tried to think through some of the problems of practice at a conceptual level. That is what I mean by an "intellectuality," an understanding of the large sort of problems facing statistical experts, and the limitations of the answers they can provide. Perhaps I over-use the word, but I want to distinguish paradigm from method, ways of thinking from thinking within established ways; creativity in how to approach a problem, rather than creativity (although just as important) within an approach.

Historically, many of what we now take to be intellectual breakthroughs have been conceived by persons excluded from the official study of their subject matter. Blacks, excluded from mainstream intellectual forums, best articulated their own plight, and the reasons why their exclusion was social insanity. Women have done the same thing, not starting from positions inside the university, but *creating* such positions when their intellectuality could not be denied.

A more mundane example concerns public policy about injuries. We started by trying

---

3. Take, for example, the Dr. Atkins diet.

> After insisting Atkins was a quack for three decades, obesity experts are now finding it difficult to ignore the copious anecdotal evidence that his diet does just what he has claimed.

Gary Taubes, "What if It's All Been a Big Fat Lie?" *New York Times Magazine*, July 7, 2002, at 34.

4. See de Cani (1974), Kadane (2000), C. Mann (2000), and Wolfgang (1974) as examples.

5. See the following books: Baldus and Cole (1980), Barnes and Conley (1986), Faigman (2000), Finkelstein (1978), Finkelstein and Levin (1990), Gastwirth (1988), and Good (2001); and articles: Finkelstein (1980), F. Fisher (1980), F. Fisher (1986), and Meier (1986); and the *Reference Manual* (1994), which was revised in 2000. Cheng and Yoon (2005) call for more technical instruction for judges. I call for less.

6. Liebenson (1964) even tells the expert how to dress! Also see Moss (2003) at 53: "Experts can be dropped by their attorney . . . for dressing the wrong way."

to prevent accidents. This approach has led to safer workplaces, to straighter roads with graduated access, and to more easily read traffic-directing signs. Another approach is to ameliorate the effect of accidents on the victims thereof, which has led to roll bars, collapsible steering columns, seat belts, and air bags. It is leading to laws *requiring* that persons in moving vehicles *wear* their seat belts, that motorcyclists wear helmets; that is, state intervention in individual behavior because of a paradigm change from an individual (do what you want, we'll regulate the environment) to a public-health (what you do affects others) view of the issue. It is one thing to think that obesity is an individual health problem, that individuals should eat better and exercise more. It is another to see a correlation between obesity and poverty and ask to what extent "good" food is available to poor people. It is easy to blame individuals who fire guns, not the gun itself; but a different approach suggests that many shootings could be prevented by measures that, one can hope, will eventually be enforced by law, such as trigger locks.

It may be that "intellectuality" is what intellectuals do, but I contend that it is *how* they do what they do. Which is to say that, like "experts," some people engaged in the same activity, on the same subject matter, do not deserve that title. Some people think that, today, most "intellectuals" are found in universities. Richard Posner suggests that the gathering of intellectuals into universities, where they speak to each other more than to, uh, common people, is a sign of, or has lead to, a decline in their merit.[7] Posner is better known for throwing ideas into the fire than for stoking it to see how they burn, but surely his is intellectual activity.[8] As an "outsider," I find some law-review articles to be thoughtful, informed, and constructive; but most, not.[9] In short, being an "academic" is not the same thing as being an intellectual. Few of the former are the latter, and many of the latter are not the former.

Little of what I have referred to above as intellectual leadership—for example leadership in taking a public-health approach to sanitation, workplace and vehicle safety, even food—has been initiated by "scholars," by those employed by universities and engaged (they think) in intellectual pursuits. In a eulogy for Susan Sontag, Joan Acocella calls her

---

7. See Posner (2001a). It is not clear whether Posner thinks that academic cloistering is hazardous to intellectual health, or that the academy's choices of its intellectuals has been poor.

8. See, for example, the profile by Larissa MacFarquhar, "The Bench Burner," *The New Yorker*, December 10, 2001, at 78:

> [H]e is more attracted to rhetoric than proof. . . . He is not, in the end, interested in the sort of prudent rigor that produces watertight logic.

9. Posner (2003) criticizes "academic lawyers," at 18, for being "too casual in their analysis of democracy." I will be noting in this chapter that the academics may be law-school professors, but are not all lawyers; and democracy is not the only subject they treat too casually. Indeed, Posner (2004) also thinks that "too many [law-review] articles are too long, too dull, and too heavily annotated." In particular, "many interdisciplinary articles are published that have no merit at all." Those non-lawyers, gathered in law schools, writing for law reviews, aren't the ones keeping the intellectual flame alive. I discuss law schools further, below.

"a public intellectual"—Posner's term—but not a professor.[10] David Hemenway credits physicians with changing the emphasis from automobile accidents to injuries caused thereby. We can easily understand the original emphasis: Automobile companies stopped caring at the point of the accident, and data at one time ended with a statement about the result of the accident (injury or fatality). In contrast, the physician's task only started at that point. Ralph Nader, another non-academic, politicized this new intellectuality, changing the measure of result from the automobile to the individual, while maintaining that much of the solution did lie with the design of the vehicle.[11]

Statistical practice occurs in many forums—in research, testing, manufacture. Statistical practice is very much a real-world activity. Yet "intellectuals" in statistics are known more for their simplifications, their few-parameter models, than their real-world insights. W. Edwards Deming brought "quality control" to Japanese industry after World War II. American industry had no use for it. It was not considered an "intellectual" achievement within academia.[12] I documented the same kind of blindness about claims of race discrimination in my "Driving While Black" discussion in Chapter 8. Uninformative selection models were not only considered sufficient to "prove" biased police behavior, but worthy of publication in statistics journals.

If "intellectuality" is knowledgeable creative thought about issues, and especially if its product is nonfiction analytic writing, then whether the center of intellectuality is—or ever has been—in universities can be disputed. First, there are centers of thought that contain no students: research institutions. Many—perhaps most—are ideologically directed, but that tint should not condemn their products to derision, only to careful scrutiny. Even if we expand the concept of academia to include such institutions, which I do for one purpose below, we will leave out a large number of people who write what they contend are serious pieces on serious topics. Many of them are syndicated columnists, radio and television "personalities," or others who prefer to work outside the boundaries of academic and research institutions.[13] Many of these writings touch on or are about institutions of

---

10. Joan Acocella, "Postscript: Susan Sontag," *The New Yorker*, January 10, 2005, at 28.

11. Hemenway (2004) reviews the changes in thinking about automobile and firearm safety, indicating that the "public-health approach" is a modern paradigm for coping with urban life, going back to sanitation (an advance over prayer and condemnation) as an escape from disease. I do not mean to disparage real contributions by academics. James Doyle (2005), for example, credits Gary Wells, an academic psychologist, with shifting the attention on mistaken eyewitness identification from the witness to the procedures used to obtain the identification, the "system variables" in Wells' terms.

12. See Deming (1975). Even while reporting to statisticians, Deming is saying that his methods relate to production, not to theory.

13. In contrast with Posner (2001a), Martin Anderson (1996) sees two clear classes of intellectuals, academics and "professionals." I agree. It would be interesting to try to determine whether the institutional framework around an "intellectual" affects his intellectual product.

law. Although few are great intellectual achievements, they are not inferior to academic writing on the same subjects.

I have found at least as much intellectuality—conceptual thinking about the law and the role of statistics in law, and how to effectuate that role (how to construct a legal system in which statistical analysis assists in the determination of fact)—among attorneys and statistical practitioners as among academics. We do not have easy access to their thinking. Some non-academics produced articles for a collection edited by Joseph Gastwirth in 2000, for which Gastwirth and they deserve praise.[14] However, that was an exceptional event. Of the members of the task force of the Carnegie Commission—those who wrote its 1993 report on judicial decision making—all but two were academics, government or nonprofit employees, attorneys in private practice, or judges. The remaining two were businessmen. Of the fifteen members of the Commission itself, 68 percent were from a university, nonprofit, or government background; 18 percent were private attorneys. The remaining three (14 percent) were businessmen. No one on the Commission or its task force came from the expert community, or from state or federal attorneys' offices.

Like that of the Carnegie Commission task force, the product of the National Academy of Science's panel on statistics and law—Fienberg (1989)—was solid but dull and unimaginative. As with Carnegie, the National Academy panel contained no private-sector experts or public (federal or state) attorneys. Academics define themselves as the most important actors, and engage others who support that position. Without representation from prime performers or major users, what would one expect?

Perhaps the committee format does not induce or allow the creativity we expect from intellectual pursuits. If "intellectuality" involves breaking bounds, more of it is likely to emanate from individuals than from groups. I expect from intellectuals not only novel insights, but analysis backing those insights up, along with discourse with others, modification, refinement. As I began noting in Chapter 2, these are not the typical activities of the professional expert in litigation. These activities are supposed to characterize the academic environment, where Posner says the intellectuals reside. Judges, also, often refer to the "standards" of the academy, although I have questioned why they do. We look to the academy to serve our intellectual needs in statistics and law, as elsewhere; and the academy has failed us.

Non-Inquiring Minds

I testified in four jury-selection cases in Connecticut, each time utilizing an analysis based on the material in Chapter 5, and each time facing a different professor from Yale Univer-

---

14. See especially C. Mann (2000), Rosenblum (2000), and Zeger et al. (2000), in Gastwirth (2000).

sity. I asserted that what these professors were doing was uninformative. These so-called experts were finding fault with a procedure (selection of juries) from measuring its outcome. They presented their results as definitive, whereas outcome results might be considered at best suggestive. The "experts" were blindly following the Michael Finkelstein paradigm, using census data to describe the pool from which jurors were drawn. As we learned in Chapter 5, jurors are not drawn from such a population.

After all, it seems so scientific, this standard-deviation stuff. Roger Kuhn had written, shortly after publication of Finkelstein's classic 1966 article:

> Hopefully . . . mathematics will replace intuition in the decision of jury-discrimination cases in which the challenger seeks to establish a *prima facie* case through statistical evidence.[15]

Experts almost universally propose that courts should use the binomial test of disparity, and, despite *Castaneda* (1977), courts almost universally reject it.[16] This enthusiasm of experts for the "precision" of mathematics remains in vogue, though, as I showed in Chapter 5, in the jury-selection context it hits a dead end: We are unable to measure characteristics of persons eligible to be jurors in advance of operating that system itself.

My client prevailed in each of these four jury-selection cases. Did these professors go back to Yale and discuss their experiences? Did they compare notes and find that they all had faced the same expert, with the same conceptual approach to the question—a different approach from theirs? As far as I can determine, the answers are "no." Did they care that the court had found their approach wanting? Did they find nothing interesting about the experience?

I explain—or define—their failure to pursue the issue as a lack of curiosity. Curiosity is the sine qua non of intellectuality. For these professors, I conclude, providing expert testimony was a source of income, not of inspiration.[17]

---

15. R. Kuhn (1968) at 256.

16. *Fryar* (1997) at 242:

> The majority of courts have looked to the absolute disparity test to determine whether underrepresentation of a group is substantial.

See also Bueker (1997) at 402:

> Courts most commonly use the absolute disparity measure when evaluating jury representation.

17. Mandel (1999) at 113:

> [T]here is no doubt that the demand for economic expert witnesses represents a new flow of money coming into the economics profession.

And at 116:

> [T]he young tenured professor with a mortgage and children to put through college has little reason to turn down consulting assignments.

Anderson (1996) summarizes, at 9:

Intellectual Failure in *Gibbs* (1998)

I was particularly taken by the *Gibbs* case, discussed in the Appendix to Chapter 5. David Pollard's failure is more remarkable than that of the other Yale professors, for two reasons. First, he spent years on the topic.[18] Second, as I explain in the Appendix to Chapter 5, there *was* a bias in the state's jury-selection system, waiting to be exposed by an astute statistical analyst. Blinded by his preconceptions, Pollard missed it.

We all make mistakes, and the easiest mistake to make is just not seeing something that someone else sees. I promised my clients all through the *Gibbs* proceedings that Pollard would come to understand the bias I was pointing out in Connecticut's jury-selection rules, and that he would agree. I was wrong.

In an ex-post review, Pollard explains:

> I strongly suspected . . . that undeliverable summonses (and perhaps no-shows) would be a major part of the explanation of the low Hispanic proportions on the questionnaires [answered by jurors entering the courthouse].[19]

True enough. But this is an arithmetic answer, not a legal answer, not a statistical analytic answer. Once the court is satisfied about the basic data—that the proportion Hispanic is smaller among jurors than in the census—it wants to know why. "Why" is not *that* summonses were not delivered. "Why" is *why* summonses were not delivered. Of course Pollard had no answer. He didn't have the question!

Pollard is not alone. Consider this example, from Judge Higginbotham, referring to Michael Wachter, a professor of economics at the University of Pennsylvania, expert for defendant union:

> Wachter in essence believed that there were numerous factors (cultural, socio-economic, religious, vocational, educational, etc.) which would render in-

---

It has been quite a while since anyone spoke of the world of American higher education as a place of integrity.

It is reasonable to believe that some persons who might have been academics have turned to writing "popular" books and columns, from which they make more money. Indeed, academics do so, also, although whether to the advantage or disadvantage of their students is not known. What is clear is that "intellectual" discourse is watered down by aiming at a non-intellectual mass market. Adam Gopnik, "Standup Guys," a review of Gerald Nachman, *Seriously Funny: The Rebel Comedians of the 1950s and 1960s* (Pantheon, 2003) in *The New Yorker*, May 12, 2003, at 109:

> What really happened to the new comedy was not that it was defanged but that, as its audience broadened, it necessarily became less intellectual.

I revisit the academic's relationship to the income he can earn in litigation, where the topic is the judicial assessment of credentials, in Chapter 10.

18. Pollard worked on *Gibbs* for two years. In Pollard (2000) he refers to his prior work on *State v. King*, CR92-0137614 (Hartford Judicial District, 1996).

19. Pollard (2000) at 205.

accurate a calculation of labor pool based simply on the number of male minority individuals aged 18–65. Wachter theorized that these factors may tend to make minority individuals, for whatever reasons, less likely to possess skills needed to enter the union, to succeed in the union, or to be oriented in the first place toward operating engineer work, etc. Wachter, however, provided no analysis which sought to quantify the effects of these factors. He plainly did not offer any evidence that minority individuals disproportionately lacked the skills or availability to do operating engineer work.[20]

In the same case, Arthur Dempster of Harvard opined that "defining the labor pool might be impossible."[21] Then, what should we do? Silence. The court did not find Dempster's view any more helpful than Wachter's.[22]

We know that most research is wrong.[23] The methodology is wrong. The data may be inadequate or badly handled. In law, the statistical study may not follow the proprieties demanded by legal definitions (such as age in Age Discrimination in Employment Act cases or "assignment" in government departments). Legal studies also have the opportunity, whether correct or not, to be irrelevant.[24] An author's conclusions do not always follow from the material he has presented as supporting them. Nonetheless, people usually quote research from the stated conclusions only. When I taught, I did not allow a student to parrot that some author "found" something. Some author may claim to have found something—but did he, or did he merely say that he did?[25] I discussed this problem in Chapter 7, asking that judges question when an expert says he "explains" something. Someone needs to do the hard work, which is figuring out what the author really did

---

20. *Local 542* (1979) at 1592. Judge A. Leon Higginbotham, a circuit judge, was sitting as a district-court judge by designation. Plaintiffs' expert was Bernard Siskin.

21. *Local 542* (1979) at 1595.

22. Dempster's work supporting reverse regression in *Harris Bank* (1981) got the same reaction. See Chapter 3.

23. Foster and Huber (1997) say the same thing, equally without proof, at 83: "A surprisingly large fraction of scientific reports are wrong." I don't see why it is surprising. This is how science advances. Also,

> That various individuals can find various flaws in the thesis does not distinguish this work from nearly the entire body of published work in the scientific literature I am sorry to say.

Ronald W. McClard, a court-appointed expert, in *Hall* (1996b) at 1470. (Appendix D of this opinion is McClard's report to the court.) Again, people finding flaws in other peoples' work is how knowledge accumulates. McClard expects too much.

24. See Judge Posner's affirmation of the exclusion of both Robert Lucas and Jeffrey Perloff on the grounds that their testimony would be irrelevant, in *Drugs* (1999), for example. Most of June O'Neill's proposed testimony in *Morgan Stanley* (2004) was excluded when the court found, at 465, "that the majority of O'Neill's proposed testimony and opinions are not relevant to the claims in this case."

25. When a professional journal relies on such a "finding," the media takes it to be fact. For example, see Note (1977), in which law-review editors based their report of poor selection of judges on a study that could have "found" no such thing, despite its claim that it did. The error in the study was a biased

and what it means and how sensitive it is to his assumptions and data.

Students should be ready to take on these tasks. Do any academics bring this work back to the university? Do they use this fascinating litigation material as a teaching tool?[26] If so, do they only describe, or do they analyze? Do they let their students analyze, and give them credit if their answers are not the same as those of the professor? Do they present their adversaries' work as well as their own? In at least one case, the academics who had been experts did not even present their own work as their own. As mentioned in Chapter 3, Gwartney and others wrote about their regression approach to explaining workplace salaries. They put it forward as a valid defense against allegations of discrimination, even though their approach had failed in *James* (1975). Nowhere did the authors reveal their association with that case.[27]

David Pollard's description of his work in *Gibbs* could hardly have avoided his association with it.[28] However, in his first circulated draft, Pollard failed to inform the reader of the outcome: The judge rejected every point Pollard tried to make, as well as his client's complaint. Did Pollard think the judge's decision was not relevant to his story?

Regression Confusion

One of the failures of intellectualization in the academy is to confuse what experts know with what they need to know in the litigation situation. For example, it is common to understand that schooling generates earnings. Those with more education have more skills and also have demonstrated skill acquisition. They shop around among employers until they find one with a job that will use those skills, and compensate for them. We therefore expect education to be a factor in position and earnings upon hire. The more-educated person's income will continue to be higher, and might rise faster than persons with lower education, who could not enter the same job class.

Now we are in litigation about earnings within a single firm. Is education a relevant variable when we also control for position, in analyzing either promotion or compen-

---

selection of data (so that no district-wide generalizations about cases or judges could be drawn), similar to errors made by some experts, as discussed in Chapter 8. The *St. Louis Post-Dispatch* then reported the Note's conclusions on page 1 on October 2, 1977, under the headline, "Judges Here are Found Hostile to Civil Rights." The study's fallacies are exposed in Wasby (1978). The newspaper is as culpable as the journal for reporting that a study "found" something that it unquestionably did not find.

26. Mandel (1999) tells us that some do.

27. See Gwartney et al. (1979). The authors did learn, though. Two factors used in *James*, supervisory ratings and "skill" measured by job class, do not appear in the published example. I believe that not revealing their association with a case they cite, or that the theory they were espousing had been vilified by the appeals court, was a violation of even the most minimal standard of academic ethics.

28. See Pollard (2000).

sation? In Chapter 3 I provided examples where academic experts thought it should be. And it might be. But neither economic theory nor the research literature leads to that conclusion. Concepts that economists think are obvious, that come from multi-firm studies, might not apply at all within a firm. Promotion may be due to performance. Earnings may be due to job class. What seems like a regression issue may really be a selection issue. A single regression across many job classes may be corrupted by non-homogeneous effects.[29] Regression is the tool economists think they know, and think they have reason to use. Yet in most of the examples in Chapter 3, it was the wrong tool for the job, for answering the litigation question.

Misuse of regression is but one example of analyst sloth, of throwing variables at the problem rather than thinking about it. Either Chapter 2 or Chapter 3 could have been extended to the length of this entire book with more such examples.[30] The statistical analyst enters litigation as a technical expert. His role should be as an intellectual partner of the judge. Nothing about the process that got the expert into the courtroom leads him to see himself playing that role. The poor performance of experts is dictated by the structure into which they are thrust, as much as by who they are. It is also generated by the places experts come from: the university.

NOT OPEN FOR BUSINESS

If one route to broadening the student experience is bringing faculty activity back to campus, another route is the outside lecturer, possibly (indeed, preferably) giving a seminar as well as a broad-based talk. Joe Galloway was a widely acclaimed Vietnam War reporter. He became interested in the relationship between the media and the military, and now writes on that topic. He tells us that he has enough requests from the military, for talks and seminars, that he could make a full-time living that way. But he has never been asked to give a talk or a seminar at a journalism school. "The military is willing to learn," he concludes, leaving the rest of the thought for us to fill in.[31]

---

29. I will end this chapter with a sad counter-example, where getting a higher degree leads immediately to higher salary. It is sad because there is no indication that the higher salary is deserved. Thus, these salaries will be well related to education by design, not by productivity.

30. Analytic errors of this type are not exclusive to litigation. James Heckman annihilated attempts to refute his use of military test scores in explaining income, where in a properly specified model those scores bring the unexplained black/white income gap close to zero. Heckman also noted that when General Education Degrees (high-school equivalency) can be distinguished from four-year-high-school degrees, the latter contribute more to earnings than the former. "Intellectuality" can be just spotting little distinctions that make big differences. See Heckman (1998).

31. See H. Moore and Galloway (1992). Quotation from a panel discussion on the media and the military, broadcast live on C-SPAN on March 26, 2002.

In 1979, as part of my consulting business, I organized luncheon seminars, inviting "winning" experts and lawyers in interesting cases to town, at my expense, to talk to anyone willing to spend the time. I invited local attorneys and experts alike to attend. We created a learning community, even if outside of these events the experts, perhaps also the attorneys, were competing for clients. I know of no school where anything like this occurs.

Mistakes

Not only do we all make mistakes, we all make many of them. Being wrong on occasion does not differentiate one expert, or one intellectual, from another. The distinguishing feature is what one does when he learns that he has been wrong. The issue is whether the academy provides a place where different lines of thinking are thrown against each other, each to learn from the other; whether better ideas replace old, or if the holders of the old ideas cling to them, suppressing the new. Michael Mandel thinks that

> consulting income encourages economists who serve as expert witnesses to become locked into their opinions, thus impeding intellectual debate.[32]

Joseph Stiglitz described the problem "in the lawyer- and politician-dominated White House environment."[33]

> What occurred was often worse than Gresham's Law: it was not only that bad argument seemed to drive out good, but good economists, responding to implicit incentives, adopted bad arguments to win their battles.

Steven Moss had a similar experience as a litigation expert:

> [V]eteran experts tend to avoid doing research that could lead to an incorrect answer, lest this information fall into the wrong hands.[34]

My criticisms of traditional jury-representation analyses in Chapter 5 will become obvious enough to anyone who thinks about them. The standard analysis compares the wrong things, race of jurors with race of the population. As there is no fix within the standard paradigm, I proposed an alternative paradigm which, I am confident, will someday be seen as conventional, and be practiced as routine. Similar is my criticism of the analyses offered to support "driving while black" litigation, in Chapter 8. Thoughtful people will come to agree that, if a single-pool analysis is to be used at all, one should compare the race of those arrested for speeding with the race of speeders, defined as driving at speeds at which tickets for speeding are issued. More attention will be paid to

---

32. Mandel (1999) at 114.

33. Stiglitz (1998) at 5; following indented quotation also at 5.

34. Moss (2003).

whether a policeman can determine the race of a driver before stopping him. Yet, on these topics, as well as others, I have had only resistance from academics, locked into their opinions, adopting bad arguments in their attempts to win their battles.[35] Has any critic of the jury-size decisions discussed in Chapter 4 asked if perhaps they were wrong, if decisions from juries of six today are quite as good as those from larger juries in the past?

The Brookings Institution

Let's define "academia" broadly, to include "think tanks," into and out of which academics flow.[36] Surely, one might think, this arm of academia houses the curious, the intellectually active. When I became an associate at the Brookings Institution in September 1966, my job was to investigate the sources of the disparity in incomes between whites and blacks. Of particular interest was the role of education. If black education became equal to white education, measured as years of school, how much of the current income gap would be closed?

In Chapter 3 I explained that other estimates of the ability of education to close the black-white earnings gap were higher than mine. And I explained why: their implicit assumption of a homogeneous (race-independent) effect of education on income. The standard estimate was that, when only the quantity of black schooling was increased, leaving all other factors as they were, one-third or more of the black/white income gap would be closed. Equalizing education, it seemed, would be a powerful income equalizing policy.[37]

I located the homogeneity assumption in each methodology and, using the original author's data, revised each approach to include separate black and white income reactions to schooling. Every study, when corrected, estimated that the "income gap" would decrease

---

35. "As time went on, the facts started to become less important to me than winning the case." Moss (2003) at 54. One aspect of what Matt Taibbi calls "our culture of emboldened stupidity" is not reviewing past pronouncements that seemed penetrating at the time. See http://www.nypress.com/18/16/news&columns/taibbi.cfm. See also Frank (2000) for a review of the frailties of management gurus and "free market" prophets.

36. This is a gross simplification. Academics have relationships with industry and government as intense as those with nonprofits. Some "think tanks" serve as governments-in-waiting, as well as places for former academics to go. Indeed, the complex interweaving of academics with other institutions, some of which is dealt with below, is a subject of increasing scrutiny. See, for example, E. Campbell et al. (2004). The lack of intellectual purity in these think tanks—or my naivete in the face of it—may explain some of the story that follows.

37. If blacks would take on the relationship between education and income of whites, why would incomes not be equal? There are regional effects (blacks live where incomes are lower), age effects (educated blacks would be younger than educated whites), specialty effects (why would we assume that blacks would have the same job distribution as whites?), and other legitimate differences, as well as racial discrimination. This is also why, even if females were more educated than males, lower average female earnings would not necessarily imply discrimination against females.

by around 10 to 12 percent, the range I had estimated. Brookings is supposed to be a high-level policy-oriented institution. If ever policy had been misdirected on the basis of faulty studies, if ever policy needed to be reformulated based on a better analysis, this was it.

I wrote this material into a chapter. In so doing, it seemed to me, I had taken my proposed book out of the realm of just another econometric estimate, into a new standard. If I was right, others were wrong. In this chapter I showed *why* each prior estimate was wrong, how to correct it, and what estimate ensued.

Brookings wouldn't publish it.

Brookings offered to publish the book, but only without that chapter.[38]

Apparently, for Brookings offered no explanation, they wanted my estimates to be just more of the same; different, but no more or less credible than others'. That may have been because one of the authors of prior estimates I criticized had been published by them.[39] It may have been because politically Brookings did not want the world to know how ineffective education would be as an income policy for blacks, without some other important societal changes. There may be some other explanation, but I cannot think of one I would have accepted. I would not let them emasculate my work this way, and so my book was never published.

I cannot know if any harm came to me from my stubborn stand to have my book published my way or not at all. But there was harm to federal policy, part of the government's promise made but not fulfilled, from Brookings' refusal to allow me to substantiate my estimates. There was harm to discourse on the roots of income disparities.[40] There was harm to intellectual inquiry. And, by the way, I was right.

---

38. I remain astounded by Brookings' position, especially as what I did is a standard way to arrive at a comfortable finding of "truth" or "fact." For example, in *Corrugated* (1981c), we read, at 1326:

> Having found the methodology and assumptions of the objectors' experts flawed, the district court corrected those flaws and found that the damage estimate of those experts was not inconsistent with Dr. Hoyt's damage estimate.

This is written to support the court's decision to accept Richard Hoyt's estimates despite objections from other experts.

39. Lester Thurow, possessor of one of the quickest minds I have met, recognized the error in his method immediately. He then published a better estimate, close to mine, based on interacting race and education. He never did acknowledge my assistance, or his initial error. I appreciate academics who show that they can learn, but would appreciate them more if they indicated how they came to their new, improved knowledge or methodology, so others could benefit from it, also.

40. Unfortunately, analysis of the effects of "equal" schooling on incomes of different parts of the population, and on how to provide that "equal" input, remains inept today. For example, in Thernstrom (2004), the authors declare that equalizing schooling would equalize earnings, if not incomes, between whites and blacks—a bald assertion not only that the other factors mentioned above in footnote 37 do not exist, but that blacks and whites present themselves as equal raw material for the schools to act upon. This is a more extreme contention than the ones I found faulty almost forty years ago; and it is equally fallacious.

Chance

As Samuel Gross remarks:

> Unfortunately, what an expert says in court is generally invisible and inaudible in her own professional world. If expert witnesses were accountable to their colleagues, even informally, they might fear the consequences of irresponsible testimony far more than they do.[41]

He makes no attempt to assess why the testimony of academic experts remains invisible to academic peers. After all, there are clear means of communication within each profession. I offer the following story as an explanation for what, to Gross, is merely an observation.

Chance magazine is an official publication of the American Statistical Association. The popular-magazine format supports a discussion of professional topics. Like *Psychology Today, Chance* is its own forum, not just dumbed-down précis of more technical work. Thus, for example, there were many articles in *Chance* about "the hot hand"—the streak hitter in baseball, the guy who seems to be making shots in basketball—testing whether the phenomenon is distinguishable from random clustering of independent events.[42]

I liked *Chance*. I liked in particular a regular column by Howard Wainer, then of the Educational Testing Service, on visualizations, that is, graphics. I disagreed with Wainer— and had told him so on at least one previous occasion—but disagreement is not disrespect.[43] When David Pollard put a particularly bad example of the craft into evidence in *Gibbs*, I sent it to Wainer with a graphic I had presented in response. My graphic was not a rebuttal, but a clarification. I established a clearer graphical form of Pollard's point, so I could use it to make my own.

I thought this real-world story was best presented, in whatever way he wanted, by someone not directly involved. I did not try to influence what Wainer said about either Pollard's graphic or my own. I just pointed out that they were in the public domain (you can't copyright court testimony) and might be of public interest.

Wainer wrote an article about the graphics. After initially accepting it, *Chance* invoked its policy of not printing anything that might displease a statistician, unless that statisti-

---

41. Gross (1991) at 1178.

42. In later years the subject matter expanded, including, for example, hockey goalies. The better articles argued against the concept, but I have been on the basketball court when I had a hot hand. Statistics is not the only path to the truth. There really are times when you see, you feel, you shoot . . . you score.

43. One of the puzzling hobbies of those looking for ways to visualize data is to describe train schedules. There are a number of famous approaches, none as good as Amtrak's. The simple timetable tells you (or would if they could keep to it) exactly what you want to know: time at departure, time at destination. In other words, when a graph makes a difficult concept easier, I am all for it; but when it makes a simple concept difficult, just skip it.

cian approved. *Chance* gave Pollard the right to *veto* Howard Wainer's article! "It seems to me inconceivable that scientists would attempt to suppress publication of a paper because they disagreed with its conclusions," wrote Lynwood Yarborough to *Science* in 1992. Not to me. *Chance* pulled Wainer's article.

This is bush-league stuff. Wainer's column was just about the display of data. He took no side in the *Gibbs* case, which anyway was long over. A trade association—the American Statistical Association, publisher of *Chance*, is nothing more—exists to support and lobby for its members.[44] If the primary activity of its members was expert testimony, perhaps their association would have an interest in the quality of such activity. This trade association, dominated by academics, did not. It could not tolerate criticism even of Pollard's *graphic*!

I reproduce and explain the suppressed graphics in the appendix to this chapter. Howard Wainer's would-be *Chance* piece, revised, now appears in a collection of his articles.[45]

---

44. The Alameda-Contra Costa Medical Association had a rule designed to prevent criticism:

> When a physician does succeed another physician in charge of a case, he should not disparage, by comment or insinuation, the one who preceded him.

On the basis of that rule, the association expelled Samuel Bernstein for several "ethical violations." In one, Bernstein characterized as "very inexpert" a pathology report from another member, J. M. Ellis, when engaged to review it for litigation. The court allowed the association to enforce this rule in other circumstances, but not, I am glad to report, when it concerned an expert opinion in litigation. See *Bernstein* (1956).

The American Association of Neurological Surgeons suspended Donald C. Austin for six months, finding (after an evidentiary hearing) that he had violated its expert-witness guidelines. The existence of these guidelines indicates that the credibility of their members' expert testimony is important to other members' economic interests. In the battle between two of them, the association defended the one who prevailed at trial. Judge Bucklo concluded that "the AANS was indeed wrong," but that nonetheless it had not violated the law in its error. *Austin* (2000) at 1154. On review, Judge Posner articulated the AANS concern:

> The Association had an interest—the community at large had an interest—in Austin's not being able to use his membership to dazzle judges and juries and deflect the close and skeptical scrutiny that shoddy testimony deserves.

Austin (2001) at 972. Referring to "the *accurate* revelation of his having given irresponsible testimony under oath in a suit for medical malpractice,"—that is, disagreeing with the lower court on the merits— the circuit court affirmed the dismissal of Austin's suit. *Austin* at 974, italics in original.

John Fullerton was placed in a censure proceeding by the Florida Medical Association—of which he was not a member—for his testimony for plaintiff in a malpractice case. The three doctors against whom Fullerton testified were members of the Association, which needless to say took their word that Fullerton had behaved badly. So he proceeded to: He sued the Association, claiming that the charges were libel, and that the publicity had already damaged him. See Adam Liptak, "Doctor's Testimony Leads To A Complex Legal Fight," *New York Times*, June 20, 2004, at 16.

45. See Chapter 12 of Wainer (2003). The original article mentioned both Pollard and me by name. Wainer has chosen to leave only my name in the article, so the formulator of the awful graphic is anonymous. Badly burned, or still suffering from publisher suppression?

This Book

I started to "market" this book for publication after completing a draft. I sent letters describing it to several university and commercial presses. One editor wrote that my book would not be "appropriate."

> Our books seem to be the model of what you oppose, and the names you cite are the ones I use to evaluate proposals in this area.[46]

A publisher will not print that which contradicts other books in his line? Brookings all over again? What happened to the idea of discourse, argument, articulate disagreement?

Another publisher sent chapters to reviewers.

> As you might have suspected, the feedback on your proposal is simply too controversial for us to consider your work for publication. . . . You should know that we even contacted various editors in our trade and professional divisions; they, too, were gun-shy of your approach to the subject-matter.

Publishers are "gun-shy" of controversy! This is indeed a bad omen. One would think that reader enlightenment and publisher profit would be coincident.[47] I think they would be, that something else—catering to the professional elite—motivates such a decision. Where I walked away from Brookings, disappointed but moving on, this time I decided to pursue my project to its conclusion: I have published this book myself.

Foreign Affairs

Published by the Council on Foreign Relations, *Foreign Affairs* has long been considered a major forum for the exposition of foreign-policy ideas. Fundamental to those ideas, one would think, is the determination of fact. When Kenneth Maxwell, a Latin America specialist and a member of the Council, reviewed a book about Chile in November 2003, he noted that the United States has released facts about our relationship with that country only begrudgingly, in minimal bits and pieces. What are we hiding?

William Rogers, Secretary of State under Richard Nixon, took exception in a letter to the editor, to which Maxwell responded in the same issue. So far, this is standard practice.

---

46. I am not naming the publishers or editors here because I greatly appreciate, and do not want to inhibit, their honesty and frankness of expression.

47. Charles Babbage, inventor of the "analytical engine"—the first mechanical calculator—as well as the cowcatcher, also laid the foundation for the field of operational research.

> When he applied his new method of analysis to a study of the printing trade, his publishers were so offended that they refused to accept any more books.

Feingold (2000), this quotation from Chapter 2, available on the internet.

Then the exchange took a strange turn. Rogers wrote another letter, published in the spring of 2004. Where was Maxwell's response? *Foreign Affairs* would not publish it, whereupon Maxwell resigned (as well he should have) from the Council.

This was an important debate, involving the possible complicity of our government in the overthrow of Salvador Allende, the elected president of Chile, and the 1976 murders of Orlando Letelier and Ronnie Moffitt in the United States. On the other side—the other side from free exposure of the facts—lie Rogers and Henry Kissinger, the powers that still be and their friends on the Council.[48]

DNA and *Science*

The district-court decision in *Yee* (1991) remains a milestone in the history of "battles of experts." It included an exhaustive examination of the validity of DNA identification evidence. It's not that there is any question about the science: There is every reason to believe that, except for identical twins, each person's DNA is unique. Although one could not prove such an assertion, it would be astounding if this ever proved untrue (outside of cloning). It was not an issue in *Yee*.

The evidentiary issue arose because DNA identification is based on an interpretation of a graph made from but a small part of the DNA strand. Apart from craft errors in preparing and interpreting the gel, theoretically, two people with different DNA could appear the same. DNA could differ somewhere else, but be the same in the tested part. Because identification is from a sample and is constructed physically with some possibility of error or contamination, and because the analyst checks for duplication in a data base (a collection of DNA samples), the conclusion of identification testimony will be a probability statement.

Suggesting that the FBI Caucasian data base did not account for substructures, Richard Lewontin of Harvard University testified for defendant in *Yee* that the FBI's calculation of the probability of the match between the defendant's DNA and the evidence DNA, were they from different people, was exaggeratedly small. Lewontin's testimony, the "centerpiece of the defendant's challenge to the scientific acceptance of the Caucasian data base,"[49] had to be seriously considered. Ultimately, Judge Potter found that

> the government has met its burden of showing by a preponderance of the evidence that the general scientific community, but by no means the entire scientific community, accepts the F.B.I. protocol and procedures for determining

---

48. Rogers and Kissinger are business partners. See Scott Sherman, "The Maxwell Affair" in 278 *The Nation* 24, June 21, 2004, at 8.

49. *Yee* (1991) at 181; following indented quotation at 202.

a match of DNA fragments and estimating the likelihood of encountering a similar pattern.

Lewontin and co-witness for the defense Daniel Hartl of the Washington University School of Medicine then submitted an article to *Science*, where it was reviewed and accepted for publication. The standard policy of *Science* is to allow counter-argument to appear in succeeding issues. This time, however, they solicited a rebuttal, and placed that rebuttal in front of the original article when it was published in 1991.[50] Based on the rebuttal, *Science* also requested that changes be made to the Lewontin-Hartl article while it was in galleys. That is, they insisted on modifying an article that had been submitted, peer reviewed, and accepted, at the behest of others—one of whom had testified on the other side from these authors (i.e., for the government) in *Yee*.

Paul Giannelli not only tells us this story, but informs us that "The *Science* controversy was not an isolated incident."

> Professor Seymour Geisser, a statistician at the University of Minnesota, submitted a paper on the forensic use of DNA statistics to the *American Journal of Human Genetics*. One of the anonymous peer reviewers, who strongly recommended against publication, was Dr. Ranajit Chakraborty, who had co-authored the rebuttal article in *Science* and had been aligned with the prosecution in court cases.[51]

Chakraborty had been a frequent expert for the FBI (plaintiffs); Geiser, for defendants. What was one doing reviewing the work of the other for publication? Similarly, one of the experts in *Soto* (1996)—the New Jersey "driving while black" case I described in Chapter 8—was asked to review this book for acceptance by one publisher to which I submitted it.[52] Guess what his reaction was.

---

50. Chakraborty and Kidd (1991) is followed by an article on foreign investments, and then Lewontin and Hartl (1991). The quotation above from Yarborough can be found in the February 28, 1992, issue at 1052. Several letters were published about the controversy, as well as replies by the editor and the two original author pairs. From Steven Austad we read, at 1050:
> Ultimately at fault for the furor is our legal system, which is innocent of quantitative thinking, as well as logic, in its treatment of evidence.

51. Giannelli (1997b), in-text and indented quotations both at 407.

52. This problem is not limited to academia, or specialist publications. Bill O'Reilly, whose Fox television program, *The O'Reilly Factor*, is "the most-watched program on cable news" (*New York Daily News*, October 9, 2003, sidebar accompanying O'Reilly's commentary column), has raised the subject of appropriate reviewers. He says he would be an inappropriate reviewer of books by Jesse Jackson, for example, a person he has criticized. An interview by Terry Gross for the National Public Radio program, *Fresh Air*, taped October 7 and broadcast October 8, 2003, consisted of nothing but Gross reading from reviews of O'Reilly's latest book by people O'Reilly thought should not have been engaged in that activity. The interview ended early when O'Reilly decided he had heard enough criticism and walked out.

Climate

There is a consensus that we are in a period of "global warming." The most famous picture of this phenomenon, created by Michael Mann, is the dark central (smoothed) line in Figure 66.[53] Temperature data are derived from ice cores and variations in the width of tree rings until 1981, after which they are average direct temperature readings. The shading around the line represents "error bounds," usually interpreted as the intervals within which those who derived the figures estimate that the true values would lie most of the times one were deriving them from data such as these. Of course these error bounds are set at plus and minus two standard deviations, and no account is taken of the fact that hundreds of them have been calculated. The same rote calculations employed by litigation experts abound outside the courtroom.

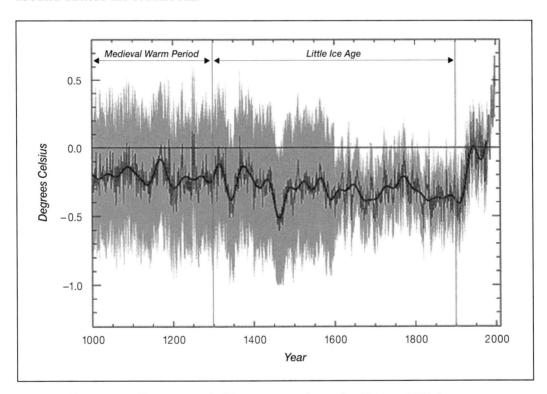

FIGURE 66: Departures in Temperature from the 1961 to 1990 Average

---

53. Figure 66 is from M. Mann et al. (1999). It has been reproduced often on the internet, from which I downloaded it. The figure was prominent in the 2001 United Nations report of the Intergovernmental Panel on Climate Change, and therefore surely is in the public domain. It originally appeared in M. Mann et al. (1998). It has been referred to as the "hockey stick" graphic, from its sharp change in slope in later years. See David Appell, "Behind The Hockey Stick," 292 *Scientific American* 3, March 2005, at 34, picture at 35.

Most scientists thought that from the sixth century AD into the fourteenth century was an exceptionally warm period—called the Holocene Maximum (or, from the ninth through the thirteenth century, the Medieval Warm Period)—warmer then than today. Then there was the "Little Ice Age." Thus Figure 66 represents a "revisionist history," to which some scientists have taken exception. The most prominent doubters, perhaps, are Willie Soon and Sallie Baliunas. I will not cite or describe in detail the ongoing debate.[54] Mann's data are limited geographically. Data are presently being collected from Alaska, Australia, and China, which may bring this debate to a consensus about Earth's temperature history.

The point of interest here is how the critique by Soon and Baliunas came to be published in *Climate Research*, and what then transpired. A paper could be submitted to any one of ten editors, who then followed a review protocol. If it passed the review, the paper would be published regardless what the other nine editors thought about it. The article by Soon and Baliunas was submitted to Chris de Freitas, an editor pre-committed to their point of view.

Several of the editors who had not been involved in reviewing the article considered the Soon and Baliunas work "fundamentally flawed." Although defending the article, the publisher restructured the editorial procedures, engaging Hans von Storch to be editor-in-chief. Von Storch drafted an editorial announcing that the Soon and Baliunas paper should not have been published, and that in the future he would determine which editor reviewed each paper. The publisher of *Climate Research* then changed the rules: This editorial would not be printed unless all ten editors agreed. Therefore Chris de Freitas could veto the editorial. He did. It was retracted. Von Storch considered that procedure unacceptable and resigned, as did four other editors.[55]

Climate Research lost half its editors in 2003 because it could not admit having published a presumably incorrectly refereed paper, and find procedures to prevent this happening again. The journal did later editorially suggest that it should have asked for revisions

---

54. The initial reply to M. Mann et al., and the article that has generated the fuss I am about to describe, is Soon and Baliunas (2003). One wonders if it is incidental that their work was supported by the American Petroleum Institute, as they acknowledge in their paper.

55. The phrase "fundamentally flawed" is from Claire Goodess, who was one of the ten editors. She tells the story in Newsletter 28 from Scientists for Global Responsibility, July, 2001, at 13. Von Storch clearly thought publication was a mistake. His suppressed editorial contains this expression:

> The major result of the Soon and Baliunas paper, "Across the world, many records reveal that the 20th century is probably not the warmest nor a uniquely extreme climatic period of the last millennium," cannot be concluded from the evidence presented in that paper, even if the statement itself may be true.

The editorial is available at http://w3g.gkss.de/G/Mitarbeiter/storch/CR-problem/CR.editorial.pdf. Von Storch, although not crediting them, later concluded that Soon and Baliunas were essentially correct. See von Storch et al. (2004).

from Soon and Baliunas. Thus, although the outcome of the large issue is in doubt, all parties agree that publication of this one article in one presumably neutral journal was misdirected by one editor, who might appropriately have recused himself.[56]

Stephen McIntyre and Ross McKitrick claimed to have recalculated the smoothed estimates by Mann displayed in Figure 66, and to have come up with quite a different picture. If they are correct, the work by Mann is faulty. However, they appear to have made their own mistake. Temperature data have to be adjusted to reflect the latitude at which they were taken. The computer program used by McIntyre and McKitrick expected latitude to be entered in radians. It seems they entered it in degrees.[57] What does peer review mean if it does not resolve issues like this?[58]

---

56. See, for example, by de Freitas: "A Critical Appraisal of the Global Warming Debate," 50 *New Zealand Geographer* 1:30 (1994); or "Are Observed Changes in the Concentration of Carbon Dioxide in the Atmosphere Really Dangerous?" 50 *Bulletin of Canadian Petroleum Geology* 2:297; or "Greenhouse Predictions Versus Climate Realities—Jury still out on global warming," 64 *New Zealand Geographic* 6 (2003).

57. A radian is the angle made by placing an arc of one radius on the circumference of a circle. As there are 360 degrees in a circle, and the circumference is $2\pi r$, one radian is: $360 \div 2\pi \approx 57.3$ degrees.

Tim Lambert disclosed the McIntyre and McKitrick error on his blog *Deltoid*; John Quiggin reviewed the data and the instructions to the SHAZAM program used by McIntyre and McKitrick, and agreed with Lambert on the *Crooked Timber* blog; it was further verified by "S2Focus" on the *Internet Infidels* discussion forum. This activity occurred on August 25 and 26, 2004, and probably can be found in those blogs' archives. I have not seen either Mann or McIntyre and McKitrick comment on this allegation.

58. See McIntyre and McKitrick (2003), who have also alleged both that M. Mann et al. were tight-fisted with their data and that they have altered their data. I downloaded the data set for 1400 to 1995 from ftp://holocene.evsc.virginia.edu/pub/sdr/temp/nature/MANNETAL98/. To summarize the data, I estimated the cubic regression which generated the following graphic:

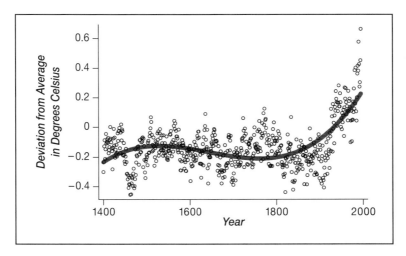

To affect Mann's general proposition, his data errors would have to be massive and biased. The shortness of the observed time period might cast doubt on the *uniqueness* of current temperatures, but not on their *strangeness*.

The climate issue is intensely political. The George W. Bush administration has dealt with environmental problems by defining them away. For example, by changing the description of mountaintops cleared by strip-mining from "waste" to "fill," environmental controls on waste were made inapplicable.[59] Similarly, our government has decided, by decree, that there are no costs generated by industrial CO_2 emissions. It does not deny the emissions themselves, only their ill effects.[60] Thus politics determines how the government will react to environmental issues not through science, but through ideology.

I need pursue this issue no further here. My point is to tell how a presumably respectable, neutral journal reconfigured itself to ally with one side of a controversy, by allowing a participant in the debate to have editorial control. And how an article slipped into another journal, passing through four referees, although incorporating the simplest kind of technical error one can make. And (in footnote 61) how notables such as a famous science-fiction author weigh in on the wrong side of this science-reality issue, either through ignorance or, again, by allowing ideology to trump science.[61]

I trust the parallel to litigation is clear: We say we want to make rational decisions based on facts. Yet we create systems for making these decisions in which facts are not valued. The political community, the body least capable to deal with science matters, has taken effective control. Like the parties in litigation, politicians seek support for their predetermined conclusions. Finding fact is not a valued skill, which is why researchers are not good at it.

---

59. This change is easily found in the rules of the Environmental Protection Agency governing enforcement of the Clean Water Act. More fundamental is the charge by the Union of Concerned Scientists that the administration distorts and manipulates "scientific" evidence to its own ideological ends. See, for example, their report, *Scientific Integrity in Policymaking*, February 2004, available at http://planetfor life.com/pdffiles/RSI_final_fullreport.pdf. The climate change issue is the first one they address, noting especially pressure exerted on the National Academy of Sciences to come out on the EPA's side. Refusing to do so, the Academy suppressed discussion of the issue entirely.

60. See Republican Policy Committee, "The Shaky Science Behind the Climate Change Sense of the Congress Resolution," included in the State Department Authorization Bill of 2003. This report was so biased that it engendered a response from Republican Senator John McCain, writing as chairman of the Senate Committee on Commerce, Science, and Transportation. I found his letter, with an appendix listing criticisms in detail, at http://ucusa.org/documents/climate-andmnt_science-dcoll(final)_JDD.pdf. I do not know its date.

61. Michael Crichton, in a speech to a joint session of the Brookings Institution and the American Enterprise Institute on January 28, 2005, mistakenly presented the McIntyre and McKitrick work as being a definitive critique of Mann. Much though I agree with the gist of Crichton's talk—that more attention should be paid to deriving and disseminating high-quality data—he seemed to have little grasp of statistics or climate issues.

A reasonable position is taken by Elizabeth Kolbert in her three-part *New Yorker* series, "The Climate of Man," starting April 25, 2005, at 56. Kolbert, correctly, finds the Mann vs. McIntyre and McKitrick debate irrelevant. What matters is first that the earth *is* warming, as indicated above at footnote

The Medical Press

Shannon Brownlee informs us about medical research:

> For the past two decades, medical research has been quietly corrupted by cash from private industry. Most doctors and academic researchers aren't corrupt in the sense of intending to defraud the public or harm patients, but rather, more insidiously, guilty of allowing the pharmaceutical and biotech industries to manipulate medical science through financial relationships, in effect tainting the system that is supposed to further the understanding of disease and protect patients from ineffective or dangerous drugs.[62]

Money corrupts. Clients get what they pay for, and the press reports it.

If clients don't get what they pay for, they get nasty. Results of the "VIGOR"—Vioxx Gastrointestinal Outcomes Research—study were published in the *New England Journal of Medicine* in November 2000. Four years later it was revealed that the data used for that study were "preliminary." Even though Merck, the manufacturer of Vioxx, knew that final data did not support the "favorable cardiovascular safety profile" indicated in that article— the Food and Drug Administration told Merck that this conclusion was "simply incomprehensible" in 2001—Merck continued to say that it did in its advertising until late 2004. It added a cardiovascular caution (but not a warning) to its label, and ultimately (in the fall of 2004) withdrew the drug.

58, and second that much of the cause is man-made. No policy question depends on whether the warming is unique.

The U.S. National Climatic Center, for example, provides us this 120-year picture of global temperature departures from the long-term mean:

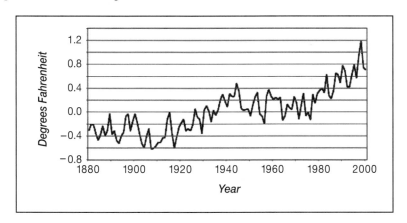

Whether Earth has been here before is not nearly as important as preparing for where it is going now.

62. Shannon Brownlee, "Doctors Without Borders: Why you can't trust medical journals anymore," *Washington Monthly*, April 2004 (http://www.washingtonmonthly.com/features/2004/0404.brownlee.html).

Gurkirpal Singh, at the Stanford School of Medicine, tried to obtain VIGOR data from Merck.

> Merck had responded to all my requests promptly and in a scientific fashion. With VIGOR, suddenly it was as if the Company had to think what questions to answer. I persisted in my enquiries—and I was warned that if I continued in this fashion, there would be serious consequences for me. I was told that Dr. Louis Sherwood, a Merck senior vice-president, and a former Chief of Medicine at a medical school, had extensive contacts within the academia and could make life "very difficult" for me at Stanford and outside.[63]

Clearly, what is published is determined by what data are available, which is controlled by the drug companies that sponsor the studies.

In his testimony, Singh indicated that company-sponsored studies are designed to avoid areas of weakness. If the study uncovers a weakness, however, it can still be hidden in the analysis. Shane Ellison refers to a review of Celebrex, published in the *Journal of the American Medical Association*:

> Pharmacia, the manufacturers of Celebrex, made it appear as if the study lasted only 6 months. In reality, the study of Celebrex lasted a year. During the last half of the year (which was unreported) almost all of the ulcer complications that occurred during the study were in Celebrex users.[64]

All of the authors of that study were employees or paid consultants of Pharmacia.

That articles in medical publications are controlled by drug companies might not implicate the publications themselves. They can only print articles that are submitted to them. Except for *reviews* of medical research:

> In [the medical] world, the author of a review article can have direct financial relationships with the manufacturers of drugs he is critiquing and still argue he has done nothing unsavory.

Although some medical journals require the revelation of conflicts of interest, others do not.[65]

---

63. Gurkirpal Singh, from a transcript of his videotaped testimony (recovering from a heart attack, he could not testify live) to the Senate Finance Committee, November 19, 2004.

64. Shane Ellison, "Pharmaceutical Scam—The Jaw-Dropping Truth," *The Chronic Pain Haven* blog, http://www.chronic-pain-haven.com/pharmaceutical-scam.html, downloaded November 21, 2004.

65. The indented quotation is from the Shannon Brownlee article referenced above, in footnote 62. The American Medical Association has called for a federal data base of clinical trials, so that drug companies could not bury those delivering unfavorable results. See Barry Meier, "A.M.A. Urges Disclosure on Drug Trials," *New York Times* (online), June 16, 2004:

> In some instances, the [AMA] report found, researchers are reluctant to submit studies unless the results are positive or significant, believing that journals will not publish them.

Let us remember what the *Journal of The American Medical Association* did when its editor, George Lundberg, published an article about what college students meant by the phrase "having sex." At the time, the President of the United States was suggesting that Monica Lewinsky's fellatio was not "having sex," and that therefore Bill Clinton had not lied under oath, saying he had not "had sex" with her. That is, Lundberg published an article that was relevant to political issues of the day. For that, in 1999, he was fired. One can debate the merits of his action vis-à-vis the journal's mission statement, but that is not my role, nor my point. What counts is that, whether as policy or as practice, the American Medical Association was not interested in contributing knowledge to a public debate—at least, not *that* public debate.

How generalizable these anecdotes are I cannot say, but representative or not, they are real. They are contrary to the concepts we think lie behind science publications.[66] They are contrary to any concept we have of "intellectuality" or "scholarship." The publisher's agenda is not the straightforward portrayal of the debate. The notion that publication raises one to an expert level—the idea fostered by the retention in *Daubert* rules of the credentialism called for by *Frye*—is dangerous.[67] It enhances the power of editors, and whatever forces lie behind them, within the litigation system. Who benefits from that? I further discuss expert credentials, and their valuation by judges, in Chapter 10.

Because federal funds subsidize the same university research that leads to new drug development, the drug companies are "in bed" with the government that is supposed to regulate them. See, for example, Marcia Angell, "The Truth About the Drug Companies," 51 *New York Review of Books* 12, July 15, 2004, at 52.

66. I have provided a deliberately naive model of "pure" science against which to contrast my stories of censorship. Caudill and Larue (2003), urging a "pragmatic" assessment of expert testimony, note, at 35, that

> there is always funding from somewhere, and there is always a social or contextual reason to study something.

True, but let's not turn away from the effects of that social context. It is beyond the interest of this book to develop a description of academic corruption engendered by commercial sponsorship of science—a description that would in any case be similar to advocate sponsorship of expert testimony. Richard Horton, editor of *The Lancet*, writes (presumably about *other* journals) in 51 *New York Review of Books* 4, March 11, 2004, at 9:

> [M]edical journals have become an important but unrecognized obstacle to scientific truth-telling. Journals have devolved into information-laundering operations for the pharmaceutical industry.

67. Kordana and O'Reilly (2001), at 2025, would have publication in "a well respected refereed economic journal" constitute "*prima facie* evidence of [a study's] admissibility, indeed of scientific rigor." They are discussing David Kaye's critique of Richard Leftwich's work in *Conwood* (2000). See Kaye (2001). Kaye's position, that the method must be valid with regard to the subject matter, is certainly correct, but no more helpful than Kordana and O'Reilly's obeisance to academic judgment.

STATISTICS

Educators in statistics acknowledge problems teaching both their majors and the masses. In a symposium in *The American Statistician*, one professor wrote:

> Few people learn from basic principles down to special cases. . . . "Theory first" in basic statistics is destined to fail—students have no idea what this is the theory of.[68]

I think this is true not only for persons studying statistics, but for persons being introduced to statistical concepts. Judges, for example.

It is also a problem among professionals. One well-credentialed applicant for a senior analyst position at my firm averred that she could do equal-employment-opportunity cases "with my hands tied behind my back." She meant that she knew the standard specification of a wage regression. I would not employ a person who thought the analysis of real issues would ever be easy. I have tried to show in this book that even the seemingly simplest issues deserve fresh thinking.

Consider this advice from the same *American Statistician* symposium:

> Statistics is primarily an applied discipline—students should have the experience of applying their learning in settings as real as possible during their education.[69]

I agree. This advice apparently comes from non-academics. I take it as similar to or confirmation of my point: Bring real-world examples into the classroom, without the attitude that you already know the answers. Let the students work it out. You might be surprised.

Statistics and Economics

Should law be part of the statistics or economics curriculum? It already is. John Campbell, we are told,

> teaches a course at Harvard that has included a segment on CMOs and their valuation.[70]

"CMOs" are collateralized mortgage obligations. Inevitably, investors sue over how such instruments were valued by brokers, creating expert-witness fees for Campbell and perhaps, in the future, for his students.

---

68. D. Moore (2001) at 1.

69. Ritter et al. (2001) at 17.

70. *Primavera* (2001) at 523.

Finance, human capital, antitrust, and epidemiology are law-related fields. Chapters 2 and 3 were devoted to the use of the tools of economists and statisticians in legal settings, some of which surely (one hopes) find their way into the classroom. In particular, at least for major papers, and I would think even for Ph.D. dissertations, re-evaluation of the economics or statistics in certain cases, or a group of cases, would be in order. There will be law-review articles telling us what *Microsoft* means in terms of antitrust law. Someone has to suggest what *Microsoft* means in the history of expert presentations in antitrust, in the history of empirical analysis of monopolies, in terms of economics.[71] These are worthy academic tasks.

John Lehoczky describes the statistics Ph.D. curriculum at Carnegie-Mellon. He tells us how important it is that "students gain experience in working on real applications," and lists eighteen projects. Despite the great experience of many Carnegie-Mellon statistics faculty with litigation, that topic is not mentioned in the text, nor included in the examples.[72]

There is no shortage of project ideas. What about evaluating the work judges are doing in *Daubert* hearings? Lloyd Dixon and Brian Gill suggest that

> One promising approach is to assemble panels of experts to evaluate expert evidence in a sample of cases. The experts would evaluate the reliability of both admitted and excluded evidence to understand how well the screening process is working. The results of such an evaluation could be the basis of a report card on how well judges are performing the gatekeeping function.[73]

They do not suggest how to fund such a "panel of experts." What about panels of students?

LAW SCHOOLS

I cannot leave the topic of education without considering the education of attorneys. I start with a bias. My father, Morris, was a sole practitioner, a trial attorney in Boston. From my visits to his courtrooms I would say he was a master of his craft. I never saw an objection of his overruled, although I did sense exasperation on the part of opposing attorneys and judges at the preciseness in following the rules to which Morris held them. He may not have been an "intellectual," but he could have taught young attorneys a thing or two about how to prepare for and conduct a trial.

---

71. Gavil (1999) says the *Microsoft* case presents "a new paradigm of complex antitrust litigation," but does not clearly describe what that paradigm is. "In the final analysis, *Microsoft*'s procedural course may be among its most enduring legacies." He means it went rather quickly. I hope it was more important than that. Both quotations at 13.

72. Lehoczky (1995).

73. Dixon and Gill (2002) at 301.

In his later years, he wanted to teach his craft, as he had for fifty years to law-school graduates who came to apprentice in his office. I remember his making disparaging remarks about law schools not being interested in the craft of lawyering, but my brother, perhaps because he *is* a law-school graduate, and therefore Morris would not make such remarks to him, has no such recollection. I find familiar the sense that law firms, law schools, and departments of statistics and economics do not treat actual litigation analyses, and the people who did them, as resources especially useful to students.[74] Except for that period when I brought experts and attorneys to open lunches in Washington, D.C., I have seen no other such activity, on or off campus.

Randy Barnett, a professor at Boston University School of Law, tells us that no school was interested in hiring him when he was applying as an Assistant Cook County Attorney. Unable to obtain an academic position, he committed to spend a year as a research fellow at the University of Chicago Law School. He had faculty offers even before he had done any work there. "Merely the change of status from county prosecutor to research fellow . . . seemed to have made the difference," he concludes.[75]

Here I turn away from the supposed intellectuality in academia with which I opened this chapter. Historically, public education arose to provide a superior working class. As many members of that class now must have college degrees, more of them are attending public universities. Law is a craft; law schools exist to teach that craft. I will return to other graduate specialties below. Let's first continue down this line of law school as a training ground for lawyers, not as a home for intellectuals.

The Rise of Law Schools

This is admittedly an old-fashioned view of the purpose of graduate schools, expressed by Oliver Wendell Holmes:

> Take the fundamental question, What constitutes the law? You will find some
> text writers telling you that it is something different from what is decided by
> the courts of Massachusetts or England, that it is a system of reason, that it is
> a deduction from the principles of ethics or admitted axioms or what not,
> which may or may not coincide with the decisions. But if we take the view of
> our friend the bad man we shall find that he does not care two straws for the

---

74. For an inside look at one law school's recruitment of entry-grade faculty, see the archives of Robert Gordon's blog now at http://www.theconglomerate.org/. Gordon, a professor of law at the University of Wisconsin, is part of the team that recruits new faculty. A series titled, "So You Want To Be A Law Professor," starts on August 24, 2004, and continues through Part V on November 17. It is not a pretty picture, if you are a law student. The emphasis is on "scholarship," not knowledge of field and ability to teach. Gordon also provides advice on how to behave during an interview.

75. Barnett is writing at *The Volokh Conspiracy*, http://volokh.com, February 2, 2005.

axioms or deductions, but that he does want to know what the Massachusetts or English courts are likely to do in fact. I am much of his mind. The prophesies of what the courts will do in fact, and nothing more pretentious, are what I mean by the law.[76]

To the lawyer, according to Holmes, law is court practice. It is the set of rules, explicit or implicit, that judges follow.[77] We go to a lawyer to find out how to articulate the mess we just got into in order to minimize the court's reaction; or to obtain redress for having been wronged; or to defend against someone seeking such redress; or to arrange a transaction invulnerable to challenge. The lawyer's job is to know his way around, and make the best case he can from the facts, the legislated law, and precedential law.[78]

In Chapter 1 I proposed that "law" is the finding of constitutional fact. I am slightly broadening—or making more explicit—the implications of that definition here. Law is constitutional, legislatively created, and precedential fact. In practice, the lawyer is not a passive recipient of the law; he is an active participant in determining what the law is. He 1) determines what law should be to most help his client's cause; 2) finds any shred of evidence that law can be interpreted that way; and 3) uses his knowledge of procedure to advance his client's cause. Court is the forum within which a lawyer argues his client's case for what the empirical facts are, what the constitutional facts should be, and how they should be applied to the empirical facts, if he is to prevail. The lawyer needs to be skilled in arguing constitutional-fact issues, and in using legislative and adjudicative fact to serve his client, but not in *finding* empirical fact. For that he "outsources" to experts.

There is a more famous Holmes quotation, from the same article, that is about the theory of law, not its practice:

> For the rational study of the law the black-letter man may be the man of the present, but the man of the future is the man of statistics and the master of economics.[79]

The study of law may be history, "why a particular rule of law has taken its particular shape"; or the science of law, the rationalization of law "to an end which it subserves."

---

76. Holmes (1897) at 460. Holmes had written, at 459, that "a bad man has as much reason as a good one for wishing to avoid an encounter with the public force." Which is why law may be a reflection of our public morality, but they are not the same thing.

77. "There are times when even a bad rule is better than no rule at all." Scalia (1989) at 1179.

78. "From this standpoint all that matters is being able to predict how the judges will rule given a particular set of facts, and this is why people consult lawyers." Posner (1997) at 1040. "I like lawyer Clark. You know, he really is my friend. He says if I just stay out of the grave, he'll make sure I stay out of the pen." From "Lawyer Clark" by Sleepy John Estes, Bluebird B8871 (1941). Holmes' view is of course not the only view of what law is. For the articulation of just one other view, see J. White (1985).

79. Holmes (1897) at 469; following in-text quotations also at 469.

Holmes predicts that the history of law will give over to the science of law, so that the historically described "dragon" (the rules) can be tamed into "a useful animal." It is the science of law, not the practice of law, that requires "the man of statistics and the master of economics."[80]

This much-celebrated essay of Holmes is taken to be the precursor of the evolution of "law and economics" and other social sciences within the law school. But the question remains, in what way does advancing the science of law (of formulating laws) assist the practicing lawyer?[81] What does the science of law have to do with the craft of law?

One could say Holmes was better at the meta-study of law—realizing that there were useful tools out there—than at evolving legal doctrine. From the point of view of this book, consider the following Supreme Court opinion by Holmes:

> But there is a point beyond which this court does not consider arguments of this sort for the purpose of invalidating the tax laws of a state on constitutional grounds. This limit has been fixed in many cases. It is that unless the party setting up the unconstitutionality of the state law belongs to the class for whose sake the constitutional protection is given, or the class primarily protected, this court does not listen to his objections, and will not go into imaginary cases, notwithstanding the seeming logic of the position that it must do so, because if, for any reason, or as against any class embraced, the law is unconstitutional, it is void as to all.[82]

That is, in the context of Chapter 5, only a black defendant (or, perhaps, a black citizen) could complain about the lack of blacks in the jury system. That was the Supreme Court's opinion in 1907, and remained so for decades. Consider this mid-1950s opinion by Justice

---

80. That this quotation is both loved and misunderstood is indicated by its use in a comment about *Daubert* (1993). See Note (1995) at 1532. Just as ignorantly, Mary Gray asks, "[A]re we in the future contemplated by Holmes?" in an article proposing guidelines to statistical experts. See "Cramming for Court: Teaching Statistics to Litigators" (2002), paper delivered at the Sixth International Conference on Teaching Statistics, Cape Town, South Africa, July 8, 2002.

81. "The Path of the Law was about the business of ordinary lawyering, not about great cases." Weinberg (1997) at 698. Posner (1997), at 1039, called Holmes "the pre-eminent figure in the history of American law." I think not. At least, I hope not.

82. *Hatch* (1907) at 160, Justice Holmes for the Court. The view expressed by Weinberg (1997), at 693, is close to mine:

> Holmes' ideas are stale. . . . [His mind] was locked in a dusty law office, where a conscientious counselor advises his client how to avoid legal liability.

Holmes was speaking from a long career as a practicing lawyer, even though, when he wrote "The Path of The Law," he had been a justice of the Massachusetts Supreme Court for over a decade. He was writing before there were codified rules of civil procedure or of evidence of which, I am sure, he would have approved. I think his years of predicting the outcomes from local courts did not prepare him to take a creative judicial role.

Clark that appears to look back to Holmes' statement, above, and reiterate that it still holds:

> This Court over the past 50 years has adhered to the view that valid grand-jury
> selection is a constitutionally protected right. The indictment of a defendant
> by a grand jury from which *members of his race* have been systematically
> excluded is a denial of his right to equal protection of the laws.[83]

Holmes was hardly a progressive. Although some characterize him this way, he was not by and large the activist dissenter whose views prevailed years later. Besides being wrong he was, as a jurist, boring.[84]

Law was not an intellectual pursuit in the first hundred years of United States history. Most lawyers, Abraham Lincoln among them, did not go to law school. They apprenticed with practicing attorneys, learning the trade.

> The American lawyer was never primarily a learned doctor of laws; he was a
> man of action and cunning, not a scholar. He played a useful role, sometimes
> admired, but rarely loved.[85]

We can count on educators to make themselves indispensable. Within a hundred years after Lincoln, it was virtually impossible to be a lawyer *without* having graduated from law school.[86] And impossible for a major law school not to have expanded into social science.

"The duty of the American law school is to train lawyers for the good of society," says Gerry Spence, who also tells us he hated law school.[87] I'm not so sure about this

---

83. *Reece* (1955) at 87, emphasis added. Only with *Peters* (1972) for race and *Taylor* (1975) for gender did the Court determine that "impartial" (the constitutional term) means "fair"—means that any defendant can complain about improperly constituted juries.

84. For example, the dictum in *Goodman* (1927) that Justice Cardozo dispensed with in *Pokora* (1934) (see footnote 9 in the Preface and footnote 83 in Chapter 8) was from Holmes, who also wrote the opinion in *Buck* (1927), allowing forced sterilization of the "feeble-minded." *Buck* at 207:

> It is better for all the world, if instead of waiting to execute degenerate offspring for crime,
> or to let them starve for their imbecility, society can prevent those who are manifestly
> unfit from continuing their kind.

However, he was more than a jurist. Indeed, that activity came late in his life. He was a philosopher— Posner (2003), in footnote 23 at 33, calls him "the American Nietzsche"—and a conceptualizer about law, such as in his theory of contracts.

85. Friedman (1985) at 304. Singer (1992), at 9, describes a former slave, grandfather of the successful Tin Pan Alley lyricist Andy Razaf:

> Late in 1874 he received an admiring offer from a prominent Cedar Rapids judge to join
> the man's law firm. Three years later, having apprenticed with the judge, John Waller
> passed his bar examination in an otherwise all-white class and was granted his certificate
> to practice law.

86. John Rawls, who was born in 1921, went to law school and became a noted law professor. His father had earned his license to practice law through apprenticeship.

87. Quotation from Spence (1989) at 235; hating law school at 240.

"for the good of society" part. Just train lawyers in their craft.

I leave to others to describe the history of law-school diversification. I think it happened as they have taken on several missions. Thirty years after Holmes wrote his most famous essay, training lawyers still seemed paramount.

> The lawyer must understand how to ascertain the existing law, and how to predict the development of it through judicial decisions; he must acquire the technique of presenting to courts the kind of argument likely to prevail; and he must learn to advise his clients how to adapt their behavior to the law as it exists or as it is likely to be developed or modified by judicial decision.[88]

In this Holmesian view,[89] law schools exist to turn out practitioners of the law. Formulators of the law are other people. However, if law is predicting what judges do then, as Posner points out, judges themselves cannot do that. Arthur Miller had made much the same point:

> If judges unavoidably must be forward-looking as much as they search for existing doctrine, then the way in which the judicial mind is informed becomes a matter of critical import.[90]

The law *judges* do must be based on more than received doctrine. It is judges and legislators, not attorneys, who can use a dose of social science. Much though statisticians like to quote Holmes as predicting or justifying the rise of the expert witness, Holmes did nothing of the sort. He predicted—urged—that rules of law would be formulated starting at the desired outcome and working backward to procedure. He predicted—urged—that social science would be brought in to help in this task, not in the courtroom itself.

Law schools in the United States have always turned out both law users and law makers, even though what these different students need to know may be very different.[91] Robert Hale, in 1927, did not advocate that law schools should mind only their practitioner business. Legal science is "an understanding of the effect of actual or possible legal arrangements on the various interests promoted or retarded thereby."[92] It may be required for rule making, but need not be part of the practitioner's curriculum. He suggested:

---

88. R. Hale (1927) at 131.

89. Holmes (1897) at 458:

> [A] legal duty so called is nothing but a prediction that if a man does or omits certain things he will be made to suffer in this or that way by judgment of the court.

90. Miller (1968) at 210. Posner (1997) at 1041: "[W]hat judges do is not law in any sense that the legal professional will recognize."

91. I have not done research on the form of legal training in other countries, but I believe some Asian countries—Japan and South Korea for example—have schools for judges separate from those for lawyers.

92. R. Hale (1927) at 131; following indented quotation at 142.

> For if the learning of the leaders of the bar included training in legal and eco-
> nomic science, it would be less likely than it is now for the ignorant utterances
> of politicians and bankers and diplomats to pass as enlightened economic
> statesmanship; and the leaders of the bar might less frequently than at present
> set an example of ignorance to the laymen.

So Hale thought that law schools should employ social scientists to give their future law-
maker students the background they need. This defines the alternative goals of law schools:
They train lawyers, judges, and legislators; law users and law refiners and law makers.[93]

More than forty years later, Ovid Lewis chafed at the reins:

> Occasionally there are course offerings in social sciences, but the bulk of the
> curriculum, especially at the middle-range law schools, remains dedicated to
> the traditional courses as though the schools were totally committed to the
> policy expressed in Samuel Hoffenstein's immortal "Come weal, come woe,
> my status is quo."[94]

Studying legal "doctrine" is boring. Lewis did not want lawyers just to practice law, but to
advance law. The situation has so turned around that Richard Posner apparently thinks law
students now are holding the university back:

> The vast majority of law students are interested only in studies that will con-
> tribute directly to their success as practicing lawyers.[95]

The vast majority of law-school students apparently want the school to do what it traditionally did—train lawyers. But now the faculty does not! Posner advocates

> the appointment of more economists, of philosophers, and perhaps of other
> nonlegal scholars such as anthropologists, sociologists, and statisticians, to
> full-time positions on law school faculties.

Posner distinguishes between the "internal" evolution of law (that engineered by lawyers) and the "external" evolution (that engineered by theorists). He thinks little of the former, and so proposes to increase the presence of social scientists on law-school faculty.[96]
I'm all for "advancing" law, but first, let's train the lawyers. What we need do is honor
Holmes' distinction, teach the craft to those who want to learn it, and utilize other skills to
enhance the evolution of law itself.

---

93. We should credit attorneys for pushing out the boundaries as much as or more than judges. It was
a Louis D. Brandeis, a Thurgood Marshall who proposed, the courts that heard them and disposed. But
I do not think social-science training helped these distinguished attorneys, or any others, in their progressive attack on current legal boundaries. On the contrary, as discussed in Chapter 1, Brandeis and
Marshall used social scientists to do their bidding, creating the tradition of the expert as hired hand.

94. Lewis (1970) at 149.

95. Posner (1981) at 1121; following indented quotation at 1129.

96. See Posner (2001b).

Posner speaks from his "law and economics" background. That field of study may well have contributed to legal theory; but I don't know that learning it makes for better lawyers, that is, in the context of this book, better clients for experts. I see nothing in the opinions of judges, as described in Chapter 7, that requires a sure understanding of social science. Rather, as I stressed there, it is by sticking with the procedures social scientists use—something familiar to law—that judges best assess social-science expertise.[97] Though Posner thinks that "the challenge is to make the law school a comfortable habitat for a diverse group of disciplines,"[98] it is not clear what these non-lawyers would do there. Fortunately, they would not try to teach statistics to future lawyers and judges:

> I do *not* propose that juries or, for that matter, judges be instructed in the elements of Bayesian theory or mathematical probability more generally—or any other theory of probability or evidence.[99]

The Mission of Law Schools

We should give up producing special materials from which attorneys and judges would "learn" statistics. They are lawyers and judges *because* they do not take well to statistics.

> Fewer than 10 percent of all students attending law school have undergraduate degrees in fields that require substantial math and science training, such as the natural sciences, math and statistics, computer science and engineering. Not only do they not have training in the particular subject, they have a more profound disability: most lawyers have little or no appreciation for the scientific method and lack the ability to judge whether proffered research is good science, bad science, or science at all.[100]

Attorneys and judges need to stay with procedure, at which they excel. If the primary challenge of the law school is to educate future lawyers, then social scientists, at least as currently employed, do not help. We need lawyers better trained to prepare and present a case, to assist their experts to communicate with the judge, to understand that statistical analysis is evidence, not proof.

My view about lawyers in real-world situations accommodates this view of lawyers in law schools. My presentation of the Social Rehabilitation Services case in Chapter 6 was about this subject: Lawyers will not be expert at creating or utilizing data bases. They would

---

97. Brewer (1998) thinks just the opposite, that ordinary judges are not capable of understanding scientific method, scientific procedure. Perhaps they do not come to the bench trained in it, but they can learn scientific procedure more easily than they can learn science.

98. Posner (1981) at 1130.

99. Posner (1999a) at 1469.

100. Faigman (2000) at 53.

do better by engaging experts earlier in the proceedings, and monitoring them more closely. They need to know how to communicate with the expert, not how to do his work.

The Harvard Center for Law and Education was being formed when I was on the faculty of the Graduate School of Education. It was to be a backup center to assist Legal Services field offices. I suggested—well nigh insisted—that it not be composed only of attorneys and secretaries. It should include someone with technical research skills and knowledge. I knew just the person to fill that position, Paul Smith, a technically sophisticated and wise graduate student. Paul got the job and proved that I had been correct, that the Center needed analytic, statistical skills to keep it on course.[101]

Law schools vie with business schools (and perhaps schools of government) to be the graduate liberal-arts schools of today. To the extent that they engage in the real world, their core faculty for the most part argue appeals. Most law schools engage practicing attorneys to teach practical courses, although Spence tells us that

> most of the training of young lawyers in this country has been entrusted to professors who have never engaged in the actual practice of law or, if they have, have abandoned it after a short and usually disillusioning exposure for the more sedate life within the university.[102]

The difference is "adjunct" professors, practitioners called in for a special purpose, but not to fully join the faculty. The law student gets least contact with the instructors he needs most.[103] The law student is in a merger of three schools: one turning out lawyers; one turning out law makers (legislators); and one turning out people who just want more liberal-arts education. Whether these schools have merged comfortably is not for me to say, but if I am correct that most training of future attorneys is undertaken by faculty with a marginal connection to the school, I infer that it has achieved second-class status.

---

101. Paul left the Harvard Center for Law and Education to complete his doctorate, and then went with Marian Wright Edelman to the Children's Defense Fund in Washington, D.C., where he has been in charge of getting facts right ever since. Whatever criticisms I have seen of the Fund's operation, or its advocacy, I have never seen a hint that its data were not accurate and reasonably interpreted. Not that Paul wouldn't have operated as well otherwise, but I like to credit his experience with legal issues as having some effect on this data accuracy. Marian, also, should get credit for understanding how critical to her operation it has been to have an expert in charge of data.

102. Spence (1989) at 52.

103. This phenomenon, using marginal faculty to teach basic courses, is not restricted to law schools. Scheaffer and Stasny (2004), at 269,

> estimate that fewer than 50% of the faculty teaching statistics courses in mathematics departments have at least a masters degree in statistics, a situation that is much worse in two-year colleges.

This is not true in statistics departments, but most students enrolled in undergraduate statistics courses are taking them in mathematics departments.

A School for Judges

An obvious conclusion from the above discussion is that judges need different training, additional to that required of lawyers. I do not demean the practical experience that attorneys get, which is a usual requirement for judgeship. Quite the contrary. I have been laudatory of experience throughout this book. My Ph.D. was merely a platform for, an entry point to, my real education. I see no reason to think that lawyers are different. But what they need to be lawyers—schooling and experience in the craft of law—is inadequate preparation for being a judge.

Institutions are currently in place to provide schooling for judges in the United States. They do not approach the subject as I would have them do it. Nor is attendance required for any judgeship. The National College of the State Judiciary has been training state judges since 1964. The Federal Judicial Center, as one of its many functions, produces federal judge training. The American Law Institute produces training sessions for judges. Hundreds of judges have passed through courses at the Law and Economics Center at George Mason University and at other, similar institutions. In the late 1970s I taught one "course" for the Federal Judicial Center, on statistics. My students were judges in the Fifth Circuit. I concluded then that the judges needed something else, not a primer. At the time I could not articulate what that something else was, but now I see it as training in how to see *through* the statistics to the underlying issues, not training in statistics.

For example, in the New Jersey case discussed under "Driving While Black" in Chapter 8, the judge notes that those speeding on the New Jersey Turnpike—defined as driving faster than sixty miles per hour—are 98.1 percent of all cars.[104] The percentage black among those "speeders" is compared with the percentage black among those stopped for speeding. A judge might ask whether 98.1 percent of all cars on the road is the population at risk for being fairly stopped for speeding. The judge does not need to know the statistics procedure used to compare speeders with stops. He does not need to evaluate the survey for accuracy in execution (although he should know to ask about it). He needs to know that this survey of speeders says nothing about the people we think of as speeders, those who pass us when we are driving ten or fifteen miles per hour over the posted limit. We need the kind of judicial training that would encourage a judge to take judicial notice of a more practical definition of "speeding," and throw out this survey for lack of relevance.

Here is another example. In *Forehand* (1996), an Eleventh Circuit panel defines an "ideal" promotion analysis, when there are two kinds of promotion, competitive and noncompetitive:

---

104. *Soto* (1996) at 70.

> The parties do not explain why they chose not to emphasize what we have
> characterized the "ideal" analysis—i.e.: first, comparing applicants for com-
> petitive promotions to those granted competitive promotions; and, second,
> comparing employees eligible for noncompetitive promotions to those grant-
> ed noncompetitive promotions.[105]

The word "compare" is general enough that, I think we can agree, the panel got it right.
In the text to which this is a footnote, however, they would "compare the percentage of
blacks in the work force to the percentage granted noncompetitive promotions." Surely that
is wrong. Any analysis, be it overt multiple-pools or survival analysis—both explained in
Chapter 2—would define those who might have been promoted each time someone was.
The Eleventh Circuit should have substituted its footnote language for that in the text, and
added that it wants to see a summary calculation. Then leave it to the experts to determine
how these "comparisons" should be made. Judges need to be taught to tell the experts what
they want (the concept), and to let the experts do their work (the method).

As was implied by my raising the issue in Chapter 1, how judges come to knowledge is
a matter of great sensitivity to attorneys. Judge Sporkin was removed from the *Microsoft*
case for relying more on a book he read than on evidence from the parties.[106] Judge Boggs
was asked to recuse himself from one case because of his participation in a seminar. I agree
with his response:

> To the extent that a judge remains interested at all in the events of society, a
> judge will inevitably be exposed to matters relating, in greater or lesser degree,
> to interesting areas of the law on which the judge may be called to rule. How-
> ever, such general knowledge does not constitute extra-judicial knowledge of
> disputed evidentiary facts.[107]

I would have *mandatory* training, at full salary, for some months between appointment
to a judgeship and assuming its duties. It is in this course that these students, almost all
lawyers, could study the history and science of law, indeed, with social scientists, if they
would help. These neophyte judges would study aspects of their new craft, such as case
management, and discuss with senior judges the pros and cons of different levels of
involvement with complex cases.

> Intelligence aside, judges vary considerably in how they view their role in the
> courtroom; active or passive, dominating or deferential to counsel, prone to
> independent inquiry or content to let the lawyers try the case.[108]

---

105. *Forehand* (1996), footnote 24 at 1572. The definition of an "ideal" analysis, also referred to here, is
also at 1572, in text.

106. See *Microsoft I* (1995).

107. *Bonds* (1994) at 1331.

108. Walsh (1999) at 144.

Is there no wisdom to impart to new judges about the consequences of these different approaches?

Sanctions may be imposed for failing to comply with a scheduling order under Federal Rule of Civil Procedure 37. The expert can be excluded unless the failure to disclose information is harmless. Thus any attempt to exclude an expert under Rule 37 will produce its own litigation. Part of "case management" training is learning how to write such an order. For example, discovery was closed on December 30, 1998 in *Sherrod* (2000), but plaintiff relied on Rule 26, which sets the deadline for submission of an expert's report ninety days before trial. No trial date had been set, and the "close of discovery" order did not specifically refer to expert reports. Plaintiff had given notice who his experts would be, and provided preliminary reports, but defendant, by delaying responses until close to the deadline, could prevent plaintiffs' experts from having the benefit of its discovery. Better scheduling is called for.[109]

Rather than learn science in this special training, judges would hone their skills at penetrating through the technicalities of expert analyses, to their conceptual core. Lawyers could take this additional training at any time, or perhaps in evening courses. Most lawyers would not take this training. Judges and Justices might require that their clerks have it, because the clerk comes directly into a judge-like setting.[110]

I make this suggestion from my experiences with under-trained lawyers, the Joel Kleins of the world, who think their academic excellence allows them to make a mess of a trial.[111] And under-trained judges who, I think, gain little but confusion from the materials presented to them to help them through "scientific" cases. The Carnegie Commission advocates more training of judges, but avoids the important question, what they intend the content of that training to be.[112] My judge course could include training on handling science experts, which is to say training in the assessment of statistical presentations, but not in science or statistics itself. As we will see in an education example at the end of this chapter, one can know what a statistic is—that is, what information it provides—and therefore why one would calculate it, without knowing how to calculate it oneself. Most material meant to "educate" judges confuses these tasks, causing the student to spend too much time learning how to do something he will never be called upon to do in practice.

---

109. The Seventh Circuit was surely correct to reverse the exclusion of plaintiff's experts in that situation.

110. Many other countries, Japan in particular, have recognized the different skills that law schools might impart, to different participants, and have arranged "tracks" accordingly. I do not necessarily recommend any one of these models, but I do recommend thinking about them.

111. Since his antitrust days, Klein has become chancellor of New York City schools, where he continues to operate as though intelligence can substitute for skill, attitude can substitute for excellence.

112. See Carnegie (1993).

The Meta-Law School

Training lawyers and judges involves limited use of social scientists, although the latter would have more use for them than the former. Even the student who wants to learn his craft can use a course or two in the history or evolution of law. If the common law of England is "the grand reservoir of all our jurisprudence," then even the practicing attorney might benefit from knowing something about it.[113] Yet there is a third function, the evolution of legal theory itself, that law schools exercise.[114] Advocates like Posner confuse the use of history, economics, and other social sciences in advancing legal theory with their very limited use in educating lawyers or judges. It may be that the same institution can house all three functions, but unless it learns to see them as separate, it will continue to turn out attorneys who deal with experts as commodities, as automatons who have nothing conceptually to contribute to their case. Having been so considered and so selected, that is what those experts will be.

Other Graduate Schools

What about other departments, especially statistics and economics? Of the two, statistics is surely the more craft-oriented, whereas economics has more intellectual pretensions. Yet most economists will do well to have learned some basic principles, and how to apply them. Most schools call for no more from their students. Ultimately such schools turn out candidates for jobs. Thus graduate schools are and perhaps should be schools of craft. If they are the repository of intellectuality, as Posner asserts, it is a sad statement about both intellectuals and graduate schools.

That statistical studies in litigation show few signs of intellectual inquiry—where the opportunity is there for it—I attribute to the training and selection of those who take on the task. Yet I advocate that their training should be in craft. What is missing?

What is missing is, in a sense, Black Mountain College in its earliest years, the spirit of intellectual inquiry, of creativity, rather than preparation for economic success. We cannot ask colleges, and especially graduate schools, to be other than craft schools— and I do not intend to demean this as their goal. It is not surprising that Black Mountain

---

113. *Wonson* (1812) at 750. Justice Story says it is the English common law that is referred to in the Seventh Amendment to the United States Constitution. Wolfram (1973) quotes Justice Story's interpretation favorably, at 641.

114. Heise (1999) at 810:

> For better or worse (or, more precisely, for better and worse), law professors produce most legal scholarship.

That is, most legal scholarship to which others have access—most published articles.

College did not survive. I am not suggesting any way in which, economically, it might have.[115] I am suggesting only that we understand what lies behind the stupidity that characterizes much of litigation analysis I have described in this book. It is the natural outcome of the institutions we have, which are the natural outcome of the role they play in our economic system. Law students come to school to learn how to be lawyers, the lowest priority of the law-school faculty. Statistics and economics students similarly want to adopt the title of their graduate education, be statisticians, be economists. None of that calls for them to be intellectuals. And so they are not.

One could ask that graduate schools look more for intellectuality and conceptual creativity in their appointments, but I have expended enough energy throwing lightning into that dark night. I have done well enough, I think, to suggest how judges can get the training they need—not the training statisticians advocate—and what they can do with it. I cannot undertake a review of the entire education system here. Experts will continue to be mundane technicians, devoted to the cause of their clients, while pretending to be honest, neutral, and oh, so sophisticated. Except for recommendations I make in Chapter 10, I offer no suggestion that would lead to different experts or different expert behavior. My suggestions have been and will be focused on the judge, on his training and his authority, and, ultimately, on his behavior.

THE MEDIA

It may be a stretch to include popular media within the context of "education," but exposure to newspapers, magazines, and television is the closest most people get to adult education. Others, though not as many as I would have expected, have written about the media's difficulty with statistical argument.[116] I include two examples of media failure in this chapter on "education" to question not their ability, but their attitude.

The *Washington Post*

"Driving While Black" in Chapter 8 was initiated by a newspaper article promising statistical "proof" of police bias in arresting speeders.[117] I suggested that its conclusion was not

---

115. In Black Mountain College's later years, liberation turned to decadence, freedom turned to sloth. That, too, is an important lesson, indicating how difficult it is to monitor an environment in which "creativity" is encouraged. Perhaps it has been for managerial sanity that such initially free-spirited institutions as Reed College and Bard College have striven to acquire, and have achieved, a more boring normalcy.

116. Huff (1954) is the classic exposé of bad statistical argument. More current and more to the point— more focused on media—is Best (2001), although Best makes mistakes of his own.

117. Lamberth (1998).

supported by the data. Shortly after that article was published, I submitted a response containing my demonstration that the facts as offered could easily justify the police behavior as described. I never received a reply. Perhaps the *Washington Post* editors share the bias of their writers. Perhaps they just don't want to be embarrassed by having apparently taken sides in what should be seen as a technical dispute.[118]

Remember, from Chapter 3, it was an erroneous article in the *Washington Post* that started me down this litigation path, in the 1960s, culminating in *Hobson II*. John Lamberth's article on speeding was a real-world statistical presentation about an important issue. I do not question its publication. Why the *Post* wanted to present such bad statistical argument *and not expose it for what it was* is the mystery. More disdain for controversy?

CNN

The nation experienced some of the difficulty in the use of probabilistic evidence in court during the preliminary hearing in which O. J. Simpson was accused of a double murder. The court and CNN viewers were first told about the results of blood tests on July 8, 1994. The occurrence of the different blood types each had a probability, determined from ten years of typing by the Los Angeles police. The percentage of the population with these characteristics—Simpson was one such person, the victims were not—was purported to be 0.53, about one-half of one percent, or one out of two hundred people. Under a different assumption, the figure might be 1 percent.

Defense attorneys were on it. In *Collins* (1968), as many books and articles have pointed out, multiplication of probabilities was incorrect because the probabilities were not independent.[119] Did the Los Angeles medical examiner know that these types were independent? And what kind of a sample had they collected? Certainly it was not a representative sample of the population in Los Angeles, having been culled from victims and suspects. And it was exclusionary evidence at best, not identifying anyone, just excluding many people from being suspects.

The CNN commentators also swung into action. One of them declared that this kind of evidence was sufficient to identify four hundred to eight hundred murderers in the stands at a UCLA-USC football game (with eighty thousand in attendance). I sent a fax to CNN:

---

118. In their defense, the editors might note that Lamberth (1998) represented the winning side in litigation. But, as I demonstrated in Chapter 8, later data confirmed my suspicions about facts buried in Lamberth's New Jersey data, and later cases exposed errors in Lamberth's methods. My criticism was more than reasonable: It was correct. The *Post* simply was not interested in a discussion, only in a headline.

119. For example, see Tribe (1971a). *Collins* (1968) and a similar case, *Sneed* (1966), are both discussed in Chapter 1 of this book at footnote 88. The issue comes up often. See, for example, *Veysey* (2003) at 604.

It doesn't help to have commentators who distort the evidence more than either witnesses or attorneys. The blood probabilities do not, under any circumstances, mean that at a UCLA-USC football game "there are 400 murderers in the stands" out of 80,000. We do not know if there are 400 murderers in the world. The probabilities indicate that if you believe there is a murderer in the stands, and if you have everyone's blood types, you can dismiss 79,200 or more of the game attendees and concentrate your search on the remaining 400–800. Quite a different meaning from that given by your commentator.

I cared enough to send that comment from the same motivation by which I have cared enough to write this book. I just want to help get it right. Needless to say, CNN neither responded to my fax nor made any attempt to correct its errors.

ENTERING THE ACADEMY

I was offered an assistant professorship at Harvard in 1968 at the then entry rate of $9,500 a year. Entry rate? I had taught two years at Reed College and written a book, albeit unpublished, in two years at Brookings. I would not accept the loss of those four years in calculating my salary. But that is all they could offer for a tenure-track position. *Tenure track*?

I said, "You mean I am to give up thousands of dollars a year in exchange for your promise only to consider me for a position I might not want and might not get—seven years from now? Why would I do that?"

They replied, "You mean you are willing to give up a tenure-track position for one in all other ways the same, except for its higher pay?"

And so we agreed on a salary of $15,000.

The tenure-track promise of future consideration is mostly a way to get assistant professors to work hard and toe the line for long enough that they forget they are doing it. You don't see rebels on college faculties because they are weeded out or the rebellion is beaten out of them.

> The academy, ever more academized in the sense of professionalized, bureaucratized, and rationalized in the Weberian sense, is becoming ever less congenial to the free spirit, the gadfly ("tenured gadfly" sounds like an oxymoron), the scoffer—"someone," as Edward Said puts it, "whose place it is publicly to raise embarrassing questions, to confront orthodoxy and dogma (rather than to produce them), to be someone who cannot easily be co-opted by governments or corporations."[120]

---

120. Posner (2001a) at 30, quoting Edward W. Said, *Representations of the Intellectual: The 1993 Reith Lectures 11* (1994). Ormerod (1994) tells us in his preface, at x: "I have been fortunate in being able to

Or lawyers. This easy co-optation may be one of the reasons tenured academics do not do well in court. The tenure track promise of "academic freedom" is a lie, because those who would need its protection do not get it. My willingness to forego tenure created the freedom most people forget how to use, when they get there. I was a member of the Union for Radical Political Economics (URPE). No tenure-track member of URPE got tenure at Harvard, and seeing that, no additional junior faculty joined.[121]

It is easy to gang up on Harvard both because of its frequent administrative and academic stumbles, and because of the publicity they receive. Moss tells us there was a "Harvard economist" in the room when he was interviewed to be an expert.

> Pointing at one of the assertions, he made a statement that had nothing to do with it and told the lawyers that what was written on the board could be used to prove their case.[122]

In 1961 the Harvard administration tried to cancel a student-council invitation to Pete Seeger, finally compromising by imposing the condition that he refrain from political speech. In the fall of 2002 an invitation to Irish poet Tom Paulin was withdrawn so he would not express his anti-Israel views. The students at the law school seem to have similar problems with free expression, including, according to Professor Charles Fried, "a hysterical, ridiculous overreaction" to some of it.[123]

---

combine academic research with a business career, which has removed the formidable pressures to conform which are faced by full-time academics." That is the story behind *this* book, also.

121. In the 1960s and 1970s Harvard continued the practice it had initiated in the 1950s, of not firing tenured faulty who veered left, but not re-appointing junior faculty with any such taint. Robert N. Bellah, in a letter to the *New York Review of Books*, February 10, 2005, describes "a record not of Harvard's being a bulwark against McCarthyism, but of abject cowardice." I dispute his suggestion that, with McCarthy's Senate censure and death, Harvard changed.

122. Moss (2003) at 52. Is it piling on to note that the four most noteworthy instances of academic plagiarism that have come to light in the past few years—surely known to readers of this book—all involve persons associated with Harvard: Doris Kearns Goodwin, Alan Dershowitz, Charles Ogletree, and Laurence Tribe? Or that three of them are at the Harvard Law School?

123. On turmoil at Harvard in the fall of 2002, see Jeffrey Toobin, "Letter From Cambridge: Speechless," *The New Yorker*, January 27, 2003. Fried is quoted at 38. The information about the 1961 incident comes from a letter in response to the Toobin article by Lewis Auerbach, *The New Yorker*, March 3, 2003. Economics students have petitioned to have Professor Stephen Marglin formulate an alternative introductory course. Marglin, who got tenure before he got religion, is the only 1960s radical who survived on the Harvard faculty. See "Econ Number Crunching," *Newsweek*, March 24, 2003, at 9.

In January 2005, Harvard President Larry Summers proposed three possibilities to explain the paucity of females in the sciences: 1) discrimination; 2) the difficult schedule, given other female roles; and 3) innate differences, given that the highest scorers on science tests are males. A storm of protest followed. However, except for the omission of early-childhood socialization, Summers' speculations constitute an agenda for research, a reasonable university role. That the storm raged outside academia is no surprise, but that it raged at Harvard is yet another disgrace. See "Summerstime, and the living ain't easy," 374 *The Economist* 8415, article dated February 24, 2005.

In the economics department, it was technical finesse, not intellectuality, that gained prominence in the 1970s. While the old guard in the economics department was claiming that it had no basis by which to assess the work of radicals, it hired mathematical economists and econometricians whose works were equally unfathomable to them. *The Economist* also has noted that

> the place of econometricians at the centre of economics is now confirmed. Indeed, there now seems to be a dearth of the grand theorists of days past. . . . But then a good plumber is in greater demand than any poet.[124]

It should not be surprising, when one looks at the development of universities over the past thirty or forty years, that the failings of the analyses presented by experts in litigation have been more in concept than method. By and large their single-pool-selection statistics were calculated correctly, except that they ought to have been multiple-pools statistics; their irrelevant regressions looked the same as those found in textbooks, except that they assumed homogeneity and often were based on an inappropriately framed question. One writer, arguing that subject-matter experts may lack technique, claims that

> statisticians are trained to combine data generated by disparate processes given only a formal description of those data—even in the absence of any deep understanding of what the data represent.[125]

I hope that statisticians would disown this generality, but it accords with my experience. "Deep understanding" is not what lawyers want, not what they will pay for, and seldom what they get. Universities, by endorsing technical advances and shunning careful thought, have sent advanced-degreed plumbers into the litigation world, where much of their work has been technically adept but empirically absurd.[126]

---

124. 369 *The Economist* 8345, October 11, 2003, at 94. Although having no pretense to be a "grand theorist," I might have placed this quotation in Chapter 4, in my discussion of the passing of graphical analysis from the economist's repertory. Anderson (1996) has a similar view, decrying, at 1, "the plunge into intellectual mediocrity that took place during the 1970s and 1980s." Ormerod (1994) at 20:

> An internal culture has developed within academic economics which positively extols esoteric irrelevance.

C. R. Rao notes:

> The courses in statistics given in the universities are mostly theoretical in nature. The relevance of statistics in solving practical problems is not emphasized.

"Statistics: Reflections on the Past and Visions for the Future," *Amstat News* 327:2 (September 2004) at 3.

125. Abramson (2001) at 738.

126. I am not alone in these observations. In writing about the Chicago economist Steven Levitt, in the *New York Times Magazine*, August 3, 2003, Stephen J. Dubner quotes Colin Camerer from the California Institute of Technology:

> [Levitt] represents something that everyone thinks they will be when they go to grad school in econ, but usually they have the creative spark bored out of them by endless math—namely, a kind of intellectual detective trying to figure stuff out.

The attitude of the academic expert, in court, is usually, "Just believe me, your honor, like my students do." I sat incredulous in the courtroom as Fletcher Blanchard from Smith College asserted that he was an expert in the relationship between background (ethnicity, race) and jury verdict, based on his having studied articles about the impact of background on other group behavior. He never had conducted research on the topic nor, apparently, had he consulted the legal—as opposed to sociological (his field)—literature. Judge Nevas was not impressed, either.[127] Blanchard will return to campus where the administration will note how active their faculty is in the real world, as Spence would have it, "for the good of society."

It may be that, in some areas, academic research is the best place to go to get as much correct information as possible. Some countries have followed academic advice in formulating fiscal or monetary policy, and some have done well by it. Others have fared badly. Until recently, there was no competitive profession to draw such advice from. Henry Kissinger did not return to academia after being President Nixon's Secretary of State. He built a large consulting business doing what professors used to do and, my view would predict, doing it better. Then, others followed: There is now an industry where, thirty years ago, there were only university faculty and think-tank "associates."[128]

---

127. See *Pugliano* (2004), which excluded Blanchard's testimony. Blanchard testified that minorities, had there been any on the jury, would have gone easier on the defendant. He made no reference to the civil research by Eisenberg and Wells (2002): "Overall, we find little evidence of consistent demographic effects on trial outcomes." At 1840.

128. In December 2002, Kissinger was named as chairman of—and then resigned from—the commission to investigate government failure to protect us from "9/11" attacks. George Mitchell was named co-chairman, but also quickly resigned. I do not mean to imply that either would have performed well, but both found the government position onerous, given their private-sector work. Government, academia, and nonprofit organizations may be considered all the same thing —I combined them in my accounting for members of the Carnegie Commission and its task force—but the private sector is something else. It may be that government will find it more and more difficult to recruit the best people in any field.

I am not alone in observing the drift of intellectual work away from universities. Professor Meir Kohn, introducing a talk by Daniel Pipes at Dartmouth in January 2005, noting that Pipes had left academia, remarked:

> By the way, it is striking how large a part of the best work on both foreign and domestic policy is being done today, not in universities, but in think tanks.

He continued:

> I have tried for years to get Dartmouth to extend Dr. Pipes an invitation. But I was always told that it would be "too controversial."

See http://www.dartlog.net/2005/01/professor-kohn-on-free-expression.php.

George Will, in his column of January 27, 2005 (*Washington Post* at A19), responded to Larry Summers' comments, mentioned above in footnote 123, about possible genetic differences between males and females:

> He thought he was speaking in a place that encourages uncircumscribed intellectual explorations. He was not. He was on a university campus. He was at Harvard, where

I sent a draft copy of my work in *Kouba* (1981) to Arthur Goldberger at the University of Wisconsin. He had written about reverse regression, and we had struck up a distant friendship. He was impressed by the depth of work that I could accomplish in a limited time.

"I had a lot of resources," I said, meaning money.

"It doesn't matter," he replied. "We could not get that kind of work done in an academic setting."

Back to Teaching

I took a position as adjunct professor at the University of Maryland, teaching basic business statistics to adults in a masters degree program. Consistent with my views about teaching lawyers, I could see no reason to drill formulas into these middle-management heads. They might profitably learn some statistical concepts, but they had no need to make calculations. They should understand them enough to direct or question them. At the next class session following one in which I had taught about the standard deviation as a "natural" metric of variation, I posed this question: "Wayne Gretsky is more superior to other hockey players than any athlete has ever been compared with other people in his sport, regardless of sport. Gretsky is more better than anyone. How would one know that?"

I was faced with blank stares, and no, not in reaction to my grammar. Gamesmanship alone, I thought, would have led at least one student to guess that this was a follow-up to last week's class. I wanted to establish quickly that this was a practical standard-deviation exercise, and then discuss data: What was the metric? Points? Goals only? Points per unit of playing time? With whom would you compare Gretsky? Centers? Front lines? First front lines only? With whom do you compare a center fielder, a shortstop, a clean-up hitter? Yes, there is a clever way to compare what seems incomparable, but it requires a lot of thought. My lesson plan stressed the kind of information and questions these people would have on the job. The concept, not the formula.

I was disappointed that I could not engage my students in what I thought would be more to their interest than some textbook example. I was not trying to impose intellectuality on them, only craft. The craft I thought they needed in their jobs.

---

he is president. Since then he has become a serial apologizer and accomplished groveler. Soon he may be in a Khmer Rouge-style re-education camp somewhere in New England, relearning this: In today's academy, no social solecism is as unforgivable as the expression of a hypothesis that offends someone's "progressive" sensibilities.

Will and others think that universities are dominated by left-think, but that is their misunderstanding. Universities are dominated by "correct" think, which is also "bad think" or "no think." The thoughtful left, as I indicated above, has been excluded.

Ultimately, the class and I discussed it. Why were they there? Most of them were employed by the government or large firms in which a master's degree led immediately to a raise in pay. They were there for the money, not the education. OK, but couldn't learning a few ideas be a bonus? Well, the problem was the final exam. If I would tell them to learn some formulas, and then ask for the formulas on the exam, they would be all right with that. An exam testing whether they had learned some statistical ideas was too chancy for them.

All was not lost. Several members of the class said they preferred my view: They would rather attend a school trying to educate them. But it was too hard, in the context of the program they were in, for this one class to be so different. It was more important to know how to calculate a standard deviation than when or why one should. They understood the intellectual poverty of that position, but they were striving for success within a bureaucracy. For that they needed the degree. For the degree they needed a B average. For a B average they needed to know in advance what would be on the final exam. A C in my course would require getting an A in another. My course, it seemed, would sink some of them.

I did not change my approach. I gave a few Cs. One student induced a dean to call me to ask me to change it, not because I had scored the exam badly, but because this grade hurt this student's record. I refused. I won't play a game in which the university makes it easy for students to get a master's degree so it will continue to receive low-cost (no facilities expense, no faculty benefits) tuition payments, while the students get a meaningless piece of paper and a raise in salary. I was not invited back.

10

Procedure

As I complete this book in late 2005, there is no perceived crisis in the judicial system. The finance-capital market is another story. We have watched Enron, Tyco, Global Crossing, WorldCom, Health South, and others fail not as those companies pursued their interests, but as their executives pursued *their* interests. Brokerages lied about the value of these companies, to obtain their business. Investment companies managed funds more for their own interests than for the interests of their clients. Mutual-fund companies allowed large clients to make off-hours deals, to the disadvantage of people like you and me. Insurance brokers would recommend the policy that was best for them, not the one that was best for you.[1] What a surprise! The "system" had relied on the rationality of competition, civil supervision by the Securities and Exchange Commission, criminal supervision by the Department of Justice, the independence of auditors like Arthur Andersen, and honest, rational assessment by brokerage analysts. Every piece of that structure failed.

Government regulators think businesses should, for the most part, "work it out" among themselves. Auditing firms strive to acquire and retain clients. Clients want agreement, not supervision; compliance, not honesty. Brokerage houses want new-issue business, which calls for favorable reviews by their analysts. (Have we forgotten that the only "research" that found no ill effects from tobacco use was funded by tobacco companies?) Mutual-fund managers want to manage more funds, insurance-company executives want to sell more policies. The actions of corporate management, in robbing their companies and their clients, in bribing others to join the robbery, in engaging accountants to bless the robbery, in generating fraudulent "research" to justify the robbery, did not always serve their companies' interests. That is the way "systems" actually work, because it is the way people within systems work, private or public.

---

1. See the Reuters story, "Marsh Executive Pleads Guilty," *New York Times* (online), January 6, 2005. "The scheme . . . maximized Marsh's fees," referring to Marsh and McLennan.

The judicial system is different only in structure, not in incentives. Its actors pursue their own interests. The system's purpose, its mandate, is part opportunity, part constraint. One structural difference is that, where government agencies can decide to what extent to be involved in capital markets, as the Supreme Court can decide which cases to take, a trial judge has no choice. Another is the decentralized nature of the judiciary. Where the income of the largest accounting firm (Deloitte and Touche) is 24 percent higher than the fourth-largest (KPMG), that fourth-largest has more than four times the income of the fifth-largest (BDO International).[2] There is a "Big Four." Other firms are too small to handle the accounts of multinational corporations. Although courts differ in experience, no federal district court is too small for any federal case.

In this chapter I will discuss the rules and procedures under which judges resolve "science" issues. I have assumed that most judges *want* to make "good" decisions, although I showed in Chapter 7 (and will more so in this chapter) that many do not achieve that goal. Honesty, integrity, and curiosity may not be universal judicial traits, but in my experience they are common. Judges by and large are rewarded (promoted) by being honest and competent, if also by having approved political views. The judge's problem is what to do with the material presented to him within the constraints of the laws under which he works and the precedents of his circuit or state. We know two things: 1) The judge should not rely on experts put forward by the parties for much assistance; 2) he doesn't.

I have been fired by private and public attorneys for plaintiffs and defendants, dropped by United States Attorneys and hounded out of a major case by opposing attorneys with the complicity of the judge and my own client. All for telling my clients—attorneys—that they were wrong, when they were. No ultimate client benefited. The Navy was not better off defending its discrimination against females in promotion. Blacks in New York were not better off for the Legal Defense Fund's prosecution of a case I told them they would lose—and they lost. AAA of Michigan was not better off defending the age-discrimination case I told them they would lose—and they lost. The Dalkon Shield claimants were not better off with an expert whose damage estimates were unrealistically high. David Copus' deep-pocket client would have been better off with an expert who could help it reform. Enron was not better off because Andersen looked the other way, although perhaps individuals at Enron were. Honesty and competence are not valued by those people who get to hire accountants or experts. They might be valued by the "system," but the "system" does not get to choose.

Judges and attorneys both view experts as whores, their opinions paid for and directed

---

2. My calculations from data in a table in 373 *The Economist* 8402, November 20, 2004, at 72. This concentration does not imply good or bad quality of service. *The Economist* also shows a chart of settlements, some in the hundreds of millions of dollars, of claims by clients against their Big Four auditors.

by adversarial clients.[3] By and large, that view is correct. In this chapter I will suggest ways in which judges can encourage parties to bring forward more competent and honest experts. More important, I will suggest ways in which judges can see through experts, and use them to derive information that will assist judicial decision making.

One benefit from recent capital-market failings is the understanding—even free-market conservatives have come reluctantly to agree—that capitalism is not self-correcting. It works not because there is that economist's delusion, "perfect competition," but because there are forums in which people can seek redress.[4] Regulation is too bound up in politics. Only litigation, civil and criminal, can restore faith in capital markets. Only judges and juries stand between the corrupt expert system and loss of faith that courts can handle complex cases. Like corporate executives' tendency to steal, the system's incentives toward engaging corrupt experts will not disappear. The judge has to make something out of this.

Who Is in the Club?

Attorneys and judges think that only they should have anything to say about the rules by which their club operates. That others do business within the club does not, in the minds of club members, give them any status to affect the rules that govern that relationship. It is the same logic by which women can play golf at Augusta National, when invited, but may not be members. Unlike a golf club, the courts belong to the people. In theory.

In a series of articles in the 1980s, John Monahan and Laurens Walker tried to re-formulate the organization of fact in law articulated by Kenneth Culp Davis in the 1940s.[5] Noting that in *Muller* (1908) the Supreme Court had declined to accord social-science fact status as "authority," but that in *Brown* (1954) it did, Monahan and Walker proposed:

---

3. Indeed, attorneys count on it. See Spence (1989) who, at 272, refers to

> the whore, euphemistically referred to as the "professional witness," who will testify to anything for anybody who provides the price.

4. This was the lesson of Tigar and Levy (1977). Milton Friedman's famous *Capitalism and Freedom* (University of Chicago Press, second edition, 1963) is misdirected. The book should have been about "Democracy and Freedom," in which judicial redress of capitalism's excesses would have played a larger part. Thomas Frank (2000), at 87, credits other actors, not the courts:

> The universal, democratic prosperity that Americans now look back to with such nostalgia was achieved only by a colossal reining in of markets, by the gargantuan effort of mass, popular organizations like labor unions and of the people themselves, working through a series of democratically elected governments not daunted by myths of the market.

Surely we are better off with the Food and Drug Administration, the Environmental Protection Agency, etc. than without, even if they are corrupted by presidential appointment and business bribery. Yet, considering three institutions—capitalism, elected government, and the courts—I still think it is judicial enforcement of the principle that he who causes damage pays for it that offers the citizen the most protection.

5. See K. Davis (1942) and (1955).

> We argue that courts should treat social-science research relevant to creating
> a rule of law as a source of authority rather than as a source of facts.[6]

Some writers have found Monahan and Walker's reformulation useful.[7] I do not, for many reasons. The reason of importance here is that if social science (in legislative fact only) is legal "authority," then social scientists become members of the club. That will not happen.

I have written freely about the law. Any American can do that, but why should others read it? To many, I am simply not "qualified," even if, as Richard Posner tells us, "there is a remarkable isomorphism between legal doctrine and economic theory." I presume I write with Posner's blessing:

> The economist who wants to work on legal questions needs to know some-
> thing about law, but he does not need a J.D.[8]

This book should be read because it is good: informative, instructive, creative. I have provided not just novel analyses, but novel—I contend, superior—ways of approaching many kinds of questions statistical experts are called upon to answer. Yet, as described in Chapter 9, those with the mandate to present such work to others—publishers—relying on highly credentialed experts, find my work threatening. Once again, personal interest trumps doing the right thing.

I argued in Chapters 7 and 8, and will again in this chapter, that judges should ignore expert credentials. The expert's success in his world has no bearing on how well he contributes to the judge's world. The value of this book cannot be assessed from my credentials in economics, statistics, and expert testimony. Yes, I have worked at prestigious academic and research institutions, and within the legal system for close to four decades. So what? I might have been sleepwalking, as I contend most experts are. This book itself is my credential to have written it. It is my testimony. It should be assessed on its merits.

---

6. Monahan and Walker (1986) at 488. The other articles in the trilogy are Walker and Monahan (1987) and Walker and Monahan (1988). Despite my rejection of their classification, their description of the intellectual history and their articulation of issues are worth the read. The difference in treatment of social science research between *Muller* and *Brown* can easily be explained by the fact that it was offered to the high court *de nouveau* in *Muller*, but came up through trial testimony and cross-examination in *Brown*.

7. See Saks (1990) and Erickson and Simon (1998), for example.

8. Posner (1981) at 1130; preceding in-text quotation, Posner (1999b) at 91. Justice Scalia (1989) at 1176 praises the judicial qualities of Louis IX of France and King Solomon, though both operated "without benefit of a law degree." In contrast, Helmholz (1999) tells us, at 298, that "habitual indifference to standards of justice" played a role in the dissolution of King John's authority, leading to Magna Carta. But then so did losing a battle to France in 1214.

Posner's concession of turf is exceptional. Consider, for example, the letter by the Historians' Committee for Fairness, whatever that is, as posted on the *History News Network* (http://hnn.us) on September 1, 2004. Wanting to criticize Michelle Malkin's writing on the World War II internment of Japanese in the United States, they write "Malkin is not a historian." So?

My main concern is with the quality of statistical analysis behind social-science evidence, and judicial evaluation thereof. Along the way I have presented three notions about the people who bring this evidence into the courtroom. One is that, though this generality has no application in any specific case, the professional expert is likely to be more skilled than the academic. He gets to improve his craft, like any skilled worker, with repeat business. The second is that the best analysts, be they academics or professionals, are systematically driven from the field because attorneys do not seek them out. Attorneys want support for their position, so they can keep their clients, win or lose, for having put up a good fight. That, then, implies the third notion, that if the once-honest expert has not been excluded, or not walked away, he has been compromised by the process. The attorney has little incentive to get a "good" expert, the expert has little incentive to be "good" in a scientific sense, and the academic expert seldom will be.

We will have more accounting crises, even though Arthur Andersen is gone. In 2004, executives of Royal Dutch Shell had to explain why its proven reserves were actually far below the levels they had consistently reported. In 2005, unable to get it right, they reduced reported reserves again. Computer Associates assured us that it no longer back-dates orders to get each quarter to the level expected on Wall St. Firing its executives, Fannie Mae's board claimed that they had rigged the timing of events to keep the stock value up and, by the way, meet their bonus benchmarks. Coca-Cola did much the same thing in Japan. Krispy Kreme had been shipping more doughnuts than stores ordered, booking the sales, then taking unsold product back. Profit in one quarter would be offset by loss in the next; but meanwhile, insiders sold stock the price of which had been based on the phony sales.[9]

As "the market" and "business" invade the political system, it takes on their characteristics. We learn that President Bush and Prime Minister Blair conspired to invent a war in Iraq, perhaps for oil, but certainly not because Iraq harbored weapons of mass destruction. Even the apologist excuse that Bush and Blair thought it did is no longer tenable. Knowing who "Deep Throat" of the Watergate era is leads us to wonder if any publisher would extend itself now as the *Washington Post* did then, even if its two young reporters were backed by a high FBI official. If anything, truth seeking has diminished.

Although the "system" asks for clarity, the future for auditors and experts alike is to

---

9. From an editorial in the *Washington Post*, September 27, 2004, at A18:
> Fannie Mae's auditor, KPMG, apparently felt unable to challenge the lender's use of unorthodox accounting techniques; an employee who questioned these techniques was ignored. The upshot was that the final word on Fannie Mae's accounting methods seems to have come from the top managers: The same group of people that set Fannie's earnings targets and stood to benefit from meeting them.

See "Coca-Cola–SEC Settle Accounting Probe," *New York Times* (online), April 18, 2005. See also Andrew Countryman, "Investors left in a glaze with Krispy Kreme restatement," *Chicago Tribune* (online) January 5, 2005.

become more skilled in subterfuge, less skilled in revelation. Accountants lobby against rules that would say they have to report fraud when they find it. Don't the regulators understand? Accounting is not what accountants are hired for. Judges understand: Analysis is not what experts are paid to do.

Similarly, I have decried the lack of "intellectuality," the absence of large-scale principled reasoning, where statistics is applied to law; but where is the reward for such activity? Not in litigation. Courts will increasingly get more-articulate but less-imaginative and less-skilled advice from experts.[10] Judges should be skeptical, but not derisive, as even the least-competent or most-corrupt expert could stumble on to a case in which his method (or even his bias) reveals information the court should have. That experts care little for the truth does not mean that everything they say is false. It just makes the judge's job difficult.

DISCOVERY

In preparing for trial in *Harris Bank* (1981), Harry Roberts suggested that experts should exchange all documents they produced. Draft reports, memos to staff, printouts, and scribbles thereon. Full disclosure. It was a really bad idea. It requires a definition of "document" that, whatever it is, attorneys will find ways to get around. One strategy would be to tell an expert not to put any staff instructions in writing. Are notes counted if made by professional staff? By a secretary? A contrasting strategy would be to generate reams of paper just to inundate the other side, to consume their time and budget. Not just memos, but drafts of memos; not just reports, but drafts of reports; not just the printouts behind calculations presented in court, but printouts behind all calculations ever made in connection with this case. "We gave them everything, your honor. They have nothing to complain about."[11]

Stephen Easton also suggests that each expert turn over all materials to the other, without clarifying what that means.[12] I don't want to spend my time and my client's money that way. It's still a bad idea.

In Chapter 7 I described the special master's instructions to David Peterson, telling him

---

10. As explained in Chapter 6, on some objective basis statistical analysts have improved because statistics is better and, more important, because data and computer programs are both better and more easily available. The ineluctable trend, however, is as I state it.

11. For example, the Sixth Circuit, explaining why on remand it wants a new judge assigned, tells us:

> [T]he district court scheduled argument on Mitsubishi's motion for summary judgment for May 21, 1999—just seventeen days after the 29,000 documents were ordered disclosed.

Nemir (2004) at 544. These documents all related to buyers' complaints about partial latching of seat belts, a subject on which Mitsubishi at first claimed it had no documents at all.

12. See Easton (2000). His proposed amendment to Rule of Civil Procedure 26A is an appendix, beginning at 610.

how to calculate damages in *Mister* (1986). Peterson created a parameter not found in the master's script, and didn't mention it in his description. My staff found it by laboriously reviewing every line of Peterson's code. Exchange of litigation materials was an effective check on Peterson's work. However, I cared only about this program, not others; and only in its final version. I did not want to know what Peterson considered, only what he did.

That Harry Roberts had considered "mini regressions" estimated on cohorts, and that he had never aggregated his results across the firm, was easily discoverable in deposition. It did not come up at trial, because he did not present it. Roberts was looking for an approach that would exonerate his client. Is this news? It would have been news only had he found one. I care what the expert will say, not every thought he has had. So the other side's expert knew about and suppressed analyses that did not support his client. Who is surprised by this behavior? Who is helped by knowing the details?

Fire-Department Promotions

The fire chief of the District of Columbia appeared to have rigged the ratings scores of firemen at one rank, vying for promotion to the next rank. Each candidate was scored in several ways, from exams and evaluations and, finally, from Chief Coleman's review. He knew the race of the candidates and what scores they had obtained before he added his. He used his points to promote blacks over whites who, otherwise, had higher scores. White firefighters sued.

I showed that the race composition of the winners, given their other scores, would have been a highly improbable result of chance.[13] Of course it was not chance, but it did not appear to be merit, either, that determined the winners. It was race.

I attended Chief Coleman's deposition. "This list of proposed promotions that you sent to the mayor," asked my client, Frank Petramalo, referring to the only list we had seen, the one from which I had done my analysis. "This list of proposed promotions, was it the only such list you made?"

"No," answered the fire chief.

Chief Coleman had first made a more honest list, which he then modified to change the racial composition of the promotees.[14] The parties settled, retaining the promotions

---

13. See *Foster* (1987). A graphic from this case is reproduced in the Appendix to Chapter 9 of this book as Figure 82. The position sought was battalion fire chief.

14. Rebecca Klemm produced a client-oriented, incorrect "analysis" of these selections, defending the chief's actions. I trust she learned from this experience, as she apparently had not as a member of my firm, that the expert's job sometimes is to be the honest bearer of bad news. More likely, she learned that the quality of an expert's analysis is not at issue. What counts is whether it supports her client. This time, she got caught; but did her inability to discern the race bias in selection, later admitted, deter her client from engaging her again? I doubt it.

granted, and also promoting the whites who had been skipped over. Something like the second gold medals presented to the Canadian ice skating pair in the 2002 Olympics, after learning that the French judge had scored dishonestly. I would have preferred, in both situations, that only the rightful winners should win.

I asked Frank if he had known or suspected that there had been another list, a list with fewer black promotions. "No, I had no idea," he said. "This is just good lawyering." Indeed it was.

Through questions such as this, unless the witness is willing to lie, one party can learn all it wants to about the processes in which the other side's expert had engaged before coming to final conclusions.[15] It requires good lawyering, and time spent with one's expert reviewing the other expert's work, to formulate reasonable questions about what has been shown and what has not been shown. This will be far less time than each expert would consume reviewing all of the opposing expert's discarded paper. And it will get what the other expert has to say about what he did, not just the fact of what he did, on the record.

Disclosure

Clearly, I find mischievous the 1993 revision of the Federal Rules of Civil Procedure (as described in Chapter 6), instructing the expert to produce all documents or data he has "considered." The rule is applied only to litigation experts, allowing other experts to pursue any path the client wants, undiscovered.

Citing "the potential chilling effect that litigation can have on scientific inquiry," Judge Jack Weinstein dismisses allegations that the National Academy of Sciences

> failed to adequately review scientific evidence concerning the association between the herbicide Agent Orange exposure and illnesses among Vietnam veterans.[16]

This decision—supported by similar decisions from other courts that Judge Weinstein carefully documents—leaves the National Academy's report in the public domain, while keeping hidden all information about what it "considered." Heaven forbid that the (pause here for emphasis) National Academy should be held to the same standards as (lying, cheating, whoring) experts!

The Federal Rules change to "considered" from "relied on" was made, I think, because

---

15. To be caught lying would end a professional expert's career. Although some people draw their ethical lines in strange places, I have never known a professional expert to answer a well-phrased question in a way he knew was false. I have quoted from judges who think that is what they got, but at least in terms of statistical analysis, they are more likely to have gotten a client-oriented approach and incompetence than outright mendacity. If the question is not precisely and correctly phrased, most good witnesses can give false impressions without lying.

16. *McMillan* (2003) at 306; preceding in-text quotation at 317.

most attorneys have no way to challenge an expert other than by innuendo.[17] Rather than looking for a contrarian view amongst the expert's papers, just ask him. Does he know of any? Has he done any such work himself? It is an expert's responsibility to know the literature. If the expert being deposed, or cross-examined, knows about opposing views, he will say so. Not to know about them impugns his expertise. The self-serving answer is an honest answer.

Melvin Kraft recommends engaging "non-testifying" experts, people who can know more and advise better than the testifying expert, as the latter must be protected from knowing anything the party does not want disclosed at trial. David Peterson and John Conley suggest that Federal Rule of Civil Procedure 26(b)(4)(B) be revised to include discovery of the existence of non-testifying experts. They characterize their suggestion as "radical," and describe adverse reactions they have gotten to it. In essence, they would move from the expert to the party the obligation to reveal all that he has "considered."[18]

I agree. Unless asked for more, each expert should say only what his opinions are, and how he came to them. The attorney, however, should list all expert opinions *he* considered, or at the least (because he will deny that other experts had yet formed opinions) the names of those experts with whom he has consulted. When a party can "shop" for opinions, it will take the most favorable one, and present it as the only one it found. We have seen that doing so creates a statistical fallacy: Probabilities assuming one look are incorrect when there have been several looks, whether by one analyst or many.[19]

Peterson and Conley modified their proposal to exempt a preliminary exploration by

---

17. Attorneys will say that information the expert had but did *not* rely on is informative, because it shows the other half of his thought process. If so, then it would be more important had Joan Haworth said she had read Gastwirth and Haber's view of weighting availability areas than if she admitted that she had not. See *Nassau* (1992) and my discussion in Chapter 6. I don't think it matters. If she did not consider weighting areas, she should have, and not doing so indicated that her "market" measure was invalid. Attorneys focus on the way the expert made a decision, whereas I care only about the quality of the decision itself.

18. See Kraft (1982) and Peterson and Conley (2001). Posner (1999a) had made a suggestion similar to Peterson and Conley's, but he did not formulate a rule.

19. David Bernstein (2003) considers this problem in class-action tort claims at 15. He reports his understanding that

> some attorneys will pass an X-ray around to numerous radiologists until they find one who is willing to say that the X-ray shows symptoms of an asbestos-related disease.

Because "a defendant cannot ask how many experts the plaintiff spoke to or what they said," Bernstein concludes:

> The best solution to this problem would be if courts would appoint panels of neutral experts, perhaps three experts, to review each X-ray.

Perhaps there is a role for neutral experts here, but first the rules should be changed to allow the defendant to determine how many adverse opinions were rejected before the testifying expert was found.

an attorney before deciding to take a case. This modification seems to exempt only plaintiffs. If the goal of the attorney is to retain his client, most defendant attorneys are already committed to defend. Both sides' attorneys are shopping for favorable opinions. The court should know how difficult they were to find for plaintiffs and defendants alike.

Early in *Mister*, before I became plaintiffs' expert, David Peterson did an alternative analysis, using standard plaintiff assumptions, for defendant. He says he did it to offer to his clients a "worst-case scenario," a glimpse at what they were fighting against. It was not, he says, a methodology he considered using himself. I believe him. The circuit court did not, however, throwing back in his face the fact that he had utilized the same methodology he was criticizing plaintiffs for using. What Peterson did was a service to his client. The judicial system should not have castigated him for it.[20]

My report as it is *now* is in the appropriate case folder on my computer. It will be different tomorrow, when today's version will disappear forever. This is how I avoid clutter and keep a semblance of organization. It is how I wrote this book. I retain no earlier draft. If the argument between the parties devolves into how each word came to be what it was—not the meaning of the words as they are—then the process of coming to a resolution will hinder finding one.

I list at the end of this book, as I do in a report, cases and documents referenced. I did not retain and could not construct a list of the additional hundreds of cases and documents I have read. I do not try to remember the content if I find the material useless, but I must have "considered" it to make that decision. Strictly speaking, I could never comply with the current rules. This is not a game experts should be asked to play.

Non-Disclosure

Attorney-client privilege was discussed in Chapter 6. We know that the murderer can tell his attorney, "Yeah, I did it, now get me off," without fear that this information will get to the court.[21] The defendant's attorney, however, had better not say to his fingerprint expert, "My guy did it; now let's get him off." Yet the district attorney can and in essence *does* say to *his* forensic expert, "This is the guy we think did it; now let's prove it." The district attorney may not *say* that, but he provides only one set of rolled (that is, professionally taken) prints—those of the suspect—to the forensic "scientist." The solution should be to produce several unidentified sets of prints, drawn by an expert other than the forensic identifier to resemble the latent prints, and provided to the examiner as possible matches.

---

20. Perhaps defendant Illinois Central Gulf Railroad was contemplating settlement. Can it be in anyone's interest to ridicule such an effort?

21. This was a correct assumption before John Ashcroft became Attorney General. It is not clear what the rules are now.

To tell an identification expert who is the suspect is like telling the eyewitness, during a lineup, "We think the third guy from the left did it—what do you think?" But to withhold information from one's statistical expert is like hiring a private detective and saying, "You have to solve this case, but I can tell you nothing about it." Some experts should be told nothing; others, everything. We need to construct a classification of experts, and articulate differences in the courts' orders that pertain to them. As the rules stand, there is but one kind of expert, and "confidential" information becomes public if he learns it.

> Many courts today hold that even information otherwise protected as core work product or attorney/client material becomes discoverable when disclosed to an expert witness.[22]

It is worth at least thinking about having whatever rules apply to the attorney apply also to the (non-forensic) science expert. If the expert has concluded that his client's client is in the wrong, he will not be testifying anyway. What the rules do is prevent the honest and completely informed expert from testifying, lest some piece of information he acquired become exposed to public view through him. Forcing the expert to reveal all that he considered provides ammunition and rationale to cross-examine on what the expert knew but did *not* say. It is an attorney's tool to turn the fact finder's focus from the expert's testimony to his character.

Had I seen accounts of improper behavior of Allstate training personnel with regard to female trainees, I could not have testified as a statistical expert.[23] Would such accounts have had an impact on my analysis of compensation? They might have. I was pursuing a model in which females, although assessed individually, were expected to perform less well than males. And they did. My model required that training salaries be determined in a particular way. My job *should* have included an examination of the presumptions underlying my model. I tried to, but could not follow this simple research path for the attorneys' fear of what else I might discover and therefore would have been discoverable through me.

I cannot dissuade attorneys from their fiction that the privilege of silence is the client's alone.[24] Let them think that it is, and find a rule by which it achieves transitivity—information remains privileged when shared with an expert. The attorney is the last person to

---

22. Allgood (2001) at 51. See Mickus (1994) for an argument that, if it is not this way, it should be.

23. I refer to *Kouba* (1981), in which I did not testify only because the parties settled. I do not know that there were such reports—I never saw any—but I was told that a prime reason for settling was to suppress individual stories. It may be that the stories were not true, but Allstate did not want them publicly told, whatever they were.

24. The attorney-client privilege extends the client's privilege against self-incrimination so that the attorney, also, does not have to reveal condemnatory information. Let us say that privilege = 1 and non-privilege = 0. The client has a value 1, as does the attorney, but the expert has the value 0. Client-attorney interaction is $1 \times 1 = 1$, privileged. Attorney-expert interaction is $1 \times 0 = 0$, not privileged. Client-

understand what information I need to consider, what I don't. The best policy for the honest firm that wants my advice is to let me search for whatever information I can find, and let me decide what I will use. This would also be the best policy for the court, but it is the worst policy for the advocate attorney. Discovery rules virtually prohibit it.

> [M]any courts will conclude that any document or fact put into expert's possession is fair game for discovery; it is imperative that you proceed cautiously and in a carefully considered way before revealing sensitive information to the expert.

> [B]y controlling the information and assignments given to various experts, a party can ensure that the testifying expert is unaware that the testimony he or she gives is unreliable.[25]

And then attorneys complain that the (other side's) expert has been ill informed!

Data Exchange

Data should be exchanged, checked, revised. Data should not be an issue, and judges should not tolerate their becoming one. As discussed in Chapters 6 and 8, the experts may disagree on the appropriate *conceptual basis* of data. For any concept there usually should be agreement on the numbers long before they are brought to a trial.

Data exchange requires negotiation. The medium of exchange must be defined, the language, the names of data sets, the data elements. Besides understanding where they came from, how they were generated, the recipient has to know their format, their order, their language. No party should just "give" data to the other. There should be an agreement on substance and form.

Judges traditionally say, "Turn over what you have," and walk away. To be useful, data usually have to be processed. For example, personnel data may contain start date and leave information, but not seniority. "Seniority" is an analytic construct, for which there may be idiosyncratic rules. In human-resource systems, seniority is a calculation, not a number. Leave time may or may not be subtracted in full, for example. The code for that calculation may be proprietary. It is written in a human-resources data-base language, not the statistical-analysis language with which the expert is familiar.

If defendant used "seniority" in its analysis, or if plaintiff wants to, then a variable that defendant will agree represents "seniority" as used by the firm should be provided by defen-

---

attorney-expert interaction is $1 \times 1 \times 0 = 0$, not privileged. The privilege to communicate cannot be assigned to the client alone. It occurs when there is interaction between the client and the attorney. It is as much the attorney's as the client's. I propose assigning a "1" to statistical experts, not to encourage dishonesty (defending the guilty, assisting a sham complaint), but to encourage openness between attorney and expert.

25. Daniels (1985) at 53, then Peterson and Conley (2001) at 215.

dant. Plaintiff's expert needs the rules in English (that is, the policy), the raw data, and defendant's results for an agreed-upon day. Plaintiffs, in turn, need to demonstrate that they have programmed seniority correctly, by replicating the calculation provided by defendant.[26] I refer to such data elements as "analytic" data. Defendant's attorney states, "We provided every data element we retain." Then, at trial, he argues that plaintiffs' calculation is incorrect, as if he is not at least partly responsible for the error, as if he did not do everything he could to induce it. The trial then becomes a test of expert calculations, not an assessment of fact under law.

In Chapter 8 I referred to *McReynolds* (2004), in which both sides complained that the other mismeasured "promotions." Such a word should relate to data that correctly describe how that word is used in that firm. It should be the obligation of defendant to provide the data that way, certifying that if plaintiffs apply these words to these data elements, defendants will not object. If it turns out that the actions (or inactions) about which the plaintiffs are complaining are not covered by the words they used, they should amend their complaint.

This is the kind of detail judges shun. Data exchange is currently viewed by the parties as a contest. One expert provided data to me in a different form than we had agreed upon. "I just thought it would be more convenient this way," he said. The proper response of the court should have been to prevent his appearance as a witness. When judges say, "Work it out," they give power to the meanest or most ignorant combatant. In this case, we *had* worked it out, but the other side's expert could not keep his word. The judge should follow through, perhaps demand a joint glossary of terms, and punish anyone who reneges on the deal.

The Carnegie Commission supports active management by judges, but takes more space to say why than to say what that entails.[27] I think judges need training in case management far more than they need training in statistics. As noted above, I have had data provided in obscure modulo arithmetic. I have had data provided raw with computer code indicating how to transform them to analytic data. I did not write in that computer language, and their code referred to data bases by the name they had at their computer facility. The transmission was useless. I have had data presented on media for which I had no read device. In each of these instances I heard, "Yes, we provided the data." As my client

---

26. In Chapter 8 I described how, as defendant's expert for the Department of State, I worked hard to deliver a "stipulated" data base to plaintiffs, who otherwise were misusing the term "assignment." My intention was to have everyone using the same language for the same events. Although courts are not sensitive to the language problem—what words are appropriately used to describe certain data elements—they do assume that when defendant produces data, it certifies the data. For example, in *Tyler* (2002), at 393, defendant Unocal got nowhere criticizing its own data as unreliable.

27. Carnegie (1993) at 50.

could not understand the issue, and the judge did not want it to become one, that was essentially the end of it. A bad end.

In the trenches, each expert is trying to screw the other. The judge *should* want to know if one side is unnecessarily making work difficult. We need just a few cases in which a witness is severely sanctioned for playing these games, to straighten it all out. We need a few judges to care about how the game is played outside their courtrooms, the dirt each party slung at the other before they cleaned up for trial. "It's hardball," I am told. No, it's spitball. It should not be tolerated.

WRITTEN REPORTS

The exchange of written reports is now mandated by the Federal Rules of Civil Procedure. The legal profession still seems tentative about structuring that exchange.[28] I would like to see more.

I have seen newly "revised" reports brought into court on the day of the trial. What should the judge do? It might seem that he is best served by having the latest, clearest thinking of the expert in front of him. Unless the delay in revision was caused by the behavior of the opposing party, justice is better served by rejecting it.[29] The *Nassau* (1992) trial started before Joan Haworth produced her data series on "market wages." David Pollard opened his testimony at the *Gibbs* (1998) trial with graphics that neither I nor my clients had ever seen. In *Pugliano* (2004), Gene Fisher had modified population by voter-registration figures for which, as noted in Chapter 8, I praised him in my response. One day before the hearing he produced—and at the hearing testified to—unmodified population figures.

The judge needs to schedule expert exchanges: data, reports, court exhibits. And he needs to enforce his schedule. In *Semi-Tech* (2004), discovery was to be closed on Decem-

---

28. The sanction for failing to provide such a report should be exclusion of the witness, as provided in Federal Rules of Civil Procedure 26(a) and 37(c), and as effectuated in a Seventh Circuit decision, *Musser* (2004), for example. Witnesses had been disclosed and deposed, but not designated as experts. The First Circuit, in contrast, does not hold the parties to this procedural standard. In *Beniquez* (2004), at 37 and then 38, forensic experts were allowed to testify although not having been designated as such:

> In particular, the government had informed defendants before trial that both pathologists would be testifying about several autopsies and provided the defendants with copies of all of these autopsy reports.

> [The government] did inform the defendants that Maldonado would be testifying about ballistics and provided the defense with all of Maldonado's notes on his testimony.

29. See, for example, *Sherrod* (2000) at 613 where,

> because both sides were at fault for the difficulties in scheduling depositions, which pushed discovery up to the December deadline, the delay in finishing the experts' reports was partially justified.

ber 31, 2003. Plaintiff disclosed the identity of two experts on December 19, and offered their reports on December 31, leaving no time for rebuttal reports. Judge Kaplan nonetheless allowed the witnesses into the case, provided that they would be deposed by January 31, 2004. Nowhere did the judge take responsibility for an insufficient scheduling order, which should have specified an earlier date for affirmative reports. How would a party otherwise know how much time the judge thought was reasonable for preparation of rebuttal?

Judge Stagg did not allow plaintiffs to produce a last-minute statistical expert, where the trial rules clearly mandated that defendant have early notice of such a witness and his exhibits. The case went forward on the attorney's presentation.

> Thus, accurate statistical comparison is impossible due to plaintiffs' poor preparation of their statistical case.[30]

So be it. If a party is harmed by his attorney's malfeasance, he should sue the attorney. This is not the other side's responsibility.

Plaintiffs in another case stated that they were prepared to go forward to trial, and "do not require further discovery."[31] Then they complained when the district judge took them at their word and scheduled the trial. The $5,000 fine imposed by Judge Wolin was reversed by the Third Circuit. Wrong lesson. Consider this:

> Plaintiff has repeatedly ignored this Court's deadlines, has filed numerous eleventh-hour motions, has identified and then withdrawn a succession of expert witnesses, and, in general, has exhibited a cavalier disregard for the deadlines and orders entered by this court. . . . Incredibly, this pending motion *in limine* was filed *four years* after this Court's deadline for the filing of *in limine* motions concerning expert witnesses had passed, and after several opportunities to object to this witness's qualifications in a timely manner had been ignored.[32]

The parties need to keep to the schedules. The sanction on the offending party must be greater than just, "No, you cannot offer that exhibit, because it was not prepared in time." The sanction needs to be to prevent the malefactor attorney from offering that expert.

In *Brennan* (2004), defendant's expert Douglas Tymkiw contended that plaintiff's expert William Legier had used the wrong data, but voiced no objection to his calculation method. With proper scheduling, Legier would have had the time to redo his calculations on the correct data, and submit his results for review. All of that would occur prior to trial, so no data dispute would ever have come before the jury.

---

30. *Johnson* (1976) at 539.

31. *Anjelino* (1999) at 100.

32. *Sara Lee* (2002) at 372. Defendant disclosed a witness late in *Pride* (2000). He was not allowed to testify.

[A] bit less than a week before trial, Legier then provided his own supplemental report in which he used the adjusted attendance data that Tymkiw said
were correct.[33]

However, Legier failed to provide Tymkiw with his revised calculations. Although recognizing that this late delivery violated a standing order, the judge let it in.

The judge then gave Tymkiw an hour in which to look at the papers and discuss them with the defendants' attorneys.

The Fifth Circuit, impressed with how much less the jury awarded plaintiff than Legier
had calculated, concluded that Tymkiw had provided a "powerful" rebuttal. Given the current loose state of affairs, I fault neither the trial judge nor the circuit court for allowing
the testimony. In a more scheduled world, however, the order to produce the revised report
and its documentation would have been stricter, and failure to comply should have been
punished by exclusion.

The National Academy statistical panel took on this issue:

The panel recommends that, to facilitate understanding of statistical procedures and analyses, the legal profession should adopt procedures designed to
(1) narrow statistical disputes prior to trial, particularly with respect to the
accuracy and scope of the data and (2) disclose to the maximum extent feasible the methods of analysis to be used by the testifying experts.[34]

Any such rules must have teeth, as Harry Roberts' flouting of the judge's instruction to disclose what he was doing in *Harris Bank* (1981) illustrates.[35]

---

33. *Brennan* (2004) at 373; following indented quotation and "powerful" quoted in text below also
at 373. Legier also modified his calculation at the last minute based on the jury's previous-day determination that only one of two Dickie Brennan restaurants should generate damages. That kind of adjustment—keeping the calculation within what has suddenly become the law of the case—surely is
permissible, but again review by the opposing expert should have been allowed for.

34. This is the panel's third recommendation. See Fienberg (1989) at 13.

35. For his failure to disclose, Roberts was prevented from presenting direct testimony. However, he
made his complete presentation as rebuttal. He should have been excluded as a witness. See Chapter 3
on regression, especially on reverse regression, and citation there to *Penk* (1985).

In *China* (2004), from footnote 12 at 182:

[D]efendants' [expert] disclosure was a month late, and did not adhere to the expert disclosure requirements [of the federal rules]. . . . [Judge Chin] ruled that because of defendants' failure to timely and properly disclose, their expert would only be permitted to testify if Bank of China's expert testified.

The First Circuit, apparently unaware of the *Harris Bank* (1981) history, seems to think that this is a sufficient sanction, telling us this story only while discussing whether another witness for the Bank of China
should have been considered to be an expert. The bank should not have had to anticipate whether its
strategy would trigger the appearance of an opposition expert witness whose existence had not properly been disclosed. That witness should have been excluded.

In *Reid* (2001), plaintiffs' expert produced an admittedly flawed report and then asked for a time extension to correct it. Judge Forrester was right not to allow that extension, but might better have excluded plaintiffs' expert entirely. In *Venator* (2002), plaintiffs' expert had to revise her report as defendant had supplemented its data delivery. Judge Schwartz correctly accepted the revised report, but should have assessed costs on defendant at the same time. In *Tremblay* (2003), defendant requested—and was granted—time and funds from the court to revise his expert's work after receiving my affidavit for the state.[36] What happened to the notion that each expert gets only one shot?[37]

In *Chavez* (1998), a "driving while black" case discussed in Chapter 8, defendants sent data to Temple University's Center for Public Policy, where summaries were prepared for plaintiffs' expert, Martin Shapiro. After Shapiro had filed his report, he discovered that Temple's work had not been correct. Plaintiffs requested a stay of defendant's motion for summary judgment, which was granted on the theory that revisions might obviate the issue. Plaintiffs thought the revisions helped them, and moved to substitute a new declaration from Shapiro, and new answers to defendant's motion.

Judge Manning then ruled that "statistical evidence cannot be used to satisfy the Equal Protection Clause's similarly situated requirement."[38]

> This means that . . . consideration of the revised analysis would not affect the court's disposition of the equal protection claims. For these reasons, the plaintiffs' motion to withdraw and substitute the revised Shapiro declaration and corresponding materials is denied.

Couldn't this legal meta-decision have been made first, before plaintiffs bore the expense of work that, even if correct, would have been ineffectual? In any event, that Shapiro subcontracted with Temple is irrelevant. The work was properly considered to be his. Within the schedule, his work was unacceptable. It should have been excluded on that basis.

---

36. Defendant's attorney was a public defender. Although the Connecticut Public Defender's Office—which handled the *Gibbs* (1998) case—has its own expert budget, apparently Rhode Island's does not.

37. See *Weisgram* (2000) at 455:

> It is implausible to suggest, post-*Daubert*, that parties will initially present less than their best expert evidence in the expectation of a second chance should their first try fail.

This is written in the context of arguing for a new trial, but should be equally applicable to repetitive testimony. It should also apply to replacing an excluded expert with another. In *McLeod* (2000), a scheduling order was revised to accommodate plaintiff's new expert, because his appearance was caused by defendant's successful motion to exclude their first expert. The error in *McLeod*, not seen by any court, was that the first expert was excluded on the basis of his credentials. Had the first expert been excluded on the basis of his proffered testimony, plaintiffs should not have been given a second chance. *Weisgram* should apply.

38. *Chavez* (1998) at 1065; following indented quotation also at 1065.

The requirement for a report—a complete report, no late submissions—should be sufficient. Rules and schedules requiring that reports and data be exchanged, and be complete, would have prevented Joan Haworth from releasing her secret "market" measure only during her testimony, or Harry Roberts from abandoning "mini regressions" in favor of reverse regression, or David Pollard from opening his testimony with graphics and an argument the other side had never heard before, or Gene Fisher from deciding at the last minute to un-revise his data.[39] Judges let this game playing, expert chicanery, meanness, occur because they cannot be bothered to intervene. And because they fear reversal. If judges were instructed to control the pre-trial exchange of data and reports by the experts, and given the tools and training *and appeals court support* to do so, the parties would be better behaved.

Response

The point of exchanging reports should not be just to inform, but to reduce the need for judicial determination. For this to happen, I would build a response time into the process.

There is an obvious logic to making the plaintiffs state their complaint, the plaintiffs' expert present his evidence, before the defendant has to defend. Samuel Gross suggests that

> Experts could be required to submit their reports sufficiently in advance of trial
> to permit the opposing lawyers and experts to ask them thoughtful questions,
> in writing, and to permit the reporting experts to respond thoughtfully.[40]

I would consider a face-to-face meeting well before trial, also. Finis Welch caught my interpretation error in *Miller* (1980), as I described in Chapter 6. It was the absence of direct expert interchange that allowed my client to blackmail defendant with a threat of a "battle of experts," when the experts in fact agreed.

Some experts are predetermined to support their client, and probably are not competent to engage in a technical discussion. Mark Berkman would not concede, when we met with attorneys, that his regression in *Crow* implied nothing about the impact of Montana's severance tax (see Chapter 3). If ever there was a conceptually hopeless and miserably performed regression analysis, Berkman's was it; but, though he made no attempt to defend his study, neither would he admit error. A meeting may accomplish nothing. However, had this meeting occurred under the auspices of the judge, it might have had a more efficacious outcome.

After the exchange of reports and depositions, I would structure short, written responses to be submitted in the same order. Then there would be a deadline for filing

---

39. For Haworth, see *Nassau* (1992); for Roberts, see *Harris Bank* (1981); for Pollard see *Gibbs* (1998). Fisher testified in *Pugliano* (2004), although his testimony has not been the subject of an opinion.

40. Gross (1991) at 1215.

revised reports. Each attorney, and each expert, would be well versed in the objections to be raised by the other side's experts by the time of a *Daubert* hearing or trial. I submit that imposing and enforcing a schedule like this would eliminate many trials.

In *Allapatah* (1999) Exxon's expert, Joseph Kalt, criticized the affidavit submitted by plaintiffs' expert, Raymond Fishe. Fishe then submitted a revised and amplified report, directly responding to Kalt's criticisms, clarifying his data and methods. "Exxon then moved to preclude the testimony by Plaintiffs' expert on analysis not contained in his final report,"[41] on the basis that the deadline for the expert's report had passed. It would make no sense to allow criticism and not a response; but that response might have come at trial, not in the form of another report, if that was the rule of the case. A better rule would be to allow each expert to submit one revision. Judge Golod did accept Fishe's revised report, but he was making it up one decision at a time, reading briefs the parties had to prepare to argue every turn in the road. It is sloppy and expensive for the parties not to know the rules in advance.

Should the Parties' Experts be Heard?

The *Daubert* hearing is now well established. Reports in hand, the parties move to exclude their opponents' experts for lack of verifiable science, for bad data, bad methodology, bad effectuation, or inappropriate conclusions. The judge is to decide not on the merits of the experts' presentations vis-à-vis one another, but on the sufficiency of their merits vis-à-vis some threshold of "reliability."[42]

---

41. *Allapatah* (1999) at 1337.

42. The extent to which a *Daubert* assessment should be made at the class-certification stage is in dispute. The Supreme Court has not taken up this issue, although it has been asked to. When it does, I presume it will admonish that an expert should be truly expert, his work truly scientific—though not necessarily correct—regardless of the stage at which he is testifying. For now, though, most courts assess an expert's work at the low level of "not so fatally flawed as to be inadmissible as a matter of law." With that standard, Bernard Siskin's analysis stands and defendant fails to get summary judgment in *Anderson* (2004) at 530. Similar language appeared in *Visa* (2000) at 76 and *Visa* (2001) at 135. In *Robinson* (1997) at 48, Judge Rakoff referred to "infirmities in the statistics" produced by plaintiffs' expert Harriet Zellner, denying class certification. He was reversed, partly because this decision defied an earlier reversal, but also because the Second Circuit thought he came too close to weighing the merits of the experts' arguments, In *Cruz* (1998), also denying class certification, Judge Rakoff refers in footnote 3 to a "purported expert" whose work *is* "fatally flawed."

In *DeMarco* (2004a), again denying plaintiffs a class, and no doubt trying to pre-empt another reversal, Judge Rakoff lays into plaintiffs' expert's work (at 249):

> [T]he net is that Torchio's conclusions are both so facially unreliable as to be inadmissable under Fed. R. Evid. 702 and so plainly irrelevant as to be inadmissible under Fed. R. Evid. 401.

Whatever the Second Circuit makes of that will occur well after publication of this book.

The Federal Rules of Evidence

James Bradley Thayer, in 1898, not only articulated the distinction between fact and law but called for a code of rules under which courts would operate in finding fact. Forty years later, there still being no such rules, Edmund Morgan and John Maguire reiterated that call.[43] The Supreme Court may intrinsically have the power to make rules for the federal judiciary, but Congress formalized the Court's authority to propose, the legislature's authority to dispose, in the Rules Enabling Act of 1934.[44] The American Law Institute started drafting such a code shortly thereafter. Kenneth Culp Davis refers disparagingly to a second draft of that code.[45] The Institute's model code was later completed, but never accepted. In 1961 the Judicial Conference of the United States suggested the formation of a committee, which was established in 1965. It reported first in 1970, and then in 1974, with a proposed code for the admission of evidence.[46]

Thus the Federal Rules of Evidence became established only in 1975. They are modified regularly. *Daubert* (1993) essentially told trial courts to follow the rules regarding the presentation of expert testimony.[47] Rule 701 disallows lay testimony "based on scientific, technical, or other specialized knowledge." That evidence is covered by Rule 702, on experts.

Rule 702 says that a person

> qualified as an expert by knowledge, skill, experience, training, or education
> may testify thereto in the form of an opinion.

As only experts can testify on the results of a "scientific" inquiry—lay people cannot—the judge assumes that he must first determine whether the person whose testimony has been proffered is in fact an expert. We have already seen that judges always had the authority to exclude evidence, but Rule 702 is the origin of the current discussion of the judge as

---

43. Morgan and Maguire (1937) at 922. They quote from Thayer, *A Preliminary Treatise On Evidence* (1898). K. Davis (1942) then, at 369, quotes Morgan and Maguire quoting Thayer, who had been writing about evidence for many years before his *Treatise*.

44. Congress can veto rule changes which otherwise, upon transmission from the Supreme Court, will go into effect. Congress has no rule-*making* mechanism. The judicial system does.

45. See K. Davis (1942).

46. There is much more to this story, of course, including congressional and Justice Department attempts to control—at least influence—the rules. For more on the history and politics of the Rules of Evidence see Giannelli (1993) or Scallen (2002).

47. Some observers think *Daubert* changed the rules:

> *Daubert* changed the law of evidence by establishing a "gatekeeper" function for trial judges under Federal Rule of Evidence 702.

The Tenth Circuit in *Goebel* (2000) at 1087. I think they are wrong. *Daubert* changed the *procedures* of evidence, and perhaps the perception of some lower-court judges, but not the law.

"gatekeeper," screening experts for their worthiness to testify. Yet, I contend, determination whether the witness is an expert should not be made independent of what he is about to say. *Daubert* called for gatekeeping on the basis of the testimony, not the witness. The implications of this difference are not understood, and form the basis for much that follows in this chapter.

The Expert's Credentials

From Rule 703, expert witnesses may base their opinion on facts not otherwise in evidence (or even admissible). Until 2000, this ability to voice an adjudicative-fact opinion was the *only* distinguishing characteristic of "expert" testimony.[48] Proposed experts always have had to demonstrate their expertise in other matters, before they would be heard in this one. Persons put forward to inform the court about legislative facts relevant to understanding other testimony may be denied that opportunity because they are not experts *in* the field. That exclusion is pernicious. Like those analysts of whom I wrote in Chapter 4, they may be experts *on* the field.

For example, Lawrence Dubin, for over twenty years a professor of law at the University of Detroit Mercy School of Law, with many publications to his credit, was not qualified to present an opinion about the Michigan Rules of Professional Conduct. Why?

> Unlike professions with a more technical bent, the court takes notice that an article in a law review is typically the product of only the author, and that it undergoes no more serious critique than the grammatical and citation checking done by the law students who run the journals and select the articles.[49]

I agree that Dubin's credentials alone did not prove his expertise. Unfortunately, the judge did not inquire into Dubin's affidavit to determine whether, credentials or no, he had something to offer in this case.

Assessing the legislative-fact "expert" presents interesting challenges which I will try to delineate, and then avoid, as a self-imposed limitation on this book. Let's for now stay with the easier case, the adjudicative-fact expert. Wood Herron, a general practitioner, "did not purport to be an expert on either industrial medicine or the care and treatment of women." The other side's expert, Nace Cohen, had been "an obstetrician and gynecologist for more than 20 years."[50] Allowing both to testify, Judge Johnson found

---

48. *Williams* (1996) at 1442:

> The difference between an expert witness and an ordinary witness is that the former is allowed to offer an opinion, while the latter is confined to testifying from personal knowledge.

49. *Cicero* (2001) at 747.

50. *Cheatwood* (1969), both quotations at 758 (2 FEP Cases at 35); following indented quotation from footnote 3 at 760 (2 FEP Cases at 36).

> that the experience of Dr. Cohen is more specifically related to the problem at
> hand, that his testimony tends to be more detailed and relevant, and that his
> conclusions are more persuasive.

Was Cohen's testimony more persuasive because of his superior credentials, or because it appeared to fit the facts better than that of Herron? Wouldn't the answer be the same, wouldn't Cohen's testimony still have been more persuasive, without any concern for his credentials?

Judge Vratil lashes out at Richard Hoyt, plaintiffs' expert: "Dr. Hoyt is an expert for hire," she says. Hoyt lists 121 cases on his resume; defendant's expert lists only six.[51]

> Here, likewise [citing *Rice* (1995)] plaintiffs call upon Dr. Hoyt not to supply
> specialized knowledge, but to plug evidentiary holes in plaintiffs' case, to spec-
> ulate, and to surmise. One does not need an expert economist to do what Dr.
> Hoyt proposes to do.

Hoyt presented a deficient, client-oriented study; but was that because he made his living as an expert?[52] Consider the academic Louis St. Peter, whose data came from ninety-two of 250 employees, although he generalized to all of Eagle Iron Works; who tried to infer flow (hires) information from stock (employees) data; of whom ultimately the court said:

> The lack of a satisfactory basis for his opinion and the obvious willingness of
> the witness to attribute more authenticity to the statistics than they possessed,
> cast doubts upon the value of Dr. St. Peter's opinions.[53]

Or consider the chairman of the department of finance at the University of Illinois Urbana, plaintiffs' expert:

---

51. *Phosphide* (1995) at 1500; following indented quotation at 1506.

52. In a case noted in Chapter 8, the Eighth Circuit had a different impression of the implication of an expert's prior trial experience. The expert, H. Boulter Kelsey, was a mechanical engineer who had "previously testified in approximately forty pneumatic nail gun cases." *Lauzon* (2001) at 685. At 689:

> Instead of detracting from reliability . . . this factor weighs heavily in favor of admitting
> the testimony of Kelsey as an expert witness.

In *Hooten* (1986), an expert claimed to have testified in three hundred cases. The majority of the Mississippi Supreme Court, remanding the case because her testimony had been excluded, concluded, at 948:

> Her practical experience in the examination of questioned documents, and frequent court
> appearances to testify in similar cases places her clearly within the ambit of our rules
> regarding experts.

The dissenters condemned the system, concluding, at 958:

> If this witness has indeed testified over 300 times as an expert on discovering spurious
> handwriting as she claimed, it is an astonishing indictment on the gullibility of lawyers
> and judges.

53. *Eagle* (1976) at 247 (14 FEP Cases at 542). Because of labor turnover, one cannot determine from current employees what kind of people were hired some time ago.

Professor Bryan provided nothing but conclusions—no facts, no hint of an inferential process, no discussion of hypotheses considered and rejected.[54]

The question was about the appropriateness of certain Exchange National Bank procedures. "Bryan offered the court his CV rather than his economic skills," says Judge Easterbrook, affirming summary judgment for defendant. "Professor Bryan cast aside his scholar's mantle and became a shill for [plaintiff] Mid-State."[55] Acting like a hired hand, having "client-oriented" opinions, being influenced by the "delirious sirens of lucre," is not limited to professionals.[56]

Judge Weinstein wrote that Barry Singer

is board certified in internal medicine, hematology, and oncology. . . . He bases his opinion on his medical background, a review of the literature on the biomedical effects of Agent Orange, and an examination of the individual affidavits.[57]

Singer was not an expert in epidemiology, the skill he should have had to be drawing conclusions about the relationship between Agent Orange and specific maladies. In contrast, plaintiffs' other expert, Samuel Epstein,

has been specially trained in the fields of pathology, bacteriology, and public health. . . . His credentials clearly suffice to qualify him as an expert pursuant to Rule 702 of the Federal Rules of Evidence.

Despite disparaging remarks about Singer's qualifications, Judge Weinstein treated the two experts alike. He allowed Singer to testify, and determined that his

conclusory allegations lack any foundation in fact. His analysis, in addition to being speculative, is so guarded as to be worthless.

But Epstein, though he had appropriate credentials, fared no better. Weinstein found that

the testimony of Doctors Singer and Epstein is insufficiently grounded in any reliable evidence.

Neither witness, it turned out, was an expert, regardless what their résumés implied.

---

54. *Mid-State* (1989) at 1339.

55. *Mid-State* (1989) at 1340, both quotations.

56. "Delirious sirens of lucre" is from Spence (1989) at 243. As I suggested in Chapter 6, and as Perrin (1995) notes, at 1445, "Lawyers are just as susceptible as experts to the lure of the almighty dollar."

Gerry Spence demonstrates the typical attorney's ignorance of all things statistical, especially in criticizing the way in which reliability is maintained in the Law School Admissions Test. But he has captured the essence of some problems in the judicial system, from law school to law firm to judicial appointment; from lay to expert testimony.

57. *Agent Orange* (1985) at 1235; following two indented quotations both at 1238; fourth indented quotation at 1250.

The Fifth Circuit understood before *Daubert* that, although it must check credentials,

> inquiry into the qualifications of an expert should not be a substitute for scrutinizing an expert's reasoning or methodology.[58]

That is, credentials are necessary but not sufficient. However, they are *not* necessary. Rule 702 could be interpreted so that a determination of expertise is made from the proffered testimony itself. As no judge will interpret it that way, Rule 702 should be rewritten to make qualification coincident with and dependent on the *Daubert*-hearing testimony. If the witness has something of value to offer the fact finder, then he is an expert. If he does not, then he is not.

Highly credentialed expert testimony is often rejected. Of plaintiff's primary expert, Lennart Hardell, Judge Blake wrote:

> His education, experience, and training, considered by themselves, establish his qualifications to provide opinion testimony in the fields of oncology and epidemiology, if those opinions otherwise satisfy the *Daubert* standards.[59]

The basis of his opinions did *not* meet *Daubert* standards, and so his testimony was disallowed. Another court, after disparaging the expert's credentials, made clear that its ultimate rejection was based on methodology,

> even if we assume that Dr. Johnstone has the expertise to give testimony on issues of epidemiology and pharmacology.[60]

The internal contradiction should be obvious. The exclusion itself is a decision that the witness demonstrated no such expertise in this case.

Although the district-court judge accepted Daniel Teitelbaum's testimony, the Tenth Circuit noted that

> We are unable to discern whether the court was referring to the professional credentials of the witness as opposed to assessing the reasoning and methodology relied upon by the witness. It is axiomatic that an expert, no matter how good his credentials, is not permitted to speculate.[61]

It remanded the case "for a new trial." But the judge wrote a *Daubert* opinion instead, allowing Teitelbaum's testimony. The Tenth Circuit then affirmed. In dissent, Judge Hartz could not find the science behind the testimony:

---

58. *Christophersen* (1991) at 1110. It found the plaintiffs' methodology lacking. As defense attorney Bert Black (1994) commented, at 2132:
> The expert testimony in *Christophersen* exemplifies the worst of what plaintiffs sometimes attempt to pass off as science.

59. *Newman* (2002) at 775.

60. *Cloud* (2001) at 1132.

61. *Goebel* (2000) at 1088.

He has an impressive résumé. But science is no respecter of résumés.[62]

The issue therefore became the circuit court's standard of review. Reversal requires that the judge has abused his discretion. Why the reviewing court's determination that the testimony lacked scientific validity does not establish such abuse, I do not know.

Affirming the primacy of the testimony, an Arizona Supreme Court justice wrote:

> We would not allow a Nobel laureate in physics to testify that, based upon his experience, the earth is flat.[63]

If some judge did, the airline pilot put up by the other side to describe the earth's curvature, as he sees it every day, might be deemed unqualified to offer rebuttal.[64]

A solution that has occurred to several judges, in cases that will not go before a jury, is to pass all experts through the *Daubert* hearing. Accepting an expert might be appealed, but excluding one is sure to be. Most reversals are of exclusions. So we get this kind of runaround from Judge Weinstein:

> The opinions of defendant's experts were unreliable. They were not consistent with other evidence in the case. Assuming for the sake of this memorandum

---

62. *Goebel* (2003) at 1001.

63. *Logerquist* (2000), Justice Martone in dissent, at footnote 2. Recall that in Chapter 8 I discussed several cases in which Franklin Fisher's testimony was rejected, although no court would ever reject his qualifications. The elimination of an expert for lack of credentials is the larger issue than the rejection of testimony from a "qualified" expert.

64. Lawyers will point out that the airline pilot might be allowed to testify, under Rule 701, as a lay witness. Judge Guy, in *Berry* (1994), at 1350, would allow him as an expert:

> [I]f one wanted to prove that bumblebees always take off into the wind, a beekeeper with no scientific training at all would be an acceptable expert witness if a proper foundation were laid for his conclusions. The foundation would not relate to his formal training, but to his firsthand observations. In other words, the beekeeper does not know any more about flight principles than the jurors, but he has seen a lot more bumblebees than they have.

That is, in terms that will be defined below, the beekeeper is not a science witness. He is a craft witness, as would be the pilot. As a craft witness, he would have to produce evidence of his reliability. As Justice Steigmann of the Illinois Appellate Court pointed out in *Harris* (1999), at 369:

> [T]he *Berry* court noted that the beekeeper's testimony could be used to prove that bumblebees always take off into the wind, but the court did not address exactly what testimony the beekeeper could give to prove that proposition—that is, how he reached his conclusion regarding bumblebee flight patterns.

Judge Guy would rely on his credentials. I would rely on evidence that he excels in his craft. Not that he has been in it for a long time, but that he does it well. That other observations of his have been shown to be correct. The *Harris* court correctly perceived that the beekeeper's testimony would not be science. Then, rather than determining that some non-*Frye* (for *Frye* is the applicable standard in Illinois) screening device needed to be devised, the court determined that this non-scientific evidence would not have to be screened at all! As long as the witness disclaims that his testimony is "science," he cannot be excluded because it incorporates bad science?

that their opinions met the *Daubert* test, they were not credible and were unpersuasive.[65]

What test was it that they are assumed to have met? Weinstein consistently waves off *Daubert*. He isn't going to get bogged down excluding experts:

> The jury then sat for six weeks examining highly technical statistical and other studies with the aid of qualified *Daubert*ized experts from the fields of statistics, merchandising, and criminology; large data sources; extensive video depositions; government reports; and other proof.[66]

If many judges adopt this attitude, the *Daubert* hearing will become a sham. As Timothy Perrin writes:

> It is rare for a trial court to exclude an expert witness because of a failure to qualify, and rarer yet for an appellate court to disturb the trial judge's decision.[67]

Credentials always look impressive. They present no opportunity to discriminate between the competent and the incompetent. Yet not only are they utilized by judges to evaluate forthcoming testimony, they are recommended to jurors for the same purpose.[68] If qualifications are not a valid screen, let's not waste time with them. Judges should take the *Daubert* gatekeeping mandate seriously.[69] My proposals below—to substitute, in *Daubert* hearings, a serious review of the expert's testimony for his credentials—are designed to bring more discernment to the initial screening process.

The Field's Credentials

Here is a different view:

> It is one thing to evaluate the truthfulness of lay witnesses on issues of adjudicative fact by resorting to their credibility. But the existence or meaning

---

65. *Gigante II* at 148.

66. *Acusport* (2003) at 465.

67. *Perrin* (1995) at 1395. As time has passed, this statement has become less true. We find reversals for inclusion and for exclusion of experts. But what remains true is that the discussion is about the expert's qualifications, not his testimony.

68. Vidmar and Diamond (2001) tell us, at 1131, that at least one state and

> federal instructions point to the credentials of the expert witness as an appropriate source of information for the jurors to use in evaluating the witness's testimony. . . . It is not surprising that education and experience figure prominently in jury instructions. Judges use them to decide whether to permit an expert to testify.

69. Abramson (2001) would have judges assess expert credentials because, at 762,

> The assessment of expert credentials, unlike the assessment of scientific merit, does lie within the broad realm of judicial competence.

We agree on the bottom line, that judges are competent to perform *Daubert* gatekeeping tasks, but we get there from different reasoning, and ask for different assessments by the judges.

of a body of asserted scientific knowledge does not depend on the credibility of the witness. Such a stance betrays not only ignorance of the scientific subject matter but also hopelessness about ever being able to understand it.[70]

On this argument, Michael Saks would exclude all handwriting experts based on finding as legislative fact that they cannot do what they say they do. At least one court agrees:

> Once a trial court has decided that proffered expert scientific testimony is scientifically valid and has admitted such evidence for the particular purpose to which it is directed, and that decision is affirmed by this court in a published opinion, it will become precedent controlling subsequent trials.[71]

This is wrong. Acceptance of one expert's use of some named methodology in one case should have no bearing on evidence purporting to use the same methodology, even if by the same expert, in another case.[72] A Maryland court explained the rationale for a legislative-fact finding this way:

> The answer to the question about the reliability of a scientific technique or process does not vary according to the circumstances of each case. It is therefore inappropriate to view this threshold question of reliability as a matter within each trial judge's individual discretion.[73]

Reliability of a method is not the issue unless one can say, with certainty, that a particular methodology is *never* correct, beyond random coincidence. Rather, the question should be whether a particular application of a particular methodology can assist in discerning the facts of this case. All parties may agree that the method in other hands is unreliable—not generally correct some boundary proportion of the time—and yet disagree as to whether it is correct (and useful) in this particular application. This court

---

70. Saks (1998) at 1112.

71. *O'Key* (1995) at 293. The court is the Supreme Court of Oregon.

72. Adina Schwartz, one of the few commentators who argues that *Daubert* is fatally flawed ("based on a fundamental misunderstanding of the history and philosophy of science"), also takes an exclusively legislative-fact view. She opposes the notion that judges can evaluate science because she thinks they must understand large science concepts and theories. A *Frye*-based standard is preferred, she says, because "scientists' opinions provide the sole rational basis for deciding on the scientific status of work." Her elitist conclusion is mistaken in part because her legislative-fact approach is mistaken. See Schwartz (1997), quotations at 237 and 219.

    Kaye (2001) also would leave the affirmation of the validity of an expert's methodology in the hands of the field. It is not clear if, to Kaye, failing to use a generally accepted methodology should be sufficient grounds for exclusion. Using such a methodology, however, would obviate exclusion. If others have been using the wrong methodology, Kaye would have an expert flirt with exclusion by going against the tide. As Kordana and O'Reilly (2001) point out, at 2023: "It is not clear that Kaye's criticisms . . . support Kaye's agenda." He shows, rather—as I will emphasize below is a characteristic of "science" testimony"—that he can refute another expert's testimony within the confines of this case.

73. *Reed* (1978) at 381.

prescribes laziness, to have the judgment about whether this testimony should be accepted in this case be based on other testimony about other applications of the methodology in other cases.

Mark Brodin continues the argument for a legislative-fact determination about the field, asserting that some extreme fact-finding methods exist. But he does not use the word "correct":

> Where, for example, a discipline itself lacks reliability, as in the case of astrology, general acceptance among practitioners carries little weight.[74]

The hangover of *Frye* (1923) standards into *Daubert* (1993) rears its ugly head. If we ask for "general acceptance among practitioners," then yes, we should be concerned with who those practitioners are, whether the court should credit them. Let's, instead, abandon "general acceptance" once and for all, and have trial courts make determinations of scientific merit specific to each case at hand.

Prior to *Daubert*, the Fourth Circuit maintained a "per se exclusionary rule," by which it did not allow polygraph evidence with respect to witness credibility. Would such automatic exclusion, Judge Hamilton asks, be

> consistent with the principles concerning the admission of scientific or technical evidence enunciated in *Daubert*?[75]

He continues:

> That question, which is finally squarely before the court, must be answered in the negative.

Correct though he is, his comment is made in dissent. The Fourth Circuit upheld exclusion of all such evidence, regardless what demonstration might be made of the reliability of the practitioner presenting it.

What these judges and writers are afraid of is apparent inconsistency among courts. Surely we are smart enough to see around labels, to understand that just because methods offered in different cases carry the same name, they are not necessarily equivalent. I could find no redeeming value for "reverse regression" in Chapter 3, but did not propose that all testimony bearing that name be suppressed. Some would have the name of the meth-

---

74. Brodin (2004) at 21. He argues against "syndrome" testimony, the legislative-fact assertion that some people react to some events in a uniform, disturbed way. "[T]here is serious question as to whether such testimony tells the jurors anything they do not already know," he writes, at 37. Jane Moriarty (2001) tells us that syndrome testimony helped convict witches in Salem, and David McCord (1986), arguing against syndrome testimony, shows that any behavior at all can be described as consistent with child sexual abuse. Yet I see no reason why syndrome testimony should be excluded as a general proposition. The judgment that specific proffered testimony is too diffuse or unreliable is always available.

75. *Prince-Oyibo* (2003) at 502.

odology substitute for its content. I say, allow the proponent an opportunity to demonstrate the usefulness of the proffered testimony.

In addition to the potential error from such all-encompassing exclusions, there is no need for them. They appear to assume that higher-level courts embody more wisdom than trial courts. By definition, the higher the court, the more "correct" (for now) its opinion about law; but not about fact. Higher-level courts should never declare some types of evidence, by their name, unacceptable.[76]

Erica Beecher-Monas and Edgar Garcia-Rill come close to sweeping generalization about psychologist predictions of future violence and the lingering effects of *Barefoot* (1983):

> If *Daubert* standards were applied to the kinds of clinical predictions currently offered in our courts, they would not be admitted because they do not meet any of the criteria for scientific validity.[77]

Of course *Daubert* standards should apply. They should apply singly, to each individual

---

76. For example, *Reed* (1978) was first a declaration by the Maryland Court of Appeals that the principles of *Frye* (1923) would hold, and second:

> We therefore hold that testimony based on "voiceprints" or spectrograms is, for the present, inadmissible in Maryland courts as evidence of voice identification.

At 399. I recommend this case not for its majority opinion, but for the remarkable dissent by Judge Smith (starting at 400), who argues that *Frye* is interpreted incorrectly (it only affirmed a judge's use of his discretion), that as used it is bad law, that voiceprint nonetheless passes the *Frye* test, and that courts should not make such sweeping pronouncements on scientific method. At 422:

> Although the accuracy of firearms identification is common knowledge today, the Illinois Supreme Court at one point labeled the claims of ballistics experts as "preposterous."

Literature citation omitted. The Illinois case is *People v. Berkman*, 307 Ill. 492 (1923).

77. Beecher-Monas and Garcia-Rill (2003) at 1859. Consider, at 1847:

> An astrologer, for example, would not be permitted to testify about future dangerousness, either as a constitutional matter or under rules of evidence, because the testimony would be misleading.

Is the point that psychologists should be excluded a priori also? Wouldn't it be better to subject individual witnesses to assessments of accuracy, permitting those who can show that they can predict to do so? It may be that neither astrologers nor psychologists would qualify, but it ill behooves the legal profession to prejudge them.

Mark Brodin (2004) asserts, at 13, that

> it is highly unlikely that the legendary doll studies [of Kenneth Clark, in *Brown* (1954)] would meet the standards set by *Daubert*.

I concur, but not because social scientists cannot perform valid studies. I concur because Clark could not relate his findings to school segregation, and therefore his studies should have been excluded as irrelevant. Beecher-Monas and Garcia-Rill ultimately support empirically based testimony assessing the probability of future dangerousness. The expert would not be allowed to assert a binary conclusion. I agree. However, they suggest that acceptable testimony will come from valid instruments (assess the field), whereas I suggest that it will come from valid instruments appropriately used by the expert before the court (assess this testimony).

expert's proffered testimony, on the basis of that expert's analysis. The challenge, then, is to offer a basis upon which to evaluate expert testimony in a *Daubert* hearing. I take on that challenge under my framework, offered below.

Prior Testimony

One aspect of an expert's résumé that interests judges is how other judges have reacted to him. Richard Hoyt, as noted above, was considered suspect for having testified often. A Sixth Circuit panel noted that

> Rappeport has been criticized by other courts for the employment of faulty methodologies and the presentation of unreliable results.[78]

This observation apparently bolstered their courage to criticize his study in the case at issue. Similarly, Judge Gleeson in New York referred to Bernard Siskin as "a nationally recognized labor economist,"[79] a notation quoted by Judge Eagen, in Oklahoma, opening a one-paragraph encomium on Siskin.[80] A few paragraphs later, Siskin's résumé is utilized to reject Boeing's motion to have his testimony barred:

> Based on Siskin's education, experience, and descriptions of the methodology utilized in conducting his statistical analyses of compensation at Boeing in Oklahoma, the Court finds that his testimony is not so fatally flawed as to be inadmissible as a matter of law.

It is almost amusing that a judge, lacking confidence to assess statistical studies, relies on other judges, few of whom have more capability, and are assessing different work.[81] The key to implementing the evaluation criteria I espouse here is understanding that there are different kinds of experts, who require different kinds of evaluation. The correctness of prior testimony should matter for craft experts, as we will see in my framework, below, but must, under *Daubert*, be irrelevant in assessing an expert's science testimony.

It may be that an expert is not very good, and the court may note that. Not being a sharp analyst in other cases, however, should not be grounds for exclusion from this case. For example, Judge Posner writes about a criminologist, Lindsay Hayes:

---

78. *Autozone* (2004) at 799, footnote 2.

79. *Sheppard* (2002) at *3.

80. *Anderson* (2004) at 527; following indented quotation at 529. For the record, Siskin is not a labor economist, although he minored in economics through college and graduate school. He is, as Judge Frye commented many years earlier, "one of the nation's leading experts on the application of statistics to Title VII cases." *Penk* (1985) at *14.

81. John Beyer, we are informed in *DeLoach* (2002) at 563, "has been involved in roughly 20 class action price-fixing cases." Not only is that the only credential referenced by Judge Osteen, this summary is quoted by Judge Lungstrum in *Telephone* (2004), at 674, as Beyer's only credential of note. The implication is clear: Other judges credited Beyer, so I (Judge Osteen) will, also.

He is a reputable criminologist, but in this case, as in two others we've discovered, his evidence was useless and should have been excluded under the *Daubert* standard.[82]

Posner goes on to explain why Hayes' testimony fails *in this case*:

It is not the number of suicides that is a meaningful index of suicide risk and therefore of governmental responsibility, but the suicide rate; and it is not even the rate by itself, but rather the rate relative to the "background" suicide rate in the relevant free population (the population of the area from which the jail draws its inmates) and to the rate in other jails. No evidence was presented that would have enabled an estimate of any of these rates—not even the population of Brown County was put into the record.

Prior testimony is a credential, of which proffering attorneys make much, and judges should make nothing. The judicial error in considering an expert's prior court appearances is is a specific example of the larger error of considering credentials of any kind. When the substance of the testimony is science, credentials should play no role—positive, as in Siskin's case, or negative, as in Hoyt's. The court must, and should only, assess expert's work in the case at hand.

Credentials in What Field?

Plaintiffs had purchased a motor boat which, they alleged, was faulty and not properly repaired. In a breach-of-warranty claim, they offered the testimony of Ramón Echeandía to establish that the fuel-management system was faulty in design.

Defendants contended that Echeandía could not properly be qualified as an expert because he lacked education, training, and experience with fuel management systems, including marine systems.[83]

In *Ruff* (2001), Terry McLendon, who worked for Shephard Miller Inc. (that is, was a professional), co-authored the "SMI Report" and testified. As in all toxic tort litigation, plaintiffs must produce a trail of evidence from the defendant to the toxic substance to the plaintiff to the malady. Each expert has a piece of the puzzle, and each relies on others. Opposing counsel therefore tries to break this chain anywhere it can.

Defendants . . . argue that Dr. McLendon does not have sufficient expertise with the explosives compound RDX to render a reliable dose estimation opinion in this case.[84]

---

82. *Boncher* (2001) at 486; following indented quotation also at 486. Citations to other cases are omitted from both quotations.

83. *Correa* (2002) at *24.

84. *Ruff* (2001) at 1232.

The first time I prepared an employment-discrimination case in which a bank was a defendant, though I was one of the most experienced equal-employment-opportunity experts a party could employ, I was challenged for not having investigated a bank before. In a breach-of-contract case,

> Defendants also contend that expert Greenwald's testimony was insufficient to establish lost profits because he lacked prior experience with movie theaters.[85]

The Sixth Circuit characterized Robert Greenwald as follows:

> Greenwald specialized in damages analysis such as the one performed in this case. He is a certified public accountant, a certified business appraiser, a shareholder and director of litigation support group of an accounting firm, and he has offered testimony in at least fifty court cases.

Similarly, we learn that

> Dr. George Mundy, has been a practicing veterinarian in Kentucky since 1983 and has extensive experience diagnosing and treating horses.

However, he had never performed a modified Forsell's procedure, on which basis his testimony was excluded by Judge Hood.[86] The Sixth Circuit vacated that exclusion. Judge Blake describes a similar complaint:

> The plaintiffs primary argument to exclude the defense experts (particularly Dr. Stampfer and Dr. Israel) focuses on those experts' lack of specific experience in the field of radio frequency radiation.[87]

Judge Alesia, concerning an insurance company's objection to a claimant's roofing expert:

> St. Paul further claims that Diederich's opinion is outside the scope of his expertise because it incorporates engineering and aerodynamics principles.[88]

Under current rules, attorneys *must* make such insipid challenges. Not to do so might be malpractice. I advocate that such a line of questioning be restricted to cross-examination at trial, to affect the weight of the testimony however the fact finder takes it. The real question is lost in such challenges: How expert is the current work of these experts? By arguing whether he is black or white, the expert's shade of grey is obscured.

I testified against the bank, and my client prevailed. Greenwald, Mundy, Stampfer, and

---

85. *Regal* (2004) at 833; following indented quotation also at 833.

86. Preceding indented quotation, *Jahn* (2000) at 387. At 389:
> The fact that Dr. Mundy had never performed a modified Forsell's procedure would cast doubt on any criticisms he had regarding the performance of the surgery, but he did not criticize the surgical procedure.

87. *Newman* (2002) at 782.

88. *Spearman* (2001) at 1096.

Israel were allowed to testify, as was Bruce Diederich. Motions for summary judgment and exclusion of McLendon were denied. Echeandía's credentials were questioned in terms of his *scientific* expertise. His expertise, though surely covered by *Daubert*, was something else, which I will discuss below as "technical" or "craft." He, too, testified, and his client prevailed.

In *Hill* (1997), Judge Murphy put his response in a footnote:

> The Court finds unpersuasive Defendants' argument that Dr. Jackson's report is inadmissible because his only familiarity with the poultry industry arose in light of this litigation.[89]

Reid Jr. (2001) provides an illustration of credentialism run amuck. Judge Parker appointed his own statistical expert, William Schucany, to comment on the credentials of both parties' experts (as well as their analyses). Judge Parker framed the question in the language of Rule 702, and got his answer from Schucany just that way:

> In my professional opinion Dr. Daymont does not deserve to be qualified in statistical science simply by virtue of his formal education and training. His Ph.D. in sociology is not adequate preparation for such statistical analyses. His C.V. does not provide convincing support in this regard. He is not a member of the American Statistical Association. Furthermore his published refereed journal articles on the specific topic of employment history comparisons are insufficient to raise his credentials to that level. The quantitative studies that he has published are fundamentally different from the methodology required here. He lists no peer-reviewed articles since 1992.[90]

Not a member of the American Statistical Association?[91] Methodology not used in his publications? Most professional experts would be barred from most of their cases by these

---

89. *Hill* (1997) at *4, footnote 5.

90. From Schucany's report, quoted in *Reid Jr.* (2001) at 501; "C.V." is the witness's curriculum vitae. Schucany goes on to allow that Daymont just might have acquired enough experience in

> the 11 federal suits in which he testified and perhaps on some other cases about which he may have been consulted. However without easy access to that testimony I cannot judge the nature or quality of his statistical analyses.

If the court's academic expert cannot assess qualifications except from academic writings—why not from his expert report?—perhaps the court needs different assistance. Perhaps a professional in litigation.

Defendant's assertion in *Electric* (2004) at 228, contesting the expertise of plaintiffs' expert Fred Dunbar, is almost equally absurd:

> Dunbar did not use regression analysis or any other econometric technique in reaching his conclusions on liability.

Although Magistrate Judge Francis did not exclude Dunbar's testimony on these grounds, he did take the criticism seriously.

91. Although I was once a member, I no longer am. Has my expertise been diminished thereby? A president of the American Statistical Association, though not using the word "expert," had a kinder, gentler, more appropriate view:

criteria. I could not have used survival analysis nor introduced the multiple-pools selection methods that educated and were soon adopted by other experts.

Assessing the Work

Had Judge Parker applied the standards enunciated by Judge Vratil about Richard Hoyt, then Thomas Daymont, for his lack of experience, would have been considered the *more* qualified expert.[92] As described in Chapter 2, Daymont used a single-pool analysis, whereas Bernard Siskin used a more appropriate multiple-pools analysis to test the age effect of layoffs at Albermarle. Daymont counted layoffs of persons above or below the median age, the amateur error of making up his own metric rather than deriving one from the law. It was easy enough to assess his analysis, unnecessary to assess his credentials.

Richard Hoyt said he would derive competitive prices for aluminum phosphide from a "before and after" study. Prices were falling due to patent expirations and Hoyt, to calculate damages for plaintiffs, chose to use only the low "after" prices. It doesn't matter how many times the man has testified. His work was poor on its face. He did it for money, yes, but he did it badly. That is all that counts.

Professional or academic, many experts fail to make sense, never mind fail to be convincing. Louise Robbins

> easily met the qualification standards for an expert witness: university appointment, doctorate in anthropology, and board certification in forensic anthropology by the American Board of Forensic Anthropology.[93]

She had created her own measures, her own method of identifying bootprints, in a manner no one else could replicate or verify. A panel of anthropologists and attorneys called

---

> [S]tatistics is the generation and effective use of knowledge from data—data with all their uncertainty, fallibility, and variability. Statisticians, at least to me, are those who have special expertise in any aspect of this practice, from developing theories to data mining, whatever may be their professional or disciplinary field.

Miron Straf in 304 *Amstat News* 2 (October 2002).

92. The Third Circuit was faced with the argument that

> the probative value of the exceptionally well-qualified expert's testimony is outweighed by unfair prejudice caused solely by his stellar qualifications.

Rutland (2004) at 546. Although conceding that this was a novel argument, the court concluded, again at 546: "This Court will not limit an expert's testimony based merely upon the expert's qualifications."

93. Giannelli (1997a) at 461; following in-text quotations also at 461. Discussing the fact that Robbins was well-known to fabricate evidence for her client, the Seventh Circuit concluded, "Neither shopping for a favorable witness nor hiring a practitioner of junk science is actionable." *Buckley* (1994) at 796. Thus Buckley, who had languished in jail for two years because of Robbins' testimony and was suing for damages, could get no recompense from the prosecutor for having based his case on her fabrication.

her method (and testimony) "unreliable." Paul Giannelli concluded that "such testimony should never be admitted in a capital case," although, given her credentials, it was. Of another expert a judge wrote:

> Dr. Morrison impressed me as capable of testifying to anything, absolutely anything.[94]

Do her credentials matter?

Because it is uninformative, assessing credentials is unnecessary. "Admissibility does not imply utility."[95] *Au contraire*. Utility is exactly what admissibility *should* imply. As I started arguing in Chapter 7, in a *Daubert* hearing, a party should be able to put forward anyone as an expert, to receive this privilege to assert an opinion.[96] The point of the hearing is to determine those who will be considered to be experts at trial, whose opinion is worth hearing. If it is, why are we censoring the person it comes from? If it is not, why do we care whose opinion it is? The single inference a fact finder should be able to take from the admission of expert testimony is that it is likely to be useful, whether it is determined to be correct or not.

The Third Circuit reversed

> the district court's exclusion of the opinion of Dr. Janette D. Sherman insofar as it was grounded on the conclusion that she was an unqualified expert.[97]

It then affirmed the district court's rejection of her testimony about "those plaintiffs whom she did not examine and whose medical history she did not take." The testimony was faulty, even if the testifier was not. The resources spent assessing her qualifications, appealing, assessing again, were wasted.

INTRODUCTION TO A FRAMEWORK

In summary, what *Daubert* (1993) did, or should have done, was change the focus from the witness to the testimony; from the legislative-fact concept of the testimony (is there merit to this field of expertise?) to the adjudicative-fact question (is there merit to *this testimony?*). Long before *Daubert*, Judge Markey suggested:

---

94. District-court judge quoted by the appeals court in *Davis* (1985) at 1342.

95. *Mid-State* (1989) at 1339. This case precedes *Daubert*. It might have been decided more easily, but not differently, under post-*Daubert* procedures.

96. I offer the motion picture *My Cousin Vinnie* (20th Century Fox, 1991) as my final piece of evidence on this point.

97. *Paoli II* (1994) at 733; following in-text quotation also at 733.

> We have no rules specifically designed to help judges understand the testimony
> of conflicting experts. . . . Perhaps what is needed are the Federal Rules of
> Technological-Sociological Adjudication.[98]

Although the Supreme Court was surely correct to bring other than strictly "science" expertise under a kind of *Daubert* umbrella in *Kumho* (1999), what was needed was a framework for doing so.[99] That framework should have differentiated among different aspects of what is now called "science" testimony, and prescribed different treatments for them.

The notion that the Supreme Court's broad "science" category does not allow the formulation of evaluation rules that judges can follow is not unique to me. John Jansonius and Andrew Gould, after essentially equating "science" testimony with verifiability, understand that non-verifiable "expert" testimony still should fall under the *Daubert* purview:

> Reliability of opinion testimony is vital to all fields of expertise presented in
> American courtrooms and the gatekeeping role prescribed in *Daubert* should
> be applied to subjects of science and non-science alike.[100]

This is their final sentence. They suggest no way to proceed, only urging that we do.

Editors of the *Yale Law Journal* noted that

> While *Kumho* may have resolved the debate over *Daubert*'s scope, it did little
> to clarify how *Daubert*'s factors might be applied to social-science evidence.[101]

Similarly, Jason Borenstein complained that

> the underlying assumption seems to be that the merits of all scientific expert
> testimony can be assessed adequately by relying upon a single set of overar-
> ching criteria. Yet the *Daubert* factors alone cannot enable the courts to eval-
> uate scientific evidence adequately.[102]

---

98. Markey (1978) at 215. Judge Markey starts, at 209, distinguishing science from technology: "Science has no place in court. Science is neither fact nor law. It is a search." Science is the questioning process, technology is the answer. Fortunately, he did not maintain this distinction throughout this article, and no one else has taken it up.

99. In his majority opinion in *Kumho* (1999), at 141, Justice Breyer follows Federal Rule of Evidence 702 in not distinguishing (except by naming them) between "scientific" and "technical" knowledge. As the point of *Kumho* was to bring technical knowledge under the *Daubert* umbrella, failing to say how it could be dealt with—not just that it should be—is understandable. But it did leave this hole, which I propose to fill.

100. Jansonius and Gould (1998) at 331. These authors badly needed a framework. "[D]istrict judges ought to take verifiability into account when ruling on admissibility," they write, at 328. Yet they suggest neither that all non-verifiable (non-science) testimony should be excluded, nor how the judge should proceed to evaluate it.

101. Case Note (2001) at 1537.

102. Borenstein (2001) at 993.

Editors of the *Harvard Law Review* defined eight categories of expert.[103] They described the judicial qualities that I have been arguing allow creditable assessment of expert testimony:

> [T]he judiciary's expertise is in deconstructing an argument: assessing the logic of the argument, the validity of its premises, the rigor with which the witness applied the technique, the faithfulness of the witness's application of the methodology to her description of it, the magnitude of the inference drawn by the witness in forming her opinion, and the sufficiency of the facts to support the inference.

The reader might want to contrast the *Harvard Law Review* editors' approach to a taxonomy of expertise, with mine. Here is their own summary:

> This Note proposes a two-axis taxonomy that divides expertise according to whether it offers opinions on social or on physical phenomena, and according to the degree to which it relies on experimentation as opposed to a witness's acquired experience.

They discuss

> the factors judges consider in evaluating the testimony. Among the most important criteria to establish the soundness of these factors is their general acceptance in the legal community.

These editors would impose a *Frye* criterion on how judges perform their *Daubert* assessment! Their taxonomy, perhaps influenced by an earlier false differentiation between physical and social science, is a failure.[104] Therefore, so are their solutions. However, they

---

103. See Note (2003), arguing, at 2142, that

> distinct analytic frameworks with which to analyze disparate forms of expertise are necessary to enable reliable admissibility decisions.

Thus these authors use the word "framework" to represent the manner by which each category of expert will be assessed under *Daubert* (1993). My concept of "framework" includes theirs, but subsumes also their "taxonomy." I call both the necessary distinctions and what to do with them my "framework." Following indented quotations at 2150, 2155, and 2149.

104. Although not referenced in Note (2003), consider the discussion by Neil Postman (1988). In his first essay, "Social Science as Moral Theology," Postman distinguishes between studies of physical laws and studies of human creations or behavior. At 7:

> The scientist uses mathematics to assist in uncovering and describing the structure of nature. At best, the sociologist (to take one example) uses quantification merely to give some precision to his ideas. But there is nothing especially scientific in that.

Both physical science and social science test models, suppositions about how things work. The universe is not centered around the sun, but that is a better model than that it is centered around the earth, and so our understanding evolved. Light is affected by gravity, the general price level is affected by the supply of money, and the value of homes is affected by the perceived quality of public-school education. The social-science part (developing the model, hypothesizing the relationships) may not be science, but the statistical analysis that distinguishes one model from another is very much like that in the physical sciences.

well articulate the *issue* of how to assess different types of expertise.

Post-*Daubert* writing on this topic has wanted a framework, struggling to assess statistical studies of the effect of Bendectin on pregnant women and the opinion of a tire mechanic about the cause of a blow-out in the same way.[105] A Sixth Circuit view of what *Daubert* should cover may seem obsolete now, having been written before *Kumho*, but it provides us a necessary step towards understanding how to apply *Daubert* outside strictly science testimony:

> *Daubert* provides a "flexible" framework to aid district courts in determining whether expert scientific testimony is reliable. If that framework were to be extended to outside the scientific realm, many types of relevant and reliable expert testimony—that derived substantially from practical experience—would be excluded. Such a result truly would turn *Daubert,* a case intended to relax the admissibility requirements for expert scientific evidence, on its head.[106]

The "expertise" referred to here is identification through handwriting, which may or may not be a craft, but surely is not science. What this court refers to as a "flexible framework" is based on a "falsifiable" concept that craft testimony, as they note, would fail. However, the court instructs, correctly, that it be included. It made the correct decision, but was unable to explain why. *Daubert* and its progeny provide a mandate without a method, a goal without a plan to achieve it.

Daubert is not the only decision to spawn an internet site (as mentioned earlier, in footnote 164 of Chapter 1)—there is one on *Brown* (1954), for example—but its site is the most important.[107] As district courts are bound by the precedent only of their own circuit courts of appeals, when there is no Supreme Court ruling on a particular issue, it is not surprising that cases on this site are organized by circuit. Not surprising but, for most purposes, not helpful, either.[108]

---

105. Caudill and Redding (2000) contend that post-*Daubert* confusion has been engendered by a poorly articulated philosophy of science. Unfortunately, even though, at 716, they use the word "framework," their discussion does not advance solution of the problem, providing the district-court judge some help in evaluating the "science" that parades in front of him. We agree, though, that judges have proved up to the task. At 699:

> Rather than appearing baffled, judges demonstrate new-found familiarity with scientific evidence from various fields.

106. *Jones* (1997) at 1158.

107. http://daubertontheweb.com.

108. Cases are also sorted by an attempt to denote the field of the expert. However, economists will be found under "accountants," although statisticians are a separate category, as are sociologists. There is no "forensic" category, but there is one for marine biologists. Most forensic expertise is found under the heading of "criminologist," although "fire experts" are distinguished. In short, the categorization of expertise at this web site appears haphazard, not well thought out.

Should this (or another) site produce a cross-classification of cases following a framework of more intrinsic interest, it would go far towards establishing that classification system as one to which judges should pay attention. Such a classification should help develop ways to determine what kind of expert issue is before the court, and how to assess it.

The framework I offer is a step toward defining those different kinds of expert issues, and structuring materials to assist the court in its *Daubert* determination. It will also help us understand the frustration of many writers on this topic who have disparaged judicial acceptance of forensic-science evidence which they deem fails the *Daubert* science test. That may not be the appropriate test to apply to this kind of testimony. Disparate forms of expert analyses have been brought together under one heading. Now that we know the scope of expertise covered by *Daubert*, we need to devise ways to assess it—different methods of assessment for different kinds of analysis. Here is my suggestion.

A *Daubert* Framework

Four kinds of expert are assessed at *Daubert* hearings:

Science. The science expert will report results of a study of the issues, using data relevant to the case, and a specified method. The appropriateness of the data and method can be contested, but the other side must be able to replicate his work as it is. To dispute it, they must show where in that work he made an error that, if corrected, would reverse the result. A science expert will always present his findings as having some probability of error, that is, with uncertainty.

Engineering. The engineering expert will have produced a device that purports to solve a problem or achieve a goal relevant to the issues in the case. The device can be tested and a judgment made how well it performs its objectives, or indicates that an improved device along these lines could do so.

The commonality of science and engineering experts is that their work is specific to the case at hand and testable on its merits. Both are predicting what would have happened if—if something were different. But they are not speculating. They produce a study (a model tested with data) the sufficiency or relevance of which can be challenged.

Engineers who merely opine about the adequacy of something they did not design themselves, without demonstrating the flaw physically or by computer modeling, should not qualify to testify, regardless what credentials they bear. Science and engineering may be rebutted by a demonstration—not speculation, not opinion—that the science or engineering offered by the other side is incorrect. For example, if one wants to argue that the other side's expert omitted "critical" variables, one would have the burden of providing data (which would not be admissible if it had not been timely provided to all), arguing for its validity, and demonstrating that it has the stated effect in use.

> **Technical.** The technical or "craft" expert will form an adjudicative opinion based on his mastery of certain skilled activities. He has a methodology which he can articulate and apply to other circumstances. It need not be the same methodology as anyone else. Others may or may not be able to replicate his outcomes using his "methods." They may not have his skill, or he may not have theirs. Although he may justify his opinion with science terms or algorithms, ultimately there is a judgment in this testimony that can be defended and disputed but, in its own terms, neither proved nor disproved.

> **Wisdom.** The wisdom expert will educate the fact finder about ways of thinking and research findings concerning the subject at hand. He will not offer a conclusion on the adjudicative facts at issue, and usually will not even refer to them. His knowledge may come from training or experience in the science or craft, or may come from academic-type study of it.

The key distinction here is that the accuracy of the specific testimony of science and engineering experts can be tested. One assumption or one data point at a time can be altered, the result of that alteration not being in dispute (though its appropriateness may be). Neither technical nor wisdom expert testimony allows direct testing, although one can conceive of examples in which such testimony is refuted by scientific or engineering testimony. That does not mean that technical or wisdom testimony is useless. Nor should it mean that technical experts should be reduced to wisdom experts, imparting education but not conclusions, although some courts have done that.

Testing only the testimony, not the witness, is the logical end of the direction in which courts are taking science and engineering testimony. Many *Daubert*-hearing orders are partial: the expert may say this, but not that. These should be substance-based, not credentials-based restrictions. Neither should a minimum set of expert credentials be required for science or engineering testimony, nor should too many credentials prevent it.

Once this distinction is made, we see that my plea to abandon a credentials test applies *only* to science and engineering testimony. The importance of classifying the proffered testimony, then, is that different criteria apply to assessing different kinds of witnesses. As a defining characteristic of experts is their ability to express an adjudicative-fact opinion, it may be that purveyors of "wisdom" should not be called experts. Perhaps we should invent a new name, such as "information" witness.

Allowing cross-examination of qualifications in either the *Daubert* hearing or the trial is insulting to experts offering a scientific or engineering analysis (of course, it is intended to be) and also to the intelligence of anyone (judge or jury) listening. The credibility of science testimony should be judged by the expertness with which a methodology was selected and effectuated, not by who did it. Engineering testimony should be judged by the engineered product. If we cannot test it, it is not science or engineering.

If not science or engineering, the testimony still may be helpful. It should be subject to judicial gatekeeping. Its conclusions should be stated probabilistically. The questions are how that gatekeeping is to be effectuated, how the probability of error is to be determined. I answer those questions below.

The *Daubert* Hearing

The *Daubert* hearing "furthers both case-processing efficiency and economy."[109]

> Whether the standard is labeled *Frye* or *Daubert*, it is clear that judges must decide whether to admit expert witnesses. Perhaps the greatest contribution of *Daubert* was to underscore this forcefully and to emphasize that judges must draw lines between expert testimony that is "reliable enough" or "valid enough" and expert testimony that is "not reliable enough" or "not valid enough."[110]

It is the testimony, not the expert, that is being judged for trial fitness. Although my view is both correct and sensible, I will lose this argument. The rules will not be re-interpreted or changed to eliminate the credentials screen. As second-best, here is a procedural suggestion for the *Daubert* hearing: The judge can ask if a party intends to object to a proffered expert or to his proposed testimony. If the judge makes clear that he will not tolerate frivolous objections to qualifications, then, in very few cases in which the presentation is of science evidence, will an attorney try to disqualify the expert. This suggestion can be filed under "judge training," the idea initiated in Chapter 7, amplified in Chapter 9, and re-iterated above, that training judges in case management would be more helpful than training them in science.

Understanding these distinctions, the opposing attorney can agree that the expertise claimed is science or engineering, his objection is to the substance of the testimony, not the credentials of the expert. (If the testimony is craft or wisdom, other procedures, suggested below, would hold.) The judge could encourage such a stipulation by announcing a *very* liberal standard for assessing qualifications. Critics of my proposal to eliminate the credentials stage *for science and engineering testimony only* think courts would be inundated by crackpots, charlatans, and incompetents. That would be different from now in what way?

---

109. M. Berger (2001) at 296.

110. Foster and Huber (1997) at 252.

The Science Expert

One commentator tried to define the science expert this way:

> The scientific witness is an expert precisely because he has intensively studied the literature in that field.[111]

He has it backwards. This is a description of the "wisdom" expert, the information witness. The scientific witness is an expert if he did good science. If he did it badly, he is not an expert, and can be rejected in a *Daubert* hearing regardless of his knowledge of the literature. If he did it well, his knowledge of others who have done it, also, is immaterial.

Joseph Kadane and Caroline Mitchell describe a revealing difference between science and law:

> In law, precedent is very important, because it makes the law more predictable. . . . Scientific thinking, by contrast, regards the most recent work as the most reliable guide.[112]

The *Frye* standard, therefore—wanting science in court to have been pre-approved by the profession it pretends to represent—was understandably lawyerly, but counter-scientific. Science in court should not be tested by whether it looks like science elsewhere, but by whether it is science, here.

If two science witnesses disagree, it should be their responsibility to articulate exactly why: Data? Variables? Mathematics (statistical method)? Interpretation? In Chapter 3 I explained my disagreement with a published regression by Craig Bolon, showing the effect of my alternative (but still regression) approach. I also demonstrated in detail the unacceptability of regressions offered in litigation by Mark Killingsworth in one case, by Mark Berkman and Fred Dunbar in another. In the former case I offered alternative regressions; in the latter, I explained why regression was inappropriate. Rebuttal of science must incorporate science. In this context, I find the following extract, typical of this Judge Weinstein opinion, unsatisfactory:

> 204. Ms. Allen found a statistically significant relationship between the decline in homicides in various states (the "crime states") and the decline in dealers with firearms traced in those states. Her conclusions were acceptable and sound.
>
> 205. Defendants' expert, Dr. Wecker, performed Ms. Allen's regression analysis doing what she claimed she did, i.e., excluding traces of firearms originat-

---

111. Imwinkelried (1988) at 9.

112. Kadane and Mitchell (2000) at 260. There is no shortage of law/science contrasts in the literature. Erickson and Simon (1998) at 7, for example:

> Where the law presents its findings as certainties, science attaches a permanent contingency to its results.

ing in the "crime state," and found no statistically significant relationship existed between the decline in homicides and the decline in traced guns originating from out-of-state. The court accepts Ms. Allen's conclusions as more accurate and useful than Dr. Wecker's.[113]

As noted above, Judge Weinstein's current approach is to let all experts testify, weighing their conclusions as he sees fit. Surely Wecker and Allen, if required to do so, could have and may have articulated why they disagreed. Had Weinstein understood that it is the testimony, not the expert, that counts in this decision, he might have considered himself obliged to tell us on what basis he thinks Allen was correct, Wecker not. In the context of a long opinion in which plaintiff's experts are always considered to have provided the superior statistical analysis, never with explanation, Weinstein appears to be driven by his inability to impose liability on gun manufacturers for gun-related crime. He would have been more credible issuing a meta-decision—that plaintiffs could not win no matter what evidence they presented—than pretending to evaluate the expert presentations.

That science testimony must be criticized or defended on its own terms—where technical judgments, we will see, cannot be—places a burden on the judge to articulate the reasons for his choice. Those reasons cannot be the demeanor or credentials of the witness. Neither, however, need they be the equivalent of a journal referee's comments, those of another scientist. Science in court—at least the science discussed throughout this book—can be evaluated by the procedures used to create it, by whether words have the meaning ascribed to them (validity), whether relevant questions were asked in constructing the data, and then in analyzing them. The specifics of science method can be argued by the experts. What the court wants to know, and tell those who read its opinions, is what it means in the context of this case. Appeals courts should remand decisions in which we are told who "wins," but not why.

THE ENGINEERING EXPERT

John Noettl, an "accident reconstruction/design engineer, was to testify that the truck was defectively designed" following an accident.[114]

> Noettl posited two hypotheses. His first hypothesis was that the front bumper's design should have included either bracketry or a brace system that would have increased the bumper's rigidity, prevented the truck from ramping, and deflected the vehicle back onto the roadway after impact with the guard rail. His second hypothesis was that thicker and/or ribbed metal on the flooring

---

113. *Acusport* (2003) at 515.

114. *Oddi* (2000) at 146; following indented quotation at 156.

of the cab would have retained the integrity of the cab. However, Noettl quite candidly testified that he never tested either hypothesis.

Noettl is like a *Kumho* witness, ascribing causation after the fact. He differs in that his theory, that minor reinforcement of the front bumper could have prevented the "ramping" (climbing the guard rail and eventually flipping over), was testable. Noettl would never have been qualified as a "scientist." He would have been an engineer had he made a product and shown how it behaved differently from the allegedly defective product. As he was put forward as a science expert, his testimony was properly excluded.[115]

Similarly, Richard Thomas asserted that a Black & Decker toaster oven had started a fire. Although it was presented as engineering testimony, it was not. He provided no support for his hypothesis, which might have made it engineering:

> Thomas never conducted any testing to determine the maximum temperature that might be reached in the toaster oven. Nor did he test his hypothesis by placing the toaster oven in an unregulated condition to determine whether it would start a fire under such circumstances. Thomas did not conduct any testing or make a model of the kind of thermal cut-off device he believed should have been incorporated into the toaster oven.[116]

Nor did Thomas present evidence that his opinion on such matters had been correct previously, which is how craft testimony will be evaluated. Summary judgment was granted to defendant.

Paul Walker was the engineering expert for David Masters, whose right arm had been chewed up by a Hesston 5600 hay baler. Masters suggested that the baler should have come with a guard.

> Walker did not analyze the impact of any proposed guards on the 5600's function. He did no design work, no testing, and no measurements of a proposed guard. He merely sketched a guard in response to questioning at his deposition and estimated that the guard should be from 3 to 24 inches off the ground.[117]

Walker's testimony was excluded, as it should have been.

Consider Larry Bihlmeyer's assertion that

> the design and roof support structures in the accident vehicle were defective because they permitted excessive roof crush. He then pinpointed areas of the

---

115. *Oddi* argued that *Kumho* should not apply. The Third Circuit said it did, failing to see that *Kumho* was irrelevant, despite the facial similarity. The application of *Daubert* to Noettl's testimony does not require *Kumho*, as the testimony itself is testable.

116. *Booth* (2001) at 218, excluding references to transcripts. This case was also referred to in Chapter 7.

117. *Masters* (2002) at 993. Circuit-judge Evans notes, at 991:

> [I]t is clear to us that Walker is no hayseed. He is a registered professional engineer and a professor of agricultural engineering at Penn State University.

roof structure where, in his expert opinion, additional support was required. To correct the alleged defects, Mr. Bihlmeyer testified he would. . . .[118]

He constructed no model, but was allowed to testify:

> Although expressing doubts about his credibility, the court ultimately determined Mr. Bihlmeyer met the qualifications for expert testimony under Federal Rule of Evidence 702.

As an engineering witness, Bihlmeyer's assertions should have been tested. His hypothetical assertions could have been made as a technical expert, but would have to be evaluated as I describe below. Trial-judge Belot had no framework within which he could exclude bad work, given the "expert's" credentials.

Hurt by an unguarded stump cutter, Mark Pestel engaged an engineer, Keith Vidal, to design a guard for it. Vidal did not perfect the guard, but he demonstrated that one could be made and mounted on this stump cutter. Vermeer, the manufacturer defendant, showed that the prototype was inadequate, as Mr. Vidal, admitted; but not that its basic concept was faulty. Indeed, Vermeer indicated what changes it would make for the protective guard to function, and Vidal testified how he himself would improve his original design.

> Mr. Vidal was hired to show that a guard could be made which would have prevented the injury from occurring. He was not prepared, however, to show that such a guard was ready for the market—his design was not finished. Therefore, his fabricated guard was not relevant to show that a guard could be made that would offer protection, and yet not inhibit the use or practicality of the machine. . . .
>
> With respect to peer review and publication, the [trial] Court noted that the expert had not contacted others in the industry to see if they had attempted to create a similar type of guard. He had not subjected his concept to any manufacturers, academicians, or engineering professors, for scrutiny.[119]

This absurd opinion came from applying *Daubert* science standards, inappropriate to this fact situation and this expert. The standard Vidal should have to meet—and did meet—is showing that a functional guard *could* have been included with the product. Whether that

---

118. *Compton* (1996) at 1516; following indented quotation at 1517. This pre-*Kumho* case is not considered good law today, because the judge thought that *Daubert* was inapplicable and the Tenth Circuit panel implicitly agreed. They were at least correct that the testimony was not "science." Nor is it engineering. The expert did not show what it would take to support the roof as he recommended—either in structure or in expense—leaving an abstract standard that Judge Belot thought, at 1516,

> seems more applicable to a Sherman tank than to any vehicle which the ordinary consumer would drive.

It is not good law because it allows an engineering opinion from an "expert" as if he were a craft expert. Engineering testimony should be testable. Bihlmeyer's was not.

119. *Pestel* (1995) at 384.

showing then required the manufacturer to provide one is not Vidal's issue, nor mine. It was not Vidal's job to perfect a product for the defendant manufacturer, only to show (not opine) that one could be made.

In some cases legislative-fact (wisdom) testimony can substitute for engineering. Suppose other stump cutters, similar in design to Vermeer's, had been modified to include safety guards.

> [Jerry] Purswell highlighted the feasibility of the guarding proposal by noting that John Deere previously had adopted similar modifications to its model 510 closed-throat baler. Elaborating on Purswell's testimony, [William] Kennedy referenced a guarding device on Vermeer's model 504-C closed-throat baler, maintaining such a guard easily could have been adapted to the Gehl 1870 baler and could have prevented Kinser's death.[120]

Were Pestel's attorney and Keith Vidal unaware that Vermeer had acted to protect other machines in the way they proposed the stump cutter should have been protected? Not all engineering situations require novel engineering solutions. If the strategic decision is made to offer such testimony, under *Daubert* it should include testability, but only to the level of proof that the engineering problem can be solved. Another route to that conclusion is available through wisdom testimony, through informing the court that similar guards have been utilized by this manufacturer on other machines—or, if this be the case, by other manufacturers.

Alan Cantor, a working, professional engineer, designer of a NASA escape hatch and the holder of a patent on an occupant safety feature used by the United States Army, was engaged by Thomas Bowersfield, plaintiff, to investigate the safety of riding in the rear cargo area of the 1992 Suzuki Samurai.

> Mr. Cantor explained that the best remedy for the hazards in the 1992 Samurai was the installation of seats with three-point seat belts in the rear area of the vehicle. At the *Daubert* hearing, he produced drawings and photographs of various ways to do so. For instance, he explained how the roll cage could be extended and modified to provide an anchor for the seat belts, and pro-

---

120. *Kinser* (1999) at 1266. My conclusions, of course, are not definitive. I could not study each case to the extent that the respective judges and juries did. For example, at 1266:

> In its defense, Gehl . . . offered testimony questioning the feasibility of plaintiff's proposed shielding/guarding designs, highlighted the dissimilarities in designs between the 1870 baler and other closed-throat balers employing various shielding/guarding devices.

Thus there were genuine factual issues about the extensibility of design concepts effectuated on other machines. My point survives, whether it is applicable to this case or not. It remains that the engineering expert must do more than opine. Plaintiff prevailed by analogy, but the *Kinser* decision would have been more convincing had an engineer showed what it would take to develop the obviously desired safety features recommended by plaintiff's experts for the machine at issue.

vided photographs, technical drawings, and calculations of the proposed modifications.[121]

In principle, showing how the vehicle could have been modified would be insufficient without showing the result of that modification. Cantor did more than Paul Walker, but I think not sufficiently more. His assertion that three-point seat belts were safer might be acceptable as legislative-fact "wisdom," but not as engineering. He applied legislative-fact knowledge to the particulars of this case, but did not generate adjudicative knowledge.

As the role of the engineer was not understood, and Cantor's "best remedy" was not questioned, his task became to show that this solution was feasible in this vehicle. That, he could accomplish with drawings. Whereas Walker's baler guard would have affected the operation of the baler, and therefore required that he construct one and test it, Cantor's seat belts would not have affected anything more than passenger safety. However, we are left not knowing *how much* they would have affected safety, especially in the particular type of crash at issue. Installation of his proposed device, followed by some tests, would not have been prohibitively expensive. That three-point seat belts are superior to two-point belts is legislative fact, wisdom. The court should have demanded an engineering demonstration that they would have prevented or ameliorated plaintiff's injury. What it got in the adjudicative realm was speculation, which should have been excluded.

Brian Yarusso became a quadriplegic as the result of an off-road motorcycle crash. He sued the helmet manufacturer, Bell, for breach of implied contract. Bell's warranty includes the warning that the helmet cannot prevent injury in all circumstances. Bell also brought in experts to argue that this helmet met all applicable standards, that in the kind of motocross accident that crippled Yarusso, the ground, not the helmet, absorbs the energy.

> Expert evidence was presented, however, that a helmet could be designed with a softer liner that would, in theory, limit the amount of force placed on the user's neck, thereby reducing the probability of partial-load direct downward neck injuries, particularly upon impact with harder surfaces.[122]

The expert making these assertions, Richard Stalnaker,

---

121. *Bowersfield* (2001) at 630. A standard can be found in *Muller* (2001) at *7:

> If Plaintiff's experts wish to testify about an alternative design of the CSLP, they are required to offer more than mere subjective belief or unsupported speculation.

The CSLP is a cervical-spine locking plate. How much more must be offered can be debated, but the point is that the engineering expert is not providing wisdom (legislative fact). He must provide adjudicative fact, a particular solution to the problem plaintiff contends exists in the manufactured product.

122. *Yarusso* (2000) at 584; following indented quotation at 588. Other cases in which engineering testimony was excluded for lack of relevance, or perhaps diligence, include *Watkins* (1997) (expert "did not even make any drawings or perform any calculations," at 992); *Brooks* (2000) (no testing of either the boat at issue or the proposed modification); and *Zaremba* (2004) (reliance on general Motors tests for other purposes was insufficient).

offered testimony that testing and research has been conducted by other scientists in the industry in support of a theory that helmets can, in specific
instances, protect users from neck injuries.

Stalnaker's testimony was considered by the Superior Court judge to have been "critical."
However, Stalnaker produced no helmet that would absorb the sixty foot-pounds of pressure he estimated that Yarusso's body put on his neck. All experts apparently were admitted based on their credentials. Under my framework, if Stalnaker could not come into
court with models and tests thereon (perhaps demonstrations filmed in the presence of
defendant's personnel), his adjudicative testimony should not have been allowed. His
description of knowledge in the field was wisdom, not engineering. His force estimate
should have been excluded because he had no engineering solution for it, particularly none
that would have made Bell liable for its failure to effectuate it. He should not have been
allowed to refer to the facts of the case or draw an adjudicative conclusion.

O. J. Hahn testified about the safety hazard of the two-piece tire rim. One solution he
posited was to bolt the two pieces together, as is done on some large airplanes.

> On cross-examination, Dr. Hahn was directly asked, "[H]ave you ever used a
> B-52 bolting system and tried it in the multi-piece trucking industry?" Dr.
> Hahn replied that he had not.[123]

Engineering is not science, but it has the science characteristic of being adjudicatively
testable. If the engineer brings nothing to test, then he is offering only an untestable
opinion.[124] Hahn had two precedents: Goodyear had looked at a bolted system in the
1930s, and it was used on airplanes. As Goodyear abandoned it for trucks, Hahn, as an
engineering expert, should have attempted to show that such a design was feasible. Keith
Vidal did exactly that with the stump-cutter guard. Failing to demonstrate his opinions
with a product, offering no more than speculation, Hahn's proposed testimony was properly rejected.

Plaintiff's expert Thomas Horton found that he could put seat belts, of the model that
had been in plaintiff's automobile, into a "partial-latch" position. He then provided data
on the force required to pull the belt apart, providing forty-six measures covering six belts.

---

123. *Goodyear* (2000) at 581.

124. Referring to plaintiff's expert, Paul Stephens:

> Stephens also did not perform any substantive testing of either the allegedly defective
> design or of his proposed alternative in connection with this litigation. Nor did he pro-
> duce any diagrams or perform any calculations which would illustrate his claims.

And therefore his testimony was excluded. *Milanowicz* (2001) at 539. Similarly,

> Mr. Court reached his conclusion without performing any testing on the actual ladder
> at issue or even an exemplar ladder.

Higginbotham (2004) at 915.

Although Horton's presentation failed to come up to the standards I espouse for the engineering expert, a more telling problem was the lack of conceptualization about what test was required. Judge Feikens writes:

> Plaintiff provides no evidence to support the assertion that Horton's methods
> can be duplicated by inadvertence.[125]

Horton might have been an acceptable engineering witness discussing the belt design, but estimating the likelihood that the belt would partially latch with ordinary use by a driver, such as plaintiff, should have followed from a more carefully controlled study. Plaintiff did not understand the need for a statistical expert to set the platform on which his engineering expert might have proved useful.[126]

Similarly, Malcolm Newman, a highly credentialed engineer, discussing the victim of a single-car crash,

> opined that Babcock was either not wearing a seat belt or the seat belt was
> defective. From examining the seat belt itself, Dr. Newman concluded that it
> had been used just prior to impact.[127]

Newman also provided what appears to be an engineering opinion that the General Motors seat belt is subject to partial latching whereas, for example, the Volvo seat belt is not. As the vehicle in question was made by General Motors, Newman

> testified that in his opinion, the seat belt unbuckled because of false latching,
> otherwise known as "partial engagement."

Newman's first conclusion, that the victim had utilized the seat belt, was not science or engineering, but a craft opinion of the kind discussed below. It should have been accompanied by a probability assessment of Newman's accuracy in knowing such things. His second conclusion, on partial latching, was accompanied by a demonstration of "how false latching can occur." Like Thomas Horton, Newman did not state its likelihood. The jury had no basis to assess his conclusion that false latching was operative in this case. His knowledge of the engineering of seat belts might well have aided the jury if presented as wisdom, stripped of all adjudicative conclusions.

---

125. *Nemir* (1999) at 669. Horton had videotaped a deposition in which he explained his method of latching and measuring separation force. However, he did not videotape the actual test.

126. Nor did the Sixth Circuit which, on remand in *Nemir* (2004), instructed that Horton could also testify about his twenty attempts to latch the very belt worn in the accident, failing to do so on two of them. Or was he, in fact, trying *not* to latch the belt? The test should not have been conducted by Horton himself. His role should have been to design the test, in conjunction with a statistician.

Other factors overwhelmed this relatively subtle question of how seat belts should be tested for partial latching. Defendant Mitsubishi was unresponsive to discovery requests, and Judge Feikens' rulings were prejudicial to plaintiff Nemir. In 2004 the case was remanded for retrial under a different judge.

127. *Babcock* (2002) at 68; following indented quotation and then in-text quotation also at 68.

The seat-belt cases lead us to recognize the importance of specialization, and give credit to expert teams. For example, Waymon Johnston, a safety engineer, described four features which, in his opinion, should have been installed on the machine that crushed plaintiff's fingers.[128] He offered no designs incorporating those features, and on that ground was not permitted to testify. Plaintiffs had bifurcated their evidence, first arguing that the machine *should* have been so equipped, and then, from other evidence, arguing that it *could* have been. The Ninth Circuit agreed that plaintiffs had the burden to provide engineering details about their proposed changes, but correctly vacated the lower court's exclusion of Johnston because that was not his role.

THE TECHNICAL OR CRAFT EXPERT

Rochelle Dreyfuss misses the point:

> The *Daubert* Court was wrong to think of science as a special case.[129]

True, we use the word "opinion" to describe the testimony of scientists and other experts. But there *is* something special about science. There is no better way to explain this than to show why technical or craft testimony is entirely different.

Ramón Echeandía's marine-engine testimony, described above, could be believed or not, but it could not be tested. Trial Judge Casellas spent some time determining if Echeandía knew "how a marine fuel-injection engine differs from an automobile fuel-injection engine."[130] This expert testimony was surely not scientific testimony, but rather the craft testimony covered by *Kumho* (1999). Thus we have a defining distinction and a procedure: Scientific testimony can and should be judged on its own merits. The craft expert's testimony cannot be evaluated on its own merits, so the judge *must* test the expert himself.[131] The reviewing court noted:

> Although plaintiffs' expert might not have qualified as an expert based solely on his educational background in marine engines, his experience repairing various marine and fuel-injection engines for over twenty years provided a basis for the district court to find him qualified to opine on the function of plaintiffs' marine engines.[132]

---

128. *Furry* (2002).

129. Dreyfuss (1995) at 1804.

130. *Correa* (2002) at 25.

131. Saks (1998) at 1100:

> If there are no data confirming the validity of a field's claims, then it is not difficult to insist on empirical data demonstrating the special skills of the particular witness.

132. *Correa* (2002) at 24.

Courts, because they think credentials make the expert, are discussing *which* credentials are to be considered. Once again, this is the wrong approach.

As I alluded to above, Bruce Diederich, a roofing expert, was allowed to testify that a storm caused a roof collapse even though (like Dennis Carlson, the proffered expert in *Kumho*, and like Echeandía) he had not seen the roof (the tire, the boat) prior to the storm (the accident).

> Although Diederich's opinion may not be derived from "hard science," his opinions are based on his specialized knowledge of roofing and roofing materials, and his extensive practical experience endows him with the kind of expertise recognized by the Seventh Circuit.[133]

This kind of ruling aggravates law-review critics of judicial acceptance of technical expertise. They—and I—would essentially define science testimony as being accompanied by a probability calculation, a statement of probable error. In my framework, however, this is not science testimony. It should not pretend to be. As Erica Beecher-Monas summarizes,

> Genuine testability in science means not only that a hypothesis can be verified or falsified by observation and experiment, but also that the hypothesis has precise logical consequences that are incompatible with alternative hypotheses.[134]

That is science. This isn't. No assessment of probable error can be derived from Diederich's testimony. One could imagine a more engineering-based demonstration of the difference between a roof that would not collapse and this roof. An engineer could supervise construction of different roofs, and measure each one's ability to withstand wind (measuring miles per hour at failure, similar to testing structures for weight loads). However, I would not ban a craft expert just because one can think of a better way for plaintiff to argue his case. If plaintiff's attorney produces a craft expert, the problem becomes how to assess him.

Expert-opinion testimony must have probability associated with it. Where does this probability come from? The testimony cannot be challenged as provably incorrect, but the witness can be challenged as being demonstrably fallible. Where science probability is associated with the testimony, technical probability is associated with the expert. If Diederich could not show engineering models and their consequences, if the testimony is to be his opinion, then the fact finder needs to know how good his opinion generally is.

My approach is at odds with some received wisdom. For example:

> The *Kumho* Court explained that the language of Rule 702 makes no relevant distinction between "scientific" knowledge and "technical" or "other specialized

---

133. *Spearman* (2001) at 1097

134. Beecher-Monas (1998) at 68.

knowledge." Moreover, such a distinction would be hard to draw, since there is no clear line that divides scientific from other types of expert knowledge.[135]

I say this distinction can be drawn and must be drawn. Furthermore, doing so is not usually difficult. If one kind of knowledge cannot be distinguished from another, one kind of testimony can be. The answer to whether this testimony is adjudicatively testable should branch the *Daubert* hearing to one of two different procedures, one for science, one for craft.

Testing the Craft

Judge McKenna correctly distinguished document identification (handwriting analysis) as being technical, not science, concluding that

> forensic document examination, which clothes itself with the trappings of science, does not rest on carefully articulated postulates, does not employ rigorous methodology, and has not convincingly documented the accuracy of its determinations.[136]

This is a statement about the field in general, but what about this witness?

> Such experts, who acquire their skills through practical training, apprenticeships, and long years of practice, are generally not expected to be able to articulate and justify the theoretical bases underlying their practice, to expose their techniques to a larger community of practitioners through peer-reviewed publication, or to subject those techniques to extensive testing.

It is not the techniques but the witness who *must* be subjected to extensive testing, for how else would we judge his opinions? The Supreme Court alludes to this possibility, though not understanding its unique application to technical (as opposed to science or engineering) experts:

> In certain cases, it will be appropriate for the trial judge to ask, for example, how often an engineering expert's experience-based methodology has produced erroneous results.[137]

Measuring the expert's past success is a test strictly for technical experts. Does it matter how many times the Wright brothers failed, before they could fly? What difference would

---

135. Weinstein (2001) at §702.05 [2] [b].

136. *Starzecpyzel* (1995) at 1028; following indented quotation at 1029. This case was decided before *Kumho* (1999), allowing the judge to determine, incorrectly, that *Daubert* was inapplicable. The issue here is *how* should *Daubert* be applied. As Borenstein (2001) summarizes, at 1000:

> [D]etermining whether claims are "scientific" is largely an irrelevant consideration; what the courts need to do is determine whether proffered claims are well-supported by evidence.

137. *Kumho* (1999) at 151.

it make had Einstein promulgated many incorrect theories before general relativity? Jonas Salk failed to develop several vaccines before developing the one that bears his name. Francis Crick did not fare well trying to discover the underlying structure of consciousness, despite his Nobel prize for co-discovering the underlying structure of DNA. In science, each work stands alone. In craft, as in art, one creates and is judged by a "body of work."

Judge McKenna discusses "those techniques" as if the question he is to answer is one of legislative fact: Can forensic document examiners (FDEs) detect forgeries?

> The Court considered only the reliability of the particular expertise claimed here—that given a large number of genuine signatures, an FDE might be able to determine whether particular questioned signatures were genuine ("forgery detection").[138]

Michael Saks, while disagreeing with Judge McKenna's finding, supports this approach.[139] It is not fruitful. When a technical expert appears in a court, all that matters is whether that expert can discern A from B, under what conditions, with what accuracy. I don't care how many carpenters cannot frame a house so it is square. I care only if mine can. The best evidence that he can, short of engaging him to do it and then testing, is that he has done so in the past.

Michael Risinger does not understand how this can be done:

---

138. *Starzecpyzel* (1995) at 1043. The Arizona Supreme Court, which is critical of the *Daubert* line, at least understands that where the *Frye* standard put a general question about a methodology, *Daubert* requires adjudicative attention:

> Further, while a *Frye* order establishes general acceptance of a theory for all cases, under *Daubert/Kumho* each trial judge in any case involving disputed expert testimony would have to review the eight or nine *Daubert/Kumho* factors so far revealed to us in case-specific pretrial testimonial hearings to determine reliability of the expert's techniques, experience, observation, methodology, and conclusions.

139. There was tradition behind this legislative-fact approach. The Supreme Court of Illinois:

> We are disposed to hold . . . that there is a scientific basis for the system of finger print identification, and that the courts are justified in admitting this class of evidence."

Jennings (1911) at 549. To Saks the legislative-fact approach was acceptable, the specific finding in *Starzecpyzel*, not. He had testified at the *Daubert* hearing for defendant, arguing that forensic document evaluation was not a science. Saks (1998) therefore is understandably disappointed at the outcome—the testimony was allowed. Saks might have fared better had he argued that the court needed to test this individual's ability to make the distinctions he claims to make.

From Risinger (2000), at 781, one might think that the *Starzecpyzel* decision was adjudicative, that it was about the facts of this case only:

> Judge McKenna makes clear that his analysis does not apply to any *other* asserted skill or global claim of expertise. Later courts and commentators, who have tended to treat *Starzecpyzel* as if it dealt with global validity, have generally missed this point. [Emphasis added.]

The decision was about handwriting, not other forensic sciences; but it was about handwriting analysis in general. Whatever distinction Risinger is making is different from the one I am making.

> Unlike the harbor pilot, who either arrives at the right dock or does not, and knows it, a person making a forensic bite-mark identification, for example, usually only knows if his conclusion was right or wrong by whether or not a jury agrees with him.[140]

The test of the technical expert's error is *not* agreement by a jury. It is agreement with fact, either in situations in which fact can be determined, or in test situations where fact is known. Jury agreement may indicate that the expert was persuasive, but is not evidence that he was correct. It is irrelevant if other experts are often wrong, and a waste of effort to try to determine whether the technical expert is right or wrong this time. If we knew the answer from more reliable means, he would not have been called. Rather, we need to know how right this expert is in general, in similar tasks. The expert should provide that information, along with his opinion, to the fact determiner.

Anyone can get lucky. If left on his own, the technical expert will show the court only his most successful work. The best assessment of how well he does it is how many times he has succeeded, how many times he has failed, in the past, over all of his work (including, perhaps, an assessment of trend, how much better he is getting).

Although it seems to speak to efficiency, getting rid of whole areas by fiat, the legislative-fact conclusion that no expert can do what the one presented to the court purports to do is more of a *Frye* test (acceptance by others) than a *Daubert* test (reliable in this instance). I would not worry about whole areas, "fields," and would not allow them to become the focus of the debate. Judges do not like to conclude beyond their reach, and only this case's experts are within that reach.

Police: An Example of Craft

The Fourth Amendment debate on probable cause for search and seizure could and should be viewed under this same concept of technical skill. The classic case in this literature, the base from which further Supreme Court reasoning flows, is *Terry* (1964). Virtually the entire discussion in *Terry* is about the reasonableness of the search that found the concealed weapons that lead to Terry's conviction. Reasonable *to whom*? Officer McFadden testified

> that he had been a policeman for 39 years and a detective for 35 and that he had been assigned to patrol this vicinity of downtown Cleveland for shoplifters and pickpockets for 30 years. He explained that he had developed routine habits of observation over the years and that he would "stand and watch people or walk and watch people at many intervals of the day."[141]

---

140. Risinger (2000) at 771.

141. *Terry* (1964) at 5. Police officers testify as "fact" witnesses, i.e., as lay witnesses. I am suggesting that they should be seen as testifying in two roles, one as fact witnesses, the other as technical experts subject to exclusion under *Daubert*.

That is, he asserted that he had special skills, that "probable cause" could occur to him on different grounds than to others. In effect, the Court accepted this view:

> [I]n determining whether the officer acted reasonably in such circumstances, due weight must be given . . . to the specific reasonable inferences which he is entitled to draw from the facts in light of his experience.[142]

Post-*Daubert*, it would be better to ask not if this officer was experienced, but if he was expert; if his method of determining whom to stop and frisk produced a number or proportion of arrests that qualifies him as expert in this field. It would not be hard to develop data that assessed police. For example, the study of traffic stops by Volusia County (Florida) sheriffs, discussed in Chapter 8, revealed that only 1 percent of the stops, supposedly for traffic violations, resulted in traffic citations. If the traffic stops were pretexts for drug searches, they should be assessed by the quantity of drugs they uncovered, at what cost. In determining probable cause, these sheriffs should not be allowed to testify, as they are clearly inexpert at what they purported to do. Similarly, perhaps *Atwater* (2001), upholding a policeman's arrest of a (literally) soccer mom for not wearing a seat belt, would have been decided differently had the Court inquired into the arresting officer's expertise.[143]

The thrust of my position is that when an expert is not credibly representing his work as scientific or the product of engineering, we should not walk away from the "testability" aspect to which we hold such evidence. Rather, we turn to the witness himself, and ask him to provide evidence that he can make the distinctions he claims to make, beyond that which anyone might do from lay experience or chance. A credentials threshold or an assessment of the "field" provides an excuse for a judge to avoid putting the expert to that test. It is correct to accept that there are non-scientific crafts. It is incorrect to confuse craft with science, to think that this effectuation of expertise can be evaluated.[144] It is equally

---

142. *Terry* (1964) at 27. David Harris (1994) misunderstands *Terry*. "For the first time, the Court allowed a criminal search and seizure without probable cause," he writes, at 659. That's not what the Court thought. It elevated a policeman's "reasonable suspicion" to probable cause, in effect accepting the police officer as a craft expert. Why would we would expect police to be trained and expert at what they do, and then evaluate them by amateur standards? See *Brown* (1979) and *Cortez* (1981). Still, the officer's expertise should be evaluated. Meeks (2000) discusses the harm unbridled "*Terry* stops" can do. If each such stop becomes part of that policeman's record, which can then be discovered in litigation to question his expertise, officers might be more circumspect.

143. It is not unusual to admit police as experts. See, for example, *Pearce* (1990). It is somewhat unusual, but allowed, to have the same police officer testify as a fact witness and as an expert. See, for example, *Thomas* (1996). It seems to be unheard of to assess the police officer's expert testimony under *Daubert*.

144. This statement is too stark, a necessary trim for the text. Of course an opposing attorney and the judge should inquire of a craft expert how he performed *this* task, how long it took, what he did, whether he did anything different from those tasks that make up his error record. Thus, in a footnote, I can easily accede that this particular craft opinion deserves attention. But the contrast in the text stands as the defining difference between craft and science.

incorrect to think that the individual craftsperson should be assessed by how well others in his field perform his task. The assessment must be of this expert's historical expertise at doing what he says he does.

Repressed Memory

Judge Harrington, ruling on the recall of "repressed memories," wrote:

> For the law to reject a diagnostic category generally accepted by those who practice the art and science of psychiatry would be folly.[145]

Many courts have rejected "science" testimony, and repressed-memory testimony in particular.[146] Although the hesitance of a judge to rule against a profession is understandable, the judge need not "reject a diagnostic category." His challenge is more limited.

Plaintiff Ann Shahzade had asserted that she had been sexually abused by her cousin many years earlier, but had repressed that knowledge. Not having been able to bring charges is critical to surviving defendant's motion to dismiss because, had she been capable, the charges would now be barred by the statute of limitations.[147]

First, Judge Harrington found that

> the plaintiff's expert, Dr. Bessel van der Kolk, is not only qualified as an expert in the field of memory, but that he is one of the country's most renowned psychiatrists in this specialty.[148]

On the other hand,

> defendant's expert, Dr. Bodkin . . . does not specialize in the field of memory. Nor do his credentials and expertise in the area of memory compare with those of Dr. van der Kolk. Furthermore, Dr. Bodkin did not claim that the theory of repressed memory was invalid, he merely stated that, in his opinion,

---

145. *Shahzade* (1996) at 290.

146. Some of these cases refer more to the method of recovering memory than to the "repression" phenomenon. I include in this discussion cases of hypnotically induced recall, rejected because hypnotism cannot be validated, such as *Borawick* (1995).

147. Silberg (1993) at 1601:

> In most states, the statutory limitations period for personal injury actions is one to three years after the cause of action accrues, the date of accrual generally being the date of injury. This statutory time period may be tolled if a person is a minor or is operating under a disability at the time the cause of action arises. In such situations, the limitations period begins to run when the disability is removed or when the individual reaches majority.

Repressed-memory plaintiffs claim that their lack of memory of the harm was such a disability, and the time period should start upon recall. Paul Shanley, the Boston priest convicted of child abuse on February 7, 2005, faced one such accuser. All others had been time-barred.

148. *Shahzade* (1996) at 287; following indented quotation at 288.

the 52 studies relating to repressed memories which he critiqued contained methodological deficiencies and therefore could not serve to validate the theory.

Both the credentials and the critique were about the field, not the technical ability of the expert. Had there been a framework with which to assess the proffered testimony, van der Kolk would have been assessed as a technical expert. Bodkin would have been a wisdom witness, and as such should have been allowed to testify, although only about legislative fact.

People forget.[149] The notion that they can forget that they forgot—that they repress memories not only of what happened, but that there was a happening at all—goes back to Freud, over a hundred years ago. Consider one study endorsed by van der Kolk as "the best study on all this."[150] Linda Williams had interviewed sexually abused children in the 1970s and, seventeen years later, re-interviewed half of them. Of 129 subjects, forty-nine, or 38 percent, did not mention the abuse on re-interview.[151] This study is put forward as evidence that memories can be repressed.

People also invent, amplify, misremember. It is easy to accept "repressed memory" as a legislative fact, but to accept it as adjudicative evidence we need more. There may be a scientific question whether some people who were abused repress the memory; but the *litigation* question is the probability that *this* person, claiming to remember, after many years, that she had been "abused," is recalling fact. That cannot be measured by counting people who forget that fact, after many years, and not counting people who claim they forgot what they now are fabricating.

Some statistical analysts will assert that determining how accurate later recall is in general may cast light on whether van der Kolk's diagnosis of repressed memory has been correct. Williams might have interviewed her former subjects' peers who had *not* been abused, to see if any later claimed that they had been. Was van der Kolk testifying that *all* persons

---

149. In another context, Judge Posner, in *Krist* (1990), at 297, has summarized the literature:

> The basic findings are: accuracy of recollection decreases at a geometric rather than arithmetic rate (so passage of time has a *highly* distorting effect on recollection); accuracy of recollection is not highly correlated with the recollector's confidence; and memory is highly suggestible—people are easily "reminded" of events that never happened, and having been "reminded" may thereafter hold the false recollection as tenaciously as they would a true one.

However, Posner relies heavily on the work of Elizabeth Loftus who, we will see in a later footnote, is not necessarily the definitive voice in this field.

150. *Shahzade* (1996) at 288, quoting plaintiff's expert witness. See Williams (1994).

151. Either van der Kolk or Judge Harrington did not read Williams' study carefully. The judge says, at 288, that they "no longer remembered the abuse," but that is an interpretation, Williams' as well as the judge's. What we know is that they did not mention it. We do not know why.

who claim recall are correct?[152] If he is providing wisdom testimony, legislative fact, we are looking for some evidence on the proportion of times they are.[153] As he is providing craft testimony, then we need evidence on how often *his* judgment has been correct.

Courts should be careful about applying general associations to particular cases. The counter-argument is that only if the general association can be made at all, can it be made in this particular case. I think that argument is essentially impossible to sustain, and is a deflection from the issue at hand. Even a negative showing in the literature—X *never* causes or is associated with Y—might not be fatal to any assertion that this relationship holds in this particular case. Even DNA non-matches, as close to an absolute negative as one gets in science, might in a particular case be incorrect.[154]

Showing that X *can* cause Y at most becomes only a platform for showing that X *did* cause Y in this instance.[155] This holds in both science and craft testimony. If the court

---

152. We care only about false positives. McAlister (1996) at 59:

> Studies conducted on the veracity of recovered memories of abuse have concluded that while memory repression does occur, some memories of abuse are almost certainly false.

153. So was the New Hampshire Supreme Court in *Hungerford* (1997) at 131 (928): "It is difficult to estimate the number or rate of recovered memories that are 'false.'"

154. DNA assessment is subject to many craft errors, including by contamination in the laboratory and analyst assessment. Although over a decade old, one of the best descriptions of craft errors remains Deftos (1994). As Lempert (1991) notes, at 316:

> [T]o conclude that the defendant is not the source of the evidence DNA ["S"] and so deserves to be acquitted risks the danger of a mistaken exclusion, a risk that increases with the prior odds on S.

See also Moenssens (1993) and Giannelli (1993), and the discussion of DNA under "Forensic Science," below. Or, the perpetrator might be a chimera.

155. As in many aspects of the application of *Daubert*, courts flounder about the importance of establishing general causation when making a specific causation argument. For example, the Texas Court of Appeals, the majority *en banc*, in *Coastal* (2002) declared, at 608, that "a differential diagnosis can only 'rule out,' but does not itself 'rule in,' the possible causes of an illness." That is, this specific causation methodology must be backed by an affirmative general finding. Judge Brister, concurring, blasts the majority. He writes, at 616, that "plaintiffs are now informed they must prove both general and specific causation in all toxic tort cases." The majority cites *Moore* (1998), and *Moore* can be read that way. *Amorgianos* (2002) is a clear expression of just this requirement in New York courts. See also Note (2000).

It is certainly advantageous to have evidence that X *can* cause Y, when claiming that it does so. See *Nelson* (2001), where the court accuses the expert, in the absence of general causation literature, of circular reasoning. But how much X is required to cause Y, and was the plaintiff exposed to that amount of X? Inability to answer these questions led to plaintiffs' experts' exclusion in *Goeb* (1999).

Other courts hold that specific causation can be shown in the absence of general causation evidence. "Thus, we hold that a reliable differential diagnosis provides a valid foundation for an expert opinion." *Westberry* (1999) at 263. A legislative-fact finding about the method, differential analysis, allowed an adjudicative-fact finding about specific causation regardless of the lack of general causation literature. Unfortunately, this is not a good example for my position that the adjudicative case does not require the legislative case, because it is about method, not relationship, and because it accepted a poor method. For a description of the inherent weaknesses of differential diagnosis see Poulter (1992) at 231–235.

believes that some experts can discern real from false memory, the question before the court is about the extent to which the present expert can do so. If the court believes that there is no such field, that persons who pretend to make this distinction cannot do so, that general skepticism informs but does not alter the present question: How much credibility should accompany *this testimony*?

The New Hampshire Supreme Court understood the controversy in the field, but stuck to the issues of its case. Affirming the lower court's suppression of the testimony even of the name plaintiffs, the Court concluded:

> The indicia of reliability present in the particular memories in these cases do not rise to such a level that they overcome the divisive state of the scientific debate on the issue.[156]

Most writers in this field agree with the New Hampshire court's dependence on corroborating evidence:

> There is no empirical evidence to support the assertion that experts can identify accurate recall. . . . The only way to test the accuracy of an individual's memory is to rely upon external indicators of reliability.[157]

However, the testimony of the "victim" of sexual abuse, who recalls that abuse years later, is lay testimony, indeed, eyewitness testimony, be it true or false. If the court waives the statute of limitations, that witness usually may testify.[158] Whether the recollection is "true," one might think, would be a matter for the ultimate fact finder (usually a jury) to determine. The function of the corroborating evidence would be to bolster the eyewitness testimony.[159]

That was the state of New Hampshire's argument. More usually, when an eyewitness

---

156. *Hungerford* (1997) at 134 (930). Similarly, referring to recollection through hypnosis, the Second Circuit referred to "the inherent incredibility of Borawick's allegations" in *Borawick* (1995) at 609.

157. Spadaro (1998) at 1192. Allegations of sexual abuse based on recall of repressed memory seems to have been a phenomenon of the 1980s and '90s. For example, the web site of the False Memory Syndrome Foundation, www.fmsf.com, a support group for persons allegedly falsely accused, contains (as of May 21, 2005) no reference dated after 1999.

158. See, for example, *Doe* (1999), in which the Supreme Court of Indiana credited Doe's expert's testimony sufficiently to overturn a summary judgment and let the trial proceed. In *Johnson* (1988), a federal court interpreted Illinois law to leave the application of the statute of limitations to a trial determination of fact. In *Tyson* (1986), at 79, the Washington Supreme Court gave the plaintiff only "until 3 years beyond the age of majority to bring an action." However, the Washington legislature revised the statute of limitations to allow later memory recovery (Washington Revised Code Chapter 144, revision of 1988).

Carro and Hatala (1996) argue that legislatures and courts should lean in the other direction. Their solution to the uncertainty of newly discovered "memories" is to maintain the "crime's" statute of limitations without waiver.

159. The truth of an allegation where there are no witnesses other than the accuser and defendant is determined by assessing their credibility. Under any circumstance, but especially if the accuser is or was a child at the time of the event, his memory might be tainted:

testifies that "He did it," the "it" has been established. Here, the question is whether there was an "it," and how to establish that premise. At least one reviewer thinks that, without corroborating evidence, even the "victim" should *not* be allowed to testify:

> Because the truth of retrieved repressed memories cannot be proven or disproven, evidence of such memories should not be admitted unless there is outside corroboration.[160]

The New Hampshire Supreme Court agreed, rejecting the state's position. As explained by the trial judge:

> It is . . . the phenomenon of that memory and the process of which that memory is the product, which is to be subjected to the test of scientific acceptance and reliability. Testimony that is dependent upon recovery of a repressed memory through therapy cannot be logically disassociated from the underlying scientific concept or the technique of recovery.[161]

Perhaps the threshold question, whether to waive the statute of limitations, must be made by the court. Wisdom experts can debate the legislative-fact question, whether trauma can induce repression of memory, before the court. *Daubert* should be no impediment to the court's hearing this information. What we still need, as I will discuss below, is a way to assess the wisdom experts who provide it.

To testify regarding *this plaintiff's* repressed memory is to express a craft opinion. The burden is on the proffered expert to show how accurately he has made this distinction in the past. Dealing at the legislative-fact level, courts have divided on both how to assess repressed-memory testimony and what their assessment is. As late as 2000 we find the Arizona Supreme court saying that neither *Frye* nor *Daubert* applies, and that van der Kolk should be allowed to testify.[162] That court's confusion is most clearly articulated by a lower court's later decision on another kind of expertise, also denying a *Frye* hearing:

> Taint is the implantation of false memories or the distortion of real memories caused by interview techniques of law enforcement, social service personnel, and other interested adults, that are so unduly suggestive and coercive as to infect the memory of the child, rendering that child incompetent to testify.

Delbridge (2003) at 35. Some courts make much of the difference between competence and credibility, reserving to the jury the sole right to determine the latter, not to be "usurped" by expert testimony. Where expert testimony is not allowed to bear on credibility, the statement in text is incorrect. I will address this judicial folly, preventing jurors from hearing legislative fact (or a debate thereon) in their assessment of eyewitness testimony, further, below.

160. McAlister (1996) at 57.

161. *Hungerford* (1995) at *1.

162. The Arizona case is *Logerquist* (2000). South Carolina has allowed such testimony in *Moriarty* (1999), and California has in *Doe* (1999). Rhode Island suppressed it in *Quadrocchi* (1999). All discussion is on a legislative-fact level. One solution was generated in *Isely* (1995). Plaintiff's expert, Carol Hartman,

> Unlike DNA and other types of "scientific" evidence, these risk-assessment tools do not have an aura of scientific infallibility.[163]

That is, a witness who disclaims science will be held to less-rigorous standards.

The fallacy is thinking of "scientific" evidence as infallible. All science and all craft evidence should be associated with the probability of error. If courts would assess repressed-memory doctors as craft experts, and demand a record of their judgments against some criterion of fact—that is, demand that each produce a validity assessment—adjudicative-fact experts affirming or disputing repressed-memory allegations would be excluded.[164]

> will be permitted to testify as to whether Mr. Isely's behavior is consistent with someone who is suffering repressed memory or post-traumatic stress disorder.

At 1069. However,

> she should not be permitted to testify that she either believes Mr. Isely or believes that the incidents he alleges occurred.

This becomes adjudicative-fact testimony disguised as legislative-fact testimony. It is like asking if Microsoft's behavior was "like" that of a monopolist, without asking the expert to conclude that it was a monopolist or was not. Judges come up with such half-baked solutions because they have not learned to subject the expert to a validity test—to produce a probability-of-error calculation based on history and "factual" assessment.

163. *Romley* (2001) at 89. The issue was using published data to make an assessment of the likelihood of recidivism. The complainants wanted individualized assessments. The court goes on, at 89:

> We perceive no reason why the trial court should be allowed to screen this evidence pursuant to *Frye* before it is presented to the jury, the ultimate arbiter of truth.

They should have concluded exactly the opposite, that adjudicative craft opinions should be accompanied by data on errors, and assessed by the judge for sufficiency for trial.

164. Like any other "field," repressed memory has developed entrenched positions. Elizabeth Loftus leads the faction that set out to determine whether persons could be induced to "remember" something that never happened, such as being lost, as a child, in a shopping mall. See Loftus and Pickrell (1995). Lynn Crook, who was a successful plaintiff in a repressed-memory case (in which Loftus testified for the defendant), has set her course on debunking the debunkers. Except for one case, she questions whether the shopping-mall "memory" was ever implanted, in Crook and Dean (1999). In addition, she has investigated the testimony of retractors, persons who at one time said they had recovered memory, and later concluded it was not memory but the false implantations of their therapists. Crook (2002) does not believe the retractions. Even if Loftus is correct, that false memory can be implanted, there seems to be no special technical expertise that can provide evidence that it was or was not in a particular case.

"Proof" of repressed memory seemed to appear in the story of Eileen Franklin-Lipsker, whose testimony convicted her father in 1991 of having murdered a friend of hers when both girls were very young. As every fact to which Franklin-Lipsker testified as personal memory had been reported in the press of the day, and as proof of publication had not been allowed as evidence at the trial, his conviction was overturned. See *Franklin* (1995). The basic fact of suppression and then recall cannot be established, and the accuracy of that "recall" cannot be assessed. There is neither science nor evaluatable craft in this field. Judge Harrington was wrong. Although each proffered adjudicative expert should be assessed on his own merits, none can pass a *Daubert* screen for proven validity. No court should allow expert testimony, except that which would say the subject is in dispute, not because it considers the field bogus, as a legislative fact, but because these "experts" cannot show adjudicative fact.

The proper end—the disappearance of adjudicative expert testimony on repressed memory—would thereby be achieved without any court drawing a sweeping conclusion about an entire "field" of study.

Assessing the Expert

Can the antitrust expert conclude, from his evidence, that there was conspiracy or collusion? Can the handwriting or fingerprint expert determine that the latent prints are those of the defendant? Can the psychologist state with certainty, in a sentencing hearing, that a defendant is irremediable, implying that he should never be freed? What kind of an outcome do these hearings call for?

Michael Saks criticizes fields that do not provide a testing basis for qualifying experts:

> Some disciplines concern themselves with empirical questions and have well-developed traditions of self-testing—that is, they have behaved like sciences. Other fields, like handwriting identification, also concern themselves with empirical questions, but have done so little testing that it is impossible to know what expert judgments are dependable.[165]

No matter how tied to judicial processes they may be, academic disciplines are not controlled by the court. The court cannot reject all evidence just because some professional society has not provided the basis for some expert (who may not be a member of that society) to testify. Nor should a court accept evidence because it comes from a reliable "field."

Starting with the individual witness, Saks provides a clue to the answer:

> [F]or such fields, individual proffered expert witnesses might be required to provide evidence of well-designed, independently and honestly conducted tests of their own skills. Whether the proffered expert is a physician, a plumber, a handwriting expert, or an astrologer, it is not difficult to devise tests of whether the individual practitioner has the proficiency to perform specified and empirically verifiable tasks relevant to the specific expertise proffered.[166]

Saks does not take his own idea as far as I would. The result of such testing would be to permit the expert to state the probability associated with his conclusion, and the basis of that probability calculation. If the expert has been tested for fingerprint identifications

---

165. Saks (2000a) at 238. See also Risinger and Saks (1996).

166. Saks (2000a) at 239. He calls this the "black box" approach. We care only about how well the expert does, not how he does it. As Caudill (2002) explains, at 1796:

> The term "black box" in science studies refers to the tendency, in idealized accounts of scientific practice, to ignore or set aside the social, institutional, and rhetorical aspects of science in order to focus on input (hypothesis, data) and output (results of experiment, conclusion).

against known identities, then we have an accuracy metric. Why not require that metric to be part of his testimony?

"I think this is the fingerprint of X, and I have been certified to be correct 92 percent of the time in such situations."

"So," goes the cross-examination, "Eight times out of one hundred that you say the print belongs to X, it does not belong to X. Is that correct?"

It may not be.[167] After analysis of the test and clarification of its findings, the finder of fact has the witness's opinion *and* has a way to evaluate that opinion. The finder of fact now has information to help determine to what extent the testimony is fit to be believed.[168]

In the *Kumho* hearing, Dennis Carlson admitted "that he does not know whether his previous analyses of failed tires have been correct or incorrect."[169] He was appropriately not allowed to express his opinion about the cause of the tire failure. Plaintiff in *Joiner* presented several experts.[170] Judge Evans found that

> the testimony of Plaintiffs' experts manifestly does not fit the facts of this case, and is therefore inadmissible.[171]

---

167. As was critical to the jury-size discussion of Chapter 4, and as any statistician will be happy to explain, there are two types of error. It could be that this expert's errors were failures to identify—false negatives—as opposed to false positives. I am calling for a *clear* exposition of the accuracy of the witness' skills, which means separate assessments of Type I and Type II error. This summary statement by the Alaska Supreme Court in *Coon* (1999) at 401, therefore, is insufficient:

> [Expert Steve] Cain also testified that research studies have calculated the known error rate for voice spectrographic analysis to be less than one percent when the technique is performed properly by a scientist skilled in the technique.

The three FBI agents who wrongly identified Brandon Mayfield from a fingerprint related to the terror bombing in Madrid in 2004, for example, should have a false positive identification on their records. See Jennifer L. Mnookin, "The Achilles' Heel of Fingerprints," *Washington Post*, May 29, 2004, at A27; and Dan Eggen, "Justice to Probe FBI Role in Lawyer's Arrest," *Washington Post*, September 14, 2004, at A5.

168. The nature of the test is an important consideration. It may not reflect the kind of conclusion being presented here. Thus cross-examination can delve into the characteristics of the procedures that provided this expert with his probability credential. "So you correctly identified only 85 percent of the correct fingerprints when they were much clearer than are those in this case. Yet you want the jury to apply that 85 percent figure to your likelihood of error here. Isn't that misleading?"

169. *Kumho* (1996) at 1521. Judge Butler did not rule on Carlson's qualifications, but assumed, at 1519, that he was qualified to get to the point that his testimony was unreliable.

170. Plaintiff's experts included Arthur L. Frank (M.D.), Arnold Schecter (M.D.), Daniel Teitelbaum (M.D.), and Larry Robertson (Ph.D.). Joiner alleged that exposure to PCBs had "promoted" his lung cancer. This is an identification problem. A tobacco chewer who no longer has a tongue or jaw? Easy. Most cases are more difficult. Surely data could have been applied to Joiner's situation, including the relationship between his exposure to PCBs and that to other carcinogens. Joiner's experts might have been able to come up with a probabilistic answer. If so, they should have been allowed to present it. Their testimony, however, consisted of judgments expressed as facts, properly excluded by the trial court in *Joiner* (1994) and then the Supreme Court in *Joiner* (1997).

171. *Joiner* (1994) at 1332.

This flaw could not have been corrected by stating either current or previous expert results probabilistically.[172]

Of the defendant, who had been found guilty of murder, the state's psychiatrist

> stated unequivocally that, in his expert opinion, Satterwhite "will present a continuing threat to society by continuing acts of violence." He explained that Satterwhite has "a lack of conscience" and is "as severe a sociopath as you can be." To illustrate his point, he testified that on a scale of 1 to 10—where "ones" are mild sociopaths and "tens" are individuals with complete disregard for human life—Satterwhite is a "ten plus."[173]

The sentence was reversed not because no assessment was made of this psychiatrist's fallibility, but because the defendant had been examined by this psychiatrist without benefit of counsel. In the absence of such procedural errors, this kind of testimony has always been deemed acceptable—though it never should be—based on the credentials of the expert.[174]

The certainty with which the expert holds his opinion is irrelevant. John Monahan has reviewed studies comparing subsequent violent behavior with assessments of "high" and "low" probability thereof. Those assessed to be dangerous were more likely to commit violent acts than those assessed not to be dangerous, but not very accurately. He reports the comparison from four studies, listed in Figure 67.[175]

---

172. Of the Joiners' experts, the Eleventh Circuit majority wrote:
> Teitelbaum stated that his methodology "has been the basis of diagnosis for hundreds of years." Schecter described his methodology as one "usually and generally followed by physicians and scientists."

Joiner (1996) at 532. So what? Nothing in the record indicates that these experts had ever correctly assessed the *causes* of the illnesses they may have correctly identified.

173. *Satterwhite* (1988) at 259. The expert psychiatrist was James Grigson, who had also been involved in *Smith* (1981).

174. La Fontaine (2002) at 208:
> As of 1994, Dr. Grigson had appeared in at least 150 capital trials on behalf of the state, and his predictions of future dangerousness had been used to help convict at least one-third of all Texas death-row inmates.

175. Monahan (2000), reporting findings from other studies cited there, at 903, 904, 905, and 907. The subjects apparently were males. Monahan also reports a study in which there was no difference in recidivism by how the patients were assessed, those patients being female. Finally, in one of the four studies cited as evidence for the "validity" of assessment, the assessments were made by hospital nurses. Thus it may be that future dangerousness can be assessed, with some accuracy, but it may also be that this assessment can be done as well by lay observers as by "experts."

Sorensen and Pilgrim (2000) use logit (see Chapter 2 of this book) to estimate recurrence of violence by inmates convicted of murder. At 1257: "As in free society, age has been found to be the major determinant of rule-violating behavior in prison." That is, if juries want to minimize recidivism, they will give longer (or death) sentences to the young. I suggest, rather, that juries should look into the factors the witness uses to come to his assessment.

	Assessed "High"	Assessed "Low"
1	39 percent	26 percent
2	53 percent	36 percent
3	40 percent	10 percent
4	57 percent	29 percent

FIGURE 67: Percent Committing Future Violent Acts

No measure of the "certainty" with which these assessments were held is reported, but there is an implicit validity to them, a correlation between the estimate of future behavior and that behavior itself. There are also many false positives, assertions of violent future behavior that does not occur. I do not see the benefit in adopting either extreme position, that such assessments should never be accepted, or that they always should be accepted. The jury can have such information about the accuracy of assessments of future behavior, in general, through wisdom testimony. It should also have information specific to the craft witness making the assessment, as part of his testimony.

Many stockbrokers are certain about the future success of their next pick. A client wants to know how many stocks similarly touted by this broker have risen by more than the market in general. The accuracy of previous equally certain predictions is the best guide to how expert this expert is, even though it is a less certain guide to how accurate this prediction is.[176]

"Monopoly" is a legal conclusion. Does the seller have pricing power? All sellers have some pricing power.[177] Should the expert provide a measure, or a conclusion? As I noted above, both economist experts in *Microsoft* testified with certainty: yes, Microsoft had monopoly power; and no, it did not. Neither, however, defined a continuum and a metric thereof, and argued for a certain point on that continuum to be the binary decision point

---

176. Recall the indication, in footnote 33 of Chapter 8, that the relationship between certainty and accuracy is "modest" at best. La Fontaine (2002) tells us, at 210: "Dr. Grigson has been proven wrong in several cases," though, because he can always assert that the predicted bad behavior has not *yet* occurred, he will not admit to it. Calculating an error rate from predictions of future dangerousness is difficult, but necessary.

In cold calls, brokers use the following device: They tout several stocks, one per call, keeping records of to whom which stock was recommended. They then call back only those to whom they had recommended a stock that fared better than the market. As evidence of their quality they cite the only record the prospective client knows, which is one success in one try. Courts need to devise ways to discern when such deceptive "statistics" are being provided. However, surely we can agree that some stock analysts are better than others. The fact that most brokers lie need not deter us from trying to find a good one.

177. See *Drugs* (1997) at 783:

There is no general rule against the possession of market power or the use of price discrimination to exploit it.

(beyond which a firm is a monopoly). No reference is made to *Daubert* in either the district-court or the appeals-court decisions.[178] As presented, with opinion conclusions, these experts gave technical testimony. There should have been no fear that they would not pass "science" criteria, had my framework been in place. They gave no science testimony, and should not have been evaluated as if they had. They should have been evaluated as technical experts, by how correct they have been in the past. The court did not know how to assess this testimony. They were admitted as experts based on their credentials.

Courts (as well as the plain words of Rule 702) recognize that "genuine expertise may be based on experience or training," that is, can be acquired by means other than higher education.[179] In some circumstances, the proposed craft expert might be tested during the *Daubert* hearing, but surely not at trial. Consider this description of cross-examination of a handwriting expert, who was

> shown two papers so folded as to disclose only what purported to be the signature of the decedent upon each. He testified, in substance, that upon the other trial, after comparing these signatures with the standards in evidence, he had pronounced them genuine, and had sworn that all were written by the same hand. Each of the papers, when unfolded, was a total blank, and the signatures were obviously spurious. The witness was thus compelled to admit that he had been mistaken in his opinion as an expert, upon the previous trial, in relation to the signature of the decedent, and had testified that the spurious signatures were genuine.[180]

Good showmanship this may have been, but it did not provide a reliable assessment, in probabilistic terms, of this expert's ability. If the witness would admit at the outset that he could be wrong, the obvious and correct question would be, "How often?" A spur-of-the-moment test would not answer that question.

As I argue further, below, handwriting analysis is a craft, not a science. Surprise testing, as it does not place the technical expert in the modus operandi in which he does his work and comes to his conclusions, is invalid. Still, what distinguishes *craft* evidence is that the other side's expert can disagree, but cannot disprove.[181] Thus the assessment of individual fallibility that is so offensive (because it is irrelevant) when applied to science experts

---

178. Gavil (1999) speculates that neither party initiated a *Daubert* hearing because it had no firmer a foundation for its testimony than did the other. They both preferred to have two experts rather than none. I am not sure judges are well served by attorney collusion to avoid *Daubert* issues.

179. *Tyus* (1996) at 263. The jury's verdict was reversed because the judge had been wrong to exclude expert testimony without evaluating it in a *Daubert* hearing.

180. *Hoag* (1903) at 41.

181. Graham (1998), at 6, called the distinction "between 'scientific' on the one hand and 'technical or other specialized knowledge' on the other," "fuzzy." I trust my distinction is clear, and solves the problem that bothered Chief Justice Rehnquist in *Daubert* (1993) at 600:

should be considered necessary for craft experts. One approach is to find a reliable, valid, dignified form of testing. Another approach is to use the expert's own history. How probability-of-error assessments are to be determined needs to evolve. That they are necessary, and cannot be performed during testimony, needs to be understood.

Forensic Science

I introduced "forensic science" in Chapter 8, noting that experts therein were different from statistical experts, the main subject of this book. I criticized the client's controlling a statistical expert's information, but agreed that forensic experts should be told little about the prosecutor's suspicions. I did not define "forensic science," except that it is usually concerned with measuring characteristics of individuals or objects, the purpose of which usually is to identify them. If the goal is to provide independent evidence either of who did something or of how or when or where he did it, that evidence is more credible the less that expert knew in advance what others thought about the case.

Obviously "forensic" implies a legal connection. There are few other forums in which most "forensic sciences" are practiced.[182] Although they have distinct histories, I will analyze all "forensic sciences" under one heading. But what are they, and are they sciences at all?

Michael Saks provides this terminology:

> Normal forensic science does things like determining what substance something is (e.g., what is that white powder?) or measuring the quantity of something (e.g., how much alcohol is in the murder victim's blood?). Forensic individualization sciences aim to connect a crime scene object or mark to the one and only source of that object or mark to the exclusion of all others in the world.[183]

> I am at a loss to know what is meant when it is said that the scientific status of a theory depends on its "falsifiability."

We need two different procedures to evaluate all that is covered by *Daubert*, because science is (as Justice Blackmun wrote in the Court's opinion) falsifiable, capable of disproof. Technical opinion is not.

182. The Seventh Circuit (Posner for the court) called forensic science "an oxymoron" in *Braun* (1996), at 235. In *McAsey* (2002), at 1098, Robert W. Johnson was called "a forensic economist." His job was to project future earnings, but he did it badly, expecting certain life until the age of "life expectancy." A skilled economist would discount expected earnings at every age by the probability of reaching that age as well as because future income is worth less, today, than present income. Of the "forensic sciences," handwriting analysis is the most used outside of the court. Indeed, the first handwriting "experts" were bank tellers, people who compared hands (a technical term with its own curious history) in the course of work.

183. Saks (2000b) at 881. It is interesting that although forensic scientists claim to do just that, they do not take the most elementary steps to do so. Thus, for example, ballistics tests "line up" the marks on a test-

Fingerprints, handwriting. and ballistics are obvious forensic-identification methods. Other identification methods include analysis of palm prints, voiceprints, dental records, DNA, and to some extent fibers.

Most people who do these things are employed by law-enforcement agencies, although the postal service is the major employer of handwriting experts. Such persons may

> tend to identify closely with the goals of police and prosecutors, seeing themselves as part of the law-enforcement team.[184]

Courts must expect that most defense experts will not be forensic scientists themselves, much as they might have done extensive research on the subject.

Forensic "science" experts testify about the results of lie-detector examinations and tests of recent activity such as the paraffin test (association with gunfire)[185] or blood, breath, and urine tests (association with drugs or alcohol). Forensic analysis provides information such as cause and time of death. Included here are pathology and entomology. This task goes beyond identifying and measuring—Saks' "normal forensic science"—but not as far as his "individualization." Witnesses in all of these fields state their conclusions as fact. They should provide an assessment of their accuracy, not just a statement of their belief.

"Science" is a label, the purpose of which is to enhance the image of those who hold it. If forensic "science" were science, then each event, each identification, would be separably testable. If we could test the identification by other means, we would not need the forensic scientist to do it. Therefore, under *Daubert*, "forensic science" is not science. It is craft.[186]

---

fired bullet with those on the recovered bullet, without reference to a data base of marks made by other guns, and therefore with no probabilistic basis by which other guns can be excluded. The same is true of handwriting analysis, where there is no data base of handwriting that might be mistaken for the suspect's.

184. W. Thompson (1997) at 1115. Thompson, Giannelli (1993), Giannelli (1997a), and others discuss deliberate falsification of forensic evidence. I do not.

185. A paraffin test was put before the jury in *Westwood* (1936), but this test had been given to the defendant *and two others* shortly after his wife had been shot. Nicely done. Paraffin tests are now discredited because they could show false positives from substances other than gunpowder, and false negatives if the defendant had a chance to wash thoroughly. It seems to be forgotten that a negative paraffin test on a presumed suicide by bullet strongly indicates homicide. That aspect of the test was ignored, for example, in *Brooke* (1959), holding at 393 (996) that

> the result of a paraffin test, rather than being placed in the category of the accepted tests has the same reputation for unreliability as the lie detector test.

That the defendant refused such a test, therefore, could not be held against him. Surely he was not re-prosecuted, as without the negative test on the victim, there was no evidence of a crime!

186. Borenstein (2001) at 1005:

> Because of the honorific connotation of the term "science," some inquirers try to have their claims viewed as being scientific.

That forensic science is not "science," however, does not relegate it to eternal exclusion. Although Borenstein apparently would not apply this concept to forensic science, he should. At 1006:

Judicial Acceptance

Not only have different forensic methods fared differently in court, some have fared differently at different times. Some criminal defendants were convicted on evidence that would not be accepted today, and indeed conviction reversals based on DNA demonstrate that something was seriously wrong with how the evidence had been assessed.

When novel methods were introduced, they were often compared with accepted methods:

> The record is devoid of evidence tending to show a general scientific recognition that the pathometer possesses efficacy. Evidence relating to handwriting, fingerprinting, and ballistics is recognized by experts as possessing such value that reasonable certainty can follow from tests.

> There is no room for doubt now that fingerprints, palmprints, and footprints are positive means of identification. Chemical analysis of the blood or urine to determine the content of alcohol is deemed acceptably accurate.

> We hold, therefore, that the result of a paraffin test, rather than being placed in the category of the accepted tests has the same reputation for unreliability as the lie detector test.[187]

The lie detector (pathometer, polygraph) has been vilified. Rejecting defendant's proffer of a voice-stress test, one court noted that it "has a purported accuracy of 85 percent which is comparable to that of a lie detector."[188] This Maryland appeals court drew its conclusion: "A lie-detector test by any other name is still a lie-detector test." So 85 percent accuracy, however that is measured, is not accurate enough?

Does eyewitness identification do as well as crafts that have been rejected? As the eye-

---

> It is unreasonable to maintain that genuine inquiry occurs only within the sciences. There are individuals from a vast range of fields who are diligent inquirers and who make significant contributions even though they are not members of a scientific field.

187. *Forte* (1938) at 206, followed by *Brooke* (1959) at 391 and then at 393. The first court to face a palmprint identification apparently was a state court in Nevada, prompting the supreme court of that state to write an extensive history of fingerprint and palmprint identification. See *Kuhl* (1918).

188. *Smith* (1976) at 119; following indented quotation at 120. Henseler (1997) finds "accuracy" rates from 70 percent to 95 percent, the high end coming from proponents. He argues against admitting polygraph evidence, unabashedly adding to his argument at 1296 that "polygraph testing lacks the general acceptance of the relevant scientific community." Thus he adds evidence that law-review writers, unable to forget *Frye* standards and generalities, are blocked from advancing the *Daubert* ball. A federal district court in Arizona determined that "The known error rates for the science of polygraphy are remarkably low." Judge Strand accepted the error rate as 10 percent if the examiner said the examinee was lying, but 5 percent if the examiner declared the examinee to be telling the truth. See *Crumby* (1995) at 1359. In *Black* (1993), however, at 123, Judge Spatt concluded that "polygraph evidence is not sufficiently reliable to be admissible in a criminal trial or pre-trial hearing."

witness is not an expert, he will have no record. Although one could conceive of individualized tests for eyewitnesses, that is not done. The only information a jury may hear about the reliability of their perception is, in fact, about the reliability of the perception of others.

Not so the craft expert. His abilities are properly tested individually. It is the role of the wisdom witness to raise questions, based on legislative fact, about the ability of people in general to make the distinction the witness—expert or lay—is making. Such testimony may be helpful, but it can be trumped by evidence about this witness's ability to do what he says he is doing. The craft expert should bring such evidence with him into court.

Voiceprints

The military, which later fought to exclude an exonerating polygraph test in *Scheffer* (1998), had presented its own voiceprint evidence in *Wright* (1967). Their expert was Lawrence Kersta, a co-inventor of the process, who had left Bell Laboratories (where it was not enthusiastically supported) to start his own voiceprint firm.

> Mr. Kersta's testimony established that his system of voice identification had, experimentally and in practical application, demonstrated a high degree of accuracy and, further, that he was personally qualified to testify as an expert on comparisons of sound patterns made by human voices.[189]

There was adverse testimony, but "neither infallibility of result nor unanimity of opinion" is required. Kersta's testimony was accepted. Wright was convicted on essentially no other evidence.

In *Williams* (1978), the court properly focused on the particular examiner offering voiceprint analysis. Frank Lundgren came complete with data about himself, not only the instrument, and that information proved to be critical to the acceptance of his testimony. The voiceprint machine in this use was found acceptably reliable:

> The sole question is whether spectrographic analysis has reached a level of reliability sufficient to warrant its use in the courtroom. . . . The record in this case demonstrates that virtually all of the safeguards designed to assure reliability, and to prevent a misleading of the jury, were employed. . . . Spectrographic voice analysis evidence is admissible.[190]

---

189. *Wright* (1967) at 453; following in-text quotation also at 453. Solan and Tiersma (2003) at 417:

> Sound spectrography was developed in the 1940s by Bell Laboratories for teaching deaf people how to speak and was quickly pursued for use in military operations during World War II.

Deaf people could see the difference between their pronunciation and the standard. Giannelli (1997b) tells us, at 396, that Kersta named the method "voiceprint" to form an analogy with "fingerprint," which is generally regarded as an accurate method of identification; i.e., Kersta was a self-promoter.

190. *Williams* (1978). Although printed here as one quotation, these sentences are at 1198, 1200, and 1201.

Unlike in *Williams*, most assessments of voiceprint have been made only on the method itself, much justified by the "science" behind it. In *Worley* (1972), where the issue was telephoned (recorded) bomb threats, Oscar Tosi of Michigan State University and Sergeant Ernest Nash of the Michigan State Police testified that the method was reliable. In *Lykus* (1975), Tosi (who testified only in *voir dire*) and the now-Lieutenant Nash, who testified also in *Baller* (1975), made voiceprint identification of tapped telephone ransom demands. Voiceprints were admitted into evidence in these and other cases.

In *Addison* (1972), Nash testified that the person who called to report a policeman in trouble was defendant Raymond. This evidence was not critical, as the wounded officer placed Raymond and defendant Addison at the scene. While not overturning defendants' convictions, the District of Columbia Circuit Court held that

> techniques of speaker identification by spectrogram comparison have not attained the general acceptance of the scientific community to the degree required in this jurisdiction by *Frye*.[191]

A similar result occurred two years later, when the Supreme Court of California noted the potential bias in such testimony:

> Nash admitted, however, that those persons who are actually involved in voice-print work are primarily voiceprint examiners "connected with a government agency of some kind," i.e., law enforcement officers such as Nash himself.

> We have concluded that, on the record before us, the People's showing on this important issue was insufficient, and that since the voiceprint evidence at issue herein was the primary evidence of defendant's guilt, the judgment of conviction must be reversed.[192]

In *King* (1968), the government's expert, Lawrence Kersta, "defended his 'voiceprint' method of identification as having the infallibility of fingerprints," but others

> testified that the method had not reached sufficient scientific certainty to be reliable as a positive means of identification in a court of law; that Kersta did not have adequate training, qualifications, and education for interpreting and identifying voices by use of the spectrograms.[193]

The entire discussion was about the biology and physics of voiceprints, and Kersta's credentials, not about Kersta's accuracy in identification. As usual, the state appeals court compared voiceprint with other forensic identification methods:

> To this date there are several so-called scientific methods of identification acceptable as evidence in the courts. Among these now used by courts are

---

191. *Addison* (1974) at 745.

192. *Kelly* (1976) at 37, then at 28.

193. *King* (1968) at 442; following indented quotation at 445; third indented quotation at 453; fourth indented quotation at 457.

> fingerprints, footprints, handwriting exemplars, certain types of blood group-
> ings, microscopic evaluation of organic matter such as human skin, hair, bal-
> listics examinations and X-rays.

Kersta refused to put forward his analysis of the spectrographs as "science," calling it "art." It is craft, which leads one to ask how well this witness performs that craft. Faced with a barrage of adverse opinion, this reviewing court determined that Kersta's testimony should not have been admitted. It was

> not generally recognized by the scientific disciplines in the related fields of
> speech, phonetics, linguistics, and acoustics.

King's conviction was reversed for as irrelevant a reason as a court can have.

Voiceprint survived after this defeat. Nonetheless, the *King* decision is important not only because it involved the founder and major non-captive proponent of the field, but because it still held that a technical opinion needed to be infallible.

> Even if the tools (the spectrograph and spectrogram) should possess the capa-
> bility they are alleged to have, except for Kersta's subjective opinion, there was
> no showing in this case that Kersta possesses sufficient capability and expert-
> ise to analyze the results with certainty.

The issue should have been not lack of certainty, but lack of measurement of Kersta's uncertainty.

In 1978, the Sixth Circuit noted that "the trend favors" admitting voiceprint evidence.[194] That may have been so, but there has been no federal voiceprint case post-*Daubert*.[195] I think that is because, prior to the publication of this book, courts have not known where to begin to assess expert testimony. Now they do: It should not be excluded on the basis of legislative-fact assessment. It is craft testimony, requiring a record of success and failure of *this witness*.

The voiceprint story is interesting for several reasons. First, like repressed memory, for two decades the method was accepted by some courts, rejected by others. Ultimately, it seems to have disappeared, where repressed-memory "expertise" manages to stay alive.[196] Both results are undeserved, in my opinion.

---

194. *Franks* (1975) at at 33. The *Franks* court refers to *Addison* (1974) as the only predecessor circuit-court opinion. *Baller* (1975) was decided five months later.

195. Voiceprint technology was admitted in Alaska state courts under a *Daubert* standard. See *Coon* (1999). *Drones* (2000) concerns voice identification through the circuitous route of defendant alleging failure of his counsel to engage experts to question lay ability to make aural identification. The court found that all voice-identification technology was so discredited that it was not unreasonable for Drones' attorney to forego trying to use it to attack a witness' identification.

196. For example, see *Mills* (2004), allowing a man to claim that he had repressed memory of childhood sexual abuse by a local priest, occurring in the 1980s, until January 2002, when he saw television reports

Second, *Frye* calls for acceptance of a method by a "field," not an assessment of the method itself. Unable to poll its members if they could define a "field," many courts were faced with large "science" arguments instead of small expert arguments.[197] Small decisions do not contradict each other, each being made about a different expert presentation. Large decisions about the field leave one to conclude that it all depends on what courtroom you are in, what judge you have. Small decisions about particular experts provide incentives for experts and their clients to be prepared to admit that they might be wrong, and to provide measures of how wrong that is, in general.

Third, as this example shows, the reaction to voiceprints was typical of the skepticism that greeted other technologies:

> There is no testimony in the record that there is general acceptance by the medical profession or general scientific recognition of the results of a Harger Drunkometer test as accurately establishing the alcoholic content of a subject's blood and thus the extent of his intoxication.[198]

Although some will say new technologies are not greeted with enough skepticism, I say the skepticism is sufficient, but misdirected. Judge Casellas appropriately assessed Ramón Echeandía, not the field of marine mechanics, in *Correa* (2002). Still, it is reasonable for a court to inquire into the methodology being proposed. The exhaustive treatment of DNA evidence in *Yee* (1991), as an example, emanated directly from the voiceprint history. An examination of the science behind the craft is relevant. In most instances it is simpler and better to assess this craft expert's use of that methodology, and his likelihood of error.

Fourth, it is interesting to realize that voiceprint, though discredited as a form of identification in court, is widely used by the FBI, the CIA, and the news media to assess the genuineness of tape recordings that claim to be from such people as Osama bin Laden. We are told that such tapes "probably" are genuine, or "probably" are not. Better would be to tell us *how* probably, but the point is that voiceprint identification is useful, though fallible,

---

about Father Paul Shanley's misdeeds in Boston. In *Webb* (2004), a father is allowed to pursue claims that a psychologist implanted *false* repressed "memories" of childhood sexual abuse in his son. At 419:

> The court ordered an evaluation by psychologist Paul Wert, who issued a report in July 1999 most decidedly favorable to the father.

Timothy Smith failed to question the trial testimony of mental-health nurse Kim Wolfe, who found the alleged victim's claims of repressed memory "credible" and "believable," while not providing her opinion that they were true. Wolfe had not been subject to a *Daubert* hearing, and the Supreme Court of Kentucky refused to speculate what such a hearing would have concluded. Mr. Smith was sentenced to twenty years in jail for sexual misconduct with his daughter ten years earlier. See *Smith* (2004).

197. Osborne (1990), for example, notes the problem of defining the relevant "field," and assessing acceptance within it, for voiceprint testimony. See especially at 502.

198. *Morse* (1949) at 273.

in answering important questions about these communications. Yet not good enough for the courtroom? I disagree.

Fifth, and most important for continuing this discussion, those courts that rejected voiceprints identified fingerprints and handwriting as acceptable forensic identification methods. These judges did not want to be thought of as "anti-science," but as properly cautious. Are other forensic-science experts unassailable, as these judges would have us believe?

Forensic Science Under Attack

Randolph Jonakait predicted, shortly after the *Daubert* decision, that

> if *Daubert* is taken seriously, then much of forensic science is in serious trouble.[199]

The rumbling had begun before *Daubert*, with the same general questioning of the ability of courts to handle science evidence that led to *Daubert*. Adrienne Hale, noting that

> admission of bite mark evidence may result in the use of irrelevant, prejudicial evidence by the trier of fact[200]

did not suggest that it be banned, only self-regulated,

> that admissibility of bite mark evidence be barred pending the establishment of standards of admissibility by a committee of forensic odontologists.

Andre Moenssens argued against the *Frye* rule in the 1980s.[201] Bert Black noted:

> The qualification of any expert witness includes both his or her field of expertise and the level of training and experience he or she has within that field.

---

199. Jonakait (1994) at 2117. Margaret Berger (1994) expressed a similar opinion. Frederick Crews notes, in "Out, Damned Blot," a review of James M. Wood, M Teresa Nezworski, Scott O. Lillienfeld, and Howard N. Garb, *What's Wrong with the Rorschach?: Science Confronts the Controversial Inkblot Test* (Jossey-Bass, 2003), in 51 *New York Review of Books* 12 (July 15, 2004) at 22:

> Until very recently, testimony by Rorschach experts has gone largely unchallenged in our courts.

To what recent challenges could this statement refer? I reviewed over fifty cases in which a Rorschach test had been administered—between 2001 and 2004—and found only two in which one could surmise that the test had been challenged. In the only one in which an opposing expert argued against it, *Ryan* (2003) at 1049, this is Judge Kopf's description:

> Dr. Martell explained that the method of scoring was standardized by Exner in the 1970s to validate the testing and eliminate the subjective results, and that absent such scoring, the test results are not reliable.

Properly a critique of the opposing expert, this is hardly a critique of the field. Psychological evaluation is a "forensic science" in this book, that is, a craft. The field should not be at issue.

200. A. Hale (1978) at 309; following indented quotation also at 309.

201. See Moenssens (1984).

> For the kind of forensic science around which the *Frye* debate over acceptance
> versus reliability has developed, the field itself tends to be a central issue.[202]

This is a correct description of a fundamentally bad approach. The debate in law reviews
has been about the field, a focus that has extended into the courts.

The law-review model of criticizing the field of a so-called science, not the ability of
the witness to make the distinction he claims to make, appeared in a stinging attack on
handwriting analysis by Michael Risinger, Mark Denbeaux, and Michael Saks in 1989.
Risinger and Saks reiterated and updated their argument in 1996, followed shortly thereafter by Moenssens' attempt to defend it, and then a rebuttal by Risinger, Denbeaux, and
Saks. In the forensic literature, many voices were raised to protest the attack. In the law-
review literature, most writers were in Risinger's corner, notably Paul Giannelli and Edward
Imwinkelried.[203]

Yet, they all missed the point. One or two waved at it in passing, but none stopped to
examine it. Black's perceptive comment should have been a criticism of how courts evaluated forensic science, not its rationale.[204]

The 1989 Risinger, Denbeaux, and Saks article attacked the acceptance of forensic
"science" under the then-prevailing *Frye* standard. What could acceptance by practitioners in a "field" mean if the field was based on a guild, which had been formed mostly to
have guild members accepted as experts? What claim to "science" did that guild have?
Where had it been tested? With case examples and literature research, Risinger, Denbeaux,
and Saks argued that it was time to question *Frye*'s ability to handle the issues coming
under its apparent jurisdiction. Yet despite this general and trial-irrelevant line—that a self-
serving non-scientific "field" should be excluded in its entirety—Risinger, Denbeaux, and
Saks maintained a sensible fallback position:

> Still some fraction of these practitioners may, for reasons unrelated to the the-
> ories they invoke to "explain" their conclusions, be able to perceive and process

---

202. B. Black (1994) at 662.

203. See Risinger et al. (1989), Risinger and Saks (1996), Moenssens (1997), Risinger et al. (1998), Giannelli (1993), Imwinkelried (1995), and Giannelli (1997a). See also B. Black et al. (1994), Faigman et al.
(1994), Saks (1998), Mnookin (2001a), Mnookin (2001b), Case Note (2001), Epstein (2002), and Risinger
et al. (2002).

204. It is so often the case that a writer articulates the problem, but does not know that is what he has
done, that I interject another example here. Needle (1962), whom I take to be a law student (there is
an asterisk beside his name, but no asterisk and identifying information below), succinctly expressed, at
496, how jury composition was tested:

> The Supreme Court in determining racial exclusion will inquire into the results of the
> selection by jury commissioners to see if they have discriminated against racial classes.

They test a procedure from its results. How perfectly expressed—except that Needle thinks this leap of
faith is neat, a beautiful aspect of the law. It is, as I showed in Chapter 5, disastrous.

accurately in their minds individualizing characteristics of handwriting significantly better than you or I.

Thus, those courts that refuse to exclude such testimony should be more receptive to requiring that all handwriting identifications be the product of appropriately designed and presented blind tests. In these tests the exemplars of the suspected candidate for authorship ought to be presented to the expert only in the coded company of a meaningful number of other appropriately similar exemplars from people who clearly did not write the contested document.[205]

Moenssens early on pinpointed what was wrong with this discussion, that handwriting analysis was not a science, and so the arrows of Risinger, Denbeaux, and Saks were aimed at the wrong target, however accurately.

Most of the witnesses who testify as experts for the prosecution are not truly scientists, but better fit the label of "technicians."[206]

Years later, still trying to defend his field, saying that Risinger, Denbeaux, and Saks were confusing true forensic document examiners with non-expert—non-guild—graphologists,[207] Moenssens came close to bringing the debate to where it should have been.

[G]iven enough comparison writings of known origin, it is possible for skilled handwriting examiners to detect the differences between intra-writer variation and inter-writer variation, and arrive at a conclusion on whether a questioned writing was actually produced by writers whose known standards are also available for comparison.[208]

Can "enough" be determined ahead of time, or is it only determined when the forensic document examiner gets the answer right? Is this a standard or a tautology? Moenssens may have meant that the conclusion "arrived at" would always be correct, but (with a foot-

---

205. Risinger et al. (1989) at 773, then at 776. Even from these snippets, one can sense a tone of derision, the bias in the assumption that the field cannot be justified, but "still" individuals might be, though they can "explain" only in quotation marks, and not based on their methodology. Risinger, Denbeaux, and Saks continue, at 779:

> At the very least any such "expert" allowed to testify ought to be subject to some appropriately designed test on cross-examination.

Although I agree that such experts should be tested, my proposal is that the test should be in an environment similar to that of their work, not in cross-examination.

206. Moenssens (1993) at 5.

207. Graphology is

> the analysis of handwriting, a complex and intricate form of body language, to determine personality, character traits, and the emotional and mental state of the writer at the time of the writing.

Davis (1987) at 375. One could conceive of models, measures, and tests of this craft, but it has never been done. Nor has such an expert ever been accepted in court.

208. Moenssens (1998) at 320.

note dismissal of that interpretation) the other side of this debate could graciously have interpreted it as an acceptance that each individual forensic document examiner should be tested, his results presented to the court with his testimony.

Rather than move the conversation in that direction, Risinger, Denbeaux, and Saks determined to keep it broad, took no advantage of this opening, and kept fighting on an issue they had already won:

> Professor Moenssens' attempt to claim the label "science" for enterprises that do not manifest the minimum characteristics of modern science has no benefit except for the egos of the participants in those enterprises. Further, his attempt not only to win the label "science" for such expertises but also to create alternative, and virtually unfailable, "validity" criteria for them, is a double dip, which would produce very questionable results indeed.[209]

The debate to this point preceded the Supreme Court's clear broadening of the *Daubert* tent to include technical expertise, in *Kumho* (1999). Risinger, Denbeaux, and Saks were more prepared for *Kumho* than was Moenssens. But while the Court in *Kumho* asked that technical work be evaluated *by* science, it did not (as I interpret it) ask that technical work *be* science. If it did, then it shouldn't have. Moenssens, now thinking he was backed into defending handwriting analysis as science, had no chance to come to a reasonable method for judicial handling of what he had earlier identified as craft. Risinger, Denbeaux, and Saks were so bound up in demonstrating that forensic "science" wasn't science that they did not set out constructively to ask what it was, whether it was useful, and if so how to assess it in a judicial fact-finding forum.

We see the blind spot clearly in the 1996 article by Risinger and Saks. Once admitted as experts, handwriting analysts "set out to create a standard theory and practice, giving their trade the appearance of 'science'" they say.[210] Better put, they gave it the *label* "science," but the appearance of craft. Black had noted that

> when courts rely on labels, their evaluation of scientific evidence quickly becomes quixotic and inconsistent.[211]

Can label and appearance be distinguished? "Unfortunately, it is less than clear how to tell one from the other," say Risinger and Saks.[212] I have presented a simple way to make that distinction: In science, expertise (as measured by error probability) is associated with the work. In craft, it is associated with the worker. Risinger and Saks are confused by their focus on the general activity. In litigation, only specific testimony is at issue.

---

209. Risinger et al. (1998) at 435.

210. Risinger and Saks (1996) at 25.

211. B. Black (1994) at 739.

212. Risinger and Saks (1996) at 29.

Writing post-*Kumho*, Robert Epstein could have seized the moment.

> A prosecutor must be able to demonstrate the reliability of latent fingerprint identification testimony either by way of the *Daubert* factors or by some alternative criteria.[213]

So, by determining that forensic science is in fact a craft, there might be "alternative criteria" by which to assess it. But Epstein is not alluding to devising a framework that would produce new procedures under *Daubert*. He really means that fingerprint identification should be excluded, because it cannot satisfy *Daubert* criteria. I think that is neither necessary nor advisable.

The Department of Justice, stung by litigation inspired by these law-review debates, issued a request for proposals to study the validity of one of the forensic sciences, fingerprints.

> The DOJ has effectively admitted that latent fingerprint analysis fails the primary criterion of science and, by extension, the primary criterion for admissibility under *Daubert*: There has been no testing of the field's basic underlying premises.

"The so-called 'science of fingerprints' is nothing but an unfounded myth," Epstein concludes, still fighting the legislative-fact fight, instead of finding a way to make sense out of what we know: Fingerprints and handwriting, in some circumstances, in the hands of some people, can be helpful (though imperfect) identification tools. Like statistics, they should be seen as evidence, but not proof.

That courts before *Daubert* considered and made determinations about whole methods was the basis of Walker and Monahan's proposal to deal with it.

> Courts treat prior decisions on the probative value of social science evidence as if they were decisions on questions of law, with the force of precedent.[214]

They should be questions of fact, directed to individual experts and what they have to say about this particular case. Debating the merit of entire fields has been so pervasive that I must devote even more space to arguing against it.

Forensic "Science" Under *Daubert*

Soon after *Daubert*, attorneys began questioning forensic "science" experts called to associate people with physical evidence.[215] In *Starzecpyzel* (1995), Michael Saks provided a

---

213. Epstein (2002) at 621; following indented quotation at 627; then in-text quotation at 657.

214. Walker and Monahan (1988) at 885.

215. Fradella et al. (2004) offer a review of how courts have handled forensic-science experts post-*Kumho*. Their sample is unsatisfactory, in that it required the word "forensic" to be used in the court's

sweeping indictment of handwriting identification, as a witness for the defendant. That was the strategy of Saks and his co-author Mark Denbeaux, in case after case. For some years, it failed.

In *Hines* (1999), in which Denbeaux's testimony was at first proferred, then withdrawn, Judge Nancy Gertner divided the handwriting issue into two parts:

> I conclude that [FBI expert] Harrison can testify to the ways in which she has found Hines' known handwriting similar to or dissimilar from the handwriting of the robbery note.[216]

The expert could explain her "science," that is, her craft. Judge Gertner ordered that "she may not render an ultimate conclusion on who penned the unknown writing." This bifurcation comes from a mistaken notion about other identification evidence:

> There is no data that suggests that handwriting analysts can say, like DNA experts, that this person is "the" author of the document.

DNA experts can make no such assertions. As indicated above (in text and in footnote 154), DNA measures are partial, like latent prints, the fingerprints removed from objects.[217] To associate one sample with another requires an error tolerance.[218] DNA identification is always submitted with a probability that the match is a false positive. Hand-

---

decision, and thus excludes many similar cases in which that word was not used. They do point to inconsistency, but conclude, strangely, at 361:

> In spite of struggling to fit technical forensic evidence into the scientific rubric of peer review, replication, and known error rates as set forth in *Daubert*, courts are doing a remarkably good job in applying *Daubert* fairly consistently in the post-*Kumho* era.

They fail to understand that it is just this struggle to evaluate forensic evidence as science that is the problem.

216. *Hines* (1999) at 69; following in-text quotation at 71; then indented quotation at 69.

217. "DNA profiling, as powerful as it is, cannot positively identify one person." Giannelli (1997a) at 448. Asplen (1999) explains, at 148: "DNA is similar to fingerprint analysis in how matches are determined." They are similar also in that the individual who performs the analysis should be tested in his craft. Mnookin (2001a) at 49:

> DNA profiling does not claim to provide more than a probability, a statistic describing the odds that DNA taken from a random person would match the DNA in question.

Lindsey et al. (2003) at 148:

> Many forensic DNA profiles reflect only a limited number of the genotypic features that cannot reasonably be said to be unique. More than one person could have the same such DNA profile, just as more than one person could pick the same combination of numbers in a lottery, even though the probability of that particular combination winning is extremely small.

See also Pam Easton, "Houston retests DNA in hundreds of cases," *Oregonian*, March 24, 2003, at A4, reporting the release of an inmate falsely convicted from DNA-matching testimony.

218. Paterson (2000) at 1223:

writing is more complicated, because its characteristics vary, whereas biological characteristics remain the same throughout one's life. Indeed, as mentioned in Chapter 1, Benjamin Peirce's conclusion that the Howland will was a forgery came from the *lack* of variation from another, known signature. He concluded that the will's signature had been traced.[219]

We can compare examples of handwriting. We do not have a universe, and so any conclusion is probabilistic, based on data and a model. The model is inclusionary (does A look like B)—where science would call for an exclusionary component (does A *not* look like C, D, E, etc.). We assume that a full description of a person's DNA would be unique, but the location of DNA markers might not be, or might not be properly prepared or assessed.[220] The way DNA-marker evidence has become reliable is by searching through banks of individual tests and finding no duplication. That is its exclusionary element. The DNA expert refers to his data bank to conclude that the probability of the evidence DNA being that of

---

A visual match is verified by a computer measurement of the digitized pattern which determines the two samples to be a match if they fall within a specified match window of measurement variation.

One can test mitochondrial DNA (mtDNA) more precisely, in a sense, because it reports a chemical sequence. However, it reports only part of the sequence, and it reflects only DNA from one's mother. More important, duplicates have been found among unrelated individuals. See *Council* (1999) at 22. W. Thompson (1997) at 1123:

Whether a [PCR] test is interpreted as a damning incrimination or a complete exculpation may depend entirely on a subjective determination.

219. See Meier and Zabell (1980). One signature being precisely like a known true signature, when that true signature was available to the defendant, is the standard method of forensic determination of forgery. See Mnookin (2001b) for a description of the assessment of forged checks and a forged will in the 1900 murder of William Rice, the benefactor of Rice University. As usual, the judge did not want to say that he relied on expert testimony. *Rice Will* (1903) at 72:

The name of William M. Rice appears four times upon the alleged will of 1900, and upon a critical examination of these four signatures it will be found that they correspond almost exactly—a coincidence which could not possibly happen in the case of four genuine signatures of a person upwards of 80 years of age; and for this reason it does not need the testimony of experts to demonstrate that these signatures were not genuine, but tracings.

220. Here is a simplified DNA lesson from the Supreme Court of Nebraska, *Freeman* (1997) at 402:

DNA profiling is done by looking at specific loci on human DNA which are known to be highly polymorphic, that is, where the VNTR sequences are highly variable.

In criminal cases, a DNA scientist examines four loci along four separate chromosomes to find a DNA pattern. This is called RFLP DNA analysis. It is conceivable that two people could have the same VNTR sequence and number of repetitions at the same locus on the DNA strand but have different sequences at other loci on the strand which were not tested.

Thus the best we can do is say that we have not seen this same sequence on these loci on anyone else in our data base.

someone other than the suspect is a small number.[221] If the markers are different, the expert can conclude (subject to laboratory and interpretation errors) that the suspect certainly did not leave the evidence; but if they are the same, the identification itself must be probabilistic.[222]

Judge Gertner thought she lived in a binary world, in which the expert's conclusion is certainly yes, or certainly no. As Judge Goodwin later understood, we live in a probabilistic world.

> [B]ecause the results in handwriting analysis are based on identification, there must be a corresponding probability of error. In other words, it is possible to calculate the number of times a handwriting expert correctly identifies the author of a handwriting sample. This number can then be used by courts as an indicative error rate. Other qualities of handwriting analysis, such as the theory that penmanship characteristics are separable from each other, and that there is a base rate of penmanship characteristics in a population of potential authors, are also capable of measurement.[223]

That the expert's conclusion is tentative does not mean it is uninformative. But to be informative towards the fact finder's ultimate binary conclusion, we need to know how tentative it is.

---

221. Donnelly and Friedman (1999) at 932: "As of October 1998, the English database held 360,000 entries." Paterson (2000) tells us, at 1226, that, at the same time, the federal data bank of Restriction Fragment Length Polymorphism (RFLP) "fingerprints," CODIS, held the "prints" of 250,000 accused or convicted criminals. Donnelly and Friedman, at 940, provide the same figure and add, "with several hundred thousand more waiting to be analyzed." However, many states have their own CODIS-compliant data bases, which may contain redundancies, so the total number of searchable unique individual "fingerprints" is unknown. For a detailed description of the RFLP method of DNA comparison, see the Magistrate's Report appended to *Yee* (1991).

222. Deputy prosecutor Jerry Costello of Pierce County, Washington, about the murder of Melinda Mercer: "Usable DNA evidence—traceable 'to only one person on the planet'—was taken from three areas." *Oregonian*, August 14, 2002, under the headline, "Yates' crimes don't justify death penalty, lawyer argues," at C12. It may be that Robert Lee Yates' DNA is unique, but it is less likely that his markers (the limited measure we make of the DNA) are, and at any rate data do not exist to say so.

Much of science is statistics, and statistics is the opposite of certainty; it is how we infer information from uncertainty. Take, for example, the use of the DNA molecule in anthropological studies of evolution, as S. Wells (2002) describes it at 21:

> The dizzying variety of the data being generated [in the 1950s] by studies of polymorphisms needed a coherent theoretical framework to make it understandable. And statistics was about to ride to the rescue.

223. *Lewis* (2002) at 552. I have omitted citations to Risinger and Saks (1996), who set out a good foundation, which Judge Goodwin used well. Judge Goodwin is explaining why he did not allow the government's handwriting expert, John Cawley, to testify. The opinion continues,:

> Yet despite the relative ease with which such measurements could be made, the Government did not offer any evidence of reliable testing and error rates, or of any of the other *Daubert* factors through Mr. Cawley's testimony.

Statisticians always state their findings probabilistically. Why shouldn't all experts? This is what the court in *Frye* should have advocated: The lie detector can be used if there is a data base of attempts to determine the truth, when the truth is known on other grounds. Then the operator could have informed the jury how easily a subject could lie and not be detected, or not lie but be thought to have, or how reliably an operator can correctly discern truth and falsehood. Let the jury decide which one of those times this is. The *Frye* court was correct to disallow the test as a certainty, but incorrect to prevent its admission along with a scientific assessment of its accuracy, when used by this particular operator. Had no assessment of the accuracy of this machine, and this operator, been made in the five years between its invention and its proposed use in court?

Hines (1999) is referred to and quoted by Judge Pollak in *Llera Plaza I*. Fingerprint evidence could be presented:

> But no witness for any party will be permitted to testify that, in the opinion of the witness, a particular latent print is—or is not—the print of a particular person.[224]

Judge Crow was not convinced. "Research shows *Llera Plaza* stands alone in rejecting fingerprint identification opinions."[225] Judge Pollak's opinion "should be applauded," especially for the studies it will provoke, but it was overreaching. Judge Crow then specified the problem:

> The court's reading of the case law and literature on this issue leads it to believe that the real rub is with the conclusiveness in which fingerprint examiners express their opinions and with which the opinions may have been generally received by the courts and juries.

Exactly! The problem is not in stating the expert's opinion that the defendant is the culprit. If he is an expert, that is what he gets to do, state an opinion. The problem is stating it *with certainty*. Judge Crow, despite the brilliance of his understanding, did not employ it in his ruling.[226]

Kathleen Stefani provided fingerprint testimony for the government in 1996. Blood

---

224. *Llera Plaza I* (2002) at 518.

225. *Cline* (2002) at 1293; following in-text quotation at 1294; then indented quotation also at 1294. Judge Crow had allowed a handwriting expert to testify that the defendant signed someone else's name to a Western Union money order, in *Battle* (1997).

226. Judge Goodwin, in *Lewis* (2002), was also impressive. Fingerprint analysts strut an unbecoming certainty, at 554:

> Mr. Cawley said that his peers always agreed with each others' results and always got it right. Peer review in such a "Lake Woebegone" environment is not meaningful. . . . By excluding Mr. Cawley's testimony, the court did not hold that handwriting identification testimony is not reliable. Rather, the court narrowly held that handwriting analysis is susceptible to testing for reliability.

type (including secreter characteristic) and DNA evidence supported her identification of the defendant as the perpetrator of the rape.[227] Nonetheless, she should not have been allowed to express herself as

> "100% certain that the latent print on Lift No. 1 is in fact the left ring finger as indicated on the card with the name John Teixeira on it."

Although Stefani was no doubt providing her honest belief, without modification by a history in which her rate of error can be provided to the jury she has no basis upon which to be 100 percent certain as an *expert* witness. The proper statement from the expert is that she makes this identification (not "surely," not "certainly," but this is a match in her opinion), and that historically her matches are correct X percent of the time.

Judge Pollak understood that fingerprint identification is a technical skill, not a science. He did not know what to make of that distinction. He reversed himself.

Even though FBI fingerprint examiners take a test each year, the nature of that test raised questions of adequacy.

> On the record before me, the FBI examiners got very high proficiency grades, but the tests they took did not.[228]

Judge Pollak then concluded that

> there is no evidence that the error rate of certified FBI fingerprint examiners is unacceptably high.

Following a review of intensive study of fingerprint evidence use in England, as well as the FBI procedures, Judge Pollak summarized:

> I have concluded that arrangements which, subject to careful trial court oversight, are felt to be sufficiently reliable in England, ought likewise to be found sufficiently reliable in the federal courts of the United States, subject to similar measures of trial court oversight. In short, I have changed my mind.[229]

Judges Gertner once and Pollak twice didn't get it. Judge Crow did, but did not know what to do with it. Statistical experts conclude only how improbable the data would have been from a model with a specified hypothesis. It is up to the finder of fact to use that and other evidence—probabilistic all—to conclude whether the defendant broke the law.

---

227. *Teixeira* (1996); following indented quotation at 240. The quotation marks indicate that this is Stefani's direct testimony, but the court provides no citation.

228. *Llera Plaza II* (2002) at 565; following indented quotation at 566. In particular, the latent prints on the test are clearer, with more Galton points, than those from crime scenes.

229. *Llera Plaza II* (2002) at 576. Richard Posner argues that foreign decisions may be *precedent*, but they may not be *authority*. See "No Thanks, We Already Have Our Own Laws," *Legal Affairs*, July-August 2004. Posner does "not suggest that our judges should be provincial and ignore what people in other nations think and do." Justice Breyer, in a discussion with Justice Scalia at the American University on

Regarding DNA collected from a hair sample, Terry Melton

> concluded that there is a "95 percent chance that 99.93 percent of the people in North America don't have this type."

This conclusion may be erroneous, but it is well stated.[230] The function the expert "usurps" when he gives an opinion as a certainty is the fact finder's conversion of probabilistic evidence into a binary conclusion. He usurps nothing when he provides his opinion with information about its possible fallibility.

January 13, 2005, broadcast live on C-SPAN, argued that foreign decisions may be *informative*, which is something less than precedent. Some politicians ask the Court not to cite foreign decisions, but politics has lost all pretense of being an intellectual pursuit.

As they do with experts, judges will refer to foreign courts but declare that their decision is their own. We do not know how much influence foreign decisions have. In *Roper* (2005), 125 S.Ct. at 1200, Justice Kennedy, writing for the Court, notes:

> The opinion of the world community, while not controlling our outcome, does provide respected and significant confirmation for our own conclusions.

He then defends his allusion to foreign law:

> It does not lessen our fidelity to the Constitution or our pride in its origins to acknowledge that the express affirmation of certain fundamental rights by other nations and peoples simply underscores the centrality of those same rights within our own heritage of freedom.

Justice Scalia, in dissent at 1226, all too typically blows wind at a straw man:

> the basic premise of the Court's argument—that American law should conform to the laws of the rest of the world.

See also Justice Scalia's reference to "the mixed reception that the right to jury trial has been given in other countries" in defending the Court's determination that *Ring* (2002) was more a procedural than a substantive decision, in *Summerlin* (2004), 124 S.Ct. at 2525. Scalia makes sure that we know that those foreign opinions are "irrelevant to the meaning and continued existence of that right under our Constitution." In *Sosa* (2004), 124 S.Ct. at 2776, he scolds the judicial system:

> For over two decades now, unelected federal judges have been usurping this lawmaking power by converting what they regard as norms of international law into American law.

Justice Scalia confuses the search for fact with the search for law. His usual foreign references are to English law prior to 1789. It was, he says, legitimate to use foreign precedent while writing our Constitution, but not thereafter. Surely it is legitimate to utilize facts found subsequent to that date, even— especially?— if those facts appear in foreign judicial decisions. David Bernstein (1996) suggests that, concerning the subject of this book, evaluating science testimony, our courts would be well-served reviewing what foreign courts are doing. I agree as, obviously, does Judge Pollak.

230. Indented quotation, *Coleman* (2002) at 964. The estimated probability may be erroneous because it extrapolates beyond the data. It comes from an FBI data base containing 4,142 people. Although his calculation is not described in the decision, obviously Melton asked what proportion of matches there could be in the population and find none 5 percent of the time, drawing 4,142 persons randomly. Once again the 0.05 level is considered the magic line. The calculation is

$$\text{probability of no match} = 0.99934^{142} = 0.0550$$

The problem: Why would one think that the 4,142 persons in the FBI's DNA data base are representative of "the people in North America"?

The Gertner Compromise

Judge Gertner's solution, allowing the expert to educate the fact finder but not to draw conclusions, puts the witness' expertise somewhere between technical and wisdom. This is not a good place to be. Do we really think that, on the basis of superficial instruction, a jury can become proficient in fingerprint or handwriting comparison?[231] If the expert has studied the facts of this case, and has a conclusion, we should hear it—along with some information how likely he is to be incorrect. Only the wisdom expert, with only legislative-fact knowledge, should express no opinion about nor even refer to the evidence in this particular case.

Some judges have excluded forensic experts entirely. *Black* (1993), *Fujii* (2000), *Saelee* (2001), *Jacobs* (2002), *Lewis* (2002), and *Brewer* (2002) are examples. Still, if not immediately, and not universally, Judge Gertner's downgrading the forensic expert to a PowerPoint instructor caught on. We find the *Hines* solution effectuated in *Van Wyk* (2000), *Rutherford* (2000), and *Hernandez 10* (2002) on document identification, for example; and in *Filler* (2000) concerning psychiatric testimony.

In *Santillan* (1999), Susan Morton offered her expert handwriting opinion for the government.

> No tests or studies of the accuracy of such an opinion have as yet been conducted. It is noteworthy that the only support put forth for its position by the government . . . does not bear directly on the question of whether a specific opinion as to the identity of an author is or is not reliable.[232]

---

231. Not that Judge Gertner is alone in letting jurors suffer upon the shoals of ignorance. In *Smith* (2000b), hedonic damages estimates could not be presented to the jury. What they got, at 1244, was a lecture

> about the meaning of hedonic damages. The court reasoned that, as hedonic damages are explicitly allowed under New Mexico law, testimony "explaining hedonic damages and how they differ from other damages, particularly pain and suffering" would ensure hedonic damages were given the "consideration they deserve as part of the substantive law of New Mexico" and would help the jury "place a value on a loss that is difficult to quantify."

The Seventh Circuit presents the opposite view from that of Gertner, asserting that fingerprint evidence without expert interpretation is useless. In *Sutton* (2003), fingerprints had been taken from places witnesses said the robbers had touched. At 795:

> Analysis by the police fingerprint laboratory concluded, however, that the prints taken from the crime scenes did not match the defendants' fingerprints.

Defendants therefore wanted to introduce the reports as evidence.

> The district court reasoned that without an expert witness's explanation the reports were of no evidentiary value.

And the circuit court affirmed. Good for them!

232. *Santillan* (1999) at *5.

Correct. The burden is on whoever proffers the expert to provide a measure of that expert's fallibility. Judge Jensen does not say that the government cannot meet such a burden, only that it has not.

In *Van Wyk* (2000), the issue was text analysis. FBI special agent James R. Fitzgerald was allowed to testify, but not to conclude.

> [T]he Court is satisfied that Fitzgerald's testimony as to the specific similarities and idiosyncrasies between the known writings and questioned writings, as well as testimony regarding, for example, how frequently or infrequently in his experience, he has seen a particular idiosyncrasy, will aid the jury in determining the authorship of the unknown writings.[233]

Judge Bassler determines that Fitzgerald is a craft expert, but not enough of an expert to do that which experts do, under the rules, which is offer their opinions. Unfortunately, Judge Bassler reaches this conclusion from the field, not the witness:

> Because of the lack of scientific reliability of forensic stylistics, the Court is not satisfied that the jury would benefit from Fitzgerald's testimony as to his subjective opinion that the questioned writings were written by the same individual and that that individual is Defendant Roy Van Wyk.

I attach the name of the originating judge (Gertner), or the case (*Hines*), to this kind of ruling. It is a reversion to the days when judges were in fear of an expert's "usurping" the fact-finding prerogative of the jury. In 1871 we are told that

> In England, the expert is not allowed to give his opinion upon all the evidence; but certain facts and particulars in evidence may be stated to him, and he is to say what they indicate, upon the supposition that they are true.[234]

The Indiana Supreme Court concluded:

> It is not the province of an expert to draw inferences of fact from the evidence, but simply to declare his opinion upon a known or hypothetical state of facts.

More important than its historical regression, the Gertner compromise makes no sense on its own. If the witness is expert enough to point out the similarities and differences in *this* handwriting or *these* fingerprints, he should be expert enough to draw a conclusion about whose handwriting it is—as long as we know with what frequency, on the average, his conclusions are correct. Under what logic would the jury be better off without it?

---

233. *Van Wyk* (2000) at 524; following indented quotation at 523.

234. *Rush* (1871) at *3; following indented quotation at *4. The second quotation appears to be from a case I cannot access, *United States v. McGlue*, 1 Curtis C. C. 1. It is, at any rate, a statement about American law, not British. Whether Judge Pettit writes with an imperial "we" or is referring to his colleagues I do not know, but his meaning is clear, at *2:

> We are not enamored with expert testimony, however procured or presented.

If he is an expert, he should be better at this than the jurors, and therefore, it follows, of assistance to them.[235] If we cannot assess his fallibility, then why is he permitted to testify on adjudicative fact at all? He should be a legislative-fact witness, not referring to the specific facts of this case.

The Wisdom Rebuttal

As indicated above, some courts that have accepted forensic testimony, with conclusions, have had a hard time allowing legislative wisdom testimony for the defendant from professionals who have studied the subject and are skeptical that prosecution experts can make the distinctions they claim. "The defense attacks the very nature of the expertise of interpreting latent fingerprints," writes Judge Arenas, allowing the prosecution's fingerprint evidence.[236] The "very nature" attack implies that the other expert's data on how often he has been correct must itself be false. Defendant asserts that there can be no such data, because no expert can do what this expert says he has done.

The "very nature" defense is exactly that which Risinger, Saks, and Denbeaux espouse. Although I think they are empirically wrong, I see no justification for preventing a jury from hearing their side of the argument as long as it is clear that the expert's data evaluate his expertise, whereas defendant's data are generalizations about workers in the field. Although in the usual case empirical observation should be more acceptable than theoretical speculation, defendant should be allowed to attempt to counter the adjudicative craft expert with legislative-fact generalizations.

In *Velasquez* (1995), testimony of Mark Denbeaux

> was offered to educate the jury concerning the lack of published data supporting the accuracy of handwriting identification by questioned document examiners.[237]

Excluding it, the trial judge

> explained that "whether or not handwriting expertise is admissible in a courtroom" is a "legal" question that was resolved against the defense when the

---

235. Commentators get the wrong answer because they ask the wrong question. Consider this question, from Mark Brodin (2004) at 35:

> But how valid is this nearly universal (but untested) assumption that the jurors need assistance because they are not sophisticated enough to recognize that victims sometimes recant, give conflicting versions of the event, fail to report promptly, forget details, etc.?

The legislative-fact information that an expert could provide is how often victims do these things. Legal commentators ask binary questions, such as whether a witness might lie. The relevant question would be how often, how convincingly, in what circumstances, what kinds of witnesses tell what kinds of lies.

236. *Martinez* (2001) at 20.

237. Risinger and Saks (1996) at 32.

court permitted Ms. Bonjour to testify as a qualified expert in the field of handwriting analysis.[238]

Of course Denbeaux should be heard.[239] The Third Circuit correctly remanded the case with the instruction to allow Denbeaux to give his opinion that Bonjour cannot do what she says she does. If Bonjour would come to court with an assessment of how well she performs her work, the debate would then be how accurate that assessment is. That is the proper debate to have. Denbeaux's opinion, derived from his research, that no one else in the world can do it as well, might enhance Bonjour's credibility, not destroy it. Whether to offer such wisdom should be defendant's call.

Military courts and the Eleventh Circuit concluded the opposite: Denbeaux was deemed not sufficiently expert to present legislative-fact testimony for the defendant in *Ruth* (1995) and *Paul* (1999). Those courts, lacking a framework by which such wisdom would have been seen as serving their fact-finding interest, were wrong.

Conclusions are usually determined by how the discussion is framed. When the argument is presented by the attorneys as about entire fields, that is how *Daubert* assessments are determined. They need not be. In *Rutherford*,

> [forensic document examiner] Rauscher admitted that he was not given samples of anonymous writings and then given the questioned documents for the purpose of determining which one of the anonymous writers wrote the questioned documents. Instead, prior to Rauscher's analysis, the government identified the author of the exemplars (samples) and explained its theory that the writer of the exemplars and the checks was the author of the questioned documents (e.g., check and load-out sheet).[240]

Judge Bataillon seems to have been influenced by the literature about the bias created when a forensic examiner is essentially told what conclusion his employer would like him to reach. It is somewhat strange that critics stress that prior-knowledge aspect of forensic testimony. It characterizes *all* expert testimony. In Chapter 8 I stressed that a statistical expert should consider alternative explanations, not just "test" his client's theory for consistency with the facts. Similarly, we would judge more favorably the opinions of forensic examiners who had identified identical authorship from additional writings that had an air of similarity, but were not by the same writer. If some documents were detected *not* to

---

238. *Velasquez* (1995) at 846. The trial judge was Stanley S. Brotman. The government's expert was Lynn Bonjour.

239. James Starrs (1996), whose views can be taken as representative of those of "certified" forensic examiners, needless to say, disagrees. At 830:

> Denbeaux was a lawyer who was out moonlighting as a document examiner with an honesty chip on his shoulder.

240. *Rutherford* (2000) at 1193, transcript references omitted.

be from the same hand, we would be more inclined to believe a conclusion that some *were* from the same hand.[241]

Rauscher was also "precluded from testifying to opinions based on a precise degree of confidence or certainty" because no data or study leading to such a measure was offered to the judge.[242] The burden was properly placed on the party offering the expert. Failing to meet that burden, their expert should not have been permitted to reflect on adjudicative fact at all.

Sensing that forensic science is losing the battle for acceptance under *Daubert*, Jessica Sombat thinks forensic document examiner experts' interests would be served by this *Hines* approach.

> For the forensic community to stem the tide of challenges and regain a measure of certainty in its use of scientific evidence in the courtroom, courts should at least allow jury evaluations of evidence such as fingerprint evidence. Overall, this option presents a better outcome than the looming alternative— total exclusion.[243]

Supporters and critics alike are engaging in the wrong discussion, asking if forensic science is a science, finding that it isn't, and thereby concluding that it fails a *Daubert* test. The appropriate test is of technical, not scientific expertise; and that test is of the supposed craftsperson, the proffered expert, alone.

For another example, the Rhode Island Superior Court found that

> there is no quantifiable error rate regarding "false" repressed and recovered memories.[244]

Even if a repressed-memory wisdom expert estimated a field-wide error rate, it would be a measure of average craft excellence, not science, not this expert's craft. Apparently no expert took the technical role of trying to verify this plaintiff's facts. If one had, the question would have been *his* error rate. All of the wisdom experts, for both sides, agreed that the phenomenon did exist elsewhere. But does it exist here, in this case? They are wisdom

---

241. This is why "line-ups" are preferred over "show-ups" for eyewitness identification. We want the witness to say, "It's not him," about some people, to assure us there is some sense of intelligent discrimination.

242. *Rutherford* (2000) at 1194.

243. Sombat (2002) at 2867.

244. *Quattrocchi* (1999) at 11. The implication of the court's reasoning is that if enough people make false claims, they can destroy the believability of correct claims. The court's statement, at 10, finding that "repressed recollection has not been tested adequately to ensure the reliability and accuracy of the recovered memory" makes no sense, absent expert testimony affirming this memory recovery. Suppose we knew that repressed memory was 25 percent reliable—that three out of four "recovered memories" were false. Why would that information justify preventing the pursuit of this particular claim?

witnesses. They cannot say. Slavishly following legal writings about *Daubert*, the court was looking for something it could not get—a field-wide error rate—and should not have thought it needed.

I noted in Chapter 5 that the court is always faced with a continuum. What finding fact *means* in law is that the fact finder selects a binary outcome (guilty or innocent, liable or not, monopolist or competitor, did or did not discriminate, etc.) from the probabilistic evidence. Part of the solution to the *Daubert* conundrum—how to assess science and technical testimony—is to maintain that dichotomy between the expert presenter's probabilistic evidence and the fact finder's binary determination. If no probabilities are presented, then no expert adjudicative evidence can be presented. That should not exclude wisdom testimony and pursuit of claims. It just excludes science and craft.

My framework asks that both the model and statistics of verification be presented to the fact finder. Both handwriting and fingerprint identification should be allowed as probabilistic evidence, not as fact.[245] Other forensic "sciences," such as forensic entomology, seem to me to have much to offer the fact-finding process.[246] Faced with a craft expert, the court needs to know how often *he* is wrong, not how often *they* (his peers) are wrong. Showing how often *this* expert errs should be the burden of his proponent (his client), a sine qua non of his testimony. If the other side wants the fact finder to know how often *other* experts have been wrong, it should be allowed to present that information through a wisdom expert.

Letting It All In

In one tradition, all evidence either side wants to submit is allowed in a trial. The fact finder, be it judge or jury, is charged with filtering it, weighing it, and drawing a conclusion from it. In the following recent cases, forensic expert testimony was allowed, conclusion and all: *Starzecpyzel* (1995), *Velasquez* (1995), *Crumby* (1995), *Sherwood* (1996), *Jones* (1997), *Battle* (1999), *Coon* (1999), *Paul* (1999), *Havvard* (2000) and *Havvard* (Seventh Circuit, 2001), *Jolivet* (2000), *Rogers* (2001), *Joseph* (2001), *Martinez* (2001), *Mitchell* (2002), *Cline* (2002), *Hernandez 8* (2002), *Gricco* (2002), *Mooney* (2002, rejecting the Gertner compromise),

---

245. Saks (1998), the best source for outlining the history and issues in legal assessment of handwriting, fingerprint and DNA evidence, fails to realize this solution. "A vote for science is a vote to exclude fingerprint expert opinions," he writes, at 1106. Sombat (2002) seems equally unable to impose a probabilistic requirement on expert testimony. She endorses the *Llera Plaza I* solution: Let the jurors decide if the latent and exemplar prints match. These solutions deprive the professional of using, and explaining, whatever expertise he has. These writers are trying to fit craft into a science mold. I say let's accept that these experts are crafts-people, and develop procedures to deal with them.

246. Using insects found with remains to date death, for example, is a popular aspect of crime solving on television "documentary" programs. Is it wrong? See Erzinçlioğlu (2000).

Mustapha (2002) and *Mustapha* (Seventh Circuit, 2004), *Crisp* (2003), *Rutland* (2004), and *Mahone* (2004).[247] In many of these opinions we read about a "longstanding tradition" or history of accepting forensic evidence, an unwillingness to depart from "the well-traveled path." Some judges have commented on the lack of specificity in the challenge, putting the burden on the opponent to discredit the specific expert, while his only credit was his credentials and the supposed expertise of the "field." Others have utilized the liberality of *Daubert* standards to allow testimony that critics, writing in law reviews, would suppress.

Once again, we need a better framework in which to discuss these issues than the over-encompassing "science" framework. The "field" concept, left over from *Frye*, should go first. Then all proffered expert testimony would be allowed at the *Daubert* hearing, at which the judge would determine what kind of testimony this is: science, technical, engineering, or wisdom. The judge would require that probabilities be associated with the testimony (which of course can be challenged, defended, etc.): If science, then with the specific task, and if technical, then with the specific witness.

In 1834 the Supreme Court of Massachusetts admitted handwriting analysis to detect a forgery:

> On the whole, the Court are of opinion, that this species of evidence, though generally very slight, and often wholly immaterial, is competent evidence, and was properly admitted in the present case.[248]

It should have been properly admitted only with a measure of *how* slight the evidence is, for otherwise the court cannot control the impact of this evidence on the fact finder. It must require an assessment of the witness' ability in terms of the probability of his being wrong.

Gatekeeping, then, proceeds in adjudicative terms: Not *can* this expert make the distinction he claims to make, at all, but *how well* can he do so? The criterion of judicial acceptance should be comparative: It helps if the jury will perform better with it than with-

---

247. *Mitchell* (2004), affirming *Mitchell* (2002), is particularly notable in its description of the *Daubert* process in which multiple experts appeared for both sides. Also interesting is the length to which the FBI went to validate its match of Mitchell's rolled prints with latent prints from the crime. Their statistical tests may miss the mark, but that they did them at all indicates the impact the opponents of forensic testimony have had.

Mahone (2004) is also notable, in that Cynthia D. Homer, the expert in footwear analysis, gave her error rate as zero. Judge Woodcock explained, at 91, that

> the error rate of the process itself is zero, meaning any error is the result of examiner error.

Then he held that

> *Daubert* merely requires the proponent demonstrate the known or potential error rate of the methodology and the Court is satisfied the Government has done so in this case.

He has it backward. All that matters is this expert's error rate. Every forensic science has described *its* error rate as zero, regardless of the error rates of its practitioners.

248. *Moody* (1834) at 497.

out it.[249] An expert who is correct one-third of the time may be informative, if lay people are correct even less often. However correct this expert is, the state of the "field" is irrelevant at the *Daubert* hearing.[250]

In a murder trial in the late 1970s, a handwriting expert declared that a certain piece of evidence was a forgery. That would have meant that the defendant didn't do it. A fingerprint expert testified that a certain latent print was the defendant's, meaning that he did do it. Years later, after he had been found guilty, sufficient evidence was gathered to show that he was not. The reviewing court found that

> The fingerprint expert's testimony was damning—and it was false. It was unquestionably material; its significance should not be underestimated. . . . [Steven] Sedlacek's testimony . . . destroyed the credibility of the testimony of appellant's handwriting expert that the address on the envelope was forged.[251]

This handwriting expert surely contributed valuable information to the case, but Steven Sedlacek did not. One would hope that Sedlacek never again testified with certainty.

The adjudicative expert's opinion per se is almost never in doubt. Whose witness is this? Once again, attorneys are engaged in a silly game. Just as I, as an expert, knew what opinion my client wanted me to find, the jury surely knows what opinion the expert espouses about the evidence he is dissecting. Prohibited in the Gertner compromise from overtly stating that opinion, the adjudicative expert cannot provide any detailed reasoning behind it. Preventing his opinion testimony accomplishes nothing positive.

---

249. Eschewing a need for opinion surveys, Judge Styn ruled that he could determine whether advertisements were misleading:

> The judge should not have to exclude himself or herself as a person of ordinary intelligence and a reasonable consumer.

He concludes:

> Considering that the advertisement speaks for itself, the judge is in a position to determine whether it is misleading, i.e. likely to deceive, under a "reasonable consumer" standard.

Park (2003) at *5. The judge draws lines from a continuum. That is his job. However, I question whether this judge is assessing the correct continuum.

250. Even outside of the debate by professors of law, condemnation of whole fields proceeds without asking whether individuals, using methods they can explain, can discern information that can be helpful when it is correct, and can document how often that occurs. "If a psychological test cannot discriminate reliably," notes Frederick Crews in the *New York Review of Books* on July 15, 2004, at 25 (cited above in footnote 199), ". . . it is a public menace and ought to be dropped forthwith." He is stronger about this than the authors of the book he is reviewing who, he says, "take a firm stand only about the urgency of getting the Rorschach out of the courtroom." If judges understood how to evaluate technical experts, and critics understood that no other review but that of the proffered expert is necessary, perhaps such crusades would disappear.

251. *Caldwell* (1982) at 586.

The Wisdom Expert

In Chapter 8 I introduced the idea that a witness may impart knowledge that is not an assessment of adjudicative fact, that provides help in processing more than in concluding. I folded that testimony into my expert framework, above, defining a "wisdom" witness. As such a witness would not present a study of the individual circumstance, he is perforce a legislative-fact expert. He will draw no adjudicative conclusion. John Strong seems to think that all experts are wisdom experts, that

> the essential function of the expert witness is to supply propositions of general knowledge which may play a part in the reasoning of the trier of fact.[252]

This approach is unhelpful. In terms of my framework, it is wrong. The scientific, technical, or engineering expert's function is to provide specific conclusions (opinions) drawn from methodology appropriate to the issues of this case, using data from this case and perhaps more-general data also. Providing "propositions of general knowledge" defines the wisdom expert, not experts in general.

For Larry Hall, the defendant, Richard Ofshe

> would have testified about the fact that experts in his field agree that false confessions exist, that individuals can be coerced into giving false confessions, and that certain indicia can be identified to show when they are likely to occur.[253]

That is, he would have imparted information to the jury, though it could be challenged. On its own, the jury would unlikely be knowledgeable about this issue. However, Ofshe was not allowed to testify at trial. The Seventh Circuit appropriately vacated the conviction, concluding that the defendant "was entitled to present his defense to the jury with the use of expert testimony." The lower court should determine if Ofshe could provide such testimony.

Judge McDade had some trouble understanding how to follow this mandate, ultimately concluding that

> testimony which is simply not amenable to the scientific method should not be subjected to the strictures of *Daubert* and instead can pass as "specialized knowledge."[254]

---

252. Strong (1992) at 355. He elucidates, at 353:
    > In fact, knowledge of general propositions is what enables the expert to form an opinion, and it is this knowledge, not the possession of an opinion, which makes an expert an expert.

253. *Hall* (1996a) at 1341; following in-text quotation at 1346.

254. *Hall* (1997) at 1200; following two indented quotations both at 1205.

Thus the judge concluded that social psychology is a "soft" science. That freed him from *Daubert*, he thought, but not from Rule 702. Because the concept of a "field" is so ingrained in legal practice, the judge determined that

> the science of social psychology, and specifically the field involving the use of coercion in interrogations, is sufficiently developed in its methods to constitute a reliable body of specialized knowledge under Rule 702.

Ofshe could show that he was an experienced member of this "sufficiently developed" field. In other words, freed from *Daubert*, the judge used *Frye* criteria.

> Thus, he can testify that false confessions do exist, that they are associated with the use of certain police interrogation techniques, and that certain of those techniques were used in Hall's interrogation in this case. Dr. Ofshe cannot explicitly testify about matters of causation, specifically, whether the interrogation methods used in this case caused Hall to falsely confess.

Ofshe became a wisdom witness. He could say with some authority that Hall's defense was not bonkers, without saying that, in his opinion, it was true. I suggest that, with my framework in hand, the court would have gotten to this conclusion at the initial hearing, and done so under *Daubert*, not around it.

The lesson: A fact finder sometimes can benefit from hearing someone who has thought about how to think about certain issues, or simply has specialized background knowledge. This combination of analysis and fact may be thought of as the "social framework" evidence discussed by Laurens Walker and John Monahan, although such testimony may be delivered by other than social scientists.[255] Consider FBI agent James Kossler's testimony in an antitrust case:

> Kossler's testimony was, by and large, general insofar as it described organized crime's infiltration of labor unions and did not touch upon Matthews's payments to Daly or Miron or the subsequent payment to Matthews. Kossler did not mention Local 638 except to identify its trade jurisdiction; he did not mention Daly, Miron, or Giardina at all, and he did not testify at all with respect to any of the tapes on which Giardina was heard and Daly was discussed.[256]

---

255. See Walker and Monahan (1987), at 560:

> The application of social science in these disparate areas does not concern legislative fact, since no rule of law is at issue. Neither does it concern adjudicative fact, since the research does not involve the parties before the court. We propose the concept of social frameworks to refer to these uses of general conclusions from social-science research in determining factual issues in a specific case.

Clearly I use the phrase "legislative fact" differently. Distinguishing the same presentation, one of general social-science research findings, by whether it is used to support a "finding of fact" or a "ruling of law," strikes me as fatuous, especially in light of the confusion between the two discussed in Chapter 7.

256. *Daly* (1988) at 1388, Judge Kearse writing for an affirming Second Circuit panel.

Kossler's testimony today would have to be characterized as expert, then tested and found valid. Similar testimony has been sustained uncomfortably, though I think correctly, post-*Daubert*.[257]

Mark Brodin tells us that Massachusetts courts have drawn a fine line:

---

257. As Judge Pooler wrote for the Second Circuit in *Mulder* (2001), at 101:

> Labor coalitions and their goals are not well known or commonly understood. Nor are their history and tactics.

Thus experts Daniel O'Rourke and James McNamara could provide such background information. In particular, at 101, "O'Rourke did not give any specific testimony concerning BFB's activities," where BFB, Brooklyn Fight Back, is

> a labor coalition that extorted money and jobs, including no-show jobs, from contractors operating in New York City.

At 98. And, again at 101:

> McNamara suggested that placement of minority laborers at job sites by coalitions did not increase the overall percentage of minorities because the coalitions often demanded that the contractors fire existing minority workers who were not members of the threatening coalition.

> In *Lopez* (2002), a drug-smuggling case, a U.S. Customs Service agent was called upon to explain the meaning of GPS coordinates found on the boat and to explain the range of cellular telephones at sea.

At 14. His testimony was kept at the level of general information about apparatus found on the defendants' boat. Again at 14:

> Appellants have made no reasoned argument to support the claim that GPS, GPS coordinates, their level of accuracy, nautical charts, marine navigation, and the role of all of these things in drug-smuggling operations are common knowledge.

The only legitimate issue, therefore, was whether this agent possessed true wisdom, whether what he described to the jury as legislative fact was correct. That seems to be the one challenge defendants did not make.

Testifying for Morgan Stanley's defense,

> [William Bielby] may properly testify about gender stereotypes, and about how these stereotypes may have affected decisions at Morgan Stanley. He may also testify regarding whether policies and practices relating to gender bias might affect employees' utilization of an equal-employment-opportunity program, but may not seek to show that alleged deficiencies in such a program are evidence of discrimination.

Morgan Stanley (2004) at 462. Magistrate Judge Ellis has a good grasp of the limits of wisdom testimony, lacking only the language and larger framework I provide here.

Attorneys, as well as judges, need to learn these distinctions. For example, in *Spriggs* (1996), special agent Dwight Rawls is described at 1256 as a wisdom witness:

> Rawls explained drug terminology the jury would hear on undercover tapes, methods used by drug dealers to launder money, and law-enforcement efforts to detect money laundering, including "sting" operations.

However, Rawls went on to discuss adjudicative matters, such as where drugs were sold. The reviewing court agreed that he should not have, but allowed it because defendants' attorneys had not objected at the time.

> A qualified witness may testify to the general behavioral characteristics and com-
> mon clinical phenomena of sexually abused children or other victims, but may
> not directly or indirectly refer to or compare the behavior of the specific com-
> plainant because that intrudes on the jury's province of assessing credibility.[258]

The witness should not have examined the person in question. In short, Massachusetts allows psychologists as wisdom witnesses, but not as technical witnesses. Excluding all technical testimony of a kind, without allowing it to be proffered and judged in a *Daubert* hearing, makes no sense; but allowing legislative-fact testimony from wisdom witnesses makes good sense.

Indeed, expert testimony on legislative fact is so ingrained in Massachusetts law that it is not clear whether it deserves special attention after *Daubert*. For example, in 1910:

> It is settled, that a general trade usage may be introduced to supply un-
> expressed terms in a contract. . . . The witness testifies to the existence of a fact
> from actual knowledge, acquired through observation and experience in the
> business; but he cannot give his opinion.[259]

So, for example, even if a contract did not say where delivery was to take place, an expert could say that delivery at the recipient's place of business would normally satisfy the contract. He is not to say that in this case, in his opinion, delivery satisfied the contract. Similarly, more than eighty-five years later, the First Circuit reversed the exclusion of an expert who would have said that "a minority participant veto is the industry norm" in joint banking deals. Even though—or perhaps because—the proffered expert had been a vice-president of the plaintiff bank, his knowledge of such practices over forty years in the industry deserved to be heard.[260]

Mark Binder was convicted of sexual molestation. There was no physical evidence, and he denied having done it. The children testified that he had. "Experts" testified that these children were credible. As the circuit court explained, reversing:

> The testimony of the experts in this case was not limited to references to psy-
> chological literature or experience or to a discussion of a class of victims gen-
> erally. Rather the experts testified that these particular children in this par-
> ticular case could be believed.[261]

---

258. Brodin (2004) at 54.

259. *Barrie* (1910) at 264 and then at 265.

260. *Den Norske* (1996); in-text quotation at 58.

261. *Binder* (1985) at 602. Judge Skopil's opinion goes too far:
> The effect of the expert witnesses' testimony was . . . to usurp the jury's fact-finding
> function.

The jury was free to find fact as the expert saw it or not. But the jury was not informed how wrong these experts could be and had been. It had no basis on which to evaluate their testimony. *That* was the error.

If such craft testimony is to be allowed, it must be presented with an evaluation of the experts' accuracy in making such assessments. Alternatively, these experts could have provided wisdom testimony about situations like this, were they qualified to do so, without reference to the children at issue.

Julio Elvin Ruiz Cintron had been killed in a car crash while trying to pass a Pepsi-Cola truck. His heirs sued the bottling company. A toxicology report, prepared during his autopsy, revealed the presence of cocaine in his system. Judge Acosta excluded defendant's expert, who would have extrapolated from the toxicology report to determine when Ruiz Cintron might have ingested the cocaine, and how it would have impaired his driving. As long as the expert could have informed the court about his abilities (not his credentials), and they reached some level of accuracy beyond lay knowledge, he should have been allowed to testify.

There now being no expert to explain the report, Judge Acosta excluded the report itself. That action was too drastic, but the judge knew of no mechanism by which to inform the jury in legislative-fact terms what the toxicology report meant.[262] There is one: the wisdom (expert) witness.

Jack Woolley testified that the plaintiff was "within the breathing zone" of harmful fumes from hot-melt glue.[263] The three empirical questions are 1) how much fume would survive at given distances from the source (knowing how much of the toxic chemicals in the hot-melt glue evaporates in the process); 2) what harm occurs for any given amount of such fumes (over specified amounts of time); and 3) how far from the source the plaintiff was, for how long. Woolley's knowledge to answer the first question is legislative fact

---

262. The First Circuit did not find merit in this exclusion, remanding for a new trial in *Ruiz Troche* (1998). The proffered testimony of James O'Donnell, described, at 82, as "a well-credentialed pharmacologist," does seem to be a good example of technical expertise based on—though not itself—science. But let's assume that O'Donnell did not come prepared with data on the correctness of his previous interpretations. Then the notion of a wisdom expert comes into play. He can explain what data are provided in a toxicology report and the findings in the literature about what they mean.

Similarly, Fred Dunbar's testimony was excluded in *Electric* (2004), due to bias in the selection of his data. Yet, at 236:

> Dr. Dunbar's report could certainly aid the jurors by helping them understand the basic economic principles of market power, the concept of distinct markets, and other economic intricacies this case involves.

Understanding that Dunbar's biased data did not obviate other observations he might make, Magistrate Judge Francis determined, at 240:

> Dr. Dunbar may, however, offer expert testimony to the extent that it is not dependent on the biased data.

Had my categories been available to Judge Francis, he might have excluded Dunbar as a science witness, but allowed him as a wisdom witness.

263. *McCullock* (1995). Woolley's acceptance as an adjudicative-fact expert was justified by his background, at 1042–1043.

presumably within his area of expertise (engineering). He probably should have been excluded from answering the second question. That is another expert's turf. He may well have qualified as a wisdom witness, knowing nothing about this plaintiff, and therefore not being able to answer the third question. Nonetheless, he was erroneously allowed to present an adjudicative conclusion, for lack of a framework in which his testimony could have been classified and restricted.

That recordings of conversations among Gambino (crime) family members would need translation is easily believable. Who would do it? How would he be presented to the jury?

> Because the recordings contained code names and were generally vague in identifying relevant people and places (often using pronouns instead of proper nouns), the government qualified the investigating FBI agent, Gregory Hagarty, as an expert so that he could interpret the tapes for the jury.[264]

This is a role for a wisdom witness. However, Hagarty

> frequently testified about the intended references of certain pronouns and general terms. For example, when an individual on one of the recordings said "I got two different issues from two different guys," the Court permitted Agent Hagarty to state his opinion that the "two guys" were [defendants] Scala and Carneglia and the "two issues" were the two different parts of the Cherry Video extortion. The defendants argue that, because Agent Hagarty's opinion as to the meaning of these references was not based upon an interpretation of Mafia code language, the District Court should not have permitted him to testify about their intended meaning.

Defendants are surely correct, in the well-defined context of the "wisdom witness" I offer here. Under the federal rules, however, the judge has discretion to allow such wanderings between legislative and adjudicative fact, and no guidance how to administer that discretion. The appeals court let it stand. The rules should be changed so such confused roles do not occur.

I will not suggest how such wisdom testimony would be evaluated in a *Daubert* hearing. One kind of wisdom expert proposes to inform the court about legislative fact from his own studies. He claims to have done relevant science outside of this litigation. Jack Woolley was such an expert. His work, then, can be disputed by the other party and evaluated.[265]

---

264. *Carneglia* (2002) at 30; following indented quotation at 32.

265. See, for example, the *Daubert* examination of the proffered testimony of Eric Gershwin in *Allison* (1999). At 1317:

> While we do not question the scientific expertise of Dr. Gershwin, we find the district court correctly excluded his testimony.

So the proper distinction is made between the expert and his work, his exclusion being based on the latter.

Another kind of wisdom expert is the reporter, usually an academic who has studied and taught from a relevant literature.

> Social scientists in particular may be able to show that commonly accepted explanations for behavior are, when studied more closely, inaccurate. These results sometimes fly in the face of conventional wisdom.[266]

Wisdom, in other words, may or may not coincide with "conventional wisdom."

Solomon Fulero was proffered to provide wisdom about eyewitness identification. The defendant had a large, visible scar on his neck. Fulero would describe "detail salience," that people observing unusual events (in this case a bank robbery) focus on unusual characteristics. It was not his job to say that, as no witness mentioned the scar, their identification was unreliable. District-judge Cohn determined that Fulero's was "not a scientifically valid opinion," though as he had not held a *Daubert* hearing, the Sixth Circuit remanded the case (reversing the conviction) for a better determination.[267]

The Seventh Circuit reviewed the proffer of a wisdom expert, Otto Maclin, who also would have clarified problems in eyewitness identification, without assessing the accuracy of these particular identifications.

> In this case, both parties agree that Dr. Maclin utilized reasoning and methodology that was scientifically valid. The only disputed issue is thus whether this information would have been of assistance to the jury.[268]

Of course juries know that eyewitness identification is fallible, but do they know how fallible, or under what conditions it is more or less fallible? The court considered the circumstances in this case different from those of most of the eyewitness literature:

> Unlike most eyewitnesses, the eyewitnesses in this case knew the defendant very well prior to the crime.

The fit between the literature the wisdom witness is relying on and the facts of this case can be brought out in cross-examination. We do not know how Maclin would have replied to questions about this distinction. His exclusion was affirmed, I think wrongly.

Should the strength with which an eyewitness holds his opinion influence the jury's determination of its accuracy? While the jury is determining whether the identification is accurate, without guidance from a wisdom expert about characteristics of fallibility, might not a question about relationship between the witness's confidence and accuracy occur to jurors? If so, how are they to answer it? Without assistance, according to the Second Circuit, in another mistaken opinion. The Seventh Circuit also, sadly,

---

266. *Tyus* (1996) at 263.

267. *Smithers* (2000); in-text quotation at 310.

268. *Welch* (2004) at 973; following indented quotation at 974.

has a long line of cases which reflect our disfavor of expert testimony on the reliability of eyewitness identification.[269]

My distinctions never having been made before, *Daubert* litigation and literature provide no guidance on when wisdom testimony should be considered, or how it should be assessed. Perhaps legislative-fact science testimony requires some other screening entirely. The judge needs to determine how useful such testimony is likely to be in order to allow it, but this notion that correct legislative-fact information does more harm to the jury than good, even if the jury's preconceptions are erroneous, is bizarre.

> A court should not dismiss scientific knowledge about everyday subjects. Science investigates the mundane as well as the exotic. That a subject is within daily experience does not mean that jurors know it *correctly*.[270]

Not only may the researcher on a topic not claim to be an expert craftsperson, he may, like Saks and Denbeaux on handwriting analysis, think there can be no such thing. Was Solomon Fulero making up this "detail salience" concept, or would he present studies showing the frequency with which a witness would have observed such features before

---

269. Seventh Circuit quotation from the majority opinion by Judge Kanne in *Hall* (1999) at 1104. The Second Circuit opinion is *Lumpkin* (1999). At 288:

> Williams sought to offer testimony from his expert witness, Dr. Lieppe, that the degree of confidence a witness purports to have in his or her identification does not correlate to the accuracy of that identification. Specifically, during an *in limine* hearing, Dr. Lieppe relied on and summarized a series of scientific studies, all of which conclude that confidence in identification is not a good predictor of accuracy. The trial court precluded Dr. Lieppe from testifying on this issue at trial, ruling the testimony might confuse or mislead the jury.

The "finding" that the certainty of the eyewitness does not reflect the accuracy of the identification was perhaps first made by Hugo Munsterberg in the early part of the twentieth century. As Doyle (2005) summarized, at 21:

> Munsterberg's collected experiments showed that memory is . . . a complex process of perception, storage, and recall, vulnerable at every stage to suggestion, distortion, and omission. This was very bad news for legal procedure.

It led to a debate with John Henry Wigmore, as I hinted in Chapter 1, although the two were on good terms, and were pursuing the same goal. Now, one hundred years later, it is recognized as a truth of which jurors, faced with eyewitness testimony, perhaps should be made aware.

270. Judge Easterbrook, concurring in *Hall* (1999), at 1118. Easterbrook concurs because the question he would like to explore was not put forward by defendant's counsel. At 1120:

> His lawyers did not appreciate the big difference between the expert evidence considered on the first appeal and the evidence offered on remand. . . . [T]he expert testimony in the first trial was about an adjudicative fact; the proposed expert testimony in the second trial would have concerned a legislative fact.

I insert this note here for the skeptical reader who thinks that my distinctions have been unimportant, or important but commonly known. As Easterbrook could not explore this subject, we do not have the benefit of his thinking on how courts might assess the "scientific validity" of a legislative-fact presentation. However, we do have the benefit of his agreeing that it is an important issue.

anything else?[271] The court rightly considered Maclin's concept of "clothing bias" to be jargon for something we all know—that if we think we see an identifiable piece of clothing, we may wrongly identify the person wearing it—but we know it as a possibility, not a frequency. Why would the court prefer that the jury guess about the extent of one's susceptibility to it? The Second Circuit expert who relied on studies to say that the strength of an identification opinion is no indication of its reliability was not criticized as being incorrect, only as potentially confusing to the jurors. How? Would an expert explaining where in DNA analysis one might create error, without contending that such error occurred in this case, and not trying to eliminate DNA identification in theory, be unhelpful? Doubt is not necessarily confusion. The former is a proper juridical response to alleged fact.

Discussing repressed memory, earlier in this chapter, I suggested that there probably can be no technical testimony, no adjudicative evaluation of a particular "victim's" recall, because there is no way to evaluate an "expert's" ability to make such an assessment. Wisdom testimony in contrast, informing a jury by whom the notion of repressed memory is accepted, and why, could be helpful. A broader topic is the credibility of fact witnesses in general. In *Dunkle* (1992), the Supreme Court of Pennsylvania took a position against wisdom testimony for such issues:

> We hold that expert testimony concerning typical behavior patterns exhibited by sexually abused children should not have been admissible in the case before us. We also hold that it was error to permit an expert to explain why sexually abused children may not recall certain details of the assault, why they may not give complete details, and why they may delay reporting the incident.[272]

In subsequent decisions that court affirmed, expanded, and explained its position as not allowing wisdom testimony to assist jury determination of the credibility of a witness:

> Here, appellant's expert would have testified generally about the reliability of eyewitness identification. Such testimony would have given an unwarranted appearance of authority as to the subject of credibility, a subject which an ordinary juror can assess.
>
> Credibility is an issue uniquely entrusted to the common understanding of laypersons. The teaching of Dunkle is that expert testimony will not be permitted when it attempts in any way to reach the issue of credibility, and thereby usurp the function of the fact finder.[273]

---

271. Defendant Smithers was over six feet five inches tall, a characteristic every witness mentioned—although so was his brother, who had keys to the car used in the robbery, but apparently was never put in front of the witnesses. Is the scar "salient" given his height?

272. *Dunkle* (1992) at 171.

273. *Simmons* (1995) at 231, then *Delbridge* (2003) at 12. In *DJA* (2002) the Pennsylvania Superior Court differentiated between wisdom testimony and technical testimony, between legislative-fact generalities

That a "common understanding of laypersons" should not be enhanced with expert knowledge—if it *is* expert, as determined in some variant of a *Daubert* hearing—is resupinate. Fortunately, not all states hold it. The New Jersey Supreme Court took a more enlightened position, allowing wisdom experts:

> to aid the jury by explaining the coercive or suggestive propensities of the interviewing techniques employed, but not of course, to offer opinions as to the issue of a child-witness's credibility.[274]

As the literature heretofore has failed to articulate a reasonable framework within which wisdom testimony is differentiated from adjudicative-fact science, engineering, or technical testimony, states make it up as they go along. They often make it up badly because they, too, think they do not need help in that determination.

In *Elsayed* (2002),

> Dr. David Wellman, an expert witness who has devoted much of his career to investigating how racism persists without open bigotry, testified that race was a factor in CSUH's decision to deny Elsayed tenure.[275]

That is, he testified as an adjudicative expert. Wellman reached the conclusion one would expect, given this description of who he is. The Ninth Circuit panel was clearly skeptical that Wellman's testimony would be acceptable under *Daubert*, and sent the case back for Judge Wilkin to assess its "reliability." Judge Wilkin had preferred that Wellman testify only about "general factors that would lead to such decisions," but she had no framework within which to limit Wellman's testimony that way.[276] He might have been an acceptable wisdom witness, informing the jury how discrimination can occur, but surely his ad hoc analysis of this particular tenure denial cannot pass a "science" test. Just as surely, Wellman can pro-

---

and adjudicative-fact opinions (though not using this language). However, faced with an adjudicative assessment of an interviewer's having "tainted" a child's recollection, and disagreeing with the trial judge's acceptance of that finding, it reversed, citing *Dunkle* as the rule and anticipating clarification in *Delbridge*.

274. *Michaels* (1994) at 323. See also *Allen* (1996), where the appeals court affirmed, the trial court having allowed the generalized testimony of an expert on child interview techniques. At 463:

> However, the trial judge refused to allow the defense expert to comment specifically on the questions employed in the videotape itself, on the basis that such opinions would impermissibly comment on the children's credibility.

I take this to mean that wisdom testimony was allowed, but technical (adjudicative) testimony was not.

275. *Elsayed* (2002) at 1061. "CSUH" is California State University at Hayward.

276. District-court judge Wilkin, quoted in *Elsayed* (2002) at 1065. In addition to amending its earlier decision, the Ninth Circuit denied a hearing *en banc* in *Elsayed* (2003). In a vigorous dissent, Judge Reinhardt also notes that the panel has not indicated what conclusion they would expect from a full *Daubert* hearing, and argues that the remand should have been for such a hearing, not a new trial. The same problem that hampered the lower court is apparent here: There is no standard by which to assess an expert who would impart legislative-fact wisdom to the jury.

duce no record of being judged "correct" in his assessments, the requirement within my framework of a technical witness.

A corollary of this delineation of a wisdom witness is that, once such a role is established, that person cannot also be an adjudicative-fact witness. It is not possible to keep the two roles distinct. For example, in a child-sexual-assault case, the examining psychologist was

> the first person to whom the child victim disclosed the abuse, the person who reported the abuse to SRS, and far and away the State's most important witness.[277]

He was called upon to generalize about such cases, as an expert, and, having established his expertise, he then directly supported this child's credibility. Surely an examining psychologist can relate what transpired during the patient's visits, including his having reported "abuse" to the authorities.[278] An expert whose role has been defined to say that some girls who describe abuse by their fathers are truthful cannot say that this particular girl is. Justice Gibson, dissenting (arguing that the testimony should have been permitted), is confused because the appropriate categories of experts have not been articulated: A legislative-fact expert simply cannot draw an adjudicative-fact conclusion.

---

277. *Weeks* (1993) at 401.

278. McCord (1986) summarizes, at 43:

> [T]he clear weight of authority is that an expert's opinion that a child sexual abuse complainant is telling the truth should not be admissible

Although McCord writes pre-*Daubert*, this summary holds today. McCord tells us, at 44, that

> behavioral scientists themselves recognize that they have no particular expertise in evaluating the credibility of a child sexual abuse complainant.

An eyewitnesses to a robbery can say, "I believed him when he said he would shoot me," as an explanation for the witness's behavior. It is not confused with an expert opinion about the robber's credibility. We evaluate fact witnesses and experts differently. The difficult question is whether an examining psychologist or physician is an "expert" by the very nature of his work. Most courts do not allow a medical professional to express an opinion on the credibility of a particular witness, or particular witness statements, for fear that the jury will accept the expert as a "truth detector." Although McCord, at 25, thinks this judicial fear is overdone, he inveighs, at 52, against allowing expert adjudicative testimony concerning the veracity of child testimony:

> [T]he testimony should not be admitted because the importance of the testimony is very high while the reliability of the testimony is very low.

I argue here, as I have throughout this chapter, against such sweeping generalized exclusions. Technical experts should be able to testify about veracity if they come with credible evidence of their accuracy in doing so. Alternatively, as we now have a formal *Daubert* process for certifying experts, it should be easy enough for a judge to inform the jury that a particular witness who is not proffered as a technical expert (or did not pass the *Daubert* review) cannot say *as an expert* that this child was credible. Thus, once the concept of a wisdom expert is understood and accepted, it should free up others to be lay fact witnesses whose "opinions" are embedded in descriptions of their behavior.

Mary Capelli-Schellpfeffer was proffered as an adjudicative expert, part of the team of physicians that had examined the plaintiff, Richard Walker.

> She was also prepared to testify that it was not unusual for electrical injuries
> to first manifest themselves long after the electrical trauma that caused them,
> as Mr. Walker argued his did.[279]

Neither Magistrate Judge Keys, who excluded her testimony, nor the Seventh Circuit panel that reinstated it, considered the possibility that if she should not be allowed to conclude that Walker had post-traumatic stress disorder, she still might be allowed to testify to the legislative-fact proposition quoted above.

In another case of confused roles, Keith Mathis

> sought to present testimony from Dr. Geoffrey Loftus regarding the reliability
> of eyewitness identifications such as Sergeant Gubbei's.[280]

As stated, this would be wisdom testimony. However, Loftus came to adjudicative conclusions:

> In applying these principles to hypothetical questions intended to simulate the
> facts of this case, Dr. Loftus stated that "it's two to three times as likely that the
> identification in the photo montage was made based on seeing the photograph
> four weeks earlier than it was based on seeing the individual" who fled on
> October 14, 1998.

District-judge Lechner did not let Loftus testify. Although affirming the conviction despite this "harmless error," the Third Circuit reversed that exclusion. The problem here is the adjudicative conclusion, which Loftus had neither scientific reason nor technical expertise to make. Once again, the trial judge needed a clear procedure within which Loftus could discuss eyewitness identification in general, but not the specifics of this case.[281]

Fact witnesses, as the Iowa Supreme Court noted in *Grismore* (1942), may believe what they say with the same certainty professed by an expert; but they too may be wrong. Thus the possibility of error does not disqualify one from testifying in the most fundamental, life-determining situation. That is why Loftus' testimony in *Mathis* (2001) — although he does not seem to have considered that the fact witness was a policeman,

---

279. *Walker* (2000) at 588.

280. *Mathis* (2001) at 333; following indented quotation at 334.

281. We see here again why the compromise fashioned by Judge Gertner does not work. Loftus went on to claim that there was zero probability that Sergeant Grubbei's identification was correct. Judge Gertner would have allowed a discussion of adjudicative fact, but prevented Loftus from giving that opinion. A better solution is to limit Loftus' testimony to generalities, to research results. The surprise in this *Mathis* decision, however, is that it was written by Judge Louis Pollak, the district-court judge (sitting as an appeals-court judge) who had been so critical of FBI testimony on handwriting. He thinks Loftus' testimony was so clearly acceptable that the lower court erred in excluding it?

possibly an expert at identification—might have been helpful if limited to legislative fact.

Witnesses differ in their ability to make the distinction they are being called upon to make:

> The research is clear: Some people are quite good at identifying speakers from their voices, and other people are terrible at it. . . .
>
> The legal system does not recognize such differences in skill. The rules of evidence certainly do not, and we have never seen a published opinion in which this issue is raised.[282]

I hinted above that one might want to test an eyewitness for his ability to distinguish among persons of similar stature. As it stands, such witnesses can be challenged only by legislative-fact evidence on the general fallibility of assertions like theirs. A person presenting research results on the accuracy of eyewitness identification would not be a science expert, because he would be drawing no testable conclusion about this case. Nor would he be a technical expert, because he would not be offering an opinion about this case.

Consider the following:

> Dr. Greene was prepared to testify that (1) contrary to popular belief, high levels of stress impair rather than improve memory; (2) the tendency of victims to focus on the weapon used during the crime reduces their ability to recall details about the offender's appearance; (3) there is no correlation between a witness's expression of confidence in his or her identification of a suspect and the accuracy of that witness's recollection; and (4) a witness's viewing of a composite drawing or photograph can influence the witness's memory of the criminal.[283]

This information would be valuable to a jury, though it is not adjudicative "science" testimony. A wisdom witness such as Edith Greene would be subject to cross-examination. Yet

---

282. Solan and Tiersma (2003) at 401, then at 402. Solan and Tiersma so misstate the results from Bradfield and Wells (2000) that we should be skeptical of their summary of others' research. Competence is surely an important consideration in admitting wisdom testimony. It deserves as much scrutiny as in adjudicative-fact testimony.

283. *Campbell* (1991) at 4. The summary is from an offer of proof, a description of what Edith Greene *would have said* had she been allowed to testify. It was in an opinion reversing the lower court's rejection of her testimony. On remand, the trial judge again determined that Greene's testimony should be excluded, but the appeals court again reversed.

Similarly, in California,

> defendant offered the testimony of Dr. Shomer as an aid to the jurors in weighing the eyewitness identifications in this case. The People objected on the sole ground that to admit the testimony would "usurp the jury's function,"

and the judge rejected the testimony. This conviction, also, was reversed, *Frye* assessment considered inapplicable. *McDonald* (1984) at 363.

her testimony was considered unacceptable by the trial court. Greene's third point is the same as that which the Second Circuit did not want a jury to hear, as discussed above. The Supreme Court of Colorado reversed not to support such information going before the jury, but because the lower-court decision was based on *Frye*. Ultimately, it appears, Greene did get to present her wisdom testimony.

Michael Saks successfully performed this role in *Fujii* (2000). He noted that in the only independent study of identification through hand *printing*, few examiners correctly identified the writer. It should still have been possible, if she had the evidence, for Karen Cox, the government's witness, to provide the error rate with which she can make that identification. If she were demonstrably good at it, Saks' testimony that others are not would have seemed trivial. She apparently did not make such a demonstration.

Thus, though the problem has been assessing legislative-fact testimony in the same light as adjudicative science, solutions exist. My suggestion is that we start by giving such testimony a name. If "wisdom expert" is not the correct label, let's find another. An alternative, suggested above when discussing the science expert, might be "information witness." The name we apply is a promise that *that* is what this witness will provide. So let's settle on a name, and then develop an assessment procedure to determine its validity in particular circumstances.

Daubert Implications

The Supreme Court defined a "scientific" proposition as one that was "falsifiable" in *Daubert*, and then—in *Joiner* and *Kumho*—added propositions that were not falsifiable. My position is that the Court was right to subject technical or craft evidence to a test, but that it is a different test from that used to evaluate science evidence. Science can be utilized to test the craft expert's prior performance, but not in a direct evaluation of his work in this case. Although only science and engineering testimony may be "falsifiable," science, engineering, technical, and wisdom testimony are all testable. The tests are different, and therefore discerning which kind of testimony is before the bench is the critical first step in a *Daubert* assessment. Once again, the judge does not have to be a scientist to get past this question; he merely has to understand its importance and put it to the parties.

Replicating *Frye*

As we know from Thomas Kuhn's influential work,[284] individuals may change their thinking when presented with information, but *ways* of thinking usually change only over

---

284. See T. Kuhn (1970). There may be later editions, but this is the one I have.

generations. I have noted many holdovers from assessment under *Frye*, including *Daubert*'s initial formulation by the Supreme Court. Consider these four procedural steps:

> The "field" is recognized. This is an existence principle: One *could* find fact this way.

> The expert is recognized. He has credentials within the field, which almost tautologically means *from* the field. He has been certified by others to possess field knowledge.

> The expert has used the accepted methods of the field in this case, including some judgment that he has used them appropriately and/or well.

> The testimony will assist more than it will prejudice the fact determiner.

This reasoning equally follows *Daubert* or *Frye*, and so does not distinguish between them.[285] Let's see where the rules might take us if we would let them.

First, Rule 702, as amended in 2000, asks if:

> (1) the testimony is based on sufficient facts or data; (2) the testimony is the product of reliable principles and methods; and (3) the witness has applied the principles and methods reliably to the facts of the case.[286]

Nothing in this rule calls for a definition of a "field" or an assessment of its principles. Law-review writers discuss fields because their aim is purposefully broad. Judges read the law reviews and accept that framing of the issue. I have argued first that much of the science debate can be resolved by the experts themselves, and second that in most cases the experts should be able to define the conflict and their positions in lay-understandable terms. I will describe below how I think this can occur at trial. The *Daubert* hearing calls for a slightly different debate. Unless one expert challenges the other's work as "bad science," then they disagree about something else. If both sides present "good science," then let's go to trial.

Second, Rule 703 does not censor the expert's opinion, only the facts and data that are otherwise inadmissible, but may be admitted through an expert.

> Facts or data that are otherwise inadmissible shall not be disclosed to the jury by the proponent of the opinion or inference unless the court declares that their probative value in assisting the jury to evaluate the expert's opinion substantially outweighs their prejudicial effect.

When I introduced multiple-pools methods to solve selection problems, Joe Gastwirth was the only expert outside of my firm who had figured out how wrong traditional

---

285. See *Amaral* (1973), for example, excluding a wisdom witness.

286. All of the Rules of Evidence are quoted as of their latest revision, December 1, 2000. Recent revisions are not universally admired. "As an attempt to advance or clarify the law, however, their value is open to question." Brixen and Meis (2000) at 536.

selection analyses had been.[287] Our multiple-pools analyses were accepted because we had good credentials. Right result; wrong way to get there. The new paradigm should ignore credentials, ignore field designations, ignore who else in the world professes to do the same thing, or how well they do it. For all that I would make three inquiries: Has the expert framed a question the answer to which would assist in resolving the issues of this case? Does the expert have a sensible approach to answering the question? How well does this expert do what he says he does?

Judge Joyner got close:

> [T]he only issue for the experts to discuss at the *Mitchell* trial was whether or not an identification could be made by examination of the specific latent fingerprints and the record of this case.[288]

The question is not "whether or not." It is "how well."[289] The answer required data on FBI expert Duane Johnson's ability, not his credentials; not an understanding of how well others perform this task, and not faith that, because other fingerprint experts believe Johnson is one, he is.

Harvard Law Review editors got even closer:

> Instead of wholly accepting or entirely excluding fingerprint testimony, courts should determine the error rate of the particular expert or agency at issue.[290]

"Or agency?" No. How well the FBI performs this task is irrelevant. Only the error rate of the expert, in this instance Stephen Meagher, should have been at issue.

For science experts, the question must be answered by assessing the work itself. For craft experts, it must be answered by assessing the witness himself. Therefore no neophyte in a craft—who would not have a record—should ever be able to testify. Of course! Is that not implicit in the concept of "expert"?

Science and Craft

Courts have sensed that different sorts of testimony have appeared, all seemingly asking for the same *Daubert* test. They have looked for a single way to assess that testimony. Judge

---

287. See Gastwirth (1984).

288. *Mitchell* (2002) at 263.

289. Judge Seabury in *Roach* (1915) at 605:

> The fact that error may sometimes result in effecting identification, by this means [fingerprint identification], affords no reason for the exclusion of such evidence. Mistakes may also occur in effecting identification by personal appearance, casual meeting, by handwriting or by one's voice heard in the dark or over the telephone, but evidence of this character is admissible and its weight is to be determined by the jury.

290. Case Note (2002) at 2352. The case being discussed is *Havvard* (2001).

Harrington went through what he thought were the *Daubert* procedures, finding that Bessel van der Kolk's testimony satisfied them.

> Dr. van der Kolk further testified that the majority of clinical psychiatrists recognize the theory of repressed memories and do not find the theory itself controversial.[291]

This word "clinical" leads us to technical or craft testimony. "Clinical" describes people who deal with persons with a complaint. We could apply it to the *Kumho* situation, to workers who deal with the same kind of issue every day, be it a cough, a flat tire, or a dead marine engine. Many proffered medical experts are clinicians, the persons who diagnosed the plaintiffs.[292] Their knowledge of the malady and what to do about it is often confused with their suppositions about its cause.[293]

One of the standards discussed in case law is that experts use "methods that they use when they are doing their regular professional work."[294] The object of *Daubert*, Judge Posner opined,

> was to make sure that when scientists testify in court they adhere to the same standards of intellectual rigor that are demanded in their professional work.[295]

No. This approach is *not* in the spirit of *Daubert*, which specifies that the judicial system, not the university or consulting firm or journal editors, will evaluate the expert's work.[296]

---

291. *Shahzade* (1996) at 288.

292. From *Coastal* (2002) at 604: "Even with all the advances of medical science, the practice of medicine remains an art." What an unproductive view, the same view, we have seen, that Lawrence Kersta held about voiceprint analysis. Similarly, David Kaye (2001) at 1965 opines that "statistical modeling is as much art as science." Surely statistical modeling and medical diagnosis, like voiceprint analysis, are crafts, which means they have a methodology and goals the accomplishment of which can be assessed less subjectively than art. Individuals performing a diagnostic craft will have different error rates. If these activities are passed off as "art" we have no way to assess them, no basis on which to hold the bad practitioners liable for their errors.

293. For example, consider the rationale of Judge McLaughlin, writing for the Second Circuit panel, accepting plaintiff's medical expert Robert Fagelson in *McCullock* (1995), at 1043:

> Fagelson is an experienced medical doctor, who is certified by the American Board of Otolaryngology and has practiced in the specialty of ears, nose and throat since 1966. We find his background sufficient to permit his expert testimony on a throat ailment and its causes.

This is a non sequitur. Although perhaps a fine doctor, nothing in his background suggests that Dr. Fagelson is an expert in cause. His "differential etiology" is a logical but hardly conclusive method of eliminating competing explanations for symptoms. That "methodology" does not provide a measurement of error; i.e., it is not science.

294. Posner for the court in *Braun* (1996) at 235.

295. Posner for the court in *Rosen* (1996) at 318.

296. If by "professional work" Posner means academic work, one author—Lind (2003), at footnote 19—takes exception to Posner's adherence to his own standard:

In *Moore* (1997), plaintiff's experts were practicing physicians, clinicians. The presiding magistrate judge allowed them to testify as experts, but did not allow one of them, Daniel Jenkins, to testify that the illness suffered by plaintiff was *caused by* the incident at issue. Plaintiff's other expert, Antonio Alvarez, also a treating physician, was allowed to do so. Thus it was guaranteed that the case would be appealed. The jury found for defendant, so the appeal was about Jenkins' non-testimony, not Alvarez' testimony.

The Fifth Circuit panel noted that

> clinical medicine (as opposed to research and laboratory medical science) is not a hard science discipline,[297]

and looked for a standard of assessment. It concluded:

> Thus, the proffered opinion of any expert in a field of knowledge, in order to be evidentiarily reliable, must either be based soundly on the current knowledge, principles, and methodology of the expert's discipline or be soundly inferred or derived therefrom.

With the guidance provided by the recently decided *Joiner* (1997), the Fifth Circuit reviewed the standard which at least two circuits had adopted—essentially the *Frye* standard, acceptance by the field from which the expert came.

> The expert's assurances that he has utilized generally accepted scientific methodology is insufficient. . . . The inquiry authorized by Rule 702 is a flexible one; however, a scientific opinion, to have evidentiary relevance and reliability, must be based on scientifically valid principles.[298]

This, I assert, is the problem. Judges look for science *within* the testimony of the craft expert. To do that they ask what principles guide the field. Thus although they state that their inquiry is about the expert, except for credentials and assurances of conformity, it is not. My dichotomy between science and craft allows the court to use science to *assess* craft expertise, but does not ask that craft expertise masquerade as science itself. Craft experts who appear with no assessment of the accuracy of their judgments, in general, should be excluded. Craft experts who can describe their methodology, use it to draw conclusions, and show that their conclusions are correct more often than lay judgments, should be

---

It is ironic that in his decisions on the Seventh Circuit Court of Appeals, Judge Posner has been one of the most aggressive proponents of comparability review, despite his acknowledgment in academic works that nonpecuniary losses reflect real costs.

A more cogent view of *Daubert*, again by Posner, in *Tuf* (2000) at 591, is:

> The principle of *Daubert* is merely that if an expert witness is to offer an opinion based on science, it must be real science, not junk science.

297. *Moore* (1997) at 682; following indented quotation at 687. The court cites *Rosen* (1996) and *Tyus* (1996) in support.

298. *Moore* (1998) at 276.

accepted regardless whether others think their methodology is "scientific." A decision to exclude craft experts because no probability assessment can be made about *this* conclusion would assume them to be something they are not.

Most clinicians have no expertise in determining why a patient has an illness, despite being able to say with great precision what illness the patient has. The job of the clinician is to determine what is wrong, and what to do about it. Both Jenkins' and Alvarez' testimony should have been excluded because, although both physicians were apparently expert at diagnosis, neither could support expertise as to cause.[299]

Cause and Effect

The technical expert must have a method. It is not wrong to inquire how he comes to his opinions. My proposed assessment of craft testimony is not Saks' "black box" approach.[300] An astrologer has a system. If one cares to know, other astrologers can attest whether a particular one is following accepted standards. However, that is the wrong question. The right question is whether this astrologer is following *any* system. Can he describe it? Has he applied it to events other than the one at issue? What is his record?[301]

Having a replicable procedure is a sine qua non, a floor upon which the expert must build, but it says nothing about what that procedure produces. When Zenith delivered set-top boxes that were incompatible with WH-TV's signal, the television broadcaster engaged Peter Shapiro to estimate damages from lost future sales. Had Shapiro produced a statis-

---

299. David Bernstein (2003) proposes, at 18, the "reasonable patient test" (would a reasonable patient go to this doctor for diagnosis) to determine the qualifications of a doctor. Perhaps because Bernstein is steeped in asbestos litigation, where a diagnosis of the disease is essentially the same thing as identifying its cause, he is not sensitive to this difference. Besides being undeterminable, this test is unhelpful in most medical-related litigation.

300. This approach seemed to be acceptable to both Michael Saks and Mark Denbeaux in 1989:

> Such persons' conclusions might perhaps be useful, if we knew which they were. They would possess a kind of "black box" skill. We (and they) wouldn't know exactly why it works, but we could still, at least theoretically, create ways to verify that it in fact works. This is no less true for handwriting identification than for other such skills.

Risinger et al. (1989) at 773. Yet, when testifying, both Saks and Denbeaux have stressed the inexpertness of forensic examiners *in general*, not in particular.

301. In *Wichita* (2003), Judge Belot did not exclude the city's modeling expert, Michael Smith, because, at 1107, one of the defendants' "experts adopted a portion of Smith's work in their own opinions." Although a roomful of monkeys with keyboards might produce an intelligible sentence here or there, that a human might utter the same sentence would not validate the monkeys' method. According to Judge Belot, at 1108, Smith

> conceded that his modeling techniques and methodology are not based on any specific guidelines or standards, but rather on his "professional judgment."

Smith had no method. His testimony should have been excluded.

tical estimate, it might have been evaluated as science. Had he produced an estimate based on some other methodology, he might have been evaluated as a craft expert. He did neither, and therefore was neither.

> Asked repeatedly during his deposition what methods he had used to generate projections, Shapiro repeatedly answered "my expertise" or some variant ("my industry expertise", "[my] awareness," and "my curriculum vitae")—which is to say that he either had no method or could not describe one. He was relying on intuition, which won't do.
>
> Indeed, the record does not contain any hint why Shapiro preferred intuition to the empirical toolkit of the social sciences. And if Shapiro did not use these devices because he does not know how: that would just demonstrate that he's not an "expert" in the first place.
>
> A witness who invokes "my expertise" rather than analytic strategies widely used by specialists is not an expert as Rule 702 defines that term.[302]

Judge Easterbrook goes too far. An expert who does utilize a definable, describable methodology should pass to the next expert screen even if that methodology is *not* "widely used by specialists." That next screen is scientifically prepared evidence measuring how well he has performed this task elsewhere. A dissertation that astrologers cannot generally predict the future might be informative, but should not be dispositive. We need a fair (scientific) assessment of how well *this* astrologer has predicted the future, compared with some non-expert standard. If no witness can be found who can pass this test, then the "field" will disappear without any court having pronounced it unscientific.

It is not always a hopeless task to determine cause. Fire and death are often assigned a "cause" by people who call themselves "forensic" examiners. It is fair to think they are usually correct. When the fire inspector concludes that the cause was arson, and then a suspect is arrested and confesses, score one true positive for the inspector. We can imagine all possibilities—undetected arson, falsely suspected arson, and a true negative (not arson, none suspected), this last outcome requiring evidence of some other cause.

Under the circumstances of *Kumho*, where Dennis Carlson's skill was unknown, excluding his testimony was appropriate. It argues not to exclude all such experts, but to assess them. If the expert can be shown to have given effective advice about tires (when

---

302. *Zenith* (2005) at 418, then at 419. Judge Easterbrook, writing for a unanimous panel, is not completely fair to Shapiro, who had made a similar estimate concerning a television station in Mexico. Shapiro correctly analogized his Mexican estimate with WH-TV only for 2002, because he based it on a competitor's known market share. In *Zenith* (2003a) at *3:

> Shapiro does not compare his predictions relating to WH-TV's growth after 2002 with results from any other market.

A craft expert has to demonstrate skill at his craft. Shapiro's exclusion was clearly correct.

they are dangerous, when they are not) in the past, if he is demonstrably (though with some error) a craft expert, is his opinion worth *nothing* in court?

Making a cause determination in an individual case, though possible, is a daunting task, of which courts should be skeptical. Adrian Zuckerman reviews an individual plaintiff's case, *Lilley* (1986). Referring to Judge Weinstein:

> His view represents an erroneous and hard-edged statistical concept of probability, which obscures the difference between law and science. . . . [H]is approach, if it becomes dogma, will gravely incapacitate the dispute-resolving power of courts in toxic tort cases.[303]

Weinstein's view was dictated mostly by epidemiological studies, and the failure of individual plaintiff data to rise to their standard. Lilley was subject to other carcinogens while loading Agent Orange on to air planes, as well as in his personal life. How would anyone ever associate an illness of his with a single cause?[304] Weinstein's approach would not "incapacitate the dispute-resolving power of courts," but it does incapacitate careless plaintiffs, as it should.

Because assessing cause and effect in Lilley's circumstance was impossible does not mean it always is. This view goes too far:

> To a medical scientist, the question of specific causation is not only unanswerable; it is absurd. Scientists never treat causation as a yes/no question, nor do responsible ones believe that it is possible to use scientific methods to determine individual causation.[305]

"Legionnaire's disease" was traced to stagnant air-conditioning water. Do we think that finding was incorrect? Do we not think that we know that a center-fuel-tank explosion caused the failure of TWA flight 800? Or that exposed wires from rotting insulation allowed

---

303. Zuckerman (1986) at 526.

304. Attempts to find deep pockets to finance medical care is understandable, but the expenditure on experts who cannot associate the malady with a defendant's cause is not. See, for example, *Milk* (1998), where experts were not allowed to testify because they could refer to no study associating airborne particles from the contaminant in some milk samples (with which plaintiff had had some contact) with plaintiff's malady. Furthermore, from *Milk* (1999), at 861, besides being unable to rule *in* this contaminant,

> The district court was not convinced that the plaintiffs had successfully ruled out other possible alternative causes such as second-hand smoke from [plaintiff] McDougal's parents and sibling or the possibility that he was exposed through his diet to other carcinogens.

Although not offering an alternative explanation, Judge Copenhaver did a similarly careful job of finding that plaintiff's experts could not associate his terrible birth defects with his mother's use of Benlate, a plant fertilizer, while he was in her womb. The experts were not allowed to testify, and summary judgment was granted to Dupont. See *Bourne* (2002).

305. Moreno (2001) at 1062, reference omitted.

the spark that generated that explosion?[306] Or that insulation tore away at liftoff, crashing into Shuttle Columbia's wing, causing a gash through which hot gasses later entered? Is there no point to investigations of such incidents? Some people make cause-and-effect decisions often, and are confirmed or not on other grounds. Those people have data that provide a basis for assessing their expert testimony. Most of us experience this with people repairing our cars, our furnaces, even our bodies. They diagnose the problem, propose a remedy, perform the remedy, and the problem is solved or not. If they want to become testifying experts, they should keep records of these events.[307]

Social Science

Economists testify often to assess corporate behavior in antitrust litigation. When an expert constructs a model of pricing containing the assumption that a company with more than 50 percent of the market is overcharging, it is, no doubt, because he is plaintiffs' expert where defendant holds more than a 50 percent share.[308] One might argue that conclusions driven by assumptions constitute craft, because they are replicable and, over many observations, testable. But, though easily exposed, they are not science.

Valuation, a subject that appeared early in Chapter 7, is a testable craft. An expert claims to have a method which correctly projects a person's future income, on the average. He uses that method in a particular case. Why not provide that expert with data on people who, ten or fifteen years earlier, had characteristics similar to the person whose income is being estimated, presumably the victim? The estimate must be based on data known at the time—i.e., the expert must replicate his method. Or some other "test" can be devised, to which the answers are known. If "experts" say they project future incomes from an initial

---

306. This explanation is disputed by some people, but I still think it is correct to conclude that we "know" that this is what happened. Those who dispute it have some radar evidence on their side, but it, too, is forensic—ex post inference from data. Would it be better to determine what we think we know from no analysis of the data, or from conflicting analyses, where we have to decide which one to believe?

307. "Stump the Chumps," an occasional segment of the National Public Radio program *Car Talk*, is about this process. Old callers are brought back to inform us whether Click and Clack's diagnosis of a car's problem, made months earlier, had been found to be correct.

308. This is the model posited by Robert Hall, a Stanford University economist, for plaintiffs in *Concord Boat* (1998), presented briefly in Chapter 8. The Eighth Circuit understood that this was a contrivance. It concluded, in *Concord Boat* (2000) at 1047. that

> The price at which Brunswick sold its engines was therefore irrelevant for purposes of the
> formula because the overcharge amount was related solely to Brunswick's market share,

The district-court judge should have understood that the model was patently absurd, and excluded Hall's testimony, especially as defendants' professional expert, Richard Rapp, explained plaintiffs' model in these terms.

set of facts, why not try to determine how well they do it? A single estimate is not expected, ever, to be very accurate; but one expert may be shown to come closer, more often, than another. Why not calculate a mean and standard deviation of error for each expert in the case?

Psychologists examine the defendant, his own saying that he was (and is) insane, the prosecutor's saying that he was (and is) sane. I would want to know the histories of persons these experts have previously examined. How many considered sane continued to commit insane acts? How many considered insane caused no trouble again? Theirs is craft testimony, too often admitted without adequate assessment. The testimony of psychologists cannot be considered "science" under *Daubert*, but should not be excluded merely because it is not science.

That the distinctions I make here are important is exemplified by the Texas Court of Criminal Appeals' quandary in assessing testimony of FBI "behavioral-science" expert Kenneth Lanning:

> From information given about appellant, Lanning concluded that appellant was a pedophile. Lanning testified that such a person was difficult to rehabilitate.[309]

The court understood that Lanning could not reach that conclusion in the "falsifiable" sense of science. That is, the court sensed the "what is science" and "how do we assess it" dilemmas I have tried to solve.

> We do not attempt, here, to develop a rigid distinction between "hard" science, "soft" sciences, or nonscientific testimony. The present case illustrates that the distinction between various types of testimony may often be blurred.

I disagree. Lanning had "studied" over a thousand cases, but could not articulate a methodology by which he assembled information and reached a binary conclusion: "He is a pedophile." No indication is given in the court's opinion—admitting the testimony!—that any data had been kept on Lanning's prior judgment and subsequent events. Perhaps some of the people he said could not be rehabilitated had been released from prison. How many have relapsed? If none have been released, then we need to go to tests like those proposed for valuation and handwriting experts, for whom we can determine the frequency of "right" or "wrong." It may be that such behavioral scientists have knowledge that can be helpful in sentencing. But should one be allowed to present a judgment about the defendant's frame of mind and future behavior without our knowing how well this particular behavioral scientist performs this task, in general? No. Methodology is the basis of craft. An error rate is the basis of assessment of that craft. Not receiving an articulate explanation of what Lanning did, with what accuracy, the court should not have allowed his testimony.

---

309. *Nenno* (1998) at 552; following indented quotation at 561.

In addition to having a methodology, an expert should be prepared to say where it came from. Judge Kocoras was rightly indignant when David Bakken tried to add a reference supporting his opinion, which, he had previously declared, was not based on any such literature.

> We truly wonder what assistance experts can be to a lay person jury if experts such as this can be found that will tailor and alter their supposed genuine opinions to meet the precise needs of those who pay them.[310]

Unfortunately, this describes most experts. Bakken and his attorney were unprepared, as I suggested in Chapters 6 and 8 that most attorneys and experts are. And particularly clumsy.

Jack Caravanos was neither a doctor nor a specialist in xylene.

> His opinion that exposure to xylene at levels he estimated caused Mr. Amorgianos's particular set of symptoms was based on a literature search on medical databases.

> [Plaintiffs'] methodology consists of an extrapolation from existing medical evidence on the relationship between exposure to various organic solvents and various PNS and CNS conditions, buttressed by the temporal proximity of the onset of Mr. Amorgianos's alleged illness to his alleged exposure to xylene and other organic solvents.[311]

Judge Trager read the same literature and disagreed with Caravanos' summary of it. He disallowed Caravanos' testimony on causation. Affirming, the reviewing court commented:

> Although this degree of review, while commendable, may not always be necessary to evaluate whether proffered expert testimony is admissible, Judge Trager's evaluation of the fit between the experts' opinions and the scientific literature on which they relied was certainly within the broad discretion afforded to the district court under *Daubert* and its progeny, and did not impinge upon the jury's function. It is precisely such an undertaking that assures that an expert, when formulating an opinion for use in the courtroom, will employ the same level of intellectual rigor as would be expected in the scientific community.[312]

Asking for "the same level of intellectual rigor as would be expected in the scientific community" is as wrong as Posner's "same standards of intellectual rigor that are demanded in

---

310. *Stainer* (2003) at *2. Any researcher might run across literature supporting his view after declaring that he knew of none. Surely there are ways of handling this situation, including notifying the other side (and providing a copy) immediately on the discovery. If, at trial, the expert has found such support, he should be allowed to say so; but it should not be a surprise.

311. *Amorgianos* (2001) at 159, then at 163.

312. *Amorgianos* (2002) at 269. This language imitates the Supreme Court's "same level of intellectual rigor that characterizes the practice of an expert in the relevant field," from *Kumho* (1999) at 152. It is equally as circular, *Frye*-like, and irrelevant.

their professional work" that I criticized above. Under *Daubert* we should ask that the expert's literature review be accurate, regardless what standards hold elsewhere.

"Doesn't the evidence matter?" asked an incredulous Judge Nevas of Fletcher Blanchard, whose testimony on the effect of minorities on juries was described in Chapter 9. Judge Nevas had presided, ten years earlier, at the trial now being reviewed. "The evidence of [defendant's] guilt was overwhelming." Blanchard stood his ground.[313] The prosecuting attorney submitted copies of some of the articles Blanchard had reviewed, which seemed to conflict with Blanchard's summary of them. One should not expect any literature to be unanimous, but rather than defend his position as a generalization, Blanchard applied his position to the very articles that did not support it.

I have no reason to think that the court got anything different from Blanchard than his students get, that his work for the court was different from his academic work. The court properly rejected it.[314] Although one can be a "wisdom" expert from having studied a subject, reading the literature on group interaction provides no expertise to the court on the effect of minorities on juries.

We will usually not know how right the craft expert is about the case in hand. That is why we need the guidance of his past record. Learning how right he has been may not be a hopeless task.

> Science can, indeed, produce very precise, accurate, and reliable information, but scientists recognize the contingent nature of their work.
>
> Thus, the real question that courts must address is not whether science requires too much certainty, but rather how scientists can validly reach conclusions at the level of certainty the law requires.[315]

We have a curious situation in which science testimony presents itself as contingent, probabilistic, which (if technically well done) is one measure of its accuracy. Craft testimony presents itself as certain, which it is not, but it contains no intrinsic test for accuracy. The statistical analyst usually can be judged as a science expert, because his study can

---

313. Not sufficiently informed, Blanchard did not know that the background issue was a turf battle between the Mafia and the Latin Kings, a Hispanic group. In this case, a juror's characteristic—being of either Italian or Hispanic background—would likely determine his vote. That is seldom true. See my discussion of the relationship between juror characteristics and juror vote in Chapter 4. Blanchard likened the Mafia's exclusion of minorities to a golf club that might do the same—using their freedom to associate with whomever they please—whereas ethnic status here determined one's side in a war. Blanchard's view that the academic expert can or even should be unaware of the facts of the case represents the expert role I argued against in Chapter 8, as well as in this chapter.

314. See *Pugliano* (2004), excluding Blanchard's testimony. The events described occurred at a hearing I attended on January 8, 2003. I wrote the description the next day.

315. B. Black (1994) at 2129, then at 2130.

be evaluated. In the litigation context, therefore, statistics is usually science, whereas social science, like forensic science, usually is not.[316] So much for names.[317]

A Separate *Daubert* Expert

The judge might engage his own experts solely for the *Daubert* hearing.[318] Judge Jones utilized his own experts in *Hall* (1996b), and in his opinion wrote extensively about doing so. Judge Vratil engaged two experts in a complex question of the relationship between a drug and suicidal behavior.[319] Thus there are examples on both sides, good and not so good gatekeeping. A general assessment of *Daubert* in relationship to the expertise of experts, and the ability of judges to figure out what they are doing, probably could not be done at the present time. In any case, it is beyond the scope of this book.

I presented my views on what the role of the parties' experts should be in cases such as these, a much stronger role than most attorneys would like, in Chapter 8. The role of the court's expert would be quite different. I discuss a judge's trial expert, below. Here, it is

---

316. The reader surely understands that I do not include social-science statistical analysis in this statement. Rather, I mean the kind of social-science pronouncement that parades as fact without rigorous empirical support. Faigman (1989) called it "suppositional science." At 1078:

> Suppositional science assumes primarily two forms. It can be recognized easily in the form of untestable or wholly untested assertions of empirical fact. While such assertions are typically backed by numerous case studies, such observations, unaided by controlled investigation, provide little more than common sense can provide. More difficult to identify, though similarly lacking significant value to the legal process, are those empirical statements purportedly subjected to test, but which have actually received no real test at all.

Although I applaud Faigman's attempt to develop a "framework" for evaluation of social science as evidence, I think he fails. Suppositional science is not science. Some should be considered, and rejected, in the "technical" category of my framework; the rest is "wisdom," although it may not be wisdom. Faigman's categories are not clear, as he contends that there can be suppositional science about adjudicative fact, one example being a survey to detect consumer confusion in a trademark dispute. Surely this is statistical analysis, to be evaluated as "science" in my framework.

317. Although the Court delved into the academic "What is science?" literature, what is science in the world at large need not be the same as what is science for the purpose of determining how to evaluate expertise in litigation. I have been making this point with regard to legal literature such as Koukoutchos (1994), Borenstein (2001), and Brodin (2004), in text and footnotes, above. A judge needs to know how to determine what procedure to follow in evaluating expert testimony. If using the word "science" confuses that question, let's use other language.

318. Editors of the *Harvard Law Review* interpret the cryptic reference to Rule 706 in *Daubert* (1993), at 595, as:

> Courts may use Rule 706 to appoint experts who testify as witnesses at evidentiary hearings rather than at trial.

See Note (1997) at 952.

319. See *Miller* (2002). As the proposed expert's calculations could not be replicated by the court's experts, not allowing him to present them was certainly the correct decision.

sufficient to say that I think a separate judge's *Daubert* hearing expert is a good idea, worth investigating, worth trying more often.

THE TRIAL

The judicial system is not only built by but for attorneys and judges. Not for truth seeking, not for obtaining the best information possible from the people who come before it, but to establish, preserve, and enhance the privileges of attorneys in an adversarial framework.[320] After toiling in these fields for over thirty-five years, I know something about them. Class and status often prevail over good sense.

What Happens?

The expert brought to support a claim (ordinarily the plaintiff's expert) takes the stand. He and his client have worked out a presentation, a series of questions and answers, an order of submissions of exhibits. In most cases I write the questions my client will put to me.

Attorneys prefer to tie the expert's presentation to their own theatrical competence, their own flair for asking questions, as it differentiates among them. Response to questions is an appropriate form first because that is what the expert is there for, and second because the questions provide markers for the judge or jury. Left to his own devices, an expert might not make clear the relevance of what he is saying to the fact-finding task. Current procedures, however, appear to be more about empowering the attorney than empowering the judge or informing the jury. The questions should be large, the responses expansive, the judge involved. He can tell the expert when he gets lost, or thinks that the jury is.

The opposing expert may not be the next person on the witness stand. To accomplish a sense of "dialogue," the one witness would have to be the protagonist's last, and the other the opposition's first. Attorneys are free to organize their cases as they wish, and they seldom wish for this dialogue. Most often, therefore, some time intervenes between one expert and another, between assertion and rebuttal.

The opposition expert must restate for the judge the argument he wants to rebut. His statement is unlikely to satisfy the expert being summarized. Once again, time and events must elapse between that presentation and the first expert's re-taking the stand to correct the misimpression left by the second. These time lapses weaken the flow of the

---

320. Frankel (1975) at 1032:

> My theme . . . is that our adversary system rates truth too low among the values that institutions of justice are meant to serve.

debate. Also, judges (and, I presume, juries) form impressions of witnesses, through means I do not understand, but which are divorced from the merits of the arguments.[321]

Protagonist experts often make the mistake of relating their testimony to the arguments that will follow them. A fact finder may not understand references to opinions he has not heard. The rebutting expert, in contrast, can refer to the record. The opposition (usually defendant) expert has a significant advantage in this regard. That is not a defect in the system. Someone has to go first. But noting it establishes a goal: How can we have a discussion between experts? How can each one refer to the other?

Would such a discussion be desirable?

> An adversarial approach is very effective for settling many types of disputes, which is no doubt why the law is based on it, but it is not the way to reach scientific conclusions.[322]

This discussion is what is missing. Current procedures lead to the kinds of game playing, misstatements, and incompetence I have been outlining in this book. Inserting attorneys and time between expert presentations prevents the fact finder from focusing on what is important, and what is correct.

Cross-Examination

One of my points in Chapter 6 was that the judge cannot rely on the attorney's cross-examination of an expert to clarify the weaknesses in the expert's report and testimony. I have spent many an hour "training" my client to handle the kinds of answers I thought a clever expert might give to the line of questioning we had formulated. Invariably, the witness was more clever than I had been in practice, for which my client was unprepared.

It is the current requirement that only the attorney can question the other side's expert that leads to suggestions of attorney training in expert fields. Writers unhesitatingly accept it:

> Attorneys will be better able to take charge of their trial proceedings if they are familiar with statistical methods and theory.

> Expert testimony will often prove to be determinative evidence in the resolution of complex and technical issues, and so effective cross-examination is essential to protect the rights of the opposing party.[323]

---

321. For example, Gross (1991) notes that the trial judge in *Wells* (1985) was explicitly swayed by the manner and appearance of the expert witnesses.

322. Angell (1996) at 29. Although I endorse this sentiment, I do not endorse where Angell takes it. She believes the battle of the experts confuses a jury more than it would a judge, and therefore recommends taking assessment of expert presentations out of the jury's hands. I discuss this idea, below, as a procedural "reform" proposed by others. Dreyfuss (1997) didn't like the idea, either.

323. Bessey et al. (1992) at 474, then Mickus (1994) at 791.

The battle of the experts is to be decided by the skill of attorneys not in law, not even in oration, but in statistics? I think the judge should "take charge" of the trial, though of course each attorney must be allowed to make his client's case. I would not eliminate cross-examination of the other side's expert, though one benefit of the trial-procedure modifications I recommend would be to change its tone.[324] I would amplify it by direct witness-to-witness confrontation.

I am not alone in thinking that cross-examination is not the best route to clarification of expert testimony.

> [W]e can surmise that often, possibly in the majority of cases, bad evidence will not be contradicted through counter-witnesses or cross-examination. . . . The evidence . . . suggests that the difficulty with evidence quality derives from the adversarial system. It is, of course, a problem with all evidence but, as the panel's report has noted, statistical evidence is beyond the ordinary experience of legal fact finders, judge or jury, and makes evaluation more difficult.[325]

My solution is to structure a discussion between the experts, head to head, moderated by the judge.

Towards a Discussion

Rich Goldstein was plaintiffs' final rebuttal witness in *Polaroid* (1983), discussed in Chapter 2. He presented his surprise attempt to replicate my conditional logit calculations, surmising that mine were incorrect. Sensing what error Goldstein had made, I wrote—and my client asked—the cross-examination question: "Did you censor any observations?" This question meant nothing to either attorney or the judge, who wisely figured that I would explain its importance later. From Goldstein's response, "No," members of my staff were able to pass our data through the program Goldstein had used both his way (no censoring) and correctly (censoring those employees who had not been terminated), that very night. They transmitted the results to me.[326] My response was ready the next day, while Goldstein's critique was fresh in everyone's mind.

---

324. As Vidmar (1994) notes at 902:

> [T]he process of cross-examination almost invariably challenges the motives as well as the opinions of the other side's experts.

Of course. Lawyers are better at impugning motives than at understanding statistics.

325. Vidmar (1989) at 289. Vidmar's later writings, as will be demonstrated below, ask whether judges would be better decision makers than jurors, faced with scientific expert testimony. He is less pessimistic about the ability of either to absorb presentations—depending on their quality and clarity—but continues to hold the implication of this quotation, that judges and jurors do not differ in this respect.

326. Today, this process would seem elementary, except that one might not have someone else's statistical package readily available. In the early 1980s, it was a remarkable event. First, we had to locate the BMDP survival package through a mainframe service with which we had a contract. Then we had to

I explained Goldstein's error. I was, in most respects, speaking to him. The judge did not need to understand the details. He was impatient to get to my conclusions. However, I needed to describe what Goldstein should have done, to convince him that he had incorrectly instructed the computer program. Thus we engaged in a discussion between the experts, open to the judge, without interference from either attorney.

If not a discussion, it was a monologue. The one-witness-at-a-time forum did not allow Goldstein to respond. After my rebuttal testimony both sides rested, and I departed. Plaintiffs were given the opportunity to call Goldstein back to the stand, but demurred. The judge, sensing the inequity in the one-sided rebuttal, and understanding the admission implicit in Goldstein's non-return to the witness stand, forced the issue. He called Goldstein as his own witness, asked him what he thought of my presentation, to which Goldstein frankly replied, "I goofed."

One could say the procedures served truth seeking well. But they did so because of a fortunate timing that one cannot control, and that seldom occurs, especially starting with direct examination. I made an argument to Goldstein, in technical language, explaining his error. And I showed the result of that error by first replicating his result and then replicating my own, using his software for both. The judge asked me enough questions to satisfy himself, and also turned to Goldstein to obtain a response. Uncluttered by questions and objections from counsel, the judge moderated a conversation, obtaining for himself only the information he needed, while letting other information pass between the experts. This is a model on which I wish to build.

Here is a conversation that transpired between me and a statistician (HW) concerning my analysis of non-delivery of summonses in *Gibbs* (1998). This conversation occurred via mail and email subsequent to trial. We were discussing my study of census tracts within Hartford, Connecticut.[327] I showed that although a summons mailed to a Hispanic had less chance of being delivered than a summons mailed to a non-Hispanic, this difference was not due to any intrinsic ethnic characteristic, but to innocent demographic characteristics held more in Connecticut by Hispanics than by non-Hispanics. I have only slightly edited the exchange here:

HW: I have a minor quibble about whether using "isolated" as a covariate is strictly legit, since it may be just a proxy for Hispanic and hence you are covarying away the phenomenon.

learn the program well enough to instruct it, and attach our data to that instruction. Finally, to get the computer output to me required that I have a state-of-the-art receiver, which at that time was a 300-baud modem with foam cups into which I placed the telephone handset, and a thermal printing terminal which fortunately I had rented for just such an occasion. The laptop computer had not yet been invented.

327. See Chapter 3—"Regression Analysis"—and the Appendix to Chapter 5.

SM: Why wouldn't "Hispanic" be the best measure of Hispanic, and defeat the inclusion of Hispanic proxies in a regression? I kept making "Hispanic" disappear using census variables. In that sense I argued that the "failure" to get Hispanics on juries was a disparate impact phenomenon. It had nothing to do with "Hispanicness" per se, but with characteristics held by Hispanics. It is true, of course, that these characteristics are correlated with Hispanic, but they "explain" the dependent variable variation better than Hispanic. Every time.

The whole point of regression, I think, is to find which variable *better* relates to the dependent variable. I am curious why you think that when another variable wipes out Hispanic, it is somehow illegitimate. I think regression does exactly what it is supposed to do, which is pick out the independent variable that is more closely related to the dependent variable.

HW: If *The Iliad* wasn't written by Homer it was written by some other Greek of the same name. A rose by any other name would smell as sweet. If the other category explains better but is still 95 percent Hispanic, I think it is disingenuous to call it different from Hispanic. If "Isolated" equals 95 percent Hispanic plus 5 percent others, it is still mostly Hispanic.

SM: 32.6 percent of Spanish-speaking households are linguistically isolated; 29.5 percent of households with a primary language that is neither Spanish nor English are linguistically isolated. Even if 95 percent of the isolated households were Hispanic, as less than a third of Hispanics are isolated, the two measures are importantly different. In fact, only 71 percent of isolateds are Hispanic, further supporting my point: It is linguistic isolation, not being Hispanic, that leads to non-delivery of jury summonses.

This is the kind of back-and-forth I would encourage. Each expert could ask and answer questions in the way HW and I did. I believe my answers would have satisfied a judge, whether they would have satisfied another expert—or whether they did satisfy HW.

Attorneys often say that we are just making a record. The point of post-trial briefs is for each side to make its best argument from that record. Without a conversation, a back-and-forth, the record fails to reflect the debate both experts would prefer to have. I have read many a record in which issues were left dangling because of procedure-induced fragmentation.

Even though at times experts are asked to contribute to the post-trial brief, neither attorney is a truth seeker. He is not supposed to be. So the briefs are in the hands of persons who do not understand the conversation, who don't even want to. What the judge needs more than the attorneys' views about what the experts said is a forum in which the experts can speak for themselves, to each other—and to him. They can and might modify their positions when induced to do so by fact or good statistical argument. Ultimately, incentives work. In a forum where honesty and competence are rewarded, experts might turn out to be other than the evil, mendacious characters judges (often correctly) see them to be.

As explained in Chapter 6—the reason this part of the story was told there—my failure to rebut Joan Haworth's badly conceived "market" variable in *Nassau* (1992) can be laid at the step of inexperienced and inept counsel. Rebuttal in hand, I was never put back on the witness stand. I knew, as Joel Klein clearly did not, that such a rebuttal could be made *only* by an expert. Klein (and Paul Smith, the trial attorney) could not have induced Haworth to admit the non-validity of her measure in cross-examination. She is too good a witness. To affect the judge's view, Haworth would have to have been confronted with an expert who could point to the relevance of validity in this context, the harm a non-valid measure would do, how to build a valid measure of the "market," and how far hers was from being one.[328]

Informal telephone depositions in *Yoder* (1989) effectively became a discussion between the two experts, and led directly to settlement.[329] It took just an afternoon to convince plaintiffs' expert that his analysis of terminations, failing to test any explanation other than age, and analyzing all selections as if from a single competition pool, would not stand up in court. Few plaintiffs' attorneys would have allowed that informal, expert-to-expert exchange, but this attorney was correct to do so. It saved his clients a lot of expense, for which they would have achieved nothing.

The Judge As Moderator

Joseph Sanders suggests that, whereas experts stress their areas of disagreement, a judge's own expert could stress areas of agreement.[330] That may be so, but it is the disagreements that require a judicial decision. Although a neutral expert might aid in this process, I think the initial focus should be on the parties' experts talking to, arguing before, the judge.

Advances in technology support this suggestion. One should expect, today, that both experts would be armed with notebook computers, with their data bases and statistical

---

328. My measure of "market" wages, which is only slightly closer to valid than Haworth's, was discussed in Chapter 7. There, I also noted how absurd Haworth's approach was, in the sense that it would have pretended to validate clearly discriminatory wages at Stockham Valves. My presentation of that analogy would have made for informative conversation in front of Judge Glasser, who would have gotten a better view of the competence of the experts than he did through any procedure he followed.

329. *Yoder* (1989). Plaintiffs alleged age discrimination in terminations. Both experts were deposed by speaker-phone on March 30, 1989.

330. See Sanders (1998), particularly at 378.

software in the court room. Thus, in *Gibbs*, the experts could have had the discussion that HW and I had, live, in real time. David Pollard raised similar questions. His objection to "collinearity" in my data was just a stab in the dark, a theoretical notion that my work might be flawed, not a credible assertion that it was. I cannot complain about the outcome (the judge properly ignored Pollard's critique), but the attorney-controlled forum cannot be justified by its occasional success.

I would allow each expert to make his initial presentation with few guiding questions from his attorney, perhaps with a time limit, but with little tolerance for objections. Exhibits would be marked for identification. All attempts to get exhibits entered into the record would be made at the end. Cross-examination could proceed as it does now.

Then let each expert appear in rebuttal, controlled by his attorney, and then again cross-examined. All of that can happen in the order the parties' attorneys determine.

The last stage would be a discussion between two experts (or more). To facilitate this discussion, after the standard rebuttals, the judge would ask each expert to write out an agenda of criticisms of or comments on the other expert's work. Not elaborate critiques themselves: just their subject matter with a one-sentence gist of the argument. The experts would come to an agreement on (or the judge would impose) an agenda for the discussion to follow. How many backs and forths would be allowed on each topic would remain open. Some time might be set aside for preparation, and then the two experts would meet knowing which topics each would be able to raise, which topics the other would raise.

Would the discussion be endless? The judge controls that by asking such questions as, "Now, really, don't you think he [the other expert] has answered your question?" As I pointed out in Chapter 6, the expert who is going to lose a point will be more effective the quicker he does so. If he still disagrees, so be it. Under current procedures, experts are not deterred from making essentially foolish criticisms which take the court's time and energy. My suggestions will reduce them, but not eliminate them.

The agenda should pare questions down to those that remain fruitful or fundamental. Both experts should possess the same data. Both should be able to ask their questions of the data before they ask the opposing expert, and the judge can hold them to that standard. The experts can dispute what the appropriate procedure would be to get at the underlying issue, but should not disagree on the result of running a particular procedure on a given data set.

Though one might fear that my "discussion" forum would foster pointless debate, I believe it would reduce the pointless comments now made in fear of not having an answer on the record, even if the question has not yet been raised. Debates now left open can be closed. Insubstantial criticism will be dropped from the agenda. Experts who cannot come up with an immediate answer are now penalized, whereas the system should want more thoughtful responses. Attorneys select the glib over the competent expert, and are rewarded for doing so. More-contemplative procedures might call for more-contemplative experts, though that is a lot to ask.

The technology should not be underrated. In *Polaroid* (1983) I had to utilize staff to locate a mainframe service with the software that Rich Goldstein had used. Today his criticism could be answered in the courtroom, on Goldstein's own computer. I would ask, "Have you censored observations," and then, not even knowing how to do so (in his software), I would explain why he should, who receives that condition. Court might be in recess while he makes the changes in my presence. Then he would explain what he has done, for the record. The results would emerge obviously honest and unmanipulated.[331]

Without the interference of the attorneys, who add nothing to the conversation, the judge could keep each debate on track by asking each expert, "Do I have to know this?" If no, then, "Does this question require an answer from Dr. X?" The experts must advance the ball or stop kicking at it.

As skeptical as I am of expert competence and honesty, I believe that some experts would concede clearly made points some of the time. A judge, whether he understands the underlying science or not, can usually tell whose argument is on point. Again, I see no reason for each expert to "fully disclose" every thought he ever had on the topic at hand; but full response to the opposing expert's questions is called for.

In open court, I would hope the promise of such debates would bring audiences: students, if no one else. Currently, the stifling one-sidedness, coupled with intermediation by attorneys, renders most statistical expert presentations unenlightening and boring. A give-and-take debate on a published agenda might actually be interesting. The expert wants to look good in such a debate. It should embarrass no one that some questions turn out not to be criticisms. That is what questions are for: to be answered.

A JOURNAL COLUMN

Given the amount of use of statistics in courts, and the generally low quality of such use, it is interesting to note that prior to 2003 there was no regular review of it. One reason, as noted in Chapter 9, is that professional associations do not want frank, open exposure of the failings of their members. Another is that they are unaware of those failings. Much of

---

331. *Polaroid* (1983) should never have come to trial, and likely would not have had my suggested pre-trial procedures been followed. In an exchange of reports and face-to-face meeting, Goldstein would have been required to disclose his supposed re-running of my MULQUALS™ program in BMDP. I would have told him his error. He could have verified that he should have censored some observations, and that had he done so, BMDP would produce the same result as MULQUALS™. With my distinction between termination notices and termination, and Goldstein's acquiescence to my methodology, I believe plaintiffs would have abandoned their complaint.

the work I have criticized throughout this book is considered state-of-the-art, at least by the highly credentialed association member who did it.

Some commentators think lack of review is a serious impediment to inducing quality work from experts.

> The reputational costs of signing a scientifically incompetent affidavit are far lower than the costs of signing a scientifically incompetent journal article. Affidavits rarely get much public notice, and most of them vanish even from legal view once a case is over.[332]

Some, not speculating why, think academic work is more rigorously prepared than litigation work:

> We have encountered economists of the caliber of Dr. DePodwin in their academic milieu, and, knowing their fetish for rigorous analysis, cannot conceive of them (or Dr. DePodwin in his academic role) seriously positing economic conclusions based upon the kind of evidence upon which Dr. DePodwin relied in his report.[333]

For some reason, "publication" seems to enhance an expert's credentials, presumably because of the "peer-review" process used by journals.[334] In fact, litigation studies are more thoroughly reviewed than publications.[335]

---

332. Foster and Huber (1997) at 179.

333. *Zenith* (1981) at 1350.

334. Foster and Huber contend, at 171:

> The peer review process is quite efficient at screening out papers that are too speculative or where there are serious errors in the design of the study or in the analysis of data.

On the contrary, academics are not well suited to take on review of litigation studies.

335. Citing a 1990 article in the *Journal of the American Medical Association,* Judge Reed informs us that

> the average referee spends less than two hours assessing an article submitted to a biomedical journal.

Valentine (1996) at 675. And that two-hour review creates a credential for litigation? Koukoutchos (1994) agrees, at 2246:

> Publication in a peer-reviewed scientific journal is a lousy litmus test for admissibility in a court of law because publication does not certify that the study is generally accepted or even sound.

Expert reports are more thoroughly reviewed:

> Indeed, the courtroom is a far superior testing ground for scientific studies and views than a journal's peer review panel. When compared to cross-examination, "the greatest legal engine ever invented for the discovery of truth," peer review comes in a very distant second in terms of the time and resources committed, and of the depth, intensity, and range of the inquiry.

At 2251. The quoted phrase is from John Wigmore, 5 *Evidence* 1367 (third edition, 1940). Lempert (1999) tells us, at 869, that law reviews, the journals that judges read, "seldom subject social-science submissions to peer review."

Limiting his observations, I think, to legislative-fact testimony, Richard Posner thinks little of what he has heard:

> One interpretation is that academics regard the courtroom as a political forum in which concerns for accuracy should play no part; the oath be damned.[336]

As suggested in Chapter 9, the courtroom is seen by academics less as a political forum than as a source of supplementary income. Perhaps what is needed is some kind of peer review, some publicity to people who matter. These "peers" not only hold social leverage; they, too, are a route up the income ladder. The lack of professional exposure is one reason the competence level of statistical experts in courts remains as low as it is.

The National Research Council's Panel on Statistical Assessment as Evidence in the Courts produced ten feeble and quickly dismissed recommendations.[337] Not one of them went to the heart of trial procedure. They also recommended journal exposure:

> The panel recommends that legal, statistical, and scientific journals publish, on a regular basis, critical statistical reviews of expert presentations and judicial opinions in cases involving important uses of statistics.

What is interesting about this recommendation is that it is *not* that journals carry the litigation *debate*. It advocates "critical statistical reviews." By whom? This panel, being itself an elite group, conceives of reviews by people of their kind. I suggest that the goal should be to publish a discussion by the original participants, who can defend their positions or indicate why they have changed their minds.[338] A reviewer/editor might introduce the debate with a summary of the issues, and might close the debate with his viewpoint. A professional reviewer could fulfill the judge's role in a moderated discussion, so that for some cases there would be two records, one in which the experts speak to the judge, the other in which they speak to a fellow professional.

The Professional Association

Even this much will not happen. As I demonstrated in Chapter 9 and its appendix, the commissars of statistics[339] are not prepared to allow criticism of a fellow statistician with-

---

336. Posner (2001a) at 370.

337. The Panel's report is Fienberg, editor (1989). The recommendations are at pages 10–16.

338. Another advantage of the discussion forum is that single reviewers cannot be expected to be very good. 287 *Journal of the American Medical Association* 21 (June 5, 2002), devoted to assessing both medical research articles and the peer-review process, shows us how poor much peer-reviewed and published research is.

339. I have borrowed this phrase from David Hawkes, "The Evolution of Darwinism," review of Stephen Jay Gould, *The Structure of Evolutionary Theory* (Harvard University Press, 2002), in 274 *The Nation* 22:29 (June 10, 2002), at 32:

out his permission. If it does not *allow* veto-proof criticism, surely the American Statistical Association will not *sponsor* it. So it is hopeless to ask the ASA, as it is currently formulated, to advance such a flow of information. I think most ASA members do not know that they have a policy designed to prevent such exposure. It is disgraceful.

Kenneth Foster and Peter Huber think there is movement towards publication of litigation studies:

> Several societies' journals have begun to publish expert testimony offered in litigation, and have subjected it to peer review after the fact, with or without the acquiescence of the testifying expert.[340]

Typical of them, they do not name any such journal. They do hint at an important point, one I made in correspondence with *Chance* magazine. Litigation reports accepted into evidence are public documents. The magazine does not need the permission of the author to reproduce either a report or testimony. It would need the cooperation of one of the experts to do a thorough review, but Foster and Huber understand that academic reviews of litigation do not go that far:

> The reviewer rarely asks for the original data in the study and seldom repeats the author's calculations or statistical analyses.

In 2003, *Chance* initiated a regular review of litigation, by Michael Finkelstein and Bruce Levin.[341] Thus, as I expected, the review function, when it did occur, was entrusted to individual commentators, not to a discussion forum with a neutral referee. Given the veto policy described in Chapter 9, one must now ask: Do Finkelstein and Levin actually criticize expert work? Does *Chance* send preview copies of the Finkelstein-Levin article to its subjects, and excise portions when asked to? If so, are readers aware of this censorship? If not, when did this policy change, under what circumstances?

As I suggested in Chapter 9, re-assessing litigation studies could be an accepted subject of Ph.D. dissertations, or at least graduate courses and major papers therein. The combination of review by students and review in professional publications might to some extent counteract the internal logic of the litigation system, which wants affirming experts, not good ones. These suggestions focus on science testimony, analyses that can be re-examined independent of the person who originally performed them. I think these notions could be extended to craft testimony, and surely to engineering testimony, although I do not do so here.

The idea that schools in Kansas might depart from Darwinist orthodoxy induced apoplexy among the commissars of science.

340. Foster and Huber (1997) at 179; following indented quotation at 174.

341. Dalene Stangl, "Michael Finkelstein and Bruce Levin Introduce 'Chance at the Bar,'" *Amstat News*, August 2003, at 11.

Why wouldn't a university invite both side's experts to debate, in an open but professionally moderated forum (for pay, of course)? Would Schmalensee vs. Fisher, a debate between the *Microsoft* economists, not induce a full house wherever it occurred? Law schools seem so disassociated from courtrooms, it is perhaps no wonder that their graduates are so unprepared to deal with experts.

My Procedural Suggestions: Summary

My proposals, in capsule, first concern what happens before there is any formal hearing:

> The judge needs to oversee data exchange, to be sure data requested have been produced so that the other side can read them. The goal is that each side should be able to match numbers to words without dispute at that level. All data-related terms should be defined and agreed upon prior to trial.

> The judge needs to set a schedule that the parties can meet, and then keep them to it. The sanctions for missing the schedule have to be severe enough that they are not seen as just a cost of the litigation. Experts not timely noticed will be excluded, exhibits will not be accepted after the final exhibit-submission date, etc. Ultimately, disruptive behavior by expert or attorney should be fined.

> The schedule should allow for written reports *and responses*.

> The experts should meet face-to-face, with attorneys, to be sure that they agree on the data, and to articulate on what they disagree. The judge can require a joint report of such a meeting from the attorneys.

The trial, even though it has not been organized to this end, is a system for obtaining fact and applying law to it. The judge is the system's administrator. If he does not take control of it, it will take control of him. If he does not direct it toward finding fact, it will fail to do so.

In a large "science" case we can expect one party or the other to call for a *Daubert* hearing. Or the judge can call for one himself. The *Daubert* hearing could be an important judicial device to help the judge keep control of the evidence presented in the courtroom. Or it could wither away into meaninglessness. Circuit courts will determine which way it goes. If credentials play no role, as I advocate, circuit courts will have to pay more attention to the judge's opinion about substance. Judges will have to write substantive decisions justifying, not just announcing, inclusion or exclusion of experts. Circuit courts should support well-reasoned *Daubert* decisions, and remand those that proclaim, but do not explain. The more serious the *Daubert* hearing—and the opinion based thereon—the better the quality of the expert, in the long run.

Recommended *Daubert*-hearing procedures:

> Determine if science, engineering, craft, or wisdom is at issue.
>
> If science, determine the basis of and probability associated with expert's conclusion(s).
>
> If engineering, determine that testimony will be supported by a prototype (not necessarily perfected) model or adequate substitutes (such as filmed tests observed in the making by opponent's experts).
>
> If craft, determine the methodological basis of the opinion and the history of such opinions by this expert, i.e., compute the historic frequencies of errors.
>
> If wisdom, determine the accuracy and completeness of the knowledge bases from which testimony will be given.
>
> Determine the acceptability of each witness and his testimony.

The invention of Judge Gertner, allowing a witness to testify as an adjudicative-fact expert, but not present an adjudicative finding, contradicts the Rules of Evidence (if you are an expert, you *can* give an opinion about ultimate fact) and deprives the jury, which knows the expert's conclusion anyway, of facts (including fallibility assessments) by which they can assess it. Rather, the *Daubert* hearing should classify and treat the experts according to the framework I presented. The result of this classification is to require different kinds of error admissions, quantitative assessments of the fallibility of the testimony (if science or engineering) or the witness (if technical).

Then, I am concerned with trial procedures:

> Less call-and-response, more lecture without objections, in each expert's initial presentation.
>
> Rebuttal as now, but foreshortened in anticipation of the discussion forum to follow.
>
> Cross-examination to obtain specific statements, where one party thinks the other party's expert has been imprecise or incorrect, or even admissions useful to limit topics in the forthcoming debate.
>
> Groundwork for a final discussion forum, including judge-supervised agenda, and preparation time.
>
> A judge-moderated discussion forum following rebuttals.

The scientific expert presents his conclusions with their accompanying probability derived from the method itself. The engineering expert presents his solution to the engineering problem, and perhaps describes where his current solution falls short, but could be modified. The technical expert presents a binary conclusion, whereas scientific and engineering conclusions are more hedged. The technical expert should be instructed to avoid adjectival language such as "with scientific certainty."[342] We understand that the prosecutor's handwriting expert thinks the defendant wrote the ransom note, and that the defendant's expert thinks he did not. There is no point in not letting them say so. Along with that opinion, however, there must be a record of each expert's historical or test accuracy, which itself can be challenged. The wisdom witness will not comment on any of the facts of this case, only about related legislative facts.

I have suggested pre-trial publicity, inviting the public to see the debate. And I have suggested post-trial publicity on the substance of the debate, playing it one more time (now well-rehearsed) in a professional journal, moderated by a professional. Much of this requires the judge to depart from his usual role into one that I have sensed many would have liked to take. The moderator is more actively involved than the recipient. Judges may think they cannot moderate scientific debates, but I think that is exactly what they can learn to do, in the special judge training I have advocated. They can learn that task far easier and far better than they can learn science itself. And it will be more useful.

My final suggestions concern professions, not the court. Professional associations exist to collect dues and perpetuate their own myths. They throw annual parties at which people meet, network, further their professional positions. Their publications are important in generating technical discussions and disseminating technical advances. They are not a place to look for "certification" of experts. Those who rise in the hierarchies of professional organizations have demonstrated the skill to do that, not the skill to assess others' work. Indeed, the political acumen necessary to become an association officer may be the opposite of that required to make appropriate litigation assessments.

The one thing professions can do, however, is publish discussions about litigation topics. It is the one thing they should do, for the education of their own members. Without censorship. Anointing litigation gurus, the path taken by the American Statistical Association, is not the answer.

---

342. Of James Grigson's testimony about future dangerousness, we learn from Eugenia La Fontaine (2002) at 209, case references deleted:

> Dr. Grigson has testified repeatedly that he was one hundred percent certain that the defendant would be dangerous in the future; that he could testify to this fact "within reasonable psychiatric certainty;" and, in some cases, that there was "a one thousand percent chance" that the defendant would be a future danger.

It is not clear how Grigson passed through screening for expertise in his craft, but how expert he is should have been presented as separate evidence, and his self-supporting statements disallowed.

Others' Procedural Suggestions I: Experts

I turn, here, to proposals made by others for the handling of statistical expertise. The most prominent are:

> A special master who would hear the statistical debate, and report back to the judge, with recommendations for findings of fact.

> An expert or panel of experts engaged by the court, to advise the court on technical disputes between the adversarial experts.

> An expert engaged by the court who might not only mediate but could initiate, perform his own studies.

> Experts engaged by—but not controlled by—the parties.

> Panels of experts that would provide "definitive" resolution of expert disputes.

In the Federal Rules of Civil Procedure, Rule 39 specifies three ways to find fact: by jury, by the court, or with an advisory jury. When there is no right to a jury trial,

> the court, with the consent of both parties, may order a trial with a jury whose verdict has the same effect as if trial by jury had been matter of right.

As most procedural suggestions under review here have been concerned with the inadequacy of the common jury to handle science questions, I will not explore the idea of imposing a jury when the law does not provide for one by right.

Despite what appears to be the plain language of Rule 39, that an advisory jury's verdict would be definitive, Rule 52, with specific reference to the advisory jury, says otherwise. That jury's verdict is truly advisory, not binding. The subject came up in a complex case including expert statistical testimony. As the judge was Jack Weinstein, one should not be surprised to find a historical review of the advisory jury in his opinion.[343]

Special Masters

A special master may be designated by the judge, with the consent of the parties, or under Rule 53(b) of the Rules of Civil Procedure. Some judges do so under powers "inherent" in their authority to manage cases.[344] Unless the master is a magistrate (that is, already on the payroll), his cost is assessed to the parties. Although it is a difficult line to draw, the master is supposed to be concerned with factual, not legal issues. In the cases in which I

---

343. See *Acusport* (2003). The discussion about the advisory jury, which Weinstein did convene, and allowed to reach a verdict by a ten-to-two majority or better, is Section III, starting at 464.

344. See M. Farrell (1994), and the discussion of *Magistrini* (2002) below.

have been involved with a special master, liability had been determined. I think this is a valid but not inviolable generality, that court-appointed experts are used in the liability stage, and masters (who themselves might have experts) are used in the damages stage.

The court assigned a special master to take expert testimony and advise the judge in *Mister* (1987).[345] A special master was appointed to coordinate expert work and provide a neutral view of it in *Robins* (1988). Although I presume that both courts were satisfied with the process, I was not.

I discussed the special master's involvement in *Mister* in Chapter 7. In this employment discrimination case, district-judge Foreman had found for defendant. At the Seventh Circuit, Judge Easterbrook's reversal opinion was withering. David Peterson's defense methodology

> assumes what is to be proven—that differences in hiring are attributable to distance rather than race. The expert derived the weights from ICG's hiring, rather than from distance. So, if the ICG hired one person from an all-black county with a labor force of 100 and ten people from an all-white county with a labor force of 100, the expert would assign the black county a weight of 0.10 and deduce that the ICG was "expected" to hire only one person from it—even if the black county were closer to the ICG's places of work than the white county. Voila! Discrimination itself produces a statistical finding of no discrimination.[346]

The case then went back to district court for damages, where Judge Foreman allowed Peterson to present calculations based on distance! The judge then appointed a special master who also allowed Peterson to base his calculation on the very factors that had been rejected in the merits trial. Finally seeing the fallacy of that approach, the master joined the fray, suggesting his own calculations. The parties were exhausted. The settlement was not based on the master's work.

Francis McGovern, the master in *Robins* (1988), went further. McGovern had been a special master in asbestos cases in Cleveland and Texas, in Indian-rights litigation in Michigan, and in DDT cases in Alabama. I do not know how he handled his previous experiences, but for the *Robins* litigation he hired his own staff.[347] They were neither better nor worse than the parties' experts, but in theory they were neutral. Samples were drawn, data

---

345. The citations in the case list, *Mister* (1986) through *Mister* (1988), do not cover the damages stage, which is where I entered the case, and of which I write here.

346. *Mister* (1987) at 1433.

347. Although McGovern has written about these experiences, he has dealt more with their theory and results than with their mechanism. He sees the use of a master as part of aggressive judicial management, and possibly a form of alternative dispute resolution which deserves experimentation. See McGovern (1986) and McGovern (2005).

were collected and coded, analysts prepared their calculations, and a hearing was held. The master's staff resolved conflict between the parties' experts. They provided a decision-making forum with some statistical expertise.[348] Their job was to allow each side to apply its own methodology to common data. That is an excellently conceived mandate, spoiled in its practice by internecine struggles. I suggest that the master should be strong, but have more respect for the parties' experts. McGovern seemed more interested in the credit he would get for having monitored the expert proceedings, than in actually doing so; more interested in the politics among lawyers than the technical issues among experts.

In short, the special master is a fine institution. It is marred by the selection of who is to be the master. That selection is marred by a predisposition to engage only attorneys in the task.

Advisory Experts for the Courts

I have included in this book many judicial comments of disappointment (to put it mildly) at the quality of expertise brought into the courtroom. On occasion, such comments are accompanied by an analysis. Consider this quotation from Wigmore included in a California court decision. The expert's

> candid scientific opinion thus has no fair opportunity of expression, or even of formation, swerved as he is by this partisan committal. The remedy therefore seems to lie in removing this partisan feature, i.e., by bringing him in court free from any committal to either party. . . . [N]o measure can be effective which does not secure such a status for the expert witness.[349]

That the *only* experts would be those engaged by the court seems not to be a viable reform. However, courts engaging their own experts, in addition to those engaged by the parties, is a reality.

Jennifer Mnookin writes:

> A constant leitmotif in the history of expert evidence has been the call for the use of neutral experts.[350]

---

348. See Sobol (1991). Sobol devotes only thirteen pages to "the McGovern process." He does not mention McGovern's staff, and therefore says nothing about expert conflicts and resolutions.

349. *Strong* (1931) at 525, quoting Volume I, *Wigmore on Evidence* § 563. The court went on to approve, at 526, the concept of an expert

> appointed by the court and paid by the county, and who would be free from any possible sentiment of loyalty to either side or to anything except the truth as it appears to a trained mind with no partisan affiliations.

Appellant had argued that such an appointment was a function of the executive branch of government. The court found it a reasonable judicial action.

350. Mnookin (2001a) at 70.

In the Huber tradition, she provides no citation, not a single example. Aside from Wigmore, I have seen only one suggestion that a judge's expert substitute for experts put forward by the parties. Use of *only* an expert for the court has been tried in child-custody hearings in Texas. As one might expect, the experts who are utilized like it (out from under the advocate's thumb) and the judges like it (more direct contact with the expert's thought process); but the attorneys do not (loss of control).[351] This might be a good model on which to build, but I know of no movement to do so.

Although Joseph Sanders thinks there may be a turnaround in the use of court-appointed experts, "historically they have been used sparingly."[352] Jan Beyea and Daniel Berger mention the court-appointed advisor almost in passing, proposing no specific procedures (for example, not discussing the advisor's role, how active he is to be with parties, etc.). Their concern is the risk inherent if the court has only one advisor. They seem more interested in "Teams of Scientific Reviewers" (one of their subheadings):

> The foundational premise is that a jury of scientists would be the gold standard for deciding whether expert testimony should be considered scientifically valid.[353]

Their teams would be "deciding," not recommending to the judge. Beyea and Berger seem to be following Samuel Gross, who supports a single advisor but suggests "peer review of expert evidence" by a review board.[354]

In *Hall* (1996b), Judge Jones appointed one expert to recommend others, eventually selecting four specialists (none in statistics) whose written reports were fundamental in the court's exclusion of much of plaintiffs' evidence. Posner proposes a simpler process: The parties' *experts*, not the parties, not intermediate experts, would nominate the neutral expert. And then, as a judge, he goes further, essentially commanding that, on remand, the trial judge use this procedure:

> [W]e recommend that the district judge use the power that Rule 706 of the Federal Rules of Evidence expressly confers upon him to appoint his own expert witness, rather than leave himself and the jury completely at the mercy of the parties' warring experts. The main objection to this procedure and the main reason for its infrequency are that the judge cannot be confident that the expert whom he has picked is a genuine neutral. The objection can be obviated by directing the party-designated experts to agree

---

351. See Anthony Champagne, Danny Easterling, Daniel W. Shuman, Alan Tomkins, and Elizabeth Whitaker, "Are court-appointed experts the solution to the problems of expert testimony?" 84 *Judicature* 4:178 (January–February 2001). "Real experts," said the lawyers at 181, "work for lawyers."

352. Sanders (1998) at 378.

353. Beyea and Berger (2001) at 365.

354. Gross (1991) at 1213.

upon a neutral expert whom the judge will then appoint as the court's expert.[355]

Gross suggests a different reason for the "infrequency" of court-appointed experts:

> In short, court-appointed experts are not used in American trials because they are beyond the control of lawyers. As a result, they threaten the prerogatives of the trial attorneys, and they are likely to be inadequately prepared for testimony and uncomfortably unpredictable.[356]

From the Texas child-custody findings we see that Gross is correct about attorney reactions, but it is not clear why a judge would cater to the displeasure of trial attorneys. I know of no evidence that court-appointed experts are "uncomfortably unpredictable," except that, as I discussed in Chapter 4, a sample of size one maximizes the variance among potential independent responses. Part of the judicial training I have advocated would concern how to structure such a relationship.

In *Magistrini* (2002), Mark Weiss was appointed to the position of "the Court's technical advisor" to help evaluate epidemiological evidence at the *Daubert* hearing in a toxic tort litigation.

> As the Court's technical advisor, Dr. Weiss' duties were to assist and advise the Court with regard to the non-legal, technical, scientific, and medical data, literature, and testimony supplied on behalf of the parties and to assist the Court in formulating questions to assess the reliability and relevancy of the methodology used by the parties' experts. Dr. Weiss did not opine on the ultimate issues of causation or warnings and offered no evidence or testimony in the case.[357]

As I recommended above, I think this is a model many courts should consider. It frontloads litigation. Both parties brought in additional experts only for the *Daubert* hearing, experts who would not testify at trial.

Erica Beecher-Monas thinks that the judge should "examine the data in the studies proffered by experts."

---

355. *Corn Syrup* (2002) at *12, citations omitted. One cite is to Rubinfeld (1985), who makes a similar suggestion.

356. Gross (1991) at 1205.

357. *Magistrini* (2002) at 589; preceding in-text quotation also at 589. Cecil and Willging—(1994a) at 531, (1994b) at 998—explain that, in addition to Rule 706 authority is

> the broader inherent authority of the court to appoint experts who are necessary to permit the court to carry out its duties, including the authority to appoint a technical advisor.

Does this "inherent authority" have no source? Judge Jones in Oregon:

> I invoked my inherent authority as a federal district court judge to appoint independent advisors to the court.

Hall (1996b) at 1392. He cites Federal Rule of Evidence 104 as his basis.

Only by examining the data can the conclusions drawn by the studies be verified. The only way to tell if such errors are contained in an expert's report or proffered testimony is to examine the data and the statistical inferences drawn from it, not for mathematical errors but for errors in logic. Such an examination may appear a tall order for a lawyer or judge, but it is fundamental not only in assessing scientific evidence, but in analyzing information of all sorts.[358]

If the judge has an expert, surely this task would be delegated to him. But what happened to the adversarial system? Telling the judge what errors an expert has made should continue to be, in the first instance, the responsibility of other partisan experts. The role of the judge's advisor is to decide, when the initial experts deny that their data or methods are faulty, which expert makes the better argument. That is, Beecher-Monas apparently asks the judge to take the very initiative I ask him not to take. The parties' experts need to do expert work, to be evaluated by the court's agent, advising the judge.

In this light, Judge Kessler envisions a more limited role for his technical advisor:

> The scope of the expert advisor's duties will be to answer the court's technical questions regarding the meaning of terms, phrases, theories, and rationales included in or referred to in the briefs and exhibits of any of the parties.[359]

Apparently the technical advisor will not be present at the trial. Judge Kessler envisions most of this consultation occurring by telephone.

Judge Parker also uses this "technical advisor" language, asserting that, as such, his expert is not an expert witness, and will not be subject to deposition, following the examples set by Judge Jones in *Hall* (1996b), and Judge Orrick in *Mexican* (1996).[360] I disagree. I think the judge's advisor should be subject to examination by the parties, perhaps the last event of the trial.[361]

---

358. Beecher-Monas (2000) at 1602.

359. *Conservation* (2002) at 32.

360. *Reid Jr.* (2001) at 507. Mexican (2000) at 590:

> Dr. Klein was appointed by the district court as a technical advisor, but was not called as an expert witness, was not subject to cross-examination, and did not furnish an expert's report.

361. *Harvard Law Review* editors, in Note (1997), also ask for more participation of the parties with the judge's expert. They seem, at 958, not to understand the limited role some judges assign to such an expert:

> Finally, courts should allow the parties to respond to the technical advisor's written report before making an admissibility ruling.

As we have seen, not all "technical advisors" write such a report.

Rule 706 permits the parties to cross-examine the "neutral" expert, which is one reason some judges avoid it as the foundation for their appointment. Another procedure is to ignore that aspect of Rule 706, as did Judge Feikens, the Sixth Circuit informs us in *Nemir* (2004) at 548.

Another problem with this "technical advisor" concept is, who pays? Rule 706 experts are a cost that can be assessed against the losing party, but "technical advisors" are not. One would think that technical advisors would be funded by the federal judiciary itself, as valuable to the judge as any other assistant. However, the federal judiciary does not pay for experts called by the judge.[362] This is like United States Attorney's offices being able to hire only attorneys and secretaries, rather than letting each office devise its most practical staffing scheme, which might include paralegals. Many courts need budgets for judicial assistants—some of whom would be "experts"—while still allowing the judge to assess costs on the parties in any proportion.

Judge Hochberg writes:

> A study is statistically significant if the p-value attributed to that study is less than 0.05. That is, the study shows that there is only 5% probability that an observed association is due to chance alone.[363]

The two misconceptions in this statement should be obvious from the material in Chapter 7. In this decision, Judge Hochberg continues, following these offending sentences, with a correct description of what the probability shows. I therefore do not wish to quibble about his language, but to point out that, despite the absence of statisticians in this case, there was no absence of statistics. This is one place judges have yet to go: to engage neutral experts in fields *utilized* by the testifying experts, but not *defining* the testifying experts.[364]

Active Experts for the Courts

Commentators have been urging courts to appoint their own experts for over half a century.[365] The National Research Council's panel likes the judge-appointed-expert approach. This is their Recommendation 6:

---

362. *Hall* (1996b) at footnote 9:
   Although I requested federal funding for the Rule 104 experts' fees, my request was denied. The fees, approximately $76,000, have been paid by the parties.

363. *Magistrini* (2002), footnote 26 at 605.

364. Beecher-Monas (2000) at 1581:
   Statistical inference, with its concepts of probability, independence, and randomness, is basic to scientific discourse and forms the cornerstone of data analysis as well as the basis for causation and other explanatory arguments.

365. Legal commentators have been recommending neutral experts since at least Wigmore's second edition, quoted above from *Strong* (1931). Wigmore may be the originator of the concept that judges have "inherent power" to do so. See his §2484. See Sink (1956) for a major exposition of the authority and reasons for the judge to appoint his own expert, based on bias inherent in those presented by the litigants. Justice Breyer, in a speech to the American Enterprise Institute broadcast live on C-SPAN2 on December 4, 2003, suggested that *appellate* judges could engage experts, and even held out the thought, though too "far out there" for now, that the Supreme Court might do so. I think these are both

> The panel believes that judges have been unduly reluctant to appoint statisti-
> cal experts to assist the court and it recommends the increased use of court-
> appointed procedures such as those provided by Rule 706 of the Federal Rules
> of Evidence.[366]

Although there are published cases in which a judge has appointed his own expert, some of which are reviewed above as "technical advisors," Joe Cecil and Thomas Willging tell us that this practice is more common than published cases suggest. And they tell us why:

> The need for assistance in decision making often arose when the parties failed
> to present credible expert testimony, thereby failing to inform the trier of fact
> on essential issues.[367]

Margaret Berger, perhaps concerned about difficulties of communication between a legally un-savvy expert and the judge, suggests:

> A court might also consider appointing a scientifically sophisticated neutral
> lawyer to articulate for the methodological expert the issues that need to be
> addressed.[368]

Berger, an attorney, sees her kind as superior to my kind. This, as I indicated in Chapter 6, is one of the problems with lawyers. Why not appoint a sophisticated expert in the relevant field, who has knowledge of law?

In my experience, once you start building a staff, those persons want to do the analysis. The National Research Council's panel clearly does not want them to. This is their Recommendation 7:

> The panel recommends that, in general, judges should not conduct analytical
> statistical studies on their own. If a court is not satisfied with the statistical

---

bad ideas. Breyer also suggested that august bodies like the American Enterprise Institute itself prepare lists of experts from which judges should select. Another bad idea. The good idea is to allow the parties to challenge the court's expert, at the trial level, and—as Justice Breyer emphasized—that the expert always be advisory, never determinative.

Perhaps the most thorough examination of the Rule 706 expert is provided by Deason (1998). I think we agree on the basic issues, for example that such experts should be subject to examination by the parties. Kim (2001) seems to think that some commentators interpret the use of Rule 706 as allowing the judge to do his own investigation, taking this initiative away from the parties. Apparently doing battle against a straw idea, espoused by no one, suffices to generate a law-review article.

Murphy (2000), at 236, would create

> a permanent organization to provide courts with experienced, respected, and impartial
> experts in various specialized fields.

It would operate as an elite network. All such organizations always do. It shouldn't happen.

366. Fienberg (1989) at 14.

367. Cecil and Willging (1994b) at 1010. For more on the Federal Judicial Center survey that underlies the Cecil and Willging conclusions, see M. Farrell (1994).

368. M. Berger (1994) at 1362.

evidence before it, alternative means should be used to clarify matters, such as a request for additional submissions from the parties or even, in exceptional circumstances, a reopening of the case to receive additional evidence.[369]

As far as this goes, I agree. Sanders discusses the fear of parties losing control (always the lawyer's primary concern), of fundamental evidence being produced by the court itself.[370] Neither the judge nor a special master should engage in such an activity, my own experience says loud and clear. But the court's expert? I do not like the idea that the judge's own expert never gets his hands dirty with actual data analysis. He should obtain data from both parties, and at least replicate some of their analyses. He might do a different analysis, but use it only to inform himself, to ask questions of and make suggestions to the parties' experts. Robert Coulam and Stephen Fienberg describe an expert who did studies on his own, apparently to some positive effect in inducing a settlement.[371]

I find Gross' complaint compelling, his solution diaphanous:

> The essential flaw in the existing schemes for appointment of experts is the absence of incentives to use them. . . . The solution is obvious, at least in general terms: make the use of court-appointed experts mandatory.[372]

The problem with this suggestion will occur to anyone who has ever tried to write a rule about anything. How would one codify the nature of cases in which such an expert would be "mandatory"? (Some have tried. See "Rule Revisions" below.)

As with technical advisors, the major problem with engaging a judge's expert is the expense. In a dispute between titans, a patent infringement or private antitrust case, assessing the parties equally seems reasonable. In some cases the state sponsors both sides, so why not also independent advice for the judge?[373] The same reasoning applies here as above: The judge can hire clerks, secretaries, and others to help him, with judiciary-system funds. I see no reason why the judicial branch of government should not have funds to engage experts to help it in its work.

---

369. Fienberg (1989) at 15.

370. Sanders (1998) suggests that this is already occurring, that the law

> has taken steps to weaken party control over litigation by empowering judges and juries to play a more active role in the trial process.

At 357. He suggests, at 365, that attorneys and judges have exacerbated jurors' misunderstandings of expert testimony. His solution is more use of court-appointed experts. I don't disagree; I just add that the current procedures are designed to allow attorney interference with expert presentations. Perhaps judges would do better, and jurors much better, following the procedures I have outlined.

371. See Coulam and Fienberg (1986).

372. Gross (1991) at 1220.

373. The state, through the public defender's office, financed defendants' experts in *Gibbs* (1998), *Soto* (1996), *Correa* (2002), and *Tremblay* (2003), for example.

As an example, I assert the experience of Judge Suhrheinrich of the Sixth Circuit.

> [A]n intern in my chambers, who also happens to be a board-certified psychiatrist, expressed concern as to why [defendant's experts] had not directly addressed the question as to whether [defendant] did or did not exhibit symptoms of a major mental illness at the time of the crime or sentencing, and, if he did, whether the symptoms were sufficient at that point to support a diagnosis of mental illness which should have been presented as mitigating evidence at the sentencing hearing.[374]

The circuit had upheld the district court's denial of a writ of *habeas corpus*. The judge pursued this issue, determined that they had been incorrect the first time, got the case re-opened and admitted evidence that had not been presented at trial. This time, the panel vacated the district court's refusal to get involved.

It is reasonable to fear a judge's expert, especially an activist one. Experts have not earned the respect we would like an independent expert to have. And academics—we know my view—are ill suited to participate in real-world forums. Most methodological advances in statistics in the courts have been introduced by practitioners, not academics.[375] The skills will evolve, even if the pool of candidates looks bleak at the moment. The only way judges will get the assistance they need is to try. From the opinions I have seen, advisory experts generally perform well. Perhaps we should let that aspect develop before we permit or ask them to be more active in solving the litigation's puzzles.

Experts Accessible to All Parties

George Harris proposes to change the relationship between the expert and his client. Parties would select experts subject to the following restrictions:

> Trial testimony by a paid expert witness should be allowed only if the expert is identified to the opposing party prior to any case-specific discussion of the substance of the expert's opinions.
>
> Once selected and identified, a party would relinquish control of an expert. The expert would be equally accessible to both (or all) sides of the case and would be subject to being called by any party as a witness at trial. Experts would also be free to communicate with each other and attempt to reach a consensus.

---

374. *Thompson* (2004) at 692. This decision was unfortunately (and incorrectly) reversed in *Thompson* (2005). What lesson does that send to curious, involved judges?

375. Practitioners, who do not have the time to write books like this, also do not have the flow of funds or perhaps the skill to devise new methodologies. Thus, aside from MULPOOLS™ and MULQUALS™, most innovations offered by practitioners were first devised by academics. Other academics could not see the applications in the legal forum, even when invited into it. That is, in symbiosis, academics revised the theory, professionals revised the practice.

All parties would pay for their own consultation and preparation time with an expert witness at rates agreed to by the expert at the time of selection and identification by one party. The trial time of the expert would be compensated by the party or parties that called her as a witness at trial.[376]

In a footnote, Harris summarizes:

The party that initially contacted the expert would, in effect, engage the expert for all parties at terms agreeable to the expert.

The existence of such a proposal—unless it is simply further evidence of how far legal scholars will go to increase the length of their résumé—is more interesting than the proposal itself. It is, in the first place, unenforceable. Who is to say what communications took place between the expert and his client before the expert was announced as a testifying expert? In the second place, Harris actually contemplates that one party will pay for the work of an expert whose conclusions favor the other party. Why wouldn't the first party fire the expert? Is an expert to be engaged for as long as he wants to be, regardless what positions he is forming?

Harris describes his proposal as

relatively simple, largely self-executing measures that would not require proactive court management or extensive additional court supervision.

My proposals are exactly what Harris would avoid, "pro-active court management or extensive additional court supervision." The question, "What to do next?" is real. Active thought in this area, in many directions, is good. Harris' suggestion is absurd, but welcome.

Expert Panels

An early recommendation for expert panels can be found in the school-desegregation literature.[377] Judges have appointed panels of experts in class-action tort litigation. Two different judges appointed expert panels to assess the relationship between silicone breast implants and the various illnesses they were alleged to have caused. Both panels found no such relationship.

In the asbestos litigation, Judge Weinstein and Bankruptcy Judge Burton Lifland used a panel of court-appointed scientific experts to report on the future course of asbestos claims.[378]

---

376. G. Harris (2000) at 68; following indented quotation at footnote 419; third indented quotation at 74.

377. See, for example, Chesler et al. (1988).

378. Erichson (1999) at 1991. The other panels referred to were appointed by Judge Jones in *Hall* (1996b) and Judge Pointer in *Silicone* (1996). See Walker and Monahan (2000) for a detailed description of the constitution and impact of the panel in *Silicone*, with some discussion of the panel in *Hall*, also.

Whether formally a "panel" or only multiple experts from different fields, this is in general a good trend. What would make it better is more regard for the professional. This view is typical:

> The very idea of a professional expert witness is problematic. "Expertise" in any field requires substantial time to accumulate and to stay abreast of current developments—by reading, experimenting, writing, perhaps teaching, and otherwise pursuing knowledge in the specialized field of study. The problem is that much of a professional expert's time is spent in courtrooms and preparing for trial rather than pursuing expertise.[379]

This is nonsense, but it is what legal scholars write and what judges believe. The result is that judges deny themselves access to available and often superior talent.

OTHERS' PROCEDURAL SUGGESTIONS II: INSTITUTIONAL REFORM

If one way to solve the problem is by controlling or supplementing the experts, another might be by insulating the other functions of the court from them. The most prominent such proposals are:

A "Ministry of Justice," a sort of meta-Justice Department and bar-association rules committee rolled into one, which would constantly assess the justice system, prescribe remedies, and figure out what to do about these difficult science/statistics cases.

Blue-ribbon juries.

Moving some decisions from jury to judge.

A "science court," a special court to which statistical cases would be removed, staffed by statistically trained judges.

Modification of Rule 702, essentially backwards to *Frye* standards.

A Ministry of Justice

The idea of a Ministry of Justice is the contrivance of Roscoe Pound, more than eighty years ago.[380] It would be a

> branch of government which should concern itself not merely with the ongoing administration of the law, but with constant reassessment of its adequacy

---

379. Owen (2002) at 352. An equally ignorant rant could be made concerning the academic's committee and other non-scholarly activities. The question remains how the judge is to find his experts, and my fear remains that professional organizations, dominated by academics, the guilds who self-proclaim their exclusive possession of expertise, will play a pernicious role.

380. See, for example, Pound (1917) and Pound (1920).

for the time and place, the pinpointing of the failures of justice and social policy, and the prescription of remedies.[381]

The codification of rules of civil procedure and, later, rules of evidence, would probably have been considered the premier achievement of such a ministry. In a sense, the Supreme Court, as leader of the federal judiciary, has assumed this role with its various research institutions. Benjamin Cardozo took up the cause to establish a separate ministry, but I know of no individual since his time who has argued for it.[382]

It is true that, without a ministry, we have no single place to turn with suggestions for judicial-system improvement. I am not sure that is bad. The Federal Judicial Center may be as much of that ministry incarnate as we can tolerate. The Carnegie Commission turned to the Center to improve the education of judges, though in a manner I criticized in Chapters 7 and 9. But the Commission also called for more, "an independent nongovernmental Science and Justice Council of lawyers, scientists, and others" that would "monitor changes" and "initiate improvements."[383] This "Science and Justice Council" is the Ministry of Justice all over again, without the cover of government. I don't think we need more abstract supervisors. We need more experienced people. Perhaps conferences are called for, to gather the knowledge and conceptions that I believe are alive in the field, often unarticulated and almost never consolidated and discussed. But not a new bureaucracy.

The Ministry of Justice was an interesting idea in its day. Not now. Calling for it did highlight the lack of systematic updated procedure in the federal judiciary. The Ministry might have been a path toward a solution to the bewilderment of the judiciary in some cases, an institution mandated to find solutions. It would not have been a solution itself.

Blue-Ribbon Juries

A "blue-ribbon" jury is one selected in a deliberate manner, not randomly from the population. I dismissed this idea in Chapter 5, and do so again here. Many writers disparage the competence of the jury to hear complex cases, and some would screen its members. Opposition by the editors of the 1947 *Harvard Law Review* fell on deaf ears.[384] The Supreme Court's decision in *Fay* (1947) is interesting, because its logic is the opposite of that which I put forward in Chapter 5. Writing for the Court, Justice Jackson sets out the issue:

> The question is whether a warranted conviction by a jury individually accept-
> ed as fair and unbiased should be set aside on the ground that the make-up of
> the panel from which they were drawn unfairly narrows the choice of jurors

---

381. Stone (1966) at 21.

382. See Cardozo (1921).

383. Carnegie (1993) at 59, and, in the executive summary, at 18.

384. Note (1947). See the quotation from this Note in Chapter 5, page 316.

and denies defendants due process of law or equal protection of the laws in violation of the Fourteenth Amendment to the Federal Constitution.[385]

Should such a question be decided by process or by outcome? The Court looked for a comparison of the occupations of these special jurors with the occupations that a traditionally selected jury would have had, but found no such comparison on the record. In *Local 36* (1947), on the other hand, Judge Hall thinks little of the elaborate analysis offered by a nameless expert witness. Using the Department of Labor's *Dictionary of Occupation Titles*, the expert had collapsed the questionnaire responses of jurors to twelve occupational categories which could be compared with the census. In my view, selection of jurors by occupation would have made the jury unconstitutional by process alone. The Court was not amenable to comparing procedures. As today, it wanted to compare outcomes. As today, that was a bad approach.

In 1962 a second-year law student was smitten by the idea of improving jury competence by special selection.[386] However, he failed to provide an empirical argument that the decisions from such panels would be in any measurable way better than those from procedurally fair juries. As I posited in Chapter 4, it is plausible, though not provable, that juries have increased in quality so much over two hundred years that, even faced with more-difficult legislation, they are superior decision makers. Uniform random selection from participant lists solves all jury-selection problems. Any form of deliberate selection of jury personnel will only bring forth additional litigation.

As often happens, the dissenters got it right.

> The constitutional vice inherent in the type of "blue ribbon" jury panel here involved is that it rests upon intentional and systematic exclusion of certain classes of people who are admittedly qualified to serve on the general jury panel. Whatever may be the standards erected by jury officials for distinguishing between those eligible for such a "blue ribbon" panel and those who are not, the distinction itself is an invalid one. It denies the defendant his constitutional right to be tried by a jury fairly drawn from a cross-section of the community. It forces upon him a jury drawn from a panel chosen in a manner which tends to obliterate the representative basis of the jury.[387]

Yale Law Journal editors needed to reference the blue-ribbon jury in making a case for black juries, because the principle of deliberate manipulation of jury composition is the same.[388] While finding race a reasonable qualification for jury duty, they did not find skill or education to be so. As Hiroshi Fukurai, Edgar Butler, and Richard Krooth illustrate in

---

385. *Fay* (1947) at 265.

386. See Du Bois (1962).

387. *Fay* (1947) at 297.

388. Note (1970). See the quotation from this Note in Chapter 5, page 307.

their proposal for re-selecting from areas from which the system's mailings did not produce "enough" jurors, the idea of manipulating the composition of the jury will not go away.[389]

Complex litigation has brought forward calls for special juries, selected for their higher-than-average skill level. For example:

> The case for special juries in complex civil cases depends upon acceptance of a rather straightforward proposition: All people are not equally capable of learning about new concepts and applying them to the solution of difficult problems. The jury itself is premised on a similar assumption, and seeks to avoid the shortcomings of individuals through reliance upon the collective wisdom and judgment of a small group. These pooled abilities may not always be enough, however, given the difficulties posed by certain kinds of civil litigation.[390]

The authors propose to limit jury service to college graduates. In essence, they would turn all juries into "blue-ribbon" juries.

Arguing for particular skills, not just higher average skills, is another approach to the same "reform." Alan Feigenbaum, for example, discusses medical-malpractice litigation:

> Shielding physicians from frivolous lawsuits that generate large damage awards may involve altering the composition of the jury entirely.[391]

Feigenbaum's special jury would be composed of medical experts. By whose determination? Should *those* experts pass a kind of *Daubert* qualification procedure? He mounts many arguments, one of interest here being that "many jurors lack the ability to understand scientific evidence entirely." Are juries limited to their members' characteristics, or can there be a synergistic group process, the whole becoming more than the sum of its parts? As I will review immediately below, it is not clear that juries make worse decisions than real alternatives would. Most important, here, special juries are exceptions which, once permitted, would expand in the same way exceptions to taxation and trade statutes flourish. There is no principle behind the special jury. "Special" juries are elite juries, anathema to the "voice of the community" view of juries that is implied by asking that they be not only impartial, but "representative."

Substituting Judge for Jury

In the larger critique of jury decisions, popular not only in the press but in conservative politics, juror reactions to experts is taken to be a particular vulnerability. After all, "Juries hate scientific evidence."[392] Although no one suggests doing away with juries, many want

---

389. See Fukurai et al. (1993).). They are still at it: See Fukurai and Krooth (2003).

390. Luneburg and Nordenberg (1981) at 899.

391. Feigenbaum (2003) at 1364; following in-text quotation at 1394.

392. Senior chemist Stephen Copley says this in P. James (1977), at 96. Of course, this is a work of fiction!

to limit what they get to decide. Indeed, many issues are taken away from juries by pre-trial actions of judges. I have cited numerous examples of the exclusion of one party's experts, followed by a summary judgment for the other party.

The movement to disassociate the jury from determination is clearest in punitive damages. Cass Sunstein and colleagues, for example, discuss "the difficulty of mapping relatively shared and stable normative judgments onto an unbounded dollar scale."[393] Punitive damages they say—with some success—are emotions, not facts. They find that groups (in their case, mock juries) award more than "the median of individual judgments." They think that is a reason to let judges make the determination, although they provide no reason to believe that this median of individuals is a righteous standard, that it could ever be determined in a particular case, or that judge-based awards would come closer to it than juries.

Years earlier, comparing judge and jury tort awards, Kevin Clermont and Theodore Eisenberg had concluded:

> Practitioners and policymakers who believe that plaintiffs as a group always do better before juries are wrong.
>
> In two of the most controversial areas of modern tort law, product liability and medical malpractice, the win rates substantially differ from other categories' win rates and in a surprising way: plaintiffs in these two areas prevail after trial at a much higher rate before judges (48%) than they do before juries (28%). Furthermore, in medical malpractice but not in product liability, the mean recovery in judge trials is higher than the mean recovery in jury trials.[394]

Although they did not stress the jury's reaction to expert testimony, Reid Hastie and Kip Viscusi suggested that juror confusion about probabilities should lead to judges determining punitive damages in tort litigation. Richard Lempert took exception to their argument, to which they replied by restating their position (and suggesting that Lempert just did not understand it) without amplification. Neil Vidmar, agreeing with Lempert, concluded against the conventional wisdom that

> While occasionally juries appear to get it wrong, the overwhelming corpus of research findings lead to the conclusion that, at minimum, juries attempt to assess the content of the expert testimony and place it in the context of other trial evidence, as they are instructed to do by the judge.[395]

---

393. Sunstein et al. (1998) at 2131; following in-text quotation from the same three authors, listed as Schkade et al. (2000), at 1172.

394. Clermont and Eisenberg (1992) at 1172, then a restatement of their 1992 findings in Clermont and Eisenberg (2002) at 145.

395. Vidmar (2001) at 11. The initial article on punitive damages is Hastie and Viscusi (1998), followed by Lempert's critique in Lempert (1999), and a reply in Hastie and Viscusi (2002). Vidmar has a number of publications on the wisdom of jury decisions. Vidmar (2001) is an easy summary of his position, and

Expanding his earlier empirical work with Clermont, Theodore Eisenberg and his colleagues agreed:

> Juries and judges award punitive damages at about the same rate, and their
> punitive awards bear about the same relation to their compensatory awards.[396]

Hastie and Viscusi then joined forces with Sunstein and others to produce a book contending that allowing jurors to determine punitive damages was "unreliable, erratic, and unpredictable."[397] Judge Weinstein, perhaps hastily, called the Sunstein et al. book "a pathbreaking empirical multidisciplinary study."[398] Then reviews started to appear. Neal Feigenson complained that the authors over-interpreted their results, especially as they relied on achieving "optimal deterrence," ignoring "retribution for wrongs perceived to be reprehensible."[399] Catherine Sharkey also criticized the authors' "monolithic conception of punitive damages," calling it a "misconception."[400] Both reviewers praised the work, while questioning whether one can interpret it as broadly as the authors do. Sharkey, for example, called it

---

Vidmar and Robinson (2005) is the most up-to-date. See also Vidmar and Diamond (2001), for example at 1174:

> It seems clear from this review that claims about jury incompetence and irresponsibility
> in assessing and considering the testimony of scientific experts are not supported by
> research findings.

On judge-juror agreement see also Kalven and Zeisel (1966) and their table reproduced in this book as Figure 46.

See also Viscusi (1998), who makes clear his premise that bad behavior is deterred only by predictable consequences. If jury awards are unpredictable, he says, they will not deter. I see no reason why this would be true, or captured in the kinds of statistical analyses utilized by all analysts—logit and regression. It could be that only very bad behavior is severely punished, but it is so only randomly. The effect would not be captured in any study I have seen, and yet, if known, could well be a deterrent. Viscusi also complains about inferences from transformed variables—the logarithm of damages, rather than their dollar amount. I agree. See my discussions of logarithmic dependent variables in Chapter 3 and its appendix.

396. Eisenberg et al. (2002) at 779.

397. See Sunstein et al. (2002a), quotation at 241. Sunstein et al. (2002b) call jury determination of punitive damages "incoherent." Referring only to Clermont and Eisenberg (1992), they recognize that the judicial judgment might not be the standard against which to measure jury awards. At 1184 they recommend consideration of punitive-damages guidelines, "a kind of 'grid' of penalties, matched to the individual facts of diverse cases." This is a bad time to recommend civil-damages guidelines, especially if they are to effectuated by judges without fact finding by the jury. This is when the legitimacy of criminal-sentencing guidelines, which Judge Weinstein characterized as "a counterproductive overly Procrustean regime" in *Simon* (2002) at 107, is being questioned.

398. *Simon* (2002) at 106.

399. Feigenson (2003) at 245.

400. Sharkey (2003b) at 384, and then Sharkey (2003a) at footnote 386; following indented quotation, Sharkey (2003b) at 411.

without question, a laudable contribution to the body of empirical scholarship that bridges the fields of economics, behavioral psychology, and law.

Referring to the reviews by Feigenson and Sharkey, Vidmar then wrote

I am in agreement with almost all of their basic conclusions, but in this article I go much further.[401]

Where previous authors thought mock-jury research could not provide a definitive argument to exclude the jury from a role in setting punitive damages, Vidmar questions the research itself. Not the idea of mock-jury research, but its execution by these authors. He brings the debate into the realm of technical proficiency (Is this how one determines fact?) where his more deferring predecessors had kept it at interpretation (Is this what one does with fact?).

The debate is now as hot as was that between Risinger and his colleagues on the one hand, Moenssens on the other, described above under "Forensic Science." It may not matter. The prerogatives of juries and judges are being determined on other grounds. As I mentioned in Chapter 5, *Blakely* (2004) placed the finding of facts for criminal punishment on the jury. The Seventh Circuit interpreted that decision as obviating federal sentencing guidelines (in which the judge finds facts that modify the sentence). The Fourth Circuit disagreed. The Second Circuit asked for help, but the Supreme Court has provided little.[402] *Cooper* (2001b), in contrast, may have taken the matter of punitive damages *out* of the jury's hands. The Court determined that although compensatory damages are a fact, punitive damages are not. At least when determined by a jury, they are, as Sunstein et al. urged, "an expression of its moral condemnation." That is not the jury's role.[403] Apparently we have all long been confused about what is fact, what is law. Not for the first time, as we have seen in earlier chapters.

This is another large topic to which I will nod and pass on by. Although Sunstein and his colleagues tie "excess" punitive damages to the influence of experts on jurors, one cannot actually draw this connection from their work. Neil Vidmar and Shari Diamond note:

---

401. Vidmar (2005) at 1364.

402. See footnote 255 in Chapter 5, referencing *Booker* (2004), *Hammoud* (2004), and *Penaranda* (2004). In *Booker* (2005), the Court did, as expected, forbid mandatory sentencing guidelines. But in another case decided in the same opinion, it recommended that guidelines be followed. Apparently mandatory minimum sentences are unaffected by these decisions.

403. *Cooper* (2001b) at 432. On its face, Cooper is a formalistic decision about the appropriate standard of appellate review. However, Litwiller (2002) concludes, at 471, that

With a single swipe of its judicial pen, the Supreme Court has decreed that punitive damages are not a fact to be found by the jury.

Earlier, but also by judicial fiat, the California Supreme Court had limited the ratio of punitive to compensatory damages. See *Lane* (2000).

Even though the data strongly suggest that in ordinary trials jurors competently deal with expert evidence, improvements in trial procedures could increase their performance potential.[404]

My suggestion for a judge-moderated discussion among experts fits here. I did not explain it as a tool for *juror* comprehension, but I don't see why it would not be. I think jurors would respond well to a controlled debate format. They would find it easier to comprehend than the implicit but chopped-up debate that now occurs with attorney control of trial procedures.

Suggestions to take decisions out of the jury's hands are simply a reaction to the system we have, not a considered evaluation of alternatives. For example, there is no reason to believe that judges, especially elected judges, would award punitive damages more fairly, honestly, acceptably, or even differently. Furthermore, there is no standard by which we can determine the "right" amount. Not only is the determination of punitive damages not science, it isn't even craft.

A Science Court

If we remove some decisions from juries, why leave them in the hands of ordinary judges? The concept of a "science court," a court composed of specially adept and trained judges, has been suggested from time to time.[405] Edward Di Lello proposes

the creation of a new adjunct judicial office for magistrate judges who are specialists in technical fields, and the adoption of certain related procedural reforms.[406]

Di Lello considers, then rejects, court-appointed experts and special masters, using the increasing expertise of the Court of Appeals of the Federal Circuit as his example why specialist judges are called for.[407] I think his example equally well argues for my view, that ordinary judges can do the job, although I agree that it should be done at the trial level.

---

404. Vidmar and Diamond (2001) at 1178.

405. See, for example, Kantrowitz (1977).

406. Di Lello (1993) at 473. This article should be considered part of the conservative assault on jury determination of damages, the primary 1990s articulation of which is the "Quayle Report" discussed in the next subsection. Di Lello's argument relies heavily on the presumed vulnerability of jurors to professional experts, the conventional wisdom noted in the previous subsection. He makes frequent reference to "commentators," but none to data.

407. The Federal Circuit was created in 1982 to hear patent cases, and thus bring uniformity to patent law. It is the only circuit defined by subject matter. All others are defined by geography. Landes and Posner (2004) discuss, at 27, the "specialized character and resulting 'mission' orientation" of the Federal Circuit, pointing out that

A more recent incarnation is Brewer's appeal for a "scientifically trained judge or juror or agency administrator" as arbiter of science disputes in law.

> The only solution (actually, it is a family of solutions) I see requires that one and the same legal decision maker wear two hats, the hat of epistemic competence and the hat of practical legitimacy.[408]

Brewer's conclusion follows from a theoretical argument, where I would call for an empirical showing that judges currently get it wrong. That is, the precursor to Brewer's entire argument should be the kinds of student panels I advocated in Chapter 9. Only if systemic error is not conceivably correctable by the kinds of judge training I have advocated (which is very different from that imagined and rejected by Brewer) would we even look in Brewer's direction.

Essentially, his idea is that there would be an elite set of judges qualified to hear special kinds of cases. It is a blue-ribbon judiciary. Suggested by an academic, it carries the typical assumption of academic superiority in these matters. It would remove one of our most remarkable democratic institutions from the understanding of the people whom it serves. It is an idea whose time should never come.

Rule Revisions

Writing before it was clear whether *Daubert* covered technical testimony, Michael Graham was critical of *Daubert*'s uncertain coverage and standards.

> Preferably, the Advisory Committee to the Federal Rules of Evidence will amend Rule 702 to address the determination of when an explanative theory is sufficiently trustworthy; or the Supreme Court will itself modify *Daubert*.[409]

This call for a rules change, besides being vague (Graham suggests no language), was hasty. What was needed was clarification of the coverage of the general principles of *Daubert*. As noted in Chapter 1 and elsewhere, *Joiner* (1994), *Kumho* (1999), and *Weisgram* (2000) clarify *Daubert* (1993), whereas *Scheffer* (1998), a bad decision, confuses the picture.[410] Graham's request for clarification of the rules, then, was fulfilled by case law. This can be an unsatisfactory process, as it is not clear how one case's rule is to be effectuated in another.

[as] it would favor patents more than the generalist federal appellate courts, [it] may thus have been a consequence largely of interest-group politics.

There are many dangers in the concept of specialized judges, of which "group think" may be more likely than overt interest-group control. Both, however, are negative attributes.

408. Brewer (1998) at 1681; preceding in-text quotation also at 1681.

409. Graham (1998) at 18.

410. Justice Thomas wrote the plurality decision. Dery (1999) explains, at 241:

In *Barefoot* (1983), the Supreme Court seemed to say that the Federal Rules of Evidence did not allow the exclusion of testimony from any "qualified" expert. That is, there was no screen on the testimony, only on the proffered expert himself. The enunciation in *Barefoot* sparked efforts by the corporate defense bar to modify the rules to allow the judge to pre-screen testimony. The Civil Rules Advisory Committee discussed revising Rule 702 in 1991, suggesting that proffered testimony had to be "reasonably reliable" and "substantially" assist the finder of fact to find its way to trial.[411] Many prosecuting attorneys had been successful without such a screen, as *Barefoot* itself attests, and did not want a rules change to diminish their use of one of their primary tools. With pressure from both sides, the issue was too hot for the Advisory Committee to handle. The reliability screen failed to make the final draft.

Tahirih Lee, again pre-*Daubert*, suggested revising the rules

> to minimize the aura of enhanced credibility that judicial appointment may lend an expert witness.[412]

> Curiously, Justice Thomas began his own analysis by rejecting any all-or-nothing argument in favor of the defense: "A defendant's right to present relevant evidence is not unlimited, but rather is subject to reasonable restrictions." [*Scheffer* (1998) at 308.] However, ... the Court of Appeals' ruling which *Scheffer* reversed did not rely upon any such flat contention that all polygraph testimony should be admitted regardless of the circumstances. Thus, Justice Thomas began his analysis by projecting the weaknesses of his own absolutist stance onto that of the defendant.

Justice Thomas then went on to argue that the polygraph was not reliable. The Supreme Court should not be making such field-wide pronouncements. If they would read and understand this book, they would do no more of it.

The Tenth Circuit found its own way around *Scheffer* in *Paxton* (1999), at 1216:

> Because *Scheffer* specifically limited its holding to cases in which exclusion did not undermine the accused's defense or implicate other significant interests, it is inapposite here.

So if we just call staying out of jail a "significant" interest of the defendant, polygraph may be used. Except in a military court. If other courts follow, *Scheffer* will mean nothing, which would be appropriate.

411. See the proposed rules, 137 F.R.D. 53 (1991) at 156. Rule 702 would have read:

> Testimony providing scientific, technical, or other specialized information, in the form of an opinion or otherwise, may be permitted only if (1) the information is reasonably reliable and will substantially assist the trier of fact to understand the evidence or to determine a fact in issue and (2) the witness is qualified as an expert by knowledge, skill, experience, training, or education to provide such testimony. Except with leave of court for good cause shown, the witness shall not testify on direct examination in any civil action to any opinion or inference, or reason or basis therefor, that has not been seasonably disclosed as required by Rules 26(a)(2) and 26(e)(1) of the Federal Rules of Civil Procedure.

412. Lee (1988) at 482.

Lee's concerns about the "partisan" expert are well-taken, though her concern that the professional expert is in some way even less trustworthy, is not. Like Samuel Gross, cited above, Lee would do more than allow judges to appoint experts, and do less than command them to. She suggests that, when judges have an affirmative obligation, failure to appoint a court expert where one is called for could be grounds for reversal. Unlike Gross, she writes out her proposed change in the rules. She would modify Rule 706 to call for a judge-appointed neutral expert when the situation arises. Codification, then, would accrue over time, in case law; and no doubt be different among circuits. I think we do not need this pressure on judges. Rather than being coerced, they should be allowed to obtain assistance when they sense the need for it.

Judge Charles Richey called for a rule revision to eliminate the word "expert"—arguing that it assigns the aura of the judge's authority to witnesses—from the federal rules.[413] Some label is necessary to explain to the jury why this witness is appearing. The word "expert" serves that purpose, but another word could, also. Lee and Richey, although they do not say it, still think that the expert "usurps" the authority of the jury. I think my insistence that all science and technical expert testimony must be presented with a measure of fallibility is a better solution than their suggested rules changes.

The President's Council on Competitiveness, under President George H. W. Bush, was formed to alert legislators to threats to economic competitiveness. One of those threats was "overuse and abuse of the legal system," which "impose[s] tremendous costs upon American society." That is, the Council was formed to push for the kind of tort reform the 1991 Advisory Committee had failed to achieve. Their argument is spelled out in the Council's report, "Agenda for Civil Justice Reform in America."[414]

> Each year the United States spends an estimated $300 billion as an indirect cost of the civil justice system. . . .
> [Th]e average lawyer takes $1 million a year from the country's output of goods and services.

Based on such non-facts, this report created hardly a stir. Nonetheless, it did contain three straightforward proposals for revision of Federal Rule of Evidence 702. It would be unfair to ignore them because of the obvious ideological bias behind their presentation, as I have not subjected any other proposals to that test.

The ideology comes from what we might call the "corporate right wing." Companies that might better have been chagrined by the harm they were doing to the consuming public instead felt threatened by the "harm" the public could do to them, through the agency of the courts. Plaintiffs also extracted billions of dollars from such innocent manufactur-

---

413. Richey (1994) at 551.

414. Published as Quayle (1992); in-text quotation at 979; following indented quotation at 980.

ers as Dow-Corning, unwarranted by scientific evidence.[415] Peter Huber's book spear-headed the "tort reform" movement, from which the $300 billion estimate, above, was drawn.[416] In his next book, also quoted by the Council, Huber took on the experts without whose testimony tort litigation could not proceed.[417] The Council can be seen as the political encapsulation of the "movement" that was, if not generated, then most popularly articulated by Huber. In 2005 we see the same forces moving class actions out of state courts.

Under the heading "Expert Evidence Reform," the Council recommended:[418]

> Requiring expert testimony to be based on "widely accepted" theories. A party would have to prove that its expert's opinion is based on an established theory that is supported by a significant portion of experts in the relevant field.

> Banning contingency fees (compensation in return for a "successful outcome") for expert witnesses.

> Requiring courts to determine that proposed expert witnesses are legitimate experts in their field before they are permitted to testify.

The first proposal comes from a major thesis of Huber. He argues that innovations in "science" no longer come from individuals, that only team science is "real" science. One way to weed out "junk science," then, is to refuse to accept any idea not "widely accepted" by some designated group of persons-in-the-know. This is *Frye* at its worst. Although one can see the Supreme Court's taking the *Daubert* case as, in part, prodded by the success of Huber's writing, one can also interpret the *Daubert* decision itself as a partial rejection of Huber's theories and recommendations.

Huber and the Council are clearly wrong, at least in the area of concern of this book, statistics. Innovation in statistics is very individualized, and is often required to deal with the issues as framed by plaintiffs and defendants or their attorneys. This is how Michael Crichton views it:

> I regard consensus science as an extremely pernicious development that ought to be stopped cold in its tracks. Historically, the claim of consensus has been

---

415. Persons suing for harm "caused" by breast implants started winning jury awards in 1984, and a large class achieved a multi-billion-dollar settlement in 1994, although no study linked silicone with medical harm—not with cancer, not with connective-tissue disease. See Angell (1996). The myth of harm is so pervasive that Good (2001), at 232, ignorantly refers to "the rule that silicone breast implants are bad per se."

416. See Huber (1988). I do not know where the one-million-dollars-per-lawyer negative GDP estimate comes from. Quayle does not say.

417. See Huber (1991). See also reviewer comments about Huber's work in Chapter 6, footnote 78.

418. Quayle (1992) at 999.

the first refuge of scoundrels; it is a way to avoid debate by claiming that the matter is already settled. Whenever you hear the consensus of scientists agrees on something or other, reach for your wallet, because you're being had.

Let's be clear: the work of science has nothing whatever to do with consensus. Consensus is the business of politics. Science, on the contrary, requires only one investigator who happens to be right, which means that he or she has results that are verifiable by reference to the real world. In science consensus is irrelevant.[419]

New ideas should be encouraged. If they are bad, let the opposition expert demonstrate it to the judge, as I did when Harry Roberts advocated using reverse regression in employment discrimination cases.

The second proposed rule has long been in force *de facto*. It was written into the American Bar Association's Canons of Professional Ethics in 1908, and remained in its Model Code of Professional Responsibility in 1969. The Association's 1983 Model Rules of Professional Conduct (revised in 1999) bar contingency payments to experts. These are not official rules of the court, but they have weight. Most courts enforce them. An expert whose compensation is based on the outcome of the case would have no credibility.[420]

The third proposal re-introduces the problematic concept of a "field," and the power of others in that field to determine who is "legitimate." The precept that "a significant portion of experts in the relevant field" must approve the expert's "theory" (methodology?) would give other members of the field veto power over the *content* of the testimony.[421] My analyses of jury size (Chapter 4), jury representation (Chapter 5), and "driving while black" (in Chapter 8) are in opposition to views held by virtually every statistician one might poll. But I am not wrong. Judges get it. My client has prevailed in every jury-representation case I prepared following Chapter 5 principles. That driving-while-black studies do not measure a policeman's prior knowledge of race of driver means that defendant cannot show the intent required for a Fourteenth Amendment violation, as Judge Robinson realized in *Mesa-Roche* (2003) and *Duque-Nava* (2004), and Judge Crow in *Arellano* (2004). No judge has yet understood that a census of cars moving faster than the speed limit does

---

419. Michael Crichton, "Aliens Cause Global Warming," the Caltech Michelin Lecture, January 17, 2003. Available at http://www.crichton-official.com/speeches/speeches_quote04.html.

420. Perrin (1995) at 1413:

> [T]he use of contingent fee agreements with experts, which make the expert's compensation contingent upon the case's outcome, is prohibited by the ethical rules of most jurisdictions.

421. Malakoff (1999) reminds us that Bayesian statistics were once so ill-regarded that Kenneth Reckhow, making a presentation before an Environmental Protection Agency review panel, was summarily rejected for using them. The profession changes slowly, but it does change. At 1460: "Reckhow is no longer an academic outcast."

not specify the pool of those most vulnerable to arrest for speeding. Some day, one will, probably long before most statisticians figure it out. If there is a relevant field, it is statistical analysis *in law*. Few statisticians are in that field, and of those who are, most are not very good. Yet they should determine who is an "expert"? I don't think so.

The *Daubert* decision in 1993 did by edict what the rule-making process had failed to do. "Reliability" now dominates the rule. Had the rule makers understood social-science language and concepts better, the key word would have been "validity." I have argued in this book that the word "reliable," and hence the rule, refers to the proffered testimony, not some larger "field" concept. Language that was considered politically difficult in 1991 became the rule in 2000, and obviated such alternative standards as "widely accepted" and "legitimate experts." The Court's limited, adjudicative approach is the right way to go. The judge must focus on the empirical issues before him, not broad theoretical constructs. If these were the alternatives considered by the *Daubert* Court, whether to re-certify participants in the "field" or to sever that connection and rely on the judge's view of the evidence before him, we can be proud that the Court chose the latter path.

THE EXPERT GAME

Margaret Hagen is bitter about what happens to the honest expert. She is hired, in custody suits, to determine which parent is the more fit guardian of the children. As a hypothetical, she supposes that half the time her client is the more fit, and half the time not. However, the other side's expert "invariably" favors his client:

> After half the attorneys who hired me lose their cases because of my highly judgmental and prejudicial reports and testimony, whom do you think will be hired for the next disputed custody case? Me? The loose cannon who can be counted on to shoot his own client in the foot half the time? Or the other psychologist, who smoothly makes a compelling and plausible argument that the client who hired him is the superior parent.[422]

This is a strange example. Each expert's client apparently prevails only when he should. Both experts have fifty-fifty records. However, Ms. Hagen is not a statistical expert, and we get the point. It is the same point that I made with respect to my experience with Fox and Grove in Chicago: Support your client in every case or lose *all* of their business. It is the same as was made by Charles Mann, that the typical expert self-censors, provides to the court only the part of his opinion that favors his client.

To the expert, either the lawyer or the system is the villain, the bad guy. Unlike Hagen, Gross thinks the generality is made only outside of one's field:

---

422. Hagen (1997) at 207.

> Experts in other fields see lawyers as unprincipled manipulators of their disciplines, and lawyers and experts alike see expert witnesses—those members of other learned professions who will consort with lawyers—as whores.[423]

There should not be, and I think there is not, any question about incentives. For the adversarial system to bring forth expertise is inevitable—would we not let a party make its case?—but dangerous. I think it does little good to rant about what bad guys experts are, and what bad guys attorneys are for corrupting their experts, or what bad guys deep-pocket clients are for engaging the nastiest attorneys they can find, who in turn hire you-know-what as experts.

The solution, as I have outlined it, has to come in judge control, first of the schedule, second of pre-trial procedures (such as data exchange), third of evidence by holding *Daubert* hearings on the experts' proposed testimony (or, if they present technical work or wisdom, on the experts themselves), and fourth by creating a discussion forum in which the experts get to ask and answer questions, explained to the judge's satisfaction, not filtered through attorneys. In addition, like many others, I support increased use of judge's experts. I also suggest that sometimes a statistical expert is called for even if no statistical expert has been put forward by either party. The system now is directed toward eliminating good, honest experts. My proposed solutions attempt to create another set of incentives, by preventing the whore from testifying, and by honoring honest expertise in a dignified debate forum.

The "independent" auditor system has not protected shareholders because management hires firms to bless the books, or be fired. The alternative has to be worse: There has to be a harsher punishment of the auditors if the books were rigged but blessed anyway. I do not expect the Department of Justice to do that, except in a few token cases. Then the auditors and the regulators will wink and the natural incentives will operate as they did before.

Judges, though, are not so centralized, and presumably not so politicized. Judges are the only people who can make the incentives against attorneys hiring crooked experts more negative than the incentives to hire them are positive. I think judges need help, and I do not think that help is a course in statistics. I didn't think (in Chapter 9) that middle managers needed to learn the formula for a standard deviation. That, however, is what they get. They get degrees, their employers get a "more educated" work force, and the University of Maryland gets tuition payments. Neither my views nor my actions affected it. There is a long way between this book and an increase in the capabilities and ethical standards of experts. Attorneys like it the way it is. Academics don't even know how it is. Professionals have learned how to play the game. The "system" will do nothing. It's up to the judges.

---

423. Gross (1991) at 1115.

CODA

Non-Judicial Reforms

The discussion in this book has concerned the operation of the judicial system with regard to expert witnesses, especially "science" experts, and most especially those that present statistical analysis. However, I have touched on other subjects, the subjects experts study. I have expressed skepticism about the role experts play, the likelihood that truly good analyses will be presented. I have also expressed skepticism about the judicial system's interest in expert quality. It is certainly not designed to produce quality experts, as I am not nearly the first to say. Although in some ultimate sense the judicial system is a creature of Congress, in most realistic senses it is a creature of itself. The judicial system, like the statistics profession, is an in-group kind of thing.

In separate chapters I have discussed attorneys, judges, and experts. In Chapter 9 I discussed where these people came from, and Chapter 10 was about what to do with them in the judicial context. Isn't that all? No, there are other actors. This final note is about them. I deal with two topics that have loomed large in this book: selection for employment and selection of jurors. The other actors are the public, ordinary people as well as people in categories like state and local legislators and administrators, and private employers.

SELECTING EMPLOYEES

On March 10, 2002, the smartest woman in the world was asked:

> If you want to hire the 10 best available people for your company, but they all happen to be of the same race, what would you do? Would you hire these 10 applicants, or would you hire some less-qualified individuals of other races, with the over-all quality of the new hires not as high?

Here is Marilyn's reply:

> I think there's a better option. In the real world, there would be far more excellent people than I would ever be able to see. So I'd take extra time to search

until I found at least one or two people of other races who were better than some of the people already in my top group. Then I'd stop and hire this new group with a clear conscience, knowing that the competition had been fair and that I had fulfilled my goal: to encourage the advancement of all races, especially when they're not my own.[1]

This response is both misguided and racially biased. It surely recommends illegal actions.

Marilyn looked at the data contained in the observations, and did not like one characteristic, race. Whatever she does now is race-based. She assumes that eventually she will find two members of the missing race B whose quality will exceed those of the last two persons she would have hired. She does not discuss the possibility of finding, also, many more qualified members of race A, the only race currently represented among winners. We already know that, from a fairly drawn sample, the top candidates are of race A. Marilyn has taken a survey and found that only race A candidates meet her criteria. Does she think that survey was flawed? Why does Marilyn not think it is representative of the universe?

If, as with juries, we view her attempt at selection as a fair survey then, in continuing to search, Marilyn is likely to find more race A people than any others. Is she suggesting that she will ignore them, as she is searching only for race B minorities? Surely Marilyn understands that she cannot do that. She cannot overtly have an employment or hiring quota. Once again, the issue is language, for she does have a quota, but feels impelled to call it something else.

Consider the "pretty good candidate" whose plight I described in Chapter 2. Race B candidates might be pretty good, but why does Marilyn, against the evidence in front of her, think any are in the top ten? The interpretation of a selection system as a survey, which I espoused for jury selection, applies here.

If there is any doubt that continuing to search for top race B candidates is a violation of law, let me quote from the Supreme Court:

> It is clear beyond cavil that the obligation imposed by Title VII is to provide an equal opportunity for each applicant regardless of race, without regard to whether members of the applicant's race are already proportionately represented in the work force.[2]

Recall that the Court articulated this individualistic approach to civil-rights legislation in other cases around this time, the late 1970s. That rights, even if defined by group status, adhere to individuals, is as solid and unrevised a view as the Supreme Court has ever set out on any topic. More important, it is one of the most brilliant and correct views

---

1. Marilyn vos Savant, "Ask Marilyn," *Parade*, March 10, 2002, at 9.

2. *Furnco* (1978) at 579.

of the Constitution the Supreme Court has ever put forth. It is about procedure: Treat each applicant fairly, without regard for his demographic characteristics or those of other applicants.[3]

At first impression, one might think that *Grutter* (2003)—allowing race preference at the University of Michigan Law School—changes things. Referring to Justice Powell's decision in *Bakke* (1978), Justice O'Connor (for the Court) writes:

> [T]oday we endorse Justice Powell's view that student body diversity is a compelling state interest that can justify the use of race in university admissions.[4]

Is diversity in a private work force equally compelling? Some will say so. Some—large businesses and the military—already have, in briefs supporting the university. *Grutter* will require clarifying litigation. This decision—which should have gone the other way (no, race cannot be a factor), will leave courts flailing away for years. But the Court will not allow race to be a factor in private-sector employment, except as it (correctly) does now, to rectify past discrimination, with a sunset provision. Racial preferences can be used to bring an employer back to where he should have been. Then, fair hiring is called for. The courts will distinguish schools, especially state schools, from private employers. Unless Marilyn wants to claim that she has been discriminating against minorities, she should not start discriminating in their favor now.

The individualistic approach of the past thirty years remains in force. In *Adarand* (1995), the Supreme Court reiterated that employment-discrimination laws apply to everyone. A member of any race may claim to have been discriminated against on that account. That *Grutter* will not prevent members of race A from prevailing against Marilyn is clear in its companion case, *Gratz* (2003), which concerned University of Michigan undergraduate admissions:

---

3. Why I consider the Court's individualistic emphasis "brilliant" is demonstrated in an article defending affirmative action in college admissions. Liu (2002) at 1046:

> [T]hat minority applicants stand a much better chance of gaining admission to selective institutions with the existence of affirmative action . . . provides no logical basis to infer that white applicants would stand a much better chance of admission in the absence of affirmative action.

The arithmetic is correct: There are so many white applicants that allowing competition for what are now affirmative-action admissions would not increase white admissions very much. That is not the point. It simply is not "fair" to white applicants, even if, from their collective point of view, the unfairness of affirmative-action admissions is small. To the individuals who fail to be admitted because of it, the impact is huge. Liu is no doubt pleased with the decision in *Grutter* (2003), but I say that not only is allowing the use of race as an admissions factor unwise, it is constitutionally incorrect. It was out of line with the individualistic tradition that would have led the members of the Court to a correct decision, had they followed it.

4. *Grutter* (2003) at 325.

> Justice Powell's opinion in *Bakke* emphasized the importance of considering each particular applicant as an individual, assessing all of the qualities that individual possesses, and in turn, evaluating that individual's ability to contribute to the unique setting of higher education.[5]

Individualism prevails. Marilyn cannot claim that she "individually" assessed the minority applicants she is determined to find. It is clear that she is holding two slots open for them. She cannot legally do that any more than the owner of Tempel Steel could hold positions open for Polish immigrants.

More important, there is no morality behind this answer. She is declaring that some people she has not met, on the basis of nothing but their skin color, are morally superior to those she has already determined are the best applicants for the job. The initial winners played by the rules. They applied, set forth their credentials, and were judged to be the best. At least two of them will not be hired because they are race A. And this response isn't called "racist"? It is, without a doubt, discriminatory.

Marilyn missed an opportunity to deflect the discussion from "equality" in some measurable aspect of employees to fairness in their treatment. Apparently, she buys in to the outcome view that has dominated "liberal" politics for at least fifty years: Procedural principles be damned, we want the world to look a particular way. As we have seen in this book, statistical experts have jumped on that bandwagon, also. It leaves us without standards, without fair procedures, and with impoverished statistical analysis. If experts are to take sides on legal approaches—as I have urged (particularly in Chapter 8) that they should— one would think their side would be that which I have advocated, procedural equity. Selections (of students, jurors, which cars to stop) should be made from valid indicators, without regard for irrelevancies like race and gender. Marilyn vos Savant, who has produced brilliant statistical discussions over the years, has been seduced into the fallacy of outcome liberalism. She should be smarter than that.

JURORS

"What about the black kid as defendant?" The woman on the telephone was from some "equal justice" public-interest group in Hartford, Connecticut. The *Gibbs* case was long over. "He shuffles into the courtroom, baggy pants attached well below his waist. He doesn't look up. If he did he would see an all-white jury made of people who don't understand him, and don't like him."

"All right," I asked, "What about him?"

---

5. *Gratz* (2003) at 271. See also *Bakke* (1978).

"I want him to see faces on his jury that are like *his* community. I don't care if those people do not get on source lists. I don't care if they move out of the jurisdiction quickly. There are some there *now*, and they should be on the jury."

It has been a long road to disestablish the concept of a blue-ribbon jury, or at least class bias, the judging of some by others as worthy or not to participate, in this way, in our democracy. That has been accomplished perhaps to bring different points of view into the jury deliberation, but not to stigmatize individuals—by their race, gender, age, etc.—as having particular points of view. Lawrence Friedman discusses the rationale for caring about the composition of the jury:

> Underlying the new jury is a kind of pop version of post-modernism. There is no such thing as objective truth. There is white truth and black truth and Asian truth and Hispanic truth. There is male truth and female truth. Probably there is old truth and young truth, and rich truth and poor truth, too. If not truth, then at least point of view. In any event, ideas along these lines are at least implicit in the thinking of millions of people—whether or not they have ever heard of postmodernism or the social construction of reality or similar theories.[6]

The lesson from Chapter 5 is that the judicial system, the courts, should not care what the jury looks like. Of all the suggestions for deliberately composing the jury, only the 1970 *Yale Law Journal* editors, in a badly conceived Note, have suggested that the jury should be made up of people "like" the defendant. How quickly we forget: It was jurors "like" the defendants who refused to convict the murderers of Emmett Till, or of Chaney, Goodman, and Schwerner. What is the logic behind "stacking" the jury in this way? Why is this "fair"?

If there is a compositional goal for juries other than "the community," it might better be that they look like the people who have been harmed, not the accused perpetrator.[7] But the public might see it differently. My caller did. If people think a black defendant can be tried fairly only with some black representation on the jury, there are legitimate ways they can pursue that interest.

At present, computer systems are incompatible from agency to agency. The FBI and the CIA and the National Security Agency do not communicate. Nor do Marines with the Army, the Air Force with the Navy, the police with the fire department, one volunteer fire department with another. Radios are on different frequencies. Code language may differ even if it could be heard. Because we have so feared central authority, we have no standards.

---

6. Friedman (2002) at 266.

7. In some cases the jury is to determine *whether* anyone was harmed, which makes this criterion inapplicable. How would we have determined what a jury "like" pop-singer Michael Jackson "should" have looked like? He did well without trying to form such a jury.

This is true among federal agencies, and between federal and state agencies, and among state agencies. It is true in voice communication. It is true in data bases. Each agency goes its own way. Exchange of information among them is difficult.

Most judicial districts encompass many counties or towns. Each locale maintains its voter list differently. When the state tells the towns to turn over their lists to the jury administration, they do so; but it is a burden to the towns and the judicial district. Thus they are asked to do it at most once a year, a high frequency by historical standards. Voter lists have another problem: Purging them is difficult. Out of fear of having eliminated someone who is really there and, you never know, may want to vote, these lists usually contain many names of persons who no longer live where the list says they do. Drivers usually wait until their license has expired before notifying the Department of Motor Vehicles that their address has changed. The presence of former residents on source lists generates more undelivered jury notices sent to the more-mobile minorities than to others.

Though the Department of Motor Vehicles will deliver data in only one form to however many judicial districts there are, it may not be a form easily read by the judicial district, and certainly differs from voter lists.[8] Now there are two, three, four differently formatted lists that have to be merged, duplicates deleted, from yet more agencies.[9] Most jurisdictions allow several months for this process to take place, including finally preparing the list and sending out appearance notices. In those several months there has been turnover. In Kent County, Michigan, 20 to 25 percent of the mailed questionnaires either are not delivered or not returned. In Providence, Rhode Island, over 30 percent of the questionnaires mailed out are not returned.[10] What portion of this instant drop-out could have been recovered had the process taken, say, one month, I do not know. But the faster the system can process lists and send out notices, the higher the response rate will be.[11]

This leaves a place for the public to act. Activists should avoid suing for more-representative juries. Keep outcome arguments out of the courts. The state has no obligation to "make up" for different behaviors of different parts of its population. However, getting the source lists to the jury administration in uniform format can be a citizen goal. Getting

---

8. In New York State, the state itself takes on the task of merging disparate lists for the counties. Cities (which, outside of New York City, are smaller units than counties) draw from county lists. Thus localities do not have the problems of list incompatibility, but neither are they fit subjects for the citizen action I will suggest.

9. As noted in Chapter 5, Fairfax County, Virginia, has gone the other way, dropping the drivers list. See Tom Jackman, "Fairfax Uses Voter Lists, not DMV, for Jury Pools," *Washington Post*, February 15, 2003.

10. The Michigan information comes from *Smith* (2000a) at 209. The Rhode Island information comes from my own work in that state.

11. This statement should be obvious, but for evidence to support it see Pollard (2000), Figure 1, at 203 and discussion at 203–204.

the jury administration more technically capable, so it can efficiently perform the merge-purge from well-constructed lists, is the next step. Providing the jury administration with the capacity to randomize the resulting list is the next step.[12]

A system that could automate these procedures could compile a new list twice a year, maybe every month, maybe every week. How many more minorities would appear on juries, no one knows. Not as many as the reformers would like; but some. Minorities still will be absent from lists, and will still be less likely to show up if contacted. However, there is no reason other than cost not to construct jury lists more often. There is no constitutional or legislative compulsion to do it, but there could be public demand. If citizens want to act, this is the place to do it: procedure.

Lawyers and lawyer associations cannot be counted on. The American Bar Association's "American Jury Project" has produced a document containing nineteen "Principles for Juries and Jury Trials."[13] This committee wants juries to have twelve members, and decisions to be unanimous. Lawyers, like others, can want more than the minimum the Supreme Court has allowed. In Chapter 4 I posited that today's six-member juries are easily the equal of the twelve-member jury of 250 years ago; but I did not assert that quality as a standard. If twelve-member juries are even better, and the public will support them, we can have them.

Then we get to Principle No. 10:

> Courts should use open, fair, and flexible procedures to select a representative
> pool of prospective jurors.

Representative? Is this what the Constitution requires? Representative of what? How?

First, this committee calls for at least two source lists, compiled at least annually. Then they call for:

> The jury source list and the assembled jury pool should be representative and
> inclusive of the eligible population in the jurisdiction. The source list and the
> assembled jury pool are representative of the population to the extent the per-
> centages of cognizable group members on the source list and in the assembled
> jury pool are reasonably proportionate to the corresponding percentages in
> the population.[14]

---

12. Many state systems select from source lists first, to reduce the data burden. Connecticut towns, for example, do not turn over their entire voter list, but a given percentage thereof. They are instructed to select voters randomly, but there is no oversight how they do that. Finally, from the merged-purged list, selections are made, often by the "every n^{th} name" procedure, because systems have not had the capability to randomize large files.

13. The American Bar Association cannot even be counted on to place a date on their documents. I have listed this document under the name of the chair of the project, Refo (2004), where the date was provided by M. Campbell (2005).

14. Refo (2004) at 11; following in-text phrase also at 11.

The word "eligible" appears in the first sentence, but not in the second, which appears to contradict the first. How a court is to determine what its eligible population (or, indeed, its resident population) looks like is not stated. To accomplish this representation, the court may take "appropriate corrective action" when it deems jury lists or juror pools to be inadequately representative. Or perhaps that should be "substantially" inadequately represented. Where is the line?

The Bar Association demonstrates the incompetence attorneys always have when they enter this field. Their view is hopelessly outcome oriented, as it has learned to be from "experts" and attorneys alike, writing in law journals. They apparently recognize neither the faultiness of their measures nor the fallacies inherent in their standards. Perhaps, from reading this book, attorneys and law professors will learn how wrong they have been. Principle No. 10 should be rejected.

Legislation by outcome is no better than judicial review by outcome. But *motivation* by outcome is understandable. Just because juries of six are allowed does not mean juries *should* be six. It only means they *can* be six.[15] That a single four-year-old voter list is acceptable to the courts does not mean it has to be acceptable to the public as a basis for juries. Like the American Bar Association, the public can want—and in theory can get—twelve-member juries drawn from fresh lists. The public should not want—and should not be able to get—juries that fit some predetermined racial composition.

Advocate improvement, but don't litigate about it.[16] Advocate improved procedures, not specific outcomes. You can ask statisticians for help in devising clever ways to construct and randomize lists. Don't ask them to testify that the lists are faulty if they don't produce the kinds of juries you want. Too many statistical "experts" have been sucked into that game. Let's have no more of it.

---

15. "First, all federal district courts should return to twelve-member juries." Lempert (1981) at 115. Lempert is parroting the standard criticism, not enunciating a political preference. He does not understand how that criticism is—as I demonstrated in Chapter 4—faulty.

16. Wasby (2000) advocates a combined strategy of litigation and lobbying for civil rights reform, but confuses procedural reform with outcome determination. All "reforms," as all litigation, should focus on procedure. Perhaps there are occasions when Wasby's solution is appropriate—litigate *and* legislate. There are also times when it is not, when choices, not rights, are at issue; when litigation is sure to fail, but progress towards equal opportunity can be made politically.

APPENDICES TO CHAPTERS

APPENDIX TO CHAPTER 2

On Conditional Logit Estimation

This appendix is a slightly edited version of Appendices B and D of my report entitled "A Study of Hiring of the City of Gallup," in *Gallup* (1985). Finis Welch, the opposing expert, had questioned my methods, suggesting particularly that the number of applicants should affect the statistics. I took the opportunity to explain the mathematics to him, and use that explanation here as it demonstrates the method in a specific litigation context.

Conditional logit estimators are derived by maximum-likelihood methods. Where there is one variable (for race) and one selection per pool, the likelihood L is

$$L = e^{bS} \prod \frac{1}{I_j e^b + N_j}$$

where b is the race coefficient to be estimated; I_j is the number of American Indians in the jth pool; N_j is the number of non-Indians in the jth pool; and S is the number of pools with an American Indian selection. There are two kinds of candidates, I for Indians and N for those who are not Indians; and one variable, b, that is being estimated to distinguish selections from these two groups.

The likelihood, L, is maximized when the logarithm of the likelihood is maximized:

$$\ln(L) = Sb - \sum_j \ln(I_j e^b + N_j)$$

To maximize this log likelihood, we set its first derivative with respect to b, which is

$$\frac{\partial \ln(L)}{\partial b} = S - \sum_j \frac{I_j e^b}{I_j e^b + N_j}$$

equal to zero. It is obvious that the number of Indians and non-Indians plays no role in the estimate of b. To see this, just multiply both I and N by a factor F. We will find F in both numerator and denominator, cancelling. Thus the number of applicants in a pool does not affect our estimate of b.

The standard error of conditional logit estimates, as with traditional logit estimates, is calculated from the second derivative:

$$\text{Var}(b) = \frac{1}{\dfrac{-\partial^2 \ln(L)}{\partial b^2}} \Bigg| \hat{b}$$

$$\frac{\partial^2 \ln(L)}{\partial b^2} = -\Sigma_j \frac{N_j I_j e^b}{(I_j e^b + N_j)^2}$$

This expression is also immune to the multiplication of the applicants by a factor F. We find F^2 in both numerator and denominator, cancelling. Thus the number of people in a pool does not affect the standard error of my estimates. The results stated here hold exactly when additional variables are considered, and approximately when there is more than one selection per pool.

Through the discovery proceedings in *United States v. Gallup*, there has been an implicit conversation between experts. In depositions and reports, each expert has stated his view of the appropriate way to handle the data, conceptualize the issues, and perform relevant calculations.

I was initially optimistic that defendant's expert would accept the multiple-pools methods that my colleagues and I at Longbranch Research Associates (LRA) have adapted for use in equal-employment-opportunity litigation. We have used these procedures in many cases. Opposing experts have invariably agreed with our approach and with our effectuation of that approach. Indeed, I informed Welch years ago that LRA had developed an exact calculation of the probability distribution used for the univariate analysis in this report.

As the discussion in this case began, Welch expressed doubt that LRA did, in fact, calculate this multiple-pools exact test utilizing the statistics of "sampling without replacement." He expressed, in short, a *technological* reservation. I think Welch now understands that our multiple-pools exact-test program, MULPOOLS™, does perform the Fisher's exact test (sampling without replacement) for all pools with multiple selections. It does so efficiently, without "smoking all the time."[1] Welch says that "it should be honored as a trade secret." Thus we appear to be past the first technological hurdle.

Our multivariate multiple-pools method, conditional logit (as it appears in our MULQUALS™ program) is an exact calculation only for pools with one selection. For multiple-selection pools, it utilizes a widely recognized and accepted approximation. Few pools in this case have multiple selections. Even if there were many such pools, the approximation in MULQUALS™ would have a negligible effect.

---

1. Finis Welch, "Third Deposition," in *Gallup* (1985), at 87; following in-text quotation at 89.

Recently, knowing that LRA can make the calculations it says it makes, Welch asks whether we should. In the abstract, such a question is always well taken. It would have had more force had he raised it initially. Welch appeared to regard the multiple-pools approach as well-conceived, but impossible to execute. Now that it is clear that we do execute it, he asserts that it is misconceived. He is incorrect.

Welch has raised the possibility that our "computer standard errors would be somewhat smaller than [his] and erroneous."[2] He suggests, therefore, that one should inflate conditional logit standard errors to account for "positive serial correlation," that is, seeing the same person in.successive pools.

Welch's error is evident in his example:

> Well, if each application, let's say, is viewed 10 times on the average by him and let's say 10 percent of the applicants are hired, then he computes a hire rate of one percent because he is counting each person 10 times. So his log odds calculation would have . . . 0.01 over 0.99 for Michelson. Ours would be 0.1 over 0.9.

In fact, I never compute the hire rate or the log odds. I am concerned only with relative hire rates, or the log odds *ratio*. As shown above, neither the estimated American Indian coefficient (b) nor its standard error is affected by the number of persons in a pool.

We can express R, the relative probabilities of selecting an Indian compared with a non-Indian, from a pool in which there is one selection:

$$R = \frac{\dfrac{e^b}{Ie^b + N}}{\dfrac{1}{Ie^b + N}} = e^b$$

where I is the number of Indians and N is the number of non-Indians in the pool. Should Welch look only at the numerator or denominator of this expression, the effect he noted will occur. But the coefficient I estimate is invariant with respect to "inflation" of the pool.

Welch apparently confuses logit, in which his point would be meaningful, with conditional logit, in which it is not. In a logit equation one estimates e^{a+bx}, which is equivalent to—and I will write as—Ae^{bx}. The parameters a (or A) and b are estimated such that for an individual i, the estimated probability of being hired is:

$$\text{estimated probability of being hired} = \frac{Ae^{bx_i}}{1 + Ae^{bx_i}}$$

and the odds of person i being hired are:

---

2. Welch, "Third Deposition," at 92; following indented quotation also at 92.

$$\text{odds of being hired} = \frac{\dfrac{Ae^{bx_i}}{1 + Ae^{bx_i}}}{\dfrac{1}{1 + Ae^{bx_i}}} = Ae^{bx_i}$$

A "baseline" person is defined as one whose x value is zero. The odds of this baseline person being hired is A. I have just shown that the odds of the ith person being hired is Ae^{bx_i}. The odds ratio between these two people is the ratio of the odds of the ith person and this baseline person, or

$$\text{odds ratio} = \frac{Ae^{bx_i}}{A}$$

The "A"s cancel, and the odds ratio is e^{bx_i}. This is also the expression for the relative probabilities (its inverse is the "relative preference" for non-Indians) where the value of x_i is 1. That is precisely this case, in which x takes the value one for Indians, zero for non-Indians.

In conditional logit we know only this odds ratio, because we have conditioned on applicant pool. We have provided each pool with its own A. There is no A, or constant, over all. We do not estimate the probability of a person's being hired. We calculate the relative probability, compared with an individual all of whose variables have the value zero. Whether the absolute probability of this baseline person being hired is 0.01 or 0.1—to use Welch's example—is immaterial. The problem does not arise because the expression estimated is the odds ratio or relative risk, not the probability or odds of an individual's being hired.

I also showed above that the standard error of the conditional logit estimate is invariant to "inflation" of the pool. As a criticism of the conditional logit method, Welch's assertion to the contrary is incorrect.

More disturbing is Welch's objection to LRA's standard error in the context of serial correlation. Welch wants to "correct" for the fact that a person who is rejected in one pool appears likely to be rejected from the next pool. In an appropriate sense, my model has done that: At the second pool, the application is older. It less represents an "applicant" than a fresh, later application. Applications lose their viability quickly in these equations. A once-failed application adds less and less information to successive pools. This down-weighting of persons previously observed is analogous to traditional corrections for serial correlation.

Welch's criticism, however, appears to be based on a less appropriate sense of the issue. Suppose the City of Gallup discriminatorily hires non-Indians but not Indians. Rejected Indians reapply, and continue to be rejected. Welch apparently asks us to assume that the initial rejection was based on merit, so that when we see subsequent rejection we are seeing the same lack of merit. Welch must *assume* non-discrimination to assert this interpretation of the observed serial correlation.

Welch is correct that *if* Indians are rejected on the basis of merit to a greater extent than non-Indians, and therefore re-apply (fruitlessly) more than non-Indians, a court might mistakenly find discrimination. Equally, if Indians are rejected based on their race, and (fruitlessly) re-apply more than non-Indians, Welch would ask the court to mistakenly find that Indian applicants are inferior.

As Welch has often noted, one could hope for more information from which to resolve possibly conflicting interpretations of the data. The analyst, however, should not resolve the fundamental question of the investigation by assuming that applicant quality is correlated with race. I believe that, unless there is evidence to the contrary, the analyst must assume that Indian and non-Indian applicants have the same distributions of abilities, for the jobs for which they apply.

I am not alone in this opinion:

> Both equitable considerations and, in Title VII cases, the policy of the statute, support a rebuttable presumption of an equal distribution of qualifications between minority and majority group applicants when data are unavailable.[3]

Data should describe the qualifications of the applicants, not Gallup's reactions to the qualifications of some of the applicants. Besides, re-application does not necessarily imply prior rejection. Some applications do not become hires because no hire into a relevant job category was made while the application was "alive." Re-application is not an exogenous characteristic of the applicant.

As David Baldus and James Cole, quoted above, continue:

> When a plaintiff has done the best that can be done with available data, and those data create an inference of likely disparate treatment, the defendant should be required to explain the disparity.

I do not think that Welch's assumption that rejected applicants are inferior is such an explanation.

---

3. Baldus and Cole (1980) at 195; following indented quotation also at 195.

APPENDIX TO CHAPTER 3

Regression Technicalities

Although I try to spare attorneys and to a large extent judges the technical details of regression, I do not minimize the importance of getting it right. Most of what "getting it right" means is in the concepts that the regressions are supposed to elucidate. That is the proper focus of Chapter 3. But part of what "getting it right" means involves the mechanics of regression. This appendix is on that subject.

PRINTOUTS

Details that do not appear on a regression graphic are available on the standard regression printout. The equation that generated the dashed line in Figure 22 looks like Figure 68.

Source	SS	df	MS		
				Number of Obs	47
				F(5, 41)	72.39
Model	6408.5842	5	1281.7168	Prob > F	0.0000
Residual	725.9761	41	17.7067	R²	0.8982
Total	7134.5603	46	155.0991	Adjusted R²	0.8858
				Root MSE	4.2079

Adjavg9	Coefficient	Standard Error	t	P > |t|	[95% Conf. Interval]	
Perlimit	−0.3753	0.1167	−3.217	0.003	−0.6109	−0.1397
Percapy	1.1945	0.1421	8.408	0.000	−0.9076	1.4815
Exam	18.7313	2.5105	7.461	0.000	13.6613	23.8015
Bosnoex	−7.6935	3.4634	−2.221	0.032	−14.6880	−0.6990
Voc	−3.7411	1.4682	−2.548	0.015	−6.7062	−0.7759
_Cons	205.5568	3.3646	61.094	0.000	198.7619	212.3517

FIGURE 68: The Boston Schools Regression of Figure 22

Some Boston schools admit only the highest scorers on an entrance exam. These schools have the value one on the variable "Exam." Non-exam Boston schools are identified by "Bosnoex." No surprise: Students who did well on an entrance exam score well on later exams. Boston's non-exam schools fall below the pattern established by all schools, even considering Boston's low per-capita income. "Creaming" comes to mind—taking the best students out of regular schools reduces their average scores as it increases the scores of schools requiring the exam. That vocational students taking this academic test scored low would not be a surprise, either, but we do not know whether they did. The variable "voc" has the value one if the school offers a vocational course.[1] "Perlimit" counts children with limited command of English, which not surprisingly correlates negatively with test score.

My coefficient for "Percapy"—per-capita income—is 30 percent lower than Craig Bolon's income-only approach would suggest. I contend that my model uses the data better than his original model, and leaves room to think that policy just might affect test scores, at least on the margin.[2]

Diagnostics tell us about each coefficient and the fit of the equation to the data. For example, R^2 is a measure of "goodness of fit." It has a minimum value of 0.00 and a maximum value of 1.00. It is adjusted (lowered) to the extent that more variables are added. Thus explaining variation with as few variables as possible is rewarded. Use of individual-variable diagnostic measures helps guide the analyst to his final "specification," the final equation. Complete output should be provided to the opposing expert, of course, and is routinely provided also to the court. A judge for whom the details are more confusing than elucidating should ignore them.[3] It is up to the experts to explain anything that needs to be understood, either in support of one expert's position or in criticism of the other's. And, as I urge in Chapter 10, the judge should ask questions.

The important point of the regression should be communicated simply, and usually graphically. In Figure 22 the point is that the original author's cavalier dismissal of all "explanations" other than income left a false impression that an academic test was a means test only. My specification tells us, from the same data, that income and academic success are correlated, but not necessarily perniciously or exclusively so.

---

1. We know only that students in schools with vocational programs scored lower. The only variable available indicated whether there were such students, not how many there were, or how many took the exam.

2. I published my critique in the same forum as Craig Bolon's original article, Bolon (2001). See Michelson (2001).

3. This seemingly innocent suggestion will be controversial. Judges think they must understand everything that is presented to them. I think that is a hopeless goal that should be abandoned before it consumes too much time. The parties are responsible for telling the court, in their briefs, what they want the court to consider, and in turn for rebutting such assertions in reply briefs. The conversation between the experts is properly part of the record, but their supporting material is best ignored by the court.

Specification

There is much confusion about how to arrive at a specification. I deal here with two issues. These are correct statements:

> The order in which one has entered dependent variables makes no difference to the estimation of their coefficients in any specification.

> Coefficient values and even signs may change in different specifications. This is not a flaw. It just means one is measuring different things with different specifications.

Order of Entry

It is not clear whether Phillip Good is confused, or if it is just his presentation that is confusing. In discussing collinearity—a correlation between independent variables—Good says that

> the values of the coefficients will depend on the order in which the variables are entered into the model.[4]

He then describes two methods of determining a specification that arose in the early years of mainframe computers, but have no application today.

> In the *forwards* method, a variable at a time is introduced into the model and only the variables yielding the highest values of R^2 are retained at each step. In the *backwards* method, one starts with all the variables at once in any order and then the variable making the least contribution to R^2 is removed at each step.

The description of backwards stepping is correct. Good has confused forwards stepping with another method, search for maximum adjusted R^2. In forwards stepping the question is which variable is added next. All previously entered variables are retained. One may never achieve the highest adjusted R^2 using either procedure, although maximizing R^2 is not necessarily a good criterion for choosing the final specification.

Deriving a specification by forward or backward stepping arose when time on a mainframe computer was scarce. A researcher would submit a job, then wait some hours for the result. It was tedious and inefficient to put in one specification, wait for the results, guess at an appropriate adjustment, submit another specification and wait again. Programmers devised a way to let the computer provide some alternatives in one pass, by calculating at each step which variable would increase R^2 the most, and adding it (forward); or decrease

---

4. Good (2001) at 185; following indented quotation also at 185, italics in original.

R² the least, and deleting it. In that one computer run, it would calculate many steps, each forward step or each backwards step building on the previous step. One was not bound to accept any specification so mechanistically devised, but it made good use of the few runs a researcher could make in a day to have "educated guesses" generated by the computer.

A generation of analysts learned forward and backward stepping as if they were methods of craft. They were methods of convenience. So, for example, Bolon, in his reply to my criticisms of his use of the Boston schools data, argues:

> [Michelson] does not provide stepwise or combinatorial analysis for the incremental association of variance.[5]

Apparently Bolon does not like how I came to my specification. Nothing could matter less.

The Sign of the Coefficient

Consider two regressions estimating personal income from a number of personal characteristics (say, age and education), and the following race variables:

1. Income = f(. . . black-female)
2. Income = f(. . . black, female, black-female)

Equation 1 has just a single race variable: "black-female." Equation 2 has two additional variables: "black" and "female." In most data sets, within an employer or among employers, the variable "black-female" in equation 1 will be associated negatively with income. Black females earn less than others, even "controlling" for obvious variables, i.e., comparing statistically "like" employees. But anyone experienced with this kind of regression expects that, in equation 2, the "black-female" coefficient will be positive.

What? Black females earn more than others? No. Black females appear in all three variables. They are black, they are female, and they are the interaction of black and female. The income loss from being black and female is smaller than the sum of the two independent negative effects of being black and being female. The positive black-female coefficient in equation 2 should say, to a judge in a wage-discrimination case, "Do not award back-pay to black females based on the black and the female coefficients. They have been harmed more than blacks, and more than females, but not as much as the sum of those two effects."

No "expert" should be bothered by the fact that coefficients have different signs in different specifications. Nonetheless, we will meet one—indeed, a professor of statistics!—in the Appendix to Chapter 5. When individuals fall into several categories contained within a regression, one needs to interpret one coefficient with an eye on the others. Collinearity—Good's problem—may or may not be an issue. Understanding always is.

---

5. Bolon (2002), under "Michelson's Complaints."

CROW COAL

My critique of the regressions by Mark Berkman and Fred Dunbar in *Crow II* goes far beyond that which I presented in Chapter 3. Some additional points are made here for the reader interested in a more technical discussion of the failure of their regression analysis.

Goodness of Fit 1

National Economic Research Associates, Inc. reports a very high fit between their equation and the data—$R^2 = 0.938$—after adjustment for degrees of freedom.[6] However, what NERA is reporting is not the equation's fit to the data. It is the R^2 on NERA's printout. Sometimes that statistic is meaningless. NERA fit a transformation of the data, and reports goodness of fit to that transformation, not to the data. They are quite different. Figure 69 compares the R^2 calculated from the data—that is, the proportion of variation from the mean "explained" by the equation—to that reported by NERA.

Fit to Data	NERA
0.352	0.938

FIGURE 69: R^2 from NERA's Equation

NERA's R^2 was incorrectly calculated even from the transformed data. As I could not replicate their equation from their data, I could not exactly replicate their R^2. The only way I came close was by estimating an equation without a constant, then inserting a constant derived as part of the autocorrelation correction. There is nothing wrong with that form of estimation, but it is well known that the R^2 a computer program calculates from a no-constant regression is meaningless. Thus NERA presented a statistic that did not even tell us how well their equation fit their transformed data. Had they done so, that statistic still would not have informed us how well their equation estimated the actual data.[7]

---

6. "Expert Witness Report," corrected version, by Mark Berkman and Fred C. Dunbar, dated January 6, 1984, in *Crow II*, Table A-2 at A10.

7. That "goodness of fit" should be measured with respect to an equation's ability to estimate the actual data, not a transformation thereof (even if that transformation was used in the estimation) seems to be an obvious point, but is missed by many. For example, Finkelstein (1973, reprinted in 1978) compared two equations, one estimating cost in dollars, the other estimating the logarithm of that cost. The "R^2 of the linear equation was 0.92, while that of the multiplicative equation was 0.81." At 1450 in 1973, 220 in 1978. He then suggested that the expert should have justified his use of the "multiplicative" (logarithmic) equation, given its lower R^2. Of course any expert should justify his estimating equation, but these figures do not increase his obligation to do so. Though suggesting several ways one might justify

Goodness of Fit 2

NERA's equation fails to capture the effect of the very event it is meant to analyze, the 1975 Montana tax increase. That is, a general "goodness of fit" statistic is not how their estimation should be evaluated. A time variable will generate an estimate close to the data. Where the analysis is trying to uncover the response to a particular event, we should look for some other way to ask if the model helps us understand the facts.[8]

If R^2 is not a good measure of fit to an equation in which time is a variable, what is? Contending that taxes "regulate" output, NERA must show not just a fit of their equation close to the data, but a concordance of tax changes with output changes. Consider assessing who is a good stock analyst. Anyone can predict that, over a long period of time, the Dow Jones stock index will rise. We give an analyst no credit for telling us that. Rather, we ask, *when* will it rise and when fall? Can the analyst predict *changes* in direction, not just the overall upward trend?

Figure 70 summarizes the differences between the ratio and NERA's estimates of it.

	Data	Estimate	Tax Difference	Time
1972–1973	Up	Down	Up	Up
1973–1974	Up	Down	Down	Up
1974–1975	Up	Down	Up	Up
1975–1976	Down	Up	Down	Up
1976–1977	Down	Down	Up	Up
1977–1978	Down	Down	Down	Up
1978–1979	Up	Down	Down	Up
1979–1980	Down	Down		Up
1980–1981	Up	Down		Up
1981–1982	Down	Down		Up

FIGURE 70: Misestimation in NERA's Regression

Starting in 1972, NERA's ratio increases in three consecutive years, while NERA's estimate of the ratio is decreasing. From 1975 to 1976 the ratio declines, but NERA's estimate

---

using the equation with the lower R^2, that the logarithmic equation fit the original data better was not one of them. Apparently neither Finkelstein nor the nameless expert calculated the goodness of fit of transformed equation estimates, converted back to dollars, to *the data*.

8. Meyer and Kadane (1992) at 298:

> In any situation the metric of goodness of fit needs to be sensitive to how the inference will be used.

of it increases. For two years, then, from 1976 through 1978, both the data and NERA's estimate decline. NERA predicts a sharp reduction in the rate of decline, which is not reflected in the data, from 1977 to 1978. From 1978 to 1979 the ratio turns up, but NERA's estimate goes down. That pattern is repeated from 1980 to 1981.

Of ten inter-year differences, NERA misestimates six. The relationship is supposed to be inverse: when tax difference goes up, the ratio goes down (two years later). Seven times the tax difference is not constant. Of these, it moves in the same direction as the ratio—the wrong direction from NERA's perspective—four times. Three times there is no change in tax difference, but a decline in the estimate, and a secular decline in Montana's "share." NERA explains that this reflects the continuing effect of a past change in tax difference. Their explanation does not come from their equation, and is not credible. There is essentially a chance relationship—a coin flip—between coal production and taxes, and nothing else. Tax difference did not affect Montana's share when it varied. Why should we assume it affects Montana's share when it does not vary?

Time is a better predictor than tax difference of Montana's "share." It successfully predicts movements in NERA's ratio five times out of ten. It obviously is an unsatisfactory explainer of the decline in Montana's production relative to Wyoming (also indistinguishable from chance), but so was tax difference. Time—not tax difference—predicts the general decline in NERA's ratio. Nothing NERA has studied tells us why that decline is happening.

Autocorrelation

Berkman and Dunbar claim that they corrected for autocorrelation. All correction methods require the estimation of a correction factor, rho or ρ. Some analysts set $\rho = 1$. That assumption leads to an estimate based on first differences in the variables. However, I can estimate ρ in the *Crow* data and, when I do, I find that I cannot distinguish it from $\rho = 0$. It is not close to 1. My analysis of the correlation of residuals is reproduced here in Figure 71.

Method	ρ	Subsequent Correlation
Stipulate $\rho = 0$	0.0000	−0.0411
Cchrane-Orcutt	−0.0178	−0.0421
Correlation of Residuals	0.0371	−0.0392
Coefficient, Residual on Lag	0.0211	−0.0400
Durbin Method	0.0660	−0.0377
Theil-Nagar DW Modification	0.3693	−0.0390
Stipulate $\rho = 1$	1.0000	0.8149

FIGURE 71: Different Serial Correlation Corrections

Material like this should *not* appear in the text of a report to the court. However, reports, as well as a presentation to the court, are a conversation between the experts—or they should be. This is the kind of material that should be in an appendix, which is where I put it in my critique of NERA.[9] The judge can then ask each expert about the other's appendices, without thinking that he, the judge, has to understand everything in them.

A Note on Truth

The truth that the NERA analysis tried to hide under the obfuscation of statistical analysis is a phenomenon of some interest today. Between the growing scarcity of oil and the increased use of low-sulphur coal encouraged by the Clean Air Act, coal flows out of the Powder River Basin as freely as water flows out of the Mississippi River. It does so by rail. A description of this process can be found in a two-part series by John McPhee in *The New Yorker*. McPhee does not mention taxes or, for that matter, Montana. This is a Wyoming phenomenon. Of course I am disturbed that Mark Berkman and Fred Dunbar corrupted my profession by claiming to "show" that Wyoming's success was "caused" by Montana's tax rate. But there will always be Berkmans and Dunbars. The solution is to educate the judiciary to see through such client-oriented work. The NERA study should have been rejected as not scientific. If it had been clear that this level of work was not acceptable, perhaps Berkman and Dunbar would have become better experts.

---

9. Stephan Michelson, "The NERA Statistical Analysis: A Critical Review," June 10, 1993, in *Crow III*.

10. John McPhee, "Coal Train," *The New Yorker*, Part 1, October 3, 2005, at 72; Part 2, October 17, 2005, at 62.

APPENDIX TO CHAPTER 4

Mathematical Models of Jury Decisions

The argument that a six-member jury will make more errors than a twelve-member jury comes from a mathematical model of the jury decision. There are two such models in the literature: the one-parameter model and the two-parameter model. If most references appear old from the perspective of the twenty-first century, it is because the issue came and went in the 1970s. Small-group decisions are still being studied and their applications to juries are obvious, but hardly anyone discusses the size of the jury, about which there is no longer any litigation.

Historically, this subject is interesting for two reasons. It was the first issue (to my knowledge) about which there was substantial review and criticism of the Supreme Court by a non-lawyer academic community, certainly by the mathematically inclined. More important, perhaps, the Court listened to this criticism, referring to it extensively in its opinion in *Ballew* (1978), which put an end to the issue. How well the Court fared, according to the critics, was well-voiced at the time. And that opinion stands unrebutted until now. I show in Chapter 4 that the Supreme Court did not turn to the social-science community for advice in determining the consequences of juries of different sizes, but that if they had done so, the advice they would have received would have been erroneous. Social-science "experts" got it wrong.

This is a bold assertion, but one that will become familiar in this book. Although I think I have proved my case in Chapter 4, in this appendix I will:

Compare the one-parameter and two-parameter models, deriving a precise mathematical relationship between them;[1]

Demonstrate why the critics of the Court concluded from these models that a reduction in jury size increases jury error;

---

1. For a more comprehensive review of jury models, including the issue of non-unanimous vote, see Grofman (1981).

> Demonstrate that the Court's critics should not have drawn the conclusions they did from their models, that we remain far from understanding the implications of the size of the jury for jury processes and the differences in process for jury outcomes; and

> Establish basic features of a realistic model of jury decision, especially the translation from some fluid judgment to a firm decision; and show that this transition step is missing in the critics' jury models.

The One-Parameter Model

The one-parameter in this model of the jury decision is g, where $0 < g \leq 1$. We assume that independent jurors are selected randomly from a population in which g represents the frequency of the jurors' willingness to vote "guilty" in the particular case at issue. As actual guilt is a two-valued function (zero if innocent, one if guilty), whatever g is, it is not that. William Feinberg would define g as the appearance of guilt, or the complement of the ability of the defendant to convince the jury that he or she is not guilty. David Walbert has an almost behavioral version of a similar concept, where g is the fraction of the jurors who

> would be inclined to consider the defendant guilty at the conclusion of the courtroom proceedings, immediately prior to deliberation.[2]

Behaviorally, one can approximate Walbert's concept by taking a jury ballot before there is any discussion. Either the same measure can be made of Feinberg's definition or his has no empirical content.

The parameter g represents a frequency of guilty votes that would occur in a particular case, within a population. The question becomes, drawing randomly from that population, for a given g, what is the chance of getting twelve out of twelve guilty votes, versus six out of six? For example, if g = 0.5, then on average any size jury will be split. However, on some draws there will be six or twelve consecutive guilty votes. How often will this occur? The probability of drawing s consecutive independent guilty votes from a large population in which g is the fraction of guilty votes can be calculated for different g and s. A jury of size s will convict if there are no votes to acquit:

$$\text{probability of convicting} = 1 - (1 - g)^s$$

The relevant values of s are six and twelve. Some values of the probability of conviction given s and g are shown in Figure 72.

---

2. Walbert (1971) at 540. See also Feinberg (1971).

Value of g	Jury of Six	Jury of Twelve
0.750	0.1780	0.0317
0.800	0.2621	0.0687
0.900	0.5314	0.2824
0.950	0.7351	0.5404
0.975	0.8591	0.7380
0.990	0.9415	0.8864

FIGURE 72: One-Parameter Probability of Initial Unanimous Guilty Vote

What seems most startling from Figure 72 is how difficult it is (assuming, as this calculation does, no interaction among jurors) to convict someone who has an appearance of guilt which, by most common sense understanding, would be "beyond a reasonable doubt." If a 0.975 appearance of guilt means that 97.5 percent of the people who looked and had to decide would declare a person guilty, that person still has a better than one in four chance of not being convicted by a twelve-member non-interacting jury requiring a unanimous vote. There is a deliberate asymmetry here, in that there is essentially no chance that a person who appeared innocent to 97.5 percent of the people would be found guilty—the chance is about one in 6×10^{20}. Herbert Friedman alone among the commentators worries that the greater representativeness of the larger jury, combined with the veto power granted to each juror under a unanimous-decision rule, acquits too many people who have an overwhelming appearance of guilt. Friedman implies that a non-unanimous vote for conviction is a good solution to the problem of convicting overwhelmingly guilty-appearing people.[3] However, the problem here may not be the jury, but the mathematical assumption of independence required for this calculation. That assumption is violated by jury deliberation.

Walbert proposes a solution. His model allows people to change their minds; specifically, he assumes that a majority vote for conviction will prevail even when unanimity is required.[4] This leads us to ask what is the probability of selecting at least four out of six—or at least seven out of twelve—jury members who will vote to convict, for a given g? The calculation is made from the binomial distribution

$$\text{probability of conviction} = \sum_{i=m}^{s} \binom{s}{i} g^i (1-g)^{s-i}$$

where s is the size of the jury, m is the minimum required for a majority (seven in the twelve-member jury, four in the six-member jury), and i varies from m to s.

---

3. Friedman (1972).

4. See Walbert (1971) at 242–245.

Walbert distributes half of the ties to conviction, half to acquittal, but no qualitative difference occurs when we just require a majority to convict.[5] One can imagine different jury instructions acting to distribute tie votes in different ways, but there is no reason to venture into that level of detail here. Probabilities of conviction if the majority persuades the minority, allowing ties to be hung juries (thus non-convictions), are listed in Figure 73.

Value of g	Jury of Six	Jury of Twelve
0.750	0.8306	0.9456
0.800	0.9011	0.9806
0.900	0.9842	0.9995
0.950	0.9978	1.0000
0.975	0.9997	1.0000
0.990	1.0000	1.0000

FIGURE 73: One-Parameter Probability of Initial Majority Guilty Vote

Those who presented the one-parameter model considered Type I error to be conviction of someone with a value of $g < 0.5$, and Type II error to be acquittal of someone with a value of $g > 0.5$. From this they conclude that fewer apparent Type I errors are made, for a given g, than Type II errors for $1 - g$. We will see that this view does not work, but let us proceed as though it did.

Using the majority-rules calculation, it appears that the smaller jury makes more errors. If $g = 0.2$ should lead to *acquittal*, that it will lead to *conviction* almost five times as often from the majority-ruled six-member jury as from the majority-ruled twelve-member jury is disturbing. Similarly, although nineteen out of every one thousand malefactors who come to trial with $g = 0.8$ are acquitted by a twelve-member jury, over five times as many are set free by the six-member jury. If the majority rules—or persuades—then the six-person jury makes more errors than the twelve-person jury. That is the implication of the one-parameter model, with which the Court's critics felt so enlightened as to condemn the Court for not seeing it.

This model produces the same aggravation one gets when plans are disrupted because, after an indicator warned of a malfunction in one's car or airplane, it was determined that the only malfunction was in the indicator itself. The *ex post* "fix" of converting a majority vote to a unanimous vote, however done, makes a mockery of the debate and court deci-

---

5. The chance of a tie is

$$\binom{6}{3}(g^3 \times (1 - g)^3) \quad \text{or} \quad \binom{12}{6}(g^6 \times (1 - g)^6)$$

depending on the size of the jury. Walbert then distributes this probability to convictions and acquittals. Nagel and Neef (1977) take the more sensible position of counting hung juries as acquits.

sions about non-unanimous votes.[6] Walbert's argument for majority persuasion comes from Harry Kalven and Hans Zeisel:

> [I]n the instances when there is an initial majority either for conviction or for acquittal, the jury in roughly nine out of ten cases decides in the direction of the initial majority. . . . With very few exceptions the first ballot decides the outcome of the verdict.[7]

The exceptions, however, are of great interest. Some would say they are the reason to have juries in the first place.

Friedman does distinguish between unanimous and non-unanimous votes. From Friedman's unanimous model, as in Figure 72 above, a defendant always has a higher probability of conviction from the smaller jury. If we are worried about people with g = 0.8 being acquitted by the larger jury, the unanimous small jury convicts 3.8 times as many of them, while still protecting people with low g from excessive convictions. Friedman shows that the oddball individual who will frustrate the will of the preponderant majority is more rare on a smaller jury. This is the other side of the representation argument: The more representation there is, the greater is the chance of getting someone whose values are at odds with most of the community. This may not always work to favor the defense.[8] Thus, there is a sense in which the gamble for everyone is larger with the larger jury.

Zeisel argued that the gamble is bigger with the *smaller* jury. If g is defined as the proportion of all possible juries that would convict, then the chance of getting an exceptional jury—one that would not decide the way most juries would decide—is greater the smaller is the jury. However, it is exactly here that Friedman's model differs: There is no gamble for the clearly innocent person, and the chance of an odd outcome is greater with the larger jury (unanimous vote, no persuasion) for high values of g. Thus, although the models of Figures 72 and 73 both show that twelve-member and six-member juries are different, each model's characteristics are determined by assumptions about how juries reach unanimity. The results look impressively mathematical, but they contradict each other. The contradictions emanate from assumptions that only emphasize the nescience of the models. As social science, as analyses of judicial procedures, these models are failures.

---

6. See *Johnson* (1972) and *Apodaca* (1972).

7. Kalven and Zeisel (1966) at 488, based on 225 observations. Walbert (1971) understands how critical this assumption is to his model, and he presents other justifications for it. He mentions, in note 48 at 542, that the non-unanimous vote is at issue as he is writing his article, but does not reveal that his model cannot distinguish between majority and unanimous votes. Zeisel (1971) adds that persuasion works best against a lone dissenter, more likely in the six-member-jury situation. Therefore, there should be fewer hung juries from the smaller jury size. The evidence seems to confirm this expectation.

8. For example, Mintz (1978) tells us about a lone juror holdout for conviction, who exhausted the other jurors until they accepted a "guilty" verdict on a reduced charge. Penrod and Hastie (1979) note that, if most jurors can assess guilt accurately, the guilty defendant will benefit most from the unanimous large jury. See 467–468.

THE TWO-PARAMETER MODEL

The problem that emerges from the one-parameter model is that g is expected to characterize both the defendant and the juror. Separating the probability of guilt from the juror's ability to perceive it should allow us to proceed with less circular reasoning. Alan Gelfand and Herbert Solomon define their parameters as follows:

> θ = probability before trial that the accused is guilty. The value of θ is a commentary on the legal system in the society which eventually brings an accused to trial as a result of arrest, arraignment, and indictment. Its value also reflects the prevailing social climate in the country at the time of the analysis. It is *not* in any way intended to represent the proportion of the population that would view the accused as guilty as a result of the evidence.

> μ = probability that a juror will *not* vote for the wrong verdict, that is, the probability that a juror will *not* err.[9]

Although μ (lower-case Greek mu) is defined as the ability of the juror correctly to judge the defendant, θ (lower-case Greek theta) is specifically *not* defined as the ability of the defendant to defend himself (Feinberg and Friedman) or the mean outcome of all possible jury decisions (Walbert). Estimates of θ differ only slightly from the proportion of all accused who are found guilty, and this comparison is made explicitly.

In their second article,[10] Gelfand and Solomon calculate the probability of conviction from twelve-person and six-person juries with different values of θ and μ. It bears emphasis here that they intend this estimate to be independent of the particular case. That is, it is the probability of the *randomly selected* defendant's being convicted, not that of a particular defendant with a characteristic such as "appearance of guilt" described by one of the parameters.

> Note that the differences between T (probability of convicting by twelve-person jury) and S (probability of convicting by six-person jury) are negligible over the whole range of values of μ and θ. In fact for $\mu = 0.9$ and $\theta = 0.7$ as suggested by our previous results the values of T and S are 0.7004 and 0.6962 respectively. This reinforces the judicial decision that there is essentially no difference in the prospects for conviction of an accused before a six-man jury vs. a twelve-man jury.[11]

Vaclav Fabian contrasted this statement with the vehement argument by Walbert and others that six-member juries and twelve-member juries are different. In reply, Gelfand and

---

9. The identical language appears in Gelfand and Solomon (1974) at 32, and in Gelfand and Solomon (1977a) at 305, except that in the latter the word "not" is never emphasized.

10. See Gelfand and Solomon (1974) and (1975).

11. Gelfand and Solomon (1974) at 36.

Solomon showed joint probabilities of conviction and guilty, conviction and innocent, etc., from which they reached a conclusion similar to Walbert's. Fabian had also commented that

> the probability of a guilty opinion would depend on the strength of evidence presented in court.[12]

Abandoning their carefully honed definitions, Gelfand and Solomon replied that the probability of conviction "is increasing in θ (provided $\mu > \frac{1}{2}$, which is surely the case),"[13] and recanted their indifference to jury size. Disdain for the Court's decisions was once again unanimous.

Although one could develop a theoretical multi-parameter model based on Walbert-type definitions, Gelfand and Solomon cannot have it both ways: Since they scrupulously deny that "guilt" to them has any connection to the defendant, they should not interpret their conditional probabilities as indicating correct jury decisions. As a matter of interpretation, Gelfand and Solomon can only say that the results from individual small juries are less likely to be predictable from knowledge of system-wide parameters than the individual results, trial by trial, of large juries. That is not a statement about whether small juries make more or fewer errors.

ONE-PARAMETER AND TWO-PARAMETER MODELS COMPARED

The basis for the careful definitions by Gelfand and Solomon is their attempt to estimate their parameters. The mathematics of their model is to an extent independent of the labels given the variables. It is instructive to see the mathematical relationship between the one-parameter and two-parameter models. We can start by looking at the expression for the probability of conviction in the two-parameter model:[14]

$$\text{probability of conviction} = \theta\sum_{i=m}^{s}\binom{s}{i}\mu^i(1-\mu)^{s-i} + (1-\theta)\sum_{i=m}^{s}\binom{s}{i}(1-\mu)^i\mu^{s-1}$$

where again s is the size of the jury, and m is the minimum majority required to convict. The simplicity of the mathematics will be obscured if the cumulative binomial expression is written out each time. I will substitute the expression B( ) where the parentheses contain the term with i as its exponent.

$$\text{probability of conviction} = \theta B(\mu) + (1-\theta)B(1-\mu)$$

The probability of conviction is the sum of the two joint probabilities conviction if guilty

---

12. Fabian (1977) at 536

13. Gelfand and Solomon (1977b) at 537.

14. Gelfand and Solomon present their model in terms of votes for acquittal. I have transposed it here to accord with my presentation of the one-parameter model. In addition, I do not distribute tie votes, effectively assuming that ties do not result in convictions.

and conviction if innocent.[15] It should now be obvious that the Walbert model is the Gelfand and Solomon model when everyone brought to trial is guilty, where $\theta = 1$.[16] Curiously, although from the definitions one might think g was meant to incorporate θ, the a priori probability of guilt, it actually describes only μ, the overall "correctness" of jurors. When $\theta = 1$ there are no truly innocent people, the marginal probability of conviction is identical to the joint probability of conviction and guilty, and the conditional probability guilty given conviction is one.

Put another way, the one-parameter model cannot show Type I error, innocent given conviction, because it implicitly assumes that all defendants are guilty. Saying that small values of g represents innocent people in the one-parameter model is wrong. Small g represents stupid jurors, badly presented evidence, or a propensity toward jury nullification. The juries that committed Type II error by acquitting O. J. Simpson or, in June 2005, former Health South CEO Richard Scrushy, would be examples. All critics of the Court who used that model to discuss Type I error were wrong to do so.

In the two-parameter model, the probability of making a Type I error, from the system's point of view, is

probability of an innocent defendant being convicted $= (1 - \theta)\,B\,(1 - \mu)$

Values of this probability, for different values of θ, μ, and jury size, are found in Figure 74. To generate Type I error the person must be not guilty $(1- \theta)$ and the jury must get it wrong $(1 - \mu)$. So, for example, from Figure 74 we can see that the smaller jury gives us more Type I error than the larger jury, although for high values of μ the difference is negligible.

μ	$\theta = 0.60$		$\theta = 0.70$		$\theta = 0.80$	
	Jury of Six	Jury of Twelve	Jury of Six	Jury of Twelve	Jury of Six	Jury of Twelve
0.20	0.3604	0.3922	0.2703	0.2942	0.1802	0.1961
0.40	0.2177	0.2661	0.1633	0.1996	0.1089	0.1330
0.60	0.0717	0.0633	0.0538	0.0475	0.0358	0.0316
0.80	0.0068	0.0016	0.0051	0.0012	0.0034	0.0008
0.90	0.0005	0.0000	0.0004	0.0000	0.0003	0.0000
0.95	0.0000	0.0000	0.0000	0.0000	0.0000	0.0000

FIGURE 74: Type 1 Error As Parameters and Jury Size Vary

15. It is important that θ and μ are independent. Then the joint probability of conviction and guilt is the probability of conviction, $B(\mu)$ times the probability of guilt, θ; and the joint probability of acquittal and innocence involves the complements of θ and μ.

16. Both models give a probability of conviction in the interval [0,1]. Thus, at any given value of g, the two models can be set equal. However, one cannot then solve for both θ and μ. An infinite combination of parameters in the two-parameter model can produce any p(conviction), except at the extreme

When θ increases, for a given μ, the relative error (Type I error from a six-person jury divided by Type I error from a twelve-person jury) stays the same. When μ increases, the relative error also increases. According to this model, the six-member jury commits more Type I error relative to the twelve-member jury *the better are the jurors!*[17]

We could view error from the defendant's point of view. Let us express this error of convicting the innocent as a proportion of innocent defendants. This will tell us the probability that an innocent defendant will be convicted (i.e., the conditional probability convicted though innocent). This is perhaps a more common measure of Type I jury error:

$$\text{probability of an innocent defendant being convicted} = \frac{(1-\theta)\,B(1-\mu)}{(1-\theta)} = B(1-\mu)$$

The system makes more errors if θ is low, but the innocent defendant's probability of being wrongly convicted depends only on μ. It is irrelevant to him how good the system is in general, in bringing people to trial who are guilty. We see that these models are silly, really. We are supposed to believe that the line between conviction and acquittal is the perception of the jurors, as described by the single parameter μ. That belief has led to the "jury consultant." I would not argue against the notion that, on the margin, informed selection (effected by peremptory challenges) can make a difference. I doubt, however, that jury consultants intend to or do maximize the value of μ. As with the use of statistical experts, the attorney is looking for a favorable decision, not a correct one. While analysts fight about μ, attorneys fight about something else entirely. Then the analysts want the Court to base its decisions on their concerns, regardless whoever else holds them.

Even at high values of θ, low values of μ present a picture of society I prefer not to believe, unless it represents reasoned juror nullification. For high values of μ—that is, a good ability of jurors to discern guilt—we would find many times more innocent people in jail with the six-member jury than with the twelve-member jury, according to the two-parameter model.[18] Should that conclusion lead us to reject smaller juries, or the model?

Finally, Gelfand and Solomon modify the assumption of majority persuasion, by adding a "social decision scheme" adapted from J. H. Davis.[19] For each possible number of

---

points. Each combination would produce a different value for each cell in Figure 73, but maintain the marginals. Interpreting the one-parameter model as the two-parameter model when θ = 1 equates the cell values as well as the marginals.

17. Grofman (1975) presents a model of group decisions which allows a trade-off between average μ and group size. The result, complementary to that above in the text, is that sometimes a group can improve its decision-making ability by accepting additional—even though inferior—people.

18. This relationship is obscured by the many decimal places it takes to present these figures as probabilities. When μ > 0.9, the six-person jury makes over twenty-five times more errors than the twelve-person jury.

19. See J. Davis (1969), and Gelfand and Solomon (1977a) at 310. Estimates modified by this social decision scheme appear in Gelfand and Solomon (1977b).

first-ballot votes to convict, they write out the fraction of times the jury will finally vote conviction. They can then weight each term in the binomial summation estimation of conviction by the proportion of times that initial vote represents a final conviction. This allows an analytical difference between majority vote and unanimous vote, though that difference turns out to be small. No conclusion about the difference between six-member and twelve-member juries is changed by this innovation; therefore, I will only tip my hat to it, and move on.

USING MODELS FOR THE DEBATE ABOUT JURY SIZE

These models do not satisfactorily consider all the elements we might care about when jury size is allowed to vary.[20] I will not attempt to construct a model of jury behavior here. However, from this review, missing elements of current models can be identified. As the focus of this book is on the ability of social science to aid the court, a more relevant question than "What would a more complete model look like?" is "Would a more complete model answer the court's question about the functional relationship between benefits (and their societal value) and jury size?" I think the answer is no, not directly. What we need is empirical research. If there were the possibility of obtaining adequate data, however, we would want to have well-defined models from which data-collection forms would be derived. Thus, in the long run, it should pay to summarize what we might like to know about juries.

We need to establish some terminology:

a Guilt of a particular defendant ($a = 1$ if guilty, $a = 0$ if not guilty).

$g(a)$ The appearance of guilt, such that $E[g(a = 1)] > E[g(a = 0)]$. Values of $g(a)$ can be juror opinions, and can be expressed $g_i(a)$ for the ith juror.[21]

$g°$ $g° = E[g_i(a)]$ for all possible independent jurors. Similar expressions could be formed to denote the value of $g_i(a)$ after deliberation, and some expected value of all possible jurors after deliberation in all possible juries.

g^* A critical level such that only if $g_i(a) > g^*$ should the juror vote guilty.

---

20. The work of Penrod and Hastie (1979 and 1980) is directed toward simulating the jury discussion. They do not account for the valuation of decisions by the public.

21. That is, the expected value of g is higher for guilty people then for innocent people. Feinberg (1971) shows this graphically by drawing two distributions of defendants along an axis that shows the ability to defend oneself. To the extent the distributions overlap, jury members make real decisions, and their quality and the luck of the draw both matter.

R   A rule (perhaps a judge's instruction to jurors) that generates g* in the mind of each juror.

μ_i Juror error in estimation of g. If the standard is g°, then $\mu_i = g° - g_i$ and $E[\mu_i] = 0$.

θ Proportion of persons brought to trial who are guilty as most persons would judge it not from applying R to the facts before the actual jury, but in absolute terms, knowing "all" the facts.

I have three major difficulties with most jury models. First, they do not deal well with deliberation. The creators of the models have been forthright in understanding this weakness. Second, the "value of the benefits" concept, society's weighting of correct and incorrect decisions (as opposed to the probability of those decisions themselves), is missing, as I showed in Chapter 4. There is no weighting of the value to society of the various outcomes. Third, there is no overt translation from the analog concept of "probability of guilt" to the juror's binary-valued outcome, a vote of guilty or innocent. Although the application of a "social decision scheme" to the majority persuasion argument does allow one to differentiate between unanimous and majority voting, it makes no attempt to identify those situations in which a minority can persuade a majority (or the hung-jury case, in which the majority cannot persuade the minority, but is not persuaded itself).[22]

The work of Steven Penrod and Reid Hastie has advanced modeling of jury decisions, but has not incorporated the concept of a "rule." The rule is given by the judge. It is the system's instruction to the juror how to map his uncertainty into a vote about the value of a. We think that different rules produce different results—jury instructions generate much ancillary litigation—yet no study of jury outcome in which size has varied has explicitly considered the rule problem.[23]

---

22. I have in my files a typescript of an article by William Fairley, "Notes on Models for Jury Balloting and Verdicts," dated February 1973. Mine is a photocopy of a marked-up version, I presume edited by Fairley himself. At page 36:

> We can suppose that each juror arrives in effect at a personal probability that a defendant is guilty. Call this probability Π. And we can suppose that each juror has a translation of the conviction standard of beyond a reasonable doubt into a probability value Π_0. If $\Pi > \Pi_0$ then the juror votes to convict.

I have no recollection of this paper, and do not know what became of it (e.g., whether it was published). Fairley was starting down a productive path, adding an element missed by previous modelers.

23. Shafer (1976) devises some theorems about how a juror may weight evidence to come to a determination. He assumes that the ultimate decision is the weighted sum of independent decisions (about different aspects of the case presented). Even given this simplification, the mathematics are complex. However, surely no one thinks that a juror's decision comes about this way. Shafer does not attempt to discuss a rule (the judge's instructions, by which the juror's weights are to be formed) or deliberation (the interaction among jurors).

Neilson and Winter (2002) model only jury deliberation, using the word "rule" to mean whether

A rule can be formulated by weighting the four possible outcomes:[24]

	Guilty	*Innocent*
Convict	w_{11}	w_{12}
Acquit	w_{21}	w_{22}

Where do such weights come from? Are they independent of θ? That is, do we value correct and incorrect juror decisions regardless how well the system does in bringing only the guilty to trial? These questions need to be addressed in any model that pretends to inform the Court about juries of different sizes.

How can we effectuate this weighting? That is the function of the rule. Such a rule would set $g^{\star}$, the probability below which there can be a "reasonable doubt." The more one values convicting the guilty relative to the other possible outcomes (i.e., the higher w_{11}), the lower $g^{\star}$ would be. The more one values acquitting the innocent, the higher $g^{\star}$ would be.[25] A judge's instruction to the jury is exactly the stuff about which debate can and should occur, and Supreme Court decisions can, should be and are made. However, defining μ_i with respect to g° instead of with respect to a guilty or innocent vote allows us to look at two places for explanations of non-unanimous votes: estimates of g°, and applications of different values of $g^{\star}$.[26] In addition, it allows a policy regarding jury instructions to overcome a bias produced by smaller juries, if that bias can be shown to exist (and if the instructions can be shown to influence the outcome).

Development of a jury model with an explicit rule function would not be easy, but its

---

the system requires a unanimous decision. Here, individual jurors take on different weights, reflecting their impact on other jurors. Assuming that those weights are constant, they describe the deliberation process as a Markov chain. Although the early models discussed in this appendix concern the "accuracy" of the jury's verdict, Neilson and Winter discuss only how individuals are affected by others, bringing the group (sometimes) to a consensus. They are unable to assess that consensus from the view of the public's like for correct verdicts and dislike for incorrect verdicts.

In Simon (1967) different sets of instructions on the legal definition of insanity given to jurors were associated with different outcomes (the acceptance of the insanity defense). Empirical studies implicitly attempt to control for judge instructions when they hold the type of case and the judge constant. Jury nullification occurs when the jurors deliberately ignore the judge's instructions. Therefore a complete model would incorporate not only my rule, but the probability of a juror following it.

24. M. Fried et al. (1975) present this formulation in relation to juror utility, asking how the juror translates his $g_i(a)$ value into a vote.

25. Setting $w_{22} = 100$ raises $g^{\star}$ to 0.991. It should be obvious that one needs to set three of the four values. Nagel and Neef (1977) make their second fundamental error in setting only two values.

26. Gelfand and Solomon (1977a) anticipate this issue, at 301

> An error in a juror's decision may result from either assessing the evidence poorly or from requiring too high or low a probability for conviction, or both.

The only way this rule error evidences itself in their model, if I understand it, is if the rule is set so that $g^{\star} = \theta$; but there is no reason why society should prefer this value of $g^{\star}$.

direction should be obvious.[27] From an analysis in which $g*$ varied, interest would focus more on the shape of the distribution of $g_i(a)$, and less on its expected value. If any difference between the twelve-person and six-person jury were found, the natural question would be, "Can it be rectified by different rules?"[28] The critics might have said, "*If* you allow the six-person jury, be sure to include the following procedural changes." Not, "Oh, that was a bad mistake."

Helping the Court

The Supreme Court was stung by criticism of its cavalier attitude toward jury size. Perhaps it believed that the criticism was correct. Most likely the court had no way to assess the work of the critics, and just wanted to hear no more from them.

The "duck and cover" action of the Court was reasonable, but more than thirty years later someone has to say it: That criticism was incorrect. The analysts hardly proved the Court wrong. That models fail to weight possible outcomes is a somewhat typical example of economists saying that statisticians, left to themselves, maximize the wrong thing. What counts here is society's valuation of the probabilities of convicting the guilty vs. convicting the innocent or letting either the innocent or guilty go free, not the probabilities themselves.

Would a well-developed model incorporating societal weights, juror interactions, and non-independence among parameters have assisted the Court in deciding whether the Constitution allowed juries smaller than twelve? I think not. I think the argument in Chapter 4, that modern jurors are better able to assess evidence, that juries of six today are as capable as juries of twelve were two hundred years earlier, is closer to the kind of argument the Court could understand and use. But that conclusion, though it is interesting and as defendable as any conclusion reached by the Court's critics, rests on little and haphazardly available data.

In short, it seems easy for academics to criticize the Court's reasoning, but difficult for them to reason better, and even more difficult for them to provide help the court can use. I doubt that either side, the academic critics or the judges and justices, understand how incorrect "expert" advice often is. The unanimous criticisms of the Court were themselves incorrect. Whether through wisdom or ignorance, the Court did better by ignoring the "experts" than it would have by listening to them.

---

27. Grofman (1981) reviews jury models from the point of view of signal-detection theory. In his work, $g*$ is related to a Bayesian prior probability. Grofman follows J. Kaplan (1968) in discussing the internal utility to the juror of his decision. Neither discusses formal system rules designed to affect $g*$. See also Penrod and Hastie (1980).

28. My list of attributes is not meant to be complete. As noted above, jurors will differ in their willingness or ability to incorporate R into their g. There would be distributions of this attribute, etc.

APPENDIX TO CHAPTER 5

Selecting Jurors in Connecticut and Rhode Island

I developed the concepts of Chapter 5 in litigation, over many years, trying to provide a better way to ask whether jury-selection systems were functioning "properly" than the ways I found in the literature and saw being used by other experts. Finding a "problem" from outcomes alone, the standard analysis provided no direct path to a remedy. I thought the proper focus should be procedure, that "fairness" is an event, not a situation. I needed to devise my own way to determine if there was a problem in the first place. If so, a procedural analysis would indicate the remedy at the same time.

Although they came to it late, states did randomize and automate and drop discretion. Convinced by outcome analysts that they still had a problem, states added more source lists. Aside from playing games with weighting, and deliberate race-conscious construction of juries, having multiple source lists was the only proposal alive in the law-review literature. If lack of minorities was a problem, additional source lists have failed as a solution. They have only increased the cost of obtaining juries, as few additional minorities found on the additional lists have proved eligible for or willing to perform jury service. This is not an unexpected result from solving what was not a problem to begin with.

When faced with an articulate alternative view, judges understand that procedural fairness is all that is required and, indeed, that catering to outcome demands is both procedurally unfair and ultimately unconstitutional. Yet the judges who have listened to my viewpoint, and accepted it in defense of jury-selection systems, have not laid out the new terms under which they have made their decision. They have masked their system-defending decisions as if made the old-fashioned way. In a top-down system, where following the Supreme Court is de rigueur, that is their safest course. I thought it might be interesting for the reader to get a sense of how I both promoted the new ideas of Chapter 5 and gave judges enough grist to feed their conventional mills. That is what I do in this appendix.

CONNECTICUT: ISSUES AND CHARACTERS[1]

The Connecticut Judicial Information Services collects samples of names from driver's-license and voter-registration lists.[2] The first mailing from the master list is a summons, specifying a date at which the addressee is to appear at a particular courthouse. He is asked to respond to his summons, saying that he is ineligible or that he will appear. Unless the envelope was returned as undeliverable, the system considers the person fit at least to show up at the courthouse to which he had been assigned, even if he has not responded. Connecticut allows deferral of service for up to a year, which means that persons summoned last year may be appearing this year, and persons summoned this year may not appear until next year. To analyze the rate of appearance over any period of time requires the reasonable assumption that persons who defer out of one time period are similar to persons who appear from another.

An ineligible addressee could return the summons with a claim for disqualification, or appear at the courthouse and explain why he should not serve on a jury. Many who are called fail to appear without ever having acknowledged receipt of the summons. We do not know from the data how many of them would have been disqualified, or for what reason. It is easy to infer from the mailing addresses that disproportionately many failures of mail delivery, and then the no-shows, were notices sent to Hispanics.

The Jury Challenge

In setting out his "Third Amended Challenge to the Jury Array," defendant's counsel, Michael Courtney, described a

> comprehensive and multifaceted study of over four years of data supplied by the state, the Bureau of the Census, and from a court-ordered survey. . . . [T]he defendant has examined the workings of the entire summoning system and is asserting diverse defects in the system, each of which contributes to systematic underrepresentation of Hispanics.[3]

These "defects" were:

> Over 30 percent of summonses sent to Hispanics are undeliverable, compared with under 13 percent of those sent to non-Hispanics.

> " 'No-shows' are disproportionately Hispanics."

---

1. The Connecticut discussion in this chapter concerns *Gibbs* (1998).

2. Since this litigation, but not because of it, other lists have been added.

3. Michael Courtney, "Third Amended Challenge to the Jury Array," March 13, 1997, at 9, omitting references.

"Defects in the construction of this master list result in an overweighting of those potential venirepersons who are both registered voters and licensed drivers, i.e. motor voters. The proportion of Hispanics amongst motor voters is less than the proportion of Hispanics on either of the single lists (voter and DMV)."

"Hispanics made up 6.56 percent of the over-age-eighteen population of the district . . . according to the 1990 Census." They were 4.2 percent of respondents to a juror survey.

Outcomes are called procedures, "defects in the system." One might think that Courtney's first two points were the state's to make, and indeed, as an agent of the state, I did make them. In *Castaneda* (1977), the Supreme Court wanted an explanation for the lack of Hispanic jurors. The strategy of Connecticut's defense was to offer that explanation, in the form of my analysis of the difference between the "population" and the "community."

Defendant's third point did cause some concern. I read testimony by the jury commissioner from a previous case, describing the merge-purge process for eliminating duplicates from the voter and driver lists, the source lists then in use in Connecticut. What he described under oath—and told me in a private telephone conversation—was mathematically biased. I reported back to my clients that the challenger appeared to be on to something. My clients then did a thorough review of the merge-purge process and determined that the commissioner's description was in error, the process was not. They invited defendant's counsel and expert to a meeting where commission staff, correctly describing their procedures, put the issue to rest.

Defendant then was left with a bottom-line comparison between jurors and the census population (the fourth "defect"), and two notions of how that bottom-line disparity in percent Hispanic came about: Hispanics did not receive first-class mail, and among those who did many did not respond. In a ruling on a jury challenge over a decade earlier, the Connecticut Supreme Court had decided to "enter the statistical morass that has developed in this area."[4] It then decided that which method of calculation was appropriate was case-specific, but in that case they would use the "substantial impact" test. The definition of "substantial" remains elusive.[5] Thus, when the Connecticut Supreme Court wrote, "it becomes clear that the defendant cannot establish substantial impact,"[6] it was clear only to them. The state's attorney, Harry Weller, eventually agreed not to cater to the "substantial

---

4. *Castonguay* (1984) at 426.

5. See Jenkins (1974), in which the Second Circuit opined at 65 that, as blacks were shy of census proportionality by only one person per venire, the deficit was not "substantial enough to deprive appellants of their constitutional or statutory rights."

6. *Castonguay* (1984) at 430.

impact" test, but to argue that, procedurally, the state had done nothing wrong regardless what the outcome was or how it was measured.

The Connecticut Challenger's Expert

People learn from their experiences and thus, it is often observed, they "fight the last war." David Pollard, the challenger's expert, a professor of statistics at Yale, had testified in a previous jury challenge. In that case he apparently was unable to convince the court that he could identify the race and ethnicity of those called to be jurors, and/or those who became jurors. Thus he entered this case determined to establish race identity, his measure of which the state, as long as I was their expert, would not dispute. My approach was to explain what happened to Hispanics, not to question that it did. Pollard never looked for explanations. He took as his job only to measure the bottom-line difference between actual jurors and "expected" jurors, where his expectation came from the U.S. Census.[7]

Pollard did an extensive "geocoding" of the mailed summonses into census tracts in the twenty-nine towns in the Hartford–New Britain judicial district of Connecticut. He also used census "last name" identification to derive a different view of who in the jury data might be Hispanic.[8] I accepted Pollard's raw numbers. What he did with them was something else. Just as Pollard's work was overkill, so was my criticism of it. I wrote a separate report analyzing Pollard's work, henceforth referred to as my "Critique."[9]

The Connecticut System

In the Connecticut juror-selection system, unless the summons is returned by the Postal Service as undeliverable, the jury system assumes that it has been delivered. Unless some-

---

7. To what extent Pollard's approach was dictated by his ignorance of the law (of the court's requirement that defendant specify a procedural flaw, and of the willingness of the court to accept explanations for disproportionalities), or by his understanding that the discrepancies he presented *were* easily explained, I do not know. In a hearing on January 13, 1997, Pollard stated that he had investigated explanatory variables. Transcript at 19:

> But I don't see that I'm being asked to go beyond the stage of saying well why is this rate what it is. I'm just saying this is what the undeliverable rate is; this is what the disqualification rate is; this is what the—and so on.

8. The Census Bureau has long studied the possibility of identifying the number of Hispanics in a group by their names. The names are treated probabilistically: From their samples, the bureau determines what percent of people with each name are Hispanic. See Working Paper (1996). Pollard did an exceptionally careful job, again probably in ignorance: I had used a census-based Hispanic-name match in a jury challenge a decade before. I was not about to object to his doing the same thing.

9. Stephan Michelson, "Critique," a review of David Pollard's "Connecticut Juror Selection," drafts of December 12 and 30, 1996, and January 5, 1997; "Amended Draft," January 8, 1997; "Final Version," April 16, 1997; "Resolved Problems Crossed Out by D. P.," December 19, 1997; and "Testimony by David Pollard," January, 1998 (dated May 15, 1997, and January 12, 1998).

one calls to say he is not qualified, the jury system assumes that he is. These are some of the bad decisions made by jury-selection-system data managers with no understanding of their consequence in the hands of litigation analysts. Many non-responders were non-recipients. Others were not eligible. The system, not having screened them, did not know that, if tested, they would be found unqualified. All, under Pollard's terminology, are listed as "OK" until the day of trial. Those who are never called are never found to be not qualified or not present. The Connecticut system can be diagramed as in Figure 75.[10]

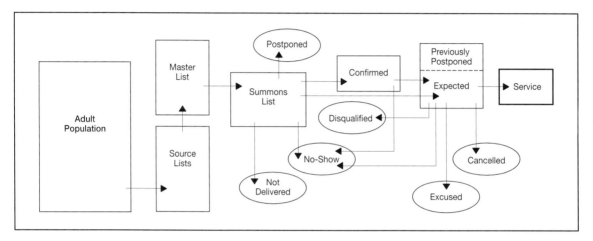

FIGURE 75: Connecticut Juror-Selection System

"Juror" Survey

Despite having devised estimates of juror ethnicity from Spanish-surname analysis, and both race and ethnicity from geocoding, Pollard persisted in estimating the composition of jurors from a courthouse survey. As he explained in a preliminary hearing, the survey was administered to all people showing up for jury duty at most courthouses, the exceptions being where judges did not cooperate. Juror identification number and self-identified race and Hispanic status were collected. However, a righteous Pollard assured the court, he never used the juror number from the questionnaire to merge this self-identification data with other juror data. He was going to use this survey to calculate the percent Hispanic among "OK" jurors, and nothing else.[11]

His approach made no sense. First, those who appear will not be a random sample of

---

10. Michelson, "Critique" at 10, Figure 2.

11. David Pollard, "Connecticut Juror Selection," April 16, 1997. Referring to earlier work in another trial, and an earlier survey questionnaire, Pollard says, at 12:

> They [questionnaire respondents] were also asked to give their juror ID numbers, and sign their names, but I made no use of those two pieces of information.

Pollard had testified, however, that he had wanted to use the name on the questionnaire to match self-

those who have been told to. Second, not all people showing in response to a summons are properly in the jury pool. Many will be disqualified at the courthouse after they complete the questionnaire.[12] Some failed to get the notice that their summons had been cancelled, and appeared in error. They would not be processed at the courthouse. We could never determine if they would have been disqualified.

Another purpose that could be served by the juror survey, without paring it down to those qualified, would be to validate Pollard's geographic and last-name imputations. Survey respondents would not be seen as "jurors," but as persons who appear in two data bases, one with self-enumerated ethnic status, one with name and address from which ethnic status was inferred. With validated or corrected ethnicity imputations, Pollard should have returned to the jury data to make his inference about the percent Hispanic among OK jurors.

Although the state accepted Pollard's race identifications a priori, we were curious what error to ascribe to that assignation. Pollard gave no indication that he was going to examine that question. Getting the idea from questions asked by state's attorney Mike O'Hare in cross-examination, Pollard later went on to do a reasonable study on this very subject.[13]

Not only was Pollard's sample obviously flawed. So was his basic "OK" concept. As I summarized in my "Critique":

> Half of Pollard's "OK" jurors have not been asked to serve. Had they been asked, some would not have appeared, could not be surveyed, and would have changed status to not OK. But they are OK in Pollard's data, even though he cannot capture them in his survey. Furthermore, and more important, these OK who have not served and would not be captured in his survey do not "look like" those who have served, would be captured. OK contains two distinct populations, of which Pollard's survey samples only one.[14]

---

enumeration with last-name identification, but was prevented from doing so by bad handwriting and careless transcription. Matching on juror number would have solved that problem.

Hearing transcript, January 13, 1997, at 1:

> The questionnaires were filled out by people who came into the courthouse. So what I was measuring was the response that those persons who came into the courthouse gave. But I was treating it as a sample . . . from the group that were the "okays" in my terminology. So this could be people who either appeared at the courthouse or were cancelled but who would have been labeled "okay."

12. Pollard did not seem to understand that, because there was no preliminary questionnaire, qualification occurred at the courthouse. "I am sampling the people who were qualified by the process," he said in a hearing on January 7, 1997,

> qualified in the sense that they hadn't been disqualified for one of the reasons and that they were not ultimately to be classified as no-shows.

Transcript at 97.

13. David Pollard, "Final Report," Appendix D.

14. Michelson, "Critique" at 16.

This comment can be seen in Figure 75 in the composition of those the system "expects" to show up. Some people appear there simply because they had been sent a summons, without further review or action.

RHODE ISLAND: ISSUES AND CHARACTERS[15]

Defendant Tremblay's alleged crime was murder. The state's crime, according to his attorney, was "racism in the criminal justice system."[16] The statistical analysis by defendant's expert, Andrew Beveridge of the sociology department at Queens College in New York, will

> compel the legal conclusion that the process is unconstitutional and in violation of Rhode Island law.[17]

Not only is there "gross under-representation" of minorities, but everyone knows it. "The evidence was anecdotal, but overwhelming." Although not telling us where in the system the state acted to create this under-representation, defendant implored the state to

> join in seeking a remedy . . . rather than occluding the issue by interposing objections predicated on the type of statistical tests to be employed.

A remedy to what?

Presumably Andrew Beveridge would tell us. Beveridge compared the proportion of "potential jurors" from each town with the census proportion of adults from that town, for the nineteen towns comprising the Providence–Bristol judicial district. He did the same for serving grand jurors, in a time period from August 5, 1996, through May 30, 2000. He never defined "potential jurors" in the context of the procedures used for jury selection. "In short," he concluded, "there are many too few grand jurors from Providence."[18] He found "massive geographic bias" among "potential jurors."

> This results in an unrepresentative set of panels, which massively and systematically under represent the voting age minority, black, and Hispanic population.[19]

---

15. The Rhode Island discussion in this chapter concerns *Tremblay* (2003).

16. See Robert B. Mann, "Memorandum of Law by Defendant's Counsel," February 20, 2001.

17. Mann, "Memorandum of Law," at 1; following in-text quotation at 2; then indented quotation at 1.

18. Andrew A. Beveridge, "Affirmation in Support of Defendant's Motion," February 17, 2001, at 7; following in-text phrases at 12.

19. Beveridge, "Affirmation in Support," at 18; following indented quotations both at 22. Beveridge defined "minority" from 1990 U.S. Census data as black plus Hispanics minus black-Hispanics. It is difficult to count Hispanics by race, as many Hispanics did not answer the race question. I would have appreciated some indication from Beveridge that he understood the data problems, but they should not have prevented him from proceeding as he did.

Beveridge applied standard binomial tests on proportion minority (jury vs. census) coming from the different towns.

> The gross geographical disparities could not have occurred by chance, rather they are the result of some systematic bias in the jury wheel process, which comes after the lists used for such selection.

Beveridge concluded that

> About 60 percent of each [minority] group is excluded from jury service due to the selection system.

The Rhode Island System

I presented a picture of the Rhode Island jury-selection system's procedures, reproduced here as Figure 76.[20] As in the figures in Chapter 5, square boxes represent the path of staying in the system. Elliptical boxes represent leaving the system. Green (appearing shaded in black-and-white photocopies) represents decisions by the jury-selection system. Blue (clear in black-and-white photocopies) represents decisions made by individuals. Red (heavy) frames show on what elements I had data. Dashed frames indicate elements for which I might have had data, but for reasons explained in my affidavit, I did not.

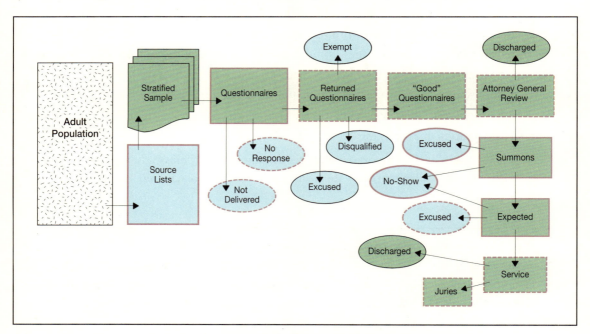

FIGURE 76: Rhode Island Juror-Selection System

---

20. Figure 76 is Figure 1 of "Affidavit of Stephan Michelson," October 26, 2001, at 14.

Source lists are driver's-license and voter-registration lists, merged and purged. They are gathered every year, and retained in town order. An "every nth observation" randomization was used.[21] Defendant and his expert found no fault with this process.

Minorities appear in excess (relative to the census) on source lists, even though non-citizens are disproportionately minority. Though questionnaires are mailed disproportionately to minorities, they are undelivered even more disproportionately. Fewer than half the questionnaires sent out are completed and returned. Rhode Island has the good sense not to expect persons to appear for trial if they have not responded to the system's mailing.

Notice that, in Figure 76, excuse and qualification is a clerical function, performed from the questionnaire responses (as well as from telephone calls). Persons can be excused from jury duty in three different places, although many of the excuses after summons are temporary (it is an excuse from this particular service date, not from jury service). If these decisions were exercised to minimize minority representation on juries, defendant would have to allege that the bias was in favor of minorities—in favor of granting them excuses they asked for.

CONNECTICUT: ANALYSIS

Understanding that all David Pollard ever presented was the idea that Hispanics were not present in juries to the extent he "expected" from census data, I will cover only one other presentation point here. Pollard did not organize the Judicial Information Services data in the order that events occurred. In Figure 77 I do, but I retain the numbers Pollard presented. "Undeliverable Subsequent" is a second notice that Judicial Information Services sends out to those who have not responded to the first, though unless returned by the Postal Service, that person is still expected to show up for trial, is still "OK" in Pollard's data. The other column headings should be obvious.

When presenting responses to a survey, one should calculate the percentage of each allowable response based on those people who answered it, or at least *might have* answered it. Pollard calculated the percentages in Figure 77 from a base of all summonses sent. In a household survey, for example, one might ask each individual, "Did you drive a car in the last year?" Surely in reporting driving differences in traffic citations (say, by race),

---

21. If there are one hundred thousand observations and we want a sample of one thousand, then starting from a random number less than one hundred (the "key number" of Chapter 5), selecting every hundredth observation will give us one thousand. If the observations had been shuffled, so that adjacent observations may or may not still be adjacent, the selection is considered random. Here, the shuffling occurs by a sort within each town.

a typical analyst would exclude from the denominator those who had not driven, as well as those who refused to participate in the survey at all. Pollard, however, would include them.[22]

	Undeliverable Summons	Not in Jurisdiction	Citizenship	Language	Over Seventy	Hardship	Other	Undeliverable Subsequent	No-Show
Hispanic	36%	2%	2%	11%	2%	3%	3%	5%	10%
Non-Hispanic	13%	6%	2%	1%	12%	7%	7%	1%	4%

FIGURE 77: Pollard's Rate of "Loss" in 1994–95

In Figure 78 I redo Pollard's figures, showing that if one wants to retrieve a behavioral picture from these data, some conceptual work is required. Hispanics exhibited different behavior from non-Hispanics, caused by their mobility. Hispanics were less securely part of the "community" than non-Hispanics, as indicated by their high rate of movement into and out of the jurisdiction, and their failure to show up when called.

	Undeliverable Summons	Not in Jurisdiction	Citizenship	Language	Over Seventy	Hardship	Other	Undeliverable Subsequent	No-Show
Hispanic	36.0%	3.1%	3.2%	17.7%	4.1%	6.1%	6.1%	12.2%	27.8%
Non-Hispanic	13.0%	6.9%	2.5%	2.5%	15.4%	9.0%	9.0%	1.9%	7.8%
Basis of Calculations	All Mailed Summons	Presumed Delivered	Presumed Delivered and in Jurisdiction		English-Speaking Citizens			Not Disqualified	All Remaining

FIGURE 78: Michelson's Rate of "Loss" in 1994–95

Pollard appears to tell us, in Figure 77, that Hispanics and non-Hispanics are disqualified for non-citizenship at the same rate. As Figure 78 shows, that is not the case. Accounting only for the non-deliveries and those not in the jurisdiction, we find a higher rate of non-citizenship among Hispanics than among non-Hispanics, which is what one would have expected from census data. Surely many more Hispanics notified to appear would have been disqualified for lack of citizenship had they received notices that were mailed to them. If the point is to infer information about those to whom notices were sent, Pollard's approach is a failure.

---

22. The percentages in Figure 77 do not add to 100 percent, because the remainder (26 percent of the Hispanics, 47 percent of the non-Hispanics) are "OK" jurors.

Similarly, Pollard would have us believe that Hispanics fail to show (the last column on the right of Figure 77) at a rate two and a half times that of non-Hispanics. Again, far more Hispanics do not reach this point. Hispanics whose summonses are otherwise alive fail to show at a rate over three and a half times that of non-Hispanics, a ratio 40 percent higher than that which Pollard displays.

Rebuttal

I submitted four reports. My "Critique" has been discussed above. The second contained my own analysis of jury selection.[23] The third contained three studies of "movement out" of the Hartford–New Britain judicial district.[24] Establishing the higher leaving rate of Hispanics was the key to my conclusion that there was no available "remedy" should one think that a "lack" of Hispanics on juries was a "flaw" in the system. The fourth report was what I call a "service" document for my clients. It contained calculations of the "disparities" described in Chapter 5, the various calculations courts have made to compare jurors to the census population.[25] Someone in my position should serve his clients, including providing to them statistical summaries that they want. However, submitting traditional disparity measures to the court undercut the point we were making, that such measures meant nothing. I made no outcome calculations in Rhode Island.

Judge Arthur L. Spada had been raised in Hartford, in a part of town that in his youth was almost exclusively Italian. At the time of trial, it was almost exclusively Hispanic. He was personally aware of the immigrant story. The first generation does not speak the language of the government, does not participate (drive, vote). In a generation or two, they will acculturate and succeed. My analysis started with a showing that although Hispanics were "missing" from juries, considering their presence in the population, it was not their "Hispanic-ness" that created this difference. I presented a regression estimate of the number of persons found qualified in Judicial Information Services data. The equation is in Figure 79. Being Hispanic is not related to becoming a qualified juror.

Judging from his dissent in *Castaneda* (1977), Chief Justice Burger would appreciate this little study. But from Chapter 5 we know that it must be wrong, or at least not precisely correct. My point about Burger's call for use of the selection model from eligibles is that we cannot know eligibles outside of the jury system's own determination. What did I do? What is my variable "Eligible"?

---

23. Stephan Michelson, "An Empirical Analysis of the Connecticut Jury System," April 2, 1997 (revised January 2, 1998).

24. Stephan Michelson, "Movement Out of the Hartford–New Britain Judicial District," May 21 and December 16, 1997.

25. Stephan Michelson, "Traditional Measures of Jury Disparity," January 12, 1998.

Variable	Coefficient	P > |t|
Eligible	0.143	0.000
Hispanics	−0.001	−0.972
Population	−0.071	−0.040

Adjusted R^2 = 0.991

FIGURE 79: Regression Estimating Qualified Jurors

I created a proxy measure for "eligible" for the sole purpose of showing that one should know that Hispanics would legitimately drop out of the jury-selection process. My counts cannot be taken literally, but the direction of change from the population can be. This is my definition of "eligible" for this Connecticut study:

> I subtract the number of adult non-citizens from the number of adults in each town, where "adult" is defined as age eighteen or higher as counted in the census;

> I subtract the number of institutionalized adults, assuming mutual exclusivity, i.e., that none of them are non-citizens; and

> I subtract one-half of the number of adults who do not speak English well, assuming that only the other half of them are non-citizens or institutionalized.[26]

I concluded that although Hispanics are disproportionately ineligible, it is not because they are Hispanic (the Hispanic coefficient is zero), but because they have disqualifying characteristics. I proceeded to show that census characteristics other than ethnicity or race predicted qualification failure better than ethnicity did, for every such screen. Being Hispanic was incidental. Who the Hispanics were, in terms of their citizenship, mobility, and language fluency, is what made them ineligible for jury duty.

Finally, I provided estimates of the effects of various stages in the jury-selection system on the percent Hispanic. These are reproduced here as Figures 80 and 81, in which I show my estimate of the percent Hispanic after every stage in the process.[27]

---

26. Michelson, "An Empirical Analysis" at 20, parenthetical statements omitted. Making some adjustment to get a more accurate count of eligibles cannot be a difficult concept. In *Esquivel* (1996) the Ninth Circuit requested and received a breakdown of citizenship status between Hispanics and non-Hispanics. The absolute disparity fell from 14.5 to 4.9. At 727:

> This means that Esquivel's computation, based on the total population of Hispanics, is inaccurate and overestimated.

27. Michelson, "An Empirical Analysis" at 42 (Figure 80) and 43 (Figure 81).

	Population	Source List	Master List	Delivery	Invalid
Percent after Stage	6.57	5.38	6.73	5.12	5.48

FIGURE 80: Hispanics through the Mechanics

	Citizenship and Language	Age and Hardship	No Notice	Excused	No-Show
Percent after Stage	4.53	5.37	4.95	5.00	4.05

FIGURE 81: Hispanics through the Qualification and Behavior Screens

In these tables we first see that Hispanics do not make it to the source lists in proportion to their presence in the population. Then they are *over*-sampled on to the master list, but fail to get their mail delivered. The over-sampling, as directed by the Connecticut legislature, is explained below. The "invalid" category is persons who demonstrate that they should not have been sent a summons. Those people have moved, are under age, are convicted felons, are state officials, or have recently served or been summoned. These figures should not imply, though Pollard argued that they did, that non-Hispanics are more likely to move, or be felons. Non-Hispanics in these categories are more likely to inform the system. Hispanics were younger, and therefore were not disqualified for old age. Hispanics were less likely to receive a second notice when mailed to them, and far less likely to show up when they were expected.

Once again, the point is that the state did not deny that Hispanics appeared on juries in smaller proportions than they held in the population. Rather, it embraced that conclusion. Given the history of the law in this area, that was a radical and, for the state, courageous strategy. More important, it was honest. Most important, it showed that Judicial Information Services did nothing wrong. Without a procedural error, there was nothing to correct.

Mobility

Most of my empirical work was summarized in my third report, on mobility. Pollard would insist that the failure of Hispanics to receive mail and appear for trials was a remediable fault of the jury-selection system. My argument was that the missing Hispanics were not there. They had left the jurisdiction. No fault, no "remedy."

Consider driver's-license-renewal data. I obtained and processed over six million license records. This is my description of what I did:

I defined the set of all licenses in the Hartford–New Britain judicial district that were valid on June 25, 1994—the date of the system conversion—and, at that date, were due to expire in 1996. As I had a record of every transaction in 1996, I should know whether each of these licenses was renewed or was no longer valid at the beginning of April, 1997. A license holder is supposed to notify the DMV within 72 hours of an address change. I doubted that happened all the time. Rather, I presume addresses are changed largely at renewal. That was why it was important to wait for renewal dates to pass before reviewing the address again. Whenever it occurred, I tried to discern who notified DMV, who just disappeared. Had the license been transferred to another state, the receiving state would have sent it back to Connecticut, and Connecticut would have noted that state's receipt. Finally, if the license holder moved within Connecticut, I would find a valid Connecticut license at the end, but at a different address.[28]

The data had been provided without name or address, but with Zip code. As I could obtain census data by Zip code also, it was easy to use the fifty-six Zip codes in the judicial district as observations in regressions. I found:

> Eighty-one percent of Connecticut drivers renewed their driver's licenses in the same judicial district. This is a high figure (compared with Postal Service change-of-address data), indicating that those who obtain licenses are more stable than average to begin with.

> Hispanics (that is, people in Zip codes containing many Hispanics) were less likely to obtain driver's licenses than non-Hispanics, verifying my earlier analysis by town to this effect.

> Hispanics were less likely to renew their licenses than non-Hispanics.

> Of those that did not renew, Hispanics were less likely to notify the DMV.

I obtained Postal Service change-of-address data covering the period from March 1994 to March 1997, also by Zip code. From a regression in which the dependent variable was change of address from apartment or "other" (as the Postal Service categorizes it), I found:

> The regression coefficients imply that if you start with a population in 1990, then, on the margin, for every additional 1,000 non-Hispanics, 344 will move in this period. For every additional 1,000 Hispanics, 765 will move in this period. Of course we realize this could be multiple turnover, persons coming into and leaving the same units. However it is generated, Hispanics move at over 2.2 times the rate of non-Hispanics.[29]

Change of address may be filed by the individual or by the postal delivery person, who indicates, "moved, left no forwarding address." I determined:

---

28. Michelson, "Movement Out" at 15.

29. Michelson, "Movement Out" at 10; following indented quotation at 13.

Controlling for both the total number of moves and the total population (which includes Hispanics), Hispanics are seen to leave no forwarding address considerably more often than non-Hispanics.

Hispanics are more likely to move, and among movers are more likely to leave no information that they had done so. They become jury delivery failures and no-shows.

I also related percent Hispanic to percent of housing units that are rented, and also percent that are vacant. Vacancies, after all, occur with turnover. The point is that the *count* of Hispanics may be stable, even increasing, but the individuals are changing places. Renters predict mobility quite well. The race or ethnic group found to have a high percentage of renters will have a high percentage of movers. They will appear on source lists less frequently and those on such lists will less frequently comply with a jury summons.

RHODE ISLAND: ANALYSIS

Unlike Connecticut's, Rhode Island's jury-system data were not computerized. However, following their concept of stratified sampling (by town), all typed lists, throughout the process, were maintained by town. And they were numbered from beginning to end. I retrieved census data for the nineteen towns in the Providence–Bristol jurisdiction, which I combined with my counts of persons from each town on each jury list (aggregated over a complete year), to form a data base. I estimated the number of persons on each list, from each town, in two ways, as indicated in Figure 82.

	Source List	Sent Questionnaire	Delivered Questionnaire	Sent Summons
Majority	1.162	0.041	0.038	0.016
Minority	1.456	0.051	0.020	−0.018
Constant	1388.4	48.9	25.5	18.2
Majority	1.293	0.046	0.044	0.020
Minority	2.086	0.073	0.040	0.001
Rentals	−0.559	−0.020	−0.031	−0.015
Non-Citizens	−0.665	−0.023	−0.003	−0.023
Constant	1076.5	38.0	6.9	9.7

FIGURE 82: Regressions Estimating Counts on Lists

One can look at the ratio of the "minority" coefficient to the "majority" coefficient—the relative likelihood of a minority being in the count denoted by the dependent variable—or more generally compare the majority and minority coefficients from stage to stage. The ratio minority to majority decreases over stages. As these are grouped data—we have data by town, not by individual—the interpretation that they apply to individuals is some-what loose. It could be others—neither blacks nor Hispanics—who happen to live where blacks and Hispanics live, who are creating these differences. But the most reasonable interpretation is that these relationships apply to majority and minority members, even if also to other people. Minorities fall out of the system.

Majority and minority coefficients are greater than 1.0 when we estimate numbers on source lists from census counts. Are we to believe that the presence of an additional one hundred minority adults increases the merged source list by over 145 persons? Two possible explanations are that the population in this judicial district has increased in the eight years since April 1990, when the census data were gathered; or that lists are not purged. If the latter explanation is correct, as Andrew Beveridge argued in a later document, then one should expect massive non-delivery, especially of questionnaires mailed to the more-mobile minorities.

The numbers in Figure 82 are coefficients from eight separate regressions. The four dependent variables are column heads. The first set of regression coefficients—with only majority and minority estimating the number of persons on the source lists, sent questionnaires, delivered questionnaires, and sent summonses—show clearly the decline in minority representation over these stages. The second set of regressions includes a variable measuring the percent of occupied housing units that are rental units, and one measuring the number of non-citizens. I showed separately that both of these variables are correlated with minority: If renters and non-citizens leave the jury system, then minorities leave the jury system. More on renters later, but non-citizens are obvious: They are eligible to drive, but not to serve on juries. That is why using additional source lists has not affected jury composition.

The first regressions are descriptions. The second set are explanations. Using these coefficients to more decimal places than shown, minorities are more than nineteen times more likely than majority members *not* to receive a questionnaire mailed to them. Minorities are even less likely to receive a summons. The intervening stages include non-response and disqualification. Non-citizens are dropped in the disqualification stage, to the extent that they returned the questionnaire. It should not be surprising, and should not be considered invidious, that minorities fall out of the process this way.

Renting is associated with mobility. In Connecticut I had the resources to demonstrate this association in several ways, in adjudicative fact. In Rhode Island I showed this association in legislative fact, using "Current Population Report" data from the Census Bureau, as in Figure 83.[30]

Nationally, one-third of renters move in a single year. One-third of *them* move beyond

---

30. U.S. Census Bureau, "Geographic Mobility," Current Population Report P20-520, January 2000.

	Percent Who Move	Percent Who Move Beyond the County Boundary
Owner	8.2	3.1
Renter	33.4	11.7

FIGURE 83: National Mobility Statistics

the county boundary. Home owners are not nearly as inclined to move. Neither of these measures includes persons in group quarters, including dormitory residents. Although one can improve the prediction (a renter who is single, for example, is more likely to move than a renter head of a family), the relationship between rental units in a place and mobility into and out of that place is strong. It doesn't matter that similar people move in to replace those who move out. Neither is available for jury duty, the immigrant because he is not yet on a list, the emigrant because he is no longer there. The census count may be stable, but the people being counted are not.

Who are renters? I first estimate the number of rental units as a function of the number of occupied housing units and its square. That projection is the solid line in Figure 84. By adding the squared term I recognize that larger cities will have more rental units regardless of the race of their occupants. Larger cities have a higher *proportion* of rentals among housing units, not just more of them. The dashed line is from the same variables plus a count of minorities. It "explains" the few anomalous observations from the first regression. Obviously minorities are consumers of rental units.

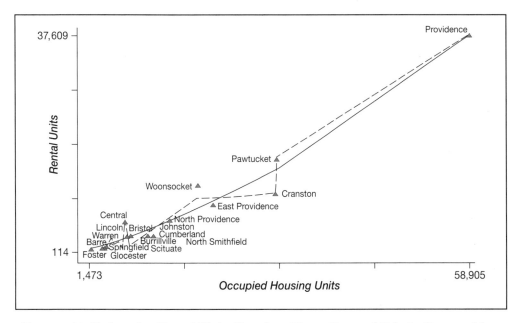

FIGURE 84: Estimating Rental Units Based on Town Size and Ethnic Composition

Ineligibility and Mobility

In all of Rhode Island there were 44,294 adult non-citizens in 1990. More than half of them were in two cities, Providence and Pawtucket. These two cities contain approximately 23 percent of the population of the state, and so have more than twice their proportional share of non-citizens. Under state law, those people could not have been on juries, but are unaccounted for in Beveridge's strong conclusions about a flawed system. Like Pollard in Connecticut, Beveridge's *Castaneda*-type study described no flaw in the jury-selection system, no state action causing jurors to be excluded.

In Rhode Island, minorities, or at least persons in towns where minorities live, were *more* likely (in 1998) to be on source lists than others. The mechanism lies in something we do not see when we analyze voters and drivers separately: The list from the department of motor vehicles is far larger than the voter-registration list. In Providence, in 1998, the merged list was 83 percent larger than the voter list, but only 46 percent larger than the DMV list. In Pawtucket and Woonsocket, the merged list was more than 84 percent larger than the voter list, but around 30 percent larger than the DMV list. In Central Falls, the merged list was over twice as large as the voter list, but 34.5 percent larger than the DMV list. In a few towns, such as Glocester, the relative addition to the voter list was larger, but over all towns the merged list was 66 percent larger than the voter list, and only 36 percent larger than the DMV list.

Some people vote but do not drive. What is more important is how many people drive who do not vote. What is more important still is how many of them *could* not vote, because they are ineligible. In Rhode Island, the addition of the driver list to the voter list created the impression that minorities could join the jury system, when they could not.

Who does not receive a mailed questionnaire? The more minorities in a town, the fewer deliveries there were, accounting for the number of questionnaires mailed. It is reasonable to infer that minorities disproportionately do not get the questionnaire. We can measure the drop-out from mailing through response and qualification, from the distribution of summonses. In Figure 85 we see that it is minorities who were brought into the system through driver's licenses, who quickly leave the system from non-delivery, non-return, and not being eligible for jury service. Summonses mailed are expressed as a percent of questionnaires. The more minority, the lower that percent.

At each stage, minorities (as "geocoded" from their towns) dropped out more than non-minorities. I concluded that the "community" from which Rhode Island drew its juries simply had a lower proportion minority than was indicated by a census count of adults. The system was old-fashioned and inefficient, and allowed clerks to make judgments usually reserved for judges, but there was no evidence that those judgments or any other part of the system was discriminatory. There was evidence that Hispanics were ineligible and mobile.

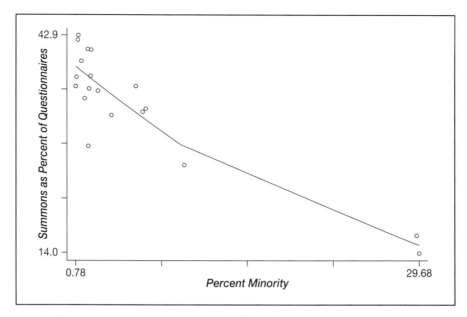

FIGURE 85: Minorities Decline from Source List to Summons

CONNECTICUT: DECISION

How did Hispanics get "over-sampled" on to the master list in Connecticut? Participation (voter and driver) is lowest in the large towns such as Hartford. These are also the towns with the most Hispanics. Suppose we just add together all the voters and drivers (subtracting duplicates) in the twenty-nine district towns, and then randomly sample for jurors, as is done in Rhode Island. Let's say there is no difference in the propensity to participate between Hispanics and non-Hispanics, but there is a difference in this propensity, unrelated to race or ethnicity, related only to size of town. The larger towns have more transient (non-voting) people who have little need to drive. We would expect, therefore, from this "natural" weighting, to find fewer people from Hartford on jury lists than their percent in the population. In the judicial district we would get fewer Hispanics than *their* percent in the population, because Hispanics live in Hartford and Hartford is, in this sense, "under"-represented.

Yet that would be the "fair" sampling of participants. It would be a uniform-random sampling from approved and reasonable source lists: It gives every participant the same chance to be selected. Instead, the Connecticut legislature instructed that the proportion from Hartford on the list be the same as the proportion of the total population from Hartford in the district.[31] To accomplish that, they have to sample from Hartford at a higher

---

31. The Connecticut system follows the precepts of Fukurai et al. (1993), although I do not know if either party knew about the other. The current system was undoubtedly established after the previous system was rebuked in *Alston* (1985), at 995:

rate than from other towns. For example, suppose Hartford has 20 percent of the population, but 17 percent of the participants. To get 20 percent of the master list from 17 percent of the participants on the source lists obviously requires that one sample Hartford more intensively. As an illustration, if every member of the source list from Hartford were on the master list, only 82 percent of those from other towns would be on the master list, in Connecticut's weighting scheme. A Hartford resident would have a 1.22:1 chance of being called for jury service, compared with a resident elsewhere in the judicial district.

This bias holds true under the assumption that, in Hartford, Hispanics and non-Hispanics participated equally, just at a lower rate than elsewhere. In a search for Hispanics, the state "taxes" Hispanics (and everyone else in Hartford) who participate, by giving them a higher probability of being called for jury service. I estimated that this tax was between 17 and 35 percent, depending on the mix between the voter list and the driver list in the merged source list. The hypothetical figures above show how easily a small difference in participation rates (and age of population: Connecticut weights are based on everyone, not just adults) creates a tax this large.

The real world is more complicated in that, within Hartford, Hispanics are less likely to participate. As a result, non-Hispanic participants are especially taxed for the lack of participation of Hispanics. They are penalized for living where non-participants live. But as most Hispanics in Connecticut are in Hartford, and Hartford is over-sampled onto the master list, therefore participating Hispanics also are over-sampled.

After insisting through the trial that Hispanics were *under*-represented on jury lists, David Pollard finally capitulated. On the witness stand he said he disagreed with my calculation (providing no alternative), but agreed with the fact and direction of the bias: Hispanics were *over*-represented, exactly the opposite of his client's complaint. In two years of intensive study of the trees, Pollard had failed to see the forest.

The Court's View

Understanding that the towns were weighted in merging source lists, Judge Spada decided that population was not an unconstitutional factor to use in jury selection. That is, he rejected uniform-random as a required basis of representative, that anything else violates equal protection, even though both experts had asserted this standard.

> The Connecticut statute in question assigns towns falling within a specified population range a fixed quota of jurors that each town must fill in supplying jurors to the county jury array. The town quota system, however, does not fix the quota of jurors in proportion to the size of the town's population.

The court, and then the legislature by following the court, both got it wrong. What counts is the numbers of persons eligible for jury duty and, better, among them only those who will cooperate (i.e., show up). Setting these numbers beforehand will never achieve a truly fair system.

As Judge Spada noted, Pollard had criticized my regressions, though never offering improvements or alternatives.

> Pollard discussed the assumptions inherent in regression models and the difficulty of interpretation. Pollard specifically pointed to the city of Hartford as an influencing factor that could affect the regression outcome. Pollard also illustrated the difficulty of relying on regression by pointing to state's exhibits 32a and 32g in which Michelson performed different multivariate regressions using the isolated factor; the sign flipped, meaning that the number of linguistically isolated households had a positive effect on undeliverables in one equation and a negative effect in the other.[32]

I discussed this "sign flipping" in the Appendix to Chapter 3. There is no mystery about it, and no flaw in it. The coefficients came from different specifications which describe different things. As some of those who were linguistically isolated were also non-citizens, the linguistic-isolation factor quite reasonably had different signs in different regressions. Although Hispanics had a lower propensity to vote than others, in a regression with explanatory variables the Hispanic coefficient was positive. Interpretation is simple: Hispanics who can, register. Many are not allowed to register based on their characteristics, such as not being citizens. The sign differs depending on what else the equation is measuring.

It could be that David Pollard does not understand regression—he gave no evidence of such comprehension in this litigation—but I suspect another explanation: Pollard was into the fight. He would say anything that might convince the judge of his goodness and my badness, even if he knew it was statistical folly. The apparent advantage of the naive academic, that he earns his primary living elsewhere, and therefore is striving honestly to find fact, disappears in the heat of battle.

The trial court found for the state. Ultimately, Judge Spada criticized defendant for

> [putting] forth no evidence that the jury officials acted in ways which deliberately excluded Hispanics,

either in the mailing or in

> intervening events between a potential juror's receipt of summons and his failure to report for jury duty.[33]

The opinion not only refused to grant that defendant had made a *prima facie* case, it concluded with this blast at defendant and, implicitly, his expert:

> A concern for husbanding precious judicial resources dictates that a decision, in the future, to challenge the array anew be predicated on facts warranting judicial intervention.

---

32. *Gibbs* (1998) at *20.

33. *Gibbs* (1998) at *22; preceding indented quotation also at *22; following indented quotation at *28.

The Connecticut Supreme Court upheld the lower-court decision.[34] The Connecticut jury system was declared constitutional. Gibbs was convicted of murder and sentenced to life in prison.

RHODE ISLAND: DECISION

Mr. Tremblay, also, failed to make a *prima facie* case. Then he pled guilty.

Andrew Beveridge responded to my analysis with speculation[35] and the passion for his client's cause with which he began. Another academic caught up in the heat of battle. Although permission to file a second analysis was granted on his promise that he would re-analyze the Providence–Bristol juries based on data from the 2000 U.S. Census, reporting that re-analysis (in which no conclusion was altered) took just one footnote of his seventeen-page paper. The remainder was a harangue against my analysis, which, he objected, was not like his. About that, he was correct. I did not respond.

In the framework that courts follow, the requirement for a procedural showing comes in the third prong of the test imposed by *Duren* (1979).

> The defendants, through Dr. Beveridge, have tendered an array of statistics and charts. These calibrations not only fail to meet *Duren*'s second requisite fair cross-section element, they do not by themselves at all satisfy the defendants' burden of demonstrating systematic exclusion, *Duren*'s third necessary prong.[36]

With their calculations of absolute disparity, assessed by no known standard, judges waste their time applying outcome concepts to a process question. Judges are mired in precedent. Judge Krause went through the *Duren* logic and the disparity calculations as if they scripted a religious ceremony. In a sense the judge is a priest, determining which ceremony to follow, and then following it as closely as he can. Are judges taught not to be creative, not to understand fundamental failings of received doctrine? The judicial training I envision in Chapters 7, 9, and 10 would not operate that way.

---

34. See *Gibbs* (2000). In *Ferguson* (2002), that court extended the *Gibbs* decision to cover the entire state of Connecticut, cutting off further jury-composition litigation.

35. For example, he concludes, from no evidence of which I am aware, that the surplus of source-list names are duplicates, rather than names of persons who have moved away and not notified the department of motor vehicles or the voter registry. As I had shown that the additional names were of minorities—which fits better a model of population "churning" than duplication—I cannot understand what Beveridge's problem is. See "Supplementary Affirmation of Dr. Andrew A. Beveridge in Support of Defendant's Motion," November 2, 2002.

36. *Tremblay* (2003) at *6.

Common Sense

My procedural view, applied to the third prong, doomed both of these complaints. Because my procedural analysis prevails every time, I cannot say the courts are getting it wrong. But as they both listen and deny that they are doing so, they sure do look foolish.

A refreshingly insightful handling of these issues can be found in *Artero* (1997), a Ninth Circuit decision. John Weeks was defendant's expert. The appeals court wrote:

> The right question is whether Hispanics eligible to serve on federal juries were unreasonably underrepresented because of systematic exclusion. But Dr. Weeks did not provide any data responsive to that question. He provided an answer to a different question, whether Hispanics, whether eligible to serve on federal juries or not, were represented in jury wheels at a lower rate than their proportion of the population as a whole. Irrelevant question, irrelevant answer.[37]

The court is not asking for a precise measurement of eligibles, just some understanding on the part of defendant's expert that population is the wrong metric, that outcome comparison is unhelpful. This case was available to both David Pollard and Andrew Beveridge, telling them their approach was disastrous. Apparently, they just didn't look.

Misleading Language

Thomas Frank, describing how the "market" came to be accepted as "the solution" to all problems, discusses escalation in language:

> In the "grand argument" in which business literature imagines itself engaged, "inevitability" served as a sort of logical atom bomb to be dropped on foes like unions, liberals, and environmentalists when conventional talk of "democracy" failed.[38]

He quotes Lester Thurow, Kevin Kelly, Thomas Friedman, and George Gilder to this effect.[39]

> "These are not mere prophesies," the ever-humble Gilder wrote. "They are the imperious facts of life."[40]

---

37. *Artero* (1997) at 1261.

38. Frank (2000) at 344.

39. Thurow claims that "genetic engineering . . . will 'inevitably' triumph over its doubters," and "Europeans . . . 'will have to adjust to the realities of a global economy.'" Frank (2000) at 345, from Thurow, *Building Wealth: The New Rules for Individuals, Companies and Nations in a Knowledge-Based Economy* (1999), at 33 and 97. Friedman is quoted from *The Lexus and The Olive Tree* (1999), Kevin Kelly from *New Rules for the New Economy* (1998), and Gilder from *Microcosm: Into the Quantum Era of Economics and Technology* (1989).

40. Frank (2000) at 347, quoting Gilder, *Microcosm*, at 369.

I will now quote from documents submitted to a federal district court in January 2005, pursuant to defendant's challenge to the jury-selection system.[41] Defendant's expert has done the usual. He compares measures of jurors (from questionnaires identifying race) with measures of the population's adults (from census data). He writes that "three conclusions are inescapable." He describes the "deviation between the actual and ideal distribution of summoned individuals," and determines that "these disparities could not have occurred by chance." He is certain that reality is different from the "ideal," that "chance" is not an explanation, that this is a problem that the state must solve.

In his memorandum supporting his motion, the expert's client, the defendant's attorney, translates these findings to this:

> The African-American representation on Master Jury Wheels . . . has been less than half of what it should be.

Thus we have a poor guess at the kinds of jurors uniform-random selection might produce called "ideal" by the expert, and "what it should be" by the attorney. Differences from that "ideal" are posited as indicating a problem, something that shouldn't have occurred, although neither the expert nor the attorney identifies why it did. The expert's calculations are limited to the "bottom line," to comparing the first element in Figure 51 of this book—the population—to one of the last elements in Figure 54.[42] Under this logic, it is left to the prosecuting attorney to sponsor the analysis that would show, as I did in Connecticut and Rhode Island, where the differences are found.

I present this work as further evidence that I have not created a "straw man" to destroy. What I say all other experts do is what all other experts do. The logic of Chapter 5 is different, and badly needed. More important, here, these participants explain what they do as obvious and certain, when it is crude and speculative. A better adjective would be "wrong." Extreme language like theirs is uncalled for. It is not the language of a reasoned, thoughtful analysis. It is the language of advocacy.

Although defendant did not prove enough for a *prima facie* constitutional disparity, he captured Judge Gertner's attention under applicable federal laws. She was, frankly, duped by false outcome comparisons, failed by bad statistical expert work. In *Castaneda* (1977) the Court asked the state to explain the jury/population disparities. Only two years later, in *Duren* (1979), that burden shifted to the complaining party. Or did it? Twenty-six years on, this defendant, his attorney, his expert, and even the judge do not think so.

---

41. Unpublished documents submitted in *Green* (2005).

42. Not everyone on the master wheel would have answered a questionnaire identifying race. Indeed, not everyone on the mailing list, which is what "Master Jury Wheel" refers to here, received his questionnaire; and of those who did, not all returned it. So it is not clear to what construct this expert refers.

APPENDIX TO CHAPTER 9

A Note on Graphics

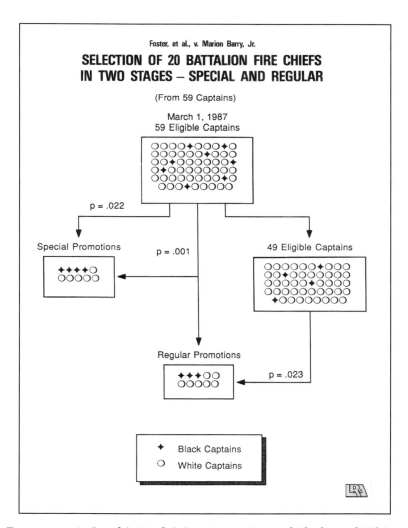

FIGURE 86: A Graphic Explaining Promotions of Blacks and Whites

As difficult as it is to perform good (relevant as well as technically sophisticated) empirical analyses in litigation, it is equally difficult, and equally important, to explain them well. As explanations of my work have shown (see, for example, Chapter 5 and its appendix, or discussions of regression in Chapter 3), pictures can be of great assistance. Graphics well done can elucidate. Graphics badly done can confuse.

From eight eligible blacks and fifty-one eligible whites, seven blacks were promoted from fire captain to battalion fire chief in Washington, D.C.[1] There were two routes to promotion—"special" and "regular." Figure 86 is my summary of the unlikelihood of the events that occurred, had race or something correlated with race not been a factor in the decisions.

Had blacks and whites been distributed equally in qualifications, the resulting race composition would have occurred one time in a thousand. This low probability is not "proof" of racial bias. In Chapter 10 I explain the (black) fire chief's role in this selection. The point of Figure 86 is to show that the 0.001 probability is the result of two improbable occurrences, the race of those receiving special promotions and then regular promotions from those captains remaining after the special promotions. Each alone is improbable— $p = 0.02$—had race not been a factor. Together, they are even less likely, $p = 0.001$. The graphic shows the pools, the selections, and their associated probabilities. I submit that this graphic establishes a standard of clarity for all litigation graphics to meet.

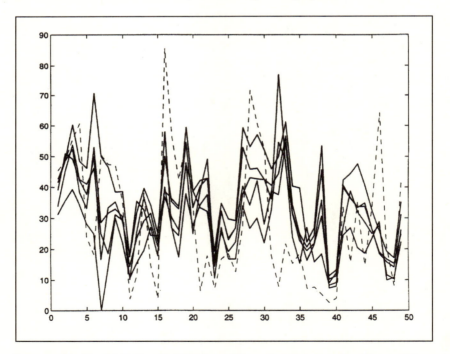

FIGURE 87: David Pollard's Display of Jury Summonses by Census Tract

---

1. See *Foster* (1987), and discussion in Chapter 10.

David Pollard introduced Figure 87 as Defendant's Exhibit X-15 in *Gibbs* (1998). He ordered the horizontal axis by the last two digits of the Hartford area census-tract number, from zero to forty-nine. The vertical axis is percentage, either percent Hispanic or percent of summonses sent which were undelivered. Pollard joined the percent Hispanic data with a dashed line, and each year's percent non-delivered with a solid line.

The graphic in Figure 87 fails any clarity test. What could Pollard be trying to show from such a jumble of lines? He told Howard Wainer that

> the goal of this display was to reveal that there is some consistency, across time, of the likelihood of a court summons being delivered in any particular census tract.[2]

That goal would not call for plotting the percent Hispanic, but whether Pollard was confused in his graphing or in his description is not for me to say.

I agreed that if one considered *only* ethnic origin as a reason why summonses were undeliverable, one would associate that phenomenon with Hispanics. By clarifying Pollard's graphic, and adding a regression line using only his single variable, Hispanic, I built a platform on which I could expand with additional variables, later. My initial graphic for the year 1993–94 is Figure 88.

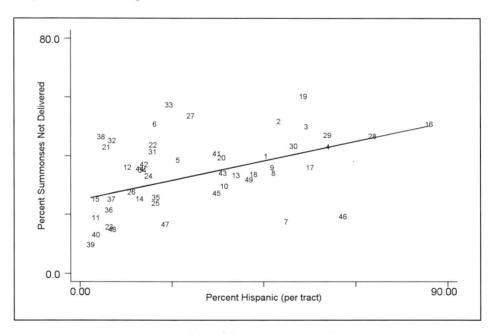

FIGURE 88: My Display of Jury Summonses by Census Tract

---

2. In Wainer's original unpublished column for *Chance*, and now in Wainer (2003), paraphrasing a communication from Pollard.

Where Pollard's x-axis was defined by an arbitrary identifier, my x-axis was the percent Hispanic, which has a natural order. I then used the tract number as a plotting symbol. Figure 88 is typical. Pollard was trying to crowd too much information into one chart. A more simple view of the concordance of the five years can come from a plot of all regression lines together. Here they are as Figure 89. I had only four complete years of data.

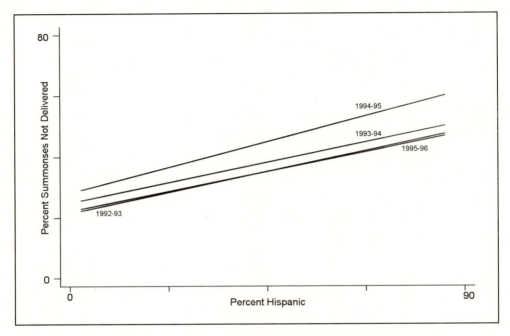

FIGURE 89: Summary of Four Years of Summons Data

The association of Hispanics with non-delivery of summonses was never in doubt. Was the ethnicity "Hispanic" the *cause* of the high non-delivery? In addition to ethnicity, I let percent renters, percent linguistically isolated, and either percent of housing units vacant or percent single person households "explain" the percent not delivered.

Using the same year, 1993–94, as an example, Figure 90 adds to Figure 88 a plot of one such multivariate regression. The locus of the relationship between Hispanic and delivery is now essentially flat.[3] Non-delivery is more strongly associated with mobility, with renters who are likely to have moved away, than with ethnic origin. It is true that Hispanics more than other identifiable segments of the population have this mobility characteristic, but it is their mobility, not their being Hispanic, that generates non-delivery.

Although I rearranged Pollard's graphic to suit my own end, it would have suited *his* end better than his own graphic did. His graphic was a bad presentation of his own idea.

---

3. The slope of the multivariate regression line is negative in Figure 90. However, the t-statistic for the variable "Hispanic" is below 0.5. Most analysts would consider the slope indistinguishable from zero.

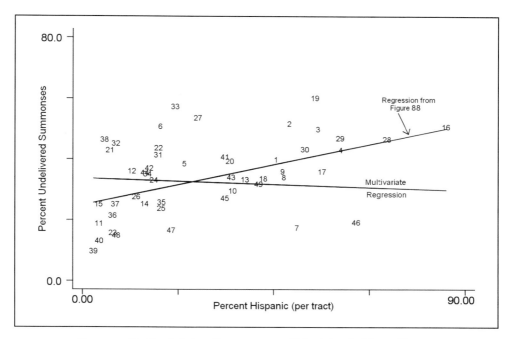

FIGURE 90: Explaining Summonses: Ethnicity Is Not a Factor

As told in Chapter 9, *Chance* magazine suppressed these graphics. Two had been reproduced in a proposed column by Howard Wainer, which *Chance* at first said it would run, but then killed. He has now published a revised version of his comments.[4]

   Although Wainer's columns did not run automatically, and few ran without editing, this column had been enthusiastically accepted. *Chance* cannot claim that I am exposing merely the daily business of a journal using its discretion to reject a submission. This is about a journal suppressing a column that, on its merits, the magazine declared itself happy to present to the world. The suppression came later, in response to David Pollard's discomfort. They should, instead, have offered Pollard space to present his own comments. A publication that will suppress an article because it is critical of someone's work, and a professional organization that will sponsor such a publication, are embarrassments to the concept of the free exchange of ideas. The American Statistical Association should issue a policy statement renouncing such a practice. *Chance* should apologize to its readers and, to establish its credibility, belatedly print Wainer's article.

---

4. See Wainer (2003), Chapter 12.

REFERENCES

List of Cases Cited

Numbers in brackets [ ] at the end of each entry refer to the chapters in which the item is referenced; a number followed by "A" denotes an appendix. "P" denotes the Preface, "I" the Introduction, and "C" the Coda.

Acusport (2003)

> *National Association for the Advancement of Colored People v. Acusport, Inc.*, 271 F.Supp.2d 435 (E.D. N.Y. 2003) [4, 10].

Adams (1998)

> *Adams v. Indiana Bell Telephone Co., Inc.*, 2 F.Supp.2d 1077 (S.D. Ind. 1998); affirmed in part, reversed in part, and remanded, 231 F.3d 414 (7th Cir. 2000) [8].

Adarand (1995)

> *Adarand Constructors, Inc. v. Pe*, 515 U.S. 200 (1995); on remand as *Adarand Constructors, Inc. v. Slater*, 228 F.3d 1147 (10th Cir. 2000) [5, C].

Addison (1972)

> *United States v. Addison*, 337 F.Supp. 641 (D. D.C. 1972); affirmed, 498 F.2d 741 (D.C. Cir. 1974) [10].

AFSCME (1985)

> *American Federation of State, County, and Municipal Employees v. State of Washington*, 578 F.Supp. 846 (W.D. Wash. 1983); reversed, 770 F.2d 1401 (9th Cir. 1985) [6].

Agent Orange I

> *In re "Agent Orange" Product Liability Litigation*, 597 F.Supp. 740 (E.D. N.Y. 1984); affirmed 818 F.2d 145 (2nd Cir. 1987a) [1, 8, 10].

Agent Orange II

> *In re "Agent Orange" Product Liability Litigation*, 611 F.Supp. 1223 (E.D. N.Y. 1985); affirmed 818 F.2d 187 (2nd Cir. 1987b) [1, 8, 10].

Akins (1945)

> *Akins v. Texas*, 325 U.S. 398 (1945) [2, 5].

Albers (1983)

    Albers v. Church of the Nazarene, 698 F.2d 852 (7th Cir. 1983) [8].

Alen (1992)

    Alen v. State, 596 So.2d 1083 (3rd District, Florida Court of Appeal 1992); affirmed, 616 So.2d 452 (Supreme Court of Florida 1993) [5, 7].

Alexander (1972)

    Alexander v. Louisiana, 405 U.S. 625 (1972) [5].

Allapatah (1999)

    Allapattah Services Inc. v. Exxon Corporation, 61 F.Supp.2d 1335 (S.D. Fla. 1999) [10].

Allen (1971)

    Allen v. City of Mobile, 331 F.Supp. 1134 (D. Ala. 1971); affirmed, 466 F.2d 122 (5th Cir. 1979) [2].

Allen (1996)

    Commonwealth of Massachusetts v. Allen, 40 Mass.App.Ct. 458, 665 N.E.2d 105 (Massachusetts Appeals Court 1996) [10].

Allison (1999)

    Allison v. Mcghan Medical Corporation et al., 184 F.3d 1300 (11th Cir. 1999) [10].

Alston (1985)

    Alston v. Lopes, 621 F.Supp. 992 (D. Conn. 1985); affirmed as *Alston v. Manson*, 791 F.2d 255 (2nd Cir. 1986) [5A].

Amaral (1973)

    United States v. Amaral, 488 F.2d 1148 (9th Cir. 1973) [8, 10].

AmNat (1979)

    Equal Employment Opportunity Commission v. American National Bank, summary judgment for defendant granted, 420 F.Supp. 181 (E.D. Va. 1976); vacated and remanded, 574 F.2d 1173 (4th Cir. 1978); on remand, 21 FEP Cases 1532 (E.D. Va. 1979); reversed and remanded, 652 F.2d 1176, 26 FEP Cases 472 (4th Cir. 1981); *certiorari* denied, 459 U.S. 923 (1982) [2].

Amoco-Cadiz (1992)

    In the Matter of Oil Spill by the Amoco-Cadiz off the Coast of France on March 16, 1978, 954 F.2d 1279 (7th Cir. 1992) [6, 8].

Amorgianos (2001)

    Amorgianos v. National Railroad Passenger Corporation, 137 F.Supp.2d 147 (E.D. N.Y. 2001), affirmed, 303 F.3d 256 (2nd Cir. 2002) [10].

Anderson (1994)

    Anderson v. Douglas and Lomason Co., 1987 WL 46935 (N.D. Miss. 1987), class certified; class expanded, 122 F.R.D. 502 (N.D. Miss. 1988); unpublished bench trial, finding for defendant; affirmed, 26 F.3d 1277, 69 FEP Cases 131 (5th Cir. 1994); *certiorari* denied, 513 U.S. 1149 (1995) [2].

Anderson (2004)

    Anderson v. Boeing, 222 F.R.D. 521 (N.D. Okla. 2004) [10].

Anjelino (1999)

> *Anjelino v. New York Times Co.*, 1993 WL 170209 (D. N.J. 1993), dismissed for failure to exhaust administrative remedies; affirmed in part, reversed in part, and remanded, 200 F.3d 73 (3rd Cir. 1999) [10].

Apodaca (1972)

> *Apodaca et al. v. Oregon*, 406 U.S. 404 (1972) [4, 4A].

Appalachian (1998)

> *Appalachian Power Company v. Environmental Protection Agency*, 135 F.3d 791 (D.C. Cir. 1998) [3].

Apprendi (2000)

> *Apprendi v. New Jersey*, 530 U.S. 466 (2000) [5].

Arellano (2004)

> *United States v. Alcaraz-Arellano*, 302 F.Supp.2d 1217 (D. Kan. 2004) [8, 10].

Arkansas (1970)

> *Arkansas Teachers Association v. Board of Education, Portland, Arkansas, School District*, 3 FEP Cases 798 (W.D. Ark. 1970); vacated and remanded, 446 F.2d 763 (8th Cir. 1971) [3, 8].

Armstrong (1996)

> *United States v. Armstrong*, 48 F.3d 1508 (9th Cir. 1995); reversed, 517 U.S. 456 (1996) [8].

Armstrong (2002)

> *In re: Armstrong World Industries, Inc., et al., Debtors*, 285 B.R. 864 (Court of Bankruptcy, Delaware 2002) [8].

Arnold (1964)

> *Arnold v. North Carolina*, 376 U.S. 773 (1964) [5].

Arriaga (2003)

> *Commonwealth v. Arriaga*, 438 Mass. 556, 781 N.E.2d 1253 (Supreme Court of Massachusetts 2003) [5].

Arrington (1969)

> *Arrington v. Massachusetts Bay Transportation Authority*, 306 F.Supp 1355, 2 FEP Cases 371 (D. Mass. 1969) [2].

Artero (1997)

> *United States v. Artero*, 121 F.3d 1256 (9th Cir. 1997); *certiorari* denied, 522 U.S. 1133 (1998) [5A].

Atkins (2002)

> *Atkins v. Virginia*, 536 U.S. 304 (2002) [P, 5].

Atonio I

> *Atonio v. Wards Cove Packing Co.*, unpublished district-court opinion dismissing most class action claims; reversed and remanded with respect to Wards Cove as defendant, 703 F.2d 329 (9th Cir. 1982); on remand, district court dismissed (unpublished), declining to apply disparate-impact analysis; affirmed, 768 F.2d 1120 (9th Cir. 1985), then withdrawn for *en*

banc review; disparate-impact analysis may be applied to subjective employment practices in employment-discrimination actions, 810 F.2d 1477 (9th Cir. 1987a), *en banc*, returning case to panel; vacate dated and remanded, 827 F.2d 439 (9th Cir. 1987b); statistics in this case unable to establish disparate-impact claim, though such a claim may be made, reversed and remanded, 490 U.S. 642 (1989). Note: The Civil Rights Act of 1991 reversed this Supreme Court decision, but excluded *Atonio* from the new standards [3, 6].

Atonio II

Atonio v. Wards Cove Packing Co., finding for defendant, 1991 WL 67529 (W.D. Wash. 1991); affirmed in part, vacated in part, and remanded with instructions, 10 F.3d 1485 (9th Cir. 1993); *certiorari* denied, 513 U.S. 809 (1994); on subsequent appeal affirmed, 275 F.3d 797 (2001) [3].

Atwater (2001)

Atwater v. City of Lago Vista, 532 U.S. 318 (2001) [10].

Austin (2000)

Austin v. American Association of Neurological Surgeons, 120 F.Supp.2d 1151 (N.D. Ill. 2000); affirmed, 253 F.3d 967 (7th Cir. 2001); *certiorari* denied, 534 U.S. 1078 (2002) [9].

Autozone (2001)

Autozone v. Tandy Corporation, 174 F.Supp.2d 718 (M.D. Tenn. 2001); affirmed, 373 F.3d 786 (6th Cir. 2004) [8, 10].

Avery (1953)

Avery v. Georgia, 345 U.S. 559 (1953) [5].

Babcock (2002)

Babcock v. General Motors Corporation, 299 F.3d 60 (1st Cir. 2002) [10].

Bacon (2001)

Bacon et al. v. Honda of America Corporation, 205 F.R.D. 466 (S.D. Ohio 2001), denial of class certification; affirmed, 370 F.3d 565 (6th Cir. 2004); *certiorari* denied, ___ U.S. ___, 125 S.Ct. 1334 (2005) [8].

Bailey (1996)

United States v. Bailey, 76 F.3d 320 (10th Cir. 1996); *certiorari* denied, 517 U.S. 1239 (1996) [5].

Baker (1996)

Baker v. General Motors Corporation, 86 F.3d 811 (8th Cir. 1996), reversing jury award because "full faith and credit" clause should have prevented testimony of one expert; but that decision was wrong, 522 U.S. 222 (1998a), reversing and remanding; remanded to the district court for a new trial, 138 F.3d 1225 (8th Cir. 1998b); an attorney's notes impeaching his own witness ordered turned over to plaintiffs, 197 F.R.D. 376 (W.D. Mo. 1999); affirmed and rehearing *en banc* denied, 209 F.3d 1051 (8th Cir. 2000) [6].

Bakke (1978)

Regents of the University of California v. Bakke, 438 U.S. 265 (1978) [5, C].

Ballard (1946)

Ballard v. United States, 329 U.S. 187 (1946) [5].

Baller (1975)

    United States v. Baller, 519 F.2d 463 (4th Cir. 1975) [10].

Ballew (1978)

    Ballew v. Georgia, 435 U.S. 223 (1978) [4, 4A].

Barefoot (1983)

    Barefoot v. Estelle, 697 F.2d 593 (5th Cir. 1983), denying stay and thus implicitly affirming district court; affirmed, 463 U.S. 880 (1983) [1, 5, 10].

Barksdale (1980)

    United States ex rel. Barksdale v. Blackburn, 610 F.2d 253 (5th Cir. 1980), reverses *State v. Barksdale*, 247 La. 198, 170 So.2d 374 (Supreme Court of Louisiana 1964); *en banc*, 639 F.2d 1115 (5th Cir. 1981), original state decision affirmed [5].

Barlow (2002)

    United States v. Barlow, 310 F.3d 1007 (7th Cir. 2002), on remand, 2004 WL 1243872 (N.D. Ill. 2004) [8].

Barnard (1973)

    United States v. Barnard, 490 F.2d 907 (9th Cir. 1973); *certiorari* denied, 416 U.S. 959 (1974) [1].

Barrie (1910)

    Barrie v. Quimby, 206 Mass. 259 (Supreme Court of Massachusetts 1910) [10].

Batson (1986)

    Batson v. Kentucky, 476 U.S. 79 (1986) [P, 4, 5].

Battle (1997)

    United States v. Battle, 1997 WL 447814 (D. Kan. 1997); affirmed, 188 F.3d 519 (10th Cir. 1999) [10].

Bazemore (1982)

    Bazemore v. Friday, unpublished (E.D. N.C. 1982); affirmed, 751 F.2d 662, 36 FEP Cases 834 (4th Cir. 1984); reversed, 478 U.S. 385, 41 FEP Cases 92 (1986); on remand, 848 F.2d 476, 46 FEP Cases 1717 (4th Cir. 1988) [1, 2, 3, 6, 7, 8].

Beazer (1979)

    New York Transit Authority v. Beazer, 440 U.S. 568 (1979) [1].

Bechtel (1984)

    Bechtel v. Allstate Insurance Company, C81-105 (N.D. Ohio 1984) [6].

Beck (2004)

    Beck v. Haik, 377 F.3d 624, 2004 WL 1687959 (6th Cir. 2004) [7].

Beckman (2000)

    Beckman v. CBS, 192 F.R.D. 608, 90 FEP Cases 1379 (D. Minn. 2000) [6].

Behrens (1973)

    Hodgson v. Behrens Drug Co., 20 WH Cases 375 (E.D. Tex. 1972); affirmed, 475 F.2d 1041, 9 FEP Cases 816 (5th Cir. 1973); *certiorari* denied, 414 U.S. 827 (1973) [3].

Beniquez (2004)

    United States v. Soto-Beniquez et al., 356 F.3d 1 (1st Cir. 2004) [10].

Berkemer (1984)

   Berkemer v. McCarty, 468 U.S. 420 (1984) [1].

Bernstein (1956)

   Bernstein v. Alameda–Contra Costa Medical Association, 139 Cal.App.2d 241 (1st District, Court of Appeal of California 1956) [9].

Berry (1994)

   Berry v. City of Detroit, 25 F.3d 1342 (6th Cir. 1994) [10].

Biaggi (1990)

   United States v. Biaggi, 909 F.2d 662 (2nd Cir. 1990) [5].

Bickerstaff (1998)

   Bickerstaff v. Vassar College, 992 F.Supp. 372, 76 FEP Cases 440 (S.D. N.Y. 1998); affirmed, 196 F.3d 435, 81 FEP Cases 624 (2nd Cir. 1999) [3, 8].

Biggers (1972)

   Neil v. Biggers, 409 U.S. 188 (1972) [7].

Binder (1985)

   United States v. Binder, 769 F.2d 595 (9th Cir. 1985) [10].

Bireley's (1951)

   United States v. 88 Cases, More or Less, Containing Bireley's Orange Beverage, 187 F.2d 967 (3rd Cir. 1951) [1].

Black (1993)

   United States v. Black, 831 F.Supp. 120 (E.D. N.Y. 1993) [10].

Black (1999)

   Black v. Food Lion, 171 F.3d 308 (5th Cir. 1999) [7].

Blakely (2004)

   Blakely v. State of Washington, 124 S.Ct. 2531, 542 U.S. 296 (2004) [1, 4, 5].

Blue Dane (1999)

   Blue Dane Simmental Corp. v. American Simmental Association, 178 F.3d 1035 (8th Cir. 1999) [8].

Boncher (2001)

   Boncher v. Brown County, 272 F.3d 484 (7th Cir. 2001) [10].

Bonds (1994)

   United States v. John Ray Bonds, 18 F.3d 1327 (6th Cir. 1994), order denying recusal [9].

Bonton (2004)

   Bonton v. City of New York, 2004 WL 2453603 (S.D. N.Y. 2004), not reported in F.Supp.2d [6, 8].

Booker (2004)

   United States v. Booker, 375 F.3d 508 (7th Cir. 2004), asserting that *Blakely* (2004) invalidates sentencing guidelines; decided jointly with *United States v. Fanfan*, ___ U.S. ___, 125 S.Ct. 738 (2005), determining that sentencing facts must be found by a jury, affirms that sentencing guidelines may not be mandatory, but suggests that they may be followed as advisory [5, 10].

Booksellers (2001)

American Booksellers Association, Inc. v. Barnes & Noble, Inc., 135 F.Supp.2d 1031 (N.D. Cal. 2001) [8].

Booth (2001)

Booth v. Black & Decker, Inc., 166 F.Supp.2d 215 (E.D. Pa. 2001) [7, 10].

Borawick (1994)

Borawick v. Shay, 842 F.Supp. 1501 (D. Conn. 1994); affirmed, 68 F.3d 597 (2nd Cir. 1995) [10].

Bormack (2003)

Commonwealth of Pennsylvania v. Bormack, 827 A.2d 503 (Pennsylvania Superior Court 2003) [8].

Bourne (2002)

Bourne v. E. I. DuPont de Nemours & Company, Inc., 189 F.Supp.2d 482 (S.D. W.Va. 2002); affirmed, 85 Fed.Appx. 964 (4th Cir. 2004) [10].

Bowersfield (2001)

Bowersfield v. Suzuki Motor Corporation, 151 F.Supp.2d 625 (E.D. Pa. 2001) [10].

Boxhorn (1986)

Boxhorn's Big Muskego Gun Club, Inc. v. Electrical Workers Local 494, 798 F.2d 1016 (7th Cir. 1986) [7].

Bradley (1976)

Bradley, Mayor, City of Los Angeles, et al. v. Judges of the Superior Court for the County of Los Angeles, State of California, 531 F.2d 413 (9th Cir. 1976) [5].

Branion (1988)

Branion v. Gramly, 855 F.2d 1256 (7th Cir. 1988) [5].

Braun (1996)

Braun v. Lorillard, 84 F.3d 230 (7th Cir. 1996); certiorari denied, 519 U.S. 992 (1996) [10].

Brecht (1993)

Brecht v. Abrahamson, 507 U.S. 619 (1993) [5].

Brennan (2004)

Brennan's, Inc. v. Dickie Brennan and Co., 376 F.3d 356 (5th Cir. 2004) [10].

Brewer (2002)

United States v. Brewer, 2002 WL 596365 (N.D. Ill. 2002) [10].

Brick (1977)

Illinois Brick Co. v. Illinois, 431 U.S. 720 (1977) [5].

Broadcasters (2001)

MD/DC/DE Broadcasters Association et al. v. Federal Communications Commission, 236 F.3d 13 (D.C. Cir. 2001) [2].

Brooke (1959)

Brooke v. People of the State of Colorado, 139 Colo. 388, 339 P.2d 993 (Supreme Court of Colorado 1959) [10].

Brooks (1965)

    Brooks v. Beto, 241 F.Supp. 743 (S.D. Tex. 1965), denies writ of *habeas corpus*; affirmed, 366 F.2d 1 (5th Cir. 1966) [5].

Brooks (2000)

    Brooks v. Outboard Marine Corporation, 234 F.3d 89 (1st Cir. 2000) [10].

Brown (1953)

    Brown v. Allen, 344 U.S. 443 (1953) [5].

Brown (1954)

    Brown v. Board of Education, 347 U.S. 483 (1954) [P, I, 1, 6, 10].

Brown (1979)

    Brown v. Texas, 443 U.S. 47 (1979) [10].

Brown (1980)

    Brown v. Delta Air Lines, Inc., 522 F.Supp. 1218 (S.D. Tex. 1980) [2].

Bryan (1980)

    Bryan v. Koch, 492 F.Supp. 212 (S.D. N.Y. 1980); affirmed, 627 F.2d 612 (2nd Cir. 1980) [6, 8].

Bryant (1968)

    United States v. Bryant, 291 F.Supp. 542 (S.D. Me. 1968); affirmed as *Butera v. United States*, 420 F.2d 564 (1st Cir. 1970) [5].

Buchanan (1985)

    Buchanan v. Commonwealth of Kentucky, 691 S.W.2d 210 (Supreme Court of Kentucky 1985); affirmed, 483 U.S. 402 (1987) [5].

Buck (1927)

    Buck v. Bell, 274 U.S. 200 (1927) [9].

Buckley (1993)

    Buckley v. Fitzsimmons, 509 U.S. 259 (1993); on remand, 20 F.3d 789 (7th Cir. 1994) [10].

Burch (1979)

    Burch v. State of Louisiana, 441 U.S. 130 (1979) [4].

Bush (2000)

    Gore v. Harris, unpublished opinion by Leon County, Florida trial court, stopping vote recount; certified by Florida Court of Appeal for Supreme Court of Florida review (2000a); reversed and remanded, 772 So.2d 1243 (Supreme Court of Florida 2000b); Florida decision stayed pending further action as *Bush v. Gore*, 531 U.S. 1046 (2000c); reversed and remanded, 531 U.S. 98 (2000d) [I, 1, 6].

Cage (1990)

    Cage v. Louisiana, 498 U.S. 39 (1990) [1].

Cain-Sloan (1973)

    Hodgson v. Cain-Sloan Co., 9 FEP Cases 831 (M.D. Tenn. 1973); affirmed in part and vacated and remanded in part as *Brennan v. Cain-Sloan Co.*, 502 F.2d 200 (6th Cir. 1974); original decision affirmed on remand, 9 FEP Cases 998 (M.D. Tenn. 1974) [3].

Caldwell (1982)

    State of Minnesota v. Caldwell, 322 N.W.2d 574 (Supreme Court of Minnesota 1982) [10].

Calhoun (2003)

> *Calhoun v. Yamaha Motor Corporation*, 350 F.3d 316 (3rd Cir. 2003) [8].

Campbell (1991)

> *People v. Campbell*, 785 P.2d 153 (Colorado Court of Appeals 1989), upheld trial court's non-admission of expert testimony on fallibility of eyewitness identification; reversed and remanded, 814 P.2d 1 (Supreme Court of Colorado 1991); discretion left to trial judge, who again did not admit the testimony; reversed and remanded for a new trial, 847 P.2d 228 (Colorado Court of Appeals 1992); convicted again, Campbell again appealed; the conviction was affirmed, 885 P.2d 327 (Colorado Court of Appeals 1994) [10].

Capaci (1983)

> *Capaci v. Katz and Besthoff*, 711 F.2d 647 (5th Cir. 1983) [2].

Cardizem (2001)

> *In re Cardizem CD antitrust litigation*, 200 F.R.D. 326 (E.D. Mich. 2001) [3].

Caridad (1999)

> *Caridad v. Metro North Commuter Railroad*, 191 F.3d 283 (2nd Cir. 1999) [2, 8].

Carneglia (2002)

> *United States v. Carneglia*, 47 Fed.Appx. 27 (2nd Cir. 2002) [10].

Carpenter (2004)

> *Carpenter v. Boeing*, 2004 WL 2661691 (D. Kan. 2004) [8].

Carter (1900)

> *Carter v. Texas*, 177 U.S. 442 (1900) [5].

Carter (1970)

> *Carter v. Jury Commission of Greene County*, 396 U.S. 320 (1970) [5].

Carter (1998)

> *State of Nebraska v. Carter*, 255 Neb. 591, 586 N.W.2d 818 (Supreme Court of Nebraska 1998) [1].

Carty (2002)

> *New Jersey v. Carty*, 170 N.J. 632, 790 A.2d 903 (Supreme Court of New Jersey 2002) [8].

Cassell (1950)

> *Cassell v. Texas*, 339 U.S. 282 (1950) [5].

Castaneda (1977)

> Conviction affirmed as *Partida v. State*, 506 S.W.2d 209 (Court of Criminal Appeals of Texas, 1974a); *habeas corpus* denied, 384 F.Supp. 79 (S.D. Tex. 1974b); reversed, 524 F.2d 481 (5th Cir. 1975); affirmed as *Castaneda v. Partida*, 430 U.S. 482 (1977) [1, 2, 4, 5, 9, 5A].

Castonguay (1984)

> *State v. Castonguay*, 194 Conn. 416 (Supreme Court of Connecticut 1984) [5A].

Catharine (1854)

> *The Schooner Catharine v. Noah Dickinson and Others*, 58 U.S. 170 (1854) [1].

Caulfield (1979)

> *Caulfield v. Board of Education of the City of New York*, 486 F.Supp. 862 (E.D. N.Y. 1979); affirmed, 632 F.2d 999 (2nd Cir. 1980); *certiorari* denied, 450 U.S. 1030 (1981) [7].

CB&Q (1907)
> *Chicago, Burlington, & Quincy Railway Company v. Babcock*, 204 U.S. 585 (1907) [8].

Chambers (1966)
> *Chambers v. Hendersonville City Board of Education*, 364 F.2d 189 (4th Cir. 1966) [2, 6].

Champ (2001)
> *State of Nebraska v. Champ*, 2001 WL 273071 (Court of Appeals of Nebraska 2001), not reported in N.W.2d [8].

Chance (1963)
> *Chance v. United States*, 322 F.2d 201 (5th Cir. 1963); *certiorari* denied, 379 U.S. 83 (1964) [5].

Chance (1971)
> *Chance v. Board of Examiners*, 330 F.Supp. 203 (D. N.Y. 1971); affirmed, 458 F.2d 1167 (2nd Cir. 1972) [2].

Chang (1985)
> *Chang v. University of Rhode Island*, 606 F.Supp 1161 (D. R.I. 1985) [1].

Chapman (1967)
> *Chapman v. State of California*, 386 U.S. 18 (1967) [5].

Chavez (1998)
> *Chavez v. Illinois State Police*, 27 F.Supp.2d 1053 (N.D. Ill. 1998); 1999 WL 754681 (N.D. Ill. 1999); 2000 WL 91918 (N.D. Ill. 2000); affirmed, 251 F.3d 612 (7th Cir. 2001) [8, 10].

Cheatwood (1969)
> *Cheatwood v. South Central Bell Telephone*, 303 F.Supp. 754 (D. Ala. 1969) [10].

China (2004)
> *Bank of China, New York Branch v. NBM, L.L.C., et al.*, 359 F.3d 171 (2nd Cir. 2004), reversing jury decision partly because judge had improperly allowed expert-type opinions from lay witness [10].

Christensen (1977)
> *Christensen v. State of Iowa*, 563 F.2d 353, 16 FEP Cases 232 (8th Cir. 1977) [7].

Christophersen (1991)
> *Christophersen v. Allied Signal Corp.*, 939 F.2d 1106 (5th Cir. 1991), *en banc*; *certiorari* denied, 503 U.S. 912 (1992) [10].

Cicero (2001)
> *Cicero v. Borg-Warner Automotive, Inc.*, 163 F.Supp.2d 743 (E.D. Mich. 2001) [10].

Citizens (2004)
> *Citizens Financial Group, Inc. v. Citizens National Bank of Evans City* (3rd Cir. 2004) [8].

Civil Rights (1883)
> *Civil Rights Cases*, 109 U.S. 3 (1883) [I].

Clifford (1981)
> *United States v. Clifford*, 640 F.2d 150 (8th Cir. 1981) [5].

Cline (2002)
> *United States v. Cline*, 188 F.Supp.2d 1287 (D. Kan. 2002) [10].

Cloud (2001)

    Cloud ex rel. Cloud v. Pfizer, 198 F.Supp.2d 1118 (D. Ariz. 2001) [10].

Coastal (2002)

    Coastal Tankships, U.S.A., Inc. v. Anderson, 87 S.W.3d 591 (1st District, Court of Civil Appeals of Texas 2002) [10].

Coker (1991)

    Coker v. Charleston County School District, No. 2:84-2162-2 (D. S.C. 1991); affirmed, 2 F.3d 1149 (table) (4th Cir. 1993) [8].

Coleman (2002)

    United States v. Coleman, 202 F.Supp.2d 962 (E.D. Mo. 2002) [10].

Colgrove (1973)

    Colgrove v. Battin, 413 U.S. 149 (1973) [4].

Collins (1964)

    Collins v. Walker, 329 F.2d 100 (5th Cir. 1964) [5].

Collins (1968)

    People v. Collins, 68 Cal.2d 319, 66 Cal.Rptr. 497 (Supreme Court of California 1968) [1, 9].

Collins (1994)

    Callins v. Collins, 510 U.S. 1141 (1994), denying petition for *certiorari* [P].

Colorado (1963)

    Colorado Anti-Discrimination Commission v. Continental Air Lines, Inc., 372 U.S. 714 (1963) [2].

Combustion (2003)

    In re Combustion Engineering, Inc., 295 B.R. 459 (D. Del. 2003) [3].

Compton (1996)

    Compton v. Subaru of America, Inc., 82 F.3d 1513 (10th Cir. 1996) [10].

Concord Boat (1998)

    Concord Boat Corp. v. Brunswick Corp., 21 F.Supp.2d 923 (E.D. Ark. 1998); reversed, vacated, and remanded, 207 F.3d 1039 (8th Cir. 2000) [8, 10].

Conservation (2002)

    Conservation Law Foundation v. Evans, 203 F.Supp.2d 27 (D. D.C. 2002) [10].

Construction (2002)

    Construction Industries Services Corp. v. The Hanover Insurance Co., 206 F.R.D. 43 (E.D. N.Y. 2001); adhered to on reconsideration, January 25, 2002 [6].

Continental (1993)

    Continental Airlines, Inc. v. American Airlines, Inc., 824 F.Supp. 689 (S.D. Tex. 1993) [8].

Conwood (2000)

    Conwood Co. v. United States Tobacco Co., 2000 WL 33176054 (W.D. Ky. 2000); affirmed, 290 F.3d 768 (6th Cir. 2002), *certiorari* denied, 537 U.S. 1148 (2003) [3, 8, 9].

Coon (1999)

    State of Alaska v. Coon, 974 P.2d 386 (Supreme Court of Alaska 1999) [1, 10].

Cooper (2001a)

   Cooper v. Smith & Nephew, Inc., 259 F.3d 194 (4th Cir. 2001) [8].

Cooper (2001b)

   Cooper Industries, Inc. v. Leatherman Tool Group, Inc., 532 U.S. 424 (2001); on remand, award reduced from $4.5 million to $0.5 million, 285 F.3d 1146 (9th Cir. 2002) [10].

Cooper (2001c)

   Cooper v. Southern Company, 205 F.R.D. 596 (N.D. Ga. 2001), class certification denied; affirmed, 390 F.3d 695 (11th Cir. 2004) [2].

Coppage (1915)

   Coppage v. Kansas, 236 U.S. 1 (1915) [1].

Corn Syrup (2002)

   In re High Fructose Corn Syrup Antitrust Litigation, 2002 WL 1315285 (7th Cir. 2002) [10].

Coronado (1932)

   Burnet v. Coronado Oil and Gas Co., 285 U.S. 393 (1932) [P].

Correa (2002)

   Correa v. Cruisers, 298 F.3d 13 (1st Cir. 2002) [10].

Corrugated (1977)

   In re Corrugated Container Antitrust Litigation, 441 F.Supp. 921 (Judicial Panel on Multi-District Litigation 310 1977); (after much intervening litigation) settlement remanded with instructions, 643 F.2d 195 (5th Cir. 1981a); lower-court decision following instructions, 1 Trade Cases (CCH) P 64,114 (S.D. Tex. 1981b); circuit court accepts settlement as lower court explained it following instructions, 659 F.2d 1322 (5th Cir. 1981c) [3, 9].

Cortez (1981)

   United States v. Cortez, 449 U.S. 411 (1981) [10].

Cotton (1989)

   Cotton Petroleum Corporation v. New Mexico, 490 U.S. 163 (1989) [3].

Council (1999)

   State of South Carolina v. Council, 335 S.C. 1, 515 S.E.2d 508 (Supreme Court of South Carolina 1999); *certiorari* denied, 528 U.S. 1050 (1999) [10].

Craik (1984)

   Craik v. Minnesota State University Board, 731 F.2d 465, 34 FEP Cases 649 (8th Cir. 1984) [2, 3].

Crawford (1909)

   Crawford v. United States, 212 U.S. 183 (1909) [5].

Crisp (2003)

   United States v. Crisp, 324 F.3d 261 (4th Cir. 2003) [10].

Croson (1989)

   Richmond v. J. A. Croson, Inc., 488 U.S. 469 (1989) [5].

Crow I

   Crow Tribe v. United States, 650 F.2d 1104 (9th Cir. 1981); amended, 665 F.2d 1390 (9th Cir. 1982) [3, 8].

Crow II

    Crow Tribe v. United States, 657 F.Supp. 573 (D. Mont. 1985); reversed *Crow Tribe v. Montana*, 819 F.2d 895 (9th Cir. 1987); affirmed, 484 U.S. 997 (1988) [3, 7, 3A].

Crow III

    Crow Tribe of Indians v. State of Montana, 969 F.2d 848 (9th Cir. 1992) [3].

Crow IV

    Crow Tribe of Indians v. State of Montana, CV-78-110-BLG, unpublished (D. Mont. 1994); reversed, 92 F.3d 826 (9th Cir. 1996); reversed and remanded, 523 U.S. 696 (1998) [3].

Crowley (1904)

    Crowley v. United States, 194 U.S. 461 (1904) [5].

Crumby (1995)

    United States v. Crumby, 895 F.Supp. 1354 (D. Ariz. 1995) [10].

Cruz (1998)

    Cruz v. Coach Stores, Inc., 1998 WL 812045 (S.D. N.Y. 1998), summary judgment for defendant; affirmed in all respects but one, 202 F.3d 560 (2nd Cir. 2000) [10].

Cruzan (1990)

    Cruzan v. Director, Missouri Department of Health, 497 U.S. 261 (1990) [1].

CSX (2004)

    CSX Transportation, Inc. v. The Board of Public Works of the State of West Virginia, 312 F.Supp.2d 839 (S.D. W.Va. 2004) [8].

Cypress (1967)

    Cypress v. Newport News Hospital Association, 375 F.2d 648 (4th Cir. 1967) [6].

Daly (1988)

    United States v. Daly, 842 F.2d 1380 (2nd Cir. 1988) [10].

Daubert (1989)

    Daubert v. Merrill Dow Pharmaceuticals, Inc., 727 F.Supp. 570 (S.D. Cal. 1989), summary judgment granted for defendant; affirmed, 951 F.2d 1128 (9th Cir. 1991); vacated and remanded, 509 U.S. 579 (1993); summary judgment affirmed on remand, 43 F.3d 1311 (9th Cir. 1995); *certiorari* denied, 516 U.S. 869 (1995) [P, I, 1, 2, 5, 6, 7, 8, 10].

Davis (1969)

    Davis v. Mississippi, 394 U.S. 721 (1969) [1].

Davis (1984)

    State of New Jersey v. Davis, 96 N.J. 611, 477 A.2d 308 (Supreme Court of New Jersey 1984) [8].

Davis (1985)

    United States v. Davis, 772 F.2d 1339 (7th Cir. 1985); *certiorari* denied, 474 U.S. 1036 (1985) [7, 10].

Davis (1992)

    Davis v. Davis, 842 S.W.2d 588 (Tenn. 1992) [1].

DeBerardinis (2004)

    Commonwealth v. DeBerardinis, 2004 WL 1171242 (Superior Court of Massachusetts 2004); also reported in 17 Mass. Law Reporter 641, for which pagination is not available [8].

Delaware (2004)

   United States v. State of Delaware, 2004 WL 609331 (D. Del. 2004) [2, 3, 7].

Delbridge (2003)

   Commonwealth of Pennsylvania v. Delbridge, 855 A.2d 27 (Supreme Court of Pennsylvania 2003) [10].

DeLoach (2002)

   DeLoach v. Phillip Morris Companies, 206 F.R.D. 551 (M.D. N.C. 2002) [10].

DeMarco (2004)

   DeMarco v. Lehman Brothers, Inc., 222 F.R.D. 243 (S.D. N.Y. 2004a), denying class certification; summary judgment for defendant, 2004 WL 2674611 (S.D. N.Y. 2004b), not reported in F.Supp.2d [6, 8, 10].

Dennis (1950)

   United States v. Dennis, 183 F.2d 201 (2nd Cir. 1950); affirmed, 341 U.S. 484 (1951) [5].

Den Norske (1996)

   Den Norske Bank v. The First National Bank of Boston, 75 F.3d 49 (1st Cir. 1996) [10].

Dentsply (2003)

   United States v. Dentsply International, Inc., 277 F.Supp.2d 387 (D. Del. 2003) [2, 5, 6, 7, 8].

Diamond (1980)

   Diamond v. Chakrabarty, 447 U.S. 303 (1980) [1].

Dickerson (1977)

   Dickerson v. U.S. Steel, 439 F.Supp. 55 (E.D. Pa. 1977) [2].

Diehl (1996)

   Diehl v. Xerox Corp., 933 F.Supp. 1157 (W.D. N.Y. 1996) [3, 7].

Diesel (1978)

   Movement For Opportunity v. Detroit Diesel, 18 FEP Cases 557 (S.D. Ind. 1978) [2].

DJA (2002)

   Commonwealth of Pennsylvania v. D. J. A., 800 A.2d 965 (Superior Court of Pennsylvania 2002) [10].

Doe (1999)

   Doe v. Shults-Lewis Child and Family Services, Inc., 718 N.E.2d 738 (Supreme Court of Indiana 1999) [10].

Doleszny (1986)

   State v. Doleszny, 146 Vt. 621, 508 A.2d 693 (Supreme Court of Vermont 1986) [5].

Donaldson (1971)

   Donaldson v. California, 404 U.S. 968 (1971) [5].

Dothard (1977)

   Dothard v. Rawlinson, 433 U.S. 321 (1977) [1, 2].

Downing (1985)

   United States v. Downing, 753 F.2d 1224 (3rd Cir. 1985) [1].

Doyle (1976)

   Doyle v. Ohio, 426 U.S. 610 (1976) [5].

Drake (2005)

> *Drake v. Delta Air Lines, Inc.*, 2005 WL 1743816 (E.D. N.Y. 2005) [8].

Drones (2000)

> *United States v. Drones*, 218 F.3d 496 (5th Cir. 2000) [10].

Drugs (1997)

> *In re Brand Name Prescription Drugs Antitrust Litigation*, 123 F.3d 599 (7th Cir. 1997), reversing district-court opinion; appeal from decision after remand, affirmed in part, vacated in part, and remanded, 186 F.3d 781 (7th Cir. 1999) [8, 9, 10].

Dukes (2004)

> *Dukes v. Wal-Mart*, 222 F.R.D. 137 (N.D. Cal. 2004), granting class certification [2].

Dunkle (1992)

> *Commonwealth of Pennsylvania v. Dunkle*, 529 Pa. 168 (Supreme Court of Pennsylvania 1992) [10].

Duque-Nava (2004)

> *United States v. Duque-Nava*, Omnibus Order Denying Defendant's Motions for Discovery, Dismissal, and Suppression, 315 F.Supp.2d 1144 (D. Kan. 2004) [8, 10].

Duren (1979)

> *Duren v. Missouri*, 439 U.S. 357 (1979) [5].

Eagle (1976)

> *Equal Employment Opportunity Commission v. Eagle Iron Works*, 424 F.Supp. 240 (S.D. Iowa 1976) [6, 10].

Eastland (1983)

> *Eastland v. Tennessee Valley Authority*, 704 F.2d 613 (11th Cir. 1983) [6].

EHOC (2001)

> *Metropolitan St. Louis Equal Housing Opportunity Council et al. v. Gordon A. Gundaker Real Estate Co., Inc.*, 130 F.Supp.2d 1074 (E.D. Mo. 2001) [6, 8].

Electric (2004)

> *U.S. Information Systems, Inc., et al. v. International Brotherhood of Electrical Workers Local Union Number 3*, 313 F.Supp.2d 213 (S.D. N.Y. 2004) [8, 10].

Elsayed (2002)

> *Mohamed Osman Elsayed Mukhtar v. California State University, Hayward*, 299 F.3d 1053 (9th Cir. 2002); amendments and order, 299 F.3d 1053 (9th Cir. 2003) [10].

Esquivel (1996)

> *United States v. Esquivel*, 88 F.3d 722 (9th Cir. 1996); *certiorari* denied, 519 U.S. 985 (1996) [5A].

Ethan Allen (2003)

> *Equal Employment Opportunity Commission v. Ethan Allen, Inc.*, 259 F.Supp.2d 625 (N.D. Ohio 2003) [7].

Eubanks (1958)

> *Eubanks v. Louisiana*, 356 U.S. 584 (1958) [5].

Eymard (1986)

> *In re Air Crash Disaster at New Orleans, La. (Eymard)*, 795 F.2d 1230 (5th Cir. 1986) [1, 7].

Fahy (1963)

   Fahy v. State of Connecticut, 375 U.S. 85 (1963) [5].

Farris (1941)

   Farris v. Interstate Circuit, 116 F.2d 409 (5th Cir. 1941) [8].

Fay (1946)

   People v. Fay, 296 N.Y. 510 (New York Court of Appeals 1946); affirmed 68 N.E.2d 453 (Supreme Court of New York 1946); affirmed as *Fay v. New York*, 332 U.S. 261 (1947) [5, 10].

Ferebee (1984)

   Ferebee, Jr., et al. v. Chevron Chemical Company, 736 F.2d 1529 (D.C. Cir. 1984) [1].

Ferguson (2002)

   State of Connecticut v. Geoffrey K. Ferguson, 260 Conn. 339, 796 A.2d 1118 (Supreme Court of Connecticut 2002) [5, 5A].

Fields (1995)

   United States v. Fields, No. 3:94CR-258(PCD) (D. Conn. 1995), no reported decision, date is of hearing on the composition of the jury [P].

Filler (2000)

   United States v. Filler, 210 F.3d 386, 2000 WL 123446 (9th Cir. 2000) [10].

Firestone (1981)

   Firestone v. Marshall, 507 F.Supp. 1330 (E.D. Tex. 1981) [6, 8].

Firestone (1987)

   Equal Employment Opportunity Commission v. Firestone, 650 F.Supp. 1561 (W.D. Tenn. 1987) [6].

Fleming (2003)

   State v. Fleming, 846 So.2d 114, 2003 WL 1950194 (4th Circuit, Louisiana Court of Appeal 2003) [5].

Flynn (1954)

   United States v. Flynn, 216 F.2d 354 (2nd Cir. 1954) [5].

Forehand (1996)

   Forehand v. Florida State Hospital at Chattahoochee, 89 F.3d 1562 (11th Cir. 1996) [9].

Forte (1938)

   People v. Forte, 279 N.Y. 204 (New York Court of Appeals 1938) [10].

Foster (1975)

   Foster v. Sparks, 506 F.2d 805 (5th Cir. 1975) [5].

Foster (1987)

   Foster v. Barry, C.A. 87-0635, procedural order, 1987 WL 18744 (D. D.C. 1987); rejection of motion to dismiss, 1987 WL 28477 (D. D.C. 1987) [7, 10, 9A].

Franklin (1995)

   Franklin v. Duncan, 884 F.Supp. 1435 (N.D. Cal. 1995) [10].

Franks (1975)

   United States v. Franks, 511 F.2d 25 (6th Cir. 1975) [10].

Freeman (1997)

    State of Nebraska v. Freeman, 253 Neb. 385, 571 N.W.2d 276 (Supreme Court of Nebraska 1997) [1, 10].

Freeman (2000)

    United States v. Freeman, 209 F.3d 464 (6th Cir. 2000) [8].

Friend (1977)

    Friend v. Leidinger, 446 F.Supp. 361, 18 FEP Cases 1030 (E.D. Va. 1977); affirmed, 588 F.2d 61 (4th Cir. 1978) [1, 2, 8].

Fryar (1997)

    Commonwealth v. Fryar, 425 Mass. 237, 680 N.E.2d 901 (Supreme Court of Massachusetts 1997); *certiorari* denied, 522 U.S. 1033 (1997) [9].

Frye (1923)

    Frye v. United States, 293 F. 1013 (D.C. Cir. 1923) [1, 7, 8, 10].

Fujii (2000)

    United States v. Fujii, 152 F.Supp.2d 939 (N.D. Ill. 2000) [10].

Fulminante (1991)

    Arizona v. Fulminante, 499 U.S. 279 (1991) [5].

Furman (1972)

    Furman v. Georgia, 408 U.S. 238 (1972) [P, 5].

Furnco (1978)

    Furnco Construction Corp. v. Waters, 438 U.S. 567, 17 FEP Cases 1062 (1978) [C].

Furry (2002)

    Furry v. Bielomatik, Inc., 32 Fed.Appx. 882, 2002 WL 464607 (9th Cir. 2002) [10].

Gallup (1986)

    United States v. City of Gallup, C.A. 83 1395-M (D. N.M. 1986), settled, no published opinion [2, 5, 6, 2A].

GenTel (1985)

    Equal Employment Opportunity Commission v. General Telephone Company, 40 FEP Cases 1533 (W.D. Wash. 1985); reversed and remanded, 885 F.2d 575 (9th Cir. 1989) [7].

Gerena (1987)

    United States of America v. Gerena, 677 F.Supp. 1266 (D. Conn. 1987); affirmed as *United States v. Maldonado-Rivera*, 922 F.2d 934 (2nd Cir. 1990) [5, 8].

Gerlib (2002)

    Gerlib v. R. R. Donnelley & Sons Company, No. 95 C 7401, not reported; 2002 WL 1182434 (N.D. Ill. 2002), not reported in F.Supp.2d [7, 8].

Gibbs (1998)

    Connecticut v. Gibbs, 1998 WL 351903 (Connecticut Superior Court 1998); affirmed, 254 Conn. 578, 758 A.2d 327 (Supreme Court of Connecticut 2000) [P, 5, 6, 9, 10, 5A, 9A].

Gibson (1896)

    Gibson v. Mississippi, 162 U.S. 565 (1896) [5].

Gigante II

United States v. Gigante, 982 F.Supp. 140 (E.D. N.Y. 1997); affirmed, 166 F.3d 75 (2nd Cir. 1999) [10].

Gingles (1984)

Gingles v. Edmisten, 590 F.Supp. 345 (E.D. N.C. 1984); affirmed in the part that is of interest here as Thornburg v. Gingles, 478 U.S. 30 (1986) [3].

Glasser (1942)

Glasser v. United States, 315 U.S. 60 (1942) [5].

Glickman (1974)

Commonwealth of Pennsylvania v. Glickman, 370 F.Supp. 724, 7 FEP Cases 598 (W.D. Pa. 1974) [6].

Goeb (1999)

Goeb v. Theraldson, 1999 WL 561956 (Minnesota Court of Appeals 1999); affirmed, 615 N.W.2d 800 (Supreme Court of Minnesota 2000) [1, 10].

Goebel (2000)

Goebel v. Denver and Rio Grande Western Railroad Company, reversing and remanding jury decision for plaintiff, 215 F.3d 1083 (10th Cir. 2000), for Daubert decision on plaintiff's expert; district-court judge allows testimony, parties stipulate to original jury verdict to allow appeal; affirmed, 346 F.3d 987 (10th Cir. 2003) [10].

Goins (1968)

Goins v. Allgood, 391 F.2d 692 (5th Cir. 1968) [5].

Goldsby (1959)

United States ex rel. Goldsby v. Harpole, 263 F.2d 71 (5th Cir. 1959) [5].

Goldston (1977)

Commonwealth v. Goldston, 366 N.E.2d 744 (Supreme Court of Massachusetts 1977) [1].

Goodman (1927)

Baltimore & Ohio Railroad Co. v. Goodman, 275 U.S. 66 (1927) [P, 9].

Goodridge (2003)

Goodridge v. Department of Public Health, 798 N.E.2d 941 (Supreme Court of Massachusetts 2003) [1].

Goodyear (2000)

Goodyear Tire and Rubber Company v. Thompson, 11 S.W.3d 575 (Supreme Court of Kentucky 2000) [10].

Gordon (1980)

United States v. Gordon, 493 F.Supp. 814 (N.D. N.Y. 1980); affirmed, 655 F.2d 478 (2nd Cir. 1981) [5].

Gorin (1963)

Gorin v. United States, 313 F.2d 641 (1st Cir. 1963) [5].

Granholm (2005)

Granholm v. Heald, ___ U.S.___, 125 S.Ct. 1885 (2005) [1].

Gratz (1999)

Gratz v. Bollinger, 188 F.3d 394 (6th Cir. 1999); reversed, 539 U.S. 244 (2003) [C].

Green (2005)

   United States v. Green, ___ F.Supp.2nd. ___, 2005 WL 2109114 (2005) [5, 5A].

Greenberg (1961)

   United States v. Greenberg, 200 F.Supp. 382 (S.D. N.Y. 1961) [5].

Greenholtz (1976)

   Inmates of the Nebraska Penal and Correctional Complex v. Greenholtz, 436 F.Supp. 432 (D. Neb. 1976); reversed, 567 F.2d 1368 (8th Cir. 1977); *certiorari* denied, 439 U.S. 841 (1978) [5].

Greenspan (1980)

   Greenspan v. Automobile Club of Michigan, 495 F.Supp. 1021 (E.D. Mich. 1980) [1, 3, 6].

Greer (1995)

   United States v. Greer, 900 F.Supp. 952 (N.D. Ill. 1995) [5].

Gricco (2002)

   United States v. Gricco, 2002 WL 746037 (E.D. Pa. 2002) [10].

Griggs (1968)

   Griggs v. Duke Power Co., 292 F.Supp. 243 (W.D. N.C. 1968); affirmed in part and reversed in part, 420 F.2d 1225 (4th Cir. 1970); reversed, 401 U.S. 424 (1971) [1, 2, 5, 6].

Grisham (1994)

   United States v. Grisham, 841 F.Supp. 1138 (N.D. Ala. 1994); affirmed, 63 F.3d 1074 (11th Cir. 1995); *certiorari* denied, 516 U.S. 1084 (1995) [5].

Grismore (1942)

   Grismore v. Consolidated Products Co., 5 N.W.2d 646 (Supreme Court of Iowa 1942) [1, 8, 10].

Grutter (2001)

   Grutter v. Bollinger, 137 F.Supp.2d 821 (D. Mich. 2001); reversed, 288 F.3d 732 (6th Cir. 2002); affirmed, 539 U.S. 306 (2003) [1, 2, 3, 5, C].

Hackley Bank

   Office of Federal Contract Compliance Programs v. Hackley Bank, an administrative proceeding in the 1980s, resolution unknown [2].

Hall (1878)

   Hall v. DeCuir, 95 U.S. 547 (1878) [2].

Hall (1996a)

   United States v. Larry D. Hall, 93 F.3d 1337 (7th Cir. 1996), remanding for *Daubert* determination; 974 F.Supp. 1198 (C.D. Ill. 1997), allowing the expert testimony that had initially been excluded [8, 10].

Hall (1996b)

   Hall v. Baxter Healthcare Corp., 947 F.Supp. 1387 (D. Ore. 1996) [9, 10].

Hall (1999)

   United States v. Hall, 165 F.3d 1095 (7th Cir. 1999) [10].

Hambsch (1984)

   Hambsch v. New York Transit Authority, 63 N.Y.2d 723, 480 N.Y.S.2d 195 (New York Court of Appeals 1984) [9].

Hamling (1974)

>   *Hamling v. United States*, 418 U.S. 87 (1974) [5].

Hammoud (2004)

>   *United States v. Hammoud*, 2004 WL 2005622 (4th Cir. 2004), affirming conviction, denying that *Blakely* (2004) invalidates sentencing guidelines [5, 10].

Harcros (1995)

>   *City of Tuscaloosa v. Harcros Chemicals, Inc.*, 877 F.Supp 1504 (N.D. Ala. 1995); vacated and remanded, 158 F.3d 548 (11th Cir. 1998) [8].

Hare (2004)

>   *United States v. Hare*, 308 F.Supp.2d 955 (D. Neb. 2004) [5, 8].

Harrington (1969)

>   *Harrington v. State of California*, 395 U.S. 250 (1969) [5].

Harris (1999)

>   *Harris v. Cropmate Company*, 302 Ill.App.3d 364 (4th District, Appellate Court of Illinois 1999) [10].

Harris Bank (1981)

>   *United States Department of the Treasury v. Harris Trust and Savings Bank*, U.S. Department of Labor Administrative Proceeding, Case No. 78-OFCCP-2, administrative law judge finding for plaintiff (1981); remand by Secretary of Labor, 31 FEP Cases 1223 (1983); original finding sustained (1986) [1, 3, 8, 9, 10].

Harrison (1982)

>   *Harrison v. Lewis*, C.A. 79-1816 (D. D.C. 1982), unpublished order on the merits, June 2, 1982; relief order, 559 F.Supp. 943 (D. D.C. 1983) [2, 7].

Hartman (1988)

>   *DeMedina v. Reinhardt*, 1979 WL 39, 21 FEP Cases 75 (D. D.C. 1979); reversed, 686 F.2d 997 (D.C. Cir. 1982); order on liability following reversal as *Hartman v. Wick*, 600 F.Supp. 361 (D. D.C. 1984); final orders, 678 F.Supp. 312 (D. D.C. 1988) [7].

Hatch (1907)

>   *People of the State of New York ex rel. Albert J. Hatch v. Edward Reardon, a Peace Officer of the County of New York*, 204 U.S. 152 (1907) [9].

Hauling (2000)

>   *Smithers v. C & G Custom Module Hauling*, 172 F.Supp.2d 765 (E.D. Va. 2000) [7].

Havvard (2000)

>   *United States v. Havvard*, 117 F.Supp.2d 848 (S.D. Ind. 2000); affirmed, 260 F.3d 597 (7th Cir. 2001) [10].

Hazelwood (1975)

>   *United States v. Hazelwood School District*, 392 F.Supp. 1276 (E.D. Mo. 1975); reversed, 534 F.2d 805 (8th Cir. 1976); affirmed, 433 U.S. 299 (1977) [1, 6, 8].

Healy (1973)

>   *Healy v. Edwards*, 363 F.Supp. 1110 (E.D. La. 1973); vacated, 421 U.S. 772 (1975) [P, 5].

Helvering (1938)

>   *Helvering v. Mountain Producers Corporation*, 303 U.S. 376 (1938) [P].

Hernandez (1954)

   Hernandez v. Texas, 347 U.S. 475 (1954) [5].

Hernandez (1991)

   Hernandez v. New York, 500 U.S. 352 (1991) [5].

Hernandez 8 (2002)

   United States v. Hernandez, 299 F.3d 984 (8th Cir. 2002) [10].

Hernandez 10 (2002)

   United States v. Hernandez, 42 Fed.Appx. 173 (10th Cir. 2002) [10].

Hexamedics (2003)

   Hexamedics v. Guidant Corporation, not reported, 2003 WL 21012179 (D. Minn. 2003) [8].

Higginbotham (2004)

   Higginbotham v. KCS International, Inc., 85 Fed.Appx. 911 (4th Cir. 2004) [8, 10].

Highland Park (1961)

   City of Highland Park et al. v. Fair Employment Practices Commission, 364 Mich 508 (Supreme Court of Michigan 1961) [2].

Hiibel (2004)

   Hiibel v. Sixth Judicial District Court of Nevada, 124 S.Ct. 2451, 542 U.S. 177 (2004) [1].

Hill (1942)

   Hill v. Texas, 316 U.S. 400 (1942) [5].

Hill (1997)

   Estate of Bud Hill et al. v. Conagra Poultry Co., not reported, 1997 WL 538887 (N.D. Ga. 1997) [10].

Hill (1999)

   Hill v. Ross, 183 F.3d 586 (7th Cir. 1999) [7].

Hillery (1983)

   Hillery v. Pulley, 563 F.Supp. 1228 (E.D. Cal. 1983); affirmed, 733 F.2d 644 (9th Cir. 1984); affirmed as *Vasquez v. Hillery*, 474 U.S. 254 (1986) [5].

Hines (1999)

   United States v. Hines, 55 F.Supp.2d 62 (D. Mass. 1999) [10].

Hiss (1950)

   United States v. Hiss, 88 F.Supp. 559 (S.D. N.Y. 1950) [1].

Hoag (1903)

   Hoag v. Wright, 174 N.Y. 36, 66 N.E. 579 (New York Court of Appeals 1903) [10].

Hobson I

   Hobson v. Hansen, 265 F.Supp. 902 (D. D.C. 1967); decree in accordance with opinion, 269 F.Supp. 401 (D. D.C. 1967); appeal dismissed, 393 U.S. 801 (1968); affirmed as *Smuck v. Hansen*, 408 F.2d 175 (D.C. Cir. 1969); further relief, 320 F.Supp. 409 (D. D.C. 1970) [P, 3].

Hobson II

   Hobson v. Hansen, 327 F.Supp. 844 (D. D.C. 1971) [P, 3, 6].

Holden (1898)

   Holden v. Hardy, 169 U.S. 366 (1898) [1].

Holden (1987)

    Holden v. Burlington Northern Railroad, 665 F.Supp. 1398 (D. Minn. 1987) [2, 3, 6].

Holiday (2002)

    Holiday Wholesale Grocery v. Philip Morris, 231 F.Supp.2d 1253 (N.D. Ga. 2002); affirmed as *Williamson Oil Co. v. Philip Morris*, 346 F.3d 1287 (11th Cir. 2003) [3, 8].

Holland (1990)

    Holland v. Illinois, 493 U.S. 474 (1990) [5].

Holloway (1978)

    Holloway v. Arkansas, 435 U.S. 475 (1978) [5].

Hooten (1986)

    Hooten v. State of Mississippi, 492 So.2d 948 (Supreme Court of Mississippi 1986) [10].

Howard (1998)

    Howard v. Wal-Mart Stores, Inc., 160 F.3d 358 (7th Cir. 1998) [8].

Howland (1868)

    Robinson v. Mandell, 20 F. Cas. 1027 (CCD Mass. 1868) No. 11,959 [1].

Hoyt (1961)

    Hoyt v. Florida, 368 U.S. 57 (1961) [5].

Hubbard (1996)

    People v. Hubbard, 217 Mich.App. 459, 552 N.W.2d 493 (Michigan Court of Appeals 1996) [5].

Hughes (1950)

    Hughes v. Superior Court, State of California, 399 U.S. 460 (1950) [2].

Hungerford (1995)

    State of New Hampshire v. Hungerford, 1995 WL 378571 (New Hampshire Superior Court 1995); affirmed, 142 N.H. 110, 697 A.2d 916 (Supreme Court of New Hampshire 1997) [10].

Hunt (1999)

    Hunt v. Cromartie, 526 U.S. 541 (1999); on remand, 133 F.Supp.2d 407 (E.D. N.C. 2000); reversed, 532 U.S. 234 (2001) [1, 6].

Hutchinson (1991)

    Hutchinson v. Groskin, 927 F.2d 722 (2nd Cir. 1991) [9].

ILA (1971)

    United States v. International Longshoremen's Association, 334 F.Supp. 976 (S.D. Tex 1971); reversed and remanded as *Equal Employment Opportunity Commission v. International Longshoremen's Association*, 511 F.2d 273 (5th Cir. 1975); *certiorari* denied, 423 U.S. 994 (1975) [2].

I-NET

    Office of Federal Contract Compliance Programs v. I-NET Corporation, an administrative proceeding in the 1990s, resolution unknown [3, 6, 7].

Ireland (1995)

    United States v. Ireland, 62 F.3d 227 (8th Cir. 1995) [5].

Irvin (1953)

    Irvin v. State, 66 So.2d 288 (Supreme Court of Florida 1953) [1].

Isely (1995)

Isely v. Capuchin Province, 877 F.Supp. 1055 (E.D. Mich. 1995) [10].

Jackman (1995)

United States v. Jackman, 46 F.3d 1240 (2nd Cir. 1995) [5].

Jacobs (2002)

Jacobs v. Government of the Virgin Islands, 53 Fed.Appx. 651 (3rd Cir. 2002) [10].

Jahn (2000)

Jahn v. Equine Services, 233 F.3d 382 (6th Cir. 2000) [10].

James (1975)

James v. Stockham Valves, 394 F.Supp. 434 (N.D. Ala. 1975); reversed, 559 F.2d 310 (5th Cir. 1977); *certiorari* denied, 434 U.S. 1034 (1978) [1, 3, 6, 7].

Janes (2002)

Janes v. Chicago Board of Education, not reported, 2002 WL 31557619 (N.D. Ill. 2002) [6, 8].

JEB (1994)

J. E. B. v. Alabama ex rel. T. B., 511 U.S. 127 (1994) [5].

Jefferson (1992)

Jefferson v. Morgan, 962 F.2d 1185 (6th Cir. 1992); *certiorari* denied, 506 U.S. 905 (1992) [5].

Jenkins (1974)

United States v. Jenkins, 496 F.2d 57 (2nd Cir. 1974); *certiorari* denied, 420 U.S. 925 (1975) [5A].

Jennings (1911)

People v. Jennings, 252 Ill. 534, 96 N.E. 1077 (Supreme Court of Illinois 1911) [1, 10].

Johnson (1972)

Johnson v. Louisiana, 406 U.S. 356 (1972) [4, 4A].

Johnson (1976)

Johnson v. Shreveport Garment Co., 422 F.Supp. 526, 13 FEP Cases 1677 (W.D. La. 1976); affirmed, 577 F.2d 1132 (5th Cir. 1978) [10].

Johnson (1987)

Johnson v. Transportation Agency, Santa Clara County, California, 480 U.S. 616 (1987) [2].

Johnson (1988)

Johnson v. Johnson, 701 F.Supp. 1363 (N.D. Ill. 1988) [10].

Johnson (1997)

United States v. Johnson, 973 F.Supp. 1111 (D. Neb. 1997) [5].

Johnson (1998)

United States v. Johnson, 21 F.Supp.2d 329 (S.D. N.Y. 1998) [5].

Johnson (2003)

Johnson v. Crooks, 326 F.3d 995 (8th Cir. 2003) [8].

Johnston (2000)

Johnston v. Bowersox, 119 F.Supp.2d 971 (E.D. Mo. 2000); affirmed, 288 F.3d 1048 (8th Cir. 2002) [5].

Joiner (1994)

Joiner v. General Electric Company, 864 F.Supp. 1310 (N.D. Ga. 1994); reversed and remanded, 78 F.3d 524 (11th Cir. 1996); reversed and remanded, 522 U.S. 136 (1997) [1, 10].

Jolivet (2000)

United States v. Jolivet, 224 F.3d 902 (8th Cir. 2000) [10].

Jones (1997)

United States v. Jones, 107 F.3d 1147 (6th Cir. 1997) [5, 10].

Jones (1999)

Jones v. United States, 526 U.S. 227 (1999) [5].

Joseph (2001)

United States v. Joseph, 2001 WL 515213 (E.D. La. 2001) [10].

Joy (1993)

Joy v. Bell Helicopter Textron, Inc., et al., Allison Gas Turbine Division of General Motors Corp., 999 F.2d 549 (D. D.C. 1993) [7].

Kadas (2001)

Kadas v. MCI Systemhouse Corp., 255 F.3d 359 (7th Cir. 2001) [7].

Kaminsky (1980)

Kaminsky v. Hertz, 94 Mich.App. 356, 288 N.W.2d 426 (Michigan Court of Appeals 1979), released for publication 1980 [8].

Keegan (1899)

Keegan v. Minneapolis & St. Louis Railway Co., 76 Minn. 90, 78 N.W. 965 (1899) [1].

Kelly (1976)

People v. Kelly, 17 Cal.3d 24 (Supreme Court of California 1976) [10].

Key (1982)

Key v. Gillette, 50 FEP Cases 1613 (D. Mass. 1982); decertification vacated, unpublished (1st Cir. 1983); class certification denied, 104 F.R.D. 139 (D. Mass. 1985); affirmed, 782 F.2d 5 (1st Cir. 1986) [3].

Keyes (1976)

Keyes v. Lenoir Rhyne College, 15 FEP Cases 914 (D. N.C. 1976); affirmed, 552 F.2d 579 (4th Cir. 1977); certiorari denied, 434 U.S. 904 (1977) [3].

King (1968)

People v. King, 266 Cal.App.2d 437 (2nd District, Court of Appeal of California 1968) [10].

Kinser (1999)

Kinser v. Gehl Company, 184 F.3d 1259 (10th Cir. 1999) [10].

Kinsey (1974)

Kinsey v. Legg, Mason & Co., 10 FEP Cases 1013 (D. D.C. 1974) [7].

Kline (1988)

Thomas J. Kline, Inc. v. Lorillard, Inc., 674 F.Supp. 183 (D. Md. 1987); reversed, 878 F.2d 791 (4th Cir. 1989); certiorari denied, 493 U.S. 1073 (1990) [7].

Knight (1836)

Knight v. Marquess of Waterford, 2 Y. and C. Ex. 22, 160 English Reports 296 [6].

Koger (1994)

> *Koger v. Reno*, 64 FEP Cases 577 (D. D.C. 1994); affirmed, 98 F.3rd 631, 73 FEP Cases 1855 (D.C. Cir. 1996) [2, 6, 7].

Koretz (1947)

> *State v. Koritz*, 227 N.C. 552, 43 S.E.2d 77 (Supreme Court of North Carolina 1947) [5].

Kotteakos (1945)

> *United States v. Lekacos*, 151 F.2d 170 (2nd Cir. 1945); reversed as *Kotteakos et al. v. United States*, 328 U.S. 750 (1946) [5].

Kouba (1981)

> *Kouba v. Allstate*, 523 F.Supp. 148 (E.D. Cal. 1981); reversed and remanded, 691 F.2d 873 (9th Cir. 1982); then settled [6, 9, 10].

Krist (1990)

> *Krist v. Eli Lilly and Company*, 897 F.2d 293 (7th Cir. 1990) [10].

Kuhl (1918)

> *State v. Kuhl*, 175 P. 190 (Supreme Court of Nevada 1918) [10].

Kumho (1996)

> *Carmichael v. Samyang Tires, Inc.*, 923 F.Supp. 1514 (S.D. Al. 1996); reversed and remanded, 131 F.3d 1433 (11th Cir. 1997); reversed as *Kumho Tire Co. v. Carmichael*, 526 U.S. 137 (1999) [1, 10].

Kyriazi (1978)

> *Kyriazi v. Western Electric Co.*, 461 F.Supp. 894 (D. N.J. 1978); vacated in part, 473 F.Supp. 786 (D. N.J. 1979) [3, 6].

Labat (1966)

> *Labat v. Bennett*, 365 F.2d 698 (5th Cir. 1966), *en banc*; *certiorari* denied, 386 U.S. 991 (1967) [5].

LaMere (2000)

> *State v. LaMere*, 298 Mont. 358 (Supreme Court of Montana 2000) [5].

Lamp (1985)

> *Equal Employment Opportunity Commission v. Chicago Miniature Lamp*, 622 F.Supp. 1281, 39 FEP Cases 297 (N.D. Ill. 1985); reversed, 947 F.2d 292, 57 FEP Cases 408 (7th Cir. 1991) [1, 6, 7, 8].

Lane (2000)

> *Lane v. Huges Aircraft Company*, 22 Cal.4th 405, 993 P.2d 388, 93 Cal.Rptr.2d 60 (Supreme Court of California 2000) [10].

Larsen (1938)

> *People v. Larsen*, 5 N.Y.S.2d 55 (Court of Special Sessions, Bronx County, New York 1938) [1].

Lauzon (2001)

> *Lauzon v. Senco Products, Inc.*, 270 F.3d 681 (8th Cir. 2001) [8, 10].

League (1976)

> *League of United Latin American Citizens v. The City of Santa Ana*, 410 F.Supp. 873, 12 FEP Cases 651 (C.D. Cal. 1976) [2].

Levine (1994)

    Levine v. Central Florida Medical Affiliates, Inc., 864 F.Supp. 1175 (M.D. Fla. 1994); affirmed, 72 F.3d 1538 (11th Cir. 1996) [8].

Lewis (2002)

    United States v. Lewis, 220 F.Supp.2d 548 (S.D. W.Va. 2002) [10].

Lilley (1985)

    Lilley v. Dow Chemical, 611 F.Supp. 1267 (E.D. N.Y. 1985), part of the Agent Orange multi-district litigation [10].

Llera Plaza I

    United States v. Llera Plaza, Acosta, and Rodriguez, 179 F.Supp.2d 492 (E.D. Pa. 2002a) [10].

Llera Plaza II

    United States v. Llera Plaza, Acosta, and Rodriguez, 188 F.Supp.2d 549 (E.D. Pa. 2002b) [10].

Local 36 (1947)

    United States v. Local 36, International Fisheries and Allied Workers, 70 F.Supp. 782 (S.D. Cal. 1947); affirmed, 177 F.2d 320 (9th Cir. 1949) [4, 5, 8, 10].

Local 38 (1969)

    United States v. Local 38, International Brotherhood of Electrical Workers, 1 FEP Cases 673 (N.D. Ohio 1969); reversed and remanded, 428 F.2d 144 (6th Cir. 1970); *certiorari* denied, 400 U.S. 943 (1970); on remand, 3 FEP Cases 362 (N.D. Ohio 1971) [7].

Local 542 (1979)

    Commonwealth v. Local 542, International Union of Operating Engineers, 18 FEP Cases 1560 (E.D. Pa. 1979) [7, 9].

Local 638 (1975)

    Equal Employment Opportunity Commission v. Local 638, Sheet Metal Workers International Association, 401 F.Supp. 467, 12 FEP Cases 712 (S.D. N.Y. 1975) [1].

Lochner (1905)

    Lochner v. State of New York, 198 U.S. 45 (1905) [1, 6].

Logerquist (2000)

    Logerquist v. McVey, 196 Ariz. 470, 1 P.3d 113 (Supreme Court of Arizona 2000) [1, 10].

Lopez (2002)

    United States v. Lopez-Lopez et al., 282 F.3d 1 (1st Cir. 2002) [10].

Louis (1974)

    Louis v. Pennsylvania Development Authority, 371 F.Supp. 877, 7 FEP Cases 49 (E.D. Pa. 1974); affirmed, 505 F.2d 730 (table) (3rd Cir. 1974); *certiorari* denied, 420 U.S. 993 (1975) [2].

Louisiana (1965)

    Louisiana v. United States, 380 U.S. 145 (1965) [5].

Lumpkin (1999)

    United States v. Lumpkin, 192 F.3d 280 (2nd Cir. 1999) [10].

Luong (2003)

    United States v. Luong, 255 F.Supp.2d 1123 (E.D. Cal. 2003) [5].

Lust (1996)

> *Lust v. Merrell Dow Pharmaceuticals, Inc.*, 89 F.3d 594 (9th Cir. 1996) [8].

Lust (2003)

> *Lust v. Sealy, Inc.*, 277 F.Supp.2d 973 (W.D. Wisc. 2003), denying defendant's motions after jury award to plaintiff; affirmed, though award reduced, 383 F.3d 580 (7th Cir. 2004) [5].

Lykus (1975)

> *Commonwealth v. Lykus*, 327 N.E.2d 671 (Supreme Court of Massachusetts 1975) [10].

MacDissi (1988)

> *MacDissi v. Valmont Industres, Inc.*, 856 F.2d 1054 (8th Cir. 1988) [2, 7].

Magistrini (2002)

> *Magistrini v. One Hour Martinizing Dry Cleaning*, 180 F.Supp.2d 584 (D. N.J. 2002); affirmed, 68 Fed.Appx. 356 (3rd Cir. 2003) [7, 10].

Mahone (2004)

> *United States v. Mahone*, 328 F.Supp.2d 77 (D. Me. 2004) [10].

Maiorana (1993)

> *In re Joint Eastern and Southern District Asbestos Litigation (Mariorana)*, 827 F.Supp. 1014 (S.D. N.Y. 1993); reversed in part, affirmed in part, and remanded, 52 F.3d 1124 (2nd Cir. 1995) [1].

Manhart (1978)

> *Los Angeles Department of Water & Power v. Manhart*, 435 U.S. 702 (1978) [5, 6].

Marbury (1803)

> *Marbury v. Madison*, 5 U.S. 107 (1803) [4].

Markey (1982)

> *Markey v. Tenneco Oil Co.*, 439 F.Supp. 219 (E.D. La. 1977), deciding for defendant but creating labor-market estimate based on employees; that labor-market concept rejected, 635 F.2d 497; on remand, 32 FEP Cases 145 (E.D. La. 1982); affirmed, 707 F.2d 172 (5th Cir. 1983) [7].

Marisol (1996)

> *Marisol v. Giuliani*, 929 F.Supp. 662 (S.D. N.Y. 1996) [6].

Marshall (2003)

> *Marshall v. City of Hobbs*, 345 F.3d 1157 (10th Cir. 2003) [8].

Martin (2004)

> *Martin v. Dyas*, 896 So.2d 436 (Supreme Court of Alabama 2004) [1].

Martinez (1999)

> *United States v. Martinez-Salazar*, 146 F.3d 653 (9th Cir. 1999); reversed, 528 U.S. 304 (2000) [5].

Martinez (2001)

> *United States v. Martinez-Cintron*, 136 F.Supp.2d 17 (D. Puerto Rico 2001) [10].

Masters (2001)

> *Masters v. Hesston Corp.*, not reported, 2001 WL 567736 (N.D. Ill. 2001); affirmed, 291 F.3d 985 (7th Cir. 2002) [10].

Mastie (1976)

    Mastie v. Great Lakes Steel Corp., 424 F.Supp. 1299 (E.D. Mich. 1976) [2, 6, 8].

Mathis (2001)

    United States v. Mathis, 264 F.3d 321 (3rd Cir. 2001); *certiorari* denied, 535 U.S. 908 (2002) [10].

Mattson (2002)

    Mattson v. Maloney, not reported, 2002 WL 1803728 (D. Mass. 2002) [1].

Maxwell (1900)

    Maxwell v. Dow, 176 U.S. 581 (1900) [4].

Maxwell (1966)

    Maxwell v. Bishop, 257 F.Supp. 710 (E.D. Ark. 1966); affirmed, 98 F.2d 138 (8th Cir. 1968); vacated and remanded on other grounds, 398 U.S. 262 (1970) [1, 8].

McAnderson (1990)

    United States v. McAnderson, 914 F.2d 934 (7th Cir. 1990) [5].

McAsey (2002)

    McAsey v. United States Department of Navy, 201 F.Supp.2d 1081 (N.D. Cal. 2002) [1, 10].

McCarthy (1983)

    Equal Employment Opportunity Commission v. McCarthy, 578 F.Supp. 45 (D. Mass. 1983); affirmed, 768 F.2d 1 (1st Cir. 1985) [3, 7].

McCleskey (1987)

    McCleskey v. Kemp, 481 U.S. 279 (1987) [1, 8].

McConnell (2003)

    McConnell v. Federal Election Commission, 540 U.S. 93 (2003) [1].

McCorvey (2002)

    McCorvey v. Baxter Healthcare Corporation, 298 F.3d 1253 (11th Cir. 2002) [8].

McCullock (1995)

    McCullock v. H. B. Fuller Company, 61 F.3d 1038 (2nd Cir. 1995) [10].

McDonald (1984)

    People v. McDonald, 37 Cal.3d 351 (Supreme Court of California 1984) [10].

McGautha (1971)

    McGautha v. California, 402 U.S. 183 (1971) [P].

McLaurin (2004)

    McLaurin v. National Railroad Passenger Corporation ("Amtrak"), 311 F.Supp.2d 61 (D. D.C. 2004) [8].

McLemore (2003)

    Mississippi Transportation Commission v. McLemore, 863 So.2d 31 (Supreme Court of Mississippi 2003) [1].

McLeod (2000)

    In re Porter McLeod, Inc. v. Porter, 196 F.R.D. 389 (D. Colo. 2000) [10].

McMillan (2003)

    McMillan v. National Academy of Sciences et al., 294 F.Supp.2d 305 (E.D. N.Y. 2003) [1, 7, 10].

McReynolds (2004a)

   McReynolds v. Sodexho Marriott Services, Inc., 349 F.Supp.2d 1 (D. D.C. 2004), denying defendant's motion for summary judgment [7, 8, 10].

McReynolds (2004b)

   McReynolds v. Sodexho Marriott Services, Inc., 349 F.Supp.2d 30 (D. D.C. 2004), denying defendant's motion to exclude testimony of plaintiffs' expert [8, 10].

MD-NAACP (1999)

   Maryland State Conference of NAACP Branches et al. v. Maryland Department of State Police, 72 F.Supp.2d 560 (D. Md. 1999) [8].

Melani (1983)

   Melani v. Board of Education of the City of New York, 561 F.Supp. 769 (S.D. N.Y. 1983) [3].

Merit (1977)

   Merit Motors v. Chrysler Corp., 569 F.2d 666 (D.C. Cir. 1977) [8].

Mesa-Roche (2003)

   United States v. Mesa-Roche, 288 F.Supp.2d 1172 (D. Kan. 2003) [8, 10].

Metro (1990)

   Metro Broadcasting Inc. v. Federal Communications Commission, 497 U.S. 547 (1990) [5].

Mexican (1996)

   Association of Mexican-American Educators v. State of California, 937 F.Supp. 1397, 80 FEP Cases 476 (N.D. Cal. 1996); affirmed *en banc*, 231 F.3d 572 (9th Cir. 2000) [2, 10].

Michaels (1994)

   State of New Jersey v. Michaels, 136 N.J. 299, 642 A.2d 1372 (New Jersey Supreme Court 1994) [10].

Microsoft I

   United States v. Microsoft Corporation, order, not reported, 1995 WL 505998 (D. D.C. 1995); denying consent decree, 159 F.R.D. 318 (D. D.C. 1995); remanded, 56 F.3d 1448 (D.C. Cir. 1995) [1, 9].

Microsoft II

   United States v. Microsoft Corporation, 980 F.Supp. 537 (D. D.C. 1997); reversed and remanded, 147 F.3d 935 (D.C. Cir. 1998) [1, 8].

Microsoft III

   United State v. Microsoft Corporation, Findings of Fact, 84 F.Supp.2d 9 (D. D.C. 1999); Conclusions of Law, 87 F.Supp.2d 30 (D. D.C. 2000); Final Order, 97 F.Supp.2d 59 (D. D.C. 2000); affirmed in part, reversed in part, and remanded in part, 253 F.3d 34 (D.C. Cir. 2001) [1, 8].

Microsoft IV

   United States v. Microsoft Corporation, Revised Proposed Final Judgment, November 6, 2001; conditional approval, 231 F.Supp.2d 144 (D. D.C. 2002) [1].

Mid-State (1989)

   Mid-State Fertilizer Co. v. Exchange National Bank, 877 F.2d 1333 (7th Cir. 1989) [7, 10].

Milanowicz (2001)

   Milanowicz v. The Raymond Corporation, 148 F.Supp.2d 525 (D. N.J. 2001) [10].

Milk (1998)

> *National Bank of Commerce v. Associated Milk Producers, Inc.*, 22 F.Supp.2d 942 (E.D. Ark. 1998); affirmed, 191 F.3d 858 (8th Cir. 1999) [10].

Miller (1980)

> *Miller v. Staats*, C.A. 73-996 (D. D.C.), consent decree (1980); case discussed on appeal concerning attorney fees, 706 F.2d 336 (D.C. Cir. 1983), in which plaintiffs are considered the prevailing party [6].

Miller (1997)

> *United States v. Miller*, 116 F.3d 641 (2nd Cir. 1997); *certiorari* denied as *Arroyo v. United States*, 524 U.S. 905 (1998) [5].

Miller (2002)

> *Miller v. Pfizer, Inc.*, 196 F.Supp.2d 1062 (D. Kan. 2002) [10].

Miller-El (2003)

> *Miller-El v. Cockrell*, 537 U.S. 322 (2003) [3, 10].

Mills (2004)

> *Mills v. Deehr*, 2004 WL 1047720 (8th District, Court of Appeals of Ohio 2004), not reported in N.E.2d [10].

Milton (1972)

> *Milton v. Wainright*, 407 U.S. 371 (1972) [5].

Minner (2000)

> *Minner v. American Mortgage and Guaranty Company*, 791 A.2d 826 (Superior Court of Delaware 2000) [1, 8].

Miranda (1966)

> *Miranda v. Arizona*, 384 U.S. 436 (1966) [5].

Mister (1986)

> *Mister v. Illinois Central Gulf Railroad Company*, 639 F.Supp. 1560 (S.D. Ill. 1986); affirmed in part and reversed in part, 832 F.2d 1427 (7th Cir. 1987); stay denied, 680 F.Supp. 297 (S.D. Ill. 1987); *certiorari* denied, 485 U.S. 1035 (1988) [1, 7, 8, 10].

Mitchell (1998)

> *United States v. Mitchell*, 145 F.3d 572 (3rd Cir. 1998); after second trial, denying motion for a third, 199 F.Supp.2d 262 (E.D. Pa. 2002); affirmed, 365 F.3d 215 (3rd Cir. 2004) [8, 10].

Montgomery (1969)

> *United States v. Montgomery County Board of Education*, 395 U.S. 225 (1969) [3, 6].

Montgomery (1979)

> *United States v. City of Montgomery*, 21 FEP Cases 484 (M.D. Ala. 1979) [2].

Moody (1834)

> *Moody v. Rowell*, 34 Mass. 490 (Supreme Court of Massachusetts 1834) [1, 10].

Mooney (2002)

> *United States v. Mooney*, 315 F.3d 54 (1st Cir. 2002) [10].

Moore (1981)

> *Moore v. Naval Air Rework Facility*, C.A. C-81-0905 (N.D. Cal.), unpublished district-court decision; affirmed, 772 F.2d 912 (9th Cir. 1985) [2, 6].

Moore (1997)

> *Moore v. Ashland Chemical, Inc.*, 126 F.3d 679 (5th Cir. 1997), reversing the lower court's jury verdict; reversed *en banc*, thus affirming the jury verdict, 151 F.3d 269 (5th Cir. 1998) [10].

Morgan Stanley (2004)

> *Equal Employment Opportunity Commission et al. v. Morgan Stanley and Co.*, 324 F.Supp.2d 451 (S.D. N.Y. 2004) [7, 8, 9, 10].

Moriarty (1999)

> *Moriarty v. Garden Sanctuary Church of God*, 334 S.C. 150, 511 S.E.2d 699 (South Carolina Court of Appeals 1999); affirmed, 341 S.C. 320, 534 S.E.2d 672 (Supreme Court of South Carolina 2000) [10].

Morse (1949)

> *People v. Morse*, 325 Mich. 270, 38 N.W.2d 322 (Supreme Court of Michigan 1949) [10].

Motes (1900)

> *Motes v. United States*, 178 U.S. 458 (1900) [5].

Moultrie (1982)

> *Moultrie v. Martin*, 690 F.2d 1078 (4th Cir. 1982) [8].

Mulder (2001)

> *United States v. Mulder*, 273 F.3d 91 (2nd Cir. 2001) [10].

Muller (1908)

> *Muller v. Oregon*, 208 U.S. 412 (1908) [1, 5, 6, 8, 10].

Muller (2001)

> *Muller v. Synthes Corp.*, not reported, 2001 WL 521390 (N.D. Ill. 2001) [1, 8, 10].

Muñoz (2000)

> *Muñoz v. Orr*, 200 F.3d 291 (5th Cir. 2000) [8].

Musser (2004)

> *Musser v. Gentiva Health Services*, 356 F.3d 751 (7th Cir. 2004) [10].

Mustapha (2002)

> *United States v. George and Mustapha*, not reported, 2002 WL 1727334 (N.D. Ill. 2002), district court denies post-conviction motions for judgment of acquittal; affirmed, 363 F.3d 666 (7th Cir. 2004) [10].

Nassau (1992)

> *American Federation of State, County, and Municipal Employees v. Nassau County*, 799 F.Supp. 1370 (E.D. N.Y. 1992); reversed in part, 96 F.3rd 644 (2nd Cir. 1996); *certiorari* denied, 520 U.S. 1104 (1997) [1, 6, 7, 8, 10].

Neal (1880)

> *Neal v. Delaware*, 103 U.S. 370 (1880) [5].

Nelson (2001)

> *Nelson v. Tennessee Gas Pipeline Co.*, 243 F.3d 244 (6th Cir. 2001) [10].

Nelson (2002)

> *United States v. Nelson*: United States' motions to treat Lemrick Nelson as an adult denied by district court; reversed, remanded for reconsideration, 68 F.3d 583 (2nd Cir. 1995); Judge Trager rules that Nelson will be tried as an adult, 921 F.Supp. 105 (E.D. N.Y. 1996a); affirmed, 90 F.3d 636 (2nd Cir. 1996b); *certiorari* denied, 520 U.S. 1122 (1997); found guilty, Nelson appeals on procedural grounds, reversed, 277 F.3d 164 (2nd Cir. 2002a); *certiorari* denied, 537 U.S. 835 (2002b) [5].

Nemir (1999)

> *Nemir v. Mitsubishi Motor Sales of America*, 60 F.Supp.2d 660 (E.D. Mich. 1999), jury finding and summary judgment for defendant; some rulings affirmed, others reversed, and remanded, 6 Fed.Appx. 266 (6th Cir. 2001); judge determines fact that circuit court wanted presented to jury, 201 F.Supp.2d 779 (E.D. Mich. 2002); circuit court remands for new trial under a different judge, 381 F.3d 540 (6th Cir. 2004) [10].

Nenno (1998)

> *Nenno v. State of Texas*, 970 S.W.2d 549 (Court of Criminal Appeals of Texas 1998); overruled by *Terrazas* (1999) as to "voluntariness" of witness statements [10].

New Energy (1997)

> *New Energy Company of Indiana v. Limbach*, 513 N.E.2d 258 (Supreme Court of Ohio 1987); reversed 486 U.S. 269 (1988) [1].

Newman (2002)

> *Newman v. Motorola*, 218 F.Supp.2d 769 (D. Md. 2002) [10].

NJ Consent (1999)

> Consent Decree between the United States and Division of State Police of the New Jersey Department of Law and Public Safety, in Civil No. 99-5970 (MLC) (D. N.J. 1999) [8].

Norris (1935)

> *Norris v. Alabama*, 294 U.S. 587 (1935) [5].

Ochoa (1971)

> *Ochoa v. Monsanto Co.*, 335 F.Supp. 53 (S.D. Tex. 1971); affirmed, 473 F.2d 318 (5th Cir. 1973) [6].

Oddi (2000)

> *Oddi v. Ford Motor Company*, 234 F.3d 136 (3rd Cir. 2000) [10].

O'Keefe (1996)

> *United States ex rel. Daniel G. O'Keefe v. McDonnell Douglas Corporation*, 918 F.Supp. 1338 (E.D. Mo. 1996) denies motion to dismiss, grants motion to compel discovery; see also 132 F.3d 1252 (8th Cir. 1998), affirming a different (unpublished) opinion [3, 6, 8].

O'Key (1995)

> *State of Oregon v. O'Key*, 321 Ore. 285, 899 P.2d 663 (Supreme Court of Oregon 1995) [10].

Olvis (1996)

> *United States v. Olvis*, 97 F.3d 739 (4th Cir. 1996) [8].

O'Neal (1995)

> *O'Neal v. Delo*, 44 F.3d 655 (8th Cir. 1995), rehearing and suggestion for rehearing denied; *certiorari* denied as *O'Neal v. Bowersox*, 516 U.S. 843 (1995) [5].

O'Neill (1972)

> *Commonwealth v. O'Neill*, 348 F.Supp. 1084, 4 FEP Cases 970 (D. Pa. 1972); vacated in part and remanded, 473 F.2d 1029, 5 FEP Cases 713 (3rd Cir. 1973) [2].

Oneonta (2000)

> *Brown et al. v. City of Oneonta*, 221 F.3d 329 (2nd Cir. 2000) [5].

Ortiz (1995)

> *United States v. Ortiz*, 897 F.Supp. 199 (E.D. Pa. 1995) [5].

Osorio (1992)

> *United States v. Luis Colon Osorio*, 801 F.Supp. 966 (D. Conn. 1992) [5].

Ottaviani (1988)

> *Ottaviani v. State University of New York at New Paltz*, 679 F.Supp. 288 (S.D. N.Y. 1988); affirmed, 875 F.2d 365 (2nd Cir. 1989) [2, 3].

Ovalle (1998)

> *United States v. Ovalle*, 136 F.3d 1092 (6th Cir. 1998) [5].

Oxendine (1996)

> *Oxendine v. Merrell Dow Pharmaceuticals, Inc.*, not reported, 1996 WL 680992 (D.C. Superior Court 1996) [8].

Page (2001)

> *United States v. Page*, 154 F.Supp.2d 1316 (M.D. Tenn. 2001) [8].

Paige (2002)

> *Paige v. State of California*, 291 F.3d 1141 (9th Cir. 2002) [2].

Paoli II (1994)

> *In re Paoli Railroad Yard PCB Litigation*, 35 F.3d 717 (3rd Cir. 1994); *certiorari* denied, 513 U.S. 1190 (1995) [1, 10].

Park (2003)

> *Park v. Cytodyne Technologies, Inc.*, not reported, 2003 WL 21283814 (California Superior Court 2003) [10].

Patterson (1976)

> *Patterson v. Western Development Labs*, 13 FEP Cases 772 (N.D. Cal. 1976) [2].

Patton (1930)

> *Patton v. United States*, 281 U.S. 276 (1930) [4].

Paul (1999)

> *United States v. G. Paul*, 175 F.3d 906 (11th Cir. 1999) [8, 10].

Paxton (1999)

> *Paxton v. Ward*, 199 F.3d 1197 (10th Cir. 1999) [10].

Pearce (1990)

> *United States v. Pearce*, 912 F.2d 159 (6th Cir. 1990); *certiorari* denied, 498 U.S. 1093 (1991) [10].

Pedraza (1995)

> *Pedraza v. Jones, Rosenquest, and Smejkal*, 71 F.3d 194 (5th Cir. 1995) [8].

Penaranda (2004)

    United States v. Penaranda, 375 F.3d 238 (2nd Cir. 2004), asking Supreme Court to determine whether *Blakely* (2004) invalidates sentencing guidelines [5, 10].

Penk (1985)

    Penk v. Oregon State Board of Higher Education, 1985 WL 25631, 48 FEP Cases 1724 (D. Ore. 1985); affirmed, 816 F.2d 458, 48 FEP Cases 1878 (9th Cir. 1987) [3, 10].

Penry (1989)

    Penry v. Lynaugh, 492 U.S. 302 (1989) [P].

PEPCO (1962)

    Potomac Electric Power Company v. Washington Chapter of Congress of Racial Equality et al., 209 F.Supp. 559 (D. D.C. 1962) [2].

Pervoe (1984)

    People of the State of California v. Pervoe, 161 Cal.App.3d 342 (1st District, Court of Appeal of California 1984) [5].

Pestel (1995)

    Pestel v. Vermeer Manufacturing Company, 64 F.3d 382 (8th Cir. 1995) [10].

Peteet (1989)

    Peteet v. Dow Chemical Corp., 868 F.2d 1428 (5th Cir. 1989) [1].

Peters (1972)

    Peters v. Kiff, 407 U.S. 493 (1972) [5, 9].

Petruzzi (1993)

    Petruzzi's IGA Supermarkets, Inc. v. Darling-Delaware Company, Inc., 998 F.2d 1224 (3rd Cir. 1993) [2].

Pettway (1967)

    Pettway v. American Cast Iron Pipe, unpublished dismissal (N.D. Ala. 1967); reversed and remanded, 406 F.2d 399 (5th Cir. 1969); unpublished relief denial (N.D. Ala. 1969); reversed and remanded, 411 F.2d 998 (5th Cir. 1969); defendant's compliance plan approved, 332 F.Supp. 811 (N.D. Ala. 1970); reversed and remanded, 494 F.2d 211 (5th Cir. 1974); unpublished judgments and denial of change of counsel (N.D. Ala. 1975); reversed in part and remanded, 576 F.2d 1157 (5th Cir. 1978) [2].

Phelps (1985)

    Phelps v. Duckworth, 757 F.2d 811 (7th Cir. 1985); reversed *en banc*, 772 F.2d 1410 (7th Cir. 1987) [5].

Phosphide (1995)

    In re Aluminum Phosphide Antitrust Litigation, 893 F.Supp. 1497 (D. Kan. 1995) [10].

Plessy (1896)

    Plessy v. Ferguson, 163 U.S. 537 (1896) [P, 1, 5].

Pokora (1934)

    Pokora v. Wabash Railway Co., 292 U.S. 98 (1934) [P, 8, 9].

Polaroid (1981)

    Mateza v. Polaroid Corporation, No. 76-3379 (Massachusetts Superior Court 1981) [2, 3].

Polaroid (1983)

Robinson et al. v. Polaroid Corporation, 567 F.Supp. 192 (D. Mass. 1983); affirmed, 732 F.2d 1010 (1st Cir. 1984) [2, 6, 7, 8, 10].

Pope (1967)

Pope v. United States, 372 F.2d 710 (8th cir. 1967) [5].

Porter (1970)

United States v. H. K. Porter Co., Inc., 296 F.Supp. 40 (D. Ala. 1970) [2].

Porter (1992)

Porter v. Whitehall Laboratory, 791 F.Supp. 1335 (S.D. Ind. 1992); affirmed, 9 F.3d 607 (7th Cir. 1993) [8].

Powell (1888)

Powell v. Pennsylvania, 127 U.S. 678 (1888) [1].

Powers (1991)

Powers v. Ohio, 499 U.S. 400 (1991) [5].

Presseisen (1977)

Presseisen v. Swarthmore College, 442 F.Supp. 593 (E.D. Pa. 1977); affirmed, 582 F.2d 1275 (3rd Cir. 1982) [2, 3].

Pride (2000)

Pride v. BIC Corporation, 218 F.3d 566 (6th Cir. 2000) [10].

Primavera (2001)

Primavera Familienstifung v. David J. Askin et al., 130 F.Supp.2d 450 (S.D. N.Y. 2001); motion for reconsideration granted in part and denied in part (without consequence to *Daubert* rulings) as to defendant Donaldson Lufkin and Jenrette Securities Corporation, 137 F.Supp.2d 438 (S.D. N.Y. 2001) [8, 9].

Prince-Oyibo (2003)

United States v. Prince-Oyibo, 320 F.3d 494 (4th Cir. 2003) [10].

Pugliano (2004)

United States v. Louis Pugliano, 315 F.Supp.2d 197 (D. Conn. 2004), *habeas corpus* petition hearing (jury challenge), excluding expert testimony [8, 9, 10].

Purdy (1996)

United States v. Purdy, 946 F.Supp. 1094 (D. Conn. 1996); affirmed, 144 F.3d 241 (1st Cir. 1998) [5].

Purkett (1995)

Purkett v. Elem, 514 U.S. 765 (1995), revises the *Batson* (1986) rule about peremptory juror challenges [4].

Quarles (1968)

Quarles v. Philip Morris, Inc., 279 F.Supp. 505 (E.D. Va. 1968) [6].

Quattrocchi (1999)

State v. Quattrocchi, not reported, (Rhode Island Superior Court 1999) [10].

Queen (1978)

Queen v. Dresser Industries, 456 F.Supp. 257 (D. Md. 1978); affirmed, 609 F.2d 509 (4th Cir. 1979) [6, 8].

Rabinowitz (1966)

   Rabinowitz v. United States, 366 F.2d 34 (5th Cir. 1966) [5].

Ramseur (1992)

   Ramseur v. Beyer, 983 F.2d 1215 (3rd Cir. 1992) [5].

Readers Digest (1974)

   Smith v. Readers Digest Association, 13 FEP Cases 853 (S.D. N.Y. 1974) [3].

Rebel (1998)

   Rebel Oil Company, Inc. v. Atlantic Richfield Company, 146 F.3d 1088 (9th Cir. 1998) [8].

Reece (1955)

   Reece v. State of Georgia, 350 U.S. 85 (1955) [9].

Reed (1978)

   Reed v. State of Maryland, 283 Md. 374 (Maryland Court of Appeals 1978) [10].

Regal (2004)

   Regal Cinemas, Inc. v. W & M Properties, 90 Fed.Appx. 824, 2004 WL 187528 (6th Cir. 2004) [10].

Reid (2001)

   Reid v. Lockheed Martin Aeronautics Co., 205 F.R.D. 655 (N.D. Ala. 2001) [8, 10].

Reid Jr. (2001)

   Robert C. Reid, Jr., et al. v. Albemarle Corporation, 207 F.Supp.2d 499 (M.D. La. 2001) [2, 7, 10].

Remigio (1985)

   United States v. Remigio, 767 F.2d 730 (10th Cir. 1985) [5].

Rendon (1989)

   Rendon v. AT&T Technologies, 883 F.2d 388, 50 FEP Cases 1587 (5th Cir. 1989) [2].

Reyes (1996)

   United States v. Reyes, 934 F.Supp. 553 (S.D. N.Y. 1996) [5].

Reynolds (1964)

   Reynolds v. Sims, 377 U.S. 533 (1964) [1].

Reynolds (2004)

   Reynolds v. Giuliani, 2004 WL 3017014 (S.D. N.Y. 2004); superceded by essentially the same opinion, 2005 WL 342106 (S.D. N.Y. 2005) [8].

Rhodes (2002)

   Rhodes et al. v. Cracker Barrel Old Country Store, Inc., not reported, 2002 WL 32058462 (N.D. Ga. 2002), magistrate's report; motion for class certification denied, magistrate's report accepted, 213 F.R.D. 619 (N.D. Ga. 2003) [2, 7].

Rice (1995)

   United States v. Rice, 52 F.3d 843 (10th Cir. 1995) [10].

Rice Will (1903)

   In Re Rice's Will, 81 N.Y.S. 68 (Supreme Court, Appellate Division, New York 1903) [10].

Ring (2002)

   Ring v. Arizona, 536 U.S. 548 (2002) [5, 10].

Rioux (1996)

> *United States v. Rioux*, 930 F.Supp. 1558 (D. Conn. 1995); affirmed, 97 F.3d 648 (2nd Cir. 1996) [P, 5].

Risley (1915)

> *People v. Risley*, 214 N.Y. 75 (New York Court of Appeals 1915) [1].

Rives (1879)

> *Virginia v. Rives*, 100 U.S. 313 (1879) [4].

Rizzo (1979)

> *Commonwealth of Pennsylvania v. Rizzo*, 466 F.Supp. 1219, 20 FEP Cases 130 (E.D. Pa. 1979) [2].

Roach (1915)

> *People v. Roach*, 215 N.Y. 592 (New York Court of Appeals 1915), affirming murder conviction [10].

Robins (1988)

> *In re A. H. Robins, Inc.*, 88 B.R. 742 (E.D. Va. 1988); affirmed, 880 F.2d 709 (4th Cir. 1989); *certiorari* denied, 493 U.S. 959 (1989) [1, 6, 7, 10].

Robinson (1973)

> *Robinson v. Cahill*, 62 N.J. 473, 303 A.2d 273 (Supreme Court of New Jersey 1973) [1].

Robinson (1997)

> *Robinson v. Metro North Commuter Railroad*, 175 F.R.D. 46 (S.D. N.Y. 1997), denying class certification; reversed in *Caridad* (1999); class certification denied again on remand, 197 F.R.D. 85 (S.D. N.Y. 2000); reversed again, with instruction to certify class, 267 F.3d 147 (2nd Cir. 2001) [2, 10].

Robledo (2002)

> *People v. Robledo and Medrano*, unpublished, 2002 WL 557766 (2nd District, Court of Appeal of California 2002) [5].

Rock (1987)

> *Rock v. Arkansas*, 483 U.S. 44 (1987) [1].

Rodriguez (1973)

> *San Antonio Independent School District v. Rodriguez*, 411 U.S. 1 (1973) [1].

Rogers (2001)

> *United States v. Rogers*, 26 Fed.Appx. 171 (4th Cir. N.C. 2001) [10].

Roman (1976)

> *Roman v. ESB, Inc.*, 550 F.2d 1343, 14 FEP Cases 235 (4th Cir. 1976) [6].

Roman (1987)

> *Roman v. Abrams*, 822 F.2d 214 (2nd Cir. 1987) [5].

Romley (2001)

> *State of Arizona, ex rel. Richard M. Romley v. Fields*, 201 Ariz. 321, 35 P.3d 82 (Court of Appeals of Arizona 2001) [10].

Roper (2005)

> *Roper v. Simmons*, 543 U.S. ___, 125 S.Ct. 1183 (2005) [P, 10].

Rosen (1996)

    Rosen v. Ciba-Geigy Corp., 78 F.3d 316 (7th Cir. 1996) [10].

Rowe (2003)

    Rowe Entertainment, Inc., et al. v. The William Morris Agency, Inc., not reported, 2003 WL 22124991 (S.D. N.Y. 2003) [8].

Royal (1988)

    United States v. James E. Royal, 7 F.Supp.2d 96 (D. Mass. 1998); affirmed, 174 F.3d 1 (1st Cir. 1999) [5].

Rubanick (1988)

    Rubanick v. Witco Chemical Corp., 225 N.J.Super. 485, 542 A.2d 975 (Middlesex County Superior Court of New Jersey 1988), excluding expert whose explanation of cause was not "generally accepted;" reversed and remanded, 242 N.J.Super. 36, 576 A.2d 4 (New Jersey Superior Court 1990); accepting the Superior Court's new standards, but remanded for finding, 125 N.J. 421, 593 A.2d 733, 1991 WL 148239 (Supreme Court of New Jersey 1991) [1, 8].

Rudebusch (2002)

    Rudebusch v. Hughes, 313 F.3d 506 (9th Cir. 2002) [7].

Ruiz Troche (1997)

    Ruiz Troche v. Pepsi Cola Bottling Company, 177 F.R.D. 82 (D. Puerto Rico 1997); reversed and remanded, 161 F.3d 77 (1st Cir. 1998) [10].

Ruff (2001)

    Ruff v. Ensign-Bickford Industries, Inc., 171 F.Supp.2d 1226 (D. Utah 2001) [10].

Rush (1871)

    Rush v. Megee, 1871 WL 4994, 36 Ind. 69 (Supreme Court of Indiana 1871) [10].

Ruth (1995)

    United States v. Ruth, 42 M.J. 730 (Military Court of Criminal Appeals 1995) [10].

Rutherford (2000)

    United States v. Rutherford, 104 F.Supp.2d 1190 (D. Neb. 2000) [10].

Rutland (2004)

    United States v. Rutland, 372 F.3d 543 (3rd Cir. 2004) [10].

Ryan (2003)

    Ryan v. Clarke, 281 F.Supp.2d 1008 (D. Neb. 2003) [10].

Saelee (2001)

    United States v. Saelee, 162 F.Supp.2d 1097 (D. Ak. 2001) [10].

Santillan (1999)

    United States v. Santillan, not reported, 1999 WL 1201765 (N.D. Cal. 1999) [10].

Sara Lee (2002)

    Lithuanian Commerce Corp. v. Sara Lee Hosiery, 202 F.Supp.2d 371 (D. N.J. 2002) [10].

Satterwhite (1986)

    Satterwhite v. Texas, 726 S.W.2d 81 (Court of Criminal Appeals of Texas 1986), affirming conviction and death sentence; reversed and remanded for new punishment hearing, 486

U.S. 249 (1988); remand for new trial, as no separate punishment hearing called for in Texas law, 759 S.W.2d 436 (Court of Criminal Appeals of Texas 1988); convicted and sentenced to death again; affirmed, 858 S.W.2d 412 (Court of Criminal Appeals of Texas 1993); *certiorari* denied, 510 U.S. 970 (1993) [5, 10].

Schanbarger (1996)

Schanbarger v. Macy, 77 F.3d 1424 (2nd Cir. 1996) [5].

Scheffer (1998)

United States v. Scheffer, 523 U.S. 303 (1998) [1, 10].

Schiavo (2005)

Schiavo ex rel. Schindler v. Schiavo, 357 F.Supp.2d 1378 (M.D. Fla. 2005); affirmed 403 F.3d 1223 (11th Cir. 2005) [1].

Schmerling (1999)

Schmerling v. Danek Medical, Inc., not reported, 1999 WL 712591 (E.D. Pa. 1999) [8].

Schollenberger (1898)

Schollenberger v. Pennsylvania and *Paul v. Pennsylvania*, 171 U.S. 1 (1898) [1].

Schwabe (1962)

Herman Schwabe, Inc. v. United Shoe Machinery Corporation, 297 F.2d 906 (2nd Cir. 1962) [3].

Sears (1986)

Equal Employment Opportunity Commission v. Sears, Roebuck & Co., 628 F.Supp. 1264 (N.D. Ill. 1986); affirmed, 839 F.2d 302 (7th Cir. 1988) [6, 8].

Seminole (1996)

Seminole Tribe of Florida v. Florida, 517 U.S. 44 (1996) [P].

Semi-Tech (2004)

Semi-Tech Litigation, L.L.C. v. Bankers Trust Company, 219 F.R.D. 324 (S.D. N.Y. 2004) [10].

Serrano (1971)

Serrano v. Priest, 5 Cal.3d 584, 487 P.2d 601 (Supreme Court of California 1971) [1].

Shahzade (1996)

Shahzade v. Gregory, 923 F.Supp. 286 (D.Mass. 1996) [10].

Shaw (1993)

Shaw v. Reno, 509 U.S. 630 (1993); 517 U.S. 899 (1996) [1].

Sheehan (1997)

Sheehan v. Daily Racing Form, Inc., 104 F.3d 940 (7th Cir. 1997) [1, 8].

Sheppard (2002)

Sheppard v. Consolidated Edison of New York, not reported, 2002 WL 2003206 (E.D. N.Y. 2002) [5, 10].

Sherrod (2000)

Sherrod v. Lingle et al., 223 F.3d 605 (7th Cir. 2000) [9, 10].

Sherwood (1996)

United States v. Sherwood, 98 F.3d 402 (9th Cir. 1996) [10].

Shield Club (1974)

Shield Club v. City of Cleveland, 13 FEP Cases 533 (N.D. Ohio 1974) [2].

Shoe (1953)

    United States v. United Shoe Machinery Corp., 110 F.Supp. 295 (D. Mass. 1953) [1].

Shulton (1983)

    Pence v. Shulton, C.A. 81-2311, and *Hart v. Shulton*, C.A. 81-2454 (D. N.J. 1983), jury decision for defendant in two cases tried together [7].

Silicone (1996)

    In re Silicone Gel Breast Implants Products Liability Litigation, No. CV92-P-10000-S, MDL 926 (N.D. Ala.); see Order No. 31, May 31, 1996, establishing a science panel, and subsequent orders constituting it. A summary of the panel's report, dated November 30, 1998, can be found at http://www.fjc.gov/breimlit/science/summary.htm [10].

Simmons (1995)

    Commonwealth of Pennsylvania v. Simmons, 541 Pa. 211 (Supreme Court of Pennsylvania 1995); execution stayed pending *certiorari*, 542 Pa. 554 (Supreme Court of Pennsylvania 1995); *certiorari* denied, 516 U.S. 1128 (1996) [10].

Simon (2002)

    In re Simon II Litigation, 211 F.R.D. 86 (E.D. N.Y. 2002), class certification order; vacated and remanded, 407 F.3d 125 (2nd Cir. 2005) [10].

Singleton (1974)

    Singleton v. Estelle, 492 F.2d 671 (5th Cir. 1974) [5].

Six (1995)

    Six v. Delo, 885 F.Supp. 1265 (E.D. Mo. 1995); affirmed, 94 F.3d 469 (8th Cir. 1996); rehearing and suggestion for rehearing denied; *certiorari* denied as *Six v. Bowersox*, 520 U.S. 1255 (1997) [5].

Smith (1940)

    Smith v. Texas, 311 U.S. 128 (1940) [1, 4, 5].

Smith (1945)

    Smith v. Rapid Transit, 317 Mass. 469, 58 N.E.2d 754 (Supreme Court of Massachusetts 1945) [8].

Smith (1976)

    Smith v. State of Maryland, 31 Md.App. 106, 355 A.2d 527 (Maryland Court of Special Appeals 1976) [10].

Smith (1982)

    Smith v. Lubbers, 28 FEP Cases 324 (D. D.C. 1982); affirmed, 713 F.2d 865 (D.C. Cir. 1983); *certiorari* denied, 464 U.S. 996 (1983) [2].

Smith (2000a)

    People v. Smith, 463 Mich. 199, 615 N.W.2d 1 (Supreme Court of Michigan 2000) [5, C].

Smith (2000b)

    Smith v. Ingersoll-Rand Company, 214 F.3d 1235 (10th Cir. 2000) [10].

Smith (2004)

    Smith v. Commonwealth of Kentucky, not reported, 2004 WL 535975 (Supreme Court of Kentucky 2004) [10].

Smithers (2000)

United States v. Smithers, 212 F.3d 306 (6th Cir. 2000) [10].

SMS (1999)

SMS Systems Maintenance Services v. Digital Equipment Corp., 188 F.3d 11 (1st Cir. 1999) [7].

Sneed (1966)

State of New Mexico v. Sneed, 76 N.M. 349, 414 P.2d 858 (Supreme Court of New Mexico 1966) [1, 9].

Soares (1979)

Commonwealth v. Soares, 387 N.E.2d 499, 377 Mass. 461 (Supreme Court of Massachusetts 1979); *certiorari* denied, 444 U.S. 881 (1979) [5].

Sobel (1983)

Sobel v. Yeshiva University, 566 F.Supp. 839 (S.D. N.Y. 1983); reversed and remanded, 797 F.2d 1479 (2nd Cir. 1986); decision on remand, 656 F.Supp. 587 (S.D. N.Y. 1987); reversed and remanded, 839 F.2d 18 (2nd Cir. 1988); *certiorari* denied, 490 U.S. 1105 (1989) [3].

Sosa (2004)

Sosa v. Alvarez-Machain, 542 U.S. 692, 124 S.Ct. 2739 (2004) [10].

Soto (1996)

New Jersey v. Soto et al., 324 N.J.Super. 66, 734 A.2d 350 (Superior Court of New Jersey 1996) [7, 8, 9, 10].

Spearman (2001)

Spearman Industries, Inc. v. St. Paul Fire and Marine Insurance Company, 138 F.Supp.2d 1088 (N.D. Ill. 2001) [10].

Spencer (1989)

Spencer v. State of Florida, 545 So.2d 1352 (Supreme Court of Florida 1989) [5].

Spensieri (1999)

Spensieri v. Lasky, 94 N.Y.2d 231 (New York Court of Appeals 1999) [9].

Spock (1969)

United States v. Spock, 416 F.2d 165 (1st Cir. 1969) [5].

Spriggs (1996)

United States v. Spriggs, 102 F.3d 1245 (D.C. Cir. 1996), as amended, and rehearing denied; *certiorari* denied, 522 U.S. 831 (1997) [10].

Spring (1878)

Spring Co. v. Edgar, 99 U.S. 645 (1878) [1].

Stainer (2003)

Stainer v. Cracker Barrel Old Country Store, Inc., not reported, 2003 WL 1193316 (N.D. Ill. 2003) [10].

Stanford (1989)

Stanford v. Kentucky, 492 U.S. 361 (1989) [P].

Starzecpyzel (1995)

United States v. Starzecpyzel, 880 F.Supp. 1027 (S.D. N.Y. 1995) [10].

Steamship (1995)

> *Equal Employment Opportunity Commission v. Steamship Clerks Union, Local 1066*, 48 F.3d 594 (1st Cir. 1995) [2].

Stevens (2004)

> *Stevens v. Horn*, 319 F.Supp.2d 592, 2004 WL 1191668 (W.D. Pa. 2004) [8].

Strauder (1879)

> *Strauder v. West Virginia*, 100 U.S. 303 (1879) [5].

Stringfellow (1970)

> *Stringfellow v. Monsanto Co.*, 320 F.Supp. 1175 (W.D. Ark. 1970) [2].

Stone (1972)

> *Stone v. FCC*, 466 F.2d 316 (D.C. Cir. 1972) [2].

Strong (1931)

> *People v. Strong*, 114 Cal.App. 522, 300 P. 84 (2nd District, Court of Appeal of California 1931); hearing denied by the Supreme Court of California (1931) [10].

Sullivan (1993)

> *Sullivan v. Louisiana*, 508 U.S. 275 (1993) [5].

Summerlin (2004)

> *Schriro, Director, Arizona Department of Corrections v. Summerlin*, 542 U.S. 348, 124 S.Ct. 2519 (2004) [10].

Sutton (2003)

> *United States v. Sutton*, 337 F.3d 792 (7th Cir. 2003) [10].

Swain (1965)

> *Swain v. Alabama*, 380 U.S. 202 (1965) [P, 5].

Sweatt (1950)

> *Sweatt v. Painter*, 339 U.S. 629 (1950) [1].

Sweeney (1977)

> *Sweeney v. Board of Trustees of Keene State College*, 14 FEP Cases 1220 (D. N.H. 1977); affirmed, 569 F.2d 169 (1st Cir. 1978); vacated and remanded, 429 U.S. 24 (1978); reaffirmed on remand, 1979 WL 303, 20 FEP Cases 718 (D. N.H. 1979); affirmed, 604 F.2d 106 (1st Cir. 1979) [3].

Tagatz (1988)

> *Tagatz v. Marquette University*, 861 F.2d 1040, 50 FEP Cases 99 (7th Cir. 1988) [7].

Taylor (1975)

> *Taylor v. Louisiana*, 419 U.S. 522 (1975) [5, 9].

Teal (1982)

> *Connecticut v. Teal*, 457 U.S. 440 (1982) [5, 6].

Teamsters (1971)

> *International Brotherhood of Teamsters v. United States*, 335 F.Supp. 246 (S.D. Tex. 1971); remanded, 517 F.2d 299 (5th Cir. 1975); vacated and remanded, 431 U.S. 324 (1977) [1, 2, 5, 6].

Teixeira (1996)

Commonwealth v. Teixeira, 40 Mass.App.Ct. 236, 662 N.E.2d 726 (Massachusetts Appeals Court 1996) [10].

Telephone (2004)

In re Universal Service Fund Telephone Billing Practices Litigation, 219 F.R.D. 661, 2004 WL 303095 (D. Kan. 2004) [8, 10].

Terry (1995)

United States v. Terry, 60 F.3d 1541 (11th Cir. 1995); *certiorari* denied, 516 U.S. 1060 [10].

Test (1975)

United States v. Test, 399 F.Supp. 683 (D. Colo. 1975); affirmed, 550 F.2d 557 (10th Cir. 1976) [5, 8].

Theil (1946)

Thiel v. Southern Pacific Co., 328 U.S. 217 (1946) [5].

Thomas (1991)

Thomas v. Baker, 717 F.Supp. 878 (D. D.C. 1989); affirmed, 925 F.2d 1523 (D.C. Cir. 1991), individual discharge only, no published class opinion [8].

Thomas (1996)

United States v. Thomas, 74 F.3d 676 (6th Cir. 1996); *certiorari* denied, 517 U.S. 1162 (1996) [10].

Thompson (1898)

Thompson v. Utah, 170 U.S. 343 (1898) [4].

Thompson (1974)

Thompson v. Shepphard, 490 F.2d 830 (5th Cir. 1974) [5].

Thompson (1979)

Thompson v. Boyle, 499 F.Supp. 1147, 21 FEP Cases 57 (D. D.C. 1979) [2].

Thompson (2004)

Thompson v. Bell, 373 F.3d 688 (6th Cir. 2004), reassessing and essentially withdrawing 315 F.3d 566 (6th Cir. 2003); reversed as *Bell v. Thompson*, ___ U.S. 245, 125 S.Ct. 2825 (2005) [10].

Traction (1899)

Capital Traction v. Hof, 174 U.S. 1 (1899) [4].

Tremblay (2003)

Rhode Island v. Tremblay, not reported, 2003 WL 23018762 (Providence Superior Court 2003) [5, 7, 8, 10, 5A].

Trout (1981)

Trout v. Hidalgo, 517 F.Supp. 873 (D. D.C. 1981), class certification and judgment for plaintiffs; petition for recertification denied as *Trout v. Lehman*, 28 FEP Cases 658 (D. D.C. 1982); affirmed in part, vacated and remanded in part, 702 F.2d 1094 (D.C. Cir. 1983); vacated and remanded, 465 U.S. 1056 (1984); on remand, 652 F.Supp. 144 (D. D.C. 1986), not admitting additional statistical evidence and finding for plaintiffs [6].

Truesdale (1998)

Truesdale v. Moore, 142 F.3d 749 (4th Cir. 1998) [5].

Tuf (2000)

> *Tuf Racing Products, Inc. v. American Suzuki Motor Corporation*, 223 F.3d 585 (7th Cir. 2000) [10].

Tufts (1977)

> *Equal Employment Opportunity Commission v. Tufts Institution of Learning*, 421 F.Supp. 152 (D. Mass. 1975), grants injunctive relief to one of two individual intervenors (no other opinion can be found) [3].

Turner (1970)

> *Turner v. Fouche*, 396 U.S. 346 (1970) [5].

Turner (1997)

> *United States v. Turner*, 104 F.3d 1180 (9th Cir. 1997) [8].

Tyler (2002)

> *Tyler v. Union Oil Company of California*, 304 F.3d 379 (5th Cir. 2002) [7, 10].

Tyson (1986)

> *Tyson v. Tyson*, 107 Wash.2d 72, 727 P.2d 226 (Supreme Court of Washington 1986) [10].

Tyus (1996)

> *Tyus v. Urban Search Management*, 102 F.3d 256 (7th Cir. 1996), reverses jury decision based on judge's improper exclusion of experts, improper charge, and other improper behavior [8, 10].

Union Gas (1989)

> *Pennsylvania v. Union Gas Company*, 491 U.S. 1 (1989) [P].

Utilicorp (1990)

> *Kansas v. Utilicorp United, Inc.*, 497 U.S. 199 (1990) [5].

Valentine (1968)

> *United States v. Valentine*, 288 F.Supp. 957 (D. Puerto Rico 1968) [5].

Valentine (1996)

> *Valentine v. Pioneer Chlor Alkali Company, Inc.*, 921 F.Supp. 666 (D. Nev. 1996) [8, 10].

Valentino (1981)

> *Valentino v. United States Postal Service*, 511 F.Supp. 917 (D. D.C. 1981); affirmed, 674 F.2d 56 (D.C. Cir. 1982) [3].

Van Wyk (2000)

> *United States v. Van Wyk*, 83 F.Supp.2d 515 (D. N.J. 2000) [10].

VCU (1994)

> *Smith v. Virginia Commonwealth University*, 856 F.Supp. 1088 (E.D. Va. 1994), summary judgment for defendant; reversed and remanded, 84 F.3d 672 (4th Cir. 1996) [3].

Velasquez (1995)

> *United States v. Velasquez*, 64 F.3d 844 (3rd Cir. 1995) [8, 10].

Venator (2002)

> *Equal Employment Opportunity Commission v. Venator Group*, 2002 WL 181711, 88 FEP Cases 158 (S.D. N.Y. 2002) [1, 10].

Verdell (1985)

Verdell v. Wilson, 602 F.Supp. 1427 (E.D. N.Y. 1985) [2, 6].

Vermiculite (2000)

Virginia Vermiculite, Ltd. v. W. R. Grace and Co., 98 F.Supp.2d 729 (W.D. Va. 2000) [7].

Veysey (2003)

United States v. Veysey, 334 F.3d 600 (7th Cir. 2003) [8, 9].

Villafane (1980)

Villafane v. Manson, 504 F.Supp. 78 (D. Conn. 1980); affirmed, 639 F.2d 770 (table) (2nd Cir. 1980) [5].

Virginia (1879)

Ex parte Virginia, 100 U.S. 339 (1879) [5].

Visa (2000)

In re Visa Check/Mastermoney Antitrust Litigation, 192 F.R.D. 68 (E.D. N.Y. 2000), granting class certification; affirmed, 280 F.3d 124 (2nd Cir. 2001); *certiorari* denied, 536 U.S. 917 (2002) [10].

VMI (1996)

United States v. Virginia, 518 U.S. 515 (1996) [1].

Vuyanich (1980)

Vuyanich v. Republic National Bank of Dallas, 505 F.Supp. 224 (N.D. Tex. 1980); vacated and remanded, 723 F.2d 1195 (5th Cir. 1984) [1].

Wado (1998)

Wado v. Xerox Corp., 991 F.Supp. 174, 75 FEP Cases 1807 (W.D. N.Y. 1998); affirmed as *Smith v. Xerox Corp.*, 196 F.3d 358, 81 FEP Cases 343 (2nd Cir. 1999) [3, 8].

Walker (2000)

Walker v. Soo Line Railroad Company, 208 F.3d 581 (7th Cir. 2000) [10].

Wallace (2003)

People v. Wallace, not reported in N.W.2d, 2003 WL 1439812 (Michigan Court of Appeals 2003); cited in this book as illustrative, not as establishing legal precedent [5].

Walton (1990)

Walton v. Arizona, 497 U.S. 639 (1990) [5].

Warren (1994)

United States v. Warren, 16 F.3d 247 (8th Cir. 1994) [5].

Watkins (1997)

Watkins v. Telsmith, Inc., 121 F.3d 984 (5th Cir. 1997) [10].

Watson (1988)

Watson v. Fort Worth Bank and Trust, 487 U.S. 977 (1988) [6].

Webb (2004)

Webb v. Neuroeducation, Inc., 88 P.3d 417 (Division 3, Panel 8, Court of Appeals of Washington 2004) [10].

Weeks (1993)

State of Vermont v. Weeks, 160 Vt. 393 (Supreme Court of Vermont 1993) [10].

Weisgram (2000)

> *Weisgram v. Marley Co.*, 528 U.S. 440 (2000) [10].

Welch (2004)

> *United States v. Welch*, 368 F.3d 970 (7th Cir. 2004) [10].

Wells (1985)

> *Wells v. Ortho Pharmaceutical Corp.*, 615 F.Supp. 262 (N.D. Ga. 1985); affirmed in part (damages reduced), 788 F.2d 741 (11th Cir. 1986); *certiorari* denied, 479 U.S. 950 (1986) [1, 10].

Westberry (1999)

> *Westberry v. Gislaved Gummi AB*, 178 F.3d 257 (4th Cir. 1999) [10].

Westwood (1936)

> *Commonwealth of Pennsylvania v. Westwood*, 324 Pa. 289, 188 A. 304 (Supreme Court of Pennsylvania 1936) [10].

Wexler (1983)

> *Wexler v. Thomas*, 1983 WL 481, 30 FEP Cases 1370 (D. D.C. 1983) [6].

Wheaton Glass (1970)

> *Shultz v. Wheaton Glass Co.*, 421 F.2d 259 (3rd Cir. 1970) [6].

White (1966)

> *White v. Cook*, 251 F.Supp. 401 (M.D. Ala. 1966) [5].

White (2002)

> *White v. Williams*, 179 F.Supp.2d 405 (D. N.J. 2002), 208 F.R.D. 123 (D. N.J. 2002) [8].

White (2004)

> *White and Gaskins v. BFI Waste Services*, 375 F.3d 288 (4th Cir. 2004) [7].

Whitus I

> *Whitus v. Balkcom*, *certiorari* denied from Georgia Supreme Court, 365 U.S. 831 (1961); affirms lower-court ruling that state remedy available, 299 F.29 844 (5th Cir. 1962); *certiorari* granted, judgment vacated, 370 U.S. 728 (1962); reversed and remanded, 333 F.2d 496 (5th Cir. 1964); *certiorari* denied, 379 U.S. 931 (1964) [5].

Whitus II

> *Whitus v. Georgia*, 385 U.S. 545 (1967) [5].

Whren (1996)

> *Whren v. United States*, 517 U.S. 806 (1996) [8].

Wichita (2003)

> *City of Wichita, Kansas v. Trustees of the Apco Oil Corporation Liquidating Trust*, 306 F.Supp.2d 1040 (D. Kan. 2003) [10].

Wilder I

> Complaint, *Wilder v. Sugarman*, 73 Civ. 2644 (S.D. N.Y., filed June 14, 1973); 385 F.Supp. 1013 (S.D. N.Y. 1974), three-judge panel finds for defendants; rehearing denied; decision abandoned by agreement under *Wilder II*, although rulings adopted as *stare decisis* in Order of Dismissal Upon Conditions, *Wilder v. Sugarman*, 73 Civ. 2644(RJW), dated June 2, 1978 [6].

Wilder II

> *Wilder v. Bernstein*, 499 F.Supp. 980 (S.D. N.Y. 1980), motions to dismiss granted in part and denied in part, and motion for class certification granted; stipulated settlement of many issues approved, 645 F.Supp. 1292 (S.D. N.Y. 1986); affirmed, 848 F.2d 1338 (2nd Cir. 1988) [6].

Wilder III

> 725 F.Supp. 1324 (S.D. N.Y. 1989), intervenors in *Wilder II* awarded attorney fees; reversed, 944 F.2d 1028 (2nd Cir. 1991); previous opinion vacated and remanded, 965 F.2d 1196 (2nd Cir. 1992); on remand, award increased, 1993 WL 51074 (S.D. N.Y. 1993); plaintiffs awarded fees, but not reimbursement for experts, 975 F.Supp. 276 (S.D. N.Y. 1997); reconsideration denied, 982 F.Supp. 264 (S.D. N.Y. 1997); plaintiffs awarded additional fees (for later work), 1998 WL 323492 (S.D. N.Y. 1998) [6].

Wilder IV

> Plaintiff-intervenors question scope of stipulation, 1994 WL 30480 (S.D. N.Y. 1994); they succeed on merits, stipulation does apply to kinship foster care, defendants ordered to comply, 153 F.R.D. 524 (S.D. N.Y. 1994); appeal dismissed, 49 F.3d 69 (2nd Cir. 1995); defendants' motion to terminate stipulation is denied, 1998 WL 355413 (S.D. N.Y. 1998) [6].

Wilkins (1979)

> *Wilkins v. University of Houston*, 471 F.Supp. 1054 (S.D. Tex. 1979); affirmed in part and reversed in part, 654 F.2d 388, 27 FEP Cases 1199 (5th Cir. 1981); vacated, 459 U.S. 802 (1982); on remand, 695 F.2d 134 (5th Cir. 1983); on remand, 725 F.Supp. 331 (S.D. Tex. 1989) [3, 6, 7].

Williams (1955)

> *Williams v. State of Georgia*, 349 U.S. 375 (1955) [5].

Williams (1970)

> *Williams v. Florida*, 399 U.S. 78 (1970) [4].

Williams (1978)

> *United States v. WIlliams*, 583 F.2d 1194 (2nd Cir. 1978) [10].

Williams (1996)

> *United States v. Williams*, 81 F.3d 1434 (7th Cir. 1996) [7, 10].

Williams (1999)

> *Williams v. Ford Motor Co.*, 187 F.3d 533, 80 FEP Cases 1175 (6th Cir. 1999) [2, 7, 8].

Williams (2002)

> *Williams v. CSX Corp.*, 2002 WL 31618455 (E.D. Pa. 2002) [1].

Winans (1858)

> *Winans v. New York & Erie Railroad Co.*, 62 U.S. 88 (1858) [1].

Witcher (1966)

> *Witcher v. Peyton*, 261 F.Supp. 1018 (W.D. Va. 1966), denying writ of *habeas corpus*; reversed and remanded for a hearing on the evidence, 382 F.2d 707 (4th Cir. 1967); the district court (unpublished) again denied relief, finding no deliberate discrimination in forming the jury; reversed again, trial vacated, 405 F.2d 725 (4th Cir. 1969) [5].

Wonson (1812)

United States v. Wonson, 28 F. Cas. 745 (Case No. 16,750, 1 Gall. 5) (Circuit Court, D. Mass. 1812) [9].

Wood (1936)

United States v. Wood, 299 U.S. 123 (1936) [5].

Worley (1972)

Worley v. State of Florida, 263 So.2d 613 (4th District, Florida Court of Appeal 1972) [10].

Wright (1967)

United States v. Wright, 37 C.M.R. 447, 17 USCMA 183 (Court of Military Appeals 1967) [10].

Wyche (1997)

Wyche v. Marine Midland Bank, 1997 WL 109564, 73 FEP Cases 1600 (S.D. N.Y. 1997) [2, 7].

X-It (2002)

X-It Products v. Walter Kidde Portable Equipment, Inc., 227 F.Supp.2d 494 (E.D. Va. 2002) [6, 7].

Yapp (2004)

Yapp et al. v. Union Pacific Railroad Company, 301 F.Supp.2d 1030, 2004 WL 231229 (E.D. Mo. 2004) [2, 6, 8].

Yarusso (2000)

Bell Sports, Inc. v. Yarusso, 759 A.2d 582 (Supreme Court of Delaware 2000) [10].

Yazee (1981)

United States v. Yazee, 660 F.2d 422 (10th Cir. 1981) [5].

Yee (1991)

United States v. Yee, 134 F.R.D. 161 (N.D. Ohio 1991) [9, 10].

Yoder (1989)

Yoder v. Mutual Broadcasting System, Inc., No. 88-71226 (D. Mich. 1989) [8, 10].

Young (1987)

United States v. Young, 822 F.2d 1234 (2nd Cir. 1987) [5].

Zaremba (2004)

Zaremba v. General Motors Corporation, 360 F.3d 355 (2nd Cir. 2004) [10].

Zenith (1981)

Zenith Radio Corp. v. Matsushita Electric Industrial Co., 505 F.Supp. 1313 (E.D. Pa. 1981); reversed, 723 F.2d 238 (3rd Cir. 1983); reversed and remanded, 475 U.S. 574 (1985) [6, 8, 10].

Zenith (2003)

Zenith Electronics Corporation v. WH-WH Broadcasting Corporation, 2003 WL 21506808 (N.D. Ill. 2003a), excluding expert; 2003 WL 22284326 (N.D. Ill. 2003b), partial summary judgment for Zenith; 395 F.3d 416 (7th Cir. 2005) affirmed [10].

Zottola (2002)

Zottola v. City of Oakland, 32 Fed.Appx. 307 (9th Cir. 2002), affirms unpublished opinion (N.D. Cal. 2001) [7].

Bibliography

Numbers in brackets [ ] at the end of each entry refer to the chapters in which the item is referenced; a number followed by "A" denotes an appendix. "P" denotes the Preface, "I" the Introduction, and "C" the Coda.

Abramson (2001)

Bruce Abramson, "Blue Smoke or Science? The Challenge of Assessing Expertise Offered as Advocacy," 22 *Whittier Law Review* 723 (Spring 2003) [9, 10].

Adams (1913)

Brooks Adams, *The Theory of Social Revolutions*, MacMillan (1913) [P].

Allen (1991)

Ronald J. Allen, "On the Significance of Batting Averages and Strikeout Totals: A Clarification of the 'Naked Statistical Evidence' Debate, the Meaning of 'Evidence,' and the Requirement of Proof Beyond a Reasonable Doubt," 65 *Tulane Law Review* 1093 (1991) [8].

Allgood (2001)

Davis B. "Pepper" Allgood, "Expert Witness and Consultant Discovery in Federal Court," *The Practical Litigator* 47 (July 2001) [10].

Alschuler (2002)

Albert W. Alschuler, "Racial Profiling and the Constitution," 2002 *University of Chicago Legal Forum* 163 (2002) [8].

Anderson (1996)

Martin Anderson, *Imposters in the Temple*, paper edition, Hoover Institution Press (1996); first published 1992 [9].

Angell (1996)

Marcia Angell, *Science On Trial*, W. W. Norton (1996) [10].

Annas (1992)

George Annas, "Using Genes to Define Motherhood," 326 *New England Journal of Medicine* 417 (1992) [1].

Ash (1986)

Arlene Ash, "The Perverse Logic of Reverse Regression," in Kaye and Aickin (1986) at 85 [3].

Ashman (1973)

Charles R. Ashman, *The Finest Judges Money Can Buy*, Nash Publishing (1973) [7].

Asplen (1999)

Christopher A. Asplen, "Integrating DNA Technology into the Criminal System," 83 *Judicature* 3:144 (1999) [10].

Ayres (1990)

Ian Ayres, "Playing Games with the Law," 42 *Stanford Law Review* 1291 (May 1990), a review of *Eric Rasmussen, Games and Information: An Introduction to Game Theory*, Basil Blackwell (1989) [2].

Baldus and Cole (1977)

David C. Baldus and James W. Cole, "Quantitative Proof of Intentional Discrimination," 1 *Evaluation Quarterly* 1:53 (February 1977) [1].

Baldus and Cole (1980)

David C. Baldus and James W. Cole, *Statistical Proof of Discrimination*, with updates, McGraw Hill (1980) [1, 3, 7, 9, 2A].

Barak (2002)

Aharon Barak, "The Role of a Supreme Court in a Democracy," 53 *Hastings Law Review* 1205 (2002) [7].

Barnes (1983)

David W. Barnes, *Statistics as Proof*, Little, Brown and Company (1983) [3, 7].

Barnes (2001)

David W. Barnes, "Too Many Probabilities: Statistical Evidence of Tort Causation," 64 *Law and Contemporary Problems* 4:191 (2001) [7].

Barnes and Conley (1986)

David W. Barnes and John M. Conley, *Statistical Evidence in Litigation*, Little, Brown and Company (1986) [1, 9].

Bator (1963)

Paul M. Bator, "Finality in Criminal Law and Federal *Habeas Corpus* for State Prisoners," 76 *Harvard Law Review* 441 (1963) [5].

Beale (1983)

Sara Sun Beale, "Integrating Statistical Evidence and Legal Theory to Challenge the Selection of Grand and Petit Jurors," 56 *Law and Contemporary Problems* 4:269 (Autumn 1983) [5].

Becker (1984)

Mary E. Becker, "Comparable Worth in Antidiscrimination Legislation: A Reply to Freed and Polsby," 51 *University of Chicago Law Review* 4:1112 (1984) [6].

Becker (1986)

Mary E. Becker, "Barriers Facing Women in the Wage-Labor Market and the Need for Additional Remedies: A Reply to Fischel and Lazear," 53 *University of Chicago Law Review* 3:934 (Summer 1986) [6].

Beecher-Monas (1998)

Erica Beecher-Monas, "Blinded by Science: How Judges Avoid the Science in Scientific Evidence," 71 *Temple Law Review* 55 (Spring 1998) [10].

Beecher-Monas (2000)

Erica Beecher-Monas, "The Heuristics of Intellectual Due Process: A Primer for Triers of Science," 75 *New York University Law Review* 1563 (2000) [1, 7, 10].

Beecher-Monas (2002)

Erica Beecher-Monas, "Respecting Pandora's Box," response to Caudill (2002), 23 *Cardozo Law Review* 1811 (May 2002) [7].

Beecher-Monas and Garcia-Rill (2003)

Erica Beecher-Monas and Edgar Garcia-Rill, "Danger at the Edge of Chaos: Predicting Violent Behavior in a Post-*Daubert* World," 24 *Cardozo Law Review* 1845 (May 2003) [5, 10].

M. Berger (1994)

Margaret A. Berger, "Procedural Paradigms for Applying the *Daubert* Test," 78 *Minnesota Law Review* 6:1345 (1994) [1, 10].

M. Berger (1998)

Margaret A. Berger, "Does the Search for Truth in Our Scholarship Continue in Our Classrooms?" 49 *Hastings Law Journal* 1179 (1998) [8].

M. Berger (1999)

Margaret A. Berger, review of Faigman et al. (2002), 1999 edition, and Foster and Huber (1997), 39 *Jurimetrics Journal* 3:335 (1999) [8].

M. Berger (2001)

Margaret A. Berger, "Upsetting The Balance Between Adverse Interests: The Impact of the Supreme Court's Trilogy on Expert Testimony in Toxic Tort Litigation," 64 *Law and Contemporary Problems* 2&3:289 (2001) [7, 10].

R. Berger (1979, 1997)

Raoul Berger, *Government by Judiciary: The Transformation of the Fourteenth Amendment*, second edition, Liberty Fund (1997) [I, 1, 4].

D. Bernstein (1996)

David E. Bernstein, "Junk Science in the United States and the Commonwealth," 21 *Yale Journal of International Law* 123 (Winter 1996) [10].

D. Bernstein (2001)

David E. Bernstein, "*Frye, Frye* Again: The Past, Present, and Future of the General Acceptance Test," 41 *Jurimetrics Journal* 3:385 (2001) [1, 8].

D. Bernstein (2003)

David E. Bernstein, "Keeping Junk Science Out of Asbestos Litigation," 31 *Pepperdine Law Review* 11 (2003) [1, 6, 10].

N. Bernstein (2001)

Nina Bernstein, *The Lost Children of Wilder*, Random House (2001) [6].

Bessey et al. (1992)

Barbara L. Bessey, Kevin J. Gilmartin, and Francis B. Stancavage, "A Review of Statistical Books for Use in Employment Discrimination Lawsuits," 32 *Jurimetrics Journal* 473 (Spring 1992) [10].

Best (2001)

Joel Best, *Damned Lies and Statistics: Untangling Numbers from the Media, Politicians, and Activists*, University of California Press (2001) [9].

Beyea and Berger (2001)

Jan Beyea and Daniel Berger, "Scientific Misconceptions Among *Daubert* Gatekeepers: The Need for Reform of Expert Review Procedures," 64 *Law and Contemporary Problems* 2&3:327 (2001) [10].

Bickel et al. (1975)

P. J. Bickel, E. A. Hammel, and J. W. O'Connell, "Sex Bias in Graduate Admissions: Data from Berkeley," 187 *Science* 398 (February 7, 1975) [2].

B. Black (1988)

Bert Black, "A Unified Theory of Scientific Evidence," 56 *Fordham Law Review* 595 (1988) [2].

B. Black (1994)

Bert Black, "The Supreme Court's View of Science: Has *Daubert* Exorcised the Certainty Demon?" 15 *Cardozo Law Review* 2129 (1994) [7, 10].

B. Black et al. (1994)

Bert Black, Francisco J. Ayala, and Carol Saffran-Brinks, "Science and the Law in the Wake of *Daubert*: A New Search for Scientific Knowledge," 72 *Texas Law Review* 4:715 (1994) [6, 10].

C. Black (1960)

Charles L. Black, Jr., *The People and the Court*, Macmillan (1960) [1].

S. Black and Strahan (2001)

Sandra E. Black and Philip E. Strahan, "The Division of Spoils: Rent-Sharing and Discrimination in a Regulated Industry," 91 *American Economic Review* 4:814 (September 2001) [3].

Blackstone (1783)

Sir William Blackstone, *Commentaries on the Laws of England*, ninth edition (1783), in modernized English and maintaining twelfth edition (1793) pagination, edited by Wayne Morrison, Cavendish Publishing (2001); the ninth edition was the last under Blackstone's direction [1, 5].

Boatright and Krauss

Robert Boatright and Elissa Krauss, "Jury Summit 2001," 86 *Judicature* 3:145 (November-December 2001) [5].

Bolon (2001)

Craig Bolon, "Significance of Test-Based Ratings for Metropolitan Boston Schools," 9 *Education Policy Analysis Archives* 42 (October 16, 2001) [3, 3A].

Bolon (2002)

Craig Bolon, "Response to Michelson and to Willson and Kellow," 10 *Education Policy Analysis Archives* 10 (January 28, 2002) [3, 3A].

Boot (1998)

Max Boot, *Out of Order: Arrogance, Corruption, and Incompetence on the Bench*, Basic Books (1998) [7, 9].

Borenstein (2001)

Jason Borenstein, "Science, Philosophy, and the Courts," "Keynote Address," in Bioethics Symposium Issue, 13 *St. Thomas Law Review* 979 (Summer 2001) [10].

Box and Draper (1987)

George Box and Norman Draper, *Empirical Model Building and Response Surfaces*, John Wiley (1987) [I].

Bradfield and Wells (2000)

Amy L. Bradfield and Gary L. Wells, "The Perceived Validity of Eyewitness Identification Testimony: A Test of the Five *Biggers* Criteria," 24 *Law and Human Behavior* 5:581 (October 2000) [8, 10].

Brewer (1998)

Scott Brewer, "Scientific Expert Testimony and Intellectual Due Process," 107 *Yale Law Journal* 1535 (1998) [7, 9, 10].

Brixen and Meis (2000)

Catherine E. Brixen and Christine E. Meis, Note, "Codifying the '*Daubert* Trilogy': The Amendment to Federal Rule of Evidence 702," 40 *Jurimetrics Journal* 4:527 (2000) [10].

Brodin (2004)

Mark S. Brodin, "Behavioral Science Evidence in the Age of *Daubert*: Reflections of a Skeptic," *Boston College Law School Research Paper No. 48* (2004), available from the Social Science Research Network [10].

Brody (1995)

David C. Brody, "Sparf and Dougherty Revisited: Why the Court Should Instruct the Jury of Its Nullification Right," 33 *American Criminal Law Review* 89 (1995) [4].

Brown (1943)

Ray A. Brown, "Fact and Law in Judicial Review," 56 *Harvard Law Review* 899 (1943) [4].

Browne (1993)

Kingsley R. Browne, "Statistical Proof of Discrimination: Beyond 'Damned Lies,'" 68 *Washington Law Review* 477 (1993) [8].

Bueker (1997)

John P. Bueker, "Jury Source Lists: Does Supplementation Really Work?" 82 *Cornell Law Review* 390 (January 1997) [5, 7, 9].

Callen (1991)

Craig R. Callen, "Adjudication and the Appearance of Statistical Evidence," 65 *Tulane Law Review* 457 (1991) [8].

E. Campbell et al. (2004)

Eric G. Campbell, Greg Koski, and David Blumenthal, *The Triple Helix: University, Government, and Industry Relationships in the Life Sciences*, AEI-Brookings Joint Center for Regulatory Studies (2004) [9].

M. Campbell (2005)

Mary Catherine Campbell, "Black, White, and Grey: The American Jury Project and Representative Juries," 18 *Georgetown Journal of Legal Ethics* 625 (Summer 2005) [C].

T. Campbell (1984)

Thomas J. Campbell, "Regression Analysis in Title VII Cases: Minimum Standards, Comparable Worth, and Other Issues Where Law and Statistics Meet," 36 *Stanford Law Review* 1299 (1984) [3].

Cappalli (2002)

Richard B. Cappalli, "Bringing Internet Information to Court: Of 'Legislative Facts,'" 75 *Temple Law Review* 99 (Spring 2002) [1].

Cardozo (1921)

Benjamin N. Cardozo, "A Ministry of Justice," 35 *Harvard Law Review* 2:113 (1921) [4, 10].

Carnegie (1993)

Carnegie Commission on Science, Technology, and Government, *Science and Technology in Judicial Decision Making*, Carnegie Corporation (1993) [7, 9, 10].

Carro and Hatala (1996)

Jorge L. Carro and Joseph V. Hatala, "Recovered Memories, Extended Statutes of Limitations, and Discovery Exceptions in Childhood Sexual Abuse Cases: Have We Gone Too Far?" 23 *Pepperdine Law Review* 1239 (1996) [10].

Carter (1993)

Linda E. Carter, "Harmless Error in the Penalty Phase of a Capital Case: A Doctrine Misunderstood and Misapplied," 28 *Georgia Law Review* 125 (Fall 1993) [5].

Case Note (2001)

"Past Imperfect," review of *Irving v. Penguin Books Ltd.*, 2000 WL 362478 (Queens Bench Division April 11), 110 *Yale Law Journal* 1531 (June 2001) [1, 10].

Case Note (2002)

"Seventh Circuit Upholds the Reliability of Expert Testimony Regarding the Source of a Latent Fingerprint, *United States v. Havvard*, 260 F.3d 597 (7th Cir. 2001)," 115 *Harvard Law Review* 2349 (June 2002) [8, 10].

Caudill and Redding (2000)

David S. Caudill and Richard E. Redding, "Junk Philosophy of Science?: The Paradox of Expertise and Interdisciplinarity in Federal Courts," 57 *Washington and Lee Law Review* 685 (Summer 2000) [1, 10].

Caudill (2002)

David S. Caudill, "Barely Opening, Then Slamming Shut, Science's 'Black Box' in Law: A Response to Beecher-Monas's Heuristics," 23 *Cardozo Law Review* 1795 (May 2002) [10].

Caudill and LaRue (2003)

David S. Caudill and Lewis H. LaRue, "Why Judges Applying the *Daubert* Trilogy Need to Know about the Social, Institutional, and Rhetorical—and Not Just the Methodological—Aspects of Science," 45 *Boston College Law Review* 1 (December 2003) [9].

Cecil and Willging (1994a)

Joe S. Cecil and Thomas E. Willging, "Court-Appointed Experts," in *Reference Manual* (1994) at 526 [10].

Cecil and Willging (1994b)

Joe S. Cecil and Thomas E. Willging, "Accepting *Daubert*'s Invitation: Defining a Role for Court-Appointed Experts in Assessing Scientific Validity," 43 *Emory Law Journal* 995 (Summer 1994) [10].

Chakraborty and Kidd (1991)

Ranajit Chakraborty and Kenneth R. Kidd, "The Utility of DNA Typing in Forensic Work," 254 *Science* 1735 (December 20, 1991) [9].

Cheesebro (1993)

Kenneth J. Cheesebro, "Gallileo's Retort: Peter Huber's Junk Scholarship," 42 *American University Law Review* 4:1637 (1993) [1, 6].

Cheng and Yoon (2005)

Edward K. Cheng and Albert H. Yoon, "Does *Frye* or *Daubert* Matter? A Study of Scientific Admissibility Standards," 91 *Virginia Law Review* 471 (2005) [1, 8, 9].

Chesler et al. (1988)

Mark A. Chesler, Joseph Sanders, and Debra S. Kalmuss, *Social Science in Court: Mobilizing Experts in the School Desegregation Cases*, University of Wisconsin Press (1988) [1, 8, 10].

K. Clark (1953)

Kenneth B. Clark, "The Social Scientist as an Expert Witness in Civil Rights Litigation," 1 *Social Problems* 1:5 (1953) [1].

S. Clark (1999)

Sherman J. Clark, "The Courage of Our Convictions," 97 *Michigan Law Review* 2381 (August 1999) [5].

Clermont and Eisenberg (1992)

Kevin M. Clermont and Theodore Eisenberg, "Trial by Jury or Judge: Transcending Empiricism," 77 *Cornell Law Review* 1124 (July 1992) [10].

Clermont and Eisenberg (2002)

Kevin M. Clermont and Theodore Eisenberg, "Litigation Realities," 88 *Cornell Law Review* 119 (November 2002) [P, 10].

Coase (1988)

R. H. Coase, *The Firm, the Market, and the Law*, University of Chicago Press (1988) [I].

N. Cohen (1985)

Neil B. Cohen, "Confidence in Probability: Burdens of Persuasion in a World of Imperfect Knowledge," 60 *New York University Law Review* 385 (1985) [8].

N. Cohen (1987)

Neil B. Cohen, "Conceptualizing Proof and Calculating Probabilities: A Response to Professor Kaye," 73 *Cornell Law Review* 78 (1987) [8].

S. Cohen (2003)

Stanley Cohen, *The Wrong Men*, Carroll & Graf (2003) [4].

Cohn (1968)

Elchanan Cohn, "Economies of Scale in Iowa High School Operations," *Journal of Human Resources* (1968) [3].

Collins (1978)

Sharon M. Collins, "The Use of Social Research in the Courts," in *Knowledge and Policy: The Uncertain Connection*, Study Project on Social Research and Development, Volume 5, National Research Council, National Academy of Sciences (1978) [1].

Commager (1943)

Henry Steele Commager, "Judicial Review and Democracy," XIX *The Virginia Quarterly* 417 (1943); reprinted in Levy (1967) at 64 [I].

Comment (1966)

"*Swain v. Alabama*: A Constitutional Blueprint for the Perpetuation of the All-White Jury," 52 *Virginia Law Review* 1157 (1966) [5].

Committee (2002)

Committee on National Statistics, *The Polygraph and Lie Detection*, National Academies Press (2002) [1].

Connolly et al. (2001)

Walter B. Connolly, Jr., David W. Peterson, and Michael J. Connolly, *Use of Statistics in Equal Employment Opportunity Litigation*, Law Journal Press (2001) [7].

Conrad (1998)

Clay S. Conrad, *Jury Nullification: The Evolution of a Doctrine*, Carolina Academic Press (1998) [4].

Conway and Roberts (1986)

Delores A. Conway and Harry V. Roberts, "Regression Analysis in Employment Discrimination Cases," in DeGroot et al. (1986) at 107 [3].

Corwin (1925)

Edward S. Corwin, "The Progress of Constitutional Theory Between the Declaration of Independence and the Meeting of the Philadelphia Convention," 30 *American Historical Review* 3:511 (April 1925); reprinted in Alpheus T. Mason and Gerald Garvey, editors, *American Constitutional History: Essays by Edward S. Corwin*, Harper Torchbooks (1964); reprinted also in Richard Loss, editor, *Corwin on the Constitution*, Cornell University Press (1981), at 56 [4].

Coulam and Fienberg (1986)

Robert F. Coulam and Stephen E. Fienberg, "The Use of Court-Appointed Statistical Experts: A Case Study," in DeGroot et al. (1986) at 305 [10].

A. Cox (1987)

Archibald Cox, *The Court and the Constitution*, Houghton Mifflin (1987) [I].

D. Cox (1972)

D. R. Cox, "Regression Models and Life Tables," 34 *Journal of the Royal Statistical Society B* 187 (1972) [2].

Crook (2002)

Lynn S. Crook, "Inadequate Legal Representation of Therapists Accused of Implanting False Memories: Three Case Studies," paper presented at the 19th Annual Conference of the International Society for the Study of Dissociation, Baltimore (November 9, 2002) [10].

Crook and Dean (1999)

Lynn S. Crook and Martha C. Dean, "'Lost in a Shopping Mall': A Breach of Professional Ethics," 9 *Ethics & Behavior* 1:39 (1999) [10].

Crosskey (1953)

William Winslow Crosskey, *Politics and the Constitution in the History of the United States*, University of Chicago Press (1953) [4].

Cwiklo (1979)

William E. Cwiklo, *Computers in Litigation Support*, Petrocelli (1979) [1].

Dahl (1957)

Robert A. Dahl, "Decision-Making in a Democracy: The Supreme Court as a National Policy-Maker," 6 *Journal of Public Law* (Fall 1957) 279; reprinted in Levy (1967) at 105 [1].

Dahl (2002)

Robert A. Dahl, *How Democratic Is the American Constitution?* Yale University Press (2002) [I].

Daniels (1985)

James E. Daniels, "Protecting Your Expert During Discovery," 71 *ABA Journal* 50 (September 1985) [10].

Danner and Varn (2002)

Douglas Danner and Larry L. Varn, *Expert Witness Checklists*, third edition, West Group (2002).

J. Davis (1969)

James H. Davis, *Group Performance*, Addison-Wesley (1969) [4A].

K. Davis (1942)

Kenneth Culp Davis, "An Approach to Problems of Evidence in the Administrative Process," 55 *Harvard Law Review* 3:364 (1942) [1, 10].

K. Davis (1955)

Kenneth Culp Davis, "Judicial Notice," 55 *Columbia Law Review* 7:945 (1955) [1, 10].

P. Davis (1987)

Peggy C. Davis, "'There Is a Book out . . .': An Analysis of Judicial Absorption of Legislative Facts," 100 *Harvard Law Review* 1539 (1987) [1].

Deason (1998)

Ellen E. Deason, "Court-Appointed Expert Witnesses: Scientific Positivism Meets Bias and Deference," 77 *Oregon Law Review* 59 (Spring 1998) [10].

de Cani (1974)

John S. de Cani, "Statistical Evidence in Jury Discrimination Cases," 65 *Journal of Criminal Law and Criminology* 2:234 (1974) [5, 9].

Deftos (1994)

Leonard J. Deftos, "*Daubert* & *Frye*: Compounding the Controversy Over the Forensic Use of DNA Testing," 15 *Whittier Law Review* 955 (1994) [10].

DeGroot et al. (1986)

Morris H. DeGroot, Stephen E. Fienberg, and Joseph B. Kadane, editors, *Statistics and the Law*, John Wiley (1986) [3, 5].

Deming (1975)

W. Edwards Deming, "On Probability as a Basis for Action," 29 *American Statistician* 4:146 (1975) [9].

Dershowitz (2001)

Alan Dershowitz, *Supreme Injustice: How the High Court Hijacked Election 2000*, Oxford University Press (2001) [I].

Dery (1999)

George M. Dery, III, "Mouse Hunting with an Elephant Gun: The Supreme Court's Overkill in Upholding a Categorical Rejection to Polygraph Evidence in *United States v. Scheffer*," 26 *American Journal of Criminal Law* 2:227 (1999) [10].

Detre (1994)

Peter A. Detre, "A Proposal for Measuring Underrepresentation in the Composition of the Jury Wheel," "Note," in 103 *Yale Law Journal* 1913 (1994) [5, 7].

Devine et al. (2001)

Dennis J. Devine, Laura Clayton, Benjamin Dunford, Rasmy Seying, and Jennifer Pryce, "Jury Decision Making: 45 Years of Empirical Research on Deliberating Groups," 7 *Psychology, Public Policy, and Law* 622 (2001) [4].

Diamond (1974)

Bernard L. Diamond, "The Psychiatric Prediction of Dangerousness," 123 *University of Pennsylvania Law Review* 439 (December 1974) [I].

Di Lello (1993)

Edward V. Di Lello, "Fighting Fire with Firefighters: A Proposal for Expert Judges at the Trial Level," 93 *Columbia Law Review* 473 (March 1993) [10].

Dixon and Gill (2002)

Lloyd Dixon and Brian Gill, "Changes in the Standards for Admitting Expert Evidence in Federal Civil Cases since the *Daubert* Decision," 8 *Psychology, Public Policy, and Law* 251 (2002) [1, 7, 9].

Donaher et al. (1974)

William A. Donaher, Henry R. Piehler, Aaron D. Twerski, and Alvin S. Weinstein, "The Technological Expert on Products Liability Litigation," 52 *Texas Law Review* 7:1303 (1974) [6, 7].

Donnelly and Friedman (1999)

Peter Donnelly and Richard D. Friedman, "DNA Database Searches and the Legal Consumption of Scientific Evidence," 97 *Michigan Law Review* 931 (February 1999) [7, 10].

Doyle (2005)

James M. Doyle, *True Witness: Cops, Courts, Science, and the Battle Against Misidentification*, MacMillan, Palgrave (2005) [9, 10].

Dreyfuss (1995)

Rochelle Cooper Dreyfuss, "Is Science a Special Case? The Admissibility of Scientific Evidence after *Daubert v. Merrell Dow*," 73 *Texas Law Review* 1779 (June 1995) [10].

Dreyfuss (1997)

Rochelle Cooper Dreyfuss, "Galileo's Tribute: Using Medical Evidence in Court," book review, 95 *Michigan Law Review* 2055 (May 1997) [10].

Du Bois (1962)

Grant P. Du Bois, Jr., "Desirability of Blue Ribbon Juries," 13 *Hastings Law Journal* 479 (May 1962) [10].

Easton (2000)

Stephen D. Easton, "Ammunition for the Shoot-Out with the Hired Gun's Hired Gun: A Proposal for Full Expert Witness Disclosure," 32 *Arizona State Law Journal* 2:465 (2000) [6, 10].

Eisenberg et al. (2002)

Theodore Eisenberg, Neil LaFountain, Brian Ostrom, David Rottman, and Martin T. Wells, "Juries, Judges, and Punitive Damages: An Empirical Study," 87 *Cornell Law Review* 743 (March 2002) [10].

Eisenberg and Wells (2002)

Theodore Eisenberg and Martin T. Wells, "Trial Outcomes and Demographics: Is There a Bronx Effect?" 80 *Texas Law Review* 1839 (June 2002) [9].

Ellis and Diamond (2003)

Leslie Ellis and Shari Seidman Diamond, "Race, Diversity, and Jury Composition: Battering and Bolstering Legitimacy," 78 *Chicago-Kent Law Review* 1033 (2003) [5].

Epstein (2002)

Robert Epstein, "Fingerprints Meet *Daubert*: The Myth of Fingerprint 'Science' Is Revealed," 75 *Southern California Law Review* 605 (March 2002) [8, 10].

Erichson (1999)

Howard M. Erichson, "Mass Tort Litigation and Inquisitorial Justice," 87 *Georgetown Law Journal* 1983 (June 1999) [10].

Erickson and Simon (1998)

Rosemary J. Erickson and Rita J. Simon, *The Use of Social Science Data in Supreme Court Decisions*, University of Illinois Press (1998) [P, 10].

Erzinçlioğlu (2000)

Zakaria Erzinçlioğlu, *Maggots, Murder, and Men*, Thomas Dunne Books (2000) [10].

Etzioni (1974)

Amitai Etzioni, "Creating an Imbalance," 10 *Trial* 6:28 (November-December 1974) [4].

Fabian (1977)

Vaclav Fabian, "On the Effect of Jury Size," 72 *Journal of the American Statistical Association* 359:535 (September 1977) [1, 4A].

Faigman (1989)

David L. Faigman, "To Have and Have Not: Assessing the Value of Social Science to the Law as Science and Policy," 38 *Emory Law Journal* 1005 (Fall 1989) [1, 10].

Faigman et al. (1994)

David L. Faigman, Elise Porter, and Michael J. Saks, "Check Your Crystal Ball at the Courthouse Door, Please: Exploring the Past, Understanding the Present, and Worrying About the Future of Scientific Evidence," 15 *Cardozo Law Review* 6:1799 (1994) [1, 6, 8, 10].

Faigman (2000)

David L. Faigman, *Legal Alchemy: The Use and Misuse of Science in the Law*, W. H. Freeman (1999, 2000) [I, 1, 6, 7, 9].

Faigman et al. (2002)

David L. Faigman, David H. Kaye, Michael J. Saks, and Joseph Sanders, *Modern Scientific Evidence: The Law and Science of Expert Testimony*, West Publishing (2002) [3, 7].

Fairley and Mosteller (1977)

William B. Fairley and Frederick Mosteller, *Statistics and Public Policy*, Addison-Wesley (1977) [1].

A. Farrell et al. (2003)

Amy Farrell, Jack McDevitt, Shea Cronin, and Erica Pierce, *Rhode Island Traffic Stop Statistics Act: Final Report*, Northeastern University Institute on Race and Justice (June 2003) [8].

A. Farrell et al. (2004)

Amy Farrell, Jack McDevitt, Lisa Bailey, Carsten Andresen, and Erica Pierce, *Massachusetts Racial and Gender Profiling Study: Final Report*, Northeastern University Institute on Race and Justice (May 4, 2004) [8].

M. Farrell (1994)

Margaret G. Farrell, "Coping with Scientific Evidence: The Use of Special Masters," 43 *Emory Law Journal* 927 (1994) [10].

Fedden (1950)

Robin Fedden, *Crusader Castles*, Art & Technics, London (1950) [4].

Feigenbaum (2003)

Alan Feigenbaum, "Special Juries: Deterring Spurious Medical Malpractice Litigation in State Courts," 24 *Cardozo Law Review* 1361 (March 2003) [10].

Feigenson (2003)

Neal R. Feigenson, "Can Tort Juries Punish Competently?" 78 *Chicago-Kent Law Review* 239 (2003) [10].

Feinberg (1971)

William E. Feinberg, "Teaching the Type I and Type II Errors: The Judicial Process," 25 *American Statistician* 3:30 (1971) [4, 4A].

Feingold (2000)

Howard Feingold, *Tools for Thought*, revised, MIT Press (2000) [9].

Fenner (1996)

G. Michael Fenner, "The *Daubert* Handbook: The Case, Its Essential Dilemma, and Its Progeny," 29 *Creighton Law Review* 939 (April 1996) [1].

Fienberg (1986)

Stephen E. Fienberg, "Comment" on Meier et al. (1984), in DeGroot et al. (1986) at 41 [8].

Fienberg (1989)

Stephen E. Fienberg, editor, *The Evolving Role of Statistical Assessments as Evidence in the Courts* (Panel on Statistical Assessment as Evidence in the Courts, National Research Council), Springer-Verlag (1989) [1, 3, 10].

Fienberg (2001)

Stephen E. Fienberg with Clark Glymour and Richard Scheines, "Expert Statistical Testimony and Epidemiological Evidence: The Toxic Effects of Lead Exposure on Children," undated, unpaginated, and un-ascribed though type-set paper found through www.scholar.google.com. The latest reference is to 2000, hence the date above [7].

Fienberg et al. (1995)

Stephen E. Fienberg, Samuel H. Krislov, and Miron L. Straf, "Understanding and Evaluating Statistical Evidence in Litigation," 36 *Jurimetrics Journal* 1 (1995) [5, 8].

Finkelstein (1966)

Michael O. Finkelstein, "The Application of Statistical Decision Theory to the Jury Discrimination Cases," 80 *Harvard Law Review* 2:338 (1966) [2, 5].

Finkelstein (1973)

Michael O. Finkelstein, "Regression Models in Administrative Proceedings," 86 *Harvard Law Review* 8:1442 (June 1973) [3A].

Finkelstein (1978)

Michael O. Finkelstein, *Quantitative Methods in Law*, MacMillan, The Free Press (1978) [1, 5, 9, 3A].

Finkelstein (1980)

Michael O. Finkelstein, "The Judicial Reception of Multiple Regression Studies in Race and Sex Discrimination Cases," 80 *Columbia Law Review* 4:737 (1980) [3, 9].

Finkelstein and Fairley (1970)

Michael O. Finkelstein and William B. Fairley, "A Bayesian Approach to Identification Evidence," 83 *Harvard Law Review* 3:489 (January 1970) [1, 8].

Finkelstein and Fairley (1971)

Michael O. Finkelstein and William B. Fairley, "A Comment on 'Trial by Mathematics,'" 84 *Harvard Law Review* 8:1801 (June 1971) [1, 8].

Finkelstein and Levenbach (1983)

Michael O. Finkelstein and Hans Levenbach, "Regression Estimates of Damages in Price-Fixing Cases," 46 *Law and Contemporary Problems* 4:145 (1983) [3].

Finkelstein and Levin (1990)

Michael O. Finkelstein and Bruce Levin, *Statistics for Lawyers*, Springer-Verlag (1990) [6, 7, 9].

Finkelstein and Levin (2003)

Michael O. Finkelstein and Bruce Levin, "On the Probative Value of Evidence from a Screening Search," 43 *Jurimetrics Journal* 265 (2003) [2, 6, 8].

Finkelstein and Levin (2004)

Michael O. Finkelstein and Bruce Levin, "*Bush v. Gore*: Two Neglected Lessons from a Statistical Perspective," 44 *Jurimetrics Journal* 2:181 (Winter 2004) [5].

Fischel and Lazear (1986)

Daniel Fischel and Edward Lazear, "Comparable Worth and Discrimination in the Labor Market," and "Rejoinder," 53 *University of Chicago Law Review* 891 and 950 (Summer 1986) [6].

F. Fisher (1980)

Franklin M. Fisher, "Multiple Regression in Legal Proceedings," 80 *Columbia Law Review* 4:702 (1980) [3, 9].

F. Fisher (1986)

Franklin M. Fisher, "Statisticians, Econometricians, and Adversary Proceedings," 81 *Journal of the American Statistical Association* 394:277 (June 1986) [3, 8, 9].

F. Fisher (1998)

Franklin M. Fisher, "Direct Testimony of Franklin M. Fisher," in *Microsoft* antitrust litigation, undated document available in Acrobat format from the Department of Justice antitrust web site, http://www.usdoj.gov/atr; 1998 assumed from Schmalensee (1999) [8].

R. Fisher (1948)

R. A. Fisher, "Combining Independent Tests of Significance," 2 *American Statistician* 30 (1948) [2].

Follett and Welch (1983)

Robert S. Follett and Finis Welch, "Testing for Discrimination in Employment Practices," in David W. Peterson, editor, "Statistical Inference in Litigation," 46 *Law and Contemporary Problems* 4 (Autumn 1983), at 171 [3, 8].

Forde-Mazrui (1999)

Kim Forde-Mazrui, "Jural Districting: Selecting Impartial Juries Through Community Representation," 52 *Vanderbilt Law Review* 353 (March 1999) [5].

Foster and Huber (1997)

Kenneth R. Foster and Peter W. Huber, *Judging Science: Scientific Knowledge and the Federal Courts*, MIT Press (1997) [1, 9, 10].

Fradella et al. (2004)

Henry F. Fradella, Lauren O'Neill, and Adam Fogarty, "The Impact of *Daubert* on Forensic Science," 31 *Pepperdine Law Review* 323 (January 2004) [7, 10].

Frank (2000)

Thomas Frank, *One Market Under God*, Doubleday (2000) [9, 10, 5A].

Frankel (1975)

Marvin E. Frankel, "The Search for Truth: An Umpireal View," 123 *University of Pennsylvania Law Review* 5:1031 (1975) [7, 10].

Frankfurter and Landis (1928)

Felix Frankfurter and James M. Landis, *The Business of the Supreme Court*, MacMillan (1928); reprinted by Johnson Reprint Corporation (1972) [4].

Freed and Polsby (1984)

Mayer G. Freed and Daniel D. Polsby, "Comparable Worth in the Equal Pay Act," 51 *University of Chicago Law Review* 4:1078 (1984) [6, 7].

Freund (1954)

Paul A. Freund, "Review of Facts in Constitutional Cases," in Edmond Cahn, editor, *Supreme Court and Supreme Law*, Indiana University Press (1954) at 47 [1].

C. Fried (2002)

Charles Fried, "An Unreasonable Reaction to a Reasonable Decision," Chapter 1 of Bruce Ackerman, editor, *Bush v. Gore: The Question of Legitimacy*, Yale University Press (2002) [I].

M. Fried et al. (1975)

Michael Fried, Kalman J. Kaplan, and Katherine W. Klein, "Juror Selection: An Analysis of *Voir Dire*," in Simon (1975) [4A].

H. Friedman (1972)

Herbert Friedman, "Trial by Jury: Criteria for Convictions, Jury Size, and Type I and Type II Errors," 26 *American Statistician* 2:21 (1972) [4].

L. Friedman (1985)

Lawrence M. Friedman, *A History of American Law*, second edition, Simon & Schuster (1985) [6, 9].

L. Friedman (2002)

Lawrence M. Friedman, *American Law in the 20th Century*, Yale University Press (2002) [C].

Friendly (1970)

Henry J. Friendly, "Is Innocence Irrelevant? Collateral Attack on Criminal Judgments," 38 *University of Chicago Law Review* 142 (1970) [5].

Fukurai et al. (1993)

Hiroshi Fukurai, Edgar W. Butler, and Richard Krooth, *Race and the Jury*, Plenum Press (1993) [5, 10, 5A].

Fukurai and Krooth (2003)

Hiroshi Fukurai and Richard Krooth, *Race in the Jury Box*, State University of New York Press (2003) [10].

Galanter (1994)

Marc Galanter, "Predators and Parasites: Lawyer-Bashing and Civil Justice," 28 *Georgia Law Review* 3:633 (1994) [6].

Gallai (1999)

David Gallai, "Polygraph Evidence in Federal Courts: Should It Be Admissible?" 36 *American Criminal Law Review* 1:87 (1999) [1].

Gastwirth (1984)

Joseph L. Gastwirth, "Statistical Methods for Analyzing Claims of Employment Discrimination," 38 *Industrial and Labor Relations Review* 75 (1984) [10].

Gastwirth (1981)

Joseph L. Gastwirth, "Estimating the Demographic Mix of the Available Labor Force," 104 *Monthly Labor Review* 4:50 (April 1981) [7].

Gastwirth (1988)

Joseph L. Gastwirth, *Statistical Reasoning in Law and Public Policy*, two volumes, Academic Press (1988) [2, 3, 5, 9].

Gastwirth (2000)

Joseph L. Gastwirth, editor, *Statistical Science in the Courtroom*, Springer (2000) [9].

Gastwirth and Haber (1976)

Joseph L. Gastwirth and Sheldon E. Haber, "Defining the Labor Market for Equal Employment Standards," 99 *Monthly Labor Review* 32 (1976) [7].

Gatowski et al. (2001)

Sophia I. Gatowski, Shirley A. Dobbin, James T. Richardson, Gerald P. Ginsburg, Mara L. Merlino, and Veronica Dahir, "Asking the Gatekeepers: A National Survey of Judges on Judging Expert Evidence in a Post-*Daubert* World," 25 *Law and Human Behavior* 5:433 (October 2001) [7].

Gavil (1997)

Andrew I. Gavil, "After *Daubert*: Discerning the Increasingly Fine Line Between the Admissability and Sufficiency of Expert Testimony in Antitrust Litigation," 65 *Antitrust Law Journal* 3:663 (1997) [1, 8].

Gavil (1999)

Andrew I. Gavil, "An Analysis of Some Procedural Aspects of the *Microsoft* Trial," 13 *Antitrust* 3:7 (1999) [9, 10].

Gavil (2000)

Andrew I. Gavil, "Defining Reliable Forensic Economics in the Post-*Daubert/Kumho Tire* Era: Case Studies from Antitrust," 57 *Washington and Lee Law Review* 831 (2000) [1].

Gelfand and Solomon (1973)

Alan E. Gelfand and Herbert Solomon, "A Study of Poisson's Models for Jury Verdicts in Criminal and Civil Trials," 68 *Journal of the American Statistical Association* 342:271 (June 1973) [1, 4].

Gelfand and Solomon (1974)

Alan E. Gelfand and Herbert Solomon, "Modeling Jury Verdicts in the American Legal System," 69 *Journal of the American Statistical Association* 345:32 (March 1974) [1, 4, 4A].

Gelfand and Solomon (1975)

Alan E. Gelfand and Herbert Solomon, "Analyzing the Decision-Making Process of the American Jury," 70 *Journal of the American Statistical Association* 350:305 (June 1975) [1, 4A].

Gelfand and Solomon (1977a)

Alan E. Gelfand and Herbert Solomon, "Considerations in Building Jury Behavior Models and in Comparing Jury Schemes: An Argument in Favor of 12-Member Juries," 17 *Jurimetrics Journal* 4:292 (Summer 1977) [1, 4, 4A].

Gelfand and Solomon (1977b)

Alan E. Gelfand and Herbert Solomon, "Rejoinder" to Vaclav Fabian, 72 *Journal of the American Statistical Association* 359:536 (September 1977) [1, 4A].

Gelman and Nolan (2002)

Andrew Gelman and Deborah Nolan, "You Can Load a Die, But You Can't Bias a Coin," 56 *American Statistician* 4:308 (2002) [6].

Gewin (1975)

Walter Pettus Gewin, "An Analysis of Jury Selection Decisions," published as an appendix to *Foster v. Sparks*, 506 F.2d 805 (5th Cir. 1975), at 811 [5].

Giannelli (1980)

Paul C. Giannelli, "The Admissibility of Novel Scientific Evidence: *Frye v. United States*, A Half-Century Later," 80 *Columbia Law Review* 6:1197 (1980) [1].

Giannelli (1993)

Paul C. Giannelli, "'Junk Science': The Criminal Cases," 84 *Journal of Criminal Law and Criminology* 105 (Spring 1993) [8, 10].

Giannelli (1997a)

Paul C. Giannelli, "The Abuse of Scientific Evidence in Criminal Cases: The Need for Independent Crime Laboratories," 4 *Virginia Journal of Social Policy and the Law* 439 (Winter 1997) [8, 10].

Giannelli (1997b)

Paul C. Giannelli, "The DNA Story: An Alternative View," review of Harlan Levy, *And the Blood Cried Out*, Basic Books (1996), 88 *Journal of Criminal Law and Criminology* 380 (Fall 1997) [9, 10].

Giannelli and Imwinkelried (1999)

Paul C. Giannelli and Edward J. Imwinkelreid, *Scientific Evidence*, third edition, Lexis (1999) [2].

Gibson (1950)

Hugh Gibson, "Racial Discrimination on Grand Juries," 3 *Baylor Law Review* 29 (1950) [5].

Glantz (1997)

Craig M. Glantz, "'Could' This Be the End of Fourth Amendment Protections for Motorists?" 87 *Journal of Criminal Law and Criminology* 864 (1997) [8].

Glazer (1978)

Nathan Glazer, "Should Judges Administer Social Services?" *Public Interest* 50:64 (Winter 1978) [I].

Goldberg (1980)

Steven H. Goldberg, "Harmless Error: Constitutional Sneak Thief," 71 *Journal of Criminal Law and Criminology* 421 (1980) [5].

Good (2001)

Phillip I. Good, *Applying Statistics in the Courtroom*, Chapman & Hall / CRC Press (2001) [3, 8, 9, 10, 3A].

J. Goodman (1976)

John L. Goodman, Jr., *Is Ordinary Least Squares Estimation with a Dichotomous Dependent Variable Really That Bad?* Working Paper No. 216-23, Urban Institute (September 1976) [3].

L. Goodman (1975)

Leo A. Goodman, "The Relationship Between Modified and Usual Multiple Regression Approaches to the Analysis of Dichotomous Variables," in David Heise, editor, *Sociological Methodology 1976,* Jossey Bass (1975), at 83 [3].

Graham (1998)

Michael H. Graham, "The *Daubert* Dilemma: At Last a Viable Solution?" 179 F.R.D. 1 (1998) [10].

J. Gray (1960)

John C. Gray, *The Nature and Sources of Law,* Beacon Press (1960) [1].

M. Gray (1983)

Mary Gray, "Statistics and the Law," 456 *Mathematics Magazine* 2:67 (March 1983) [5].

Greenberg (1956)

Jack Greenberg, "Social Scientists Take the Stand," 54 *Michigan Law Review* 953 (1956) [1].

Greenfield (1977)

Ester Greenfield, "From Equal to Equivalent Pay: Salary Discrimination in Academia," 6 *Journal of Law and Education* 1:41 (January 1977) [3].

Griffin (1999)

Robert M. Griffin, "News Flash: Judges Are Ideologically Motivated," review of Susan U. Phillips, *Ideology in the Language of Judges: How Judges Practice Law, Politics, and Courtroom Control,* Oxford University Press (1998), 26 *American Journal of Criminal Law* 395 (Spring 1999). [1].

Grilliches (1961)

Zvi Grilliches, "Hedonic Price Indexes for Automobiles: An Econometric Analysis of Quality Change," in *The Price Statistics of the Federal Government,* General Series No. 73, Columbia Press (1961); reprinted in Grilliches (1971b) at 55 [6].

Grilliches (1971a)

Zvi Grilliches, "Hedonic Prices Revisited," in Grilliches (1971b) at 3 [6].

Grilliches (1971b)

Zvi Grilliches, editor, *Price Indexes and Quality Change,* Harvard University Press (1971) [6].

Grilliches and Grunfield (1960)

Zvi Grilliches and Yehuda Grunfield, "Is Aggregation Necessarily Bad?" 42 *Review of Economics and Statistics* 1 (February 1960) [3].

Grofman (1975)

Bernard Grofman, "A Comment on 'Democratic' Theory: A Preliminary Mathematical Model," 21 *Public Choice* 99 (Spring 1975) [4, 4A].

Grofman (1980)

Bernard Grofman, "The Slippery Slope," 2 *Law and Policy Quarterly* 3:285 (July 1980) [4].

Grofman (1981)

Bernard Grofman, "Mathematical Models of Juror and Jury Decision-Making: The State of the Art," in Bruce D. Sales, editor, *The Trial Process*, Volume II of *Perspectives in Law and Psychology*, Plenum (1981), at 305 [4A].

Grofman (2000)

Bernard Grofman, editor, *Legacies of the 1964 Civil Rights Act*, University Press of Virginia (2000) [7, 10].

Gross (1991)

Samuel R. Gross, "Expert Evidence," 1991 *Wisconsin Law Review* 5:1113 (1991) [I, 6, 7, 8, 9, 10].

Gross and Barnes (2002)

Samuel R. Gross and Katherine Y. Barnes, "Road Work: Racial Profiling and Drug Interdiction on the Highway," 10 *Michigan Law Review* 651 (December 2002) [8].

Gross and Livingston (2002)

Samuel R. Gross and Debra Livingston, "Racial Profiling Under Attack," 102 *Columbia Law Review* 1413 (June 2002) [8].

Gwartney et al. (1979)

James Gwartney, Ephraim Asher, Charles Haworth, and Joan Haworth, "Statistics, the Law, and Title VII: An Economist's View," 54 *Notre Dame Lawyer* 633 (1979) [3, 9].

Hacking (1975)

Ian Hacking, *The Emergence of Probability*, Cambridge University Press (1975) [1].

Hagen (1997)

Margaret A. Hagen, *Whores of the Court: The Fraud of Psychiatric Testimony and the Rape of American Justice*, Regan Books, Harper Collins (1997) [8, 10].

Hager (1990)

Mark M. Hager, "Civil Compensation and its Discontents: A Response to Huber," 42 *Stanford Law Review* 539 (1990) [6].

A. Hale (1978)

Adrienne Hale, "The Admissibility of Bite Mark Evidence," 51 *Southern California Law Review* 2:309 (January 1978) [10].

R. Hale (1927)

Robert L. Hale, "Economics and Law," in William Fielding Ogburn and Alexander Goldenweiser, editors, *Social Sciences and Their Interrelations*, Houghton Mifflin (1927), at 131 [9].

Hall (1998)

Christopher Hall, "Challenging Selective Enforcement of Traffic Regulations After the Disharmonic Convergence: *Whren v. United States, United States v. Armstrong*, and the Evolution of Police Discretion," 76 *Texas Law Review* 1083 (1998) [8].

Hand (1901)

Learned Hand: "Historical and Practical Considerations Regarding Expert Testimony," 15 *Harvard Law Review* 1:40 (1901) [1].

Haney (1994)

William P. Haney, III, "Scientific Evidence in the Age of *Daubert*: A Proposal for a Dual Standard of Admissibility in Civil and Criminal Cases," 21 *Pepperdine Law Review* 1391 (1994) [8].

Harcourt (2004)

Bernard E. Harcourt, "Rethinking Racial Profiling: A Critique of the Economics, Civil Liberties, and Constitutional Literature, and of Criminal Profiling More Generally," 71 *University of Chicago Law Review* 4:1275 (Fall 2004) [8].

Harper (1981)

Gregory L. Harper, "Statistics as Evidence of Age Discrimination," 32 *Hastings Law Journal* 1347 (1981) [2].

D. Harris (1994)

David A. Harris, "Factors for Reasonable Suspicion: When Black and Poor Means Stopped and Frisked," 69 *Indiana Law Journal* 659 (1994) [10].

D. Harris (1997)

David A. Harris, "'Driving While Black' and All Other Traffic Offenses: The Supreme Court and Pretextual Traffic Stops," 87 *Journal of Criminal Law and Criminology* 544 (1997) [8].

D. Harris (1999)

David A. Harris, "The Stories, the Statistics, and the Law: Why 'Driving While Black' Matters," 84 *Minnesota Law Review* 265 (1999) [8].

G. Harris (2000)

George C. Harris, "Testimony for Sale: The Law and Ethics of Snitches and Experts," 28 *Pepperdine Law Review* 1 (2000) [6, 10].

Hastie and Viscusi (1999)

Reid Hastie and W. Kip Viscusi, "What Juries Can't Do Well: The Jury's Performance as a Risk Manager," 40 *Arizona Law Review* 901 (Fall 1998) [10].

Hastie and Viscusi (2002)

Reid Hastie and W. Kip Viscusi, "Juries, Hindsight, and Punitive Damages Awards: Reply to Richard Lempert," 51 *DePaul Law Review* 987 (Summer 2002) [10].

Heckman (1998)

James J. Heckman, "Detecting Discrimination," 12 *Journal of Economic Perspectives* 2:101 (Spring 1998) [9].

Heise (1999)

Michael Heise, "The Importance of Being Empirical," 26 *Pepperdine Law Review* 807 (May 1999) [9].

Helmholz (1999)

R. H. Helmholz, "Magna Carta and the *ius commune*," 66 *University of Chicago Law Review* 2:297 (Spring 1999) [1, 10].

Hemenway

David Hemenway, *Private Guns, Public Health*, University of Michigan Press (2004) [7, 9].

Henseler (1997)

Timothy B. Henseler, "A Critical Look at the Admissibility of Polygraph Evidence in the Wake of *Daubert*: The Lie Detector Fails the Test," 46 *Catholic University Law Review* 1247 (Summer 1997) [10].

Herbert and Shelton (1996)

Douglas C. Herbert and Lani Schweiker Shelton, "A Pragmatic Argument Against Applying the Disparate Impact Doctrine in Age Discrimination Cases," 37 *South Texas Law Review* 625 (June 1996) [7].

Holdsworth (1903)

Sir William Holdsworth, *A History of English Law*, Methuen & Co., London (1903); seventh edition (1966) [1, 4].

Holmes (1897)

Oliver Wendell Holmes, "The Path of the Law," 10 *Harvard Law Review* 8:457 (1897) [9].

Horowitz (1977)

Donald L. Horowitz, *The Courts and Social Policy*, The Brookings Institution (1977) [I, 3].

Hubbard and Bayarri (2003)

Raymond Hubbard and M. J. Bayarri, "Confusion Over Measures of Evidence (p's) Versus Errors ($\propto$'s) in Classical Statistical Testing," 57 *American Statistician* 3:171 (August 2003) [7].

Huber (1985)

Peter W. Huber, "Safety and the Second Best: The Hazards of Public Risk Management in the Courts," 85 *Columbia Law Review* 2:277 (1985) [6].

Huber (1988)

Peter W. Huber, *Liability: The Legal Revolution and Its Consequences*, Basic Books (1988); paper (1990) [6, 10].

Huber (1991)

Peter W. Huber, *Galileo's Revenge: Junk Science in the Courtroom*, Basic Books (1991) [1, 3, 6, 9, 10].

Huff (1954)

Darrell Huff, *How to Lie with Statistics*, W. W. Norton (1954); reissued (1993) [6, 7, 9].

Hyman and Tarrant (1975)

Harold M. Hyman and Catherine M. Tarrant, "Aspects of American Trial Jury History," in Simon (1975) at 21 [4].

Imwinkelried (1988)

Edward J. Imwinkelried, "The 'Bases' of Expert Testimony: The Syllogistic Structure of Scientific Testimony," 67 *North Carolina Law Review* 1 (1988) [10].

Imwinkelried (1993)

Edward J. Imwinkelried, "The *Daubert* Decision: *Frye* Is Dead, Long Live the Federal Rules of Evidence," 29 *Trial* 60 (September 1993) [1].

Imwinkelried (1995)

Edward J. Imwinkelreid, "Evidence Law Visits Jurassic Park: The Far-Reaching Implication of the *Daubert* Court's Recognition of the Uncertainty of the Scientific Enterprise," 81 *Iowa Law Review* 55 (1995) [1, 7, 8, 10].

P. James (1977)

P. D. James, *Death of an Expert Witness*, Scribner Books (1977); reprint by Warner Books (1992) [10].

R. James (1960)

Rita M. James, "Jurors' Evaluation of Expert Psychiatric Testimony," 21 *Ohio State Law Journal* 75 (1960); reprinted in part in Lawrence M. Friedman and Stewart Macaulay, *Law and the Behavioral Sciences*, Bobbs-Merrill (1969), at 684 [1].

Jansonius and Gould (1998)

John V. Jansonius and Andrew M. Gould, "Expert Witnesses in Employment Litigation: The Role of Reliability in Assessing Admissibility," 50 *Baylor Law Review* 267 (Spring 1998) [10].

Jasanoff (1995)

Sheila Jasanoff, *Science at the Bar*, Twentieth Century Fund (1995) [I, 6].

Joiner (1975)

Charles W. Joiner, "From the Bench," in Simon (1975) at 145 [4].

Jonakait (1994)

Randolph N. Jonakait, "The Meaning of *Daubert* and What That Means for Forensic Science," 15 *Cardozo Law Review* 2103 (1994) [10].

Judicial Center (1977)

Federal Judicial Center, *Annual Report* (1977) [4].

Kadane (2000)

Joseph B. Kadane, "Forensic Statistics and Multiparty Bayesianism," in Gastwirth (2000) at 353 [5, 7, 9].

Kadane and Mitchell (2000)

Joseph B. Kadane and Caroline Mitchell, "Statistics in Proof of Employment Discrimination Cases," Appendix 1 in Grofman (2000) at 241 [7, 10].

Kairys et al. (1977)

David Kairys, Joseph B. Kadane, and John P. Lehoczky, "Jury Representativeness: A Mandate for Multiple Source Lists," 65 *California Law Review* 776 (1977) [5].

Kalven and Zeisel (1966)

Harry Kalven, Jr., and Hans Zeisel, *The American Jury*, Little, Brown and Company (1966); revised edition, University of Chicago Press (1971) [4, 10, 4A].

Kantrowtiz (1977)

Arthur Kantrowitz, "The Science Court Experiment," 17 *Jurimetrics Journal* 4:332 (Summer 1977) [10].

E. Kaplan and Meier (1958)

E. L. Kaplan and Paul Meier, "Nonparametric Estimation from Incomplete Observations," 52 *Journal of the American Statistical Association* 457 (June 1958) [2].

J. Kaplan (1968)

John Kaplan, "Decision Theory and the Fact Finding Process," 20 *Stanford Law Review* 1065 (1968) [4, 4A].

Karst (1960)

Kenneth L. Karst, "Legislative Facts in Constitutional Litigation," in Philip B. Kurland, editor, *The Supreme Court Review*, University of Chicago Press (1960), at 75 [1].

Kaye (1986)

D. H. Kaye, "Statistical Evidence of Discrimination in Jury Selection," in Kaye and Aickin (1986) at 13 [5].

Kaye (1987)

D. H. Kaye, "Apples and Oranges: Confidence Coefficients and the Burden of Persuasion," 73 *Cornell Law Review* 54 (1987) [7, 8].

Kaye (2001)

D. H. Kaye, "The Dynamics of *Daubert*: Methodology, Conclusions, and Fit in Statistical and Econometric Studies," 87 *Virginia Law Review* 1933 (December 2001) [1, 9, 10].

Kaye (2003)

D. H. Kaye, "Adversarial Econometrics in *United States Tobacco Co. v. Conwood Co.*, 43 *Jurimetrics Journal* 343 (2003) [3].

Kaye and Aickin (1986)

D. H. Kaye and Mikel Aickin, editors, *Statistical Methods in Discrimination Litigation*, Marcel Dekker (1986) [5].

Kaye and Freedman (1994)

David H. Kaye and David A. Freedman, "Reference Guide on Statistics," in *Reference Manual* (1994) at 383 [7, 8].

Kennebeck (1975)

Edwin Kennebeck, "From the Jury Box," in Simon (1975) at 235 [4].

Kesan (1996)

Jay P. Kesan, "An Autopsy of Scientific Evidence in a Post-*Daubert* World," 84 *Georgetown Law Journal* 5:1985 (1996) [1].

Killingsworth (1993)

Mark R. Killingsworth, "Analyzing Employment Discrimination: From the Seminar Room to the Courtroom," 83 *American Economic Review* 2:67 (1993) [3].

Kim (2001)

Hyongsoon Kim, "Adversarialism Defended: *Daubert* and the Judge's Role in Evaluating Expert Evidence," 434 *Columbia Journal of Law and Social Problems* 223 (Spring 2001) [10].

Klerman (2003)

Daniel Klerman, "Was the Jury Ever Self-Informing?" 77 *Southern California Law Review* 1:123 (November 2003) [1].

Kluger (1975)

Richard Kluger, *Simple Justice*, Knopf (1975) [1, 6].

Knoll (1996)

Michael S. Knoll, "A Primer On Prejudgment Interest," 75 *Texas Law Review* 293 (1996) [7].

Knowles et al. (2001)

John Knowles, Nicola Persico, and Petra Todd, "Racial Bias in Motor Vehicle Searches: Theory and Evidence," 109 *Journal of Political Economy* 1:203 (February 2001) [8].

Kordana and O'Reilly (2001)

Kevin A. Kordana and Terrance O'Reilly, "*Daubert* and Litigation-Driven Econometrics," 87 *Virginia Law Review* 2019 (December 2001) [9, 10].

Koshland (1994)

Daniel E. Koshland, Jr., "Scientific Evidence in Court," 266 *Science* 1787 (1994) [5].

Koukoutchos (1994)

Brian Stuart Koukoutchos, "Solomon Meets Galileo (and Isn't Quite Sure What to Do with Him)," 15 *Cardozo Law Review* 2237 (April 1994) [10].

Kraft (1982)

Melvin D. Kraft, editor, *Using Experts in Civil Cases*, Practising Law Institute (1982) [1, 10].

R. Kuhn (1968)

Roger S. Kuhn, "Jury Discrimination: The Next Phase," 41 *Southern California Law Review* 234 (1968) [5, 9].

T. Kuhn (1970)

Thomas S. Kuhn, *The Structure of Scientific Revolutions*, second edition, enlarged (1970); first published (1962). [10].

Kurland (1970)

Philip B. Kurland, *Politics, the Constitution, and the Warren Court*, University of Chicago Press (1970) [I, 1].

La Fontaine (2002)

Eugenia T. La Fontaine, "A Dangerous Preoccupation with Future Danger: Why Expert Predictions of Future Dangerousness in Capital Cases Are Unconstitutional," 44 *Boston College Law Review* 207 (December 2002) [10].

Lamberth (1996)

John Lamberth, "Revised Statistical Analysis of the Incidence of Police Stops and Arrests of Black Drivers/Travelers on the New Jersey Turnpike Between Exits or Interchanges 1 and 3 from Years 1988 Through 1991," plaintiff's expert's report in *Soto* (1996) [8].

Lamberth (1998)

John Lamberth, "Driving While Black," *Washington Post* (August 16, 1998) at C1, continued at C5 as "Profiling" [8, 9].

Lamberth (2003)

John C. Lamberth, *Racial Profiling Study and Services: A Multijurisdictional Assessment of Traffic Enforcement and Data Collection in Kansas*, Police Foundation (2003) [8].

Landes (1971)

William Landes, "An Economic Analysis of the Courts," 14 *Journal of Law and Economics* 1:61 (April 1971) [4].

Landes and Posner (2004)

William M. Landes and Richard A. Posner, *The Political Economy of Intellectual Property Law*, AEI-Brookings Joint Center for Regulatory Studies (2004); available from AEI Press [10].

Lazear (2001)

Edward P. Lazear, "Educational Production," 116 *Quarterly Journal of Economics* 3:777 (August 2001) [3].

Lee (1988)

Tahirih V. Lee, "Court-Appointed Experts and Judicial Reluctance: A Proposal to Amend Rule 706 of the Federal Rules of Evidence," 6 *Yale Law and Policy Review* 480 (1988) [10].

Lehoczky (1995)

John Lehoczky, "Modernizing Statistics Ph.D. Programs," 49 *American Statistician* 1:12 (1995) [9].

Leipold (1998)

Andrew D. Leipold, "Constitutionalizing Jury Selection in Criminal Cases: A Critical Evaluation," 86 *Georgetown Law Journal* 945 (1998) [5].

Lempert (1981)

Richard O. Lempert, "Civil Juries and Complex Cases: Let's Not Rush to Judgment," 80 *Michigan Law Review* 1:68 (1981) [5, C].

Lempert (1985)

Richard Lempert, "Statistics in the Courtroom: Building on Rubinfeld," 85 *Columbia Law Review* 5:1098 (1985) [6, 7, 8].

Lempert (1991)

Richard Lempert, "Some Caveats Concerning DNA as Criminal Identification Evidence: With Thanks to the Reverend Bayes," 13 *Cardozo Law Review* 303 (November 1991) [7, 10].

Lempert (1999)

Richard Lempert, "Juries, Hindsight, and Punitive Damage Awards: Failures of a Social Science Case for Change," 48 *DePaul Law Review* 867 (Summer 1999) [10].

Lempert (2000)

Richard Lempert, "Befuddled Judges: Statistical Evidence in Title VII Cases," in Grofman (2000) at 263 [3, 7].

Levin and Robbins (1983)

Bruce Levin and Herbert Robbins, "Urn Models for Regression Analysis, with Application to Employment Discrimination Studies," 46 *Law and Contemporary Problems* 4:247 (Autumn 1983) [3].

Levy (1967)

Leonard W. Levy, editor, *Judicial Review and the Supreme Court*, Harper Torchbooks (1967) [1, 4].

Levy (1972)

Leonard W. Levy, editor, *The Supreme Court Under Earl Warren*, New York Times, Quadrangle Books (1972) [4].

Levy (1999)

Leonard W. Levy, *The Palladium of Justice: Origins of Trial by Jury*, Ivan R. Dee (1999) [4].

Lewin (1992)

Jeff L. Lewin, "Calabresi's Revenge? Junk Science in the Work of Peter Huber," 21 *Hofstra Law Review* 1:183 (1992) [1, 6].

Lewis (1970)

Ovid C. Lewis, "Review of Law and the Behavioral Sciences," 22 *Case Western Reserve Law Review* 1:144 (November 1970) [9].

Lewontin and Hartl (1991)

R. C. Lewontin and Daniel L. Hartl, "Population Genetics in Forensic DNA Typing," 254 *Science* 1745 (December 20, 1991) [9].

Liebenson (1962)

Harold A. Liebenson, *You, the Expert Witness*, Callaghan & Company (1962) [9].

Lind (2003)

JoEllen Lind, "The End of Trial on Damages? Intangible Losses and Comparability Review," 51 *Buffalo Law Review* 251 (Spring 2003) [10].

Lindsey et al. (2003)

Samuel Lindsey, Ralph Hertwig, and Gerd Gigerenzer, "Communicating Statistical DNA Evidence," 43 *Jurimetrics Journal* 2:147 (Winter 2003) [10].

Litwiller (2002)

Lisa Litwiller, "Has the Supreme Court Sounded the Death Knell for Jury Assessed Punitive Damages? A Critical Re-Examination of the American Jury," 36 *University of San Francisco Law Review* 411 (Winter 2002) [10].

Liu (2002)

Goodwin Liu, "The Causation Fallacy: Bakke and the Basic Arithmetic of Selective Admissions," 100 *Michigan Law Review* 1045 (March 2002) [C].

Loftus and Monahan (1980)

Elizabeth Loftus and John Monahan, "Trial by Data: Psychological Research as Legal Evidence," 35 *American Psychologist* 3:270 (March 1980) [1].

Loftus and Pickrell (1995)

Elizabeth F. Loftus and J. E. Pickrell, "The Formation of False Memories," 25 *Psychiatric Annals* 720 (1995) [10].

Louisell (1955)

David W. Louisell, "The Psychologist in Today's Legal World," 39 *Minnesota Law Review* 3:235 (February 1955) [1].

Lozowick et al. (1968)

Arnold H. Lozowick, Peter O. Steiner, and Roger Miller, "Law and Quantitative Multivariate Analysis: An Encounter," 66 *Michigan Law Review* 8:1641 (June 1968) [1].

Lundman and Kaufman (2003)

Richard J. Lundman and Robert L. Kaufman, "Driving While Black: Effects of Race, Ethnicity, and Gender on Citizen Self-Reports of Traffic Stops and Police Actions," 41 *Criminology* 195 (2003) [8].

Luneburg and Nordenberg (1981)

William V. Luneburg and Mark A. Nordenberg, "Specially Qualified Juries and Expert Non-jury Tribunals: Alternatives for Coping with the Complexities of Modern Civil Litigation," 67 *Virginia Law Review* 5:887 (1981) [10].

Lurie (1955)

Nancy Oestreich Lurie, "Problems, Opportunities, and Recommendations," 2 *Ethnohistory* 357 (1955) [1].

Mac Donald (2001)

Heather Mac Donald, "The Myth of Racial Profiling," *City Journal* (Spring 2001), http://www.city-journal.org/html/11_2_the_myth.html [8].

Mac Donald (2004)

Heather Mac Donald, "NU Profiling Study Really Proves Nothing," *The Boston Globe* (May 19, 2004) [8].

Malakoff (1999)

David Malakoff, "Bayes Offers a 'New' Way to Make Sense of Numbers," 286 *Science* 1460 (1999) [7, 10].

Mandel (1999)

Michael J. Mandel, "Going for the Gold: Economists as Expert Witnesses," 13 *Journal of Economic Perspectives* 2:113 (Spring 1999) [9].

C. Mann (1981)

Charles R. Mann, "The Original Concept of Underutilization: An Unreasonable Expectation," in *An Equal Employment Opportunity Guide, 1981*, Federal Bar Association, Washington, D.C. (1981) [2].

C. Mann (2000)

Charles R. Mann, "Statistical Consulting in the Legal Environment," in Gastwirth (2000) at 245 [8, 9].

M. Mann et al. (1998)

Michael E. Mann, Raymond S. Bradley, and Malcolm K. Hughes, "Global-Scale Temperature Patterns and Climate Forcing Over the Past Six Centuries," 392 *Nature* 779 (April 1998) [9].

M. Mann et al. (1999)

Michael E. Mann, Raymond Bradley, and Malcolm Hughes, "Northern Hemisphere Temperatures During the Past Millennium: Inferences, Uncertainties, and Limitations," 26 *Geophysical Research Letters* 759 (1999) [9].

Manning (1982)

Jean Manning, "Multiple Regression Analysis: A Statistical Approach to Assessing and Correcting Salary Inequity," 1982 *University of Illinois Law Review* 2:449 (1982) [3].

Mantel and Haenszel (1959)

Nathan Mantel and William Haenszel, "Statistical Aspects of the Analysis of Data from Retrospective Studies of Disease," 22 *Journal of the National Cancer Institute* 4:719 (1959) [2].

Markey (1978)

Howard T. Markey, "Needed: A Judicial Welcome for Technology: Star Wars or *Stare Decisis*?" 79 F.R.D. 209 (1978) [10].

Marlow (1998)

George D. Marlow, "From Black Robes to White Lab Coats: The Ethical Implications of a Judge's Sua Sponte, ex Parte Acquisition of Social and Other Scientific Evidence During the Decision-Making Process," 72 *St. John's Law Review* 291 (1998) [1].

D. Martin (1972)

Donald Martin, "The Economics of Jury Conscription," 80 *Journal of Political Economy* 4:680 (1972) [4].

G. Martin and Clay (1981)

Gerald D. Martin and William C. Clay, Jr., *How to Win Maximum Awards for Lost Earnings: A Guide to Estimating Damages Fairly and Proving Them in Court*, Executive Reports Corporation (1980); second printing (1981) [7].

Mause (1969)

Philip J. Mause, "Harmless Constitutional Error: The Implications of *Chapman v. California*," 53 *Minnesota Law Review* 519 (1969) [5].

McAlister (1996)

Cynthia V. McAlister, "The Repressed Memory Phenomenon: Are Recovered Memories Scientifically Valid Evidence under *Daubert*?" 22 *North Carolina Central Law Journal* 56 (1996) [10].

McCart (1965)

Samuel W. McCart, *Trial by Jury*, second edition, Chilton Books (1965) [5].

McCloskey (1990)

Donald N. McCloskey, *If You're So Smart: The Narrative of Economic Expertise*, University of Chicago Press (1990) [8].

McCord (1986)

David McCord, "Expert Psychological Testimony About Child Complainants in Sexual Abuse Prosecutions: A Foray into the Admissibility of Novel Psychological Evidence," 77 *Journal of Criminal Law and Criminology* 1 (Spring 1986) [10].

McGovern (1986)

Francis E. McGovern, "Toward a Functional Approach for Managing Complex Litigation," 53 *University of Chicago Law Review* 440 (Spring 1986) [10].

McGovern (2005)

Francis E. McGovern, "The What and Why of Claims Resolution Facilities," 57 *Stanford Law Review* 5:1361 (April 2005) [10].

McIntyre and McKitrick (2003)

Stephen McIntyre and Ross McKitrick, "Corrections to the Mann et al. (1998) Proxy Data Base and Northern Hemispheric Average Temperature Series," 14 *Energy and Environment* 751 (2003) [9].

McWhorter (2003)

John McWhorter, *Authentically Black*, Gotham Books (2003) [8].

Meeks (2000)

Kenneth Meeks, *Driving While Black*, Broadway Books (2000) [8, 10].

Meier (1986)

Paul Meier, "Damned Liars and Expert Witnesses," 81 *Journal of the American Statistical Association* 394:269 (June 1986) [5, 9].

Meier and Zabell (1980)

Paul Meier and Sandy Zabell, "Benjamin Peirce and the Howland Will," 75 *Journal of the American Statistical Association* 371:497 (September 1980) [1, 10].

Meier et al. (1984)

Paul Meier, Jerome Sacks, and Sandy L. Zabell, "What Happened in Hazelwood: Statistics, Employment Discrimination, and the 80% Rule," 1984 *American Bar Foundation Research Journal* 1:139; revised and reprinted in DeGroot et al. (1986) at 1 [5].

Mendelson (1967)

Wallace Mendelson, editor, *The Supreme Court: Law and Discretion*, Bobbs-Merrill (1967) [1].

Meyer and Kadane (1992)

Michael M. Meyer and Joseph B. Kadane, "Reconstructing the Adjusted Census for Florida: A Case Study in Data Examination," 1 *Journal of Computational and Graphical Statistics* 4:287 (December 1992) [3A].

Meyers and Albers (1991)

Robert L. Meyers, III, and Michael F. Albers, "The Expert Witness in Construction Litigation," in Rossi (1991) at 487 [6].

Michelson (2001)

Stephan Michelson, "Comments on 'Significance of Test-Based Ratings for Metropolitan Boston Schools' by Craig Bolon" [9 *Education Policy Analysis Archives* 42 (October 2001)], in 10 *Educational Policy Analysis Archives* 8 (January 2002), http://epaa.asu.edu/epaa/v10n8/ [3A].

Michelson (2004)

Stephan Michelson, "Driving While Black: A Skeptical Note," 44 *Jurimetrics Journal* 161 (Winter 2004) [8, 9].

Mickus (1994)

Lee Mickus, "Discovery of Work Product Disclosed to a Testifying Expert Under the 1993 Amendments to the Federal Rules of Civil Procedure," 27 *Creighton Law Review* 773 (1994) [10].

Miller (1968)

Arthur Selwyn Miller, *The Supreme Court and American Capitalism*, The Free Press (1968) [I, 1, 9].

Mills (1962)

Edwin S. Mills, "A Statistical Study of Occupations of Jurors in a United States District Court," 22 *Maryland Law Review* 205 (Spring 1962) [4].

Mintz (1978)

Morton Mintz, "'Bias, Misconduct, Incompetency' Claimed in Case of Juror Infatuated with Prosecutor," *Washington Post* (September 28, 1978) at A8 [4A].

Mitchell (1994)

Gregory Mitchell, "Against 'Overwhelming' Appellate Activism: Constraining Harmless Error Review," 82 *California Law Review* 1335 (October 1994) [5].

Mnookin (2001a)

Jennifer L. Mnookin, "Fingerprint Evidence in an Age of DNA Profiling," 67 *Brooklyn Law Review* 13 (Fall 2001) [8, 10].

Mnookin (2001b)

Jennifer L. Mnookin, "Scripting Expertise: The History of Handwriting Identification Evidence and the Judicial Construction of Reliability," 87 *Virginia Law Review* 1723 (December 2001) [8, 10].

Moenssens (1984)

Andre A. Moenssens, "Admissibility of Scientific Evidence: An Alternative to the *Frye* Rule," 25 *William and Mary Law Review* 545 (Summer 1984) [10].

Moenssens (1993)

Andre A. Moenssens, "Novel Scientific Evidence in Criminal Cases: Some Words of Caution," 84 *Journal of Criminal Law and Criminology* 1 (Spring 1993) [10].

Moenssens (1997)

Andre A. Moenssens, "Handwriting Identification Evidence in the Post-*Daubert* World," 66 *University of Missouri Kansas City Law Review* 251 (1997) [10].

Monaghan (1985)

Henry P. Monaghan, "Constitutional Fact Review," 85 *Columbia Law Review* 2:229 (1985) [1].

Monahan (2000)

John Monahan, "Violence Risk Assessment: Scientific Validity and Evidentiary Admissibility," 57 *Washingon and Lee Law Review* 901 (Summer 2000) [10].

Monahan and Walker (1986)

John Monahan and Laurens Walker, "Social Authority: Obtaining, Evaluating, and Establishing Social Science in Law," 134 *University of Pennsylvania Law Review* 477 (March 1986) [1, 10].

D. Moore (2001)

David S. Moore, "Undergraduate Programs and the Future of Academic Statistics," 55 *American Statistician* 1 (2001) [9].

H. Moore and Galloway (1992)

Harold G. Moore and Joseph L. Galloway, *We Were Soldiers Once . . . and Young: Ia Drang: The Battle That Changed the War in Vietnam*, Random House (1992) [9].

Moreno (2001)

Joelle Anne Moreno, "Beyond the Polemic Against Junk Science: Navigating the Oceans That Divide Science and Law with Justice Breyer at the Helm," 81 *Boston University Law Review* 5:1033 (December 2001) [1, 7, 10].

Morgan and Maguire (1937)

Edmund M. Morgan and John MacArthur Maguire, "Looking Backward and Forward at Evidence," 50 *Harvard Law Review* 6:909 (April 1937) [6, 10].

Moriarty (2001)

Jane Campbell Moriarty, "Wonders of the Invisible World: Prosecutorial Syndrome and Profile Evidence in the Salem Witchcraft Trials," 26 *Vermont Law Review* 43 (Fall 2001) [10].

Morris (1979)

Frank C. Morris, *Current Trends in the Use (and Misuse) of Statistics in Employment Discrimination Litigation*, second edition, Equal Employment Advisory Council (1979) [1].

Morse (1978)

Stephen J. Morse, "Crazy Behavior, Morals, and Science: An Analysis of Mental Health Law," 51 *Southern California Law Review* 3:527 (1978) [5].

Mosher (2003)

Clayton Mosher, "Vancouver Police Department: Citizen Contact Data Analysis Project, Preliminary Report," typescript, Contract Research Center, Washington State University, Vancouver, Washington (2003) [8].

Mosher et al. (2002)

Clayton Mosher, Terance D. Miethe, and Dretha M. Phillips, *The Mismeasure of Crime*, Sage (2002) [2].

Mosher et al. (2004)

Clayton Mosher, Mitch Pickerill, Nicholas Lovrich, and Michael Gaffney, "The Importance of Context in Understanding Biased Policing: State Patrol Traffic Citations in Washington State," typescript revision (2004); paper presented at the 2003 annual meeting of the American Society of Criminology [8].

Moss (2003)

Steven Moss, "Opinion for Sale: Confessions of an Expert Witness," 2 *Legal Affairs* 2:52 (March-April 2003) [9].

Mossman (1974)

Keith Mossman, "Justice and Numbers," 10 *Trial* 6 (1974) [4].

Moynihan (1969)

Daniel Patrick Moynihan, *On Understanding Poverty*, Basic Books (1969) [I].

Mueller and Kirkpatrick (1999)

Christopher B. Mueller and Laird C. Kirkpatrick, *Evidence: Practice Under the Rules*, Aspen Law & Business (1999) [8].

Munsterberg (1909)

Hugo Munsterberg, *On the Witness Stand*, Doubleday & Page (1909); reprinted several times, the last being in 1927 [1].

Murphy (2000)

Justin P. Murphy, "Expert Witnesses at Trial: Where Are the Ethics?" 14 *Georgetown Journal of Legal Ethics* 217 (Fall 2000) [10].

Nagel and Neef (1977)

Stuart S. Nagel and Marian G. Neef, *Legal Policy Analysis*, Lexington Books (1977) [4, 4A].

Needle (1962)

Gerald M. Needle, "Selection of the Jury," "Comment" in 13 *Hastings Law Journal* 495 (1962) [10].

Neilson and Winter (2002)

William S. Neilson and Harold Winter, "Consensus and Jury Deliberation," typescript (September 2002); available at http://www.tamu.edu/perc/publication/0221.pdf [4A].

Nelson and Bridges (1999)

Robert L. Nelson and William P. Bridges, *Legalizing Gender Inequality: Courts, Markets, and Unequal Pay for Women in America*, Cambridge University Press (1999) [6, 7].

Nesson (1985)

Charles Nesson, "The Evidence or the Event? On Judicial Proof and the Acceptability of Verdicts," 98 *Harvard Law Review* 7:1357 (1985) [2].

Nesson (1986)

Charles Nesson, "Agent Orange Meets the Blue Bus: Fact-Finding at the Frontier of Knowledge," 66 *Boston University Law Review* 521 (1986) [8].

J. Noonan (2002)

John T. Noonan, *Narrowing the Nation's Power*, University of California Press (2002) [P, I].

P. Noonan (1990)

Peggy Noonan, *What I Saw at the Revolution*, Random House (1990) [1].

Northrup and Larson (1979)

Herbert R. Northrup and John A. Larson, "The Impact of the AT&T–EEO Consent Decree," *Labor Relations and Public Policy Series No. 20*, The Wharton School, University of Pennsylvania (1979) [3].

Note (1947)

"The Blue Ribbon Jury," 60 *Harvard Law Review* 613 (1947) [5, 10].

Note (1948)

"Social and Economic Facts: Appraisal of Suggested Techniques for Presenting Them to the Courts," 61 *Harvard Law Review* 692 (1948) [1].

Note (1965a)

"The Defendant's Challenge to a Racial Criterion in Jury Selection: A Study in Standing, Due Process, and Equal Protection," 74 *Yale Law Journal* 919 (1965) [5].

Note (1965b)

"Fair Jury Selection Procedures," 75 *Yale Law Journal* 322 (1965) [5].

Note (1966)

"The Congress, The Court, and Jury Selection: A Critique of Titles I and II of the Civil Rights Bill of 1966," 52 *Virginia Law Review* 1069 (1966) [5].

Note (1970)

"The Case for Black Juries," 79 *Yale Law Journal* 531 (1970) [5, 10].

Note (1975)

"Beyond the *Prima Facie* Case in Employment Discrimination Law: Statistical Proof and Rebuttal," 89 *Harvard Law Review* 387 (1975) [3].

Note (1977)

"Civil Rights Enforcement and the Selection of Federal District Court Judges," 21 *Saint Louis University Law Journal* 385 (1977) [9].

Note (1995)

"Confronting the New Challenges of Scientific Evidence," Part IV of " Scientific Evidence, Standards of Admissibility, and Burdens of Proof," 108 *Harvard Law Review* 1532 (May 1995) [7, 9].

Note (1997)

"Improving Judicial Gatekeeping: Technical Advisors and Scientific Evidence," 110 *Harvard Law Review* 941 (February 1997) [10].

Note (2000)

"Navigating Uncertainty: Gatekeeping in the Absence of Hard Science," 113 *Harvard Law Review* 1467 (April 2000) [10].

Note (2003)

"Reliable Evaluation of Expert Testimony," 116 *Harvard Law Review* 2142 (May 2003) [10].

Oaxaca (1976)

Ronald Oaxaca, "Male-Female Wage Differentials in the Telephone Industry," in Wallace (1976) at 17 [3].

Ogletree (1991)

Charles J. Ogletree, "*Arizona v. Fulminante*: The Harm of Applying Harmless Error to Coerced Confessions," 105 *Harvard Law Review* 152 (November 1991) [5].

Oliver (2000)

Wesley MacNeil Oliver, "With an Evil Eye and an Unequal Hand: Pretextual Stops and Doctrinal Remedies to Racial Profiling," 74 *Tulane Law Review* 1409 (2000) [8].

Ormerod (1994)

Paul Ormerod, *The Death of Economics*, Faber and Faber (1994) [9].

Osborne (1990)

John W. Osborne, "Judicial/Technical Assessment of Novel Scientific Evidence," 1990 *University of Illinois Law Review* 497 (1990) [10].

Osburn (1970)

Donald D. Osburn, "Economies of Size Associated with Public High Schools," 52 *Review of Economics and Statistics* 113 (February 1970) [3].

Owen (2002)

David G. Owen, "A Decade of *Daubert*," 80 *Denver University Law Review* 345 (2002) [1, 10].

Pabst (1973)

William R. Pabst, Jr., "What Do Six-Member Juries Really Save?" 57 *Judicature* 1:6 (June-July 1973) [3, 4].

Pabst and Munsterman (1975)

William R. Pabst, Jr., and G. Thomas Munsterman, "The Economic Hardship of Jury Duty," 58 *Judicature* 10:494 (May 1975) [4].

Paterson (2000)

Rebecca Sasser Paterson, "DNA Databases: When Fear Goes Too Far," 37 *American Criminal Law Review* 1219 (2000) [10].

Paulos (1990)

John Allen Paulos, *Innumeracy: Mathematical Illiteracy and Its Consequences*, Vantage Books (1990) [7].

Penrod and Hastie (1979)

Steven Penrod and Reid Hastie, "Models of Jury Decision Making: A Critical Review," 86 *Psychological Bulletin* 3:462 (1979) [4, 4A].

Penrod and Hastie (1980)

Steven Penrod and Reid Hastie, "A Computer Simulation of Jury Decision Making," 87 *Psychological Review* 2:133 (1980) [4, 4A].

PERF (2001)

Lorie Fridell, Robert Lunney, Drew Diamond, and Bruce Kubu, *Racially Biased Policing: A Principled Response*, Police Executive Research Forum (2001) [8].

Perrin (1995)

L. Timothy Perrin, "Expert Witness Testimony: Back to the Future," 29 *University of Richmond Law Review* 1389 (December 1995) [6, 10].

Peters (2000)

Christopher J. Peters, "Outcomes, Reasons, and Equality," 80 *Boston University Law Review* 1095 (2000) [3].

Peterson (1986)

David W. Peterson, "Measurement Error and Regression Analysis in Employment Cases," in Kaye and Aickin (1986) at 107 [3].

Peterson and Conley (2001)

David W. Peterson and John M. Conley, "Of Cherries, Fudge, and Onions: Science and Its Courtroom Perversion," 64 *Law and Contemporary Problems* 4:213 (2001) [7, 10].

Piette and White (1999)

Michael J. Piette and Paul F. White, "Approaches for Dealing with Small Sample Sizes in Employment Discrimination Litigation," 12 *Journal of Forensic Economics* 1:43 (1999) [3].

Pollard (2000)

David Pollard, "A Connecticut Jury Array Challenge," in Gastwirth (2000) at 195 [9, C].

Posner (1972)

Richard A. Posner, *Economic Analysis of Law*, Little, Brown and Company (1972) [4].

Posner (1981)

Richard A. Posner, "The Present Situation in Legal Scholarship," 90 *Yale Law Journal* 5:1113 (1981) [9, 10].

Posner (1985)

Richard A. Posner, *The Federal Courts: Crisis and Reform*, Harvard University Press (1985) [I].

Posner (1997)

Richard A. Posner, "The Path Away from the Law," 110 *Harvard Law Review* 5:1039 (1997) [9].

Posner (1999a)

Richard A. Posner, "An Economic Approach to the Law of Evidence," 51 *Stanford Law Review* 1477 (1999) [6, 7, 9, 10].

Posner (1999b)

Richard A. Posner, "The Law and Economics of the Economic Expert Witness," 13 *Journal of Economic Perspectives* 2:91 (Spring 1999) [7, 10].

Posner (2001a)

Richard A. Posner, *Public Intellectuals: A Study of Decline*, Harvard University Press (2001) [8, 9, 10].

Posner (2001b)

Richard A. Posner, *Frontiers of Legal Theory*, Harvard University Press (2001) [6, 7, 9].

Posner (2003)

Richard A. Posner, *Law, Pragmatism, and Democracy*, Harvard University Press (2003) [I, 1, 4, 5, 9].

Posner (2004)

Richard A. Posner, "Against the Law Reviews," *Legal Affairs* (November-December 2004), http://legalaffairs.org/issues/_November-December-2004/review_posner_novdec04.html, [9].

Postman (1988)

Neil Postman, *Conscientious Objections*, Alfred A. Knopf (1988) [10].

Poulter (1992)

Susan R. Poulter, "Science and Toxic Torts: Is There a Rational Solution to the Problem of Causation?" 7 *High Technology Law Journal* (1992) [7, 10].

Pound (1917)

Roscoe Pound, "Juristic Problems of National Progress," 22 *American Journal of Sociology* 721 (1917) [10].

Pound (1920)

Roscoe Pound, "Anachronisms in Law," 3 *Journal of the American Judicature Society* 142 (1920) [10].

Primus (2003)

Richard A. Primus, "Equal Protection and Disparate Impact: Round Three," 117 *Harvard Law Review* 493 (December 2003) [1, 3, 5].

Quayle (1992)

Dan Quayle, "Agenda for Civil Justice Reform in America," a report of the President's Council on Competitiveness, 60 *University of Cincinnati Law Review* 979 (1992) [10].

Ramirez et al. (2000)

Deborah Ramirez, Jack McDevitt, and Amy Farrell, *A Resource Guide on Racial Profiling Data Collection Systems*, U.S. Department of Justice (2000) [8].

Ranii (1980)

David Ranii, "Management Consultants Take the Stand," 3 *National Law Journal* 10:1 (November 17, 1980) [1].

Raskin (2003)

Jamin B. Raskin, *Overruling Democracy: The Supreme Court vs. The American People*, Routledge (2003) [1].

Ray (1955)

Verne F. Ray, "Anthropology and Indian Claims Litigation: Introduction," 2 *Ethnohistory* 287 (1955) [1].

***Reference Manual* (1994)**

Reference Manual on Scientific Evidence, Federal Judicial Center (1994); second edition (2000) [2, 3, 7, 8, 9].

Refo (2004)

Patricia Lee Refo, chair, "Principles for Juries and Jury Trials," *American Jury Project of the American Bar Association* (October 2004); available as an Acrobat document at http://www.abanet.org/juryprojectstandards [C].

Richey (1994)

Charles R. Richey, "Proposals to Eliminate the Prejudicial Effect of the Use of the Word 'Expert' Under the Federal Rules of Evidence in Civil and Criminal Jury Trials," 154 *Federal Rules Decisions* 537 (July 1994) [6, 10].

Riew (1966)

John Riew, "Economies of Scale in High School Operation," 48 *Review of Economics and Statistics* 280 (August 1966) [3].

Riew (1972)

John Riew, "Scale Economies in Public Schools," 54 *Review of Economics and Statistics* 100 (February 1972) [3].

Risinger (2000)

D. Michael Risinger, "Defining the 'Task at Hand': Non-Science Forensic Science After *Kumho Tire Co. v. Carmichael*," 57 *Washington and Lee Law Review* 767 (Summer 2000) [10].

Risinger and Saks (1996)

D. Michael Risinger and Michael J. Saks, "Science and Nonscience in the Courts: *Daubert* Meets Handwriting Identification Expertise," 82 *Iowa Law Review* 21 (1996) [8, 10].

Risinger et al. (1989)

D. Michael Risinger, Mark Denbeaux, and Michael J. Saks, "Exorcism of Ignorance as a Proxy for Rational Knowledge: The Lessons of Handwriting Identification Expertise," 137 *University of Pennsylvania Law Review* 731 (1989) [2, 8, 10].

Risinger et al. (1998)

D. Michael Risinger, Mark P. Denbeaux, and Michael J. Saks, "Brave New 'Post-*Daubert* World': A Reply to Professor Moenssens," 29 *Seton Hall Law Review* 405 (1998) [10].

Risinger et al. (2002)

D. Michael Risinger, Michael J. Saks, William C. Thompson, and Robert Rosenthal, "The *Daubert/Kumho* Implications of Observer Effects in Forensic Science: Hidden Problems of Expectation and Suggestion," 90 *California Law Review* 1:1 (2002) [8, 10].

Ritter et al. (2001)

Mary Ann Ritter, Robert R. Starbuck, and Robert V. Hogg, "Advice from Prospective Employers on Training BS Statisticians," 55 *American Statistician* 1 (2001) [9].

Robinson (1950)

W. S. Robinson, "Bias, Probability, and Trial by Jury," 15 *American Sociological Review* 73 (February 1950) [1, 4].

Rose (1967)

Arnold M. Rose, "The Social Scientist as an Expert Witness in Court Cases," in Paul F. Lazarsfeld, William H. Sewell, and Harold L. Wilensky, editors, *The Uses of Sociology*, Basic Books (1967), at 100 [1].

L. Rosen (1977)

Lawrence Rosen, "The Anthropologist as Expert Witness," 79 *American Anthropologist* 3:555 (September 1977) [1].

P. Rosen (1972)

Paul L. Rosen, *The Supreme Court and Social Science*, University of Illinois Press (1972) [1].

Rosenblum (2000)

Marc Rosenblum, "On the Evolution of Analytical Proof, Statistics, and the Use of Experts in EEO Litigation," in Gastwirth (2000) at 161 [1, 9].

L. Rosenthal (1935)

Lloyd D. Rosenthal, "The Development of the Use of Expert Testimony," 2 *Law and Contemporary Problems* 403 (1935) [1].

R. Rosenthal (1978)

Robert Rosenthal, "Combining Results of Independent Studies, 85 *Psychological Bulletin* 185 (1978) [2].

Rossi (1991)

Faust F. Rossi, *Expert Witnesses*, American Bar Association (1991) [1, 9].

Rothstein (2002)

Paul F. Rothstein, *Federal Rules of Evidence*, third edition, West Group (2002) [8].

Rubin (2000)

Donald B. Rubin, "Statistical Issues in the Estimation of the Causal Effects of Smoking Due to the Conduct of the Tobacco Industry," in Gastwirth (2000) at 321 [1].

Rubinfeld (1985)

Daniel L. Rubinfeld, "Econometrics in the Courtroom," 85 *Columbia Law Review* 5:1048 (1985) [7, 10].

Saks (1974)

Michael J. Saks, "Ignorance of Science Is No Excuse," 10 *Trial* 6:18 (November-December 1974) [4].

Saks (1987)

Michael J. Saks, "Accuracy v. Advocacy: Expert Testimony Before the Bench," 90 *Technology Review* 6:43 (1987) [6].

Saks (1990)

Michael J. Saks, "Judicial Attention to the Way the World Works," 75 *Iowa Law Review* 1011 (May 1990) [1, 7, 10].

Saks (1998)

Michael J. Saks, "Merlin and Solomon: Lessons from the Law's Formative Encounters with Forensic Identification Science," 49 *Hastings Law Journal* 1069 (1998) [1, 8, 10].

Saks (2000a)

Michael J. Saks, "The Aftermath of *Daubert*: An Evolving Jurisprudence of Expert Evidence," 40 *Jurimetrics Journal* 2:229 (2000) [1, 10].

Saks (2000b)

Michael J. Saks, "Banishing *Ipse Dixit*: The Impact of *Kumho Tire* on Forensic Identification Science," 57 *Washington and Lee Law Review* 879 (Summer 2000) [10].

Saks and Baron (1980)

Michael J. Saks and Charles H. Baron, *The Use, Nonuse, Misuse of Applied Social Research in the Courts*, Council for Applied Social Research, Abt Books (1980) [1].

Saks and Ostrom (1975)

Michael J. Saks and Thomas M. Ostrom, "Jury Size and Consensus Requirements: The Laws of Probability v. The Laws of the Land," 1 *Journal of Contemporary Law* 163 (1975) [4].

Sammon (2001)

Bill Sammon, *At Any Cost: How Al Gore Tried to Steal the Election*, Regnery (2001) [I].

Sanders (1998)

Joseph Sanders, "Scientifically Complex Cases, Trial by Jury, and the Erosion of Adversarial Processes," 48 *DePaul Law Review* 355 (Winter 1998) [10].

Saunders (1997)

Kurt M. Saunders, "Race and Representation in Jury Service Selection," 36 *Duquesne Law Review* 49 (1997) [5].

Scalia (1989)

Antonin Scalia, "The Rule of Law as a Law of Rules," 56 *University of Chicago Law Review* 4:1175 (1989) [7, 9, 10].

Scallen (2002)

Eileen A. Scallen, "Analyzing The Politics of [Evidence] Rulemaking," 53 *Hastings Law Journal* 843 (April 2002) [10].

Scheaffer and Stasny (2004)

Richard L. Scheaffer and Elizabeth A. Stasny, "The State of Undergraduate Education in Statistics: A Report from the CBMS 2000," 58 *American Statistician* 4:265 (November 2004) [9].

Schkade et al. (2000)

David Schkade, Cass R. Sunstein, and Daniel Kahneman, "Deliberating about Dollars: The Severity Shift," 100 *Columbia Law Review* 1139 (May 2000) [10].

Schmalensee (1999)

Richard L. Schmalensee, testimony (for defendant) in *Microsoft* antitrust litigation (January 3, 1999), downloaded from Microsoft web site [8].

Schulman et al. (1973)

Jay Schulman, Philip Shaver, Robert Colman, Barbara Emrich, and Richard Christie, "Recipe for a Jury," 6 *Psychology Today* 12:44 (May 1973) [4].

Schwartz (1997)

Adina Schwartz, "A 'Dogma of Empiricism' Revisited: *Daubert v. Merrell Dow Pharmaceuticals, Inc.* and the Need to Resurrect the Philosophical Insight of *Frye v. United States*," 10 *Harvard Journal of Law and Technology* 149 (Winter 1997) [10].

Scott (1899)

Austin Scott, "Holmes vs. Walton: The New Jersey Precedent," 4 *American Historical Review* 3:456 (1899) [4].

Shafer (1976)

Glenn Shafer, *A Mathematical Theory of Evidence*, Princeton University Press (1976) [4A].

Shapard (1981)

John E. Shapard, *A Comparative Study of Jury Selection Systems*, Federal Judicial Center (1981) [5, 8].

Shapley (1974)

Deborah Shapley, "Jury Selection: Social Scientists Gamble in an Already Loaded Game," 185 *Science* 1033 (September 1974) [4].

Sharkey (2003a)

Catherine M. Sharkey, "Punitive Damages as Societal Damages," 113 *Yale Law Journal* 347 (November 2003) [10].

Sharkey (2003b)

Catherine M. Sharkey, "Punitive Damages: Should Juries Decide?" 82 *Texas Law Review* 381 (December 2003) [10].

Shaviro (1989)

Daniel N. Shaviro, "Statistical-Probability Evidence and the Appearance of Justice," 103 *Harvard Law Review* 530 (1989) [8].

Shaviro (1991)

Daniel N. Shaviro, "A Response to Professor Callen," 65 *Tulane Law Review* 499 (1991) [8].

Sigal (1969)

Paul Sigal, "Judicial Use, Misuse, and Abuse of Statistical Evidence," 47 *Journal of Urban Law* 1:165 (1969–70) [5].

Silberg (1993)

Julie Schwartz Silberg, "Memory Repression: Should It Toll the Statutory Limitations Period in Child Sexual Abuse Cases?" 39 *Wayne Law Review* 1589 (Summer 1993) [10].

Simon (1967)

Rita James Simon, *The Jury and the Defense of Insanity*, Little, Brown and Company [4A].

Simon (1975)

Rita James Simon, editor, *The Jury System in America*, Sage (1975) [4].

Singer (1992)

Barry Singer, *Black and Blue: The Life and Lyrics of Andy Razaf*, Schirmer (1992) [9].

Sink (1956)

John M. Sink, "The Unused Power of a Federal Judge to Call His Own Expert Witness," 29 *Southern California Law Review* 2:195 (1956) [6, 10].

A. Smith and Abram (1981)

Arthur B. Smith, Jr., and Thomas G. Abram, "Proof of Employment Discrimination," 1981 *University of Illinois Law Review* 1:33 (1981) [3].

W. Smith et al. (2003)

William R. Smith, Donald Tomaskovic-Devey, Matthew T. Zingraff, H. Marcinda Mason, Patricia Y. Warren, and Cynthia Pfaff Wright, *The North Carolina Highway Traffic Study*, final report to the National Institute of Justice under Grant No. 1999-MU-CX-0022 (July 21, 2003) [8].

Sobol (1991)

Richard B. Sobol, *Bending The Law: The Story of the Dalkon Shield Bankruptcy*, University of Chicago Press (1991) [6, 7, 10].

Solan and Tiersma (2003)

Lawrence M. Solan and Peter M. Tiersma, "Hearing Voices: Speaker Identification in Court," 54 *Hastings Law Journal* 2:373 (January 2003) [10].

Sombat (2002)

Jessica Sombat, "Latent Justice: *Daubert*'s Impact on the Evaluation of Fingerprint Identification Testimony," 70 *Fordham Law Review* 2819 (2002) [8, 10].

Soon and Baliunas (2003)

Willie Soon and Sallie Baliunas, "Proxy Climatic and Environmental Changes of the Past 1000 Years," 23 *Climate Research* 89 (2003) [9].

Sorensen and Pilgrim (2000)

Jonathan R. Sorensen and Rocky L. Pilgrim, "An Actuarial Risk Assessment of Violence Posed by Capital Murder Defendants," 90 *Journal of Criminal Law and Criminology* 1251 (Summer 2000) [10].

Spadaro (1998)

Joseph A. Spadaro, "An Elusive Search for the Truth: The Admissibility of Repressed and Recovered Memories in Light of *Daubert V. Merrell Dow Pharmaceuticals, Inc.*," 30 *Connecticut Law Review* 1147 (1998) [10].

Speiser (1988)

Stuart M. Speiser, *Recovery for Wrongful Death and Injury*, third edition, The Lawyers Cooperative Publishing Company (1988) [7].

Spence (1989)

Gerry Spence, *With Justice for None*, Penguin Books (1989) [P, 2, 4, 6, 7, 9, 10].

Sperlich (1979)

Peter W. Sperlich, "Trial by Jury: It May Have a Future," in Philip B. Kurland, editor, *Supreme Court Review, 1978*, University of Chicago Press (1979), at 191 [4].

Sperlich and Jaspovice (1974)

Peter W. Sperlich and Martin L. Jaspovice, "Grand Juries, Grand Jurors, and the Constitution," 1 *Hastings Constitutional Law Quarterly* 63 (1974) [5].

Sperlich and Jaspovice (1979)

Peter W. Sperlich and Martin L. Jaspovice, "Methods for the Analysis of Jury Panel Selections: Testing for Discrimination in a Series of Panels," 6 *Hastings Constitutional Law Quarterly* 787 (1979) [5, 8].

Starrs (1996)

James E. Starrs, "Recent Developments in Federal and State Rules Pertaining to Medical and Scientific Expert Testimony," 34 *Duquesne Law Review* 813 (Summer 1996) [10].

Steward (1955)

Julian H. Steward, "Theory and Application in Social Science," 2 *Ethnohistory* 292 (1955) [1].

Stiglitz (1998)

Joseph Stiglitz, "The Private Uses of Public Interests: Incentives and Institutions," "Distinguished Lecture on Economics in Government," in 12 *Journal of Economic Perspectives* 2:3 (Spring 1998) [9].

Stone (1966)

Julius Stone, *Law and the Social Sciences in the Second Half Century*, University of Minnesota Press (1968) [10].

Strodtbeck and Hook (1961)

Fred L. Strodtbeck and Harmon L. Hook, "The Social Dimensions of a Twelve-Man Jury Table," 24 *Sociometry* 4:397 (1961) [3].

Strodtbeck et al. (1957)

Fred L. Strodtbeck, Rita M. James, and Charles Hawkins, "Social Status in Jury Deliberations," 22 *American Sociological Review* 6:713 (1957) [3].

Strong (1992)

John William Strong, "Language and Logic in Expert Testimony: Limiting Expert Testimony by Restrictions of Function, Reliability, and Form," 71 *Oregon Law Review* 349 (Summer 1999) [10].

Sugrue and Fairley (1983)

Thomas J. Sugrue and William B. Fairley, "A Case of Unexamined Assumptions: The Use and Misuse of the Statistical Analysis of *Castaneda/Hazelwood* in Discrimination Litigation," 24 *Boston College Law Review* 4:925 (July 1983) [2, 5, 6].

Sunstein et al. (1998)

Cass R. Sunstein, Daniel Kahneman, and David Schkade, "Assessing Punitive Damages (With Notes on Cognition and Valuation in Law)," 107 *Yale Law Journal* 2071 (May 1998) [10].

Sunstein et al. (2002a)

Cass R. Sunstein, Reid Hastie, John W. Payne, David A. Schkade, and W. Kip Viscusi, *Punitive Damages: How Juries Decide*, University of Chicago Press (2002) [10].

Sunstein et al. (2002b)

Cass R. Sunstein, Daniel Kahneman, David Schkade, and Ilana Ritov, "Predictably Incoherent Judgments," 54 *Stanford Law Review* 1153 (June 2002) [10].

Surowiecki (2004)

James Surowiecki, *The Wisdom of Crowds*, Random House (2004) [4].

Tam Cho and Yoon (2001)

Wendy K. Tam Cho and Albert H. Yoon, "Strange Bedfellows: Politics, Courts, and Statistics: Statistical Expert Testimony in Voting Rights Cases," 10 *Cornell Journal of Law and Public Policy* 237 (Spring 2001) [7].

Tapper (2001)

Jake Tapper, *Down and Dirty: The Plot to Steal the Presidency*, Little, Brown and Company (2001) [I].

Taylor and Faust (1952)

Donald W. Taylor and William L. Faust, "Twenty Questions: Efficiency in Problem Solving as a Function of Size of Group," 44 *Journal of Experimental Psychology* 360 (1952); reprinted in A. Paul Hare, Edgar F. Borgatta, and Robert F. Bales, editors, *Small Groups: Studies in Social Interaction*, revised edition, Knopf (1966), at 513 [4].

Terrin and Kadane (1998)

Norma Terrin and Joseph B. Kadane, "Counting Cars in a Legal Case Involving Differential Enforcement," 11 *Chance* 3:25 (1998) [8].

Thernstrom (2004)

Abigail and Stephan Thernstrom, *No Excuses: Closing the Racial Gap in Learning*, Simon and Schuster (2004) [9].

Thomas (2001)

George C. Thomas, III, "Judges Are Not Economists and Other Reasons to be Skeptical of Contingent Suppression Orders: A Response to Professor Dripps," 38 *American Criminal Law Review* 47 (Winter 2001) [7].

R. Thompson (1991)

Robert S. Thompson, "Decision, Disciplined Inferences, and the Adversary Process," 13 *Cardozo Law Review* 725 (November 1991) [5, 7].

W. Thompson (1997)

William C. Thompson, "A Sociological Perspective on the Science of Forensic DNA Testing," 30 *U.C. Davis Law Review* 1113 (Summer 1997) [10].

Tigar and Levy (1977)

Michael E. Tigar and Madeleine R. Levy, *Law and the Rise of Capitalism*, Monthly Review Press (1977) [1, 10].

Tribe (1971a)

Laurence H. Tribe, "Trial by Mathematics: Precision and Ritual in the Legal Process," 84 *Harvard Law Review* 6:1329 (1971) [1, 8, 9].

Tribe (1971b)

Laurence H. Tribe, "A Further Critique of Mathematical Proof," 84 *Harvard Law Review* 8:1810 (June 1971) [1, 8].

Tribe (2001)

Laurence H. Tribe: "*Bush v. Gore* and Its Disguises: Freeing *Bush v. Gore* from Its Hall of Mirrors," 115 *Harvard Law Review* 1:170 (2001) [I].

Tucker (1966)

S. W. Tucker, "Discrimination in Virginia Jury Selection," 52 *Virginia Law Review* 736 (1966) [5].

Tuckman et al. (1977)

Howard P. Tuckman, James H. Gapinski, and Robert Hagemann, "Faculty Skills and the Salary Structure in Academe: A Market Perspective," 67 *American Economic Review* 4:692 (1977) [3].

Vidmar (1989)

Neil Vidmar, "Assessing the Impact of Statistical Evidence in the Legal System, a Social Science Perspective," in Fienberg (1989) at 279 [10].

Vidmar (1994)

Neil Vidmar, "Are Juries Competent to Decide Liability in Tort Cases Involving Scientific/Medical Issues? Some Data from Medical Malpractice," 43 *Emory Law Journal* 885 (1994) [10].

Vidmar (2001)

Neil Vidmar, "Juries, Judges, and Civil Justice," paper presented at the Forum for State Judges, Roscoe Pound Institute (July 2001) [1, 10].

Vidmar (2004)

Neil Vidmar, "Experimental Simulations and Tort Reform: Avoidance, Error, and Over-reaching in Sunstein et al.'s Punitive Damages (2002)," 53 *Emory Law Journal* 3:1359 (2004) [10].

Vidmar and Diamond (2001)

Neil Vidmar and Shari Seidman Diamond, "Juries and Expert Evidence," 66 *Brooklyn Law Review* 1121 (Summer 2001) [1, 10].

Vidmar and Robinson (2005)

Neil Vidmar and Russell M. Robinson, II, "Expert Evidence, the Adversary System, and the Jury," 95 *American Journal of Public Health* 137 (July 2005) [10].

Viscusi (1998)

W. Kip Viscusi, "Why There Is No Defense of Punitive Damages," 87 *Georgetown Law Journal* 381 (November 1998) [10].

Von Storch et al. (2004)

Hans von Storch, Eduardo Zorita, Julie M. Jones, Yegor Dimitriev, Fidel González-Rouco, and Simon F. B. Tett, "Reconstructing Past Climate from Noisy Data," 306 *Science* 5696:679 (October 22, 2004) [9].

Wainer (2003)

Howard Wainer, *A Trout in the Milk and Other Tales of Visual Discovery*, Princeton University Press (2003) [9, 9A].

Walbert (1971)

David F. Walbert, "The Effect of Jury Size on the Probability of Conviction: An Evaluation of *Williams v. Florida*," 22 Case *Western Reserve Law Review* 3:529 (April 1971) [4, 4A].

Walker and Monahan (1987)

Laurens Walker and John Monahan, "Social Frameworks: A New Use of Social Science in Law," 73 *Virginia Law Review* 559 (April 1987) [1, 10].

Walker and Monahan (1988)

Laurens Walker and John Monahan, "Social Facts: Scientific Methodology as Legal Precedent," 76 *California Law Review* 877 (July 1988) [1, 10].

Walker and Monahan (2000)

Laurens Walker and John Monahan, "Scientific Authority: The Breast Implant Litigation and Beyond," 80 *Virginia Law Review* 801 (May 2000) [10].

Wallace (1976)

Phyllis A. Wallace, editor, *Equal Employment Opportunity and the AT&T Case*, MIT Press (1976) [3].

Walsh (1999)

Joseph T. Walsh, "Keeping the Gate: The Evolving Role of the Judiciary in Admitting Scientific Evidence," 83 *Judicature* 3:140 (1999) [1, 9].

Wasby (1978)

Stephen L. Wasby, "A Little Social Science Is a Dangerous Thing: A Response to 'Civil Rights Enforcement and The Selection of Federal Judges,'" 22 *Saint Louis University Law Journal* 1:91 (1978) [9].

Wasby (2000)

Stephen L. Wasby, "Litigation and Lobbying and Complementary Strategies for Civil Rights," in Grofman (2000) at 65 [C].

Weinberg (1997)

Louise Weinberg, "Holmes' Failure," 96 *Michigan Law Review* 3:691 (1997) [9].

Weinstein (1986)

Jack B. Weinstein, "Improving Expert Testimony," 20 *University of Richmond Law Review* 473 (1986) [1, 6, 7].

Weinstein (2001)

Joseph M. McLaughlin, general editor, *Weinstein's Federal Evidence*, second edition, Matthew Bender & Co., Inc. (2001) [1, 8, 10].

C. Wells (1911)

Charles L. Wells, "The Origin of the Petit Jury," 27 *Law Quarterly Review* 347 (1911) [1, 4].

S. Wells (2002)

Spencer Wells, *The Journey of Man: A Genetic Odyssey*, Princeton University Press (2002) [10].

Wenger and Hoffman (2003)

Kaimipono David Wenger and David A. Hoffman, "Nullificatory Juries," 2003 *Wisconsin Law Review* 1115 (2003) [4].

J. White (1985)

James Boyd White, "Law as Rhetoric, Rhetoric as Law: The Arts of Cultural and Communal Life," 52 *University of Chicago Law Review* 3:684 (Summer 1985) [9].

P. White and Piette (1998)

Paul F. White and Michael J. Piette, "The Use of 'Reverse Regression' in Employment Discrimination Analysis," 11 *Journal of Forensic Economics* 2:127 (1998) [3].

Widacki and Horvath (1978)

J. Widacki and F. Horvath, "An Experimental Investigation of the Relative Validity and Utility of the Polygraph Technique and Three Other Common Methods of Criminal Identification," 23 *Journal of Forensic Sciences* 3:596 (1978) [1].

Wigmore (1909)

John Henry Wigmore, "Professor Muensterberg and the Psychology of Testimony," 3 *Illinois Law Review* 7:399 (1909) [1].

Wigmore (1935)

John Henry Wigmore, *Evidence in Trials at Common Law* (also known as "Wigmore on Evidence"), Little, Brown and Company, first edition (1904). Different volumes exist—there are now eleven plus a 2002 supplement—edited by different authors at different times [8].

Williams (1994)

Linda Myer Williams, "Recall of Childhood Trauma: A Prospective Study of Women's Memories of Child Sexual Abuse," 62 *Journal of Consulting and Clinical Psychology* 1167 (1994) [10].

Wilson (1995)

Paul E. Wilson, *A Time to Lose: Representing Kansas in Brown v. Board of Education*, University Press of Kansas (1995) [6].

Wolf (1976)

Eleanor P. Wolf, "Social Science and the Courts: The Detroit Schools Case," *Public Interest* 102 (Winter 1976) [I].

Wolf (1978)

Eleanor P. Wolf, "Northern School Desegregation and Residential Choice," in Philip B. Kurland and Gerhard Casper, editors, *The Supreme Court Review, 1977*, University of Chicago Press (1978), at 63 [I].

Wolfgang (1974)

Marvin E. Wolfgang, "The Social Scientist in Court," 65 *Journal of Criminal Law and Criminology* 2:239 (1974) [1, 8, 9].

Wolfram (1973)

Charles W. Wolfram, "The Constitutional History of the Seventh Amendment," 57 *Minnesota Law Review* 639 (1973) [9].

Wolins (1978)

Leroy Wolins, "Sex Differentials in Salaries: Faults in Analysis of Covariance," 200 *Science* 19 (May 1978) [3].

Wolter et al. (2003)

Kirk Wolter, Diana Jergovic, Whitney Moore, Joe Murphy, and Colm O'Muircheartaigh, "Reliability of the Uncertified Ballots in the 2000 Presidential Election in Florida," 57 *American Statistician* 1:1 (February 2003) [1].

Working Paper (1996)

Building A Spanish Surname List for the 1990s: A New Approach to an Old Problem, Technical Working Paper #13, U.S. Bureau of the Census, Population Division (March 1996) [5A].

Zeger et al. (2000)

Scott L. Zeger, Timothy Wyant, Leonard Miller, and Jonathan Samet, "Statistical Testimony on Damages in *Minnesota v. Tobacco Industry*," in Gastwirth (2000) at 303 [1, 9].

Zeisel (1969)

Hans Zeisel, "Dr. Spock and the Case of the Vanishing Women Jurors," 37 *University of Chicago Law Review* 1 (1969) [5].

Zeisel (1971)

Hans Zeisel, ". . . And Then There Were None: The Diminution of the Federal Jury," 38 *University of Chicago Law Review* 710 (1971) [4, 4A].

Zeisel and Diamond (1974)

Hans Zeisel and Shari Seidman Diamond, "'Convincing Empirical Evidence' on the Six Member Jury," 41 *University of Chicago Law Review* 281 (1974) [4].

Zeisel and Diamond (1978)

Hans Zeisel and Shari Seidman Diamond, "The Effect of Peremptory Challenges on Jury and Verdict: An Experiment in a Federal District Court," 30 *Stanford Law Review* 491 (February 1978) [4].

Zeisel and Kaye (1997)

Hans Zeisel and David Kaye, *Prove It with Figures: Empirical Methods in Law and Litigation*, Springer (1997) [4, 5].

Ziliak and McCloskey (2004)

Stephen T. Ziliak and Diedre N. McCloskey, "Size Matters: The Standard Error of Regressions in the *American Economic Review*," 1 *Econ Journal Watch* 2:331 (2004) [7].

Zingraff et al. (2000)

Matthew T. Zingraff, H. Marcinda Mason, William R. Smith, Donald Tomaskovic-Devey, Patricia Warren, Harvey L. McMurray, and C. Robert Fenlon, *Evaluating North Carolina State Highway Patrol Data: Citations, Warnings, and Searches in 1998*, report submitted to the North Carolina Department of Crime Control and Public Safety and North Carolina State Highway Patrol (November 1, 2000) http://www.nccrimecontrol.org/shp/ncshpreport.htm [8].

Zuckerman (1986)

Adrian A. S. Zuckerman, "Law, Fact or Justice?" 66 *Boston University Law Review* 487 (1986) [2, 8, 10].

Index of Experts

Numbers in brackets [ ] following each name refer to the chapters in which the person is referenced as an expert; a number followed by "A" denotes an appendix. "P" denotes the Preface, "I" the Introduction, and "C" the Coda.

THE EXPERT: The Statistical Analyst in Litigation has been designed and produced by John Laursen at Press-22 in Portland, Oregon. The typeface employed for both text and display is Minion, a contemporary face based upon classical, old-style typefaces of the late Renaissance, created for electronic composition by Robert Slimbach; the typeface in the figures is Helvetica Neue. The paper is 60# acid-free Torchglow Colonial White. The printing was done by Millcross Litho, with imposition and imagesetting by Revere Graphics. The books have been Smythe-sewn and bound by Lincoln & Allen.